Handbook of Legislative Research

Handbook of
Legislative Research

Edited by

Gerhard Loewenberg
Samuel C. Patterson
Malcolm E. Jewell

HARVARD UNIVERSITY PRESS
Cambridge, Massachusetts, and London, England   1985

Copyright © 1983, 1984, and 1985 by the Comparative Legislative Research Center

All rights reserved

Printed in the United States of America

10 9 8 7 6 5 4 3 2 1

This book is printed on acid-free paper, and its binding materials have been chosen for strength and durability.

Library of Congress Cataloging in Publication Data

Main entry under title:

Handbook of legislative research.

Includes bibliographies and index.
1. Legislative bodies—Addresses, essays, lectures. 2. Legislators—Addresses, essays, lectures. 3. Comparative government—Addresses, essays, lectures. I. Loewenberg, Gerhard. II. Patterson, Samuel Charles, 1931-   . III. Jewell, Malcolm E., 1928-   .
JF501.H35   1985   328'.3'072   84-29059
ISBN 0-674-37075-9 (alk. paper)

Preface

This *Handbook* offers an inventory of research on one of the central institutions of politics. That institution, commonly referred to as the "legislature" in the United States and by various other names elsewhere, has been the focal point of study by scholars so attentive to each other's work that they constitute something of an informal academic community. As a result, research on legislatures has produced an organized body of knowledge which can be usefully summarized. The editors believed that a coherent presentation of this research was not only possible but would itself promote further research and help that research to advance cumulative knowledge.

Research on legislatures has been particularly prolific in the last 25 years, although it is heir to a long tradition, as Heinz Eulau indicates in the introduction to this *Handbook*. No other field of political science except voting behavior has attracted similarly focussed research efforts. This is perhaps due to the centrality of legislatures in political systems, to the relatively clear definition of their boundaries as subjects of research, and to their characteristic openness to study.

The accelerated pace of legislative research has produced a body of knowledge which defies description by any single scholar. Recognizing this, the National Science Foundation supported a conference among some of the leading practitioners of legislative research to enable them to take stock of the field. The conference took place at the University of Iowa in 1982, organized by the editors of this volume together with Roger Davidson of the Congressional Research Service and Heinz Eulau of Stanford University. Eighteen leading scholars prepared papers, each of which dealt with one of the major subfields of legislative research. The papers had been commissioned by the conference organizers from among 40 proposals submitted in response to a call for contributors. At the conference, the papers were the subject of written critiques prepared by a group of distinguished commentators: Aage R. Clausen (Ohio State University), Joseph Cooper (Rice University), Roger Davidson (Congressional Research Service), Lawrence C. Dodd (Indiana University), Richard F. Fenno, Jr. (University of Rochester), Morris P. Fiorina

(Harvard University), Barbara Hinckley (University of Wisconsin), Charles O. Jones (University of Virginia), Chong Lim Kim (University of Iowa), Anthony King (University of Essex), John W. Kingdon (University of Michigan), Thomas E. Mann (American Political Science Association), Samuel C. Patterson (University of Iowa), Kenneth A. Shepsle (Washington University, St. Louis), and Joel H. Silbey (Cornell University). Other participants in the conference were W.O. Aydelotte (University of Iowa), G.R. Boynton (University of Iowa), and Robert X Browning (Purdue University).

Discussion and commentaries at the conference and thereafter led to substantial revision of the original papers, the addition of a paper on "Committee Selection" by Heinz Eulau, and the initial publication of the papers during 1983 and 1984 in the *Legislative Studies Quarterly*. Further revised and corrected, they are now presented here as a compendium for scholars interested in legislative behavior, processes, and organization.

The chapters of this *Handbook* have been written by leaders in this field of study, and have had the benefit of advice from a larger company of scholars. They do not purport to be syntheses of research findings. That is the task of textbooks. Rather, they are extensive bibliographical essays, offering disinterested surveys of the principal subfields of legislative research. They comprise a stock-taking which brings us up-to-date on what has been accomplished and suggests future research directions. Each chapter enumerates the major studies which have been done, particularly in the last generation, and interprets their findings in terms of the theoretical traditions guiding the work, the research questions which constituted the point of departure, and the available data.

Despite its endeavor to be comprehensive, this *Handbook* reflects the shortcomings of contemporary legislative research in the United States. It does not fully take into account scholarship published outside the United States, studies of non-American legislative institutions, research on pre-twentieth century legislatures, and the work of historians. The omission of that body of scholarship is not meant to disparage its importance. Rather, its omission reminds us all of the need to keep encouraging the development of a genuinely interdisciplinary and international research community, which alone can produce the theoretically grounded comparative research to which we all aspire.

The desirability of a *Handbook of Legislative Research* was first expressed by Heinz Eulau at a meeting of the "Legislative Studies Group" of the American Political Science Association in 1980. Eulau planted the idea, nurtured it, worked on its development, is author of one of the *Handbook's* chapters and co-author of another, and wrote the introduction. He is clearly the "first among equals" in the set of industrious and illustrious contributors to this volume. They made the task of the editors easy.

Bringing this *Handbook* from idea to reality in so short a span of time is the result of the effort of the dedicated, skilled, and talented staff of the Comparative Legislative Research Center which publishes the *Legislative Studies Quarterly.* Suzanne R. Gendler, Jane W. Jennings, and Joan E. Kellogg worked at various stages of publication. Mary Beth Kaminski played a major part in the composition of manuscripts and the checking of bibliographical entries in the text and the index. Barbara Yerkes performed a superb job of copy-editing the manuscripts and prepared the indispensable index. Michelle L. Wiegand managed the entire enterprise, as she has managed the Center and the *Quarterly* for nearly a decade, with rare conscientiousness and a devotion to the highest standards of publishing. The *Handbook,* like the field of knowledge it describes, has been a genuinely cooperative venture.

Gerhard Loewenberg
Samuel C. Patterson
Malcolm E. Jewell

Iowa City, Iowa
February 12, 1985

Contents

Handbook of Legislative Research

Introduction:
Legislative Research
In Historical Perspective

by

HEINZ EULAU

"Politics without history has no roots," Sir Frederick Pollock, the constitutional historian, observed long ago. The inventories of published research on legislative institutions, processes, policies, and behavior in this *Handbook* take stock of the field's scholarly accomplishments, but also failures, over the last 35 years or so. They attest to the veracity of Sir Frederick's admonition: even though there are often discontinuities in scientific development, research builds on research; and research impervious to its antecedents is footless and rootless. This recognition gives warrant to the kind of periodic reviewing of the relevant literature found in the chapters of this volume. However, while recent work on legislatures has been both prodigious and elaborate by any previous standards, it rests on important predecessors and, in turn, calls for some historical sensitivity. I therefore propose to consider here the problem of history in research on legislatures.

Three questions should be distinguished at the outset. First, what can political scientists—who are preeminently interested in contemporary legislative behavior, institutions, and policies—learn from modern historians who have produced important and interesting work on the origins, evolution, and historical contexts of legislative assemblies? Second, what can we still learn from the nineteenth- and early twentieth-century writers on legislative institutions? Third, how and why has the study of legislative institutions changed over time?

Recent Historical Research

Although their work is not always well known to political scientists, a substantial community of historians study the development of legislative assemblies in time—as they emerged in the Middle Ages, became established after 1500, and flowered in the nineteenth century. Historical scholarship on legislatures is important, as demonstrated in this *Handbook* by Margaret Susan Thompson and Joel H. Silbey, who survey research on nineteenth-century legislatures. While their chapter chiefly covers the U.S. Congress and the

1

British Parliament, modern historical scholarship is not limited to these institutions. Indeed, a separate chapter might well have been devoted to historical scholarship on continental European legislatures.

The interested political scientist has two readily available sources to draw on. One is the volume on *The History of Parliamentary Behavior*, edited by William O. Adyelotte (1977), which includes behavioral-historical studies on legislatures in Denmark, France, Britain, Sweden, Mexico, and Norway. Aydelotte's own introductory essay (pp. 3-26) is required reading for any legislative scholar who aspires to more than a historically flat understanding of the ways of parliaments. A recent special issue of the *Legislative Studies Quarterly*, edited by John B. Henneman (1982), includes seven fascinating articles on various aspects of medieval and modern European representative assemblies. Henneman's introduction (pp. 161-180) is of interest because it deals with some of the conceptual and definitional problems faced, for more than 40 years, in the historical studies sponsored by the International Commission for the History of Representative and Parliamentary Institutions.

The complaint is sometimes made that a younger generation of political scientists has lost a sense of history and that, in avoiding historical topics, scholars have impoverished their understanding of political institutions and processes. The complaint is unfounded. Contemporary political scientists in fact use longitudinal time-series data whenever it is available and have formulated questions which require the study of legislative institutions and processes over time. Moreover, given the division of labor within the social sciences, with their specialties and subspecialties, it makes eminently good sense for political scientists to rely on the "new historians" who, in their study of legislatures, have generously acknowledged their debt on matters of theory and method to the behaviorally-oriented political scientists.

The Results of Earlier Research

Methodological Development

Contemporary students of legislatures ignore at their peril the modes of inquiry which characterized earlier scholarship. It is from the historical and constitutional modes of the nineteenth century that the institutional and behavioral modes of the twentieth century have developed. This transformation has been less cataclysmic than is sometimes assumed. The transition was gradual, and there was, in fact, a "transition period," from about 1900 to 1950, which deserves more attention if contemporary modes of legislative analysis are to be properly understood. And to appreciate the transition period, one should know something about nineteenth-century constitutional scholarship. It is not unusual to refer to this work as "legalistic," at times in a rather contemptuous manner. What those using the term have in mind is by no means clear, but it presumably refers to the alleged hair-splitting, nit-picking nature of law-related discourse. But behind the hair-splitting and nit-picking loomed the great constitutional issues of parliamentary government as it emerged in the nineteenth century, notably the conflicts over representation and the separation of powers. The very best of the constitutional writers on these matters—Dicey (1889) in England, Jellinek (1900) in Germany, Esmein (1903) in France, and others—were concerned with the place of representative assemblies in the grand scheme of constitutional things, not a minor matter in a political perspective.

A transition period is of course circumscribed by what is "old," as just suggested, and what is presumably "new." If one seeks a name, at least in the U.S. context, this period may be best characterized by the adjective "pragmatic"; it was part of a much larger and widespread "revolt" (rather than revolution) against formalism and positivism, on the one hand, and idealism and moralism, on the other hand—all orientations that pervaded the new discipline of political science before the Second World War. In the legislative field, in particular, the "pragmatic revolt" found expression in two confluent trends—one toward a pluralistic interpretation of politics, the other toward realistic description. The former discovered the forces external to the legislature that impinge on its processes and products—the "pressure" or "interest" groups. Insofar as there was theoretical stimulus, it did not really come from Bentley (1908) whose work was largely ignored until Truman (1951) rediscovered it, but rather from the European pluralist writers who were frequently discussed in the theoretical literature in the United States (and severely criticized by Elliott, 1928, and Hsiao, 1927). However, not being doctrinaire as the European pluralists were, the U.S. scholars interested in "group politics" were not in search of a pluralistic utopia but strove for an empirically-based "new realism." Among the best of the relevant works are those of E. Pendleton Herring (1929) and Elmer E. Schattschneider (1935). This genre dominated legislative thinking well into the early 1950s when it was still articulated in the works of Bailey (1950), Latham (1952), and Gross (1953). But if one reads these late transitional studies carefully, one cannot but notice the rising impact of the new behavioral orientations.

The behavioral approaches had, of course, their own predecessors, reaching back to the work of A. Lawrence Lowell (1902), who made use of roll calls in comparing the British House of Commons and the U.S. Congress; Stuart A. Rice (1924, 1928), who made significant substantive and methodological contributions; and the Chicago "school" of political science (Merriam, 1925). As this line of transition is well covered in some of the chapters of the *Handbook,* there is no need to dwell on it here. More important is to remark on the synthesis which occurred in the 1950s with the confluence of the group-oriented institutionalism and the quantitatively-inclined behavioralism. Although some observers then and now have seen a conflictual duality between institutional and behavioral research in political science generally, this was simply not the case in the field of legislative studies. Behavioral analyses of the legislature were necessarily "institutional" because treating legislative behavior outside its institutional constraints and environment would have made little sense. And the more institution-focused studies could not avoid taking account of the behavioral analyses. Granted that some scholars stressed more one than the other aspect of legislative life, different approaches coexisted and influenced each other without the hard feelings sometimes engendered in some of the discipline's other subfields.

Cross-National Comparison

Into the transition period also fall the first efforts to compare legislative assemblies crossnationally. The strength of these efforts was their grand design and generally elegant style of writing; their weakness was, despite Lord Bryce's plea for "facts, facts, facts," the limited empirical data base on which they could draw. The group of writers involved is usually dubbed "institutionalist," but it is a rather inappropriate term. What these scholars would say about legislative processes and structural arrangements drew on constitutional history and included a good dose of classical political theory, but it was often speculative and opinionated, based on casual observations and anecdotal experiences, including more or less careful reading of the daily press. Their "descriptions" were embedded in comprehensive texts on "comparative government," as those of A. Lawrence Lowell (1896), James Bryce (1921), or Hermann Finer (1932). This literature reached its apogee in Carl J. Friedrich's *Constitutional Government and Politics* (1937), revised in 1941 and subsequently published under the title *Constitutional Government and Democracy* (1946). It was a work of great legal, historical, and theoretical erudition; and it was, in contrast to its predecessors, notably well documented and analytical.

The Themes of the Classical Works

Friedrich's work is still of interest and use today because it is an excellent introduction to the constitutional uncertainties of representative democracies and a persuasive example of how much can still be learned from earlier scholarship. These constitutional uncertainties, as already noted, derived from the relationship between the executive and legislative powers, on the one hand, and between these powers and the expanding electorate, on the other hand—the problem of democratic representation. Neither the parliamentary nor the presidential arrangement provided obvious solutions to the constitutional uncertainty, and the literature reflected this.

Although "parliamentary government" as we know it today had emerged in Britain between 1780 and 1830, it was not understood by the British themselves until Walter Bagehot published his influential treatise on *The English Constitution* in 1872. The failure to understand the parliamentary system was largely due to the pervasive influence of Blackstone's and Montesquieu's doctrine of the separation of powers in Britain and on the continent as well as in the United States. On the continent "parliamentarism" remained controversial, as reflected, for instance, in a still significant work by Robert Redslob (1924) that dealt with the situations in Britain, Belgium, Hungary, Sweden, France, Czechoslovakia, Austria, and Germany. An up-to-date compendium of European views of parliamentarism is an anthology edited by Kluxen (1980).

In the United States, Woodrow Wilson's *Congressional Government* (1885), still widely cited today, was purposefully modeled on Bagehot's book. "My desire and ambition," he wrote, "are to treat the American constitution as Mr. Bagehot . . . has treated the English constitution. His book has inspired my whole study of our government. He brings to the work a fresh and original method. . . ." However, Wilson did not model his work after Bagehot's "fresh and original method" but after his theory of the English constitution. He interpreted U.S. political practices from the standpoint of Bagehot's theory of parliamentary or cabinet government. Bagehot, too, had taken a comparative perspective, comparing the English constitution to the U.S. presidential system. But he did so to exorcise, once and for all, the doctrine of the separation of powers from interpretations of nineteenth-century British parliamentarism and certainly not to endorse presidential government as preferable, as Wilson considered cabinet government preferable. So, while Bagehot from the outset rejected the theory of the separation of powers as inapplicable in the study of the English parliamentary system, Wilson—counter to Bagehot's "method"—accepted the theory of the "fusion of powers" as the guiding criterion in his critique of the congressional system of his time.

Despite its erroneous interpretation but because of its felicitous style, Wilson's work continues to overshadow some other studies written in the United States which were not in fact as "legalistic" as they are sometimes loosely categorized. If one discounts certain biases of a cultural sort, the work of Follett (1896) on the speaker of the House, of McConachie (1898) on congressional committees, of Alexander (1916) on the history and procedures of the House, and of Hasbrouck (1927) on party government in the House, are of interest and use to the scholar seeking to understand "how things have come to be what they are." One must include here Robert Luce's (1922, 1924, 1930, 1935) excruciatingly detailed four-volume work on the Congress. Current interest in "institutionalization" and a "new institution-alism" (see Rohde and Shepsle, 1978) warrant renewed consideration of these works.

The tortuous growth of "representative government" should be of even greater interest, both to those "conservatives" whose understanding of representation derives mainly from Edmund Burke and to those "radicals" whose understanding derives chiefly from Jean-Jacques Rousseau. For the former, a reading of Sir Lewis Namier's *The Structure of Politics at the Accession of George III* (1929) is a salubrious corrective, as are the essays of the theoretically sophisticated institutionalist Ernest Barker (1945). For the latter, the nineteenth-century U.S. and British writers spoke of "repre-sentative government," but they did so without much attention to the evolving party systems. John Stuart Mill's *Representative Government,* published in 1861, largely ignored parties. As the political sociologist Robert MacIver has argued, Mill did not recognize the "class-bound character of the states within which democracy grew," and was unaware that "before the party-system could develop, the distinction between class and party had to be made effective" (1947, p. 211). A much-neglected work by Edward M. Sait, *Political Institutions: A Preface* (1938, Chapters 19-21) is still a useful, though conservatively biased, introduction to the nineteenth-century con-troversies concerning democracy and representation. Polsby's (1975) essay on "Legislatures," written in the literary tradition of institutional analysis but in a modern perspective, is a broad-gauged review of the issues involved.

Continuity and Change in Legislative Research

Explanation

I return now to the last of the three questions I raised at the outset: how and why has the study of legislative institutions changed over time? Part of the answer is in the overview I have given of legislative studies prior to 1950. That overview shows a slow transition from the themes and methods of the late nineteenth-century to those which characterized contemporary research. To some extent it is the continuity of the study of legislative institutions which is most evident. Quite consistently, practitioners of legis-lative research have been and are among the more sober students of politics. There is a "directness" in research on legislatures that stems from the observa-tional immediacy and political openness of the legislative institution. Students of legislative behavior and processes rarely can or will wander far from the paths which interaction between the investigator and the things investigated sets out for them. One looks directly at legislators as they speak, work, deal, vote, relate to colleagues and constituents, and so on. One looks directly at a committee as it is chosen, composed, meets, negotiates, investigates, decides, and so on. One even looks directly at the legislative chamber as a whole and its products. While not all that meets the naked eye is what it seems to be, and while there are probably many things that escape the naked eye, there is on the whole in the study of legislatures a close affinity between the "knower and the known." Thus it is, to paraphrase Edmund Burke, "the happiness and glory" of legislative scholars "to live in the strictest union, the closest correspondence, and the most unreserved communication" with their subjects or objects of inquiry.

The direct observation of legislative phenomena has in a way prevented distance between the scholar and his subject, and that lack of distance has left explanation at a relatively simple theoretical level. Historical research as well as interpretations and reinterpretations of historical works force us to ask why institutions are what they are, but this is a question rarely confronted in current empirical research on legislatures. The historian's answer is, of course, that they have come to be what they are as a result of changing conditions and circumstances in the past. The answer is no more absurd than some of the more sophisticated alternatives. It is no more absurd than the answer that institutions perform "functions" for other institutions or for individuals. Indeed, the latter appears to be the prevailing notion—as when it is said, for instance, that legislative committees "serve the goals" of their members (Fenno, 1973). There is nothing more "scientific" about this sort of functional explanation than there is about historical "explanation." In general, research on legislative behavior, processes, and institutions in whatever vein has been sober—not one of the criteria normally mentioned in texts on scientific method that give warrant to judgements about social or political research.

Cumulation

Legislative research may lack a sophisticated method or theory, but its findings have cumulated and developed, perhaps as a consequence of its rather well defined boundaries. The essays assembled in this *Handbook* attest to this cumulation. Legislative research is conducted in two contexts—the changing political context of the legislative institution itself and the changing context of social science theories and methods. It is not necessarily clear, therefore, whether the institution itself has measurably changed, or whether new data or approaches have been brought to bear on essentially the "same" institution. A scholar doing an interview study in the late 1950s had at best only two or three prior studies for guidance, and both interview technology and analysis were in a rudimentary stage of development. By contrast, the scholar working in the middle 1980s can draw on a multitude of relevant studies. Similarly, when Turner (1951) and Grassmuck (1951) published their roll-call studies of Congress, they could refer to less than a handful of prior quantitative studies, and their pre-computer-age analyses were rather simple. Today's roll-call analyst, as Collie shows in this *Handbook,* has an abundance of practical experience to rely on, a variety of theoretical models to choose from, and a powerful tool, the computer, for handling huge sets of data. It is difficult to say, therefore, whether contrasting findings between the 1940s and today indicate a cumulation of knowledge or indicate change in the observed world.

One becomes particularly aware of this dilemma if one inspects the volumes of "readings" on legislative behavior, processes, and institutions which have periodically appeared through the years. Because these volumes may have been neglected in the bibliographies accompanying the chapters of the *Handbook,* at least some of the more interesting ones might be listed, beginning with *Legislative Behavior: A Reader in Theory and Research,* edited by Wahlke and Eulau (1959). The purpose of the volume, composed mostly of reprinted but also some freshly written pieces, was to smooth the transition from the "older" to the "newer" approaches and orientations in legislative studies. The volume's section titles are symptomatic—"The Historical and Institutional Context of Legislative Behavior," "The Political Bases of Legislative Behavior," and "The Social and Psychological Bases of Legislative Behavior." Another volume, *Comparative Legislative Systems: A Reader in Theory and Research,* edited by Hirsch and Hancock (1971) and organized in the systems-analytical perspective of the 1960s, has among its section titles "Inputs into the Legislative System," "The Institutional Nexus," and "Legislative Decision-Making." Among other books of readings on U.S. legislatures, those by Peabody and Polsby (1963, 1969, 1977), Patterson (1968), Rieselbach (1970), and Dodd and Oppenheimer (1977, 1981) are noteworthy. Fresh research and writing are found in a number of volumes, like *Comparative Legislative Behavior: Frontiers of Research,* edited by Patterson and Wahlke (1972a); *Legislatures in Comparative Perspective,* edited by Kornberg (1973); or *The New Congress,* edited by Mann and Ornstein (1981). These research collections are evidence of the desire at least for cumulation, and they help us to interpret how much cumulation actually exists.

Infrastructural Development

The development of legislative research is in part a result of research organization. If the publication of the *Handbook of Legislative Research* is evidence that legislative research has come of age, "infrastructural" developments contributed to its maturity. The first of these, beginning in 1955, was the Social Science Research Council sponsored State Legislative Research Project which, in 1962, led to the publication of *The Legislative System,* by John C. Wahlke and his associates (see Wahlke, Eulau, Buchanan, and Ferguson, 1962). The second, initiated in 1964, was the American Political Science Association's Study of Congress, under the direction of Ralph K. Huitt and Robert L. Peabody (see Peabody, 1969, pp. 67-70). A third development, in the late 1960s, was the founding of the Consortium for Comparative Legislative Studies which, under the auspices of the Agency for International Development, stimulated and advanced legislative research in third-world countries (for reports on this research, see Kornberg and Musolf, 1970; Boynton and Kim, 1975; Smith and Musolf, 1979; Kim, Barkan, Turan, and Jewell, 1984). Finally, at the 1977 meeting of the American Political Science Association, an informal Legislative Studies Group organized under the leadership of Samuel C. Patterson. This group brought together, for the first time, scholars working on the U.S. Congress, U.S. state and local legislatures, and legislative assemblies abroad. The group sponsored "unaffiliated" panels at the Association's annual meetings, began publishing an occasional newsletter, and issued an annual directory of scholars active in legislative research. In 1983 the group was granted formal section status within APSA as the Legislative Studies Section and now lists its panels in the formal program.

Of more immediate interest in connection with the *Handbook of Legislative Research,* because of the editorial connection involved, was the appearance in February 1976, of the *Legislative Studies Quarterly*, published by the Comparative Legislative Research Center at the University of Iowa under the editorship of Malcolm E. Jewell, with Gerhard Loewenberg as the driving force and Samuel C. Patterson as a wise counsellor. Not only would this *Quarterly* become a long-needed specialized outlet for legislative research, but through a regular department, "Comparative Legislative Studies Newsletter," edited by Michael L. Mezey, it also became an essential informational resource for legislative scholars. The "Newsletter," recently renamed "Legislative Research Reports," includes abstracts of essays presented at conferences and of articles published in other journals; it periodically lists the chapter titles of significant, recently published books and the titles of recent doctoral dissertations in the field; it announces forthcoming professional meetings and the panels to be held at these meetings; it reports on "research in progress" and provides much other useful information on the organizational life of the scholarly community interested in legislatures, both in this country and abroad.

A rudimentary analysis of the contents of the *Quarterly* provides some insight into the recent interests of legislative scholars. In the first eight years of its publication (not including the "*Handbook* series") the *Quarterly* published 206 articles. Articles on the U.S. Congress dominate— hardly a surprising result. Of the 83 congressional studies, 19 deal with elections, 9 with constituency linkages or representation, and 3 with public attitudes toward the institution. In other words, almost 40 percent of the congressional articles are geared to "popular government," as it used to be called, and attest to the importance which scholars assign to the popular foundations of the "legislative power" in the United States.

Studies of parliaments in the Western European and British Commonwealth nations are also well represented, with 51 articles altogether. About 49 articles are "comparative"—that is, they compare at least two units and include crossunit aggregative treatments. But over half of the comparative studies deal with U.S. state legislatures, while only seven compare Western European assemblies and another seven compare European legislatures with the U.S. Congress. Whatever interpretations one may attach to these figures (and one should not make too much of them because comparative studies appear in other journals as well), legislative scholars are still predominantly one-country (or one-unit) specialists. And while the relatively large number of U.S. state studies suggests that this arena is fertile ground for further exploration of and experimentation with the comparative method, one may note that only two studies compare state legislatures with the U.S. Congress—symptomatic of a division of labor not necessarily conducive to general theorizing about legislatures.

The Future

This *Handbook of Legislative Research,* then, is another landmark in the evolution of legislative studies. In the immediate future, I expect, research on legislatures and related matters is likely to be much the same as it has been in the immediate past, with some theoretical advances and methodological improvements made possible by computer technology. This prospect of gradual and uneventful development, it seems to me, provides an opportunity to reflect once again on the place of the changing legislative institution in the grand design of constitutional government—not in the manner of the nineteenth-century social philosophers and moralists or of the early twentieth-century legal positivists and political pluralists, but in the manner of an empirically-based interpretative social science. I stress that such reflection and interpretation be empirically based because I certainly do not mean opinion or statement of preferences, however well justified, if unsupported by systematic analysis of observations.

At issue, it seems to me, is not only the need to locate the research enterprise in the larger real-world context of constitutional government but also to bring to bear on this effort the weight of theoretical understanding and empirical evidence that have been amassed by the scholarly community and that make this *Handbook of Legislative Research* a practical enterprise. But unless present knowledge is also used in broad-gauged consideration and reconsideration of the legislature's role in representative government, a great opportunity for giving legislative research socially justified warrant will be lost.

Regarding the more distant future I would expect, though this is perhaps more a hope than an expectation, that legislative scholars will increasingly turn to team research and comparative intranational or cross-national studies. In contrast to the related field of electoral research, legislative studies have been unduly individualistic and parochial, some exceptions notwithstanding. Yet, the mass of data on all aspects of legislative life needed for comprehensive understanding of legislatures through space and time can no longer be the province of individual investigators. Legislative institutions the world over have grown enormously in number and complexity, requiring the coordination and collaboration of scholars. Without that coordination, the necessary division of labor would degenerate into trivial observations on one or another aspect of the legislature as a whole and its role or functions in the democratic polity. Team research and resources considerably more generous than here-to-fore made available are on the agenda of the more distant future.

Equally likely, if legislative research is to get off dead center, is the development of more and better comparative research, whether within or between nations. This development is related, of course, to the growth of team research and the availability of resources. With a few exceptions, the bulk of legislative research has involved the study of single legislatures in this country or abroad. But the proliferation of such studies does not make for either cumulation or comparison in a truly scientific manner. It is to be hoped that a new generation of scholars will have the linguistic knowledge to make collaboration with colleagues in several countries possible and thus extend the range of understanding by genuine comparison. And comparison cannot be restricted to countries where legislative institutions more or less successfully function; it needs to be extended to countries where they fail. Understanding failure, it seems to me, is necessary for understanding success. This requires the most difficult of assignments for legislative research—the comparison of dissimilarities in legislative behavior, processes, policies, and structures. I hope that some of the inventories in this *Handbook of Legislative Research* will point the way to this distant future.

REFERENCES

Alexander, DeAlva S. 1916. *History and Procedure of the House of Representatives.* Boston: Houghton-Mifflin.
Aydelotte, William O., ed. 1977. *The History of Parliamentary Behavior.* Princeton: Princeton University Press.
Bagehot, Walter. 1872. *The English Constitution.* London: Nelson.
Bailey, Stephen K. 1950. *Congress Makes a Law.* New York: Columbia University Press.
Barker, Ernest. 1945. *Essays on Government.* Oxford: The Clarendon Press.
Bentley, Arthur F. 1908. *The Process of Government: A Study of Social Pressures.* Chicago: University of Chicago Press.
Boynton, George R. and Chong Lim Kim, eds. 1975. *Legislative Systems in Developing Countries.* Durham, NC: Duke University Press.
Bryce, James. 1921. *Modern Democracies.* 2 vols. New York: Macmillan.
Dicey, Albert V. 1889. *Introduction to the Study of the Law of the Constitution.* 3d ed. London: Macmillan.
Dodd, Lawrence C. and Bruce I. Oppenheimer, eds. 1981. *Congress Reconsidered.* 2d ed. Washington, DC: Congressional Quarterly. 1st ed., 1977.
Elliott, William Y. 1928. *The Pragmatic Revolt in Politics.* New York: Macmillan.
Esmein, Adehar. 1903. *Elements de Droit Constitutionnel Francais et Compare.* 3d ed. Paris: Larose.
Fenno, Richard. 1973. *Congressmen in Committees.* Boston: Little, Brown.
Finer, Herman. 1932. *The Theory and Practice of Modern Government.* 2 vols. New York: Dial Press.
Follett, Mary P. 1896. *The Speaker of the House of Representatives.* New York: Longmans-Green.
Friedrich, Carl J. 1937. *Constitutional Government and Politics.* New York: Harper.
_____ . 1946. *Constitutional Government and Democracy.* Boston: Ginn and Company.
Grassmuck, George L. 1951. *Sectional Biases in Congress on Foreign Policy.* Baltimore: Johns Hopkins University Press.
Gross, Bertram M. 1953. *The Legislative Struggle: A Study in Social Combat.* New York: McGraw-Hill.
Hasbrouck, Paul D. 1927. *Party Government in the House of Representatives.* New York: Macmillan.
Henneman, John B. 1982. "Editor's Introduction: Studies in the History of Parliaments," *Legislative Studies Quarterly* 7:161-180.
Herring, E. Pendleton. 1929. *Group Representation before Congress.* Washington, DC: The Brookings Institution.
Hirsch, Herbert and M. Donald Hancock, eds. 1971. *Comparative Legislative Systems: A Reader in Theory and Research.* New York: The Free Press.
Hsiao, Kung C. 1927. *Political Pluralism: A Study in Contemporary Political Theory.* New York: Harcourt, Brace.

Jellinek, Georg. 1900. *Allgemeine Staatslehre*. Berlin: Haring.

Kim, Chong Lim, Joel D. Barkan, Ilter Turan, and Malcolm E. Jewell. 1984. *The Legislative Connection: The Politics of Representation in Kenya, Korea, and Turkey*. Durham, NC: Duke University Press.

Kluxen, Kurt, ed. 1980. *Parlamentarismus*. Koenigstein/Ts.: Verlagsgruppe Athenaum, Hain, Scriptor, Hanstein.

Kornberg, Allan, ed. 1973. *Legislatures in Comparative Perspective*. New York: McKay.

Kornberg, Allan and Lloyd D. Musolf, eds. 1970. *Legislatures in Developmental Perspective*. Durham, NC: Duke University Press.

Latham, Earl. 1952. *The Group Basis of Politics*. Ithaca, NY: Cornell University Press.

Lowell, A. Lawrence. 1896. *Government and Parties in Continental Europe*. Boston: Houghton-Mifflin.

————. 1902. "The Influence of Party on Legislation in England and America," *Annual Report of the American Historical Association for 1901* 1:321-545.

Luce, Robert. 1922. *Legislative Procedure*. Boston: Houghton-Mifflin.

————. 1924. *Legislative Assemblies*. Boston: Houghton-Mifflin.

————. 1930. *Legislative Principles*. Boston: Houghton-Mifflin.

————. 1935. *Legislative Problems*. Boston: Houghton-Mifflin.

MacIver, Robert M. 1947. *The Web of Government*. New York: Macmillan.

Mann, Thomas E. and Norman J. Ornstein, eds., 1981. *The New Congress*. Washington, DC: American Enterprise Institute.

McConachie, Lauros G. 1898. *Congressional Committees*. New York: Crowell.

Merriam, Charles E. 1925. *New Aspects of Politics*. Chicago: University of Chicago Press.

Mill, John Stuart, 1861. *Representative Government*. London: Oxford University Press, 1912.

Namier, Sir Lewis. 1929. *The Structure of Politics at the Accession of George III*. London: Macmillan.

Patterson, Samuel C., ed. 1968. *American Legislative Behavior: A Reader*. Princeton, NJ: Van Nostrand.

Patterson, Samuel C. and John C. Wahlke, eds. 1972a. *Comparative Legislative Behavior: Frontiers of Research*. New York: Wiley.

Peabody, Robert L. 1969. "Research on Congress: A Coming of Age," in Ralph K. Huitt and Robert L. Peabody, eds., *Congress: Two Decades of Analysis*. New York: Harper & Row, pp. 3-73.

Peabody, Robert L. and Nelson W. Polsby, eds. 1977. *New Perspectives on the House of Representatives*. 3d ed. Chicago: Rand McNally. 1st ed., 1963; 2d ed., 1969.

Polsby, Nelson W. 1975. "Legislatures," in Fred I. Greenstein and Nelson W. Polsby, eds., *Handbook of Political Science*. Vol. 5. Reading, MA.: Addison-Wesley, pp. 257-319.

Redslob, Robert. 1924. *Leg Regime Parlementaire*. Paris: Girard.

Rice, Stuart A. 1924. *Farmers and Workers in American Politics*. New York: Columbia University Press.

————. 1928. *Quantitative Methods in Politics*. New York: Appleton.

Rieselbach, Leroy N., ed. 1970. *The Congressional System: Notes and Readings*. Belmont, CA: Wadsworth.

Rohde, David W. and Kenneth A. Shepsle. 1978. "Taking Stock of Congressional Research: The New Institutionalism," Department of Political Science, Washington University in St. Louis, *Political Science Papers*.

Sait, Edward M. 1938. *Political Institutions: A Preface*. New York: Appleton-Century.

Schattschneider, Elmer E. 1935. *Politics, Pressures and the Tariff*. New York: Prentice-Hall.

Smith, Joel and Lloyd D. Musolf, eds. 1979. *Legislatures in Development*. Durham, NC: Duke University Press.

Truman, David B. 1951. *The Governmental Process*. New York: Knopf.

Turner, Julius. 1951. *Party and Constituency: Pressures on Congress*. Baltimore: Johns Hopkins University Press.

Wahlke, John C. and Heinz Eulau, eds. 1959. *Legislative Behavior: A Reader in Theory and Research*. Glencoe, Il: The Free Press.

Wahlke, John C., Heinz Eulau, William Buchanan, and LeRoy C. Ferguson. 1962. *The Legislative System: Explorations in Legislative Behavior*. New York: Wiley.

Wilson, Woodrow. 1885. *Congressional Government*. Boston: Houghton-Mifflin.

PART ONE

Legislators and Constituencies

Chapter 1

Legislative Recruitment And Legislative Careers

by

DONALD R. MATTHEWS

Who belongs to legislative assemblies and how they got there are questions which have attracted the attention of a wide variety of scholars. Researchers interested in political elites, in social stratification, in the political role of personality, in the processes of modernization, and many other large matters have studied the backgrounds and careers of legislators. And next to college sophomores, legislators may be the most accessible subjects for social science research around. The result is a large amount of research which seems, on its face, to have little to say to students of legislative institutions. (For review of this general literature, see Lasswell, Lerner, and Rothwell, 1952; Matthews, 1954a; Bell, Hill, and Wright, 1961; Keller, 1963; Marvick, 1968; Czudnowski, 1975; Putnam, 1976.)

Students of legislatures have not ignored this topic either. A good many have included information on the recruitment and careers of legislators in their writings. It seems safe to these authors to assume that the skills, attitudes, and goals of legislators are the product of their total life experiences. Thus, knowledge about who legislators are and how they got to be there should contribute to a better understanding of legislative behavior and institutions. Yet after several decades of unprecedented achievement in legislative research, this linkage is still mainly an assertion. Just as introductory comparative government textbooks have their mandatory chapters on "The Land and the People," general works on legislatures have their chapters on "The Members." Neither is taken very seriously by the authors or readers. (See the leading textbooks on U.S. and comparative legislatures: Blondel,

17

1973; Jewell and Patterson, 1977; Keefe and Ogul, 1981; Loewenberg and Patterson, 1979; Olson, 1980.)

If students of legislative recruitment and legislative careers are to progress beyond providing "interesting" descriptive material they must do a better job of demonstrating how recruitment matters. Thus, during this review of the literature on legislative recruitment and careers I shall be looking for answers to these and related questions: In what ways, if at all, do different patterns of legislative recruitment and careers affect the behavior of legislators? Do these same variables affect the legislature's capacity to resolve conflicts and make reasonable policy decisions? In what ways, if at all, do these phenomena affect the legislature's ability to build or reenforce governmental legitimacy?

While I have sought to review the literature on legislative recruitment for all times and in all places, limitations of time, space, and competence have led to a paper which emphasizes (although is not confined to) works in the English language on the United States and western Europe.

Opportunities

Studies of legislative recruitment demonstrate at least one proposition beyond doubt: opportunities to serve in legislatures are quite unevenly distributed in all societies. The magnitude and dimensions of this bias in the selection of legislators vary from one system to the next and over time, but it remains substantial almost everywhere.

Social Status and Political Recruitment

Legislators are far from being "an average assortment of ordinary men," as Harold Laski once described the British House of Commons. Almost everywhere legislators are better educated, possess higher-status occupations, and have more privileged backgrounds than the people they "represent." This has been found to be the case in the U.S. Senate[1] and House of Representatives,[2] among American state legislators,[3] and in city councils.[4] The same general findings have emerged from dozens of studies of legislatures in other advanced, industrial societies,[5] in developing countries,[6] and in contemporary Communist regimes.[7] Few generalizations have been more exhaustively supported by empirical research.

But this research has had limited explanatory power. Background attributes of legislators are collected (usually from legislative manuals and biographical directories) and tabulated, and frequencies are compared (sometimes only implicitly) with the distribution of these same personal attributes in the population at large. Sizeable divergencies suggest that the legislative recruitment process is "biased" in favor of individuals possessing "overrepresented" attributes. This procedure, by itself, does not explain why the bias exists or how the selection process works to favor some categories of persons and disadvantage others. Most of the studies have been of a single legislature in a single country over a short span of years; the possibilities of comparative analysis (over time and across cultures) have yet to be fully exploited. Few researchers in this tradition engage in much internal analysis of this data, either; crosstabulations by political party membership are about as far as most have gone.

Why and how do relatively high social status and relatively favorable opportunities to serve in legislatures go together? Prevailing explanations are not entirely satisfying.

Aberbach, Putnam, and Rockman (1981), on the basis of their major comparative study of bureaucrats and parliamentarians, conclude that inequality in access to higher education is the primary reason for this phenomenon in western Europe. But the U.S. has both a greater status gap between congressmen and citizens and a more egalitarian higher educational system than European countries. Other factors are clearly at work on this side of the Atlantic. Prewitt (1970), on the basis of his study of the recruitment of city councilmen in the San Francisco Bay area, stresses self-selection and the importance of prior political interest and political activity. With but rare exceptions, legislators tend to be chosen from among the group of politically interested, active, and involved people. Since political interest and activity is positively associated with high social status, legislators on the average end up being from higher social strata than the less active and involved people they represent.

Other processes are also at work. Private wealth can be a distinct asset to a legislative career, particularly in entrepreneurial political systems, where candidates must raise their own campaign resources. Studies of winning and losing candidates for the U.S. Congress and the Canadian Parliament find winners to be of higher social status than losers (Huckshorn and Spencer, 1971, chs. 2 and 3; Fishel, 1973, ch. 2; Kornberg and Winsborough, 1968). This suggests that voters may prefer candidates of higher status than themselves. But alternative explanations of this finding are many. A far less hazardous way to explore the role of voter preferences in the class bias of legislative recruitment would be via survey research. To my knowledge, no one has done so yet.

Variations on a Theme

While a status gap between legislators and their constituents seems a constant feature of legislative life, the magnitude of the gap can and does vary. For example:

1. The social status of the average legislator tends to be higher in national legislatures with much formal authority than in local or regional legislative bodies with less authority (see Matthews, 1954a; Putnam, 1976; Frey, 1965, 400ff). The formal position of the legislature within the political system shapes the sociological characteristics of its normal members significantly.

2. The status gap between legislature and citizens tends to be far greater in developing countries, with their often tiny, educated elites, than in more "advanced," affluent countries with higher standards of living and widespread literacy.

3. The magnitude of the status gap has narrowed substantially with the development of universal adult suffrage, the adoption of proportional representation, and the development of strong socialist parties. This "democratization" of the legislative membership has been well documented in nineteenth- and early twentieth-century Europe. Interestingly enough, there has been little discernible movement in this direction in the United States Congress. Bogue, Clubb, McKibbin, and Traugott conclude their massive study of the backgrounds of all members of the House of Representatives from 1789 to 1960 with this statement: "Little change can be observed in the characteristics and experiences of representatives before entry into House service" (1976, p. 300). And in the contemporary parliaments of at least some European countries, the historical trend toward lower-status legislators seems to be reversing as socialist parties, confronted with a shrinking constituency of manual workers, reach out for white-collar and middle-class support.

4. While legislators as a group enjoy high social status, they tend to be less atypical in their social backgrounds than chief executives, top-level civil servants, or economic elites (Aberbach, Putnam, and Rockman, 1981; Hacker, 1961; Guttsman, 1951, 1974; Matthews, 1974; Mills, 1956).

Lawyers and Other Talkers

Lawyers have constituted from 40 to 65 percent of the members of Congress since 1789 (Bogue, et al., 1976). Explanations of this phenomenon differ. Max Weber (1946) stresses the "dispensibility" of lawyers, the ease with which they can combine politics on a part-time or intermittent basis with legal practice. Combining a legislative career with other high-status occupations is usually more difficult and risky than it is for a lawyer. Other scholars stress the acquisition of skills appropriate to legislative roles in the course of legal training and experience (Lasswell and McDougal, 1948; Gold, 1961). Joseph Schlesinger (1957) points out the critical importance in the U.S. of the lawyers' monopoly over elective law enforcement and judicial offices: these offices provide incentives for political activity and avenues of political ascent not available to nonlawyers (see also Hain and Pierson, 1975). Eulau and Sprague (1964) devote a short monograph to the thesis that the "convergence" of the legal and political profession explains both why lawyers preponderate in U.S. political life and why state legislators who are lawyers do not behave very differently from state legislators with other occupations.

Where some of these factors are not present, the number of lawyers in legislatures can be small. In Denmark, for example, Pedersen (1972) points out that few lawyers engage in private practice and that the career concerns of young jurists are actually disadvantaged by service in the Folketing. The number of lawyers in parliament dropped sharply with the advent of class-based political parties and proportional representation, until in recent years only about 4 percent of the members of parliament are lawyers.

Thus the preponderance of lawyers in legislatures is mostly a U.S. phenomenon. A more constant occupational bias in the recruitment of legislators is a decided tilt toward people with verbal jobs—teachers, journalists, and bureaucrats as well as lawyers.

The Second Sex

The big losers in legislative recruitment everywhere have been women. In the United States, only 2 percent of all members of Congress (between 1917 and 1964) and only 4.5 percent of all state legislators (1920-1961) were women (Werner, 1966, 1968; Kohn, 1980; see Stewart, 1980 for local office-holding). As this chapter is being written there are 21 women in Congress (3.9 percent). Moreover, as Bullock and Heys (1972) remind us, 41 percent of all females who served in Congress prior to 1979 were appointed to vacancies created by the deaths of their husbands; these women usually dropped out of the institution quickly thereafter. "Over His Dead Body" seems to be a declining mode of access (Kincaid, 1978; Bullock, 1972; Merritt, 1977; Gertzog, 1979, 1980), and the women in Congress are coming from increasingly diverse occupations and age groups after following more conventional (i.e., male-style) careers. Still, the fact remains that lawmaking in the U.S. remains essentially a man's game.

Other countries do a little better (Duverger, 1955, p. 15; Blondel, 1973, pp. 78-79; Putnam, 1976, pp. 32-33; Kohn, 1980), but only in Scandinavia and in the Soviet Union (Hill, 1973) and some other Communist systems does the proportion of women in national parliaments begin to approach one half. Even in the Communist systems, efforts to further expand the political participation of women have not always been successful (Lapidas, 1975; Seroka, 1979; Cohen, 1980).

There is a rather large literature which attempts to explain why there are so few women politicians and legislators. Kirkpatrick, on the basis of her study of U.S. state legislators, concludes:

The principal constraints that impede women's full participation in the power processes of society appear to be rooted in prevailing role distributions rather than in anatomy, physiology, male conspiracy, or even in the basic values of society. Education, occupational experience, place of residence, average age of entry into a legislative career are all products of the sex role system (1974, p. 239).

In all these ways potential women politicians are disadvantaged in the U.S.— by lesser educational and occupational achievement, only partially offset by greater opportunities for volunteer civic activities and political party work (Welch, 1978; Merritt, 1977; Dubeck, 1976; Mezey, 1978b); by less geographical mobility and a later career start, resulting from family and child-rearing responsibilities. The "management of conventionally incompatible roles" in the U.S. is not easy, as Kirkpatrick makes abundantly clear. But it seems no easier in Britain (Comstock, 1926; Brookes, 1967; Vallance, 1979) or in many of those countries with more female legislators than the U.S.

The structure of the U.S. political system—with its weak political parties, entrepreneurial style of primary nominations, candidate-oriented election campaigns, and single-member district constituencies—seems to discriminate against women politicians. Especially at the congressional level, most women ambitious enough to try to overcome the inhibitions run underfinanced races for hopeless seats, polling a few votes less than the man who ran and lost last time (Darcy and Schramm, 1977; Deber, 1982; Van Hightower, 1972; Kelley and McAllister, 1983). In countries with stronger parties, nominations controlled by established party leaders and proportional representation elections women have a somewhat easier time of it (Brichta, 1974-1975). When this type of political system is combined with unusually positive attitudes toward sexual equality, as in Scandinavia, the result is a relatively heavy representation of women in parliaments (Haavio-Mannila, 1983; Means, 1972; Skard, 1981).

The Structure of Legislative Opportunities

Most research on legislative opportunities has focused on the impact of social structure. But the legal and institutional structure of the political system itself affects the attractiveness of legislative service.

Thus the British House of Commons may play an insignificant role in policy making, but as the only channel to top executive office it has the special attractiveness of "the only game in town" for the politically ambitious. Separated executive and legislative institutions, like those in the United States, result in multiple career lines and much competition for political talent

FIGURE 1
A Typology of Legislatures,
By Attractiveness of Service

		Opportunities for Upward Mobility	
		High	Low
	High	U.S. Senate	U.S. House of Representatives
Opportunities for Policy Influence	Low	Typical American State Legislature	Typical Small-Town Councils
		British House of Commons	

between them. Parliamentary systems in which top executives are not chosen exclusively from the national legislature may represent an intermediate position. Of course, the upward mobility potential of legislative offices do change over time—the rise of the U.S. Senate as a stepping stone to the presidency during the last 20 years is instructive on the point (Matthews, 1974; Peabody, Ornstein, and Rohde, 1976).

An opportunity to play an influential role in legislative policy making is another incentive for legislative service which is affected by the overall political arrangements. Legislatures which are dominated by executives and/or are characterized by strong party discipline may be less attractive to potential members than ones in which individual legislators can play some role beyond voting the party line. Thus Social Democrats in western Europe seem to find service in parliaments less appealing than adherents of less centralized and disciplined political parties. Long periods of weak executives (and especially of minority Governments) may make national legislatures more politically significant arenas and hence more attractive places to be (see Isberg, 1982).

When these two dimensions—opportunities for shaping public policy and for upward mobility—are combined, a preliminary typology of legislatures is the result (Figure 1). The placement of actual legislatures within that typology is, of course, highly debatable.

Such mundane factors as the size of legislatures, their terms, their level of compensation and fringe benefits, their geographical locations, and their demand of a part-time or full-time commitment, all affect the costs and benefits of legislative service to different individuals. Thus, low legislative salaries presumably favor the well-to-do, the retired, and the subsidized, while discriminating against their opposites. A full-time legislature located at a distance from major population centers may attract very different members than a part-time one located in a large city, and so on. Such matters have been little studied (but see Wiggins and Bernick, 1977; Oxendale, 1979).

Joseph Schlesinger's *Ambition and Politics: Political Careers in the United States* (1966) was the first systematic study of some of these issues. By studying the office-holding careers of U.S. politicians, Schlesinger shows that the movement of politicians in and out of national, state, and local offices in the U.S. are patterned and relatively predictable. Some public offices, for example, are highly transitory (e.g., state governor), while others are typically held for multiple terms and longer periods (U.S. senator or congressman). Some offices give their incumbents exceptional opportunities to run for other offices: the two offices may share the same electorate or the same political arena or have overlapping terms. Political ambitions are directed and focused by a structure of political opportunity. Politicians with lofty ambitions are attracted to public offices which have served as stepping-stones for others; their behavior in office is shaped by anticipated future constituencies. When political recruiters search for attractive candidates they look where they have found them before. "In the game of politics the political as well as the social system determines the players" (Schlesinger, 1966, p. 12).

Does It Matter?

Does it make any difference whether legislators are better educated, enjoy higher social status, or are far more often male than the people they represent? The research literature has yet to answer that question.

The social and political backgrounds of legislators have been linked to aspects of their behavior in office. Matthews (1960) finds that the backgrounds of U.S. senators seem to affect the rate at which new members are socialized into the Senate, their areas of specialization, their committee performance, and their chances of achieving leadership positions. Snowiss (1966) has demonstrated how the "political machine" style of political organization in Chicago leads to the recruitment of an identifiable type of congressman sharply different in legislative style from Detroit or Los Angeles Democrats. And Fiellin, in an undeservedly obscure article (1967), illustrates how the social backgrounds and prior political experiences of the New York City Democrats in the House of Representatives contributes to their ineffectiveness in Washington. Githens and Prestage (1978) find that women state legislators tend to be most active in health, education, and welfare issues, stereotypically areas of female concerns, and to be excluded from leadership positions. Kornberg and Mishler (1976) in Canada, Hellevik (1969) in Norway, and Guttsman (1951) in Britain find that parliamentary leaders have higher social status than rank and file parliamentary members. Of course, these are statistical associations, causal explanations of these behaviors would involve far more than prelegislative experiences.

The social and political backgrounds of U.S. legislators do not seem to be highly predictive of their roll-call voting. Derge (1959, 1962), for example, finds that lawyers in state legislatures vote about the same way as nonlawyers; Eulau and Sprague (1964) build their theory of the "convergence" of the legal and political professions on this same lack of difference. Even women politicians in one state legislature did not differ significantly from male state legislators on feminist policy votes (Mezey, 1978a).

The voting of legislators has not been extensively studied in assemblies with more heterogeneous memberships than U.S. legislatures have. (Legislatures with a significant number of working-class members usually have strong parties and disciplined voting, which discourages individual level analysis.) The most important exception is Soren Holmberg's study of the Swedish Riksdag (1974) which finds that working class members of parliament are, on the average, to the left of members who are farmers or from the upper and middle classes. But this relationship is reversed when examined within each of the parties; Social Democrats with upper-class backgrounds are more radical than Social Democrats from the working class (pp. 390-391). In Sweden (and one suspects elsewhere in western Europe) the left wings of all parliamentary parties have professional backgrounds, the right wings tend to be capitalists, small businessmen, and farmers, and the center of all parties tend to be workers and salaried employees.

There is a fairly sizeable literature which seeks to explain variations in the role orientations of legislators (Wahlke, Eulau, Buchanan, and Ferguson, 1962; Sorauf, 1963; Bell and Price, 1969; Kornberg, 1967; Davidson, 1969; Prewitt, Eulau, and Zisk, 1966-1967). Jewell's valuable review of this literature (1970) finds few consistent, statistically significant relationships between social background and legislative role orientations.

These scattered and inconclusive research results certainly do not add up to a finding that the social, economic, and gender biases of legislative recruitment result in a consistent policy bias of legislative institutions. The results are consistent with the lack of strong and consistent relationships between social background variables and the policy attitudes of other elite populations (Edinger and Searing, 1967). But perhaps this bias does make a difference at certain times and circumstances. Czudnowski in a recent essay on political elites (1982, pp. 5-6) suggests that the social backgrounds of elites were good predictors of elite policies until recent times, when increasing pluralism, social mobility, and the development of "catch-all" political parties with heterogeneous memberships have blurred the historic connections. He further argues that the ties between the social and class backgrounds of ruling elites and their policies may be reestablished in times of crises in the future.

Students of legislators have yet to consider whether the privileged status of most legislators affects the capacity of legislatures to deal with public problems in a reasonable way. Does the high educational levels of legislators enhance their knowledge and the institution's ability to deal with complex issues? It seems plausible to assume that the outcomes of legislative recruitment affect the legislature's success as a legitimizing agency: a British House of Commons consisting exclusively of Oxbridge graduates or a U.S. Senate made up exclusively of white male millionaires would not seem to contribute to the happy acquiescence of the masses these days. But so far, legislative studies have not spoken to these issues.

Motives, Incentives, Goals

In 1945, the Conservative party of Bergen, Norway placed the name of a local hero of the World War II Resistance Movement on their electoral list for the national elections. He was elected to parliament—and promptly sued! The Norwegian constitution explicitly states that persons elected to the Storting must serve. But the Conservative party had used Sjur Lindebraekke's name without his consent; he did not belong to the Conservative party, he did not campaign, and he did not wish to serve. The courts ruled that Lindebraekke must serve anyway. This is the only case known to me of a person becoming a legislator against his will.

Why do some people want to become legislators, while most people do not? Does it make any difference what the motives, incentives, or goals of legislators are?

The Political Personality

One of the more intriguing hypotheses in political science is that politicians have a distinctive type of personality which causes them to seek out (or to be recruited by others into) political office. Harold Lasswell (1930, 1936, 1948) has been the leading proponent of this view. Politicians, according to Lasswell, are characterized by an "intense and ungratified craving for deference" which is "displaced upon public objects" and "rationalized in terms of the public interest" (1948, p. 38). *"Power is expected to overcome low estimates of the self"* (1948, p. 39), he emphasizes. Lasswell applied these ideas in several case studies of the political behavior of historical figures, mental patients, and some local judges and politicians.

While Lasswell has many admirers, few have applied his ideas in systematic empirical research; the practical and methodological problems of studying the personalities of public figures are so severe that few have even tried.[8] McConaughy (1950) was the first to test Lasswell's ideas by studying legislators. A battery of personality and opinion tests were administered to 18 state legislators in South Carolina and to two small control groups of nonpoliticians. The results were mixed at best: the legislators proved to be less neurotic and less introverted, more self-sufficient, dominant, and lacking in inferiority feelings than the control groups. Over a decade later Browning and Jacob (1964) gave thematic aperception tests (TATs) to small groups of politically active and politically inactive persons in "Eastern City" (presumably New Haven, Connecticut) and in two Louisiana parishes. The politicians tested (including some legislators) were not clearly different from nonpoliticians. They concluded,

Simply being a politician does not entail a distinctive concern for power, or for achievement or affiliation. The data for Eastern City and the Louisiana parishes are consistent with the propositions that relatively plentiful opportunities for power and achievement in the economic arena channel strongly motivated men into economic rather than political activity; that in communities where politics and political issues are at the center of attention and interest, men attracted to politics are likely to be more strongly power- and achievement-motivated than in communities where politics commands only peripheral interest (pp. 89-90).

In a subsequent article, Browning (1968) elaborated on this finding by suggesting a model of the political recruitment process based upon the interactions of personality and political system characteristics. His model contains two major paths leading to political candidacy and office holding: self-initiative and recruitment by party leaders. He suggests that persons following these two routes to public office may have rather different personalities, motivations, and goals. Comparisons of TAT scores of small groups of politically active and politically inactive businessmen in "Eastport" (still New Haven?) support this view. Those with higher achievement and power scores tended to be self-starters, to run for offices with relatively greater power-yielding opportunities, and to aspire to higher public office.

Probably the most successful effort to relate the personalities of legislators to their behavior is James David Barber's *The Lawmakers: Recruitment and Adaptation to Legislative Life* (1965). This study, based upon interviews and questionnaire responses of first-term members in the lower house of the Connecticut legislature, divides the legislators into four types, depending upon their activity in the legislature and willingness to continue service in it.

	Willing to Return	*Not Willing*
Active in Legislature	Lawmakers	Advertisers
Not Active in Legislature	Spectators	Reluctants

Usually recruited from politically noncompetitive small towns, spectators enjoy the conviviality and excitement of the legislature but take little part in its substantive work. Advertisers are typically young, upwardly mobile lawyers from urban constituencies who are seeking occupationally beneficial contacts. Reluctants are elderly and rural members, motivated by a sense of duty; lawmakers are the interested and active good guys who make the legislature work.

   Barber's description of these types and their recruitment and adaptation to the life of the Connecticut legislature is unusually interesting and rich in insight. Individuals adapt to being legislators in ways which satisfy different personal needs. Thus, self-concept has a great deal to do with shaping the behavior of legislators. For three types—the spectators, advertisers, and reluctants—much of this behavior is compensation for low self-estimates. The lawmakers, on the other hand, tend to have higher self-estimates and to be less concerned with bolstering or protecting their egos. Recruiting and keeping a sizeable cadre of lawmakers is essential for a legislature (at least one of the U.S. type) to function well.

   Ziller, Stone, Jackson, and Terbovic (1977; see also Stone and Baril, 1979) came to somewhat contrasting conclusions. They studied two aspects of personality—self-esteem and complexity of the self-concept—and their joint effects on the success of politicians running for state legislative seats and on the behavior of these elected in the legislature. They sum up their studies in Oregon and Maine in these words:

Self-esteem and complexity of self-concept, taken together, bear a remarkably consistent relationship to political success, at least for state legislators. Two of the four self-other orientations are related to both electoral success and legislative success. These two types of self-other orientations we have labelled the pragmatist (low self-esteem, high complexity) and the ideologue (high self-esteem, low complexity) orientations. The results suggest that the state legislator who is a pragmatist is alert and responsive to the desires of his constituents while running for election and, after elected, to the desires of his legislative colleagues. On the other hand, the state legislator who is an ideologue is more issue-oriented in his candidacy and, when elected, is quite active in the legislative arena (p. 203).

   The "ideologues" described here bear some resemblance to Barber's "lawmakers" and the "pragmatist" to Barber's "advertisers," although the two works are very different. The Barber study suffers from ill-defined and unmeasured variables and a greater willingness to "listen with the third ear" than most political scientists consider prudent. Ziller and his colleagues are mechanical and unimaginative by comparison and less politically savvy, but their research, unlike Barber's, can be replicated. The later style is likely to prove more useful in the long run (see Carlson and Hyde, 1980; Jaffee, 1981).

   Almost all empirical studies of legislative personalities have been of U.S. legislators. The most important exception to this is Gordon DiRenzo's research on Italian deputies (1967a, 1967b). In 1961, DiRenzo administered a shortened version of Rokeach's dogmatism scale, standardized for Italian usage, to a representative sample (n=129) of national legislators and to a control group of nonpoliticians. He found the Italian parliamentarians had more dogmatic, power-oriented, and authoritarian personality structures than non-politicians. However, this was true only for parties of the center and right, while the Communist, Socialist, and Liberal party deputies were slightly less dogmatic than their fellow partisans in the control group. DiRenzo explains this apparent anomaly by pointing out that the Italian parties of the left have less open and democratic recruitment of parliamentary candidates than the parties of the center and right. Party leaders—either knowingly or unknowingly—tend to choose candidates who will be reliable followers. Self-recruitment in the Italian setting of the 1960s favored dogmatic and authoritarian personalities. In a subsequent study of state legislators in Michigan and Indiana, DiRenzo (1977) found that the modal personality of the U.S. legislators was less dogmatic and authoritarian than the personalities of U.S. nonpoliticians.

Empirical research on the personalities of legislators has been limited in quantity and of uncertain quality, but it has succeeded in muddying the waters considerably since Harold Lasswell's day. Certainly, the Lasswellian ego-compensation hypothesis has not been supported. What research there is leads us to expect a wide variety of personality structures among legislative politicians, depending upon such things as the dominant values of the political culture, the ways in which legislators are recruited, and the complexity of constituencies. The personalities of legislators seem to matter more at some times and in some situations than in others, and we have yet to specify these adequately.[9]

The interactions between the personalities of legislators and other explanatory variables may be so complex in the real world that we must resort to strategies of benign neglect or drastic simplification.

Incentives

One way of avoiding some of the problems of dealing with "personalities" and "motivations" without totally ignoring psychological variables is to study "incentives." This strategy has been used with some success in organizational theory and in nonlegislative research settings.[10] The principal advocates of incentive analysis for legislators have been James Payne and Oliver Woshinsky (Payne and Woshinsky, 1972) who between them have published studies of the incentives of members of the Colombian Congress (Payne, 1968), national political leaders in the Dominican Republic (Payne, 1972), and French deputies (Woshinsky, 1973).

Incentives, as conceived by Payne and Woshinsky, are not the same thing as goals, but are quite specific and pronounced emotional needs which are satisfied by political participation. Politics is a demanding and risky business. Persons who take part at the highest levels must gain much personal satisfaction therefrom or they would spend their time and energy doing something easier, more enjoyable, less risky. Politicians are driven people and incentives are the things which drive them.

The number of incentives that Payne and Woshinsky have found in their studies is small. Payne (1968) found only two in Colombia; Woshinsky (1973) only four among French deputies. Other studies have led them to posit that seven incentives are the most important ones for high-level politicians, such as legislators (Payne, 1972, p. 3):

Incentive	Satisfaction
Program	Working upon specific, concrete public policies
Status	Attaining and exhibiting prestige
Adulation	Receiving the affection and praise of others
Mission	Committing oneself to a transcendental cause
Obligation	Relieving anxieties of conscience
Conviviality	Pleasing others and being accepted by them
Game	Competing with others in highly structured interactions

The bulk of Payne and Woshinsky's published work has been devoted to fleshing out and illustrating these types (especially the first five) by quotations from their intensive interviews with legislators and other politicians. While this material is persuasive, most readers probably will wish that Payne and Woshinsky had conducted more extensive and systematic reliability checks on their coding than seems to have been the case. Their finding that "almost invariably" politicians have but one incentive is hard to accept without more support.

Nonetheless, what evidence there is suggests that legislators behave in a fashion consistent with their primary incentive and that the dominant incentive(s) of legislators affect legislative institutions, and vice versa. In Colombia, for example, Payne (1968, ch. 11) found the primary incentive among congressmen to be "status," and he argues that a legislature dominated by status incentive will be characterized by chronic absenteeism, inactive committees, few research facilities, disruptive and conflict-provoking patterns of behavior, and ineffective legislating. Woshinsky's study of the members of the French National Assembly suggests many interesting connections between incentive type and the legislator's role conceptions, attitudes, and orientations toward politics, and patterns of behavior in the legislature (see 1973, pp. 16-19 for summary table).

Rational Office Seeking

"Ambition lies at the heart of politics," Schlesinger writes in his *Ambition and Politics*. "Politics thrives on the hope of preferment and the drive for office" (1966, p. 1). Political ambition can take several forms: it may be discrete (a desire for a specific office for a single term), static (a desire to make a long-run career out of a particular office), or progressive (a desire to hold an office more important than the one now held or sought). No matter which, Schlesinger assumes that the politician's behavior is a rational response to his office goals. Thus, a state legislator who wishes to become governor will behave differently from one who is happy where he is or who wants to go back home.

Schlesinger's book came at a time when "economic," deductive theorizing about politics as rational goal seeking had recently been introduced by Downs, Riker, and others. He demonstrated how the same approach might be applied to empirical research in a somewhat different field. The result has been a literature testing and elaborating Schlesinger's original ideas and findings.

The City Council Research Project at Stanford University spawned a number of these articles. Prewitt and Nowlin (1969), on the basis of interviews with city councilmen in the San Francisco Bay area, found that ambitious councilmen tended to adopt the perspective and attitudes associated with the higher offices to which they aspired—a partial confirmation of a key Schlesinger assumption. Gordon Black, using the same data on Bay-area councilmen but a more ponderous set of concepts, found a similar difference between the ambitious and nonambitious councilmen (1970). Black's "A Theory of Political Ambition" (1972) formalizes the calculations of the rational office seeker in this formula:

$$U(0) = (PB) - C$$

where B = the benefit that an individual will receive from achieving an office;

P = the candidate's estimate of the probability that he can obtain an office should he attempt to seek it;

C = the cost required during a campaign to obtain an office; and

U(0) = the utility of an office for the individual prior to the elections.

Rational office seekers will not run for office unless $U(0)$ is positive and greater than the utility that might be derived from alternative ways of investing their resources $[U(0) > U(A_i)]$.

Several hypotheses are derived from this cost/benefit model and partially tested with Bay Area Study data. For example, both the size of a community and the degree of competition in its local elections affect the risks (P) which politicians face and the investment that is required (C) to win office. Thus, only those expecting large benefits (B) will run for office in large, competitive districts.

Students of Congress were also quick to follow Schlesinger's lead. In 1970, Mezey published the first description of the opportunity structure for the House of Representatives, based upon the careers of more than a thousand members serving between 1949 and 1967. A year later, Fishel (1971) brought out an article examining the ambitions of all nonincumbent candidates for the House of Representatives in the election of 1964.

Mayhew's *Congress: The Electoral Connection* (1974) focuses on static political ambition—the desire for reelection—and how it affects the behavior of congressmen and the processes and outcomes of congressional politics. He begins with the assumption that all congressmen are single-minded and rational seekers of reelection. What kind of activity does that goal imply? The resulting picture, presented in one of the most influential essays in recent years, depicts behavior and institutional practices which are strikingly familiar to Congress-watchers. A great deal of what transpires on Capitol Hill can be explained by the static ambitions of congressmen. If Congress becomes less attractive to its members—as seems to be happening in recent years—one can expect some important changes in institutional ways to follow.

Schlesinger began his study of political ambition by looking at persons who behaved ambitiously. Virtually all studies of political ambition have followed in this retrospective tradition. David Rohde's "Risk-Bearing and Progressive Ambition" (1979) represents a significant advance, since it develops a model to predict which members of the U.S. House of Representatives will run for higher office (i.e., for state governor or U.S. senator). The variables included in the model are the probability of winning the higher office, the value of the higher office, the value of the present office, and the "risk-taking" propensity of members. Rohde assumes that all members of the House are progressively ambitious—that is, would accept a Senate seat or governorship if it were offered without cost or risk. "Thus static ambition is not something chosen a priori, but is a behavior manifested by a member because of the risks of the particular opportunity structure he finds himself in, and his unwillingness to take these risks" (p. 3). The article develops a number of (mostly nonobvious) hypotheses about the conditions under which congressmen will, or will not, run for higher office. A preliminary testing of these hypotheses with data from 1954-1974 (when there were 3,040 opportunities for House members to run for higher office and 111 of these opportunities, or 3.7 percent, were taken) tends to support his hypotheses.

Studies of legislative recruitment which assume that legislators are rational goal seekers have become popular in the U.S. The results of this trend toward a more "economic," deductive, and formal approach to legislative studies have been impressive. So far, though, students of non-U.S. legislatures have manifest little interest in this mode of analysis.

Processes

How do people become legislators? The short answer to this question for almost all contemporary legislatures is "by popular election." A less formal and more realistic answer would be "by a lengthy process with several stages, the last of which is usually some kind of popular election." The number of these stages, their proper descriptions, and their relative importance are subjects about which scholars disagree.

Seligman, King, Kim, and Smith (1974, ch. 2) divide the process into three stages: certification, selection, and role assignment. Prewitt (1970) compares the process of selecting leaders to a Chinese box puzzle with smaller and smaller boxes nesting in one another, an image which indicates the narrowing of the total population to a few governors.

More important than the number of stages and their labelling is the point that becoming a legislator involves several selective stages after becoming "eligible" or "certified" or "politically active" but before the final electoral contest. It is the literature on this stage in the selection process which we shall now review. Legislative elections will not be covered in this essay.

The Initial Decision to Run

Without persons willing to serve in them, legislative assemblies cannot survive. Without some competition for these seats, the legislators' claim to "represent" the people is problematical. It is therefore surprising that the initial decision to run for legislatures has been little studied. Formal models of the decision-process have been proposed, but empirical studies are few.

Huckshorn and Spencer's *The Politics of Defeat: Campaigning for Congress* (1971) and Fishel's *Party and Opposition: Congressional Challenges in American Politics* (1973) do look at the people who run for Congress and their reasons for running. Both studies are based primarily upon mail questionnaires returned by nonincumbent candidates for the House in 1962 (Huckshorn and Spencer) and 1964 (Fishel). Huckshorn and Spencer divide their subjects into candidates from marginal districts (who had some chance of winning) and "all losers," whose statistical chances of winning were very poor. Huckshorn and Spencer stay very close to their questionnaire data, which is mainly concerned with nominations and campaigning. Fishel's work is more speculative and wide-ranging, providing a multifaceted picture of congressional challenges in a most atypical election year. Fishel also follows the winning candidates into their early years of service in the House.

Kazee (1980) interviewed 25 unsuccessful congressional challengers, each of whom had been defeated at least twice, about their experiences. While there were differences between them, their overall response to defeat was surprisingly upbeat. Running for Congress was a personally rewarding experience to many of these experienced losers. Even the most negative aspect of the situation—the overwhelming electoral advantages of incumbents—contributed to the attractiveness of a seat in Congress as a career goal for them.

The competitive situation within congressional districts is not a constant; "off year" elections tend to favor candidates from the "out" party, and national events can lead to electoral tides favoring one party or another. Jacobson and Kernell (1981) argue persuasively that the anticipations of national electoral trends by local elites lead directly to the behavior that fulfills those expectations. "More and better candidates appear when signs are favorable; worse and fewer when they are unfavorable" (p. 34). Strategic resources—money, personnel, publicity—tend to flow to candidates who look like winners. Thus highly decentralized and uncoordinated recruitment processes end up responding to national forces.

Studies of the initiation of candidacies at the state and local levels are more numerous and detailed. Frank Sorauf's *Party and Representation* (1963) is a landmark study of the role of political parties in the recruitment and election of candidates in Pennsylvania in the late 1950s. In that state, Sorauf concludes,

the political party dominates the candidate and legislator selection system. In addition to exercising its classic role in the general election, it intervenes freely in the primary elections and supervises the preprimary recruiting activities. . . . Plainly, Pennsylvania parties, strong and vital by any standard, have not been greatly discomforted by the primary. In fact, one can reasonably argue that they have turned it to their purposes by making it another hurdle for the unanointed candidate (pp. 118-119).

Seligman et al. (1974) depict a very different picture in their detailed and conceptually innovative study of legislative nominations in Oregon. They write:

Among the variety of groups and individuals that sponsor legislative candidates (primary groups, interest groups, civic associations, political party leaders, factional leaders and legislative leaders), political parties are neither the most important nor are they even first among equals. To be sure, the direct primary prevents a political party from officially endorsing particular candidates. Yet, even sub rosa, party leaders do not exercise much influence in instigating candidates, except in the case of the minority party in the districts with one dominant party (p. 185).

Primary groups—friends, family, acquaintances—and interest groups are important in encouraging candidacies. These ties are reinforced in the process of campaigning, since the candidate's sponsors serve as the nucleus of his or her campaign organization, and the successful candidate's sponsorship becomes a determinant of his behavior in power. (These groups are the legislator's "personal" and "primary" constituencies, in the terminology of Fenno's *Home Style* [1978].)

Prewitt's theoretically-oriented case study of the recruitment of city councilmen (1970) was carried out in a nonpartisan setting. When asked about how they became local legislators, the California councilmen frequently mentioned the influence of other persons—friends and family, community activists, and incumbent councilmen and public officials. Over half had served in nonelective posts in city government and civic groups. An informal apprenticeship and cooptation system had developed to fill the vacuum created by the absence of party leaders (p. 114).

The role of political parties in recruiting candidates for U.S. legislatures obviously varies from one jurisdiction to the next. The major determinants of that variation discussed in the literature are electoral laws: whether the election is partisan or nonpartisan, whether nominations are made by open or closed primaries or by conventions (see Key, 1956, ch. 6; Tobin, 1975).

The V.O. Key Hypothesis

In his classic *Southern Politics* (1949, see especially ch. 14), the late V.O. Key, Jr. argues that selecting public officials in electoral contests between numerous unscreened, unlabelled, and self-starting candidates favors certain types of politicians. This process favors incumbents and those with high name recognition, a capacity to raise campaign resources, and media skills. Such a system encourages short-time perspectives and "position taking" over the sustained pursuit of long-term policy goals. Thus the net effects of electoral politics where parties play little or no role are to favor the established and comfortable people over the less well-off segments of society. Key developed this hypothesis, which has been among the most important ideas in U.S. political science for a generation, within the unique contexts of the South and its gubernatorial politics. But Key's hypothesized linkages between political processes and public policy can be explored in a variety of settings, including legislatures. Some of the studies of nonpartisan city councils represent a start (Lee, 1960). A few scattered articles tend to find that American state legislators recruited by political parties are more professional, career-oriented politicians linked more closely to their legislative parties than those recruited in other ways (Tobin, 1975; Tobin and Keynes, 1975; Thurber, 1976; Keynes, Tobin, and Danziger, 1979). But the opportunity to test, clarify, and expand upon Key's insights has yet to be taken seriously by legislative scholars.

Selection Processes Abroad

Legislator selection processes have not been studied extensively outside the U.S. Great Britain is the main exception. Austin Ranney's *Pathways to Parliament* (1965) and Michael Rush's *The Selection of Parliamentary Candidates* (1969) provide detailed and basically similar views of this "secret garden of British politics." In the 1960s, the choice of parliamentary candidates by the major parties was made in secret by local party elites. Generally, the critical "short-listing" stage in the process was dominated by a committee of a dozen or so local activists over whom the national party had no sure control. But this decentralized process did not result in undisciplined legislative parties, as it does in the U.S. The local party machinery was "manned by activists primarily loyal to the national parties' leaders and causes. Each is established for one essentially national purpose: to elect a Member of Parliament" (Ranney, 1965, pp. 281-282). Local control in the British system has very different results from local control in the U.S. system.

Bochel and Denver (1983) have recently published a major study of the selection conferences which pick parliamentary candidates in the Labour party. They are interested in the apparent paradox in that party whereby "left-wing local activists produce by their choices a right-dominated parliamentary party" (p. 68). This seems to have occurred because most selectors are concerned primarily with "vote-getting ability and the personal qualities of candidates" rather than their ideology. Furthermore, the selectors want to win and know the electorate is more middle-of-the-road than themselves.

British politics is changing in a number of other respects (see Norton, 1980). There have been scattered experiments with closed primaries in both the Labour and Conservative parties (Holland, 1981) and the Liberal party has gone even further toward opening up the selection process to full meetings of constituency members (Beaumont, 1974). Party cohesion in Parliament is not what it used to be, and there are signs that a different type of person is finding his way into national prominence (King, 1974, 1981). It is time for a replication and updating of Ranney and Rush. And the selection process for local councillors in the United Kingdom has scarcely been studied at all (for an exception, see Brand, 1973).

The selection of candidates for the Canadian Parliament displays a mixture of qualities found in the U.S. and Britain (Kornberg and Winsborough, 1968; Mishler, 1978). The process is decentralized into the hands of constituency party leaders, but stresses the candidate's personal qualities and campaigning ability more than does the process in Britain. The relative influence of candidates and local party leaders in the selection process is shifted somewhat towards the candidates in Canada, but remains a far cry from the candidate-dominated U.S. system.

Outside the Anglo-American democracies, the literature becomes very sparse. Valen's research on nominations to the Norwegian parliament (1966) is one of the few empirical studies which looks at how local party leaders put together electoral lists in a proportional representation system. These processes have consequences: candidates on the top of party lists in Norway are systematically different from candidates near the bottom, who have no chance of election without massive electoral shifts. The top positions on electoral lists tend to be heavy with incumbents, candidates holding local public office, and candidates from areas in which their respective parties have strong local organizations. The social status of the normal candidate goes up toward the top of the list of middle-class parties; top Labour and Communist nominees display increasing degrees of involvement in "the movement." The inexperienced, the young, women, and persons of marginal status in their respective parties have easier access to the lower (i.e., losing) list positions. This, however, is probably better than those individuals would do in a two-party, single-member district electoral system.

Czudnowski's valuable analyses of legislative recruitment in Israel (1970, 1972) concludes that proportional representation encourages group-oriented recruitment rather than recruitment focused on the skills, qualities, and loyalties of individual candidates. The recruitment process in Israel can be thought of as having two stages: 1) a decision concerning the eligibility of a group for a position on the list and 2) the selection of a candidate to represent that group. He proposes a number of variables which determine political party control over the process of determining group eligibility and candidate selection.

Obler's two articles on the selection of parliamentary candidates in Belgium (1973, 1974) provide an excellent analysis of the difficulties of putting together lists of candidates for proportional representation elections in a socially and linguistically divided country. As in Britain and the U.S., in Belgium the national legislative nominations are made at the local constituency level. But competition for the few places near the top of each party's list can be fiercely zero sum, leading to serious threats to party unity which the national party leadership must seek to resolve. Many of the local nominating decisions in Belgium are made by private, intraorganization elections in which dues-paying party members decide the slate. The results of these "primaries" often do not fully represent the array of interests needed to maximize support in the general election, and then national leaders may manipulate or override primaries to insure socially balanced electoral lists.

Despite this handful of good studies, it seems safe to say that the study of legislative nominations in multiparty systems with proportional representation elections has scarcely begun.

Careers

Serving in a national legislature has become a full-time job almost everywhere; legislators often hold office for a significant part of their lives. Modern-day national legislators are becoming "professionals" or "careerists." Even at the subnational level the trend is toward longer periods of service and greater stability of membership (see Shin and Jackson, 1979, for American state legislatures). A sizeable literature (mostly on the U.S. Congress) attempts to describe this "professionalization" of legislatures and to probe its causes and consequences.

From Amateurs to Careerists

"In the beginning," H. Douglas Price writes, "all American legislative bodies were quite non-professional" (1975, p. 3). Legislative service was a short-term, part-time, and nonrecurring commitment. Under the Articles of Confederation, rotation in legislative office was obligatory; by law, members of the Continental Congress could serve only three of every six years. A strong suspicion of legislative careerism persisted in the U.S. well into the nineteenth century, and local rotation agreements limiting the length of service in Congress to one or two terms were common (Kernell, 1977; Struble, 1979-1980).

The distinguished senators of the 1st Congress set the early career patterns for that chamber: they fled the Capital—not yet located in Washington—almost as fast as humanly possible. Five of the original twenty-six hastened to resign even before completing their initial terms, most of which were for only two or four years (they had drawn lots to determine who would serve two-, four-, or six-year terms). One chanced to die in office, and two who had been selected for short-terms had the unusual misfortune to seek re-election and fail. Eight were re-elected, but six of these had been on short-terms. The remaining ten managed to serve out their terms (or sentences to obscurity), but did not seek another round. By the time the Capital was moved from Philadelphia to the swamps of Washington, only two of the original twenty-six senators remained, and in two more years they were gone (Price, 1975, p. 5).

While the House of Representatives got off to a somewhat better start, it too was characterized by very high turnover, most of it the result of voluntary retirements. There were 465 departures from the House of Representatives between 1811 and 1820, and only 49 of these could be attributed to electoral defeat (Price, 1975, p. 9).

How and why did the U.S. Congress change into a highly professionalized body?

Research on this question began with Stuart Rice's *Quantitative Methods in Politics* (1929). The goal of this book was to persuade political scientists of the utility of statistical methods. One of Rice's illustrations was a 1790 to 1924 time series on the age and lengths of service of members of the House of Representatives. But it was over 35 years before students of Congress saw anything very interesting in Rice's long array of numbers. Then in the 1960s H. Douglas Price, Richard Witmer, and Nelson Polsby finally did.

Price, beginning with an unpublished but widely circulated paper written in 1964, prepared a series of influential articles (Price, 1971, 1975, 1977) describing the U.S. Congress in the early nineteenth century and comparing it with the same institution in the post-World-War-II years. Very high turnover, frequent resignations, and frequent and unpredictable changes in the internal distributions of power characterized both House and Senate throughout the entire pre-Civil-War period (see also Young, 1966). The

Senate first achieved a reasonable degree of membership stability after the end of Reconstruction. Price credits this development to the growing importance of political parties and the Senate's constitutional powers over federal patronage. Certainly by the 1860s the Senate had become an attractive place for a politician to be (see Rothman, 1966).

The House of Representatives, according to Price, did not achieve a comparable degree of "professionalization" until after the party realignment of 1896, which increased the number of safe seats drastically. The spread of the Australian ballot system at about the same time reduced the likelihood of minority party congressmen losing their seats in purely partisan "contested election" proceedings, a common occurrence earlier in the nineteenth century. Taken together, these changes lowered the risks and increased the attractiveness of congressional service to the politically ambitious.

Witmer (1964) made a less promising start. Observing the drastic increase in tenure of congressmen in the late nineteenth and early twentieth centuries, he tried to explain much of it on the basis of increasing life expectancy of members and decreasing average age of entry. Such an actuarial approach would have made more sense if more members had died in office, but the high turnover of the early years was mostly the result of other factors.

Polsby (1968) interpreted the growing tenure of congressmen as one element of a larger phenomenon, the "institutionalization" of the House of Representatives. Successful organizations in the modern world must be "institutionalized" he argued. All institutionalized organizations have three major characteristics: clearly defined boundaries, internal complexity with a division of labor, and a commitment to universalism (rather than particularism) and automatic (rather than discretionary) means of conducting its internal business. The growing number of careerists in the House signifies a clarification and "hardening" of boundaries between the House of Representatives and other parts of the system. The development of powerful standing committees and the increasing utilization of seniority as a means of choosing committee chairmanships (Polsby, Gallaher, and Rundquist, 1969) are further indications of the "institutionalization" of the House of Representatives.

Polsby's work is unnecessarily teleological: the same developments which he sees as a successful adaptation to environmental change can be viewed as signs of institutional decay (see Huntington, 1973). But taken together with Price's research, Polsby's two articles add up to a powerful historical explanation of how long and continuous service in the House became both possible and highly desirable.

There have been several efforts to revise and extend Price's and Polsby's work. Fiorina, Rohde, and Wissel have published a useful article on historical change in House turnover (1975) which points out that the measure of congressional turnover used by Rice and Polsby (percentage of the total membership in their first terms) tended to inflate turnover until the House of Representatives reached its current size in 1917. Each new addition of seats added new members who were not replacements for members of the previous Congress. They propose a new measure ("percent replacements"), recalculate the time series developed by Rice and Polsby, and reexamine the causes of turnover.

Kernell (1977) has studied three factors which reduced House turnover between 1820 and 1910: the reduction in party competition; the increasingly attractive nature of careers in the House, which led more members to seek reelection; and the decline in frequency of voluntary rotation agreements in the congressional districts. Using some ingenious indirect measures, he finds that all three factors contributed to membership stability in the House, but that the primary cause was the growing desire of members to serve there.

Price and Polsby, Gallaher, and Rundquist tend to focus on the declining number of newcomers in the House during the nineteenth century. Bullock (1972) reverses that perspective and focuses on the growing number of senior House members—those winning more than 10 elections—since 1910. These "careerists," he points out, have increased from 2.8 percent of the House in 1911 to 20.0 percent in 1971. He also finds a growing electoral vulnerability of House careerists, apparently as the result of the emergence of new political issues and conflicts in the late 1960s. Research on the reelection chances of incumbent senators points to a similar vulnerability to electoral defeat of the more senior senators in recent years (see Matthews, 1960, p. 241; Hinckley, 1970, pp. 839-840; Kostroski, 1978; Tuckel, 1983).

Research on the "professionalization" of legislatures has been conducted almost entirely in the U.S. House of Representatives. Pedersen's work on the Danish Folketing (1976, 1977) is an exception. He finds evidence to support the view that the Danish parliament has tended to become more "institutionalized" between 1849 and 1960. Kjell Eliassen and Pedersen (1978) have done a comparative study of the professionalization of the Norwegian Storting and the Danish Folketing which finds some similarities and puzzling differences between the rates, timing, and levels of legislative professionalization in these two countries. Finally, James Q. Graham (1982) has recently conducted a study of careers in the French Chamber of Deputies and the U.S. House of Representatives. While the effects of greater regime instability in France are manifest in the patterns of legislative careers, the similarities between the two countries are perhaps even more impressive.

While not based on systematic data, Anthony King's recent essay on career politicians in Britain (1981) adds to the conclusion that studies of the "professionalization" of legislative careers in non-U.S. settings might do much to add to our understanding of the relationship between legislative careers and institutional change.

The Decision to Retire

In every Congress since 1966 except one, voluntary retirement from the House of Representatives has increased. A similar, though less pronounced, trend can be seen in U.S. senatorial careers. The development toward a more "careerist" Congress seems to have halted or even reversed in the 1960s. There have been a number of attempts to find out why.

Cooper and West (1977, 1981-1982) look at the traditional explanations of retirement from Congress—age, political vulnerability, and higher political ambition—and find that none of them explain this new trend. The average age of the retirees has been declining, along with the average age of all House members. Most of the voluntary retirees have come from safe districts; indeed the electoral vulnerability of House members has gone down as retirements have increased. There has been only a modest increase in the number of House retirees who run for higher office, usually the Senate. The primary reason for the increase in retirements from the House, Cooper and West argue, has been a growing dissatisfaction with service in the House. Ironically, many of the changes in the House which contribute to the incumbent congressmen's electoral advantage over challengers have made the job of congressman more onerous and unpleasant than it was a few decades ago.

Stephen Frantzich (1978a, 1978b), after studying the careers of 358 congressmen retiring between 1965 and 1974, comes to much the same conclusion: while the causes of voluntary retirements are multiple, job frustration is the dynamic new element in the picture. John Hibbing (1982a, 1982b), on the basis of interviews with House retirees in 1978, finds that both the direct costs and opportunity costs of serving in the House of Representatives have increased in recent years. And recent internal reforms—especially the weakening of the seniority role in selecting committee and subcommittee chairs—have reduced the benefits of long continuous service. Hibbing quotes from one of his interviews:

It used to be no one wanted to quit because they were always getting closer to the brass ring. Today they figure "why wait around for fifteen years when it might not do any good?" Besides, most members these days have as much power in their second term as they will in their eighth (Hibbing, 1982b, p. 69).

The study of legislative retirements has been confined almost exclusively to the U.S. Congress. The relatively high turnover in American state legislatures (Hyneman, 1938; Hyneman and Lay, 1938; Rosenthal, 1974; Ray, 1974; Hain, 1974; Shin and Jackson, 1979) has resulted in some applied research on how service in them might be made more attractive (Wiggins and Bernick, 1977; Oxendale, 1979).

Outside the U.S., the only comparable studies have been of drop-outs and careerists in British local government councils and in the Dutch parliament (Budge and Farlie, 1975; Farlie, Budge, and Irwin, 1977; Irwin, Budge, and Farlie, 1979; Budge, Farlie, and Irwin, 1981).

Legislative Careers and Institutional Change

Over the last decade or so, some progress has been made in demonstrating how changes in political recruitment and career patterns affect legislative institutions and vice versa. Indeed Swenson (1982), in an important article on the structure of power in the U.S. House, argues that congressional recruitment practices are the single most important explanation of institutional change in the Congress during the late nineteenth and early twentieth centuries. From 1870 to 1910, power was increasingly concentrated in the hands of the Speaker; after 1910, power was gradually dispersed as committees and individual members grew more independent. During the late nineteenth century, local party machines came to dominate recruitment process; they selected party careerists as congressional candidates, loyal to the organization and willing to accept the authority of congressional leaders. The twentieth century saw the decline of party organizational control over nominations and the emergence of the entrepreneurial congressman who won his seat on his own. Once in the House, these congressmen reorganized the institution to suit their own individualistic styles and reelection goals.

The systematic evidence in support of this interpretation is not overwhelming, but the theory is more than plausible. And at least some of its propositions are testable through empirical study of contemporary legislatures.

Some Concluding Comments

We began this essay by asking whether legislative recruitment really mattered. This review of the literature has not led to a clear answer to the question.

We have found a large, descriptive literature on the socioeconomic and psychological characteristics of individual legislators. While this line of research has contributed to knowledge in a number of other fields, it has made little direct contribution to the study of legislative institutions and processes. Relationships between the personal backgrounds of legislators and their attitudes and behavior in office have been demonstrated in numerous studies, but these associations are complex and severely bound in time and space. More often than not, other modes of explanation prove more economical and plausible. Thus, viewed as independent variables explaining the behavior of legislators or as inputs shaping legislative systems, recruitment has been pretty much a wash. But perhaps this is not the best way to look at the recruitment of legislators.

Recently a number of studies have appeared which view legislative recruitment largely as dependent or intervening processes rather than as independent variables (or inputs). These studies focus on legislative careers rather than static attributes of legislators, on institutions rather than individual behavior, and on change rather than stability. These shifts in the orientation of legislative recruitment studies may well be a part of what March and Olsen (1984) call "the new institutionalism" in political science. Be that as it may, these studies seem to show (or in some cases just assume) a greater autonomy for legislative institutions than was previously the fashion.

Legislative institutions themselves, their organization and their manner of conducting business, have major effects on the type of men and women who are elected to them. Persons who "fit" the legislature tend to stay on; the misfits exit, voluntarily or otherwise. Thus selective recruitment and derecruitment tend to reinforce the institutional status quo. But legislative institutions change along with the types of people attracted to serve in them, and students of the U.S. Congress have begun to depict these interactions between an institution and its members. Viewed in this way, legislative recruitment studies move much closer to center stage.

NOTES

I wish to thank Barbara Gehrels for research assistance, C.L. Kim and Anthony King for their helpful comments, and the Institutt for samfunnsforskning, Oslo, Norway, for a congenial setting for the preparation of the final draft of this paper.

1. Haynes, 1938, Vol. 2, ch. 20; Matthews, 1954b, 1960, ch. 2, 1961; Rothman, 1966, ch. 4.

2. McKinney, 1942; Davidson, 1969, ch. 2; Bogue, Clubb, McKibbin, and Traugott, 1976; Ornstein, Mann, Malbin, and Bibby, 1982, ch. 1.

3. Hyneman, 1940; Epstein, 1958, ch. 6; Wahlke, Eulau, Buchanan, and Ferguson, 1962, Appendix 5; Sorauf, 1963; Barber, 1965; Seligman, 1974.

4. Dahl, 1961; Prewitt, 1970.

5. *Great Britain:* Namier, 1929; Ross, 1948; Berrington and Finer, 1961; Guttsman, 1963; Buck, 1963; Mellors, 1978. *France:* Dogan, 1961; Hamon, 1961; Beck, 1974; Cayrol and Perrineau, 1982. *Germany:* Kirchheimer, 1950; Loewenberg, 1967, ch. 3; Fishel, 1972; Herzog, 1975. *Italy:* Sartori, 1961a, 1961b, 1963, 1967; Cotta, 1982. *The Netherlands:* Daadler and S. Hubee-Boonzaaijer, 1970; Daadler and van den Berg, 1982. *Sweden:* Holmberg, 1974, chs. 8-10. *Norway:* Valen, 1966; Hellevik, 1969; Eliassen and Pedersen, 1978. *Denmark:* Pedersen, 1972, 1976, 1977; Eliassen and Pedersen, 1978. *Finland:* Noponen and Pesonen, 1964; Pesonen, 1972. *Spain:* de Campo, Tezanos, and Santin, 1982. *Israel:* Akzin, 1961, 1967; Seligman, 1964; Czudnowski, 1972. *Canada:* Kornberg and Thomas, 1965-1966; Kornberg, 1967, ch. 3; Kornberg and Winsborough, 1968; Kornberg, Clarke, and Watson, 1973; Kornberg, Falcone, and Mishler, 1973; March, 1974; Kornberg and Mishler, 1976. *Australia:* Martin, 1956.

6. *Turkey:* Frey, 1965. *Syria:* Winder, 1962, 1963. *Iran:* Schulz, 1973. *Afghanistan:* Dupree, 1971. *French Speaking West Africa:* LeVine, 1968. *Nigeria:* Kurtz, 1976. *Uganda:* Byrd, 1963. *India:* Morris-Jones, 1957; Robins, 1967; Singhvi,

1970; Sisson and Shrader, 1977. *Ceylon:* Singer, 1964. *Burma:* Pye, 1962. *Malaysia:* Glick, 1966. *Philippines:* Stauffer, 1966. *Chile:* Agor, 1971a. *Argentina:* Ranis, 1971. *Guatemala:* Verner, 1971. *Jamaica:* Bell, 1964.

      7. *U.S.S.R.:* Gubin, 1961; Abrams, 1967-1968; Clarke, 1967-1968; Hill, 1973; Vanneman, 1977; White, 1980. *Poland:* Simon and Olson, 1977. *Yugoslavia:* Seroka, 1979; Cohen, 1980. *Comparative Communist Systems:* Lammich, 1977.

      8. Alexander and Juliette George, *Woodrow Wilson and Colonel House* (1956), is generally considered the best case study of a political figure using a Lasswellian perspective. George (1968) argues that the methodological problems of this approach are less difficult than is generally realized, at least in intensive studies of a single historical figure.

      9. See Greenstein (1967) for a good, but highly generalized, beginning.

      10. See for example Clark and Wilson, 1961; Wilson, 1962; Downs, 1967; Wildavsky, 1965.

REFERENCES

Aberbach, Joel D., Robert D. Putnam, and Bert A. Rockman. 1981. *Bureaucrats and Politicians in Western Democracies.* Cambridge: Harvard University Press.

Abrams, Robert. 1967-1968. "Political Recruitment and Local Government: The Local Soviets of the R.S.F.S.R., 1918-21," *Soviet Studies* 19:573-580.

Agor, Weston. 1971a. *The Chilean Senate.* Austin: University of Texas Press.

————, ed. 1971b. *Latin American Legislatures: Their Role and Influence.* New York: Praeger.

Akzin, Benjamin. 1961. "The Knesset," *International Social Science Journal* 8:567-582.

————. 1967. "The Knesset in Israel" in *Decision-Makers in the Modern World.* Paris: UNESCO, pp. 144-146.

Barber, James David. 1965. *The Lawmakers.* New Haven: Yale University Press.

Beaumont, Lord. 1974. "The Selection of Parliamentary Candidates," *Political Quarterly* 45:123-124.

Beck, T.D. 1974. *French Legislators, 1800-1834.* Berkeley: University of California Press.

Bell, Charles G. and Charles M. Price. 1969. "Pre-Legislative Sources of Representational Roles," *Midwest Journal of Political Science* 13:254-270.

————. 1975. *The First Term: A Study of Legislative Socialization.* Beverly Hills, CA: Sage.

Bell, Wendell. 1964. *Jamaican Leaders: Political Attitudes in a New Nation.* Berkeley: University of California Press.

Bell, Wendell, Richard J. Hill, and Charles R. Wright. 1961. *Public Leadership: A Critical Review.* San Francisco: Chandler.

Berrington, Hugh B. and Samuel E. Finer. 1961. "The British House of Commons," *International Social Science Journal* 8:600-619.

Black, Gordon. 1970. "A Theory of Professionalization in Politics," *American Political Science Review* 64:865-878.

————. 1972. "A Theory of Political Ambition: Career Choice and the Role of Structural Incentives," *American Political Science Review* 66:144-159.

Blondel, Jean. 1973. *Comparative Legislatures.* Englewood Cliffs, NJ: Prentice-Hall.

Bochel, John and David Denver. 1983. "Candidate Selection in the Labour Party: What the Selectors Seek," *British Journal of Political Science* 13:45-69.

Bogue, Allan G., Jerome M. Clubb, Carroll R. McKibbin, and Santa A. Traugott. 1976. "Members of the House of Representatives and the Processes of Modernization, 1789-1960," *Journal of American History* 63:275-302.

Brand, Jack. 1973. "Party Organization and the Recruitment of Councillors," *British Journal of Political Science* 3:473-486.

Brichta, Aviaham. 1974-1975. "Women in the Knesset: 1949-1969," *Parliamentary Affairs* 28:31-50.

Brookes, Pamela. 1967. *Women at Westminster*. London: Peter Davies.

Browning, Rufus B. 1968. "The Interaction of Personality and Political System in Decisions to Run for Office: Some Data and a Simulation Technique," *Journal of Social Issues* 24:93-109.

Browning, Rufus P. and Herbert Jacob. 1964. "Power Motivation and the Political Personality," *Public Opinion Quarterly* 28:75-90.

Buck, Philip W. 1963. *Amateurs and Professionals in British Politics, 1918-1959*. Chicago: University of Chicago Press.

Budge, Ian and Dennis Farlie. 1975. "Political Recruitment and Drop-out: Predictive Success of Background Characteristics over Five British Localities," *British Journal of Political Science* 5:33-68.

Budge, Ian, Dennis Farlie, and Galen Irwin. 1981. "Predicting Parliamentary Careers—A Quantitative Index Generated and Tested with Dutch Data," *European Journal of Political Research* 9:201-208.

Bullock, Charles S. III. 1972. "House Careerists: Changing Patterns of Longevity and Attrition," *American Political Science Review* 66:1295-1305.

Bullock, Charles S. III and Patricia L.F. Heys. 1972. "Recruitment of Women for U.S. Congress: A Research Note," *Western Political Quarterly* 25:416-423.

Byrd, Robert O. 1963. "Characteristics of Candidates for Election in a Country Approaching Independence: The Case of Uganda," *Midwest Journal of Political Science* 7:1-27.

Carlson, James M. and Mark S. Hyde. 1980. "Personality and Political Recruitment: Actualization or Compensation," *Journal of Psychology* 106:117-120.

Cayrol, Roland and Pasal Perrineau. 1982. "Governing Elites in a Changing Industrial Society: The Case of France," in Moshe Czudnowski, ed., *Does Who Governs Matter?* DeKalb: Northern Illinois University Press, pp. 90-124.

Clark, Peter B. and James Q. Wilson. 1961. "Incentive Systems: A Theory of Organizations," *Administrative Science Quarterly* 6:129-166.

Clarke, Roger A. 1967-1968. "The Composition of the USSR Supreme Soviet 1958-1966," *Soviet Studies* 19:53-65.

Cohen, Lenard J. 1980. "Politics as an Avocation: Legislative Professionalization and Participation in Yugoslavia," *Legislative Studies Quarterly* 5:175-209.

Comstock, Alzada. 1926. "Women Members of European Parliaments," *American Political Science Review* 20:379-384.

Cooper, Joseph and William West. 1981. "The Congressional Career in the 1970's," in Lawrence C. Dodd and Bruce I. Oppenheimer, eds., *Congress Reconsidered*, 2d ed. Washington, DC: Congressional Quarterly Press, pp. 83-106.

————. 1981-1982. "Voluntary Retirement, Incumbency and the Modern House," *Political Science Quarterly* 96:279-300.

Cotta, Maurizio. 1982. "The Italian Political Class in the Twentieth Century: Continuities and Discontinuities," in Moshe Czudnowski, ed., *Does Who Governs Matter?* DeKalb: Northern Illinois University Press, pp. 154-187.

Czudnowski, Moshe M. 1970. "Legislative Recruitment under Proportional Representation in Israel: A Model and a Case Study," *Midwest Journal of Political Science* 14:216-248.

————. 1972. "Sociocultural Variables and Legislative Recruitment," *Comparative Politics* 4:561-588.

Hacker, Andrew. 1961. "The Elected and the Anointed," *American Political Science Review* 55:539-549.

Hain, Paul L. 1974. "Age, Ambitions, and Political Careers: The Middle-Age Crisis," *Western Political Quarterly* 27:265-274.

Hain, Paul and James E. Pierson. 1975. "Lawyers and Politics Revisited: Structural Advantages of Lawyers-Politicians," *American Journal of Political Science* 19:41-51.

Hamon, Leo. 1961. "Members of the French Parliament," *International Social Science Journal* 13:545-566.

Haynes, George H. 1938. *The Senate of the United States: Its History and Practice.* Boston: Houghton-Mifflin.

Hellevik, Ottar. 1969. *Stortinget: en sosial elite?* Oslo: Pax Forlag A/S.

Hermann, Margaret G. and Thomas W. Milburn. 1977. *A Psychological Examination of Political Leaders.* New York: The Free Press.

Herzog, Dietrich. 1975. *Politische Karrieren: Selektion und Professionalsierung Politischer Fuehrungsgruppen.* Berlin: The Free University Institute of Social Science Research.

Hibbing, John R. 1982a. "Voluntary Retirements from the U.S. House of Representatives: Who Quits?" *American Journal of Political Science* 26:467-484.

——————. 1982b. "Voluntary Retirement from the U.S. House: The Costs of Congressional Service," *Legislative Studies Quarterly* 7:57-73.

Hill, Robert J. 1973. "Patterns of Deputy Selection to Local Soviets," *Soviet Studies* 25:196-212.

Hinckley, Barbara. 1970. "Incumbency and the Presidential Vote in Senate Elections," *American Political Science Review* 64:836-842.

Holland, M. 1981. "The Selection of Parliamentary Candidates—Contemporary Developments and the Impact of the European-Elections," *Parliamentary Affairs* 34:28-46.

Holmberg, Soren. 1974. *Riksdagen Representerar Svenska Folket.* Lund, Sweden: Student-literatur.

Huckshorn, Robert J. and R.C. Spencer. 1971. *The Politics of Defeat: Campaigning for Congress.* Amherst: University of Massachusetts Press.

Huntington, Samuel P. 1973. "Congressional Responses to the Twentieth Century," in David B. Truman, ed., *The Congress and America's Future.* 2d ed. Englewood Cliffs, NJ: Prentice-Hall, pp. 6-38.

Hyneman, Charles S. 1938. "Tenure and Turnover of Legislative Personnel," *Annals of the American Academy of Political and Social Science* 23:21-31.

——————. 1940. "Who Makes Our Laws?" *Political Science Quarterly* 55:556-581.

Hyneman, Charles S. and H. Lay. 1938. "Tenure and Turnover of the Indiana General Assembly," *American Political Science Review* 32:55-57.

Irwin, Galen, Ian Budge, and Dennis Farlie. 1979. "Social Background vs. Motivational Determinants of Legislative Careers in the Netherlands," *Legislative Studies Quarterly* 4:447-465.

Isberg, Magnus. 1982. *The First Decade of the Unicameral Riksdag: The Role of the Swedish Parliament in the 1970's.* Stockholm: Stockholm University Research Reports.

Jacob, Herbert. 1962. "Initial Recruitment of Elected Offices in the U.S.—A Model," *Journal of Politics* 24:703-716.

Jacobson, Gary C. and Samuel Kernell. 1981. *Strategy and Choice in Congressional Elections.* New Haven: Yale University Press.

Jaffe, Alan M. 1981. "Comparison of State Legislators with a Control Group on Maslow's 'Security-Insecurity' Measure," *Psychological Reports* 48:41-42.

Jewell, Malcolm E. 1970. "Attitudinal Determinants of Legislative Behavior: The Utility of Role Analysis," in Allan Kornberg and Lloyd D. Musolf, eds., *Legislatures in Developmental Perspective*. Durham, NC: Duke University Press, pp. 460-500.

Jewell, Malcolm E. and Samuel C. Patterson. 1977. *The Legislative Process in the United States*. 3d ed. New York: Random House.

Kazee, Thomas. 1980. "The Decisions to Run for the U.S. Congress: Challenger Attitudes in the 1970s," *Legislative Studies Quarterly* 5:79-100.

Keefe, William J. and Morris S. Ogul. 1981. *The American Legislative Process*. 5th ed. Englewood Cliffs, NJ: Prentice-Hall.

Keller, Suzanne I. 1963. *Beyond the Ruling Class: Strategic Elites in Modern Society*. New York: Random House.

Kelley, Jonathan and Ian McAllister. 1983. "The Electoral Consequences of Gender in Australia," *British Journal of Political Science* 13:365-377.

Kernell, Samuel. 1977. "Toward Understanding 19th Century Congressional Careers: Ambition, Competition and Rotation," *American Journal of Political Science* 21:669-693.

Key, V.O., Jr. 1949. *Southern Politics in State and Nation*. New York: Knopf.

————. 1956. *American State Politics: An Introduction*. New York: Knopf.

Keynes, Edward, Richard J. Tobin, and Robert Danziger. 1979. "Institutional Effects on Elite Recruitment: The Case of State Nominating Systems," *American Politics Quarterly* 7:283-302.

Kincaid, Diane D. 1978. "Over His Dead Body: A Positive Perspective on Widows in the U.S. Congress," *Western Political Quarterly* 31:96-104.

King, Anthony. 1974. *British Members of Parliament: A Self Portrait*. London: Macmillan and Granada Television.

————. 1981. "The Rise of the Career Politician in Britain—And Its Consequences," *British Journal of Political Science* 11:249-285.

Kirchheimer, Otto. 1950. "Composition of the German Bundestag, 1950," *Western Political Quarterly* 3:590-601.

Kirkpatrick, Jeanne J. 1974. *Political Women*. New York: Basic Books.

Kohn, Walter S.G. 1980. *Women in National Legislatures: A Comparative Study of Six Countries*. New York: Praeger.

Kornberg, Allan. 1967. *Canadian Legislative Behavior*. New York: Holt, Rinehart, and Winston.

————, ed. 1973. *Legislatures in Comparative Perspective*. New York: McKay.

Kornberg, Allan and William Mishler. 1976. *Influence in Parliament: Canada*. Durham, NC: Duke University Press.

Kornberg, Allan and Lloyd D. Musolf, eds. 1970. *Legislatures in Developmental Perspective*. Durham, NC: Duke University Press.

Kornberg, Allan and Norman Thomas. 1965. "The Political Socialization of National Legislative Elites in the United States and Canada," *Journal of Politics* 27: 761-775.

————. 1965-1966. "Representative Democracy and Political Elites in Canada and the United States," *Parliamentary Affairs* 19:91-102.

Kornberg, Allan and Hal H. Winsborough. 1968. "Recruitment of Candidates for the Canadian House of Commons," *American Political Science Review* 62:1242-1257.

Kornberg, Allan, Harold D. Clarke, and George L. Watson. 1973. "Toward a Model of Parliamentary Recruitment in Canada," in Allan Kornberg, ed., *Legislatures in Comparative Perspective*. New York: McKay, pp. 250-281.

Kornberg, Allan, David Falcone, and William Mishler. 1973. "Legislatures and Social Change: The Case of Canada," *Sage Research Papers in the Social Sciences.* Beverly Hills, CA: Sage.

Kostroski, Warner. 1978. "The Effect of Number of Terms on the Reelection of Senators, 1920-1970," *Journal of Politics* 40:488-497.

Kurtz, Donn M. 1976. "Nigerian Ministers and Parliamentarians, 1954-1965," *Journal of African Studies* 3:101-124.

Lammich, S. 1977. *Grundzuge des Sozialistichen Parlamentarismus.* Baden-Baden: Nomos Verlagesellschaft.

Lapidus, Gail Warshofsky. 1975. "Political Mobilization, Participation, and Leadership: Women in Soviet Politics," *Comparative Politics* 8:90-118.

Lasswell, Harold D. 1930. *Psychopathology and Politics.* Chicago: University of Chicago Press.

————. 1936. *Politics: Who Gets What, When, How.* New York: McGraw-Hill.

————. 1948. *Power and Personality.* New York: Norton.

Lasswell, Harold D. and Myres S. McDougal. 1948. "Legal Education and Public Policy: Professional Training in the Public Interest," in Harold D. Lasswell, ed., *The Analysis of Political Behavior: An Empirical Approach.* London: Kegan Paul, pp. 21-119.

Lasswell, Harold D., Daniel Lerner, and C. Easton Rothwell. 1952. *The Comparative Study of Elites: An Introduction and Bibliography.* Stanford, CA: Stanford University Press.

Lee, Eugene C. 1960. *The Politics of Nonpartisanship.* Berkeley: University of California Press.

LeVine, V.T. 1968. "Political Elite Recruitment and Political Structure in French Speaking Africa," *Cahiers d'Etudes Africaines* 8:369-389.

Loewenberg, Gerhard. 1967. *Parliament and the German Political System.* Ithaca, NY: Cornell University Press.

Loewenberg, Gerhard and Samuel C. Patterson. 1979. *Comparing Legislatures.* Boston: Little, Brown.

March, James G. and Johan P. Olsen. 1984. "The New Institutionalism: Organizational Factors in Political Life," *American Political Science Review* 78:734-749.

March, R. 1974. *The Myth of Parliament.* Scarborough: Prentice-Hall.

Martin, A.W. 1956. "The Legislative Assembly of New South Wales, 1856-1900," *Australian Journal of Politics and History* 2:46-67.

Marvick, Dwaine. 1968. "Political Recruitment and Careers," in *International Encyclopedia of the Social Sciences. Vol. 12.* New York: Crowell Collier and Macmillan, pp. 273-282.

Matthews, Donald R. 1954a. *The Social Background of Political Decision-Makers.* New York: Random House.

————. 1954b. "United States Senators and the Class Structure," *Public Opinion Quarterly* 18:5-22.

————. 1960. *U.S. Senators and Their World.* New York: Vintage Press.

————. 1961. "United States Senators: A Collective Portrait," *International Social Science Journal* 8:620-634.

————. 1974. "Presidential Nominations: Process and Outcomes," in J.D. Barber, ed., *Choosing the President.* New York: Prentice-Hall, pp. 35-70.

Mayhew, David R. 1974. *Congress: The Electoral Connection.* New Haven: Yale University Press.

McConaughy, John B. 1950. "Certain Personality Factors of State Legislators in South Carolina," *American Political Science Review* 45:897-903.

McKinney, Madge. 1942. "The Personnel of the 77th Congress," *American Political Science Review* 36:67-75.

Means, Ingunn Norderval. 1972. "Political Recruitment of Women in Norway," *Western Political Quarterly* 25:491-521.

Mellors, Colin. 1978. *The British MP: A Socio-Economic Study of the House of Commons.* Westmead: Saxon House.

Merritt, Sharyne. 1977. "Winners & Losers: Sex Differences in Municipal Elections," *American Journal of Political Science* 21:731-743.

Mezey, Michael. 1970. "Ambition Theory and the Office of Congressmen," *Journal of Politics* 32:563-579.

Mezey, Susan Gluck. 1978a. "Women and Representation: The Case of Hawaii," *Journal of Politics* 40:369-385.

––––––– . 1978b. "Does Sex Make a Difference? A Case Study of Women in Politics," *Western Political Quarterly* 31:492-501.

Mills, C. Wright. 1956. *The Power Elite.* New York: Oxford University Press.

Mishler, William. 1978. "Nominating Attractive Candidates for Parliament: Recruitment to the Canadian House of Commons," *Legislative Studies Quarterly* 3:581-599.

Morris-Jones, W.H. 1957. *Parliament in India.* Philadelphia: University of Pennsylvania Press.

Namier, L.B. 1929. *The Structure of Politics at the Accession of George III.* London: Macmillan.

Noponen, Martti and Pertti Pesonen. 1964. "The Legislative Career in Finland," in Erik Allardt and Yrgö Littunen, eds., *Cleavages, Ideologies, and Party Systems: Contributions to Comparative Sociology.* Helsinki: Westermarck Society Transactions, no. 10.

Norton, Philip. 1980. "The Changing Face of the British House of Commons in the 1970s," *Legislative Studies Quarterly* 5:333-357.

Obler, J. 1973. "The Role of National Party Leaders in Selection of Party Leaders in Selection of Parliamentary Candidates–The Belgian Case," *Comparative Politics* 5:157-184.

––––––– . 1974. "Intraparty Democracy and Selection of Parliamentary Candidates–The Belgian Case," *British Journal of Political Science* 4:163-185.

Olson, David M. 1980. *The Legislative Process: A Comparative Approach.* New York: Harper and Row, ch. 3.

Ornstein, Norman J., Thomas E. Mann, Michael J. Malbin, and John F. Bibby, eds. 1982. *Vital Statistics on Congress.* Washington, DC: American Enterprise Institute.

Oxendale, James R., Jr. 1979. "Compensation and Turnover in State Legislative Lower Chambers," *State and Local Government Review* 11:60-63.

Patterson, Samuel C. and G.R. Boynton. 1969. "Legislative Recruitment in a Civic Culture," *Social Science Quarterly* 50:243-263.

Payne, James L. 1968. *Patterns of Conflict in Colombia.* New Haven: Yale University Press.

––––––– . 1972. *Incentive Theory and Political Process: Motivation and Leadership in the Dominican Republic.* Lexington, MA: Lexington Books.

Payne, James L. and Oliver H. Woshinsky. 1972. "Incentives for Political Participation," *World Politics* 24:518-546.

Peabody, Robert L., Norman J. Ornstein, and David W. Rohde. 1976. "The U.S. Senate as a Presidential Incubator: Many Are Called But Few Are Chosen," *Political Science Quarterly* 91:237-258.

Pedersen, Mogens N. 1972. "Lawyers in Politics: The Danish Folketing and United States Legislatures," in Samuel C. Patterson and John C. Wahlke, eds., *Comparative Legislative Behavior*. New York: Wiley, pp. 25-63.

—————. 1975. "Geographical Matrix and Parliamentary Representation—A Spatial Model of Political Recruitment," *European Journal of Political Research* 3:1-19.

—————. 1976. *Political Development and Elite Transformation in Denmark.* Beverly Hills, CA: Sage.

—————. 1977. "The Personal Circulation of a Legislative: The Danish Folketing, 1849-1968," in William O. Aydelotte, ed., *The History of Parliamentary Behavior*. Princeton: Princeton University Press, pp. 63-101.

Pesonen, Pertti. 1972. "Political Parties in the Finnish Eduskunta," in Samuel C. Patterson and John C. Wahlke, eds., *Comparative Legislative Behavior*. New York: Wiley, pp. 199-233.

Polsby, Nelson. 1968. "The Institutionalization of the U.S. House of Representatives," *American Political Science Review* 62:144-168.

Polsby, Nelson W., Miriam Gallaher, and Barry Spencer Rundquist. 1969. "The Growth of the Seniority System in the U.S. House of Representatives," *American Political Science Review* 63:787-807.

Prewitt, Kenneth. 1965. "Political Socialization and Leadership Selection," *The Annals of the American Academy of Political and Social Science* 361:96-111.

—————. 1970. *The Recruitment of Political Leaders: A Study of Citizen-Politicians.* Indianapolis: Bobbs-Merrill.

Prewitt, Kenneth and Heinz Eulau. 1971. "Social Bias in Leadership Selection: Political Recruitment and Electoral Context," *Journal of Politics* 33:293-315.

Prewitt, Kenneth and William Nowlin. 1969. "Political Ambitions and the Behavior of Incumbent Politicians," *Western Political Quarterly* 22:298-308.

Prewitt, Kenneth, Heinz Eulau, and Betty H. Zisk. 1966-1967. "Political Socialization and Political Roles," *Public Opinion Quarterly* 30:569-582.

Price, Douglas. 1971. "The Congressional Career: Then and Now," in Nelson Polsby, ed., *Congressional Behavior*. New York: Random House, pp. 14-27.

—————. 1975. "Congress and the Evolution of Legislative 'Professionalism'," in Norman J. Ornstein, ed., *Congress in Change: Evolution and Reform.* New York: Praeger, pp. 2-23.

—————. 1977. "Careers and Committees in the American Congress: The Problem of Structural Change," in William O. Aydelotte, ed., *The History of Parliamentary Behavior*. Princeton: Princeton University Press, pp. 28-62.

Putnam, Robert D. 1976. *The Comparative Study of Political Elites.* Englewood Cliffs, NJ: Prentice-Hall.

Pye, Lucian W. 1962. *Politics, Personality, and Nation Building: Burma's Search for Identity*. New Haven: Yale University Press.

Ranis, Peter. 1971. "Profile Variables Among Argentine Legislators," in Weston Agor, ed., *Latin American Legislatures: Their Role and Influence*. New York: Praeger.

Ranney, Austin. 1965. *Pathways to Parliament: Candidate Selection in Britain.* Madison: University of Wisconsin Press.

Ray, David. 1974. "Membership Stability in Three State Legislatures: 1893-1969," *American Political Science Review* 68:106-112.

Rice, Stuart A. 1929. *Quantitative Methods in Politics.* New York: Knopf.

Robins, Robert S. 1967. "Political Elite Formation in Rural India," *Journal of Politics* 29:838-860.

Rohde, David W. 1979. "Risk-Bearing and Progressive Ambition: The Case of the US House of Representatives," *American Journal of Political Science* 23:1-26.

Rosenthal, Alan. 1974. "Turnover in State Legislatures," *American Journal of Political Science* 18:609-616.

Ross, J.F.S. 1948. *Parliamentary Representation.* London: Eyre and Spottiswoode.

Rothman, David J. 1966. *Politics and Power: The United States Senate 1869-1901.* Cambridge: Harvard University Press.

Rush, Michael. 1969. *The Selection of Parliamentary Candidates.* London: Nelson.

Sartori, Giovanni. 1961a. "Parliamentarians in Italy," *International Social Sciences Journal* 8:583-599.

_____ . 1961b. "La Sociologia del Parlemento," *Studi Politica* 8:131-159.

_____ . 1963. *Il Parlamento Italiano: 1946-1963.* Naples: Edizioni Scientifiche Italiane.

_____ . 1967. "Italy: Members of Parliament," *Decisions and Decision-Makers in the Modern State.* Paris: UNESCO, pp. 156-173.

Schlesinger, Joseph A. 1957. "Lawyers and American Politics: A Clarified View," *Midwest Journal of Political Science* 1:26-39.

_____ . 1960. "The Structure of Competition for Office in the American States," *Behavioral Science* 5:197-210.

_____ . 1966. *Ambition and Politics: Political Careers in the United States.* Chicago: Rand McNally.

_____ . 1967. "Political Careers and Party Leadership," in Lewis J. Edinger, ed., *Political Leadership in Industrialized Societies.* New York: Wiley, pp. 266-293.

Schulz, Ann T. 1973. "A Cross-National Examination of Legislators," *The Journal of Developing Areas* 7:571-590.

Seligman, Lester G. 1964. *Leadership in a New Nation: Political Development in Israel.* New York: Atherton Press.

Seligman, Lester G., Michael King, Chong Lim Kim, and Roland Smith. 1974. *Patterns of Recruitment: A State Chooses Its Lawmakers.* Chicago: Rand McNally.

Seroka, James H. 1979. "Legislative Recruitment and Political Change in Yugoslavia," *Legislative Studies Quarterly* 4:105-120.

Shin, Kwang S. and John S. Jackson III. 1979. "Membership Turnover in U.S. State Legislatures: 1931-1976," *Legislative Studies Quarterly* 4:95-104.

Simon, Maurice D. and David M. Olson. 1977. "Evolution of a Minimal Parliament: Membership and Committee Changes in the Polish Sejm," *Legislative Studies Quarterly* 5:211-232.

Singer, Marshall R. 1964. *The Emerging Elite: A Study of Political Leadership in Ceylon.* Cambridge, MA: MIT Press.

Singhvi, L.M. 1970. "Parliament in the Indian Political System," in Allan Kornberg and Lloyd D. Musolf, eds., *Legislatures in Developmental Perspective.* Durham, NC: Duke University Press, pp. 179-227.

Sisson, Richard and Lawrence L. Shrader. 1977. "Social Representation and Political Integration in an Indian State: The Legislative Dimension," in Albert F. Eldridge, ed., *Legislatures in Plural Societies.* Durham, NC: Duke University Press, pp. 54-94.

Skard, Torild. 1981. "Progress for Women: Increased Female Representation in Political Elites in Norway," in Cynthia Fuchs Epstein and Rose Lamb Coser, eds., *Access to Power: Cross-National Studies of Women and Elites.* London: Allen and Unwin.

Snowiss, Leo M. 1966. "Congressional Recruitment and Representation," *American Political Science Review* 60:627-639.

Sorauf, Frank J. 1963. *Party and Representation*. New York: Atherton Press.

Stauffer, Robert. 1966. "Philippine Legislatures and Their Changing Universe," *Journal of Politics* 28:556-591.

Stewart, Debra W., ed. 1980. *Women in Local Politics*. Metuchen, NJ and London: Scarecrow Press.

Stone, William F. and G.L. Baril. 1979. "Self-Other Orientation and Legislative Behavior," *Journal of Personality* 47:162-176.

Struble, Robert, Jr. 1979-1980. "House Turnover and the Principle of Rotation," *Political Science Quarterly* 94:649-667.

Swenson, Peter. 1982. "The Influence of Recruitment on the Structure of Power in the U.S. House, 1870-1940," *Legislative Studies Quarterly* 7:7-36.

Thurber, James A. 1976. "The Impact of Party Recruitment Activity upon Legislative Role Orientations: A Path Analysis," *Legislative Studies Quarterly* 1:533-550.

Tobin, Richard J. 1975. "The Influence of Nominating Systems on the Political Experiences of State Legislators," *Western Political Quarterly* 28:553-566.

Tobin, Richard J. and Edward Keynes. 1975. "Institutional Differences in the Recruitment Process: A Four-State Study," *American Journal of Political Science* 19:667-682.

Tuckel, Peter. 1983. "Length of Incumbency and the Reelection Chances of U.S. Senators," *Legislative Studies Quarterly* 8:283-288.

Valen, Henry. 1966. "The Recruitment of Parliamentary Nominees in Norway," *Scandinavian Political Studies* 1:121-166.

Vallance, Elizabeth. 1979. *Women in the House: A Study of Women Members of Parliament*. London: The Athlone Press.

Van Hightower, Nikki R. 1972. "The Recruitment of Women for Public Office," *American Politics Quarterly* 5:301-314.

Vanneman, Peter. 1977. *The Supreme Soviet: Politics and the Legislative Process in the Soviet Political System*. Durham, NC: Duke University Press.

Verner, Joel G. 1971. "The Guatemalan National Congress: An Elite Analysis," in Weston Agor, ed., *Latin American Legislatures: Their Role and Influence*. New York: Praeger, ch. 7.

Wahlke, John C., Heinz Eulau, William Buchanan, and LeRoy C. Ferguson. 1962. *The Legislative System: Explorations in Legislative Behavior*. New York: Wiley.

Weber, Max. 1946. "Politics as a Vocation," in H.H. Gerth and C.W. Mills, eds., *From Max Weber: Essays in Sociology*. New York: Oxford University Press, pp. 77-125.

Welch, Susan. 1978. "Recruitment of Women to Public Office: A Discriminant Analysis," *Western Political Quarterly* 31:372-380.

Werner, Emmy E. 1966. "Women in Congress: 1917-1964," *Western Political Quarterly* 19:16-30.

————. 1968. "Women in the State Legislatures," *Western Political Quarterly* 21:40-50.

White, Stephen. 1980. "The USSR Supreme Soviet: A Developmental Perspective," *Legislative Studies Quarterly* 5:247-274.

Wiggins, Charles W. and E. Lee Bernick. 1977. "Legislative Turnover Reconsidered," *Policy Studies Journal* 5:419-424.

Wildavsky, Aaron. 1965. "The Goldwater Phenomenon: Purists, Politicians and the Two-Party System," *The Review of Politics* 27:386-413.

Wilson, James Q. 1962. *The Amateur Democrat*. Chicago: University of Chicago Press.

Winder, R. Bayley. 1962. "Syrian Deputies and Cabinet Members, 1919-1959. Part I," *The Middle East Journal* 16:407-429.

_____ . 1963. "Syrian Deputies and Cabinet Members, 1919-1950. Part II," *The Middle East Journal* 17:35-53.

Witmer, T. Richard. 1964. "The Aging of the House," *Political Science Quarterly* 79: 526-541.

Woshinsky, Oliver. 1973. *The French Deputy: Incentives and Behavior in the National Assembly*. Lexington, MA: Heath.

Young, James S. 1966. *The Washington Community: 1800-1828*. New York: Columbia University Press.

Ziller, Robert C., William F. Stone, Robert M. Jackson, and Natalie J. Terbovic. 1977. "Self-Other Orientations and Political Behavior," in Margaret G. Hermann and Thomas W. Milburn, eds., *A Psychological Examination of Political Leaders*. New York: The Free Press, pp. 174-204.

Chapter 2

Legislative Elections
And Electoral Responsiveness

by

LYN RAGSDALE

Legislative elections, touted in political folklore as hallowed rites, have been treated in scholarly lore as rather obscure curiosities. Only recently have scholars begun to examine the electoral link between legislators and citizens. An extensive literature exists on representation as a link between legislators and citizens, but the electoral association, often the source of representation, has received much less attention. Within the legislative election field, there is a kind of Orwellian problem: some elections have been treated more equally than others. Of the many elections for national legislatures and regional assemblies, some of which are highly competitive, some minimally competitive, some token, only the U.S. congressional election has been intensively studied. So, the question can rightly be asked, "What do we know about legislative elections?" and an answer is by no means obvious.

One, only partly cynical response might be that we know nothing. Numerous legislative elections, many involving long-standing exchanges among parties, have received little or no scholarly attention. Those which have are often treated in isolation, with comparisons neither stated nor implied, leaving the literature rather disparate. Much of the work remains descriptive, outlining for a specific election who votes and who wins. Moreover, the heavy emphasis on American congressional elections tells us a good deal about a rather atypical set of electoral contests. Few other national legislative elections have separate ballots for the legislature and the executive; in the U.S., these provide an "independence of choice" and a legislative autonomy which make it "difficult to discern what a national election decides" (Key, 1964, p. 545). By contrast, no such difficulty is apparent in the more prevalent parliamentary systems, where legislative elections are executive elections, executive elections are legislative elections, and electors often make but one choice. Few other legislative elections involve similar levels of attention to individual candidates, distinct from collective lists of candidates drawn up by parties. So, we know something of several legislative elections treated separately and a great deal about one somewhat peculiar set of legislative elections, but overall there has been no attempt to draw together what is known into a relevant framework for legislative elections.

Although a general treatment of legislative elections may be absent, the task does not appear to be a matter of hopeless guesswork. Despite the lopsided attention given U.S. congressional elections, research on an increasing number of legislative elections in other nations and in the American states is taking place, some comparing elections across several contexts. Further, the extensive information available on U.S. congressional elections may provide a baseline for a more general comparative design. Comparison implies neither that the objects being compared are alike in all measures, nor that they are different in all respects. Indeed, if they were all alike or all different, the comparison would be either uninteresting or implausible. Although differences can be expected, a comparative design may also uncover basic commonalities which identify key electoral components, not specific to a nation, but more generally legislative.

So, while the disparateness of legislative election research invites clarification, the clarification seems both possible and worthwhile. Scholarship on legislative elections can be canvassed for its central themes as elements of a broader comparative design. Such a design may provide general statements about legislative elections, allow crossnational contrasts, and detail the ramifications of elections on other aspects of legislative activity. We may then have more knowledge of legislative elections than we might first have thought.

Electoral Responsiveness

To shape this design, we can first note that legislative elections all rest on a simple premise: that they link the legislature and the citizenry, allowing citizens to participate, albeit indirectly, in legislative decision making. Clearly, this link can be made with more or less success. In some elections several candidates or parties may compete, in others one candidate or party may always win, and in still others only one candidate or party may ever run. However, what all these elections are or are not doing effectively is allowing citizen preferences and choices to determine the makeup of the legislature and, therefore, the content of its decisions. "Once the scale of society makes direct popular rule impossible and the complexity of political life renders selection by lot unacceptable, representation based on popular election preserves the elements of popular participation, direction, and control" (Katz, 1980, p. 1).

We can call this link electoral responsiveness. All legislative elections are thus devices for translating, with varying degrees of precision, citizen desires into legislative action. The idea is familiar to studies of representation; legislators act "in the interest of the represented, in a manner responsive to them" (Pitkin, 1967, p. 209). Responsiveness is an elementary but overarching concept, within which legislative elections can be understood. Indeed, because it is elementary, all studies of legislative elections have examined, either implicitly or explicitly, this link. Three important features of legislative elections bear upon electoral responsiveness: the nature of the collective choice, the extent of competitive change, and patterns of voter preferences.

Studies of collective choice consider the legislature as an entire body chosen by the electorate as a whole. Elections ultimately involve global outcomes: the National party retains control of the lower house in New Zealand; Republicans gain control of the U.S. Senate; Socialists win a clear-cut victory across France. Thus, those exploring collective choice target the aggregate distribution of votes, the distribution of seats, or some relation between the two. As Rose asserts, "many studies of voting terminate with statements about the preferences of individual voters. The most important political phenomena are not individual choices, but the aggregate distribution of seats in the national parliament, affecting control of executive government" (1974, p. 8). While all researchers would not agree that this phenomenon is "most important," none would disagree that the aggregate composition of the legislature is an important political outcome. At this level, responsiveness is indicated by the electorate's collective evaluation of the performance of the legislature.

Studies of competitive change unmask responsiveness by virtue of the opportunity voters have to change the composition of the legislature. The degree of competitiveness among parties or candidates determines the extent of change from one election to the next. Whether and at what rate the "ins" go out becomes the focus of research. Thus, scholars move from a global perspective to a vantage point at the margins. They examine changes in the votes, changes in seats, the influx of new members, and the stability of old members. The extent of the electorate's control—and hence the degree of responsiveness—depends on the margin of change in the composition of the legislature.

Studies of voter preference view responsiveness as a quality of the one-to-one relationship between individual voters and individual candidates or local parties. In their campaigns, candidates and parties may stress their ability to meet the concerns, interests, and demands of the voters or may create those concerns themselves. Voters may then evaluate these individual performances in accord with their own partisan dispositions, social class outlooks, evaluations of candidates, and positions on issues. The central interest for researchers is the match between the campaign efforts and voter attitudes. Ultimately, individual voters control the composition of the legislature to some degree by preferring one party or candidate and not another.

Analyses of each aspect of legislative elections—collective choice, competitive change, voter preference—can be thought of as asking questions the others leave unanswered. Elections determine the composition of the legislature (collective choice), provide changes in that composition through partisan competition (competitive change), or involve the decisions of individual voters within the partisan campaign context (voter preference). Although there are no hard and fast boundaries separating the three, each offers insights into legislative elections which do not depend on the legislature involved.

Election Laws, Election Outcomes

Responsiveness ultimately rests on matters of law. Seemingly mundane decisions of geography and arithmetic which establish district types, ballot orders, and vote-seat formulae may affect the electoral choices that can be made and that ultimately are made. Analyzing the impact of election laws on election results, Rae (1967) notes that in virtually all of the 115 electoral systems he examines, seat allocations disproportionately benefit parties that obtain large shares of the popular vote. In Duverger's words, the systems act as "brakes" on the fractionalization of parties, promoting a few large parties at the expense of many smaller ones (1963, p. 205). While the redistributive effect in favor of large parties appears universal, there are differences in degree. Both Rae and Duverger argue that plurality and majority systems, more than proportional representation systems, tend to magnify the relative advantage of strong parties. Variation also exists among similar systems: proportional representation plans, in particular, provide numerous and varied translations of votes to seats (see Rae, Ch. 6). Both authors are careful to place these effects of electoral arrangements in perspective, noting that other factors—social, economic, ideological, or partisan—are likely to be stronger determinants of election outcomes.

Still, if electoral laws exert an influence on electoral outcomes, researchers must be cautious in designing comparative studies. Different systems may affect responsiveness in particular ways, as they facilitate certain outcomes and inhibit others. Yet similarities have been observed across systems—the pattern of major party bias, for instance. So research seems to face a predicament of comparability: To avoid being simple-minded or contrived, comparisons must allow for systemic differences. Yet the most interesting comparisons may be those across different types of systems. Work on electoral laws provides evidence that the predicament, while real, does not preempt studies comparing election outcomes across systems and nations.

Collective Choice

Electoral systems create the boundaries within which a collective electoral choice is made. In making this collective choice, the national electorate evaluates the legislature in relation to national events and conditions. From this perspective, legislative elections are national elections; responsiveness is a national result.

Nationalization of Legislative Elections

Research on collective choice of legislative elections has examined the impact of national influences on election outcomes. Stokes (1976) charts national, constituency, and state or regional factors and determines the degree to which each type explains U.S. and British elections. As determinants of voter turnout in U.S. House elections from 1952 to 1960, national effects outweigh the other factors; however, constituency factors have a greater influence than national or state factors on the partisan division of the vote. Even stronger indications of nationalization exist in Great Britain, where, unlike in the United States, national factors exceed constituency and regional factors in their influence on the party vote between 1958 and 1966.[1] "Britain," he concludes, "may well provide an extreme case of the nationalization of political attitude in the western world" (p. 521).

Yet as Katz (1980) observes, other legislative elections involve national factors to an even greater extent than do those in Britain. Using an approach slightly different from Stokes's, Katz traces the effects of national factors on the party vote in Italy, Ireland, and Great Britain from 1948 through 1972. The importance of national factors for Britain is confirmed. But, interestingly, national factors explain somewhat more of the Irish vote and considerably more of the Italian vote, than they do of the British vote.

Contrasting Stokes's study with Katz's points out the pitfalls but also the values of comparisons among legislative elections. Claims about any one legislature can be made only within the confines of the other cases studied. The differences and similarities of electoral laws, social characteristics, and political history between nations may make comparisons more or less apt. But apt comparisons increase our knowledge of legislative elections: the apparent uniqueness of Great Britain fades and a noteworthy sameness appears among four nations where electoral outcomes involve a substantial national component. To be sure, there are variations among the countries. Yet, now national factors appear to be one element common to legislative elections.

Economic Performance and Collective Choice

Beyond noting that national factors influence legislative elections, research has sought to identify these factors. By far the greatest attention has been given the impact of macroeconomic conditions. Elections are examined as collective judgements on the governing party's handling of economic matters, in which their current performance is compared with the past and potential performances of other parties. In a major early work, Kramer (1971) examines the impact of economic factors on U.S. House election results from 1896 to 1964. Analyzing the Republican share of the vote across the period, he observes that change in real per capita income (not inflation or unemployment) is the key predictor of the party vote. In addition to the economic effects, presidential coattails also influence the results.

In a similar vein, Tufte (1975, 1978) considers House elections from 1948 through 1976, predicting the standardized vote loss for the president's party in a given election. Like Kramer, Tufte finds clear electoral consequences for changes in real per capita income for both midterm and on-year congressional results (see also Jacobson, 1983). He also notes the significant effect of presidential popularity (using levels of approval obtained from Gallup poll data) on the midterm vote. Thus, the model emerging from this research is that congressional elections, whether at the midterm or during presidential election years, are essentially referenda on the performance in office of the incumbent (read presidential) party. The collective choice being made, then, reflects voters' satisfaction or dissatisfaction with that party's performance.

Questions have been raised and refinements have been offered on this economic performance model. Arcelus and Meltzer (1975), altering several methodological flaws they see in Kramer's analysis, find little evidence of the effect of real income on electoral outcomes (see also Stigler, 1973). Bloom and Price (1975) modify Kramer's conclusion that an "economic upturn [helps] the congressional candidate of the incumbent party, and economic decline [benefits] the opposition" (Kramer, 1971, p. 141). Considering the effects of party identification and of changes in real per capita income on the Republican vote, they find that income influences election outcomes only during economic downturns (years of declining real income). Party identification alone significantly affects the results in years of rising income. Thus, economic bad times spell trouble for the in-party, but prosperity shows no effect on party fortunes.

Providing other refinements, Hibbing and Alford (1981) maintain that changes in real disposable per capita income strongly and negatively affect the vote only for in-party incumbents during postwar House elections (1946-1978). Open-seat candidates and incumbents of the out-party are not affected. Comparing House and Senate elections, the authors discover that while there are significant economic effects on in-party votes and in-party seats for the House, "Senate elections are far more responsive to short-term fluctuations in economic conditions" (Hibbing and Alford, 1982, p. 513). In sum, U.S. House and particularly Senate elections are influenced by economic conditions, and at least for the House these conditions tend to affect in-party incumbents more than other candidates and to have a strong impact during years of economic decline but not during periods of prosperity.

Some crossnational attention has also been given to the effect of economic conditions on legislative elections. Lewis-Beck and Bellucci (1982) observe that in French and Italian legislative elections economic adversity enhances the leftist vote and diminishes support for the coalition of parties in power. Specifically, in France from 1965 through 1978, rising unemployment and declining real per capita income increase the vote for parties of the left. In Italy (1953-1979) inflation boosts support of the Communist party. Thus, the French and Italian results closely parallel the American findings. Whether in multiparty systems or two-party systems, economic decline adversely affects those governing.

Examining Great Britain and West Germany, Hibbs (1982b) devises a dynamic model of economic performance, theorizing that voters evaluate the performance of the in-party against the prior performance of the opposition. He observes that economic conditions, specifically unemployment, inflation, and real income growth, have significant independent effects on vote intention in Great Britain (1959-1972) and West Germany (1957-1978).[2] The effects, similar for both nations, are not static, but are instead derived partly from conditions present during prior governments. In addition to economic influences, vote intention in each instance is strongly predicted by stable partisan loyalties (see also Hibbs, 1982a). Baker, Dalton, and Hildebrandt (1981) also observe the impact of economic conditions on West German vote intentions, but they find that the effect lessens across the period from 1950 to 1976 as German prosperity expands.

Finally, Ames (1970) provides evidence on the electoral consequences of the government performance of Mexico's dominant party, the Partido Revolucionario Institucional (PRI). Taking an approach different from the other studies, Ames monitors the effect not of economic conditions, but of the party's distribution of benefits from 1952 to 1967. The distribution of these benefits favors urban areas and effectively lessens an erosion of PRI support when other parties become more active in the urban centers.

To assess these studies, let us contrast key assumptions of the economic performance model with the analyses designed to test it. The model says that legislative elections are referenda in which the electorate decide on the success or failure of the incumbent parties. Three assumptions construct the model. First, individual voting patterns contribute to the referendum. Second, the economy is the key criterion used in the electorate's evaluation. Third, the evaluation of the incumbent party links executive and legislative politics.

The first assumption suggests that individual voters reward or punish the incumbent party by casting their legislative votes in accord with their evaluations of the economy. These evaluations collectively make up the referendum. But while the model says something about individual voters' preferences, the data used in testing the model say nothing about these opinions. As Tufte acknowledges, "all we observe in these data is the totally aggregated outcome of the individual performances of the voters.... Aggregate studies provide evidence about aggregates" (1975, p. 826). Thus, these studies, although often alluding to individual voters' rationales, actually explain only the collective decision made by all voters as a group. The question remains how the collective referendum and individual voter decisions may be linked.

The investigation of individual voters itself has produced mixed results. Fiorina (1978, 1981) finds no indication of personal economic situations affecting voter choice in congressional elections from 1956 through 1974 (see also Kuklinski and West, 1981). In contrast, Hibbing and Alford (1981) uncover some evidence of this personal retrospective voting, but only in districts with in-party incumbents. Others note that assessments of national economic conditions, not personal financial situations, have a modest influence on congressional voting (Kinder and Kiewiet, 1979, 1981; Kiewiet, 1981). Work in Great Britain (Butler and Stokes, 1976) reveals that individual economic well-being affects voters' decisions, particularly when they feel their situations have worsened. A close relationship also exists between voters' approval of the incumbent party's handling of the economy and their vote intentions.

Thus, the evidence, less strong at the individual level, nevertheless can be linked to the aggregate results. Much was made early in the individual studies of an incongruity between the collective choice and the individual decisions: a robust effect of the economy on one level, little relationship on the other. Yet the disparity apparently results from looking for the link in the wrong place. Personal economic conditions do not have an effect across the board, but are likely to affect voting decisions only for in-party incumbents in U.S. House elections. The effect for British parliamentary elections is most likely when personal situations are deteriorating. Beyond this, national conditions also have an impact in both the U.S. and Britain. Thus, the individual studies suggest that modifications of the collective model are in order. The referendum may be less one on the in-party as a whole than on its incumbents, and it may be shaped by voters' perceptions of both personal and national economic circumstances.

Second, besides stressing the importance of economic conditions in the model, the research identifies several other factors which affect legislative election outcomes. Kramer points to the influences of presidential coattails, Tufte to presidential performance, Bloom and Price to party identification, and Hibbs to partisan loyalties. At the individual level, partisanship is a far stronger indicator than either attitudes on national economic conditions (Kinder and Kiewiet, 1981) or personal economic conditions, even in in-party races (Hibbing and Alford, 1981). Further, other researchers, dealing more directly with the impact of noneconomic factors on collective choice, point to the importance of partisanship (Kostroski, 1973), incumbency (Hinckley, 1970; Kostroski, 1973), and presidential coattails (Hinckley, 1967, 1970). So noneconomic elements—aspects of executive politics and partisan influences—shape the collective choice. The economy has an effect, but not the only effect. Unhappily, we do not know what might be the result of taking into account economic conditions, party loyalties, executive performance, the prosperity of the period, and the status of the candidates involved within a single model. Inferring from the combined findings of current research, this seems to be the key question worth asking.

Third, the model assumes and research has indeed found a link between executive and legislative politics. Within the model, the "incumbent party"—the executive and legislators of the executive's party—is the referendum target. Testing the model reveals that evaluations of executive performance have some effect on national election outcomes (Tufte, 1975, 1978). But treating this link within a comparative design reveals both a central analytic and a contrasting empirical problem. As part of a comparative analysis, attention needs to be paid to the variations in the overlap between executive and legislative politics across several settings. In Italy, Great Britain, West Germany, and Mexico, the interrelation between executive and legislative politics is systemic, assured by electoral laws and the structures of the parties. We can then speak of the incumbent party and hence government performance with little difficulty. In the U.S., where the party of the president need not be the party of the House or Senate and where references to the incumbent party can be more confusing than helpful, the executive-legislative connection is less clear.

Ironically, empirical research has examined the link most thoroughly in the American context. And the examination points to the limits of the American executive-legislative connection. Studies note a decline in the degree of coincidence between presidential and congressional voting (Cummings, 1966; Burnham, 1975). Jacobson (1983), reanalyzing Tufte's economic-presidential popularity model of congressional elections, finds that with the addition of a variable distinguishing the past elective experience of congressional challengers, presidential popularity no longer significantly affects the aggregate midterm outcome. Other researchers investigating individual voters' evaluations of presidents discover a fairly tenuous link to the congressional contest. Kernell (1977) maintains that midterm congressional results (1946-1966) are influenced by voter disapproval of the president, but this "negative voting" is minimal. Piereson (1975) notes an impact of presidential approval only for independents. Considering president approval with congressional variables (candidate evaluations, party, incumbency), Ragsdale (1980) observes very limited evidence of presidential influence. Again, the link based on presidential approval like that observed through presidential voting, is modest at best.

By contrast, executive performance, or the performance of the government, has not yet been measured as a factor influencing the collective choices of electorates outside the American context (but see Finer, 1980, pp. 131-133, for an indicator of perceived government performance in Britain). Researchers have found that individual voters' decisions are affected by their perceptions of party leaders in France (Campbell, 1974) and Canada (LeDuc, Clarke, Jenson, and Pammett, 1980), prime ministerial candidates in Britain (Butler and Stokes, 1976), and the prime minister and other government ministers in Ireland (Sinnott, 1978). But research has not examined how these individual attitudes on executives may translate to collective outcomes linking executives and legislatures. In short, the executive-legislative link has been studied most in a nation where the connection may be least strong.

On balance, research examining the economic performance model provides intermediate evidence that legislative elections are sensitive to national economic conditions. Yet so few nations have been explored that a crossnational assessment remains tentative. Moreover, studies have only begun to pinpoint what are most likely to be the influences and how important they may be compared to noneconomic matters. The referendum concept, so often discussed as a simple matter of satisfaction or dissatisfaction with the economy, perhaps should be viewed more intricately as a statement on other government agendas as well (see Ames, 1970). Moreover, the evaluation of overall government performance derives in part from loyalties and not directly from the performance itself. Research has identified economic concerns as a key element of legislative elections generally. Placing that statement in an appropriate perspective now becomes the task, which it seems is of equal consequence and greater difficulty.

Competitive Change

Research also considers legislative elections as sources of change. In this sense, electoral responsiveness depends on the degree of competitiveness among parties vying for legislative seats. As an introduction, it is important to consider what is meant by competition and how change can be monitored. Definitions of competition are at times offered, at other times assumed, and often left unclear. Three approaches seem most common. At its most elementary level, competition is indicated by opposition, by the number of contests in which two or more parties or candidates challenge one another. Studies of U.S. state legislative elections often use the presence of opposing candidates as a minimal indicator of competitiveness, since parties frequently proceed to victory unopposed. At a second level, when there is opposition, competition is typically indicated by the closeness of an individual race. Research on Britain often identifies competitive "marginal" constituencies as those in which a party wins by no more than 5 percent of the vote (as an example, see Rush, 1969, p. 69). Finally, on a national scale, competition is denoted by the closeness of national vote or the seat totals across the parties and by changes in the margins from previous elections.

Swings and Swing Ratios

In this last vein, studies have measured the extent of partisan change either by changes in votes and in seats from one election to the next or by associations between changes in votes and changes in seats. Comparing Great Britain, Ireland, and Italy (1946-1972), Katz finds that interelection change (measured either by percentage changes in votes or by seats) is more substantial in Britain than, in turn, Ireland and Italy (1980, pp. 70-73). Stokes (1976) examines changes in votes as the mean "swing" from one party to the other across all constituencies in the U.S. from 1952 through 1960 and in Great Britain for various years from 1892 through 1966. In a comparison of the standard deviations of the swings for the two countries, Stokes shows far greater uniformity of change across British constituencies between elections (i.e., small standard deviations) than across constituencies in the U.S., where greater heterogeneity is apparent. There are then different sources of change: in Great Britain, uniform national change, in the United States, the diversity of local factors. This is consistent with Stokes's discussion, noted earlier, of the greater importance of national factors in British elections. These patterns continue for both countries into the 1970s (see Burnham, 1975; Mann, 1978; Mayhew, 1974a).

Ultimately, the change in votes can be correlated with the change in seats as measures of party competition. This relationship, "the swing ratio," is the percentage change in seats associated with a 1 percent change in the nationwide legislative vote for a party (see Tufte, 1975, p. 823). As a simple linear relationship between votes and seats, it indicates the "responsiveness of the partisan composition of parliamentary bodies to changes in the partisan division of the vote" (Tufte, 1973, p. 542).

Dahl (1956) measures this swing ratio for U.S. House and Senate elections from 1928 to 1954. He observes that in House elections a 1 percent net shift in votes from one party to the other results in a net gain of 2.5

percent of the seats for the benefited party, in Senate elections a net gain of 3 percent of the seats (pp. 146-149). Expanding Dahl's research, Tufte (1973) records the swing ratio of six two-party systems (Great Britain, New Zealand, the United States, Michigan, New Jersey, New York). During comparable periods, Great Britain has the greatest swing ratio among the three nations (a 1 percent net shift in votes for a party yielding a 2.8 percent shift in seats, compared to 2.3 percent for New Zealand and 1.9 percent for the United States). The state legislatures examined show a fairly strong relationship between seats and votes, with the largest swing ratio being in New Jersey (a ratio of 3.7, compared to 2.1 for Michigan and 1.3 for New York). Spafford (1970) observes a translation rate (comparable to a swing ratio) of 3.0 in Canada from 1921 to 1965. Canadian legislative outcomes, then, are much like those of Great Britain.

What does the relative size of the swing ratio reflect? Tufte discusses the connection between the swings of an election and the swing ratio. "The more uniform electoral swings are across the nation, the greater will be the swing ratio" (1973, p. 547). Thus, the comparatively high swing ratio in Britain relative to the U.S. is not surprising, given the partisan swings themselves. The greater impact of national factors in British parliamentary elections produces higher swing ratios. By contrast, the proportionately stronger constituency influence in U.S. congressional elections results in lower swing ratios.

The size of the swing ratio also indicates the potential for turnover in the legislature. The smaller the swing ratio, the less responsive the partisan distribution of seats is to voter preferences, the less frequently turnover of a seat will occur. Tufte charts a close association between the swing ratio and turnover for the U.S. House, observing the decline of both from relatively high figures during the period 1870-1890 to their lowest points in 1970. Their concomitant decline denotes an overall decrease in the competitiveness of congressional seats.

Studies of vote-seat relationships indicate at the margin how resilient a legislative electoral system is to change in voter preferences. As the swing ratio drops, votes have less and less effect on seats, and the consequence is a less competitive system. Parties vie for seats but have a more limited opportunity to attain them. This lessened competition means less turnover of seats and greater stability of the current membership within the legislature. As Mayhew notes, variations in swings and swing ratios have significant consequences for electoral responsiveness, as the electorate attempts change in the legislature's composition. The electoral changes provide at least

a rotation of government elites that has policy consequences; at the most there is some detectable relation between what such temporarily empowered elites do and what popular wishes are. Over time the working of the seat swing has sometimes given a dialectical cast to national policy-making with successive elites making successive policy approximations. . . . Because of all the translation uncertainties, the House seats swing has been a decidedly blunt voter instrument, but it has been a noteworthy instrument nonetheless (1974a, p. 296).

Turnover and Competition

While the partisan swings and swing ratios illustrate the change that does occur with legislative elections, they do not directly measure the number of new members entering the legislature, through the retirement or defeat of old members. Available research permits a crossnational comparison of this turnover of legislative seats (measured by the percentage of new members) in six countries. Turnover rates in the United States, Italy, and Great Britain are all similar. In the U.S. from 1946 to 1980, 17 percent of the total House membership are incoming freshmen (adapted from Hinckley, 1981, p. 39). Mean turnover in Italy from 1953 to 1972 is 18 percent (adapted from Katz, 1980, p. 75). Mellors observes that British parliamentary turnover averages 19 percent across elections from 1950 to 1974 (1978, pp. 16-18). Turnover rates in Ireland, France, and West Germany appear somewhat higher. Irish Dail turnover between 1948 and 1973 averages 23 percent (adapted from Katz, 1981, p. 75). In the early Fifth Republic (1951-1968), Woshinsky (1973) notes, new members make up 36 percent of the French National Assembly. From 1957 to 1976, new members of the German Bundestag range from 25 to 30 percent of the body (Loewenberg and Patterson, 1979, p. 112).

Most striking is the considerable stability of membership: in each case, the number of returning members is rather high. As Loewenberg and Patterson point out, turnover declines as legislatures develop stable institutional patterns. Thereafter, the percentage of new members remains relatively low and stable, except during periods of major social, economic, or constitutional change (1979, pp. 106-113). Turnover thus provides an indication of both the extent and the limits of change in the composition of a legislature.

The principal work on turnover has been undertaken on U.S. state legislative elections. Indeed, while state legislative election research is still embryonic, much of what is known about state outcomes concerns membership turnover. Jewell (1982) provides basic information on levels of state legislative turnover. A downward trend in turnover is apparent; the average proportion of incoming freshmen legislators in lower houses declined from 45 percent in the 1950s to 37 percent in the 1970s (pp. 25-26). Turnover is still considerably higher, however, than that for the U.S. House.

Rosenthal (1974) analyzes factors affecting turnover from 1963 through 1971 for 50 state senates and houses, taken as groups. Opportunities for higher offices increase turnover for both houses; compensation (salary and expenses) more strongly affects turnover in the lower houses, while the electoral system (the number of years between elections) has greater influence in the upper houses. Shin and Jackson (1979) report the turnover for the 50 state upper and lower houses on a state-by-state basis. Exploring the period from 1931 through 1976, they observe wide variations and no real trends across time. The one trend that does exist, but not for all states, is a decline of turnover after 1960. The study provides a caution for state legislative election research: the generalizations which can be drawn may be as numerous as the states from which they are drawn. The different results of the Shin and Jackson study and the Rosenthal study suggest that patterns found for all state elections may vary considerably from patterns in any one of those elections.

Studies have also delineated the two elements of turnover: voluntary retirement and defeat. Ray (1976) traces both factors in the lower houses of eight states from 1897 through 1967. Again, there is some problem of identifying patterns across the states. In three states, voluntary retirement exceeds defeat as the largest component of turnover; in five states, defeat exceeds retirement. There are observable trends downward in voluntary retirement for each state, although no trend is apparent for defeats. Examining 29 states from 1966 to 1976, Calvert (1979) also finds a drop in voluntary retirement for both upper and lower houses, with a leveling off after 1968. Compensation, particularly for the Senate, is the greatest influence on retirement rates. Defeats during the period make up a much smaller portion of overall turnover and there is no apparent temporal change. Unlike state legislatures, the U.S. House in the 1970s has had a significant increase in voluntary retirements, an increase that follows a steady decline from the 1920s to the 1960s. Hibbing (1982b) finds that uncertainties in the seniority system and questions of salary increases promote more retirements (see also Hibbing, 1982a, 1982c; Cooper and West, 1981).

Aspects of Competition

Others have detailed more fully the competitiveness which may prompt specific levels of turnover. A good deal of research is available on intraparty competition in primaries for state legislatures and, to a lesser extent, for Congress. As noted earlier, the studies gauge competitiveness by the number of races involving opposition between two or more candidates. Key (1956), observing state legislative primaries in Missouri, Indiana, and Ohio, identifies three circumstances under which the competitiveness of the primaries varies. First, primaries in which an incumbent seeks renomination are less likely to involve competition than those in which an incumbent is not running. Second, competition in rural districts is lower than in more urban districts. Third, and Key finds most important, intraparty competition increases as the chances of general election victory for the party improve. In other words, the greater the strength of the party in interparty contests, the more intraparty activity.

The influences examined by Key have continued to be explored in most later research on state legislative primaries. Studying eight Southern states, Jewell (1967) confirms the pattern noted by Key. Races with incumbents are less often contested, especially those with more senior legislators seeking renomination; metropolitan districts are more competitive than rural districts; and where general election chances of victory are good, primary competition tends to be high.

Grau (1981) investigates lower house primaries in 15 Southern and non-Southern states from 1972 through 1978 and finds much the same overall picture observed by Key and Jewell, despite some state-by-state variations. The presence of an incumbent lessens the likelihood of candidates entering a race in both safe and marginal districts of a party. Interestingly, this is true for the opposition party as well as the incumbent's party. Thus, incumbents scare away competitors in their own primaries and discourage active primaries for the opposing party. Metropolitanism is again a factor, as is the party's strength in the general election. Unlike Key, who found the strength of the party in the general election the most important factor, Grau suggests that the presence or absence of an incumbent is the principal determinant of primary competition for both parties.

The little that is known about congressional primaries indicates major similarities to state legislative primaries. Charting House primaries from 1956 through 1974, Schantz (1980) notes that congressional incumbents, like state legislative incumbents, deter primary contests. He also underscores the interaction between party strength and incumbency analyzed by Grau. Party prospects in the general election affect primary contests only in races without incumbents. With incumbents running, primary contests are diminished, regardless of party strength. Unlike state legislative primaries, congressional primaries are not more likely to be contested in urban districts.

Some attention has been given interparty competition, most notably in U.S. state legislative elections. Examining the closeness of contests in eight states, Jewell shows that party competition is greatest in Indiana and Colorado, with over half the seats won by 60 percent of the vote or less. In California and Ohio, less than 40 percent of the districts are closely contested (1982, pp. 43-46). Early studies explored urbanism as one factor related to interparty competition (see Eulau, 1957; Gold and Schmidhauser, 1960; Jewell, 1967). However, there is no current research on factors affecting interparty competition.

The growing research on state legislative elections provides the most comprehensive information available on electoral turnover and competition.

more substantial. Using estimates of weekly caseloads obtained from congressional staffs, Johannes and McAdams (1981) detect no significant impact of casework on aggregate vote totals. Nor do they find any influence on individual voters' decisions. Fiorina (1981) presents a counterclaim that personal satisfaction with casework has a small, although conventionally insignificant, effect (p = .10). Unlike Yiannakis, Fiorina finds that those dissatisfied with the efforts are affected. Travel and mail have also been examined as aspects of members' constituency styles, but how these activities may affect members' reelection chances is as yet unknown (see Parker, 1980b; Cover, 1980).

Finally, scholars have investigated changes in voter behavior, distinct from incumbent behavior, as an explanation of the U.S. House advantage. Cover (1977), examining the period from 1958 to 1974, identifies an increase in partisan defections after 1964-1966 favoring incumbents. There is a steady increase in defection rates for people of the challenger's party, particularly after 1964. Defections for incumbent partisans are much less prevalent and much more erratic (see also Nelson, 1978).

In these many debates on how U.S. House incumbents have become more advantaged, each author attempts to shed light on one or another of a variety of potential incumbent resources: travel, franking, constituency service both in the legislature and at home, changes in voter behavior. Others try to determine when the advantage is most likely to occur: in the freshman term, at all levels, across generations, moving from marginal to safe seats. Yet, the claims are often contradicted by counterclaims and much ground remains unexplored. Home styles may be more important now because political scientists are now more sensitive to their existence. The value of casework may vary less in the eyes of voters than in the eyes of scholars. Voters may have always been positively disposed toward constituency service and critical of its absence or blatant mismanagement. The evidence on partisan defections leaves unsettled reasons for those defections. Did incumbents prompt them or merely benefit from them? In all, incumbents may be more safe, but we are still left wondering why.

Party Strength and Incumbent Success. In the extensive scholarly treatment of congressional incumbent strength and its increase, another factor in incumbent reelections has been lost sight of: party strength within a state or district. Perhaps this factor has received little attention because it is difficult to measure party support adequately, especially at the district level (see Kostroski, 1973, pp. 1225-1226; Owens and Olson, 1977, pp. 499-500). It may also be that concern about the decline of parties and partisanship has made studies of party strength less than interesting. Some studies are, however, available. Kostroski (1973) shows an erratic tradeoff between the impacts of party strength and of incumbency on Senate elections from 1948 to 1970. Interestingly, the matter has been pursued in state legislative research, where Caldeira and Patterson (1982) reveal that party strength is a more influential electoral determinant than is incumbency in upper and lower house races in Iowa and California (see also Owens and Olson, 1977; Welch, 1976). Yet beyond this, little is known. So the relative contribution of incumbents and parties to congressional election outcomes awaits future study.

Incumbency beyond the United States. Despite the dilemmas left unresolved, congressional research is valuable within the current comparative context. It is less important that a House incumbency advantage has increased than it is that such an advantage, specific to a member, exists at all. This raises a central question of how appropriate it is to consider such an effect in other legislative settings. Prevailing views suggest that incumbent strength, distinct from party strength, within an electoral system is an American oddity. In parliamentary systems, well-organized parties select candidates and voters decide among the parties. Incumbents may be easily returned to office, but it is the party, not the legislator, that has prompted the victory. As Barnes notes for Italy, "the party [is] in almost complete control over who is and who is not elected" (1977, p. 38; for similar views see Döring and Smith, 1982, on West Germany; Hancock, 1972, on Sweden; Weil, 1970, on the Netherlands).

Work on Great Britain provides a useful example on this point. Research demonstrates party control of the candidate selection process and the presumed lack of candidate control over the election process. Ranney (1965) sums up much of the research by concluding that as a result of the selection process, the qualities of incumbents and other candidates are of little consequence (see also Butler and Stokes, 1976). Research has also developed several measures of the safeness of party seats; these measures show stable party strength to be the prime factor accounting for incumbent reelections (see Finer, Berrington, and Bartholomew, 1961; Jones, 1963-1964; Rasmussen, 1969; Rush, 1969). In short, legislators' continued electoral success is based on party, not personal, strength.

Yet despite its widespread acceptance, there is an incongruity between this view of incumbents' inability to affect their electoral fates and the views of incumbents themselves. Legislators in Great Britain (Cain, Ferejohn, and Fiorina, 1979), Canada (Clarke, 1978), Ireland (Chubb, 1982), and Italy (Katz, 1980) all perceive their constituency service as beneficial for reelection. Cain, Ferejohn, and Fiorina note that of the MPs they interviewed, all felt that "doing well on cases could help protect them from national electoral swings" (1979, p. 519). Beyond legislators' own beliefs, there is added evidence that voters may favor incumbents. This is particularly apparent in Ireland, where deputies enjoy a personal edge over their running mates in preference voting, a result of their emphasizing local service (see

Gallagher, 1980, pp. 491-492; Chubb, 1982). Also, in the 1974 Assembly elections in Kenya, members who satisfactorily meet constituent needs are more likely to win reelection than those with whom constituents are dissatisfied (Loewenberg and Patterson, 1979, p. 108). In Great Britain, Ragsdale (1983) notes that voters are more likely to know incumbent MPs than their challengers, that the MPs' activities are positively perceived, and that these views affect voters' decisions.

This evidence modifies to a degree the traditional belief that parliamentary elections are exclusively party affairs. There may be an incremental advantage provided by an incumbent for a party within a constituency. The increment may not be large; it may not be as large as that found in legislative races in the United States; but it may be large enough to help secure a safe victory for the party and retain the seat in the legislature. As one indication of this, Williams (1966-1967), in a study of the swing in marginal British constituencies from 1950 to 1966, observes that established MPs (those serving at least eight years) are likely to garner an additional 1.5 to 3.5 percent of the vote for their party, regardless of the direction of the national swing (see also Cain, 1983). To be sure, research on the incumbency advantage requires a balanced perspective. As Barnes states, "the role of the party remains great even if the impact of the individual representative can be demonstrated" (1977, p. 136). Nevertheless, the demonstration does suggest that a party's victory may be aided by its incumbents running.

Overall, research on U.S. congressional elections may benefit from greater attention to party strength as a source of incumbent reelection success; research on parliamentary elections may profit from greater attention to incumbent strength. Still, incumbent strength and party strength, in whatever combinations, are factors limiting electoral change. Both reveal limits to competition and resulting stability within the legislature.

Electoral Change, Continuity, and Responsiveness

Research on electoral change has successfully monitored changes in votes and seats in many legislative settings. Research on incumbent strength and party strength has shown that these changes are limited by incumbent reelections. But the electoral margin that denotes change or continuity is ill-defined. In gauging this margin, scholars are faced with a central question: how much change is change enough? How many seats must change hands before we are willing (or able) to say that the election has produced substantive change? Indeed, is change a necessary condition for electoral responsiveness? There are, of course, clear-cut instances of electoral change, when enough seats change to change the government or the majority party. In these cases, the electorate is able to alter the direction of the legislature and thus maintain responsiveness.

But there are also less dramatic forms of change. A dominant party or a majority party may gain or lose seats without a change in government. There may be occasions of little change at all, when a stable popular vote yields few changes in the governing coalition. These instances make us ask whether electoral continuity aids or inhibits responsiveness. Continual success of the majority party or the governing party or coalition may mean that the electorate is satisfied with the course of the legislature, its individual members, or the party balance. Such an explanation, if warranted, expands the notion of responsiveness, since it means that limits to change need not be limits to citizen participation and control.

Yet, it may be that continuity reflects ineffective party competition. Parties may be unable to effectively challenge a major party in a district for reasons unrelated to the achievements of the party or its legislators. Change that might otherwise occur suffers for want of that challenge. Such a situation would diminish legislative responsiveness, since ineffective party competition preempts the possibility of change. These differing, yet equally plausible, interpretations of how continuity limits change and determines responsiveness suggests the work needed to clarify the rather muddled meaning of electoral margins.

Voter Preference

In legislative elections, the issue of responsiveness can influence the decisions made by parties, candidates, and voters. During the campaign, parties and candidates may attempt to convince voters that they are responsive to their interests. Voters may make parties' and candidates' responsiveness the underlying criterion when they decide on their votes. This links individual voters' decisions to the activities of parties and candidates, with the campaign as a focus of analysis.

Legislative Election Campaigns

Legislative election campaigns can be conducted within three political settings: within active party organizations, developing party organizations, or inactive party organizations. Barnes observes that among a sample of newly-elected and returning Italian deputies in 1968, a significant proportion recall their parties' help in gaining preference votes, a finding which indicates that the parties are fairly active (1977, pp. 144-155). Especially for the Communist and Christian Democratic deputies, the parties organized meetings and rallies, as well as providing specific information to party activists and voters on how they should assign their preference votes. Italian candidates also stress their "party program" in the campaign (see Katz, 1980, p. 88). Britain also provides a clear example of active party organizations (see Kavanagh, 1970; Rush, 1969; Ranney, 1965).

As in Italy, campaigns are relatively party-centered in India, but involve what might be considered developing party organizations. Although party efforts are established, they occur within a context of uncertainty. Mehta (1975) provides evidence of the extent of party efforts in an in-depth study of campaigning in a single constituency during the 1971 elections. Election meetings and posters are key sources of information, as is door-to-door canvassing. Yet, as Eldersveld and Ahmed (1978) caution, the parties have mobilized and the masses have accepted parties and elections only recently, since independence in 1947, in a period often marked by conflict and violence. Thus, citizens have been exposed to campaign activities, but in varying degrees and least among those who are illiterate and from the lower castes (1978, p. 24, pp. 224-228). And in the post independence period, "the Indian public remains primarily an illiterate, poor, and overwhelmingly rural and caste society" (1978, p. 9).

In contrast to these party-centric campaigns, American legislative campaigns are more nearly candidate-centric. Indeed, a theme emerges in the research: party efforts vary and candidates need personal campaign organizations to compensate for party shortcomings. Leuthold (1968) observes that in the 1962 congressional campaigns in the San Francisco Bay area, the support of party leaders and party resources (money, training, research) are most often channeled into competitive campaigns. Candidates with little chance of winning receive little party help. Seligman, King, Kim, and Smith (1974) find much the same focus of party attention on competitive districts in Oregon legislative races. In their analysis of defeated congressional candidates in 1962, Huckshorn and Spencer (1971) conclude that while party leaders are the key impetus in the candidates' decisions to run, party follow-through is inadequate. The candidates themselves see the weakness of party organization and erratic party support as the central reasons for their defeats.

Party ineffectiveness thus places an inordinate burden on the candidates' personal organizations. For incumbents, these are frequently well organized, ongoing extensions of activities in office. For less experienced candidates, the organizations are far more temporary and often have "no antecedent and probably a limited future" (Huckshorn and Spencer, 1971, p. 229; see also Jacobson, 1983, pp. 49-74). These weak personal organizations, as Fowler (1980) notes, leave challengers reliant on subjective information and intuition in making campaign decisions, with little understanding of how a winning electoral coalition could best be formed (see also Maisel, 1982). Ultimately, American legislative candidates' perceptions of the effectiveness of their campaigns is heavily colored by whether they win or lose. Kingdon, in a principal study of state legislative candidates and congressional candidates, observes that winners "tend to emphasize the dynamic manipulable variables that affect votes at the margin," with the campaign therefore making a difference (1966, p. 35). Losers, however, see the matter as out of their control, the outcome resting instead on a blind vote for party.

The Costs of Campaigns

The decisions made within party and candidate organizations on who should run and how they should run are often tied to the money used to run. The impact of campaign funding and expenditures has been examined in several legislative contexts. Rosenthal (1981, p. 33) reports 1978 campaign spending in state legislative races for the upper and lower houses of nine states. Not surprisingly, despite variation across the states, winners spend more than losers and state Senate candidates spend more that House candidates. Caldeira and Patterson (1982) observe a curvilinear relationship between campaign spending and state legislative election outcomes in Iowa and California. The more money, the more votes, until a threshold is reached, after which spending has a diminishing impact (see also Welch, 1976). Examining spending in races for the California Assembly (1972-1974), Glantz, Abramowitz, and Burkhart (1976) show that challenger expenditures influence electoral outcomes, when the analysis is controlled for party registration and incumbent expenditures (see also Owens and Olson, 1977). For California incumbents, the more they spend, the less well they do, incumbent spending being wholly reactive to challenger strength and spending.

This is also true in U.S. House campaigns (Jacobson, 1978, 1980). The more the challenger spends, the greater is voter recognition and support. Again for House incumbents, as they spend more their victory margins tend to decrease. For the Senate, results are less clear. Senate challengers do not enjoy the same spending boost in recognition and votes as do House challengers, since they start from a less disadvantaged position—with stronger personal organizations, more attention from party organizations, and more money (see Fenno, 1982). The resources available for various congressional candidates may be tied to national political trends. Jacobson and Kernell (1981) offer the argument that contributors, knowing the trends favoring one party or another, are more likely to support the advantaged party. Unhappily, efforts have not yet been undertaken to analyze the impact of campaign spending on the decisions of voters in other national legislative contests.

Voters and Campaigns

What bearing might the campaign have on voter preferences? Pulzer remarks that "it is one thing to dragoon, another to persuade." Campaigners must "go on the assumption that most people's minds are made up: an election campaign makes sense only on the assumption that some are not" (1967, p. 89). Much depends on two key aspects of voter preference: voters' standing commitments to parties or groups and the information voters have about specific candidates and issues in a race.

Voters' Standing Commitments. Numerous studies have explored the extent to which partisanship, viewed as an established loyalty to a party, may be useful in explaining electors' decisions. There are three central issues in research examining the electoral relevance or irrelevance of partisan attitudes. First, do voters report an identification with a party? Second, does the party identification have meaning independent of party voting? Third, is party voting stable? (For a lucid elaboration of the three points, see Baker, Dalton, and Hildebrandt, 1982, pp. 195-196.)

Scholars have attempted to test whether party identification is a valid concept in several nations with varied results. The importance of partisanship continues to be well documented among voters in U.S. legislative elections. Even with the decline of parties in America, many voters continue to identify with a party, use the party affiliation to cast their vote, and vote for the same party fairly consistently (for a full discussion of party and congressional voters, see Hinckley, 1981, pp. 61-77; Jacobson, 1983, pp. 75-122; for state legislative voters, see Owens and Olson, 1977). In an early study on party affiliation in Norway, Campbell and Valen (1966) suggest that Norwegians also identify with several political parties. At the time, party voting appears to have been more stable in Norway than in the United States. Borre (1980), however, shows increasing instability from 1950 to 1977 in Norway, as well as in Denmark, Finland, and Sweden. Among Italians, there appears to be an increase in partisan attitudes from the late 1950s to the late 1960s; party voting is also highly stable (Barnes, 1977, pp. 71-74). A similar pattern appears to have existed in France (see Inglehart and Hochstein, 1972; Campbell, 1974; and MacRae, 1967, pp. 232-242).

Butler and Stokes (1976) observe great stability in party voting over successive British elections. Drawing a comparison with the United States, they find that the stability is nearly identical in the two nations: 79 percent in Britain and 78 percent in the U.S. However, British electors tend to change their party affiliation to match their vote (but see Cain and Ferejohn, 1981). Americans, by contrast, are more likely to keep their affiliation with one party while voting for the opposite party. Nonetheless, party affiliation appears to have some meaning in the British context distinct from party choice at the time of a specific election. Specifically, Crewe, Särlvik, and Alt (1977) chart party identification and party support as separate aspects of partisan dealignment in Britain from 1964 through 1974.

Identification declines only after 1970, while stability of voting shows a continuous erosion beginning in the 1950s (see also Zucherman and Lichbach, 1977).

Partisanship appears less relevant in other legislative settings, including the Netherlands (Thomassen, 1976) and West Germany (Kasse, 1976; Baker, Dalton, and Hildebrandt, 1982). For the Dutch and the Germans, party affiliation appears to reflect vote choice rather than influence it. Indeed, Budge and Farlie conclude in an eight-nation study that "the very predictive success of party identification . . . leads one to suspect its empirical independence of voting choice, its conceptual antecedence, and its explanatory capacity" (1976, p. 123).

To alleviate some of the difficulties surrounding the partisanship concept, Campbell (1974) adapts Key's notion of a "standing commitment," so that it includes ideological and religious dimensions in addition to a partisan dimension. Campbell finds this to accommodate more adequately the impact of long-term affiliations on French voter choice. This or other adaptations may help minimize the difficulties of interpreting the role of partisanship in legislative elections.

Although questions exist on the extent to which legislative voters have long-standing loyalties to a party, there is little doubt that commitments to socioeconomic groups or classes shape legislative voter preferences, particularly in British and European settings. Indeed, this is often the distinction made between the U.S. and these settings. As much as it has been a truism that party is a major influence on voters' choices in U.S. legislative elections, it has been a truism that class is the major influence in other countries. And like party, class voting and its change over time is the subject of controversy.

In a classic study, Alford (1963) finds that between 1952 and 1962 class voting (with class indicated by occupations) is most prevalent in Great Britain and successively less important in Australia, the United States, and Canada. Butler and Stokes (1976) observe the decline of the importance of social class ties, indicated by occupation, as determinants of British party preferences and party voting across elections from 1963 through 1974. Franklin and Mughan (1978) suggest that when class is assumed to precede other variables (union membership, phone ownership, tenancy) in time, it has both direct and indirect effects on vote choice. They, like Butler and Stokes, observe an erosion in class voting from 1966 to 1970.

Investigating a somewhat broader period, 1945 to 1974, Zucherman and Lichbach (1977) draw a conclusion contrary to Franklin and Mughan's: that the working class support for the Conservative and middle class support for Labour has remained fairly stable across the time frame. Beyond Great Britain, Zucherman and Lichbach find that given the degree of social heterogeneity within West Germany, parties remain similar from the 1950s through the 1970s. In Sweden, heterogeneity increases somewhat, but there is no evidence of any party becoming a "catch-all" party (see also Särlvik, 1969). Even in U.S. congressional elections, where catch-all parties are most likely present, there is some indication of differences between working class and middle class voters. Weatherford (1978) observes, when he has controlled for party, that economic conditions have a greater impact on working class voter choice than on middle class voter decisions. Social cleavages, defined by occupation and sector, are also important determinants of party voting in Israel (see Burstein, 1978).

There are, however, limits to the effects of social class on voter preference when considered with other factors. Lijphart (1979) analyzes the impacts of social class, language, and religion on voter choice in four countries—Belgium, Canada, Switzerland, and South Africa. In each case, language and religion are more important than social class. In fact, language and religion are mutually reinforcing, rather than crosscutting, determinants of party choice in Belgium, Switzerland, and Canada.

Voter Information. Beyond loyalties to party and class, voters may make decisions on the basis of their knowledge of party candidates and current issues. A consensus emerges in recent research on legislative elections that voters' information, while limited, is nonetheless sufficient to influence their choices. For American congressional voters, knowledge of the candidates is neither overwhelming nor absent (Stokes and Miller, 1966; Hinckley, 1976; compare these with Ferejohn, 1977; Mann, 1978). Congressional voters often provide general evaluations of the candidates, their experience, personal qualities, and leadership characteristics (see Hinckley, Hofstetter, and Kessel, 1974; Wright, 1974; Ragsdale, 1980; Parker, 1980a, 1981). The information congressional voters have, however, is likely to favor incumbent candidates more than their challengers (see Hinckley, 1980; Jacobson, 1981a; Mann and Wolfinger, 1980). House incumbents are also better liked than their opponents, whom voters treat indifferently. This appears to be the result of incumbents' own popularity, measured by their district attentiveness, personal helpfulness, and vote positions (see Jacobson, 1981b; Parker, 1981), and of the invisibility of their challengers (Hinckley, 1980) and the reciprocal influence of popularity and invisibility on voter choice (Ragsdale, 1981).

A comparison of British and American voters reveals that, like their American counterparts, British electors are more aware of incumbent MPs than of their opponents (see Ragsdale, 1983). Members of Parliament are perceived as favorably as are members of Congress. And, like American electoral choices, British voters' decisions are influenced by their knowledge of incumbents and challengers and their opinion on members' job performance.

Pierce and Converse (1981) show that candidate visibility in France is generally related to incumbency. Incumbents are better known than, in turn, former deputies, and candidates with no parliamentary experience. Yet, in examining the joint effect of parliamentary experience and electoral success on voters' familiarity, the authors find some intricacies. Among losers, the general pattern holds: incumbents, former deputies, and inexperienced losers are successively less known. But among winners, there is no difference in familiarity across the three groups. "The determining force affecting candidate visibility among winners appears to be the simple fact of electoral victory itself, and that force completely washes out the effect of differences in previous parliamentary experience" (p. 342). The authors note that French voters are more likely than Americans to remember candidates' names and candidates' parties. Additionally, familiarity hinges most directly on victory in France, but it is more directly linked to incumbency status in the U.S.

French voters' decisions are influenced by their attitudes toward the candidates. As Campbell observes, opinions on local candidates, as well as on national leaders and issues, shape choices among significant groups of voters with limited standing commitments to ideology, party, or religion (1974, p. 80). This is not true for those with stronger commitments. A similar pattern is seen in Canada by LeDuc et al. Measuring the effects of attitudes toward local candidates, party leaders, and issues on the 1974 vote, they show that views of local candidates modestly influence voting behavior, but only among electors with variable party commitments (1980, p. 40). Thus, it appears that the influence of the campaign, including efforts of the legislative candidates, depends on the extent of voter commitments to partisan or other affiliations. Among voters with abiding commitments, attitudes about specific campaign factors are likely to have little bearing on their vote. Among voters with less durable loyalties, the views become more important.

As the studies by Campbell and LeDuc et al. reveal, research has examined voters' familiarity with issues, in addition to their familiarity with candidates. Indeed, the more studies probe voters' knowledge of issues, the more it appears they know. This knowledge also influences their electoral choices. In both the Campbell and the LeDuc et al. studies, the impact of issues on voter preference is actually greater than that of local candidates or party leaders. Additionally, Alt, Särlvik, and Crewe (1976), examining the effect of issues on the 1974 British election, observe that the perceived distance between a voter's position on an issue and that of the party has an impact on electoral choice. "Electors" they conclude "are not as politically illiterate as is often assumed" (p. 274). Much the same view is taken by Studler (1978), who finds that the colored immigration issue is important in the British election in 1970, but not in 1964 or 1977. In the United States, Wright (1976) finds that when candidates clearly diverge on the issues involved, issues are more likely to have an impact, thereby decreasing congressional voters' reliance on incumbency. Finally, Baker, Dalton, and Hildebrandt (1982) show that German voter decisions are influenced by the perceived competence of the parties on such issues as education, price stability, and U.S. relations (1961-1972).

Legislative Voters

In the countries where information is available, it indicates that voters adopt stable party choices partly on the basis of long-standing identifications with class or party, that they pay some attention to issues, and that they know legislative candidates, although they may not know them well. Two aspects of this picture stand out. First, studies of party and class point to both commonalities and variations across legislative settings. Party and class affiliations provide ways in which voters make stable party choices across successive elections. Barring crosscutting cleavages which may result from clashes between party and class (see Butler and Stokes, 1976), legislative voters appear to be creatures of comfortable political habit. Indeed, perhaps the most central observation in these studies is the great consistency with which voters make party choices from one election to the next. Still, the relative importance of party and class in creating this stability also varies across legislative settings. In some contexts, class more than party defines the result; in others, party is the stronger determinant. So stability and these variations in stability afford topics for future comparative research.

Second, the comparative design provides some evidence on responsiveness as a general criterion in voters' preferences, but also indicates what is yet unknown. In U.S. legislatures, responsiveness as a link between individual voters and individual candidates seems to merit study. The evaluations voters have of candidates are specific enough to suggest the qualities they identify with responsiveness: positive personal characteristics, experience, leadership. This is consonant with the emphasis placed on personal attributes by candidates in their campaigns (see Kingdon, 1966; Leuthold, 1968). It also parallels the ways incumbents choose to convey their empathy and identity with voters and their qualifications for office (Fenno, 1978). Voters then seek and candidates stress responsiveness to policy claims, to district or personal problems, or to feelings of satisfaction.

What is less clear is how in other contexts such responsiveness might link voters with candidates or, more especially, parties. Responsiveness to local concerns appears to be a particularly important criterion in candidate appeals and voter decisions in Ireland (Chubb, 1982). There is also some indication that French voters and deputies share common desires to protect local interests from central government control (Woshinsky, 1973). But beyond this, little evidence is available on the ways candidates may emphasize responsiveness and the ways voters may wish to see it emphasized. Additionally, responsiveness may be a criterion voters use to evaluate parties in some settings. The link may rest on the party's accommodation of class interests, language concerns, religious beliefs, or issue stands. West German voters' impressions of the parties' issue competence provides some information on the form of this party responsiveness, but little else is known (Baker, Dalton, and Hildebrandt, 1982). So, as a whole the research provides substantial, albeit preliminary, evidence on legislative voters and elements of their electoral preferences.

Comparative Legislative Elections

Having pooled the significant studies on legislative elections in several nations and the American states, we can offer a general account of the parallels and the differences which emerge. The elections are structured at the outset by electoral laws that bias outcomes in favor of several large parties and minimize the fractionalization of partisan interests. The bias, observed in virtually all electoral systems, varies relatively across the systems. The effects of electoral arrangements, however, are more modest than those of other factors. One such factor is the performance of the national economy. In periods of economic decline, the electoral fortunes of the incumbent party in two-party and multi-party systems post a corresponding diminution. Economic changes may then affect the competitiveness among parties seeking seats in the legislature. There are variations in this competitiveness as vote changes, seat changes, and swing ratios differ in magnitude among electoral settings.

Despite the differences in the degree of marginal change, the margin itself remains a rather small one. Whether as a result of members' own political strength or the strength of their parties, legislators gain reelection with considerable ease. Continuity, then, more than change, characterizes legislative election outcomes and may limit the degree of responsiveness. This continuity is in part a measure of the stable party choices made by voters. Standing commitments to party, ideology, religion, or class prompt voters to act again as before. Depending on the strength of these attachments, voters may also gauge their preferences according to more short-range views drawn from the campaign. Voters, faced with party-centric campaigns or more candidate-centric efforts, are informed about the candidates but—equally important—their information tends to be minimal. Voter attitudes toward these candidates and voter opinions on party leaders and issues are most likely to affect their electoral preferences when standing commitments are weak. In sum, the choices voters ultimately make are not formed only during the campaign, nor do they end with the closing of the polls. They reflect evolving and devolving patterns of the economy, political demography, political organizations, social outlooks, and personal opinions.

These empirical statements offer a first step in ordering existing research on legislative elections within a comparative framework. They provide touchstones to underscore the value of the three analytic approaches to responsiveness present in the research. Looking ahead, it would be tempting to propose more studies of more nations, more elections. Many electoral settings have not been investigated and among those that have, often only a single election has been explored. Consequently, discussions are incomplete on how elections compare across several settings at any one time and how they may change over time.

Yet simply supplying an inventory of research items which have not been done, which could be done again for another election or another country, or which could be done for the elections of several countries begs a more fundamental question: what effect do legislative elections have? Do legislative elections make a difference for the electors, the elected, the parties, and the decisions and procedures of the legislature? This question, left aside in many legislative election studies, poses a serious challenge not only to scholars of legislative elections, but also to those interested in legislatures. It asks about the ways in which the institution and its members may affect and be affected by citizen decisions. It allows us to consider electoral responsiveness beyond the immediate election context. If we pursue this question, a research agenda may emerge which, while tied to the existing research, nonetheless expands our view of legislative elections.

On a fundamental level, we can examine whether legislative elections affect the activities of the legislature. Do elections determine which party controls the government or is designated as the majority party? In some nations there is an automatic link between election outcomes and government composition; while in others the election merely defines the stakes for interparty bargaining following the contest (see King, 1981, pp. 298-299). A connection between election choices and the formation of the government might offer one concrete indicator of electoral responsiveness. Among systems with a direct link, the people and parties voters choose will be reflected in the composition of the executive. In settings without the link, voters' choices bear a more tenuous relationship to who governs.

Do elections actually shape legislative policy decisions? In some instances, the electorally-established distribution of seats among the parties may influence levels of government expenditures or economic, social welfare, or defense programs. In other cases, however, the composition of the legislature may not affect policies as much as social or economic factors do (for a clear discussion of studies observing both outcomes, see King, 1981, pp. 300-320).

The link between election and policy or between election and government formation may provide ways of moving research beyond merely descriptive categories of elections, such as two-party and multiparty parliamentary and presidential systems. Instead, legislative settings can be classified according to the degree of responsiveness which exists, based on the presence or absence of each link.

What effect do elections have on representation within the legislature? Voters are not merely electing legislators, they are choosing representatives responsive to them. The interests and concerns of voters may shape the way legislators act. Research on representation has long explored a one-to-one policy agreement between citizens and legislators, expecting it to be the key aspect of representation, yet has often found little evidence of such a policy congruence (for a survey of this problem, see Eulau and Karps, 1977). Election studies help explain this result. Attention to constituency business, more than the accommodation of constituency policy preferences, appears to be the most general activity of legislators in numerous legislative bodies and an activity assessed by voters (see Clarke, 1978). Additionally, the importance of group affiliations of class, religion, or language for voters suggests that legislators may represent groups within a constituency or within the entire nation. Thus, a one-to-one policy congruence between legislators and individual citizens or between legislators and a single constituency becomes an unlikely result (see Weissberg, 1978).

How do elections intertwine with the institution of the legislature, its norms, procedures, and structures? The elections may affect the leadership, committees, staff, and organization of the body; reciprocally, the institution may influence the reelection chances of members and the safeness of seats. Key institutional arrangements may insulate individual members or the incumbent party from defeat or provide opportunities to develop constituent contacts and to promote local or group concerns.

Do elections affect party systems? Certainly, party systems structure elections; the number of parties may determine whether there will be clear winners and losers or whether coalitions are formed. But it is also important to consider how elections may influence party systems by altering or strengthening allegiances among the parties over time. The controversies and candidacies in an election may shift alignments among the parties and modify party organizations. Do elections influence the agenda of the media? If elections are considered major national events, media time and space would be consumed accordingly. Investigating the election coverage by various forms of media also raises issues of how the media may set agendas for the elections. Little is yet known on the effect of the mass media on legislative elections, including the impact of news coverage, advertising, and editorial positions.

Finally, a paradoxical situation can be posed in which elections are regularly held, but have no effect on the legislature beyond establishing its composition. The policies adopted, the activities of the members, and the institutional arrangements established procede independent of the election results. Are elections rituals? Whether or not elections place any constraints on lawmakers, they can offer symbolic assurance to the participants. Voters may feel that their participation and decisions have some effect on legislative outcomes, even if in fact they do not. The media may also portray the elections as consequential. The elections thus serve as public ceremonies and voting becomes a ritualized expression of belonging and commitment.

The effect of legislative elections, then, is a central issue for any electoral system. What, if anything, have voters accomplished by entering the polling booth? The universality of the issue suggests that it can be most effectively addressed within a comparative framework. Comparisons across various types of electoral systems can be made which suggest what effects of elections on the broader legislative setting are most likely. This may also provide insight into how these various aspects of the legislative setting affect elections. The information gained may then add to the general empirical statements offered by current research.

Legislative elections are not, then, mysterious enterprises defined solely by the idiosyncracies of individual nations, their electoral laws, and traditions. Notable similarities exist which broadly define components common to almost all legislative elections. Legislative election research, which might have seemed equally mysterious, defines instead an area of comparative study. Knowledge of legislative elections is more than knowledge of U.S. congressional elections. Material is sufficient for crossnational references to be made and classification schemes to be explored. So while much is left to be done, the ground is far from unbroken. And the ground that has been broken suggests that the study of comparative legislative elections is not arcane or misnamed but is a relevant addition to comparative legislative research.

NOTES

An earlier version of this piece was presented at the Legislative Research Conference at the University of Iowa, October, 1982. My thanks to Gerhard Loewenberg for his graciousness during the conference and to Samuel C. Patterson for his insightful editorial help and criticism. I am also grateful to Thomas Mann, Roger Davidson, Heinz Eulau, and Barbara Hinckley for their comments.

1. Stokes presents no corresponding data for turnout in Great Britain. Research on voter turnout is at least as extensive as that on voter choice. Certainly issues of turnout address a basic dimension of the responsiveness of legislative elections— whether voters, with the choices available and the likely results, will have any impact on legislators. Space constraints prohibit treatment of the material. For a useful essay which employs a comparative perspective, see Crewe, 1981 (see also Powell, 1980).

2. Note that the study involves vote intention, not the vote. However, Whiteley (1979) has studied the relationship between vote intention and the vote in Great Britain. He finds great stability in the vote intention measure and a strong influence of intention on the vote.

REFERENCES

Alford, John R. and John R. Hibbing. 1981. "Increased Incumbency Advantage in the House," *Journal of Politics* 43: 1042-1061.

Alford, Robert. 1963. *Party and Society*. Chicago: Rand McNally.

Alt, James, Bo Särlvik, and Ivor Crewe. 1976. "Partisanship and Policy Choice: Issue Preferences in the British Electorate, February, 1974," *British Journal of Political Science* 6: 279-290.

Ames, Barry. 1970. "Bases of Support for Mexico's Dominant Party," *American Political Science Review* 64: 153-167.

Arcelus, Francisco and Allan Meltzer. 1975. "The Effect of Aggregate Economic Variables on Congressional Elections," *American Political Science Review* 69: 1232-1239.

Baker, Kendall, Russell Dalton, and Kai Hildebrandt. 1981. *Germany Transformed*. Cambridge: Harvard University Press.

Barnes, Samuel. 1977. *Representation in Italy*. Chicago: University of Chicago Press.

Bloom, Howard and H. Douglas Price. 1975. "Voter Response to Short-Run Economic Conditions: The Asymmetric Effect of Prosperity and Recession," *American Political Science Review* 69: 1240-1254.

Born, Richard. 1979. "Generational Replacement and the Growth of Incumbent Reelection Margins in the U.S. House," *American Political Science Review* 73: 811-817.

Borre, Ole. 1980. "Electoral Instability in Four Nordic Countries, 1950-1977," *Comparative Political Studies* 13: 141-171.

Budge, Ian and Dennis Farlie. 1976. "A Comparative Analysis of Factors Correlated with Turnout and Voting Choice," in Ian Budge, Ivor Crewe, and Dennis Farlie, eds., *Party Identification and Beyond*. London: John Wiley, pp. 103-126.

Burnham, Walter. 1975. "Insulation and Responsiveness in Congressional Elections," *Political Science Quarterly* 90: 411-435.

Burstein, Paul. 1978. "Social Cleavages and Party Choice in Israel: A Log-Linear Analysis," *American Political Science Review* 72: 96-109.

Butler, David and Dennis Kavanaugh. 1974. *The British General Election of February 1974*. London: Macmillan.

Butler, David, Howard Penniman, and Austin Ranney, eds. 1981. *Democracy at the Polls*. Washington, DC: American Enterprise Institute.

Butler, David and Donald Stokes. 1976. *Political Change in Britain*. New York: St. Martin's Press.

Cain, Bruce. 1983. "Blessed Be the Tie That Unbinds: Constituency Work and Vote Swing in Great Britain," *Political Studies* 31: 103-111.

Cain, Bruce and John Ferejohn. 1981. "Party Identification in the United States and Great Britain," *Comparative Political Studies* 14: 31-47.

Cain, Bruce, John Ferejohn, and Morris Fiorina. 1979. "The House is Not a Home: British MPs in their Constituencies," *Legislative Studies Quarterly* 4: 501-523.

Caldeira, Gregory and Samuel C. Patterson. 1982. "Bringing Home the Votes: Electoral Outcomes in State Legislative Races," *Political Behavior* 4:33-67.

Calvert, Jerry. 1979. "Revolving Doors: Volunteerism in State Legislatures," *State Government* 52: 174-181.

Campbell, Angus and Henry Valen. 1966. "Party Identification in Norway and the United States," in Angus Campbell, Philip Converse, Warren Miller, and Donald Stokes, eds., *Elections and the Political Order.* New York: John Wiley, pp. 245-268.

Campbell, Bruce. 1974. "The Future of the Gaullist Majority: An Analysis of French Electoral Politics," *American Journal of Political Science* 28: 67-94.

Chubb, Basil. 1982. *The Government and Politics of Ireland.* Stanford: Stanford University Press.

Clarke, Harold. 1978. "Determinants of Provincial Constituency Service Behavior: A Multivariate Analysis," *Legislative Studies Quarterly* 3: 601-628.

Collie, Melissa. 1981. "Incumbency, Electoral Safety, and Turnover in the House of Representatives 1952-1976," *American Political Science Review* 75: 119-131.

Cooper, Joseph and William West. 1981. "The Congressional Career in the 1970's" in Lawrence Dodd and Bruce Oppenheimer, eds., *Congress Reconsidered.* 2d ed. Washington, DC: Congressional Quarterly Press, pp. 83-106.

Cover, Albert. 1977. "One Good Term Deserves Another: The Advantage of Incumbency in Congressional Elections," *American Journal of Political Science* 21: 523-541.

———. 1980. "Contacting Congressional Constituents: Some Patterns of Perquisite Use," *American Journal of Political Science* 24: 125-135.

Cover, Albert and David Mayhew. 1977. "Congressional Dynamics and the Decline of Competitive Congressional Elections," in Lawrence Dodd and Bruce Oppenheimer, eds., *Congress Revisited.* New York: Praeger, pp. 54-72.

Crewe, Ivor. 1981. "Electoral Participation," in David Butler, Howard R. Penniman, and Austin Ranney, eds., *Democracy at the Polls.* Washington, DC: American Enterprise Institute, pp. 216-263.

Crewe, Ivor, Bo Särlvik, and James Alt. 1977. "Partisan Dealignment in Britain 1964-1974," *British Journal of Political Science* 7:129-190.

Cummings, Milton. 1966. *Congressmen and the Electorate.* New York: Free Press.

Dahl, Robert. 1956. *A Preface to Democratic Theory.* Chicago: University of Chicago Press.

Döring, Herbert and Gordon Smith, eds. 1982. *Party Government and Political Culture in West Germany.* London: Macmillan.

Duverger, Maurice. 1963. *Political Parties.* New York: John Wiley.

Eldersveld, Samuel and Bashiruddin Ahmed. 1978. *Citizens and Politics: Mass Political Behavior in India.* Chicago: University of Chicago Press.

Erikson, Robert. 1971. "The Advantage of Incumbency in Congressional Elections," *Polity* 3: 395-405.

———. 1972. "Malapportionment, Gerrymandering, and Party Fortunes in Congressional Elections," *American Political Science Review* 66: 1234-1245.

———. 1978. "Constituency Opinion and Congressional Behavior," *American Journal of Political Science* 22: 511-535.

Eulau, Heinz. 1957. "The Ecological Basis of Party Systems: The Case of Ohio," *Midwest Journal of Political Science* 1: 125-135.

Eulau, Heinz and Paul Karps. 1977. "The Puzzle of Representation: Specifying Comments on Responsiveness," *Legislative Studies Quarterly* 2: 233-254.

Europa Year Book 1982. 2 vols. London: Europa Publications, 1982.

Fenno, Richard. 1978. *Home Style.* Boston: Little, Brown.

_____. 1982. *The United States Senate: A Bicameral Perspective.* Washington, DC: American Enterprise Institute.

Ferejohn, John. 1977. "On the Decline of Competition in Congressional Elections," *American Political Science Review* 71: 166-176.

Finer, Samuel E. 1980. *The Changing British Party System, 1945-1979.* Washington, DC: American Enterprise Institute.

Finer, Samuel E., H.B. Berrington, and D.J. Bartholomew. 1961. *Backbench Opinion in the House of Commons, 1955-1959.* London: Pergamon Press.

Fiorina, Morris. 1977a. "The Case of the Vanishing Marginals: The Bureaucracy Did It," *American Political Science Review* 71: 177-181.

_____. 1977b. *Congress Keystone of the Washington Establishment.* New Haven: Yale University Press.

_____. 1978. "Economic Retrospective Voting In American National Elections: A Micro Analysis," *American Journal of Political Science* 22: 426-443.

_____. 1981. "Some Problems in Studying the Effects of Resource Allocation in Congressional Elections," *American Journal of Political Science* 25: 543-567.

Fowler, Linda. 1980. "Candidate Perceptions of Electoral Conditions," *American Political Quarterly* 8: 483-494.

Franklin, Mark and Anthony Mughan. 1978. "The Decline of Class Voting in Britain: Problems of Analysis and Interpretation," *American Political Science Review* 72: 523-534.

Gallagher, Michael. 1980. "Candidate Selection in Ireland: The Impact of Localism and the Electoral System," *British Journal of Political Science* 10: 489-503.

Glantz, Stanton, Alan Abramowitz, and Michael Burkhart. 1976. "Election Outcomes: Whose Money Matters?" *Journal of Politics* 38: 1033-1038.

Gold, David and John Schmidhauser. 1960. "Urbanization and Party Competition: The Case of Iowa," *Midwest Journal of Political Science* 4: 62-75.

Grau, Craig. 1981. "Competition in State Legislative Primaries," *Legislative Studies Quarterly* 6: 35-54.

Hancock, M. Donald. 1972. *Sweden, the Politics of Postindustrial Change.* Hinsdale, IL: Dryden Press.

Hibbing, John. 1982a. *Choosing to Leave: Voluntary Retirement from the U.S. House of Representatives.* Washington, DC: University Press of America.

_____. 1982b. "Voluntary Retirement from the House in the Twentieth Century," *Journal of Politics* 44: 1020-1034.

_____. 1982c. "Voluntary Retirement from the U.S. House of Representatives: Who Quits," *American Journal of Political Science* 26: 467-484.

Hibbing, John R. and John R. Alford. 1981. "The Electoral Impact of Economic Conditions: Who Is Held Responsible," *American Journal of Political Science* 25: 423-439.

Hibbing, John R. and John R. Alford. 1982. "Economic Conditions and the Forgotten Side of Congress, A Foray into U.S. Senate Elections," *British Journal of Political Science* 12: 505-513.

Hibbs, Douglas. 1982a. "Economic Outcomes and Political Support for British Governments Among Occupational Classes: A Dynamic Analysis," *American Political Science Review* 76: 259-279.

_____ . 1982b. "On the Demand for Economic Outcomes: Macroeconomic Performance and Mass Political Support in the United States, Great Britain, and Germany," *Journal of Politics* 44: 426-462.

Hill, Keith. 1974. "Belgium: Political Change in a Segmented Society," in Richard Rose, ed., *Electoral Behavior: A Comparative Handbook*. New York: Free Press, pp. 29-108.

Hinckley, Barbara. 1967. "Interpreting House Midterm Elections: Toward a Measurement of the In-Party's 'Expected' Loss of Seats," *American Political Science Review* 61: 694-700.

_____ . 1970. "Incumbency and the Presidential Vote in Senate Elections: Defining Parameters of Subpresidential Voting," *American Political Science Review* 64: 836-842.

_____ . 1976. "Issues, Information Costs, and Congressional Elections," *American Politics Quarterly* 4: 131-152.

_____ . 1980. "House Reelections and Senate Defeats: The Role of the Challenger," *British Journal of Political Science* 10: 441-460.

_____ . 1981. *Congressional Elections*. Washington, DC: Congressional Quarterly Press.

Hinckley, Barbara, Richard Hofstetter, and John Kessel. 1974. "Information and the Vote: A Comparative Election Study," *American Politics Quarterly* 2: 131-156.

Huckshorn, Robert and Robert Spencer. 1971. *The Politics of Defeat*. Boston: University of Massachusetts Press.

Ingelhart, Ronald and Auram Hochstein. 1972. "Alignment and Dealignment of the Electorate in France and the United States," *Comparative Political Studies* 5: 343-372.

Jacobson, Gary. 1978. "The Effects of Campaign Spending in Congressional Elections," *American Political Science Review* 72: 469-491.

_____ . 1980. *Money in Congressional Elections*. New Haven: Yale University Press.

_____ . 1981a. "Congressional Elections, 1978: The Case of the Vanishing Challengers," in Louis Maisel and Joseph Cooper, eds., *Congressional Elections*. Beverly Hills, CA: Sage Publications, pp. 219-247.

_____ . 1981b. "Incumbents' Advantages in the 1978 U.S. Congressional Elections," *Legislative Studies Quarterly* 6: 183-200.

_____ . 1983. *The Politics of Congressional Elections*. Boston: Little, Brown.

Jacobson, Gary and Samuel Kernell. 1981. *Strategy and Choice in Congressional Elections*. New Haven: Yale University Press.

Jewell, Malcolm. 1967. *Legislative Representation in the Contemporary South*. Durham, NC: Duke University Press.

_____ . 1978. "Legislative Studies in Western Democracies: A Comparative Perspective," *Legislative Studies Quarterly* 3: 537-554.

_____ . 1982. *Representation in State Legislatures*. Lexington: University Press of Kentucky.

Jewell, Malcolm and Gerhard Loewenberg. 1979. "Toward a New Model of Legislative Representation," *Legislative Studies Quarterly* 4: 485-497.

Jewell, Malcolm and David Olson. 1982. *American State Political Parties and Elections*. Homewood, IL: Dorsey Press.

Johannes, John and John McAdams. 1981. "The Congressional Incumbency Effect: Is It Casework, Policy Compatibility, or Something Else?" *American Journal of Political Science* 25: 512-542.

Jones, Charles O. 1963-1964. "Inter-Party Competition in Britain–1950-1959," *Parliamentary Affairs* 17: 50-56.

Kaase, Max. 1976. "Party Identification and Voting Behavior in the West German Election of 1969," in Ian Budge, Ivor Crewe, and Dennis Farlie, eds., *Party Identification and Beyond.* London: John Wiley, pp. 81-102.

Katz, Richard. 1980. *A Theory of Parties and Electoral Systems.* Baltimore: Johns Hopkins Press.

Katz, Richard and Luciano Bardi. 1980. "Preference Voting and Turnout in Italian Parliamentary Elections," *American Journal of Political Science* 24: 97-114.

Kavanagh, D.A. 1970. *Constituency Electioneering In Britain.* London: Longmans.

Kernell, Samuel. 1977. "Presidential Popularity and Negative Voting," *American Political Science Review* 71: 44-66.

Key, V.O., Jr. 1956. *American State Politics.* New York: Knopf.

_____ . 1964. *Politics, Parties, and Pressure Groups.* New York: Crowell.

Kiewiet, Roderick. 1981. "Policy-Oriented Voting in Responses to Economic Issues," *American Political Science Review* 75: 448-459.

Kinder, Donald and Roderick Kiewiet. 1979. "Economic Discontent and Political Behavior: The Role of Personal Grievances and Collective Economic Judgement in Congressional Voting," *American Journal of Political Science* 23: 495-527.

_____ . 1981. "Sociotropic Politics: The American Case," *British Journal of Political Science* 11: 129-161.

King, Anthony. 1981. "What Do Elections Decide?" in David Butler, Howard Penniman, and Austin Ranney, eds., *Democracy at the Polls.* Washington, DC: American Enterprise Institute, pp. 293-324.

Kingdon, John. 1966. *Candidates for Office.* New York: Random House.

Kostroski, Warren. 1973. "Party and Incumbency in Postwar Senate Elections: Trends, Patterns, and Models," *American Political Science Review* 67: 1213-1234.

Kramer, Gerald. 1971. "Short-term Fluctuations in U.S. Voting Behavior, 1896-1964," *American Political Science Review* 65: 131-143.

Kuklinski, James and Darrell West. 1981. "Economic Expectations and Voting Behavior in U.S. House and Senate Elections," *American Political Science Review* 75: 436-447.

LeDuc, Lawrence, Harold Clarke, Jane Jenson, and Jon Pammett. 1980. "Partisanship, Voting Behavior, and Election Outcomes in Canada," *Comparative Politics* 12: 401-418.

Leuthold, David. 1968. *Electioneering in a Democracy.* New York: John Wiley.

Lewis-Beck, Michael and Paolo Bellucci. 1982. "Economic Influence on Legislative Elections in Multiparty Systems: France and Italy," *Political Behavior* 4: 93-107.

Lijphart, Arend. 1979. "Religious v. Linguistic v. Class Voting: The 'Crucial Experiment' of Comparing Belgium, Canada, South Africa, and Switzerland," *American Political Science Review* 73: 442-458.

Loewenberg, Gerhard and Samuel C. Patterson. 1979. *Comparing Legislatures.* Boston: Little, Brown.

MacRae, Duncan. 1967. *Parliament, Parties, and Society in France, 1946-1958.* New York: St. Martin's Press.

Maisel, S. Louis. 1982. *From Obscurity to Oblivion: Congressional Primary Elections in 1978.* Knoxville: University of Tennessee Press.

Maisel, S. Louis and Joseph Cooper, eds. 1981. *Congressional Elections*. Beverly Hills, CA: Sage Publications.

Mann, Thomas. 1978. *Unsafe at Any Margin*. Washington, DC: American Enterprise Institute.

Mann, Thomas and Raymond Wolfinger. 1980. "Candidates and Parties in Congressional Elections," *American Political Science Review* 74: 617-632.

Mayhew, David. 1974a. "Congressional Elections: The Case of the Vanishing Marginals," *Polity* 6: 295-317.

————. 1974b. *Congress: The Electoral Connection*. New Haven: Yale University Press.

Mehta, Prayag. 1975. *Election Campaign (Anatomy of Mass Influence)*. Delhi: National Publishing House.

Mellors, Colin. 1978. *The British MP*. London: Saxon House.

Mezey, Michael. 1979. *Comparative Legislatures*. Durham, NC: Duke University Press.

Miller, Warren and Donald Stokes. 1963. "Constituency Influence in Congress," *American Political Science Review* 57: 45-57.

Milnor, A.J. 1969. *Elections and Political Stability*. Boston: Little, Brown.

Mughan, Anthony. 1978. "Electoral Change in Britain: The Campaign Reassessed," *British Journal of Political Science* 8: 245-253.

Nelson, Candice. 1978-1979. "The Effect of Incumbency on Voting in Congressional Elections, 1964-1974," *Political Science Quarterly* 93: 665-678.

Nie, Norman, Sidney Verba, and John Petrocik. 1976. *The Changing American Voter*. Cambridge: Harvard University Press.

Owens, John and Edward Olson. 1977. "Campaign Spending and the Electoral Process in California 1966-1974," *Western Political Quarterly* 30: 493-512.

Parker, Glenn. 1980a. "The Advantage to Incumbency in House Elections," *American Politics Quarterly* 8: 449-464.

————. 1980b. "Sources of Change in Congressional District Attentiveness," *American Journal of Political Science* 24: 115-124.

————. 1981. "Incumbent Popularity and Electoral Success," in Louis Maisel and Joseph Cooper, eds., *Congressional Elections*. Beverly Hills, CA: Sage Publications, pp. 249-279.

Pierce, Roy and Philip Converse. 1981. "Candidate Visibility in France and the United States," *Legislative Studies Quarterly* 6: 339-371.

Piereson, John. 1975. "Presidential Popularity and Midterm Voting at Different Electoral Levels," *American Journal of Political Science* 19: 683-693.

Pitkin, Hanna. 1967. *The Concept of Representation*. Berkeley: University of California Press.

Powell, G. Bingham. 1980. "Voting Turnout in Thirty Democracies: Partisan, Legal, and Socioeconomic Influences," in Richard Rose, ed., *Electoral Participation: A Comparative Analysis*. Beverly Hills, CA: Sage Publications, pp. 5-34.

Pulzer, Peter. 1967. *Political Representation and Elections*. New York: Praeger.

Rae, Douglas. 1967. *The Political Consequences of Electoral Laws*. New Haven: Yale University Press.

Ragsdale, Lyn. 1980. "The Fiction of Congressional Elections as Presidential Events," *American Politics Quarterly* 8: 375-398.

————. 1981. "Incumbent Popularity, Challenger Invisibility, and Congressional Voters," *Legislative Studies Quarterly* 6: 201-218.

————. 1983. "The Many Meanings of Incumbency: Great Britain and the United States." Delivered at the Annual Meeting of the Midwest Political Science Association, Chicago.

Ranney, Austin. 1965. *Pathways to Parliament*. Madison: University of Wisconsin Press.

Rasmussen, Jorgen. 1969. "The Implications of Safe Seats for British Democracy," in Richard Rose, ed., *Policymaking in Britain*. New York: Free Press, pp. 30-47.

Ray, David. 1976. "Voluntary Retirement and Electoral Defeat in Eight State Legislatures," *Journal of Politics* 38: 426-433.

Richardson, Bradley. 1975. "Party Loyalties and Party Saliency in Japan," *Comparative Political Studies* 8: 32-57.

Rose, Richard. 1974. "Comparability in Electoral Studies," in Richard Rose, ed., *Electoral Behavior: A Comparative Handbook*. New York: Free Press, pp. 2-10.

———, ed. 1974. *Electoral Behavior: A Comparative Handbook*. New York: Free Press.

Rosenthal, Alan. 1974. "Turnovers in State Legislatures," *American Journal of Political Science* 18: 609-616.

———. 1981. *Legislative Life*. New York: Harper & Row.

Rush, Michael. 1969. *The Selection of Parliamentary Candidates*. London: Nelson.

Särlvik, Bo. 1969. "Socioeconomic Determinants of Voting Behavior in the Swedish Electorate," *Comparative Political Studies* 2: 99-135.

Schantz, Harvey. 1980. "Contested and Uncontested Primaries for the U.S. House," *Legislative Studies Quarterly* 5: 545-562.

Seligman, Lester, Michael R. King, Chong Lim Kim, and Roland E. Smith. 1974. *Patterns of Recruitment*. Chicago: Rand McNally.

Shin, Kwang and John Jackson III. 1979. "Membership Turnover in U.S. State Legislatures 1931-1976," *Legislative Studies Quarterly* 4: 95-104.

Sinnott, Richard. 1978. "The Electorate," in Howard Penniman, ed., *Ireland at the Polls: The Dail Elections of 1977*. Washington, DC: American Enterprise Institute, pp. 35-67.

Spafford, Duff. 1970. "The Electoral System of Canada," *American Political Science Review* 64: 168-176.

Stigler, George. 1973. "Micropolitics and Macroeconomics: General Economic Conditions and National Elections," *American Economic Review* 63: 160-167.

Stokes, Donald. 1976. "Parties and the Nationalization of Electoral Forces," in Richard G. Niemi and Howard F. Weisberg, eds., *Controversies in American Voting Behavior*. San Francisco: Freeman, pp. 514-531.

Stokes, Donald and Warren Miller. 1962. "Party Government and the Salience of Congress," *Public Opinion Quarterly* 26: 531-546.

Studler, Donley. 1978. "Policy Voting in Britain: The Colored Immigration Issue in the 1964, 1966, and 1970 General Elections," *American Political Science Review* 72: 46-64.

Thomassen, Jacques. 1976. "Party Identification as a Cross-National Concept: Its Meaning in the Netherlands," in Ian Budge, Ivor Crewe, and Dennis Farlie, eds., *Party Identification and Beyond*. London: John Wiley, pp. 63-79.

Tufte, Edward. 1973. "The Relationship Between Seats and Votes in Two-Party Systems," *American Political Science Review* 67: 540-554.

———. 1975. "Determinants of Midterm Congressional Elections," *American Political Science Review* 69: 812-826.

———. 1978. *Political Control of the Economy*. Princeton: Princeton University Press.

Weatherford, M. Stephen. 1978. "Economic Conditions and Electoral Outcomes: Class Differences in the Political Response to Recession," *American Journal of Political Science* 22: 917-938.

Weil, Gordon. 1970. *The Benelux Nations, The Politics of Small Country Democracies.* New York: Holt, Rinehart.

Weissberg, Robert. 1978. "Collective and Dyadic Representation in Congress," *American Political Science Review* 72: 535-547.

Welch, William. 1976. "The Effectiveness of Expenditures in State Legislative Races," *American Politics Quarterly* 4: 333-356.

Whiteley, Paul. 1979. "Electoral Forecasting from Poll Data: The British Case," *British Journal of Political Science* 9: 219-236.

Williams, Philip. 1966-1967. "Two Notes on the British Electoral System," *Parliamentary Affairs* 20: 13-30.

Woshinsky, Oliver. 1973. *The French Deputy.* Lexington, MA: D. C. Heath.

Wright, Gerald. 1974. *Electoral Choice in America.* Chapel Hill; NC: Institute for Research in Social Science.

_____. 1976. "Candidates' Policy Position and Voting in U.S. Congressional Elections," *Legislative Studies Quarterly* 1: 445-464.

Yiannakis, Diane. 1981. "The Grateful Electorate: Casework and Congressional Elections," *American Journal of Political Science* 25: 568-580.

Zariski, Raphael. 1972. *Italy, The Politics of Uneven Development.* Hinsdale, IL: Dryden Press.

Zuckerman, Alan and Mark Lichbach. 1977. "Stability and Change in European Electorates," *World Politics* 29: 523-551.

Chapter 3

Legislators and Constituents
In the Representative Process

by

MALCOLM E. JEWELL

This essay begins with a definition of the scope and meaning of the word "representation" and surveys research in the following areas:

1. normative and theoretical studies of representation;
2. empirical studies of the representative character of legislative bodies;
3. empirical studies of legislators' styles of representation or roles as representatives relating to their variously defined constituencies;
4. studies of public expectations of and support for the legislature;
5. studies of the allocation and service components of representation;
6. studies of policy responsiveness, including the methodological problems of measuring congruence between the views of constituents and the action of representatives.

The conclusion assesses the state of research and the unanswered questions in the field of legislative representation.

Defining Representation

Representation has been defined in many ways. For the purposes of this essay it is not necessary to review the range of definitions used by political theorists; it is enough to define the boundaries of the subject and thus determine what literature should be reviewed in this survey.

Traditionally the term "representation" has referred to the relationship between legislators and constituents on policy matters, but in recent years we have defined the topic more broadly. Eulau and Karps (1977, pp. 242-245) have defined four components of representation.

Service responsiveness: "the advantages and benefits which the representative is able to obtain for particular constituents."

Allocation responsiveness: "legislative allocations of public projects [that] involve advantages and benefits presumably accruing to a representative's district as a whole."

Policy responsiveness: the interaction of "the representative and the represented . . . with respect to the making of public policy."

Symbolic responsiveness: a relationship "built on trust and confidence expressed in the support that the represented give to the representative and to which he responds by symbolic, significant gestures, in order to, in turn, generate and maintain continuing support."

Studies of the first three components will be summarized in the last two sections of this literature review; symbolic representation is a more diffuse concept, aspects of which will be considered in analyzing individual styles of representation and public support for the legislature.

Most of the literature which defines representation has been devoted to policy responsiveness. Pitkin (1967, ch. 3) summarizes this literature in great detail and argues that most of the classic definitions are incomplete and unrealistic and thus of limited value. She criticizes as "formalistic" Thomas Hobbes's concept of "authorization," representation as a formal arrangement authorizing one person to act on behalf of another. She criticizes as equally formalistic the diametrically opposed concept of "accountability," according to which the representative must answer to another for what he does. "Neither (concept) can tell us anything about what goes on during representation, how a representative ought to act or what he is expected to do, how to tell whether he has represented well or badly" (p. 58). She also criticizes as unrealistic the concept of "descriptive representation," according to which the legislature is a mirror image of the population. She describes as incomplete the notion of "symbolic representation."

Most recent writers have accepted Pitkin's focus on representation as activity; a number of them have borrowed her definition of representation, a useful definition for the policy component of representation in this survey.

Representation here means acting in the interest of the represented, in a manner responsive to them. The representative must act independently; his action must involve discretion and judgement; he must be the one who acts. . . . And, despite the resulting potential for conflict between representative and represented about what is to be done, that conflict must not normally take place. The representative must act in such a way that there is no conflict, or if it occurs an explanation is called for (Pitkin, 1967, pp. 209-210).

In addition to describing the service, allocative, and policy components of representation, the literature analyzes the individual legislator's style of representation, his method of communicating with the district (in Fenno's terms, his "home style"), and his representational role. The literature on each of these will be examined, as well as a closely related subject, theories of legislative decision making at the individual level.

However, some related subjects will not be included. Some aspects of legislative elections are pertinent to representation but are beyond the boundaries of this survey. Studies of legislators' characteristics are described by Pitkin as the "mirror image" of representation studies but are excluded here. Roll-call analysis is mentioned only where it is directly pertinent to the question of congruence between legislators and constituents.

Normative and Theoretical Approaches

Most of the theoretical writing about representation deals with a normative question: what should the relationship be between the representative and the represented? The most comprehensive analysis and criticism of normative theories of representation is Pitkin's *The Concept of Representation* (1967). The study criticizes (in ways already mentioned) theories that define representation as authorization or as accountability and the notions of symbolic and descriptive representation. After a careful analysis of Burke and the mandate-independence controversy, she concludes that the prolonged debate has failed to produce any solution because in a sense both positions are correct. Moreover, if either position is advanced to its logical extreme, the result is not actually representation. In the concluding chapter she defines political representation, exploring the obligations that a representative has to his constituency: he must both exercise independent judgment and explain to the constituency any conflict between its wishes and his perception of its interests. This analysis of representation recognizes both its individual and its institutional dimensions.

Pennock and Chapman (1968), in a volume simply titled *Representation*, have collected essays on a number of aspects of representation. There are several papers on the meaning of representation and its normative components, a brief historical section on controversies over the subject, a section on constitutional aspects, and some attention to representation in nonelected governmental bodies, such as the bureaucracy.

Another scholar critical of traditional theories of representation, Heinz Eulau, argues that "in spite of many centuries of theoretical effort, we cannot say what representation is" and asserts that "our common conceptions of representation are obsolete" (1967, p. 54). Eulau summarizes the work of some classic theorists, particularly Edmund Burke, and concludes that they offer little toward an understanding of representation in modern societies. Eulau focuses on two problems: making representatives responsive to huge numbers of constituents with diverse interests and demands and holding representatives responsible for policy decisions in a modern electoral system. Wahlke (1971) is more explicit about the weaknesses of traditional notions of democratic representation. He emphasizes that most citizens do not have clear policy demands or well-thought-out positions on public issues and that relatively few communicate with their representatives or take any interest in the policy-making process (p. 273).

Analysis of the Representative Character of Institutions

Despite Pitkin's (1967, p. 221) assertion that representation is "primarily a public, institutionalized arrangement," nearly all research on representation has focused on the relationship between the individual legislator and the constituency. There are several obvious reasons for this. Institutional analysis requires comparisons—either among legislatures or within one legislature over time. Either research design is expensive and time-consuming. Moreover, the study of representation requires extensive interviews—with legislators and perhaps even with lobbyists, constituents, and other actors in the legislative system; it may also require detailed observation of legislators' behavior. It is difficult to generalize about representation in an entire institution on the basis of interviews with and observations of individual legislators— particularly if there are wide variations in attitudes and behavior within the institution. As Loewenberg and Kim (1978, p. 30) point out, "we are much less adept at observing groups" than in surveying individuals, and consequently we must often transform individual-level into group-level data.

The pioneering effort at institutional analysis of legislative bodies was undertaken by Eulau and Prewitt (1973), who interviewed 435 councilmen on 82 city councils in the San Francisco Bay area. The authors used the interview data to classify each of the councils according to a large number of criteria, covering many aspects of the decision-making process. One aspect of that study involved the representative character of the councils. The authors defined representativeness as "the relationship between council and community when the former governs in a manner responsive to the expressed interests of the latter." Eulau and Prewitt classified the councils into two broad categories; slightly under half were nonresponsive, while slightly over half were responsive. Among the responsive councils, some considered the expressed preferences of permanent interest groups in the community; a slightly larger number responded primarily to transitory, ad hoc issue groups. Members of the responsive councils (both categories of them) perceived constituents to be more attentive to public affairs; these councilors were also more likely to provide services for constituents than other councilors were. Most significantly, the responsive councils were more likely to be in communities where the electoral conditions maximized accountability of the councilors.

A second example of institutional analysis is the six-nation study reported by Loewenberg and Kim (1978). The data came from two separate and largely unrelated research projects at the University of Iowa; one covered Kenya, Korea, and Turkey, and another Belgium, Italy, and Switzerland. In each of the countries, MPs were asked how they perceived their constituencies, which were then categorized as organized or unorganized; they were asked about the extent of communication with the constituency; and they were given a series of questions to measure their receptivity to the constituency. From the answers to these questions, the authors constructed a five-part typology of parliamentary representativeness: participatory (Belgium and Italy), elitist (Switzerland), parochial (Kenya), authorized (Korea), and limited (Turkey). The authors discuss a number of systemic variables likely to affect the types of representativeness that predominate, giving particular attention to the number of MPs per constituency, the extent of party organization, the political culture, and the size of the legislature.

There is no example in the scholarly literature of an institutional analysis of any number of American state legislatures. The closest approximation is a report by the Citizens Conference on State Legislatures (1971). The purpose of that study was reformist rather than scholarly. The organization collected data on legislative structure and process in the 50 states and rank-ordered the states on five criteria, one of which was representativeness. This criterion was defined by several aspects, including single-member districting, diversity in the characteristics of members, and the effectiveness of individual members. The study also found that the states ranking as most representative were more likely to be industrialized and urbanized, with competitive parties and relatively professional legislatures.

Legislators' Styles of Representation

Home Style: Communicating with Constituents

One important aspect of representation concerns the legislator's perception of, and communication with, the constituency. It was a largely neglected topic, at least in American legislative studies, until the publication of *Home Style* by Richard Fenno (1978). Fenno describes the congressman's constituency as a number of concentric circles: the geographic, reelection, primary, and personal constituencies. He describes a variety of styles in which members present themselves to the district to gain trust and build a base of political support. Fenno shows how these styles may change over the course of a congressional career. One of Fenno's contributions is to show how the activities of the congressman in the district contribute to representation:

"Nearly everything he does to win and hold support—allocating, reaching, presenting, responding, communicating, explaining, assuring—involves representation" (p. 240). Fenno's research technique is noteworthy: he observed a number of members at work in their district and interviewed them at length. While there are obvious problems of generalization and replication, the study provides a much richer portrait of congressmen in their districts than we have had before.

Lewis Dexter (1956, 1957, 1960) has studied how congressmen's perceptions of their constituency affect communications with the district. These perceptions affect what members hear from constituents, how they interpret it, and how much they are influenced by the specific demands of constituents. A congressman often has considerable flexibility in determining which issues to emphasize and which constituents to listen to. Dexter's data on congressional-constituent relations came from a large-scale study of reciprocal trade legislation (Bauer, Pool, and Dexter, 1968), which contains extensive case study material on how congressmen respond to constituent influence on that issue.

Jewell (1982), in a study of representation in nine state legislatures, has described the techniques that state legislators use to gain visibility and communicate with constituents. A surprising number of them use relatively sophisticated techniques such as newspaper columns, radio tapes, newsletters, and opinion polls to maintain contact. Jewell did not find, however, that many state legislators perceive their constituencies in terms of various levels of support, as Fenno found in his congressional research.

Almost no efforts have been made to determine the accuracy or effectiveness of congressional or legislative efforts to monitor the views of constituents. One such study, by Stolarek, Rood, and Taylor (1981), assessed the reliability of a mail survey sent out by a congressman, comparing that survey with a public opinion poll in the district which used the same questions. The authors conclude that the congressman's survey provides a distorted picture of overall constituent opinion but provides a much better picture of the views of his primary or supportive constituency (in Fenno's terms).

Cain, Ferejohn, and Fiorina (1979) have examined the "home styles" of a number of British MPs. They found that there are a variety of styles used in dealing with constituents, some of which closely resemble those Fenno found. Most MPs pay considerable attention to the district. British MPs also identify various levels of supportive constituencies, similar to those outlined by Fenno.

The increased research on legislatures in less developed countries has emphasized the attention given by legislators to their constituents. Although much of that research has concentrated on constituent service and district projects (to be discussed later), some information has been collected concerning the ways in which legislators perceive their district and maintain contact with it. Some of these studies are primarily descriptive. A study of Malaysian MPs (Ong, 1976) describes in some detail visits of members to their districts, emphasizing urban-rural differences. Some studies provide more systematic data on communication patterns. Narain and Puri (1976) have measured the frequency and methods of contact between constituents and members of an Indian legislature. A study in the Indian state of Rajasthan (Sisson and Shrader, 1977) provides data on the members' perceptions of the constituency affairs. A study of members of the national parliament in India (Maheshwari, 1976) provides data on the amount of time MPs spend in the district and the numbers of communications of various kinds they receive from constituents. A recent study of Malaysia (Musolf and Springer, 1979) describes the methods by which legislators maintain district contacts and the frequency of such contacts as letters and visits; it also describes the priorities MPs assign to various types of activity within the district.

The most detailed study of constituency communication patterns comes from a survey of legislators in Kenya, Korea, and Turkey (Kim, Barkan, Turan, and Jewell, 1983). The data come from interviews with legislators and with constituents and local elites in legislator-constituent communications. Although the level of attention to the district is relatively high, the data show variations among legislators and among the countries in the priority accorded to the district.

Only limited attention has been paid to the district activities of legislators in western countries. In addition to the study of British "home style" already cited (Cain, Ferejohn, and Fiorina, 1979), there are two studies that devote some space to the activities of British backbenchers in their districts (Richards, 1972; Leonard and Herman, 1972). A study of the Canadian parliament (Kornberg and Mishler, 1976, pp. 191-199), devoted primarily to measuring influence within the institution, contains some statistical information on constituency communications. The data show that the levels of mail and other contacts from constituents are relatively high, and that these contacts are mostly requests for assistance. MPs are found to use newsletters, questionnaires, town meetings, and other forms of contact extensively and communicate with local elites such as party workers to get a sense of local opinion. The data on information sources and communication patterns are broken down by party.

Legislative Roles

Compared to any other aspect of representational studies, the literature on the roles played by legislators is enormous. This can be attributed directly to the influence of *The Legislative System* (Wahlke, Eulau, Buchanan, and Ferguson, 1962), a study of four state legislatures. In this study, role was the organizing concept, a concept which could integrate behavioral and institutional findings and define the boundaries of the legislative system. The study defines a number of role sectors (including representational, areal, partisan, and purposive roles) and specific role orientations (such as the trustee, the politico, and the delegate). It demonstrates that a large proportion of legislators do in fact have role orientations, and it provides data on the proportion of legislators in each state with each orientation. There are also tables showing the interrelationships of several roles—such as the representational and areal roles. The study does not attempt to explain why legislators choose particular role orientations nor to measure the behavioral consequences of these orientations.

In the years since the publication of *The Legislative System,* studies of legislative role have proliferated, not only in the United States at the state and national level but also in a number of other countries. This should have made possible extensive comparative analyses, but researchers have been handicapped by methodological problems. Although the role concept seems to be well understood by most of those using it, there are many different approaches to operationalizing it. The data reported in *The Legislative System* were based on open-ended questions, and some other studies of role have used the same technique. Although this is a technique that gives respondents maximum flexibility in answering, it creates coding problems that make replication difficult. Most studies of role have been based on more structured questions, but there is no uniformity in the questions used for defining a trustee or a delegate, for example. This raises doubts about tabular comparisons of the proportion of delegates and trustees in a variety of legislatures. There is also disagreement among researchers about whether role orientations should be viewed in discrete terms or in terms of a continuum or dimension (see Francis, 1965). Where roles are conceptualized, defined, and measured differently, the chances of meaningful comparison are obviously reduced.

Most of the research on legislative role has simply classified legislators according to their role orientations. There have been a few efforts to identify variables that may help to explain particular role orientations, and very few efforts to identify behavioral consequences of role orientations. Most studies of roles have been based solely on questions to legislators, but there are a few examples of constituents being asked about the roles that legislators should play.

Representational Role. The largest proportion of research on legislative role orientations has been devoted to representational roles, perhaps because the distinction between delegate and trustee roles is so central to the study of representation. An article several years ago (Jewell, 1970) summarized the findings of a number of studies concerning variables that had the strongest effect in explaining the legislator's choice of a representational role. No single variable predominated, but several turned out to be significant in one or more studies. Legislators are more likely to be trustees if they are well educated and have more legislative experience. There is some evidence that the nature of the district affects representational role, with trustees more likely to come from less competitive districts and from at-large rather than single-member districts. (For original sources, see Friedman and Stokes, 1965; Wahlke, Eulau, Buchanan, and Ferguson, 1962; Sorauf, 1963; Kornberg, 1967; Prewitt, Eulau and Zisk, 1966-1967.) Bell and Price (1975) have traced changes in California legislators' roles during their first term in office. They found a shift in direction toward a trustee orientation. They also found that previous political activity, such as running for office, was associated with an early trustee orientation. Similarly, by conducting a panel study, Clarke and Price (1981) have measured changes in the representational roles of Canadian MPs during the first term in office. They find that rural MPs tend to give increasing emphasis to a constituency delegate style and a constituency focus during their term, while MPs with progressive ambitions give decreasing emphasis to the constituency.

Studies in a number of countries have found that the representational role is a meaningful concept; these studies make it possible to compare the proportion of trustees, politicos, and delegates in a wide variety of legislatures, but it should be remembered that these comparisons are imprecise because the criteria and measuring techniques are not consistent from study to study. Davidson (1969, p. 117) found that the largest proportion of congressmen were classified as politicos. Wahlke et al. (1962, p. 281) found that the trustee orientation was the most common one in four American states, with less than 20 percent classified as delegates. Studies in several other American state legislatures since that time have found more politicos and trustees in California, more trustees in Iowa, more delegates in Wisconsin and North Carolina, and nearly even divisions among categories in Pennsylvania and Michigan (Bell and Price, 1975, pp. 92, 94; Sorauf, 1963, p. 124; summary of other studies in Jewell and Patterson, 1977, p. 362).

Mezey (1979, p. 172) has summarized a number of studies of representational role in other countries; trustees were more common in the Philippines, Japan, an Indian state, Belgium, Switzerland, and Kenya; delegates predominated in a Japanese province, Canada, and Korea; there were more politicos in Colombia. A comparative study of legislators in Kenya, Korea, and Turkey (Kim et al., 1982, ch. 6) showed that delegates were most common in Kenya, while trustees were in the majority in Korea and Turkey.

Other studies have shown that Scottish and Welsh members of the British House of Commons are predominantly trustees (Mishler and Mughan, 1978, p. 338); French deputies are more often trustees, with variations by party (Cayrol, Parodi, and Ysmal, 1976, p. 77); Dutch legislators are also more likely to be trustees, though many are sensitive to party pressures (Daalder and Rusk, 1972). A study of Canada (Kornberg and Mishler, 1976, pp. 86-94) provides a more elaborate analysis of representation roles, one that emphasizes the MP's conscience, district constituents, and party leadership and colleagues in the House; it also indicates some significant variations by party. Generally, the more thoroughly representative roles are explored, the more complex the relationships become and the less useful it seems to simply classify legislators in terms of the traditional trustee-politico-delegate categories.

Efforts to determine what effect representative roles have on legislative behavior have encountered a number of difficulties. There is no reason to anticipate that trustees or delegates would vote in support of particular policies. There have been some efforts to determine whether delegates make more effort to determine the views of constituents or more accurately perceive those views. Hedlund and Friesema (1972) found that trustees in Iowa were better able than delegates to predict the opinions of their constituents on referenda issues; a similar finding emerged from a study of referenda issues in Florida (Erikson, Luttbeg, and Holloway, 1975). It is difficult to collect the data on constituency preferences needed to test whether delegates are more likely to vote in accord with constituency preferences. Gross (1978), using data from the 1958 representation study, concluded that delegates make a greater effort to discern district opinion, but that they were not consistently more likely to vote in accord with constituent preferences. Friesema and Hedlund (1974) found that delegates had voting records less consistent with constituents on referenda issues than did trustees or politicos. Kuklinski and Ellington (1977), using voting scales based on referenda and roll-call votes, found that delegates voted more consistently with constituents than trustees did, but only on issues most salient to constituents. McCrone and Kuklinski (1979) add another condition—the issue must be one on which constituencies provide consistent cues to legislators.

Areal Role. While the study of representational roles has generally been directed to the relationships between legislators and their constituents in individual districts, studies of the focus of representation examine the member's relationship to partisan and group interests that extend beyond the boundaries of a district. Such analyses are particularly pertinent in political systems where parties are strong and where legislators are elected by proportional representation and list systems.

One of the roles identified in *The Legislative System* is an areal one: the choice between representing the district and representing a larger entity, such as the state or nation. In countries which do not have single-member districts or in which party loyalties are very strong, we would not expect to find strong loyalties to the district, though this relationship has rarely been explored. In their study of the American state legislators, Wahlke et al. (1962) found that the district orientation predominated, and that has been the finding in most studies of state legislatures (Jewell and Patterson, 1977, pp. 352-353) and of Congress (Davidson, 1969, p. 122). This coincides with our expectation that most legislators would give priority to the interests of their district if conflicts arise with other interests. A study of Canada (Kornberg, 1967, p. 108), however, showed that more MPs had a national than a local role orientation. It is also possible that the areal focus of representation is more complicated than can be described in district-state terms. Some state legislators in metropolitan areas perceive themselves as representing the whole area, some a section such as the central city, and some a specific district or locality; the choice is affected in part by the districting system used (Jewell, 1970, p. 482; 1982, pp. 87-95).

Partisan Role. The partisan role might be expected to vary among legislatures and among parties within legislatures, and a limited number of studies have examined such variations. Partisan loyalties have been shown to be relatively strong in New Jersey, Ohio, Wisconsin, and Massachusetts, and weaker in Pennsylvania, California, and Tennessee (Jewell and Patterson, 1977, p. 355-357; Sorauf, 1963, p. 124; Wahlke et al. 1962, p. 371). In one study of the French parliament several measures of partisan role demonstrated that party loyalties are much stronger among Communist and Socialist deputies than among others (Cayrol, Parodi, and Ysmal, 1976). Another study (Converse and Pierce, 1979) of French deputies confirmed that the sense of party loyalty was much stronger among Communists and Socialists and was moderately strong among Gaullists. Those deputies who did not give priority to the party were more likely to defect from the party; within this group the deputies were inclined to follow their own conscience more than the views of constituents.

A study of the Vienna City Council (Gerlich, 1972) showed that even in a legislative body where party loyalties are strong the strength of partisanship varies. A study of partisanship in the Dutch parliament (Daalder and Rusk, 1972) demonstrated some differences in strength of loyalties by party and also explored legislators' attitudes toward party in some depth, including their views on how decisions should be made within party groups. In Italy, the political party is clearly the dominant reference point for deputies from all parties, but this is most strongly the case for Communist deputies; it is also clear that the parliamentary party takes precedence over the party organization in the constituency (Barnes, 1977, pp. 128-132). In Canada (Kornberg and Mishler, 1976) MPs were asked about the importance of the party compared to that of other groups to which they might be accountable. Despite the evident strength of Canadian parties, the partisan role generally ranked below the district and the MP's conscience. There were some variations by party, particularly in the importance members attached to the party organization in the district.

Davidson (1969, ch. 5) has explored in some detail the partisan roles of American congressmen and has defined four types: loyalist, super-loyalist, neutral, and maverick, in order of frequency. Differences between the parties were rather small, though more Republicans were superloyalists. The most loyal members tended to be more junior and, in the case of Democrats, to come from more marginal districts; this is presumably because the less loyal Southern Democrats come from safe districts, or did in the 1960s. It should be obvious that partisan roles must be understood within the legislative context and that a U.S. congressman identified as a superloyalist might appear to be more independent in a legislative body where expectations of party loyalty were generally higher.

Measuring the behavioral consequences of partisan role orientations should be relatively easy; it is necessary merely to correlate roles with voting behavior on partisan issues. But very little research has been done along these lines. Ferguson and Klein (1967), using data from the four-state study by Wahlke et al. (1962), found that party loyalists were more likely to support the party in roll-call votes in four of the legislatures; the opposite effect was found in two houses, and there appeared to be little relationship in the other two. Hadley (1977) measured the impact of the partisan roles on Indiana legislators' support for their party and for the governor on pertinent roll calls. They found that the relationships were generally weak and inconsistent, particularly when the effect of other variables was taken into account; the relationships were slightly higher for members of the minority party. However, party discipline was so strong on partisan issues that there was little variance in roll-call behavior. It would be useful to measure the effect of partisan roles in some legislature where party discipline is weaker. Outside of the United States, the strong party discipline that is evident in some legislatures makes roll-call analysis inappropriate. In the French parliament, however, Converse and Pierce (1979) found relatively high correlations between the partisan roles of deputies and their rate of defection from the party on roll calls.

Interest Group Representation

Organized interests have an influence on decision making in every democratic legislature. That influence may be exercised through linkages to legislative parties or leadership or, in parliamentary systems, to the cabinet. Detailed studies of such linkages have been conducted in Britain (Beer, 1969; Stewart, 1958), West Germany (Hirsch-Weber, 1958), and France (Brown, 1963), among other countries. It may also be exercised through relationships directly with individual legislators, who in some sense represent these interest groups. That relationship may be established because the legislator belongs to the group or shares its views or because the group played a significant role in the legislator's nomination or election. Pertinent studies have been done in Britain (Roth, 1972) and Germany (Loewenberg, 1967).

In political systems with single-member districts the relationship of legislator to interest group is likely to be stronger if the group is a significant force in the legislator's district, although some legislators have ties to groups outside the district. In a list or proportional representation system, the linkages between groups and members may be more direct and are not limited by district boundaries. Where party discipline is strong the linkage is likely to occur within the framework of the legislative party, and legislators with ties to groups that are not allied with their party are faced with serious cross pressures, usually settled in favor of the party (Stewart, 1958; Muller, 1973).

Despite the importance of this topic, relatively little research has been devoted directly to the question of how legislators represent interest groups: how do they define their roles, what choices must they make between groups, and what pressures or sanctions do they feel? Wahlke et al. (1962) defined a pressure-group role and classified members by their attitude toward and knowledge of interest groups. Such a classification is so elementary that it adds little to our understanding of such roles. The most detailed study of interactions between legislators and lobbyists in American states (Zeigler and Baer, 1969) sheds some light on the topic but does not explicitly deal with legislative roles. A number of the more complex and subtle aspects of representing interest groups in Congress are described in Bauer, Pool, and Dexter (1968). One of the most insightful analyses of ways in which legislators defend themselves against lobbyists is found in Matthews (1960, ch. 8). The problems faced by German legislators who are closely linked to interest groups is discussed in Braunthal (1965).

The representation of interests varies from one legislative system to another, and this is a major theme of Loewenberg and associates (forthcoming), who compare members of parliament in Belgium, Italy, and Switzerland. The members who were interviewed were asked how they defined their constituency, whether geographically or in terms of political or other types of groups. In Belgium and Switzerland the legislators most frequently said they represented interest groups; in Italy (where interest groups was not one of the choices) they most often mentioned social class. A relatively small proportion in any of these countries defined representation in geographic terms.

The Legislator and the Public

In recent years there has been considerable research on the perceptions of both legislators and the public about the responsibilities of the legislative job. A closely related area of study is public support for the legislature, which we would expect to be partly dependent on the congruence between legislator and public perceptions of these responsibilities.

Purposive Roles

Wahlke et al. (1962) used the term "purposive role" to describe legislators' perceptions of their most important responsibilities as legislators. The categories were based heavily on the question, "How would you describe the job of being a legislator—what are the most important things you should do here?" (p. 465). They defined five roles: ritualist (the most common), tribune, inventor, broker, and opportunist. These categories proved to be useful, and similar results were found by other researchers in several other states. Barber (1965), in his study of motivations for legislative service in Connecticut, used a different technique but defined somewhat similar roles: lawmakers, reluctants, spectators, and advertisers. Davidson (1969, pp. 79-97) analyzed congressmen, using the categories established by Wahlke et al., and found that the tribune and ritualist categories were the most common. However, he noted that the term "tribune" is "extremely inclusive" (p. 80) and those congressmen who emphasized constituency service were included under it.

Purposive role is a useful concept for differentiating among members of a legislature; it is even more valuable for comparing legislatures—particularly along crossnational lines. One of the best ways of understanding how the functions of legislatures differ is to study the priorities that their members give to various aspects of their job. Several studies of nonwestern legislatures used the purposive role categories developed in *The Legislative System*. This is the case in an analysis of roles of Japanese prefectural assemblymen (Kim, 1969) and in a survey of parliamentary members in Singapore (Chee, 1976).

However, most studies of legislative systems outside the United States have preferred other categories or purposive roles. Kornberg and Mishler (1976, pp. 235-239) distinguish three types of Canadian MPs: insiders, the parliamentary professionals who dominate debate; gadflies, who introduce most of the private bills; and committee activists, who keep busy with committee work but appear to be amateurs. Woshinsky (1973) defines three types of French deputies, based on their motivation: mission participants, concerned principally with ideology; program participants, interested in gaining higher positions; and obligation participants, concerned with the moral aspects of politics. He provides data on differences among the types in party, floor, and committee activity; leadership career patterns; and other aspects of legislative activity. Gerlich (1972), in his study of the Vienna City Council, sticks more closely to the purposive roles delineated by Wahlke et al. but also specifies errand boy and communication roles, both directly related to constituents. In their study of Scottish and Welsh MPs, Mishler and Mughan (1978) define purposive roles that emphasize legislative activities, party loyalty, and social work and pork-barrel activities on behalf of the constituency.

One of the strongest themes that emerges from studies of legislatures in developing countries is the importance that a majority of legislators—often a large majority—attach to constituency service. Mezey (1979, p. 174) cites studies that confirm such findings in the Philippines, Mexico, and several states in India. The importance of constituency service as a purposive role might be inferred from the actual time and effort devoted to it by legislatures in a number of other countries to be discussed later.

A comparative study of legislatures in Kenya, Korea, and Turkey (Kim et al., 1983, chs. 5, 6) shows that legislators in all three countries emphasized the formal function of law making but that relatively few mentioned policy making. Some legislators were classified as internals and some as externals (or constituency-oriented). A second major responsibility was representing the voters, particularly in Kenya. An indirect measure of purposive role was provided by a question about activities MPs thought they should devote more time to. Large numbers of MPs responded by naming three activities directly related to the constituency: obtaining government projects for the district (particularly in Kenya), interceding with the bureaucracy to help constituents, and expressing the views of people in the district. A similar question asked of Malaysian MPs showed that they thought it most important to spend more time on the same three activities (Musolf and Springer, 1979, p. 49). A study in Tanzania (Hopkins, 1970) showed that legislators were most likely to define three responsibilities: explaining government policies to the constituency, promoting the constituency, and (where appropriate) serving as members of the government.

Public Expectations

What roles do constituents expect their legislators to perform? Do they have clearly defined expectations? Relatively few efforts have been made to answer these questions, presumably because of the cost and difficulty of obtaining the necessary survey data. Parker and Davidson (1979) found that constituents evaluate Congress by criteria different from those they apply to congressmen. They evaluate Congress, often negatively, on its policy making, but they judge congressmen, usually positively, largely on their service to the district. Davidson (1970, p. 654) learned from a national sample that tribune and ritualist were the purposive roles mentioned most frequently by the public as well as by congressmen. A study of Iowa constituents (Patterson, Hedlund, and Boynton, 1975, p. 139) showed that, when asked to make choices in paired comparisons about representative roles a substantial majority preferred to have legislators exercise their own judgment, but constituents also thought that district and state interests should rank ahead of other group interests.

The comparative study of Kenya, Korea, and Turkey (Kim et al., 1983, chs. 5, 6) includes data on how constituents rank the tasks of legislators, data comparable to that gathered from legislators. As might be expected, constituents and local elites both gave priority to those activities directly related to the constituency: expressing the views of constituents, getting projects for the district, interceding with civil servants on behalf of constituents, and visiting the district. These preferences were particularly strong in Kenya. In Korea and Turkey the constituents gave less priority than MPs did to purely legislative activities. Interestingly, constituents tended to agree with legislators about representational style; those in Kenya emphasized the delegate role, while those in Korea and Turkey were more likely to stress the trustee role. When asked about the focus of representation, Kenyan and Korean constituents emphasized the electoral district, and gave less priority to the party or the executive branch than legislators did. Barnes (1977, pp. 131-133) reports that in Italy the public believes that deputies should follow the wishes of the voters rather than their own judgment. Most also believe that the deputies should vote with their party rather than following their own judgment, but this is not true for followers of right-wing parties.

Public Support for Legislatures

The study of public support for political institutions, including legislatures, is fraught with methodological difficulties. The distinction between diffuse and specific support may be clear in theory (Easton, 1975), but it is difficult to operationalize in research. In those countries where the level of support is relatively high, it may be difficult to find enough variation in levels of support to be worth investigation. In countries where it appears to be low, there are practical difficulties in asking respondents about their attitude toward political institutions. Under any conditions, it is difficult to develop questions that adequately measure levels of support.

It is only a slight exaggeration to say that we know more about legislative support and the variables affecting it in Iowa than in all the rest of the world. The study by Patterson, Hedlund, and Boynton (1975) compared the views of legislators, lobbyists, local party leaders, attentive constituents, and the general public about the state legislature. Generally, high status individuals were found to be more supportive. Among the most supportive respondents were ones who perceived that the legislature did a good job of representing the citizens and effecting compromise. The authors of the Iowa study also included comparative data from 13 states on support of the legislature and briefly assessed explanatory variables.

The study by Kim et al. (1983) of Kenya, Korea, and Turkey includes data on how much both constituents and local elites support the legislature. Support was generally higher from the local elites, and from the higher and more modernized strata of the general public. Support was also higher from those for whom the legislature was more salient and those who were more satisfied with its performance. The salience of, and satisfaction with, one's own legislator, however, had no significant effect.

One other noteworthy study (Boynton and Loewenberg, 1973) measured the growth of support for the West German parliament during the crucial period of the 1950s. They found higher support among those who thought that MPs would be responsive to constituent problems and those who had a more favorable attitude toward the government in office, though the effect of this latter factor decreased over time as those less favorable grew more supportive. Support from younger respondents grew disproportionately over time.

Allocation and Service Components of Representation

The allocation and service aspects of representation, after years of neglect by scholars, have recently begun to receive attention in the literature. It has long been recognized that U.S. congressmen devote much of their effort and even more of their staff resources to gaining projects and benefits for their district and to serving the needs of individual constituents. Recent research has described this activity in more detail and analyzed its consequences. Increasing legislative research in other countries, both western and nonwestern, has demonstrated that allocation and service activities are major responsibilities of most legislators, even though they lack the staff resources of American congressmen.

A major theme of recent research on congressional allocation and service has been the effect of these activities on the success of incumbents in winning reelection, often by comfortable margins (the so-called "vanishing marginals"). The electoral impact of these activities on behalf of the constituency is beyond the scope of this essay, however. Despite the attention researchers have given to district projects and constituency service and despite their speculation about the consequences, there is relatively little detailed description or quantitative analysis of these activities; some of it is scattered across unpublished papers and congressional documents. Cavanaugh (1979) has measured how congressmen allocate their resources for these purposes. Johannes (1980) has collected data on the casework load (both district projects and individual service) of senatorial and congressional offices. Finding wide variation in the size of the caseload, he explains differences in terms of the seniority of representatives and the legislative activism of senators. He also finds that districts and states in the East generate more cases.

Johannes (1979) has assessed the utility of congressional casework as a means of administrative oversight. He finds it provides a direct and relatively inexpensive form of oversight and contributes to internal agency supervision. Its effects are limited by a number of factors, including members' motivations, their committee responsibilities, and the availability of staff. Elling (1979), in a parallel study in state legislatures, reaches similar conclusions but stresses the limitations of this form of oversight, particularly because of the limits of legislator motivations, opportunities, and staff.

Jewell (1982, ch. 6) has analyzed the allocation and service roles of legislators in nine American states, finding that most legislators are active in getting district benefits but that they vary in the extent of their constituency service. Legislators who are most service oriented are found in states where constituency service norms are strong and more staff resources are available and in single-member districts where constituency demand is high. The legislator's own sense of priorities is also an important variable.

Research on legislatures in other western countries has devoted relatively little attention to allocation and service activities of members; even basic descriptive information is missing in many cases. Cain, Ferejohn, and Fiorina (1979) provide some information on service activities in the context of brief case studies of MPs. Richards (1972, ch. 8), Barker and Rush (1972), and Dowse (1972) describe briefly the service activities performed by British MPs in their "surgeries." More information is available on the service role of Canadian legislators, particularly at the provincial level. Studies at the provincial level (Clarke, Price and Krause, 1975; Clarke, 1978) show that Canadian legislators devote substantial time to constituency service but some much more than others. Some differences are explained by party membership and the two-party balance in the legislature. Other differences are individual, depending on representative and purposive roles, career motivations, socioeconomic status, and ideological orientations.

The major finding of the research on constituency activities in nonwestern and developing countries has been that most legislators devote considerable amounts of their time and give high priority to seeking projects and benefits for their districts and acting as intermediaries between their constituents and the bureaucracy. In those legislative bodies that have minimal policy-making functions, this may be the most important activity performed by legislators. Those legislatures where these activities have been shown to be important include Tanzania (Hopkins, 1970), Afghanistan (Weinbaum, 1977), national and state levels in India (Maheshwari, 1976; Narain and Puri, 1976), Bangladesh (Jahan, 1976), Malaysia (Ong, 1976; Musolf and Springer, 1979, pp. 50-55), and South Vietnam (Goodman, 1975).

Several surveys of allocation and service responsiveness provide additional analysis of the causes or consequences of these activities. Goodman (1975) found that in the late 1960s about one-third of the legislators in South Vietnam had initiated constituency service work. A multiple regression analysis failed to define variables with an important effect, though other analysis suggested that those deputies opposing the government and those trying to bolster their political influence were most active. Weinbaum (1977) found that in Afghanistan the legislator's service activities made him an intermediary between the citizens and the national and provincial governments, thereby adding some support to the fragile parliamentary system. Kim et al. (1983, ch. 9) describe in some detail the resource allocation and constituency service activities of legislators in Kenya, Korea, and Turkey. Data are presented on legislators' perceptions of constituency needs, the types of services performed, and constituent awareness of services. The authors argue that, in performing these roles, legislators are an important linkage between the central government and local communities, a linkage which may enhance support for the government.

Although the scope of this essay does not extend to electoral questions, it should be noted that the political and electoral consequences of providing services to the constituency (or failing to provide them) may be considerable. Evidence from several countries to support this assertion has been summarized by Mezey (1979, pp. 175-179).

Policy Responsiveness: Methodological Problems and Substantive Findings

The literature on policy responsiveness has concentrated on efforts to measure the congruence between the interests and opinions of constituents, on the one hand, and the views and voting behavior of legislators, on the other. Measuring congruence involves serious methodological problems, which must be examined here before substantive findings about congruence can be presented. There is an intermediate variable—the legislator's perception of constituency opinion—that assumes so much importance in policy responsiveness that it should be dealt with separately; in fact, it is a logical place to begin.

The Problem of Perception

Earlier in this essay, reference was made to Dexter's (1956, 1957, 1960) findings that the perceptions of congressmen affect their communications with the district. In defining the areal role, this essay also noted that such a role derives from the legislator's perception of his constituency, a constituency which may be narrower or broader than the geographical boundary of the district. This latter point becomes pertinent when we try to measure congruence between the legislator and his constituency. Presumably congruence is more likely if a legislator's perception of constituency opinion is accurate. However, a legislator who does not appear to have an accurate perception of district opinion may in fact accurately perceive the opinions of those constituents whom he believes he ought to be representing.

If perceptual accuracy is a significant ingredient in policy responsiveness, it becomes important to understand why legislators' perceptions are sometimes not accurate. Clausen (1977) has thoroughly summarized and analyzed findings of political scientists on the perceptual accuracy of legislators and findings of social scientists generally on the perceptual accuracy of political leaders. In addition, he points out the problems of measuring perceptual accuracy. He notes that such research often shows that legislators are likely to perceive constituent opinion as being closer to their own than is actually the case. A number of contextual factors affect accuracy: perceptions are more likely to be accurate when the district is heterogeneous and when issues are salient to constituents. Party and interest group ties may also enhance perceptual accuracy, depending on how broadly the constituency is defined. There is also some evidence that delegates are less accurate in their perceptions than are trustees. Specific studies of legislators' perceptual accuracy that consider salience include Miller and Stokes (1963), Brand (1972), Erikson, Luttbeg, and Holloway (1975), and Hedlund and Friesema (1972); party and interest group ties are explored by Hedlund and Friesema (1972); delegate-trustee differences are noted by Hedlund and Friesema (1972) and Erikson, Luttbeg, and Holloway (1975).

Uslaner and Weber (1979) have compared state legislators' perceptions of constituent opinion with statewide opinion estimated by computer simulation. They conclude that legislators represent their perception of opinion better than they represent actual opinion. They explore several explanations for misperception and find most support for the theory that legislators at the state level are in a poor position to estimate what opinion actually is. There is also some support for the thesis that members are more likely to have opinions congruent with perceived preferences when they believe that they know what constituents think and when they come from typical districts.

Problems of Measuring Congruence

A number of scholars have discussed the problems of measuring or estimating the congruence between the opinions of constituents in a district and the views and behavior of the legislator. The problems are now well known; the solutions remain generally elusive. The easiest method of estimating opinion is to collect demographic data on a district and use that data as a surrogate for opinion data. There seems to be consensus that this approach is fraught with too many problems to be useful (Weissberg, 1979). Another approach, used quite successfully by Kuklinski (1978), is to make referenda a measure of opinion. However, referenda votes are not only rare but untypical of most issues, providing legislators with unusually precise measurements of opinion on unusually salient issues (Weissberg, 1979). A number of scholars have used national opinion survey data and state or district demographic data to simulate opinion at the state or congressional district level (Uslaner and Weber, 1977, 1979; Weber, Hopkins, Mezey, and Munger, 1972). This technique has been criticized on a number of grounds: among other things, it assumes that opinions at the state or district level are unaffected by local, nondemographic factors and it is very difficult to apply to units as small as state legislative districts (Jewell and Loewenberg, 1979; Kuklinski, 1977).

Miller and Stokes (1963) inaugurated a research design that is generally recognized as having greater potential for accurate measurement; it is based on the collection of constituent opinion survey data in each sampled district, data which are compared to the perceptions, views, and actions of the legislator from the district. Despite the theoretical advantages of this approach, it is beset by many practical problems. Erikson (1978, 1981) has discussed the problems created by very small samples in each district and the methods of coping with these problems. Weissberg (1979) has discussed a variety of problems of aggregating opinions in the district; these range from the difficulties of using simple averages to the effects of salient issues and intense opinions. A number of scholars (Achen, 1977, 1978; Kuklinski, 1979; Stone, 1979; Weissberg, 1979) have described the weakness of correlation techniques for comparing constituent and legislator opinion; the principal problem is that the opinion scales are not equivalent. There seems to be consensus that some form of proximity measure is more suitable, such as that used by Uslaner and Weber (1979).

While some of the methodological problems raised are quite technical, others are fundamental questions about the feasibility of comparing constituent opinion and legislative opinion and behavior. Weissberg (1979) has emphasized the fundamental difference between the general attitudes expressed by constituents in surveys and the specific policy questions that face legislators on roll calls. Can scaling techniques be developed to overcome this difficulty? Stone (1979) suggests that "our concept of representation builds in non-equivalence of the sort attacked when survey items do not 'match' roll call indicators" (p. 625). In other words, if we are measuring representation or policy congruence we cannot expect perfect equivalence.

One of the fundamental problems of studying congruence arises from the complexity of all but the smallest legislative districts. There may be a substantial degree of congruence between the opinions of the representative and most constituents on broad, general approaches to government, but on a daily basis the representative must make decisions about questions that are salient only to quite narrow groups within the constituency. We have noted earlier Fenno's (1978) point that, from the legislator's perspective, the constituency is seen as concentric circles with varied levels of support and often varied interests. Fiorina (1974) has emphasized the effect that the homogeneity or heterogeneity of a district has on a legislator's calculations, and Clausen (1977) has stressed the importance of defining what part of the constituency a congressman represents. As Stone (1979) has pointed out, it is often necessary to measure opinions of subgroups in a district, because the legislator may be responsive on some issues to particular subgroups, but such efforts run into severe problems of small sample size.

Another fundamental criticism of much research on policy congruence, raised by Kuklinski (1979) and Stone (1979), is its generally static quality. Stone (1979) has sought to add a dynamic feature by measuring congruence over a number of years. Karps and Eulau (1978) have reanalyzed the 1958 congressional survey data, adding a dynamic dimension by tracking relationships among congressmen's preferences and their votes and constituency preferences between 1956 and 1960.

Substantive Findings on Policy Congruence

Although the study of decision-making processes of legislators is a broader topic than can be included in this essay, it is pertinent to note how the representation of the constituency is treated by those who write about decision making. Fiorina (1974) has developed a sophisticated theory about the influence of constituency on legislator's voting decisions. It is based on a rational approach to decision making, and distinguishes between legislators who are maximizers and those who are maintainers. As was noted earlier, he emphasizes the distinct effect that homogeneity or heterogeneity of the district has on the member's calculations. Kingdon (1977, 1981) has developed a model in which the legislator establishes a pattern of decision making based on major goals; these goals become important when conflicts arise among the groups that are sources of voting cues. "The congressman considers the constituency first" (Kingdon, 1977, p. 587), when he decides not to vote with the constituency; his first consideration is whether the issue is salient to the constituency.

Roll-call studies are beyond the scope of this essay. A number of these studies have used demographic variables to measure the impact of constituency on roll-call voting and on specific aspects such as party loyalty. Some degree of constituency influence, generally varying by issue, has been found in many of these studies. The literature is summarized in Jewell and Patterson (1977, pp. 403-410) and Fiorina (1977, pp. 1-23). Our concern in this essay is only with those roll-call studies in which some attempt is made to estimate or measure constituent opinion and to relate it to the views and voting record of legislators. Despite the methodological problems involved in such research, a number of studies have been done, most of them in American legislatures, as might be expected. It should be kept in mind that in most of these studies at least some of the methodological problems outlined above have not been fully solved.

The first of these, and by far the most ambitious, was the 1958 study by the Michigan Survey Research Center, which included incumbent congressmen, their opponents, and a sample of constituents in 116 districts. The survey produced information on the views of constituents on issues and on the congressmens' views, perceptions of constituent views, and roll-call voting records. Attention was focused on three sets of issues: civil rights, social welfare, and foreign policy. One major finding of the study (reported in Miller and Stokes, 1963; Miller, 1964) was that congruence varied with the salience of the issue. Congressmen were most likely to perceive opinion correctly and to vote in accordance with opinion on civil rights and least likely to do so on foreign policy. With regard to both civil rights and social welfare policies, congruence was greater in safe districts with respect to constituents belonging to the majority party, than it was in marginal districts with respect to any group of constituents.

The value of the 1958 representation study lay less in its specific findings than in its bold and imaginative methodology. One might have expected the research design to be duplicated in subsequent election years, but it has not been. One discouraging factor was the large cost of replicating such a survey; another was the widespread belief (Erikson, 1978; Fiorina, 1974, p. 17) that the sample size per district was much too small to be reliable and that any future survey would require a much larger, and prohibitively expensive, sample.

Several scholars have done further analysis of the 1958 survey data. Erikson (1978) used simulated district constituency opinion, drawn from a 1956-1958 SRC panel survey, to make comparisons with congressional behavior. He found considerably higher correlations than in the Miller-Stokes study between constituent opinion and congressmens' attitudes and votes, at least on domestic issues. These relationships were found to result partly from legislator's perception of constituent opinion and partly from the election of candidates who agreed with constituent opinion. As noted earlier, Gross (1978) used the 1958 data to measure the intervening effects of role and found those effects to be limited. Other efforts to determine the effect of role on policy congruence and legislative perceptions were cited in the section on roles.

Stone (1979) has replicated some components of the Miller-Stokes study over an extended period (1956-1972). He has used SRC/CPS election survey data, broken down by district, and compared it to the congressman's roll-call record on issues covered by the opinion survey; within each district he separates constituents into Democrats and Republicans. He does not have longitudinal data on the congressmen's views or on their perceptions of constituent opinion. He finds generally strong correlations between constituency opinion and roll-call behavior on civil rights issues and, for those constituents identified with the congressman's party, on domestic welfare issues. He also emphasizes that constituent opinion tends to change over time; as a result, the district is often polarized and minority-party constituents are less well represented. Stone's research emphasizes the importance of dynamic rather than static analysis of policy congruence.

Other efforts to measure policy congruence have not followed the Miller-Stokes research design; most have used either data on referenda or simulated district opinion, not district survey data. One of the earliest studies (preceding the 1958 SRC survey) was Crane's (1960) study, comparing a Wisconsin legislative vote and a referendum on daylight saving time. He found most representatives voted consistently with their district's subsequent vote, and very few voted contrary to what they perceived opinion on that issue to be. Not only was the issue unusually salient, but constituent preferences were probably well known; in short, it was untypical.

In an extensive study of voting in California on issues that went to a referendum, referendum and roll-call votes were compared on scales covering particular policy dimensions (Kuklinski, 1978; McCrone and Kuklinski, 1979). Although the general level of policy agreement between roll calls and constituency opinion is low, it is higher on issues most salient to constituents (as measured by turnout in the referenda); these are primarily "contemporary liberalism" issues. On these issues, legislators also have reasonably accurate perceptions of constituency opinion. Policy congruence also tends to be higher when constituencies provide consistent cues to legislators and when legislators have a delegate role orientation. Kuklinski also found that senators were more likely to vote in accordance with the views of constituents during the last two years of their four-year term, as the next election approached.

A somewhat similar effort has been made at the national level to investigate whether legislators change their voting patterns to conform to opinion in their district. Elling (1982) has studied the roll-call voting pattern of U.S. senators over the course of their six-year term, using a liberal-conservative index, and finds that (except for southern Democrats) they generally shift to a position that is ideologically more moderate in the last part of the term. Although Elling does not have data on constituent opinion, and thus is not actually measuring congruence, it is plausible to believe that senators are shifting toward what they perceive is the opinion of constituents. The fact that southern Democrats (presumably representing more conservative districts) did not shift in that direction supports the thesis.

In contrast to these studies, which attempt to measure congruence between the views of constituents in individual districts and the views and votes of individual legislators, several studies have surveyed the opinions of national or state constituents and compared them with the collective views and/or voting record of members of Congress or of a state legislature. The problems of measurement are obviously much simpler. The findings provide much more general information about policy congruence and of course do not make it possible to determine how much variation in congruence there is among districts or the reasons for such variation.

At the national level, Backstrom (1977) compared the views of congressmen with a national sample of public opinion and found relatively small differences of opinion and little variation by issue in the size of differences. Moreover, partisans in the general public tended to agree with members of their party in Congress. Uslaner and Weber (1977, 1979) used national surveys to develop simulated public opinions for each state and used an ambitious mail survey to determine the views of a sample of legislators in each state. Their broad conclusions are that the views of American state legislators do not correspond closely with those of their constituents, and that legislators frequently misperceive opinion in their states. This is true even though legislators were compared with those constituents who identified with their party.

Another type of study was conducted in four southwestern states by Ingram, Laney, and McCain (1980). In each state, the views of the general public (measured through a mail survey) were compared with those of legislators in that state. The authors found that the strength of congruence depended on the policy dimensions or "issue clusters" involved. Legislators were more responsive on those issue clusters on which voters have broad, cohesive policy beliefs. Congruence was greatest on the issue cluster defined as ideological and partisan. Legislators were least inclined to follow opinion that was inconsistent or appeared to be unrealistic. Detailed findings were presented on environmental and water use issues.

Generally, those who have analyzed policy congruence at the institutional rather than the district level seem to have done so because of the difficulty of obtaining constituency opinion data at the district level. Weissberg (1978), however, analyzes policy congruence collectively because of his belief that collective representation is a concept as legitimate and important as individual representation. Moreover, he asserts that citizen opinion is often better represented at the collective level than at the individual level. Using the 1958 SRC data, he shows that the aggregate differences between the opinions of citizens and legislators are smaller than the differences calculated on a district-by-district basis. When the legislature is viewed as a whole, there is a tendency for instances of extreme misrepresentation (very liberal congressmen-very conservative constituents and the reverse) to cancel each other out. Hurley (1982) uses data from the 1978 SRC/CPS opinion survey and finds that, compared to district-level or dyadic analysis, an aggregate analysis improves representation for both district majorities and minorities. In a critique of Weissberg, however, Hurley describes some of the problems of operationalizing policy congruence collectively. If collective representation is defined not as having one's view represented in the legislature, but as being satisfied with the outcome, collective representation may be better only when the policy outcome of legislative voting reflects the majority public preference.

These analyses of policy congruence have all been of U.S. legislatures at either the congressional or state level. Why have scholars studying non-American legislatures ignored this issue that seems to intrigue American scholars so much? One reason, of course, is that many legislatures have large multi-member districts or at-large elections, systems in which the concept of congruence with district opinion loses much of its meaning. Another important reason is that in many legislative systems the political party is so strong and party discipline is usually so tight that the question of congruence with district opinion seldom arises. Where party lines are not so strong, legislators may owe loyalties to interest groups or factions rather than to the constituency. In other words, in many non-American legislative systems legislators demonstrate their responsiveness to those partisan constituents who elected them by maintaining loyalty to the political party and to the program that it originally presented to the voters. One final reason why the non-American literature on policy congruence is so thin is that some legislative bodies simply rubber-stamp the policy initiatives of the executive branch or the cabinet.

Converse and Pierce (1979) collected opinion survey data from 86 constituencies in France and compared it with the voting of deputies on 445 roll calls from 1967 to 1973 covering a dozen policy domains. The major substantive finding is that defections from party discipline result in an increase in the congruence between constituent views and the voting record of deputies. Barnes (1977) has compared the views on major issues of Italian parliamentary deputies and constituents. The data are analyzed by district, but the districts are large multi-member ones; within each district the views of deputies are compared with constituents identified with the same party. The correlations are generally strong on most issues. Comparisons are also made at the national level and show that the strongest agreement on issues between deputies and the general public occurs among Communists, the next strongest among Socialists. Brand (1972), in a study of three Scottish cities, found that agreement between councilors and residents of their own wards was relatively low, but in two of the three cities was higher at the ward level than at the city level. When councilors were asked their perception of constituent opinion, substantial numbers did not know and on some issues less than half of those having any perception were accurate.

The comparative analysis of legislatures in Kenya, Korea, and Turkey (Kim et al., 1982, ch. 5) includes district-level data on the attitudes of legislators, local elites, and constituents toward several broad issues of development, quality of resource distribution, and democratization. Generally correlations between the views of constituents and elites on the one hand and legislators on the other were low; the few strong correlations were often negative rather than positive, particularly in Korea.

Although district-level analysis of congruence is lacking in Canada, Kornberg, Mishler, and Smith (1975) compared the positions of MPs with samples of elite and mass public opinion on a number of major issues. Although the opinions of each group were correlated by party, the level of congruence between MPs and both other groups was relatively low. MPs were more likely to make decisions along ideological lines; constituents were more influenced by party and by government-opposition differences.

An Agenda for Future Research

Theoretical Studies

It seems obvious that Eulau (1967) and other critics are right in arguing that too much theoretical work on representation has been devoted to the Burkean dispute over delegates and trustees. There is a lack of theoretical work pertinent to the highly complex problems of modern representation: the choices forced on a representative by multiple demands and the various forms of linkages between representatives and constituents. Our ambiguities about the theory of representation are well illustrated by the confusion about single- and multi-member districts and the representation of minorities.

We have learned a considerable amount about how legislators actually represent constituents, but our theoretical efforts have lagged behind our empirical research.

Studies of Institutions

The most obvious comment on empirical research into representation at the institutional level is that so little has been done. It is equally obvious that well designed comparative studies of legislative institutions are extensive and expensive undertakings. Comparative studies would be most feasible between state legislatures. Moreover, we do not know very much about how to compare institutions. The three studies cited in this essay, involving local councils (Eulau and Prewitt, 1973), state legislatures (Citizens Conference on State Legislatures, 1971), and national legislatures (Loewenberg and Kim, 1978), are fundamentally different in research design, goals, and specific techniques.

Before new efforts are undertaken to compare representation in different legislative institutions, some serious theoretical efforts should be made to clarify the purposes of such studies. For example, what do we mean when we say that an institution is highly representative? What categories for classifying legislatures in terms of representation make theoretical sense? Parenthetically, it is not clear why the San Francisco Bay area study of councils by Eulau and Prewitt, which is rich in concepts and classifications, has not been followed up by other scholars, if only on a limited scale, as the study by Wahlke et al. of roles in legislative systems was.

Styles of Representation

If we are to understand the home style of representatives—how they develop contacts and communicate with their constituents, how they measure opinions, and how they build a political base—we are going to have to carry out research in the districts. Fenno's research technique for *Home Style* has been criticized because it is difficult to replicate, but there do not appear to be any short cuts available for gaining information and insights into representation in the districts. We need simple descriptive information and analysis about the home style of legislators in all countries. As we begin to accumulate such information, it should be possible to develop a more systematic analysis of the varied home styles of legislators and the reasons for these variations.

Research on legislative roles in a number of countries has demonstrated that role is a useful research tool for the study of representation. We have learned that there are some variations in representative role orientations in American legislatures. In comparing other nations, the variations that emerge reflect the sharp difference in the importance of party, interest groups, and constituent interests, among other factors. Comparison from one legislature to another of the purposive role orientations of members is particularly valuable because it helps us to understand how the functions of legislatures differ and how well institutionalized these legislatures are.

Many of the weaknesses of legislative role studies, particularly for comparative purposes, result from differences in research design and in the specific questions and scales used to classify legislators. Some of the research on the apparent causes of variations in role within legislatures has been productive, suggesting that more work should be done along that line. It would be equally valuable to explore more systematically the differences in role orientations between legislatures. The most obvious gap in role studies concerns the consequences of varied role orientations. To date, the efforts to understand the consequences of role orientations have had only limited success, partly because role orientations are often too complex to be measured by simple questions and to be stereotyped for systematic analysis. In addition, not enough thought has been given to developing plausible and logical hypotheses about the consequences of specific role orientations.

Allocation and Service Responsiveness

We have learned in recent years that legislators in most countries devote considerable time and effort to serving constituents individually and gaining benefits for their districts. In many cases, that is all we have learned. In most countries, and even in the U.S., we need more accurate descriptions of the scope and variety of services performed by legislators; where there are great variations among legislators in these activities, we need to know why. Not much is known about the consequences of this activity, and in congressional studies the only consequence that has attracted much attention has been the electoral one. We need to know how much impact legislators' efforts have on the distribution of services to districts. Particularly in countries where the legislature is weak and the bureaucracy is powerful, we need to find out what—if anything—makes legislators successful in gaining benefits.

Policy Responsiveness

A quarter of a century after the Michigan SRC study of representation was undertaken, no comparable study of policy congruence has been undertaken in this country. Because such a study would be so costly, it would be prudent to begin with extensive discussions about goals and research techniques. What is the goal of research on policy responsiveness or congruence?

If the goal is simply to measure generally the level of agreement between legislators and constituents on issues, it should be possible to do so by measuring policy congruence collectively or through a simulation of district opinions based on national (or state) surveys. If we want to learn what conditions affect congruence, how it varies by issue and by district, and how much agreement there is between legislators and particular subgroups in the districts, the task is much more difficult and short cuts seem unlikely to accomplish these goals.

What is needed is a comprehensive survey in a substantial number of districts of the attitudes legislators, local elites, and constituents hold toward issues—with constituents being sampled in large enough number to permit a within-district analysis. The research needs to be carried out several times over a period of years. It needs to be combined with in-depth studies of the characteristics and political processes in the sampled districts. We need to learn why representatives change their views or behavior, how they respond to particular subgroups on particular issues, how they react to changing constituency attitudes on issues, and whether they have any impact in changing such attitudes. We already know a great deal about how legislators are constrained by the general pattern of attitudes in their district, and we do not need an elaborate research project to confirm what is known. There is little point in undertaking extensive research in the field of policy congruence unless the research design is one that can provide answers to these more detailed questions.

REFERENCES

Achen, Christopher. 1977. "Measuring Representation: Perils of the Correlation Coefficient," *American Journal of Political Science* 21: 805-815.
——— . 1978. "Measuring Representatives," *American Journal of Political Science* 22: 475-510.
Backstrom, Charles H. 1977. "Congress and the Public: How Representative Is One of the Other?" *American Politics Quarterly* 5: 411-436.
Barber, James David. 1965. *The Lawmakers.* New Haven: Yale University Press.
Barker, Anthony and Michael Rush. 1970. *The Member of Parliament and His Information.* London: Allen and Unwin.
Barnes, Samuel H. 1977. *Representation in Italy.* Chicago: University of Chicago Press.
Bauer, Raymond, Ithiel de Sola Pool, and Lewis A. Dexter. 1968. *American Business and Public Policy.* New York: Atherton Press.
Beer, Samuel H. 1969. *British Politics in the Collectivist Age.* New York: Vintage Books.
Bell, Charles G. and Charles M. Price. 1975. *The First Term: A Study of Legislative Socialization.* Beverly Hills, CA: Sage Publications.

Boynton, G.R. and Gerhard Loewenberg. 1973. "The Development of Public Support for Parliament in Germany, 1951-59," *British Journal of Political Science* 3: 169-189.

Brand, John A. 1972. "Councillors, Activists, and Electors: Democratic Relationships in Scottish Cities," in Samuel C. Patterson and John C. Wahlke, eds., *Comparative Legislative Behavior: Frontiers of Research*. New York: John Wiley.

Braunthal, Gerhard. 1965. *The Federation of German Industry in Politics*. Ithaca, NY: Cornell University Press.

Brown, Bernard E. 1963. "Pressure Politics in the Fifth Republic." *Journal of Politics* 25: 509-525.

Cain, Bruce E., John A. Ferejohn, and Morris P. Fiorina. 1979. "A House Is Not a Home: British MPs in Their Constituencies," *Legislative Studies Quarterly* 4: 501-524.

Cavanaugh, Thomas E. 1979. "Rational Allocation of Congressional Resources: Member Time and Staff Use in the House," in Douglas W. Rae and Theodore J. Eismeier, eds., *Public Policy and Public Choice*. Beverly Hills, CA: Sage Publications, pp. 206-247.

Cayrol, Roland, Jean-Luc Parodi, and Colette Ysmal. 1976. "French Deputies and the Political System," *Legislative Studies Quarterly* 1: 67-100.

Chee, Chan Heng. 1976. "The Role of Parliamentary Politicians in Singapore," *Legislative Studies Quarterly* 1: 423-439.

Citizens Conference on State Legislatures. 1971. *State Legislatures: An Evaluation of Their Effectiveness*. New York: Praeger.

Clarke, Harold. 1978. "Determinants of Provincial Constituency Service Behavior: A Multivariate Analysis," *Legislative Studies Quarterly* 3: 601-628.

Clarke, Harold D. and Richard G. Price. 1981. "Parliamentary Experience and Representational Role Orientations in Canada," *Legislative Studies Quarterly* 6: 373-390.

Clarke, Harold D., Richard G. Price, and Robert Krause. 1975. "Constituency Service Among Canadian Provincial Legislators: Basic Findings and a Test of the Three Hypotheses," *Canadian Journal of Political Science* 8: 520-542.

Clausen, Aage R. 1973. *How Congressmen Decide: A Policy Focus*. New York: St. Martin's Press.

————. 1977. "The Accuracy of Leader Perceptions of Constituency Views," *Legislative Studies Quarterly* 2: 361-384.

Converse, Philip E. and Roy Pierce. 1979. "Representative Roles and Legislative Behavior in France," *Legislative Studies Quarterly* 4: 525-562.

Crane, Wilder. 1960. "Do Representatives Represent?" *Journal of Politics* 22: 295-299.

Daalder, Hans and Jerrold G. Rusk. 1972. "Perceptions of Party in the Dutch Parliament," in Samuel C. Patterson and John C. Wahlke, eds., *Comparative Legislative Behavior: Frontiers of Research*. New York: John Wiley, pp. 143-198.

Davidson, Roger H. 1969. *The Role of the Congressman*. New York: Pegasus.

Dexter, Lewis A. 1956. "What Do Congressmen Hear: The Mail," *Public Opinion* 20: 16-27.

————. 1957. "The Representative and His District," *Human Organization* 16: 2-13.

————. 1960. *Sociology and the Politics of Congress*. Chicago: Rand McNally.

Dowse, R. E. 1972. "The M.P. and His Surgery," in Dick Leonard and Valentine Herman, eds., *The Backbencher and Parliament*. London: Macmillan.

Easton, David. 1975. "A Re-Assessment of the Concept of Political Support," *British Journal of Political Science* 5: 435-457.

Elling, Richard C. 1979. "The Utility of State Legislative Casework as a Means of Oversight," *Legislative Studies Quarterly* 4: 353-380.

————. 1982. "Ideological Change in the U.S. Senate: Time and Electoral Responsiveness," *Legislative Studies Quarterly* 7: 75-92.

Erikson, Robert S. 1978. "Constituency Opinion and Congressional Behavior: A Reexamination of the Miller-Stokes Representation Data," *American Journal of Political Science* 22: 511-535.

————. 1981. "Measuring Constituency Opinion: The 1978 U.S. Congressional Election Survey," *Legislative Studies Quarterly* 6: 235-246.

Erikson, Robert S., Norman R. Luttbeg, and William V. Holloway. 1975. "Knowing One's District: How Legislators Predict Referendum Voting," *American Journal of Political Science* 19: 231-246.

Eulau, Heinz. 1967. "Changing Views of Representation," in Ithiel de Sola Pool, ed., *Contemporary Political Science: Toward Empirical Theory*. New York: McGraw-Hill.

Eulau, Heinz and Paul D. Karps. 1977. "The Puzzle of Representation: Specifying Components of Responsiveness," *Legislative Studies Quarterly* 2: 233-254.

Eulau, Heinz and Kenneth Prewitt. 1973. *Labyrinths of Democracy: Adaptations, Linkages, Representation, and Policies in Urban Politics*. Indianapolis: Bobbs-Merrill.

Fenno, Richard E., Jr. 1978. *Home Style: House Members in Their Districts*. Boston: Little, Brown.

Ferguson, LeRoy C. and Bernard W. Klein. 1967. "An Attempt to Correlate the Voting Records of Legislators with Attitudes Toward Party," *Public Opinion Quarterly* 31: 422-426.

Fiorina, Morris P. 1974. *Representatives, Roll Calls, and Constituencies*. Lexington, MA: Heath.

Francis, Wayne. 1965. "The Role Concept in Legislatures: A Probability Model and a Note on Cognition Structure," *Journal of Politics* 27: 567-585.

Friedman, Robert S. and Sybil L. Stokes. 1965. "The Role of the Constitution-Maker as Representative," *Midwest Journal of Political Science* 9: 148-166.

Friesema, H. Paul and Ronald D. Hedlund. 1974. "The Reality of Representational Roles," in Norman R. Luttbeg, ed., *Public Opinion and Public Policy*. 2d ed. Homewood, IL: Dorsey Press, pp. 413-417.

Gerlich, Peter. 1972. "Orientations to Decision-Making in the Vienna City Council," in Samuel C. Patterson and John C. Wahlke, eds., *Comparative Legislative Behavior: Frontiers of Research*. New York: John Wiley, pp. 87-106.

Goodman, Allan E. 1975. "Correlates of Legislative Constituency Service in South Vietnam," in G.R. Boynton and Cong Lim Kim, eds., *Legislative Systems in Developing Countries*. Durham, NC: Duke University Press, pp. 181-205.

Gross, Donald A. 1978. "Representative Styles and Legislative Behavior," *Western Political Quarterly* 31: 359-371.

Hadley, David J. 1977. "Legislative Role Orientations and Support for Party and Chief Executive in the Indiana House," *Legislative Studies Quarterly* 2: 309-335.

Hedlund, Ronald D. and H. Paul Friesema. 1972. "Representatives' Perceptions of Constituency Opinion," *Journal of Politics* 34: 730-752.

Hirsch-Weber, Wolfgang. 1958. "Some Remarks on Groups in the German Federal Republic," in Henry Ehrmann, ed., *Interest Groups on Four Continents*. Pittsburgh: University of Pittsburgh Press.

Hopkins, Raymond F. 1970. "The Role of the M.P. in Tanzania," *American Political Science Review* 64: 754-771.

Hurley, Patricia A. 1982. "Collective Representation Reappraised," *Legislative Studies Quarterly* 7: 119-136.

Ingram, Helen M., Nancy K. Laney, and John R. McCain. 1980. *A Policy Approach to Representation: Lessons From the Four Corners States.* Baltimore: Johns Hopkins University Press.

Jahan, Rounaq. 1976. "Members of Parliament in Bangladesh," *Legislative Studies Quarterly* 1: 355-370.

Jewell, Malcolm E. 1970. "Attitudinal Determinants of Legislative Behavior: The Utility of Role Analysis," in Allan Kornberg and Lloyd D. Musolf, eds., *Legislatures in Developmental Perspective.* Durham, NC: Duke University Press, pp. 460-500.

_____ . 1982. *Representation in State Legislatures.* Lexington: University Press of Kentucky.

Jewell, Malcolm E. and Gerhard Loewenberg. 1979. "Editors' Introduction: Toward a New Model of Legislative Representation," *Legislative Studies Quarterly* 4: 485-498.

Jewell, Malcolm E. and Samuel C. Patterson. 1977. *The Legislative Process in the United States.* 3d ed. New York: Random House.

Johannes, John R. 1979. "Casework as a Technique of U.S. Congressional Oversight of the Executive," *Legislative Studies Quarterly* 4: 325-351.

_____ . 1980. "The Distribution of Casework in the U.S. Congress: An Uneven Burden," *Legislative Studies Quarterly* 5: 517-544.

Karps, Paul D. and Heinz Eulau. 1978. "Policy Representation as an Emergent: Toward a Situational Analysis," in Heinz Eulau and John C. Wahlke, *The Politics of Representation.* Beverly Hills, CA: Sage Publications, pp. 207-231.

Kim, Chong Lim, Joel D. Barkan, Ilter Turan, and Malcolm E. Jewell. 1983. *The Legislative Connection: The Representative and the Represented in Kenya, Korea, and Turkey.* Durham, NC: Duke University Press.

Kim, Y. C. 1969. "Role Orientations and Behavior: The Case of Japanese Prefectural Assemblymen in Chiba and Kanagawa," *Western Political Quarterly* 22: 390-410.

Kingdon, John W. 1977. "Models of Legislative Voting," *Journal of Politics* 39: 563-595.

_____ . 1981. *Congressmen's Voting Decisions.* 2d ed. New York: Harper & Row.

Kornberg, Allan. 1967. *Canadian Legislative Behavior.* New York: Holt, Rinehart, Winston.

Kornberg, Allan, and William Mishler. 1976. *Influence in Parliament: Canada.* Durham, NC: Duke University Press.

Kornberg, Allan, William Mishler, and Joel Smith. 1975. "Political Elite and Mass Perceptions of Party Locations in Issue Space: Some Tests of Two Positions," *British Journal of Political Science* 5: 161-185.

Kuklinski, James H. 1977. "Constituency Opinion: A Test of the Surrogate Model," *Public Opinion Quarterly* 41: 34-40.

_____ . 1978. "Representatives and Elections: A Policy Analysis," *American Political Science Review* 72: 165-177.

_____ . 1979. "Representative-Constituency Linkages: A Review Article," *Legislative Studies Quarterly* 4: 121-140.

Kuklinski, James H. and Richard E. Elling. 1977. "Representational Role, Constituency Opinion, and Legislative Roll-Call Behavior," *American Journal of Political Science* 21: 135-147.

Leonard, Dick and Valentine Herman, eds., 1972. *The Backbencher and Parliament.* London: Macmillan.

Loewenberg, Gerhard. 1967. *Parliament in the German Political System.* Ithaca, NY: Cornell University Press.

Loewenberg, Gerhard, and associates. *How Parliamentary Leaders Cope with Conflict: Politicians In and Outside Parliament in Belgium, Italy, and Switzerland* (forthcoming).

Loewenberg, Gerhard and Chong Lim Kim. 1978. "Comparing the Representativeness of Parliaments," *Legislative Studies Quarterly* 3: 27-50.

Maheshwari, Shriram. 1976. "Constituency Linkage of National Legislators in India," *Legislative Studies Quarterly* 1: 331-354.

Matthews, Donald R. 1960. *U.S. Senators and Their World.* New York: Vintage Books.

McCrone, Donald J. and James H. Kuklinski. 1979. "The Delegate Theory of Representation," *American Journal of Political Science* 23: 278-300.

Mezey, Michael L. 1979. *Comparative Legislatures.* Durham, NC: Duke University Press.

Miller, Warren E. 1964. "Majority Rule and the Representative System of Government," in Erik Allardt and Y. Littunen, eds., *Cleavages, Ideologies, and Party Systems.* Helsinki: Westmark Society, pp. 343-376.

Miller, Warren E. and Donald E. Stokes. 1963. "Constituency Influence in Congress," *American Political Science Review* 57: 45-56.

Mishler, William and Anthony Mughan. 1978. "Representing the Celtic Fringe: Devolution and Legislative Behavior in Scotland and Wales," *Legislative Studies Quarterly* 3: 377-408.

Mohapatra, Manindra K. 1976. "The Ombudsmanic Role of Legislators in an Indian State," *Legislative Studies Quarterly* 1: 295-314.

Musolf, Lloyd D. and J. Frederick Springer. 1979. *Malaysia's Parliamentary System: Representative Politics and Policymaking in a Divided Society.* Boulder, CO: Westview Press.

Muller, William. 1973. "Union-MP Conflict: An Overview," *Parliamentary Affairs* 26: 336-355.

Narain, Iqbal and Shashi Lata Puri. 1976. "Legislators in an Indian State: A Study of Role Images and the Pattern of Constituency Linkages," *Legislative Studies Quarterly* 1: 315-330.

Ong, Michael. 1976. "The Member of Parliament and His Constituency: The Malaysian Case," *Legislative Studies Quarterly* 1: 405-422.

Parker, Glenn R. and Roger H. Davidson. 1979. "Why Do Americans Love Their Congressmen So Much More Than Their Congress?" *Legislative Studies Quarterly* 4: 63-78.

Patterson, Samuel C., Ronald D. Hedlund, and G. Robert Boynton. 1975. *Representatives and Represented: Bases of Public Support for the American Legislatures.* New York: John Wiley.

Pennock, J. Roland and John W. Chapman, eds. 1968. *Representation.* New York: Atherton Press.

Pitkin, Hanna F. 1967. *The Concept of Representation.* Berkeley: University of California Press.

Prewitt, Kenneth, Heinz Eulau, and Betty H. Zisk. 1966-1967. "Political Socialization and Political Roles," *Public Opinion Quarterly* 30: 569-582.

Richards, P.G. 1972. *The Backbenchers.* London: Fletcher.

Roth, Andrew. 1972. *The Business Background of MPs.* Old Woking, Surrey: Gresham Press.

Sisson, Richard and Lawrence L. Shrader. 1977. "Social Representation and Political Integration in an Indian State: The Legislative Dimension," in Albert F. Eldridge, ed., *Legislatures in Plural Societies*. Durham, NC: Duke University Press, pp. 54-94.

Sorauf, Frank J. 1963. *Party and Representation.* New York: Atherton Press.

Stewart, J. D. 1958. *British Pressure Groups: Their Role in Relation to the House of Commons*. Oxford: The Clarendon Press.

Stolarek, John S., Robert M. Rood, and Marcia Whicker Taylor. 1981. "Measuring Constituency Opinion in the U.S. House: Mail Versus Random Surveys," *Legislative Studies Quarterly* 6: 589-596.

Stone, Walter J. 1979. "Measuring Constituency-Representative Linkages: Problems and Prospects," *Legislative Studies Quarterly* 4: 623-639.

Uslaner, Eric M. and Ronald E. Weber. 1977. *Patterns of Decision Making in State Legislatures*. New York: Praeger.

_____ . 1979. "U.S. State Legislators' Opinions and Perceptions of Constituency Attitudes," *Legislative Studies Quarterly* 4: 563-586.

Wahlke, John C. 1971. "Policy Demands and System Support: The Role of the Represented," *British Journal of Political Science* 1: 271-290.

Wahlke, John C., Heinz Eulau, William Buchanan, and LeRoy C. Ferguson. 1962. *The Legislative System*. New York: John Wiley.

Weber, Ronald E., Anne H. Hopkins, Michael Mezey, and Frank J. Munger. 1972. "Computer Simulation of State Electorates," *Public Opinion Quarterly* 36: 549-565.

Weinbaum, Marvin G. 1977. "The Legislator As Intermediary: Integration of the Center and Periphery in Afghanistan," in Albert G. Eldridge, ed., *Legislatures in Plural Societies*. Durham, NC: Duke University Press, pp. 95-121.

Weissberg, Robert. 1978. "Collective vs. Dyadic Representation in Congress," *American Political Science Review* 72: 535-547.

_____ . 1979. "Assessing Legislator-Constituency Policy Agreement," *Legislative Studies Quarterly* 4: 605-622.

Woshinsky, Oliver H. 1973. *The French Deputy: Incentives and Behavior in the National Assembly*. Lexington, MA: Heath.

Zeigler, Harmon and Michael A. Baer. 1969. *Lobbying: Interaction and Influence in American State Legislatures*. Belmont, CA: Wadsworth.

PART TWO

Legislative Organization And Leadership

Chapter 4

Party and Factions Within Legislatures

by

DAVID W. BRADY
CHARLES S. BULLOCK, III

Any essay purporting to deal with factions and parties in legislatures immediately confronts two serious definitional problems. First, what are the boundaries of legislatures? And second, what distinguishes parties from factions? Sartori (1976) describes the problem of defining party in legislatures: "We are traveling more and more through the ever growing jungle of party politics without really knowing where we started, let alone where we are heading" (p. 24). The literature on parties, factions, fractions, and coalitions is amazingly confused on what distinguishes factions from party, party and faction from fraction, and so on. The situation remains much as it was in 1967, when Macridis observed that classifications and typologies of party systems are characterized by a "confusion and profusion of terms" (p. 22).

Our task is made more difficult because scholars of comparative political parties and comparative legislatures have not focused on legislative groups. Party scholars have concentrated on the linkages between party in the electorate and party organization as these affect democracy and/or the political system. Studies which focus on party or faction within legislatures outside the U.S. are the exception, not the rule. Students of comparative legislatures, like students of party, classify and typologize legislatures according to a variety of variables. However, as Mezey points out, "the easiest way to stymie a conference of legislative scholars is to raise the question of what is a legislature" (1979, p. 3). Given the difficulty of defining a legislature, it is not surprising that typologies of legislatures do not include the legislative parties

135

in their schema. For example, in a serious attempt to compare legislatures, Mezey uses Easton's (1965) concept of diffuse support and the legislature's policy-making power.

Our first task is to combine two streams of highly varied, intrastream research into an organized framework. This entails devising a classificatory scheme which allows an orderly review of relevant literature. We begin with a discussion of the general comparative party literature.

Definitions

Sartori (1976, Ch. 1) instructively reviews the development of parties and factions, their theory and practice. From David Hume and Lord Bolingbroke comes the idea that faction and party (essentially interchangeable terms for both writers) are mean and inimical to government. Edmund Burke first clearly distinguished party from faction. Burke claimed that parties were a means to an end, functional associations of like-minded men pursuing similar goals. In contrast, factions were a "mean and interested struggle for emoluments." Because Burke saw parties as functional, he was the first to place parties within the political system, not outside it. However, because parties in Burke's time did not have to appeal to a broad electorate, his notion of party is inadequate for contemporary parties. In Duverger's words, "true parties—those that are divisions of the country at large—are only a century old" (1954, p. 1).

Numerous studies have followed Duverger's pioneering work on political parties. Among others, Crotty (1967), Janda (1980), Epstein (1980), Riggs (1970), and Sartori (1976) have gone to great pains to distinguish party from faction, party and faction from fraction, and all of these from interest groups. The result is somewhat confusing. American scholars, for example, use faction in a neutral sense, while Sartori and others continue to use faction in the Burkean sense. Sartori recognizes the fundamental problem of distinguishing clearly among and between these terms: "A general theory of parties requires preliminary information which, in turn, is not forthcoming 'so long as there exists no general theory' " (1976, p. 106).

Other students of parties point to similar difficulties. In an excellent essay, Sorauf (1967) says, "While on some levels the American political party—or any other political party, for that matter—is easily identifiable, on others it is amazingly elusive. The elusiveness is both definitional and empirical." Similarly Barbara Hinckley writes, "We do not know what this thing [party] is we are claiming to be important and so do not know (1) what we should or should not be linking it to and (2) what we should be comparing its importance against" (1981, p. 111; see also Cooper and Maisel, 1978). Given this confusion about parties it is not surprising that the concept of factions is also confused. In this essay, we accept Sartori's (1976, p. 64) definition of party: "A party is any political group that presents at elections, and is capable of placing through elections, candidates for public office." This definition allows us to distinguish party from faction, since factions do not run candidates for public office. Thus, members of a legislative party are members because they have run for office using the party label.

Following Sartori, we can distinguish legislative factions, which are cross-party groups (Sartori, 1976, Ch. 4), from intraparty fractions. Fractions may be ideological (Seyd, 1972, although he uses "faction" where we would use "fraction"), a tendency (Rose, 1974), personalized (Sartori, 1976, pp. 74-76), or issue specific. The important point is that the legislative party's structure and behavior can be understood in terms of its fractional subunits. The Democratic Party in the U.S. House is clearly affected by the differences between its Southern and Northern fractions. Charles O. Jones (1981, pp. 20-36) has utilized Sartori's distinctions between party, faction, and fraction to analyze reforms in the U.S. House instructively.

By "coalition" we will mean the coming together of two or more parties to form a government, and we will use the term only in reference to parliaments. Coalitions, then, are cross-party groupings designed to govern; factions are cross-party groupings which, although perhaps determining the legislative outcome of a particular policy, do not govern. A parliament may have a governing coalition, but there may also be issues on which fractions of two or more parties vote together as a faction.

A Framework

We shall, like Eulau and Hinckley (1966), separate research on legislative parties and factions into two models: the inside and the outside. The inside model describes some key structural and behavioral variables characterizing parties and factions within the legislature. The outside model describes forces and influences which are beyond the institutional boundaries of legislatures. By starting with the inside model, one can describe those characteristics of legislative parties and factions that scholars have considered important. Thus, we will describe the animal we seek to explain. Then we can review which outside variables have been thought to affect party and factional behavior within legislatures. In sum, we list variables borrowed from coalition theory which characterize legislative groups within the institution; we then derive from the comparative party literature outside variables so that we may classify types of legislative parties and factions. Having done so, we proceed to review the literature.

Coalition Theory

By restricting our scope at first to the legislature, we limit the structural and behavioral variables which characterize legislative groups. However, we still need a guide to point us to the key variables. Coalition theory describes who joins which groups for what purpose and thus seems an appropriate guide. Moreover, William Riker (1962) has argued persuasively that a science of politics should have coalitions as a central organizing concept. In a recent book, Barbara Hinckley asserts that "coalition activity is, in fact, a small measure of political activity" (1981, p. 4)—i.e., a model of politics. She writes that coalition activity implies (1) applications of political power, (2) combinations of conflict and coordination, and (3) collective activity, all of which result in "collective mixed-motive situations." Resolving such situations requires political skills—for example, bargaining, compromise, and mobilization of support. Coalition activity and the skills it requires all seem to be part and parcel of the legislative process.

Legislatures are clearly collectives of individuals representing other people, individuals who work in combinations of conflict and coordination, applying power to make decisions they favor. Indeed, from the beginning, coalition theorists have used legislatures as settings in which to test their theories.

Internal Variables

The "internal" variables—stability, range, task, power, goals, membership, and size—will each be discussed under its own heading. These variables have not all received equal attention; for example, task distribution is an important but little-studied phenomenon.

Stability of membership. Factions and parties are distinguished from one another largely by their degree of stability (Stern, Tarrow, and Williams, 1971). In a responsible two-party system representatives would belong to one of the two parties, and their party membership would determine their voting, committee assignments, rewards, etc. In a perfectly factional legislature, specific factions would determine each vote, committee assignment, etc., so that groupings might shift from issue to issue. The British parliamentary system (Schattschneider, 1948; Ranney, 1981) has often approximated a stable, responsible party system; the Louisiana legislature approximates a factional legislative system (Key, 1949; Sindler, 1955). The U.S. House of Representatives fits somewhere between these two extremes: the two major parties determine committee assignments, but cross-party factions such as the Conservative Coalition often determine voting patterns (Manley, 1973; Brady and Bullock, 1980; Sinclair, 1981).

Range of activities. The range of legislative activities covered by the coalition also distinguishes between factions and parties (Seyd, 1972). In the U.S. House, each party acts cohesively and in opposition to the other when organizing the chamber (Ripley, 1969; Jones, 1970). Thus, votes to accept the rules of the previous House (e.g., committee assignments) and the vote for the Speaker are almost always purely party votes. But different configurations characterize voting on issues. Some groups are active on only a single issue; for example, in the French Fourth Republic the MRP split with its coalitional partners over the Barange bill, which would have supported parochial schools (Williams, 1966). Such single-issue groups can form either across parties or within a party. U.S. Congressional Black Caucus members are all Democrats, but they work together to maximize benefits on issues affecting black interests. A legislative group's activities are not restricted to voting in clusters, but also include selection of leaders, committee assignments, administrative lobbying, and attempts to direct money toward certain sectors. In short, determining the range of legislative groups' behavior within legislatures is an important area of study, though not one that is easily handled.

Organizational attributes. An important aspect of a party's organization in the legislature is its distribution of tasks and power. Task distribution can be understood as the division of labor. British and Japanese legislative parties have numerous party task forces dealing with aspects of party business (Norton, 1978; Baerwald, 1974). Likewise, the Democratic and Republican parties have partisan task forces which deal with various questions; however, these task groups are heavily integrated with the committee system. Clearly, legislative groups vary greatly in how they distribute tasks.

The distribution of power in legislative parties is essentially a question of centralization of power or hierarchy. Surely there is greater hierarchy in the British Labour party (Rose, 1974, Ch. 6) and in Communist legislative parties in Western Europe (Williams, 1966) than in the American Democratic party (Ripley, 1969). In parties where power is centralized or hierarchical, a relatively small number of leaders can make policy; in decentralized parties leaders are more numerous so that more people have some say in fixing policy preferences (King, 1981, pp. 87-89). Nonpartisan factions can range from the relatively hierarchical, like the Long faction in the Louisiana legislature, to the almost casual factions found in the Texas or Georgia legislatures.

Legislatures which operate by a simple majority rule will have different combinations of task and power distribution than will legislatures which require a two-thirds majority on some or all issues. The rules themselves are not listed as variables here because they are not properties of factions and parties.

Goals. Goals also characterize legislative party configurations. The first distinction is whether faction or party goals fit within the domain of diffuse support for the regime (Easton, 1965). For example, Communist legislative parties in Western Europe often seek to overthrow the current regime; in the French Fourth Republic, both the Communists and the Gaullists sought to eliminate parliamentary government (Williams, 1966; Jackson, Atkinson, and Hart, 1977).

The mix of personal and collective goals is especially important. Sartori (1976) and others see factions as characterized by personal goals and parties as means of achieving collective benefits. Thus, the extent to which a legislative group is dominated by personal or collective goals is an important characteristic (Fenno, 1973).

Membership. Asking who joins parties, factions, and coalitions and why will also help characterize legislative groups (Stern, Tarrow, and Williams, 1971). The composition of a legislative coalition will vary from country to country and will in turn affect what coalitions do. Fiorina's (1974) distinction between heterogeneous and homogeneous constituencies can easily be applied to coalitions; clearly, a legislative party representing a heterogeneous constituency will behave differently from one representing a relatively homogeneous constituency (Fenno, 1974). Many of the differences between Republicans and Democrats in the U.S. Congress can be explained by the relatively heterogeneous constituency of the Democratic party and the relatively homogeneous constituency of the congressional Republicans. Research on European parliaments focuses on questions of who joins governing coalitions and why such coalitions succeed and fail.

Size and number. The size of coalitions in legislatures has received considerable scholarly attention, particularly the question of minimum winning coalitions. According to Riker's (1962) coalition theory, players can maximize benefits by forming a minimum winning coalition. The logic of this analysis is compelling and sheds light on why coalitions act as they do.

Scholars have also studied the number of parties in a legislature (Duverger, 1954; Sartori, 1976). While identifying the number of factions, parties, and/or coalitions in legislatures appears easy, such is not always the case (for counts of parties, see Blondel, 1969; Janda, 1980). For example, should one count the 40 or so Populist representatives in the 55th U.S. House as a third party, thus making that House multiparty? The answer is clearly no: Populists were given their committee assignments through the Democratic party, and they voted and sat with the Democrats. Should members of the British SDP be considered a fourth party in the House of Commons, or, since most were elected under the label of a different party, should they be classified as Labourites, Conservatives, or Liberals? However one answers specific questions, the basic distinction between multiparty, two-party, and one-party legislatures has long been recognized as important, and these terms refer to characteristics which affect legislative outputs and organization. Likewise, the extent to which a legislature is factionalized has long intrigued legislative scholars (Rose, 1964; Seyd, 1972; Sartori, 1976, Ch. 4; Key, 1949). However, as we shall see, the question of the number of parties in the legislative system fits best in the external model.

While it is possible to think of other characteristics of legislative groups, these seem to predominate in the literature and constitute a reasonable description of the characteristics of legislature groups. These variables are analytically distinct but empirically related. Thus, a strong two-party legislative system will more than likely be stable (have nonoverlapping membership) and the parties will have a wide range of activities. How to account for the empirical combinations of these characterizing variables has long been a question of concern to party scholars. Any student of the American Congress knows that federalism, the single-member district, the plurality electoral rule, and the diversity of the American population (Key, 1964; Sorauf, 1967; Orfield, 1975) help shape the structure and behavior of American legislative parties. Thus, the question becomes what external variables affect the structure and behavior of legislative groups.

External Variables

The literature comparing political parties abounds with classifications and schema which relate external variables to parties and to legislative groups. Terms such as "consociational democracies" (Lorwin, 1974) and "developing societies" (Boynton and Kim, 1975) are used to classify party systems. Researchers in this area range from those interested in explaining the role of parties in democratic societies to those interested in showing how parties and/or legislatures help integrate and develop nationhood in the Third World. A review of this varied and impressive literature is beyond the scope of this essay; however, we have culled from it a short list of outside variables which affect how our characterizing variables may be combined for a classification of legislative systems.

Elections have a crucial effect on party structure and behavior in legislatures. Electoral competition and electoral rules are especially important because they define linkages between the legislature and the society. For some researchers, the unique feature of a party is that it offers candidates for election under a party label (Epstein, 1967). Rae (1967) and Rae and Taylor (1971) developed a fragmentation index based on the size and number of legislative parties in a nation and used this index to classify types of party systems. While there is much disagreement over the classifications which result (see Sartori, 1976, Ch. 9, for an example), elections are important in determining the number of parties in a legislature and how they behave.

Another crucial variable is the function that the overall political system assigns the legislature. That is, what does the legislature do? The comparative literature both on legislatures and on parties emphasizes legislative functions. In *Comparative Legislatures* (1979), Mezey uses the policy-making power of legislatures as one of two typologizing variables; Loewenberg and Patterson (1979, p. 10) list this as a determining environmental factor. Blondel (1973) developed a five-point scale that assesses the strength of legislatures compared to the executive, a factor also considered by Loewenberg and Patterson (1979, p. 11). Similarly, Polsby (1975, p. 277) distinguishes between transformative and arena legislatures. Sartori (1976, pp. 121-123) argues that what matters in a classification of party systems is the governing potential. Axelrod (1970, Ch. 8) and de Swaan (1973) make essentially the same point. In short, political parties which cannot govern or do not have governing potential are less important than governing parties and should be so classified.

The relationship between the external party and the legislative party is also of interest (Epstein, 1980). In fact, the extent to which the external party organization seeks to impose or enforce its views on the legislative party is at the heart of the question of representation. In one theory, the legislative party members are considered to be Burkean representatives; in the other, the legislator is seen as an agent. Epstein (1980) argues that the relationship between the external party and the legislative party will vary with the size, ideology, and number of major parties in the system. The more programmatic the party, the greater the likelihood of external control of legislators. Likewise, the smaller the size of the party and the fewer the number of major parties, the greater the likelihood of external control. Studies of the British Labour Party (Epstein, 1980), the Australian Labour Party (Butler, 1973), and the New Zealand Labour Party (Chapman et al., 1962) reveal some of the conditions affecting external and legislative party relations within programmatic parties. Epstein (1980) also reviews literature pertaining to this relationship in other Western democracies. However, as he points out, external control derives largely from the parties' working class origins; as these origins become more remote, the control diminishes.

Classificatory Scheme

Combining legislative elections and legislative functions, we can classify legislative party systems using Sartori's (1976, p. 128) scheme. The two classificatory variables are the concentration of parties in the legislature and the dispersion of power, which taps the constituent bases of legislative parties (cf. Loewenberg and Patterson, 1979, pp. 9-10). The concentration or numerical variable has the obvious one-party, two-party, multiparty components. However, the one-party category has three classes: one party, hegemonic party, and predominant party. The multiparty category has two classes: limited pluralism and extreme pluralism. Thus, there are six classes.

Sartori (1976) uses the second variable, the dispersion of power, to measure the extent to which political parties monopolize or share political power; here we are concerned with the dispersion of legislative parties' power. In one-party systems, one can clearly distinguish, as Sartori does, systems where one party monopolizes all power (the U.S.S.R. and East Germany, for example) from hegemonic systems (Mexico, for example, where the PRI relaxes its monopoly to allow other parties to have legislative representation). However, when we turn to the two-party and multiparty systems, a problem arises, since some countries, such as France and the United States, elect an executive independently of the legislature. Thus, the question of how legislative parties share the governing function is important in all cases, from predominant party systems to polarized multiparty systems.

In one-party monopolies, whether hegemonic or not, the legislature plays little or no role in setting goals or making policy. However, in all other cases, the legislature's role varies from moderately important to important. Thus, the variables for the dispersion of power and concentration of parties are interactive, one-party monopoly systems having legislatures of little importance for policy making and all other categories having legislatures which play some role in the policy process.

In one-party predominant systems there is a legislative party which controls power, but there is legitimate and sufficient opposition, so that one could envision alternation of power. The Japanese Diet is a case in point; the Liberal Democrats have dominated the Diet since its inception, yet the Socialists and other leftist parties have the potential to govern. For these reasons, we classify Japan as a one-party predominant system, even though electorally it is a multiparty system.

The distinguishing feature of a two-party system is not whether more than two parties compete electorally but whether one or the other of two parties has an absolute majority in the legislature. Power alternates in such a system between two and only two parties. Under this schema, the British system qualifies as a two-party system while the German system does not. In Britain, either the Conservatives or Labour has a majority and governs; in Germany, neither the Socialists nor the Christian Democrats usually has a majority, and they must form cross-party coalitions in order to govern.

Multiparty systems are divided according to the amount of fragmentation of power within the legislature—i.e., the number of parties. The German Bundestag has low fragmentation, while the Italian and Finnish Parliaments have high fragmentation. There are a number of political parties spread across considerable ideological spectra in the latter two systems.

Several important definitions which underlie this typology: parties count only if they have governing potential; factions are not parties but cross-partisan groups without governing potential; fractions are intraparty groupings based on single issues, ideology, or personalism; "fragment" refers to the number of parties with governing potential. With these distinctions and the typology presented above, we can proceed to review the literature under the following headings: multiparty legislatures, distinguishing between consensual pluralistic and fragmented polarized systems; two-party systems with relatively even concentration and alternation of power; predominant party systems; and one-party monopolistic systems.

Our emphasis is on studies which compare or have comparative concepts. There are innumerable studies of parliaments in single nations; while we have tried to cull these studies for information useful to our purpose, we could not possibly cite all these studies, much less review them individually.

We shall concentrate on two-party and multiparty democratic systems, with the heaviest emphasis on Western legislatures. This focus is determined, in part, by our choice of a scheme which requires that legislative parties actively participate in policy making. Before turning to the main body of the essay, we shall briefly explain why we devote little attention to the less-developed countries.

Legislatures in Less-Developed Countries

Parties and factions in less-developed countries pose a special problem, since in most of them the legislature's function is not policy oriented. Most studies of these countries' legislatures focus on their role in representation (Jewell, 1977; Boynton and Kim, 1975; Smith and Musolf, 1979). Other studies have focused on recruitment, socialization, and training functions. While there are some studies on the legislature's role in conflict management via policy (Mezey, 1975; Hoskin, 1975), very little has been done on legislative parties and factions.

We suspect that these legislative parties draw little attention because most less-developed countries lack a well-articulated diffuse support structure. Legislative parties and factions in such countries resemble the early British Parliament and the U.S. Congress before the 1820s (see Young, 1966); the legislatures do not serve decisional or governmental functions as do Western legislatures.

Only when political systems have relatively stable diffuse support can party subsystems—parties within the system—develop. Legislative parties, as we define them, function within a framework of diffuse support; therefore they have developed a governmental or decision-making function. The development of such functions affects their stability, range, task, power, goals, membership, and size. In less-developed countries, where decisional/governmental functions are outside the legislature, parties and factions (if they exist) serve different purposes. Packenham's (1970) warning that non-Western legislatures are not strictly comparable to Western legislatures should be kept in mind. Thus, the greatest part of our essay is concerned with Western parties and factions because these serve a governmental function. Legislatures or parties which develop support for the system by representation, integration, and so on are not strictly comparable to Western legislative parties, and studies which describe them are not relevant here.

Coalitions to Form Governments

In multiparty parliamentary systems this question is the most frequently researched from a comparative perspective: how can parties form a government and then remain sufficiently cohesive for that government to remain in power? Students of parties, particularly those interested in Western democracies, have sought to develop and test theory with which to explain the formation of governing coalitions. While there are many excellent studies of party, fraction, and faction in individual countries, our emphasis here is on comparative research.

Game theory has provided a useful perspective on why prospective partners unite to form a ruling coalition. From Von Neumann and Morgenstern (1947) comes the proposition that the coalition will include only partners needed to achieve majority status. Riker's (1962) refinement is that the smallest possible coalition will be formed. Leiserson (1968) postulates that the governing coalition will be the one with the fewest parties. Axelrod (1970) and de Swaan (1973) anticipate that governing coalitions will be of minimal size and that they will be formed by parties which share policy concerns.

Students of coalition formation assume that parties join coalitions to maximize their benefits. Benefits which have been suggested include policy outputs, a share of cabinet posts, and specific cabinet posts which would enable a party to strengthen its position in the next election.

Ministerial Portfolios

It is expected that parties want, at a minimum, a proportion of cabinet positions equal to the share of the votes which they contribute to the coalition (Gamson, 1961). Browne and Franklin (1973) find strong support for this hypothesis among the 358 parties which belonged to 114 governing parliamentary coalitions in 13 western democracies for the period 1945 to 1969. The regression line has an intercept of near zero (a=-.01) and the slope is close to unity (b=1.07). Moreover, there is little variability around the regression line (r=.93).

Where there are deviations from perfect proportionality, Browne and Franklin found that small parties had received a share of the cabinet positions larger than their proportion of seats in the legislature (cf. Felsenthal, 1979). A larger partner may give up a ministry to which it is entitled because it expects great benefits from dominating the government and does not see the small party as a threat to its leadership. Such overpayment is likely only when a coalition consists of two or three members; the authors speculate that in coalitions with more members the dominant party would have less control over policy, making control of ministries more critical.

Bueno de Mesquita (1975, 1979) has challenged the Browne and Franklin proportionality rule. He has speculated that coalition partners will concentrate on obtaining the most desirable ministries, those he refers to as "redistributive ministries." To substantiate this proposition, Bueno de Mesquita shows that party size can account for substantially less than 100 percent of the variation in the distribution of the most desirable cabinet seats. He therefore hypothesizes that allocation of the very desirable ministries is determined by the bargaining skills of party leaders and not simply by party size.

Testing Bueno de Mesquita's redistribution proposition, Browne and Frendreis (1980) conclude that party size cannot account for all the variation in the distribution of the most desirable posts because it is impossible for a party's percentage of the coalition's parliamentary seats to match perfectly its share of the cabinet posts. For example, if there are 10 redistributive ministries, a party which accounts for 25 percent of the coalition's seats will receive either 20 or 30 percent of the posts.

A variant of the size principle predicts that a party's share of the ministries depends on whether its participation is essential for the coalition to achieve majority status. Coalition members whose votes are not essential to the creation or maintenance of the government are given less than their proportionate share of the portfolios (Merkl, 1970, pp. 24-25). Parties pivotal for forming a governing coalition receive a disproportionate share of the ministries.

From an analysis of coalitions in 12 European countries, Schofield (1976, pp. 24-49) suggests that the level of polarization will affect payoffs. This helps explain the Browne and Franklin (1974) and Browne and Frendreis (1980) findings concerning the fate of small parties in coalitions having few or many partners. In systems characterized by moderate polarization,

fragmentation of the resource distribution works against the larger parties. The smaller parties are able to construct pivotal subgroups to defend their position. . . . In a few situations, it may be rational for the larger parties to construct and maintain surplus coalitions (i.e., coalitions including more parties than necessary to form a government), since in a smaller minimal coalition, the bargaining strengths of parties of different sizes would be similar (Schofield, 1976, pp. 47-48).

In the absence of such equality, the larger parties will receive a disproportionate share of the cabinet positions.

While the largest partner in a coalition may not receive a proportionate share of the cabinet seats, it is usually compensated by receiving the
prime ministership (Browne and Dreijmanis, 1982). Browne and Feste (1975,
1978) show that there are a set of ministries, including the prime ministership,
usually awarded to the largest partner in a coalition. There are, however, some
coalitions in which the smaller partners reject the largest member's candidate
for prime minister (Groennings, 1970, p. 76).

Achievement Needs of Party Leaders

Bueno de Mesquita has argued that "size, or representation, is
probably one of the most important resources of political parties, but size
alone usually is not sufficient to insure success" (1974, p. 1207). He asserts
that parties participate in coalitions primarily to obtain policy payoffs and to
use their position to win additional legislative seats in subsequent elections.
The latter objective is easier to achieve if the party controls those ministries
which provide patronage, publicity, and/or useful grassroots contacts.

Competitive party leaders seek to advance their party at the expense
of their coalition partners; cooperative party leaders make fewer demands for
payoffs distributed by the coalition. Whether a party follows a competitive
or a cooperative strategy will be linked to its leaders' need for achievement.
Bueno de Mesquita, testing his theory in the context of Indian states (1974,
1975) and of European democracies (1979), concluded that the achievement
needs of party leaders are important when the most important cabinet posts
are allocated. These he calls "redistributive portfolios," since a clever leader
uses these positions to win additional seats in the next election.

Policy Considerations

A third explanation is that coalitions form primarily to produce a
particular kind of public policy. According to de Swaan, "the evidence has
clearly shown that parliamentary coalitions cannot be explained satisfactorily
in terms of the number of seats of the member actors alone: the actors'
policy positions must also be taken into account. Theories that take into
account the policy positions of the actors without exception achieve better
results than theories that ignore them" (1973, pp. 284-285). For example,
the parties which coalesced to govern France from 1932 to 1936 were primarily
those from the ideological center (Wood and Pitzer, 1979).

In bargaining over policy positions, small parties which are essential
for the formation of a government may be advantaged, just as they often are

in competing for a share of the cabinet portfolios (Merkl, 1970, p. 40). Generally the small parties' advantage in setting coalition policy will not be too significant, since coalition members infrequently display a broad ideological range. "The less conflict of interest there is in a coalition, the more likely the coalition will form" (Axelrod, 1970, p. 167); conflicts of interest should be less pronounced when the partners' policy preferences are similar. Therefore, assuming a one-dimensional policy space, Axelrod hypothesizes that ideologically adjacent parties will form coalitions.

De Swaan (1973), using data from nine Western democracies, confirms Axelrod's conclusion, based on data from Italy, that coalition partners are ideologically adjacent. De Swaan indicates that a coalition partner would consider its position optimal if there were, on either side of it ideologically in the coalition, parties equal in strength to one another.

Under certain environmental conditions, coalitions may span a wide ideological range. Such a coalition may form when a political system faces a crisis—for example, wartime all-party governments and the all-party governments which ruled in many West German states after World War II (Merkl, 1970, pp. 16-17). When there is a deep ideological cleavage, the government is likely to include all of the prosystem parties on the majority side of the left-right cleavage (Budge and Herman, 1978, pp. 472-473).

Incremental Changes in Membership

Researchers have observed a general tendency towards stability in coalition membership. Budge and Herman (1978) characterize this as an effort to include within governing coalitions parties which have normally been part of the government (cf. Laver, 1974). Often the same individuals serve in a succession of coalition cabinets, although the ministries for which they are responsible may change (Siegfried, 1956). Sani (1976) offers a further explanation for this pattern. Cleavages which have divided parties in the past may not be easily papered over. Even if party leaders are willing to join with the enemies of the past, it may be difficult to convince the rank and file that a party which was once an opponent should now be an ally (Groennings, 1970; Nyholm, 1982).

Coalition Size

Students of legislative politics have been interested in the size of the coalitions as well as in their reasons for forming. Most scholars since Von Neumann and Morgenstern (1947) have expected that coalitions will tend to be no larger than necessary to constitute a majority. To the extent that ministerial portfolios are the payoff for joining a coalition, each partner will get more cabinet slots when the number of partners is minimized. If policy is the glue which holds the coalition together, there will be less strain when the policy dimension across which the partners are arrayed is narrow (Leiserson, 1968).

Axelrod (1970) and de Swaan (1973) have postulated that coalitions will unite the minimum number of parties in adjacent policy spaces. De Swaan calls this "closed minimal range" theory because according to this theory coalitions will be oversized rather than exclude a small party bracketed by coalition members. Dodd (1974) implies that a closed range coalition which is not minimal will, in time, be reformed to exclude an unnecessary partner; thus he rejects de Swaan's criterion of closedness.

When de Swaan tests the usefulness of 13 theories of coalition formation across nine Western democracies, he finds that those theories which consider policy agreement perform better than those which consider only size (1973, pp. 148-149). Closed minimal range theory performs quite well under normal times—that is, when a country does not face a crisis.

One explanation for larger than minimal coalitions is uncertainty. If some of the participants seem to be weakly wedded to the coalition, then in the interest of stability it may be worthwhile to include additional members at the outset. This situation is more likely when there are fractions in one or more of the parties or policy disagreements among the participating parties. Perhaps because the coalitions in question were uncertain, the closed minimal range theory did not successfully predict coalitions in Fourth Republic France and, of the seven Italian coalitions not accurately predicted by Axelrod (1970, p. 178), three had more participants than expected.

According to Dodd (1974), uncertainty occasions either over- or undersized coalitions. In Dodd's schema, two factors affect whether parties have reliable information when they consider possible coalitions: the parliament's fractionalization (the number of parties and their relative strengths) and the party system's stability or continuity in the parliament across time. A third important variable is the extent to which cleavages divide parties on policy dimensions.

Dodd's analysis uses data for 17 Western parliamentary systems from the end of World War I through 1972, excluding the World War II period. He finds that coalitions larger than the minimum needed to win control tend to occur when the parliamentary system is very fractionalized and/or unstable and the cleavage conflict relatively small. Coalitions of smaller than minimum winning size are likely when the party system is highly fractionalized and/or unstable and the cleavage conflict relatively great. Minimum winning coalitions are most likely when there is less fractionalization and instability. Dodd concludes that "it is the interactive occurrence of fractionalization and instability together, and their joint interaction with cleavage conflict that seems most influential in determining cabinet coalitional status" (p. 1110), i.e., coalition size relative to the minimum needed for a majority.

A perceived threat to the stability of a system—another sort of uncertainty—also makes it more likely that larger than minimal-winning coalitions will form. Under such a threat, the coalition is likely to expand to include all prosystem parties (Budge and Herman, 1978).

Browne (1982), in a review of case studies of 11 countries, discounts uncertainty as an explanation. Instead, he points to the need for extraordinary majorities to resolve constitutional crises and the benefits for partners of oversized coalitions.

Cabinet Dissolution

In a parliamentary system, a government can fall in one of four ways. A coalition or a single governing party may fall because too many members defect on a confidence vote. A coalition may collapse if a party which has been a partner defects. A coalition may lose a confidence vote if a fraction defects from one of the coalition's parties (cf. Wood and Pitzer, 1979). Finally, a minority government may fall if a sufficient number of legislators no longer supports the government nor abstains on votes of confidence.

Individual defections may be idiosyncratic and therefore unpredictable, or back-benchers dissatisfied with the policies of the leadership may defect (Crowe, 1980). Defections of parties or fractions may be explained by the intensity of policy disagreements, the internal cohesion of the coalition's parties, the number of parties in the coalition, the ideological range of the coalition partners, the size of the anti-system parties in the legislature, and the size of the governing coalition in relation to the size of a minimal winning coalition. Fractions based on ideology, issues, or personalities impair stability.

Measurement of Coalition Durability

Durability may be a significant characteristic of coalitions, since it indicates the coalition's stability, without which the government cannot achieve its policy objectives. The presumption that a stable coalition produces important outputs has come into question, since stability may result from an avoidance of thorny issues. Instability does, however, reveal the relative strength of the legislature and the executive (Lijphart, 1982). Durability of coalitions has been measured differently by the various scholars who have been concerned with cabinet dissolution. Blondel (1968, p. 190) considered a government to have persisted so long as it had the same prime minister and the same party or parties supporting it. Dodd (1974, p. 1117) put forth a less-restrictive definition: he considered the government to have persisted so long as the coalition contained the same parties, regardless of whether there was a new prime minister. For Hurwitz (1971, p. 44), who uses a still more liberal definition, a new government comes into being when there has been an election, when there is a new prime minister, when there is a change in the parties which form the government, or when there is a cabinet shake up even if the prime minister remains the same. Sanders and Herman (1977, pp. 356-357) measure coalitions' "survival": that percentage of the time until the next required election which the cabinet actually serves. For example, if a government is elected to a four-year term and serves 36 months, its survival score is .75.

Number of Parties

Just before the turn of the century Lowell wrote, "It is an axiom in politics that, except under very peculiar circumstances, coalition ministries are short lived compared with homogeneous ones. . . . [T]he parliamentary system will give the country a strong and efficient government only in case the majority consists of a single party" (1896, pp. 70, 73; quoted in Dodd, 1974, p. 1093). Support for Lowell's proposition was offered by Taylor and Herman (1971) from their analysis of 196 governments in 19 countries from the end of World War II to 1969. They found that coalitions were more durable when there were few parties in the governing coalition. One-party governments lasted an average of 1108 days, coalition governments an average of 625 days.

Additional support comes from Warwick (1979). In this study the units of analysis are cabinets in nine European parliaments between 1918 and 1976, except the World War II years. The author finds a strong bivariate relationship indicating that when the number of parties in the government is small it is longer lasting, a relationship which holds up in multivariate models.

In an updating of Taylor and Herman, Sanders and Herman (1977) found the number of parties in the governing coalition to be negatively correlated with the duration of a cabinet and its stability. The correlations were not large and accounted for less than 4 percent of the variance. In multivariate models, the number of parties in the government is an important predictor of the government's survival and duration. In models to predict survival, the number of parties correlated negatively with survival in the equation for minority governments and in a model combining intra- and extra-parliamentary factors. The number of parties in the cabinet correlated positively, however, in the model for majority governments.

Mayer (1980) introduces what he calls a "party aggregation score," the proportion of parliamentary seats held by a coalition's largest partner divided by the number of partners. Using data from 18 countries, he finds a strong correlation between aggregation and cabinet stability.

One piece of research by Laakso and Taagepera (1979) goes against the common pattern. They put forward a measure of the "effective number of parties," defined as "the number of hypothetical *equal*-size parties that would have the same *effect* on fractionalization of the system as have the actual parties of *unequal* size" (p. 4). They conclude that "government instability . . . is not correlated with the mere effective number of parties in our sample of 15 countries" (p. 24).

Relative Size of the Coalition

Since minority cabinets always depend on the support or acceptance of some legislators whose party does not belong to the coalition, it is hardly surprising that majority governments last longer than minority ones (Sanders and Herman, 1977; Warwick, 1979).

Game theory refines our understanding of majority and minority governments and predicts that coalitions should, if the players have perfect information, be of minimal winning size. Laver (1974) suggests that coalitions of minimal winning size will be more durable than those which are over- or undersized. Dodd explains the instability of oversized coalitions thus: "The greater the deprivation parties suffer relative to a potential minimum winning size, the more quickly these parties should act to remove the deprivation" (1974, p. 1101). A central source of conflict is the award of cabinet posts to parties unnecessary to maintaining the government.

Dodd demonstrates that minimal winning coalitions are longer lived than over- or undersized coalitions and also isolates three variables related to cabinet durability. He writes that "there is a difference in the direction of cabinet deviation under different cleavage conflict conditions. If cleavage conflict is high, cabinets in a fractionalized and unstable party system will deviate toward an undersized coalitional status" (p. 113). In systems in which the party system is more stable and less fractionalized, minimum winning coalitions are the norm.

Warwick (1979) finds minimum winning coalition status to be the strongest bivariate correlate of cabinet durability. It remains a significant variable in Warwick's most successful multivariate model.

Axelrod (1970) contributes this criterion to the notion of minimal winning coalition: the coalition will be more durable if the partners are adjacent ideologically. Warwick (1979) also observed a strong bivariate relationship for this variable, using data from nine European countries. However, when he adds this term to a multivariate model which includes terms for minimum winning status and number of parties in the government, "there is no room for the ideological criterion posited by Axelrod" (1979, p. 473).

Ideological Diversity and Conflict Cleavages

From Laver (1974) comes the notion that ideological diversity within a coalition contributes to its instability. Like Axelrod's minimal connected winning coalition, Laver's ideological diversity measure is related in the expected direction to cabinet durability in a bivariate analysis, but is not an important correlate in the multivariate analysis (Warwick, 1979).

Warwick does, however, devise a variant of ideological diversity which proves quite useful, using a method like Dodd's (1976, pp. 97-115) to measure cleavage conflict. He demonstrates that two important cleavages contributed to the downfall of European parliaments: the inclusion of socialist and bourgeois parties within a coalition and the attempt to bridge the clerical/ secular split within a coalition. A term which combines the effects of these two cleavages is important in Warwick's best multivariate model for coalition stability.

Fractionalization Within the Parliament

Taylor and Herman (1971) found that governments lasted longer where there was less fractionalization among the cabinet partners (cf. Browne and Dreijmanis, 1982), among the prosystem parties in parliament, and within the opposition. Opposition fractionalization was not as important as were divisions among government supporters. In multivariate models, however, Sanders and Herman (1977) and Warwick (1979) did not find fractionalization within parliament, measured in various ways, to be an important independent variable.

Antisystem Parties

When there are relatively large parties—usually Communist or neo-Fascist—dedicated to the overthrow of the current system, there is a smaller pool of potential coalition partners. Antisystem parties create what Sartori (1976) refers to as polarized pluralism within the legislature. Sartori argues that in such a system the governing coalition or party will occupy the ideological center, challenged by parties on both the right and the left. Moreover, there are strong centrifugal forces; some parties will take extreme positions in order to differentiate themselves from their competitors.

Taylor and Herman (1971) observed a strong relationship between the strength of the antisystem parties and government stability. Indeed, this remained one of the most important variables in their multivariate model. Of the variables Sanders and Herman (1977) consider, the share of seats held by antisystem parties has the strongest bivariate relationship with government duration and government survival. The same variable also figures prominently in multivariate models estimated for the full data set and in a separate model estimated for majority governments only.

Sartori suggests that while governments may be short-lived where there are large antisystem parties, there is continuity in the composition of the governing coalitions. In polarized systems, he finds *"peripheral turnover—* peripheral in that the access to the government is limited to the center-left and/or the center-right parties only. . . . [P]eripheral turnover consists of permanently governing parties that merely change partners in their neighborhood" (1976, p. 139). So Budge and Herman found that when coalitions form "there will be a premium on including in government one or more parties which 'normally' hold office" (1978, p. 462). In contrast, in systems having moderate pluralism, there is more likely to be an alteration of power between two two-party systems (Sartori, 1976, pp. 178-179).

External Variables

Except for Sanders and Herman (1979), most of those studying the correlates of cabinet durability have ignored external variables. They find that in a multivariate model three kinds of protest activity—strikes, protest demonstrations, and the imposition of government sanctions—are significantly related to government survival.

Summary

Multivariate studies of cabinet dissolution have isolated several variables related to government duration. Cabinets last longer when they have majority backing, are in parliaments with small antisystem parties, and are supported by a minimum winning coalition composed of few parties which do not straddle major cleavages. Moreover, the scant research on external variables has shown cabinets survive where there are few political strikes but also more frequent demonstrations and government sanctions.

How useful are fractionalization measures for explaining cabinet persistence? Taylor and Herman (1971) found fractionalization of prosystem parties to be important. However, Herman, in an article he coauthored six years later, rejected that finding. "Rather surprisingly, therefore, in view of previous research, we must conclude that in the context of the intraparliamentary prediction and explanation of governmental stability, simplicity in conceptualization and measurement is more valuable than sophistication" (Sanders and Herman, 1977, p. 371).

Two-Party Systems

In two-party systems, one of two parties normally has a legislative majority and the parties alternate control over time. The two major countries with this type of system are Great Britain and the United States. Costa Rica (Baker, 1973), New Zealand, and the Philippines prior to martial law (Grossholtz, 1970) also are two-party systems. We also include Canada and the U.S. state legislatures in this section.

Britain

Studies of Great Britain have traditionally relied upon the British party model in which stable political parties compete for the right to govern. The parties are distinguished by ideologies and policy positions. Once elected, the majority party governs through the cabinet, with MPs voting cohesively to enact policy. Each election is a referendum on the governing party. Given this model, research during the 1960s and early 1970s focused on electoral behavior (Butler and Stokes, 1974). Little work was done on the parliamentary parties because their behavior was so uniform, and the studies of Commons had traditional orientations (see Patterson, 1973, for an excellent critique of these studies). However, research on Parliament, parties, and factions increased during the 1970s, beginning with research on factions and fractions in the Labour and Conservative parties.

Recent research has called into question many of the assumptions of the British party model (see Epstein, 1980, and Norton, 1980, for reviews of change in the British model and the British Parliament, respectively). One theme of this research is party "tyranny" versus responsiveness (Rose, 1974). This surprises Americans, since the British system of responsible parties represented an ideal for many American political scientists for well over a generation (Schattschneider, 1942). However, as Ranney (1981) points out, the flow of ideas is now from east to west. The push for standing committees, some form of proportional representation, and increased latitude for back-bench members of both parties testify to change within the supposedly staid House of Commons.

At first the most important work on parties in Parliament focused on the existence of fractions within the parties, then on the behavioral consequences of fraction. In an important article Seyd (1972) showed that the Conservative party's Monday Club was organized and united over a range of issues. Piper (1974), Norton (1975, 1980), Petney (1977), Leece and Berrington (1977), and Franklin and Tappin (1977), among others, showed that back-bench members of both parties did not fit the portrait of cohesive behavior. In short, the British parties were composed of members who had widely differing political views, and they behaved differently depending on the situation and their views.

Scholars used abstention (Norton, 1980), Guttman scaling of Early Day Motions (Leece and Berrington, 1977), and other nonobtrusive measures (Franklin and Tappin, 1977) to identify fractions within the parties. Wood (1982) demonstrated an ideological split over membership in the European Economic Community. Norton (1976) showed that the parties were split ideologically, not uniformly as we had been led to believe. In addition to the ideological cleavages, there were nationalist party movements, such as the Scottish Nationalist party (Mansbach, 1973).

The divisions within the Labour and the Conservative parties become manifest with the creation of the Social Democratic party. This development should not have been surprising, given the extent of fractionalism. Moreover, over 100 members of the Commons had changed parties since 1945, seeking election to Commons as members of another party (Petney, 1977). The rise of fractions within the major parties led a number of scholars to speculate about the possibility of coalitional government in Britain (Laver, 1977; Pulzer, 1977). Crewe's (1980) perceptive analysis of partisan dealignment in Britain fits well with the claim that coalition government would reflect divisions in the electorate.

However, more has changed in our perception of the British responsible party model than our belief that the parties were uniform. A major contemporary criticism of the British model is that the party system neither represents the national distribution of opinions nor enhances the problem-solving capacity on the system (Kavanaugh, 1974; Epstein, 1980). It is charged that the two parties alternate tyranny of party, not party government. Bogdanor (1981, p. ix) states, "Britain's problems can be explained as the result of a rigid party system which inhibits popular involvement in politics." King (1975) relates Britain's problems in governing to the overload which party places on government. Rose (1970) argues that because the Labour and Conservative parties practiced adversary rather than consensual politics, policy moved too far, too rapidly from left to right. Thus, neither party represented the center, where most British voters were located. The electoral system forced majority party status on minority parties, and successive prime ministers, concerned with party unity, neglected broader public interests (Waltz, 1967). In sum, scholars criticized the British model on normative policy grounds as well as on the grounds that it inaccurately portrayed the British system.

Another focus of attention was on changes in the British parliamentary system. Schwarz (1980) convincingly argued that during the 1970s back-benchers in both parties jumped the part line to change policy outcomes. King's (1977) analysis showed Labour badly split in the 1975 referendum on Britain's continued membership in the EEC. As a result of these changes,

Schwarz concluded, "it is time to reach beyond viewing [Commons] as an institution so steeped in tradition that change is next to impossible" (1980, p. 36).

The increasing evidence of fractionalism within the two major parties was accompanied by studies of the distribution of power within the legislative parties. Lynskey (1973), Seyd (1975), Norton (1978), Pinto-Duchinsky (1972), and Drucker (1981) have written on changes in the distribution of both task and power within the two major parties. King (1981) has analyzed consequences of reforms sought in Commons, including higher pay, greater staff support, and an increased role for back-benchers. The last is perhaps the most important for, as King claims, "able men and women will wish to remain in the legislature only if they have, and are seen to have, important work to do" (1981, p. 81). Closely tied to the structure of power within the parties is the advocacy of a British standing committee system, modeled in part after the American Congress (see Smith, 1981, for a review). Scholarly attention has recently focused on the Select Committee on Procedure's 1978 report, which advocated the creation of 12 standing committees and ministerial relations to such committees. Boyd-Carpenter (1971) and Ryle (1965) have written useful background articles on committees in the House of Commons.

The distribution of both task and power within the legislative parties was an important research topic in the 1970s. A very detailed description of party organization in Britain can be found in Rose's *The Problem of Party Government* (1974, Chs. 6, 7, 10). There were also studies of the role of the all-party committees in the House of Commons (Richardson and Kimber, 1972). These committees, composed of back-benchers, meet on substantive issues in a nonpartisan context both to garner information and to affect policy.

Much of the recent research shares a common theme—the relationship between the executive and the legislature—and emphasizes the decline of Parliament. From Crick (1964) to Rose (1980), scholars have studied how the tyranny of party voting increases executive power and decreases legislative power. The traditional model held that the cabinet decided policy while bureaucrats impartially applied it. With the publication of Crossman's (1975) memoirs, the role of the bureaucracy vis-à-vis cabinet ministers came into question (also see Gordon, 1971; Wright, 1977; Finer, 1980). In short, British bureaucrats, like their American counterparts, played an important role in policy making.

Research on Parliament in the 1970s refocused attention on parliamentary parties, fractions, and factions. The most surprising and relevant finding, for our purposes, was that in a five-year period the House of Commons inflicted almost 150 defeats on the Government (Schwarz, 1980). These defeats altered a pattern established over a century and thus signaled a change in norms. Schwarz sees the influx of new members and the rise of fractions as causing this change. Perceiving the breakdown of parliamentary norms and the power of bureaucrats in policy making, some scholars either contemplated or advocated coalitional government for Britain. King (1981) mentioned the German system as a useful model for Britain—more representative yet stable. In an excellent piece, Pulzer (1978) outlined the policy differences between two-party responsible systems and multiparty coalitional systems. In Britain, parties formulate policies and compete in elections to determine who will govern. In European systems, policies are formed in order to put together a government. Thus, policy in the British system precedes elections, whereas in coalitional systems it often follows elections. Pulzer argues that this difference is grounded in the historical development of parties and parliaments. Britain's 1984 elections should generate a good deal of scholarly attention on parties in the Parliament; the major question will continue to be the role of parties in the electorate and in the Commons.

The United States

While students of the British legislature focused on the tyranny of party and the development of fractions, those studying Congress continued to analyze the "ceaseless maneuvering to find coalitions capable of governing." The single greatest research topic in the 1970s was the reform of Congress. The cumulative effects of the Vietnam War, presidential impoundments, congressional scandals, and Watergate resulted in major reforms in the U.S. House of Representatives and, to a lesser extent, in the U.S. Senate. Congressional reforms limited the presidency, both domestically and in foreign affairs, limited seniority power in the House, decentralized committee power to subcommittees, increased the Speaker's power, increased staff size and support in both the House and Senate, developed a new congressional budget process, and "computerized" Congress. Some of these reforms are peripheral to our purpose, but we shall deal with the increased role of the caucus, the new role of the Rules Committees, and the incumbency advantage.

As a major effect of the 1974-1975 congressional reforms, the role played by the Democratic caucus in the U.S. House of Representatives increased. Under the new Democratic rules, the caucus removed three chairmen of committees, effecting the first major violation of the seniority principle since the days of Czar Cannon (1903-1911). The caucus also mandated subcommittees for the House Ways and Means committee and made subcommittee chairs on Appropriations exclusive and responsible to the caucus. The caucus also gave the Speaker a greater role in selecting members of the Rules Committee (Oppenheimer, 1981). Thus, the reforms centralized power in the Speaker and the caucus and at the same time decentralized power to the subcommittees. Scholars soon attempted to assess the causes of these reforms and their effects on the Congress (Davidson and Oleszek, 1977; Dodd and Oppenheimer, 1977, 1981; Rieselbach, 1978; Mann and Ornstein, 1981). While it is hard to summarize the diverse viewpoints on these reforms, scholars seem to agree on two points: the effect of the reforms was not what the reformers intended (see Jones, 1977, for an analysis of the difficulty in reforming Congress), and the reforms did more to increase the factionalization of Congress and the fractionalization of the parties than to increase party strength in Congress. Studies of specific reforms and their effects on legislative parties are, however, limited in what they can achieve without a framework which handles adaptivity (Cooper, 1981).

In one sense, most of the literature of the 1970s reflects the decline of the importance of party in Congress. The immense literature on incumbency advantage which began with studies by Erikson (1971b) and Mayhew (1974) presumes that party has declined in importance as a cue in congressional elections (see Mann and Wolfinger, 1980, for a review of the findings). When party becomes a less important determinant of voting in elections, then candidates, issues, organization, money, and the professionalization of campaign staffs become more important. Representatives elected to Congress under these conditions are less likely to follow party cues. Fiorina (1977), Parker (1980), and others have argued that representatives now engage much more in personal contact and service-oriented activities (which are inherently nonpartisan) than in policy-making activities. The result is viewed as a mad scramble for particularized policy rather than policy in the "public interest."

David Mayhew's influential *The Electoral Connection* (1974a) attempts to analyze congressional behavior in terms of members' election strategy, in which party plays a minor role. Mayhew draws a picture of representatives who are posturers and advertisers rather than responsible policy makers. Tufte (1978) also doubts whether the electoral connection makes for good policy. Passing out largesse to constituents in order to be reelected, candidates foster "a lurching, stop-and-go economy. . . . There is a bias toward policies with immediate, highly visible benefits and deferred costs—myopic policies for myopic voters" (Tufte, 1978, p. 143). One study shows that even congressional retirements are caused in part by the constituent work load which increases at the expense of party (Hibbing, 1982). Anyone reviewing the literature on elections, congressional reforms, and congressional policy making cannot fail to be impressed by the extent to which they show party declining in the United States.

Critics of the American political system have often concentrated on the absence of party government. A line of anglophiles beginning with Woodrow Wilson (1885) have criticized how frequently legislators have voted against the stands taken by their party leaders in Congress and/or by a president of their own party. Because Congress has not had higher levels of party voting, it has often made responsible party government impossible.

From the perspective of this essay, party voting in a two-party presidential system is somewhat analogous to the critical votes by which a governing coalition is approved or falls in a parliamentary system. Once a parliamentary governing coalition is in place, it will be able to enact its policies until it loses a vote of confidence. In the U.S. presidential system, partisan configurations may fluctuate greatly from roll call to roll call, so that the majority party can attain its policy objectives on some but usually not all of its agenda items. Here we will touch only briefly on differences in voting across time, caucuses, and state party systems.

The pattern of party voting in Congress has varied over time (Brady, Cooper, and Hurley, 1979). Measures of party voting are aggregate measures, and Clausen (1973) and Sinclair (1982) have shown party structures voting differently on different issue dimensions. Sinclair's (1978, 1982) work is an excellent exposition of how both issues and voting patterns change over time. Thus, the aggregate-level voting patterns conceal a variety of issue-dimension voting patterns. Brady (1982) has analyzed roll-call votes in the realignments of the Civil War and 1890s and has discovered different levels on which party structures voting on issue dimensions. At some point there is a congruence between party structuring of voting on issue dimensions and aggregate party voting scores. However, until we have longer time series of issue-dimension voting, the structuring of congressional voting will remain in skeletal portrait. Nevertheless, owing to the work of Sinclair and others, we have a much richer portrait of change in congressional voting over time than we had a decade ago. We know more about the emergence of issue dimensions and about the changing effects of both constituent and party factors on voting patterns.

During the 1970s, a multitude of new organizations sprang up in Congress. Some were bipartisan factions, others simply fractions within parties. Most have offices and paid staff, some raise and distribute campaign funds. All of them provide information, and they typically have legislative agenda (Loomis, 1981).

The forerunner of the caucuses which developed in the 1970s was the Democratic Study Group, formed during the late 1950s by liberal Democrats who chaffed under the congressional control Southern Democrats exercised. (On the development of the DSG, see Stevens, Miller, and Mann, 1974; Kofmehl, 1964.) The latter-day caucuses have also developed out of frustration with the inability to achieve policy objectives through the established congressional structure. As Loomis observes,

caucuses have generally formed because members are frustrated with the institution's arrangement for making certain types of policy; the organizational decentralization and dispersion of power provide incentives for circumventing normal policymaking bodies such as committees, subcommittees, and parties (1981, p. 217).

In some ways akin to the single-issue interest groups which are proliferating in American politics, most caucuses have a relatively narrow range of interests. (A notable exception is the Congressional Black Caucus, which in some years has responded to the president's State of the Union address with its own critique of current conditions and has provided a set of counter proposals.) In his brief analysis of three caucuses, Loomis finds that the Bipartisan Northeast-Midwest Congressional Caucus has succeeded in winning a larger share of federal funds for its part of the country. Such success stories, coupled with the breakdown of party ties and party voting, may encourage the creation of additional factions and fractions.

Parties in State Legislatures

Wahlke, Eulau, Buchanan, and Ferguson (1962) have accurately summarized the importance of state legislative parties: "Partisanship enters the legislative process in the various states in different ways and different degrees" (p. 376). Reviewing many single-state studies, Rosenthal (1981) provides a number of perspectives on this proposition. He presents statistics from several states or offers generalizations but does not test hypotheses or present statistical analyses which would account for variations in the role party plays in state legislatures.

Jewell's (1966) review of single-state studies isolates several variables which may be associated with the incidence of roll calls on which parties divide. Three clusters of variables emerge from this analysis (see Figure 1). One of these clusters consists of constituency features, such as urbanization and economic activity. The important consideration here is whether the two parties represent distinct types of constituencies. For example, the Democrats might represent urban, blue collar districts while Republicans represent rural areas and small towns. If members of the same party represent different kinds of districts, the party will vote less cohesively on roll calls. If parties have homogeneous constituencies, there may be stronger norms of party loyalty, since party members would experience fewer cross-pressures. These norms constitute a second cluster of variables.

Leadership pressures may also promote party voting. The governor, partisan legislative leaders, and the party caucus may be sources of voting cues. The relationship between leadership pressures and voting may be reciprocal, since the extent to which leaders try to exert influence will depend on whether there is a tradition of party voting (Jewell, 1966, p. 91). In some legislatures in which party is most important, leadership comes from daily caucuses of the majority party (Rosenthal, 1981, p. 169). In states in which the party organization outside the legislature is strong, the governor enjoys greater success in leading his partisans in the legislature (McCally, 1966; Morehouse, 1973).

FIGURE 1
Model of Partisan Voting in State Legislatures

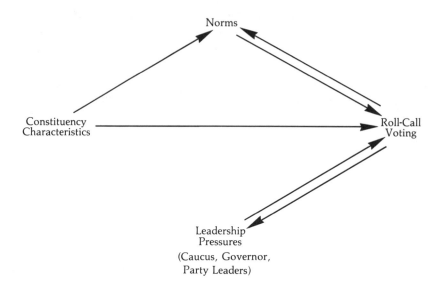

In state legislatures, as in the U.S. Congress, the incidence of partisan voting is related to the type of issue. Party loyalty is most likely on items relating to social or economic programs, party organization, or issues of critical significance to the administration, such as the budget (Jewell, 1966, pp. 92-93; LeBlanc, 1969).

In one-party states, considerations other than party may dominate. These may include urban-rural cleavages (Broach, 1972), friendship ties, or fractions. The governor, particularly during the first year or two after taking office, may be the chief cue-giver; fractionalization may become more apparent later in the term. Even in two-party states, fractions have sometimes been more important than parties, as they were in California during the 1950s (Buchanan, 1963, Ch. 7). More recently, liberal study groups have helped ideological minorities in some legislatures achieve greater strength (Keith, 1981) and have provided cues like those given by parties.

Redrawing constituency boundaries to reflect population shifts may affect the strength of legislative parties. If the portions of a polity which have experienced population growth have a different partisan configuration from those in which population has declined or remained constant, the reallocation of seats may benefit one party to the detriment of others.

The redistricting of American state legislatures in the 1960s often had this effect. In the South, the urban-based Republican party benefited (Hawkins, 1971; Jewell, 1962, pp. 28-29). In the North the allocation of seats to central cities helped Democrats, but newly created suburban seats tended to be Republican (Erikson, 1971a; O'Rourke, 1980). At the state level, redistricting increased the frequency with which partisan control of the legislative and executive branches was divided (Uslaner, 1978a). Thus, redistricting did not eliminate the incidence of divided party control which Key (1956) had attributed to malapportionment and which should affect the kinds of policy decisions reached by the legislature.

Although there is little evidence that redistricting by itself reduced partisan competition in the electorate, it seems to have contributed to heightened partisanship within legislatures. Both Robeck's (1972) study of California and Patterson's (1976) broader review conclude that party voting increased in state legislatures after redistricting.

Canada

The Canadian parliamentary system has been modeled on that of Great Britain, but two small, regional parties have frequently prevented either the Liberals or the Conservatives from obtaining a majority. In the absence of a majority, however, coalition governments rarely form. Moreover, Canadian minority governments have been more stable than the coalition governments of postwar Italy or Fourth Republic France and have initiated major policy changes, in health care for example.

This stability is due to the governing party's relatively great cohesion in voting. Kornberg's (1967) interviews with members of the 25th Parliament reveal that party voting persists despite widely differing opinions about the extent to which caucus decisions bind members. Because of shared policy preferences, social ties, norms, and the benefits of caucus participation, only 16 percent of the MPs said they would bolt the party if it took a stand at variance with their constituency's preferences. In the past, minority governments have survived partly because the Social Credit party was reluctant to bring down the government. The party feared it might lose seats in the ensuing election, and in 1980 it did indeed lose its remaining seats (Kornberg and Mishler, 1976, p. 315). Minority governments may also have survived longer because there are no major political divisions paralleling class lines (Christian and Campbell, 1974; Kornberg, Falcone, and Mishler, 1973).

While it resembles the British Parliament in its degree of party voting, the Canadian Parliament also has features associated with the U.S. Congress, such as committee work and constituency service. Committee work is largely the province of backbenchers in the Liberal party (which has dominated

Parliament with brief, infrequent lapses for more than half a century) and the New Democrats; Conservative backbenchers are more active in constituency service (Kornberg and Mishler, 1976).

Kornberg and Mishler suggest that the Liberal hegemony is due to two weaknesses in the Conservative approach. First, Conservative leaders believe that the function of Parliament is to set an agenda through substantive debate. This handicaps the Conservatives, who must largely respond to the agenda set by the government. Second, Conservative backbenchers' ad hominem attacks on French-Canadian government ministers thwart Conservative efforts to win seats in Quebec, the second most populous province. With virtually no strength in Quebec, the Conservatives have little chance of winning a majority.

Colombia and Uruguay: A Note

One can make a case for including Colombia and Uruguay in the category of two-party systems. McDonald's (1971, Ch. 4) analysis of party systems in Latin America so classifies these systems, and for most of this century they have had functioning two-party systems. The countries share one important characteristic: party identities formed along a liberal-conservative dimension before social mobilization and electoral organization grew. At times there are intense fractions within the parties in both countries (McDonald, 1978). In both systems there have been interesting changes in the way government positions are awarded to the various intraparty fractions.

Yet it is difficult to make these two systems fit our usual definitions of legislative parties and legislatures more generally. In an excellent analysis of parties in the Colombia legislature, Hoskin argues that "while such conflicts permeate the [Colombian] Congress, their generation and resolution often can be traced to political party behavior, the dynamics of which are not necessarily congruent with norms and roles associated with the legislature itself" (1975, p. 147). One cause of this disjointedness is that the president has largely usurped the legislative function, leaving Congress with a legitimizing function (Hoskin, 1975, p. 153). Whether Colombia is a two-party system in our sense of the term is beyond the ability of the authors to resolve. In Uruguay the militarization of government makes the question moot.

Summary

Research has revealed both similarities and differences in the variables which characterize parliamentary and U.S. two-party systems. In both, membership is becoming less stable, parties more fractionalized, and cross-party factions more frequent. Analyzing this phenomena in some detail, scholars have agreed that because factions are more prominent and shift more frequently, policy making has become more chaotic. Most studies of task distribution within congressional parties deal with Congress after the reforms of the 1970s. The results indicate that tasks, at least within the Democratic party, have become more decentralized. In the British system of responsible parties, task distribution has been well studied (Rose, 1974), but in general, this area needs further investigation.

Who joins fractions and factions is an important research question in both systems. In both systems representatives are elected to office on a party label, so party membership is a given. However, who joins the Democratic Study Group, the Conservative Coalition, or the Monday Club is a question of interest. In the U.S. Congress, membership in fractions or factions is a combination of both ideology and personal interest. Members' decisions to vote with the Conservative Coalition, the Democratic Study Group, or the Boll Weevils are based on ideology, and sometimes the vote cuts across party lines. However, membership in the Black Caucus or the Women's Caucus is derived from shared characteristics.

The goals of the British parties and fractions are relatively easy to ascertain. The major parties seek to govern; party fractions seek to influence the ideological direction of the major parties and achieve this goal through their representation on the cabinet. In American parties, the situation is more complex: U.S. congressmen have more individual than collective goals (Fenno, 1973; Mayhew, 1974).

One-Party States

The question of what constitutes a one-party state has generated a good deal of controversy. The controversy is over classification at different levels—whether Japan is a one-party state (see Leiserson, 1973; Sartori, 1976) but also, more generally, what constitutes a party. Our classification of party system uses electoral competition as a critical variable; without competitive elections, the party controls the society (Sartori, 1976) and legislatures and legislative parties do not have governing or decision-making functions. Thus in one-party states, such as the U.S.S.R. and Eastern European nations, these are the major research questions: what role does the legislature play in the system? Do legislatures and legislative parties have any decisional role? Studies done early in the 1970s seem to conclude—either explicitly or implicitly— that legislatures in one-party systems are of little importance. However, more recent studies seem to suggest some role for these legislatures.

The problem of classifying one-party systems persists during the 1970s. Following Sartori's lead, we break one-party systems into the following categories: one-party totalitarian, one-party authoritarian, and one-party hegemonic. In both totalitarian and authoritarian systems, party clearly dominates society; however, in the authoritarian class the control is relaxed. In the Soviet Union, for example, the system under Stalin was totalitarian; under Khruschev, it was authoritarian. One-party hegemonic states, such as Mexico and Poland, allow other parties to exist, but there remains a dominant party. Some scholars would dispute this classification. Zakrsewski (cited in Sartori, 1976, p. 231), for example, wants to call Poland a multiparty cooperative system. However, recent events in Poland clearly show the dominance of the Communist party outside the legislature and cast doubt on whether Poland can be classified as even a hegemonic system. Prezworski and Sprague (1971) argue that in Communist systems mobilizing the vote constitutes competition and therefore that one-party systems should be classified as competitive. Thus, they claim that it makes sense to speak of competition in one-party systems and even to call the Soviet Union one of the most competitive systems in the world. Our classification scheme precludes accepting this argument; such one-party states are monopolies of power in which no other group has a reasonable chance of sharing, let alone alternating, the governing function.

Another question, an immense one, arises in the literature on one-party systems. Many of the recently founded states, particularly in Africa, began as one-party systems. How should such systems be classified, when few of them lasted long (Foltz, 1973)? In a one-party state, such as Poland or Argentina, which has a history as a people or as a country, one can talk of systemic support for communities at least, if not for regimes. But such African states as Uganda, Ghana, Mali, and Chad have no such history; they are amalgams of regional and tribal loyalties existing within boundaries established by colonial powers. Where support must develop first for the community before politics itself can develop, it is unlikely that a party system will be established which could cut across old loyalties and tie the electorate to those governing. In such nations, legislative parties and factions, in our sense of those terms, do not exist. Legislatures and parties in these systems may or may not serve integrating, representing, socializing, or other functions, but they do not govern. The rise of Ghana's one-party system was closely studied by political scientists, and much was made of its rise. Yet it fell within six years, and Ghanians expressed little or no regret, since it was not an established part of the system of government. In addition, the military takeovers in these countries testify to what Sartori calls their fluid politics. Political parties are possible when they exist, as Burke described them, within the system. Even in a reasonably stable system like Kenya's (Loewenberg and Patterson, 1979), important elements of the society do not support the regime. Witness the attempted military coup in Kenya in mid-1982. Without regime stability, political party and fraction in legislatures are not likely to make governmentally relevant decisions.

We do not deny nor mean to deny the utility of studying how party systems and legislatures develop in the less developed countries. Indeed, in our conclusion, we recommend that the study of legislatures and legislative parties in Mexico, Portugal, and Spain will tell us much about how parties and legislatures develop. However, we do feel that studies of legislatures and parties in countries which do not have stable polities should ask questions quite different from those examined in this essay. Moreover, the literature which does exist on African and, to a lesser extent, on Latin American countries has been little concerned with legislative parties, even in democratic countries.

One-Party Totalitarian/Authoritarian

In *Regimes and Opposition* (1973), Dahl included three articles which deal with one-party systems in Communist countries. These articles focus on the nature of opposition, both within the party system and outside of it. Barghoorn's essay on the Soviet Union outlines patterns of opposition in three categories: factional, sectoral, and subversive. The first two are within the system, the third outside. Barghoorn argues that most factional opposition comes from within the Central Committee Presidium (after 1966, the Politburo), its Secretariat, and the Central Committee (1973, p. 50). He does not mention the Supreme Soviet as a source of factional nor of sectoral opposition. Skilling's essay on opposition in Eastern European countries distinguishes three kinds of opposition within the system: factional, fundamental, and specific. He argues that after 1948 the East European states, with the exception of Yugoslavia, assumed the totalitarian form which Russia had assumed after 1930. "Representative assemblies became nothing more than rubber stamps, and societal organizations, such as trade unions, mere transmission belts" (1973, p. 96). Opposition developed piecemeal and varied from country to country, but after Stalin opposition within the system had become manifest, and in Hungary, Yugoslavia, Czechoslovakia, and Poland second and third parties were allowed to develop within the Communist party's overriding hegemony. In spite of this liberalization, he concluded that "the representative bodies in nearly all countries (the exception is Yugoslavia) were still deprived of the real power of policy making, which remained in the hands of the organs of the party" (1973, pp. 105-106).

One could not today make a case that these one-party states have developed Western-style legislatures with full-fledged parties, fractions, and factions; however, one could argue that these legislatures have some role in decision making and that in some of them fractions and parties are important.

Many comparative scholars still claim that, except in Yugoslavia, legislatures are rubber stamps (Bertsch, 1978, p. 123). However, in an issue of *Legislative Studies Quarterly* devoted to Communist legislatures (Vol. 5, No. 2, 1980), several authors dealt with the role of these legislatures and thus with parties and fractions. Nelson's perceptive introduction to the volume clarifies the functions of legislatures in these systems. Although he focuses on the functions of representation (as contact), integration, education, and stability, he concludes that "some communist legislatures today appear to exhibit activities at the periphery of lawmaking, particularly in Yugoslavia and Poland" (Nelson, 1980, p. 171).

Simon and Olson (1980) argue that the Polish legislature has evolved into a minimal legislature. They argue that the rise of the Peasants party, the Democratic party, and the three independent Catholic groups in the Sejm has changed its composition and organization, increasing its ability to influence policy. Recent events have clearly shown how limited the possibilities are for developing a more representative assembly. Nevertheless, it remains clear that the Sejm was a focal point for opposition within the Polish system, and it may yet play a significant role in the future.

White, writing on the Supreme Soviet (1980), argues that although it has not extended its authority vis-à-vis the Central Committee, it remains an important institutional actor. Smith (1981) shows that the attention of Supreme Soviet has shifted from foreign to domestic affairs. He extends this thesis by arguing that on budgetary matters the legislators play an increasingly important role in shifting expenditures toward their constituents. Thus, there is some reason to believe that fractions within the Communist party can express themselves through the Supreme Soviet.

Scholars interested in comparative research on one-party Eastern European legislatures should read Welch's review essay, "The Status of Research on Representative Institutions in Eastern Europe" (1980). We conclude with Welch, "These changes are significant not so much because of their magnitude, but because they may be laying the groundwork for future developments of greater impact" (1980, p. 298).

One-Party Hegemonic

Sartori distinguished the ideological from the pragmatic hegemonic party by the extent to which the other party or parties are its "satellite" parties. Thus, he calls Poland an ideological hegemonic party and Mexico a pragmatic one (1976, pp. 230-231). In the latter category, as of the mid-1970s, were Mexico, Portugal, Paraguay, and South Korea. Of these, Mexico is most often studied (Padgett, 1966; Casanova, 1970; Sartori, 1976, p. 243; de la Garza, 1972; Ames, 1970).

How nonmonopolistic can a one-party system become before it becomes something else—predominant, two-party, or multiparty? Students of development have often turned to these hegemonic systems—particularly Mexico's—to observe changes in institutions and parties. The changes in Mexico's electoral laws in 1962-1963 were taken to indicate that the elite felt secure, felt they could handle more opposition—within limits. Mexican legislators serve a constituent function (de la Garza, 1972) and are expected to contact constituents regarding legislation. Moreover, those who do contact constituents seem to rise through the party hierarchy more rapidly than those who do not. Nevertheless, when all is said and done, the PRI dominates the legislature and largely determines policy outside the legislature. The minor parties in the legislature, restricted by law from being a potential majority, have little or no role in policy making. Serving in the Mexican legislature is a step to higher office in the dominant PRI (Scott, 1964), particularly because congressional deputies are limited to a single term in office.

The Yugoslavian legislature is another example of a hegemonic party system. Skilling concludes that the "idea of a multi-party system or of an opposition party was explicitly rejected" (1973, p. 91) in Yugoslavia in favor of a hegemonic system. Yugoslavia's system guaranteed substantial articulation of diverse interests. However, even in Yugoslavia's one and one-half party system, "personal competition for office has not represented opposition in terms of policy" (Skilling, 1973, p. 107). More recent work on the Yugoslavian Assembly has focused on the post-1974 reorganization (Sturanović, 1977), particularly on amateur legislators and a delegational system. Nevertheless, as Cohen (1980) points out, the crucial problem is how bureaucracy can be controlled by representative bodies. Cohen's article dealing with deprofessionalization of the legislature and its effects on policy is important. However, whether the hegemonic legislature is Communist as in Poland and Yugoslavia or democratic as in Mexico, the governing and decision-making functions are carried out at bureaucratic and executive levels. Thus, legislative parties and fractions are not a focal point for comparative scholars.

One-Party Dominant Systems

One-party dominant systems are defined as those in which one party has historically constituted a majority in the legislative body, but other parties or coalitions have some prospects of winning a majority. The Japanese, Indian, and Turkish legislatures are examples of one-party dominant systems. The Indian system has once resulted in a non-Congress majority, while Turkey has moved toward a multiparty system in recent years. The Japanese and Indian legislatures are the most frequently researched one-party dominant systems.

Since the mid-1950s the Japanese Diet has been dominated by the Liberal Democratic Party, formed by a merger of Japan's two conservative parties in 1955. Since then, the LDP has been returned as the majority party in each election; every Japanese prime minister has been the LDP president. The opposition consists of a large socialist party (Japan Socialist party) and three minor parties: the Japan Communist party, the Clean Government party, and the Democratic Socialist party.

The two main Japanese parties have been called "a labyrinth of fractions and counter-fractions" (Burks, 1961, p. 81). Similarly, Scalapino and Masumi conclude that Japanese parties are made up of factional coalitions or alliances (1971, pp. 18-19, 54), which take precedence over party and national interest. Ward (1967, pp. 65-69) and Ike (1972, pp. 81-83) conclude that both the LDP and JSP are loose coalitions or federations of fractions united for purposes of campaigning and legislating. Fukui (1970, Ch. 5) has a detailed description of fractions in the LDP. In short, the defining characteristic of Japan's legislative parties is that fractions (in our sense of the term) dominate party behavior.

The origins of the various fractions in Japan's party can be found in Japan's societal structure of vertically organized groups; the fractions within the legislative parties mirror Japanese society. Fukui (1978) offers a brief and lucid description of the transition of these structures from the imperial regime to a parliamentary system of government.

The focus of power in Japan is the presidency of the LDP, since the president is assured of being prime minister. However, both of Japan's leading political parties are fractional; in fact, both began as mergers of diverse political groups. It follows that they are tolerant and eclectic (Fukui, 1978, pp. 48-49). Both parties tend to be elitist and neither has effective mass-level organizations. Japan's electoral system encourages competition among some party candidates in multimember districts as well as competition between parties (Thayer, 1969, pp. 35-39).

The most important factor contributing to fractionalism has been the way that important party, parliamentary, and (for the LDP) cabinet and subcabinet jobs have been parcelled out. Since the LDP is the governing party, it can award positions to various fractions within the party. The JSP was divided into left and right wings ideologically but in the mid-1960s became more pragmatic (Fukui, 1978, p. 50). The contest for the presidency of the LDP is tantamount to election as prime minister. Thus, the fractions in the LDP form around contenders for the presidency. In Leiserson's words, "the factions become like army 'divisions,' headed by a 'general' who was advised by his 'General Staff.' There were 'line officers,' fixed and known memberships, officers, publications, regular sources of funds, and so forth" (1968, p. 771). These institutionalized fractions perform some of the functions of parties in multiparty coalitional governments. Most fractions maintain offices and meeting places and often hold policy seminars conducted by their member experts. Fractions in the LDP are personalized around various party strong men; ideology and policy play a lesser role. The JSP is organized in essentially the same fashion; however, ideology and policy play a larger role in its fractions than in the LDP's.

Even though fractions are personalized and leaders shift through death or retirement, membership remains stable. Fukui shows that in a 24-year period slightly over 80 percent of the LDP members in the Diet had not shifted fractions. He attributes this stability to the rule whereby members lose seniority when they shift fractions. JSP fractions are more ideological and policy oriented; thus, shifting fractions is more common. In short, the structure of the major legislative parties in the Japanese Diet is fractionalized and personal.

In regard to party functions, fractionalism is the major mechanism for allocating benefits. Party elections are intensely competitive attempts to build coalitions of fractions. Thus, a party leader is not only the leader of a fraction, but also the leader of a coalition of fractions. Dominant coalitions of fractions shift from presidential election to presidential election (Baerwald, 1974, pp. 66-69). Since no one fraction or bloc has more than about 100 members, smaller fractions have little reason to merge with larger fractions.

The winning candidate can distribute some 120 directorships and chairmanships in each House of the Diet (Kim, 1975) and, more important, 21 cabinet portfolios and 24 parliamentary vice-ministerships (Leiserson, 1968, p. 778; Fukui, 1978, p. 61). The actual distribution of these payoffs has been a question of scholarly interest. Leiserson, using a game theoretic approach, argues that prime ministers distribute cabinet posts to retain the backing of some of the factional leaders who currently support them but also to win over some current opponents by including leaders of these fractions in the government. Others, notably Fukui, argue that payoffs are given according to the size of the fractions and its relationship to the mainstream fractional coalition (1978, pp. 62-65). The awards are made to fractional leaders, who distribute the payoffs based on seniority. The struggle for leadership posts in the JSP is not as systematic nor acrimonious as in the LDP, largely because, aside from a few Diet chairmanships, no important posts are filled by the JSP. It is important to note that each fraction of the LDP collects its own money, primarily from relevant business interests, and fractional leaders disperse them freely at the time of Diet elections. Thus, both money and appointive powers flow to fraction leaders who maintain control via personal connections (Flanagan, 1971).

However, when attention turns from the structure and function of fractions to voting in committees and on the floor of the Diet, one finds that strict party voting prevails (Fukui, 1978, p. 65). Thus, the will of the main-stream fractions in the LDP has been the policy of the Japanese government. The LDP fractions, divided loosely into mainstream (prime minister's coalition) and antimainstream, have at times collided over major policy issues. When one cabinet falls in a controversy over a policy matter, another (antimainstream) replaces it, and the dominance of the LDP is assured. These changes in cabinet are usually carried out after the fact, and the new elections are called only to ratify the change.

The dominant party in the Indian Lok Sabha is the Congress party. Since its inception, the Congress party has drawn the attention of political scientists (Weiner, 1967; Huntington, 1968), largely because of its success in governing a highly plural society. However, most attention to the Indian party system has focused, rightly enough, on the problems of nation building—integration, representation, and socialization. The Congress party attempted to build a structure of political affiliations throughout the nation within the frame-work of an inherited nationalist movement. Unlike the Japanese fractional system with its many strong men, the Congress Party has always been dominated by the Nehru family. Nevertheless, India clearly has a one-party dominant system, especially since the nation changed in 1975 to a presidential form of government, with the major party dominated by fractions (Kothari, 1964).

After Nehru's death, there was no longer a personal relationship between the strong national leader and elite leaders in the states, but factional conflict based on ideology and regional coalitions with distinct organizational interests (Kothari, 1964). Some of these regional leaders joined opposition parties, thus reducing the size of Mr. Gandhi's party in Parliament. The national elections of 1971 and the state elections of 1972 returned the Congress Party to dominance. Since the 1975 changes, the party has remained an amalgam of fractional groupings split on both ideological and organizational grounds. The Indian system has been described as having a dominant center and a polycentric opposition, the dominant party providing the center around which fractional consensus is formed.

The bases of the fractions of the Congress Party in the Lok Sabha parallel the fractions in the party organization and the Council of Ministers (Brass, 1965; Carras, 1972). Nicholson (1978) argues that the prime minister is insulated from the local, state, and ideological and organizational fractions found in lower levels of the party. In his view, the fractions of the Congress party are essentially nonideological, but ideology does provide some structuring of intraparty coalitions (Nicholson, 1972, 1978).

Some members of the Council of Ministers are also insulated from fractional policies. These "uninvolved ministers," comprising about 25 percent of the Council (Nicholson, 1975), come as symbolic representatives of regions, minority communities, or professional communities.

The fractional system is hierarchically ordered. "At each level, factional [fractional] bosses depend on resources generated and disbursed to them by higher levels of government" (Nicholson, 1978, p. 182). The concentration of power in the Council and the prime minister and the discipline of the party in the Lok Sabha assure that decisions are made at the center. Thus, payoffs to coalition partners, at whatever level, are possible only through the party leaders.

In summary, at local and state levels politics are highly fractional—"amorphous factions" in Nicholson's terms (1978, p. 182). However, as one moves vertically through the system, power is concentrated in the Congress party. Controlling the Council of Ministers and the party discipline in the Lok Sabha, the party thereby controls resources and patronage at state levels. Finally, unlike the Japanese system, the Indian system makes the prime minister the decision maker. The intense fractional negotiations surrounding the election of Babadur Shastri and Indira Gandhi are similar to Japan's election of an LDP president. However, since the time of Nehru, the prime minister has had mass appeal and institutional authority which make the Indian system of party and fraction centralized rather than decentralized. Whenever this leadership tradition has been challenged, the matter has been resolved strongly in favor of the prime minister.

While India and Japan are the predominant party systems most often studied, there are studies of predominant parties in other countries. These studies vary widely because of both location and classification problems. However, worthy of mention are studies regarding changes from one-party predominant to two-party or multiparty systems. Weinbaum's (1975) study of Iran, Turkey, and Afghanistan, especially the section on Iran and Turkey, is a useful attempt to assess the causes of change. Particularly interesting is the argument that legislatures seek to shape their character and fate (pp. 63-64). Another interesting study of transition is Karpat's (1959) analysis of the change to a multiparty system in Turkey. Pollack's study (1978) of Spain's transition from a corporate state to a multiparty democracy contains a useful review of the change since Franco's death and a section on the voting patterns of parties in the legislature. This study is particularly interesting in light of Linz's classic (1973) study of government and opposition in Spain during the Franco era. Patch's (1970) study of Bolivia, from its change to a one-party system in 1952 through the 1964 military takeover, provides useful information about the roles of personal loyalties and ideological abstractions in Bolivia's changed system. In short, party systems which have changed from predominant to multiparty or two-party or whose governments have been taken over by the military should be fertile ground for students of party systems and legislators.

Research Agenda

When we started this review essay, we did not realize that the literature on parties and legislatures was so voluminous. Having sorted through a good deal of it, we have formed a number of lasting impressions. First, there is the number of excellent case studies of parties and legislatures in individual countries. The works of DiPalma (1977), Kornberg (1967), Loewenberg (1967), Williams (1968), and Rose (1974) come to mind, and there are others not mentioned. Second, the burgeoning business of comparative legislature studies has produced an important set of books out of Duke University Press (Boynton and Kim, 1975; Eldridge, 1977; Mezey, 1979; Kornberg and Musolf, 1970). Third, the theoretical classifications of comparative party systems are impressive. Here Sartori's book (1976) clearly stands out as a major achievement. Fourth, we have discovered a number of journals not normally read by American political scientists which publish important articles on parties and legislatures.

It is also important to note the shortcomings of this literature. The two most important are the amorphous case study approach much of it takes, which frustrates comparisons between systems, and the confusion of terms and classificatory schemes put forward in the truly comparative literature. Moreover, the literature on comparative parties and comparative legislatures has not merged.

In 1973, Patterson and Wahlke wrote an essay, "Trends and Prospects in Legislative Behavior Research," to conclude an international conference on comparative legislatures. We turn to their essay for guidance in summarizing the literature on parties, coalitions, fractions, and factions. Their major categories were focus, legislative system properties, and individual legislative behavior. While all of their subcategories are not appropriate for our purposes, their general categories are applicable.

Focus

Under focus, Patterson and Wahlke note the problems of territory and of unit of analysis. The territorial problem—that is, where one conducts the research—seems to us to be relevant. The studies of legislatures and parties in industrial nations are quite distinct from apparently similar studies in non-Western or Third World or less-developed countries.

Students of industrial nations focus heavily on the roles of party, coalition, fraction, and faction in forming governments and, to a lesser extent, on how party affects governmental decisions. However, even these studies fall into two groups: case studies, some rich in history, setting, and detail; and comparative studies, more sophisticated methodologically, but often weaker conceptually. In contrast, studies of nonindustrial legislatures and parties focus on the role of legislatures and, to a lesser extent, of parties in integration, representation, recruitment, and socialization. Perhaps this is as it should be, given Packenham's (1970) essay about the function of legislatures in non-Western countries. However, in this literature we found many studies which talked about how Lebanon, Ghana, Chile, Poland, or other countries had assured stability, in part through a party system or through equal representation of segmented interests in the legislature. In many of these cases, events have made the researchers poor prognosticators, particularly events in Africa. Until we know more about how stability (diffuse support?) is developed in such countries, research on parties in legislative bodies may well be off the track. The territorial problem is a conceptual one, not simply a problem of the region or country one studies.

The level of analysis problem is the problem of defining the legislative system so that it encompasses not only the legislative assembly but also components external to the system (Eulau and Hinckley, 1966). Among attempts to relate outside factors to what occurs inside the legislature, the work of Rae (1967) and Rae and Taylor (1971) on the consequences of electoral laws is significant. The work of Epstein (1967), Lijphart (1969), Lorwin (1971), Sartori (1976), and Janda (1980), linking elements of fragmentation in the society to legislative structures, is worthy of note. These studies of single legislatures have maximized richness of detail and explanation. If this richness does not carry over fully to comparative studies, it is partly because of the very nature of the comparative approach.

The problems facing industrial economies, while obviously important, have not received as much attention as we might have expected. Studies of the U.S. and Britain (Dodd and Schott, 1970; Fiorina, 1977; King, 1975; Pulzer, 1977) show the importance of this external influence. However, with the exception of Castles (1976), comparative researchers have done little in this area. Students of nonindustrial legislatures have focused on external components of the legislative system. Jewell's perceptive essay (1973) and Loewenberg and Patterson's (1979) introductory chapter outline well the basic environmental linkages.

Legislative System Properties

In this area of research, which should presumably link the legislative party to the external components, we find much to be done. The classifications are still, some 30 years after Duverger, basically his. Research on multiparty systems focuses on how governments are put together and dissolved, with little attention to whether the structure of the society is segmented-plural, consensual, or adversarial or whether the system is parliamentary or presidential.

The attempts to deal with this problem, most notably Sartori's (1976), remain classificatory rather than predictive. Also lacking are comparative works on the context of legislative decision styles, like Eulau and Prewitt's study (1973).

We found research dealing with the roles of parties and legislatures, particularly legislatures, to be confused. There was, to be sure, much done on the decline of parliament vis-à-vis the executive in various countries, on the roles of party and parliament in deciding among policy alternatives, and on the importance of different types of party structures for representing interests. However, on the basic issue of the importance of party and legislatures in governing, as our typology shows, we simply distinguished systems in terms of the role of legislative parties in governing and making policy. The problem is exacerbated when one moves to the study of legislatures in nonindustrial economies. Here our knowledge is extremely partial and is continuously relegated to history or to the scrap pile, as coups, revolution, and wars change institutions daily. The argument that legislatures appear remarkably resilient in spite of political upheavals is, in the long run, unacceptable.

The relationship between the degree of fractionalization and/or factionalization of legislative parties and the way in which parties distribute task and power has been neglected (Cooper, 1981). The broader question is, of course, how do parties accommodate and effect change in the broader system? These questions deserve more attention than they have received.

Another topic within the systemic category deserving mention is the relationship between decision rules in legislatures and policy outcomes. The work of Shepsle (1979), Steiner (1971), and Rae and Taylor (1971) stand out. In general, this question needs more attention because of its importance and its potential research payoff.

Individual Legislative Behavior

The final category used by Patterson and Wahlke was the behavior of individual legislators. Scholars concentrating on multiparty systems deal little with individual level behavior. Yet studies of legislators in Italy (Sartori, 1976; DiPalma, 1977), Japan (Fukui, 1978), and Sweden (Clausen and Holmberg, 1977) have shown the value of studying individual member behavior in systems with strong party discipline. Perhaps most impressive has been the payoff from studying individual behavior in the British House of Commons. Jackson (1968), Norton (1979), and Schwarz (1980) have shown that such study can both correct substantial misinterpretations and lead to theories of change. Studies of nonindustrial legislatures, focusing on individuals' behavior toward constituents, intermediary elites, and governmental agencies, have improved our understanding of the role legislatures and, to a lesser extent, parties play in system maintenance.

The motivations of individual legislators have proved to be useful for explaining American legislatures (Fenno, 1973, 1978; LeLoup, 1981). In other countries, high party unity appears to have dissuaded researchers from studying such motivations. We suggest that studies comparing motivational configurations in different types of legislatures—e.g., multiparty fragmented versus two-party factionalized—might well prove fruitful, regardless of whether motivation is treated as a dependent or independent variable. Surely the motives of British backbenchers have played and will continue to play an important part in determining the structure and behavior of the parliamentary system.

If this has sounded more like a review than a research agenda, the reader has been with us. Our reluctance to prescribe an agenda stems from the difficulty of doing real comparative studies. Instead of an agenda, we have two suggestions.

First, rather than endlessly increase the studies of parties and legislatures, we should stop and determine what we want to know and why we want to know it. In this review we first described the characteristics of legislative groups—parties, fractions, and factions. We borrowed from coalition theory (Hinckley, 1981) a number of characterizing variables in an attempt to sort out what we were to describe. We did not claim this list was exhaustive or even finally correct, but without such a list we could not determine what we were trying to describe. Having established these characterizing variables, we classified party systems according to the structure of legislative parties and the characteristics of parties in the external environment. Obviously in this regard, we felt Sartori's work was important. The way in which legislative groups are linked to their environments and the role that the political system assigns to the legislature deeply affect the structure and behavior of parties, coalitions, fractions, and factions. Again, our classification, taken from Sartori, is not meant to be exhaustive nor final. However, our feeling is that without some similar classification, the research payoffs will be less than they could have been.

Second, we suggest that time series be used in comparative legislative research to study the development of party systems within individual countries and to compare systems in regional cross-national research. Party systems which developed within established legislatures, as they did in the United States and Britain (see Burnham and Chambers, 1967, and Pulzer, 1978, respectively), should have linkages and degrees of stability quite different from systems which started with external parties that then moved into the legislature. The development of legislatures and parties in countries such as Spain, Portugal, and Mexico should also be fertile ground for students of legislative parties. It is even likely that studies of the development of legislatures in Europe have applications useful for students of nonindustrialized nations and vice-versa.

NOTE

The authors would like to thank John Alford, Joseph Cooper, and Barbara Sinclair for their very thoughtful comments. Dr. Bullock received summer research support from the University of Georgia to prepare this essay.

REFERENCES

Axelrod, Robert. 1970. *Conflict of Interest.* Chicago: Markham Publishing.

Ames, Barry. 1970. "Bases of Support for Mexico's Dominant Party," *American Political Science Review* 64:153-167.

Baerwald, Hans H. 1974. *Japan's Parliament: An Introduction.* New York: Cambridge University Press.

Baker, Christopher. 1973. "Costa Rican Legislative Behavior in Perspective." Ph.D. Dissertation, University of Florida.

Barghoorn, Frederick C. 1973. "Factional, Sectoral, and Subversive Opposition in Soviet Politics," in Robert A. Dahl, ed., *Regimes and Oppositions.* New Haven: Yale University Press, pp. 27-87.

Bernick, E. Lee and Charles Wiggins. 1978. "Legislative Reform and Legislative Turnover," in Leroy N. Rieselbach, ed., *Legislative Reform.* Lexington, MA: Lexington Books, pp. 23-34.

Bertsch, Gary K. 1978. *Power and Policy in Communist Systems.* New York: Wiley.

Blondel, Jean. 1968. "Party Systems and Patterns of Government in Western Democracies," *Canadian Journal of Political Science* 1:180-203.

_____ . 1969. "Legislatures' Behavior: Some Steps Towards a Cross National Measurement," *Government and Opposition* 5:67-85.

_____ . 1973. *Comparative Legislatures.* Englewood Cliffs, NJ: Prentice-Hall.

Bogdanor, Vernon. 1981. *The People and the Party System.* New York: Cambridge University Press.

Boyd-Carpenter, J. 1971. "Development of the Select Committee in the British Parliament," *The Parliamentarian* 52:101-104.

Boynton, G. R. and Chong Lim Kim. 1975. *Legislative Systems in Developing Countries.* Durham, NC: Duke University Press.

Brady, David W. 1978. "Critical Elections, Congressional Parties and Clusters of Policy Change," *British Journal of Political Science* 8:79-99.

_____ . 1982. "Congressional Party Realignment and Transformations of Public Policy in Three Realignment Eras," *American Journal of Political Science* 26:333-360.

Brady, David W. and Charles S. Bullock, III. 1980. "Is There a Conservative Coalition in the House?" *Journal of Politics* 42:549-559.

Brady, David W., Joseph Cooper, and Patricia A. Hurley. 1979. "The Decline of Party in the U.S. House of Representatives, 1887-1968," *Legislative Studies Quarterly* 4:381-407.

Brady, David W. and Naomi B. Lynn. 1973. "Switched-Seat Congressional Districts: Their Effect on Party Voting and Public Policy," *American Journal of Political Science* 17:528-543.

Brass, Paul R. 1965. *Factional Politics in an Indian State*. Berkeley: University of California Press.

_____ . 1977. "Party Systems and Government Stability in the Indian States," *American Political Science Review* 71:1384-1405.

Broach, Glen T. 1972. "A Comparative Dimensional Analysis of Partisan and Urban-Rural Voting in State Legislatures," *Journal of Politics* 34:905-921.

Browne, Eric. 1971. "Testing Theories of Coalition Formation in the European Context," *Comparative Political Studies* 3:391-410.

_____ . 1982. "Considerations on the Construction of a Theory of Cabinet Coalition Behavior," in Eric C. Browne and John Dreijmanis, eds., *Government Coalitions in Western Democracies*. New York: Longman, pp. 335-357.

Browne, Eric C. and John Dreijmanis. 1982. *Government Coalitions in Western Democracies*. New York: Longman.

Browne, Eric and Karen A. Feste. 1975. "Qualitative Dimensions of Coalition Payoffs: Evidence from European Party Governments, 1945-1970," *American Behavioral Scientist* 18:92-118.

_____ . 1978. "Scaling Ministerial Payoffs in European Governing Coalitions," *Comparative Political Studies* 11:397-408.

Browne, Eric C. and Mark N. Franklin. 1973. "Aspects of Coalition Payoffs in European Parliamentary Democracies," *American Political Science Review* 67:453-469.

Browne, Eric C. and Jon P. Frendreis. 1980. "Allocating Coalition Payoffs by Conventional Norm: An Assessment of the Evidence from Cabinet Coalition Situations," *American Journal of Political Science* 24:753-768.

Buchanan, William. 1963. *Legislative Partisanship: The Deviant Case of California*. Berkeley: University of California Press.

Budge, Ian and Valentine Herman. 1978. "Coalitions and Government Formation: An Empirically Relevant Theory," *British Journal of Political Science* 8:459-479.

Bueno de Mesquita, Bruce. 1974. "Need for Achievement and Competition as Determinants of Political Party Success in Elections and Coalitions," *American Political Science Review* 68:1207-1220.

_____ . 1975. *Strategy, Risk and Personality in Coalition Politics: The Case of India*. New York: Cambridge University Press.

_____ . 1979. "Coalition Payoffs and Electoral Performance in European Democracies," *Comparative Political Studies* 72:61-81.

Bullock, Charles S. III. 1978. "Congress in the Sunshine," in Leroy N. Rieselbach, ed., *Legislative Reform: Its Policy Impact*. Lexington, MA: Lexington Books, pp. 209-221.

Burks, Ardath W. 1961. *The Government of Japan*. New York: Crowell.

Burnham, Walter Dean and William N. Chambers. 1967. *American Party Systems*. New York: Oxford University Press.

Butler, David. 1973. *The Canberra Model*. Melbourne, Australia: Cheshire Publishing Company.

Butler, David and Donald Stokes. 1969. *Political Change in Britain: Forces Shaping Electoral Choice*. New York: St. Martin's Press.

_____ . 1974. *Political Change in Britain: The Evaluation of Electoral Choice*. New York: St. Martin's Press.

Caplow, Theodore. 1956. "A Theory of Coalitions in the Triad," *American Sociological Review* 21:489-493.

Carras, Mary. 1972. *The Dynamics of Indian Political Factions*. London: Cambridge University Press.

Casanova, Pablo Gonzales. 1970. *Democracy in Mexico.* New York: Oxford University Press.

Castles, Francis. 1976. "Policy Innovation and Institutional Stability in Sweden," *British Journal of Political Science* 6:203-217.

Chapman, Robert M., W.K. Jackson, and A.V. Mitchell. 1962. *New Zealand Politics in Action: The 1960 Election.* London: Oxford University Press.

Christian, William and Colin Campbell. 1974. *Political Review and Ideologies in Canada.* Toronto: McGraw-Hill Ryerson.

Clausen, Aage. 1973. *How Congressmen Decide: A Policy Focus.* New York: St. Martin's Press.

Clausen, Aage R. and Soren Holmberg. 1977. "Legislative Voting Analysis in Disciplined Multi-Party Systems: The Swedish Case," in William O. Aydelotte, ed., *The History of Parliamentary Behavior.* Princeton: Princeton University Press, pp. 159-185.

Cohen, Lenard J. 1980. "Politics As an Avocation: Legislative Professionalization and Participation in Yugoslavia," *Legislative Studies Quarterly* 5:175-209.

Cooper, Joseph. 1981. "Organization and Innovation in the House of Representatives," in Joseph Cooper and G. Calvin Mackenzie, eds., *The House at Work.* Austin: University of Texas Press.

Cooper, Joseph and Gary Bombardier. 1968. "Presidential Leadership and Party Success," *Journal of Politics* 30:1012-1027.

Cooper, Joseph and G. Calvin Mackenzie. 1981. *The House at Work.* Austin: University of Texas Press.

Cooper, Joseph and Louis Maisel. 1978. "Problems and Trends in Party Research: An Overview," in Louis Maisel and Joseph Cooper, eds., *Political Parties: Development and Decay.* Beverly Hills, CA: Sage Publications, pp. 7-30.

Cooper, Joseph and William West. 1981. "The Congressional Career in the 1970s," in Lawrence C. Dodd and Bruce I. Oppenheimer, eds., *Congress Reconsidered.* 2d ed. Washington, DC: Congressional Quarterly, pp. 83-106.

Crewe, Ivor. 1980. "Prospects for Party Realignment," *Comparative Politics* 12:379-400.

Crick, Bernard. 1964. *The Reform of Parliament.* London: Weidenfeld and Nicolson.

Crossman, R.H.S. 1975. *The Diaries of a Cabinet Minister.* London: Haish Hamelton.

Crotty, William. 1967. *Approaches to the Study of Party Organization.* Boston: Allyn and Bacon.

Crowe, Edward W. 1980. "Cross-Voting in the British House of Commons, 1945-1974," *Journal of Politics* 42:487-510.

Daalder, Hans. 1966. "Parties, Elites and Political Development in Western Europe," in J. LaPalombara and M. Weiner, eds., *Political Parties and Political Development.* Princeton: Princeton University Press, pp. 43-77.

Dahl, Robert A. 1973. *Regimes and Oppositions.* New Haven: Yale University Press.

Davidson, Roger H. 1981. "Subcommittee Government: New Channels for Policy," in Thomas E. Mann and Norman J. Ornstein, eds., *The New Congress.* Washington, DC: American Enterprise Institute, pp. 99-133.

Davidson, Roger H. and Walter J. Oleszek. 1977. *Congress Against Itself.* Bloomington: Indiana University Press.

Deckard, Barbara Sinclair. 1976. "Political Upheaval and Congressional Voting: The Effects of the 1960s on Voting Patterns in the House of Representatives," *Journal of Politics* 38:326-345.

de la Garza, Rudolph O. 1972. *The Mexican Chamber of Deputies as a Legitimizing Agent of the Mexican Government and Political System.* Tucson: University of Arizona Press.

de Swaan, Abram. 1973. *Coalition Theories and Cabinet Formations*. San Francisco: Jossey-Bass.

DiPalma, Giuseppe. 1977. *Surviving without Governing: The Italian Parties in Parliament*. Berkeley: University of California Press.

Dodd, Lawrence C. 1974. "Party Coalitions in Multiparty Parliaments: A Game-theoretical Analysis," *American Political Science Review* 68:1093-1118.

_____ . 1976. *Coalitions in Parliamentary Government*. Princeton: Princeton University Press.

Dodd, Lawrence C. and Bruce I. Oppenheimer, eds. 1977. *Congress Reconsidered*. New York: Praeger.

_____ . 1981. *Congress Reconsidered*. 2d ed. Washington, DC: Congressional Quarterly.

Dodd, Lawrence C. and Richard L. Schott. 1979. *Congress and the Administrative State*. New York: Wiley.

Drucker, H.M. 1981. "Changes in the Labour Party Leadership," *Parliamentary Affairs* 34:369-391.

Duverger, Maurice. 1954. *Political Parties*. New York: Wiley.

Easton, David. 1965. *A System Analysis of Political Life*. New York: Wiley.

Edwards, George C. 1980. *Presidential Influence in Congress*. San Francisco: Freeman.

Eldridge, Albert F. 1977. *Legislatures in Plural Societies*. Durham, NC: Duke University Press.

Epstein, Leon. 1967. *Political Parties in Western Democracies*. New York: Praeger.

_____ . 1980. "What Happened to the British Party Model?" *American Political Science Review* 74:9-22.

Erikson, Robert S. 1971a. "The Partisan Impact of State Legislative Reapportionment," *Midwest Journal of Political Science* 15:55-71.

_____ . 1971b. "The Advantage of Incumbency in Congressional Elections," *Polity* 3:395-404.

Eulau, Heinz and Katherine Hinckley. 1966. "Legislative Institutions and Processes," in James A. Robinson, ed., *Political Science Almanac*. Vol. 1. Indianapolis: Bobbs-Merrill, pp. 85-189.

Eulau, Heinz and Kenneth Prewitt. 1973. *Labyrinth of Democracy*. Indianapolis: Bobbs-Merrill.

Felsenthal, Dan S. 1979. "Aspects of Coalition Payoffs: The Case of Israel," *Comparative Political Studies* 12: 151-168.

Fenno, Richard. 1973. *Congressmen in Committees*. Boston: Little, Brown.

_____ . 1978. *Home Style*. Boston: Little, Brown.

Ferejohn, John A. 1977. "On the Decline of Competition in Congressional Elections," *American Political Science Review* 71:166-176.

Finer, S.E. 1980. "Princes, Parliaments and the Public Service," *Parliamentary Affairs* 33:33-53.

Fiorina, Morris P. 1974. *Representation, Roll Calls, and Constituencies*. Lexington, MA: Lexington Books.

_____ . 1977. *Congress: Keystone of the Washington Establishment*. New Haven: Yale University Press.

Fiorina, Morris P. and Charles Plott. 1978. "Committee Decisions under Majority Rule: An Experimental Study," *American Political Science Review* 77:575-598.

Fisher, Louis. 1978. *The Constitution between Friends: Congress, the President and the Law*. New York: St. Martin's Press.

Flanagan, Scott. 1971. "The Japanese Party System in Transition," *Comparative Politics* 3:231-253.

Foltz, William J. 1973. "Political Oppositions in Single-party States of Tropical Africa," in Robert A. Dahl, ed., *Regimes and Oppositions*. New Haven: Yale University Press, pp. 143-170.

Franklin, Mark and Michael Tappin. 1977. "Unobtrusive Measures of Backbench Opinion in Britain," *British Journal of Political Science* 7:49-71.

Froman, Lewis A. and Randall B. Ripley. 1965. "Conditions for Party Leadership: The Case of the House Democrats," *American Political Science Review* 59:52-63.

Fukui, Haruhiro. 1970. *Party in Power*. Berkeley: University of California Press.

————. 1978. "Japan: Factionalism in a Dominant-party System," in Frank P. Belloni and Dennis C. Beller, eds., *Faction Politics*. Santa Barbara: ABC-Clio Press, pp. 43-72.

Gamson, William. 1961. "A Theory of Coalition Formation," *American Sociological Review* 26:373-382.

Gordon, Michael. 1971. "Civil Servants, Politicians, and Parties: Shortcomings in the British Policy Process," *Comparative Politics* 1:29-58.

Groennings, Sven. 1970. "Patterns, Strategies, and Payoffs in Norwegian Coalition Formation," in Sven Groennings, E. W. Kelley, and Michael Leiserson, eds., *The Study of Coalition Behavior*. New York: Holt, Rinehart & Winston, pp. 60-79.

Grossholtz, Jean. 1970. "Integrative Factors in the Malaysian and Philippine Legislatures," *Comparative Politics* 1:93-114.

Hawkins, Brett. 1971. "Consequences of Reapportionment in Georgia," in Richard Hofferbert and Ira Sharkansky, eds., *State and Urban Politics*. Boston: Little, Brown, pp. 273-298.

Hibbing, John R. 1982. *Retired from the House*. Washington, DC: University Press of America.

Hinckley, Barbara. 1972. "Coalitions in Congress: Size and Ideological Distance," *Midwest Journal of Political Science* 16:197-207.

————. 1977. "'Stylized' Opposition in the U.S. House of Representatives: The Effects of Coalition Behavior," *Legislative Studies Quarterly* 2:5-28.

————. 1981. *Coalitions and Politics*. New York: Harcourt Brace.

Hoskin, Gary. 1975. "Dimensions of Conflict in the Colombian National Legislature," in G. R. Boynton and Chong Lim Kim, eds., *Legislative Systems in Developing Countries*. Durham, NC: Duke University Press, pp. 143-178.

Huntington, Samuel P. 1968. *Political Order in Changing Societies*. New Haven: Yale University Press.

Hurwitz, L. 1971. "An Index of Democratic Stability," *Comparative Political Studies* 4:41-68.

Ike, Nobutaka. 1972. *Japanese Politics*. New York: Knopf.

Jackson, Robert J. 1968. *Rebels and Whips: An Analysis of Dissension, Discipline and Cohesion in British Political Parties*. New York: St. Martin's Press.

Jackson, Robert J., Michael M. Atkinson, and Kenneth D. Hart. 1977. "Constitutional Conflict in France: Deputies' Attitudes Toward Executive-Legislative Relations," *Comparative Politics* 9:399-420.

Janda, Kenneth. 1980. *Political Parties: A Cross National Survey*. New York: The Free Press.

Jewell, Malcolm. 1962. *The State Legislature*. New York: Random House.

————. 1966. "The Political Settings," in Alexander Heard, ed., *State Legislatures in American Politics*. Englewood Cliffs, NJ: Prentice-Hall, pp. 70-97.

_____ . 1973. "Linkages Between Legislative Parties and External Parties," in Allan Kornberg, ed., *Legislatures in Comparative Perspective*. New York: David McKay, pp. 203-234.

_____ . 1977. "Legislative Representation and National Integration," in Albert F. Eldridge, ed., *Legislatures in Plural Societies*. Durham, NC: Duke University Press.

Jewell, Malcolm E. and Samuel C. Patterson. 1977. *The Legislative Process in the United States*. 3d ed. New York: Random House.

Jones, Charles O. 1970. *The Minority Party in Congress*. Boston: Little, Brown.

_____ . 1977. "Will Reform Change Congress?" in Lawrence C. Dodd and Bruce I. Oppenheimer, eds., *Congress Reconsidered*. 1st ed. New York: Praeger, pp. 247-260.

_____ . 1981. "Can Our Parties Survive Our Politics?" in Norman J. Ornstein, ed., *The Role of the Legislature in Western Democracies*. Washington, DC: American Enterprise Institute, pp. 20-36.

Karpat, Kemal H. 1959. *Turkey's Politics: The Transition to a Multi-party System*. Princeton: Princeton University Press.

Kavanagh, Dennis. 1974. "An American Science of British Politics," *Political Studies* 22:251-278.

Keith, Gary. 1981. "Comparing Legislative Studies Groups in Three States," *Legislative Studies Quarterly* 6:69-86.

Key, V. O., Jr. 1949. *Southern Politics in State and Nation*. New York: Knopf.

_____ . 1956. *American State Politics*. New York: Knopf.

_____ . 1964. *Parties, Politics and Pressure Groups*. 5th ed. New York: Crowell.

Kim, Young C. 1975. "The Committee System in the Japanese Diet," in G. R. Boynton and Chong Lim Kim, eds., *Legislative Systems in Developing Countries*. Durham, NC: Duke University Press, pp. 69-85.

King, Anthony. 1975. "Overload Problems of Governing in the 1970s," *Political Studies* 13:287-294.

_____ . 1977. *Britain Says Yes: The 1975 Referendum on the Common Market*. Washington, DC: American Enterprise Institute.

_____ . 1981. "How to Strengthen Legislatures: Assuming That We Want To," in Norman J. Ornstein, ed., *The Role of the Legislature in Western Democracies*. Washington, DC: American Enterprise Institute, pp. 77-89.

Koehler, David K. 1975. "Legislative Coalition Formation: The Meaning of Minimal Winning Size with Uncertain Participation," *American Journal of Political Science* 19:27-40.

Kofmehl, Kenneth. 1964. "The Institutionalization of a Voting Bloc," *Western Political Quarterly* 17:256-272.

Kornberg, Allan. 1967. *Canadian Legislative Behavior*. New York: Holt, Rinehart & Winston.

Kornberg, Allan and William Mishler. 1976. *Influences in Parliament: Canada*. Durham, NC: Duke University Press.

Kornberg, Allan and Lloyd D. Musolf. 1970. *Legislatures in Developmental Perspective*. Durham, NC: Duke University Press.

Kornberg, Allan, David J. Falcone, and William T. E. Mishler. 1973. *Legislatures and Societal Change: The Case of Canada*. Beverly Hills, CA: Sage Publications.

Kothari, Rajni. 1961. "Party System," *Economic Weekly* 13:847-854.

_____ . 1964. "The Congress Party in India," *Asian Survey* 4:1161-1173.

————. 1973. "India: Oppositions in a Consensual Polity," in Robert A. Dahl, ed., *Regimes and Oppositions*. New Haven: Yale University Press, pp. 305-340.

Laakso, Markku and Rein Taagepera. 1979. "Effective Number of Parties: A Measure with Application to West Europe," *Comparative Political Studies* 12:3-27.

Laver, Michael. 1974. "Dynamic Factors in Government Coalition Formation," *European Journal of Political Research* 2:259-270.

————. 1977. "Coalitions in Britain?" *Parliamentary Affairs* 30:107-111.

Laver, Michael and Michael Taylor. 1973. "Government Coalitions in Western Europe," *European Journal of Political Research* 1:205-248.

LeBlanc, Hugh L. 1969. "Voting in State Senates: Party and Constituency Influences," *Midwest Journal of Political Science* 13:33-57.

Leece, John and Hugh Berrington. 1977. "Measurements of Backbench Attitudes by Guttman Scaling of Early Day Motions: A Pilot Study; Labour, 1968-69," *British Journal of Political Science* 7:529-541.

Leiserson, Michael. 1968. "Factions and Coalitions in One Party Japan: An Interpretation Based on the Theory of Games," *American Political Science Review* 62:770-787.

————. 1973. "Political Opposition and Political Development in Japan," in Robert A. Dahl, ed., *Regimes and Oppositions*. New Haven: Yale University Press, pp. 341-398.

LeLoup, Lance T. 1981. *The Fiscal Congress: Legislative Control of the Budget.* Westport, CT: Greenwood Press.

Lijphart, Arend. 1969. "Consociational Democracy," *World Politics* 21:204-225.

————. 1982. "Coalition Theory and Cabinet Durability: A Critique." Delivered at the Annual Meeting of the American Political Science Association, Denver.

Linz, Juan L. 1973. "Opposition to and under an Authoritarian Regime," in Robert A. Dahl, ed., *Regimes and Oppositions*. New Haven: Yale University Press, pp. 171-260.

Loewenberg, Gerhard. 1967. *Parliament in the German Political System.* Ithaca: Cornell University Press.

Loewenberg, Gerhard and Samuel Patterson. 1979. *Comparing Legislatures.* Boston: Little, Brown.

Loomis, Burdett A. 1981. "Congressional Caucuses and the Politics of Representation," in Lawrence C. Dodd and Bruce I. Oppenheimer, eds., *Congress Reconsidered.* 2d ed. Washington, DC: Congressional Quarterly, pp. 204-220.

Lorwin, Val R. 1971. "Segmented Pluralism: Ideological Cleavages and Political Cohesion in the Smaller European Democracies," *Comparative Politics* 2:141-176.

————. 1974. "Belgium: Conflict and Compromise," in Kenneth McRae, ed., *Consociational Democracy.* Toronto: McClelland and Stewart, pp. 179-206.

Lowell, A. Lawrence. 1896. *Governments and Parties in Continental Europe.* Cambridge: Harvard University Press.

————. 1902. "The Influence of Party upon Legislation in England and America," *Annual Report of the American Historical Association for 1901* 1:321-544.

Luce, R. Duncan and Arnold A. Rogow. 1956. "A Game Theoretic Analysis of Congressional Power Distributions for a Stable Two-Party System," *Behavioral Science* 1:83-95.

Lynskey, J. J. 1973. "Backbench Tactics and Parliamentary Party Structure," *Parliamentary Affairs* 27:28-37.

Macridis, Roy, ed. 1967. *Political Parties: Contemporary Trends and Ideas.* New York: Harper & Row.

Maheshewari, S. R. 1976. "Constituency Linkage of National Legislators in India," *Legislative Studies Quarterly* 1:331-354.

Manley, John F. 1973. "The Conservative Coalition in Congress," *American Behavioral Scientist* 17:223-247.

Mann, Thomas E. and Norman J. Ornstein, eds. 1981. *The New Congress*. Washington, DC: American Enterprise Institute.

Mann, Thomas E. and Raymond E. Wolfinger. 1974. "Candidates and Parties in Congressional Elections," *American Political Science Review* 74:617-632.

Mansbach, Richard. 1973. "The Scottish National Party," *Comparative Politics* 2:185-210.

Mansfield, Harvey C. 1975. *Congress Against the President*. New York: Academy of Political Science.

Matthews, Donald R. 1960. *U.S. Senators and Their World*. New York: Vintage.

Mayer, Lawrence C. 1980. "Party Systems and Cabinet Stability," in Peter H. Merkl, ed., *Western European Party Systems: Trends and Prospects*. New York: The Free Press, pp. 335-347.

Mayhew, David R. 1966. *Party Loyalty Among Congressmen: The Difference Between Democrats and Republicans, 1947-1962*. Cambridge: Harvard University Press.

_____. 1974a. *The Electoral Connection*. New Haven: Yale University Press.

_____. 1974b. "Congressional Elections: The Case of the Vanishing Marginals," *Polity* 6:295-317.

McCally, Sarah P. 1966. "The Governor and His Legislative Party," *American Political Science Review* 60:923-942.

McDonald, Ronald H. 1971. *Party Systems and Elections in Latin America*. Chicago: Markham Publishing.

_____. 1978. "Party Factions and Modernization: A Comparative Analysis of Colombia and Uruguay," in Frank P. Belloni and Dennis C. Beller, eds., *Faction Politics*. Santa Barbara, CA: ABC-Clio, pp. 219-243.

Merkl, Peter H. 1970. "Coalition Politics in West Germany," in Sven Groennings, E.W. Kelley, and Michael Leiserson, eds., *The Study of Coalition Behavior*. New York: Holt, Rinehart & Winston, pp. 13-42.

Mezey, Michael L. 1975. "Legislative Development and Political Parties: The Case of Thailand," in G. R. Boynton and Chong Lim Kim, eds., *Legislative Systems in Developing Countries*. Durham, NC: Duke University Press, pp. 107-141.

_____. 1979. *Comparative Legislatures*. Durham: Duke University Press.

Morehouse, Sarah McCally. 1973. "The State Political Party and the Policy-Making Process," *American Political Science Review* 67:55-72.

Murray, Richard W. and Donald S. Lutz. 1974. "Redistricting Decisions in the American States: A Test of the Minimal Winning Coalition Hypothesis," *American Journal of Political Science* 18:233-256.

Nelson, Daniel N. 1980. "Editor's Introduction: Communist Legislatures and Communist Politics," *Legislative Studies Quarterly* 5:161-173.

Nicholson, Norman. 1972. "The Factional Model and the Study of Politics," *Comparative Political Studies* 5:291-314.

_____. 1975. "Integrative Strategies of a National Elite: Career Patterns in the Indian Council of Ministers," *Comparative Politics* 7:533-558.

_____. 1978. "Factionalism and Public Policy in India," in Frank P. Belloni and Dennis C. Beller, eds., *Faction Politics*. Santa Barbara, CA: ABC-Clio Press, pp. 161-188.

Norton, Philip. 1975. *Dissension in the House of Commons*. London. Macmillan.

————. 1976. "Intra-party Dissent in the House of Commons: A Case Study," *Parliamentary Affairs* 29:404-420.

————. 1977. "Private Legislation and the Influence of the Backbench M.P.," *Parliamentary Affairs* 30:356-362.

————. 1978. "Party Organization in the House of Commons," *Parliamentary Affairs* 31:406-423.

————. 1980. "The Organization of Parliamentary Parties," in S. A. Walkland, ed., *The House of Commons in the Twentieth Century*. Oxford: Clarendon Press.

Nyholm, Pekka. 1982. "Finland: A Probabilistic View of Coalition Formation," in Eric C. Browne and John Dreijmanis, eds., *Government Coalitions in Western Democracies*. New York: Longmans, pp. 71-108.

Ogul, Morris S. 1981. "Congressional Oversight: Structures and Incentives," in Lawrence C. Dodd and Bruce I. Oppenheimer, eds., *Congress Reconsidered*. 2d ed. Washington, DC: Congressional Quarterly, pp. 317-331.

Oppenheimer, Bruce I. 1978. "Policy Implications of Rules Committee Reforms," in Leroy N. Rieselbach, ed., *Legislative Reform*. Lexington, MA: Lexington Books, pp. 91-104.

————. 1981. "Congress and the New Obstructionism: Developing an Energy Program," in Lawrence C. Dodd and Bruce I. Oppenheimer, eds., *Congress Reconsidered*. 2d ed. Washington, DC: Congressional Quarterly, pp. 275-295.

Orfield, Gary. 1975. *Congressional Power*. New York: Harcourt, Brace, Jovanovich.

Ornstein, Norman J. 1981. "The House and the Senate in a New Congress," in Thomas E. Mann and Norman J. Ornstein, eds., *The New Congress*. Washington, DC: American Enterprise Institute, pp. 363-383.

O'Rourke, Timothy. 1980. *The Impact of Reapportionment*. New Brunswick, NJ: Transaction Books.

Packenham, Robert. 1970. "Legislatures and Political Development," in Allan Kornberg and Lloyd D. Musolf, eds., *Legislatures in Developmental Perspective*. Durham, NC: Duke University Press.

Padgett, L. Vincent. 1966. *The Mexican Political System*. Boston: Houghton Mifflin.

Parker, Glenn R. 1980. "Cycles in Congressional District Attention," *Journal of Politics* 42:540-548.

Paltiel, K. Z. 1975. "The Israeli Coalition System," *Government and Opposition* 10: 397-414.

Patch, Richard W. 1970. "The Bolivian Revolution," in Robert D. Tomasek, ed., *Latin American Politics*. Garden City, NY: Anchor Books, pp. 344-374.

Patterson, Samuel. 1973. "The British House of Commons as a Focus for Political Research," *British Journal of Political Science* 3:363-382.

————. 1976. "American State Legislatures and Public Policy," in Herbert Jacob and Kenneth Vines, eds., *Politics in the American States*. 3d ed. Boston: Little, Brown.

Patterson, Samuel C. and John C. Wahlke, eds. 1972. *Comparative Legislative Behavior: Frontiers of Research*. New York: Wiley Interscience.

Peabody, Robert L. 1975. *Leadership in Congress: Stability, Succession, and Change*. Boston: Little, Brown.

————. 1981. "House Party Leadership in the 1970s," in Lawrence C. Dodd and Bruce I. Oppenheimer, eds., *Congress Reconsidered*. 2d ed. Washington, DC: Congressional Quarterly, pp. 137-155.

Petney, John. 1977. "Worms That Turned: The Inter-party Mobility of British Parliamentary Candidates Since 1945," *Parliamentary Affairs* 30:363-372.

Pinto-Duchinsky, Michael. 1972. "Central Office and Power in the Conservative Party," *Political Studies* 10:1-17.

Piper, J. R. 1974. "Backbench Rebellion, Party Government and Concensus Politics: The Case of the Parliamentary Labour Party, 1966-1970," *Parliamentary Affairs* 27:384-396.

Pollack, Benny. 1978. "Spain: From Corporate State to Parliamentary Democracy," *Parliamentary Affairs* 31:52-66.

Polsby, Nelson. 1975. "Legislatures," in Fred Greenstein and Nelson Polsby, eds., *Handbook of Political Science*. Reading, MA: Addison-Wesley.

Prezworski, Adam and John Sprague. 1971. "Concepts in Search of Explicit Formulation," *Midwest Journal of Political Science* 40:183-218.

Pulzer, Peter S. 1977. "Will England Have Coalitions?" *Parliamentary Affairs* 30:69-79.

_____ . 1978. "Responsible Party Government and Stable Coalition: The Case of the German Federal Republic," *Political Studies* 26:181-208.

Rae, Douglas. 1976. *Political Consequences of Electoral Laws*. New Haven: Yale University Press.

Rae, Douglas and M. S. Taylor. 1971. "Decision, Rules, and Policy Outcomes," *British Journal of Political Science* 1:71-91.

Ranney, Austin. 1981. "The Working Conditions of Members of Parliament and Congress: Changing the Tools Changes the Job," in Norman J. Ornstein, ed., *The Role of the Legislature in Western Democracies*. Washington, DC: American Enterprise Institute, pp. 67-76.

Richardson, J. J. and Richard Kimber. 1972. "The Role of All-Party Committees in the House of Commons," *Parliamentary Affairs* 25:339-350.

Rieselbach, Leroy N. 1978. *Legislative Reform: The Policy Impact*. Lexington, MA: Lexington Books.

Riggs, Fred. 1970. *Administrative Reform and Political Responsiveness*. Beverly Hills, CA: Sage Publications.

Riker, William H. 1962. *The Theory of Political Coalitions*. New Haven: Yale University Press.

Ripley, Randall. 1967. *Party Leaders in the House of Representatives*. Washington, DC: Brookings Institution.

_____ . 1969. *Majority Party Leadership in Congress*. Boston: Little, Brown.

Robeck, Bruce W. 1972. "Legislative Partisanship, Constituency and Malapportionment: The Case of California," *American Political Science Review* 66:1234-1245.

Rohde, David W. and Kenneth A. Shepsle. 1978. "Thinking About Legislative Reform," in Leroy N. Rieselbach, ed., *Legislative Reform*. Lexington, MA: Lexington Books.

Rose, Richard. 1964. "Parties, Factions and Tendencies in Britain," *Political Studies* 12:33-46.

_____ . 1970. *People in Politics*. New York: Basic Books.

_____ . 1974. *The Problem of Party Government*. London:Macmillan.

_____ . 1980. *Do Parties Make a Difference?* Chatham, NJ: Chatham House.

Rosenthal, Alan. 1981. *Legislative Life*. New York: Harper & Row.

Ryle, M. 1965. "Committees of the House of Commons," *Political Quarterly* 36:295-308.

Sanders, David and Valentine Herman. 1977. "The Stability and Survival of Governments in Western Democracies," *Acta Politica* 12:346-377.

Sani, Giacomo. 1976. "Mass Constraints on Political Realignments: Perceptions of Anti-Systems Parties in Italy," *British Journal of Political Science* 6:1-32.

Sartori, Giovanni. 1976. *Parties and Party Systems: A Framework for Analysis*. New York: Cambridge University Press.

Sayari, Sabri. 1978. "The Turkish Party System in Transition," *Government and Opposition* 13:39-57.

Scalapino, Ria and J. Masumi. 1971. *Parties and Politics in Contemporary Japan*. Berkeley: University of California Press.

Schattschneider, E. E. 1942. *Party Government*. New York: Holt, Rinehart & Winston.

Schick, Allen. 1981. "The Three-Ring Budget Process: The Appropriations, Tax, and Budget Committees in Congress," in Thomas E. Mann and Norman J. Ornstein, eds., *The New Congress*. Washington, DC: American Enterprise Institute, pp. 288-328.

Schofield, Norman. 1976. "The Kernel and Payoffs in European Government Coalitions," *Public Choice* 26:29-49.

Schwarz, John E. 1980. "Exploring a New Role in Policy Making: The British House of Commons in the 1970s," *American Political Science Review* 74:22-37.

Scott, Robert. 1964. *Mexican Government in Transition*. Urbana: University of Illinois Press.

Seyd, Patrick. 1972. "Factionalism within the Conservative Party: The Monday Club," *Government and Opposition* 7:464-487.

————. 1975. "Democracy within the Conservative Party," *Government and Opposition* 10:219-237.

Shepsle, Kenneth. 1979. "Institutional Arrangements and Equilibrium in Multidimensional Voting Models," *American Journal of Political Science* 23:27-59.

Siegfried, Andre. 1956. "Stable Instability in France," *Foreign Affairs* 34:394-404.

Simon, Maurice D. and David M. Olson. 1980. "Evolution of a Minimal Parliament: Membership and Committee Changes in the Polish Sejm," *Legislative Studies Quarterly* 5:211-232.

Sinclair, Barbara Deckard. 1977. "Who Wins in the House of Representatives: The Effect of Declining Party Cohesion on Policy Outputs, 1959-1970," *Social Science Quarterly* 58:121-128.

————. 1978. "From Party Voting to Regional Fragmentation: The House of Representatives," *American Politics Quarterly* 6:125-146.

————. 1981a. "Coping with Uncertainty: Building Coalitions in the House and the Senate," in Thomas E. Mann and Norman J. Ornstein, eds., *The New Congress*. Washington, DC: American Enterprise Institute, pp. 178-220.

————. 1981b. "Agenda and Alignment Change: The House of Representatives, 1925-1978," in Lawrence C. Dodd and Bruce I. Oppenheimer, eds., *Congress Reconsidered*. 2d ed. Washington, DC: Congressional Quarterly, pp. 221-245.

————. 1982. *Congressional Realignment, 1925-1978*. Austin: University of Texas Press.

Sindler, Allan P. 1955. "Bifactional Rivalry as an Alternative to Two-party Competition in Louisiana," *American Political Science Review* 49:641-662.

Skilling, H. Gordon. 1973. "Opposition in Communist East Europe," in Robert A. Dahl, ed., *Regimes and Oppositions*. New Haven: Yale University Press, pp. 89-119.

Smith, Geoffrey. 1981. "Parliamentary Change in Britain," in Norman J. Ornstein, ed., *The Role of the Legislature in Western Democracies*. Washington, DC: American Enterprise Institute, pp. 37-49.

Smith, Joel and Lloyd D. Musolf. 1979. *Legislatures in Development: Dynamic of Change in New and Old States*. Durham, NC: Duke University Press.

Sorauf, Frank. 1967. "Political Parties and Political Analysis," in Walter Dean Burnham and William Chambers, eds., *American Party Systems*. New York: Oxford University Press.

Steiner, Jurg. 1971. "The Principles of Majority and Proportionality," *Comparative Political Studies* 1:63-70.

Stern, Alan J., Sidney Tarrow, and Mary F. Williams. 1971. "Factions and Opinion Groups in European Mass Parties," *Comparative Politics* 3:529-559.

Stevens, Arthur, Arthur Miller, and Thomas Mann. 1974. "Mobilization of Liberal Strength in the House, 1955-1970," *American Political Science Review* 68:667-681.

Sturanovic, Radovan. 1977. "The Assembly of the Socialist Federal Republic of Yugoslavia," *Yugoslav Survey* 18:3-34.

Sundquist, James L. 1981. *The Decline and Resurgence of Congress*. Washington, DC: Brookings Institution.

Taylor, Michael and Valentine H. Herman. 1971. "Party Systems and Government Stability," *American Political Science Review* 65:28-37.

Thayer, Nathaniel B. 1969. *How the Conservatives Rule Japan*. Princeton: Princeton University Press.

Tufte, Edward R. 1973. "The Relationship between Seats and Votes in Two-Party Systems," *American Political Science Review* 67:540-554.

_____ . 1978. *Political Control of the Economy*. Princeton: Princeton University Press.

Turner, Julius. 1951. *Party and Constituency: Pressures on Congress*. Baltimore: The Johns Hopkins Press.

Turner, Julius and Edward V. Schnier, Jr. 1970. *Party and Constituency: Pressures on Congress*. Rev. ed. Baltimore: The Johns Hopkins Press.

Uslaner, Eric M. 1978a. "Comparative State Policy Formation, Interparty Competition, and Malapportionment: A New Look at V.O. Key's Hypotheses," *Journal of Politics* 40:409-432.

_____ . 1978b. "Policy Entrepreneurs and Amateur Democrats in the House of Representatives: Toward a More Party-Oriented Congress," in Leroy N. Rieselbach, ed., *Legislative Reform*. Lexington, MA: Lexington Books, pp. 106-116.

Von Neumann, John and Oskar Morgenstern. 1947. *Theory of Games and Economic Behavior*. Princeton: Princeton University Press.

Wahlke, John, Heinz Eulau, William Buchanan, and Leroy C. Ferguson. 1962. *The Legislative System*. New York: Wiley.

Waltz, Kenneth. 1967. *Foreign Policy and Domestic Politics*. Boston: Little, Brown.

Ward, Robert E. 1967. *Japan's Political System*. Englewood Cliffs, NJ: Prentice-Hall.

Warwick, Paul. 1979. "The Durability of Coalition Governments in Parliamentary Democracies," *Comparative Political Science* 11:465-498.

Weinbaum, Marvin G. 1975. "Classification and Change in Legislative Systems: With Particular Application to Iran, Turkey, and Afghanistan," in G. R. Boynton and Chong Lim Kim, eds., *Legislative Systems in Developing Countries*. Durham, NC: Duke University Press, pp. 31-68.

Weiner, Myron. 1967. *Party Building in a New Nation: The Indian National Congress*. Chicago: University of Chicago Press.

Weingast, Barry R. 1979. "A Rational Choice Perspective on Congressional Norms," *American Journal of Political Science* 23:245-262.

Welch, William A. 1980. "The Status of Research on Representative Institutions in Eastern Europe," *Legislative Studies Quarterly* 5:275-307.

White, Stephen. 1980. "The USSR Supreme Soviet: A Developmental Perspective," *Legislative Studies Quarterly* 5:247-274.

Williams, Philip M. 1966. *Crisis and Compromise: Politics in the Fourth Republic.* Garden City, NY: Anchor Books.

――――――― . 1968. *The French Parliament: Politics in the Fifth Republic.* New York: Praeger.

Wilson, Woodrow. 1885. *Congressional Government.* Gloucester, MA: Peter Smith.

Wood, David M. 1973. "Responsibility for the Fall of Cabinets in the French Fourth Republic, 1951-1955," *American Journal of Political Science* 17:767-780.

――――――― . 1982. "Comparing Parliamentary Voting on European Issues in France and Britain," *Legislative Studies Quarterly* 7:101-117.

Wood, David M. and Jack T. Pitzer. 1979. "Parties, Coalitions, and Cleavages: A Comparison of Two Legislatures in Two French Republics," *Legislative Studies Quarterly* 4:197-226.

Wright, Maurice. 1977. "Ministers and Civil Servants: Relations and Responsibilities," *Parliamentary Affairs* 30:293-311.

Young, James. 1966. *The Washington Community.* New York: Columbia University Press.

Chapter 5

Committee Selection

by

HEINZ EULAU

Given the centrality of standing committees in democratic legislatures, especially in the U.S. Congress, committee assignments would seem to
be the high road to legislators' influence and success as participants in the
governmental process, with important consequences for the functions and performance of committees, for the interests affected by committee decisions
inside and outside of government, and for the public policies that emanate
from the legislature. Yet intensive, systematic, and theory-driven investigation
of the complexities involved in the committee assignment process is of rather
recent vintage. Moreover, most of the research conducted in the last 20 years
has dealt with assignments in the U.S. House of Representatives and, for
reasons that will become clear, with Democratic assignments. A few studies
cover the U.S. Senate and some U.S. state legislatures.[1] There is no research
literature to speak of on assignments in non-U.S. legislative bodies.[2] Why
committee assignments and the process involved have been neglected in the
case of the Senate is difficult to say, though it is possible to say that research
on the Senate generally has been neglected in comparison to the House. It
has been suggested that the greater number of "cases" available in the House
proved so attractive that little attention has been given to the Senate or that
the unavailability of "request data" for senatorial assignments may be blamed
for the absence of research. Neither suggestion is persuasive. More plausible
is the explanation that the Senate does not have the "size problem" that, as
will be noted, looms large in the House. As Fenno (1973) has pointed out,
the "most marked characteristic" of Senate committees is "their permeability.
They are not kept exclusive in their membership or autonomous in their

191

operating procedures. . . . Every Senator serves on at least two and often three committees. . . . These multiple assignments keep committees interlocked and help to dilute the importance a Senator will attach to any one committee membership" (p. 148).

Development: From Simplicity to Complexity

In order to appreciate the poverty of research on committee assignments in the early 1950s and the progress made since then, one need only inspect the most authoritative text of its time on the U.S. Congress. Galloway (1953) devotes only a handful of paragraphs to the subject, mostly dealing with formal arrangements. Although there are some "data" in his description, he is able to refer to only one solid piece of research, a doctoral dissertation by Marvick (1950). Referring to the Agriculture, Interior, and Merchant Marine committees, he informs the reader that "the committees of Congress vary in their representative character, some being fairly representative of the House or Senate, others being dominated by members from particular regions or economic interests. . . . Congressmen naturally seek assignment to committees having jurisdiction over matters of major concern to their district and states" (p. 281).

How disciplined imagination can drive the research process is demonstrated by the first genuinely behavioral study of the assignment process—Huitt's (1957) "deviant case analysis" of how the Republicans denied Senator Wayne Morse his committee seats after he failed to support the party's 1952 presidential ticket. Huitt's interest, at least initially, was not in the assignment process as such but rather in those informal norms by which legislators are expected to abide if they wish to be effective. Difficult as norms are to investigate, Huitt assumed that particular conflict situations may furnish clues about the norms that affect behavior, and that "it should be possible to make valid, if crude, inferences about norms of behavior from the printed record" (p. 315).[3] Of interest from the research perspective is Huitt's use of the case; he does not treat it anecdotally to "make a point," but as a stimulus for the theoretical imagination. At issue, it appeared, were not the norms guiding committee assignments themselves but rather whose interpretation of the norms should prevail. Among several tentative conclusions offered as "hypotheses for further testing," Huitt states, "The response of senators under cross-pressures of claims of friendship or ideological allegiance, on the one hand, and loyalty to the party leadership on the other, will depend on the structuring of the situation" (p. 329).

Prior to the first study exclusively devoted to the committee assignment process, two investigators touched on it more or less directly—Goodwin (1959) in connection with a study of seniority and Matthews (1960) in connection with an effort to understand the committee system in the Senate as a stratification system. Goodwin's study is particularly noteworthy on two grounds: first, its distinguishing between congressional and committee seniority as these two aspects may affect assignments (a major point of controversy in Huitt's study of the Morse assignment case); and, second, its developing a mode of classifying committees on the basis of "hard data" on transfer assignments. Largely descriptive in approach, the study does not really deal with the assignment process or assignment preferences but rather with the demographic outcomes of assignments in the two houses of Congress, notably as they affect chairmanships. Still writing in the reformist style of the early postwar period and addressing reform concerns, Goodwin reports that "statistical analysis does not make as clear a case against seniority as many of the critics of the system seem to claim" (p. 430). He later extended his analysis of seniority and related matters in a book-length study of congressional committees (Goodwin, 1970).

Matthews's (1960) chapter on committees in his book on the U.S. Senate was the first theoretically sophisticated quantitative study of assignments, very much influenced by the sociological literature on social stratification. Taking committee seniority for granted, Matthews seems to have been interested in them initially as indicators of committee prestige or status. Both Goodwin's and Matthews's methods of rank-ordering committees in terms of assignments will be more fully discussed below. Suffice it here to report some of Matthews's observations. He argues that "the consensus on committee desirability reinforces the seniority system by making it more 'functional' than it otherwise would be"; this in turn means that "senators from competitive two-party states are seldom able to achieve chairmanships or senior positions on important committees." Inspecting the rankings of the "interest" committees, so-called, he suggests that the "ranking of committee desirability is undoubtedly influenced by the relative power of these groups in the senators' constituencies, but the senators' ranking of these committees tends to reinforce the relative power of these groups outside the Senate" (p. 152).

However, Matthews continues, "in order to discover the influences of senators' committee preferences, we must go considerably beyond the crude notion of political advantage" (p. 154). He finds that "occupational differences between the Senate committees hold up even when the effect of the senators' constituencies are held constant" (p. 156). Career type—previously identified as professional, patrician, agitator, and amateur—is also found to be related to committee preference, and seniority creates "a class bias in the recruitment of committee chairmen," just as it places "a premium upon regular re-election" (p. 163).

Matthews's study of committee assignments in the Senate has never been brought up to date or extended, and it stands as a locus classicus of sociological, rather than psychoeconomic, investigation of committee assignments and careers. Masters's (1961) study of committee assignments in the House of Representatives, the first one of its kind and highly influential for more than two decades, remains significant on three grounds: first, it challenged the seniority hypothesis insofar as it was believed to explain committee assignments; second, it formulated a hypothesis that became later known as the "Masters-Clapp re-election hypothesis" (and which will be treated more fully below); and third, perhaps most important, it set an agenda for future reesrach that, in fact, has been followed by many investigators. As to seniority, Masters concedes that continuous service "insures a member his place on a committee once he is assigned," but he challenges the "supposition that these assignments are made primarily on the basis of seniority." He sees in this supposition at least one reason why, until then, "the processes and patterns of committee assignments have been only generally discussed." But, he argues, "seniority may have very little to do with transfers to other committees, and it has virtually nothing to do with the assignment of freshman members" (p. 345).

Having issued the challenge and taking off from Goodwin (1959) whose statement concerning factors affecting assignments "leaves significant questions unanswered," Masters presents his agenda:

What, for example, is meant by geographical distribution or balance? Is every section or region represented in each party on each committee? Or does the committee's subject matter jurisdiction guide the type of geographical representation the committee-on-committees considers? Is the number of assignments allotted to a state party delegation on particular committees restricted? Do state party delegations develop a "vested interest" in certain committees and attempt to maintain continuous representation on them? What groups actively seek representation for their interests on the various committees by campaigning for an individual congressman to fill a vacancy? How influential are they? The study of committee assignments should also throw light on party factionalism, the differences between the parties in performing this organizational task, and the importance attached to the professional and group backgrounds of legislators (p. 345).

In addition to its agenda-setting importance, Masters's study was novel in two other respects: first, it was the first systematic empirical investigation of the committee assignment process in the House;[4] and, second, it was a theory-driven attempt to consolidate various micro and macro aspects of the assignment process. The theory involved concerns the federalistic nature of the U.S. system of representation. While Masters himself does not articulate the theory explicitly, it shines through, for instance, in his treatment of the procedures for assigning members in the parties' committees-on-committees. In the case of the Democrats' committee-on-committees, members are given "geographical zones," and the deans of state party delegations are important "auxiliary actors." Yet, because seniority remains a crucial constant in the case of the Ways and Means Committee (then performing the assignment function), the continuity of its membership "makes it ill-designed for flexibility and responsiveness to electoral changes and public opinion trends." In the case of the Republicans, the federalistic procedure of allowing each state to be represented on their committee-on-committees makes the committee "much more responsible (responsive?) to electoral changes"; but as each member can cast as many votes as there are Republicans in his delegation, the method "concentrates power over committee assignments in the hands of the senior members from the large state delegations" (p. 348).

Following the publication of Masters's article there was a hiatus in research development. His work was cited or referred to widely for over a decade as if it gave contemporary information. A chapter on committee assignments in Clapp (1964, pp. 207-240) reported on round-table discussions with congressmen at the Brookings Institution that supplied many anecdotes more useful as sources of hypotheses than as evidence, especially because the "evidence" may have been biased by the liberal cast of the personnel involved. Eulau (1967), in an admittedly "normative" piece, argued the case for a functional view of the committee assignment process. The major committee case studies by Fenno (1966) and Manley (1970) provided information about assignments to the Appropriations and Ways and Means committees respectively. But only one study of a systematic sort (Gawthrop, 1966) was reported between 1961 and 1969, when a more or less cumulative "research tradition" can be said to have begun. Nevertheless, as late as 1973, Bullock would observe that "our knowledge of circumstances surrounding committee recruitment remains far from complete. Except for the few committees for which case studies exist, the primary sources of information about committee appointments are Nicholas A. Masters's pioneering article, now a decade old, and a chapter in Charles Clapp's *The Congressman*" (Bullock, 1973, p. 87).

Within a few years after Bullock's observation, a research tradition had come into existence—and a tradition to which Bullock himself had made significant contributions (Bullock, 1970, 1971, 1972, 1973, 1976; Bullock and Sprague, 1969). This tradition is evident in Shepsle's (1978) masterful, book-length study exclusively devoted to "the giant jigsaw puzzle," a theoretical-empirical tour de force through Democratic committee assignments in the modern House of Representatives, in which the author frankly acknowledges or makes use of the work of others during the 1970s.[5] Some of Shepsle's study will be referred to in various parts of the next section and again more comprehensively in the concluding section. While Shepsle, in an "Epilogue" (pp. 262-281), took note of recent reforms in the 94th (1975-1976) Congress, his study largely covers Democratic assignment requests and assignments from the 86th (1959-1960) to the 93d (1973-1974) Congresses. For the impact of the reforms one must go to Smith and Ray (1983) and relevant sections in Smith and Deering (1984). As Smith and Deering point out, "there is no strong evidence that the decisions of the committee on committees (now called the Steering and Policy Committee, and in no way resembling the old Ways and Means Committee's Democratic component) have changed in any systematic way" (p. 245).

The Assignment Kaleidoscope: Stability and Change

This inventory and review of assignment studies could have been organized in any number of ways. The mode adopted here is "topical," centered in "themes" that seem to be at the focus of a given study's research attention and relying on authors' own references to prior studies that pertain to one or another theme. This approach again emphasizes research development and should make it possible to determine whether there has been cumulation in research findings. Of course, studies often include several, more or less connected themes, and this makes topical treatment at times appear to be quite kaleidoscopic rather than categoric; but the various aspects of the committee assignment process in the "real world" are difficult to capture in clean, exclusive categories. The emphasis will be on theoretical and methodological developments, and only "findings" germane to theories and methods will be reported. All of the studies reviewed here contain a good deal of "information" that a comprehensive portrayal of the assignment process would want to take into account, but this is not the task at hand.

Committee Size Manipulation as Leadership Strategy

Political units are more likely to increase than decrease in size, and efforts to reduce their size are invariably offset by tendencies toward growth, as if growth were a law of nature. Yet, if there are any "laws" concerning a unit's growth or optimum size, they have still to be discovered. There is reason to believe, however, that whatever regularities exist are not "immanent" tendencies but that they are determined by the behavior of those who are in a position to manipulate a unit's size. In the case of legislative committees, their size is a function of the assignment process and of the actors involved— those who seek assignments and those who do the assigning (committees-on-committees and party leaders).

In the early, anecdotal phase of concern with the relationship between committee size and assignment, the process seemed rather simple and unproblematic. The party leaders would get together at the beginning of each new congress and, depending on the proportion of party seats won or lost in the election, negotiate committee membership quotas which would then set the assignment process in motion. While there were hints at the "politics" ("horse-trading") and underlying conflicts involved in these leader negotiations, committee size did not seem to be a theoretically or empirically exciting problem. In the more recent period of research, a spectacular controversy first called attention to the essentially manipulable aspects of the decisions concerning committee size. Cummings and Peabody (1963) and Peabody (1963), in two minutely descriptive case studies, examined the immediate conditions and short-term consequences of a controversy over the enlargement of the Rules Committee in the House of Representatives. But until the mid-1970s neither case nor systematic studies paid much attention to the interlocking of committee size decisions and party leader strategies in assigning members to committees. As late as 1970, Goodwin (1970) devoted only two and a half pages to "committee size" in the House (pp. 66-69) and a similar space to committee size in the Senate (pp. 80-83).

Inadvertent evidence of the relationship between committee size and assignments first appeared in a study by Gawthrop (1966) concerning "changing membership patterns" in the House. Its point of departure is the empirical observation that from the 80th (1947-1948) through the 89th (1965-1966) Congresses there was a "gradual but steady increase in the number of double committee assignments" or, correlatively, a decline in single assignments (p. 366). Gawthrop notes that "admittedly, six of every ten House members still had only one committee assignment in 1965," but compared to 1949, when 90 percent held only one committee seat, "a decrease of this extent deserves close examination" (p. 371). He offers as "the most apparent cause" of double assignments the increasing size of most House committees and suggests that this increase was "in response to a wide range of increasing demands." He says nothing about these demands and merely notes that "more empirical investigations are needed to determine the exact nature of these demands" (pp. 371-372). But increasing committee size is not a "cause" of double assignments; rather, it is a collinear artifact of the fixed number of House members available for assignment, and it is more plausible to assume that double assignments are the "cause" of increase in committee size.

The first systematic treatment of committee size and the assignment process did not appear until Westefield (1974) sought to account for the relationship in terms of majority party leadership strategy. Westefield notes, first, that over two time periods for which he aggregated the data on committee assignments, 1927-1945 and 1947-1971, there was a monotonic increase in committee sizes; and, second, that with some exceptions these increases occurred more on committees in the middle to upper range of the committee prestige structure. His theoretical point of departure is the assumption that party leaders use the committee system as a resource to accommodate member demands for assignments "in order to gain leverage with the members. To gain leverage the leaders must guarantee a steady supply of resources–i.e., party positions on committees" (p. 1593). Underlying this assumption are two further assumptions about motivations. First, "the members want 'good' assignments. Because the demand for 'good' assignments most often exceeds the supply, these resources are scarce. The members want these scarce resources." Second, "the majority party leaders want compliant behavior on the part of the members. They perceive that by accommodating the followers (dispensing 'good' assignments) they, the leaders, can reward past loyalty or encourage such behavior in the future" (p. 1594). From these assumptions Westefield derives three propositions:

I. The leaders expand their resource base by increasing the number of committee positions they can dispense (p. 1595).

II. The leaders, in expanding their resource base, will concentrate the increase in the middle to upper range of the committee prestige ordering (p. 1599).

III. In time the currency (committee positions) will be devalued to the point where the system of resources must be overhauled (pp. 1601-1602).

While, except for the prestigious "top" committees where leaders conserve their resource by not increasing committee size, these are plausible propositions, they are only indirectly connected with the aggregate data that Westefield can use, as he puts it, to "evaluate" them (p. 1595). His evaluation criterion is invariably the "consistency" between the data and their "explanation," but it is not clear whether Westefield seeks to "explain" the data or whether the data are used to "test" the theory. The analytic problem is, of course, that the data are macro or aggregate, while the theory is micro or individualistic, based as it is on assumed motivations and perceptions. Indeed, as he proceeds with the analysis Westefield has to introduce further assumptions, such as that "the leaders of the majority party are concerned, first and foremost, with the committee preferences of their party members" (p. 1599). Other assumptions made throughout the study suggest that the theory far outruns the data. For instance, "benefits (member compliance) increase with the expected prestige of the new position (in the case of transfers). But costs (depletion of seat value) also increase with the prestige of the new seat to be created" (p. 1599).

Westefield's version of the leadership accommodation theory was accepted by Shepsle (1978), who characterizes his analysis as "a modest extension" of Westefield's "reasoning," and suggests that the use of assignment request data permits him "to focus more accurately on an important set of pressures on the leadership than Westefield's reliance on the public record permitted" (p. 298, n. 1). Shepsle conceives of an "equilibrium committee structure" that emerges as "the product of two sets of forces, one pressing for expanded committee sizes, the other seeking to limit expansion" (p. 112).

Three considerations make for expansionist pressures: first, "probably the most compelling partisan pressure on party leaders is to protect the committee positions of returning members"; second, "freshman first-preference and nonfreshman transfer requests"; and third, "freshman lower-order requests and nonfreshman dual-service requests" (pp. 114-115). In support of the leadership accommodation theory, Shepsle points out that "the committee structure is negotiated, that is, sizes and party shares are established, *after* member preferences have been submitted" to the committee-on-committees (p. 115). However, as "some excess demand for committee berths remains after committee sizes and party shares are determined," the committees-on-committees "must perform their allocation tasks under a scarcity constraint" (p. 117).

If party leaders do not "adjust perfectly" to the excess demand and maintain scarcity for some committee slots, Shepsle argues, it must be due to "counterexpansionist pressures." Three sets of actors bringing this pressure are identified: first, members on some committees will "wish to prevent the dissipation of their own monopoly on access to a policy subgovernment" and other privileges; second, "particular policy coalitions will oppose expansion because of their fear that it will be used in ways contrary to their preferences"; and third, the majority leadership may fear that the committee system will become unmanageable, since in the course of "currency inflation" each assignment "possesses less value in exchange" (pp. 118-119).

In testing his propositions by way of two statistical models Shepsle warns that the models "allow us to examine the impact of expansionist pressures directly but counterexpansionist pressures only indirectly" (p. 120). The first model, with change in Democratic seats from the previous congress as the dependent variable, includes such variables as chamber ratio change, freshman first-preference demand and lower-preference demand, nonfreshman demand, vacancies created by electoral defeat, potential vacancies stemming from nonfreshman transfers, and minority party "needs." Analysis shows that "the theory of leadership responsiveness is given strong empirical support" (p. 127). The second model, with change in committee size over and above that implied by the change in the party ratio, is less successful. Shepsle suggests that one source of misspecification may be related to the presence of countervailing pressures. But inclusion of transfer data in the model shows that "the countervailing-pressures argument is given only modest support." However, Shepsle finds "strong support" for two "important conclusions." First, "party leaders do pay strong attention to freshman lower-order requests," but not for those committees with high rankings on the transfer index (exclusive committees were excluded from the analysis). Second, especially on the high-ranking committees, "majority party leaders rarely accommodate minority needs outright; rather their financing of these needs involves extra seats for the majority party as well" (pp. 133-134).

Westefield's and Shepsle's work has been challenged by Whiteman (1983) on the ground that "serious anomalies exist within the current theory of committee size" (p. 49). He finds Shepsle's interpretation of his second model "somewhat unsettling. Found to be most strongly related to Democratic deviation from committee seat entitlements is Republican deviation from committee seat entitlement. But, since the sizes of Democratic and Republican delegations are negotiated simultaneously, this leaves the cause of both deviations still in doubt" (p. 52). Whiteman also deals with "two serious and unexamined anomalies within Westefield's original theory"—the fact that "many decisions to increase committee size create only minority party seats" and the fact that "most expansion in the last decade has been concentrated in the less prestigious committees" (p. 52).

Whiteman constructs and estimates a model based on both aggregate and committee-level data for the 81st (1949-1950) through the 95th (1977-1978) Congresses, giving him 298 individual cases of committee size decisions. The model is to test a "party ratio proposition" which takes account of both "a baseline level of existing seat commitments on every committee" and changes in the House party ratio: "The greater the change in House party ratio and the higher the level of baseline commitments, the greater the increase in committee seats" (pp. 55-56). This proposition is said to provide "an explanation for growth by committees with high baseline levels," but many increases occur on low prestige committees "whose membership is so transient that size increases are not likely to have been caused by high baseline levels" (p. 57).

Also counter to Westefield's assumption that members seek "good" assignments "where good is defined by the aggregate preferences of all members," Whiteman argues that "from the individual member's viewpoint, *any* additional committee assignment might be highly valued" (p. 57). This is so because "members demand additional committee seats to maintain the same electoral and legislative advantages as other members." However, growth in dual assignments will eventually imply decline because demand "is the product of two component factors: the intensity of member desire for second assignments and the number of members with such a desire. Both of these factors are functions of the proportion of members with dual assignments.... Demand, therefore, as the product of these two factors, continues to rise until the dwindling number of members without dual assignments causes it to decline" (p. 59).

The data seem to support the argument. Between 1955 and 1969 dual assignments gradually increased by 25 percent (from 25 percent to 50 percent); in the following six years they "jumped" by 30 percent; and "the modest 1977 increase, by which time 80% of the members had two seats, is also consistent with this account. With much of the demand for dual assignments apparently satisfied, the 1977 increase was the smallest in over a decade" (p. 60). Whiteman therefore formulates a "dual assignment proposition" which also takes account of the House rule that dual assignments are permissible only when one or both committees have low prestige. "As an increasing proportion of House members acquired two committee seats, these rules channeled much of the resulting committee size increase into the low-prestige committees. The organization of the House, in effect, created an artificial demand for seats on low prestige committees" (p. 61).

In the most recent contribution to the study of committee size and the assignment process, Ray and Smith (1984) argue that Westefield's theory of leadership accommodation requires "refinement" on theoretical grounds and that both his and Shepsle's studies, before aggregating the data, should have distinguished between the regimes of various House Speakers. Against Westefield they argue that leaders dispense committee assignments through size decisions not to obtain leverage and compliance but rather to maintain "party harmony." They reject the leverage thesis because, "except in the most unusual circumstances, members are never removed from committees against their will, [and] leaders retain little leverage over members once assignments have been made" (p. 680). As to Westefield's first proposition, they find that when majority and minority seats are kept separate, "majority seat losses approximate changes in the party ratio within the House, although House majority party leaders seldom reduce their members' individual shares" (p. 681). In regard to Westefield's second proposition, they find that "there is no tendency for more frequent expansion in the middle to upper range of prestige ordering." However, the least prestigious committees "exhibit more seat losses than other committees." This "strongly implies," Ray and Smith hold, "that leaders are more concerned about avoiding the wrath of members seeking coveted seats than they are about purchasing their support with seats" (p. 683). Finally, in regard to Westefield's third proposition, Ray and Smith present "three related pieces of circumstantial evidence ... that House Democrats have exceeded the point at which ... reform is necessary but have not seriously considered restructuring of even their own allotment of seats" (pp. 683-684). First, as the number of Democratic slots on nonexclusive committees of the 97th (1981-1982) Congress was twice the number of eligible members, "temporaries," so-called, received a third appointment. Second, there was in that Congress very little competition for assignments, and in half of the "contests" assignments were made by unanimous consent. And third, the Democratic leadership greatly overestimated the number of seats presumably needed to give all eligible Democrats a second assignment. Ray and Smith conclude from all this that the leaders "are unwilling or unable to disturb the norms of accommodation" (p. 686); that, counter to Westefield's "manipulative interpretation" of leaders' size decisions, "leaders do not reorganize committees or reduce the numbers of seats in order to make assignments more valuable"; and that there appears to be no evidence of leaders seeking to halt the devaluation of committee seats (p. 687).

Using request data from the 86th (1959-1960) through the 97th (1981-1982) Congresses, but not including the 91st, Ray and Smith report that their findings "are consistent with Shepsle's and based on a longer time series," but they challenge Shepsle's "questionable assumption that the relative importance of demand, changes in party strength, and other possible explanatory factors is constant over time" (p. 689). They therefore describe in some detail the circumstances under which the four recent Speakers sought to influence committee size decisions and estimate their model's parameters separately for each Speaker's regime. The findings

indicate that speakers have differed substantially in their approach to setting the size of the Democratic contingents on committees. It is not clear from this evidence, of course, whether the difference can be attributed to differences in leadership style or to differences in the political circumstances faced by the speakers, although other evidence strongly favors the latter interpretation. In either case, there is good reason to suspect that simple assumptions about a manipulating leadership do not capture the strategic considerations—or lack thereof—of leaders in the process of readjusting the committee system every two years. The party's electoral fortunes and the accommodation of rank-and-file demands are much more important determinants of change in the size of individual committees than is the desire of majority party leaders to have leverage over the rank and file (pp. 692-693).

Committee Stratification and Transfer Preferences

That legislative committee systems are stratified and that the status order of a committee system is not unrelated to the assignment process was part of conventional wisdom long before the relationship came to be systematically examined. The formal rules of legislatures often recognize more or less well rank-ordered categories of committee importance, sometimes giving some committees privileges denied to others. Similarly, limitations on multiple committee memberships point to the relative importance of committees with different jurisdictions. Interviews with legislators have shown that they are themselves more or less agreed, at least at a given time, on differences in the attractiveness of committee assignments. By far the most widely used technique to obtain an "objective" index of committee prestige is to examine transfer patterns from one committee to another. The index is thus predicated on the simple assumption that members prefer committees "higher" in a committee status system to those that are "lower." Whether members in fact hold the preferences they are assumed to hold required, as a first step, that the committee status system could be "objectively" established. To measure and somehow classify a legislature's committee stratification can therefore be considered an important research task in its own right.[6]

Whereas Goodwin (1959) limited himself to "net transfers per unit of membership," aggregated for the 81st (1949-1950) through 85th (1957-1958) Congresses, Matthews (1960) examined the net gains and losses of senatorial committee memberships through transfers from the 80th (1947-1948) through 84th (1955-1956) Congresses by way of a net turnover analysis. He found that transfers pointed to a pecking order, "each committee tending to lose members to those ranked above it while tending to gain members from those ranking below." The pattern, he notes, "is by no means perfect, but there is sufficient agreement in committee preferences to say that the committees are clearly stratified." The pecking order emerging from the study of transfer patterns is not the sole explanation of committee preferences, however. As Matthews points out, the existence of a status system "does not mean that all senators agree on their committee preferences" (p. 152), and he proceeds to other "influences" on assignment preferences (pp. 152-158).

Bullock and Sprague (1969), building on Goodwin and Matthews in trying to develop a more complex model of committee assignments, also proceed from the assumption that legislators are motivated to seek transfer from less to more desirable committees, but they seem to have been aware of the dilemma involved in imputing motivations from prestige rankings. Defining the assignment process as "the interaction between leaders and their strategies and members and their career aspirations," Bullock and Sprague build their theory on three variables—party seniority, committee prestige, and committee seniority. Party seniority is interpreted as a measure of individual influence or "clout." Committee seniority provides "a measure of the cost of a transfer or alternatively, a measure of investment in a committee career." And committee prestige is taken as "a measure of committee desirability and furnishes a means of imputing motivation to the participants in the transfer process" (pp. 494-495).[7]

To test a number of derivative propositions, Bullock and Sprague present data on the transfer behavior of Southern Democratic congressmen for the 80th (1947-1948) through 89th (1965-1966) Congresses. Comparison shows that the "preferred" committees of Southern Democrats are slightly different from those of other Democrats and Republicans, but the differences are slight (rho = .80 and .86 respectively). In summarizing their findings, Bullock and Sprague report that "motivation to seek committee reassignment is in part a function of differences in committee prestige" (p. 511); that "motivation to seek reassignment is in part a function of investment in a committee career"; and that "accumulated service in the House contributes to obtaining reassignments of high quality" (p. 512). Of course, data on failed attempts to transfer are missing.

Bullock (1973), following the procedures reported by Bullock and Sprague (1969) and treating reassignment as the dependent variable, examines its relationship with transfers' House and committee seniority, several constituency characteristics, and district electoral competition. In theoretical perspective, transfers are conceived as "occurring at the juncture of motivation and opportunity curves":

> A congressman may seek a new assignment to gain the power and prestige it offers, to serve his constituents' interests better, or to exert influences over matters which interest him. Opportunities for transfer may be conditioned by seniority and electoral security. Seniority may operate in two opposing fashions. As a congressman's seniority increases, his opportunities for transferring expand. Seats on the highly-prized, exclusive committees . . . are largely unattainable by congressmen who have not served an apprenticeship. For other committees, House experience, while not essential, may enhance one's position vis-a-vis any other claimants, although there is no certainty that it will do so (pp. 89-90).

Extending coverage from the 80th (1947-1948) to the 91st (1969-1970) Congresses, Bullock reports somewhat lower correlations for the comparisons between Southern Democrats and other Democrats and Republicans than had been found in his earlier study with Sprague (rho = .73 for Southern and other Democrats; .72 for Southern Democrats and Republicans; and .59 for non-Southern Democrats and Republicans).

Not all of Bullock's results can be indicated here. He finds an inverse relationship between committee seniority and frequency of transfer (p. 97). Congressmen are locked into their committee assignments early in their careers; those with less prestigious initial assignments are more likely to transfer; and Southern Democrats, who as freshmen are less likely to receive desired assignments, transfer in greater proportions than Northern Democrats or Republicans (pp. 97-100). Congressmen with low-prestige initial assignments are granted "promotions" earlier than their colleagues with better initial assignments, while the latter may transfer if they lack committee seniority (pp. 101-103). Southern Democrats appear to be more willing to leave committees on which they have accrued significant seniority—perhaps "because they could—at least in the past—anticipate longer House careers than other congressmen. Also with turnover rates lower among Southern Democrats, members of this group may have to wait longer for delegation or regional vacancies to occur on desired committees" (pp. 102-103).

An approach somewhat different from that of their predecessors in the study of committee stratification and transfer behavior appeared in research by Jewell and Chi-hung (1974). Raising essentially the same questions asked earlier, they made a novel contribution by tracing the movement of transfers from one committee to another on eight "levels"—from low to high—presumably indicative of committee attractiveness. The study is based on 180 transfer cases for the 88th (1963-1964) through 92d (1971-1972) Congresses. Jewell and Chi-hung worked with three separate measures: 1) the pattern of membership movement; 2) the "drawing power" of each committee; and 3) the "holding power" of each committee. In regard to the first measure,

FIGURE 1

Pattern of Movements Among U.S. House Committees,
88th-92d Congresses[a]

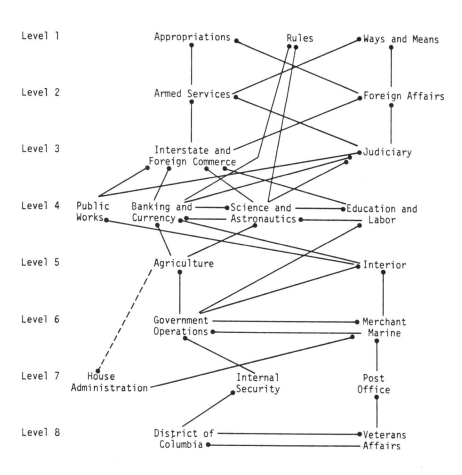

[a]Reprinted from Jewell and Chi-hung, 1974.

"each committee lost members only to committees on a higher level and got members only from lower-level committees," except for a few cases of lateral transfer on the same level (pp. 435-436). The diagram emerging from the analysis is reproduced in Figure 1.

Because the cost of transfer varies with seniority, the index of drawing power simultaneously measures the proportion of vacancies filled by transfers (rather than freshmen) and the amount of seniority given up by the transfers. Comparing the results of the drawing power index with the level of movement measure, Jewell and Chi-hung find that "the top seven committees (on the drawing power index) are the same ones found in the three top levels of Figure 1, and the rank order among these seven committees is generally the same in both. . . . Two committees, Ways and Means and Appropriations, attracted more than one-third of those shifting committees and over half of those giving up more than one term of seniority" (p. 439).

The purpose of the third measure, holding power, is to determine the likelihood that "a member will stay on a committee as long as he remains in Congress and what the variations are among committees." The index is the turnover rate, which "takes account of the size of the committee, while excluding from consideration members who left the Congress." Not surprisingly, the most attractive committees are also the most stable: "The top three committees had no losses. . . . The next four committees are the same ones that ranked high in drawing power and were in the second and third level of Figure 1, and the rankings among them have changed only slightly. The rankings of the 13 remaining committees for holding power, however, do not coincide very well with either the rankings for drawing power or the levels in tracing patterns of movement (pp. 439-440).

Jewell and Chi-hung offer several reasons for the last result—a member's willingness to sacrifice seniority, or willingness to give up two lower-ranked committees for the opportunity to move to a third; avoidance of undue work load on two major committees; or the rule that service on two committees is permissible only if one of them is a minor or nonexclusive committee. In short, "the index of holding power is a less precise measure of committee attractiveness than drawing power because members often are forced to leave a middle-range committee in order to gain membership on a higher ranking one" (p. 440).

Previous studies of transfer behavior, writes Shepsle (1978), "with the notable exception of Jewell and Chi-hung (1974), give a very static and simplified view of mobility in the committee opportunity structure" (p. 58). Shepsle finds it "useful to regard a committee as a 'queue' and to conceive of nonfreshman request decisions as involving a consideration of the benefits and costs of queue-switching" (p. 43). The process is presumably "dynamic" because "the costs and benefits of the queue . . . are constantly changing"

(p. 58). The queue analogy is elaborated: "length of continuous committee service determines queue position; movement along the queue depends upon a member's own survival characteristics and those of his colleagues ahead of him in the queue; the benefits of waiting in the queue depend on one's goals and queue position, the latter of which, in turn, depends on continuous time in the queue; and the real costs of waiting in the queue are the foregone opportunities offered by other queues" (p. 43). Queue switching reveals a transfer preference that has one of several sources—dissatisfaction with a freshman assignment; discounted "interest" as a freshman due to competition and, therefore, requests that are insincere; a nonfreshman's greater ability to act upon his interest; and, most obviously, changing goals. In a first test, Shepsle hypothesizes that "freshman request lists will tend to be longer than nonfreshman request lists." He finds, aggregating the data over eight congresses from 1959 to 1974, that "while more than nine out of every ten nonfreshmen seeking transfers submit short lists (two or fewer requests), only 39% of all freshmen behave similarly" (pp. 50-51).

In contrast to other studies of committee transfers, Shepsle's research deals with revealed preference for transfer. Actual transfers, "are only the tip of the iceberg. While about half of those who request transfers have their requests honored . . ., half do not" (p. 54). Moreover, not all transfers have been requested, since some members are asked to transfer by the committee-on-committees or the leadership. Rank-ordering the committees according to "relative popularity," Shepsle finds that "the general pattern of revealed transfers is unidirectional: committees lower down on the list serve as suppliers for those higher up." However, "despite this general pattern, the rank ordering, per se, does not always have an unequivocal meaning" (p. 55). "The popularity ordering, though an aggregate indicator, does not imply homogeneity of tastes, interests, or objectives" (p. 56). Analysis of transfer opportunities shows that a declining proportion of members seek transfers over time, and that those seeking them are "more likely to seek exclusive committee transfers if they seek any at all" (p. 57). After examining some typical and atypical cases, Shepsle reaches two conclusions. First, initial assignments do not lock members into particular institutional careers—for whatever reasons, "opportunities to alter one's committee portfolio are available and frequently taken advantage of." Second, committee personnel is highly variable and shifting from congress to congress—"nearly 40 percent of all committee personnel changes are due to internal movement . . . [that] portray the committees of Congress as a system in flux. As in other 'ambition systems', the patterns of career mobility are myriad" (pp. 61-62).

Addressing the argument more formally, Shepsle tests three propositions:

I. The proportion of members maintaining the status quo is a declining function of time (number of opportunities).

II. The proportion of members taking the status quo option is an increasing function of wealth. The "wealth effect" is a decreasing function of time (number of opportunities).

III. The status of the queue for which a transfer preference is revealed is an increasing function of wealth and time (number of opportunities) (pp. 94-95).

Three reasons are offered for the first proposition: acquisitiveness, changing objectives, and learning (pp. 96-98). Analysis shows that "*opportunities matter*. Independently of other factors, with increasing opportunities a member is less likely to maintain his 'freshman wealth'. . . . Use of both dual service and transfer options increases with opportunities as expected" (pp. 98-99). In regard to the second proposition, "wealth," subjectively defined, also has the expected effect: "the wealthy stay put and the poor try to move." If a "wealthy" member moves, he "faces substantial opportunity costs in seeking change, namely, accrued seniority" (p. 99). The third proposition means that "the rich and senior will transfer only for the big prizes." The data provide empirical support: "there is a monotonically increasing relationship between wealth and proportion of exclusive-committee revealed preferences. The wealthy seek the exclusive committees at a 58% rate, the moderately wealthy at a 40% rate, and the poor at a 35% rate" (p. 101).

Assignments, Reelection, and Constituency Interests

Among the many considerations presumably guiding the committees-on-committees in making assignments, none has proved to be more fragile than the "re-election hypothesis," so-called, also sometimes referred to, after its original exponents, as the "Masters-Clapp hypothesis." Basing his statement of the hypothesis on interview data, Masters (1961) was emphatic in asserting that "the most important single factor in distributing assignments to all other [i.e., nonexclusive] committees is whether a particular place will help to insure the reelection of the member in question" (p. 354). Clapp (1964) qualifies the hypothesis somewhat but seems to have it found confirmed in his round-table discussions with congressmen: "Where competition for vacancies exists, choice assignments are often given to members representing 'marginal' congressional districts as opposed to those from districts firmly held by their party" (p. 234).

The Masters-Clapp hypothesis remained unchallenged until it was systematically examined by Bullock (1972) in a study of freshman assignments and, subsequently, in a study of nonfreshman reassignments (Bullock, 1973). Bullock (1972) initially tests the null hypothesis that "narrowly elected and safe freshmen are given 'good' assignments at the same rates" (p. 1002). Rejection of the hypothesis would support the Masters-Clapp hypothesis.

Examining 830 assignments for 688 freshman House members from the 80th (1947-1948) through 90th (1967-1968) Congresses, Bullock found 366 to be narrowly elected, accounting for 435 assignments. In regard to the "top, duty, and public works" committees, he analyzes the assignments of all freshmen. For these committees, he finds, "there is only one instance in which the null hypothesis can be rejected, and it does not support Masters-Clapp" (1972, p. 1002). Testing the hypothesis was problematic, however, because reelection is not independent of a congressman's "constituency interest," which, in fact, is another criterion for freshman assignments. It seemed desirable, therefore, to control for the interest variable. Bullock selects five committees—Agriculture, Merchant Marine and Fisheries, Banking and Currency, Interior, and Education and Labor—which permit identification of members as "interesteds" and others. "If a significantly larger proportion of narrowly elected interesteds than safe interesteds is assigned to the committee, we have support for the Masters-Clapp re-election promotion hypothesis, that is, that assignments are made to improve re-election chances" (p. 998). Rather than relying on the method for ranking committees and defining a "good" appointment accordingly, Bullock thus treats constituency interest as the choice criterion. Looking only at the narrowly-elected and safely-elected "interesteds," then, Bullock finds that "a significant difference occurred only for the Democratic appointees to Education and Labor. [Moreover], safe rather than marginal Democrats are overrepresented on the committee." Although there were some tendentious but statistically not significant differences, "the data do not support the Masters-Clapp generalization" (p. 1002). In regard to the duty committees, Bullock is also unable to reject the null hypothesis: "That narrowly elected and safe freshmen are equally likely to begin service on these committees is further evidence that the Masters-Clapp hypothesis is inaccurate" (pp. 1003-1004).

In a subsequent study, Bullock (1973) also finds no support for the reelection hypothesis in the case of nonfreshman transfers. He suggests that the findings "raise serious questions about the accuracy of the assertion that congressmen from marginal districts are denied seats on the most prestigious committees" (p. 107). As he also points out, "while 73 percent of the congressmen placed on Appropriations and 83 percent of the Ways and Means appointees were from safe districts,[8] the same is true of 81 percent of those transferring to low-prestige committees" (p. 107). Bullock again seeks reasons why the reelection hypothesis may have held sway. First, "perhaps the interview responses upon which the Masters generalization is based are rationalizations offered by those who for other reasons had their claims for reassignment to an exclusive committee rejected." Second, "electoral security does not seem to determine the quality of one's reassignment, perhaps because more than 90 percent of the incumbents typically triumph in re-election bids" (pp. 107-108).

Bullock's negative findings concerning the reelection hypothesis seemed to be persuasive, but they were soon somewhat contradicted by findings that were based on legislators' requests rather than on assignments alone. Rohde and Shepsle (1973), looking at the assignment process from the perspective of the Democratic Committee-on-Committees, said to be interested in "party maintenance," argue that "it is in the interest of most Committee members [i.e., of the CC] to help insure the reelection of party colleagues" and that "clearly, the members most in need of help are those who were elected by the smallest margin" (p. 900). Basing their analysis on request data for 106 freshmen and 89 nonfreshmen in the 86th (1959-1960) through 88th (1963-1964) and the 90th (1967-1968) Congresses, they find that "marginal freshmen are slightly less likely to fail to receive a requested committee and are much more likely to receive their first choice than are safe freshmen." Moreover, "marginal nonfreshmen are *much* less likely to receive no choice than are safe nonfreshmen, but they are about equally likely to receive their first choice as are safe nonfreshmen." In regard to first choice, "safe freshmen are treated about the same as marginal nonfreshmen." Rohde and Shepsle comment that "when one recalls that these nonfreshmen, even though they are marginal, have demonstrated (at least once) their ability to get re-elected, it does not seem surprising that these two groups are about equally successful" (p. 900).

To test the hypothesis that "good" committee assignments promote reelection, Bullock (1972) compares the reelection rates of marginal freshmen with those having other appointments. Analysis failed "to produce a single statistically significant difference in the re-election rates of marginal freshmen depending on their committee assignments. . . . Rarely do committee assignments seem to help the narrowly elected win second terms" (p. 1004). Fowler, Douglass, and Clark (1980) adopt a somewhat different research design "by treating electoral margins as the dependent rather than independent variable" (pp. 311-312). Employing request data for all members, freshmen and nonfreshmen, in the 86th (1959-1960) through 94th (1975-1976) Congresses, they test the hypothesis that "success in obtaining committee requests exerts little direct effect on electoral margins" (p. 312), having stated earlier that "opportunities for winning voter approval are so widely available to members of Congress that committee choice per se would exert little systematic influence on electoral outcomes" (p. 309). On having obtained rather meager results, they conclude that "the wide availability of opportunities for members of the House of Representatives to curry favor with constituents creates difficulties in assessing the electoral impact of any one institutional feature—even one so distinctive as the committee system" (p. 319).

The discrepancy between the cognitive data obtained in interviews and the behavioral request or actual assignment data is evident in a study by

Smith and Ray (1983). Reporting a tally of the comments made about nominees in committee-on-committee discussion for all committees (except Appropriations and Ways and Means) in the post-reform 97th (1981-1982) Congress, Smith and Ray find that "paralleling Masters' (1961) interview results for the 1950s, the electoral needs of nominees were the most common argument made on their behalf" (p. 222). In their own mammoth regression model for Democratic committee assignments in the 95th (1977-1978) through 97th (1981-1982) Congresses, a model which introduces some 25 variables, they find "surprisingly, only one additional factor, electoral marginality, is significant for non-freshmen in contested decisions and, even more surprisingly, it is of the unexpected sign" (p. 235). The finding seems to have been a "surprise" only because the investigators' expectation was evidently based on the previous cognitive datum that "electoral needs" were arguments put forward in support of members' assignment requests.

While the reelection hypothesis has been shattered, there is every reason to believe that legislators' "constituency concerns" give guidance to both assignment seekers and the committees-on-committees. The evidence is both negative and positive. On the one hand, some committees are purposefully composed of members who, if at all possible, do not have a constituency stake in a committee's work. On the other hand, some committees are composed of members from constituencies which have a direct interest in a committee's jurisdiction, and their members are "expected" to represent these constituency interests on the committee. This has been recognized since Masters (1961, pp. 353-355) wrote about it. If constituency interest and committee specialization are matched, reelection may be more likely, but it can just as well be argued that the "match" is functionally plausible or desirable. As Masters pointed out in regard to the explosive issues before the Education and Labor Committee of the 1950s, assignment to the committee "has called for the most careful attention to the constituencies of the applicants. . . . This assignment is no place for a neutral when there are so many belligerents around" (p. 354).

The disjunction between committee assignments and reelection considerations thus does not negate a relationship between assignments and constituency considerations that may exist for representational reasons. While freshmen have little chance to be appointed to the exclusive committees, Bullock (1972) points out, "other assignments draw the attention of representatives with certain types of districts" (p. 999). He finds that in the case of a number of "special appeal committees," freshmen placed on the committees "for which constituency characteristics were isolated typically represent districts evincing the relevant feature" (p. 1000). Again, in his study of transfers, Bullock (1973) reports that while congressmen generally seek to transfer from less to more prestigious committees, "a second basis is the desire to work on a committee which offers an opportunity to serve one's district" (p. 109). Over time, he suggests, constituency considerations guiding committee selection may "dissipate"; but he also intimates that his findings "suggest some possible implications for the policy-making activities of committees"—a theme which he does not pursue. Rohde and Shepsle (1973), though emphasizing reelection as a "goal," report that "we can classify members according to the kinds of districts they represent in order to demonstrate the extent to which 'committee popularity' varies with constituency types" (p. 893).

One of the difficulties involved in relevant research is the crudeness of the indicators used to characterize "constituency interests"—something recognized by most investigators. For instance, Shepsle classifies districts according to region and population per square mile to get at the "interest" variable. A frequent example for the "utility" of such measures is invariably the Interior Committee; for instance, Rohde and Shepsle (1973) report that this committee "was the most requested for both Midwestern and Western congressmen from sparsely populated districts." And, they continue, "the reason is clear: Congressmen from these constituencies can probably serve the interests of their districts better on that committee than on any other" (p. 894). But regions are not "constituencies," and it is easy to see why "representation" in any other than its descriptive-statistical sense seems to have little purchasing power in the committee assignment studies.

Not the unfolding of representation but "committee attractiveness" has therefore been the focus of most assignment studies, as it is in Rohde and Shepsle's research. For instance, after partitioning members requesting assignments to five committees (Banking and Currency, Education and Labor, Armed Services, Interior, and Agriculture) into "interesteds" and "indifferents," Rohde and Shepsle report that "although the relationships between ascribed interest and request behavior varies from committee to committee, it is always in the predicted direction and quite strong" (1973, pp. 895-896). As "government-by-committee" is being supplemented by "government-by-subcommittee," one should expect representation to be an even more critical issue. Davidson (1981) who has carefully monitored changes at the committee system level, anticipates the shape of things to come.

Under pressure from members and factions desiring representation, party leaders not only have allowed assignments to proliferate but have tended to accede to members' preferences for assignments. Inevitably, this means that legislators gravitate to those committees with which they, or their constituents, have the greatest affinity. Thus, many congressional workgroups are not microcosms of the parent houses, but are biased in one way or another (p. 111).

Constituency interest and the "goal of reelection" appear to be so closely linked that separating one out from the other is difficult indeed. At issue, from a causal point of view, is what comes first. Careful examination of Fenno's (1973) treatment of the Post Office and Interior committees, and especially of the latter, symptomizes the difficulty. Congressmen seeking membership on these committees "have the primary goal of helping their constituents and thereby insuring their re-election," Fenno writes (p. 5). The causal proposition seems quite explicit; the more a representative helps his constituents by service on a committee relevant to the interests of his district or constituency, the more likely it is that his reelection is insured. Making constituency service a "function of" the "goal" of reelection is a teleological procedure. In fact, all of Fenno's subsequent discussion of the Interior Committee points to the representational more than to the electoral link between this committee's members and their constituencies.

In view of these difficulties, it is most interesting to note, perhaps emphasize, that in a recent text on *Committees in Congress* (Smith and Deering, 1984), the authors, though in general following Fenno's three types of "member goals," bid farewell to the "reelection label," and that they do so without much ado. Referring to a table reporting their own research on "Committee Preference Motivation Combinations, 1982," they write, "The 'constituency' label has replaced the 'reelection' label . . . because many members mention a richer set of constituency-oriented motivations than the reelection label suggests" (p. 85). As if somewhat embarrassed by this sleight-of-hand substitution of labels (whose conceptual content and meaning should be important), they immediately add, rather apologetically, "Even so, the vast majority of constituency-oriented motivations are defined in terms of electoral needs" (p. 85). Presumably, what they mean by "are defined in terms of" are the definitions given by the respondents, but this only suggests that what words "say" and what they "mean" are not necessarily the same thing. Of course, reelection is not just a necessary condition, it is the necessary condition for anything else, including achieving influence in a legislature, or making policy there, or representing, in one way or another, clientele or constituency interests. To elevate reelection into a "goal" constitutes a truism, as if one were to say that eating or sleeping are "goals." Because legislators recite reelection as a "goal" over and over again, whether their reelection is really in jeopardy or not, even sophisticated political scientists seem to believe that reelection can serve as an independent variable in a model of committee assignments. The evidence, especially from Bullock (1972, 1973), is contrary. Even Fenno (1973) finally concedes, "Objectively, it might be noted, there is no clear evidence that Interior membership has an 'appreciable impact' on a Westerner's re-election chances" (p. 272).

A number of studies conducted in the 1970s have been concerned with constituency interest representation on particular committees and the distribution of benefits that may or may not accrue to certain types of districts. While some studies find that constituency representation on particular committees seems to determine the geographic distribution of federal spending, others seem to show no such effect. However, these studies are not directly concerned with the assignment process but rather with the effect of extant committee membership composition on policy outcomes. One exception is research by Ray (1980) which raises the question of "whether the pre-existing geographic distribution of federal spending dictates representatives' committee assignments" (p. 495). This "recruitment hypothesis," Ray argues, "places the geographic distribution of federal outlays and congressional committee assignments in the correct causal relationship" (p. 496).

Ray's dependent variable is assignment requests, ignoring their preference orderings, made by House Democratic freshmen in the 92d (1971-1972) to 94th (1975-1976) Congresses. The independent variable is federal outlays in congressional districts for the preceding election years. For the purpose of analysis, each spending area is paired with the relevant committee (Agriculture, Armed Services, Education and Labor, Banking and Currency, Interior, and Veterans Affairs). If the recruitment hypothesis is valid, "the geographic distribution of federal spending within each of these domains should predict which freshmen will, and which will not, request assignment to the associated committees" (p. 497).

Straightforward comparisons show, as a first finding and as hypothesized, that "there is a tendency for members from districts with greater-than-average involvements in a committee's jurisdiction to be over-represented among those seeking assignments" (p. 498). The "fit" is best for Agriculture and Education and Labor (72 and 63 percent, respectively); it "reflects" the weighted average of 57 percent for all congresses in the cases of Armed Services and Veterans Affairs (56 and 55 percent, respectively); but it is relatively poor for Interior (50 percent) and very poor for Banking and Currency (37 percent). Plausible explanations are given for the poor fits:

Most of the incorrect predictions for Banking involved representatives from suburban districts . . . [who] may be just as concerned with HUD activities as those representing central cities since entire metropolitan areas are affected by outlays for urban redevelopment. The poor fit for Interior results from the extraordinary large number of freshmen who made this request in the 94th Congress. Since this was the first class elected after the OPEC oil embargo, the requests which do not fit the hypothesis may reflect heightened constituent (and member) concern about the energy crisis (p. 498).

Given these findings, Ray infers that the correlation between the geographic distribution of federal spending and committee assignments "may in fact exist because representatives follow district interest, rather than because they alter the expenditure process to favor their own constituencies" (p. 498).

However, a second requirement in testing the recruitment hypothesis is to show that "those elected from districts with the largest investments in

given spending areas submit the 'appropriate' requests" (pp. 498-500). To test
for this requirement, Ray introduces into a probit analysis three control
variables—electoral insecurity, delegation membership, and intradelegation
competition. Separate equations for each committee support the hypothesis
that freshman committee requests are determined by district interests. Ray
reports R^2s which, in each instance, are quite low (ranging from .01 to .27).
However, "never less than three-quarters of the freshmen's preferences and
non-preferences were predicted correctly. In one case (Veterans Affairs) this
percentage reaches 93. Overall, the proportion predicted accurately is .83"
(p. 506). Ray concludes:

Considering the multitude of motivations for selecting committee assignments and the
competing claims that pull members toward several different assignments, district interests have been demonstrated to be a viable, and frequently used, determinant of committee selection. The "base," i.e., the existing geographic distribution of federal spending,
strongly affects which institutional positions Congress members prefer and secure. It
appears that, as a general rule, powerful positions are acquired because of the congressional district's involvement in federal activities, rather than the reverse as is commonly
believed (pp. 507-508).

Motivations, Preferences, Goals

Many of the studies reviewed so far as well as others still to be considered make assumptions about the motivations, preferences, and goals of
legislators requesting particular assignments. As one examines the literature,
one is impressed by the lack of sharp definitions of the concepts, their often
interchanged usage, and the questionable character of the assumptions made
concerning them. Only the studies based on requests interpreted as revealed
preferences are unambiguous as long as they do not go beyond what the data
themselves say, but when they do they seem to make for an even longer chain
of inferences about motivations and/or goals than the studies based only on
assignment information alone.

The three concepts refer to three quite different, if interlocking,
components of a psychology of assignments which, moreover, are temporally
distinct. Motivations are stimuli for behavior or "predispositions" which are
of the "past." Preferences are contemporary statements of choice to the
effect that something is valued "over" something else. Finally, goals refer
to the "end" toward which behavior is directed and are, therefore, a matter
of the future. Just as motivations or predispositions may or may not be linked
to preferences, so the preference order may or may not be linked to the goals
that are sought or actually obtained. Different motivations may facilitate or
hinder the translation of preferences into goals. Given the complexity of the
psychological and behavioral processes involved, only hinted at here, it is
important to pay close attention to the use made of the three concepts in
studies of committee assignments.

Fenno (1973) posited that "of all the goals espoused by members of the House, three are basic. They are *re-election, influence within the House, and good public policy*." He suggests that "all congressmen probably hold all three goals. But each congressman has his own mix of priorities and intensities—a mix which may, of course, change over time." He points out that "the opportunity to achieve the three goals varies widely among committees." From these two premises Fenno deduces that "House members, therefore, match their individual patterns of aspiration (read: goals) to the diverse patterns of opportunity presented by House committees. The matching process usually takes place as a congressman seeks an original assignment or a transfer to a committee he believes well suited to his goals." However, he immediately and significantly qualifies: "But it [the matching] may occur when a congressman adjusts his personal aspirations, temporarily or permanently, to fit the opportunities offered by the committee where he happens to be" (pp. 1-2). The conceptual problem should be clear: if the prediction made in the qualifying statement comes true, what has taken place is also a change in the legislator's preference structure. Only a nonpreferred committee would stimulate an "adjustment" of personal goals or aspirations; or, put another way, a member who obtained his preferred committee would have no reason to change his goals.

In fact, the three goal variables Fenno posits have little to do with his own analysis of recruitment to committees, something largely ignored by investigators trying to use the goal typology in studying assignments to committees. He develops a typology of "recruitment methods" that classifies committee members into four categories: 1) the "co-opted" who "are taken off the committee on which they sit, without their request, and assigned to another committee"; 2) "self-starters" who "decide on their own to seek a committee assignment"; 3) "inner circle choices" who "have the idea (of seeking a certain assignment) suggested to them by someone else"; and 4) "assigned members" who "are placed on a committee they did not request" (pp. 20-21). Overall, of 179 cases, 115 or 64 percent were "self-starters"; it is to them alone, then, that the triple-goal typology might be applied. However, Fenno himself uses the recruitment typology as sparingly as the goal typology when he is concerned with the assignment process. He notes that behavioral style—being cooperative, reasonable, responsive, and so on— seems to have more to do with assignment to the money committees than do preassignment goals (which are not even mentioned).

Some of the conceptual difficulties involved in subsequent studies of either the motivations, goals, or preferences of members as they seek assignments undoubtedly stem from inadvertent misuse of Fenno's typology of member goals. Although, as noted, Fenno himself uses the typology only sparingly in his very limited observations on recruitment to one or another committee, later investigations (like Bullock, 1976) are said "to test Richard Fenno's (1973) well-known typology of committee motivations" (Smith and Deering, 1983, p. 271). Apart from the confusion of "goals" and "motivations" here, it is by no means clear that Fenno considered the goal typology a useful means for studying assignments as such because, for that purpose and as noted, he introduced the "recruitment method typology." Moreover, there is simply no way to determine whether the "goals" which Fenno elicited in his interviews referred to the goals members may have had when entering Congress or seeking a transfer or whether they referred to their goals at the time of the interview, when they had served for more or less time on a committee.

Just what difficulties are inherent in Fenno's goal typology when the effort is made to apply it in a study of committee recruitment using systematically collected quantitative data is evident in a case study by Perkins (1981) of the Judiciary Committee, called a "mixed goals committee." Perkins's starting point is the empirical observation that beginning with the 93d (1973-1974) Congress "unexpected" recruitment problems came to characterize a committee that "has traditionally been a choice committee" (p. 348). After suggesting some "explanations" for the committee's new unpopularity—its having to deal with politically unattractive issues, and so on—Perkins offers an additional explanation which, she says, "relies" on Fenno (pp. 349-350).

Interviews were conducted with 36 members of the Judiciary Committee from the 92d (1971-1972) and 93d (1973-1974) Congresses, as well as with staff members, legal counsels, lobbyists, and reporters. Perkins asked a battery of questions considerably more detailed than the questions asked by Fenno (1973) and Bullock (1976). What puzzled Perkins was that, on the one hand, a large group of Judiciary members was primarily interested in reelection and constituency service but that, on the other hand, this goal "could not be advanced much through their membership in the Judiciary Committee" (p. 352). Moreover, Perkins finds no support for Fenno's "explanation" of "adjusted aspirations."

After illustrating that members may choose or stay on a committee like Judiciary for reasons of prestige, training, or seniority, Perkins suggests that "the lack of fit between Judiciary Committee jurisdiction and the goals of large numbers of members attracted to the committee was important to the drop in Judiciary Committee desirability after the 92nd Congress" (pp. 359-360). She then discovers "the final piece of the puzzle" in the departure of chairman Emanuel Celler and the ascension to the chair of Peter Rodino. She concludes that "an important factor in the committee's drop in popularity was its change from a policy oriented chairman to a re-election oriented one in the 93rd Congress. . . . Committee prestige began to change, partisanship rose, and even in the 93rd Congress the word was verbally passed around that all freshman members were not on the committee at their own request" (pp. 361-362).

Bullock (1976), also taking off from Fenno's typology of goals in a study of 52 freshmen during Fall 1971,[9] speaks of "motivations" rather than "goals." He suggests that Fenno "may have slightly biased his results by assuming that his respondents all sought the committees they sat on by asking, 'Why did you want to get on the _____ committee in the first place?' . . . If the questioner assumes that the respondent wanted a particular assignment, the respondent may feel compelled to offer some rationale" (p. 202). Insofar as Bullock is correct, then, what Fenno reported, at least as far as assignments are concerned, are postappointment rationalizations which, indeed, are difficult to interpret as "motivations" (or, for that matter, as "goals").

Bullock claims to be "building" on Fenno's work, though his focus is on a class of freshmen rather than on members of particular committees. This approach "permits learning about a range of preferences and the motives behind each." He also emphasizes that he asked somewhat different questions: "What committees did you want to serve on? Why?" Bullock argues that in contrast to Fenno's design, "which led to the conclusion that each committee is desired by some set of legislators, the approach followed here will indicate whether some committees are generally perceived as having little value" (p. 202). Some of the answers, Bullock reports, included preferences that were not formally submitted "because freshmen were convinced that there was no chance of the request being honored." Bullock, then, proposes to analyze what he calls "preference motives" by way of Fenno's goal typology (p. 203). As in his earlier studies (1972, 1973), Bullock finds that "although re-election was highly ranked, it was not the most common motivation expressed by freshmen in explaining their committee preferences" (p. 205). To explore this matter further, Bullock divides the freshmen into four categories from electorally least to electorally most secure. He hypothesizes and finds that "overall, the general pattern is for the frequency of the re-election promotion motive to increase with electoral marginality" (p. 207).

That Shepsle's (1978) treatment of the issues involved in the motivation-preference-goal syndrome would be more sophisticated than that of his predecessors is not surprising: he had the benefit of their errors but also the benefit of a genuine theory of social choice and an excellent empirical data base. It is difficult and perhaps dangerous to extract relevant passages from Shepsle's tightly reasoned and complex modeling of the entire assignment process. The point to be made here is that he clearly distinguishes between "revealed preferences" (requests) on the one hand and "preferences" on the other hand. The member's request list must therefore be distinguished from his "real" preferences, for the request list is "a complicated mix of individual goals and ambitions, modified by newly acquired advice and information, and tempered by political realities." But both preferences and requests must not be confused with motivations. "Member requests are motivated chiefly by the kind of district they represent and their personal background and experiences" (p. 40). Revealed preferences (requests) "reflect the operational compromises and tradeoffs of instrumental behavior in a context of competition for scarce committee berths" (p. 41).

Shepsle clearly rejects the rather simple-minded view of a symmetry between requests for assignments and goals that others have read into Fenno's triple-goal typology. The diversity of freshman requests "mirrors the variety of goals, interests, and concerns entertained by members that are differentially served by the committees. Moreover, even for those members who share goals in common, it is not unusual to find them revealing preferences for different committees" (p. 47). In developing a model for freshman requests, therefore, Shepsle suggests that two estimation problems are involved in the freshman's request decision: first, a "value problem" which relates to "discovering which committees will serve as useful vehicles for the accomplishment of personal goals and objectives"; and, second, a "discounting problem" which concerns "how much weight he should attach to these valuations in his final request list in light of assignment likelihoods" (p. 63).

Again in connection with the request behavior of nonfreshmen, Shepsle emphasizes the heterogeneity of those seeking transfers. "With the possible exception of the general gravitation toward the exclusive committees, it is the diversity of interests, and the differing extent to which committees are believed to serve those diverse interests, that is the important point" (p. 103). Comparing freshman and nonfreshman requests he characterizes the several themes of his request analysis

as a system that is both complex and dynamic. Freshman requests are a one-shot affair; the temporal dimension plays no significant role either in affecting behavior or explaining it. The complexity of freshman requests, moreover, derives not from the heterogeneity of *objectives* (most freshmen single-mindedly seek reelection), but rather from the heterogeneity of *interests* that endow the reelection objective with behavioral meaning. With nonfreshman transfer and dual-service behavior, on the other hand, we have a more complicated pattern of changing interests, changing objectives, multiplying opportunities, and an increased number of behavioral options (pp. 103-104).

The most significant aspect of Shepsle's analysis of whatever considerations may be underlying requests—whether we think of motivations, preferences, or goals—is that his final assessment of the effect of personal characteristics on assignment success is "primarily negative" (p. 198).

Shepsle's structural argument was put to a test in a study of freshman preferences and assignments in the 97th (1981-1982) Congress by Smith and Deering (1983), though it is more directly a replication, modification, and extension of Bullock's (1976) analysis of freshmen in the 92d (1971-1972)

Congress. In any case, the reforms of the 1970s had presumably created a different structural environment and also changed the structure of the assignment process itself. In their own words, Smith and Deering wanted to find out "whether changes in House procedures and policy agendas had affected the reasons why members seek their committee assignments" and "how clearly the three motivations examined by Fenno and Bullock (reelection, policy, prestige) could be distinguished as motives for seeking these appointments" (p. 271). They are most explicit in emphasizing that "the central question . . . is why members prefer the committees they do, rather than why they request the committees they actually request or what goals they pursue after assignment" (p. 272). The latter question is the one that had been left most ambiguous in Fenno's discussion of assignments.

Smith and Deering offer "at least three important reasons" for expecting changes to have occurred in the motives of new congressmen for preferring some committees over others as a result of the 1970s reforms:

First, the leadership role played by full committee chairmen has been weakened, hence, there are weaker constraints on the goals that committee members can pursue. Second, more and better committee seats are available for members of Congress; hence, members— especially House Democrats have more reason to consider the full range of their goals when they calculate the value of assignments. Third, and perhaps most important, the policy agendas of several committees have changed; hence, the mix of goals envisioned by new members of these committees may have changed, since issues structure the opportunities to pursue certain goals (pp. 271-272).

Turning to "several ambiguities" in the triple-goal typology, Smith and Deering report "a richer set of district-oriented motivations . . . than the straightforward label 'reelection' suggests. Members mentioned two other district-oriented motivations: predecessor clues and a delegate-model philosophy." Smith and Deering claim to have found these differences in district-oriented motivations because they "inquired about motives for preferring a committee assignment rather than about goals pursued after assignment." However, they qualify, "Despite these variations, the vast majority of district-oriented motivations have reelection in view," in two senses. "In the most frequent, positive sense, members seek to do something on the sought-after committee which will benefit their districts and for which they can claim credit (Mayhew, 1974). In the negative sense, however, some members clearly believe that their chances for reelection will be appreciably reduced by failure to obtain a particular assignment" (p. 273).

Norms, Rules, Practices

In his agenda-setting study of the committee assignment process, Masters (1961) challenged the long-held supposition that assignments "are made primarily on the basis of seniority." Continuous service, he pointed out, "insures a member of his place on a committee once he is assigned, but seniority may have very little to do with transfers to other committees, and it has virtually nothing to do with the assignment of freshman members" (p. 345). There are, of course, many "rules" (formal regulations) and "practices" (informal patterns of behavior) that shape the assignment process. These rules and practices are subject to more or less frequent changes, and they are described in more or less detail in the literature on assignments, in most detail by Shepsle (1978), but also for the early decades of the congressional committee system by Cooper (1970). However, with some rare exceptions, norms, rules, and practices are seldom treated as variables in systematic studies of the assignment process. This makes it difficult to compare studies across time, even when they are based on time-series data.

Concepts like "practice," "rule," "custom," or "norm" are often used interchangeably without sharp definitions having been given; and, perhaps, no sharp definitions are possible, though intuitively one would expect practices to be most flexible, rules to be amendable, customs to be relatively immutable, and norms to be least violable. Hinckley (1978), for instance, writes that "legislatures, like other human organizations, are social systems characterized by stable patterns of action and by widely shared standards of what that action should be. These standards are norms. Norms are informal rules, frequently unspoken because they need not be spoken, which may govern more effectively than any written rule. They prescribe 'how things are done around here'" (p. 59). But just what a "norm" in the evaluative sense is cannot be simply inferred from "stable patterns of action" or, as one can say, from those behavioral regularities which are "normal" in the statistical sense. There is, of course, a subtle interchange between norms as "values" and norms as "regularities," but the interplay remains something of an unknown. The study of norms as "widely shared standards" for appropriate behavior is, therefore, facilitated by a situation in which a norm has been violated, and the violation leads to sanctions. Huitt's (1957) study of the "Morse Committee Assignment Controversy" is the classical study of such a situation. In general, then, norms in the evaluative sense are difficult to identify, and only a few studies of a systematic character have ventured into this terra incognita. Of course, when there is a massive insurrection against prevailing practices, as there was in the House of Representatives in the middle 1970s in regard to committee assignments and especially chair selection, the norm structure might also change; but there is also some evidence that the "old" norms reassert themselves and prevail.

A study by Swanson (1969) is one of the few that venture into the uncharted territory of norms in the assignment process, and its emphasis is characteristically on the "nonconformist legislator." The study seeks to test the allegation once made by Senator Joseph S. Clark (1963) that liberal

Senate Democrats, "particularly those liberals who fall in the nonconformist category," are discriminated against when committee assignments are made. By nonconformist behavior is meant behavior that is not "cooperative," or that "evinces a lack of respect for Senate tradition" (see Huitt, 1961).

Swanson studies 44 Democrats still serving in the 88th (1963-1964) Congress. He concludes that "those individuals who consciously use the Senate as a forum to publicize their liberal ideas, with little regard for cherished norms, may have to pay a heavy price in terms of the potential influence that conformity would generate. As our data indicated, major committee posts come most easily to the 'responsible' legislator" (p. 94).

Bullock (1970) seeks to test the effect of an alleged "apprenticeship norm" in the committee assignment process. From the norm he deduces a model which holds that "freshmen are generally appointed to mediocre committees" (p. 717). To test the model, average House and committee seniority per member was computed for each standing committee at the beginning of 12 congresses, the 80th (1947-1948) to the 91st (1969-1970). Bullock then tests the hypothesis that the rank-ordering of House committees according to average seniority will remain stable from one congress to the next. Why he undertakes this complicated exercise is not made clear. One's common sense (which may admittedly be false) would suggest that if an apprenticeship norm operates in the assignment of freshman members, one can simply look directly at the assignment of freshmen and compare them with the assignments of other members. Bullock finds, of course, that the rank correlation coefficients are consistently high and suggests that "the apprenticeship model is more helpful in explaining initial assignments than subsequent ones" (p. 718).

Bullock also finds that in addition to consistency from congress to congress, there is substantial change between the 80th and 91st Congresses. Though each congress resembles its predecessor and successor, there is incremental change over the whole period. In fact, "change has been so large that the rankings for the Ninety-first Congress only faintly resemble those found 22 years earlier" (p. 719). To explain this secular change, Bullock suggests that "a possible source of variation is the large periodic influx of freshmen whom a party must distribute across committees" (p. 719). He therefore proposes as a second hypothesis that variations in the rank-order correlations of committees "were a product of the mean seniority of congressmen not returning from the previous session." He finds that "while the relationship was in the expected direction, it was not large" (pp. 719-720). It is difficult to accept Bullock's conclusion that "the apprenticeship model is useful in understanding committee assignments despite the changing values of some of the variables in the assignment process" (p. 720).

Another study of the apprenticeship norm by Asher (1975) was a by-product of a more general study of "the learning of legislative norms" (see Asher, 1973). In this study, based on January and February interviews with 30 freshmen in the opening 91st (1969-1970) Congress, of whom 24 were reinterviewed in May of 1969, and based as well on interviews with 65 nonfreshmen, Asher (1975) found that "nonfreshman representatives did not consider apprenticeship as mandatory for newcomers and the newcomers themselves indicated low adherence to the norm. Support for the norm of apprenticeship declined among freshmen in the early months of their House service and those newcomers who thought it necessary to serve an apprenticeship talked in terms of a period of months, not years" (p. 217). Asher offers a number of "plausible explanations" for the discrepancy between the interview and actual assignment data which cannot be summarized here. He seems to hold that it was not the assignment process as it had been practiced that contributed to the changed status of freshmen and the decline of an apprenticeship norm, but rather that it was the changed status and the decline of the norm that contributed to better assignments for freshmen. Asher is writing, it must be remembered, during the period of reform that followed the time when he documented the "changing status" of the freshman congressman.

That freshman committee preferences ought to be respected as a norm in its own right can be inferred from a study by Gertzog (1976) concerning "routinization" in the assignment process that, in many respects, is a cousin of Polsby's (1968, 1969) studies of "institutionalization" in the House of Representatives. Although not directly cast as a study of a norm, Gertzog's analysis sheds light on how a norm may come about. His initial concern is scholarly "disagreement about the frequency with which new members of the House are assigned to the committees they most prefer . . . , and the alleged motivations prompting members to refrain from requesting transfers once they have accumulated a reasonable amount of seniority" (p. 694).

Interviews were conducted with 53 congressmen in the 89th (1965-1966), with 44 in the 90th (1967-1968), and with 32 in the 91st (1969-1970) Congress, asking them about their preferences when first entering the House. Examining denials of preferred assignments in the congressmen's first, third, and fifth years, Gertzog finds perceptible decrease over time. Detailed analysis of assignment patterns and examination of deviant cases showed that those at no time transferring to their initially preferred committees fail to do so "not so much because they wish to retain accumulated seniority on a less desirable committee, but because they were ambivalent about which committee they preferred to begin with, or because they perceived little difference between two or more committees in which interest was expressed, or because they had gained the enmity or distrust of delegation and party leaders" (p. 704).

As significant as the empirical research itself is Gertzog's interpretation of the findings. Early satisfaction of the newcomers' preferences in the period covered, from 1965-1970, is interpreted to mean that the assignment process "has become an essentially routine, nondiscretionary procedure." This "routinization" is further articulated in a theoretical manner not often found in other studies of the assignment process: "a more routinized committee assignment process is likely to affect the speed with which freshmen gain access to important policymaking opportunities. It is likely to affect the psychic gratification and sense of accomplishment they experience in their first terms, as well as the rhetoric and content of their early reelection campaigns." As if he were anticipating developments from the middle 1970s on, Gertzog suggests that "routinization is likely also to reduce the rewards to House leaders interested in securing the loyalty of new members, and undermine further a party leadership hierarchy in that chamber which is already both tenuous and intermittently expressed" (p. 705). While other authors expected the House reforms to permit party leaders to regain some power, Gertzog is essentially correct: power in the House continued to become more, not less, decentralized.

Auxiliary Actors: Interest Groups and Delegations

Little is systematically known about actors in the assignment process other than position-seeking legislators themselves and those who make committee appointments, such as interest groups and their lobbyists or state delegations.[10] (In the case of the U.S. Congress, one may also wonder whether its many special "caucuses" have a hand in the assignment process.) This lack of research attention to "auxiliary actors" may simply be due, in the case of interest groups, to their not in fact being participants in the assignment process. Masters (1961) asserted that "organized groups, with occasional exceptions, appear to refrain from direct intervention in committee assignments." But he also stated that "the influence of such groups is thought to be important, but little evidence is available on its nature and extent (p. 355). He gives four examples of "exceptions" and then speculates that

overt intrusion is apt to be resented and to be self-defeating. Rather, they [interest groups] have certain "expectations" about the type of person who should be selected for the vacancies on committees which affect their interests. Each group usually counts several members "friendly" or responsive to their needs. Organized interests do not often concern themselves too much with the selection of a particular member of the "friendly" group so long as one of them is eventually chosen (p. 355).

Nevertheless, it is difficult to fathom why interest groups, not reluctant to intrude on other aspects of the legislative process, would be shy in connection with committee assignments. Even Shepsle (1978), in his book-length treatment of the assignment process, makes only a handful of references to "interested others," and they do not figure in his analytic equations. His most salient reference echoes the anecdotal writers:

A number of groups and individuals outside the House are interested in the business of various committees and thus occasionally pay some attention to the committee assignment process. They tend, however, to play a relatively minor role in that process and are certainly not regarded very seriously by members of the CC unless their preferences happen to reinforce those of more important actors in the CC's environment. At any rate they do not appear to lobby openly for particular committee assignments (pp. 162-163).

Shepsle then quotes a member of the Committee-on-Committees about appointments to Education and Labor to the effect that "over a two-Congress period the letters of endorsement contained in the files of another CC member revealed the relative inactivity of interest groups: as few as 2.6% of the letters received (3 of 116) were sent by organized groups." He claims that "the more usual arrangement for 'interested others' is to work through other members of Congress," and gives one example of how ex-Congressman Andrew Biemiller, the chief lobbyist for the AFL/CIO, made use of his "friendship and influence" with the Speaker and the chairman of the Congressional Campaign Committee to have "some input into CC decisions on Education and Labor" (p. 163).

All of this anecdotal testimony would suggest that there is simply nothing to study because what does not "exist" cannot be studied, but the absence of "evidence" still leaves open the question of whether there exists material that has not been mined. This ambiguity is reinforced by the fact that there is not much more evidence in the case of the state party delegations which, the anecdotal writers are agreed, are "important" participants in the assignment process. Masters (1961) reported that in the assignment negotiations the dean or senior member of the delegation "plays a crucially important role in securing assignments" (p. 346). Clapp (1964) lists the state party delegations among the "decisive factors" in assignments: as especially large delegations feel "entitled" to one or more seats on the more important committees, "designation by the delegation generally suffices to ensure election to fill 'our' vacancy regardless of seniority claims of other candidates" (p. 238).

In spite of the anecdotal consensus (or, perhaps, because of it), there is only one systematic study, by Bullock (1971), on the influence of state party delegations on House committee assignments. Bullock's measure of influence is "long-term possession of a committee seat," though he also observes that, "like other norms, this one is not immune to violation. In time some delegations acquire committee seats while others lose theirs" (p. 527). The study covers the period from 1947 to 1968, "perhaps a time span insufficient to establish conclusively which delegations have rights to which committee seats, but certainly adequate for some tentative inferences" (p. 528).

Bullock thus looks at "protracted seat control" (p. 527) for 51 state party delegations—31 Democratic and 20 Republican. There are three types of seat control: maintenance of a delegation member on a committee for the entire period; maintenance for all but 1 of the 11 congresses; and "one-man occupancy" for at least 20 of the 22 years. In regard to the first type, "typically the greater the turnover among holders of the delegation's seat, the more conclusive the evidence that the seat 'belongs' to the delegation" (p. 528). Bullock finds that of 536 House committee seats, 205 met the criteria of delegation control. Excluding the one-man occupancy seats "shows 28 percent of the House committee seats to be delegation held. A less stringent definition of delegation control . . . might well reveal that as many as half of all committee seats are subject to the same state rule." He also finds that "delegation held seats on constituency committees are more common than on duty committees but less frequent than on top committees" (p. 532). Techniques of seat control may involve filling the vacancy "by rewarding a member with moderate seniority" or "inheritance"—seats given to congressmen from particular districts—or a "mixture of chance and planning" which "involves the frequent rotation of freshmen onto a minor committee" (p. 530).

Seat control, Bullock also finds, "is to some extent a product" of a delegation's size. The correlation between delegation size and number of prescriptive seats is .93, but only .53 for the relationship between proportion of prescriptive seats per delegation and size. He therefore reasons that other factors are involved as well, especially as delegations of the same size "differ greatly in the number of seats which they command" (pp. 532, 534). While these other factors "are not easily quantifiable," Bullock speculates that

qualities associated with delegation leadership, i.e., desire to maintain representation on specific committees, persuasiveness in prevailing upon members to forego personal preferences in the best interests of the delegation, and the quality of accesss to other influentials, are important in determining whether claims to seats are honored. Also relevant is the homogeneity or heterogeneity of the districts represented in a delegation, the presence of an ideological—as opposed to a state—strategy in personnel placement, and the imponderables of personality and individual aspirations (pp. 534-535).

Consequences for Public Policies

The great bulk of research on committee assignments treats either the process itself or its outcomes as dependent variables. Yet, ironically, the stimulus for this research has been that committee assignments "matter" and, therefore, are worthy of inquiry because they have an effect on "something." This "something" has not always or often been articulated with clarity or precision. Apart from some illustrative case studies involving the policy consequences of denying a particular committee seat to a particular person, the effect of assignments on public policies has not been high on the

agenda of research, unless one includes the research on the alleged effect of
committee composition after assignments have been made, notably the many
studies testing for the impact of committee membership on the distribution
of federal expenditures to particular districts represented on relevant committees (see above, pp. 609-610). Nevertheless, as Cook (1983) rightly
points out, "virtually every writing on the committee assignment process
emphasizes its potential impact on policymaking. Yet to my knowledge,
there has never been an empirical test of the proposition that the committee
assignment process itself makes a difference, beyond the recruitment of
interested requesters" (p. 1028). Cook therefore proposes to study "one aspect of the potential influence of the assignment process upon policy by
examining whether individuals with particular ideological stances were consistently advantaged by the assignment process for seats on particular committees" (p. 1029).

Cook's data are the assignment requests, regardless of preference
ordering, made by House Democrats for the 87th (1961-1962) through 90th
(1967-1968) and 92d (1971-1972) through 94th (1975-1976) Congresses.
The study's dependent variable is the "contest" (Achen and Stolarek, 1974).
In each of the one-on-one contests one can observe, therefore, "which candidate the Committee on Committees ultimately preferred, and whether he or
she was the more liberal or the more conservative of the two" (p. 1030).
The measures used were the ratings of various Congress-watching groups like
Americans for Democratic Action, Americans for Constitutional Action,
and others.

Cook's results were largely random: "The impact of the assignment
process itself upon the ideological composition of a committee rarely differs
from that which would be obtained by a series of coin tosses" (p. 1031).
What, then, Cook asks, "has been the impact of the committee assignment
process upon policymaking and policy change in Congress?" He answers that
the process "does not appear to have a decisive influence upon the policy
orientations of the committees, measured by ideological or issue-specific
voting scales" (p. 1034). But Cook's study, its pretensions notwithstanding,
does not really address the effect of assignments on committee policy making.

A Brief Appraisal

For whatever reasons one may consider the legislative committee
assignment process socially or politically significant, and for whatever scientific purposes one may make it a topic of investigation, the development of
relevant studies over the last 30 years is an exemplar of what a serious "science
of politics" in fact looks like, not what it might or should be. There are
evidently "stages of development," but these stages are by no means temporally

consecutive, one replacing another; rather, they may overlap and even be repeated as new data sources become available, new substantive interests arise, new methods of discovery and analysis are invented, and one theoretical fashion is replaced by another. As a result, the development of studies dealing in one way or another with committee assignments has been "messy," but it has also been "progressive" without necessarily being linear. Nevertheless, one may speak of "stages of development."

Development in the study of committee assignments—the locus and focus largely being the U.S. Congress—begins with narratives mainly based on formal documentation which, however, is not systematically used, and on the most casual, often hear-say observations (Galloway, 1953; Gross, 1953; Healy, 1973), and they are much influenced by considerations of legislative reform notable in a period. Unusual or episodic events give rise to more intensive, yet still largely anecdotal case studies which may or may not be cast in a more or less explicit conceptual framework (Huitt, 1957; Cummings and Peabody, 1963; Peabody, 1963). As particular topics come to fascinate particular investigators, such as the relationship between committee assignments and seniority, committee prestige, or committee size, a "natural history" stage of development sets in that no longer relies on anecdotal information and tends to be quantitative but remains largely descriptive (Goodwin, 1959; Gawthrop, 1966; Swanson, 1969), though it may also be theoretically oriented (Matthews, 1960). Along comes an investigator who locates a particular analysis in a descriptive framework of what, at the time, is "known" about the assignment process and provides both an "authoritative" statement that for a decade or more influences the textbooks and an agenda for future research (Masters, 1961). The scientific component of this research is mainly classification of committees in terms of a sociological theory of stratification which, it can easily be noted, creates difficulties: assignment transfers are assumed to express preferences, and the classification of committees based on transfers is then used to explain preferences.

The need to overcome such difficulties gradually gives rise to theoretical considerations, sometimes suggested by anomalies in a classification, sometimes by analogical possibilities. At this point, theoretical and methodological innovations initially outside the research arena of assignments influence developments inside. In the study of assignments, in particular, the "economic theory of democracy" and the "computer revolution" of the mid-1960s occasion the first theoretically sophisticated study (Bullock and Sprague, 1969) of the process. On the side of method, also, new means of data collection, management, and analysis enrich the foundations on which theoretical knowledge can be built. Unstructured interviewing is replaced by structured interviews, though compared with studies based on actual assignments there are very few systematic interview studies (Asher, 1975; Bullock, 1976; Gertzog, 1976; Perkins, 1981; Smith and Deering, 1983).

The most significant boost in the development of the assignment studies came with the discovery of the early 1970s—"discovery" in the literal sense—of actual member requests for appointments and applicants' preference orderings. This discovery opened up a rich mine of data which also permitted the legitimate and direct application of social choice theory in an understanding of the assignment process (Rohde and Shepsle, 1973; Shepsle, 1978). Even more recently, previously unavailable Democratic Committee-on-Committees ballot tallies could be used by Smith and Ray (1983) to good effect. As these investigators write, "the data permit us to peer into the 'black box' of the assignment process and to avoid questionable assumptions about who is nominated and the mechanism by which they are elected" (p. 220).

There are, then, important continuities in the study of committee assignments and the assignment process but also discontinuities. As one theoretical mode replaces another, there may also occur a displacement of one empirical interest by another, with the result that reliance is placed on assumptions (such as "motivations") that could be empirically validated or falsified. An emphasis on "process" may involve a neglect of "structure," and significant structural changes may introduce apparent anomalies in the assignment process that could be resolved by structural interpretation. A number of such difficulties have been mentioned throughout this review. To repeat, time-series analysis that fails to take note of structural changes may lead to false conclusions or "implications" of the findings. (For instance, only one investigator—Westefield, 1974—pushes analysis far enough back, to 1927, to take account of structural change; and only one study, by Ray and Smith, 1984, shows how "Speaker regimes" affect the assignment process and must therefore be taken into account in the interpretation of time-series data.)

In turn, of course, structural analysis neglectful of secular change creates analytic problems. It is for this reason that replication of a structural study—like Ray's (1982) replication of Jewell and Chi-hung (1974)—can be useful. But secular change may also appear to be "real" when in fact it is an artifact of changing research methodology or conceptual innovation. But cumulation of findings may be hindered by the use of ambiguous concepts because conceptual ambiguity may lead to a good deal of collinearity in the variables used in analysis. Moreover, the use of really noncommensurable indicators, especially when the data come from interviews, occasions index instability (as noted in reference to Fenno, 1973; Bullock, 1976; Perkins, 1981) and makes comparison of doubtful validity. Index ambiguity and index instability thus obstruct the cumulation of findings. Besides, false starts are at times simply abandoned altogether rather than rectified, with the result that they may be inadvertently repeated at a later time. What "rectification" (rather than replication) can accomplish appears in the cumulative study of the relationship between assignments and committee size (Westefield, 1974; Shepsle, 1978; Whiteman, 1983; Ray and Smith, 1984).

In general, much has been learned about various aspects of the committee assignment process, especially in the U.S. House of Representatives. It also has made "synthesis" the more difficult. But if a synthesis were to be attempted (which was not an objective of this review), the resulting "profile" would surely look very different from the descriptions one finds in the texts of the prebehavioral research era. Synthesis would be difficult, however, because the empirical "findings" are so enmeshed in theoretical paradigms and methodological approaches (which is all to the good) that sorting out "truth" from "falsehood" requires the most careful attention to both theory and method as well as a sophisticated use of the research findings.

A sophisticated synthesis of what is "known" would, of course, also have to be theory-driven. To what extent Shepsle's (1978) notion of the assignment process as an "interest-advocacy-accommodation syndrome" can serve as a comprehensive theoretical framework, within which all that has been empirically learned can be located, remains to be seen. The very elegance of Shepsle's model may also be its most severe limitation from a synthetic perspective because it is satisfied by assumptions and/or inferences that themselves require empirical inquiry and documentation. Shepsle's argument that the interest-advocacy-accommodation syndrome cannot be isolated from the institution spawning it is obviously in point; but his conclusion that, while serving the individual needs of the legislature's members, it does not serve institutional needs, is more in the nature of a normative than a scientific statement. On the other hand, an attempt made by Uslaner (1974) to construct a normative-institutional model of the assignment process on the basis of a scientifically-inspired linear programming approach seems to defy what is known about Congress as an aggregate of individual-goods maximizing, reelection-oriented members.

Perhaps synthesis is impossible at this stage of research development. Perhaps, before synthesis can be attempted, it is necessary to formulate once more a research agenda that will pinpoint what is yet to be discovered and demonstrated in the "real world"—and a changing world it is—of legislative committee assignments. As the overwhelming bulk of studies has been concerned with the U.S. House of Representatives, the resultant knowledge is necessarily parochial. Certainly, the Senate, the U.S. state legislatures, and the parliaments of the constitutional democracies deserve to be investigated. Moreover, one can only be impressed by the absence of a "college" of investigators (as one finds it, for instance, in the study of electoral processes and behavior). As a glance at the Appendix listing quantitative research on assignments shows, many more studies are one-shot than long-range projects. Except for Bullock and Shepsle and, more recently, perhaps a collaborative team centered in Smith (Smith and Deering, 1983; Smith and Ray, 1983; Ray and Smith, 1984), most investigators do not seem to have a continuing interest in the committee assignment process or some aspect of it. It may well be that investigators would be discouraged by Smith and Ray's (1983) conclusion that, in spite of reform, "overall ... there are few detectable differences between pre- and post-reform periods" (p. 238). If so, research should address the question of why this is the case.

APPENDIX
Inventory of Quantitative Studies of Committee Assignments

Date Published	Author	Congress	Years	Chamber	Data Type	Main Theme
1959	Goodwin	81-85	1949-1958	Senate	Actual	Seniority
1960	Matthews	80-84	1947-1956	Senate	Actual Interview	Prestige
1961	Masters	80-86	1947-1960	House	Actual Interview	Process
1966	Gawthrop	80-89	1947-1966	House	Actual	Dual Assignments
1969	Swanson	85-88	1957-1964	Senate	Actual	Nonconformism
	Bullock & Sprague	80-89	1947-1966	House	Actual	Transfer Strategy
1970	Bullock	80-91	1947-1970	House	Actual	Apprentice
1971	Bullock	80-90	1947-1968	House	Actual	Delegations
1972	Bullock	80-90	1947-1968	House	Actual	Freshman Reelection
1973	Bullock	80-91	1947-1970	House	Actual	Transfers
	Rohde & Shepsle	86-88 90	1959-1968	House House	Request	Choice Strategy

APPENDIX (continued)

Date Published	Author	Congress	Years	Chamber	Data Type	Main Theme
1974	Jewell & Chi-hung	88-92	1963-1972	House	Actual	Transfer Patterns
	Westefield	70-92	1927-1972	House	Actual	Leadership
	Uslaner	91	1969-1970	House	Actual	Model
1975	Asher	86-93	1959-1974	House	Actual Interview	Apprentice Norm
1976	Bullock	92	1971-1972	House	Interview	Freshman
	Gertzog	89-91	1965-1970	House	Actual Interview	Routinization
1978	Shepsle	86-93	1959-1974	House	Request	Social Choice
1980	Ray	92-94	1971-1976	House	Request	Federal Spending
	Fowler	86-94	1959-1976	House	Request	Electoral
1981	Perkins	92-93	1971-1974	House	Interview	Judiciary
1982	Ray	93-97	1973-1981	House	Actual	Transfers
1983	Smith & Deering	87	1981-1982	House	Interview	Changing Motives
	Smith & Ray	95-97	1977-1982	House	Actual	Reform Impact
	Whiteman	81-95	1949-1978	House	Actual	Size
	Cook	87-94	1961-1976	House	Request	Ideology
1984	Ray & Smith	86-97	1959-1982	House	Request	Size & Leadership

NOTES

I want to acknowledge the assistance of Vera McCluggage, who wrote a number of memoranda on the committee assignment studies in an early phase of preparation for this review.

1. Among the state studies specifically dealing with committee assignments that came to attention in preparing this review, see Beth and Havard, 1961; Robeck, 1971; Sokolow and Brandsma, 1971; and Basehart, 1980. There may of course be others.

2. The volume edited by Lees and Shaw (1979), comparing eight national legislatures, has no index entry for committee assignments, though the process is described for the United States, relying on a few studies reviewed in this essay. Under "Committees" there is a subentry entitled "socialization and recruitment" referring to two pages in the volume's "Conclusion" (pp. 428-429).

3. Huitt (1957) also reports interviewing persons "who had first-hand participant knowledge of the controversy." He informs the reader that the conclusions derived from the printed record "did not have to be altered as a result of the interviews" (p. 315).

4. Survey data, derived from unstructured interviews with members and staffs of various committees, covered (retrospectively) the 80th (1947-1948) through 86th (1959-1960) Congresses, with special attention to the 86th Congress. The interviews included members of the committees-on-committees, deans of state delegations, and affected members. In addition, use was made of personal letters and similar papers, official documents, and personal observations.

5. Shepsle (1978) acknowledges that the title of his book was "provided by Goodwin, 1970 (p. viii)." Actually Goodwin had used the concept in his 1959 article (p. 414).

6. It is all too often forgotten that classification by way of "mere description" of the phenomena to be classified is a necessary step in scientific development. In a world of phenomena that constantly undergo change, as social and political relations do, classifications require constant revision. This, unfortunately, is not often the case in the social sciences in general, just as it is not the case in research on committee systems. As a result, the error may be made that the committee stratification or prestige system is not a relevant or significant variable when an obsolete classification scheme does not yield meaningfully interpretable results.

7. Leadership strategies were declared as being beyond the scope of Bullock and Sprague's research.

8. Bullock (1973) here relies on and cites Fenno (1966, p. 58) and Manley (1970, p. 51).

9. Bullock's data in this connection are rather suspect. His "target data set," as he puts it, was 53 congressmen, all freshmen. He reports interviews having been conducted in 52 of these congressmen's "offices." Of those interviewed in the offices, 18 were elected members of Congress, and interviews with five other freshmen were made available to Bullock by another scholar. Sixty-eight interviews were conducted with staff members, and these interviews are treated in the analysis as if they had been interviews with the "missing" 29 congressmen (52−(18+5)=29). It is difficult to accept that one person can serve as a surrogate or agent for another when it comes to a psychological variable like "motivation."

10. Although there are a number of specialized delegation studies (Truman, 1956; Fiellin, 1962; Kessel, 1964; Deckard, 1972), these studies have not dealt with the role of the state party delegations in the committee assignment process.

REFERENCES

Achen, Christopher H. and John S. Stolarek. 1974. "The Resolution of Congressional Committee Assignment Contests: Factors Influencing the Democratic Committee on Committees." Delivered at the Annual Meeting of the American Political Science Association, Washington, DC.

Asher, Herbert B. 1973. "The Learning of Legislative Norms," *American Political Science Review* 67:499-513.

————. 1974. "Committees and the Norm of Specialization," *Annals of the American Academy of Political and Social Science* 411:63-74.

————. 1975. "The Changing Status of the Freshman Representative," in Norman J. Ornstein, ed., *Congress in Change: Evolution and Reform.* New York: Praeger, pp. 216-239.

Basehart, Hubert H. 1980. "The Effect of Membership Stability on Continuity and Experience in U.S. State Legislative Committees," *Legislative Studies Quarterly* 5:55-68.

Beth, Loren P. and William C. Havard. 1961. "Committee Stacking and Political Power in Florida," *Journal of Politics* 23:57-83.

Bullock, Charles S. III. 1970. "Apprenticeship and Committee Assignments in the House of Representatives," *Journal of Politics* 32:717-720.

————. 1971. "The Influence of State Party Delegations on House Committee Assignments," *Midwest Journal of Political Science* 15:525-546.

————. 1972. "Freshman Committee Assignments and Re-election in the United States House of Representatives," *American Political Science Review* 66:996-1007.

————. 1973. "Committee Transfers in the United States House of Representatives," *Journal of Politics* 35:85-120.

————. 1976. "Motivations for U.S. Congressional Committee Preferences: Freshmen of the 92nd Congress," *Legislative Studies Quarterly* 1:201-212.

Bullock, Charles and John Sprague. 1969. "A Research Note on the Committee Reassignments of Southern Democratic Congressmen," *Journal of Politics* 31:493-512.

Clapp, Charles L. 1964. *The Congressman: His Work as He Sees It.* Garden City, NY: Doubleday.

Clark, Joseph S. 1963. *The Senate Establishment.* New York: Hill and Wang.

Cook, Timothy E. 1983. "The Policy Impact of the Committee Assignment Process in the House," *Journal of Politics* 45:1027-1036.

Cooper, Joseph. 1970. *The Origins of the Standing Committees and the Development of the Modern House.* Rice University Studies, Vol. 56, No. 3. Houston: Rice University Press.

Cummings, Milton C., Jr. and Robert L. Peabody. 1963. "The Decision to Enlarge the Committee on Rules: An Analysis of the 1961 Vote," in Robert L. Peabody and Nelson W. Polsby, eds., *New Perspectives on the House of Representatives.* Chicago: Rand McNally, pp. 167-194.

Davidson, Roger H. 1981. "Subcommittee Government: New Channels for Policy Making," in Thomas E. Mann and Norman J. Ornstein, eds., *The New Congress.* Washington, DC: American Enterprise Institute, pp. 99-133.

Deckard, Barbara. 1972. "State Party Delegations in the U.S. House of Representatives— A Comparative Study of Group Cohesion," *Journal of Politics* 34:199-222.

Eulau, Heinz. 1967. "The Committees in a Revitalized Congress," in Alfred de Grazia, ed., *Congress: The First Branch of Government.* Garden City, NY: Doubleday, pp. 204-243.

Fenno, Richard F., Jr. 1966. *The Power of the Purse: Appropriations Politics in Congress.* Boston: Little, Brown.

———. 1973. *Congressmen in Committees.* Boston: Little, Brown.

———. 1978. *Home Style: House Members in Their Districts.* Boston: Little, Brown.

Fiellin, Alan. 1962. "The Functions of Informal Groups in Legislative Institutions," *Journal of Politics* 24:72-91.

Fiorina, Morris P. 1977. *Congress: Keystone of the Washington Establishment.* New Haven: Yale University Press.

Fowler, Linda L., Scott R. Douglass, and Wesley D. Clark, Jr. 1980. "The Electoral Effects of House Committee Assignments," *Journal of Politics* 42:307-319.

Galloway, George B. 1953. *The Legislative Process in Congress.* New York: Crowell.

Gawthrop, Louis C. 1966. "Changing Membership Patterns in House Committees," *American Political Science Review* 60:366-373.

Gertzog, Irwin N. 1976. "The Routinization of Committee Assignments in the U.S. House of Representatives," *American Journal of Political Science* 20:693-712.

Goodwin, George, Jr. 1959. "The Seniority System in Congress," *American Political Science Review* 55:412-436.

———. 1970. *The Little Legislatures: Committees on Congress.* Amherst: University of Massachusetts Press.

Gross, Bertram M. 1953. *The Legislative Struggle: A Study of Social Combat.* New York: McGraw-Hill.

Healy, Robert. 1973. "Committees and the Politics of Assignments," in Sven Groennings and Jonathan P. Hawley, eds., *To Be a Congressman: The Promise and the Power.* Washington, DC: Acropolis Books, pp. 99-120.

Hinckley, Barbara. 1971. *The Seniority System in Congress.* Bloomington: Indiana University Press.

———. 1978. *Stability and Change in Congress.* 2d ed. New York: Harper & Row.

Huitt, Ralph K. 1957. "The Morse Committee Assignment Controversy: A Study in Senate Norms," *American Political Science Review* 51:313-329.

———. 1961. "The Outsider in the Senate—An Alternative Role," *American Political Science Review* 55:566-575.

Jewell, Malcolm E. and Chu Chi-hung. 1974. "Membership Movement and Committee Attractiveness in the U.S. House of Representatives, 1963-1971," *Midwest Journal of Political Science* 18:433-441.

Kessel, John H. 1964. "The Washington Congressional Delegation," *Midwest Journal of Political Science* 8:1-21.

Lees, John D. and Malcolm Shaw. 1979. *Committees in Legislatures: A Comparative Analysis.* Durham, NC: Duke University Press.

LeLoup, Lance T. 1979. "Process Versus Policy: The U.S. House Budget Committee," *Legislative Studies Quarterly* 4:227-254.

Manley, John F. 1970. *The Politics of Finance: The House Committee on Ways and Means.* Boston: Little, Brown.

Marvick, Dwaine. 1950. "A Quantitative Technique for Analyzing Congressional Alignments." Ph.D. dissertation, Columbia University.

Masters, Nicholas A. 1961. "Committee Assignments in the House of Representatives," *American Political Science Review* 55:345-357.

Matthews, Donald R. 1960. *U.S. Senators and Their World.* Chapel Hill: University of North Carolina Press.

Mayhew, David R. 1974. *Congress: The Electoral Connection.* New Haven: Yale University Press.

Peabody, Robert L. 1963. "The Enlarged Rules Committee," in Robert L. Peabody and Nelson W. Polsby, eds., *New Perspectives on the House of Representatives.* Chicago: Rand McNally, pp. 129-164.

Perkins, Lynette P. 1980. "Influences of Members' Goals on Their Committee Behavior: The U.S. House Judiciary Committee," *Legislative Studies Quarterly* 5:373-392.

_____. 1981. "Member Recruitment to a Mixed Goal Committee: The House Judiciary Committee," *Journal of Politics* 43:348-364.

Polsby, Nelson W. 1968. "The Institutionalization of the U.S. House of Representatives," *American Political Science Review* 62:144-168.

Polsby, Nelson W., Miriam Gallaher, and Barry S. Rundquist. 1969. "The Growth of the Seniority System in the U.S. House of Representatives," *American Political Science Review* 63:787-807.

Ray, Bruce A. 1980. "Federal Spending and the Selection of Committee Assignments in the U.S. House of Representatives," *American Journal of Political Science* 24:494-510.

_____. 1982. "Committee Attractiveness in the U.S. House, 1963-1981," *American Journal of Political Science* 26:609-613.

Ray, Bruce A. and Steven S. Smith. 1984. "Committee Size in the U.S. Congress," *Legislative Studies Quarterly* 9:679-695.

Robeck, Bruce W. 1971. "Committee Assignments in the California Senate: Seniority, Party, or Ideology?" *Western Political Quarterly* 24:527-539.

Rohde, David W. and Kenneth A. Shepsle. 1973. "Democratic Committee Assignments in the House of Representatives: Strategic Aspects of a Social Choice Process," *American Political Science Review* 67:889-905.

Shepsle, Kenneth A. 1978. *The Giant Jigsaw Puzzle: Democratic Committee Assignments in the Modern House.* Chicago: University of Chicago Press.

Smith, Steven S. and Christopher J. Deering. 1983. "Changing Motives for Committee Preferences of New Members of the U.S. House," *Legislative Studies Quarterly* 8:271-281.

_____. 1984. *Committees in Congress.* Washington, DC: Congressional Quarterly.

Smith, Steven S. and Bruce A. Ray. 1983. "The Impact of Congressional Reform: House Democratic Committee Assignments," *Congress & The Presidency* 10:219-240.

Sokolow, Alvin D. and Richard W. Brandsma. 1971. "Partisanship and Seniority in Legislative Committee Assignments," *Western Political Quarterly* 24:740-760.

Swanson, Wayne R. 1969. "Committee Assignments and the Nonconformist Legislator: Democrats in the U.S. Senate," *Midwest Journal of Political Science* 13:84-94.

Truman, David B. 1956. "The State Delegations and the Structure of Party Voting in the United States House of Representatives," *American Political Science Review* 50:1023-1045.

Uslaner, Eric M. 1974. *Congressional Committee Assignments: Alternative Models for Behavior.* Beverly Hills, CA: Sage Publications.

Vogler, David J. 1980. *The Politics of Congress.* Boston: Allyn and Bacon.

Westefield, Louis P. 1974. "Majority Party Leadership and the Committee System in the House of Representatives," *American Political Science Review* 68:1593-1604.

Whiteman, David. 1983. "A Theory of Congressional Organization: Committee Size in the U.S. House of Representatives," *American Politics Quarterly* 11:49-70.

Chapter 6

Leadership in Legislatures: Evolution, Selection, and Functions

by

ROBERT L. PEABODY

"Empirical science," as Carl G. Hempel once observed, "has two major objectives: to describe particular phenomena in the world of our experience and to establish general principles by means of which they can be explained and predicted" (1952, p. 1). The primary task of this essay is more limited, namely to provide an inventory of contemporary research on leadership in and of legislatures.[1] In the process some general principles, worthy of further empirical testing should emerge. Until about two decades ago the study of leadership in legislatures tended to concentrate on "the actions of a few eminent politicians, whose careers are apt to be documented extensively, and to discuss their attitudes, preferences and decisions" (Aydelotte, 1977, p. 6). The techniques of modern social science, including intensive observation, interviewing, and quantitative analysis, such as roll-call studies, have broadened research on leadership until it includes the whole legislature, followers as well as leaders. But unless each legislature is sui generis, and some seem to argue so, there is much that remains to be done by way of comparative analysis. Leadership, which is common to all legislatures, seems to provide an appropriate vehicle for developing comparisons and generalizations beyond single-nation settings.

This review of the literature on legislative leadership will be divided into four main sections: (1) historical studies, especially those treating the origins and evolution of legislative leadership; (2) research on the selection of leaders, on how top party and legislative officials are chosen; (3) descriptions and analysis of tasks and functions performed; and (4) the state of the subfield, with possible future research agendas. Before turning to this literature, several definitional problems must be set forth and discussed.

Definitions of Leadership

Definitions of leadership are almost as ubiquitous as the phenomenon itself. By way of illustration, a mid-1970 review of the research on leadership, primarily from a social-psychological perspective, totaled more than 600 pages. More than a quarter of the book was devoted to bibliographical references (Stogdill, 1974). Almost all of the social science disciplines—anthropology, psychology, sociology, political science, and managerial sciences—have their own, often overlapping, sometimes contradictory, perspectives on leadership. As research continues on this fundamental process, changes in meaning are probably unavoidable. Hypotheses undergo reformulation, with scholars hoping to arrive at more detailed concepts and theories (Bass, 1981).

There are probably no definitions of leadership applicable to all settings, let alone all seasons. Still, some acceptable definitions, cutting across a wide range of experiences, have been achieved. Certain core elements or "essential attributes" can be specified. Typically, such a definition takes the form: "X is leadership if, and only if, X satisfies conditions $C_1, C_2, \ldots C_n$" (Hempel, 1952, p. 7). There appears to be some agreement in political science, at least, that "leadership" consists of a relationship between two or more individuals such that one imposes his will upon another; the other can accept or reject the imposition (Weber, in Gerth and Mills, 1958; Dahl, 1957). Other social scientists would relax this requirement to allow for facilitative leaders who sometimes moderate their own wills in order to secure cooperation from subordinates (Barnard, 1938; Merriam, 1945; Burns, 1978; Tucker, 1981).[2] One of the more comprehensive and sensible explications has been set forth by social psychologist Cecil A. Gibb:

Definition of the simplest unit of leadership as 'the act of leading' ... [leads] to the identification of four basic elements in the relationship: (1) the *leader,* with his characteristics of ability and personality and his 'resources relevant to goal attainment ... '; (2) the *followers,* who also have relevant abilities, personality characteristics and resources; (3) the *situation* within which the relationship occurs; and (4) the *task* with which the interacting individuals are confronted (Gibb, 1968, p. 91).

Legislative Settings

Compared with the agony of sorting out leadership definitions, the identification and explication of such key terms as "legislator" and "legislation" are relatively simple. It suffices, here, to note that by mid-twentieth century, "legislature" had become the generic term for representative assemblies. Thus, Wheare (1963) launched his classic study as follows: "Parliaments and congresses and other similar assemblies are commonly called 'legislatures'." Loewenberg has provided a more complex and useful definition. The conditions which underlie parliaments or legislative bodies, he argues, are two-fold:

(1) "their members are formally equal to each other in status, distinguishing parliaments from hierarchically-ordered organizations," and (2) "the authority of their members depends on their claim to representing the rest of the community in some sense of that protean concept, representation" (1971, p. 3).

A third definitional component, already implied by this analysis, is that legislatures are bodies which promulgate laws, that is to say, authenticate and legitimate commands as to what citizens of a state can or cannot do. Indeed, an early Blackstone Commentary observes that "legislature . . . is the greatest act of superiority that can be exercised by one being over another" (Oxford English Dictionary, s.v. "legislature").

To sum up, "legislatures" have three principal characteristics.
1. Members are equal in status (at a minimum each has one vote).
2. Law-making, the promulgation of authoritative commands to the citizenry, is their chief (but not exclusive) function.
3. Their authority to make laws stems from a constitutional and representational base (usually dependent upon free and periodic elections).

Obviously, any number of exceptions could be identified among the legislatures of some 150 countries, let alone their subdivisions.[3]

More refined classifications of legislatures are still in their formative stages (Patterson and Wahlke, 1972; Mezey, 1979). Polsby makes an important distinction between legislation in open regimes which mainly function as arenas, such as the British House of Commons, and those which are transformative institutions, such as the U.S. Senate and House of Representatives.

The crucial question we must ask of arenas is exemplified by Sir Lewis Namier's celebrated inquiry about eighteenth-century Britain—why men *went* into Parliament—in short the question of political recruitment, which significantly is not a study of the acquisition or exercise of power once they got there (Polsby, 1975, p. 278).

If, on the other hand, legislatures possess "the independent capacity, frequently exercised, to mold and transform proposals from whatever source into laws" (Polsby, 1975, p. 277), then the study of internal structure and allocation of tasks, especially between leaders and followers, becomes all the more significant.

Typologies of Legislative Leadership

Formal-Informal

One major distinction suggested in the literature is that between formal and informal leadership. The former is usually equated with office-holding or authority; the latter with influence or personal persuasion. The U.S. Senate of the 1950s provided a classic illustration of the two types of leadership—Lyndon B. Johnson of Texas, the youthful, assertive, formal leader; and Richard B. Russell of Georgia, the senior, taciturn, mainly behind-the-scenes leader (White, 1956; Evans and Novak, 1966; Kearns, 1976). Of course, much of Russell's influence rested upon his lengthy experience, his occupancy of a powerful Senate chair, and his ability to influence the votes of many of his Southern colleagues. Informal and formal leadership are frequently fused in practice.

A closely related distinction has been set forth by organizational psychologist Alex Bavelas—the idea of leadership as a personal quality rather than an organizational function.

The first refers to a special combination of personal characteristics; the second refers to a distribution throughout an organization of decision-making powers. The first leads us to look at the qualities and abilities of individuals; the second leads us to look at the patterns of power and authority in organization. Both of these ideas or definitions are useful, but it is important to know which one is being talked about, and to know under what conditions the two must be considered together in order to understand a specific organizational situation (Bavelas, 1960, p. 491; cf. Peabody, 1964).

In most legislatures, if not all, personal skills become significant primarily in an organization context (Jones, 1981, pp. 118-119).

Cooper and Brady expand on these same themes in their analysis of U.S. House speakers from Cannon to Rayburn. As they conclude,

first, institutional context rather than personal skill is the prime determinant of leadership power in the House. . . . Skill cannot fully compensate for deficiencies in the quality or quantity of inducements. . . .

Second, institutional context rather than personal traits primarily determines leadership style in the House (1981, p. 423).

Party and Committee Leadership

In all legislatures of any complexity, a further delegation of power has become characteristic, namely, the allocation of members to committees, usually segmented along jurisdictional subject matters—finance, foreign policy, commerce, and the like. Although committee structures have been most refined in the U.S. Congress, they have become important vehicles for considering, modifying, and sometimes defeating legislation in most modern parliaments. Research on the activities of committee chairmen in the U.S. Congress, although scattered, is beginning to accumulate (Robinson, 1963; Peabody and Polsby, 1963; Manley, 1970; Fenno, 1973; Oppenheimer, 1977; Price, 1977; Unekis and Rieselbach, 1983). The primary focus of this essay, however, will be on party leaders, most typically designated as speakers, prime ministers, floor leaders, caucus chairmen, party whips, and the like.

Internal and External Leadership

Another important distinction is that between internal and external leadership. As legislative leaders rise in the legislative hierarchy of the party, their responsibilities increasingly lead them to interactions with "outsiders"— the executive branch, the news media, interest group leaders, and the like (Peabody, 1981, pp. 90-100).

Distinctions between internal and external facets of leadership became all the more important when one shifts from a presidential-congressional system to parliamentary forms of government. Prime ministers are legislative leaders in both senses—they guide their parties' programs within the legislature, but their main functions are external and they are more frequently compared to presidents and other heads of state than to congressional leaders (Bradshaw and Pring, 1972; Rose and Suleiman, 1980).

All such analytical distinctions aside, the critical questions addressed, but by no means resolved, in this review essay are (1) why do some members (leaders) of a legislature become more equal than others (followers) and (2) what are the consequences for task performance, individually and collectively, over time? Put slightly differently, why have legislatures, by definition collectivities of more or less equal members, come to be characterized by permanent leadership structures? And what difference does legislative leadership make for the goals of the institution, its environmental setting, and the broader political system?

Origins and Evolution

Recall Loewenberg's basic criteria for distinguishing parliaments from other, more hierarchically ordered organizations: "members are formally equal to each other in status" (1971, p. 3). Simply put, a member of a legislature typically has one vote, like all other members of the body. As parliaments evolved, however, some members became "more equal" than others, achieved higher status, took on positions of formal authority. How did such positions evolve? Equally important, how were such positions institutionalized in the representative assemblies of various countries?

Most modern scholarship on legislative leadership starts from the development of the English parliament in the early thirteenth century (Pasquet, 1914; McIlwain, 1910; Pollard, 1920). In 1215, King John was forced temporarily to acknowledge the claims of the barons, resulting in the Great Charter or Magna Carta (Thompson, 1972). As the parliament evolved from the king's court and became more independent, routine positions of legislative leadership evolved (Marsden, 1966; Moore and Horwitz, 1971). Fundamentally, there were and still are two main types: officers of the Parliament, such as speakers and clerks, typically but not always nonpartisan; and political leaders charged with representing factions or parties within the legislature to other, external power holders, such as the king (Carter, 1956; Marsden, 1966; King, 1969). Occasionally, as with the U.S. speaker, an amalgam emerged (Follett, 1896; Ripley, 1967; Peabody, 1976).

Another major analytical and practical distinction emerged from late eighteenth-century developments, namely the evolution of two types of governmental systems: the presidential-congressional and the parliamentary. Regardless of how power is segmented, in every legislature some party leaders are mainly concerned with internal matters of the legislature—for example, getting out the vote on legislative matters. Other party leaders, especially top leaders, must allocate more time to shared or external functions—for example, most prime ministers in parliamentary systems, or speakers and floor leaders in the U.S. Congress. The full thrust of such distinctions will become clearer when the selection and functions of legislative leaders are reviewed, below.

Historical Treatment of a Core Position: Speakers

Every legislature of any complexity requires someone to preside over its deliberations. In the United States, in most countries of the British Commonwealth, and in many European and African parliaments, the legislative positions and practices can be traced to the British House of Commons, appropriately regarded as "the mother of parliaments." Perhaps nowhere is this more clearly revealed than in the evolution and institutionalization of a core office—the speakership.

Most authorities concur that the first speaker "known to have been chosen by the Commons from among themselves and to have acted for the duration of a parliament" was Sir Peter de la Mare in the Good Parliament of 1376 (Roskell, 1965, p. vii; cf. Laundy, 1964). Since French was still the dominant language of the court, de la Mare was known as a "prelocutor," hence "speaker." His principal function was to represent—that is, to speak for—his fellow commoners to the king and his advisors, as well as to report back the king's directives. The first "speaker" to be designated as such was de la Mare's successor, Sir Thomas Hungerford. "It was not until the year 1377, toward the end of Edward III's reign, that the continuing line of identifiable Speakers was first founded" (Marsden, 1966, p. 94). Other officers of the British House of Commons predate the speaker by only a few years—the first clerk of the Commons was Robert de Melton, first appointed in 1363 (Marsden, 1966, p. 30). The position of Serjeant-at-Arms, the man charged with enforcing parliamentary privileges, can be traced back even earlier. Not until 1415 did the king grant to the Commons an individual, one Nicholas Maudit, charged "during his life to attend upon all his Parliament and the Parliaments of his heirs so long as they should last as Serjeant-at-Arms for the Commons" (Marsden, 1966, p. 79).

By the late sixteenth century, the time of *The Elizabethan House of Commons* (Neale, 1949), there were "three officers in the pay of the Crown— the Speaker, the Clerk, and the Serjeant-at-Arms. By ancient usage, which can be traced back to 1485, the Speaker received a fee of £100 for each session of Parliament" (p. 332). But for all three officers, salaries and gifts from the queen were only a minor part of their overall benefits. Only the speaker remains a legislative leader as this essay defines that term, although officers of legislatures help ensure continuity, preserving the body's precedents and traditions. For example, speakers were "entitled to £5 for every private bill before the first reading—'before he deliver it out of his hand' " (p. 336). Neale estimates that by the end of the sixteenth century, in a year in which Parliament met, the speaker's "official salary could have constituted no more than one-eighth or one-tenth of his total earnings" (p. 348). (By these criteria, a speaker of the Elizabethan age had more political discretion, if not tempta- tion, than his modern-day counterparts.) Thus, fees for legislative favors could, and sometimes did, amount to bribery.

In his last work, *The House of Commons, 1604-1610,* Wallace Notestein, another eminent parliamentary historian, provides a succinct description of the duties of a speaker. Sir Edward Phelips—"not one of the distinguished Speakers, nor one of the more popular, his personality had, nevertheless, to be reckoned with" (1971, p. 475)—served during the years Notestein writes of. By the early seventeenth century, it had become cus- tomary for speakers to discharge such duties as arranging the order of the day's proceedings, putting the form of the question to the House at the close of debate, and deciding whether or not an orator should be taken off his feet. The speaker also had responsibility for maintaining the privileges of the House as, for example, when a member or his servant might be arrested for failure to pay debts. It was also the duty of the speaker to assist in the scheduling of the House and to oversee the functioning of a nascent committee system. Still, the "Speaker's main function was to preside over debate" (Notestein, 1971, p. 486).

Gradually, the speaker of the House of Commons moved out from beneath the dominance of the Crown. By the mid-nineteenth century, speakers came under the appointive influence of emerging political parties. Even as late as the mid-eighteenth century, Namier (1929) notes, little attention was de- voted to the activities of formal officers of the House of Commons. Namier's predominant interest was the decisions of men to enter into the electoral politics of that period. The biographical compilations of Namier and his associates remain a basic storehouse of information on the history of parliaments and their membership (Namier and Brooke, 1964).

The American Speaker

Compared to the extensive treatment of the speaker of the House of Commons, capped by a number of personal accounts such as Selwyn Lloyd's *Mr. Speaker, Sir* (1976), the literature on U.S. speakers is somewhat limited. Follett's study of *The Speaker of the House of Representatives* (1896), despite its datedness, remains the best written analysis of the U.S. experience with this office. Tracing the roots of the office to the British system, Follett begins her book with a historical examination of the office in the House of Commons. "It was not until [the nineteenth] century that the just and impartial character which we attribute to the presiding officer of the House of Commons became a reality" (pp. 11-12).

Among the political customs and traditions which the American colonists brought with them from the old world, one of the most important was English parliamentary procedures, including the use of a presiding officer called the speaker. But as Follett notes, "all of these institutions were altered and modified by new conditions, the Speaker in the colonies developed into a very different officer from the Speaker of the House of Commons" (p. 12). Colonial speakers, initially selected by their respective houses with the approval of the British governors, gradually developed into independent sources of power. When the founding fathers met in Philadelphia in 1789 to draft a constitution, they included a clause in Article I: "The House of Representatives shall chuse their Speaker and other officers." The first speaker of the first congress (1789-1791) was Frederick A.C. Muhlenberg, a former presiding officer for the Pennsylvania state legislature. In the first several congresses little partisanship was attached to the position. Only later would the speaker evolve into the leader of the majority party, invested with substantial parliamentary powers (Josephy, 1975, pp. 22-23).

For Follett, "the Speakership is not only an institution, it is an opportunity, in which men of strong character have shown their leadership" (1896, p. 64). Her treatments of the growth of the speaker's legislative prerogatives and her sketches of strong speakers, such as Henry Clay of Kentucky (1811-1814, 1815-1820, 1823-1825) and Thomas B. Reed of Maine (1889-1891, 1895-1899), remain models of historical analysis.

Chiu's attempt to update Follett, *The Speaker of the House of Representatives Since 1896* (1928), never quite escapes from its doctoral trappings. However, when bolstered by other accounts (Thompson, 1906; Alexander, 1916; Brown, 1922; Hasbrouck, 1927), a fairly clear picture of

U.S. congressional leadership at the turn of the century emerges. What is perhaps the critical event in the evolution of the speaker's powers—the 1910 revolt against Joseph Cannon of Illinois—has also received extensive treatment from historians and political scientists (Atkinson, 1911; Busby, 1927; Hechler, 1940; Galloway, 1962). Another critical episode in the development of the speaker's powers—the 1961 floor vote on the enlargement of the House Committee on Rules and the aftermath of that vote—has also been well documented (MacNeil, 1963; Peabody and Polsby, 1963; *A History of the Committee on Rules,* 1983).

In addition, a number of historical treatments of the functions of speakers and other party leaders have been set forth in the works of Galloway (1953, 1962), Jones (1968, 1970, 1981), and Ripley (1967, 1969a, 1983). Ronald M. Peters (1982), the director of the Carl Albert Congressional Research Center at the University of Oklahoma, has begun to publish portions of his research on contemporary House speakers, Rayburn to O'Neill.

Most full-length studies of western European parliaments also touch upon the development and functions of parliamentary leadership positions—for example, Loewenberg (1967, pp. 10-15) or MacRae (1967, pp. 45-47). Studies of the role of political oppositions in western democracies (Dahl, 1966, 1973) also provide rich and illustrative case studies in different regimes. With the important exception of Japan (Fukui, 1970; Ike, 1972; Thayer, 1971), treatment of the evolution and institutionalization of legislative leadership in non-Western countries is rather isolated and fragmentary.

Selection Processes

How and why are legislative leaders chosen? Every legislative body, from the smallest city council to the largest, most complex, national legislature is stocked with aspiring leaders, if not consummate politicians. Almost all members consider themselves worthy of leadership of their faction or party, but only a handful in any legislative body are selected by their peers to provide formal leadership. Leadership selection is often routine, with little or no competition; in many legislatures top leaders groom their successors. Occasionally, however, fascinating and multifaceted political struggles between two or more candidates occur. In such contests the stakes are high, the dynamics complex, and the competition potentially fierce. The outcomes of such leadership struggles occasionally determine the paths of political careers and affect legislative policy for years to come (Peabody, 1967, 1976).

Local and State Leaders

Systematic studies of leadership selection in legislatures are rare at the local level, relatively sparse at the state level, and only slightly more prevalent for parliamentary institutions.

In the U.S., for example, much of the literature on local government and its patterns of leadership is inexorably tied to examinations of macro-societal trends, urbanization, bureaucratization, centralization of power, and professionalism. Recall Merton's famous distinction between the manifest and latent functions of the cities' political machines. According to Merton, "the key structural function of the Boss is to organize, centralize and maintain in good working condition 'the scattered fragments of power' which are presently dispersed through our political organizations" (1957, p. 72). In addition to stimulating further theoretical developments in functional analysis, Merton's paper (first written in 1948) also contributed to the ferment which later came to characterize community power analysis. Within that extensive and controversial literature, there are fragments of research on the roles of city councilmen in their "power structures," as well as on the relationships among mayors, councils, and other community decision makers (see, for example, Hunter, 1953; Dahl, 1961; Bachrach and Baratz, 1962; Polsby, 1963a, 1968a; Jennings, 1964; Wilson, 1968; Banfield, 1969; Eulau and Prewitt, 1973; Wolfinger, 1974).

U.S. State Leaders

The typology of party leadership positions in the 50 U.S. state legislatures is, not surprisingly, very uniform. A number of colonial legislatures served as models for the national legislature; the constitutions of others were, in turn, shaped by national practices. As in the U.S. Congress, in U.S. state legislatures the major positions are likely to be the speaker and majority and minority leaders for the more populous house or assembly and the president, president pro tempore, and majority and minority leaders in the Senate. (Only one state, Nebraska, has a unicameral legislature.)

Selection of leaders in the first instance hinges on vacancies in leadership positions. Perhaps the prevailing pattern in most legislatures of any complexity is to reelect leaders. Jewell and Patterson (1977) note that the more professionalized state legislatures—those with higher pay, larger staffs, and longer and more frequent meetings, such as the legislatures in California, Michigan, or New York—"tend to give longer tenure to their leaders, but the pattern is not a consistent one." They reviewed tenure patterns for house speakers and for the top elective officer of the the senates in the 50 state legislatures from 1947 to 1976 (a period covering 15 two-year terms), finding a total of "six lower houses and eight upper houses in which there was a change of leadership every two years throughout the period" (pp. 135-136). They found that about one-fifth of the state legislatures' principals might serve for 6 terms or more out of a possible 15 in the period examined (see also Chaffey and Jewell, 1972). In contrast, there is some evidence that a few state party leaders have amassed extraordinarily lengthy tenures. Rosenthal singles out two South Carolina legislators, each of whose leadership careers spanned two decades or more (1981, p. 154). But the Browns and Blatts of South Carolina, like the Rayburns and Mansfields of the U.S. Congress, are becoming anachronisms. As with their congressional counterparts, surveys of state legislative leadership patterns in the 1970s indicate decreasing tenure across the board.

Although "the selection of legislative leaders has great significance for the distribution of power and the representation of interests in legislatures," Keefe and Ogul were forced to conclude that, surprisingly, "political scientists have given . . . little systematic attention to change in the composition of legislative party elite" (1977, pp. 282-283).

U.S. Congress

Patterns of party leadership selection and operations in the U.S. Congress have undergone considerable scrutiny over two distinct periods. Beginning about the turn of the century, a number of authors pursued leadership selection and functions in Congress: Follett (1896), Thompson (1906), Brown (1922), Hasbrouck (1927), and Chiu (1928). These early studies were mainly anecdotal and descriptive, with little or no effort to develop generalizations about the selection process, let alone its theoretical implications for policy formation. Follett is the exception. Her chapter on "Choice of the Speaker" not only depicts a number of the major contests during the nineteenth century but also outlines some "principles of choice" guiding the selection of speakers: parliamentary knowledge and experience, congressional service, reelection patterns, sectional advantage, special interests, prospects of places on committee, political motivations, and the personal character and popularity of the leading candidates (1896, pp. 27-63).

A second, more systematic and cumulative, wave of research on congressional leadership came following World War II. While this literature is far too extensive to be reviewed in detail, several of its important findings about leadership selection can be highlighted here. Truman's middleman hypothesis— "that a general qualification for the choice of a floor leader and for his effective performance is that he should be a 'middle' man," not only "in the sense of a negotiator but also in a literal [voting] structural sense" (1959, p. 106, p. 112)—finds further confirmation as well as some qualification in the research of Patterson (1963) and Sullivan (1975). Beginning with Polsby's intensive case study of the contest for House majority leader in 1962, a number of scholars have explored House and Senate leadership contests in detail (Polsby, 1963b; Peabody, 1966; Romans, 1977; Oppenheimer and Peabody, 1977). From such an approach more theoretical schemes have been developed for analyzing the conditions affecting congressional leadership change (Peabody, 1967, 1976; Nelson, 1977).

Case studies of major congressional leadership contests are not only rich in personal psychology and strategic planning; they can also have far-reaching implications for individual careers and for the political environment. Consider the fortunes of House minority leader Gerald R. Ford, appointed vice-president in 1973 by President Richard M. Nixon to take the place of Spiro Agnew, who had been forced to resign. Within a year, Nixon had to step down under the threat of congressional impeachment, and Ford advanced to the presidency of the United States. Ford's selection as vice-president and, later, his elevation to the nation's highest executive position would never have occurred had he not first achieved national recognition as minority leader for the House Republicans (Peabody, 1966, 1976, Ch. 4).

Unlike the prime ministers of parliamentary regimes, few U.S. presidents had first held formal leadership positions in the national legislature. Gerald Ford was one exception; former Senate Democratic Floor Leader Lyndon B. Johnson, former House Floor Leader James A. Garfield, and former Speaker James K. Polk complete the list. Yet many presidential and vice-presidential contenders, especially since the Civil War, have been members, if not formal leaders, of Congress. Of the 40 presidents of the United States, 15 (40 percent) had formerly served in the Senate. Second in frequency of election to the presidency were governors of U.S. states (Peabody, Ornstein, and Rohde, 1976).

Selection of Leaders: Parliaments

What inspires members of Parliament to move to the forefront, some as internal leaders, such as speakers (Laundy, 1964), floor leaders, and whips,[4] others as the highest elected and appointed leaders of the country: ministers of the cabinet and, above all, prime ministers (Wilson, 1959; Rose, 1974)?

Who are the British political elite? Who runs for parliament, secures a cabinet post, becomes prime minister? Guttsman (1968) presents class backgrounds, age of entry, and education and career patterns for British political leaders from 1830 to 1955. Johnson (1973) extends this analysis from 1955 to 1972, singling out "the decline of working-class elite representation" as the most striking characteristic of the post-World-War-II evolution of the British ruling class (p. 68).

Max Weber, more noted for his study of bureaucracies than of parliamentary leaders, nevertheless provides some important insights in his classic essay on "Politics as a Vocation": "How does the selection of these strong leaders take place? . . . Next to the qualities of will—decisive all over the world—naturally the force of demagogic speech is above all decisive." Noting that the quality of rhetoric had changed over the centuries, Weber argued that it was the highly developed system of committee work and floor deliberation which made an effective training ground for future leaders. "All important ministers of recent decades have this very real and effective work-training as a background" (Weber, in Gerth and Mills, 1958, p. 107).

Initially, of course, ministers were not required to be members of Parliament. They were king's men, "appointed by him and . . . responsible to him alone" (Carter, 1956, p. 15). The modern office of prime minister grew from that of the first lord of the Treasury—still the legal title of the prime minister. According to Philip Marsden,

it was not until Walpole asserted himself so forcibly in the Commons in the years following 1721 that any *one* of the King's ministers assumed an importance greater than that of his colleagues. Walpole was the first 'prime' minister (1966, p. 60).

During the sixteenth and seventeenth centuries, the king began "to choose his chief ministers from those political leaders who were best able to secure the support of Parliament" (George B. Adams, quoted in Carter, 1956, p. 18). With the adoption of the Reform Act of 1832, the cabinet became more responsible to Parliament and party leaders found it more necessary to make national appeals to an increasingly participatory electorate. All these developments greatly enhanced the powers of the prime minister, both in the cabinet and in the Parliament.

In his masterful study of *British Political Parties* (1964), McKenzie examines the rise to power of Conservative and Labour party leaders from the late nineteenth century to the 1960s. For the selection of Conservative party leaders from Salisbury to Macmillan (1885 to 1963), he notes that "the most striking fact . . . is that each leader has been selected by acclamation; no ballot, nor any formal contest of any kind, has ever taken place." Instead, when meetings are called to select a new Conservative leader, a kind-of-Quaker-like consensus develops. "It appears to be established practice that the most important of his possible rivals (as well as the elder statesmen of the party) . . . send messages urging his election or else . . . move or second the resolution offering him the leadership" (McKenzie, 1964, p. 51). In contrast, the selection of leaders in the British Labour Party has from time to time been characterized by spirited contests—for example in 1906, 1922, 1935, 1955, and 1963. The Labour leader, except when he serves as prime minister, is formally subject to periodic reelection (McKenzie, 1964, pp. 602, 630). But it is notably a number of Conservative leaders—Balfour (1910), Austen Chamberlain (1922), and Neville Chamberlain (1940)—who have been forced out of office (Bradshaw and Pring, 1972, p. 17).

No man or woman of either party can expect to occupy the office of prime minister without extensive time in Parliament and service in a number of junior ministries. By way of illustration, the 10 prime ministers who served from 1894 to 1953 averaged 24.3 years in the House of Commons prior to assuming top leadership (Carter, 1956, p. 63).

One characteristic which seems to distinguish legislative leaders from corporate and presidential leaders is their relatively lengthy service in office. Long tenure is often crucial both to the selection and to the effectiveness of leaders in most complex legislatures. Unfortunately, as this review has emphasized, comparisons of leadership styles of two or more legislative leaders are still relatively rare, but see Laundy (1964), King (1969), Jones (1968), Ripley (1969b), and Peabody (1981).

So centralized and powerful has the office of prime minister become in Britain and other parliamentary countries, it has sometimes been contrasted and compared with the U.S. presidency. Although the presidency is a unique institution, the president has a number of tasks in common with other heads of governments (Rose and Suleiman, 1980). Among the most important of these are the initiation and implementation of their own legislative programs (Neustadt, 1960; Kearns, 1976; Greenstein, 1982). As Richard Neustadt has observed, "Americans are bound to glimpse a long-familiar pattern in the conduct of an activist Prime Minister. It is the pattern of a President maneuvering around or through the power-men in his Administration *and* in Congress" (1969, p. 143). Moreover, as already noted, U.S. presidents have frequently been recruited from Congress. Of the eight postwar presidents, five had previously served in Congress, two as floor leaders; four of the five had also been vice-president.

Leadership Functions

Most studies of leadership in legislatures primarily describe and analyze leadership functions—what leaders do. Careful, systematic descriptions of leadership tasks, preferably based on case studies of two or more leaders who have held the same position, can provide a sense of the range of alternative behaviors appropriate to a given position. Strong leaders not only "fill" a position, they are also likely to expand its parameters, take on new responsibilities, seek ways to enhance the scope of their powers. For congressional leaders, the lines of demarcation between internal and external powers are blurred, hence the opportunities to expand powers are greater. In most parliamentary systems, in contrast, the tasks which belong to external leaders, such as cabinet ministers, are more clearly delineated from those which belong to internal party officials, such as floor leaders.

Congressional Leadership

The U.S. Constitution (Article I) establishes only three positions of congressional leadership; these are held by the speaker of the House, the president of the Senate (a post filled by the vice-president of the United States), and the president pro tempore of the Senate. The first speaker, Frederick A.C. Muhlenberg of Pennsylvania, and the first president pro tempore of the Senate, John Langdon of New Hampshire, were selected almost as soon as the newly-formed House and Senate obtained quorums (Josephy, 1975, pp. 23-26; De Pauw, 1972, Vol. 1, p. 7; Vol. 3, p. 7). By the early 1800s all four congressional parties had formed caucuses or conferences, and they often named chairmen to preside over their deliberations, including their nominations to committees. More than a century would elapse before other major party leadership positions—such as floor leaders and party whips—evolved (Haynes, 1960; Galloway, 1962; Riddick, 1971; Oleszek, 1972; Swanstrom, 1961; Rothman, 1966; Ripley, 1969a; Munk, 1974).

In the modern British House of Commons, the speaker is "a very ordinary member elected to the chair because he has taken no prominent part in controversy" (Jennings, 1969, p. 15); but in the United States, the speaker is the principal party leader in the House of Representatives, almost always at the center of controversy and the focal point of policy making. The two speakers recognized as the most active partisans, hellbent on accruing power for themselves and the office, were Thomas B. Reed of Maine (1889-1891, 1895-1899) and Joseph G. Cannon of Illinois (1903-1911). Both chaired the Committee on Rules, made committee assignments, presided over the House, and exercised almost unlimited powers of recognition.

Emphasizing the important distinction between institutional context and leadership style, Cooper and Brady (1981) trace the transition of House leadership from Speaker Cannon to Speaker Rayburn. They contend that there is no straightforward relationship between leadership style and effectiveness; instead, style and effectiveness are contingent upon the situation. Accordingly, "Rayburn was not and could not be as powerful a Speaker as Cannon or Reed" (p. 423).

In more modern times, party leaders in the House have been responsible for six major legislative functions:

(1) organizing the party, (2) scheduling the business of the House, (3) promoting attendance of members for important votes on the floor, (4) distributing and collecting information, (5) persuading members to act in accord with their wishes, and (6) maintaining liaison with the President and his top advisors (Ripley, 1967, p. 54).

Although the basic functions of congressional leadership may have changed but little over the past century, leaders have had to adopt different strategies in different eras. Sinclair describes Speaker Thomas P. O'Neill's strategies in the postreform House, most notably his use of ad hoc task forces to implement legislation (1981b, pp. 409-410). Although party leaders may be consumed by their responsibilities as national figures, they cannot afford to ignore their basic responsibility, common to all 435 members of the House, to carefully nurture their home constituencies as a means of insuring reelection (Mayhew, 1974; Fiorina, 1977; Fenno, 1978).

U.S. Senate

Transactional leadership, defined by Burns (1978), "conceives of leader and follower as exchanging gratifications in a political marketplace. they are bargainers seeking to maximize their political and psychic profits" (p. 258). Such a definition has its roots in sociological "exchange theory" (Homans, 1961; Blau, 1964; Coleman, 1970). For Burns, "the classic seat of transactional leadership is the 'free' legislature" and the "consummate transactional leader of legislation" Senate Majority Leader Lyndon B. Johnson (1978, pp. 344-345). If one accepts the assumptions underlying Burns's definition of a "transactional leader," then Ralph K. Huitt provides the definitive explication of the term in his classic article "Democratic Party Leadership in the Senate," primarily a case study of Johnson's performance as "the most skillful and successful [Senate floor leader] in the memory of living observers" (Huitt, 1969, p. 144). Johnson's performance, first as Democratic minority leader (1953-1955) and then as majority leader (1955-1961), has been extensively analyzed (Evans and Novak, 1966; Stewart, 1971; Peabody, 1976, pp. 333-345). In an overview of "Senate Party Leadership: From the 1950s to the 1980s," Peabody (1981) identified five somewhat overlapping primary tasks of Senate majority leaders: (1) managing party organizational machinery, (2) supervising the scheduling of legislation, (3) implementing the flow of the Senate's business, (4) contributing to policy innovation, and (5) enhancing the electoral opportunities of their colleagues in order to maintain control of the Senate.

In the short run, factors such as the size of the chamber, the methods of selecting members, and the length of the members' tenure, will all affect what leaders can expect of members and vice versa. Most close observers of the U.S. Congress agree that leadership in the House is almost inevitably more unwieldy, complicated, and dependent on formal methods of control than is leadership in the smaller, more collegial Senate (Ripley, 1967, 1969a, 1969b, 1983; Jones, 1970, 1981, 1982; Davidson and Oleszek, 1981). In the longer run, such factors as historical traditions, a decentralized two-party system, and the characteristic operations of a representative and law-making body limit what party leaders can hope to accomplish. Context, especially membership constraints, become more important than personal style or persuasion.

Leadership in Parliamentary Systems

Probably more books have been written about the British parliament than about any legislative institution, save perhaps the U.S. Congress. And sometimes, as in the classic works of Bagehot (1867) and Wilson (1885), a treatise on one system begets another. More contemporary books upon parliaments typically include a chapter on membership, followed closely by a chapter on party organization. Thus, Jennings (1939), in his authoritative treatment of the British Parliament, sets forth in his chapter on "Parties and Officials," the obligations of majorities and minorities, the duties of the speaker and his deputies, and the roles of the prime minister, the leader of the opposition, and the whips. Like studies of the U.S. Congress undertaken in the 1960s and especially in the 1970s, studies of the British parliament have become more empirical and quantitative, including several which concentrate on the attitudes and activities of followers as distinct from leaders (Finer, Berrington, and Bartholomew, 1961; Jackson, 1968; Richards, 1972; Punnett, 1973; Norton, 1978, 1980).[5]

Comparative analyses of leadership in legislatures are exceedingly rare. An effort by Bradshaw and Pring (1972), two British parliamentary staffers, illustrates both the advantages and the possible pitfalls of such an approach. Their study, *Parliament and Congress,* opens with several basic assumptions about legislative leadership.

Of major importance in such a study is the way in which power is wielded. Leadership in each legislature is, then, the first subject to be considered. Once elected or constituted an assembly must have leaders to focus its energies and crystallize its will. The leaders in their turn must direct, or oversee the direction of, the governmental machinery which gives effect to that will (p. 8).

From their institutional perspective, the two authors see a "line of responsibility from the electorate to that executive machinery" which is "clear and direct" in the British case but "by no means so clear" in the United States (pp. 8-9). "Concentration of power in the British system and its diffusion in the American" (p. 10) becomes an unfortunate rubric for almost every comparison made in this study. However exemplary their treatment of British parliamentary practices, Bradshaw and Pring's examination of House and Senate leadership is based primarily upon the institutional, descriptive, and reform-oriented literature of the 1950s. Riddick (1949), Griffith (1951), and Galloway (1953) serve as the patron saints here, only occasionally tempered by Clapp (1963) and Ripley (1967).

Almost every European parliament, as well as legislative bodies in many other countries, has been the subject of at least one book which, in part, describes its leadership, organization, and functions. The best of this genre would include Loewenberg's study of the German parliament (1967), and MacRae's (1967) and Williams's (1968) studies of the French parliament. Also notable are Di Palma's excellent analysis of the Italian parliament, *Surviving Without Governing* (1977), from which he finds that "the government's duty/ right to govern and concurrence by the opposition have found no clear acceptance and no way to coexist in an effective operational code" (p. 155).

Attempts at truly comparative analyses of leadership functions in two or more legislatures are rare. Unfortunately, such efforts too often degenerate into compendiums of essays by scholars from various countries, focusing mainly upon their own specific subfields. These collections, however, have contributed much in the way of formal critiques and more informal discussions among scholars of comparative legislatures (Kornberg and Musolf, 1970; Hirsch and Hancock, 1971; Patterson and Wahlke, 1972; Kornberg, 1973; Boynton and Kim, 1975; Smith and Musolf, 1979). Such publications, many of them resulting from conferences sponsored by the Consortium for Comparative Legislative Studies and published under the general editorship of Malcolm E. Jewell, have significantly advanced the study of "legislative systems, institutions, behavior, and outputs that are cross-national in scope as well as studies of single nations that test and develop hypotheses which are significant for comparative research" (Jewell, 1975). Their substantive contribution to the analysis of leadership in legislatures has been peripheral.

According to Dahl,

the three great milestones in the development of democratic institutions [are] the right to participate in governmental decisions by casting a vote, the right to be represented, and the right of an organized opposition to appeal for votes against the government in elections and in parliament (1966, p. xi).

In recent years, those studies of legislative behavior which examine the role of the opposition in the electorate and in the legislature have been among the most productive (see, for example, Dahl, 1973; Milnor and Franklin, 1973). The role of the parliamentary opposition has perhaps come under closest scrutiny in the British House of Commons (Punnett, 1973; Norton, 1975, 1978; Searing, 1982).

Attempts to evaluate research on leadership functions in non-Western legislatures are more hazardous for two reasons: there are far fewer empirical studies as yet and the research tends to be more uneven. These caveats aside, one might single out Agor's treatment of *Latin American Legislatures* (1971), Bihari's analysis in *Socialist Representative Institutions* (1970), Likhovski's description of the workings of the Israeli Knesset (1971), and a number of works treating of the Japanese Diet, including Fukui's (1970), Thayer's (1971), and a recent collection of essays by leading Japanese and American scholars, edited by Valeo and Morrison (1982).

An even more difficult area to assess is the research on leadership in Communist countries, especially the Union of Soviet Socialist Republics and the People's Republic of China. It is not a matter merely of language barriers but rather of fundamental conceptual differences between East and West as to what a "legislature" is and does. Simple, but objective, descriptions of the workings of the legislatures in these and other Communist countries are provided in such standard reference works as the *Political Handbook of the*

World (1981) and *Parliaments of the World* (1976). For Russia, but less so for China, U.S. and European scholars have written a number of texts, typically devoting a chapter or two to the Presidium, the Supreme Soviet, and other constitutional instruments. However, systematic studies of leadership in such institutions are rare (Brzezinski and Huntington, 1964; Guillermaz, 1977).

Other Areas of Study

Still another arena for research on legislative leadership is in international organizations, rapidly proliferating and ranging from the Andean Group, with headquarters in Lima, to any of the United Nations' councils, assemblies, and commissions. Here again, research must distinguish between officers or secretariats and political leaders, usually heads or delegates of country missions.

Another promising concentration of research is coalition building, sometimes focusing on parties within individual parliaments, sometimes extending to the formation of coalitions within regional groups (Dahl, 1966; DeSwann, 1973; Dodd, 1976; Browne and Feste, 1978; Katz, 1980). A further encouraging development in elite studies has come about through the establishment of the *International Yearbook for Studies of Leaders and Leadership* under the general editorship of Moshe M. Czudnowski (1982) and Heinz Eulau.

Specific studies of international leaders are scattered, save for biographies of major officials such as secretaries general of the United Nations. Since Claude (1964), a number of scholars have written about international organizations in a broader context. Two of the more comprehensive studies, both utilizing more quantitative techniques, are Alker and Russett (1965) and Holsti, Hopmann, and Sullivan (1973).

Conclusions

What can be said by way of final observations on the state of research on legislative leadership as of the early 1980s? What might be the most promising avenues for future research?

First, the past several decades have witnessed a surge of interest in the comparative study of legislative institutions. Sponsored and encouraged by such diverse organizations as the Social Science Research Council, the National Science Foundation, the Consortium for Comparative Legislative Studies, and the Comparative Legislative Research Center, the results are surfacing through the publication of an increasing number of scholarly monographs and articles. Setting the highest standards have been a number of excellent studies of the organization and operations of legislatures in individual countries, for example, Matthews (1960), Kornberg (1967), Loewenberg

(1967), MacRae (1967), Williams (1968), Rose (1974), and Di Palma (1977). Although most of these works analyzed the legislative polities of a single country, there have been increasing efforts to incorporate single-nation studies into a broader, comparative context.

Second, most of the leadership studies cited in this review have examined one or more incumbents of a single leadership position (such as speaker, floor leader, or prime minister), in a single country's legislative institution, usually over a limited time. The sheer number of studies of leadership in legislatures has increased dramatically. Save for the historical analysis of the British Parliament and, to a lesser extent, of the U.S. Congress, studies of legislative leadership were rather sparse before World War II. Over the past three decades, and especially since 1970, research on leadership in legislatures has undergone an additional surge. Some 500 references, the great majority dating from 1960, were amassed for this review, of which only about one-half are actually included here. There are other more comprehensive, bibliographical attempts, such as the Inter-Parliamentary Union's *World-Wide Bibliography on Parliaments* (1978, 1980). Even so, material on leadership in non-Western legislatures is especially difficult to uncover, let alone analyze.

Third, in common with social science research in general, the published research on legislative leadership has become increasingly sophisticated—in its ability to isolate a focus, its methodological techniques, the quality of its empirical findings, and its potential for addressing broader, systemic questions. As in every discipline or area, a few scholars have made extraordinary contributions. One singles them out at the risk of neglecting other equally valuable research contributions.

—Almost every scholar of leadership, especially in the United States, but also abroad, is indebted to the contributions of Ralph K. Huitt (1961; Huitt and Peabody, 1969) and Donald R. Matthews (1960). Huitt has been especially adept at capturing the roles of different Senate types; Matthews's book remains the best comprehensive treatment of this complex institution.

—Among the studies of leadership in the U.S. Congress, the works of Charles O. Jones (1968, 1970, 1981, 1982) and Randall B. Ripley (1967, 1969a, 1969b, 1983) have proven to be invaluable, both for their in-depth analysis and the placing of leaders in a broader theoretical and historical context.

—Perhaps no one scholar of the U.S. Congress has provided more formative theoretical constructs, especially as to the goals, attitudes, and behavior of committee leaders and followers, than Richard F. Fenno, Jr. (1966, 1973, 1978).

—The literature on prime ministers, cabinet leaders, and backbenchers in the British House of Commons has also undergone rapid expansion.

For examples of studies in the best historical and institutional mode, see Carter (1956), Laundy (1964), Roskell (1965), Marsden (1966), Jackson (1968), King (1969), and Crossman (1976).

—In research on Canada, Allan Kornberg (1966, 1967; Kornberg and Mishler, 1976) has been especially innovative, but other scholars have written solid analyses of the Canadian parliamentary experiences—for example, Matheson (1976), Punnett (1973), and Campbell (1978).

Most of these works are primarily historical and qualitative in approach, while later studies, for example those by Richards (1972), Punnett (1973), and Norton (1978), rely on more sophisticated quantitative techniques.

Fourth, research on leadership in legislatures has tended to over-emphasize the behavior of leaders and to neglect the perceptions and actions of followers. Still, a number of more quantitatively-oriented U.S. scholars have cast a broader net and have looked at membership performance, especially through roll-call techniques—for example, Turner (1951, 1970), MacRae (1956, 1958, 1970), Truman (1959), Wahlke, Eulau, Buchanan, and Ferguson (1962), Miller and Stokes (1963), Mayhew (1966), Olson and Nonidez (1972), Clausen (1973), Matthews and Stimson (1975), and Kingdon (1981). Obviously, methodological techniques which shed light on the behavior of small elites will not, alone, be adequate for the analysis of large groups of followers (Aydelotte, 1977, p. 6). Moreover, as every user of roll-call or member-constituency analysis soon becomes aware, such techniques have their limitations. Scholars who wish to develop generalizations about the performance of party leaders, the activities of committee spokesmen, and the behavior of rank-and-file members—let alone explore the internal and external constraints which envelop them—must inevitably adopt multifaceted research strategies.

Despite a plethora of new empirical efforts, a number of basic questions about legislative leadership remain only partially resolved or even unanswered. Chief among these are (1) the question of trait analysis, or how leaders differ from their followers;[6] (2) problems of leadership style, or what makes some leaders more effective than others;[7] (3) analysis of contextual variables, or what makes legislative leadership similar to or different from leadership in other situations;[8] (4) linkage or systemic questions, or how leaders interface with and represent their legislatures in the broader political environment in which they so frequently play a major role;[9] and, finally, (5) the age-old questions of comparative analysis—how is it possible to compare leadership or committees or staffing across institutions and nation-states?[10]

From Sir Lewis Namier, who almost single-handedly inspired a major breakthrough in the understanding of British parliamentary politics, I would like to borrow a final observation. He quotes Aeschylus, who thus provides an apt metaphor for what seems to me to be our individual and collaborative tasks:

I took pains to determine the flight of crook-taloned birds, marking which were of the right by nature and which of the left, and what were their ways of living, each after his kind, and the enmities and affections that were between them, and how they consorted together (Namier, 1929, epigraph).

Most scholars seem to agree that leadership, so fundamental to human organizations, will continue to be a central, if evasive, focus of political science and related disciplines. The close analysis of leadership, let alone its understanding, will demand a sensitivity to variables which, for the most part, will remain essentially unquantifiable. What kept Churchill in the British Parliament, isolated if not ostracized, until his particular blend of skills was needed in 1940? What personal characteristics conjoined with the resources of their followers and the climate of the time to bring on "great speakers"— Clay, Reed, Cannon, Rayburn, possibly O'Neill—in the U.S. House of Representatives? What situational variables act on leaders in emergent parliaments and what on formal party leadership in advanced, industrialized nation-states? For those who elect to concentrate on these and other elusive leader-follower relationships in legislatures around the world, the rewards may be late-blooming, if not forged by frustration. More likely, they will be highly rewarding, rich in both the challenges and achievements. Where go the "crook-taloned birds" and how, indeed, do they "consort" together?

NOTES

Writing a review essay for a broader audience is inherently a collective effort. I would like to acknowledge the assistance and support of a number of friends and colleagues: Heinz Eulau, Ken Kato, Richard Katz, Norman Ornstein, Evelyn Scheulen, Evelyn Stoller, and, especially, Ellen Moran and Catherine Grover.

1. Charles O. Jones made this important distinction as well as providing other helpful comments in his critique of my paper at the University of Iowa Legislative Research Conference, 24-27 October 1982. I would also like to acknowledge the suggestions of other conference participants, especially Roger Davidson and Kenneth Shepsle. In the preparation of this revised version the comments of the editors of *Legislative Studies Quarterly,* especially Gerhard Loewenberg, were invaluable.

2. "The most general strategic factor in human cooperation is executive capacity. In the nature of the physical world and of the social world as well, opportunities and ideals outrun the immediate motives and interests of and the practical abilities that are required of leaders" (Barnard, 1938, p. 282).

"The precise nature of political leadership is one of the most difficult problems in the domain of politics or, indeed, in social action, yet it is one of the most real phenomena in political and social behavior" (Merriam, 1945, 1957, p. 107).

"Leadership is one of the most observed and least understood phenomena on earth.... Leadership as a concept has dissolved into small and discrete meanings" (Burns, 1978, p. 2).

After reviewing these and other attempts at defining and explaining leadership as a relational aspect, Tucker concludes that the "most fruitful way to start is the question of what it is that leaders do, or try to do, in their capacities as leaders, what functions do they perform in the process of exerting influence upon their followers?" (1981, p. 13).

3. *The Political Handbook of the World: 1981* lists and briefly identifies and describes the heads of state, the government and politics, political parties and legislative structures of more than 150 countries, from the 250-member unicameral People's Assembly of Albania to the 40-member Senate and 100-member House of Assembly of Zimbabwe.

4. In the British House of Commons "the need for an impartial speaker rules out the candidate of a high temperature or strongly partisan member. . . . On being selected, he forswears political connections and ceases to be a member of his party" (Bradshaw and Pring, 1972, p. 51).

For several centuries, of course, speakers of the House of Commons, as well as kings' ministers, were appointed by royal decree. Notestein provides a droll description of the election as speaker of Sir Edward Phelips in 1604, a man whose nomination "came as a surprise to Commons." It was "doubtful if anyone outside of the Privy Council had thought of him as a possible presiding official." After Phelips was nominated, "The motion was followed by silence, 'the House not naming any'."

> At last he being named again, some few cried, 'A Phelips,' some cried
> 'No, no,' but then an ancient Parliament man, directing the House,
> said it was not sufficient to say 'No,' but they must propound some
> other. So some cry, 'Phelips' again, some one or two cry, 'Sir Edward
> Hoby'; some one, some another. But it is being put to the question,
> 'as many as will have a Phelips say 'I',' most cried 'I,' and the rest
> 'No'; some five (?) cried 'No' (Notestein, 1971, p. 475).

5. Patterson (1973) provides an extensive review of books on the British House of Commons from the early 1960s through 1972.

6. More than 60 years ago, Max Weber put forth "three pre-eminent qualities . . . decisive for the politician: passion, a feeling of responsibility, and a sense of proportion" (Weber, in Gerth and Mills, 1958, p. 115). That kind of analysis, more in vogue a generation ago, may yet warrant rediscovery. Polsby observes that, in the 1962 contest for the House majority leadership, "the mysteries of how men interact with one another, of what leads people into enmity, jealousy, friendship, all . . . played a very significant part" (1963b, pp. 243-244). And Greenstein has commented that "personality variations will be more evident to the degree that the individual occupies a position free 'from elaborate expectations of fixed content'. Typically, these are leadership positions" (1969, p. 56).

7. Froman and Ripley (1965) outlined a number of variables conditioning success of leadership for House Democrats in the early 1960s, but there has been little follow-up or parallel research.

8. Shepsle has suggested an alternative to analysis like Weber's, which focused on the traits, qualities, and motivations of leaders. Shepsle sees leadership as "an *agency relationship* between a legislative group, party or caucus (the principals) and their leader (the agent)." This theory of agency, with its obvious parallels to "leader-follower" analysis, has already had broad application in the fields of industrial organization and legal scholarship (Shepsle, personal communication).

9. Several of the best examples of this type of analysis have been written by Sundquist (1968, 1981).

10. Neustadt, in his comparisons of "White House and Whitehall" (1969, p. 133), puts forth a useful suggestion for would-be comparative scholars: "I find no functions in the British system for which ours lacks at least nascent counterparts. But it is rare when institutions with the same names in both systems do the same work for precisely the same purpose. We make ourselves much trouble, analytically, by letting nomenclature dictate our analogies."

REFERENCES

Agor, Weston H., ed. 1971. *Latin American Legislatures: Their Role and Influence.* New York: Praeger.

Alexander, DeAlva S. 1916. *History and Procedure of the House of Representatives.* Boston: Houghton Mifflin.

Alker, Hayward R. and Bruce M. Russett. 1965. *World Politics in the General Assembly.* New Haven: Yale University Press.

Atkinson, C.R. 1911. *The Committee on Rules and the Overthrow of Speaker Cannon.* New York: Columbia University Press.

Aydelotte, William O., ed. 1977. *The History of Parliamentary Behavior.* Princeton: Princeton University Press.

Bachrach, Peter and Morton S. Baratz. 1962. "The Two Faces of Power," *American Political Science Review* 57: 947-952.

Bagehot, Walter. 1867. *The English Constitution.* London: Chapman and Hall.

Banfield, Edward C., ed. 1969. *Urban Government.* Rev. Ed. New York: The Free Press.

Banks, Arthur S. and William Overstreet, eds. 1981. *Political Handbook of the World: 1981.* New York: McGraw-Hill.

Barnard, Chester I. 1938. *The Functions of the Executive.* Cambridge: Harvard University Press.

Bass, Bernard M., ed. 1981. *Stogdill's Handbook of Leadership: A Survey of Theory and Research.* New York: The Free Press.

Bavelas, Alex. 1960. "Leadership, Man and Function," *Administrative Science Quarterly* 4:491-498.

Beer, Samuel H. 1965. *British Politics in the Collectivist Age.* New York: Knopf.

Bihari, Otto. 1970. *Socialist Representative Institutions.* Budapest: Akademiai Kiado.

Blau, Peter M. 1964. *Exchange and Power in Social Life.* New York: Wiley.

Bolling, Richard. 1965. *House Out of Order.* New York: Dutton.

————. 1968. *Power in the House.* New York: Dutton.

Boynton, G.R. and Chong Lim Kim, eds. 1975. *Legislative Systems in Developing Countries.* Durham, NC: Duke University Press.

Bradshaw, Kenneth and David Pring. 1972. *Parliament and Congress.* Austin: University of Texas Press.

Brady, David. 1972. "Congressional Leadership and Party Voting in the McKinley Era: A Comparison to the Modern House," *Midwest Journal of Political Science* 16:439-459.

Brown, George R. 1922. *The Leadership of Congress.* Indianapolis: Bobbs-Merrill.

Browne, Eric C. and Karen Ann Feste. 1978. "Scaling Ministerial Payoffs in European Governing Coalitions," *Comparative Political Studies* 11:397-408.

Brzezinski, Zbigniew and Samuel P. Huntington. 1964. *Political Power: USA/USSR.* New York: Viking.

Burns, James MacGregor. 1978. *Leadership.* New York: Harper & Row.

Busby, L. White. 1927. *Uncle Joe Cannon.* New York: Henry Holt.

Butt, Ronald. 1967. *The Power of Parliament*. London: Constable.

Campbell, E. Colin. 1978. *The Canadian Senate: A Lobby-from-Within*. Toronto: Macmillan.

Carter, Byrum E. 1956. *The Office of Prime Minister*. Princeton: Princeton University Press.

Chaffey, Douglas C. and Malcolm E. Jewell. 1972. "Selection and Tenure of State Legislative Party Leaders: A Comparative Analysis," *Journal of Politics* 34:1278-1286.

Chiu, Chang-wei. 1928. *The Speakers of the House of Representatives Since 1896*. New York: Columbia University Press.

Clapp, Charles L. 1963. *The Congressman: His Job As He Sees It*. Washington, DC: The Brookings Institution.

Claude, Inis L., Jr. 1964. *Swords into Plowshares. The Problems and Progress of International Organization*. 3d ed. New York: Random House.

Clausen, A.R. 1973. *How Congressmen Decide: A Policy Focus*. New York: St. Martin's Press.

Coleman, James S. 1970. "Political Money," *American Political Science Review* 64: 1074-1087.

Cooper, Joseph and David W. Brady. 1981. "Institutional Context and Leadership Style: The House from Cannon to Rayburn," *American Political Science Review* 75:411-425.

Crossman, Richard. 1976. *The Diaries of a Cabinet Minister*. 2 vols. London: Hamish Hamilton.

Czudnowski, Moshe M., ed. 1982a. *Does Who Governs Matter?* DeKalb: Northern Illinois University Press.

_____, ed. 1982b. *International Yearbook for Studies of Leaders and Leadership*. DeKalb: Northern Illinois University Press.

_____, ed. 1983. *Political Elites and Social Change*. DeKalb: Northern Illinois University Press.

Dahl, Robert A. 1957. "The Concept of Power," *Behavioral Science* 2:201-215.

_____. 1961. *Who Governs?* New Haven: Yale University Press.

_____, ed. 1966. *Political Oppositions in Western Democracies*. New Haven: Yale University Press.

_____, ed. 1973. *Regimes and Oppositions*. New Haven: Yale University Press.

Dasent, Arthur Irwin. 1911. *The Speakers of the House of Commons*. London: John Lane.

Davidson, Roger H. 1981. "Congressional Leaders as Agents of Change," in Frank H. Mackaman, ed., *Understanding Congressional Leadership*. Washington, DC: Congressional Quarterly Press.

Davidson, Roger H. and Walter J. Oleszek. 1981. *Congress and Its Members*. Washington, DC: Congressional Quarterly Press.

DePauw, Linda G., ed. 1972. *Documentary History of the First Federal Congress, 1789-1791*. Baltimore: The Johns Hopkins University Press.

DeSwaan, Abram. 1973. *Coalition Theories and Cabinet Formations*. Amsterdam: Elsevier Scientific Publishing.

Di Palma, Giuseppe. 1977. *Surviving Without Governing: The Italian Parties in Parliament*. Berkeley: University of California Press.

Dodd, Lawrence C. 1976. *Coalitions in Parliamentary Government*. Princeton: Princeton University Press.

_____. 1979. "The Expanded Role of the House Whip System: 93rd and 94th Congresses," *Congressional Studies* 7:17-56.

Dodd, Lawrence C. and Bruce I. Oppenheimer, eds. 1981. *Congress Reconsidered.* 2d ed. Washington, DC: Congressional Quarterly Press. (1st ed., Praeger, 1977.)

Dogan, Mattei. 1979. "How to Become a Cabinet Minister in France: Career Pathways, 1870-1978," *Comparative Politics* 12:1-25.

Eulau, Heinz. 1962. "Bases of Authority in Legislative Bodies: A Comparative Analysis," *Administrative Science Quarterly* 7:309-321.

Eulau, Heinz and Kenneth Prewitt. 1973. *Labyrinths of Democracy: Adaptations, Linkages, Representation and Policies in Urban Politics.* Indianapolis: Bobbs-Merrill.

Evans, Rowland and Robert Novak. 1966. *Lyndon B. Johnson: The Exercise of Power.* New York: The New American Library.

Fenno, Richard F., Jr. 1966. *The Power of the Purse: Appropriations Politics in Congress.* Boston: Little, Brown.

————. 1973. *Congressmen in Committees.* Boston: Little, Brown.

————. 1978. *Home Style: House Members in Their Districts.* Boston: Little, Brown.

Finer, S.E., H.B. Berrington, and D.J. Bartholomew. 1961. *Backbench Opinion in the House of Commons, 1955-59.* Oxford: Pergamon Press.

Fiorina, Morris P. 1977. *Congress: Keystone of the Washington Establishment.* New Haven: Yale University Press.

Follett, Mary Parker. 1896. *The Speaker of the House of Representatives.* New York: Longmans, Green.

Froman, Lewis and Randall Ripley. 1965. "Conditions for Party Leadership: The Case of the House Democrats," *American Political Science Review* 59:52-63.

Fukui, Haruhiro. 1970. *Party in Power: The Japanese Liberal-Democrats and Policy-Making.* Berkeley: University of California Press.

Fuller, Herbert B. 1909. *The Speakers of the House.* Boston: Little, Brown.

Galloway, George. 1953. *The Legislative Process in Congress.* New York: Crowell.

————. 1962. *History of the House of Representatives.* New York: Crowell.

Gerth, H.H. and C. Wright Mills, eds. 1958. *From Max Weber: Essays in Sociology.* New York: Oxford University Press.

Gibb, Cecil A. 1968. "Leadership: Psychological Aspects," *International Encyclopedia of the Social Sciences* 9:91-101.

Greenstein, Fred I. 1969. *Personality and Politics.* Chicago: Markham.

————. 1982. *The Hidden-Hand Presidency: Eisenhower as Leader.* New York: Basic Books.

Griffith, Ernest S. 1951. *Congress: Its Contemporary Role.* New York: New York University Press.

Guillermaz, Jacques. 1977. *The Chinese Communist Party in Power, 1949-1976.* Boulder, CO: Westview Press.

Guttsman, W.L. 1968. *The British Political Elite.* London: MacGibbon and Kee.

Hasbrouck, Paul D. 1927. *Party Government in the House of Representatives.* New York: Macmillan.

Haynes, George H. 1960. *The Senate of the United States.* 2 vols. New York: Russell & Russell.

Hechler, Kenneth W. 1940. *Insurgency.* New York: Columbia University Press.

Hempel, Carl G. 1952. *Fundamentals of Concept Formation in Empirical Science.* Chicago: University of Chicago Press.

Herman, Valentine and Francoise Mendel. 1976. *Parliaments of the World: A Reference Compendium.* Edited by Inter-Parliamentary Union. Berlin and New York: Walter De Gruyter.

Hinckley, Barbara. 1970. "Congressional Leadership Selection and Support: A Comparative Analysis," *Journal of Politics* 32:268-287.

Hirsch, Herbert and M. Donald Hancock, eds. 1971. *Comparative Legislative Systems.* New York: The Free Press.

A History of the Committee on Rules. 1983. Washington, DC: U.S. Government Printing Office.

Holsti, Ole R., P. Terrence Hopmann, and John D. Sullivan. 1973. *Unity and Disintegration in International Alliances.* New York: Wiley.

Homans, George. 1961. *Social Behavior: Its Elementary Forms.* New York: Harcourt, Brace & World.

Huitt, Ralph K. 1961. "Democratic Party Leadership in the Senate," *American Political Science Review* 55:333-344.

Huitt, Ralph K. and Robert L. Peabody. 1969. *Congress: Two Decades of Analysis.* New York: Harper & Row.

Hunter, Floyd. 1953. *Community Power Structure.* Chapel Hill: University of North Carolina Press.

Huntington, Samuel P. 1969. *Political Order in Changing Societies.* New Haven: Yale University Press.

Ike, Nobutake. 1972. *Japanese Politics: Patron Client Democracy.* New York: Knopf.

Inter-Parliamentary Union. 1978, 1980. *World-Wide Bibliography on Parliaments.* Vols. I, II. Geneva: International Centre for Parliamentary Documentation.

Jackson, John E. 1974. *Constituencies and Leaders in Congress.* Cambridge: Harvard University Press.

Jackson, Robert. 1968. *Rebels and Whips: Discipline and Cohesion in British Political Parties Since 1945.* London: Macmillan.

Jennings, M. Kent. 1964. *Community Influentials: The Elites of Atlanta.* New York: The Free Press.

Jennings, W. Ivor. 1939. *Parliament.* Cambridge: The University Press. (2d ed. 1957.)

Jewell Malcolm E. 1975. "Foreword," *Legislative Systems in Developing Countries.* Durham, NC: Duke University Press.

_____ . 1978. "Legislative Studies in Western Democracies: A Comparative Perspective," *Legislative Studies Quarterly* 3:537-554.

Jewell, Malcolm E. and Gerhard Loewenberg. 1981. "The State of United States Legislative Research," *Legislative Studies Quarterly* 6:1-25.

Jewell, Malcolm E. and Samuel C. Patterson. 1977. *The Legislative Process in the United States.* 3d ed. New York: Random House.

Johnson, R.W. 1973. "The British Political Elite, 1955-1972," *Archives Européenes de Sociologie* 14:35-77.

Jones, Charles O. 1968. "Joseph G. Cannon and Howard W. Smith: An Essay on the Limits of Leadership in the House of Representatives," *Journal of Politics* 30:617-646.

_____ . 1970. *The Minority Party in Congress.* Boston: Little, Brown.

_____ . 1981. "House Leadership in an Age of Reform," in Frank H. Mackaman, ed., *Understanding Congressional Leadership.* Washington, DC: Congressional Quarterly Press, Ch. 3.

_____ . 1982. *The United States Congress: People, Place, and Policy.* Homewood, IL: The Dorsey Press.

Josephy, Alvin M., Jr. 1975. *The American Heritage History of the Congress of the United States.* New York: American Heritage Publishing.

de Jouvenel, Bertrand. 1959. *Sovereignty: An Inquiry into the Political Good.* Chicago: University of Chicago Press.

Kaplan, Abraham. 1964. *The Conduct of Inquiry; Methodology for Behavioral Science.* San Francisco: Chandler.

Katz, Richard S. 1980. *A Theory of Parties and Electoral Systems.* Baltimore: The Johns Hopkins University Press.

Kearns, Doris. 1976. *Lyndon Johnson and the American Dream.* New York: Harper & Row.

Keefe, William J. and Morris S. Ogul. 1977. *The American Legislative Process: Congress and the States.* 4th ed. Englewood Cliffs, NJ: Prentice-Hall.

King, Anthony S., ed. 1969. *The British Prime Minister.* London: Macmillan.

Kingdon, John W. 1981. *Congressmen's Voting Decisions.* 2d ed. New York: Harper & Row.

Kornberg, Allan. 1966. "Caucus and Cohesion in Canadian Parliamentary Parties," *American Political Science Review* 60:83-92.

——————. 1967. *Canadian Legislative Behavior.* New York: Holt, Rinehart & Winston.

——————, ed. 1973. *Legislatures in Comparative Perspective.* New York: McKay.

Kornberg, Allan and Colin Campbell. 1978. "Parliament in Canada: A Decade of Published Research," *Legislative Studies Quarterly* 3:555-580.

Kornberg, Allan and William Mishler. 1976. *Influence in Parliament: Canada.* Durham, NC: Duke University Press.

Kornberg, Allan and Lloyd D. Musolf, eds. 1970. *Legislatures in Developmental Perspective.* Durham, NC: Duke University Press.

Laundy, Philip. 1964. *The Office of Speaker.* London: Cassell.

Leonard, Dick and Valentine Herman, eds. 1972. *The Backbencher and Parliament.* London: Macmillan.

Likhovski, E.S. 1971. *Israel's Parliament.* Oxford: Clarendon Press.

Lloyd, Selwyn. 1976. *Mr. Speaker, Sir.* London: Jonathan Cape.

Loewenberg, Gerhard. 1967. *Parliament in the German Political System.* Ithaca, NY: Cornell University Press.

——————, ed. 1971. *Modern Parliaments: Change or Decline.* Chicago: Aldine-Atherton.

Mackaman, Frank H., ed. 1981. *Understanding Congressional Leadership.* Washington, DC: Congressional Quarterly Press.

Makintosh, J.P. 1962. *The British Cabinet.* London: Methuen.

MacNeil, Neil. 1963. *Forge of Democracy.* New York: McKay.

MacRae, Duncan, Jr. 1956. "Roll Call Votes and Leadership," *Public Opinion Quarterly* 20:543-558.

——————. 1958. *Dimensions of Congressional Voting.* University of California Publications in Sociology and Social Institutions, vol. 1, no. 3. Berkeley: University of California Press.

——————. 1967. *Parliament Parties and Society in France 1946-1958.* New York: St. Martin's Press.

——————. 1970. *Issues and Parties in Legislative Voting: Methods of Statistical Analysis.* New York: Harper & Row.

Manley, John F. 1970. *The Politics of Finance: The House Committee on Ways and Means.* Boston: Little, Brown.

Mann, Thomas and Norman Ornstein, eds. 1981. *The New Congress.* Washington, DC: American Enterprise Institute.

Marsden, Philip. 1966. *The Officers of the Commons, 1363-1965.* London: Barrie and Rockliff.

Matheson, W.A. 1976. *The Prime Minister and the Cabinet.* Toronto: Methuen.

Matthews, Donald R. 1960. *U.S. Senators and Their World.* Chapel Hill: University of North Carolina Press.

Matthews, Donald R. and James A. Stimson. 1975. *Yeas and Nays: Normal Decision-Making in the U.S. House of Representatives.* New York: Wiley.

Mayhew, David R. 1966. *Party Loyalty Among Congressmen.* Cambridge: Harvard University Press.

_____. 1974. *Congress: The Electoral Connection.* New Haven: Yale University Press.

McIlwain, C.H. 1910. *The High Court of Parliament and Its Supremacy.* New Haven: Yale University Press.

McKenzie, Robert T. 1964. *British Political Parties.* 2d ed. London: Macmillan.

Merriam, Charles E. 1945. *Systematic Politics.* Chicago: University of Chicago Press.

Merton, Robert K. 1957. *Social Structure and Social Theory.* New York: The Free Press.

Mezey, Michael L. 1975. "Legislative Development and Political Parties: The Case of Thailand," in G.R. Boynton and Chong Lim Kim, eds., *Legislative Systems in Developing Countries.* Durham, NC: Duke University Press, pp. 107-141.

_____. 1979. *Comparative Legislatures.* Durham, NC: Duke University Press.

Miller, Warren E. and Donald E. Stokes. 1963. "Constituency Influence in Congress," *American Political Science Review* 57:45-56.

Milnor, Andrew J. and Mark N. Franklin. 1973. "Patterns of Opposition Behavior in Modern Legislatures," in Allan Kornberg, ed., *Legislatures in Comparative Perspective.* New York: McKay.

Moore, T.K. and Henry Horwitz. 1971. "Who Runs the House? Aspects of Parliamentary Organization in the Later Seventeenth Century," *Journal of Modern History* 43:205-227.

Morgan, Janet. 1981. "The House of Lords in the 1980s," *The Parliamentarian* 62:18-26.

Munk, Margaret. 1974. "Origin and Development of the Party Floor Leadership in the United States Senate," *Capital Studies* 2, no. 2:23-41.

Namier, Lewis. 1929. *The Structure of Politics at the Accession of George III.* London: Macmillan. (2d ed. 1957.)

Namier, Lewis and John Brooke. 1964. *The House of Commons, 1754-1790.* 3 vols. New York: History of Parliament Trust.

Neale, J.E. 1949. *The Elizabethan House of Commons.* London: Jonathan Cape.

Nelson, Garrison. 1977. "Partisan Patterns of House Leadership Change, 1789-1977," *American Political Science Review* 71:918-939.

Neustadt, Richard E. 1960. *Presidential Power: The Politics of Leadership.* New York: Wiley.

_____. 1969. "White House and Whitehall," in Anthony King, ed., *The British Prime Minister.* London: Macmillan, pp. 131-147.

Norton, Philip. 1975. *Dissension in the House of Commons: Intra-party Dissent in the House of Commons' Division Lobbies, 1945-1974.* London: Macmillan.

_____. 1978. *Conservative Dissidents: Dissent Within the Parliamentary Conservative Party 1970-1974.* London: Temple Smith.

_____. 1980. *Dissension in the House of Commons, 1974-1979.* Oxford: Clarendon Press.

Notestein, Wallace. 1971. *The House of Commons, 1604-1610.* New Haven: Yale University Press.

Oleszek, Walter J. 1972. *Majority and Minority Whips of the Senate.* Senate Document 92-86, 92d Congress, 1st session. Washington, DC: U.S. Government Printing Office.

Olson, David M. and Cynthia T. Nonidez. 1972. "Measures of Legislative Performance in the U.S. House of Representatives," *Midwest Journal of Political Science* 16:269-277.

Oppenheimer, Bruce I. 1977. "The Rules Committee: New Arm of the Leadership in a Decentralized House," in Lawrence C. Dodd and Bruce I. Oppenheimer, eds., *Congress Reconsidered*. 1st ed. New York: Praeger, pp. 96-116.

Oppenheimer, Bruce I. and Robert L. Peabody. 1977. "How the Race for House Majority Leadership Was Won—By One Vote," *The Washington Monthly* 9:46-56.

Ornstein, Norman, ed. 1981. *The Role of the Legislature in Western Democracies*. Washington, DC: American Enterprise Institute.

Ornstein, Norman J., Robert L. Peabody, and David W. Rohde. 1977. "The Contemporary Senate: Into the 1980s," in Lawrence C. Dodd and Bruce Oppenheimer, eds., *Congress Reconsidered*. 1st ed. New York: Praeger.

Paige, Glenn D. 1977. *The Scientific Study of Political Leadership*. New York: The Free Press.

Pasquet, D. 1914. *Essai sur les origines de la Chambre des Communes*. Paris: Colin.

Patterson, Samuel C. 1963. "Legislative Leadership and Political Behavior," *Public Opinion Quarterly* 27:399-410.

————— . 1973. "Review Article: The British House of Commons as a Focus for Political Research," *British Journal of Political Science* 3:363-381.

————— . 1978. "The Semi-Sovereign Congress," in Anthony King, ed., *The New American Political System*. Washington, DC: American Enterprise Institute.

Patterson, Samuel C. and John C. Wahlke, eds. 1972. *Comparative Legislative Behavior*. New York: Wiley.

Peabody, Robert L. 1964. *Organizational Authority*. New York: Atherton Press.

————— . 1966. *The Ford-Halleck Minority Leadership Contest, 1965*. New York: McGraw-Hill Book Company, Inc.

————— . 1967. "Party Leadership Change in the United States House of Representatives," *American Political Science Review* 61:675-693.

————— . 1968. "Authority," in *International Encyclopedia of the Social Sciences*. New York: Macmillan and The Free Press.

————— . 1969. "Research on Congress: A Coming of Age," in Ralph K. Huitt and Robert L. Peabody, eds., *Congress: Two Decades of Analysis*. New York: Harper & Row.

————— . 1976. *Leadership in Congress: Stability, Succession and Change*. Boston: Little, Brown.

————— . 1981. "Senate Party Leadership: From the 1950s to the 1980s," in Frank H. Mackaman, ed., *Understanding Congressional Leadership*. Washington, DC: Congressional Quarterly Press, Ch. 2.

————— . 1981-1982. "Research on Congress: The 1970s and Beyond," *Congress and the Presidency: A Journal of Capital Studies* 9:1-15.

Peabody, Robert L. and Nelson W. Polsby. 1977. *New Perspectives on the House of Representatives*. 3d ed. Chicago: Rand McNally. (1st ed., 1963; 2d ed., 1969.)

Peabody, Robert L., Norman J. Ornstein, and David W. Rohde. 1976. "The United States Senate as a Presidential Incubator: Many Are Called But Few Are Chosen," *Political Science Quarterly* 91:237-258.

Peters, Ronald M. 1982. "The Theoretical and Constitutional Foundations of the Speakership of the United States House of Representatives." Delivered at the Annual Meeting of the American Political Science Association, Denver.

Political Handbook of the World. 1981. Binghamton, NY: Center for Comparative Political Research, State University of New York, Binghamton.

Pollard, A.F. 1920. *The Evolution of Parliament*. London: Longmans, Green.

Polsby, Nelson W. 1963a. *Community Power and Political Theory*. New Haven: Yale University Press.

_____ . 1963b. "Two Strategies of Influence: Choosing a Majority Leader, 1962," in Robert L. Peabody and Nelson W. Polsby, eds., *New Perspectives on the House of Representatives*. 1st ed. Chicago: Rand McNally, pp. 237-270.

_____ . 1968a. "Community: The Study of Community Power," in *International Encyclopedia of the Social Sciences*. New York: Macmillan and The Free Press.

_____ . 1968b. "The Institutionalization of the U.S. House of Representatives," *American Political Science Review* 62:144-168.

_____ . 1975. "Legislatures," in Fred Greenstein and Nelson W. Polsby, eds., *Handbook of Political Science*. Vol. 5. Reading, MA: Addison-Wesley.

Polsby, Nelson W., Miriam Gallaher, and Barry Spencer Rundquist. 1969. "The Growth of Seniority in the U.S. House of Representatives," *American Political Science Review* 63:787-807.

Price, Douglas. 1977. "Careers and Committees in the American Congress: The Problem of Structural Change," in William O. Aydelotte, ed., *The History of Parliamentary Behavior*. Princeton: Princeton University Press.

Punnett, R.M. 1973. *Front Bench Opposition: The Role of the Leader of the Opposition, the Shadow Cabinet and Shadow Government in British Politics*. London: Heinemann; New York: St. Martin's Press.

Richards, Peter G. 1972. *The Backbenchers*. London: Faber and Faber.

Riddick, Floyd M. 1949. *The United States Congress: Organization and Procedure*. Manassas, VA: National Capitol Publications.

_____ . 1971. *Majority and Minority Leaders of the U.S. Senate: History and Development of the Offices of Floor Leaders*. Senate Document 92-42, 92d Congress, 1st session. Washington, DC: U.S. Government Printing Office.

Ripley, Randall B. 1964. "The Party Whip Organization in the United States House of Representatives," *American Political Science Review* 58:561-576.

_____ . 1967. *Party Leaders in the House of Representatives*. Washington, DC: Brookings.

_____ . 1969a. *Majority Party Leadership in Congress*. Boston: Little, Brown.

_____ . 1969b. *Power in the Senate*. New York: St. Martin's Press.

_____ . 1983. *Congress: Process and Policy*. 3d ed. New York: Norton.

Robinson, James A. 1963. *The House Rules Committee*. New York: Bobbs-Merrill.

Rohde, David W., Norman J. Ornstein, and Robert L. Peabody. 1974. "Political and Legislative Norms in the United States Senate." Delivered at the Annual Meeting of the American Political Science Association, Chicago.

Romans, Maureen Roberts. 1977. "Republican Leadership Fights in the House of Representatives: The Causes of Conflict, 1895-1911." Delivered at the Annual Meeting of the American Political Science Association, Washington, DC.

Rose, Richard. 1971. "The Making of Cabinet Ministers," *British Journal of Political Science* 1:394-414.

_____ . 1974. *The Problem of Party Government*. London: Macmillan.

Rose, Richard and Ezra N. Suleiman, eds. 1980. *Presidents and Prime Ministers*. Washington, DC: American Enterprise Institute.

Rosenthal, Alan. 1981. *Legislative Life*. New York: Harper & Row.

Roskell, J.S. 1965. *The Commons and Their Speakers in English Parliaments, 1376-1523*. New York: Barnes & Noble.

Rothman, David. 1966. *Politics and Power: The U.S. Senate 1869-1901*. Cambridge: Harvard University Press.

Russett, Bruce and Harvey Starr. 1981. *World Politics: A Menu for Choice*. San Francisco: Freeman.

Sartori, Giovanni. 1968. "Representational Systems," in *International Encyclopedia of the Social Sciences.* New York: Macmillan and The Free Press.

Searing, Donald D. 1982. "Rules of the Game in Britain: Can the Politicians be Trusted?" *American Political Science Review* 76:239-258.

Seligman, Lester G. 1975. "Political Risk and Legislative Behavior in Non-Western Countries," in G.R. Boynton and Chong Lim Kim, eds., *Legislative Systems in Developing Countries.* Durham, NC: Duke University Press.

Sherif, Mustapher, ed. 1962. *Intergroup Relations and Leadership: Approaches and Research in Industrial, Ethnic, Cultural and Political Areas.* New York: Wiley.

Sims, Catherine S. 1939. "The Speaker of the House of Commons," *American Historical Review* 45:90-95.

Sinclair, Barbara. 1981a. "Majority Party Leadership Strategies for Coping with the New U.S. House," *Legislative Studies Quarterly* 6:391-414.

_____ . 1981b. "The Speaker's Task Force in the Post-Reform House of Representatives," *American Political Science Review* 75:397-410.

_____ . 1983. *Majority Leadership in the U.S. House.* Baltimore: The Johns Hopkins University Press.

Smith, Joel and Lloyd D. Musolf, eds. 1979. *Legislatures in Development: Dynamics of Change in New and Old States.* Durham, NC: Duke University Press.

Stewart, John G. 1971. "Two Strategies of Leadership: Johnson and Mansfield," in Nelson W. Polsby, ed., *Congressional Behavior.* New York: Random House, pp. 61-92.

Stogdill, Ralph M. 1974. *Handbook of Leadership: A Survey of Theory and Research.* New York: The Free Press.

Sullivan, William E. 1975. "Criteria for Selecting Party Leadership in Congress: An Empirical Test," *American Politics Quarterly* 3:25-44.

Sundquist, James L. 1968. *Politics and Policy: The Eisenhower, Kennedy and Johnson Years.* Washington, DC: The Brookings Institution.

_____ . 1981. *The Decline and Resurgence of Congress.* Washington, DC: The Brookings Institution.

Swanstrom, Roy. 1961. "The United States Senate, 1787-1801." (Ph.D. dissertation, University of California.) Senate Document 87-64, 87th Congress, 1st session. Washington, DC: U.S. Government Printing Office.

Thayer, Nathanial B. 1971. *How the Conservatives Rule Japan.* Princeton: Princeton University Press.

Thomas, Paul G. 1982. "The Role of House Leaders in the Canadian House of Commons," *Canadian Journal of Political Science* 15:125-144.

Thompson, Charles Willis. 1906. *Party Leaders of the Time.* New York: Dillingham.

Thompson, Faith. 1972. *Magna Carta.* New York: Octagon Books.

Truman, David B. 1959. *The Congressional Party.* New York: Wiley.

Tucker, Robert C. 1981. *Politics as Leadership.* Columbia: University of Missouri Press.

Turner, Julius. 1951. *Party and Constituency: Pressures on Congress.* Baltimore: The Johns Hopkins University Press. (Rev. ed. by Edward V. Schneier, Jr., 1970.)

Unekis, Joseph K. and Leroy N. Rieselbach. 1983. "Congressional Committee Leadership, 1971-1978," *Legislative Studies Quarterly* 8:251-270.

Valeo, Francis R. and Charles E. Morrison, eds. 1982. *The Japanese Diet and the U.S. Congress.* Boulder, CO: Westview Press.

Wahlke, John C., Heinz Eulau, William Buchanan, and LeRoy C. Ferguson. 1962. *The Legislative System.* New York: Wiley.

Waldman, Sidney. 1980. "Majority Leadership in the House of Representatives," *Political Science Quarterly* 95:373-393.

Wheare, K.C. 1963. *Legislatures.* London: Oxford University Press.

White, William S. 1956. *The Citadel: The Story of the United States Senate.* New York: Harper & Row.

Williams, Philip M. 1968. *The French Parliament, 1958-1967.* London: Allen and Unwin.

Wilson, F.M.G. 1959. "The Routes of Entry to New Members of the British Cabinet," *Political Studies* 76:222-232.

Wilson, James Q. 1968. *City Politics and Public Policy.* New York: Wiley.

Wilson, Woodrow. 1885. *Congressional Government.* Boston: Houghton Mifflin.

Wolfinger, Raymond. 1974. *The Politics of Progress.* Englewood Cliffs, NJ: Prentice-Hall.

Chapter 7

Legislative Staffs

by

SUSAN WEBB HAMMOND

Legislatures have recently undergone extensive change and reform: especially during the past two decades, state and national legislative staffs have increased rapidly in size and become more specialized and differentiated. At the same time, both the external and internal environments of legislatures have become increasingly complex.

This essay focuses on the literature on legislative staffing. In this literature, the changes in types of data, methods of analysis, and research questions are similar to the changes in political science generally. There has been a shift from a descriptive, institutional approach to the systematic collection of quantitative data and, in some instances, to testing hypotheses. Researchers have become increasingly interested in describing and analyzing the activities, role, and impact of legislative staffs and in the causes and consequences of legislative staffing change.

Three subfields have been particularly important in research on legislative staffing: comparative studies, and especially comparative studies of development; studies of American state politics; and studies of the U.S. Congress. The influence of public administration is evident, especially in the comparative development staffing literature; more recently, state politics scholars, and most recently, congressional scholars, have drawn on public administration and organization theory. Perhaps because much of the literature developed "geographically" (as studies of the U.S. Congress or of U.S. state legislatures or of other national legislatures), there has not been much borrowing—at least until recently—of concepts from one research area to another, and comparative studies are infrequent.

Prior to 1960 the legislative staffing literature was largely descriptive and prescriptive. The decade of the 1960s was transitional: many studies continued to be largely descriptive, others developed hypotheses and reported data used by later scholars. Also in this decade a generation of younger scholars published case studies which, although not focused on staff, reported systematic data and reached insightful conclusions about legislative staffing (Clapp, 1963; Fenno, 1966; Manley, 1966; Ripley, 1969). And several major studies of Congress suggested research agendas which included studies of staffing (Huitt, 1965, 1966; Matthews, 1960). After about 1970, staffing studies were characterized by more systematic data gathering and analysis and by efforts to develop conceptual approaches and theoretical constructs.[1]

A normative theme runs through much of the staffing literature. This is particularly true of the congressional literature of the 1940s and the 1950s and also of various state studies. But current studies also raise normative questions (e.g., Malbin, 1980). Two other motifs—legislative information needs and legislative reform—are also important.

Finally, much of the literature on legislative staffing continues to be written by American scholars, with a few notable exceptions. Even much of the comparative literature has been authored by Americans. As legislatures in other countries establish legislative service agencies and increase levels of staffing, scholarly interests appear to be changing too, and scholars in other countries are beginning to conduct research on legislative staffing.

Legislative Staffing Literature Before 1960

Although articles occasionally appeared earlier (e.g., Lee, 1929), the literature on legislative staffing might be said to begin about 1940, when articles began to appear with increasing frequency and a body of literature began to build. The early studies are primarily descriptive, reporting data on demographic characteristics and tenure (Rogers, 1941; Kammerer, 1949, 1951a, 1951b), recruitment and turnover (Kammerer, 1949, 1951a, 1951b; Kampelman, 1954; Elder, 1957), and partisanship (Kampelman, 1954) of U.S. congressional staff. Galloway (1946, 1951, 1953) reports staff numbers, positions, and salaries. Systematic interviews, supplemented by congressional documents, serve as data sources.

The works are often evaluative and judgmental. Kammerer (1951b), for example, considers "strongly staffed committees" to be those appointing expert staff (their expertise measured by education and experience) without regard to party affiliation and with minimal turnover even when party control changes. Galloway judges staffing against his standard for congressional reform and his passionate belief that Congress needs expert, nonpolitical staff.

The concerns of these studies foreshadow the work of later political scientists. Rogers (1941) distinguishes between power and influence. Kampelman (1954) focuses on whether staff in a political institution can have nonpolitical objectivity. Gross (1953) questions the efficacy of some staffing reforms, noting that staff may increase rather than reduce the workload because "imaginative staff aides often uncovered new problems, new opportunities and new challenges. They tend to create—or at least attract—heavier burdens" (p. 422). Included in Bailey's (1950) case study of the Full Employment Act of 1946 is sophisticated analysis of staff activity and function (Ch. 4).

Two state studies (Lentz, 1957; Siffin, 1959) are descriptive. Meller's 1952 article, although primarily descriptive, is unique in suggesting a conceptual framework for thinking about legislative staffing. He suggests that legislative service agencies be viewed functionally and that different types of agencies have a differential impact: some agencies assemble data; others weigh information; still others participate in definitive action processes. The proposed categories might be arrayed on a continuum, based on the increasing need for value judgments by staff.[2]

1960-1969: A Decade of Transition

The 1960s are a decade of transition in the research on legislative staffing. Descriptive studies continue (Graves, 1961; Crane and Watts, 1968; Lacy, 1967), as do prescriptive studies (McInnis, 1966). The state reform movement shifted into high gear, and the movement for further congressional reforms accelerated; staff "reform"—including more staff, more expert staff, and a different distribution of staff resources—is a major component. As in the 1940s and 1950s, during this decade academics often evaluated and prescribed, as well as studied, legislative staffs (e.g., Butler, 1966). The state reform movement resulted in comprehensive surveys and the collection of massive data bases, including legislative staffing data (Greene and Avery, 1962; Clark, 1967; Council of State Governments, 1963; data base reported by Citizen's Conference on State Legislatures, 1971). The 1965 hearings held by the Joint Committee on the Organization of Congress amassed a similar data base for Congress, and the committee made specific recommendations for closing the congressional "information gap" through staffing changes (U.S. Congress, 1965).

However, the approach to research on legislative staffing was changing. Prescription was grounded in theory (de Grazia, 1966; U.S. Congress, 1965). Case studies generated hypotheses (Bibby, 1966; Manley, 1966). Leading students of legislatures suggested that staff influenced the behavior of legislators, that they had a direct as well as indirect effect on the policy process, and that they deserved study by scholars (Huitt, 1966; Jewell and Patterson, 1966; Matthews, 1960). Case studies of committees (Fenno, 1966; Green and Rosenthal, 1963; Manley, 1966), of the policy process (Sundquist, 1968), and of the individual member (Clapp, 1963) reported data on the activities, functions, and effect of staff. Comparative crossnational research was encouraged by the formation of the Consortium on Comparative Studies. The basis was laid for subsequent research which focused on staffs.

Prescriptive Studies

Several essays in the de Grazia (1966) volume on the U.S. Congress are relevant to legislative staffing. In his essay on committees in that volume, Eulau proposes a redivision of functions between staff and member, so that a professional but "different and nonpartisan" committee staff would handle technical, routinized, and nonpolitical matters. In his essay, Robinson distinguishes between information for current matters and information for emerging issues. In the same volume, Olson reports on case loads, requests for assistance, and mail volume in offices, arguing that improved hiring and training procedures for constituent staffs will "heighten the capability of Congress to carry out its deliberative and supervisory responsibilities" (p. 325).

Robinson (p. 796ff.) and Jones (p. 724ff.) suggested to the Joint Committee on the Organization of Congress (U.S. Congress, 1965) that staffing reforms may have unanticipated consequences and that collection of data (e.g., a staff time-use survey, as Jones recommends) is needed.

On-going Themes

Staff partisanship (Cochrane, 1964) and the effect of increased staff numbers (Butler, 1966; Meller, 1967) are continuing themes during the 1960s. Cochrane (1964) analyzes factors affecting committee staff partisanship and affecting the manifestation and impact of partisanship. On highly partisan staffs, political affiliation is important in selection, minority and majority distinction is sharp, not all staffs serve all members, and "intrastaff cooperation may be non-existent." The committee's subject matter, the chairman's attitude toward the staff, the intensity of members' partisan differences, personal animosities, and committee tradition affect staff partisanship. Cochrane's insights and suggestions—including the suggestion that different distributions of staff resources impact differentially—offer hypotheses for later research.

Meller's (1967) article is comparative and conceptual. Using data on central service staff in Hawaii and Japan and on personal staff in California, he demonstrates that more staff does not ensure less work for the legislature. He develops further his 1952 legislative staff typology (p. 384). The vertical axis is labeled "personal identification" and ranges from personal involvement to anonymous objectivity. The horizontal axis is the clientele axis; at one extreme the staff, or the staff aide, works for an entire legislature, at its other extreme for an individual legislator. Groups of staff and individual staff aides can thus be categorized. The measures of staff impact are crude (the increase in legislation introduced and in requests for assistance) and the typology is unlikely to lead to overarching theory, but both suggest directions for later research.

Case Studies

As parts of larger studies. During the 1960s, several scholars studying the U.S. Congress dealt with legislative staff as part of a larger study. Clapp (1963), using data from the Brookings Round Table Conference on Congress (a panel of 19 Democrats and another of 17 Republicans, each meeting separately eight times between January and June 1959), discusses variations in House office organization and staff recruitment. He reports that offices were often overwhelmed by "nonlegislative work" and that representatives wanted legislative help from personal staff. Fenno's (1966) appropriations study reports data on staff recruitment, organization, and activities; he makes some comparisons between Senate and House staff—for example, that information networks of Senate staff are wider than those of House staff. He finds that committee staff contribute to committee integration and also serve as linkages between the House and the Senate and to the wider political system.

Ripley's (1969) study of the Senate is drawn from Brookings Round Table discussions in 1968, with 11 Democratic senators and 6 Republican senators, each meeting five times, and 14 Democratic staff aides and 16 Republican staff aides, each meeting twice. Ripley hypothesizes that the power of staff, as distinct from their influence, depends on the power of the senator: "The pattern of power distribution among senators at any given time helps to determine how much legislative power personal and committee staff members can develop" (pp. 187-188). Findings suggest directions for further study: Republicans used personal staff for legislative duties more than Democrats, apparently because they did not control committee staff; impact is affected by timing—the staff aide must offer information at the right time, and it must be the type of information the senator then needs. Ripley finds personal staff most influential on "matters of secondary importance" and matters which are before a committee on which the senator does not serve. Minority staff are more influential than majority staff; staff of junior members are more influential than those of senior members, although senior members—and therefore, their aides—have more clout; and aides to senators from small states have more influence than aides to those from large states. On committees, staff influence varies with partisanship and responsibility. There is a gap between the power of Senate committee staff aides and their perception of their power, and "it also seems safe to say that they are less influential on legislative matters than personal staff members" (p. 212). The latter is a remarkable and startling finding which appears to have been refuted in the 1970s; certainly it is a hypothesis to be explored further with some quite specific measures.

Committee case studies. Two committee studies offer insights and generate research hypotheses. Bibby (1966) suggests that committee staffing practices affect the conduct and the incidence of committee oversight. Manley's (1966) purpose is to "analyze the role of one staff in the policy process." His data are drawn from extensive interviews and observation. He finds that staff have two main functions: to filter demands and information and to link House with Senate and Congress with the executive and interest groups. He also concludes that staff on the Finance and the Ways and Means committees hold norms of objectivity, bipartisanship, and neutrality and that staff norms and function may vary over time.

Manley suggests several variables which affect the role of staff: the committee subject matter (the more complex the subject matter, the more staff are needed); the scope of the decision ("the more salient the issue . . . the less likely the judgment of the staff will direct the decision"); personal factors, such as the management style of the staff director; unstable committee membership and stable staff; staff organization (centralized or decentralized); and the norm of anonymity. The findings from the study are important in themselves. The hypotheses generated deserve further research, and comparative studies of committees within and across legislatures would be useful.

Institutional Study

Kofmehl's major study of staff in the U.S. Congress, although not published until 1962, is in the genre of the evaluative studies of the 1950s. The study covers the 80th through the 82d Congresses, the three congresses following the passage of the Legislative Reorganization Act of 1946, and provides detailed description of the characteristics, activities, and organization of committee staff, personal staff of senators, and the Offices of Legislative Counsel. The strength of the work lies in the fact that it is the first comprehensive research on legislative staffs. Staff are viewed as actors in a political system, and their interrelationships with other actors are important. There is excellent coverage of the history of staffing (updated to 1976 with the introduction to the third edition), systematic interviews, and comments which are often insightful; there is some useful categorization—as for example of the attributes needed by professional staff. The study, however, lacks an organizing conceptual framework to link the data more generally to legislative behavior.

Saloma's (1969) study reports personal staff time-use data, based on staff recall. He reports that in an average week staff spend nearly 25 percent of their time on constituency service, 41 percent on correspondence, 14 percent on legislative support, and 10 percent on education and publicity. He also reports time spent on specific staff activities: for example, time spent with the member in committee or on case work. Subsequent time-use studies focus on senators and representatives; Saloma's is the only staff survey.

The 1960s: Summary

By the end of the 1960s there are a growing data base and a number of hypotheses about factors which affect staff activity, function, and effectiveness, although different level factors are not distinguished analytically. Some definition and measurement of key concepts occurs (e.g., Fenno, 1966; Matthews, 1960; Meller, 1967). The comments of Matthews (1960) and Huitt (1965, 1966) serve as a basis for some of the research in the 1960s and, even more, to focus the attention of scholars on legislative staffs after 1970. Matthews describes variations in office organization and suggests that "the way a senator staffs and organizes his office is a kind of political Rorschach test which when studied with some care, tells a great deal about him as a man, what his problems and preoccupations are, and how he defines his role" (p. 83). On routine matters the personal staffs of senators are particularly important, and on other matters much of the influence of staff comes from their position in the communications and information process. Huitt (1965) suggests that "one dimension of power in the Senate which is subtle and complex but largely unexplored is the influence on their principals of members of professional staffs."

Legislative Staffing Research: 1970 and After

The legislative staffing literature of the 1970s and early 1980s is characterized by (1) a multiplicity of perspectives, foci, and methodologies; (2) some comparative study of staff in similar legislatures (e.g., state legislatures, legislatures in developing countries, House and Senate in the U.S. Congress), but rarely comparison across these divisions; and (3) some "borrowing" of approaches and perspectives across these divisions. Collection of quantitative data on staff characteristics and activities continues more systematically.

Researchers are interested in categorizing and conceptualizing staff differentiation and function. Following the pre-1970 tradition, discussions of legislative staffing are often tied to assumptions about legislators' information needs, but there is also recognition that staff does more than process information or assist constituents (e.g., Malbin, 1977, 1980, 1981; Fox and Hammond, 1975a, 1977). Studies which focus on legislators' information needs and resources (e.g., Wissel, O'Connor, and King, 1976) and legislative reform (e.g., Hammond and Langbein, 1982) can shed light on legislative staffing, as can studies of legislative performance which use staff levels as a measure of structural capacity (e.g., Rosenthal's work).

Contextual factors are important. Professional committee staff capabilities are used only in the context of constraints posed by the internal and external congressional environment (Patterson, 1970a, 1970b). Price (1971) studies committee staff in the context of the committee environment. Hammond (1981) argues that the distribution of staff resources in the U.S. House of Representatives is governed to a large degree by the collegial nature of the organization and the ties which the individual representatives have to their own constituencies. Malbin's (1980) central thesis rests on the importance of the representative function and the constituency. Wolman and Wolman (1977) study staff perception of constituency views. By 1970, researchers accept the political aspect of staffing, and some studies examine this explicitly (see especially Macartney, 1982).

Focus on the Individual

Two kinds of studies focus on the individual in legislative systems: those in which the individual staff aide is the unit of analysis and those which analyse the individual legislator's disposition of resources. The common conceptual framework is built around the individual actor in the congressional system. In contrast to the pre-1970 period, comparisons are made across legislative subunits—for example, Fox and Hammond (1977) compare Senate and House personal and committee staff, and Patterson (1970a, 1970b) compares committees; the impact and effect of staff on legislative outcomes is also of interest. The context of staff work is important, and staff are considered an important intervening variable in the legislative process.[3]

The individual staff aide: background, recruitment and career patterns, and activities. Research by individuals and by several U.S. congressional committees has produced rich data on the characteristics and activities of legislative staff. The data are primarily from the U.S. and mostly from Congress, although there are also some U.S. state studies.

Hammond (1975) reports data on personal staff of the members of the U.S. House of Representatives, the data drawn from interviews with the professional staff and most representatives in a sample of 25 House offices during the 92d Congress (1971-1972). Staff background, training, and tenure vary in the different staff jobs. Administrative assistants are older than other personal staff professionals; their average tenure is nine years, in contrast to 2.3 years for legislative aides. Legislative assistants have more formal training than other aides (93 percent hold a B.A. or an advanced degree, in contrast to 76 percent of the administrative assistants) and more are lawyers. Press aides have journalism training and specialized media experience. Recruitment patterns also vary: most administrative assistants come from the representative's district and have often worked on the first campaign; press aides also generally have district ties. In contrast, other professional aides in the more specialized positions are as likely to have been recruited from other Capitol Hill offices. Few (only 25 percent) personal staff aides have had federal executive branch experience; 12 percent had worked in state government. Hammond proposes a typology of staff career orientations, and concludes that "[personal] staff jobs are filled primarily by men and women with a legislative and local orientation, reflecting . . . their bosses' experience" (p. 73). Variation in staff demographics according to party and seniority differences of the representative is also examined. Hammond suggests that there is differential impact on staff activities and on legislative output, but the data do not permit this analysis.

Evidence has been presented that staff background varies by job position (Hammond, 1975) and by type of staff (Balutis, 1975d), and that there is differentiation among staff. The consequences of that differentiation have not been explored however. Balutis assumes but does not demonstrate that different backgrounds result in different norms and constraints. Rosenthal (1981) reports data on recruitment, characteristics, and career patterns of state legislative staff.

Fox and Hammond (1975b, 1977) identify five professional staff roles or activity patterns, drawing on data from Fox's questionnaire survey of professionals on U.S. Senate personal staffs: the "interactors" (often the administrative assistants) handle constituent federal projects and casework and meet with lobbyists or special interest groups; the "supporters" (generally legislative assistants) work on legislative research and bills and draft speeches and floor remarks; the "corresponders" handle requests for information and draft correspondence; the "advertisers" (press aides) assist on presswork; the "investigators" (often legislative assistants or the administrative assistants) handle legislative issues, meet with lobbyists, and are active in investigations and oversight. Rather than starting with the typical staff positions and asking what activities were associated with each position, Fox began with the general set of activities performed in Senate offices and through factor analysis determined how they were grouped into staff positions. Such a perspective might be especially useful for comparing different legislative institutions or, more broadly, for comparing legislative and nonlegislative governmental institutions. For the U.S. Congress, the roles he identifies are typical staff positions.

Fox and Hammond (1977) present additional and quite extensive data on the background and activities of legislative staff. (They are also concerned with subunits—e.g., personal offices and committees—and legislative outputs, both to be discussed in later sections of this article.) In addition to documentary data, their primary data sources are Hammond's House of Representatives interviews, Fox's Senate questionnaires and interviews, and a questionnaire returned by 35.2 percent of all professional staff on Senate, House, and joint committees in 1974. They report data on the age, education, sex, legal residence, and tenure of Senate and House personal staff and committee staff. There is differentiation among positions (e.g., the position of administrative assistant and of legislative assistant) and among types of staff: Senate aides are younger than House aides; two-thirds of personal staff professionals have legal residence in the state their senator represents, while two-thirds of committee staff professionals are from the Washington, D.C. area. Staffs are partisan: 97 percent of personal staff and of committee staff have a "strong" or "very strong" party preference. And Fox found that the political ideology of Senate personal staff is similar to that of the senators for whom they work. Using the Bales "Interpersonal Rating Form," self-administered by a subpopulation of Senate personal staff, he also found that the typical aide is a task-oriented leader, with high social-interaction skills. The results are not surprising to observers of congressional staff, but systematic analysis is useful.

Fox and Hammond also present data on recruitment patterns and document communication patterns and information sources within offices, between offices, and between Congress and other institutions and groups. Similar data on staff activities are reported and analysed. The data set is rich; replication, comparison with other staff populations, and further work on the consequences of these characteristics and patterns would be useful and could shed light on the policy process, on legislative change, and on the operations of subsystems and policy networks.

Walsh (1976) describes the conditions of employment for some Senate staff. Data on education, tenure, salary, sex, job position, and previous employment of House staff are reported with extensive analysis by the Commission on Administrative Review, the Obey Commission (U.S. House, 1977). Brady (1981) analyses the same data in the context of the work environment in the House. He argues that context is important: the political character and collegial nature of the House affect the autonomy and working conditions of subunits and personnel systems. Unfortunately, the Commission data and the Fox and Hammond data are not really comparable; if they were, analysis of legislative change would be facilitated. Studies focusing on congressional activities—casework, oversight—are also sources for data on both individual and subunit level staffing (see, for example, Breslin, 1976, and Johannes, 1979, 1981, on casework; and Ogul, 1976, and Kaiser, 1977, on oversight).

Systematic analysis of staff characteristics across governmental institutions, and in comparison with the private sector, has not been done and would be useful. It may be that organizational characteristics affect staff characteristics: the conditions of employment which govern legislative jobs may result in a large group of young, inexperienced aides. We need analysis to demonstrate what staff differences occur between organizations. Then, with staff as the intervening variable, we need exploration of the effect, if any, of differing characteristics of staff.

Staff role and functions. The studies of legislative staff roles and norms comprise a unified body of work within the legislative staffing literature. They are unique in that they share a conceptual framework and develop earlier analyses—for example, Price (1971, 1972) builds on Patterson's (1970a, 1970b) earlier analysis. And in a shift from the pre-1970 staffing studies, the contextual has a major effect on staff "capabilities and constraints," to use Patterson's phrase; besides Patterson and Price, Burks and Cole (1978) especially focus on the interactions of environment (including structure) and staff activity.

Patterson's article (1970a) on "The Professional Staffs of Congressional Committees" is important for its findings and for suggesting a theoretical construct and framework for further analysis. The data are also reported in Patterson (1970b) and in Jewell and Patterson (1973, 1977). The study is based on focused interviews with 40 professional staff of 15 House and 7 Senate committees in 1965-1966. Data on the increase in the number of aides and the size of committee staffs are presented; Patterson suggests that these are a consequence of an increased congressional workload and greater institutional complexity. He briefly outlines the utilization of committee staff by committee members, individual members of Congress, executive agencies, and lobbyists, summarizing data from Saloma (1969), Fenno (1966), and Green and Rosenthal (1963) among others.

The heart of the study, and its great contribution, is the discussion of staff functions, capabilities, and constraints. Patterson uses the Almond (1965) typology to organize the material on staff capability—a major shift in perspective which is an important contribution. He finds that "providing information is probably the central characteristic of the role definition of the professional staff members" (p. 26); that staff promote intracommittee, interchamber, and interinstitution (executive-legislative) integration; that the extent of innovation varies and depends on the issues under committee jurisdiction, the committee leadership, and the staff style; and that staff have influence through information gathering and processing, drafting legislation, and so forth.

The discussion is based on quotations from interviews rather than on systematic presentation of data. A similar presentation characterizes most studies during the 1970s: the data are gathered systematically but do not lend themselves to frequency distributions or to sophisticated quantitative analysis. As scholars pursue the concept of influence, it would be useful to find some way to measure the concept empirically, perhaps by specifying components and measuring those.

Factors identified as promoting staff capability include pay; high morale; professional status; expertise and specialization; a relationship with the committee chairman which is characterized by mutual loyalty, trust, and confidence; and generally stable tenure. Patterson finds that "the more non-partisan the committee, the greater the support for staff performance capability" (p. 28)—a finding which has not been tested by other studies.

Staff constraints are "limitations on staff capabilities resulting from the institutional environment"; through these constraints, "Congress shapes the behavior of professional staffs of committees" (p. 29). Staff reflect the legislative goals of committee members; Appropriations Committee staff, for example, want to "cut the budget and guard the Treasury." Staff norms are identified: limited advocacy, loyalty to the committee chairman, deference to members of Congress, anonymity, specialization, and limited partisanship. Other factors constrain committee staff: the committee chairman ("the staff must learn to anticipate the reactions of a chairman," p. 31) and on some committees the ranking minority member; staff organization; the nonpartisan tendencies of some committee staffs; isolation ("staff loyalties and identifications are specific to committees"); and specialization (e.g., subject matter expertise). Patterson suggests a number of consequences of these constraints: that staff performance is probably "more effective" in hierarchical committees; that nonpartisan staff is probably more effective than partisan; that isolation results in information gaps and duplication, probably increases staff influence and committee integration, but "works against" integration within each chamber and between each chamber; and that isolation "may promote policy innovations in a narrow sense although (probably) impeding innovation of far-reaching consequence" (pp. 34-35). He concludes that staff have actual or potential influence, contribute to integration of policy subsystems, and contribute to innovation.

Price (1971) focuses on one of the capabilities of staff: innovation. He assumes that Congress needs innovation for policy formulation, argues that the information search process affects innovation, and asks whether an expert ability to amass facts competently but neutrally is sufficient. Interviews, observation, and congressional documents were used for intensive study of three Senate committees—Commerce, Finance, and Labor and Public Welfare—during the 88th Congress. Price's book, *Who Makes the Laws* (1972), reports the results of the broad study; the 1971 article, "Professionals and 'Entrepreneurs'," focuses on the orientations and activities of committee staff. He finds "the character of the staff of considerable independent importance" in developing and passing legislation.

Price identifies three possible staff orientations. The "pure policy entrepreneurs" are activist, partisan, and "committed to a continual search for policy gaps and opportunities" (p. 335). The committee permits the staff to search for new initiatives and to push proposals; constraints exist, but limits are wide. "Mixed" entrepreneurs serve committees with somewhat less "slack"; aides suggest and push proposals, but with less area for maneuver. "Professionals" are nonpartisan, with neutral competence; they use their expertise to analyze and present alternatives; their orientation is reactive. The goals and orientations of the committee chairman and most members are major factors in shaping staff orientation and activity (cf. Matthews, 1960, and Patterson, 1970a). A major contribution of the analysis is the identification of different staff types and data on differential impact of the types. The analysis is contextual (although that is not the focus); scholars could usefully explore further the conditions which facilitate entrepreneurial or professional activity and the consequences, both functional and dysfunctional.

One state study (Balutis, 1975b, 1975c, 1975d) employs the Patterson framework and finds that all New York state legislative aides, whether on a personal, committee, or legislative service group staff, share norms identified by Kofmehl (1962) and Patterson (1970a, 1970b). Reporting staff and legislator perceptions of influence, Balutis supports Patterson on staff function: New York State legislative staffs are important in intelligence, integration (committee, interchamber, and executive-legislative), innovation, and influence. The data may be intrinsically interesting, but some comparison with previous studies would be useful in building a body of empirically grounded research.

Burks and Cole (1978) pursued the entrepreneur-professional dichotomy in their 1974 questionnaire survey of the role orientations of congressional aides. They found that most aides perceive themselves as a mixture of professional and entrepreneur. Entrepreneurs tend to be young and more partisan than professionals. They perceive themselves as influential at all stages of the legislative process, and especially (unlike professionals' perceptions of influence) in developing floor support for committee legislation.

In this subset of literature, scholars have identified staff norms, developed typologies of staff function, and suggested factors which systematically result in differentiation of staff function and roles. Staff characteristics, and perception of influence, differ in the different roles. Data is gathered from interviews, questionnaires, and congressional documents. More comparative research and further work on the various hypotheses generated (e.g., the effect of partisanship, of different models of organization, of isolation) would be useful.

Legislator-staff perceptions: convergent or divergent? Fox's findings (reported in Fox and Hammond, 1977) that Senate personal staff held ideological views similar to, and in some cases more intense than, their principals has not been replicated, but several studies have explored various aspects of legislator-staff perceptions.

Worman (1975) interviewed Florida staff and legislators to determine whether they held similar expectations regarding aides' activities (drafting legislation, public relations, constituent assistance, personal chores, official representation, campaigning) and whether legislators communicated those expectations to aides. He found agreement on activities related to the legislative function but less agreement about activities closely related to constituent work (e.g., expressing a legislator's opinion to a constituent). Worman's central concern is the way legislators' expectations shape aides' roles. The study is descriptive; the activities identified seem chosen rather randomly, although it may be that they simply reflect aides' activities in the Florida legislature at that time.

Huwa and Rosenthal (1977) compared legislator and staff roles after an extensive study of 20 standing committees in five state legislatures (Connecticut, Florida, Louisiana, Minnesota, and New Jersey) in 1975-1976. The authors find that legislators and staff differed in prelegislative experience: more legislators were trained as lawyers and had been involved in private careers, public service, and politics; staff were more academic, trained in social science, and had less varied experience (three-fourths had worked only in the legislature). Orientations also differ: in contrast to legislators, staff focus their loyalties on one committee or legislative service bureau and their career aspirations are varied. (Most legislators aspire to a career in politics and expect to run for higher office.) Legislators work in "several areas—often simultaneously"; "take account of multiple factors" (pp. 7-8); and are concerned with political factors—"[technical] information is only one factor in [their] decision-making." Their work product is legislation. Staff are more focused and less distracted; they are specialists; their work product is "research, and the transmission of information" (p. 8). Huwa and Rosenthal find that much of the staff work relates to procedural matters (bill analysis, summarizing views, etc.) rather than policy; this is what legislators want and need. Other researchers have had similar findings (Balutis, 1975a, 1975b, 1975c, 1975d; Feller, King, Menzel, O'Connor, and Ingersoll, 1975; Porter, 1970). All of these are state studies, and the findings may be specific to states. It would be useful to compare data from other states and national subunits as well as from national legislatures and to analyse further the implications of divergent (or similar) roles and orientations.

Wolman and Wolman (1977) are also concerned with the extent to which staff and member perceptions are similar. In 1972, they surveyed members and principal aides of the U.S. Senate Labor and Public Welfare Committee regarding their views and constituents' views on population and family planning policy (a low salience and low activity issue within the jurisdiction of the committee). They suggest four models of staff influence on policy: (1) staff is an intervening variable between constituency attitude and a congressman's perception of constituency attitude; (2) staff is an independent variable with "direct impact on the congressman's attitude on roll call behavior"; (3) staff is an independent variable with direct impact on public policy; and (4) staff may perceive the constituency's attitude incorrectly, even when the congressman perceives it correctly, and act for the congressman. Both senators and staff erred in their perceptions of constituency opinion (by 3.7 percent of possible error, p. 287); they especially underestimated the profamily planning views. For all staff-senator pairs, the staff accurately perceived the senator's views 71 percent of the time; when attitudes diverged, 50 percent of the time the staff did not know it. The authors conclude that staff "do not appear greatly to affect either their senator's perception of public opinion or the senator's personal attitudes," although it is not clear that the data they present support this conclusion as to causality. They point out that the findings raise questions about the opinion linkage process and the role of staff. The models of staff influence (effect) are plausible, and useful, but not tested. The research in this area offers a number of interesting findings. With comparative data (for similar subunits of nations and of legislatures) it would be possible to asssess whether characteristics are unique or general. The effect, and implications, of convergence or divergence patterns also deserve futher analysis.

The legislator: staff utilization. Several studies focus on the individual legislator's utilization of staff. Ornstein (1975) analysed staff in the U.S. Congress. In addition to using documentary data, he uses data from 60 interviews conducted with staff and legislators in 20 Senate and 20 House Offices in 1969-1970. Inter- and intrainstitutional comparison is therefore possible. Those members in both chambers who use personal staff most heavily on legislative work are identified: they are Northern Democrats, less senior, more liberal, and more active (activism measured by the number of bills cosponsored), and they represent the more urban districts or states. He finds that House personal staff aides are used primarily for clerical and constituent service work; in the Senate, personal staff are "an integral part of the Senate decision making process." Size is the variable which best explains these differences, Ornstein suggests.

Fenno's (1978) and Cavanaugh's (1981) studies do not focus primarily on legislative staff, but staff utilization is a component of the broader studies. As in Ornstein's (1975) studies, staff is the dependent variable—a quite different perspective from other staff studies. Fenno's seminal study has resulted in major scholarly attention to legislators-in-constituencies. For this survey his analysis of staff in district offices, a component of members' "home style," is of interest. Seniority, electoral margin, family residence, and distance from Washington do not make a difference in how members allocate staff resources (measured by 1973 expenditures) between the district and Washington, D.C. Region, however, has a "substantial effect on home style" (staff allocation patterns) (p. 44). Representatives from southern and border states have small district staffs, eastern representatives have large district staffs. There are also state patterns: he suggests that state delegations are an important factor, a finding similar to Fox and Hammond's (1977). Cavanaugh (1979, 1981) presents data on functional and geographic (D.C. and district) allocations of staff (e.g., resource allocation) to test his model of congressional behavior: the institutional and electoral arenas offer different and conflicting incentives. Congressmen resolve the conflict by allocating staff resources to constituent service work; they expand their attention to legislation as they become more senior; with more attention to legislative work (the institutional arena) they obtain assistance from a new set of resources: committee staff. Cavanaugh uses data from the survey of House members conducted by the House of Representatives' Commission on Administrative Review. The relevance here is in the explanation offered for resource allocation patterns. Schiff and Smith (1983) study utilization of personal staff by three House cohorts (elected pre-1960; 1960-1967; and 1968-1978), comparing decentralization to the district and time spent on various activities by Washington and district staff. They too suggest that larger staffs have enabled representatives to pursue policy and reelection goals simultaneously. The perception (staff as resources) and the assumption regarding the direction of causality (staff as the dependent variable) especially distinguish this subset of the legislative staffing literature. As with other studies, context is important.

Individual level studies have resulted in rich but uneven data on staff characteristics, activity patterns, norms, and functions. Researchers have identified environmental variables affecting staff, legislator-staff similarities and differences, and staff utilization patterns. In the future, research might be directed toward (1) filling gaps in the data base (e.g., other states, other national legislatures) so that comparative analysis can proceed; (2) gathering data for longitudinal analysis (e.g., data on changes in congressional staffing over time, to supplement the informed comment we now have); and (3) assessing the impact of observed patterns and testing the generated hypotheses.

Focus on Subunits in Legislatures

A number of studies of legislative staff focus on legislative subunits: committees, personal staff offices, central legislative service organizations, and other institutional subgroups. Most of the studies compare staff across a particular subunit (e.g., Rosenthal, 1974) or compare different subunit staff

(Rosenthal, 1973a). Most recently, Salisbury and Shepsle (1981a, 1981b) have studied all staff (personal and committee) controlled by one member of Congress. This group of studies includes literature on U.S. state legislatures and the U.S. Congress. Although some of the comparative literature treats different types of staff groups, the focus in those studies differs: it is primarily on the institution and its staff, rather than on the subunit staff in the institution. The studies discussed in this section focus on legislative subunits, but the contextual environment in which subunits work is important: interactions with other subunits, relationships with the outside environment (e.g., the executive branch, constituents) and the impact of variables external to the subunit on the subunit and subunit staff are tacitly—if not explicitly—recognized.

Personal staff offices. Case studies can shed light on the operation of legislative subunits. Bibby and Davidson (1972, Ch. 3) describe the work of staff employed by Senator Abraham Ribicoff and by Representative John Anderson, focusing especially on casework, legislative support, and the relationship of staff and member. The chapter is part of their more general study of Congress and the legislative process. Caro (1982) describes Lyndon Johnson's work as a staff aide and his own House and Senate offices.

Fox and Hammond (1975b, 1977) find three typologies of personal office organization: hierarchical, coordinative, and individualist. Office organization in both chambers varies by region, but not by party or by policy attitude. Seniority affects House but not Senate organization: the most senior members of the House have hierarchical organizations; the least senior members have larger staffs, more professionals, and either coordinative or individualistic offices. In the House, the authors also find that organization varies according to the member's background; the Senate data are not run by background. The authors hypothesize, but do not examine, that member perceptions, ambitions, and goals may affect the number of staff and organization of offices (cf. Matthews, 1960), and that offices organized differently impact differently on legislative output. They also compare Senate and House, finding that in both chambers staff have become increasingly specialized and formally organized. Data on communication patterns indicate more communication between personal offices in the House than in the Senate and more frequent communications with those outside Congress, especially the White House and interest groups, by Senate aides (1975b, pp. 161-162). Hammond's study for the Commission on the Operation of the Senate (1976) describes the organization and operation of senators' offices. It finds that increasing departmentalization, an increase in the average number of legislative aides (0.7 per member in 1960; 5.3 in 1975) and press aides, and the need for management assistance characterize these offices.

Loomis (1979) views the personal office as a group which can assist representatives in pursuing goals of reelection, policy making, and institutional power (see Fenno, 1973). Questionnaires and interviews with the 70 Democratic freshman elected in 1974 (the "Watergate class") reveal that the expanded personal staff resources of the contemporary House permitted legislators to balance the demands of apparently conflicting goals (reelection; policy). He also finds (cf. Hammond, 1975; Fox and Hammond, 1977) increasingly formal organization characterized by hierarchy, specialization, decentralization, and formalization. He views the office as a "small business," which advertises the member as a product. He raises theoretical questions about the effect on the representative and policy functions. In a sense, he anticipates the perspective of Salisbury and Shepsle (1981a, 1981b) discussed below.

Macartney (1982) focuses on the organization, operation, and activities of congressional district offices. He finds that staff activities include political "organizing" and "surveillance"—as staff aides keep in touch with district concerns, issues of importance to constituents, and the constituency's perception of the senator or representative. Macartney's focus on district offices and on the political component of staff activity is unique and a valuable addition to understanding the role and functions of staff. The larger study from which the 1982 article is taken covers all district offices in the Los Angeles region: municipal, state legislature, and U.S. Congress field staff.[4] The functional approach is a fine example of how comparisons of apparently disparate offices across governmental levels can contribute to understanding and to theory building.

Committees and comparable subunits. Studies of committee staff groups range from case studies to major comparative studies, from purely descriptive works to sophisticated efforts to operationalize output and effectiveness and to set the study of staffing firmly in a conceptual framework.

Case Studies: The appropriations function is common to legislatures, and fiscal staff are among the first type of staff authorized as legislatures move to increase their information processing capability. Perhaps this explains why several studies of legislative fiscal staff have been conducted (Balutis and Butler, 1975; Kayali, 1977). The separate essays in Balutis and Butler (1975) draw on previous studies of U.S. state legislatures and the U.S. Congress for organizing concepts. In a concluding essay, the editors summarize the work of legislative fiscal staffs, using Patterson's typology: intelligence is served through both substantive and political information; integration occurs, especially intralegislature conflict management; innovation is a consequence of presenting legislatures with policy alternatives, aides' activities, and staff working closely with legislators. Moreover, innovation is assumed if staff contribute to intelligence, innovation, and integration—although the authors acknowledge that measurement of staff influence is a difficult problem. Four essays in this volume by legislators describe organization and operations of legislative fiscal staffs in New Mexico (Budtke, 1975), Florida (Kyle, 1975), Michigan (Farnum, 1975), and Illinois (Kent, 1975). Hartmark (1975) describes the organization and work of legislative budget staff in Wisconsin (technically a central legislative service group, but working as staff to committees). The data sources are not indicated. Context is important: the economy of the state, the relationship of the legislature to the governor, and the partisan control of the legislature all affect the perspective and impact of the fiscal staff.

Staff influence is a central concern of Butler's (1975) essay on the Texas Legislative Budget Board and Balutis's (1975c) essay on the New York legislature's fiscal staff. Butler argues that the anticipated reactions of the executive branch are evidence of staff influence; integration (see Fenno, 1966) is indicated by similar perceptions of the budget and the budget process held by staff and principals.

The Balutis-Butler book broadens the data set on legislative staffing, and, by using typologies previously suggested (Fenno, 1966; Patterson, 1970a, 1970b; Rosenthal, 1971), builds on previous research. It does not break new ground conceptually—indeed, many of the essays are descriptive and lack a theoretical framework—and does not synthesize comparative data.

Case studies, although not systematically comparative, can shed light on staff activities and influence. Davidson and Oleszek's (1977) study of the House Select Committee on Committees (the Bolling Committee) is not a staffing study—their focus is on the work of the committee—but in analysing that work they present considerable evidence of how staff can affect policy outcomes through background research and shaping and presenting alternatives. Rosenthal's (1970) study of party caucus staff in Wisconsin, discussed below, is similarly useful.

Comparative Studies: Since 1970, some comparative work has been published, including a major comparative and integrative study. In papers prepared for the Bolling Committee in the U.S. House of Representatives (U.S. House, 1973), Kofmehl, Patterson, Saloma, and Robinson discuss issues of minority staffing, staff norms and constraints, and diversification of staff resources. All recognize that committee variation means different staffing needs. Saloma (pp. 681-682) recommends an Annual Survey of Congressional Staff Requirements and Resources (which would give legislative scholars a superb data set).

Machowsky (1978), drawing on the *Congressional Staff Directory* and Reports of the Clerk of the House and the Secretary of the Senate, documents patterns of committee staff growth from 1947-1977: majority and minority, professional and clerical, by committees and in the aggregate. He concludes that it is important to look at staff differentiation and variations in patterns of staff increase as well as at aggregate data.

Malbin's articles (1977, 1981) and major book (1980) are an important body of work. Although the focus of his 1981 article shifts toward the institutional—for he is concerned with the effect of staff on the institution—his evidence and conclusions in this, as in his other writings on staff, are based on intensive study through interviews and observation of committee staff. His central concern is with the role and influence of committee staff, especially the increasingly personalized and entrepreneurial staff system, and the problem for democratic theory of "unelected representatives" making policy. In his book (1980), using case studies of different committee staffs he examines the activities, role, and impact of staff at various stages of the policy process. Agenda setting, "shepherding" legislation through a chamber, negotiation of details (and on quite numerous occasions agreement on new policy), and oversight are analysed. Different kinds of staff are described: the entrepreneurial staff of the Senate Commerce Committee, the nonpartisan technocrats of the Joint Committee on Internal Revenue Taxation, and the nonpartisan bureaucrats of the congressional support agencies. He demonstrates how different kinds of staff use similar information differently and are "anything but neutral information conduits" (p. 163).

The study is comparative in the sense that different committees and different types of committee staff are examined. It is not systematically comparative, as the analysis does not, for example, cover different staffs at the same stage in the legislative process or the same staff at different points in the process. Malbin concludes (Ch. 10) that staff are "middle-men," keeping senators and representatives from "face-to-face negotiations and deliberations." Congress gets more information from the professional staffs, but it does not necessarily get better information, as it is not forced to focus on the assumptions behind the (ever more technical) information. Personalized, entrepreneurial staff have "helped Congress retain its position as a key initiator of federal policy" (p. 240). Staff impact on policy by bringing to Congress new ideas from small groups without political clout. Malbin argues that these groups have access because staffers are interested in a career in the issue network later, but it seems as plausible that they assist their principals in the representative function by giving small groups a hearing. Staff also craft complex legislation which is more inclusive and responsive to more interests because staff aides are oriented toward process and legislation and want negotiation to succeed. Staff career goals shape staff behavior (many are thinking of their next noncongressional job); large committee staffs make more work for congressmen, who must process ideas and work devised by staff; both interface with the deliberative function of Congress. Malbin's central thesis raises important questions about the function of staff in a representative legislature. A number of his conclusions deserve further systematic empirical analysis.

Central Legislative Support Agencies: Two kinds of studies of central legislative agencies exist: state level studies of legislative staffing, which include comparative analysis of central staff agencies (discussed in the next section) and national level case studies of the legislative support agencies of the U.S. Congress. This reflects the extent of development of legislative staffs: only the U.S. Congress has major central legislative support agencies and staff groups sufficiently large and differentiated to invite separate case study analysis.

The studies of the American congressional legislative support agencies are quite different from other staffing studies: less behavioral, more "institutional," and in some instances more typical of the public administration literature (Carroll, 1976; Pois, 1976; Skolnikoff, 1976; Capron, 1976; Griffith, 1976, for the Commission on the Operation of the Senate; Goodrum, 1982). Thurber's studies (1977, 1981) report variations in utilization and perception of the support agencies by members and other legislative staff. Two recent studies (Pois, 1979; Mosher, 1979) of the GAO have focused on its operations as a bureaucratic agency, analysing a government bureau and its largely executive branch work.

Comparative studies of staff of different types of subunits. Rosenthal was one of the first to insist that different types of legislative staff "have different consequences" (1971, p. 74). In a 1973 study (1973a; see also 1971, 1973b) he draws primarily on data from Wisconsin, which in the mid-1960s staffed party caucuses and the Joint Finance Committee. He found that the "rank and file" benefitted most from personal staff and "not much" from legislative service groups (e.g., committee or central research bureau staff) which gave institutional groups first priority. The caucus staffs in Wisconsin increased the power of party leaders and also gave individual legislators alternative sources of information. He concludes that increasing staff may distribute power differently, both among legislators and between legislators and legislative bureaucracy (such as permanent committee staff).

Caucus staffs also increased partisanship in an already partisan legislature. Fiscal staff "strengthened legislative budget cutting." He concludes that staff reinforce, but do not transform, the legislative process.

Rosenthal (1971) also concludes insightfully that increased staff often results in more, not less, work ("the more competent the staff, the more alternatives it will uncover," p. 82) (cf. Gross, 1953). Nor does more staff mean greater efficiency, "especially if [that] means getting the job done with less effort and resources"; however, efficiency is improved if that means "better methods by which legislatures reach informed policy decisions" (p. 82).

More legislative staff often is a result of legislative reform; assessing staff changes permits some assessment of reform. Rosenthal (1973b) ingeniously grapples with measurement of reform and staff effectiveness; he uses a number of different variables, measured prior to and subsequent to staffing reforms in Wisconsin, to serve as "operational indicators." Since press releases were prepared by party caucus staff, he determines staff effectiveness by measuring (1) the production of press releases (covering individual members or party leaders and "safe seat" or marginal members) and (2) the use of press releases by 66 newspapers in a sample of 16 assembly districts. He found a rise in coverage given to local legislators: the number of articles increased more than 150 percent, the number of column lines more than 100 percent; separate articles on members, legislative names in headlines, and first page placement of articles on legislators all doubled. Using multiple regression to measure the impact of staff effectiveness on the individual legislator (with the number of press releases in 1967 and 1968, the 1966 percentage of vote for incumbents, and the 1968 percentage of vote for their party's gubernatorial candidate as independent variables), he found that press releases had little effect except in some marginal districts.

Evidence of staff impact on legislative decision making is derived from a survey of legislators regarding the effectiveness of different staff groups. A strong association between effectiveness of staff and the (perceived) effectiveness of the group for which staff works is hypothesized as positive evidence of staff impact. Rosenthal finds a strong association between the perceived effectiveness of caucus staff and party leadership (gamma=+.45) and party caucuses (gamma=+.45), a weak association between effectiveness of caucus staff and standing committees (gamma=+.11), and a strong association between fiscal committee staff and committee effectiveness (gamma=+.56). Interview data support the findings, as do data on newspaper coverage. Using party cohesion scores and multiple sponsorship of amendments to the 1963 and 1967 budget bills, he measures staff impact on integration. Similar measures are used to assess the impact of staff on legislative performance: the number of changes in higher education and public welfare budget items, the number of amendments to bills (interview data revealed many were staff assisted), and measures from newspaper coverage and interview data. It is an ingenious use of data and of measurement. The concepts, the operational indicators, and the measures can be employed for other legislatures: U.S. state legislatures, the U.S. Congress, and other national legislatures.

Hammond (1978) makes a point similar to Rosenthal's (1973a, 1973b): the consequences of increasing different types of staff will differ. In the U.S. Congress, distributing staff resources more widely to subcommittee and individual members has contributed to fragmentation and legislative delay; Balutis's study (reported 1975b, 1975c, 1975d, 1977, 1979) is also a comparative subunit study.

Fox and Hammond's (1977) subunit data permit comparisons of committee and personal office staff in both Senate and House. Of particular comparative interest are questions regarding staff communications activity and information patterns. What variables affect these patterns: the stage of the legislative process? same- or split-party control of the Senate or the House and the White House? Longitudinal data, as well as comparable House data, would be useful. At the time their studies were conducted, it was useful to study whether personal staff was involved in legislative decision making and policy formulation. Now, it would be useful to specify, and operationalize and measure more systematically, the components of influence and effect.

Legislative subunits: congressman as enterprise. Recently, Salisbury and Shepsle (1981a, 1981b) have suggested a different perspective on legislative staffing, applicable to the U.S. Congress and perhaps to other legislatures with high levels of staffing. They view the senator or representative and all the staff he controls, whether personal or committee, as a separate subunit, an "enterprise." The concept of congressman as enterprise cuts across the traditional and more typical view of congressional subunits as member and committee offices and reflects the reality of committee staff control by individual members. Staff are considered member-specific resources.

In the first of two articles (1981a), the authors examine patterns of recruitment and turnover for personal and committee staff. Analysis of elite circulation in enterprises is important to understanding Congress and to broader questions of policy making and democratic theory. They suggest three explanations for staff turnover. The first includes the motives of individual staff members; the authors posit a curvilinear pattern of turnover, with an increasing number of resignations in the first four years of tenure as staff who use their employment for "credentialling" leave and a slowly decreasing number of resignations (to 20 years or so) as the incentives of more responsibility and generous retirement benefits increase. They suggest that as staff numbers increase rapidly and young, inexperienced aides are hired, turnover also increases, because the pool of probable turnovers increases: "Growth and turnover go hand-in-hand, though possibly with some lag" (p. 383). The second explanation is the staff's relationship with members; the authors assume close ties to the employing members. Consequently, staff aides move when the member moves to a committee or to the other chamber and staff are less likely to move between members. The third explanation comprises situational features, which include member turnover, staff growth, situational change (e.g., an increase or decrease in the number of committees or subcommittees), executive branch growth, change in partisan control of the executive branch, and growth in the Washington community, which opens up new job opportunities off the Hill. Data were drawn from the *Congressional Staff Directory,* 1962-1978. Observations and interviews served as additional data sources.

Using time series data for each chamber, Salisbury and Shepsle test the hypotheses on staff turnover and also test the "echo" effects of staff growth on turnover. They do not, as they note, have data to examine individual motives and ambition. They find an association, similar for House and Senate, between growth and turnover; contemporaneous association is larger than the lagged relationships.

Examination of the "ties-that-bind" hypothesis (the second explanation) reveals that a large number (89 percent in 1979) of representatives' personal staffs moved to the Senate when representatives won Senate election. New representatives and senators recruit their staffs from off the Hill: only about 25 percent have Hill experience. Committee data present a somewhat different picture. Salisbury and Shepsle assume that all committee staff are chairman's staff, an assumption which, as they note, may understate the ties-that-bind for staff who actually are chairman's staff (although it may overstate reality). From 1962 to 1978, the period of their study, there is little staff change or staff director change even when the chair changes. They conclude that the ties-that-bind are more important for personal staff and that committee staff display some characteristics of a permanent bureaucracy.

Mean staff turnover and turnover in staff directors are compared before and after 1970 (i.e., a period of quiet versus a period of rapid institutional change); there is higher turnover during the 1970s. Salisbury and Shepsle conclude that elections (institutional change) make some difference. Staff loyalty to members probably increases fragmentation of policy making, and staff are a "giant recruitment pool" for public service. A great strength of the article is in the conceptual approach and the hypothesis testing. As the authors point out, the data are somewhat less than full or completely reliable. And the assumption that committee staff are a member-specific resource for chairmen may skew reality somewhat.

The second article (1981b) carries the analysis of congressmen as enterprises further. Primarily theoretical (and less empirical), it offers a number of interesting ideas about perspectives on Congress and about congressional behavior and outputs. The enterprise concept is extended beyond the immediate staff to the "extended enterprise"—staff alumni in other staff positions on the Hill, in the executive branch, or in private sector employment. They ask what it means to the member to head an enterprise and how enterprises affect Congress as an institution. They speculate that enterprises enable members to pursue the goals of reelection, policy, and power in Congress simultaneously. The survival and success of the enterprise is of major importance; staff ambition and style affect enterprises. The authors suggest (but do not have data to prove) that there are fewer professionals and entrepreneurs on staffs now than 20 years ago and that there are many more staff politicos whose primary goal is advancing the career of the member. They suggest areas for further research: the effect of enterprise on the number of bills, amendments, and laws and on the amount of bargaining; on policy fragmentation and on distributive politics; and on vertical integration of different functions (election, policy oversight). The perspective links the member and the institutional structure, the micro and the macro, and gives promise of useful theoretical constructs.

Much of the legislative staffing literature focuses on legislative sub-units. Most research is based on standard data sources: published legislative documents, questionnaires, and interviews. Although the literature is not cumulative, more recent studies (Fox and Hammond, 1977; Loomis, 1979; Malbin, 1980) draw on earlier studies. Researchers have begun to develop, define, operationalize, and measure concepts and to test hypotheses (e.g., Rosenthal, 1971, 1973a, 1973b, 1974; Salisbury and Shepsle, 1981a). The approach permits systematic comparison and links the micro and the macro levels—important elements in theory building.

Studies with an Institutional Focus

The comparative subfield, particularly comparative development, has contributed disproportionately to staffing studies with an institutional-level focus; this fact reflects both subfield perspective and the less elaborate staffing patterns in non-U.S. national legislatures. Organization theory and occasionally public administration theory are drawn on for a conceptual framework.[5]

Baaklini (1975) and Baaklini and Heaphey (1975) report data on newly established central staff agencies of nonpartisan professionals serving the entire legislature in Brazil, Costa Rica, and Lebanon; their data are drawn from parliamentary documents, interviews, observation, and consultant-participation. Staff are civil servants insulated from partisanship, although as in Western European countries there are separate legislative personnel systems. They work on "generally legislative" matters, assembling information, and not on private bills, constituency service, or reelection-assisting issues.

Baaklini recognizes the political nature of the environment and of legislative decision making. He finds that "neutral" staff may not be adequately responsive to legislators' needs nor sufficiently sensitive politically. "Expert" staff identified with legislators who had similar training and considered most legislators "not worth helping"; such attitudes are often typical of developing countries, Baaklini notes (1975). As a result, staff lose influence because legislators won't work with them or the legislative process is undermined. There is a contradiction between "political legislative values and bureaucratic administrative values"; neutral, nonpartisan professionals in central staff agencies "may end up weakening the institution they were supposed to strengthen" (p. 236). Neutral staff may even weaken the linkage between legislators and constituents (Baaklini and Heaphey, 1975, p. 48). Thus, staffing patterns typical of many developing countries may be dysfunctional and "development of a staff unit needs to [take into account] the total setting" (Baaklini and Heaphey, 1975).

The information needs of legislatures and the effect of different staffing patterns are also of concern to Patterson (1973), Robinson (1970,

1973a), Harder and Davis (1979), and Solomon (1978). Robinson suggests (1970) that legislative information requirements may vary according to the stage of development; important variables are the "legislature's prominence vis-à-vis other institutions of government," the opposition parties, and the "affluence" of the society. The place of the legislature in the political system and the institution's efficiency also shape Burns's (1971) perspective and the recommendations of the Citizen's Conference on State Legislatures.

European parliaments have introduced legislative staff later than the U.S. Congress, perhaps because of differences in organization and in member-party relationships. There is relatively little scholarly analysis in English of legislative staffing in these parliaments. Three articles published in 1981 in *Legislative Studies Quarterly* describe legislative staff in Britain, France, and Germany. The authors' perspective is institutional: staff structure and operation reflect the role of the legislature in the political system. All argue that staff developed to increase the efficiency and effectiveness of the legislature and of the individual members; as in the United States, staff increases have occurred incrementally in response to demands of members. All three parliaments have central agencies staffed by legislative civil servants and some provision for personal staff.

Ryle (1981) describes the organization, operation, and increased need for coordination of the five departments of the House of Commons staff. Study of staffing changes on the select committees established in 1979 may be of particular interest to those interested in parliamentary reform. Ryle concludes that fragmented and incremental responses to demands for staff have resulted in fragmented staff organization. Campbell and LaPorte (1981) describe a dramatic increase in French parliamentary staff since 1945, including provision for two personal assistants for each member. The autonomy of the parliament is enhanced by staff and reflected in the tradition of an autonomous legislative bureaucracy responsible to the parliament. Blischke (1981) finds that Germany's Bundestag staff—developed since 1969 and numbering 1500—also enhance the autonomy and independence of the institution and its members. Central staff, committee and party staff, and members' aides provide various research and system-linkage services. Bundestag members may call on neutral or partisan experts for information and analysis. The data and the conclusions of the three articles suggest interesting and important questions for further research. How do the political system and traditions affect legislative staffing? How does legislative staffing affect the political system and the place of the legislature in that system? Are there patterns of evolution for legislative staffing? What is the role, and effect, of legislative civil servants in contrast to personal assistants? The development of legislative staff in non-U.S. parliaments offers an important opportunity for comparative study.

A state case study explores some of these questions. Davis (1975) studied the process of change and institutionalization in the California legislature, using structural indicators (numbers and types of staff, expenditures for staff) and case studies. He draws on propositions from organization and exchange theory: "Legislative staff are used by the legislature to buffer it from outside influences which it seeks to avoid or control" (p. 202); "In a complex environment, the legislature's dependence upon staff is exchanged for access and influence" (p. 215). The data and discussion demonstrate that the propositions seem accurate, although hypotheses are not formally tested. The perspective and propositions are useful in thinking about staffing.

Another California study (Wyner, 1973) finds that increased staff, a major component of legislative reform, has increased legislative information and strengthened the legislature's autonomy and independence. From his data (quantitative measures of output, interviews, and observations) he also concludes that legislative-interest group and executive branch interaction changed, with staff an important new actor. A study of Kansas (Harder and Davis, 1979) and two national studies, Solomon's on Australia (1978) and Clarke, Campbell, Quo, and Goddard's on Canada (1980) focus on some of these questions.

Meller's (1973) central concern is also legislative institutionalization and the autonomy and independence of legislatures and individual members, in this instance in developing countries. In his study of Pacific Basin legislatures, he concludes that legislative staff can significantly enhance progress toward institutionalization; staff help maintain procedures and give the institution more visibility and autonomy. Staff are especially important in premodern legislatures; in those, members have few other sources of aid (such as interest groups or political parties) and legislatures are generally undifferentiated from other political subsystems. He suggests a 16-cell paradigm for research on staff (pp. 331-332). This paradigm distinguishes two system variables: the form of government (presidential or parliamentary) and the level of legislative institutionalization. It also distinguishes two staffing variables: "supportive identification" with legislator (personal identification or anonymous objectivity) and the organizational position of the staff group assisting the legislator or the legislature. As with his earlier work, the effort to measure, categorize, and compare and to develop theoretical constructs is particularly useful.

Several other studies (Roberts, 1975; Turnbull, 1977; Walker, 1979; Flemming, 1981; Ranney, 1981) touch on the interaction of legislative staff and institution and suggest some interesting hypotheses. Ranney, for example, although his study does not focus on staff, makes the point that changing staff support will change the legislator's job, and changing the job requires different levels of staff support: giving (more) staff to parliamentary backbenchers could result in more intraparty splits.

The studies with an institutional focus are particularly interesting, for there are more comparative studies and the case studies, although not comparative, often use similar conceptual frameworks. The findings of the studies are not, perhaps, as conclusive as subunit or individual studies, but the hypotheses generated offer opportunity for integrative, comparative work and theory building.

Legislative Staff and Legislative Information Needs

Arguments for establishing or increasing legislative staff are generally tied to the information needs of legislatures. And most studies of staffing include analysis of the "intelligence" function of aides. Several recent studies focus not on staff but on legislators' information requirements; however, the data and the hypotheses are relevant to a survey of legislative staffing.[6] Case studies predominate (Barker and Rush, 1970; Rush and Shaw, 1974; Van Schendelen, 1976; Maisel, 1981), although four are comparative across states (Porter, 1974, 1975; Wissel, O'Connor, and King, 1976; Bradley, 1980).

Studies of the information needs and resources of the British Parliament have been conducted by Barker and Rush (1970) and Rush and Shaw (1974). Van Schendelen (1976) found variation in patterns of staff use in the Dutch Parliament. Members generally considered staff information highly reliable; specialist MPs from middle-sized and government parties especially rely on legislative staff.

The Obey Commission gathered extensive data on the types of information needed by U.S. representatives and on information sources (U.S. House of Representatives, 1977). Personal staff, committee staff, and non-official groups were identified as major sources of information. Maisel (1981) suggests that information needs and sources vary at different stages of the legislative process. He discusses the role of legislative staff in information analysis, pointing out that key legislative assistants do not have time for "detailed policy analysis" yet such analysis is often needed for complex legislative decision making. Variations in information needs and the structural placement of different types of staff experts are important questions for legislatures.

Porter (1974, 1975) also finds reliance on staff by state legislators in Michigan and Virginia. Sixty percent of Virginia legislators in 1974 found personal staff a "very useful" information source, with delegates rating research on legislation among the most important activities of aides. Porter, as well as Huwa and Rosenthal (1977), finds that procedural information is more often requested than policy information (see also Rosenthal, 1981, pp. 217-224). Wissel, O'Connor, and King (1976) report that in their study of eight state legislatures, in well-staffed legislatures, members relied primarily on internal and especially staff, information sources; in poorly staffed legislatures, external information sources were most important. Their study examines an interesting proposition, that existing information search patterns affect legislative staffing reform proposals. They arrayed states along a "developmental continuum" according to staffing patterns (eight stages from generalist, centralized, liaison to specialized, decentralized, processing staff), and examined state staffing reform proposals, finding that the modal recommendation reflects the existing information search (staffing) arrangement. They predict that staffing change will be incremental and will follow the development continuum; they also discuss the difficulty of disentangling causal variables. It is an interesting approach, useful to pursue. Bradley (1980) also found that Nevada legislators, surveyed in 1968, relied heavily on legislative staff for scientific and technical information, and that different sources are complementary and valued for different reasons.

Legislative Staff and Legislative Output

Factors affecting legislative performance and legislative output are of interest to all legislative scholars. Various studies have used legislative staffing levels as an intervening or independent variable affecting the output and/or performance of legislatures or legislative subunits. Most but not all the studies are at the state level. Although legislative staffing is peripheral to researchers' central concerns, it is useful to focus on some studies briefly, especially to assess concepts and approaches which might be particularly relevant to the study of legislative staffing.

Ornstein (1975), in studying staff utilization by American senators and representatives, finds an association between both staff size and legislative use of staff and the activity of congressmen (measured by the number of bills cosponsored): those with the highest number of cosponsored bills use staff the most on legislative tasks and also have the largest legislative staffs. In Ornstein's study, staff size and utilization are dependent variables, although his data show an association and do not indicate the direction of causality. Fox and Hammond (1977, Ch. 9), also studying the U.S. Congress, found a "rough correlation" between staff size and committee activity: committees with larger staffs generally held more hearings and more meetings and were likely to communicate more frequently with others in the policy system. Representatives with the largest number of professionals and with the largest staffs cosponsored the most bills. Hammond and Langbein (1982) use committee staff levels as a measure of committee resources to test the impact of complexity and reform on congressional output (measured by number and length of bills which became public law). Hamm and Moncrief's (1982) study of five state legislative chambers also uses committee research staff as one (of two) measures of legislative support services.

Rosenthal's work on legislative staff is important and a major contribution to thinking about staff: the differentiation of staff groups; the interaction of staff and legislative development; operationalizing and measuring "effectiveness"—he grapples with a number of the most difficult conceptual problems, tries to overcome the atheoretical approach to staffing of much of the literature, and in the process shapes the approach and thinking of later scholars. His research is state-level; the concepts, and the findings, are transferable to U.S. national and to crossnational research. His focus is primarily on legislative subunits, mostly committees. His work on different types of staff groups has been discussed; here, the focus is on his comparative committee work: the 1971 article on "Legislative Committee Systems" and the 1974 book *Legislative Performance in the States,* comparing and assessing committee systems. Neither is technically a staffing study; rather, they are comparative committee studies, with committee staff an important variable. They are included in this summary of staffing literature because the concepts and the measures shed light on the concerns of legislative staffing scholars, and we can learn from the approach. The contextual environment is important: committees are subsystems embedded in a larger legislative system and the broader political and social environment.

In the 1971 article Rosenthal's objective is to "compare committee systems among the fifty states, and to suggest how and why they vary in terms of their effectiveness from one legislature to another" (p. 252). Committee effectiveness is defined as "the degree to which committee systems perform the functions expected of them as legislative agencies" (p. 252) and is measured on two dimensions: policy formulation and policy control (i.e., oversight). Rosenthal assumes that an effective committee exercises independent judgment and that independent judgment means that changes are made by committees. There are several operationalized measurements of effectiveness: (1) the number of bills referred to committees (more bills mean a more effective committee); (2) the proportions of referred bills reported favorably, not reported, or reported negatively (less effective committees report most bills favorably); (3) the number of changes in bills made by committee (more effective committees make more changes); (4) the "extent to which committees shape the passage of legislation," measured by whether bills are blocked from consideration or amended or rejected on the floor (the less change, the more effective the committee); (5) activity during the interim or recess (more effective committees study issues and develop legislation during this period). In this model, the effective committee is activist (like the entrepreneurs in Price's classification of committee staff). It is, of course, possible that independent judgment results in few or no changes or in favorable reports on bills.

The data base includes December 1970 telephone interviews with state legislators who attended Eagleton Institute Conferences and the massive survey of indicators by the Citizen's Conference on State Legislatures. Committee effectiveness is the dependent variable. Institutional power and institutional capacity are independent variables. Institutional capacity can be measured by committee resources; one resource is the number of professional staff, a dichotomized variable with 15 or more staff defined as a larger staff and fewer than 15 a smaller staff. Committees are grouped as more effective, somewhat effective, and less effective. He finds no association (.04 gamma coefficient) between size of staff and committee system effectiveness—a finding which seems intuitively wrong, and is therefore all the more important. Rosenthal is well aware of the "primitive nature" (p. 253) of his measures, and of legislative records which make it difficult to operationalize effectiveness and to conduct comparative studies. The assumptions which must be made to perform the analysis pose problems; for example, he assumes that an "effective" committee system is autonomous and independent from the executive, from the central leadership in legislatures, and from other committees. But his attempt is very useful, particularly in specifying more precisely the components of effectiveness and in operationalizing and measuring these.

The 1974 book draws on additional studies and on interviews and survey data from legislatures in 50 states. Of particular relevance here are the operationalization and measurement of concepts of performance (inputs, output, procedures, functions) and the chapter on legislative staffing. Rosenthal considers staff an input, one measure of legislative capacity. He continues his concern with the validity of quantitative measures, noting a problem with the assumption that "material resources determine the quality of legislatures." Furthermore, measuring the quantity of output (as of laws) does not capture differences in quality, and even if it were possible to measure quality (as of public policy outputs) it cannot be assumed that the effects are all due to the legislature. He distinguishes between nominal output (e.g., the number of laws passed) and "real" output (the impact on citizens). He again reports no association between size of staff and committee system performance (pp. 52-53) in policy formulation (although institutional capacity, including staff, is important). Professional staff is one of the variables associated with committee performance of the policy control (oversight) function (p. 102), but he later drops it in his analysis, as less important than four other variables. In a section studying the impact of reform in the New Jersey legislature, he examines the hypothesis that committees with larger staffs screen more bills and report fewer bills favorably; however, he finds no pattern and no confirmation of the hypothesis. Staff make a difference on amendments; committees with larger staffs propose more amendments and modifications and have greater floor success (pp. 138-141). Rosenthal also suggests that the type of staff organization (central service agency or decentralized to committees) and staff orientation (established by committee or set by staff) are "central issues" in committee and legislative performance. These studies and scattered others (e.g., Kingdon, 1973, 1981, esp. Ch. 7; Rosenthal, 1981) begin to assess staff impact and influence; all use quantitative measures. Before legislative staffing is understood, research must focus more fully on this very important question.

Conclusion

Legislative staffing research has matured along with the political science discipline; research also reflects a larger and more differentiated legislative staff. Scholars approach the study of staffing from a variety of perspectives. The level of analysis differs; studies may focus on the individual aide, subunit staff groups, or institutions.

The theoretical viewpoint varies: role theory, organization theory, exchange theory, decision- and policy-making frameworks, and other concepts drawn from sociology and psychology as well as from political science inform the research. An increasing number of studies are technically sophisticated, both in analysis and hypothesis testing. Different kinds of data are used by researchers. Systematic interviewing of a random sample of a large population (e.g., the U.S. House of Representatives) or a universe (e.g., all members of a subcommittee), often supplemented by observation and/or participation, continues to be the predominant method of gathering data. Questionnaire surveys and quantitative data (as on staff levels or expenditures, committee activity, bill cosponsorship) derived from legislative documents are also used. Although it is pluralistic and informed by a variety of perspectives, theory building is progressing on the role and functions of staff, the impact of staff on legislatures and policy making, and the effects of legislators and of legislatures on staff.

Studying one legislature or subunits in a legislature continues to be the modus operandi of most researchers. There are few integrative comparative studies across national or state legislatures or across legislative levels (e.g., state-level and national). As Bradley (1980) notes, there are pitfalls in comparisons: apparently similar institutions—legislatures, committees, staff agencies—may actually be quite different. Nevertheless, integrative and synthesizing comparative studies seem a fruitful area for future research; without comparative studies we are less likely to make much progress in theory building. There are other gaps: few studies explicitly link the micro and the macro levels. There is not much borrowing of concepts from one study to another; the literature on functions, norms, and constraints of staff is the major exception. Nor is there much integration of previous studies into later research. There are few longitudinal studies.

Research Problems

Scholars studying legislative staff face problems of definition, of data, and of measurement.

Definition. Concepts used by researchers–"professionalism," "expert information," "bureaucracy"–need precise definition. Although there may be agreement on the attributes of bureaucracy, congressional scholars disagree on whether staff bureaucracies exist in the U.S. Congress, for example. If large size, differentiation, and specialization are the test, the answer will be yes; if hierarchy and formal authority patterns are required, many would argue that legislative staff groups are not bureaucracies. Similarly, information can be partisan or nonpartisan, technical, political or strategic, procedural or substantive, and so forth; such distinctions are important, but precise definition is needed, and use of the same typologies by scholars would be helpful. Other terms–e.g., "work load," "output"–which may be used in staff analysis studies also require specification.

Data. Legislative scholars are well aware of data problems. There are data gaps. Few congressional committees, for example, keep data on subcommittee activity (hearings, meetings, staff levels, or even bills referred), and yet the subcommittee should be a major focus for analysis. Historical records are not kept, or are inaccessible, making longitudinal analysis impossible. Some legislatures keep only summaries of debate and votes. It is not possible to gather data on changes in the number of caseworkers or press aides in the U.S. Congress, because until recently names but not titles of staff aides were reported by Congress. Available data are not always comparable across subunits within a legislature or between legislatures. Data may be unclear: should interns employed as aides be counted as regular staff? Or, a body of data may be built by different researchers using different decision rules. How reliable can the data set then be considered?

Interviews are generally conducted with a sample or an entire population. Although the data are gathered systematically, often the interviews are drawn on to provide illustrative examples and nonsystematic evidence. Lack of data and noncomparability of data shape staffing research: some questions may not be researched and some theoretical frameworks may not be used because they do not lend themselves to analysis with the data available.

Systematic use of available data may overcome some of these problems. For example, Price's (1972) legislative process typology, specifying analytically distinct stages, enables him to use interview and observation data to compare three Senate committees systematically.

Measurement. Problems in measuring concepts and testing hypotheses are linked to problems of data availability. Measures of structural capacity used in the state literature are often quite general: level of expenditure for staff, for example. Similarly, researchers interested in the effect of environmental variables on legislative staffing often must use very general measures and often must make a number of assumptions (e.g., that the number of government agencies is a good surrogate for governmental complexity). And finally, only some measures of output are available: the number of bills reported from committees or number of laws. Legislatures do not keep data on other output: constituent contacts or staff memoranda. If researchers want to use quantitative measures, they often must use surrogates for the phenomenon they are tapping.

Research Findings, Hypotheses, and Legislative Staffing Models

At the individual, subunit, and institutional levels, there is an increasing data set on legislative staff. There are data on demographic characteristics, recruitment, communications and activity patterns, norms, and role perception. There has been some analysis of the effect of environmental variables on staff and of the impact of staff characteristics on activity patterns and roles, for example. At the subunit level, there is comparative study of staffing patterns, of staff function in the subunit, and of staff effect on variation in subunit output. At the institutional level, studies focus on the effect of staff on the legislative institution, the "stage" of staffing in the context of legislative development, and the differential effects of specialized staff groups. The contextual now informs analysis, although perhaps not precisely, and most studies assume a micro-macro level linkage, although it may not be made explicit. Scholars agree on the importance of staff as actors in the policy process and the legislative system. A subtle but important shift in research direction has occurred quite recently: toward analysis of factors affecting variation in staff work and influence and toward assessment and measurement of staff influence and impact.

In thinking about legislative staff and staffing patterns, various typologies have been suggested and may offer a basis for further research. At the individual level, classifications which distinguish between, for example professionals and entrepreneurs (Price, 1971) or between Hill professionals and Hill specialists (Hammond, 1975) and categories based on variation in background and/or position suggest research approaches. At the subunit level, staff groups have been categorized according to function (Jewell and Patterson, 1973), position in the legislative structure, partisanship (e.g., Cochrane, 1964; Malbin, 1981; Patterson, 1970a; Price, 1971), and organization (Patterson, 1970a; Fox and Hammond, 1977). It has been suggested that these variables, among others, affect staff function, innovation and initiative, and legislative policy. Legislator role orientations (e.g., Matthews, 1960), ideology, and the nature of the district may also have an independent effect on staff. At the institutional level, the focus has been on legislative (or system) development and institutionalization or on staff-legislature interaction.

Jones suggests a contextual model for differentiating the perspective and effect of staff groups, based on whether the problem or demand is characterized by a "state and local perspective" or by a "public policy, law-making perspective" (1982, p. 146). Meller's development of a 16-cell paradigm takes into account differences among legislatures, among staff groups, and among individual legislative aides. Heaphey's (1975) approach has similar theoretical and linkage possibilities: "Legislatures are lateral, not scalar organizations. [Such] organizations are [less] able to deal with long-range problems, decisions . . . are more narrow . . . and reached faster . . . [,] loyalty is highly personalized . . . and [the organizations are] more flexible and adaptable. . . . Some suborganizations within legislatures will be scalar." Heaphey suggests there be study of the "extent to which such scalar organizations function . . . unresponsively to the needs of the legislature as a lateral organization" (pp. 10-13).

Just as the availability of data shapes research, so does the level of analysis. And research designs are shaped by the general focus: on staff, on reform (an important subtheme in the staffing literature), or on information and the mobilization of expertise. The last provides opportunity for expansion of analysis beyond the legislature to include executive branch and interest group personnel, for example.

Case studies will continue to be important, to advance our knowledge of a specific institution or legislative subunit, and to serve as a basis for systematic comparison. There continues to be a need to "map the terrain" and to fill in data gaps. Surveys of staff recruitment, characteristics, and activities are similarly useful. But in case studies and surveys, as in staffing research generally, there is need to build on earlier studies and to work with similar questions and hypotheses. Data on staff career patterns would, for example, assist analysis of interest group functions or of the operation of policy networks. There are data which indicate that certain professionals—those in foreign policy issue areas, for example—now move on and off Capitol Hill with ease. But there is little data on recruitment and post-congressional employment of other professionals. With that data, it would be possible to explore systematically the implications of new patterns of personnel movement for policy making. What, for example, is the effect of similar perceptions, goals, and socialization of professionals in traditionally separate and differing institutions? Has the traditional subsystem government expanded as staff mobility has changed? What is the role of expertise, and of expert knowledge, in the policy process?

There is need for longitudinal analysis. From research done in the 1960s and 1970s, there is a fairly extensive data base on the recruitment, turnover, attributes, and activities of legislative staff in the U.S. Congress, some U.S. state legislatures, and some non-U.S. legislatures. Have these changed and if so how? Longitudinal analysis not only helps map the terrain but also sheds light on the causes and consequences of legislative change and reform (cf. Hammond and Langbein, 1982).

There is especially need for systematic comparative analysis. There is little data on and almost no comparison of national legislatures other than the U.S. Congress. Studies of the American states and especially of subnational units elsewhere are also infrequent. All of these need study if we are to understand legislative staffing. And understanding would be enhanced by systematic comparative analysis of subunits and staff groups within legislatures, of similar subunits and staff groups between legislatures, and of legislative staff and similar groups outside legislatures (cf. Aberbach, Putnam, and Rockman, 1981, on political executives). Studies of staff of new subunits, such as informal caucuses, would also be useful. These might especially focus on relationships with established subunits (committees, party caucus) and with subsystem personnel. What are the structural implications? What are the policy consequences?

Scholars might explore hypotheses generated by the rich research on legislative subunits. Does the type of committee (Fenno, 1973) affect staff recruitment, attributes, activities, role, or function? Does staff assistance on procedural information (Porter, 1974; Rosenthal, 1981) vary systematically by type of committee? Or does it vary by "enterprise" (Salisbury and Shepsle, 1981a, 1981b)? What is the effect of staff in constituencies on, for example, the representative function of the institution? Crossnational comparison might serve as a surrogate for longitudinal analysis on this aspect of staffing. What are the similarities, or differences, between different types of staff groups, and how are they to be explained?

At the institutional level, researchers might explore whether different types of legislatures have different requirements for expertise or whether they organize differently to mobilize expertise. What variables affect the kind of expert, or the kind of expert group, mobilized (e.g., staff vs. experts outside the legislature)? Do recruitment and career patterns differ among legislatures, and if so why, and what is the effect? Do the functions performed by a legislature shape staffing; for example, is staffing affected by a legislature's role in conflict resolution? In the absence of staff, how are staff functions fulfilled? In many countries, the opposition has little capacity to influence events (see Baaklini, 1975). Or backbenchers may serve as staff to senior members (Ranney, 1981; King, 1981). Does staffing differ according to the type of legislature (for various classifications, see Polsby, 1975, and Loewenberg and Patterson, 1979)? What is the effect of structural differences between legislatures (parliamentary or separation of powers; single member or multi-member districts), of developmental stages, or of modernization?

With systematic comparative analysis, it should be possible to identify commonalities and differences, and to specify much more precisely the factors which affect these. Inevitably, scholars will be concerned with the contextual, and they should be. Context shapes the perceptions and behavior of legislators and staff (see, for example, Cooper and Mackenzie, 1981; Patterson, 1982). Conversely, the effect of staff on institution is also an important empirical question.

Systematic comparative inquiry would also inform discussion of normative questions (e.g., Malbin, 1980) regarding the role of staff. The differential impact and influence of different types of staff (see Rosenthal, 1974, 1981; Malbin, 1980, 1981) and subunit work load and output should be considered. Reconceptualizing can also contribute to the discussion: it may be that in the present era a legislature should be less concerned with increased levels of staffing than with managing staff so that major decision making rests with elected representatives.

Important questions are the impact and influence of staff on legislative institutions and functions and on output, decision making, and policy. Studies describing patterns and variations, and identifying important variables affecting these, will contribute to the answers. But the questions should also be addressed directly. Careful definition of concepts, development and precise statement of hypotheses, and specificity of measurements are required.

Other aspects of legislative staffing deserve research attention. The theoretical approach based on the purposive behavior of legislators has informed congressional research during much of the past decade (see Fenno, 1973; Mayhew, 1974). This approach might also be applied to staffing studies. Fox found that the ideology of personal staff aides tends to match that of the senators for whom they work (Fox and Hammond, 1977); Malbin (1980) argues that staff career goals shape staff behavior. What is the "fit" between the goals of principals and staff, and how does this affect staff function and influence? Some work has been done on staff perceptions (e.g., Huwa and Rosenthal, 1977). How do different perceptions among staff impact on staff activity and function? What effect do different legislator-staff perceptions (see, for example, Wolman and Wolman, 1977) have on legislative agendas? or on policy information? or on legislative decisions?

There is need for (1) longitudinal analysis, (2) integrative comparative analysis, (3) work which links the micro and the macro levels, (4) development of conceptual frameworks, and (5) theory building. We especially need to develop a theory of legislative behavior which incorporates staffing into the dynamics of the institution and which explains staffing patterns and roles over time. There are interesting and significant questions to be explored.

NOTES

I am grateful for comments and suggestions on an earlier version of this essay to Norman Ornstein, to my colleagues at the Legislative Research Conference at The University of Iowa in October 1982, and especially to Samuel C. Patterson for his commentary paper at the conference and for subsequent suggestions.

1. This essay covers research published in English. Dissertations, journalistic articles, and unpublished manuscripts are not included.

2. In a footnote, Meller suggests other ways legislative service agencies might be categorized: by organizational type (legislative staff, committee staff, executive department staff); by primary purpose (formulation of a presession program; legal representation; reference and library service); and by functional type (fiscal, legal, general research, and so forth).

3. Redman's (1973) delightful account of a staff aide's work in the U.S. Senate and BeVier's (1979) insightful participant-observer case study of California should also be noted as individual level studies. Mark Twain's vignettes of congressmen and descriptions of Congress, where he served as private secretary to Senator Stewart of Nevada in 1867-1868, is perhaps the first staff commentary (see Anderson, Frank, and Sanderson, 1975); I am indebted to Ken Shepsle and Robert Salisbury for bringing Twain's congressional writings to my attention.

4. John D. Macartney, "Political Staffing: A View from the District." Unpublished Ph.D. dissertation, University of California, Los Angeles, 1975.

5. These perspectives may overlap, but are not similar (cf. Davis, 1975 and Baaklini, 1975).

6. In these studies staff and information is a major subtheme; of course most of the literature on legislative information needs and resources focuses on members, not staff.

REFERENCES

Aberbach, Joel D., Robert Putnam, and Bert A. Rockman. 1981. *Bureaucrats and Politicians in Western Democracies.* Cambridge: Harvard University Press.

Almond, Gabriel. 1965. "A Developmental Approach to Political Systems," *World Politics* 17:183-214.

Anderson, Frederick, Michael B. Frank, and Kenneth M. Sanderson, eds. 1975. *Mark Twain's Notebooks & Journals. Vol. 1 (1855-1873).* Berkeley: University of California Press.

Baaklini, Abdo I. 1975. "Legislative Staffing Patterns in Developing Countries," in James J. Heaphey and Alan P. Balutis, eds., *Legislative Staffing: A Comparative Perspective.* New York: Wiley.

Baaklini, Abdo I. and James J. Heaphey. 1975. *Legislative Institution Building in Brazil, Costa Rica, and Lebanon.* Sage Professional Papers in Administrative and Policy Studies, no. 03-27. Beverly Hills, CA: Sage Publications.

Bailey, Stephen Kemp. 1950. *Congress Makes a Law.* New York: Columbia University Press.

Balutis, Alan P. 1975a. "Legislative Staffing: A Review of Current Trends," in James J. Heaphey and Alan P. Balutis, eds., *Legislative Staffing: A Comparative Perspective*. New York: Wiley.

_____ . 1975b. "Legislative Staffing: A View From the States," in James J. Heaphey and Alan P. Balutis, eds., *Legislative Staffing: A Comparative Perspective*. New York: Wiley.

_____ . 1975c. "The Budgetary Process in New York State: The Role of the Legislative Staff," in Alan P. Balutis and Daron K. Butler, eds., *The Political Pursestrings*. New York: Wiley.

_____ . 1975d. "The Role of Staff in the Legislature: The Case of New York," *Public Administration Review* 35:357-360.

_____ . 1977. "Legislative Executive Integration," *State and Local Government Review* 9:88-94.

_____ . 1979. "Legislative Staffing: Does It Make a Difference?" in Susan Welch and John Peters, eds., *Legislative Reform and Public Policy*. New York: Praeger.

Balutis, Alan P. and Daron K. Butler, eds. 1975. *The Political Pursestrings: The Role of the Legislature in the Budgetary Process*. New York: Wiley.

Balutis, Alan P. and James J. Heaphey. 1974. *Public Administration and the Legislative Process*. Sage Professional Papers in Administrative and Policy Studies, no. 03-24. Beverly Hills, CA: Sage Publications.

Barker, Anthony and Michael Rush. 1970. *The Member of Parliament and His Information*. London: Allen and Unwin.

BeVier, Michael J. 1979. *Politics Backstage: Inside the California Legislature*. Philadelphia: Temple University Press.

Bibby, John F. 1966. "Committee Characteristics and Legislative Oversight of Administration," *Midwest Journal of Political Science* 10:78-98.

Bibby, John F. and Roger H. Davidson. 1972. *On Capitol Hill: Studies in the Legislative Process*. 2d ed. Hinsdale, IL: The Dryden Press. (1st ed. 1967. New York: Holt, Rinehart and Winston.)

Blischke, Werner. 1981. "Parliamentary Staffs in the German Bundestag," *Legislative Studies Quarterly* 6:533-558.

Bradley, Robert B. 1980. "Motivations in Legislative Information Use," *Legislative Studies Quarterly* 5:393-406.

Brady, David W. 1981. "Personnel Management in the House," in Joseph Cooper and G. Calvin Mackenzie, eds., *The House at Work*. Austin: University of Texas Press.

Breslin, Janet. 1976. "Constituent Service," in U.S. Senate, Commission on the Operation of the Senate, 94th Congress, 2d Session, *Studies*. 7 vols. Washington, DC: Committee Prints.

Budtke, Maralyn S. 1975. "The Legislative Fiscal Staff's Role in the Budgetary Process—New Mexico," in Alan P. Balutis and Daron K. Butler, eds., *The Political Pursestrings*. New York: Wiley.

Burks, Stephen W. and Richard I. Cole. 1978. "Congressional Staff Personnel Role Orientations," *Georgia Political Science Association Journal* 6:17-37.

Burns, John. 1971. *The Sometime Governments*. New York: Bantam.

Butler, Daron K. 1975. "The Legislative Budget in Texas," in Alan P. Balutis and Daron K. Butler, eds., *The Political Pursestrings*. New York: Wiley.

Butler, Warren H. 1966. "Administering Congress: The Role of Staff," *Public Administration Review* 26:3-13.

Campbell, Stanley and Jean LaPorte. 1981. "The Staff of the Parliamentary Assemblies in France," *Legislative Studies Quarterly* 6:521-532.

Capron, William M. 1976. "The CBO," in U.S. Senate, Commission on the Operation of the Senate, 94th Congress, 2d Session, *Studies.* 7 vols. Washington, DC: Committee Prints.

Caro, Robert A. 1982. *The Path to Power: The Years of Lyndon Johnson.* New York: Knopf.

Carroll, James D. 1976. "Policy Analysis for Congress: A Review of the CRS," in U.S. Senate, Commission on the Operation of the Senate, 94th Congress, 2d Session, *Studies.* 7 vols. Washington, DC: Committee Prints.

Cavanaugh, Thomas E. 1979. "Rational Allocation of Congressional Resources: Member Time and Staff Use in the House," in D.W. Rae and T.J. Eismeier, eds., *Public Policy and Public Choice.* Beverly Hills, CA: Sage Publications.

——————. 1981. "The Two Arenas of Congress," in Joseph Cooper and G. Calvin Mackenzie, eds., *The House at Work.* Austin: University of Texas Press.

Citizen's Conference on State Legislatures. 1971. *State Legislatures: An Evaluation of Their Effectiveness.* New York: Praeger.

——————. 1972. "Legislatures Move to Improve Their Effectiveness." Research Memorandum No. 15. Kansas City, MO: Citizen's Conference on State Legislatures.

Clapp, Charles. 1963. *The Congressman: His Work As He Sees It.* Washington, DC: The Brookings Institution.

Clark, Calvin. 1967. "A Summary of Legislative Services in the Fifty States." Kansas City, MO: Citizen's Conference on State Legislatures.

Clarke, Harold D., Colin Campbell, F.Q. Quo, and Arthur Goddard, eds. 1980. *Parliament, Policy and Representation.* Toronto: Methuen.

Cleveland, James C. 1966. "The Need for Increased Minority Staffing," in Mary McInnis, ed., *We Propose: A Modern Congress.* New York: McGraw-Hill.

Cochrane, James D. 1964. "Partisan Aspects of Congressional Committee Staffing," *Western Political Quarterly* 27:338-348.

Cooper, Joseph and G. Calvin Mackenzie, eds. 1981. *The House at Work.* Austin: University of Texas Press.

Council of State Governments. 1963. *Legislative Staff Improvement Study.* Lexington, KY: Council of State Governments.

Crane, Wilder, Jr. and Meredith W. Watts, Jr. 1968. *State Legislative Systems.* Englewood Cliffs, NJ: Prentice-Hall.

Davidson, Roger H. and Walter J. Oleszek. 1977. *Congress Against Itself.* Bloomington: University of Indiana Press.

Davis, Raymond. 1975. "The Evolution of California Legislative Staff," in James J. Heaphey and Alan P. Balutis, eds., *Legislative Staff: A Comparative Perspective.* New York: Wiley.

de Grazia, Alfred, ed. 1966. *Congress: The First Branch of Government.* Washington, DC: American Enterprise Institute. (Paperback ed. 1967. Garden City, NY: Doubleday, Anchor Books.)

Elder, Robert E. 1957. "The Foreign Affairs Division of the Legislative Reference Service: Organization and Functions of a Professional Staff," *Western Political Quarterly* 10:169-179.

Elliott, William Y. 1965. "Committee Staffing," in U.S. Congress, Joint Committee on the Organization of Congress, 89th Congress, 1st Session, *Hearings; Symposium; Interim Reports; Final Report.* Washington, DC: Government Printing Office.

Eulau, Heinz. 1966. "The Committees in a Revitalized Congress," in Alfred de Grazia, ed., *Congress: The First Branch of Government*. Washington, DC: American Enterprise Institute.

Farnum, Eugene. 1975. "The Legislative Fiscal Staff's Role in the Budgetary Process in Michigan," in Alan P. Balutis and Daron K. Butler, eds., *The Political Purse-strings*. New York: Wiley.

Feller, I., M. King, D. Menzel, R. O'Connor, and T. Ingersoll. 1975. *Sources and Uses of Scientific and Technological Information in State Legislatures*. State College: Pennsylvania State University Press.

Fenno, Richard F. 1966. *The Power of the Purse*. Boston: Little, Brown.

_____. 1973. *Congressmen in Committees*. Boston: Little, Brown.

_____. 1978. *Home Style*. Boston: Little, Brown.

Flemming, Robert J., ed. 1981. *Canadian Legislatures: The 1981 Comparative Study*. Toronto: Office of the Assembly.

Fox, Harrison W., Jr. and Susan Webb Hammond. 1975a. "The Growth of Congressional Staffs," in Harvey C. Mansfield, ed., *Congress Against the President*. New York: Praeger.

_____. 1975b. "Congressional Staff and Congressional Change," in James J. Heaphey and Alan P. Balutis, eds., *Legislative Staffing: A Comparative Perspective*. New York: Wiley.

_____. 1977. *Congressional Staffs: The Invisible Force in American Lawmaking*. New York: Free Press.

Galloway, George B. 1946. *Congress at the Crossroads*. New York: Crowell.

_____. 1951. "The Operation of the Legislative Reorganization Act of 1946," *American Political Science Review* 45:41-68.

_____. 1953. *The Legislative Process In Congress*. New York: Crowell.

Goodrum, Charles. 1982. *The Library of Congress*. 2d ed. Boulder, CO: Westview Press. (1st ed. 1974. New York: Praeger.)

Graves, W. Brooke. 1961. "Legislative Reference Service for the Congress of the United States," *American Political Science Review* 41:289-293.

Green, Harold P. and Alan Rosenthal. 1963. *Government of the Atom*. New York: Atherton.

Greene, Lee Seifert and Robert Sterling Avery. 1962. *Government in Tennessee*. Knoxville: The University of Tennessee Press.

Griffith, Ernest. 1976. "Four Agency Comparative Study," in U.S. Senate, Commission on the Operation of the Senate, 94th Congress, 2d Session, *Studies*. 7 vols. Washington, DC: Committee Prints.

Gross, Bertram. 1953. *The Legislative Struggle: A Study in Social Combat*. New York: McGraw-Hill.

Hamm, Keith E. and Gary Moncrief. 1982. "Effects of Structural Change in Legislative Committee Systems on Their Performance in U.S. States," *Legislative Studies Quarterly* 7:383-400.

Hammond, Susan Webb. 1975. "Characteristics of Congressional Staffers," in James J. Heaphey and Alan P. Balutis, eds., *Legislative Staffing: A Comparative Perspective*. New York: Wiley.

_____. 1976. "The Operation of Senators' Offices," in U.S. Senate, Commission on the Operation of the Senate, 94th Congress, 2d Session, *Studies*. 7 vols. Washington, DC: Committee Prints. Also in D. Kozak and J. Macartney, eds., *Congress and Public Policy*. 1982. Homewood, IL: Dorsey Press.

_____. 1978. "Congressional Change and Reform: Staffing the Congress," in Leroy Rieselbach, ed., *Legislative Reform*. Lexington, MA: Heath.

—————. 1981. "The Management of Legislative Offices," in Joseph Cooper and G. Calvin Mackenzie, eds., *The House at Work*. Austin: University of Texas Press.

Hammond, Susan Webb and Laura Irwin Langbein. 1982. "The Impact of Complexity and Reform on Congressional Committee Output," *Political Behavior* 4:237-263.

Harder, Marvin and Ramond G. Davis. 1979. *The Legislature as an Organization: A Study of the Kansas Legislature*. Lawrence: Regents of Kansas.

Hartmark, Leif S. 1975. "The Role of the Legislative Budget Staff in the Budgetary Process in Wisconsin," in Alan P. Balutis and Daron K. Butler, eds., *The Political Pursestrings*. New York: Wiley.

Heaphey, James J. 1975. "Legislative Staffing: Organizational and Philosophical Considerations," in James J. Heaphey and Alan P. Balutis, eds., *Legislative Staffing: A Comparative Perspective*. New York: Wiley.

Heaphey, James J. and Alan P. Balutis, eds. 1975. *Legislative Staffing: A Comparative Perspective*. New York: Wiley.

Herzberg, Donald G. and Alan Rosenthal, eds. 1971. *Strengthening the States: Essays on Legislative Reform*. Garden City, NY: Doubleday.

Huitt, Ralph. 1965. "The Internal Distribution of Influence: The Senate," in David Truman, ed., *The Congress and America's Future*. (2d ed. 1973.) Englewood Cliffs, NJ: Prentice-Hall.

—————. 1966. "Congress: The Durable Partner," in Ralph Huitt and Robert L. Peabody, eds., *Congress: Two Decades of Analysis*. New York: Harper & Row.

Huwa, Randy and Alan Rosenthal. 1977. *Politicians and Professionals: Interactions Between Committee and Staff in State Legislatures*. New Brunswick, NJ: Center for State Legislative Research and Service, Eagleton Institute of Politics, Rutgers University.

Hyneman, Charles. 1938. "Tenure and Turnover of Legislative Personnel," *Annals of the American Academy of Political and Social Science* 195:21-31.

Illinois Commission on the Organization of the General Assembly. 1967. *Improving the State Legislature*. Evanston: University of Illinois Press.

Jewell, Malcolm E. and Samuel C. Patterson. 1966. *The Legislative Process in the United States*. 1st ed. New York: Random House. (2d ed. 1973, 3d ed. 1977.)

Johannes, John R. 1979. "Casework as a Technique of U.S. Congressional Oversight," *Legislative Studies Quarterly* 4:325-351.

—————. 1981. "Casework in the House," in Joseph Cooper and G. Calvin Mackenzie, eds., *The House at Work*. Austin: University of Texas Press.

Jones, Charles O. 1965. "Committee Staffing," in U.S. Congress, Joint Committee on the Organization of Congress, 89th Congress, 1st Session, *Hearings; Symposium; Interim Reports; Final Report*. Washington, DC: Government Printing Office.

—————. 1982. *The United States Congress: People, Place and Policy*. Homewood, IL: Dorsey Press.

Kaiser, Fred. 1977. "Oversight of Foreign Policy: The U.S. House Committee on International Relations," *Legislative Studies Quarterly* 2:255-279.

Kammerer, Gladys M. 1949. *The Staffing of the Congress*. Lexington: University of Kentucky.

—————. 1951a. *Congressional Committee Staffing Since 1946*. Lexington: Bureau of Government Research, University of Kentucky.

—————. 1951b. "The Record of Congress in Committee Staffing," *American Political Science Review* 55:1126-1136.

Kampelman, Max. 1954. "The Legislative Bureaucracy: Its Response to Political Change, 1953," *Journal of Politics* 16:539-550.

Kayali, Khaled M. 1977. "Patterns of Congressional Staffing: The House Committee on Appropriations," in Abdo I. Baaklini and James J. Heaphey, eds., *Comparative Legislative Reforms and Innovations.* Albany: Comparative Development Studies Center, State University of New York.

Kent, James D. 1975. "Legislative Fiscal Staffing in Illinois," in Alan P. Balutis and Daron K. Butler, eds., *The Political Pursestrings.* New York: Wiley.

King, Anthony. 1981. "How to Strengthen Legislatures," in Norman J. Ornstein, ed., *The Role of the Legislature in Western Democracies.* Washington, DC: American Enterprise Institute.

Kingdon, John W. 1981. *Congressman's Voting Decisions.* 2d ed. New York: Harper & Row. (1st ed. 1973).

Kofmehl, Kenneth. 1973. "Three Major Aspects of House Committee Staffing," in U.S. House of Representatives, Select Committee on Committees, 95th Congress, *Hearings,* "Committee Organization in the House." H. Doc. 94-186. Washington, DC: Government Printing Office.

_____ . 1977. *Professional Staff of Congress.* 3d ed. West Lafayette, IN: Purdue University Press. (1st ed. 1962, 2d ed. 1969.)

Kurtz, Karl T. 1974. "The State Legislatures," in *The Book of the States.* Lexington, KY: Council of State Governments.

Kyle, Joseph F. 1975. "Florida Legislative Budget Review Process," in Alan P. Balutis and Daron K. Butler, eds., *The Political Pursestrings.* New York: Wiley.

Lacy, Alex B., ed. 1967. *Power in American State Legislatures.* New Orleans: Tulane University Press.

Lee, Frederic P. 1929. "The Office of the Legislative Counsel," *Columbia Law Review* 29:397-399.

Lees, John D. and Malcolm Shaw, eds. 1979. *Committees in Legislatures: A Comparative Analysis.* Durham, NC: Duke University Press.

Lentz, Gilbert G. 1957. "Better State Government Through Better Legislative Services," *Western Political Quarterly* 10:448.

Loewenberg, Gerhard and Samuel C. Patterson. 1979. *Comparing Legislatures.* Boston: Little, Brown.

Loomis, Burdett A. 1979. "The Congressional Office as a Small (?) Business: New Members Set Up Shop," *Publius* 9:35-55.

Macartney, John. 1982. "Congressional Staff: The View From the District," in David C. Kozak and John D. Macartney, eds., *Congress and Public Policy.* Homewood, IL: Dorsey Press.

Machowsky, Martin. 1978. "On the Growth of Congressional Standing Committee Staff: Decentralization of Control and Access." St. Louis: Washington University Political Science Papers.

Maisel, Louis Sandy. 1981. "Congressional Information Sources," in Joseph Cooper and G. Calvin Mackenzie, eds., *The House at Work.* Austin: University of Texas Press.

Malbin, Michael J. 1977. "Congressional Committee Staffs: Who's In Charge Here?" *The Public Interest,* No. 47:16-40.

_____ . 1980. *Unelected Representatives: Congressional Staff and the Future of Representative Government.* New York: Basic Books.

_____ . 1981. "Delegation, Deliberation, and the New Role of Congressional Staff," in Thomas E. Mann and Norman J. Ornstein, eds., *The New Congress.* Washington, DC: American Enterprise Institute.

Manley, John F. 1966. "Congressional Staff and Public Policy-Making," *Journal of Politics* 30:1046-1067.

Matthews, Donald R. 1960. *U.S. Senators and Their World.* Chapel Hill: University of North Carolina Press.

Mayhew, David R. 1974. *Congress: The Electoral Connection.* New Haven: Yale University Press.

McInnis, Mary, ed. 1966. *We Propose: A Modern Congress.* New York: McGraw-Hill.

Meller, Norman. 1952. "The Policy Position of Legislative Service Agencies," *Western Political Quarterly* 5:109-123.

——————. 1967. "Legislative Staff Services: Toxin, Specific, or Placebo for the Legislature's Ills," *Western Political Quarterly* 20:381-389.

——————. 1973. "Legislative Staff in Oceania as a Focus for Research," in Allan Kornberg, ed., *Legislatures in Comparative Perspective.* New York: McKay.

Mosher, Frederick C. 1979. *The GAO: The Quest for Accountability in American Government.* Boulder, CO: Westview Press.

Ogul, Morris S. 1976. *Congress Oversees the Bureaucracy.* Pittsburgh: University of Pittsburgh Press.

Olson, Kenneth G. 1966. "The Service Function of the U.S. Congress," in Alfred de Grazia, ed., *Congress: The First Branch of Government.* Washington, DC: American Enterprise Institute.

Ornstein, Norman J. 1975. "Legislative Behavior and Legislative Structures: A Comparative Look at House and Senate Resource Utilization," in James J. Heaphey and Alan P. Balutis, eds., *Legislative Staffing: A Comparative Perspective.* New York: Wiley.

Ornstein, Norman J. and David Rohde. 1976. "Resource Usage, Information and Policy Making in the Senate," in U.S. Senate, Commission on the Operation of the Senate, 94th Congress, 2d Session, *Studies.* 7 vols. Washington, DC: Committee Prints. Also in D. Kozak and J. Macartney, eds., *Congress and Public Policy.* 1982. Homewood, IL: Dorsey Press.

Patterson, Samuel C. 1970a. "The Professional Staffs of Congressional Committees," *Administrative Science Quarterly* 15:22-37.

——————. 1970b. "Congressional Committee Professional Staffing: Capabilities and Constraints," in Allan P. Kornberg and Lloyd D. Musolf, eds., *Legislatures in Developmental Perspective.* Durham, NC: Duke University Press.

——————. 1973. "Staffing House Committees," in U.S. House of Representatives, Select Committee on Committees, 95th Congress, *Hearings,* "Committee Organization in the House." H. Doc. 94-186. Washington, DC: Government Printing Office.

——————. 1982. "Staffing as a Focus for Legislative Research: A Comment." Delivered at the Legislative Research Conference, Iowa City, Iowa.

Patterson, Samuel C., Gerhard Loewenberg, and Malcolm E. Jewell. 1981. "Editors' Introduction," *Legislative Studies Quarterly* 6:489-494.

Pois, Joseph. 1976. "The GAO as a Congressional Resource," in U.S. Senate, Commission on the Operation of the Senate, 94th Congress, 2d Session, *Studies.* 7 vols. Washington, DC: Committee Prints.

——————. 1979. *Watchdog on the Potomac: A Study of the Comptroller General of the U.S.* Washington, DC: University Press of America.

Pollock, James. 1965. "Congressional Staffing," in U.S. Congress, Joint Committee on the Organization of Congress, 89th Congress, 1st Session, *Hearings; Symposium; Interim Reports; Final Report.* Washington, DC: Government Printing Office.

Polsby, Nelson. 1975. "Legislatures," in Fred Greenstein and Nelson Polsby, eds., *Handbook of Political Science*. Vol. 5. Reading, MA: Addison-Wesley.

Porter, H. Owen. 1974. "Legislative Experts and Outsiders: The Two Step Flow of Communications," *Journal of Politics* 36:703-730.

_____. 1975. "Legislative Information Needs and Staff Resources in the American States," in James J. Heaphey and Alan P. Balutis, eds., *Legislative Staffing: A Comparative Perspective*. New York: Wiley.

Price, David E. 1971. "Professionals and 'Entrepreneurs': Staff Orientations and Policy-Making on Three Senate Committees," *Journal of Politics* 33:316-336.

_____. 1972. *Who Makes the Laws?* Cambridge, MA: Schenckman.

Ranney, Austin. 1981. "The Working Conditions of Members of Parliament and Congress: Changing the Tools Changes the Job," in Norman J. Ornstein, ed., *The Role of the Legislature in Western Democracies*. Washington, DC: American Enterprise Institute.

Redman, Eric. 1973. *The Dance of Legislation*. New York: Simon and Schuster.

Ripley, Randall B. 1969. "The Power of Staff," in *Power in the Senate*, Chap. 8. New York: St. Martin's Press.

Ritt, Leonard G. 1973. "State Legislative Reform: Does It Matter?" *American Politics Quarterly* 1:499-510.

Roberts, Albert B. 1975. "American State Legislatures: The Staff Environment," *Public Administration Review* 35:501-504.

Robinson, James A. 1965. "Staffing Congress," in U.S. Congress, Joint Committee on the Organization of Congress, 89th Congress, 1st Session, *Hearings; Symposium; Interim Reports; Final Report*. Washington, DC: Government Printing Office.

_____. 1966. "Decisionmaking in Congress," in Alfred de Grazia, ed., *Congress: The First Branch of Government*. Washington, DC: American Enterprise Institute.

_____. 1970. "Legislative Staffing," in Allan Kornberg and Lloyd D. Musolf, eds., *Legislatures in Developmental Perspective*. Durham, NC: Duke University Press.

_____. 1973a. *State Legislative Innovation*. New York: Praeger.

_____. 1973b. "Statement on Committee Staffing," in U.S. House of Representatives, Select Committee on Committees, 95th Congress, *Hearings*, "Committee Organization in the House." H. Doc. 94-186. Washington, DC: Government Printing Office.

Rogers, Lindsay. 1941. "The Staffing of Congress," *Political Science Quarterly* 55:7-22.

Rosenthal, Alan. 1970. "An Analysis of Institutional Effects: Staffing Legislative Parties in Wisconsin," *Journal of Politics* 32:531-562.

_____. 1971. "The Consequences of Legislative Staffing," in D.G. Herzberg and Alan Rosenthal, eds., *Strengthening the States: Essays on Legislative Reform*. Garden City, NY: Doubleday, Anchor Books.

_____. 1973a. "Professional Staff and Legislative Influence in Wisconsin," in James A. Robinson, ed., *State Legislative Innovation*. New York: Praeger.

_____. 1973b. "Legislative Committee Systems: An Exploratory Analysis," *Western Political Quarterly* 46:252-262.

_____. 1974. *Legislative Performance in the States: Explorations of Committee Behavior*. New York: Free Press.

_____. 1981. *Legislative Life: People, Process and Performance in the States*. New York: Harper & Row.

Rush, Michael and Malcolm Shaw. 1974. *The House of Commons: Services and Facilities*. London: Allen and Unwin.

Ryle, Michael T. 1981. "The Legislative Staff of the British House of Commons," *Legislative Studies Quarterly* 6:497-520.

Salisbury, Robert H. and Kenneth A. Shepsle. 1981a. "Congressional Staff Turnover and the Ties-That-Bind," *American Political Science Review* 75:381-396.

_____ . 1981b. "U.S. Congressmen as Enterprise," *Legislative Studies Quarterly* 6:559-576.

Saloma, John S. III. 1969. *Congress and the New Politics.* Boston: Little, Brown.

_____ . 1973. "Proposals for Meeting Congressional Staff Needs," in U.S. House of Representatives, Select Committee on Committees, 95th Congress, *Hearings,* "Committee Organization in the House." H. Doc. 94-186. Washington, DC: Government Printing Office.

Schiff, Steven H. and Steven S. Smith. 1983. "Generational Change and the Allocation of Staff in the U.S. Congress," *Legislative Studies Quarterly* 8:457-468.

Siffin, William J. 1959. *The Legislative Councils in the American States.* Bloomington: Indiana University Press.

Skolnikoff, E.B. 1976. "The OTA," in U.S. Senate, Commission on the Operation of the Senate, 94th Congress, 2d Session, *Studies.* 7 vols. Washington, DC: Committee Prints.

Solomon, David. 1978. *Inside the Australian Parliament.* Sydney: Allen and Unwin.

Sundquist, James L. 1968. *Politics and Policy.* Washington, DC: The Brookings Institution.

Thurber, James A. 1977. "Policy Analysis on Capitol Hill: Issues Facing the Four Analytic Support Agencies of Congress," *Policy Studies Journal* 6:101-111.

_____ . 1981. "The Evolving Role and Effectiveness of the Congressional Research Agencies," in Joseph Cooper and G. Calvin Mackenzie, eds., *The House at Work.* Austin: University of Texas Press.

Turnbull, Augustus. 1977. "Staff Impact on Policy Development in the Florida Legislature," *Policy Studies Journal* 5:450-454.

U.S. Congress. 1965. Joint Committee on the Organization of Congress, 89th Congress, 1st Session, *Hearings; Symposium; Interim Reports; Final Report.* Washington, DC: Government Printing Office.

U.S. House of Representatives. 1973. Select Committee on Committees, 93rd Congress, *Hearings,* "Committee Organization in the House." H. Doc. 94-187. Washington, DC: Government Printing Office.

_____ . 1977. Commission on Administrative Review, 95th Congress. *Final Report.* H. Doc. 95-272. Washington, DC: Government Printing Office.

U.S. Senate. 1976. Commission on the Operation of the Senate, 94th Congress, 2d Session, *Studies.* 7 vols. Washington, DC: Committee Prints.

_____ . 1977. Temporary Select Committee to Study the Senate Committee System, 94th Congress. *First Staff Report.* Washington, DC: Committee Prints.

Van Schendelen, M.P.C.M. 1976. "Information and Decision Making in the Dutch Parliament," *Legislative Studies Quarterly* 1:231-250.

Wahlke, John C. 1961. "Organization and Procedure," in Alexander Heard, ed., *State Legislatures in American Politics.* Englewood Cliffs, NJ: Prentice-Hall.

Walker, David. 1979. "Legislative Underlaborers," *Political Quarterly* 50:482-492.

Walsh, Samuel. 1976. "Personnel Practices and Policies," in U.S. Senate, Commission on the Operation of the Senate, 94th Congress, 2d Session, *Studies.* 7 vols. Washington, DC: Committee Prints.

Welch, Susan and John Peters, eds. 1979. *Legislative Reform and Public Policy.* New York: Praeger.

Wissel, Peter, R. O'Connor, and M. King. 1976. "The Hunting of the Legislative Snark: Information Searches and Reforms in U.S. State Legislatures," *Legislative Studies Quarterly* 1:251-267.

Wolman, Harold L. and Dianne M. Wolman. 1977. "The Role of the U.S. Senate Staff in the Opinion Linkage Process: Population Policy," *Legislative Studies Quarterly* 2:281-293.

Worman, Michael A. 1975. "Role Consensus and Conflict in Legislative Staffing," in James J. Heaphey and Alan P. Balutis, eds., *Legislative Staffing: A Comparative Perspective.* New York: Wiley.

Wyner, Alan J. 1973. "Legislative Reform and Politics in California: What Happened, Why? and So What?" in James A. Robinson, ed., *State Legislative Innovation.* New York: Praeger.

Chapter 8

Organizational Attributes
Of Legislative Institutions:
Structure, Rules, Norms, Resources

by

RONALD D. HEDLUND

The behavioral approach to the study of legislatures has resulted in research on new types of legislative phenomena, the specification of new variables to account for these phenomena, and the adoption of nontraditional methods to study them.

Perhaps the greatest single difference emerging in behavioral-era research was the focus on the individual actor (legislators, lobbyists, constituents, bureaucrats, and so on). Two consequences are that research problems began to be phrased in terms of individual phenomena rather than legalistic and/or structural ones and that the variables studied were on the individual level rather than organizational or structural. One common outcome is that structural and organizational concerns were "ignored" or "overlooked." Regarding the impact of this trend, Cooper and Brady note that

institutional analysis has lagged behind behavioral analysis since the advent of the behavioral revolution in the early 1950's. Our ability to handle questions that posit individuals, whether in small numbers or large aggregates, as the units of analysis is far greater than our ability to handle questions that posit institutionalized collectivities in complex environments as the units of analysis (1981a, p. 994).

Further, Harder and Davis point out,

in a relative sense, the organizational characteristics of legislatures have been neglected by both political and organizational analysts. The former, influenced by the perspective called behavioralism, have tended to minimize the importance of organizational structure and procedure in explaining patterns of influence. The latter have concentrated their efforts toward understanding private and public organizations commonly thought of as being bureaucratic. The result has been a paucity of information in scholarly literature about the organizational aspects of American state legislatures (1979, p. 2).

Few would question that prebehavioral legislative research tended to concentrate on formal descriptions and structural explanations, excluding other important factors; however, much behavioral legislative research seems to omit organizational and situational variables as possible explanatory factors, and this omission may have been premature and ill advised.

Following a brief discussion of organizational characteristics in a legislature, this review summarizes approaches to the study of legislative organization. The main body of this review considers how these characteristics have been described in the literature, what factors have been identified as affecting these characteristics, and what relationships have been found between organizational characteristics and other legislative variables.

Legislative Organizational Characteristics

A variety of legislative traits have been described as "organizational" in nature. From studies of general organizations as well as studies of legislatures, five categories of organizational characteristics can be identified: personnel, technology, structure, task, and environment. However, only factors related to legislative structure and technology will be discussed here (Hedlund and Freeman, 1981; Hellriegel and Slocum, 1979). Taken together, structure and technology include several component parts of an organization whose purposes are to define the boundaries of individual action in the organization, to facilitate member interaction in performing their organizational roles, and to perpetuate the organization. Structure may be seen as the arrangement (anatomy) of organizational components. Technology refers to the means—"the sequence of man-machine systems" (Gerwin, 1981, p. 5)—used by an organization within its structural arrangements to seek its goals and to acquire necessary resources. Included for discussion here are an organization's formal features, its rules and procedures, its power and influence arrangements, its physical setting, and its resources.

A legislature's formal features (its structural components) are traits which can be identified without specific reference to individual members. These traits help set the boundaries and define the context in which member behavior takes place; they are usually established in chartering documents which specify the organization's basic features. In large part, these formal characteristics define the organization and set the framework for subsequent action (Wahlke, 1966; Meller, 1960). Included as formal features for a legislature are traits like size (the number of members), complexity (the units and subunits within the legislature), and the arrangements among units, levels, or divisions (their autonomy and hierarchical ordering).

If formal features create the boundaries and establish the framework for action, rules and procedures set the ways in which things are done within the organization. Assuming that goals are set for an organization, the rules and procedures specify how (the means) these goals are to be pursued and achieved. Rules and procedures indicate what specific behaviors, individual as well as group and formal as well as informal, are acceptable to that organization and what sequence of steps is to be used for accomplishing specific tasks.

The arrangements of formal power and influence relationships among members are an additional aspect of structure. They create the basis for members' interactions. Included here are such features as the centralization of authority and the degree of control held by members. (Typically, an organization's leadership is one aspect of power and influence relationships; however, leadership is excluded from treatment in this review.) While such arrangements may be altered in important ways by the behavior of members as they interact, the manner in which these relationships have been stated and established is an important organizational characteristic.

The fourth structural component is the organization's setting—its physical setting and its history. Factors related to organizational setting create much of the environment within which behavior takes place (Patterson and Wahlke, 1972).

Resources, the time and materials made available to an organization by its environments, comprise the final structural aspect to be discussed here. Resources are the "raw materials" required for organizational activity and their availability affects the success an organization is likely to experience in meeting its goals.

In reviewing the literature on legislative organizations, varying amounts of discussion can be found for each of these characteristics. As noted above, greater attention seems to have been given organizational characteristics prior to the widespread acceptance of the behavioral approach; however, treatment of organizational variables during that time period was largely descriptive and value-laden and offered little critical analysis or explanation of the roles played by these legislative features (Worthley and Crane, 1976).

In pre- as well as postbehavioral legislative literature, four functions of organizational characteristics have been identified.

First, organizational factors establish the way the legislature will operate in its goal seeking and specify this for organizational members and legislative observers alike by defining what can be done, how it can be accomplished, and what types of strategies can be used (Jones, 1982; Keefe and Ogul, 1977; Bibby and Davidson, 1972).

Second, organizational factors affect the policy outcome of the decision-making process. *"How* things are done may well affect *what* is done in the United States Congress. The rules and procedures may have a significant bearing on the final outcome, either by impeding or facilitating the success of the various participants in the legislative process" (Chelf, 1977, p. 57; see also Polsby, 1975b).

Third, these factors determine the division of power in the legislature and thereby channel and restrain activity. "A good case can be made that the political function of rules is vastly more significant than the function of 'regularizing' or 'ordering' legislative processes" (Keefe and Ogul, 1977, p. 49; see also Rogers, 1921).

Fourth, these factors enhance the legitimacy and acceptance of legislative activity by nonmembers.

A legislature would be unable to make collective decisions if it were merely an assemblage of men and women from all over the country who meet at intervals in the Nation's capital. What converts these individuals into a body able to act is a structure for the organization of work and a set of rules by which it can proceed (Loewenberg and Patterson, 1979, p. 117; see also Jones, 1982).

Approaches to the Study of Organizational Characteristics

Two approaches can be found in the literature for studying organizational characteristics and their effect on legislatures. One is based on evidence provided in specific studies of legislatures and legislative activity, while the other uses one of several theoretical orientations to argue the importance of organizational characteristics.

Case Studies

Perhaps the richest sources of information on the impact of organizational characteristics on a legislature are case studies. In each, a specific legislative procedure or feature is described and its effects on individual behavior and/or policy making.

Berman's (1966) book on the passage of the Civil Rights Act of 1960 treats a number of obstacles, both procedural and structural, which were used to delay and alter civil rights legislation. The use of the filibuster by Southern senators to defeat or retard progress on civil rights legislation is well documented here, and Berman indicates how this procedure resulted in compromise and change ("watering down") in the content of legislation. (See also Oleszek, 1978; Congressional Quarterly, 1976a; Wolfinger, 1971; Froman, 1968; Shuman, 1957; Burdette, 1940.)

The House Rules Committee can also affect legislative activity. In his classic study on the passage of the Employment Act of 1946, Bailey

(1950) indicates how a rule handed down by the Rules Committee so structured the decision making that alternative proposals were unlikely to be adopted by the entire House. (See also Oleszek, 1978; Matsunaga and Chen, 1976; Orfield, 1975; Robinson, 1963.)

The powers of committee chairpersons to affect deliberations on bills and policy outcomes is one of the topics of Bendiner (1964) in his study of congressional action on federal aid to elementary and secondary schools.

The possible effects of committee referral of the Depressed-Areas Bill to an unfriendly committee is discussed by Bibby and Davidson (1972). The results were acceptance of substantive amendments altering the bill's provisions in order to prevent committee jurisdictional questions from stopping the bill's floor consideration.

The role of the Conference Committee in adjusting differences in legislation so as to secure compromises on bill content is described by Reid (1980) with reference to legislation regarding inland waterways. Speaker O'Neill, utilizing Conference Committee action, was able to secure several important changes in the bill's provisions in order to obtain a common bill for both House and Senate.

Keynes (1969) indicates how the Senate rules in general were used in handling the Dirksen constitutional amendment on legislative reapportionment. His conclusion is that "the rules were also employed as tools in the legislative process to bargain over substantive changes in the proposed legislation" (p. 139).

The impact of increasing decentralization of power in the House during the 1970s and the impact of this decentralization on oil and gas legislation is discussed by Oppenheimer (1974, 1980).

In his book on river and harbor legislation considered by Congress between 1947 and 1968, Ferejohn (1974) illustrates how the voting rules and procedures in committees and on the floor affected what was done as well as how it was done, as did the strategies used for coalition formation.

These legislative case studies have considered different legislation at different points in time and have all identified instances in which the organization's characteristics have affected subsequent legislative activity, including the content of bills. (See also BeVier, 1979; Derthick, 1979; Redman, 1973; Bauer, de Sola Pool, and Dexter, 1964.)

Theoretical Approaches to the Study of Structural Factors

Four theoretical orientations have been used in the legislative literature to explain why and how structural characteristics affect the organization: structural-functional analysis, role analysis, game theory-social choice theory, and organization theory.

Structural-functional analysis. Structural-functional analysis emerged in the social sciences as a framework for describing and understanding social systems. In political science it has been especially prevalent in comparative politics for studying political activity across different political systems. In what is probably the most thorough effort to explain the application of structural-functional analysis to legislatures, Riggs (1973) points out that while many structural-functional analyses have concentrated on the functions performed by political systems, structures cannot be overlooked. "Functions cannot be performed except by structures. Moreover, the characteristics of structures in any system affect the degree to which any functions are performed—indeed, whether they can be performed at all" (p. 39). There has been some limited use of structural-functional analysis in the study of non-U.S. legislatures, where its primary purpose seems to be sensitizing the reader to the distinction between a legislative institution and legislative functions (Cotta, 1974).

Role analysis. One of the early efforts at a behavioral approach to legislatures applied role theory to the study of four state legislatures (Wahlke, Eulau, Buchanan, and Ferguson, 1962). In the opening chapter, the authors argue that by using the role concept and its integral relationship with organizational positions, the political scientist is able to interrelate structural characteristics as constraints on the behavior of individuals. In this conception, the nature of the legislative organization, including its structural features, is a determinant of legislative role; therefore, one must consider the organization's structure to understand the development of role orientations. The authors specifically refer to structural variables, such as those noted above, as "situational landmarks" which demarcate and influence behavior via the roles assumed by individual members. The limited ability of role variables to explain much variance in individual or group behavior has led to their use in subsequent research primarily as descriptive factors (Jewell, 1970).

Game theory-social choice theory. Researchers have also used game theory or social choice theory and deductive analysis to evaluate collective decision making and goal-oriented behavior. Basically the argument advanced is that the nature of the organization's structure, rules, and procedures— especially voting rules—affect collective decision making. Using logic, deductive analysis, and abstract models of simple legislatures rather than empirical data, Shepsle (1979a, 1979b), Ferejohn and Fiorina (1975), Blydenburgh (1971), Buchanan and Tullock (1962), Riker (1958), and others have shown that the decisional rules used in a legislature do have some impact on the amalgamation of individual preferences into collective legislative decisions. The results of empirical tests for these formulations have provided only mixed support (Ferejohn and Fiorina, 1975).

Organization theory. Concern with organizational structure and technology is evident across the range of organization theory, even though this umbrella term actually includes a series of discrete theoretical perspectives on organizations. Researchers from one of these orientations, comparative organizational analysis, define structure "as the pattern of relationships among people which facilitate accomplishment of an organization's tasks" (Gerwin, 1981, p. 9) and identify four structural attributes which characterize organizations: complexity, formalization, centralization, and configuration. Based on studies of several private sector organizations, researchers have found organizational performance and goal attainment to be related in various ways to structural characteristics in these four categories and to the organization's technology (Gerwin, 1981; Hellriegel and Slocum, 1979; Ivancevich, Szilagyi, and Wallace, 1977; Evan, 1976; Price, 1968).

Several studies have explicitly applied organizational theory to legislatures and have also used associated concepts, propositions, and variables (Cooper, 1975, 1977, 1981; Cooper and Brady, 1981a; Hedlund and Freeman, 1981; Moncrief and Jewell, 1980; Harder and Davis, 1979; Hedlund, 1978; Hedlund and Hamm, 1976, 1977, 1978a; Davidson and Oleszek, 1976; Froman, 1968). Collectively this work demonstrates, first, that concepts derived from organizational theory can be applied to legislatures. These concepts include organizational autonomy, division of labor, task environment, organizational technology, "buffering" between inputs and outputs, institutional "imperatives," organizational uncertainty, adaptation, consolidation, organizational elaboration, organizational productivity, organizational expeditiousness, and organizational efficiency (Cooper, 1975, 1981; Harder and Davis, 1979; Hedlund and Hamm, 1977, 1978a; Davidson and Oleszek, 1976).

Second, such works demonstrate that propositions and hypotheses suggested by organizational theory can be tested in legislative settings. These hypotheses concern expectations that structural innovation by an organization grows from environmental stress or internal organizational dynamics, that individual goals for organizational change relate to more general organizational goals, that organizations will adapt to stress and strain by increasing their organizational capacity or changing expectations for that organization, that a highly differentiated environment will enhance an organization's status, and that increased environmental pressure on an organization will foster a more elaborate leadership structure (Cooper, 1977, 1981; Moncrief and Jewell, 1980; Davidson and Oleszek, 1976; Froman, 1968).

Third, this work demonstrates that explanations for organizational phenomena must consider organizational goals and environmental constraints; further, the relationship between an organization and its environments, which is both a context for performance and a basis of performance (Cooper, 1975, 1977), can be germane for legislatures.

Fourth, this work demonstrates that measures and indicators for organizational traits and phenomena can be applied to legislatures. This includes organizational personnel, organizational technology and product use, formal organizational structure, support work groups, leadership consideration, leadership initiating structure, member role ambiguity, member satisfaction, organizational productivity, organizational expeditiousness, and organizational efficiency (Hedlund and Freeman, 1981; Hedlund, 1978; Hedlund and Hamm, 1977, 1978a).

Reservations Regarding the Use of Organizational Characteristics

As this brief review suggests, widespread support can be found for concluding that organizational characteristics are important features for understanding individual and group behavior and that they do systematically differentiate among social science phenomena. However, reservations have been expressed. For example, both Wahlke (1966) and Keefe (1971) indicate that changes in a legislative organization's characteristics (session length, formal features, or rules and procedures) may not necessarily result in the improvements in legislative performance or output anticipated by legislative reformers. Hirsch and Hancock (1971) conclude that structural characteristics are of minor importance at best. Patterson states that "so-called organization theory has never informed legislative research very effectively, I think mainly because it was conceived with the bureaucracy, or the firm, in mind. The theory is not sufficiently general, so legislative organizations do not fit its rubrics well; the fit is strained at best" (1981, p. 1008). In reflecting on the evolution and development of legislatures, Sait (1938) notes that their patterns of change resemble more the nonplanned, random growth of a "coral island" (quoted in Patterson, 1981). Toll (1928) points to a widespread belief that structure and procedural changes devoid of concern regarding who "sits" as a legislator will not lead to improvements in legislation or legislative operations. Additionally, Kostroski minimizes the impact of organizational characteristics in light of other, more immediate and important, factors.

Any legislative reform that fails to take into account the profound and pervasive effect of elections on policy decisions and legislative performance will almost surely have little effect or go astray. Structures, rules, and procedures "internal" to a legislature do affect behavior and outcomes, but only at the margins. Their influence pales by comparison to two types of "external" electoral phenomena: electoral recruitment and reelection calculus" (1977, p. 414).

This view is reinforced somewhat by Rohde and Shepsle's (1978) empirical analysis and theoretical formulation showing the absence of consistent relationships among procedural changes, membership changes, and policy changes. They conclude that three types of factors must be considered.

In general, policy outcomes are the consequences of three factors: the rules under which decisions are made, the preferences of the decision makers, and the situation or circumstances in which the decision makers find themselves. . . . In any given area of decision, the rules divide the set of conceivable outcomes into those that are feasible and those that are not. Some results are made easy to achieve, while others are rendered virtually impossible; the preferences of some actors are advantaged, while those of others are disadvantaged. Similarly, the changing preferences of actors (or replacement of the actors themselves) are important in determining outcomes in different policy areas. Finally, varying circumstances can lead the same decision makers to one outcome at one time and to another at some other time (p. 13).

Descriptions of Organizational Characteristics in Legislatures

Describing a legislative organization and how it works has been one long standing and primary goal of political science literature. Several different types of descriptions can be found in the literature. Attention to each is useful for categorizing how political scientists have studied legislative organizational factors and for illustrating how legislative descriptions may provide a basis for more general and theoretically useful analysis.

Historical Descriptions

In their recent analysis of diachronic (across-time) studies of Congress, Cooper and Brady (1981a) offer a useful typology which may be applied to historical studies of all legislatures. Their first category, diachronic analysis, considers the nature and level of a single legislative feature across time. The distinguishing feature of these studies is their application of "a related set of concepts and measures to the analysis of change over an extended period" (p. 989). Studies of this type examine one legislative feature across time, assessing change in that feature and in its impact upon other aspects of the legislature. The primary example cited by Cooper and Brady is Polsby's (1968) study of the institutionalization of the U.S. House of Representatives. In addition, they discuss studies relating to tenure and turnover, seniority, party voting, and leadership. Their second category of across-time analysis is general historical treatments of Congress. This literature provides generic consideration of a legislature or some legislative feature in a broad historical perspective. Two examples are Galloway's (1961) study of the U.S. House and the Congressional Quarterly's (1976a) treatment of congressional origins. This type of analysis provides much useful information regarding the development of an organization, including its formal features, rules and procedures, power and influence arrangements, physical setting, and resources. The third type of historical description covers a single particular historical period—for example, Congress before 1840. More recently, Dodd and Oppenheimer (1981), Ornstein (1981), Ornstein, Peabody, and Rohde (1981), and Shaw (1981) have all discussed the development of the U.S. Senate and House during the most recent period of major change, the internal congressional reforms of the 1970s. The primary purpose in each was to describe the changes taking place in Congress and assess the impact of these changes on the legislature's role and operations.

The primary subject of literature in the diachronic mode is the U.S. Congress, where varied and useful studies are available. (See Cooper and Brady, 1981a, for a listing and analysis.) However, much less is apparent for subnational units (states and local legislatures) and for non-U.S. legislatures. Admittedly, useful historical studies may be available for a specific state or country, but usually these are noncomparative, contain limited analysis and interpretation, and follow a step-by-step developmental approach for the evolution of organizational characteristics.

A review of past historical studies suggests distinguishing among three levels in the focus of historical legislative analyses: change with regard to specific legislative procedures or characteristics, change with regard to general patterns in a legislature, and macro-level organizational evolution. A brief review of congressional studies with regard to each one of these three should prove useful for illustrative purposes and also for demonstrating what historical analysis can tell one about legislatures.

The House Rules Committee. The Rules Committee in the U.S. House is an example of one organizational characteristic whose change is apparent in an across-time study of Congress. While reviewing the role of the House Rules Committee in contemporary Congress, Matsunaga and Chen (1976) discuss changes in the committee. In the 1955 to 1960 period, the committee, because of its power to set the agenda and because of a six-to-six conservative-liberal tie in membership, became independent from the Democratic leadership in its ability to affect legislative action.

Smith [the chairman of the committee during this period] succeeded in withholding action on an average of thirty bills per Congress, and 31 percent of the Committee Democrats voted consistently to disagree with the leadership, that is to say, 2½ out of the 8 Democrats were invariably in disagreement with the leadership.... These Democrats, voting in concert with the four Republicans, were able to block, in the Rules Committee, most of the legislation desired by the Democratic leadership (p. 139).

The election of President Kennedy in 1960 and the enlargement of the committee set the stage for change; however, the chairman continued to be able to use his power to frustrate the goals of the Democratic leadership. Even after Smith's electoral defeat, there continued to be a pattern for Democratic members of the Rules Committee voting against the leadership. It was not until 1973, with the replacement of the chairman by a Democratic "loyalist," that the Rules Committee became more supportive of the Democratic leadership. This change was short-lived: the committee reasserted itself and became more independent of the leadership. The election of 75 new Democratic members of the House for the 94th Congress provided new strength to the movement for controlling the independence of the Rules Committee. This analysis of how the Rules Committee and its independent role in influencing legislative activity in the U.S. House changed is typical of many historical analyses, each highlighting the evolution of one aspect of the organizational characteristics for a legislature and the impact of these alterations on the legislature itself. Other examples would include the filibuster (Wolfinger, 1971), the proliferation of "work groups" (Davidson, 1981a, 1981b; Shaw, 1981; Ornstein, 1981), the dramatic increase in legislative staff (Shaw, 1981; Ornstein, 1981; Malbin, 1981; Salisbury and Shepsle, 1981a, 1981b; Fox and Hammond, 1977), and the role of seniority (Shaw, 1981; Price, 1972; Hinckley, 1971; Polsby, Gallaher, and Rundquist, 1969; Abram and Cooper, 1968).

   Decentralization. A second type of change detectable from historical analysis has been alterations in more general patterns within a legislative body. One of the most important in recent years has been the growing decentralization of power in Congress, especially in the House during the 1970s. Rather than focusing on change in one specific feature, studies of pattern change involves alterations in several interrelated features; for example, the decentralization of power in Congress has been attributed to the enhanced "power orientation" of individual members, the "relaxation" of deference/ apprenticeship norms, the weakened role of committee chairpersons, the growing independence of subcommittees, the "dispersal" of power, the growth in the number of legislative groups, and the increased autonomy of individual members. Studies of decentralization describe how this pattern has increased the time and bargaining involved in decision making, heightened the trend toward piecemeal policy formation, increased the accessibility of Congress to particularistic interests, heightened power dispersal in the legislature, and increased power held by informal groups and individual members (Whalen, 1982; Davidson, 1981a; Loomis, 1981a; Ornstein, 1981; Ornstein, Peabody, and Rohde, 1981; Shaw, 1981; Sundquist, 1981; Oppenheimer, 1980; Hinckley, 1978; Oleszek, 1978; Ripley, 1978; Dodd, 1977; Rieselbach, 1977). Other general trends cited for Congress in recent years include increased openness in procedures (Whalen, 1982; Dodd and Oppenheimer, 1981; Bullock, 1978; Davidson and Oleszek, 1977), enhanced accountability for individual member decisions (Shaw, 1981; Davidson and Oleszek, 1977), greater democratization of procedures and proceedings (Davidson, 1981a; Ornstein, 1981), and declining careerism among members (Hibbing, 1982a, 1982b; Cooper and West, 1981; Frantzich, 1978a, 1978b).

Institutionalization. Perhaps the most significant across-time descriptive analysis has been of macro-level organizational trends. Probably the best known is Polsby's (1968) work on institutionalization. In this path-breaking study, Polsby called institutionalization a basic component for describing and assessing legislative organization. When it is institutionalized, an organization has clear boundaries which separate it from other organizations and its environments; is relatively complex in terms of the division of labor, the role structure, and the interdependence of units; and is more universalistic and automatic in all its operations. In describing the U.S. House across time using indicators for these features, Polsby concluded that the House has become much more institutionalized in recent years. As a result, it has become a more attractive organization for career-oriented individuals, has developed increased influence, and has evolved a more professional set of norms for activity therein. The concept of institutionalization, but with somewhat different operational indicators, has appeared subsequently in theoretical orientations to the legislative process (Grumm, 1973a, 1973b), in descriptive studies of state legislatures (Harder and Davis, 1979; Chaffey, 1970), and in several analyses of non-U.S. legislatures (Jewell and Eldridge, 1977; Gerlich, 1973; Loewenberg, 1973; Sisson, 1966, 1973). Another macro-level organizational trend has been the changing nature of legislative relations with the executive (Whalen, 1982; Congressional Quarterly, 1976b; Ogul, 1976).

General Descriptions

Several different types of more general, nonhistorical, and noncase study descriptions can be found in the literature of legislative organizations and processes. While the research areas below generally began with a series of detailed descriptive studies, the work in each area has been (or can be) elaborated in subsequent work into more general, theoretically-oriented explanatory studies. Included here are treatments of entire legislative organizations, informal legislative processes (i.e., legislative norms and seniority), and more formal legislative processes (i.e., the lawmaking process and the legislator as head of an enterprise).

Legislative organizations. Virtually every legislative text contains much descriptive information about legislatures in general and even specific legislative bodies. (For examples, see Jones, 1982; Rosenthal, 1981b; Olson, 1980; Loewenberg and Patterson, 1979; Mezey, 1979; Ripley, 1978; Jewell and Patterson, 1977; Keefe and Ogul, 1977; Van der Slik, 1977; Jewell, 1969.) The most extensive of this literature deals with the U.S. Congress and the British Parliament. Less adequate general descriptive material is available about most U.S. state legislatures and legislatures in other political systems. The least adequate descriptive material is available at the subnational level for virtually all political systems.

In addition to the generalized descriptions of legislative organizations found in textbooks, there are more specialized treatments available in a variety of formats. These descriptions tend to concentrate on a single legislative organization and provide only minimal comparisons across legislative bodies. The most impressive array is available for the U.S. Congress. (See for example, weekly reports from Congressional Quarterly; the biennial summary of congressional statistics in Ornstein, Mann, Malbin, and Bibby, 1982, and Bibby, Mann, and Ornstein, 1980; Jones, 1982; Oleszek, 1978; Congressional Quarterly, 1976b; Froman, 1967.)

Early literature on this topic tended to provide minute detail regarding rules, procedures, and structural characteristics and to indicate how each of these had been used to advantage by one person or other (Galloway, 1953; Riddick, 1949; Burdette, 1940; Luce, 1922; Alexander, 1916). These descriptive statements do not depict a legislature's structural characteristics, rules, and procedures as neutral features which treat all equally; rather, these traits give advantage to some and disadvantage to others.

Few rules and procedures are neutral, politically, in their efforts. That is, rules and procedures define the conditions under which the 'game' will be played. When there is conflict among the players in the game, as there is in most important pieces of legislation in Congress, the rules and procedures lay out the conditions for the conflict and provide certain processes, sometimes alternative processes, under which proponents and opponents may 'make moves' in the 'game.' But some rules and procedures will favor one side. Some rules and procedures will favor the other side. Strategies and tactics will be built around the rules and procedures which will be most favorable to one side or the other (Froman, 1967, p. 188).

In this literature, political scientists have extensive descriptive information about Congress's organizational features, rules, and procedures.

Complementing these descriptions of Congress, several comparable studies are available for state legislatures in the United States, with the goal of delineating the legislative process in that particular setting with regard to its organizational features, rules, and procedures. (See BeVier, 1979; Kirkpatrick, 1978; Craft, 1973; Flinn, 1973; Gatlin, 1973; Gove, 1973; Wyner, 1973; Chartock and Berking, 1970; Buchanan, 1963; Havard and Beth, 1962; Sorauf, 1963; Wahlke et al., 1962; Steiner and Gove, 1960; Lockard, 1959; Zeller, 1954; Farmer, 1949.) Further, the American Political Science Association, through a grant from the Ford Foundation, produced a series of state legislative manuals as a part of the State Legislative Service Project. Although each of the manuals produced is slightly different, each details a state's legislative process for the purpose of orienting newly elected members. The material is largely descriptive and usually includes topics like committees, pressure groups, the press, the role of political parties, relationships with the governor, and the problems of adjusting to being a legislator in addition to discussing the legislature's structure and rules of procedure. Many of these manuals also indicate how legislators can maximize their impact on the legislature and on legislation and the informal rules governing behavior in that legislature. While these manuals were written by political scientists, there was heavy reliance in each case on experience provided by sitting members in the state legislatures (Pettit, Hayes, Hary, Horen, and Treachout, 1974; Chelf, 1973; Fischer, Price, and Bell, 1973; Palmer, Hayes, Hary, Horen, and Treachout, 1973; Gere, 1972; Harder and Rampey, 1972; Kirkpatrick and Cathey, 1972; Pierce, Frey, and Pengelly, 1972; Radway, 1972; Best, 1971; Hedlund and Crane, 1971; Chance, 1970; Cornwell, Goodman, DeNuccio, and Mosca, 1970; McGraw, 1970; Wiggins, 1970; Gove and Carlson, 1968). (See also Tacheron and Udall, 1970, and Clapp, 1963, for comparable material on Congress.) In addition, two organizations concerned with communications among practitioners at the state legislative level produce periodicals and regular reviews containing useful descriptions and analytical articles on state legislatures–*State Legislatures* from the National Conference of State Legislatures and *State Government* and the biennial *Book of the States* from the Council of State Governments.

Although much basic information about non-U.S. legislatures is still unavailable, progress is evident; several descriptions have now been published in both monograph and article form. (See for example Norton, 1980; Welsh, 1980; Franks, 1978; Opello, 1978; DiPalma, 1976, 1977; Vanneman, 1977; Weinbaum, 1972; Agor, 1971; Baker, 1971; Singhvi, 1970; Loewenberg, 1967; Gertzel, 1966; Gupta, 1966; Lee, 1963.)

From this descriptive literature, several interesting and useful portrayals of legislative features have emerged. In fact, this literature has identified and described many important legislative features which have become critical factors for subsequent rigorous research. Legislative norms, seniority, the lawmaking process, and legislators as heads of an "enterprise" are four of the more important ones.

Legislative norms. Based on research in the early and middle 1950s, three researchers have reported about a very important, but informal activity in the U.S. Senate: the setting of legislative norms (White, 1956; Huitt, 1957, 1961; Matthews, 1959, 1960). In his description of the Senate, White identifies an elite, the "inner club," who set norms for the entire Senate and thereby amassed extra influence in the body. Elaborating on this theme, Huitt (1957, 1961) provides two case studies of senators (Wayne Morse and William Proxmire, respectively) whose behavior violated many of the Senate's norms: fostering cooperation with other members, serving an apprenticeship, prudent action, and minimal involvement in debate. In each case, Huitt describes the senator's behavior in terms of these norms, especially how these norms were violated, why they were violated, and the responses of other members. The picture of the Senate which emerges from these three studies is of an organization which has extensive norms, known to all members and followed by those seeking greater influence. Deviation from these norms results in a cost to "trespassers."

In an effort to be more systematic, Matthews methodically collected information regarding the norms operating in the U.S. Senate. His work provides greater scope and more thorough treatment of norms and relates norm behavior to subsequent activity. Matthews points out that norms exist in every group and that the U.S. Senate is no exception. Six norms are identified: apprenticeship, legislative work (show horses and work horses), specialization, courtesy, reciprocity, and institutional patriotism (1960, pp. 92-103).

They [the informal rules] provide motivation for the performance of legislative duties that, perhaps, would not otherwise be performed. They discourage long-windedness in a chamber of 100 highly verbal men, dependent on publicity, and unrestrained by any formal limitations on debate. They encourage the development of expertise and division of labor and discourage those who would challenge it. They soften the inevitable personal conflict of a legislative body so that adversaries and competitors can meet (at the very least) in an atmosphere of antagonistic cooperation or (at best) in an atmosphere of friendship and mutual respect. They encourage senators to become "compromisers" and "bargainers" and use their substantial powers with caution and restraint. Without these folkways, the Senate could hardly operate in anything like its present form (1959, p. 1074).

The consequences thought to follow from adherence to the rules were greater respect and confidence from other members as well as effectiveness in legislative activity. In measuring effectiveness, Matthews considered the proportion of all public bills and resolutions passed which a member introduced and how often a senator talked on the floor.

The less a senator talks on the floor, and the narrower a senator's areas of legislative interest and activity, the greater is his "effectiveness." Moreover, the types of senators who, as we have already seen, tend not to conform have considerably less impact on the chamber's legislative output than the conformists.... Conformity to the Senate folkways does, therefore, seem to "pay off" in concrete legislative results (1959, p. 1086).

Although subsequent political scientists have criticized Matthews in his use of proportion of bills passed as a measure of effectiveness (e.g., Huitt, 1961), this evidence does suggest that following the norms may have some impact on certain limited forms of subsequent behavior. In his more extensive treatment of this same subject, Matthews (1960) speculates about what background factors may be related to a senator's adopting Senate norms. These include prior occupational experiences (governors of states tend to encounter more difficulty in adjusting to the norms), ambitions for higher public office, difficulties with one's own constituency (especially electoral insecurity), and political ideology.

Beginning with this work, a generation of political scientists has continued to investigate the rules of the game in various legislative settings.

The status of knowledge regarding legislative norms may be conveyed by reviewing 11 questions considered in the literature.

Do rules of the game exist in legislative organizations? The unanimous answer in the literature is yes, rules of the game do exist. No study, regardless of the cultural setting or the unit of government, failed to identify rules of the game. Only the earliest literature on unwritten rules of the game spent much time dealing with their existence (Wahlke et al., 1962; Matthews, 1960; Huitt, 1957; White, 1956).

What unwritten rules of the game are observed in legislative settings? Despite the considerable literature available, two lists of norms tend to predominate—the set of norms Matthews found for the U.S. Senate (1960) and the Wahlke et al. formulation (1962). Matthews's list of six norms in the Senate (apprenticeship, legislative work, specialization, courtesy, reciprocity, and institutional patriotism) is much more general than that formulated in Wahlke et al., which identified 42 separate rules of the game. Patterson (1961) and Searing (1982) have used different approaches to the rules of the game, so that their lists are somewhat at variance with those above.

What degree of consensus exists regarding the content of norms? A cursory examination of most tabular presentations reveals great agreement among members of a legislative body on many rules of the game, especially those regarding general interpersonal behavior—respecting one another, keeping one's word, and so on (Kirkpatrick and McLemore, 1977; Hebert and McLemore, 1972; Hedlund and Wiggins, 1967; Kornberg, 1964; Wahlke et al., 1962). Bernick and Wiggins (1983) found even greater emphasis on norms prescribing interpersonal behavior in 11 state senates. Modest levels of agreement have been found for certain political and partisan norms and even lower levels of agreement on norms for member independence (Kirkpatrick and McLemore, 1977; Hebert and McLemore, 1972).

Are these rules of the game the same across all legislative settings? Great comparability has generally been found in the norms cited for many different legislatures. Two studies of non-U.S. legislatures—Canada (Kornberg, 1964) and Chile (Agor, 1970)—both identify similarities between the rules of the game operating in these legislatures and those in U.S. state and national legislatures. Differences have also been found across members of the Iowa legislative chambers with regard to the structuring of norm perceptions (Hebert and McLemore, 1972) and in Oklahoma with regard to levels of congruity (Kirkpatrick and McLemore, 1977). Recently, Bernick and Wiggins found 13 of 19 norms "accepted" in more than one of the states studied and four "accepted" in at least 10 state senates (1983).

How do legislative rules of the game differ from those found in other organizations? Many authors have noted the similarity of legislative norms to norms found in other organizations (Bernick and Wiggins, 1983; Price and

Bell, 1970; Wahlke et al., 1962). In fact, one study found that delegates to six state constitutional conventions perceived norms very similar to legislative norms; only four of the 42 rules cited in Wahlke et al. were not mentioned by constitutional convention delegates (Carroll and English, 1981). Thus, many legislative norms probably reflect a more general set of social interaction expectations.

What functions do rules of the game have in an organization? Hinckley (1978) argues that norms are especially important in elected bodies because they compensate for the absence of common experience or uniform anticipatory socialization on the part of members. Wahlke et al. (1962) identify six functions performed by these rules; they promote group cohesion and solidarity, promote predictability of legislative behavior, channel and restrain conflict, expedite legislative business, give special advantages to individual members, and promote desirable personal qualities to facilitate interaction. Loomis (1981b) points out that the erosion of certain norms in Congress during the 1970s increased the unpredictability of legislative behavior and of the House in general. With regard to Congress, Hinckley writes:

Norms are not neutral. In assigning value to certain actions, they may exert a decisive impact on the organization of influence and on policy. Congressional norms have definite political implications. Specialization and reciprocity strengthen the committee system, reinforce decentralized decision-making and distribute influence widely through Senate and House. . . . At the same time these norms work against corporate decision-making (1978, pp. 69-70).

Experiences reported from non-U.S. legislatures where general norm acceptance can be much less pervasive suggest that the absence of norms regarding debate and member interaction produces exchanges which are blunt and often threatening (Weinbaum, 1972).

How constant are rules of the game in one legislature across time? While comparatively little systematic analysis has been done on this question, some fragmentary survey evidence suggests that rules of the game can and do change in the same legislature (Jewell and Patterson, 1977, pp. 342-343). Further, while a relatively great consistency exists across time for congressional norms, changes have taken place for apprenticeship and possibly for legislative work and specialization (Ornstein, Peabody, and Rohde, 1977, 1981; Hinckley, 1978; Asher, 1973, 1975). Polsby (1975a), for example, noted that many of the norms associated with the "Senate Club" had eroded or disappeared, so that the inner club itself described by White was gone by the early 1970s. (See also Davidson, 1981a.)

To explain the changing nature of norms, some recent research directs attention to organizational factors like the power distribution in the legislature (Loomis, 1981a; Ornstein, Peabody, and Rohde, 1977, 1981). Specifically, these studies find that as power in the Senate and House was distributed more widely among members, limited benefit norms (i.e., those affecting members differentially, like seniority and apprenticeship) began to weaken and disappear while general benefit norms (i.e., those affecting members equally, like courtesy and reciprocity) remained.

Does a legislator's perception of norms remain constant across time? In their study of freshman members of the California Assembly, Price and Bell (1970) suggest that perceptions of norms do change somewhat during the member's first term, but that any change (learning) takes place very quickly. On the other hand, Asher (1973) notes relatively little formal learning with regard to norms in the first six months for members of the 91st Congress.

What factors are related to an individual's perception of the legislative rules of the game? In spite of the substantial consensus noted for many rules of the game, political scientists have speculated that all individuals do not have similar perceptions of appropriate legislative norms. Partisan differences have been found to be related to norm perception (Wahlke et al., 1962), to initial rule sophistication (Price and Bell, 1970), and to articulation of rules (Kornberg, 1964). In addition, rural-urban experiences and occupation are related to norm sensitivity (Wahlke et al., 1962), and ideology is related to initial rule sophistication (Price and Bell, 1970). However, other individual-level variables, such as education and prior experience in the legislature, have not been found to be related to norm sensitivity (Wahlke et al., 1962); length of service is not related to rule articulation (Kornberg, 1964); and education, occupation, and prior community activity are not related to initial rule sophistication (Price and Bell, 1970).

One primary question concerns the relationship of rule perception to a legislator's subsequent effectiveness, influence, and assignment to important committees. While White (1956) and Matthews (1959, 1960) provide evidence that there is a relationship between these and behavior consistent with the accepted rules of the game, Wahlke et al. (1962) and Price and Bell (1970) offer evidence to the contrary.

How do members learn the norms for a legislative organization? Although there are suggestions throughout the literature that much of the socialization a person experiences in general organizational settings is transferable to a legislature, consensus seems to be that postselection socialization is also important (Price and Bell, 1970; Monsma, 1969).

What are the consequences for deviation from a legislature's norms? In the four-state study, Wahlke et al. (1962) found that sanctions are salient to most members with regard to behavior that is inconsistent with the norms. This finding is generally reinforced in every other study; however, as Huitt and Hinckley point out, deviance from norms is tolerated but is not rewarded (Hinckley, 1978; Huitt, 1957, 1961).

In reviewing this literature, it is obvious that political scientists know a great deal about legislative rules of the game and how they develop. While much of this is descriptive information with little, if any, critical analysis or interpretation, some useful investigation regarding the role of norms in the legislative process has appeared.

Seniority. The literature describing the origins and development of seniority during the early twentieth century is thorough and provides a good treatment of how seniority began and evolved (Hinckley, 1971; Polsby, Gallaher, and Rundquist, 1969; Abram and Cooper, 1968; MacNeil, 1963; Galloway, 1961; Goodwin, 1959; Martin, 1960; Chamberlain, 1936; Alexander, 1916). Seniority became the primary means for selecting committee and later subcommittee chairpersons in the early twentieth century, when members reacted to the erosion of the speaker's control over appointing committee chairpersons. This weakened congressional leadership created a vacuum regarding leadership selection which had to be solved. Seniority had the advantage of being a more "universalistic" selection method (i.e., routine, automatic, and more "impersonal") and one relatively immune to personal manipulation. It further decentralized power by taking it away from some leaders and giving it to others. In addition, seniority provided incentives for members to remain in Congress, making this service a career while also stimulating specialization of members on committees. Subsequent studies in non-U.S. legislatures suggest that fostering or requiring rotation of members through committees does in fact decrease member specialization (Weinbaum, 1972; Baker, 1971). For 50 or 60 years, seniority in Congress was used primarily as the means for selecting committee and subcommittee chairpersons as well as for assigning office space, for determining the "rankings" of members (especially on committees), and to a lesser degree for making committee assignments.

Careful review of seniority from the 1920s through the early 1970s resulted in the development of a long list of supposed consequences and implications. Although the evidence presented to support the relationship of seniority to each supposed consequence varied greatly, this approach resulted in seniority achieving great notoriety as a "basic shortcoming" in the congressional system. The political science literature suggested the following negative and positive consequences:

—insulating members from constituencies, pressures, and public opinion, thus giving greater freedom to members and retarding their responsiveness and accountability (Davidson, 1981b; Hinckley, 1971; Bolling, 1965; Congressional Quarterly, 1963);

—reducing party cohesion by freeing members from many of their traditional partisan ties (Hinckley, 1971; Bailey, 1966; Congressional Quarterly, 1963; Goodwin, 1959; Griffith, 1961; Burns, 1949; Galloway, 1946);

—enhancing the power of members who were most "out of touch" with the Congress and the country (Goodwin, 1959; Young, 1958; Galloway, 1946);

—providing powerful benefits to regions of the country dominated by a one-party system (Bailey, 1966; Goodwin, 1959; Burns, 1949);

—increasing the power of members representing electorally "safe" districts (Hinckley, 1971; Congressional Quarterly, 1963; Matthews, 1960; Goodwin, 1959);

—avoiding disruptive and potentially destructive struggles for selecting committee chairpersons, thus promoting harmony among members (Davidson, 1981b; Berg, 1977; Hinckley, 1971; Polsby, Gallaher, and Rundquist, 1969; Goodwin, 1959; Young, 1958; Galloway, 1946);

—stimulating longer service in the Congress, thus fostering more careerism among members (Hinckley, 1971; Goodwin, 1959); and

—advancing member specialization in relatively "narrow" topics through extended service on a committee (Berg, 1977; Blondel, 1973; Hinckley, 1971; Polsby, Gallaher, and Rundquist, 1969; Witmer, 1964).

Subsequent, more detailed and careful analysis of data, especially the consideration of other factors, resulted in a modification of views on the impact of seniority on Congress in the late 1960s and early 1970s. For example, it was found that

—committee chairs were actually fairly representative of the entire membership for their party in terms of region, state size, rural-urban district, etc. (Hinckley, 1971, pp. 35-63);

—use of seniority did restrict development of power for districts subject to electoral shifts and increase the time necessary for newly developing coalitions and factions to establish a committee power base (Hinckley, 1971, pp. 109-110); and

—service as a committee chair or ranking member as well as seniority itself had less to do with explaining the amount of federal money spent in a district than did committee membership (Ritt, 1976).

Political scientists chronicled how in the 1960s and 1970s Congress moved away from seniority as the sole criterion for selecting committee and subcommittee chairs in response to pressure from the larger numbers of new, younger members (Jones, 1982; Shaw, 1981; Dodd and Oppenheimer, 1977b, 1981; Mann and Ornstein, 1981; Cooper and Mackenzie, 1981; Keefe, 1980; Hinckley, 1978; Rieselbach, 1977). Subsequent research has attributed many expected and unexpected consequences to this change, including

—the development of greater "policy individualism" and of more innovative committees in the House (Stanga and Farnsworth, 1978);

—a greater propensity for freshman members to receive more "desirable" committee assignments (Asher, 1975);

—the selection of more liberal, younger, and Northern members as chairs (Berg, 1977);

—a larger gap developing between liberals and conservatives in the Democratic party (Davidson, 1981b);

—a greater openness by chairs in committee operations (Berg, 1977);

—a larger number of voluntary retirements due to changing incentives (Cooper and West, 1981);

—a reduction in the level of member expertise on subcommittees (Malbin, 1976);

—a greater responsiveness in decision making to influence from outside the legislature (Ornstein, 1981);

—an accelerating decentralization of power, with stronger, more independent subunits (Cooper and West, 1981; Davidson, 1981a; Asher, 1975); and

—a greater fragmentation among members (Cooper and West, 1981).

Law-making process. Political scientists studying legislatures have been concerned with how adequately these legislative organizations meet the goals set for them. Since for many legislative bodies law making is one of the primary purposes, descriptions of legislatures functioning in this capacity have been common. Most case studies of law making provide the reader with the author's perspective on the adequacy with which that legislative body enacts legislation. (See for example Bailey, 1950.) Many of the reform-oriented treatments of legislatures also discuss the organization's adequacy in achieving this goal, while advocating a set of structures and procedures which will maximize "effective law making" (see for example Citizens Conference on State Legislatures, 1971). A third orientation to law making can be identified as a macro-organizational one. Recent studies from this perspective tend to be more objective and quantitative in their treatments, while remaining largely descriptive (Rosenthal and Forth, 1978). However, some recent analysis has adopted a more rigorous and theoretic base for studying the law-making process.

In one of the earliest "rigorous" studies of the law-making process, Fletcher (1938) described a technique whereby IBM cards were coded so that analysis would indicate how bills were treated at various stages in the legislative process. Based on this research, she was able to conclude:

the committee system is poorly organized. The committees failed to function as well as they should. The amount of activity of individual members vary greatly, with results that do not follow partisan lines. The output is small in comparison with the proposed legislation introduced, and the length of time consumed by the process seems to be much greater than should be necessary (Fletcher, 1938, p. 85).

Her perceptions were shared by large numbers of political scientists and legislative observers, but the evidence she provided was much more systematic than that produced by many of her time.

More recently, Rakoff and Sarner (1975) looked at bill histories in the New York Senate to assess legislative action at various points in the legislative decision-making process. They created a flow chart of the six major decision points for accepting or rejecting proposed legislation and viewed bill histories through a six-stage stochastic branching model. Rakoff and Sarner concluded that a Markov assumption of equal probability at each decision point was not an accurate picture for the New York Senate. Rather, more bills were "killed" at the committee stage than at any other point.

Legislative bodies have sometimes been compared to machines whose purpose it is to pass laws (Polsby, 1969; Riddick, 1949). In a recent description of the law-making process in 50 states, Rosenthal and Forth (1978) reintroduced the idea of a legislature being a "bill-passing machine."

Another approach for analyzing law making (Hedlund and Freeman, 1981; Hedlund and Hamm, 1977, 1978a) uses concepts and measures based on organization theory. Its objective is to assess the impact of environment and of organizational factors including personnel, technology, structure, and task variables on the effectiveness of state legislatures as they consider and enact legislation. The earlier work of Hedlund and Hamm (1977, 1978a) specified dimensions of effectiveness for legislative chambers considering bills (expeditiousness, productivity, efficiency) and compared performance levels under differing "organizational conditions" before and after rule and structure changes, using a quasi-experimental across-time research design. They concluded that the chambers did work at different levels across the two time periods—generally being more expeditious, productive, and efficient after rule and structure change—and that interest sectors were generally affected differently by these changes. In more recent work (Hedlund and Freeman, 1981), these authors treat organizational factors for a legislative chamber separately in a multivariate model. The conclusions, while somewhat different, are compatible with the earlier findings; certain variables—technology use, interpersonal relations, and leadership style as well as some rule and procedure variables—are found to have an impact on the levels of performance effectiveness, while variables identified with the state legislative reform movement have mixed relationships. The contributions of these studies are fourfold: the design and testing of systematic measurement and treatment procedures of characteristics (personnel, organizational, and environmental) at the legislative chamber level; procedures for and collection of wide-ranging perceptual and factual data; specification and measurement of legislative chamber performance measures; and approaches for and implementation of analysis of data across time. However, major limitations are apparent due to the limited number of cases analyzed, the questions raised regarding the importance of the dependent variables studied for legislative research, and the possible biases due to autocorrelation of variables.

Legislator as head of an enterprise. One final approach to the formal aspect of the legislative organization which may prove useful for future research is the conception of legislators as heads of an "enterprise." Studies by Loomis (1979) and Fox and Hammond (1977) culminated in the work of Salisbury and Shepsle (1981a, 1981b), which describes members of Congress as heads of an emerging "cottage industry." In this last article, the authors focus on the degree to which the office and operation of each member of Congress has become a small "enterprise," headed by the legislator. They attribute this trend to structural reform in Congress and the growth of staff. With each member of Congress as the head of a small semiautonomous enterprise, the casework of legislators, their policy proposals, and the operation of the legislature are all affected.

Factors Affecting Organizational Features

Organizational characteristics, such as those under consideration here, do not appear spontaneously and remain constant over time; rather they are the product of planning and discussion by the persons involved in creating the legislative organization and reflect a variety of environmental, personnel, and situational factors. This section summarizes evidence and speculation regarding the development of various legislative traits. In this the topics of legislative change and reform will inevitably be included, since factors producing change are in fact related to the adoption of certain organizational characteristics. Two of the great shortcomings in this literature are the absence of rigorous data and of explicit comparisons across legislative organizations at different stages of their development.

General Political-Social Environment

The first set of factors affecting the organizational characteristics of a legislature stems from the environment in which the legislature is situated. In reviewing the development of U.S. state legislatures, Rosenthal (1981b) notes that "legislatures are interwoven in the fabric of their states; and the legislative process cannot be considered in isolation from the prevailing ethos, the political ethics, and the capital community in the state in which it operates" (p. 111). Thus, a legislature will reflect the political culture in a state or nation (e.g., the Progressive tradition in Wisconsin), the ethics expected of public figures (e.g., entrepreneurship and profit in Louisiana politics), and the physical features of the state (e.g., the ability to commute from home in small states like New Jersey and Rhode Island).

Regarding the nature of the political system itself, Hoskin concludes that in the Colombian Congress:

the role of Congress in the political system, especially its institutional autonomy, is determined to a great extent by the structure of power prevailing in the society. With the crisis of "oligarchical hegemony" in the late 1920's, Congress assumed a significant role, due to politics or compromise, in the alterations that occurred in terms of power relationships. Accompanying this strategy, the locus of political power shifted increasingly to the executive branch of government. This trend reached a climax with the passage of the 1968 constitutional reforms which the National Front government successfully pushed through a docile Congress (1975, pp. 173-174).

Organization theory also suggests that the general environment surrounding an organization should affect its characteristics. For example, Froman (1968) points out 1) that a highly differentiated political-social setting should be related to a legislative organization which is very salient to all citizens, highly decentralized in structure and authority, and composed of very committed members and which has high levels of internal communications; 2) that a setting in which high pressure levels exist should have a highly complex legislative leadership structure; and 3) that a low conflict setting should be related to lower cohesion among groups within the legislature and low levels of authority among members. Thus, using organization theory, he is able to link theoretically seven important characteristics of Congress to three features of the general political-social setting.

In a more extensive and elaborate review of organizational theory, Cooper (1977, 1981) also connects environment and organization. He emphasizes a tie between input and output (i.e., between resources provided and expectations satisfied) and the organization's adaptiveness to changes in the environment. Within the specific environmental factors affecting the structure and operation of the U.S. House, he differentiates between fixed parameters and situational variables. He identifies (1981) "five parameters that limit the organizational flexibility of the House." First, it has "limited institutional control over the character of the workforce and the distribution of tasks"—that is, over the selection and retention of its members and their independence from many organizational constraints. Second, it has "limited institutional control over the dimensions and mix of output goals" since societal forces or individual members have great influence on these. Third, it has "limited institutional tolerance for hierarchy"; much depends on the willing cooperation of members and their limited control over their colleagues. Fourth, it has "limited institutional capacity to rely on objective standards or measures"; inherent in legislatures are disagreements over ends and means which limit the use of objective criteria or performance measures. Finally, the House has "limited institutional capacity to motivate organizational identification"; unlike other institutions, legislatures cannot compel their members to identify with the organization and may even have members who are quite independent of it (pp. 328-330). He also identifies four situational variables for the U.S. House which are "more fluid and more concrete facets of environmental values" than are the fixed parameters: environmental demand, electoral politics, executive roles and resources, and democratic decision-making values (1981, pp. 332-336).

History

A second set of factors relates to the historical tradition and evolution for that system. For example, several political scientists have noted the
heavy borrowing from other political systems when legislative organizations
are established. Despite the Revolutionary War, the Constitutional Convention
of 1787 agreed to a compromise plan creating a bicameral legislative body in
which only one chamber was popularly elected, clearly reflecting prior colonial experience and the British tradition (Congressional Quarterly, 1976a).
In creating their legislative bodies, several former colonies blended their own
precolonial values and processes with legislative features adapted from other
political systems (Stauffer, 1970; Stultz, 1970). When commenting on several
parliamentary practices which appear "out of place" in Canada, Jackson and
Atkinson (1974) note the British legacy and the Canadian tendency to adapt
procedures "blindly" simply because they were British. Thus, the nature of
a political system's prior experiences and legacies from other systems profound-
ly affect the organizational characteristics in a legislative body (Loewenberg
and Patterson, 1979; Patterson and Wahlke, 1972; Wahlke, 1966).

Demographic Composition

A third set of characteristics relates to the demographic composition
of the political system in which the legislature is situated. For example,
Roeder (1979) relates urbanism and industrialization to rankings of the
legislative bodies for structural characteristics, using both Citizens Conference
on State Legislature (1971) rankings and the Grumm (1970) index. He speculates that urban industrial environments have different expectations for
organizations and are more likely to have complex legislative organizations
emerge than are other types of environments. Also, Tatalovich (1978), using
a combined ranking for the 50 state legislatures on the CCSL characteristics,
concludes that "linkages between societal conditions, legislative quality, and
public policies were found. Quality legislatures [judged on a multidimensional
index created from the CCSL's five individual rankings] exist in states with
higher socioeconomic status, a 'moralist' political culture, and greater non-
racial diversity" (Tatalovich, 1978, p. 231). Although these latter findings
must be tempered in light of the widespread criticism for the CCSL rankings
and of the simple bivariate nature of the analysis undertaken, evidence has
been provided that the composition of a political system may affect the
nature of the legislative organization.

Situational Factors

Another set of elements contributing to the nature of an organization's characteristics will be situational, especially the level of stress apparent

in the environment. In applying the tenets of organizational theory to the study of legislatures, Davidson and Oleszek (1976) note that legislative organizations, like all organizations, must adjust to changes in the external environment.

The structure of demands shifts as technology develops, resources are exploited or depleted, and public attitudes change. Relationships with other institutions, too, are dynamic and impose varying degrees of stress upon the organization. . . . No organization, the House included, can retain its autonomy and vitality if it fails to respond to its changing external environment (pp. 39-40).

Other examples can be cited regarding the effects of external stress on an organization and its features, including the work of Griffith (1944). He noted the difficulties Congress had in responding to the stress of World War II in both its policy decisions and its procedures, and he suggested the directions for change.

In addition to external situational factors, a number of features within a legislative organization can also produce an atmosphere conducive to the emergence of one set of organizational characteristics. For example, the continuing inability of the majority party to bring its legislation to a vote led members of the Wisconsin Assembly to implement differing procedures for bill consideration (Hedlund and Hamm, 1977, 1978a, 1978b). Thus, both internal and external situational features have been viewed as having some impact on organizational characteristics.

The Organization Itself

Characteristics of the organization itself are also seen as having an impact on its features. For example, an organization's membership size has subsequent impact on the organizational characteristics. The larger size of membership for the U.S. House is in part responsible for its more restrictive procedures governing debate, its greater reliance on the committee system, and its more formalized set of procedures (Congressional Quarterly, 1976a, pp. 81-82).

Bicameralism is another characteristic affecting legislative organizations. Much of the early political science literature on bicameralism concentrated on describing the conditions surrounding its establishment (Page, 1978; Congressional Quarterly, 1976a; Galloway, 1961; Riddick, 1949; Luce, 1922; Alexander, 1916), assessing its impact on legislative operations (Galloway, 1953; Riddick, 1949; Fletcher, 1938; Rousse, 1937), and advocating its adoption in other political settings (Rousse, 1937). Among the organizational effects noted from a bicameral legislature are the enhancement of "check points and decision making units" provided to prevent excesses and haste in the actions of the "other body" (Page, 1978; Cotta, 1974;

Rousse, 1937), the greater elaboration of organizational units thus enhancing the division of labor (Page, 1978; Cotta, 1974), and the increased requirement for coordination and "sequencing" units in the organization to facilitate action (Page, 1978).

Members of an Organization

The traits found among an organization's members and changes which take place in these traits have sometimes been related to the organization's structural and procedural characteristics. For example, Engstrom and O'Connor (1980) found lawyers in legislatures more supportive of changes in the organizational characteristics when those changes enhance legislative independence.

Studies of legislative change frequently note alterations in organizational characteristics after the recruitment of many new members for a legislative body. For example, reform in the U.S. House in the 1970s is frequently attributed to the election of many new members in 1970 (Congressional Quarterly, 1976a, pp. 153-161). Further, Swenson (1982) concludes from a review of recruitment patterns for members of the U.S. House from 1870 to 1940 that recruitment at the local level, especially the role played by party organizations, had much to do with what kinds of people were selected and what views they took with regard to the structure of that organization.

Another reason for a legislature having certain characteristics or undergoing change to acquire certain characteristics is the perceived payoffs such a set of characteristics will have for individual members. Mayhew (1974) argues that members of Congress have as their primary goal reelection to office and that they are assisted in this by the structure and organization of Congress.

The organization of Congress meets remarkably well the electoral needs of its members. To put it another way, if a group of planners sat down and tried to design a pair of American national assemblies with the goal of serving members' electoral needs year in and year out, they would be hard pressed to improve on what exists. The second point is that satisfaction of electoral needs requires remarkably little zero-sum conflict among members. That is, one member's gain is not another member's loss; to a remarkable degree members can successfully engage in electorally useful activities without denying other members the opportunity successfully to engage in them (pp. 81-82).

But if members of Congress were concerned only with reelection, they would leave all of the decision-making activities to others and concentrate on reelection. Dodd (1977) posits that members of Congress, like all politicians, tend to enter politics in order to obtain the influence necessary to affect policy decisions and that this influence in turn gives them power vis-à-vis others, including their constituents. To attain this influence in Congress, new members quickly learn that reelection is a prerequisite. As a consequence, Congress is organized to permit the widest possible dispersion of power among members in order to facilitate their reelection.

Impact of Organizational Characteristics on Legislative Operations and Performance

It is assumed that the purpose and role of organizational character-istics is to structure the interaction of members and consequently affect organizational activity. Therefore, the next four sections of this review consider the impact of a legislature's formal features, rules and procedures, power and influence patterns, setting, and resources on its operations and performance, public policy decisions, member behavior, and nonlegislative factors. In each section, attention will be directed first to the major themes occurring in the literature for each type of organizational activity. This will be followed by a selective summary of relevant findings.

The initial area on which we expect organizational characteristics to have some impact is legislative operations and performance—that is, the kind and scope of activities by which an organization pursues its goals. These are distinguished here from policy consequences, from purely individual-level behavior, and from impact on the relationships of the organization with its environments.

Legislative Performance

A common topic in much prebehavioral legislative literature was the performance of legislatures in pursuing various tasks. It was not uncommon to find references to inefficiency (Haines, 1917), efficiency and economy in processing legislation (Baker, 1940), and a better flow of business on the floor (Perkins, 1946). The troubling aspect in most of this work, however, was a failure to specify or define operationally the indicators for these perfor-mance variables.

Recognition of the shortcomings in prior performance-oriented research led to a series of specific proposals for establishing measures of legis-lative-level activity vis-à-vis legislation by Blondel et al. (1969). The measures proposed reflected a concern for the quantity of legislative output, the aims and relative importance of various legislation, and the role of the legislature (initiating, "preventing," and reacting) in relation to legislation. Their efforts were directed toward assessing the "viscosity" (i.e., resistance) of a legislative body in its law making.

A recent discussion of legislative accountability broadened the con-cerns of Blondel et al. with legislative performance levels and demonstrated that the Lazarsfeld (1958) approach can be used to operationalize performance concepts and specify observable indicators (Hedlund and Hamm, 1978b). Here, the authors describe seven legislative goals for which performance measures could be developed: policy responsiveness, formal decision making, oversight of the administration, constituent representation in policy formation, constituent relations-education-advocacy, solidarity building, and problem investigation; they also suggest specific operational-level indicators for each. While this effort is tentative and in need of elaboration and development, the process of formulating measures is instructive. A somewhat similar process can be found for Congress in Saloma (1969). In addition, several studies have offered suggestions regarding measurement for more specific aspects of legislative performance. (See for example Hedlund and Freeman, 1981; Hedlund and Hamm, 1977, 1978a; Jackson and Atkinson, 1974; CCSL, 1971; Grumm, 1970, 1973b; Lovink, 1973; Kornberg, 1970.) For example, three studies of policy making in the Canadian Parliament made use of legislative activity level measures indicating that concern with legislative-level phenomena is relatively widespread. Lovink (1973) suggests using five largely "impressionistic" measures of parliamentary activities. Kornberg (1970) developed several additional, more objective measures of legislative activity in the Canadian House of Commons and provided an across-time analysis of trends indicated by these data. Jackson and Atkinson (1974) elaborated on Kornberg's interpretation and measures on both an across-time and type-of-government basis.

Number of Structural Units

Once any organization grows beyond a relatively small number of members, subunits begin to appear and a division of labor across subunits becomes evident. Recent studies of Congress, for example, have pointed out the high degree of elaboration with regard to component units and the roles each plays in the legislative process. The existence, growth, and use of subunits in a legislative organization to assist in the processing of work is seen as a natural consequence of an increasing workload and a growing complexity (Francis and Riddlesperger, 1982; Cooper, 1981; Davidson, 1981a; Salisbury and Shepsle, 1981a; Loomis, 1979). In addition, many of these units have overlapping or competing responsibilities, so that a complex division of labor is apparent. This multifaceted nature of most legislative organizations creates the potential for fragmentation of responsibility as well as for noncoherent action. To the extent that multiple subunits become autonomous or semi-autonomous, the disintegrative tendencies of the entire organization are increased.

Political scientists have assessed the degree of autonomy residing in legislative subunits, especially the power residing in committees and subcommittees (Davidson, 1981b; Sundquist, 1981; Oleszek, 1978; Rieselbach,

1977; Malbin, 1976). One consequence of growing autonomy among subunits has been increased factionalism and weakened leadership (Malbin, 1976). The proliferation of informal groupings (caucuses) and congressional offices has added more subunits. These trends together with the recent enhancement of legislative staffs—especially in the U.S. Congress—suggest that legislative organizations are complex and elaborate and will likely continue to be so.

Decentralized and Fragmented Responsibilities

A third major theme regarding legislative organizations is the decentralized and fragmented nature of legislative responsibilities. This is a natural outgrowth from the large number of units existing in legislative organizations. To the extent that its decision-making responsibilities are divided across many structural units, an organization has multiple access points for influence on its goal-seeking activities. Further, the demise of seniority, the increased democratization of legislatures, and the growing bureaucratization of legislative staff have all heightened the decentralization of legislatures. This decentralization is more extensive than that found in most nonlegislative organizations and has increased, as noted above, with recent changes in most legislatures (Whalen, 1982; Cooper, 1981; Davidson, 1981a; Ornstein, 1975, 1981; Shaw, 1981; Sundquist, 1981; Keefe, 1980; Oppenheimer, 1980; Dodd and Schott, 1979; Hinckley, 1978; Oleszek, 1978; Patterson, 1978; Ripley, 1978). Regarding decentralization and fragmentation, Oleszek notes that

structural decentralization means that policymaking is subject to various disintegrative processes. Broad issues are divided into smaller sub-issues for consideration by the committees. Overlapping and fragmentation of committee responsibilities can impede the development of comprehensive and coordinated national policies. More than a dozen House committees, for example, consider some aspect of the energy issue. Jurisdictional controversies occur as committees fight to protect their "turf." Finally, committees develop special relationships with pressure groups and executive agencies. . . . Committees, then, become advocates of policies and not simply impartial instruments of the House or Senate (1978, p. 13).

One of the consequences attributed to decentralization (and to the consequent weakening of party discipline) is the use of bargaining, compromise, and "log rolling" in legislative activities (Davidson, 1981a). As decentralization increases, legislators must develop strategies to generate support sufficient to pass proposals through the multiple decision-making points in the decentralized organization (Rieselbach, 1977, p. 17).

Specialization by Generalists

One of the consequences of a decentralized legislature with its division of labor is the development of specialization in terms of areas of impact.

Legislative subunits as well as legislators specialize in order to acquire the expertise necessary for decision making, to build the capacity required for dealing with issues, and to develop the ability to wield influence and power (Cooper, 1981; Chelf, 1977; Volger, 1974). The irony is that members must also be generalists in order to participate in the broad range of decision making and in the wide variety of activities associated with any legislature. As a consequence, specialization is adopted while strategies are developed for coping with the broad range of issues; this has important consequences for legislative activity in considering legislative proposals.

"Slow Moving" and Open Decision Making

One persistent theme for legislative organizations is that they are slow moving and deliberate. Virtually every case study has pointed out that the procedures in that legislative body for considering legislation require a great amount of time and patience.

From the beginning, the Congress has shown that its most deep-seated fear is not of obstruction but of quick majoritarian decisions, and its structures and procedures have evolved accordingly. Committees, and later subcommittees, were created for the thorough consideration of legislation, each with the right to proceed with virtual autonomy at its own unhurried pace, to act or not to act, as it might choose. The Senate adopted a rule of unlimited debate, a principal so cherished that even after the circumstances of the 20th Century forced members to reconsider and modify it, the votes of three-fifths of the body's membership are still required to terminate debate. And, of course, the constitutional division of the American legislature into two independent houses compounds its difficulties in attaining "decision" and "dispatch" (Sundquist, 1981, pp. 156-157).

One factor contributing to this languor is the degree to which certain legislative processes and procedures—especially those associated with bill consideration—are specified in great detail so as to leave little room for flexibility. And, whenever flexibility is required, it usually involves a unanimous vote or an extraordinary majority vote.

Another characteristic of decision making in legislative organizations is the degree to which it is "open" to public view. Since legislative bodies are public in nature, they cannot be closed in their operations like corporations and other private groups. Based on accumulated case studies, however, it becomes obvious that great variation exists across legislatures and across time regarding their degree of openness. Legislatures which stress openness are thought to be more likely to experience delays in decision making, more susceptible to external influence, more difficult to lead, and more democratic in their decision making. One theme in recent assessments of Congress has been increased openness because of changes in chamber procedures, including a "freeing up" of the amendment process, opening up sessions of committees and subcommittees, using recorded teller votes, providing more television coverage, publishing committee notes, and so on (Whalen, 1982; Ornstein, 1981; Oleszek, 1978; Shaw, 1981). Similar trends have become apparent in state legislatures with comparable results.

Legislative Resources

Although resources are generally considered to be a most important factor for an organization to meet its goals, comparatively little treatment has been given this topic per se in legislative literature. Instead, attention has been given to certain factors which many would consider a resource—for example, type of members and size and expertise of staff—without necessarily labeling them as resources. Other commonly cited resources like time, money, and technology are frequently ignored or given little attention. Such trends pose problems to the extent that separate or inadequate treatment fails to sensitize researchers and their audiences to actual resource use by legislative bodies.

In their recent anthology on the work setting in the U.S. House, Cooper and Mackenzie (1981) specifically differentiate between the productive system (that is, those units, individuals, and processes doing the work of the organization in meeting its goals) and the support system (that is, those units, individuals, and processes obtaining the resources and allocating them to the productive system). The performance of the productive system is dependent on the support system, even though there is great overlap between the two. The support system has severe limitations imposed on its scope of activities, leading the authors to describe its nature as underdeveloped and undifferentiated in the U.S. House. A similar characterization is probably accurate for most other legislative bodies.

Regarding one widely discussed resource, new technologies, Cooper (1975) notes the limited extent to which "modern and innovative" techniques and machines are adopted by Congress or other legislatures. He attributes this in part to the nature of the legislature.

It remains true that because the most critical aspects of Congress' work are political in nature, its productive processes cannot be as highly routinized or mechanized as they are in an automobile or steel factory, nor as highly regulated by logical or analytical search procedures, as they are in a hospital or engineering firm. Congress, in short, has been and remains a custom or unit producer of highly intangible outputs (p. 329; see also Wissel, O'Connor, and King, 1976).

In spite of this assessment, however, recent political science literature has described the adoption of certain new technologies by some legislatures. Although most of these studies analyze a single legislative case, the accumulated work indicates what technologies have been adopted and suggests possible consequences. A modest number of studies have considered how adoption of a new technology could or does help legislative operations. For example,

Worthley and Overstreet (1978) showed that ombudsman/computerized follow-up procedures helped Florida legislators in their oversight of the executive, and several researchers have shown that computerized legislative information systems assisted in processing and updating needed data (Goldberg, 1981; Maisel, 1981; Worthley, 1977a, 1977b). Other studies have considered what factors affect the adoption of new technology: Frantzich (1979a) considered member characteristics, Worthley (1977a, 1977b) organizational structure. Still other studies have determined what might happen to a legislative body with the adoption of new technology: greater efficiency and lower costs (Worthley, 1977a; Hedlund and Freeman, 1981), greater "fiscalization" in legislative analysis and debate (Goldberg, 1981), greater career security as well as increased legislative capacity and redistributed power (Frantzich, 1979b), and better public perception (Robinson, 1975).

Information has been treated as a resource of great importance to legislative organizations (Feller, King, Menzel, O'Connor, Wissel, and Ingersoll, 1979; Zwier, 1979; Porter, 1974; Citizens Conference on State Legislatures, 1971; Janda, 1968). In fact, developing the capacity to collect and independently assess information has become an underlying theme of the legislative change (reform) movement in Congress and the U.S. state legislatures. Further, a review of more "practice-oriented" studies of legislative bodies by organizations like the National Conference of State Legislatures reinforces the conclusion that collecting and analyzing information has become an important legislative activity; yet, contemporary political science literature is incomplete in its treatment of information use by legislatures.

Overview

A review of the literature regarding relationships between organizational characteristics and the legislature's operations and performance is detailed in Appendix 1. This overview shows that of the formal features of a legislature, its size and bicameral nature seem to have received greatest attention, in part because each is an attribute that distinguishes legislatures from other public and private organizations. Research on seniority, norms, and reforms in procedures appear to dominate the study of relationships between legislative rules or procedures and subsequent legislative operations and performance. Furthermore, decentralization and factors affecting the amount of power held by units like committees have an impact on many aspects of legislative operation and performance.

Impact of Organizational Characteristics on Public Policy

Behavioral-era legislative studies have been criticized for a general deemphasis on public policy and policy making. From this policy-making literature as a whole, two trends are evident—legislative decision making is increasingly seen as "piecemeal" and policy outputs and outcomes are being studied in terms of relationships with legislative organizational factors.

Piecemeal Policy Making

Studies at almost every level of government indicate that legislative decision making tends to be piecemeal in nature and approach. Rather than developing or adopting a comprehensive policy on a topic, legislative decision making seems to involve breaking a proposal into component parts and dealing with each part rather than dealing with the entire proposal (Oppenheimer, 1980). In addition, policy making is incremental and each step tends to be small. As a consequence, a single, small change in policy seems to be the preferred strategy for legislators (Ripley, 1978; Dodd, 1977). Viewed in this context, legislative involvement in decision making fits well with the decentralized and deliberate policy-making process described above. As one result of this trend, political scientists have concentrated on analyzing portions or parts of legislative decision making rather than on considering the broad scope or overall views of the process.

Most studies about the incremental nature of legislative policy making are case studies with limited comparisons and virtually no theoretic orientation. While this approach provides in-depth treatment of one policy-making sequence, we know very little about how typical the process is; exceptions are some work regarding congressional decision making (Kingdon, 1981; Clausen, 1973) and the work on policy outputs and outcomes discussed below.

Policy Outputs and Outcomes

Concern with policy outputs and outcomes from a rigorous, non-case-study perspective in contemporary political science began with Dawson and Robinson (1963) and continued with Dye (1966), Hofferbert (1966), and Sharkansky (1967). These researchers examined the impact of political versus social and economic factors on policy outputs and outcomes as measured by expenditure data. Beginning with the work of Dye (1966), certain legislative organizational variables have been used to explain state expenditure levels for various purposes, such as education and welfare. The general conclusion of these early studies was that environmental, especially economic, factors were most important for "explaining" state expenditures. These findings were based on relatively simplistic "political" measures used to represent governmental (often legislative) structural and institutional factors. Much subsequent work has criticized this research for the nature of factors used and the types of analysis undertaken (LeLoup, 1978; Grumm, 1971, 1977; Munns, 1975; Carmines, 1974).

Studies conducted on the state level after the legislative reforms of the early 1970s proposed and used several new and separate indicators for variables related to legislative structure, operation, and decision making. The goal of this research remained the same: to evaluate the impact of organizational and institutional factors on policy outputs and outcomes. The earlier studies generally identified individual indicators (for example, party composition of the legislature) and used these as measures of the nature of legislative operations or performance (Dye, 1966; Hofferbert, 1966); more recent ones combined individual indicators into indices (for example, legislative professionalism) and used such constructed variables in their analysis (Grumm, 1970, 1971, 1973a, 1977; Uslaner and Weber, 1975; CCSL, 1971). In addition to using different measures for organizational variables, these more recent studies have also tended to use different indicators for policy outputs and outcomes and different analysis strategies.

The earlier studies generally concluded that the so-called "political variables" had little, if any, independent effect on policies, especially on state expenditures, when the analysis was controlled for social and economic variables. The conclusions from the more recent studies are more mixed. Studies using Grumm's measures of legislative professionalism have tended to find differences in welfare policies, in a state's capacity to respond to welfare needs, and in a state's fiscal redistribution policies when the analysis was controlled for social and economic factors (Grumm, 1970, 1971, 1973a, 1973b, 1977; Carmines, 1974; Asher and Van Meter, 1973; Booms and Halldorsen, 1973; Sullivan, 1972; Fry and Winters, 1970). On the other hand, studies utilizing the CCSL measures of legislative capability have generally found no relationships between them and public policies when the analysis was controlled for social and economic factors (Wohlenberg, 1980; Ritt, 1973, 1977; Karnig and Sigelman, 1975). These latter studies counter earlier findings from CCSL which had reported large numbers of statistically significant relationships but had introduced no controls for social and economic variables (CCSL, 1971). One reason for this difference in findings between the Grumm and CCSL indices may be the apparent absence of a relationship between these measures. While professionalism and capability are not necessarily synonymous, the nonrelationship of these two indices has been troubling to many researchers; and questions have been raised about the data collection techniques and the procedures used by CCSL to combine indicators into indices (Patterson, 1972). Using a completely different research approach, Shepsle (1979b) demonstrated deductively that certain aspects of legislative structure (division of labor, specialization of labor, and a monitoring mechanism) affect policy equilibrium and outcomes. (See also Shepsle, 1979a.) Similarly, other research, summarized above, shows a relationship between structure and policy (Hedlund and Hamm, 1976, 1978a). Such analysis provides some modest support for concluding that a legislature's institutional arrangements do affect policy outcomes.

Overview

In addition to the piecemeal focus, several studies .iave appeared which report on actual or expected relationships between organizational variables and public policy making by legislative bodies. Several of these relationships are summarized in Appendix 2. This appendix contains notably fewer findings than Appendix 1, suggesting either that less research has been completed regarding public policies or that organizational characteristics have fewer relationships with these types of variables. The former conclusion seems more plausible given the considerable number of case studies indicating that a legislature's organization affects the nature of public policy. The distribution of power has been identified as one organizational characteristic affecting legislative policy making.

Impact of Organizational Characteristics on Legislators

Aside from individual case studies, relatively few systematic studies have been published about how individual legislator behavior has been affected by organizational characteristics. The information available is very general and of limited use in developing an overall perspective on this question. The major tasks seem to be conceptualizing how the organization affects individual behavior, developing appropriate indicators, and implementing a research agenda for more systematic investigations of these relationships. For example, as has been pointed out above, congressional reforms as well as increasing staff are attributed with creating enterprises around members of Congress which alter individual behavior; electronic voting in the U.S. House is credited with enhancing cue giving and cue taking in roll-call voting and at the same time with introducing more openness regarding member behavior. The decentralization of power and the weakening of committee chairpersons in the U.S. House are seen as giving many less senior members more responsibility and influence in decision making, thus altering their behavior. And the increasing democratization of the legislature has led many legislators to reconsider their commitment to legislative service and to consider nonlegislative careers.

One question posed by many researchers has been the effect of legislative organizational factors on legislators' decisions to retire from a legislative body. The argument is that the nature of the legislative organization itself, especially its differences from other types of organizations, becomes an increasing source of aggravation and frustration and that voluntary exit from legislative office is one consequence (Hibbing, 1982a, 1982b; Frantzich,

1978a, 1978b; Bernick and Wiggins, 1978). Recent systematic analysis has indicated that, indeed, legislative changes to reduce the role of seniority and related norms in Congress did seem to have some impact on the decision to retire voluntarily from service (Hibbing, 1982a, 1982b); however, nonorganizational factors like political ambition, legislative salaries, and personal concerns have also been found to affect legislative turnover levels (Hibbing, 1982a, 1982b; Frantzich, 1978a, 1978b; Bernick and Wiggins, 1978).

Impact of Organizational Characteristics on Legislative Relations with Other Branches of Government and with the Public

The final area in which legislative characteristics are considered in this review is their effects on groups and individuals outside the legislature. Although relatively little systematic information has been collected, the available findings suggest that a decentralized legislative organization permits executives and administrative agencies to assume greater influence in the formation of policy demands and their aggregation into an agenda, greater involvement in specifying policy alternatives, and wider latitude in altering policy impact through the implementation process. Further, the nature of the legislative organization and its difficulties in projecting a dynamic and active image have weakened it in the public's eyes. Thus, many members adopt a style in which they "work against" the institution and seek reelection by running against Congress as an organization (Davidson, 1981a; Loomis, 1981b; Fenno, 1975). Indeed, the low esteem held by many citizens for Congress is attributed to its image and its deliberate nature (Parker, 1981).

Concluding Observations

This review has considered the nature of factors conceptualized as characteristics of a legislative organization, presented the rationale for and reservations expressed regarding the use of organizational characteristics in the study of legislatures, traced the origins of various legislative organizational characteristics, and evaluated how a legislature's formal features, rules and procedures, authority and influence, setting, and resources affect its activities and performance, public policies, individual members, and interactions with nonlegislative forces. Certain concluding observations seem in order.

First, organizational characteristics are important features of a legislature because they define the situation in which legislative activity takes place, structure legislative behavior and activity, and establish the ways in which legislatures operate. Despite the emphasis on individual-level variables and analysis, legislative-level research continues to be important. The impact of such organizational factors has been seen in both direct and indirect ways;

however, more systematic, rigorous, and comparative research regarding these factors is needed.

Second, the effects of organizational characteristics on subsequent legislative activity is a recurring theme in the numerous legislative case studies in the political science literature. Several different organizational characteristics have been identified through case studies as having some impact on legislatures or legislators in a variety of legislative settings. This research reinforces the conclusion that how a legislature is structured does affect what it does. Future research must be expanded beyond the inherent limitations of case studies and must continue to focus on the effects of alternative organizational arrangements.

Third, several different theoretical orientations—structural-functionalism, role theory, game theory-social choice, and organization theory, as well as individual rationality-purposive action—have all included the features of an organization as a critical factor in accounting for legislative and legislator behavior. Additional explorations using and expanding these theoretical orientations must have high priority among political scientists.

Fourth, reservations have been expressed about the utility of theoretical orientations based on organizational characteristics and about the overall importance of organization-based variables. Other factors, especially member selection and election, member predispositions, and the general sociopolitical setting, are viewed by some as being more important explanatory variables. However, no one has concluded that organizational features have no impact on subsequent legislative or legislator activity; rather, concern is with how much effect the organizational factors have. Research investigating the overall contributions of organizational factors in comparison with other factors should be encouraged.

Fifth, uneven levels of descriptive and analytical information is available for various legislatures. One legislative body—the U.S. Congress—has received significantly greater treatment. Very little has appeared on legislatures at the local level. These differences in coverage must be reduced by increasing the level of research and publication regarding U.S. state, local, and non-U.S. national legislatures to that level found for Congress.

Sixth, treatments of organizational characteristics, whether descriptive or analytical, tend to concentrate on single legislatures. Comparative analysis across legislative bodies, as well as between legislative bodies and other organizations, is necessary.

Overall, the accumulated literature, as presented in this review, clearly indicates in a variety of ways that organizational characteristics are an important concern for serious study, but attention to these characteristics has often been less systematic, rigorous, and comparative than is required for an adequate evaluation of their impact. The failure to resolve the status of legislative organizational characteristics is primarily a product of the limited nature and scope of existing research. To overcome these shortcomings, political scientists must carefully pursue a research agenda utilizing a theoretical base with systematic and comparative data.

APPENDIX 1
Studies and Sources Discussing Legislative Organizational Characteristics
And Their Relationships with Legislative Operations and Performance

Specific Feature	Type of Relationship	Study/Source
A. Formal Features		
1. Larger number of members	More resources and talent available, with members having expertise on most problems	Kornberg, 1967
	More time available to members, especially for constituent services	Blondel, 1973
	Greater complexity in organizational structure	Eulau and Prewitt, 1973
	More hierarchical organizational structure	Volger, 1974 Chelf, 1977 Keefe, 1980 Rosenthal, 1981b
	More limited debate	Rosenthal, 1981b Keefe, 1980 Wheare, 1963 Ornstein, 1981
	More unwieldly in conduct of business	Galloway, 1953 Ornstein, 1981
	Greater specialization among members	Chelf, 1977 Volger, 1974 Ornstein, 1981
	More "confusion apparent" among members	Rosenthal, 1981b
	More impersonal in operations	Rosenthal, 1981b
	Longer sessions	Kornberg, 1967

APPENDIX 1
(continued)

Specific Feature	Type of Relationship	Study/Source
1. Larger number of members (continued)	Less individual participation in legislative operations	Kornberg, 1967
	Less opportunity to "experiment" with informal procedures	Oleszek, 1978
	More formal relationships among units and members	Volger, 1974
	Greater number of subunits (e.g., committees)	Volger, 1974 Froman, 1968 Francis and Riddlesperger, 1982 Francis, 1982
	Less floor consideration	Volger, 1974
	More bargaining in decision making	Eulau and Prewitt, 1973
	More coalition formation	Eulau and Prewitt, 1973 Francis, 1970 Groennings, 1970
	Fewer "general" exchanges among entire council	Eulau and Prewitt, 1973
	More "limited" exchanges among portions of council	Eulau and Prewitt, 1973
	More rigid rules for conducting business	Keefe, 1980 Rosenthal, 1981b Volger, 1974 Froman, 1968 Dodd and Oppenheimer, 1981
	Less power for individual members	Keefe, 1980 Rosenthal, 1981b
	"Adjusted" rather than "minimal" winning coalition more likely	Francis, 1970
2. Bicameral legislature	More bargaining and compromise	Rosenthal, 1981b
	Less accountability for operations	Unruh, 1971 Rousse, 1937

APPENDIX 1
(continued)

Specific Feature	Type of Relationship	Study/Source
2. Bicameral legislature (continued)	More costly	Galloway, 1953 Rousse, 1937 Unruh, 1971
	More delays in handling legislation	Loewenberg and Patterson, 1979 Rousse, 1937 Unruh, 1971 Page, 1978 Cotta, 1974
	More "expeditious" in treatment of bills	Galloway, 1953
	Greater review of legislation	Galloway, 1953 Page, 1978
	Additional access points	Loewenberg and Patterson, 1979
3. Bicameral size ratio (indicating less diversity across two chambers)	Larger majorities in decision making	Crain and Tollison, 1980
4. Short sessions	Larger majorities in decision making	Crain and Tollison, 1980
5. Less frequent sessions	Larger majorites in decision making	Crain and Tollison, 1980
6. Annual sessions of legislature	Better workload across session	Perkins, 1946
	Less chaos at end of session	Wyner, 1973
7. No time limit on session	Business expanded to meet time available	Rosenthal, 1981b
	More debate and deliberation	Jewell and Patterson, 1977 Jewell, 1969
	Weaker committees	Jewell and Patterson, 1977 Jewell, 1969
8. Members popularly elected from geographical constituency	Increased fragmentation	Ripley, 1978
9. Legislative organization "open" to influence from diverse groups	Increased fragmentation	Ripley, 1978

APPENDIX 1
(continued)

Specific Feature	Type of Relationship	Study/Source
10. Large number of units	Increased fragmentation	Ripley, 1978
11. Weak political parties	Increased fragmentation	Ripley, 1978
12. Strong personal goals for members	Increased fragmentation	Ripley, 1978
13. Institutionalization (well-established boundaries, complex organization, universalistic rather than particularistic criteria, automatic rather than discretionary methods)	More decentralized power More professionalized norms Increased influence of organization and individual in decision making	Polsby, 1968 Polsby, 1968 Polsby, 1968
14. Institutionalization (legislative structure including apportionment, expenditures for legislative research, turnover, length of session)	Increased response capacity of legislature to "public needs"	Grumm, 1973b
15. Less professional legislature (limited session length, limited staff, limited facilities, large number of freshmen)	Greater importance of committees for decision making Less debate Fewer partisan caucuses	Chaffey, 1970 Chaffey, 1970 Chaffey, 1970
16. Labor intensive legislature (high number of bills in relation to time/experience/facilities)	Use of seniority system in committee and strong committees	Chaffey, 1970
17. Labor permissive (small number of bills in proportion to time/experience/facilities)	Strong party caucuses with weak committees	Chaffey, 1970
18. Professional legislature (longer sessions, higher salaries, better facilities, lower turnover)	More automated internal decision-making devices (scheduling legislation) but seniority used less for committee appointments unless committees and chairpersons are powerful	Chaffey, 1970
19. Division of labor	Prevalence of bargaining Greater specialization and concentration on few issues	Davidson and Oleszek, 1976 Polsby, 1970

APPENDIX 1
(continued)

Specific Feature	Type of Relationship	Study/Source
20. Reduction in the number of committees/subcommittees	Greater efficiency, alleviating members' schedules	Parris, 1979
	Stronger jurisdiction for committees	Parris, 1979
B. Rules and Procedures		
1. Rules in general	Power and prerogatives of committees protected	Ripley, 1978
	Multiple veto points	Ripley, 1978
	Enhanced bargaining	Ripley, 1978
2. Informal norms (rules of the game)	Increased predictability (continuity) for legislature	Loomis, 1981b
Jackson and Atkinson, 1974
3. Legislative norms followed	Group cohesion and solidarity promoted	Wahlke et al., 1962
	Conflict channeled	Wahlke et al., 1962
	Law making expedited	Wahlke et al., 1962
4. Norms for member specialization and reciprocity	Committees stronger, more autonomous	Hinckley, 1978
Davidson, 1981b
	Decentralized decision making reinforced	Hinckley, 1978
	Influence distributed more widely in legislature	Hinckley, 1978
	Corporate decision making in the legislature retarded	Hinckley, 1978
5. Restrictive (rigid) rules and procedures	More delay in decision making	Jewell and Patterson, 1977
	Proliferation of strategies to to get around rules and procedures	Jewell and Patterson, 1977
	Decision making in more informal (flexible) settings (e.g., subcommittees)	Ornstein, 1981
7. Procedures with fewer obstructions to decision making and debate	More discussion in legislature	Franks, 1978
	More responsive government	Franks, 1978
	Increased session length	Rogers, 1921
8. Rules permitting extended debate by individual members and strengthening individuals	Decreased possibility for decision making in public	Kane, 1971

APPENDIX 1
(continued)

Specific Feature	Type of Relationship	Study/Source
9. Rules which give majority more power by strengthening leadership and preventing delays	More productive in considering bills	Hedlund and Hamm, 1977
	More expeditious in handling bills	Hedlund and Hamm, 1977
	More efficient in use of time resources	Hedlund and Hamm, 1977
10. Rules removing time restrictions and simplifying process	Larger number of pages in journal for bills per day	Jackson and Atkinson, 1974
	Makes more time available to legislature	Jackson and Atkinson, 1974
11. Use of seniority in member appointments	Communications concentrated	Chelf, 1977 Witmer, 1964
	Power concentrated in the the hands of a few	Goodwin, 1959 Orfield, 1975 Oleszek, 1978 Abram and Cooper, 1968 Polsby et al., 1969 Price, 1978 Hinckley, 1971
	Party cohesion reduced	Hinckley, 1971 Burns, 1949 Bailey, 1966
	Enhanced party responsibility	Goodwin, 1959
	Enhanced division of labor	Polsby et al., 1969
	Expertise allowed to build in legislature	Goodwin, 1959
	Power decentralized	Hinckley, 1971
	"Harmony" promoted in decision making through "automatic selection" rule	Goodwin, 1959 Polsby, 1968 Berg, 1977 Abram and Cooper, 1968 Polsby et al., 1969
12. Decline in use of seniority in member appointments	Chairs continued to have seniority	Stanga and Farnsworth, 1978
	Levels of chamber expertise reduced	Malbin, 1976
	Greater decentralization of power	Asher, 1975
13. Anonymous voting (unrecorded teller)	Stronger role for leadership in roll calls	Wheare, 1963

APPENDIX 1
(continued)

Specific Feature	Type of Relationship	Study/Source
13. Anonymous voting (unrecorded teller) (continued)	Challenges on floor discouraged	Davidson, 1981b
	Less time voting	Shaw, 1981
14. Democratization of legislature	More "inefficiency" in legislative process	Rieselbach, 1975
	More difficult for legislature to act quickly	Rieselbach, 1975
	Norms providing limited benefits (e.g., apprenticeship) will disappear	Loomis, 1981b
15. Congressional reform, 1970-1976 (subcommittee bill of rights, weaker committee chairs, elected committee chairs, active democratic caucus, committee assignments from steering and policy committee, Democratic members of Rules Committee appointed by speaker, congressional budget reorganization)	Decentralized decision making	Shaw, 1981 Dodd and Oppenheimer, 1981 Rieselbach, 1977 Dodd and Oppenheimer, 1977b Hinckley, 1978 Oleszek, 1978 Oppenheimer, 1980 Sundquist, 1981 Hibbing, 1982a Ripley, 1978 Davidson, 1981a
	Narrow policy jurisdictions of units	Oppenheimer, 1980
	Chairs unable to pressure members	Oppenheimer, 1980
	Chairs more responsible	Ornstein and Rohde, 1977
	Much legislation at a standstill (slower process)	Hibbing, 1982a Ornstein, 1981 Shaw, 1981
	More committee work	Thurber, 1978
	More time in legislative day (longer days)	Malbin, 1976
	More democratic decision making	Davidson, 1981a Ornstein, 1981
	Increased accountability of legislature	Oppenheimer, 1980
	Piecemeal processing of bills	Oppenheimer, 1980
	Greater number of votes taken	Ornstein and Rohde, 1977 Shaw, 1981 Whalen, 1982 Malbin, 1976

APPENDIX 1
(continued)

Specific Feature	Type of Relationship	Study/Source
15. Congressional reform, 1970-1976 (continued)	Committee recommendations more vulnerable on the floor	Ornstein and Rohde, 1977
	House less specialized	Ornstein, 1981
	More member participation, even in debate	Whalen, 1982
	Much less predictable decision-making environment	Sinclair, 1981b
16. Legislative reform syndrome	Lower perceived performance	Hedlund and Freeman, 1981
	Lower perceived performance in legislative operations	Hedlund and Freeman, 1981
	Less expeditious treatment of bills	Hedlund and Freeman, 1981
	Mixed effects with regard to efficiency in decision making	Hedlund and Freeman, 1981
	Lower levels of productivity	Hedlund and Freeman, 1981
17. Numerous rules regarding procedures	More bargaining and coalition formation	Ripley, 1978
18. Increased openness in legislative process	More floor amendments to legislation	Whalen, 1982
	Decreased party discipline	Shaw, 1981
	Legislature "slowed down"	Shaw, 1981
	Committee chairs less able to block action	Rohde, 1974
19. Specialization in legislature	Fragmented decision making	Asher, 1974
	Resolution of conflict fostered	Asher, 1974
20. Open caucuses	Increased delays in decision making	Bullock, 1978
C. Power and Influence Factors		
1. Numerous decision points in the law-making process	Easier to defeat bills	Oleszek, 1978
	Easier to change bills	Oleszek, 1978
	More bargaining and coalition formation	Oleszek, 1978
2. Decentralization	More informal groups formed among members which must be overcome	Stevens, et al., 1981

APPENDIX 1
(continued)

Specific Feature	Type of Relationship	Study/Source
2. Decentralization (continued)	Increased time needed for decision making	Sundquist, 1981 Oppenheimer, 1980 Hinckley, 1978 Oleszek, 1978 Ripley, 1978 Dodd, 1977 Rieselbach, 1977 Shaw, 1981
	Decreased party discipline	Davidson, 1981a
	Weaker committee chairs	Whalen, 1982 Shaw, 1981
	Stronger subcommittee chairs	Whalen, 1982
	More floor amendments	Whalen, 1982
	More openness in legislative process	Whalen, 1982
	Increased bargaining	Sundquist, 1981 Oppenheimer, 1980 Hinckley, 1978 Oleszek, 1978 Ripley, 1978 Dodd, 1977 Rieselbach, 1977 Whalen, 1982
3. Strengthened role of subcommittee in decision making	Increased factionalism	Malbin, 1976
4. Strong leadership	Greater expeditiousness in law making	Hedlund and Freeman, 1981
	Greater efficiency in law making	Hedlund and Freeman, 1981
5. Absence of hierarchy	Prevalence of bargaining	Davidson and Oleszek, 1976
D. Setting		
1. Physical arrangement of chamber so that opposing parties face one another (an oblong rather than theatre seating)	More debate and confrontation	Wahlke, 1966 Loewenberg and Patterson, 1979 Wheare, 1963
	More partisan-oriented behavior	Patterson, 1972 Loewenberg and Patterson, 1979 Wheare, 1963

APPENDIX 1
(continued)

Specific Feature	Type of Relationship	Study/Source
1. Physical arrangement of chamber so that opposing parties face one another (continued)	More unity and cohesion in each party	Wheare, 1963
	Different communications patterns with more cliques	Loewenberg and Patterson, 1979 Patterson, 1972
2. Concentrated seating among parties under specific feature	More partisan behavior More cliques	Patterson, 1972 Patterson, 1972
3. Theatre seating	Passive membership	Wahlke, 1966 Vanneman, 1977
4. Speaking from the rostrum	Speaking rather than debate encouraged	Wheare, 1963
5. Office space adequate for members	Greater ability to complete functions and tasks	Wahlke, 1966 Citizens Conference on State Legislatures, 1971
6. Use of air conditioning in summer	Longer sessions	Martin, 1960
7. Electronic voting	Secrecy removed	Bullock, 1978
E. Resources		
1. Greater expenditures and resources for the legislature	Large number of bills introduced	Rosenthal, 1981b Rosenthal and Forth, 1978
	Moderate increase in bill passage	Rosenthal, 1981b Rosenthal and Forth, 1978
	Greater independence from "government" in a parliament	Ranney, 1981
2. Higher levels of technology use	Higher level of perceived legislative performance (general and avoiding conflict)	Hedlund and Freeman, 1981
	More expeditious law making	Hedlund and Freeman, 1981
3. Increased information collecting and processing capacity	Greater specialization	Janda, 1968
	Greater division of labor	Janda, 1968
	Greater "fiscalization" in legislative analysis and debate	Goldberg, 1981
	Greater attention to district impact of legislation	Goldberg, 1981
	Increased legislative capacity for making decisions	Frantzich, 1979b

APPENDIX 2
Studies and Sources Discussing Legislative Organizational Characteristics
And Their Relationships with Public Policy

Specific Feature	Type of Relationship	Study/Source
A. Formal Features		
1. Type of legislature (parliamentary or separate executive)	Policies regarding air pollution different	Lundquist, 1974
2. Large number of subunits	More policy-making activity More "radical" policies	Price, 1972 Price, 1972
3. Level of legislative professionalism (Grumm index, legislator compensation, session length, legislative expenditures on research, level of legislative services, number of bills introduced)	More liberal policies regarding social welfare issues	Grumm, 1970 Grumm, 1971 Asher and Van Meter, 1973
	More receptive to demands from constituents	Grumm, 1971
	Not related to policies regarding size of government	Grumm, 1970
	Not related to financial centralization	Grumm, 1970
	Not related to progressive taxation	Grumm, 1970
	Not related to government expansion policies	Grumm, 1970
	Financial redistribution in state fiscal policy	Fry and Winters, 1970 Sullivan, 1972 Booms and Halldorson, 1973
	Stronger relationship between party competition and welfare policy in high professionalism states	Carmines, 1974
4. Legislative professionalism (Uslaner and Weber index, compensation, session length, legislative expenditure on research, number of bills introduced)	More liberal policies regarding fiscal redistribution	Uslaner and Weber, 1975
5. Legislative capability (CCSL/ LEGIS 50 index overall as well as FAIIR)	More "innovative" in various policy areas	Citizens Conference on State Legislatures, 1971
	More "generous" in welfare	CCSL, 1971
	More "generous" in educational spending and services	CCSL, 1971
	More "interventionist" in scope of powers and responsibilities	CCSL, 1971

APPENDIX 2
(continued)

Specific Feature	Type of Relationship	Study/Source
6. Reformed legislative organization and structure (CCSL indices)	No differences in expenditure policies, education, welfare, highways, and health	Ritt, 1973
	Modest relationship to welfare expenditures	Ritt, 1977
	No differences in policies for per pupil expenditure, welfare and education expenditures per capita, general revenue expenditures, scope of power and responsibilities, or innovation when controlled for income and political culture	Karnig and Sigelman, 1975
	No difference in ratification for ERA	Wohlenberg, 1980
7. Legislative capability (CCSL indices)	Among legislatures with less legislative capability, stronger relationship between interparty competition and progressive, activist policies than among states with strong legislative capability	Le Loup, 1978
8. Institutionalization of legislature (Grumm index, apportionment of legislative districts, expenditures for legislative research and information agencies, legislative turnover, length of legislative sessions, index of party composition)	Greater responsiveness to welfare needs	Grumm, 1973b
	Very modest responsiveness to educational needs	Grumm, 1973b
	Very small responsiveness to health needs	Grumm, 1973b
9. Legislative reforms (frequency of sessions, limit on length of sessions, restrictions on special sessions, bill carryover provision, total number of committees, total number of joint committees, open committee hearings, requirement for committee reports, compensation of members, expenditure for legislative services)	Greater effectiveness (in meeting needs of residents) in welfare policy	Grumm, 1977
	More efficient resource use for welfare policy	Grumm, 1977
	No differences in effectiveness or efficiency for education or health policy	Grumm, 1977

APPENDIX 2
(continued)

Specific Feature	Type of Relationship	Study/Source
10. Legislative modernization (compensation, expenditures on legislative services, number of bills produced, session length, legislative services score)	Greater continuity in policy output so that appropriations seem to follow incremental model	Grumm, 1973a
	Less relationship to the economic deficiencies in terms of policy formulation	Grumm, 1973a
11. Legislative reform (longer sessions and annual sessions type of relationship)	No effect on innovativeness, no increased number of decisions made	McDowell, 1977
12. Reform of legislative structure	No differences in policies	Gove, 1973 Wyner, 1973 Gove, 1977
13. Bicameral legislature	Fewer errors in legislation	Cotta, 1974
	Formulation of policy alternatives not considered in other chamber	Gross, 1982
	More "moderate" content of policy enactments	Reid, 1980 Cotta, 1974
	Easier to block legislation	Shapley and Shubik, 1954
	Fewer "errors" in legislation enacted	Galloway, 1953 Loewenberg and Patterson, 1979 Page, 1978
	Less "care" in preparing bills	Rousse, 1937
14. Division of labor (committees), specialization of labor (jurisdictional arrangement), and monitoring mechanism (amendment control rule)	Enhances policy equilibria	Shepsle, 1979b
15. Annual session of legislature	More policies (bills) passed	Wyner, 1973
16. No time limit on session	More policies (bills) passed	Rosenthal, 1981b
17. Requirement that state legislature deal with local issues	More bills considered with greater inefficiency	Haines, 1917
B. Rules and Procedures		
1. Deliberateness in rules and procedures	Advantage to policies maintaining the status quo	Oppenheimer, 1974

APPENDIX 2
(continued)

Specific Feature	Type of Relationship	Study/Source
2. Limitations on member prerogatives (limited debate, limited subject matter, committees, limited individual involvement)	More likely to pass the "government's" program	Kornberg, 1967
	Low visibility for individual members	Kornberg, 1967
3. Rule changes to give majority party more power, strength, and leaders and to prevent delays	Differential effects on groups requesting legislation, with greater success going to some groups than to others	Hedlund and Hamm, 1978a
	Greater differences between success rates for successful requesters than for less successful requesters after change	Hedlund and Hamm, 1978a
	Differential impact on various committees	Hedlund and Hamm, 1978a
4. Direct power to pass legislation to committees, with strong protection for individuals, very weak parties, little input from government, strong minorities, no priority for government bills	Legislature unable to handle divisive and controversial issues	DiPalma, 1976
	Legislature able to pass only specific, routine legislation	DiPalma, 1976
	Legislative proposals framed in very specific terms	DiPalma, 1976
5. Universalist legislative "rules" rather than minimum winning coalition	Large majorities observed in passing legislation	Weingast, 1979
6. Filibuster and threats for filibusters	Delay, defeat, "watering down" of legislation	Oppenheimer, 1974 Berman, 1966 Froman, 1968 Oleszek, 1978 Wolfinger, 1971
7. Norms of specialization and less talk in debate	More personal influence on bill content	Matthews, 1959 Matthews, 1960 White, 1956
8. "Strong" Rules Committee with conservative members controlling bills to floor	Fewer "liberal" bills to floor	Oleszek, 1978 Matsunaga and Chen, 1976 Orfield, 1975 Robinson, 1963 Bailey, 1950
9. Congressional reform, 1970-1976	More piecemeal legislation	Oppenheimer, 1980 Oppenheimer, 1974

APPENDIX 2
(continued)

Specific Feature	Type of Relationship	Study/Source
9. Congressional reform, 1970-1976 (continued)	Increased particularism in policy making	Davidson, 1981a
10. Use of seniority in member appointments	Committees that react in policies and policy making rather than innovating	Stanga and Farnsworth, 1978
11. Decline in use of seniority in member appointments	More policy individualism	Stanga and Farnsworth, 1978
12. Specialization in legislature	Legislature able to make decisions on more complex issues	Asher, 1974
13. Specialized work groups	Longer, more complicated legislation	Davidson, 1981b
C. Power and Influence		
1. Decentralized power	Problems dealt with in a piecemeal fashion rather than in an integrated and unified manner	Sundquist, 1980 Oppenheimer, 1980 Hinckley, 1978 Oleszek, 1978 Ripley, 1978 Dodd, 1977 Rieselbach, 1977 Huitt, 1976 Oppenheimer, 1974
2. Fragmentation	Stable policy which changes slowly and in small increments	Ripley, 1978
	More passive policy role	Ripley, 1978
	Most policy distributive	Ripley, 1978
3. Stronger subcommittees (subcommittee bill of rights and independence from committees)	More restrictive policies toward agencies	Kaiser, 1978

NOTES

I would like to acknowledge the assistance of Samuel C. Patterson, Gerhard Loewenberg, Joseph Cooper, John Bibby, Eric Uslaner, Rodger Davidson, Ellen Hedlund, Margaret Hassel, and Mary Tracy.

REFERENCES

Abram, Michael and Joseph Cooper. 1968. "The Rise of Seniority in the House of Representatives," *Polity* 1:52-85.

Agor, Weston H. 1970. "The Senate in the Chilean Political System," in Allan Kornberg and Lloyd D. Musolf, eds., *Legislatures and Developmental Perspective.* Durham, NC: Duke University Press, pp. 228-272.

————. 1971. "The Decisional Role of the Senate in the Chilean Political System," in Weston H. Agor, ed., *Latin American Legislatures: Their Role and Influence.* New York: Praeger, pp. 3-51.

Alexander, DeAlva S. 1916. *History and Procedure of the House of Representatives.* Boston: Houghton-Mifflin.

Asher, Herbert B. 1973. "The Learning of Legislative Norms," *American Political Science Review* 67:499-513.

————. 1974. "Committees and the Norms of Specialization," *Annals of the American Academy of Political and Social Science* 250:63-74.

————. 1975. "The Changing Status of the Freshman Representative," in Norman J. Ornstein, ed., *Congress in Change.* New York: Praeger, pp. 216-239.

Asher, Herbert and Donald Van Meter. 1973. *Determinants of Public Welfare Policies: A Causal Approach.* Beverly Hills, CA: Sage Publishing.

Bach, Stanley. 1982. "Germaneness Rules and Bicameral Relations in the U.S. Congress," *Legislative Studies Quarterly* 7:341-357.

Bailey, Stephen K. 1950. *Congress Makes a Law: The Story Behind the Employment Act of 1946.* New York: Columbia University Press.

————. 1966. *The New Congress.* New York: St. Martin's Press.

Baker, Christopher E. 1971. "The Costa Rican Legislative Assembly: A Preliminary Evaluation of the Decisional Function," in Weston H. Agor, ed., *Latin American Legislatures: Their Role and Influence.* New York: Praeger, pp. 53-111.

Baker, Roscoe. 1940. "The Reference Committee of the Ohio House of Representatives," *American Political Science Review* 34:306-310.

Bauer, Raymond A., Ithiel de Sola Pool, and Lewis Anthony Dexter. 1964. *American Business and Public Policy: The Politics of Foreign Trade.* New York: Atherton Press.

Bell, Roderick. 1971. "Notes for a Theory of Legislative Behavior: The Conceptual Scheme," in Herbert Hirsch and M. Donald Hancock, eds., *Comparative Legislative Systems.* New York: The Free Press, pp. 21-35.

Bendiner, Robert. 1964. *Obstacle Course on Capitol Hill.* New York: McGraw-Hill.

Berg, John C. 1977. "Reforming Seniority in the House of Representatives: Did It Make Any Difference?" *Policy Studies Journal* 5:437-443.

Berman, Daniel M. 1964. *In Congress Assembled: The Legislative Process in the National Government.* New York: Macmillan.

————. 1966. *A Bill Becomes Law: The Civil Rights Act of 1960.* 2d ed. New York: Macmillan. 1st ed., 1962.

Bernick, E. Lee and Charles W. Wiggins. 1978. "Legislative Reform and Legislative Turnover," in Leroy N. Rieselbach, ed., *Legislative Reform: The Policy Impact.* Lexington, MA: Lexington Books, pp. 23-34.

————. 1983. "Legislative Norms in Eleven States," *Legislative Studies Quarterly* 8:191-200.

Best, James J. 1971. *The Washington State Legislative Handbook.* Washington, DC: American Political Science Association.

BeVier, Michael J. 1979. *Politics Backstage: Inside the California Legislature.* Philadelphia: Temple University.

Bibby, John F. and Roger H. Davidson. 1972. *Studies in the Legislative Process on Capitol Hill.* 2d ed. Hinsdale, IL: Dryden Press.

Bibby, John F., Thomas E. Mann, and Norman J. Ornstein. 1980. *Vital Statistics on Congress: 1980.* Washington, DC: American Enterprise Institute.

Blondel, Jean. 1973. *Comparative Legislatures.* Englewood Cliffs, NJ: Prentice-Hall.

Blondel, Jean et al. 1969. "Legislative Behavior: Some Steps Toward Cross-National Measurement," *Government and Opposition* 5:67-85.

Blydenburgh, John C. 1971. "The Closed Rule and the Paradox of Voting," *Journal of Politics* 33:57-71.

Bolling, Richard. 1965. *House Out Of Order.* New York: Dutton.

Booms, Bernard H. and James R. Halldorson. 1973. "The Politics of Redistribution: A Reformation," *American Political Science Review* 67:924-933.

Bradley, Robert B. 1980. "Motivations in Legislative Information Use," *Legislative Studies Quarterly* 5:393-406.

Buchanan, James M. and Gordon Tullock. 1962. *The Calculus of Consent: Logical Foundations of Constitutional Democracy.* Ann Arbor: University of Michigan Press.

Buchanan, William. 1963. *Legislative Partisanship: The Deviant Case of California.* Berkeley: University of California Press.

Bullock, Charles S. III. 1972. "House Careerists: Changing Patterns of Longevity and Attrition," *American Political Science Review* 66:1295-1300.

_____ . 1978. "Congress in the Sunshine," in Leroy N. Rieselbach, ed., *Legislative Reform: The Policy Impact.* Lexington, MA: Lexington Books, pp. 209-221.

Burdette, Franklin L. 1940. *Filibustering in the Senate.* Princeton: Princeton University Press.

Burns, James MacGregor. 1949. *Congress on Trial.* New York: St. Martin's Press.

Carmines, Edward G. 1974. "The Mediating Influence of State Legislatures on the Linkage Between Inter-Party Competition and Welfare Policies," *American Political Science Review* 68:1118-1124.

Carroll, John J. and Arthur English. 1981. "'Rules of the Game' in Ephemeral Institutions: U.S. State Constitutional Conventions," *Legislative Studies Quarterly* 6:305-312.

Chaffey, Douglas G. 1970. "The Institutionalization of State Legislators: A Comparative Study," *Western Political Quarterly* 23:180-196.

Chamberlain, Joseph P. 1936. *Legislative Processes: National and State.* New York: Praeger. 2d ed. Washington, DC: Congressional Quarterly.

Chance, C. Williams. 1970. *A Guidebook for Ohio Legislators.* Columbus: Ohio Legislative Service Commission.

Chartock, Alan S. and Max Berking. 1970. *Strengthening the Wisconsin Legislature.* New Brunswick, NJ: Rutgers University Press.

Chelf, Carl P. 1973. *A Manual for Members of the Kentucky General Assembly.* Washington, DC: American Political Science Association.

_____ . 1977. *Congress in the American System.* Chicago: Nelson-Hall.

Citizens Conference on State Legislatures. 1971. *State Legislatures: An Evaluation of Their Effectiveness.* New York: Praeger.

Clapp, Charles L. 1963. *The Congressman: His Work As He Sees It.* Washington, DC: The Brookings Institution.

Clausen, Aage R. 1973. *How Congressmen Decide: A Policy Focus.* New York: St. Martin's Press.

Congressional Quarterly. 1963. "Congressional Reform," *Congressional Quarterly Weekly Report* 21:857-920.

————. 1976a. *Origins and Development of Congress*. Washington, DC: Congressional Quarterly.

————. 1976b. *Powers of Congress*. Washington, DC: Congressional Quarterly.

Cooper, Joseph. 1975. "Strengthening the Congress: An Organizational Analysis," *Harvard Journal on Legislation* 12:307-368.

————. 1977. "Congress in Organizational Perspectives," in Lawrence C. Dodd and Bruce I. Oppenheimer, eds., *Congress Reconsidered*. New York: Praeger, pp. 140-159.

————. 1981. "Organization and Innovation in the House of Representatives," in Joseph Cooper and G. Calvin Mackenzie, eds., *The House at Work*. Austin: University of Texas Press, pp. 319-355.

Cooper, Joseph and David W. Brady. 1981a. "Toward a Diachronic Analysis of Congress," *American Political Science Review* 75:988-1006.

————. 1981b. "Institutional Context and Leadership Style: The House From Cannon to Rayburn," *American Political Science Review* 75:411-425.

Cooper, Joseph and G. Calvin Mackenzie, eds. 1981. *The House at Work*. Austin: University of Texas Press.

Cooper, Joseph and William West. 1981. "The Congressional Career in the 1970's," in Lawrence C. Dodd and Bruce I. Oppenheimer, eds., *Congress Reconsidered*. 2d ed. Washington, DC: Congressional Quarterly, pp. 83-106.

Cornwell, Elmer E., Jr., J.S. Goodman, William J. DeNuccio, and Angelo A. Mosca, Jr. 1970. *The Rhode Island General Assembly*. Washington, DC: American Political Science Association.

Cotta, Maurizio. 1974. "A Structural-Functional Framework for the Analysis of Unicameral and Bicameral Parliaments," *European Journal of Political Research* 2:201-224.

Craft, Ralph. 1973. *Strengthening the Arkansas Legislature*. New Brunswick, NJ: Rutgers University Press.

Crain, W.M. and R.D. Tollison. 1977. "Legislative Size and Voting Rules," *Journal of Legal Studies* 6:235-240.

————. 1980. "The Sizes of Majorities," *Southern Economic Journal* 46:726-734.

Crane, Edgar G. 1977. "Legislatures as a Force for Government Accountability: Organizational Challenge of New Tools of Program Review," in Abdo I. Baaklini and James J. Heaphey, eds., *Comparative Legislative Reforms and Innovations*. Albany: State University of New York at Albany, pp. 115-153.

Davidson, Roger. 1981a. "The Two Congresses and How They Are Changing," in Norman J. Ornstein, ed., *The Role of the Legislature in Western Democracies*. Washington, DC: American Enterprise Institute, pp. 3-19.

————. 1981b. "Subcommittee Government: New Channels for Policy Making," in Thomas E. Mann and Norman J. Ornstein, eds., *The New Congress*. Washington, DC: American Enterprise Institute, pp. 99-133.

Davidson, Roger H. and Walter J. Oleszek. 1976. "Adaptation and Consolidation: Structural Innovation in the U.S. House of Representatives," *Legislative Studies Quarterly* 1:37-65.

————. 1977. *Congress Against Itself*. Bloomington: University of Indiana Press.

————. 1981. *Congress and Its Members*. Washington, DC: Congressional Quarterly.

Dawson, Richard E. and James A. Robinson. 1963. "Inter-Party Competition: Economic Variables and Welfare Policies in the American States," *Journal of Politics* 25:265-289.

Declerq, Eugene. 1977. "Inter-House Differences in American State Legislatures," *Journal of Politics* 39:774-785.

Derthick, Martha. 1979. *Policymaking for Social Security*. Washington, DC: The Brookings Institution.

DiPalma, Giuseppe. 1976. "Institutional Rules and Legislative Outcomes in the Italian Parliament," *Legislative Studies Quarterly* 1:147-180.

_____. 1977. *Surviving Without Governing: The Italian Parties in Parliament*. Berkeley: University of California Press.

Dodd, Lawrence C. 1977. "Congress and the Quest for Power," in Lawrence C. Dodd and Bruce I. Oppenheimer, eds., *Congress Reconsidered*. New York: Praeger, pp. 269-307.

Dodd, Lawrence C. and Bruce I. Oppenheimer, eds. 1981. *Congress Reconsidered*. 2d ed. New York: Praeger. 1st ed., 1977a, Washington, DC: Congressional Quarterly.

_____. 1977b. "The House in Transition," in Lawrence C. Dodd and Bruce I. Oppenheimer, eds., *Congress Reconsidered*. New York: Praeger, pp. 21-53.

_____. 1981. "The House in Transition: Change and Consolidation," in Lawrence C. Dodd and Bruce I. Oppenheimer, eds., *Congress Reconsidered*. 2d ed. Washington, DC: Congressional Quarterly, pp. 31-61.

Dodd, Lawrence C. and Richard L. Schott. 1979. *Congress and the Administrative State*. New York: Wiley.

Dye, Thomas R. 1961. "A Comparison of Constituency Influences in the Upper and Lower Chambers of a State Legislature," *Western Political Quarterly* 14: 473-480.

_____. 1966. *Politics, Economics, and the Public: Policy Outcomes in the American States*. Chicago: Rand McNally.

Eidenberg, Eugene and Roy D. Morey. 1969. *An Act of Congress: The Legislative Process and the Making of Education Policy*. New York: Norton.

Engstrom, Richard L. and Patrick F. O'Connor. 1980. "Lawyer-Legislators and Support for State Legislative Reform," *Journal of Politics* 42:267-276.

Eulau, Heinz and Katherine Hinckley. 1966. "Legislative Institutions and Processes," in James A. Robinson, ed., *Political Science Annual: An International Review*. Vol. I. Indianapolis: Bobbs-Merrill, pp. 85-190.

Eulau, Heinz and Kenneth Prewitt. 1973. *Labyrinths of Democracy: Adaptations, Linkages, Representation, and Policies in Urban Politics*. Indianapolis: Bobbs-Merrill.

Evan, William M. 1976. "Organizational Theory and Organizational Effectiveness: An Exploratory Analysis," in S. Lee Spray, ed., *Organizational Effectiveness*. Kent, OH: Kent State University Press, pp. 15-28.

Falcone, David J. 1979. "Legislative Change and Policy Change: A Deviant Case Analysis of the Canadian House of Commons," *Journal of Politics* 41:611-632.

Farmer, Hallie. 1949. *The Legislative Process in Alabama*. University: University of Alabama Press.

Faust, Martin L. 1928. "Results of the Split-Session System of the West Virginia Legislature," *American Political Science Review* 22:109-121.

Feller, Irwin, Michael R. King, Donald C. Menzel, Robert E. O'Connor, Peter A. Wissel, and Thomas Ingersoll. 1979. "Scientific and Technological Information in State Legislatures," *American Behavioral Scientist* 22:417-436.

Fenno, Richard F., Jr. 1973. *Congressmen in Committees*. Boston: Little, Brown.

_____. 1975. "If, As Ralph Nader Says, Congress Is 'The Broken Branch,' How Come We Love Our Congressmen So Much?" in Norman J. Ornstein, ed., *Congress in Change: Evolution and Reform*. New York: Praeger, pp. 277-287.

Ferejohn, John A. 1974. *Pork Barrel Politics: Rivers and Habors Legislation, 1947-1968.* Stanford, CA: Stanford University Press.

Ferejohn, John A. and Morris P. Fiorina. 1975. "Purposive Models of Legislative Behavior," *The American Economic Review* 65:407-414.

Fiorina, Morris. 1977. *Congress: Keystone of the Washington Establishment.* New Haven: Yale University Press.

Fischer, Joel M., Charles M. Price, and Charles G. Bell. 1973. *The Legislative Process in California.* Washington, DC: American Political Science Association.

Fletcher, Mona. 1938. "Bicameralism As Illustrated by the 19th General Assembly of Ohio: A Technique for Studying the Legislative Process," *American Political Science Review* 32:80-85.

Flinn, Thomas A. 1973. "The Ohio General Assembly: A Developmental Analysis," in James A. Robinson, ed., *State Legislative Innovation: Case Studies of Washington, Ohio, Florida, Illinois, Wisconsin, and California.* New York: Praeger, pp. 236-278.

Fox, Harrison W., Jr. and Susan Webb Hammond. 1977. *Congressional Staffs: The Invisible Force in American Lawmaking.* New York: The Free Press.

Francis, Wayne L. 1970. "Coalitions in American State Legislatures: A Prepositional Analysis," in Sven Groennings, E.U. Kelley, and Michael Leiserson, eds., *The Study of Coalition Behavior: Theoretical Perspectives and Cases From Four Continents.* New York: Holt, pp. 409-423.

——————. 1982. "Legislative Committee Systems, Optimal Committee Size, and the Costs of Decision Making," *Journal of Politics* 44:822-837.

Francis, Wayne L. and James W. Riddlesperger. 1982. "U.S. State Legislative Committees: Structure, Procedural Efficiency, and Party Control," *Legislative Studies Quarterly* 7:453-471.

Franks, C.E.S. 1978. "Procedural Reform in the Legislative Process," in William A.W. Neilson and James C. MacPherson, eds., *The Legislative Process in Canada: The Need for Reform.* Toronto: Butterworth, pp. 249-259.

Frantzich, Stephen E. 1978a. "Congress by Computer," *Social Policy* 8:42-45.

——————. 1978b. "De-Recruitment: The Other Side of the Congressional Equation," *Western Political Quarterly* 31:105-126.

——————. 1979a. "Technological Innovation Among Congressmen," *Social Forces* 57:968-974.

——————. 1979b. "Technological Innovations Among Members of the House of Representatives," *Polity* 12:333-348.

——————. 1979c. "Who Makes Our Laws? The Legislative Effectiveness of Members of the U.S. Congress," *Legislative Studies Quarterly* 4:409-428.

Froman, Lewis A., Jr. 1967. *The Congressional Process: Strategies, Rules and Procedures.* Boston: Little, Brown.

——————. 1968. "Organization Theory and the Explanation of Important Characteristics of Congress," *American Political Science Review* 62:518-526.

Fry, Brian R. and Richard F. Winters. 1970. "The Politics of Redistribution," *American Political Science Review* 64:508-522.

Fuhrman, Susan and Alan Rosenthal. 1981. *Shaping Education Policy in the States.* Washington, DC: Institute for Educational Leadership.

Galloway, George B. 1946. *Congress at the Crossroads.* New York: Crowell.

——————. 1953. *The Legislative Process in Congress.* New York: Crowell.

——————. 1961. *History of the House of Representatives.* New York: Crowell.

Galloway, George B. and Sidney Wise. 1976. *History of the House of Representatives.* 2d ed. New York: Crowell.

Gatlin, Douglas S. 1973. "The Development of a Responsible Party System in the Florida Legislature," in James A. Robinson, ed., *State Legislative Innovation: Case Studies of Washington, Ohio, Florida, Illinois, Wisconsin, and California*. New York: Praeger, pp. 1-45.

Gere, Edwin Andrus. 1972. *The Massachusetts General Court: Processes and Prospects*. Washington, DC: American Political Science Association.

Gerlich, Peter. 1972. "Orientations to Decision-Making in the Vienna City Council," in Samuel C. Patterson and John C. Wahlke, eds., *Comparative Legislative Behavior: Frontiers of Research*. New York: Wiley, pp. 87-106.

_____ . 1973. "The Institutionalization of European Parliaments," in Allan Kornberg, ed., *Legislatures in Comparative Perspective*. New York: McKay, pp. 94-113.

Gertzel, Cherry. 1966. "Parliament in Independent Kenya," *Parliamentary Affairs* 19: 486-504.

Gerwin, Donald. 1981. "Relationships Between Structure and Technology," in Paul C. Nystrom and William H. Starbuck, eds., *Handbook of Organizational Design*. Vol. 2. Oxford: Oxford University Press, pp. 3-38.

Goldberg, Jeffrey A. 1981. "Computer Usage in the House," in Joseph Cooper and G. Calvin Mackenzie, eds., *The House at Work*. Austin: University of Texas Press, pp. 275-291.

Goodwin, George, Jr. 1959. "The Seniority System in Congress," *American Political Science Review* 53:412-436.

Gove, Samuel K. 1973. "Policy Implications of the Legislative Reorganization in Illinois," in James A. Robinson, ed., *State Legislative Innovation: Case Studies of Washington, Ohio, Florida, Illinois, Wisconsin, and California*. New York: Praeger, pp. 101-135.

_____ . 1977. "The Implications of Legislative Reform in Illinois," in Susan Welch and John G. Peters, eds., *Legislative Reform and Public Policy*. New York: Praeger, pp. 174-187.

Gove, Samuel K. and Richard J. Carlson. 1968. *An Introduction to the Illinois General Assembly*. Urbana, IL: Institute of Government and Public Affairs.

Griffith, Ernest S. 1944. "The Changing Pattern of Public Policy Formation," *American Political Science Review* 38:445-459.

_____ . 1961. *Congress: Its Contemporary Role*. 3d ed. New York: New York University Press.

Groennings, Sven. 1970. "Notes Toward Theories of Coalition Behavior in Multi-Party Systems: Formation and Maintenance," in Sven Groennings, E.W. Kelley, and Michael Leiserson, eds., *The Study of Coalition Behavior: Theoretical Perspectives and Cases From Four Continents*. New York: Holt, pp. 445-465.

Gross, Bertram M. 1953. *The Legislative Struggle: A Study in Social Combat*. New York: McGraw-Hill.

Gross, Donald R. 1982. "Bicameralism and the Theory of Voting," *Western Political Quarterly* 35:511-526.

Grumm, John G. 1970. "Structural Determinants of Legislative Output," in Allan Kornberg and Lloyd D. Musolf, eds., *Legislatures in Developmental Perspective*. Durham, NC: Duke University Press, pp. 429-459.

_____ . 1971. "The Effects of Legislative Structure on Legislative Performance," in Richard I. Hofferbert and Ira Sharkansky, eds., *State and Urban Politics*. Boston: Little, Brown, pp. 298-322.

_____ . 1973a. "The Legislative System as an Economic Model," in Allan Kornberg, ed., *Legislatures in Comparative Perspective*. New York: McKay, pp. 235-249.

————. 1973b. *A Paradigm for the Comparative Analysis of Legislative Systems.* Beverly Hills, CA: Sage Publications.

————. 1977. "The Consequences of Structural Change for the Performance of State Legislatures: A Quasi-Experiment," in Susan Welch and John G. Peters, eds., *Legislative Reform and Public Policy.* New York: Praeger, pp. 201-213.

Gupta, Anirudha. 1966. "The Zambian National Assembly: Study of an African Legislature," *Parliamentary Affairs* 19:48-55.

Haines, Wilder H. 1917. "Legislative Activity in Massachusetts, 1916," *American Political Science Review* 11:528-539.

Harder, Marvin A. and Raymond G. Davis. 1979. *The Legislature as an Organization: A Study of the Kansas Legislature.* Lawrence: Regents Press of Kansas.

Harder, Marvin and Carolyn Rampey. 1972. *The Kansas Legislature: Procedures, Personalities, and Problems.* Lawrence: University Press of Kansas.

Havard, William C. and Loren P. Beth. 1962. *The Politics of Mis-representation: Rural-Urban Conflict in the Florida Legislature.* Baton Rouge: Louisiana State University Press.

Hebert, F. Ted and Lelan E. McLemore. 1972. "Character and Structure of Legislative Norms: Operationalizing the Norm Concept in the Legislative Setting," *American Journal of Political Science* 17:506-527.

Hedlund, Ronald D. 1978. "A Path-Goal Approach to Explaining Leadership's Impact on Legislator Perceptions," *Social Science Quarterly* 59:178-191.

Hedlund, Ronald D. and Wilder Crane, Jr. 1971. *The Job of the Wisconsin Legislator.* Washington, DC: American Political Science Association.

Hedlund, Ronald D. and Patricia K. Freeman. 1981. "A Strategy for Measuring the Performance of Legislatures in Processing Decisions," *Legislative Studies Quarterly* 6:87-113.

Hedlund, Ronald D. and Keith E. Hamm. 1976. "Conflict and Perceived Group Benefits from Legislative Rules Changes," *Legislative Studies Quarterly* 1:181-199.

————. 1977. "Institutional Development and Legislative Effectiveness: Rules Changes in the Wisconsin Assembly," in Abdo I. Baaklini and James J. Heaphy, eds., *Comparative Legislative Reforms and Innovations.* Albany: State University of New York at Albany, pp. 173-213.

————. 1978a. "Institutional Innovation and Performance Effectiveness in Public Policy Making," in Leroy N. Rieselbach, ed., *Legislative Reform: The Policy Impact.* Lexington, MA: Lexington Books, pp. 117-132.

————. 1978b. "Reconceptualizing Legislative Accountability," in Scott Greer, Ronald D. Hedlund, and James L. Gibson, eds., *Accountability in Urban Society: Public Agencies Under Fire.* Beverly Hills, CA: Sage Publications, pp. 63-86.

Hedlund, Ronald D. and Charles W. Wiggins. 1967. "Legislative Politics in Iowa," in Samuel C. Patterson, ed., *Midwest Legislative Politics.* Iowa City, IA: Institute of Public Affairs, pp. 7-36.

Hellriegel, Don and John W. Slocum. 1979. *Organizational Behavior.* 2d ed. St. Paul, MN: West Publishing.

Hibbing, John R. 1982a. "Voluntary Retirement from the U.S. House: The Costs of Congressional Service," *Legislative Studies Quarterly* 7:57-74.

————. 1982b. "Voluntary Retirements from the House in the Twentieth Century," *Journal of Politics* 44:1020-1034.

Hinckley, Barbara. 1971. *The Seniority System in Congress.* Bloomington: Indiana University Press.

_____. 1983. *Stability and Change in Congress*. 3d ed. New York: Harper & Row. 1st ed., 1971. 2d ed., 1978.

Hirsch, Herbert and M. Donald Hancock. 1971. "Legislatures in Systemic Perspective," in Herbert Hirsch and M. Donald Hancock, eds., *Comparative Legislative Systems*. New York: The Free Press, pp. 1-20.

Hofferbert, Richard. 1966. "The Relation Between Public Policy and Some Structural and Environmental Variables in the American States," *American Political Science Review* 60:73-82.

Hoskin, Gary. 1975. "Dimensions of Conflict in the Colombian National Legislature," in G.R. Boynton and Chong Lim Kim, eds., *Legislative Systems in Developing Countries*. Durham, NC: Duke University Press, pp. 143-178.

Huddleston, Mark W. 1980. "Assessing Congressional Budget Reform: The Impact on Appropriations," *Policy Studies Journal* 9:81-86.

Huitt, Ralph K. 1957. "The Morse Committee Assignment Controversy: A Study in Senate Norms," *American Political Science Review* 51:313-329.

_____. 1961. "The Outsider in the Senate: An Alternative Role," *American Political Science Review* 55:566-575.

_____. 1976. "Congress: Retrospect and Prospect," *Journal of Politics* 38:209-227.

Hurley, Patricia, David Brady, and Joseph Cooper. 1977. "Measuring Legislative Potential for Policy Change," *Legislative Studies Quarterly* 2:385-398.

Ivancevich, John M., Andrew D. Szilagyi, Jr., and Marc J. Wallace. 1977. *Organizational Behavior and Performance*. Santa Monica, CA: Goodyear.

Jackson, Robert J. and Michael M. Atkinson. 1974. *The Canadian Legislative System: Politicians and Policy-Making*. Toronto: Macmillan.

Janda, Kenneth. 1968. "Future Improvements in Congressional Information Support," in Robert L. Chartrand, Kenneth Janda, and Michael Hugo, eds., *Information Support, Program Budgeting, and the Congress*. New York: Spartan Books, pp. 45-96.

Jewell, Malcolm E. 1969. *The State Legislature: Politics in Practice*. 2d ed. New York: Random House. 1st ed., 1962.

_____. 1970. "Attitudinal Determinants of Legislative Behavior: The Utility of Role Analysis," in Allan Kornberg and Lloyd D. Musolf, eds., *Legislatures in Developmental Perspective*. Durham, NC: Duke University Press, pp. 460-500.

Jewell, Malcolm E. and Albert F. Eldridge. 1977. "Conclusion: The Legislature as a Vehicle of National Integration," in Albert F. Eldridge, ed., *Legislatures in Plural Societies: The Search for Cohesion in National Development*. Durham, NC: Duke University Press, pp. 267-277.

Jewell, Malcolm E. and Samuel C. Patterson. 1977. *The Legislative Process in the United States*. 3d ed. New York: Random House.

Jones, Charles O. 1967. *Every Second Year*. Washington, DC: The Brookings Institution.

_____. 1977a. "How Reform Changes Congress," in Susan Welch and John G. Peters, eds., *Legislative Reform and Public Policy*. New York: Praeger. pp. 11-29.

_____. 1977b. "Will Reform Change Congress?" in Lawrence C. Dodd and Bruce I. Oppenheimer, eds., *Congress Reconsidered*. New York: Praeger, pp. 247-260.

_____. 1982. *The United States Congress: People, Place, and Policy*. Homewood, IL: Dorsey.

Junkins, Lowell L. 1978. "Changes in Legislative Procedure: The Iowa Experiment," *State Government* 51:173-179.

Kaiser, Fred M. 1977. "Structural and Policy Change: The House Committee on International Relations," *Policy Studies Journal* 5:443-450.

_____ . 1978. "Congressional Change and Foreign Policy: The House Committee on International Relations," in Leroy N. Rieselbach, ed., *Legislative Reform: The Policy Impact*. Lexington, MA: Lexington Books, pp. 61-71.

Kane, Peter E. 1971. "Extended Debate and the Rules of the United States Senate," *Quarterly Journal of Speech* 57:43-49.

Karnig, Albert K. and Lee Sigelman. 1975. "State Legislative Reform and Public Policy: Another Look," *Western Political Quarterly* 28:548-552.

Keefe, William J. 1971. "Reform and the American Legislature," in Donald G. Herzberg and Alan Rosenthal, eds., *Strengthening the States: Essays on Legislative Reform*. New York: Doubleday, pp. 183-193.

_____ . 1980. *Congress and the American People*. Englewood Cliffs, NJ: Prentice-Hall.

Keefe, William J. and Morris S. Ogul. 1977. *The American Legislative Process: Congress and the States*. 2d ed. Englewood Cliffs, NJ: Prentice-Hall.

Kernell, Sam. 1973. "Is the Senate More Liberal Than the House?" *Journal of Politics* 35:332-366.

Keynes, Edward. 1969. "The Senate Rules and the Dirksen Amendment: A Study in Legislative Strategy and Tactics," in Lawrence K. Pettit and Edward Keynes, eds., *The Legislative Process in the U.S. Senate*. Chicago: Rand McNally, pp. 107-150.

Kingdon, John W. 1981. *Congressmen's Voting Decisions*. 2d ed. New York: Harper & Row. 1st ed., 1973.

Kirkpatrick, Samuel A. 1978. *The Legislative Process in Oklahoma: Policy Making, People, and Politics*. Norman: University of Oklahoma Press.

Kirkpatrick, Samuel A. and Gary L. Cathey. 1972. *The Legislative Process in Oklahoma: Preliminary Foundations for a Legislative Manual*. Norman, OK: Bureau of Government Research.

Kirkpatrick, Samuel A. and Lelan McLemore. 1977. "Perceptual and Affective Components of Legislative Norms—Social Psychological Analysis of Congruity," *Journal of Politics* 39:685-711.

Kornberg, Allan. 1964. "The Rules of the Game in the Canadian House of Commons," *Journal of Politics* 26:358-380.

_____ . 1967. *Canadian Legislative Behavior: The Study of the Twenty-Fifth Parliament*. New York: Holt.

_____ . 1970. "Parliament in Canadian Society," in Allan Kornberg and Lloyd D. Musolf, eds., *Legislatures in Developmental Perspective*. Durham, NC: Duke University Press, pp. 55-128.

Kornberg, Allan and William Mishler. 1976. *Influence in Parliament: Canada*. Durham, NC: Duke University Press.

Kostroski, W.L. 1977. "Elections and Legislative Reform—External and Internal Influences on Legislative Behavior," *Policy Studies Journal* 5:414-418.

Lazarsfeld, Paul F. 1958. "Evidence and Inference in Social Research," *Daedalus* 87: 99-130.

Lee, J.M. 1963. "Parliament in Republican Ghana," *Parliamentary Affairs* 16:376-395.

Lees, John D. 1973. "Reorganization and Reform in Congress: Legislative Responses to Political and Social Change," *Government and Opposition* 8:195-216.

Lehnen, Robert G. 1967. "Behavior on the Senate Floor: An Analysis of Debate in the U.S. Senate," *Midwest Journal of Political Science* 11:505-521.

LeLoup, Lance T. 1978. "Reassessing the Mediating Impact of Legislative Capability," *American Political Science Review* 72:616-621.

Lockard, Duane. 1959. *New England State Politics*. Princeton: Princeton University Press.

Loewenberg, Gerhard. 1967. *Parliament in the German Political System*. Ithaca, NY: Cornell University Press.

_____ . 1973. "The Institutionalization of Parliament and Public Orientations to the Political System," in Allan Kornberg, ed., *Legislatures in Comparative Perspective*. New York: McKay, pp. 142-156.

Loewenberg, Gerhard and Samuel C. Patterson. 1979. *Comparing Legislatures*. Boston: Little, Brown.

Loomis, Burdett A. 1979. "The Congressional Office as a Small(?) Business: New Members Set Up Shop," *Publius* 9:35-55.

_____ . 1981a. "Congressional Caucuses and the Politics of Representation," in Lawrence C. Dodd and Bruce I. Oppenheimer, eds., *Congress Reconsidered*. 2d ed. Washington, DC: Congressional Quarterly, pp. 204-220.

_____ . 1981b. "The 'Me Decade' and the Changing Context of House Leadership," in Frank H. McKaman, ed., *Understanding Congressional Leadership*. Washington, DC: Congressional Quarterly, pp. 157-180.

Lovink, J.A.A. 1973. "Parliamentary Reform and Governmental Effectiveness in Canada," *Canadian Public Administration* 16:35-54.

Luce, Robert. 1922. *Legislative Procedure*. Boston: Houghton-Mifflin.

Lundquist, Lennert J. 1974. "Do Political Structures Matter in Environmental Politics? The Case of Air Pollution Control in Canada, Sweden, and the United States," *American Behavioral Scientist* 17:731-750.

Lyons, W. and L.W. Thomas. 1982. "Oversight in State Legislatures: Structural Attitudinal Interaction," *American Politics Quarterly* 10:117-133.

MacKintosh, John P. 1971. "Reform of the House of Commons: The Case for Specialization," in Gerhard Loewenberg, ed., *Modern Parliaments: Change or Decline*. Chicago: Aldine, pp. 33-63.

MacNeil, Neil. 1963. *Forge of Democracy: The House of Representatives*. New York: McKay.

Maisel, Louis Sandy. 1981. "Congressional Information Sources," in Joseph Cooper and G. Calvin Mackenzie, eds., *The House at Work*. Austin: University of Texas Press, pp. 247-274.

Malbin, Michael J. 1976. "House Reforms: The Emphasis is on Productivity, Not Power," *National Journal* 8:1731-1737.

_____ . 1981. "Delegation, Deliberation, and the New Role of Congressional Staff," in Thomas E. Mann and Norman J. Ornstein, eds., *The New Congress*. Washington, DC: American Enterprise Institute.

Mann, Thomas E. and Norman J. Ornstein, eds. 1981. *The New Congress*. Washington, DC: American Enterprise Institute.

Martin, Joseph (as told to Robert J. Donovan). 1960. *My First Fifty Years in Politics*. New York: McGraw-Hill.

Matsunaga, Spark M. and Ping Chen. 1976. *Rulemakers of the House*. Urbana: University of Illinois Press.

Matthews, Donald R. 1959. "The Folkways of the United States Senate: Conformity to Group Norms and and Legislative Effectiveness," *American Political Science Review* 53:1064-1089.

_____ . 1960. *U.S. Senators and Their World*. New York: Random House.

Mayhew, David R. 1974. *Congress: The Electoral Connection*. New Haven: Yale University Press.

McDowell, James L. 1977. "Legislative Reform in Indiana: The Promise and the Product," in Susan Welch and John G. Peters, eds., *Legislative Reform and Public Policy.* New York: Praeger, pp. 157-173.

McGraw, Darrell V., Jr. 1970. *The Role of the Lawmaker in West Virginia.* Washington, DC: American Political Science Association.

Meller, Norman. 1960. "Legislative Behavior Research," *Western Political Quarterly* 13:131-153.

Mezey, Michael L. 1979. *Comparative Legislatures.* Durham, NC: Duke University Press.

Mikva, Abner J. and Patti B. Sanis. 1983. *The American Congress: The First Branch.* New York: Franklin Watts.

Moncrief, Gary and Malcolm E. Jewell. 1980. "Legislators' Perceptions of Reform in Three States," *American Politics Quarterly* 8:106-127.

Monsma, Stephen V. 1969. "Integration and Goal Attainment as Functions of Informal Legislative Groups," *Western Political Quarterly* 22:19-28.

Munns, Joyce. 1975. "The Environment, Politics, and Policy Literature: A Critique and Reformulation," *Western Political Quarterly* 27:646-664.

Norton, Philip. 1980. "The Changing Face of the British House of Commons in the 1970's," *Legislative Studies Quarterly* 5:333-357.

_____ . 1981. "The House of Commons and the Constitution: The Challenges of the 1970's," *Parliamentary Affairs* 34:253-271.

O'Donnell, Thomas J. 1981. "Controlling Legislative Time," in Joseph Cooper and G. Calvin McKenzie, eds., *The House at Work.* Austin: University of Texas Press, pp. 127-150.

Ogul, Morris. 1976. *Congress Oversees the Bureaucracy: Studies in Legislative Supervision.* Pittsburgh: University of Pittsburgh Press.

Oleszek, Walter J. 1974. "House-Senate Relationships: Comity and Conflict," *Annals of the American Academy of Political and Social Science* 250:75-86.

_____ . 1978. *Congressional Procedures and the Policy Process.* Washington, DC: Congressional Quarterly.

Olson, David M. 1980. *The Legislative Process: A Comparative Approach.* New York: Harper & Row.

Opello, Walter C., Jr. 1978. "The New Parliament in Portugal," *Legislative Studies Quarterly* 3:309-334.

Oppenheimer, Bruce I. 1974. *Oil and the Congressional Process: The Limits of Symbolic Politics.* Lexington, MA: Lexington Books.

_____ . 1980. "Policy Effects of U.S. House Reform: Decentralization and the Capacity to Resolve Energy Issues," *Legislative Studies Quarterly* 5:5-30.

Orfield, Gary. 1975. *Congressional Power: Congress and Social Change.* New York: Harcourt Brace Jovanovich.

Ornstein, Norman J. 1975. "Causes and Consequences of Congressional Change: Subcommittee Reforms in the House of Representatives, 1970-73," in Norman J. Ornstein, ed., *Congress in Change: Evolution and Reform.* New York: Praeger, pp. 88-114.

_____ . 1981. "The House and the Senate in a New Congress," in Thomas E. Mann and Norman J. Ornstein, eds., *The New Congress.* Washington, DC: American Enterprise Institute, pp. 363-383.

Ornstein, Norman J. and David W. Rohde. 1977. "Shifting Forces, Changing Rules, and Political Outcomes: The Impact of Congressional Change on Four House Committees," in Robert L. Peabody and Nelson W. Polsby, eds., *New Perspectives on the House of Representatives.* 3d ed. New York: Rand McNally, pp. 186-270.

Ornstein, Norman J., Robert L. Peabody, and David W. Rohde. 1977. "The Changing Senate: From the 1950's to the 1970's," in Lawrence C. Dodd and Bruce I. Oppenheimer, eds., *Congress Reconsidered*. New York: Praeger, pp. 3-20.
_____ . 1981. "The Contemporary Senate: Into the 1980's," in Lawrence C. Dodd and Bruce I. Oppenheimer, eds., *Congress Reconsidered*. 2d ed. Washington, DC: Congressional Quarterly, pp. 13-30.
Ornstein, Norman J., Thomas E. Mann, Michael J. Malbin, and John F. Bibby. 1982. *Vital Statistics on Congress, 1982*. Washington, DC: American Enterprise Institute.
Page, Benjamin I. 1978. "Cooling the Legislative Tea," in Walter Dean Burnham and Martha Wagner Weinberg, eds., *American Politics and Public Policy*. Cambridge: MIT Press, pp. 171-187.
Palmer, Kenneth T., Kenneth P. Hayes, Edith L. Hary, James F. Horen, and Ronald Treachout. 1973. *The Legislative Process in Maine*. Washington, DC: American Political Science Association.
Panning, William H. 1982. "Rational Choice and Congressional Norms," *Western Political Quarterly* 35:193-203.
Parker, Glenn R. 1980a. "Sources of Change in Congressional District Attentiveness," *American Journal of Political Science* 24:115-124.
_____ . 1980b. "Cycles in Congressional District Attention," *Journal of Politics* 42:540-548.
_____ . 1981. "Can Congress Ever Be a Popular Institution?" in Joseph Cooper and G. Calvin Mackenzie, eds., *The House at Work*. Austin: University of Texas Press, pp. 31-55.
Parris, Judith H. 1979. "The Senate Reorganizes Its Committees, 1977," *Political Science Quarterly* 94:319-337.
Patterson, Samuel C. 1961. "The Role of the Deviant in the State Legislative System: The Wisconsin Assembly," *Western Political Quarterly* 14:460-472.
_____ . 1972. "Party Opposition in the Legislature: The Ecology of Legislative Institutionalization," *Polity* 4:345-366.
_____ . 1974. "Legislative Research and Legislative Reform: Evaluating Regime Policy," *Publius* 4:109-115.
_____ . 1977. "Conclusions: On the Study of Legislative Reform," in Susan Welch and John G. Peters, eds., *Legislative Reform and Public Policy*. New York: Praeger, pp. 214-222.
_____ . 1978. "The Semi-Sovereign Congress," in A. King, ed., *The New American Political System*. Washington, DC: American Enterprise Institute, pp. 125-178.
_____ . 1981. "Understanding Congress in the Long Run: A Comment on Joseph Cooper and David W. Brady, Toward a Diachronic Theory of Congress," *American Political Science Review* 75:1007-1009.
Patterson, Samuel C. and John C. Wahlke. 1972. "Trends and Prospects in Legislative Behavior Research," in Samuel C. Patterson and John C. Wahlke, eds., *Comparative Legislative Behavior: Frontiers of Research*. New York: Wiley, pp. 289-303.
Payne, James L. 1968. *Patterns of Conflict in Colombia*. New Haven: Yale University Press.
_____ . 1982. "Career Intentions and Electoral Performance of Members of the U.S. House," *Legislative Studies Quarterly* 7:93-100.
Peabody, Robert L. 1969. "Research on Congress: A Coming of Age," in Ralph K. Huitt and Robert L. Peabody, eds., *Congress: Two Decades of Analysis*. New York: Harper & Row, pp. 3-73.

Perkins, John A. 1946. "State Legislative Reorganization," *American Political Science Review* 40:510-520.

Pettit, Lawrence K. and Edward Keynes, eds. 1969. *The Legislative Process in the U.S. Senate*. Chicago: Rand McNally.

Pettit, Lawrence K., Kenneth P. Hayes, Edith L. Hary, James F. Horen, and Ronald Treachout. 1974. *Legislative Process in Montana*. Washington, DC: American Political Science Association.

Pierce, Lawrence C., Richard G. Frey, and S. Scott Pengelly. 1972. *The Freshman Legislator: Problems and Opportunities*. Washington, DC: American Political Science Association.

Polsby, Nelson W. 1968. "The Institutionalization of the U.S. House of Representatives," *The American Political Science Review* 62:144-168.

————. 1969. "Policy Analysis and Congress," *Public Policy* 18:61-74.

————. 1970. "Strengthening Congress in National Policy-Making," *Yale Review* 59:481-497.

————. 1975a. "Goodbye to the Senate's Inner Club," in Norman J. Ornstein, ed., *Congress in Change*. New York: Praeger, pp. 208-215.

————. 1975b. "Legislatures," in Fred I. Greenstein and Nelson W. Polsby, eds., *Handbook of Political Science*. Vol. 5. Reading, MA: Addison-Wesley, pp. 257-319.

Polsby, Nelson W., Miriam Gallaher, and Barry Spencer Rundquist. 1969. "The Growth of the Seniority System in the U.S. House of Representatives," *American Political Science Review* 63:787-807.

Porter, H. Owen. 1974. "Legislative Experts and Outsiders: The Two-Step Flow of Communication," *Journal of Politics* 36:703-730.

Price, Charles M. and Charles G. Bell. 1970. "The Rules of the Game: Political Fact or Academic Fancy?" *Journal of Politics* 32:839-853.

Price, David E. 1972. *Who Makes the Laws? Creativity and Power in Senate Committees*. Cambridge, MA: Schenkman Publishing.

————. 1978. "The Impact of Reform: The House Commerce Subcommittee of Oversight and Investigations," in Leroy N. Rieselbach, ed., *Legislative Reform: The Policy Impact*. Lexington, MA: Lexington Books, pp. 133-157.

Price, James L. 1968. *Organizational Effectiveness: An Inventory of Propositions*. Homewood, IL: Irwin.

Radway, Laurence I. 1972. *A Handbook for the New Hampshire General Court*. Hanover, NH: The Public Affairs Center.

Rakoff, Stuart H. and Ronald Sarner. 1975. "Bill History Analysis: A Probability Model of the State Legislative Process," *Polity* 7:402-414.

Ranney, Austin. 1981. "The Working Conditions of Members of Parliament and Congress: Changing the Tools Changes the Job," in Norman J. Ornstein, ed., *The Role of the Legislature in Western Democracies*. Washington, DC: American Enterprise Institute, pp. 67-76.

Ray, David. 1974. "Membership Stability in Three State Legislatures: 1839-1969," *American Political Science Review* 68:106-112.

Redman, Eric. 1973. *The Dance of Legislation*. New York: Simon and Schuster.

Reid, T.R. 1980. *Congressional Odyssey: The Saga of a Senate Bill*. San Francisco: Freeman.

Riddick, Floyd M. 1949. *The United States Congress: Organization and Procedure*. Manasses, VA: National Capitol Publishers.

Rieselbach, Leroy N. 1975. "Congressional Reform: Some Policy Implications," *Policy Studies Journal* 4:180-188.

_____ . 1977. *Congressional Reform in the Seventies*. Morristown, NJ: General Learning.

Riggs, Fred W. 1973. "Legislative Structures: Some Thoughts on Elected National Assemblies," in Allan Kornberg, ed., *Legislatures in Comparative Perspective*. New York: McKay, pp. 39-93.

Riker, William H. 1958. "The Paradox of Voting and Congressional Rules for Voting Amendments," *American Political Science Review* 52:349-366.

Ripley, Randall B. 1969. *Power in the Senate*. New York: St. Martin's Press.

_____ . 1978. *Congress: Process and Policy*. 2d ed. New York: Norton.

Ritt, Leonard. 1973. "State Legislative Reform: Does It Matter?" *American Politics Quarterly* 1:499-510.

_____ . 1976. "Committee Position, Seniority, and the Distribution of Government Expenditures," *Public Policy* 24:463-489.

_____ . 1977. "The Policy Impact of Legislative Reform: A 50-State Analysis," in Susan Welch and John G. Peters, eds., *Legislative Reform and Public Policy*. New York: Praeger, pp. 189-200.

Robinson, James A. 1967. *Congress and Foreign Policy-Making*. Rev. ed. Homewood, IL: Dorsey. Orig. ed., 1962.

_____ . 1963. *The House Rules Committee*. Indianapolis: Bobbs-Merrill.

Robinson, Michael J. 1975. "A Twentieth-Century Medium in a Nineteenth-Century Legislature: The Effects of Television on the American Congress," in Norman J. Ornstein, ed., *Congress in Change: Evolution and Reform*. New York: Praeger, pp. 240-261.

Roeder, P.W. 1979. "State Legislative Reform—Determinants and Policy Consequences," *American Politics Quarterly* 7:51-69.

Rogers, Lindsay. 1921. "American Government and Politics, Notes on Congressional Procedure," *American Political Science Review* 15:71-81.

Rohde, David W. 1974. "Committee Reform in the House of Representatives and the Subcommittee Bill of Rights," *Annals of the American Academy of Political and Social Sciences* 250:39-47.

Rohde, David W. and Kenneth A. Shepsle. 1978. "Thinking about Legislative Reform," in Leroy N. Rieselbach, ed., *Legislative Reform: The Policy Impact*. Lexington, MA: Lexington Books, pp. 9-21.

Rosenthal, Alan. 1981a. "Legislative Behavior and Legislative Oversight," *Legislative Studies Quarterly* 6:115-131.

_____ . 1981b. *Legislative Life: People, Process, and Performance in the States*. New York: Harper & Row.

Rosenthal, Alan and Susan Fahrman. 1981. *Legislative Education Leadership in the States*. Washington, DC: Institute for Educational Leadership.

Rosenthal, Alan and Rod Forth. 1978. "The Assembly Line: Law Production in the American States," *Legislative Studies Quarterly* 3:265-291.

Rousse, Thomas A. 1937. *Bicameralism vs. Unicameralism*. New York: Thomas Nelson.

Rudder, Catherine. 1978. "The Policy Impact of Reform of the Committee on Ways and Means," in Leroy N. Rieselbach, ed., *Legislative Reform: The Policy Impact*. Lexington, MA: Lexington Books, pp. 73-89.

Sait, Edward McChesney. 1938. *Political Institutions*. Boston: Houghton-Mifflin.

Salisbury, Robert H. and Kenneth A. Shepsle. 1981a. "U.S. Congressman as Enterprise," *Legislative Studies Quarterly* 6:559-576.

_____ . 1981b. "Congressional Staff Turnover and the Ties-That-Bind," *American Political Science Review* 75:381-396.

Saloma, John S. III. 1969. *Congress and the New Politics*. Boston: Little, Brown.

Schwab, Larry M. 1980. *Changing Patterns of Congressional Politics*. New York: Van Nostrand.

Schwarz, John E. and L. Earl Shaw. 1976. *The United States Congress in Comparative Perspective*. Hinsdale, IL: Dryden Press.

Searing, Donald D. 1982. "Rules of the Game in Britain: Can the Politicians Be Trusted?" *American Political Science Review* 76:239-257.

Shaffer, William R. and Ronald E. Weber. 1974. *Policy Responsiveness in the American States*. Beverly Hills, CA: Sage Publishing.

Shapley, L.S. and Martin Shubik. 1954. "A Method for Evaluating the Distribution of Power in a Committee System," *American Political Science Review* 48: 787-792.

Sharkansky, Ira. 1967. "Economic and Political Correlates of State Government Expenditures: General Tendencies and Deviant Cases," *Midwest Journal of Political Science* 11:173-192.

Shaw, Malcolm. 1981. "Congress in the 1970's: A Decade of Reform," *Parliamentary Affairs* 34:272-290.

Shepsle, Kenneth A. 1979a. "Institutional Arrangements and Equilibrium in Multi-Dimensional Voting Models," *American Journal of Political Science* 23:27-59.

_____ . 1979b. "The Role of Institutional Structure in the Creation of Policy Equilibrium," in Douglas W. Rae and Theodore J. Eismeir, eds., *Public Policy and Public Choice*. Beverly Hills, CA: Sage Publishing, pp. 249-281.

Shuman, Howard E. 1957. "Senate Rules and the Civil Rights Bill: A Case Study," *American Political Science Review* 51:955-975.

Simon, Maurice D. and David M. Olson. 1980. "Evolution of a Minimal Parliament: Membership and Committee Changes in the Polish Sejm," *Legislative Studies Quarterly* 5:211-232.

Sinclair, Barbara. 1981a. "Agenda and Alignment Change: The House of Representatives, 1925-1978," in Lawrence C. Dodd and Bruce I. Oppenheimer, eds., *Congress Reconsidered*. 2d ed. Washington, DC: Congressional Quarterly, pp. 221-245.

_____ . 1981b. "The Speaker's Task Force in the Post-Reform House of Representatives," *American Political Science Review* 75:397-410.

_____ . 1983. "Purposive Behavior in the U.S. Congress: A Review Essay," *Legislative Studies Quarterly* 8:117-131.

Singhvi, L.M. 1970. "Parliament in the Indian Political System," in Allan Kornberg and Lloyd D. Musolf, eds., *Legislatures in Developmental Perspective*. Durham, NC: Duke University Press, pp. 179-227.

Sisson, Richard. 1966. "Institutionalization and Style in the Rajasthan Congress," *Asian Survey* 6:605-613.

_____ . 1973. "Comparative Legislative Institutionalization: A Theoretical Exploration," in Allan Kornberg, ed., *Legislatures in Comparative Perspective*. New York: McKay, pp. 17-38.

Somit, Albert and Joseph Tanenhaus. 1967. *The Development of Political Science: From Burgess to Behavioralism*. Boston: Allyn and Bacon.

Sorauf, Frank J. 1963. *Party and Representation: Legislative Politics in Pennsylvania*. New York: Atherton.

Stanga, John E., Jr. and David N. Farnsworth. 1978. "Seniority and Democratic Reforms in the House of Representatives: Committees and Subcommittees," in Leroy N. Rieselbach, ed., *Legislative Reform: The Policy Impact*. Lexington, MA: Lexington Books, pp. 35-47.

Stauffer, Robert B. 1970. "Congress in the Philippine Political System," in Allan Kornberg and Lloyd D. Musolf, eds., *Legislatures in Developmental Perspective.* Durham, NC: Duke University Press, pp. 334-365.

Steiner, Gilbert Y. and Samuel K. Gove. 1960. *Legislative Politics in Illinois.* Urbana: University of Illinois Press.

Stevens, A.G., D.P. Mulhollan, and P.S. Rundquist. 1981. "United States Congressional Structure and Representation–The Role of Informal Groups," *Legislative Studies Quarterly* 6:415-437.

Stewart, John B. 1977. *The Canadian House of Commons: Procedures and Reform.* Toronto: McGill, Queen's University Press.

Stultz, Newell M. 1970. "The National Assembly in the Politics of Kenya," in Allan Kornberg and Lloyd D. Musolf, eds., *Legislatures in Developmental Perspective.* Durham, NC: Duke University Press, pp. 303-333.

Sullivan, John L. 1972. "A Note on Redistributive Politics," *American Political Science Review* 66:1301-1305.

Sundquist, James L. 1968. *Politics and Policy: The Eisenhower, Kennedy, and Johnson Years.* Washington, DC: The Brookings Institution.

_____ . 1980. "The Crisis of Competence in Our National Government," *Political Science Quarterly* 95:183-208.

_____ . 1981. *A Decline and Resurgence of Congress.* Washington, DC: The Brookings Institution.

Swenson, Peter. 1982. "The Influence of Recruitment on the Structure of Power in the U.S. House, 1870-1940," *Legislative Studies Quarterly* 7:7-36.

Tacheron, Donald G. and Morris K. Udall. 1970. *The Job of the Congressman.* 2d ed. Indianapolis: Bobbs-Merrill. 1st ed., 1966.

Tatalovich, Raymond. 1978. "Legislative Quality and Legislative Policy Making: Some Implications for Reform," in Leroy N. Rieselbach, ed., *Legislative Reform: The Policy Impact.* Lexington, MA: Lexington Books.

Thurber, James A. 1978. "New Powers of the Purse: An Assessment of Congressional Budget Reform," in Leroy N. Rieselbach, ed., *Legislative Reform: The Policy Impact.* Lexington, MA: Lexington Books, pp. 159-172.

Toll, Henry W. 1928. "The Work of the American Legislator's Association," *American Political Science Review* 22:127-129.

Truman, David B. 1951. *The Governmental Process: Political Interests and Public Opinion.* New York: Knopf.

Tubbesing, Carl D. 1975. "Does Changing the Rules Change the Players?" *State Government* 48:79-84.

Unruh, Jess. 1971. "Unicameralism–the Wave of the Future," in Donald G. Herzberg and Alan Rosenthal, eds., *Strengthening the States: Essays on Legislative Reform.* Garden City, NY: Doubleday, pp. 87-94.

Uslaner, Eric M. and Ronald E. Weber. 1975. "The 'Politics' of Redistribution: Towards a Model of the Policy-Making Process in the American States," *American Politics Quarterly* 3:130-170.

_____ . 1977. *Patterns of Decision Making in State Legislatures.* New York: Praeger.

Van der Slik, Jack R. 1977. *American Legislative Processes.* New York: Crowell.

Vanneman, Peter. 1977. *The Supreme Soviet: Politics and the Legislative Process in the Soviet Political System.* Durham, NC: Duke University Press.

Volger, David J. 1974. *The Politics of Congress.* Boston: Allyn and Bacon.

Wahlke, John C. 1966. "Organization and Procedure," in Alexander Heard, ed., *State Legislatures in Politics.* Englewood Cliffs, NJ: Prentice-Hall, pp. 126-153.

Wahlke, John C., Heinz Eulau, William Buchanan, and LeRoy C. Ferguson. 1962. *The Legislative System: Explorations in Legislative Behavior.* New York: Wiley.

Walsh, John. 1973. "Reform in the House: Amending the Seniority Rule," *Science* 179: 877-881.

Weinbaum, Marvin G. 1972. "Afghanistan: Non Party Parliamentary Democracy," *Journal of Developing Areas* 7:57-74.

Weingast, Barry R. 1979. "A Rational Choice Perspective on Congressional Norms," *American Journal of Political Science* 23:245-262.

Welsh, William A. 1980. "The Status of Research on Representative Institutions in Eastern Europe," *Legislative Studies Quarterly* 5:275-308.

Whalen, Charles W., Jr. 1982. *The House and Foreign Policy: The Irony of Congressional Reform.* Chapel Hill: University of North Carolina Press.

Wheare, K.C. 1963. *Legislatures.* New York: Oxford University Press.

White, Graham. 1979. "Teaching the Mongrel Dog New Tricks: Sources and Directions of Reform in the Ontario Legislature," *Journal of Canadian Studies* 2:117-132.

White, William S. 1956. *Citadel: The Story of the U.S. Senate.* New York: Harper & Row.

Wiggins, Charles W. 1970. *The Iowa Lawmaker.* Washington, DC: American Political Science Association.

Winters, Richard. 1977. "Legislative Reform and Legislative Cleavages," in Susan Welch and John G. Peters, eds., *Legislative Reform and Public Policy.* New York: Praeger, pp. 111-127.

Wissel, Peter, Robert O'Connor, and Michael King. 1976. "The Hunting of the Legislative Snark: Information Searches and Reforms in U.S. State Legislatures," *Legislative Studies Quarterly* 1:251-268.

Witmer, T. Richard. 1964. "The Aging of the House," *Political Science Quarterly* 79: 526-537.

Wohlenberg, Ernest H. 1980. "Correlates of Equal Rights Amendment Ratification," *Social Science Quarterly* 60:676-684.

Wolfinger, Raymond E. 1971. "Filibusters: Majority Rule, Presidential Leadership and Senate Norms," in Nelson W. Polsby, ed., *Congressional Behavior.* New York: Random House, pp. 111-127.

Wolfinger, Raymond E. and Joan Heifetz Hollinger. 1971. "Safe Seats, Seniority, and Power in Congress," in Raymond E. Wolfinger, ed., *Readings on Congress.* Englewood Cliffs, NJ: Prentice-Hall, pp. 36-58.

Woll, Peter. 1963. *American Bureaucracy.* New York: Norton.

Worthley, John A. 1977a. "Legislatures and Information Systems: Challenges and Responses in the States," in Abdo Baaklini and James J. Heaphey, eds., *Comparative Legislative Reforms and Innovations.* Albany: State University of New York at Albany, pp. 154-172.

————. 1977b. "Legislative Information Systems: A Review and Analysis of Recent Experience," *Western Political Quarterly* 30:418-430.

Worthley, John A. and Edgar G. Crane. 1976. "Organizational Dimensions of State Legislatures," *Midwest Review Public Administration* 10:14-30.

Worthley, John A. and Jack C. Overstreet. 1978. "Modern Technology Applied to Traditional Political Functions: The Florida Senate Ombudsman Program," *Polity* 11:280-289.

Wyner, Alan J. 1973. "Legislative Reform in Politics in California: What Happened, Why, and So What?" in James A. Robinson, ed., *State Legislative Innovation: Studies of Washington, Ohio, Florida, Illinois, Wisconsin, and California.* New York: Praeger, pp. 46-100.

Yarwood, Dean L. 1970. "Norm Observance and Legislative Integration: The U.S. Senate in 1850 and 1860," *Social Science Quarterly* 51:57-69.

Young, Roland. 1958. *The American Congress.* New York: Harper & Row.

Zeller, Belle, ed. 1954. *American State Legislatures.* New York: Harper & Row.

Zwier, Robert. 1979. "The Search for Information: Specialists and Non-Specialists in the U.S. House of Representatives," *Legislative Studies Quarterly* 4:31-42.

PART THREE

Legislative Processes

Chapter 9

Standing Committees
In Legislatures

by

HEINZ EULAU
VERA MCCLUGGAGE

Critical and meaningful examination of the plethora of now-extant legislative committee studies recommends, first, a definition of boundaries—what will be included or excluded—and, second, a preliminary overview of research development. It is only in the context of scope and development that particular studies obtain whatever theoretical, methodological, or substantive significance they may have. We shall provide this context, in highly condensed and stylized manner, after presenting a brief outline of the contents of this essay.

The essay deals solely with studies of standing committees, mainly in the Congress of the United States, to some extent in U.S. state legislatures, and to a very limited extent abroad. Not included, then, are studies of conference, joint, select, special, and investigatory committees or of informal committees and party committees. Also not included is coverage of the committee assignment process and its implications for committee structures, functions, and behavior. Finally, not included are a number of, from our standpoint, auxiliary, peripheral, and supplemental studies covered in other essays of this series, notably studies of committee-agency-interest group interactions and of legislative staffing.

There are any number of ways in which we could have organized and presented the materials. Because our accent is on research approaches, both theoretical and methodological, we found it convenient to adopt the following categories:

1. topical single-committee studies
2. integral single-committee studies
3. comparative committee case studies
4. synchronic-aggregate studies
5. diachronic-aggregate studies
6. institutional change studies
7. comparative systems studies

Committees In Level-of-Analysis Perspective

In spite of the enormous output of committee and committee-related studies, there is no definition of "committee" helpful in orienting theory and research. That the committee is a "human group" is not saying very much; that it is a "system" may be saying too much; that it is a "little legislature"—a microcosm that replicates the legislature as a whole—has been disavowed.

In the level-of-analysis perspective, legislative committees can be defined as institutionalized, specialized, interactive, interstitial, and structurally more or less similar collective units of action that intervene between the individual member, the legislator in committee, and the larger "whole," the legislature, of which both the individual member and the committee are "parts" (Eulau, 1969).[1] Each of the five properties specified in this definition points to any number of problems, observational and explanatory, that can only be solved in a multi-level perspective. The notion of the committee's interstitiality is particularly helpful in answering the question of whether studying the committee "in its own right"—or, as one might put it, at its own level of analysis—is scientifically warranted. The question was raised by Cooper (1971) in a prior review of research on congressional committees. Comparative analysis, Cooper points out, "is neither the only possible new strategy nor the only one that should be pursued"; indeed,

there is an essential range of conceptualization and empirical research that will not issue out of a focus on committees, but rather requires a higher level focus on Congress itself both in relation to the broader political system and in relation to its subsystems (p. 131).

In the level-of-analysis perspective, then, the boundaries of whole and parts are permeable, and the problem is not one of setting parts and whole off against each other but rather one of determining where to draw the line—what to include and exclude in a definition of committees. The notion of interstitiality requires exclusion, at one extreme, of units like autonomous city councils, boards, commissions, and so on. Although such units intervene between the individual member and some citizenry, electorate, or constituency in need of representation because they cannot act on their own, they are not parts of a whole as a legislative committee is part of a parent chamber.

At the other extreme, interstitiality precludes identifying committees with "elections," as formulated, for instance, by Black (1958). Both committees and elections involve voting and voting strategies, including preference structuring, coalition formation or logrolling, and so on. But these phenomena, though occurring in both contexts, do not, as such, define committees as institutionalized and interstitial units of collective action.

As parts of a whole, committees also stand in particular relationships to each other. These relationships, in turn, make for a "committee system" that can also be conceptualized as a "whole" but must not be confused with the legislature as a whole. The difference is, of course, that the legislature is a concrete structure and collective unit of action, while the committee system is an analytic structure and, as such, does not constitute a collective unit of action.

The level-of-analysis perspective calls attention to the possibility of empirically observing the committee as an "object unit" in terms of, minimally, three subject units of action—the individual legislators composing the committee, the committee itself (which, then, is both subject and object of analysis), and the legislature. The focus of observation may be on a single member (for instance, the chairman, as in Manley, 1969), though what is to be explained is not only his/her behavior but also committee behavior; or the focus may be on all members as individuals—their attributes, preferences, goals, roles, or interactions, and so on. The individual members are treated as subunits, and observations or measurements conducted on subunit variables may be used to construct a profile of the committee, either by aggregation or, in the case of observations on member interactions, by some sort of sociometric device. Aggregation is used, for instance, in measuring committee prestige out of observations on committee assignments or transfers. However, there are committee properties that are not reducible to member attributes or interactions, such as committee norms, decision rules, structural arrangements, outputs, and so on. These are properties of the committee and not of an individual member. It is the existence of such integral properties that makes the committee a collective unit rather than a mere aggregate.

Finally, the level-of-analysis perspective suggests that the committee may also be described in terms of properties attributed to it by virtue of its location in various environments. The most significant factors in the context of any one committee are other committees and the parent chamber. (There are also other significant environmental factors—bureaucratic agencies, lobbies, constituencies, and so on; but they vary from committee to committee.

Which is the most important factor is not our concern here.) The existence of other committees gives rise to the "committee system," but as the system is not a directly observable unit, its properties cannot be attributed to the committee. The committee, though a unit in the system, is not an interstitial structure between its members and the committee system, and it does not perform a function for the system, because the system itself cannot act in any meaningful sense of the word "act." The notion of the committee system calls attention to the relationships between and among committees, but it is other committees and not the committee system that constitute a context for committee behavior. We note all this because there is a good deal of confusion in the literature, especially at the macro level, where committee properties are sometimes inferred from presumed properties of the system.

"Committee system" easily rolls off the analytic tongue, often inadvertently or thoughtlessly. It is mostly used then as a summary term to refer to the aggregate of committees in a legislature that, as a result of their location in it, are assumed to share certain characteristics, properties, or qualities. In fact, the committees share only one property: the common environment of the legislature. But even this condition makes for suspect classification: their collective environment may and usually does impinge on committees in different ways, partly because the environment is itself not an undifferentiated unit and partly because different committees are differentially receptive to the same environmental factors.

Another use of the term "committee system" refers to the general functions that all committees presumably perform for the legislature, especially allowing its members to divide labor, specialize, represent, influence outcomes, and so on. Reference, then, is to the committee system as being characterized by these functions. Or the committee system is characterized in structural terms, presumably as a result of detailed observations but often only as a result of generalized impressions—centralized or decentralized, integrated or fragmented, autonomous or controlled, effective or ineffective, and so on. These generalized structural characterizations are then likely to be reified and become "properties" of the committee system, and the "system" is given more reality than is empirically tenable or theoretically warranted.

By way of contrast, the house or parent chamber, of which the committee is a part, constitutes a unit of collective action—it has decision rules, norms, organizational arrangements, and policy outputs that can be observed at its own level without recourse to either its individual members or committees. Many other house properties are, of course, reducible. For instance, committee studies sometimes refer to "house expectations" concerning desirable committee action. This is short-hand language. It refers to what some, many, or all individual members of the legislature "expect"—in a normative sense—a given committee to do or not to do. "House expectations," then, are empirically aggregative properties of the legislature. Again, they may be observed by way of interviews with the universe or a sample of house members and then aggregated, or they may be inferred from statements made by informants who may or may not be members. In practice, committee studies have relied on information from committee members themselves—that is, on committee members' perceptions of what "house expectations" are. However constructed, such perceptions of the house are treated as contextual variables and attributed to the committee by the investigator. From the standpoint of the observer, then, the house is a "superunit," while the committee and its members are subunits. Being a subunit, the committee shares with other committees the legislature as an environment whose properties constitute contextual properties of its own.

Investigators are not always explicit about the unit of analysis on which they conduct their observations, on the one hand, and the unit whose behavior they seek to explain or interpret, on the other hand. Moving from a unit at one level of analysis to a unit at another level occurs most often in case studies, whose strength and weakness stem from their multi-level character. It is less likely in studies of a quantitative sort, in which the need to specify a model's variables alerts the investigator to the problems involved. One reason for moving from one level to another is, of course, pragmatic: it is sometimes difficult or impossible to observe the unit whose behavior is to be explained. In general, the smaller the unit, the more easily it can be observed. On the other hand, in general, larger units produce and leave collective "records" not available for individuals or small groups. And as units are "nested" within each other—individual members in subcommittees, subcommittees in committees, committees in a house, with behavioral "effects" in both directions, a multi-level approach is not only plausible but also commendable.

Sensitivity to the source of data made possible by the level-of-analysis perspective is important because it helps to clarify what observations can be made for what analytic purposes, what measurements or manipulations can be performed on the data, and what extrapolations are permissible from one level to another. Just as the aggregate behavior of individual members does not permit inference to the collective behavior of the committee, so the collective behavior of the committee does not permit inference to the aggregate behavior of its members, not to say the behavior of any one member. Failure to appreciate the source and nature of data in terms of the level-of-analysis perspective tends to make for false inferences and flawed interpretations when it comes to the explanation of committee behavior.

Development: A Generational Overview

To convey a sense of both continuity and discontinuity in the development of research on legislative committees, it is convenient to think in terms of "generations" of studies. "Generation" is not used here as a strictly chronological concept. Studies "late in time" may belong, in theoretical or methodological stance and style, to an earlier generation; and studies "early in time" may anticipate a later generation. A generation of studies may well seem to "die out" at some point in time; but it may also be "regenerated" at a later point. Overlap across generations makes for continuity; but because each new generation tends to see older generations as "old-fashioned," there is also discontinuity.

The "modern era" of legislative committee research can be dated to what we shall call a "topical single-committee study" by Huitt (1954). Huitt was eminently self-conscious about his effort—or, as one must acknowledge today, his achievement. " 'Congressional government is Committee government' said Woodrow Wilson in 1884,[2] and political scientists since that day have seen no reason to disagree with him. . . . The frequency with which Wilson is quoted is as much a reflection of a lack of substantive research by later students as it is a tribute to his intuitive insights" (p. 340). Twelve years later, in his magisterial work on the congressional Appropriations Committees, Fenno (1966) also paid his respects to Wilson: "His quotable aphorisms and his forceful generalizations are copybook maxims in political science. They have dominated our monographs and our textbooks since 1885" (p. xvi). Peabody (1969) referring to the "qualitative phase of the behavioral approach" beginning about 1950, suggests that it "had its forerunner in Wilson's *Congressional Government*" and that "in his classic essay he was attempting to break away from formal and literary treatments of the Constitution to a description of how the federal government actually worked" (p. 4).

Wilson's book evidently eclipsed a work specifically dealing with congressional committees by Lauros G. McConachie, published in 1898. While occasionally cited in footnotes, especially in work dealing with institutionalization (Polsby, 1968; Cooper, 1970; Douglas Price, 1977), McConachie's book has been neglected. The book is a much more profound, better researched, and better balanced study than Wilson's, though its approach is in the Spencerian social-evolutionary mode then prominent in social science, and its language is at times quaint and often turgid in contrast to Wilson's verbal clarity and elegance.

First Generation: Role, Interaction, Group, Class

When Huitt (1954) published what is generally recognized as the first behavioral study of a committee, he drew on anthropological culture theory and sociological interaction theory. However, there was more continuity with what had gone before than later mystique acknowledged. Truman (1951) had provided the link to the past by reviving and enriching the theory of politics as "group process" that had been developed by Bentley (1908). Legislators are no longer seen as arbitrators of the "group struggle," but as participants in it. And they are seen as participating in the struggle not only as individuals linked to their constituents in characteristic ways, but as groups of their own. Huitt clearly did not find in the earlier strongly reform-oriented literature (Chamberlain, 1936; Galloway, 1946; Griffith, 1951) much that could be helpful in understanding the formal patterns in and of the committee as an arena of legislative action. He singles out Gross (1953) as providing "a realistic description of the operations of congressional com-mittees" (p. 342, fn. 9). Gross's relevant chapters are, it is true, more realistic than what one encounters in the earlier texts, but his mode of analysis is quite traditional: Gross generally makes more or less plausible assertions and generalizations which are then "substantiated" by illustrative anecdotes from historical events or situations.

Huitt's own role as a scholar bridging the generations appears in a certain ambivalence toward the committee's position in the legislative process. Following Galloway (1946), he still refers to committees as "miniature legislatures" or "microcosms" of their parent bodies, a notion which appears to have made him sufficiently uncomfortable to amend it quickly, though the amendment itself has since been amended: committees are "microcosms" of their parent bodies "not in the sense that they epitomize the larger houses, but rather that the committees are subject to the same influences and power drives, which are easier to intercept and analyze here than in the larger and more complex houses themselves" (p. 340). It has since been learned that particular committees are not only not subject to the "same influences" as the chambers as wholes, but the chambers themselves are significant environments for their committees, therefore precluding any isomorphic assumptions about similarities which the notion of the committee as a "mini-ature legislature" or "microcosm" implies.

That quality and quantity are not antagonistic characteristics of committee research appears in the second major first-generation study to be noted—a more generic, aggregative study of Senate committees by Matthews (1960), constituting a chapter in his comprehensive work on the U.S. Senate. Like Huitt's research, Matthews's study represents a break with the same past, though it follows an altogether different route, drawing on different sociological theories as well as relying on the interview and quantifiable or quantified data in both portraying committees and testing some propositions about them or their members' behavior.

Like Huitt, Matthews is self-conscious about his "departure from the traditional ways of studying the Senate or, for that matter, any other legis-lative chamber. . . . Our behavioral perspective leads us to ask somewhat different questions than did the earlier scholars" (pp. 7-8). Matthews's dependence on sociological theory appears less directly in his chapter on committees than elsewhere in his book. There are two distinct lines: first, stratification and social class approaches to both individual and collective behavior; and second, European elite theories. The pervasiveness of relevant ideas in the chapter on committees is clearly apparent. There is a concern with the committee as a "caste system," which indicates the influence of the stratification approach, and with individual and group influence, power, or effectiveness which indicates the impact of elite-theoretical notions.

Matthews was one of the first students of Congress trained in quantitative techniques, even though, at the time, the techniques were relatively simple. But for the time, his use of these techniques and their application to subject matter later intensively studied by many investigators—committee assignments, committee constituency composition, chairman selection and power, committee prestige, committee floor success, committee member effectiveness, and so on—make his work prototypical. Finally, one finds the rudiments of causal analysis which presupposes clear operationalization and specification of variables in the testing of hypotheses.

Second Generation: System, Structure, Function

By the early 1960s, "systems theory" had become the theoretical rage in political science, at least among those who thought of themselves as working at the discipline's scientific cutting edge. Originally launched in biology, systems notions, along with a structural-functional mode of analysis, had been elaborated for sociology by Parsons (1951), and a first sketch of their potential uses in political science had been drawn by Easton (1953, 1957). The idea of a "legislative system" as something more than the legislative institution, combined with role-analytic concepts, had given direction to the comparative study of four U.S. state systems by Wahlke, Eulau, Buchanan, and Ferguson, begun in 1955 and published in 1962. System ideas of various origins thus permeated the intellectual culture of political science when Fenno (1962) brought some of these ideas to the study of the House Appropriations Committee.

Ten years later, systems and/or structural-functional analysis were no longer in fashion. This makes it all the more important to inspect briefly Fenno's justification for using systems theory, but also to consider the second most significant work in this generation, a study of the House Ways and Means Committee by Manley (1965, 1970).

Fenno (1966, p. xix) gives three major reasons why "this amalgam of theoretical notions" seemed to him "especially congenial to a committee-centered description of congressional activity." First, the idea of system covers "the full range of a committee's internal and external relationships. . . . What the idea of system sacrifices in precision, therefore, is compensated for in the large number of interrelated variables that can be accommodated." Because the committee is relatively small, so that one can observe greater complexity than in larger units like city, state, or nation, "a general level of theory seems particularly useful in organizing an empirical description."

Second, Fenno finds that the idea of system is "valuable intellectual baggage" in that it forces the investigator "to ask what consequences, if any, one kind of observed activity has for other kinds of observed activity" and especially in that "the researcher may discover relationships that had not occurred to him before." Here Fenno refers to structural-functional analysis which, in its requisite version, directs attention to "a variety of survival problems." Finally, the idea of system is useful in analysis of "a set of inter-related activities which do in fact recur fairly frequently and which in fact persist for considerable periods of time." At this point Fenno makes a revealing statement—revealing because it symptomizes the intellectual climate of the early 1960s: "Most congressional committees display these properties most of the time. . . . This does not mean, however, that the notion of system precludes the analysis of change. Where a set of activities is fairly stable, most changes are incremental and small scale. And this kind of change can be identified, explained, and perhaps, predicted within the rubric of system description." Systems analysis was congenial to the quiescent political bias of the 1950s and early 1960s. By 1970, Congress was in the ferment of reform. Of course, systems theory is not a political theory, and it lingered on into the 1970s and is being revived. But by 1970 it was no longer the dominant paradigm at the frontier of research.

Manley's work is especially revealing because it shows the process of the generation's intellectual journey from systems analysis to a new model of committee behavior between the time when his article was pub-lished in 1965 and the time of his book's publication in 1970. In the article, Manley cites several of the familiar works in anthropology, sociology, and social psychology that had fertilized recent political science. Not that, in the 1970 book, he abandons systems theory and functionalism altogether. But unlike Fenno, Manley finds these approaches flawed. He describes how his study moved from the systems to the small-group literature, "when 'grand' theory, as Merton discusses it, proved too grand to be of much specific help," and how it "came to rest heavily on the inducement-contribution theory of Barnard and similar notions in the exchange theory of Homans and Blau" (p. 7).

In some respects, the marriage of the "grand theory" of systems and the individual-centered behavioralism of modern political science was always somewhat morganatic. The new vocabulary that Manley finds attractive—inducement, incentive, cost, and benefit—was already present in the "eco-nomic" models that would soon give an individual-oriented behavioralism a new boost.

Third Generation: Statistical Models and Methods

It is not easy to name the generation of theoretically heterogenous studies, probably initiated in the late 1960s but not reported until the early 1970s, that emerged as an alternative to the system and functional approaches. Two developments in social science generally contributed to the new generation of quantitative-statistical and methodological studies. Simon (1957) had challenged social scientists to think more rigorously in causal terms, and he had suggested the propinquity of the scientific notion of "cause" and the political notion of "power." Simon's work was soon followed by the "more practical" and quickly influential work of Blalock (1964) on causal inferences in nonexperimental research. The computer revolution permitted increasingly complex multivariate analyses. In the legislative field, roll-call votes, first on the floor alone (used for decades, if rather simply) but later also in committees, were available for modelling and statistical treatment, though they initially dealt with individual members and aggregates rather than committees (Fiorina, 1974).

Beginning about 1970, a series of studies seek to account for "committee floor success" in terms of independent variables, built from roll-call votes or other quantified measures, such as committee attractiveness (usually based on committee assignments or transfers), integration, partisanship, seniority (influence), or constituency similarity. These studies try to overcome the low generalizability of the single-committee case studies by dealing with many or all committees in a comparative-statistical manner, often aggregating over time data synchronically but also dealing with them diachronically.

What some of these studies lacked in theory they make up in methodological finesse. They deal either with data on committee assignments or on floor roll-call votes in efforts to explain committee behavior. The latter, more often than not, cover either a single session (Dodd, 1972) or, like Dyson and Soule (1970), several sessions in a synchronic manner, aggregating time-series data into single measures. Although claiming to be influenced by systems theory or small-group theory, their points of theoretical departure are just that: departures without arrival. Instead, implicit or explicit causal models give these studies their particular stamp. Early debate over the legitimacy of using floor roll-call votes for inferences about committee behavior was resolved, in the late 1970s and early 1980s, as investigators obtained access to votes taken in committee following the congressional reforms of the period. More recently, a number of comparative-systemic studies of U.S. state legislatures, especially by Hamm (1980) and Francis and Riddlesperger (1982), represent a revival of third-generation studies. One can also include in this generation a number of studies which use quantitative data diachronically, providing in fact a firmer basis for inference about committee activities and changes in the committee system. The *locus classicus* of these studies is Polsby's (1968; Polsby, Gallaher, and Rundquist, 1969) work on institutionalization in the House of Representatives. A study of change in five state committee systems by Hamm and Moncrief (1982) is noteworthy.

Fourth Generation: Purposive Behavior

Periods of relative stability in the real world of politics are likely to generate theories and research approaches commensurate with that stability; the first three generations of studies reflected this existential condition. When change is relatively slow, the observer will see it as a manifestation of institutionalization over time; when it is relatively fast, the observer will focus on the implications of easily visible change for behavioral and institutional patterns. While the fourth-generation studies are primarily concerned with personal goals and adaptation to change, the fifth-generation studies concentrate on institutional innovations.

Three real-world developments converged in the second half of the 1960s to give rise to the fourth generation of committee studies: first, many new members arrived in Congress who felt more or less inhibited in their personal pursuits by existing institutional arrangements and practices; second, the committees came to have more of an impact on public policy in the wake of the "Great Society" legislation than they previously had; and third, committee-processed policies were becoming more "constituency-oriented" than had been the case or had been admitted earlier.

Research on legislative committees responded to these developments by once again concentrating on the individual legislator as a purposive actor.[3] The approach was facilitated by the gradual reception in political science of "economic" models with their emphasis on "rational choice" as the guiding theoretical premise (see Mayhew, 1974; Ferejohn and Fiorina, 1975; Sinclair, 1983). Two major lines of relevant inquiry can be discerned. First, a set of studies concerned with the committee assignment process which have their *locus classicus* in an early report by Masters (1961) and culminated in a rational-choice modeled investigation by Shepsle (1978).[4] And second, beginning with an article by the economist Plott (1968), a set of studies, covered elsewhere in this series by Hamm, involves research on committee behavior and the distribution of benefits which committee members can bestow on their constituencies by virtue of their membership. These studies, to judge by criticism made of them by Arnold (1979), often arrive at contradictory conclusions about constituency effect. The issues are discussed in an article by Rundquist and Ferejohn (1975), who dub the theory "distributive" because it concerns the formation of distributive policies and the geographic distribution of governmental expenditures.

As the uses that purposive actors can make of their committee memberships for personal goals came to research attention, scholarship became sensitive to the need for systematic comparative treatment of committees, for only by controlling the committee as a variable can the particular individual purposes pursued by legislators be identified with particular committees. There emerged, as part of the fourth generation, a set of comparative studies, in some respects offspring of the second-generation integral case studies, but now influenced by theories of purposive behavior or by the growing interest in policy outcomes (rather than, as in earlier work, policy making as a process). These studies are especially concerned with the interchange between the personal goals of committee members and the institutional-structural arrangements they seek to shape in order to achieve their objectives. To explain this linkage is the critical burden of Fenno's (1973) again path-setting comparative study of six House committees. Committees, Fenno seeks to show, evolve institutional devices—decision rules or strategic premises—that facilitate the aspirations and preferences of their members. While Fenno's "purposive individualism" set the tone for much that has since been written about committees, it is by no means economic-reductionist, and it is sensitive to the autonomy of institutional constraints on behavior.

Fifth Generation: Organizational Models and Change

The rather kaleidoscopic fifth-generation committee studies were disciplinary responses to the many changes in the U.S. Congress, most of them unusually fast in historical perspective, which in the 1970s overwhelmed the observer. Indeed, one might argue that political science, at least at first, was rather unprepared to come to grips with the "New Congress," as it finally came to be called (see Mann and Ornstein, 1981). It is all the more remarkable that a few scholars succeeded in making theoretical sense of the changes that were taking place in congressional committee structures and the functioning of the committee system. What allowed them to make sense of the new structures and processes was, once again, the formulation or application of theoretical notions borrowed from sociology, especially the sociology of organizations and behavior systems. These notions are now applied to the committee system or committee interactions in the system rather than to particular committees, as they were in the second-generation studies.

Although systems theorists have always denied that their mode of analysis precludes the study of change, some scholars were uncomfortable with the apparently static concept of system. If one examines the "reasons" for change at the micro (individual) level of analysis, the purposive model can be a powerful tool of explanation. But as reforms, innovations, and changes cumulate to produce a transformation of the committee system, micro-analytic approaches appear to be more cumbersome than helpful, and the macro-analytic concepts of systems or organizational theory seem more parsimonious and efficient.

In general, one can identify and distinguish at least three kinds of studies or writings initiated either in the course of or as a consequence of the changes that overtook the Congress from about 1970 on. First, a set of largely prescriptive writings in which the scholar plays a kind of participant-observer role in explicitly giving his/her opinions or stating his/her preferences. A number of articles published under the editorship of Ornstein (1974, 1975) are largely but not exclusively of this sort. Second, a set of largely descriptive studies monitoring proposals for reform, the politics of reform, or the substantive consequences of reform. And third, a set of mature macro-theoretical writings, by no means empirically empty, which seek to cope with change in the legislative system as a whole or in part (Cooper, 1981; Davidson, 1981a; Price, 1981; Schick, 1981).

Most of the fifth-generation studies and writings are likely to overlap two and even all three of these categories. Some are empirically better grounded than others. Some strive for conceptual clarity while others do not. Some are more biased than others, explicitly or implicitly. And some of them tend to close the cycle of generations by returning to the mode of analysis in the Wilsonian tradition—literary, descriptive, anecdotal, normative, or prescriptive. All of them are more or less influenced, of course, by the contemporary notions and approaches of the intervening generations.

Topical Single-Committee Studies

A "topical" single-committee study typically selects some aspect of committee life as its focus of research attention. No attempt is made to describe or explain the committee as a whole, as an integral unit of action. Some aspect of committee behavior, structure, activity, or function is considered particularly noteworthy, for either theoretical, programmatic, or historical reasons. The topic in the *locus classicus* of these studies by Huitt (1954) is the performance of the Senate Banking and Currency Committee during its 1946 hearings concerning continuation of the wartime price-control and stabilization program. The study's theoretical frame of reference is considerably broader than the topic required but has given the study its permanent importance in the literature on legislative committees. Following Homans (1950), Huitt assumes that "each house of Congress is a human group, with leadership, a hierarchy in influence, and a set of norms which control, more or less, the behavior of its members" (p. 340). But groups as large as the houses are difficult to study in the behavioral vein. By way of contrast, the committee "is a small group, susceptible in most of its operations to close observation" (p. 341). It cannot be emphasized enough, in today's perspective, how novel Huitt's quest for "close observation" was in the early 1950s. Moreover, he sees in the study of the committee as a human group in its own right "the attractive possibility that techniques so developed will be useful in the more difficult undertaking with the larger group of which it is a part" (p. 341).

Role concepts, as formulated by the cultural anthropologist Linton (1945), provide Huitt with a second point of theoretical departure. The theory suggests to him that generalizations about the committee as a group "may be extended and refined by focusing on the behavior of individual members of the committee" (p. 344). However, it was evidently quite difficult for Huitt to use roles as analytic concepts for the purpose of examining or testing hypotheses derived from group theory about the behavior of the committee as a whole. At one point he remarks that "one way to intercept the shifting roles of the Committee members is to observe the variations in their behavior when different witnesses appear before them—representatives of the Administration, of interest groups, businesses, etc." (p. 349). And he notes that "some of the roles which might have been anticipated were not played by anybody" (p. 352), but he does not pursue a theme which occupied later students of committees—how roles taken or not taken conduce to "functional problems" of the committee, such as its integration or adaptation as a group rather than as an aggregate of persons. On the other hand, Huitt comes to a conclusion which anticipates a line of inquiry later pursued by the fourth-generation studies: "A congressional committee is an agency for the implementation of the purposes of congressmen" (p. 353).

Interestingly, the hypotheses Huitt actually set out to test do not stem from the newer behavioral theories but from the "group process" theory that derives from Bentley (1908). Huitt confronts Chamberlain's (1936, pp. 72-73, 79) notion of the committee as "the guardian of the general public interest, too large and too vague to be organized" and as a "legislative court, listening to the evidence of fact and law brought before it by interested parties, considering their suggestions," a notion which suggests to Huitt the committee's function as a fact-finding agency. This conception is opposed to that of the group theorists who consider legislators not "judges, discovering the public interest" but "themselves participants in the group struggle" (p. 342). Finding that facts are indeed screened through individual preferences and preoccupations, Huitt concludes that there is "nothing new in this conception" and that Plato's allegory of the cave "has a relevance for a theory of the group process in politics that has not been sufficiently appreciated. In the price control controversy (and surely in others like it) the senators were not sitting as arbiters of the group struggle, but as participants; it flowed through them" (p. 364).

One of the few investigators making systematic use of the printed record (in somewhat the same fashion as Huitt) makes no reference to his predecessor's work. The topic of Kingdon's (1966) modest study of a House Appropriations subcommittee is different from Huitt's but its mode of analysis is similar. The study's objective is to explore variables accounting for differential treatment of agencies by the subcommittee. The congressman's preferences for certain policies, awareness of the relative importance of agency programs, and desire to be reelected—he "can see that some agencies are likely to affect his constituents more than others"—constitute "a set of personal values" that affect his/her stance in the appropriations process. Kingdon finds that certain committee norms "are also repeatedly evident in the hearings. Committee members come to perceive that role as protector of the taxpayer and maintainer of the fiscal well-being of the entire nation" (p. 70). Administrators' conduct at the hearings influence the subcommittee's decisions, but "subcommittee perceptions of these stimuli are conditioned by the values which congressmen bring to their relations with administrators" (p. 73).

Like Huitt, then, Kingdon exploits committee hearings to identify congressmen's perceptions and values. The model of "subcommittee decision" is multi-level, however. "Objective" environmental factors—constituency or clientele interests and bureaucratic strategies—are screened through subcommittee members' perceptions, which in turn are guided by "a set of personal values." Kingdon does not deal with the question of how individual decisions come to be aggregated in the subcommittee decision, but his study, although based exclusively on public documents, anticipates later approaches (Fenno, 1973; Mayhew, 1974) to the same problem.

Committee-agency relations are also at the focus of a study by Sharkansky (1965), whose central topic is the budget strategies of four HEW agencies and an Appropriations subcommittee's responses to the initiatives taken by the agencies. As Sharkansky points out, "the discovery of differences between agency strategies should suggest the likelihood of differences in the postures that legislative committees assume vis-à-vis administrators" (p. 255).

Sharkansky employs an ingenious design. "By holding constant the Subcommittee and Department environments of the agencies, it is possible to discuss the contribution of certain factors to the agencies' budget strategies without fear that personality differences between legislators and administrative superiors might be responsible for the variations" (p. 256). In order to select the agencies, Sharkansky initially uses two "primitive" indices: an index of "agency assertiveness" (operationalized as "long-term increase in budget requests") and an index of "agency control" (operationalized as "the subcommittee's action in changing each agency's budget"). With "assertiveness of agency budget strategy" as dependent variable, Sharkansky hypothesizes that "the nature of Subcommittee support received by an agency might influence the anticipations that administrators hold about their chances for success with the Subcommittee" (p. 269). However, as Sharkansky relies for evidence on "systematic coding of published records" rather than interviews, he is precluded from "a thorough investigation of the impact from the administrators' perceptions, attitudes or beliefs upon the nature of his agency's budget strategy" (p. 269).

One study explicitly acknowledging its indebtedness to Huitt is an effort by Lutzker (1969) to apply the categories of Interaction Process Analysis—IPA, invented by Bales (1950)—to the record of committee hearings. The purpose of the study is "to test the generality of Huitt's finding concerning the nature of the hearings and the roles played by committee members" (p. 142), but this formulation is sufficiently vague to prohibit an assessment of the presumed "test." In fact, some of the Balesian categories—especially "tension" or "solidarity"—are difficult to assimilate to the congressional hearing process. Lutzker's laborious effort is disappointing. His findings— for example, that subcommittees assembled in hearings are not problem-solving groups or that there is an absence of negative social-emotional content in hearing behavior, which he calls "the single most startling finding" (p. 165)— are self-denying prophesies. Given its disappointing results and other limitations, Lutzker's call for more of this type of analysis has not been followed by other investigators.[5]

Representation as a topic is the focus of a study of the House Agriculture Committee by Jones (1961), in many respects a *locus classicus* in its own right, not only because of its contents but also because it was the first published interview study of a legislative committee. Jones observes that "there have been a number of empirical studies of representatives, few of which concentrate on specific policy fields" (p. 358). And while some prior studies have recorded the play of interests in specific legislation, this has been done "without a systematic account of the legislative committee members involved, acting in their representative capacities as they saw them" (p. 358). If, Jones asks, representatives take such roles as trustee, delegate, or politico, as suggested by Eulau, Wahlke, Buchanan, and Ferguson (1959), "how then can we tell when to expect a representative to view his role in one way rather than another?" (p. 358).

In order to come to grips with this question, Jones was the first investigator to develop and employ the concept of "policy constituency" which he defines as "those interests within his (the representative's) geographical or legal constituency which he perceives to be affected by the policy under consideration" (p. 354). His approach is two-pronged. On the one hand, he seeks to explain committee members' behavior as representatives of their policy constituencies; on the other hand, he uses this behavior to construct the committee as a behavioral system. What emerges from the analysis is a committee structure highly rationalized in terms of subcommittees corresponding to the representation of commodity interests in the committee as a whole. Moreover, Jones discovers that on classifying committee members in terms of the commodities of greatest interest to their constituencies, "almost without exception the six groups (of the classification) show an alignment between commodity interests and party allegiance," so that "consequently, different commodities will ordinarily be favored when different parties are in control" (p. 360). The committee's organization, Jones shows, is "strongly influenced by the commodity problems in agriculture" in two ways: first, "subcommittees are established to deal with currently critical commodity problems," and second, "members are assigned to commodity subcommittees on the basis of their constituency interests" (p. 360).

Jones's study is noteworthy because, though he conducted some of his investigation at the level of the individual member as the subject unit of analysis, his object unit is the committee as a structured whole (a theme which he followed up in a 1962 article). Unfortunately, his treatment of the committee as a representational institution has not been pursued by other investigators. This is probably due to Jones's own conclusion that the committee's representational and policy functions were rather indeterminate and, in the end, individualistic: "[Although] the representative has a concept of his constituency interests in legislation, there is still no reliable evidence as to how he develops it. But whether he gets it by divination, intuition, or instruction, it appears to dominate his behavior as a representative when its outline is sharp" (p. 367).

A study by Entin (1973) takes as its point of departure the concept of "interpersonal communication" and focuses on "information exchange" as its central topic. The study's approach is functional: "Information exchange operates at the committee level to check the compartmentalization of knowledge." However, the Armed Services Committee differs from other committees in that "executive branch personnel often monopolize the hearings on the defense authorization bill because, unlike other policy areas, almost all the witnesses are from the Department of Defense" (p. 430). Unlike members on "domestic" committees, "members of Armed Services are often denied countervailing private information sources" (p. 430, fn. 13). The chair is in a strategic position to influence communication among his colleagues by creating subcommittees "to rechannel the potentially disruptive effects of discontent" (p. 433) and by obtaining bipartisan legitimation of his own actions. An expert staff and committee members' trust in the staff's expertise conduce to the committee's function as an information exchange system, with consequences for the committee's impact on other congressmen's floor behavior.

In conclusion, Entin suggests that two consequences derive from the information exchange model. First, "it operates to rationalize and economize the decision-making process. . . . The specialization system diffuses power and atomizes knowledge." But this very restriction of expertise to specific groups and reliance upon them help "to neutralize the unsettling effects of compartmentalization" (p. 438). And second, "centralized control over policy coexists with structural decentralization" (p. 439).

Although Brenner (1974) deals primarily with the politics of a House-Senate conference, his study sheds some light on committee behavior in a conflict situation. Its "theory" is a curious combination of a Marxist version of elite theory, theory about the professions, and Schattschneider's (1960) conflict theory. Conflict over educational policy can be seen either as a "pork barrel concern" or as "a concern which relates to the fundamental processes of our society" (p. 88). In connection with a complex parliamentary situation that developed in the case of the Higher Education Act of 1972, Brenner identifies two aspects of the conflict—one rooted in personality differences, the other rooted in "the awareness members of Congress had of the scope of conflict" (p. 92). While following Schattschneider's theory concerning the duration and scope of conflict, Brenner does not find "traditional pluralist theory" adequate. Drawing therefore on the literature on the professions, presumably because professionals are the custodians of "objective interests," Brenner argues that congressmen share with other professionals the norm of specialization. But insofar as congressmen, like other professionals, address unarticulated interests, they seek to restrict the scope of political conflict. In particular, Brenner outlines "five characteristics of committees or of the committee system which relate to the control of conflict"—limited participation, secrecy, close interaction, seniority, and specialization (pp. 98-100). Only the last of these is of interest, because it seems to be related to Brenner's earlier concern with professionalization (even though he does not make the connection himself). Specialization, he argues, "works to diminish conflict and to discourage the participation of nonspecialists." Were committees reduced in number or given broader jurisdiction or were their members rotated, "the apparent specialization of committee members would be less convincing" (p. 100).

The relationship between a committee and its parent chamber is the topic of a study by Kaplan (1968) that raises an interesting question in regard to what is called "the most important situation"—the situation "in which a significant group in the parent chamber is dissatisfied with the actions of a committee and seeks to force a change in its behavior" (p. 647). The case in question, however—efforts to curtail the controversial House Un-American Activities Committee—is so special that its generalizability, even if treated as a deviant case, is doubtful. Working with floor roll-call votes, Kaplan specifies variables associated with opposition to the committee—both characteristics of congressmen's districts (such as urbanization, socio-economic composition, ethnicity, and so on) and characteristics of congressmen as individuals (such as religion, education, occupation, and ideological orientation). He also compares his target groups—Northern Democrats who supported and opposed the committee—in terms of "internal" variables, such as committee membership, seniority, and leadership.

Integral Single-Committee Studies

A distinction is necessary between what we call "integral single-committee studies" and mainly "descriptive" single-committee studies. The latter (for instance, Farnsworth, 1961; Robinson, 1963; Horn, 1970; Matsunaga and Chen, 1976) share with the former an ambition to describe the committee as an "entity," but they are essentially idiographic in using conventional categories of description. By way of contrast, the integral studies aspire to being nomothetic by bringing to the "case" a theoretical frame of reference that, as Fenno (1962, p. 310) put it in the *locus classicus* of the genre, permits treatment of the committee as "a discrete unit of analysis" in the context of relevant legislative processes: "appropriations politics" (Fenno, 1966), "the politics of finance" (Manley, 1970), "pork-barrel politics" (Murphy, 1974), and so on. This work, its nomothetic aspirations notwithstanding, is beset by all the familiar problems that characterize single case studies, notably the problem of generalizability.

"It's purpose," Fenno (1962) writes of his work, "is to add to our understanding of appropriations politics in Congress and to suggest the usefulness of this type of analysis for studying the activities of any congressional committee" (p. 310). And he envisages the possibility of "comparative committee analysis" (p. 324). Fenno's own odyssey from case to comparative analysis and the difficulties he encountered in the transition will be treated later on, for it also epitomizes the problem of comparing and, hence, making valid inferences about any congressional committee from the integral single-committee studies.

Fenno's version of functional analysis assumes that any social unit (unfortunately sometimes called "system") must "solve" a number of "problems," such as its internal maintenance or adaptation to the environment. The problem fascinating Fenno is "committee integration." "The necessity for integration," he writes, arises from "differentiation among sub-groups and among individual positions, together with the roles that flow therefrom" (p. 310). Because Fenno's definition of committee integration is invariably appealed or referred to in later research but often reduced or changed in meaning, full quotation is in order:

Committee integration is defined as the degree to which there is a working together or meshing together or mutual support among its roles and subgroups. Conversely, it is also defined as the degree to which a committee is able to minimize conflict among its roles and its subgroups, by heading off or resolving the conflicts that arise. A concomitant of integration is the existence of a fairly consistent set of norms, widely agreed upon and widely followed by the members. Another concomitant of integration is the existence of control mechanisms (i.e., socialization and sanctioning mechanisms) capable of maintaining reasonable conformity to norms. In other words, the more highly integrated a committee, the smaller will be the gap between expected and actual behavior (p. 310).

This definition and its implicit and explicit hypotheses give direction to the organization and interpretation of an enormous amount of qualitative (interview and documentary) materials and quantitative data about the House and, in parallel fashion, Senate Appropriations Committees, providing a widely accepted vision of these committees and making Fenno's work a model of integral single-committee research.

Fenno's analytic approach, and especially his notion of integration, had an almost immediate impact on a study of the House Agriculture Committee by Jones (1962). Jones finds that three norms specified by Fenno as conducive to integration—specialization, reciprocity, and subcommittee unity—"are much the same . . . , but the realization of these norms in the Agriculture Committee is affected by the fact that Republicans and Democrats have constituency interests in different commodities." Jones, concerned with the role of the subcommittees, feels it important "to turn to the reasons why integration has not been achieved" (p. 329).

Jones's study points to the difficulty in replication by way of case studies. Insightful in its own right, what seems to be a replication is not really a replication, for Jones gives his explanation for low integration an interesting twist by introducing a new variable—the pervasiveness of constituency commodity interests in the committee—that constitutes an essentially external or environmental constraint. Yet Fenno had not treated such an environmental variable in his early report and, in fact, initially referred to the "problem of self-integration" (Fenno, 1962, p. 310).

Ironically, while Jones (1962) does not really benefit much from adopting Fenno's theory of integration, Fenno might have benefitted from Jones's (1961) work on the Agriculture Committee as an interstitial structure in the process of representation when he came to examine the House Education and Labor Committee (Fenno, 1963; also Munger and Fenno, 1962). Perhaps because of his concern with integration stemming from systems theory and the structural-functional approach, Fenno does not see that Education and Labor's failure to resolve internal conflicts may not have been unrelated to members' representational posture (in addition to their ideological and partisan predispositions). The implications of the conflicts tearing apart the Education and Labor Committee are not theoretically exploited because representation is not allowed for in systems theory as a "functional problem" in its own right. Yet, "since they have assumed more or less unequivocal positions on federal aid before their constituents, members come to their committee work committed in advance and are denied the freedom to maneuver so basic to the production of legislative agreement" (p. 199).

Fenno makes clear throughout that the divisions on the committee were in many respects reflections of similar divisions in the House and in the country. The Committee on Education and Labor, it seems, was highly "representative"—in the descriptive sense at least—of the represented, and to expect from it behavior, norms, or processes conducive to conflict resolution and consensus-building, when there is no consensus elsewhere, is to fit a model to the data that is not appropriate.

A study of the House Ways and Means Committee by Manley (1965, 1970) is generally recognized as the most noteworthy successor of Fenno's type of analysis, in part because Manley himself defined it so: "An attempt is made to contribute to the development of an analytical framework, based on Fenno's study of the House Appropriations Committee, which may prove useful for the comparative analysis of congressional committees generally." However, Manley makes a number of contributions of his own to the understanding of committees. In particular, while Fenno began his study with a number of theoretically-derived "basic problems," Manley evidently encountered early what cannot be called so much a theoretical problem as an "empirical puzzle," to the effect that the committee is able "to process, in a bipartisan manner, political demands which its members regard as highly partisan issues" (1965, p. 927).

While Manley set out to solve this puzzle by way of a causal approach, the contemporary spell of requisite analysis asserts itself: "To perform this function the Committee must solve certain problems of internal organization and interaction." Yet he also points out that three problems he identified— instrumental interaction, affective interaction, and integration—"are affected by the type of subject matter and the external demands placed on the Committee" (p. 928). Manley's final work (1970), like Fenno's final study on appropriations, is of course much more broad-gauged in its emphasis on the process of legislation in its jurisdiction.

Manley's analysis was soon made substantively (though not theoretically) obsolete by the reforms and changes that overcame the Ways and Means Committee in the 1970s. Fortunately, in this case a fifth-generation study by Rudder (1977), reporting and assessing the changes, has updated the substance of Manley's work. According to Rudder, democratization has been successful in that power within the committee is more widely dispersed among members and its processes have been opened up. Reform of the closed rule has allowed many challenges to committee bills. More congressmen "are getting a say in Ways and Means legislation at the expense of the chairman and the committee as a whole" (p. 132). Policy output is more difficult to evaluate, but there has been a perceptible shift as "the committee is probably more liberal in fiscal policy than the old committee was" (p. 135).

The role of the committee chairman as an "independent variable" and of committee integration as presumably a dependent variable emerges in a study of the Senate Banking and Currency Committee by Bibby and Davidson (1967).[6] The committee's informal internal arrangements and formal activities varied a good deal with the chairman's leadership style—first a chairman who ran the committee in a highly centralized manner, with subcommittees existing only on paper; then a "service chairman" whose real interests were elsewhere and whose permissive style gave each subcommittee chairman an opportunity to assert leadership; and finally a "minority and restraining" chairman who "used his powers and prerogatives as chairman to restrain the committee in quiet and innocuous ways," thereby avoiding any challenge to himself (p. 177).

The Senate Banking and Currency Committee is described as not attractive "in terms of power" and as having no subject matter appeal (pp. 184-185). The conditions for integration are found lacking—membership is unstable, subject matter not of consuming interest to members, maverick behavior not uncommon, and the subject matter not given to unity and compromise. Because the committee is "responsible for a field in which traditional divisions on domestic policy can easily assert themselves with intensity," partisanship is strong (p. 192). Intra- and interparty "blocs" make for poor communication between members. Although the committee included some specialists, it "lacks the norm of strict specialization in subcommittee work and the willingness to accept readily the decisions of its subcommittees" (p. 193).

A study of the House Public Works Committee by Murphy (1974) symptomizes the shift from the structural-functional to a more reductionist-causal type of analysis yet remains sensitive to what cannot be explained at the individual level of analysis. Writing "against a backdrop of the behavior of other congressional committees" (p. 184), Murphy finds that "to a degree unknown in any congressional committee studied to date, the House Public Works committee is a partisan committee" rather than "an essentially bipartisan, backscratching committee" (pp. 184-185). Bipartisan favor trading cannot account for party conflict and cooperation in the committee: "To account for these patterns of party conflict and party cooperation, one must begin with party affiliation, not with exchange processes" (p. 169). Member partisanship, constituency, and program orientations—all individual-level variables—are mobilized by Murphy to support this premise. But pork-barreling within fixed allocation formulas cannot account for the fixed formulas. Explanation for the latter therefore shifts from structural patterns of exchange and the behavior involved to "partisan distrust" not as an individual-level but as a group-level variable.

By the time Murphy reported his research, an early (1970) version of Fenno's (1973) comparative study, with its emphasis on member goals as a source of committee behavior, had become available (see Murphy, 1974, p. 170, fn. 5). Whereas Fenno specifies reelection as one member goal, Murphy finds "constituency interest" (shared by 60 percent of his respondents) rather than reelection to be a significant consideration in members' decision-making calculus. Although these individual-level variables are used to explain, in part, conflict and cooperation on the committee, Murphy's effective explanatory unit of analysis is the partisan subgroup in the committee. Not the goals of individual members but "party goals" become crucial. As a result, "party conflict"—a structural variable—"is the committee's dominant decision-making characteristic" (p. 172).

Murphy moves in rather free-wheeling manner from one to another level of analysis, but it is always reasonably clear where the presentation is at. Without explicitly saying so, Murphy is sensitive to the problem of evidence and inference from one level to the other. On the one hand, individual-level processes—symbolized in the term "pork-barreling"—did not account for the fixed allocation formulas. On the other hand, committee success on the House floor—the House "typically adopts" committee recommendations "whether the committee is divided or not" (p. 181)—"is not perfectly correlated with committee unanimity." Therefore, "it is treacherous to infer committee power or autonomy from success" (p. 185).

The best of the integral committee studies are concerned with the relationship between the behavioral and structural properties of committees and the policies that Congress as a whole produces or fails to produce. David E. Price (1978),[7] in a study of the House and Senate Commerce Committees, argues that central as committee-related variables are, research "also must take account of the environment in which the committee subsists and of the forces impinging upon its operation" (p. 548). In search of a theoretical handle to cope with the impact of "environmental" factors, Price takes issue with Fenno's treatment in his comparative study, to the effect that Fenno's

capacity to explain differing levels of congressional interest and assertiveness is reduced by his conceptualization of environmental forces mainly in terms of the "constraints" they place on the pursuit of these independently existing "member goals." Fenno thinks of the "environment" primarily as groups of interested outsiders who must be *adapted to*. But to understand the impact of environmental factors on policy makers, one must also think of their settings as fields of incentives, opportunities, and constraints that shape their priorities and strategies (p. 549).

Price tries to work with a "rational-economic" or "maximization" model, though it is not quite clear why he needs it. Not only does he come to the conclusion that "economic rationality does not exhaust the possibilities of purposive behavior" (p. 574), but his method is explicitly inductive rather than deductive (pp. 549-550). Distinguishing between "clientele-centered" and "publicly salient" policy areas, Price's concern is with "how *differences* among the environmental forces operating in each of these policy areas are reflected in the level and content of committee output." Two "general characteristics" are said to "distinguish the Commerce Committees' environment from that of many other committees": first, "group conflict is, while sometimes intense, generally limited in scope" (p. 550), and second, there is a "relative absence of high intensity executive branch and party involvement" (p. 551).

It is in Price's analysis and interpretation of his findings that one once more encounters the generic "softness" of the case study approach. For instance, " 'public salience' refers not to any precise measure but to a rough comparative standard based on the expressed perceptions of congressional members and aides"; or "the 'conflict' variable is also imprecise but is real enough to policy makers" (p. 568). Even if, as in this study, the effort is made to be explicit and systematic in the handling of the variables, the usual indeterminacy of the case study and the difficulty of replication become again apparent, especially when it comes to some kind of causal analysis or interpretation. At issue is the relationship between the saliency and conflict variables. On the one hand, Price finds some policy areas where "the presence of conflict, after all, presupposes saliency in *some* quarter, and the conflict is more likely to be perceived in universalistic-particularistic terms in those areas that possess high public salience." On the other hand, "while the level of saliency may determine the form or arena of conflict, both high- and low-saliency policy areas range across the spectrum in the degree of conflict they entail" (p. 569).[8]

Propositions of this kind are illustrated but hardly demonstrated. What emerges is a picture of great complexity, but the complexity is not reduced to generalizable knowledge as discourse moves from one unit level of analysis to another (from the individual congressmen to the committee to the Congress) and from more or less concrete to more or less abstract statements. We say this not to be critical but to point up the intrinsic difficulties facing the case analyst who, like Price in this study of the Commerce Committees, seeks to pursue the causal path. In the end, the presumed causal statements do not differ much from the kind of functional statements that one encountered in Fenno's (1962) early work. For instance, in comparing the "relative mix" of congressional and executive responsibility for given initiatives Price picks up on Manley's discussion of "compensatory representation" but ends with the warning that "it is important not to be overly deterministic about such matters" (p. 572).

Ostrom's (1979) attempt to reappraise the theoretical foundations of the integral single-committee studies, notably Fenno's and Manley's, does not come off well. Presuming to present "an alternative to the Fenno-Manley types by contending that committee conflict as well as consensus can produce legislative achievement" (p. 430), the author refers to Ways and Means as a consensual and to Education and Labor as a conflictual committee and asserts that the former produced—in his scheme of values—"regressive" and the latter "progressive" legislation. From this it is inferred that conflict is not necessarily dysfunctional. But this line of argument hardly negates the Fenno-Manley type of analysis and, as the author shows, change occurred with the changing partisan and ideological composition of the committee. Although the author suggests that "additional research is needed to determine whether conflict generally results in more progressive legislation" (p. 438), the causal nexus may be reverse. It may be more plausible to assume that "progressive" (read, "new") legislation introduced in a committee creates conflict, and whether or how the conflict is resolved is likely to depend on just those strategic premises inside the House that Fenno, Manley, and other structural-functionalists described.

Comparative Committee Case Studies

To speak of "comparative committee case studies" is something of a paradox. "Cases" are to be compared, but their number is still likely to be too small to permit transition from nonquantitative to statistical analysis, and there is still the problem of what a case is a "case of" and why particular cases are selected in the first place. Moreover, different modes of analysis and different points of theoretical departure make cross-case comparison hazardous or impossible.

Given the influence of Fenno's earlier work, one turns with great expectation to his equally influential comparative study of six House committees: Appropriations, Ways and Means, Education and Labor, Foreign Affairs, Interior, and Post Office (Fenno, 1973). Of particular interest, of course, is how Fenno would solve the problem of comparison, for his mode of research and presentation remained essentially the same as they had been in his single-committee studies. Comparison requires a common theoretical frame of reference in the treatment of cases. Ironically, perhaps, Fenno's

FIGURE 1

Analytic Scheme for Comparing Committees

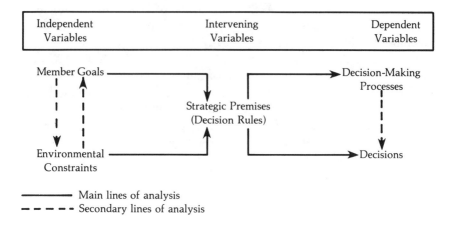

——————— Main lines of analysis
– – – – – Secondary lines of analysis

solution came by way of his jettisoning the mode of explanation that had evidently served him so well—systems theory and the structural-functional approach. Instead, as he reports,

I have made goal seeking by the members a keystone of this analysis. The resulting conceptual framework is, therefore, somewhat more individualistic than the previous one. But both are similar in their concentration on the expectations and perceptions of the participants and in their effort to view the world from the perspectives of the participants themselves. This explains why—despite the fact that one will not find 'adaptation' or 'integration' or 'roles' mentioned in the book—my earlier description of the two Appropriations Committees can easily be accommodated within this framework (p. xvii, fn. 1).

The title of Fenno's comparative study speaks of "congressmen in committees." The methodological question immediately arises whether a study of congressmen in committees can make possible comparison of committees as integral units of action, if that is the objective. As we will note, this seems to have been the objective, although it does not appear until one reaches the very end of the book. For the purpose of overall orientation, it is possible to let Fenno speak for himself, for his research design in fact constitutes a kind of causal model or, at least, an analytic scheme (see Figure 1).

According to Fenno, the ability of committees to meet the goals of their members varies widely. Since individual congressmen vary in the emphasis placed upon particular goals, different committees are sought by different congressmen. A congressman whose committee does not meet his goals, or whose goals have changed, will transfer. "By a combination of processes, then, House committees come to be characterized . . . by distinctive nonrandom distributions of individual members" (p. 2). Three goals are basic: reelection, influence within the House, and the opportunity to make "good" public policy. Fenno makes it clear, however, that though a congressman may have a primary goal, he does not hold one goal to the exclusion of others. And though members of a committee may agree upon goals, environmental constraints, imposed by groups outside the committees which have their own goals to pursue, may necessitate some compromises.

The goals and constraints of the six committees studied by Fenno are summarized here. While this summary is no substitute for Fenno's prose, it briefly lists the most important points he makes about each committee:

Committee	Members' Primary Goals	Prominent Outsiders	Nature of Policy Coalition
Appropriations	Influence within House and government	House members, executive	Executive-led
Ways and Means	Influence within House and government	House members, president's administration	Complex, partisan, administration-led
Foreign Affairs	"Good" public policy	Executive	Monolithic, executive-led
Education and Labor	"Good" public policy	Parties	Pluralistic, party-led
Interior	Constituency service for reelection	Clientele groups	Pluralistic, clientele-led
Post Office and Civil Service	Constituency service for reelection	Clientele groups (postal workers' union)	Monolithic, clientele-led

Decision-making processes on the various committees should be compatible, Fenno argues, with their strategic premises. Three variables are important to committees' decision-making structures: partisanship, participation-specialization, and leadership (p. 81). The two committees which have strategic premises calling for partisanship—Ways and Means, Education and Labor—score highest of the six on an index of partisan divergence (pp. 52-53); but there are striking differences in the way the partisanship is expressed. The decision-making processes, like the strategic premises, reflect the differences in autonomy among the six committees: "The greater the relative influence of the members, the more autonomous the committee; the greater the relative influence of outside groups, the less autonomous the committee" (p. 137).

The conclusion is reached that "when a committee's members agree on what they should do, they are more likely to be able to control their own decision-making than when they cannot agree on what to do" (p. 138).

In his final chapter Fenno returns to the problem of comparison, if only inadvertently, for the problem is by no means made explicit. Fenno's "theme," it will be recalled, was that "committees differ from one another" (p. xv). And this is precisely the conclusion reached in the book's Epilogue: "Congressional committees differ from one another" (p. 280). But, Fenno also postulates, committees "differ systematically" (p. xv). In order to cope with the problem of systematic differences, Fenno formulates a simple (and perhaps all too simple) dichotomized typology. Using what he calls "relative distinctions," Fenno purports to "find two types of House committees."

One type is identified by the House orientation of its decision rules, the autonomy of its decision-making processes, its emphasis on committee expertise, its success on the House floor, its members' sense of group identity, and the relatively higher ratio of member to nonmember satisfaction with its performance. The other type is identified by its extra-House-oriented decision rules, the permeability of its decision-making processes, the de-emphasis on committee expertise, its lack of success on the House floor, the absence of any feeling of group identification, and the relatively higher ratio of non-member to member satisfaction with its performance (pp. 278-279).

The typology, then, is an empirical one (it is "found"), and it is therefore presumably a generalization. Whether so broadly conceived a typology can serve the purpose of comparison is doubtful, for each of the two types contains so much internal differentiation that assignment of one or another committee—especially committees not studied by Fenno—to one or the other category should prove very difficult and perhaps impossible. Fenno, having derived this typology empirically, has no difficulty. Appropriations, Ways and Means, and Interior are in the first category; Post Office, Foreign Affairs, and Education and Labor are in the second.[9]

Fenno's literary approach makes it difficult to check up on his method of analysis, especially insofar as aggregation is concerned. He deals in what he calls "modal characterizations" which "are admittedly over-simplifications." He assures us that "they have sufficient validity to serve as a basis for predicting gross similarities and differences in committee behavior" (p. 14). But why should one go to the trouble of interviewing so many individuals only to be able to account for "gross similarities and differences?" Moreover, one questions whether "consensus" is a concept that can be treated as a "modality" and retain its conventional meaning. Finally, what is at issue is not the validity of such "measurement" but its reliability.

A study of the House Judiciary Committee by Perkins (1980) is characterized as "an extension and modification" of Fenno's comparative study (p. 373). The study differs from Fenno's, however, in two important respects: first, the interview data seem to have been collected in a more "structured" or "focused" mode; second, the effort is made to present the data in quantitatively more exact form rather than to deal with them in terms of modalities. Both differences create problems of comparison.

Perkins's initial concern is the high consensus on member goals which Fenno had discovered in all of his six committees—a consensus high enough to treat them as "single goal committees" (pp. 373-374). But what, she asks, "would be the consequences for a committee's strategic premises, its structure, and its behavior" if, in fact, "mixed goal committees" existed?

If one contrasts Fenno's with Perkins's questions, it is immediately evident how very much an investigator's findings are dependent on the formulation of questions in the interview and how very much differences in the questions asked undermine the validity of comparison with another investigator's findings. Fenno (1973, p. 2) relied on a single question ("Why did you want to get on the _____ committee in the first place?"). In contrast, Perkins routinely asked an entire battery of rather specific questions and also used, for the purpose of determining members' goals,"the comments of office and committee staff, reporters, interest group and executive branch representatives, and other congressmen" (p. 374). That Perkins would obtain results different from Fenno's is almost a foregone conclusion and further raises the question of comparability.

The Judiciary Committee, at the time of study, was in a phase of transition, occasioned not only by the committee reforms of the period but also by the change from a very active to a relatively inactive chairman. Further, the "new" issues coming before the committee—busing, gun control, abortion, and school prayers—made the Judiciary Committee less prestigious than it had been in an earlier period and less attractive in the assignment process. This created something of a "recruitment crisis," which Perkins explored in a second article (1981). This crisis created what Perkins calls "one theoretical problem": members' reelection as a goal "could not be advanced much through their membership in the Judiciary Committee and the question arises whether re-election is not a congressional goal rather than a Judiciary Committee goal" (p. 352).

Perkins's puzzlement seems to be rooted either in the conceptual and operational ambiguity of "consensus on goals" or a misunderstanding of Fenno's usage. The latter rather than the former appears to be the case, though both conditions may be operative. "A re-election oriented committee," she writes, "is characterized not only by a numerically dominant member goal, but also by committee activity.... The Judiciary Committee's activity, however, was not directed toward re-election" (p. 354). And more: "Since the Judiciary Committee does not contribute much to its members' re-election, it is not a re-election oriented committee" (p. 355).

As these statements indicate, Perkins seems to view "reelection activity" as an integral property of the committee as a whole that would exist quite independently of members' own private goals. However, according to Fenno, as we read him, reelection as such may be on the minds of members on some committees more than of members on other committees, but no committee has reelection endeavor on its agenda as an organized group activity.

Fenno's work had been preceded in 1972 by a complex comparative study by David Price of three Senate committees—Commerce, Finance, and Labor and Public Welfare—during the 89th (1965-1966) Congress. Price's work also raises the methodologically critical issue of how a few cases can be used, by way of comparison, to warrant generalizations about committee structures and functions in the context of a legislature's internal and external relationships. Price examines 13 more or less "major" pieces of legislation in order to determine just which actors in the policy-making process—not only Senate committees or subcommittees and their chairs but also the House, executive agencies, and interest groups—assumed and effected "responsibility" in connection with particular bills.

Price sets himself two objectives: first, "to ascertain how and to what effect legislative tasks and influence are shared in certain major areas of domestic policy and among various constellations of policy-making forces," and second, "to specify various factors which have a bearing on the division of responsibility that emerges in a given area" (p. 2). Price's major objective is the second, and for this purpose he concentrates on situational variables. The intellectual ancestry of his work is thus different from Fenno's and can be traced to the "decision-making approach" of Dahl (1960, 1967) and notably of Lasswell (1950, 1963), though there is a good deal of reconceptualization to make their formulations suit his own view of the legislative process. Price argues that his use of the term "responsibility" is appropriate because it denotes "innovative or assertive political action" (p. 337, fn. 14), but it seems to refer largely to the involvement of the various actors in six different phases of the policy-making process—instigating and publicizing issues, formulating legislative alternatives, gathering information on implications and consequences, responding to different interests by way of aggregation, mobilizing support or opposition, and modifying proposals. Examination of the detailed descriptions of the 13 bills shows that Price's functional categories are as difficult to use analytically as Lasswell's, which he had found to be "rather bloodless" (p. 5). His bill studies tend to rectify the simplistic and often stereotypic textbook image of the legislative process, but the diversity of the processes involved creates new problems for scientific generalization which the small-n approach cannot handle.

Price is sensitive to this methodological dilemma and, in the book's last chapter, attempts to pull the policy case materials together in order to give, by way of comparison, substantive content to the analytic categories and propositions initially set out and, especially, to answer the question concerning "responsibility"—what it consists of and where it is located. Price argues that, despite the evident complexity and diversity of the legislative processes involved, "certain patterns do appear" (p. 289). Yet it remains unclear just what the patterns are, for the impression prevails that the actors "responsible" for performing one or another function varied from bill to bill in rather random fashion. The discovery of patterns, one can only conclude from Price's heroic effort to discover them, would seem to require a research design that will sacrifice intensive analysis of a few for extensive analysis of many cases.

Even if Price's search for patterns remains indeterminate and no firm conclusions are reached about the roles played by the Senate committees in the over-all policy-making process, the study is rich in theoretical "points of departure" for the empirical analysis of committee phenomena. As Price (p. 10) suggests, as "a complex pattern of action and interaction, structures and norms, internal and external relationships," the committee can be conceived in terms of six "images"—a set of personalities, an organization, a social system, a representative institution, an "island of decision," and a communications center (pp. 11-24). Price's studies of the 13 bills provide rich illustrative material for all of these dimensions, just as they provide much material for the "functions" that committees have more or less in common (are "responsible for" in Price's theory) and which they share with nonlegislative actors in the policy process.

An ingenious study by Hinckley (1975) constitutes something of a bridge between the comparative case studies and comparative-aggregate studies. Her concern, referring to both modes, is that "little of this cumulates or comes together into more than a set of disparate, and at times contradictory, findings—employing widely different conceptualizations and kinds of data. Having found that 'committees vary,' we need now the kind of analysis that can order and explain this variation and that can begin to bring some of these very diverse results together" (p. 544). Whether her own study meets this objective is another matter, for Hinckley introduces her own conceptualization and kinds of data.

To cope with more than a few committees and yet provide a conceptual umbrella, Hinckley (p. 544) proposes to organize committees by subject matter or "policy content" of the legislation they consider. To test relevant hypotheses about committee or committee members' behavior, Hinckley (p. 545) introduces two "policy content dimensions": scope, which is defined as "subject matter attracting a broad versus restricted number of 'interested' actors," and stake, which is defined as "subject matter permitting positive-sum versus zero-sum solutions." Alternately, these are defined as "competitive" and "noncompetitive" solutions, respectively. The former, it appears, is akin to what is sometimes called "regulative" and "redistributive" policy, while the latter seems to be akin to "distributive" policy. Apparently in an effort to validate the two categories, Hinckley asked six scholars to place 16 committees, 8 from the House and 8 corresponding ones from the Senate, into the two-dimensional matrix of policy scope and stakes. As the numbers in parentheses in the following chart show, the typology appears to be reasonably valid in the experts' judgment.

	Stakes	
Scope	Zero-Sum (competitive)	Positive Sum (noncompetitive)
Broad	Ways and Means/Finance (6, 5)[a] Judiciary/Judiciary (4, 6)	Appropriations/ Appropriations (6, 5)
Restricted	Education and Labor/Labor (4, 5) Banking and Currency/ Banking and Currency (5, 6)	Interior/Interior (6, 5) Public Works/Public Works (4, 6) Post Office/Post Office (5, 6)

[a]Numbers in parentheses refer to the number of six judges agreeing to the placement of committees by scope and stakes, respectively.

Using the typology, Hinckley articulates three core "expectations," as follows:

If subject matter shapes membership, . . . broad-scope committees would be more attractive to members, therefore more stable in membership and possessing more senior members than restricted committees (whether competitive or noncompetitive).

If subject matter shapes behavior, . . . competitive committees should be less cohesive than noncompetitive committees (whether broad or restricted).

If subject matter is important, we would expect strong intercorrelations in the ranking of these attributes for House and Senate committees handling essentially the same jurisdiction (p. 546).

In general, Hinckley finds support for all of her hypotheses. In regard to the first, House-Senate similarity suggests that "subject matter alone is a powerful shaper of committee attractiveness and senior membership." Arraying the 16 committees on the three dimensions for 48 placements, "there would be only two errors made: Senate Interior and Senate Judiciary would be misplaced for committee stability" (p. 550). Unanimity in committee recommendations being "a kind of empirical 'norm'," Hinckley stipulates nonunanimous floor recommendations as the measure of cohesive committee behavior (making clear that this is a measure of members' behavior outside, not inside, the committee). She claims "strong support" for the second hypothesis concerning committee cohesion and subject matter stakes. And, with the exception of the House and Senate Public Works Committees, there is also support for the third hypothesis—a strong correlation on cohesion between House and Senate committees dealing with the same subject matter (p. 552).

The finding that committee attractiveness is unrelated to cohesion, Hinckley feels (pp. 553-554), "may help reconcile some of the very disparate and apparently contradictory findings of Fenno (1962) and Dyson and Soule (1970) but also Dodd (1972)." (For review of the last two studies, see below.) Neither Fenno, who found a relationship, nor Dyson and Soule, who did not, "controlled for subject matter controversy"; Dodd, who did control, "found an inverse relationship between attractiveness and cohesion in the Senate." Hinckley continues:

The present study based on committee recommendations indicates, supporting Fenno, that Appropriations is indeed exceptionally cohesive, and supporting Dyson and Soule, that House committees overall show no relationship between attractiveness and cohesion. And controlling for subject matter controversy, the study indicates some support for the inverse relationship for Senate committees that Dodd reported, and no relationship for House committees. The picture that begins to emerge, then, from these very different investigations is that attractiveness and membership attributes appear to be only coincidentally linked with cohesive behavior (p. 554).

Hinckley is perhaps more enthusiastic in her conclusions than the study itself warrants. Its two dichotomized subject-matter dimensions are extraordinarily broad and conceptually ambiguous. A typology built from such dimensions is by no means frivolous, since it helps the process of theorizing, but it remains operationally suspect. While Hinckley's panel of expert judges was reasonably consensual in placing the committees offered them, these were committees relatively easy to place. We simply note, as Hinckley reports, that "two additional committees originally offered—Armed Services and Foreign Affairs—received no consensus and were dropped from the analysis" (p. 546). How other committees would fare on being placed is an open question.

Synchronic-Aggregate Studies

A number of what we call "synchronic-aggregate studies," based on floor or committee roll-call votes, seek to test propositions largely derived from the case literature—propositions about committees' attractiveness, integration, partisanship, floor success, member effectiveness, influence, constituency interest, factional structure, and so forth.

Matthews (1960), in his seminal study of the U.S. Senate, used floor roll-call votes for the purpose of gaining insight into the behavior of legislators in committees. Matthews is painfully aware that "executive sessions, however, present an obvious barrier to the analysis of committee decision-making" (p. 166). Committee reports (at the time) did not give the final lineup of members, and "none cast much light on the preliminary votes and give-and-take that make up the process of decision."

While later investigators would usually take it for granted that they can use floor roll-call votes for the purpose of inference to legislators' behavior in committee, Matthews searches for scientific warrant. He defends the use of roll calls on the ground that inconsistent voting—"one way in the semisecrecy of the committee room and in another on the floor of the chamber"—would violate the Senate's folkways. Comparing the votes of reporting committee members with those of all other senators, he finds that "committee members tend to be more nearly agreed on what should be done in their areas of policy than is the case with the Senate as a whole" (p. 167).

Matthews's cautious use of roll-call data and conceptualization is not followed in later, more comprehensive studies. Conceptualization and measurement seem to be at loggerheads, though the conflict is not acknowledged. The problem involved can be illustrated by the uses made of the concept of "integration" which, by 1970, had come to be a staple of committee analysis. The investigators whose work is reviewed here claim to measure the same thing when using the term "integration" as the single-case analysts meant by it, but it is questionable that they actually do so.

Noting that much of the research during the 1960s focused upon single committees, Dyson and Soule (1970) take a comparative approach.[10] In order to "bring case studies on particular committees into a common theoretical framework" (p. 627), they employ the terminology and concepts of small group research. They argue that the variables in question—committee attractiveness, success, and partisanship, as well as integration—are related in a systematic way. Contrary to the authors' expectations, attractive committees are not more integrated than the less attractive committees. That more attractive committees will experience greater success at getting bills passed is also shown to be false. Committee success, Dyson and Soule conclude, is "structurally derived rather than sociometrically (attractiveness) derived" (p. 638). Interparty agreement within committees is high for the same committees which rank high on the integration scale. And while success does not vary with attractiveness, it varies with integration. Success is also related to partisanship: when the majorities of the parties on a committee agree on a bill, it stands a better chance of passing than it does when the parties disagree or when a majority of the Democrats oppose a majority of the committee. Minimal partisanship is "a key to committee success" (p. 645).

Dyson and Soule's evidence is flawed, however, on two counts. First, congressmen's roll-call voting behavior may be quite different from internal committee behavior. Second, Dyson and Soule note (in their conclusion) but do not account for the inherent divisiveness of the more attractive committees' legislation, which may explain the lack of cohesion of members of attractive committees in their floor voting on their own committees' legislation.

Dodd (1972) and Dodd and Pierce (1975) also deal with integration, but if Dyson and Soule give the concept almost no substantive content, Dodd and Pierce read more into it than is theoretically warranted. Dodd (1972), in a Senate study, is concerned with the "average committee effectiveness of committee members" (itself involving measurement problems) which, in part, is to be explained by "committee integration" defined as "agreement among group members on fundamental values" (p. 1138).[11] At issue is whether Dodd's measure is a quantification of the concept of integration as used by Fenno. The latter, it will be recalled, was using the concept "without, for the time being, having devised any precise measure of integration" (Fenno, 1962, p. 323). In fact, rather than being a variable, integration was conceived by Fenno as a "functional problem" arising out of structural difficulties such as subgroup differentiation, role conflict, or deficient internal control mechanisms.

Dodd's explication of integration is troublesome. In particular, there is the question of what values are to be considered "fundamental" and what measure is to be used. As to the latter, some kind of measure of social cohesion, based on paired voting on roll calls, can only assume that what is measured is "agreement on fundamental values." Dodd is not unaware of this, conceding that in "some specific instances" a legislator may vote against his basic values as a result of presidential influence, lobby activity, or party pressure; but he argues that "in the long run" the patterns of high and low cohesion among committee members "should indicate the existence of high and low agreement among the members on fundamental values" (pp. 1144-1145).

Dodd, in cooperation with Pierce, returns to the measurement aspects of integration in a study published three years later (Dodd and Pierce, 1975). The article reviews alternative measures of roll-call vote cohesion but now equates integration with "agreement on policy-related values" rather than "agreement on fundamental values"—a concept "which in differing contexts refers to the existence of shared committee norms, explicit committee goals, and mechanisms to control partisan conflict" (p. 388). Just why this reconceptualization is introduced and how it might affect measurement is not made clear. Substantively, Dodd and Pierce take account of the inherent divisiveness of certain bills. They feel that the roll-call method of measuring integration can be made more exact if one consideration is kept in mind: "Subject matter investigated by some committees invariably is more or less controversial than the subject matter concern of other committees. As a result, bills reported by some committees naturally produce more or less cohesion than the bills reported by other committees" (p. 389).

In a modest, descriptive study based on the floor's reaction to all 6621 bills (excluding motions and amendments), reported for the period from

1959 to 1968, Lewis (1978) demonstrates that in assessing a committee's "floor success" the critical factor is not whether a bill receives favorable or unfavorable action but whether it is acted on at all by the House. Evidently troubled by the findings of Dyson and Soule, Lewis shows that "success in getting bills acted on by the floor affects committees' success scores" (p. 465). The critical factor, then, is floor consideration in the first place. "Of all bills reported, a high percentage (94 percent) was considered on the House floor and acted on. As a rule, most standing committee reports get floor consideration. However, individual committees differ widely in terms of whether their reported bills are acted on by the floor" (p. 465).

Lewis concludes that "some propositions about committee variation in floor success with their reported bills are misleading." If the criterion of actual floor consideration is used as a control, "the differences among their success averages are so slight as to make ranking them a case of splitting hairs." Committees, then, "differ in more subtle ways. Committees are not equally adept at getting their reported bills considered," and "it remains to be seen whether they pass in the form reported by the committee" (p. 467). Unfortunately, Lewis neither speculates about the "subtle ways" in which committees get their bills on the calendar, nor does she report on amendments, nor does she seek to account for success after a bill has been considered and amended. In fact, as total variation by the revised measure of floor success on entire bills is only three percentage points, there is no elbow room for any sort of causal analysis. What seems to have been demonstrated is that all committees are, in fact, the effective decision-making centers in the House of Representatives.

Lewis's new measure of "committee success"—by which, it now appears, not even the House Education and Labor Committee fared badly—points up the dilemma of inferring from floor roll-call action the existence of prior constraint on committee behavior. The dilemma of the "prior constraint hypothesis" has been explored by Kingdon (1973, p. 126). A strong test of the hypothesis requires a real-world situation in which a committee does not misjudge House sentiment but correctly anticipates it and yet moves forward with its bill and recommendation, taking the risk of defeat. Kingdon reports a few tests of this kind in connection with the 1969 House session, in which he interviewed a sample of congressmen concerning particular votes they had cast on the floor. In these tests,

the committee majority took a position contrary to the wishes of the House majority and attempted to defend it on the floor. Generally speaking, their defense was unsuccessful. When the whole House membership had a well-formed attitude on a given measure, the committee position could not prevail against it (p. 127).

Kingdon emphasizes that these genuine test situations for the prior constraint hypothesis are "rare, isolated instances, and that the normal pattern is much different" (p. 129).

In contrast to those who have interpreted the anticipatory behavior of committees as indicative of committee dominance vis-à-vis the chamber, Kingdon is more cautious in speculating about the direction of influence: "The 'normal' pattern has the appearance of committee dominance, in part *because* committee members generally anticipate House reaction well enough that confrontations between House and committee are rare." It should be noted that Kingdon here speaks of the "appearance" of committee dominance and not just dominance. On the occasions when the "normal pattern" prevails, "it can be argued that the whole House has still a profound influence on the committee action" (p. 129). It is the House, then, that influences the committee to engage in anticipatory behavior. But there can be exceptions to the normal pattern: "In all this discussion about the importance of committee and leadership anticipation of the bulk of the House membership, it should not be forgotten that the committees still have considerable influence on policy outcomes" (pp. 131-132). And because of this inconclusiveness in the causal direction of influence, Kingdon makes clear that "the theoretical question is one of specifying the conditions under which committee influence predominates" (p. 132). Simple extrapolation from aggregate floor roll-call votes to "committee success" will not do.

Had research stood still, one would need to assess once more the problem of inference of floor roll-call votes to committee behavior. But scientific development was abetted by the congressional reforms of the 1970s which, in making committee votes public, practically wiped out much of the need to depend on inference from floor roll-call votes. In particular, it became possible to compare votes on the floor of the chamber and votes cast in committee. Unekis (1978) is the first published study testing congressmen's voting consistency and thus shedding new light on an old controversy. The study is based on votes taken in the 21 committees of the House during two Congresses, 1971-1974. Congressmen, Unekis reports, "are consistent in their voting behavior approximately ninety-two percent of the time. Eight percent of the time, however, their vote on the floor differs from their stand in committee" (p. 764).

Unekis believes that "an eight percent deviation is too large to dismiss as unimportant (thereby failing to reject) but too small to reject the null hypothesis with any degree of confidence. It may be that the size of the deviation reflects a structural factor" (p. 764). One such factor is the opportunity to vote. But he finds no relationship between the number of votes and consistency scores: "Clearly the opportunity to cast votes does not cause the consistency scores to deviate from total agreement" (p. 765). "Inconsistent" behavior, however, may be only apparent rather than real if a bill is radically amended on the floor. "When this occurs, congressmen are not voting on the same matter; what they vote on in the full Chamber is not what they voted on in committee" (p. 765). Tracing the history of the bills in order to control for the effect of floor amendments, Unekis places them into three groups: those with no amendments, those with minor amendments, and those with major amendments. He finds that "the consistency score rises slightly to .944, when bills with major amendments are omitted, leaving unexplained an inconsistency rate of approximately five percent." The remainder of inconsistency, Unekis believes, may simply be "noise" (p. 766).

In general, party-by-party and congress-by-congress analysis shows little variation in inconsistency, though there are exceptions. In the case of four committees average consistency scores vary "considerably" from congress to congress. Unekis offers several explanations for inconsistent voting, including party pressure, interest group activity, or pragmatic going along after alternatives proved unsuccessful. In conclusion Unekis notes that "there is little difference between committees with regard to levels of voting consistency. Where there are differences, analysis reveals the deviations are conditioned by circumstances. It appears the reasons for not voting consistently are simply too numerous and idiosyncratic to be reasonably categorized." This set of findings, Unekis suggests, "reinforces the position of those who argue for behavioral consistency in legislative voting behavior" (pp. 768-769).

Unekis's demonstration that floor roll-call votes on policies could be treated as valid surrogates of legislators' policy positions in committee seems to exonerate the studies that rely on roll-call votes to investigate committee phenomena. However, Unekis's "proof" cannot be taken as evidence that the earlier surrogate studies' inferences from members' floor votes to their committee behavior are valid. It may have been that prior to the 1970 reform members did differ in committee and floor behavior and that "consistency" became mandatory only when committee votes were made public.

Hamm (1982), acknowledging the need for replication of the Unekis study, raises the question whether the congressional findings can be generalized to the state legislatures. For in the latter "circumstances make voting consistency more tenuous than in Congress" (p. 474): shorter sessions, more personnel turnover, more chair rotation, multiple committee assignments, less staffing, insincere voting in committee because the party caucus is the locus of decision making, and so on. "Thus, sufficient conditions exist not to apply without question the findings of Congress to the states" (p. 474).

Hamm's research was conducted in seven chambers.[12] These chambers differ in size, size of party majorities, and committee centrality in decision making. None of these structural system variables prove viable. First, "there appears to be no one-to-one relationship between centrality of the committee system and degree of consistency"; second, "contrary to expectation, the two smallest chambers exhibited the greatest inconsistency, but the chamber with the largest membership was not far behind"; and third, "the chamber which was most dominated by a single party had the highest degree of consistency, but the chamber with the second largest number of majority members . . . had one of the lowest consistency scores." These results, Hamm asserts, "do not suggest that these variables are unimportant; they do indicate, however, that the impact of any one of these factors is neither uniform nor obvious" (p. 481).

Three factors—floor opposition, alternation in bill content, and intracommittee consensus or conflict—produce eight combinations which are arrayed according to the probability of change between committee and floor voting: "the most consistency should occur among those bills which have unanimous support in committee, no significant floor opposition, and no change in content, while the greatest change in voting patterns should occur for cases in which the reverse conditions are present" (p. 478). Hamm's tabulations indicate that "legislators in six of the seven chambers are consistent in voting between the committee and the floor in over 90 percent of the cases. . . . These overall results, however, mask substantial, important, and statistically significant differences in consistency among the eight possible combinations of conditions" (pp. 478-479). When noncontroversial legislation is excluded from analysis, "consistency scores drop significantly in all seven chambers. . . . Thus, roughly 11 to 19 percent of the legislators who cast a complete vote (committee and floor) on controversial legislation were not consistent from committee to floor" (p. 479).

Controlling for only those bills where there was 100 percent voting consistency, Hamm finds substantial variation among the eight conditions. In general, "the assumption that floor votes can be used as a surrogate of behavior in the committee is erroneous, at least at the state level" (p. 483). Moreover, changes in bill content cannot alone be assumed to make for inconsistency. Hamm therefore also examines some individual characteristics and the small-group factor. At the individual level, he finds neither a relationship between a legislator's voting frequency and consistency in any of the seven chambers nor a relationship between the number of terms served and consistency.

Hamm presents an interesting discussion in connection with a third hypothesis—that "individuals from the minority party will have higher levels of inconsistency than those of the majority party." Ambivalent individuals [read, "legislators"], he suggests, "are more inclined to behave in accord with the dominant position of a group [read, "committee"] to which they belong" (p. 485).

Hamm concludes with some methodological considerations. His "basic conclusion" is that "problems may develop if researchers use floor votes as surrogates of committee votes on nonconsensual legislation." This conclusion "reduces the probability of doing comparative state committee research in a simple, straightforward manner" because in states where committee members' votes are not available the use of floor votes may involve significant misspecification. He also warns against projecting such findings as his own (or those of Unekis, 1978) backward in time: "If the voting in committee today is more open, subject to public scrutiny, I can only suppose that the extent of voting inconsistency may actually have been greater in the past" (p. 488).

Parker and Parker (1979) exploit the new, post-1970 within-committee roll-call votes as a data base for systematic, comparative, and quantitative analysis of one aspect of committee decision structure—conflict and factionalism. They set out "to define the factional alignments in committee decision making . . . , and, in the process, illuminate the saliency of particular environmental influences within selected House committees." They start from the premise that "as a result of the differing impact of these environmental influences, cleavages or divisions develop within committees" (p. 85). Eight House committees from the 93d and 94th Congresses (1973-1976) were selected for study.[13]

Neither constituency demographics nor electoral votes proved useful in identifying the nature of factional alignments on the committees. Parker and Parker therefore limit the independent variables to member ratings by interest groups, congressional coalition scores, and presidential support scores. The accuracy and validity of what the investigators call the "visual interpretation of a committee's factional structure" can be examined by the correlates of individual committee factions (p. 88).[14]

Noteworthy in the Parkers' careful committee-by-committee analysis is their effort to compare their findings with those of prior investigators. However, in all but one committee (International Relations), party and ideology are found to structure the factional alignments in the roll-call stage of decision making; and in six committees these variables are said to be so "intertwined" that their separate effects are difficult to disentangle. Issues seem to play a firm role in structuring the factions on three committees, but are said to be "modest" or "relatively unimportant" on five. When it comes to environmental influence, the "House" is evidently "important" in all but one case (International Relations), the parties in four committees, and the administration in two. Clientele constraints are found to be explicit in only one case (Labor). Most noticeable but not apparent to the naked eye is that Parker and Parker find no effect of constituency as an environmental factor, a rather surprising nonfinding. One is given no indication why this is so.

Parker and Parker themselves seem to sense the limitations of their work as a structural study: "While knowledge of a committee's factional structure may not reveal the intricacies of committee decision-making practices, this information provides a baseline for mapping and monitoring changes in committee behavior" (p. 102). Perhaps frustrated by the indeterminate nature of their results, they invoke the need for case studies: "Case studies of individual committees then can provide additional specification of committee decision-making patterns, and further delineate some of the influences which have been obscured by party and ideology" (p. 102). Case analysts are likely to disagree, and consider roll-call analysis as at best supplemental to the discovery of a committee's factional structure.

Case analysts would also take exception to the notion that roll-call analysis of committee decisions is convenient "where interviews are difficult, if not impossible, to obtain" (p. 102). Parker and Parker's study has too many "missing data" to warrant such a suggestion. The analysis of environmental influences seems particularly deficient. The absence of a "constituency factor" where one would certainly expect it—on Agriculture, Interior, or Public Works—is troublesome. Only "labor" is identified as an outside influence on Education and Labor, but education groups are probably as much involved in the committee as labor is. The powerful postal unions seem to have nothing to do with the Post Office Committee. And "administration lobbying" seems to be surprisingly rare. Perhaps these are all "periods noneffects," but only diachronic analysis can cope with such problems.

Parker and Parker find that the House itself is a consistent and pervasive factor in the environment of committees. Committees want the House to pass their legislation, and to get legislation passed they permit themselves to be "constrained" in their recommendations. Usually, the "prior constraint" hypothesis is inferred by extrapolation. Most committees' high floor-success rates are interpreted to show that "prior constraint" must have been operating. Floor roll-call votes can be legitimately used, of course, to measure "committee success" on the chamber floor, but whether success is due to prior constraint requires separate inquiry, especially as "success" can be variously measured.

Diachronic-Aggregate Studies

Synchronic studies are temporally bound, so that it is never clear how far back in time a generalization can be extended. As Douglas Price (1977) has pointed out in another connection, in the course of time there may be "basic structural changes so sharp as to suggest the emergence of a new system of organization requiring a new analytic paradigm" (p. 28). Time-series data used diachronically are useful, however, not only to locate phenomena on the time dimension but also to make inferences from observations in time to the process of change itself.

McConachie's (1898) ancestral study of committees pointed the way toward systematic treatment of the time dimension in the development of congressional committees, but it was not until much later that a historical account of early congressional committees by Cooper (1965, 1970) provided rich contextual detail of possible use in undergirding diachronic-aggregate analysis. Unfortunately, space limitations do not permit us to summarize this original study of the birth and early development of the system of standing committees in the House of Representatives from the Jeffersonian period to about 1830. Just how useful such intensive historical study can be appears from Polsby's (1968) complaint that "a wholly satisfactory account of the historical development of the House committee system does not exist," forcing him in his own study of committee institutionalization to rely instead on "a more modest anecdotal procedure" (p. 153). The burden of Polsby's complaint is that time-series analysis can be substantively deceptive if it remains historically noncontextual. In combination, however, quantitative time-series data and anecdotal information allow Polsby to present the first and now classic systematic comparison of stages or phases of committee institutionalization in the U.S. House of Representatives.

Although only tangentially concerned with committees, Polsby's study is firmly rooted in relevant theories. Drawing on the work of Maine, Tonnies, Weber and Durkheim, Polsby (1968) points out that "the process of institutionalization is one of the grand themes of all modern social science." From these theories Polsby derives three major characteristics of an "institutionalized organization": first, differentiation from its environment; second, relative complexity stemming from a division of labor "in which roles are specified, and there are widely shared expectations about the performance of roles"; and third, the use of universalistic rather than particularistic criteria for organization and "automatic rather than discretionary methods of conducting its internal business" (pp. 144-145).

Polsby identifies four major and distinct phases in the development of congressional committees—first, "the no-committee, Hamiltonian era, in which little or no internal differentiation within the institution was visible"; second, "a Jeffersonian phase, in which factional alignments had begun to develop . . . [and] a small number of standing committees existed, but were not heavily relied upon"; third, a period of about 100 years, beginning in 1810, during which "the committee system waxed and waned more or less according to the ways in which committees were employed by the party or faction that dominated the House and elected the Speaker"; and fourth, a "decentralized" phase in which "committees have won solid institutionalized independence from party leaders both inside and outside Congress" (pp. 155-156). During this last phase, the work of the committees became "increasingly technical and specialized, and the way in which they organize internally to do their work is entirely at their own discretion," though "to a degree, the development over the last sixty years of an increasingly complex machinery of party leadership within the House cross-cuts and attenuates the independent power of committees" (p. 156).

Polsby demonstrates the institutionalization of the committee system by way of a careful, congress-by-congress analysis of the growth of seniority as a criterion determining committee rank between 1881 and 1963 (see also Polsby, Gallaher, and Rundquist, 1969). He interprets his findings:

> The increasing complexity of the division of labor presents an opportunity for individual Representatives to specialize and thereby enormously increases their influence upon a narrow range of policy outcomes in the political system at large. Considered separately, the phenomenon of specialization may strike the superficial observer as productive of narrow-minded drones. But the total impact of a cadre of public policies is a formidable asset for a political institution; and it has undoubtedly enabled the House to retain a measure of autonomy and influence that is quite exceptional for a 20th century legislature (1968, p. 166).

Haeberle (1978) is a useful, if strictly descriptive, extension of Polsby's arguments to House subcommittees. Three subcommittee properties—activity, permanency, and distinctiveness (the latter referring to whether subcommittees are named or numbered)—are used to examine subcommittee institutionalization from the 80th (1947-1948) to the 94th (1975-1976) Congress. "Although the indicators of subcommittee activity, permanency, and distinctiveness show a moderate trend towards institutionalization through the 91st Congress, each indicator 'takes off' suggesting an intensified movement toward institutionalization beginning with the 92d Congress and continuing through the 94th Congress" (pp. 1062-1063). The subcommittee is thus established as "a new unit in American government." As such, Haeberle concludes, it "is a unit capable of reshaping the existing distribution of power within the House of Representatives, and thereby altering the policy outcomes of the legislative process" (p. 1065).

Haeberle argues that the House committee reforms of the 1970s, notably the emergence of subcommittees as institutional units with considerable autonomy, follow as much as precede institutionalization; support for this argument comes from Deering's (1982) time-series study of bill management on the floor from the 86th (1959-1960) to the 95th (1977-1978) Congresses. Deering examines data at three levels—at the aggregate level of the House as a whole, at the level of the committee, and at the level of the individual bill managers. At the House level, Deering finds "strong support for the proposition that subcommittee chairs now manage most legislation." However, he also finds "substantial participation by non-full-committee chairs in all of the Congresses examined." His data indicate that "at least since 1959, committee chairs have not managed bills to the exclusion of other participants" and that subcommittee chairs "managed more legislation than full committee chairs by the 91st Congress at the latest—a full two years prior to the change in caucus rules" (pp. 536-537). At the second level, committee-by-committee analysis shows that "committees have become more decentralized internally" (p. 538). Classifying committees in terms of the percentage of bills managed by the full-committee chair, Deering finds that in the stable, low-to-moderate category "there has always been substantial bill management by subcommittee chairs" (p. 539). At the individual level, generalization is difficult, but on the whole, tendencies for more dispersion in bill management already present earlier increased with the reforms from the 93d (1973-1974) Congress on. He concludes that "the expansion of subcommittee power has not been just within the confines of the subcommittee itself but has extended to the full committee and on the floor of the House" (p. 543). But while there has been an unmistakable shift in bill management from full to subcommittee chairs, "the shift has been from a base of substantial ongoing subcommittee chair participation, and the shift has not reflected the true proportion of subcommittee chairs in the House" (p. 544).

Changes in institutions must not be confused with changes of institutions. The former may or may not be conducive to the latter. For instance, numerical increase of subcommittees does not necessarily mean that "government by committees" has been replaced by "subcommittee government." The conditions required for the emergence of subcommittee government and the question of its institutionalization are set forth by Davidson (1981b) in a theoretically and empirically sophisticated attack on these problems. After briefly reviewing what he calls "the mechanisms of change" (pp. 100-102, treated more fully in Davidson and Oleszek, 1976, and Davidson, 1981a), Davidson traces "the triumph of subcommittee government" from "the era of the committee chairmen" (pp. 103-106) and "the revolt against seniority" (pp. 106-108) to the changes of the 1970s. He concludes that "the new system of subcommittee government is very different from its predecessor, which has been so convincingly described by researchers of the 1950s and 1960s. The new system is not mature, in that not all of the details of its operation have been institutionalized. Yet it is a highly complex and articulated system" (p. 108).

To specify the broad outlines of this subcommittee government, Davidson inspects available workload data and particular cases of policy making, warning that as these cases tend to deal with highly salient and controversial issues, "they may exaggerate somewhat the leading features of the decision-making system" (p. 115).

Diachronic-aggregate inspection of "committee and subcommittee work patterns" (pp. 115-118) from the 84th (1955-1956) to the 95th (1977-1978) Congress shows a steady increase of committee and subcommittee meetings in the Senate and a dramatic rise in the House. But, Davidson notes, "this dramatic shift in meeting activity in the House occurred prior to the much-publicized subcommittee reforms of the early 1970s, which apparently served to ratify and legitimize a revolution that was already well advanced" (p. 117). On the other hand, although subcommittees may be "where the action is," this "does not mean that subcommittees are autonomous." Moreover, again inspecting data for the 1955-1978 period by congressional sessions, Davidson notes that "more workgroup activity does not necessarily mean more laws. . . . [T]he number of reports to the full chamber has actually declined over the past twenty-five years, as has the number of laws passed." However, these data are deceptive: "Those measures that are passed tend to be longer, more complex, and subject to more floor amendments than their predecessors" (p. 118).

Jurisdictional politics have led to the practice of multiple bill referrals which, Davidson argues, make for intercommittee cooperation and flexibility in the committee system and "can broaden participation . . . by breaking up the monopolistic control committees and subcommittees once exerted over legislation in 'their' jurisdiction" (p. 122). But, "at the same time, multiple referrals accentuate the decentralized, unwieldy character of congressional policy making." Through delaying and vetoing they "erect new obstacles to policy making."

Drawing on the studies of others as well as relying on his own diachronic data for hours of House and Senate sessions and number of recorded floor votes, Davidson argues that "congressional policy making is permeable not only at the early deliberative stages but also at later stages to participation on the part of a variety of members, whether or not they serve on workgroups holding jurisdiction over the legislation at hand" (pp. 124-125). He takes exception to the metaphor of "iron triangles" because it conveys a sense of closure that tends to exaggerate the system's rigidity. Many of the subsystem relationships subsumed by the metaphor, Davidson suggests, "were neither ironclad nor triangular. Today these relationships are, in fact, so complex and fluid that the metaphor may be altogether misleading" (p. 131).

Distinguishing between a "lone wolf" and a "collegial" pattern of questioning of witnesses before three full U.S. House committees (Agriculture, Banking and Currency, Foreign Affairs) from the early 1950s into the early 1970s, Payne (1982) measures change in "interposition level"— whether a congressman continues his own questioning after having received an answer or allows another committee member to interpose before resuming his own questioning. In all three committees "there has been a dramatic decline in the interposition levels over the 1950-1970 period" (p. 628). Seeking an explanation, Payne asks why congressmen would be prompted in the first place to engage in collegial questioning and suggests that "congressmen interact when they are interested in the substance of the policy being discussed," so that "the decline in the interposition level, then, would seem to reflect a lower collective interest in the substance of policy" (p. 631). On the other hand, he suggests that monopolizing the questioning may be due to "self-display" (p. 632). But as the five-minute rule has grown in importance, it may also be that the declining interposition level could be due to this institutionalization. Payne offers two objections to this: it fails to explain why the rule has grown in importance, and even when the rule is in effect, members may ignore it and engage in collegial questioning.

The availability of time-series data and their use in diachronic analysis facilitate what is more often than not extraordinarily difficult in the study of real-world politics: the application of an experimental design. A study by Rieselbach and Unekis (1981-1982) of the consequences of committee reforms and changes in four House committees during the 92d (1971-1972) and 95th (1977-1978) Congresses was made possible by the Legislative Reorganization Act of 1970, which mandated the recording of committee roll calls. The experimental design, in turn, was facilitated by the "fortunate" (from the experimental point of view) forced change of committee chairmen at the midpoint of the time series in 1975. As the investigators put it, analysis of all votes in the four committees "permits us both to trace the general course of reform and to compare directly the two Congresses prior to and the two following the ouster of the sitting chairmen" (p. 85).

Using cluster-bloc procedures, set forth in detail in an Appendix (pp. 113-114), Rieselbach and Unekis test a number of hypotheses that are carefully stated and explicated (pp. 85-86). Even before analyzing the findings separately for each of the four committees—Agriculture, Armed Services, Banking and Currency, and Ways and Means—Rieselbach and Unekis provide an overview of their findings.[15]

Our results reveal, overall, the basic stability of congressional committee politics. On three of the four panels we examine, changing chairpersons, as well as the variety of other alterations that occurred during the decade, produced shifts of degree, at most, not of kind. Only the Ways and Means Committee, the object of a wholesale assault that far transcended ousting the sitting chairman, displayed significantly different structures and behavior in the aftermath of reform. Generally, committees, as on-going political institutions—with relatively fixed member motivations and internal organizations and processes, with established relationships with environmental actors—seem highly resistant to the pragmatic, piecemeal, politically inspired change typical of the 1970s' reform movement (p. 86).

Further pursuing the theme of committee leadership in the first such study based on diachronic-aggregate data, Unekis and Rieselbach (1983) understate the importance of their work when they write that "there have been few systematic, comparative analyses of committee leadership" (p. 251). Accepting as fact that committees differ in their decision-making structures, Unekis and Rieselbach predict that leadership styles will also differ. Two linkages between committee structure and leadership need investigation: first, "to what extent committee attributes are associated with committee leadership patterns"; and second, "whether committees with distinctive leadership patterns perform in distinctive ways." The analysis is based on all nonprocedural roll calls in nine committees in the 92d (1971-1972) through 95th (1977-1978) Congresses. These roll calls are used "to identify the chairperson's place in the overall committee voting patterns, to chart the changes in leadership positions that occur over time, and to assess the relationship of leadership posture to committee performance" (p. 252). Using cluster-bloc procedures, Unekis and Rieselbach identify committee factions in each congress and, by way of correlation coefficients and interagreement scores, define the chairperson's position with respect to the factions as well as party and ideological groups. They also report on the chair's agreement with the ranking minority member.

Unekis and Rieselbach anticipate finding three possible patterns of committee leader behavior: first, drawing on studies of political parties (Patterson, 1963; MacRae, 1956), an "extremity pattern," with the leader mobilizing a dominant majority faction; second, drawing on Truman (1959), a "partisan-middleman pattern"; and third, following Fenno (1973), a "bipartisan-consensual pattern." They concede that they "cannot resolve a complex problem of causality. Roll-call data do not permit us to say whether leader behavior creates or reflects a committee's ways of conducting business" (p. 253). In reporting their findings, the investigators find support for their three categories in 34 of the 36 cases. Of more interest here, because of the diachronic nature of the data, the results "reveal both the nonrandom distribution of leadership styles and the differential impact of change, intended or otherwise, on individual committees" (p. 259).

Four committees (Armed Services, Banking, Education and Labor, Commerce) showed constant leadership patterns—something not surprising in the latter two as the same chairs sat through the four congresses. But on Armed Services and Banking, where the chairs had been replaced after the 1974 elections, the same leadership postures were taken by the new chairs—bipartisan-consensual and middleman, respectively. Two committees showed a single change over the 1971-1978 period. On Rules, there was a shift from the bipartisan strategy of a Southern conservative to an extremity posture under his liberal successor (facilitated by the new influence of the speaker over the committee). On Ways and Means, the departure of Wilbur Mills as a bipartisan-consensual leader was followed by the middleman position which his successor had to assume in order to hold the committee

Democrats together. But the remaining three committees (Agriculture, Government Operations, Post Office) "reveal more variability still." Unekis and Rieselbach conclude that "leadership emerges as a complex and fluid set of interactions between chairman and rank-and-file members, interactions that reflect both factors peculiar to single committees and changes in the broader environment of the House and American national politics" (p. 260).

Turning to what they call "committee performance," Unekis and Rieselbach test three hypotheses. A first hypothesis has it that "the extremity posture and strong partisanship should be closely related. . . . In short, moving from extremity through middleman to bipartisan leadership styles should lead to a diminution of inter-party cleavage" (p. 261). Aggregate comparison, the investigators report, supports this view as do the data for individual committees. The second hypothesis predicts that "leadership style will relate to majority party (Democratic) cohesion" (p. 261). Again, the aggregate and individual committee data are reported to "sustain" the hypothesis: average integration scores are in the expected direction along the leadership style continuum. The third hypothesis relates leadership posture to what is called "extracommittee performance, victory on the floor," and predicts that "partisan leadership—extreme or middleman variety—will be less successful on the floor than bipartisan strategies." Once again, according to the authors, "the aggregate figures tend to sustain our expectation: bipartisan committees have their position supported by a majority of the full House on 88.2 percent of all roll calls; the comparable figures for the committees with extremity and middleman leadership are 84 and 86 percent" (p. 263). A footnote seeks to make these miniscule differences statistically palatable, but there is an element of self-fulfillment in this hypothesis as well.

Using time-series data of House roll calls, Feig (1981) "seeks confirmation of the findings [by Fenno and Manley] . . . concerning the relationship between integration and partisanship, when examined with a methodology different from ones they employed" (p. 426). At best, however, the tests Feig used allowed only indirect and inferential confirmation. Like its methodological predecessors (Dyson and Soule, 1970; Dodd, 1972) the study relies on floor roll-call votes, and its conceptualizations of the measures are even more stylized.

Its conceptual and measurement problems notwithstanding, the study is noteworthy for four reasons: first, its data base covers 24 years (1947 through 1970) and involves an over-time analysis; second, by including two House committees—Ways and Means and Education and Labor—it provides for comparison over time; and third, the model (see also Feig, 1979) is dynamic in allowing for the "present *level or amount*" of integration and partisanship as dependent variables. As the author points out, "at work here is what might be called a 'saturation effect.' A committee which is already highly integrated is less likely to become even more highly integrated than is a currently less well-integrated committee, other things being equal" (p. 428). And fourth, in order to control for years of House service, party and region, variables that might affect committee voting over time, Feig identifies for every committee member a matching congressman not on the committee.

Five hypotheses are tested. First, that integration is negatively related to district electoral heterogeneity is supported for both committees. Second, that integration is negatively effected by the average "independent power" of the members is also confirmed for both committees, though in the case of Ways and Means seniority does not preclude cooperative behavior (p. 432). Third, no relationship between committee and environmental (House) partisanship is found for either committee. This finding may have been due, however, to the way in which partisanship was measured. Fourth, opposite results were expected and are obtained for the relationship between change in committee integration and change in partisanship—positive but weak in the case of Ways and Means, negative in the case of Education and Labor. Feig interprets these results to mean that "at any given point in time, the amounts of integration and partisanship will be highly dependent upon one another with . . . changes in one being compensated for by changes in the other" (p. 433). Fifth, a saturation effect is found, as expected, in Ways and Means. In Education and Labor, on the other hand, the effect of saturation is negative for change in integration but positive for change in partisanship. The author infers that "in this case large amounts of partisanship do *not* make more difficult future increases in partisanship (a 'saturation effect') but rather make such increases more *easy* (an 'acceleration effect')" (p. 434).

Institutional Change Studies

The new literature dealing with committee reform and its consequences as well as with secular institutional change that may or may not be related to reform can be partitioned into three, but by no means mutually exclusive, modes: predominantly and intentionally "prescriptive," though predicated on some analytic model of the place of committees in the legislative scheme; mainly designed to "monitor" reform proposals, reform politics, and short- or long-term changes; and essentially "interpretative" or "evaluative" of the reforms and their implications.

Prescriptive Studies

Two analytic models seem to underlie the prescriptive writings: first, a kind of zero-sum "leadership-committee interdependence" model which assumes that what is added by way of authority to one side of the power continuum will or must be taken away from the other side; and second, a "representative principle" model which is based on the "mirror theory" of representation.

According to Ripley (1974), party leadership-committee interaction exhibits either "party activist" or "committee autonomy" characteristics, with any real-world situation being a mixture. In the U.S. House of Representatives the committee autonomy pattern predominates, while the House would be better able to fulfill its functions if the leadership activist pattern prevailed. Jones (1974) recommends that committee autonomy should be curbed by party leadership because "failure to make changes may jeopardize existing congressional authority and thereby may threaten the whole democratic structure of this nation" (p. 160). Peabody (1974) also recommends strengthening party leadership, but he contends that "it may be possible to . . . enhance the organization and the effectiveness of the committees and, ultimately, to increase the overall powers of the Congress" (p. 136). While Peabody's reforms, like Jones's, would increase the dependency of committee chairmen on party leadership, they also have the potential of decentralizing power even more. As he notes himself, "the proliferation of subcommittee autonomy could lead to one hundred thirty little fiefdoms" (p. 140). Despite a desire to enhance the effectiveness of committees, the "leadership activist" modelers are concerned mainly with leadership, as opposed to committee, control of the legislative product.

A second prescriptive model is predicated on a more general theory of "representativeness." Davidson (1974) and Ornstein (1974), like Jones and Peabody, feel that committees have too much influence over legislation. The situation is best remedied, they argue, by making the committees more "representative" of the parent chamber, so that the legislation they propose will accurately reflect what the whole chamber would have proposed. Davidson as well as Ornstein recommend a number of alternative solutions to what they consider the problem of unrepresentativeness, including consolidation of committees, limitation of chairmanship tenure, or rotation of committee assignments. Both authors indicate that enlarged jurisdictions would result in a large number of subcommittees. While Davidson (p. 56) considers subcommittee proliferation a "serious drawback" to the enlarged jurisdiction plan, Ornstein seems to feel that this proliferation might be advantageous, up to a point: "Giving out more subcommittee chairs can encourage congressmen to do their legislative work. . . . Once one reaches the point of overlap at which members must chair several different units, the effects of subcommittee proliferation become negative. Until that point is reached, more subcommittees may be beneficial" (p. 153).

While the "representativeness model" may appear persuasive to those who subscribe to a "descriptive" theory of representation, it is flawed by a further premise that Davidson and Ornstein fail to articulate. They evidently assume that the composition of the House as a whole is "representative," in the mirror sense, of the nation as a whole. This premise is implicit in the guiding question which Ornstein asks: "How, then, can committees reflect the makeup of the entire body as a microcosm of the nation . . . ?" (p. 152). But the House, counter to the premise, is not a "microcosm of the nation." It is a corporation of electoral-district constituencies. The House, then, may be "representative" of these constituencies, but it is not representative of the nation. Even if it were possible to make the committees "more representative" of the constituencies represented in the House as a whole, it is difficult to see what "national interest" would guide committee policy-making. In fact, the bargaining and compromising required in "more representative"—that is, more heterogeneous—committees might aggravate the task of national consensus-building.

Monitoring Studies

As a genre, monitoring studies are predominantly descriptive. Yet, description of events such as those connected with the congressional committee reforms of the 1970s is of necessity a part of the scientific enterprise. It helps to delineate the changing context in which more explanation-conscious investigators can orient themselves. It is not appropriate, therefore, to speak of "mere" description and write it off as irrelevant. And indeed, as Oppenheimer (1980) has pointed out, "Congressional scholars have been kept busy ensuring that their colleagues are up-to-date with the extensive reforms in Congress" (p. 5).

Description is likely to focus on spectacular occurrences, but legislatures are not institutions whose normal and regular processes are often disturbed by such happenings. In the case of the U.S. Congress, for instance, only the fight over the enlargement of the House Rules Committee in 1961 and 1963 intervened as a significant episode between the Legislative Reorganization Act of 1946 and the reforms of the 1970s. In the case of the Rules Committee, a recent study by Oppenheimer (1981a) could fruitfully build on a number of prior studies, notably a comprehensive earlier account by Robinson (1963), coming to the conclusion that "less than 20 years after Robinson's book appeared, we find a very different House Rules Committee" (p. 207). Drawing on other prior research as well (Peabody, 1963; Cummings and Peabody, 1963; Fox and Clapp, 1970a, 1970b; Oppenheimer, 1977) and combining this cumulative information with his own longitudinal-quantitative data from 1956 to 1978, Oppenheimer is able to describe and possibly explain how and why the Rules Committee changed over the period. In doing so he makes use of his own earlier formulation of three new "collective" roles that the committee seems to be playing in its latest phase— " 'new' traffic cop," "dress rehearsal," and "field commander" (1977, pp. 102-113). As "traffic cop" the Rules Committee serves the leadership, for example by arranging to report leader-favored bills at the most propitious time; as "field commander" the committee takes over some of the responsibilities of whipping; and as a "dress rehearsal" forum, it provides members of other committees with an opportunity to test out their proposals in a relatively informal and unpublicized setting. Methodologically, Oppenheimer is especially sensitive to the connection between changes in an institution's subunits and the structure of the institution as a whole.

Unlike Oppenheimer's studies, a number of articles seeking to provide early overviews of the congressional committee reforms are not very satisfactory, partly because they lack sufficient information, partly because the observer is too close to the event to give it thoughtful reflection. Rohde (1974), for instance, reports on the origins of the "Subcommittee Bill of Rights," so-called, and monitors compliance with some of the reforms. Substantive compliance, he admits, "could only be determined by extensive interviewing with members of all committees—which was not done" (p. 45). Limited to examining "formal compliance," he finds many variations, but the rules making for subcommittee autonomy fared best. Ornstein (1975) largely monitors the politicking involved in the reform efforts of the 1970s. Although the article purports to be in the genre of studies designed "to look more and more at the nature and origins of institutional change" (p. 88, with reference to Polsby, 1968, and Douglas Price, 1971), its perspective is short-range.

These and other more or less "occasional" writings have been largely superceded by a comprehensive and sustained account of the entire reform movement in both House and Senate by Davidson and Oleszek (1977) which is currently the *locus classicus* of the monitoring genre of studies and the most worthy successor to the reform writings of the 1940s (such as Galloway, 1946). However, in contrast to the earlier writings, the Davidson and Oleszek report is based on and incorporates a generic theory of legislative organization and institutional change. (Because the theory is more germane to interpretation and evaluation, we shall deal with it in the next section.)

Davidson and Oleszek's work is also an exercise in advocacy. It is written from the perspective of the authors' experiences as staff members of the House Select Committee on Committees (or Bolling Committee) set up in January 1973 for the purpose of studying the House committee system and making recommendations for reform. Their account of the committee's birth, life, and demise features chairperson Bolling and a few other members as heroes and antireform opponents as villains. However, this bias notwithstanding, in no other study is the potential for reform of the congressional committee system more richly and sharply delineated.

The formidable methodological problem of monitoring change is apparent in a study of four House committees (Agriculture, Government Operations, Commerce, and International Relations) by Ornstein and Rohde (1977a). At issue is the possibility of isolating and observing the change agent so that its effects can be separated out from the effects of other stimuli which might also occur in its absence. The difficulty is that in reform incubating over several years there is no single event that can be identified and isolated as the change agent to allow a clear before-and-after comparison. Ornstein and Rohde seem to assume that all of the reforms can be treated as a kind of summated independent variable whose impact on committee behavior and policy outputs can be observed. However, the independent and dependent variables are so cumulatively intermingled that causes and effects are impossible to specify. After presenting the evidence, Ornstein and Rohde (p. 187) must settle for the rather vague assertion that "the interaction of these shifts in membership and in procedures have led to significant alterations in the power structure of the House of Representatives."

Ornstein and Rohde are sensitive to another methodological problem—within-unit/cross-time and interunit/cross-time comparisons. In regard to the former, and specifically the Government Operations Committee, they write:

Since our comparisons across time are only for the first seven months of each Congress, we must be cautious in our interpretations—the between-Congress differences might well disappear if we had information for each full two-year period—but it appears that several subcommittees underwent significant jumps in activity between the Ninety-first and Ninety-second Congresses (p. 246).

In regard to interunit, cross-time comparison, Ornstein and Rohde point to the varying base lines against which comparison of change effects must be seen:

Probably the least surprising generalization one can draw from the preceding analysis is that the impact of House turnover and reform has not been the same on all committees. The reason is that the committees were . . . themselves not all the same to begin with. The differences which existed among these committees influenced the ways in which turnover and rule changes affected them (pp. 261-262).

We cannot attempt to summarize the rich detail presented in Ornstein and Rohde's 80-page report. While the authors claim to be employing Fenno's theory of three "basic goals," the theory is not used explicitly or systematically. For instance, it is reported that "despite the fact that the Agriculture Committee has undergone enormous membership change and has been substantially affected by the reform process, little overt change in behavior or policy outputs has occurred" (p. 229). No explanation is given for this finding in comparison with the other committees.

The hazards of instant monitoring are even more obvious in a study also by Ornstein and Rohde (1977b) of the House Commerce Committee during the 94th (1975-1976) Congress. The study describes the power struggles over the new and strengthened subcommittee chairs, evidently as an "effect" of the changes occasioned by membership turnover, substantive reform and, implicitly, the personal ambitions of the actors involved. But it is difficult to specify just what is supposed to have caused what. In spite of "a striking decentralization of power and resources to the subcommittees," Ornstein and Rohde found "virtually no change in the number of committee hearings between the 93rd and 94th Congresses." In fact, the data show that "there was a substantial upsurge of activity between the 91st and the 93rd Congress" (pp. 62-63). Their attempt to account for this null effect of drastic structural change is not persuasive.

Deering and Smith (1981), in a partly well-documented, partly overwritten narrative, report on what they perceive as the interactions between the House majority party leadership and "the new House subcommittee system." Overall, "there are many more points of origin for legislation, more points of access for political causes, and more opportunities for legislators to establish individual political identities" (p. 266). Comparing party unity scores for committee and subcommittee leaders with those for all House Democrats, Deering and Smith conclude that while in the last two congresses of the period (the 95th and 96th) "the subcommittee chairs have fallen behind the full committee chairs in terms of their overall support . . . , the most important change has been the improved representativeness of committee and subcommittee leaders of the House Democrats" (p. 267).

Most of the study concerns the interactions between the majority leadership and subcommittee chairs. The factors shaping these interactions are alternatively seen from the perspective of either side during the 96th (1979-1980) Congress. Deering and Smith conclude that "on balance, the leadership has lost ground in its struggle to gain greater control of the legislative process. The lost ground, of course, has gone primarily to the subcommittees. The strength of the new subcommittee system has multiplied and extended the lines of communication through which the leadership's tasks are performed" (pp. 288-289).

Evaluative-Interpretative Studies

As Davidson and Oleszek (1976) point out, "approached with caution, the study of institutional reform can illuminate the process of organizational change and help us to comprehend the complex interactions between an organization and its environment." Bargaining being the most salient characteristic of a legislative body, "innovation in such an organization assumes a complexity and subtlety far greater than that for hierarchical structures." The organizational problem of a legislature is "whether it can maintain or perhaps increase its autonomy (control of its own decisions) and scope of operations (extent or sphere of influence)" (pp. 38-39).

To cope with this problem, Davidson and Oleszek (1976) and Davidson (1981a) present a kind of functional requisite theory of structural innovation that guides their evaluation of the changes that occurred in the U.S. House throughout the 1970s, but also occurred in the Senate in the late phase of the period (1981a, pp. 120-128). Adapting notions of organization formulated in other contexts, they proceed from the assumption that the legislature, like any organization, "must adjust both to its external environment and to its internal needs" (1976, p. 39). There are two distinctive "ideal-typical" modes of responding to these pressures: adaptation and consolidation.

Adaptation refers to shifts in practices or work habits designed to adapt to external pressures. Consolidation refers to adjustments in procedures or power relationships designed to help members realize individual goals or relieve internal tensions. These two types of innovation flow from divergent sources and exert independent effects upon the institution. What is more, adaptation and consolidation may pull in opposing directions, forcing the institution to make difficult and costly choices (1981a, pp. 109-110).

And while these modes of response are common to all organizations, "in a flatly structured organization like the House, whose norms place a premium upon behavioral stability and conflict avoidance or containment, the tilt toward consolidative as opposed to adaptive innovation will presumably be quite pronounced" (1976, p. 41).

Innovations may range from "grand designs" to marginal and incremental adjustments. Cutting through familiar polemics, Davidson and Oleszek argue that adaptive and consolidative changes are "twin organizational imperatives" because "adaptations must not overturn the organization's internal equilibrium; conversely, consolidative arrangements that impair the organization's ability to interface with its external environment will eventually cause difficulty" (p. 43).

What is called a "simplified and fragmentary" theory is more intensively used by Davidson (1981a) in a historical appraisal of House committee reorganizations and also of Senate efforts to reorganize its committees. If the real world which Davidson describes seems more complex than the theory accounts for, it is because, as Davidson points out in his conclusion on "the process of innovation," the reorganization proposals "followed a similar design," but "in final form the changes bore the imprint of each chamber. The House made minimal alterations in committee jurisdictions and none at all in controlling assignments. . . . The Senate, on the other hand, had no conceptual difficulty with such matters, even though given changes were often stoutly resisted" (p. 129).

Like Davidson, David Price (1981) introduces two stable analytic criteria for an "estimate of Congress's strengths and weaknesses"—type of issues being processed and stage of the policy-making process. These categories permit Price to provide some rectification of the exaggerated view of the "new" committee system as being out-of-hand and of the extremist version of purposive individualism. Price explicitly recognizes that the impact of committees on legislative policy-making can be examined at two levels: the level of the committee system which "both reflects and reinforces congressional particularism and fragmentation" and the level of the committees "in their particularity" (pp. 182-183).

Making his criteria types of issues and policy-making stage, Price argues that Congress is well-suited as an "issue-generating" agency in the early stages of policy making; in controversial areas of broad national scope, policies may be agitated in Congress long before they reach the presidential agenda. Therefore, "recognition of the multifaceted and cooperative character of policy-making undermines simplistic generalizations about congressional or executive domination of the process in general. . . . Congress's decentralized, committee-centered decision structure is ideally suited to the early stages of legislative initiative" (pp. 159-160).

Although initially accepting the "individualistic" interpretation of the congressional committee system as "admirably equipped to help in this regard" (p. 163), Price subsequently concedes that this perspective "seriously underestimates the independent impact the committee system has on their [legislators'] priorities and their behavior. . . . The committee system channels these desires for leverage and status into activity that serves the *institution's* needs and builds its policymaking capacities" (p. 165). However, in contrast to other critics who invariably return to strengthening the parties and the leadership, Price suggests that "here, too, committees comprise part of the solution," as shown by the integrative roles played by the Appropriations, Budget, Rules, or Ways and Means committees (p. 166).

In dealing with the "policymaking environment," Price accepts but also modifies Fenno's interpretation and refers to his own previous work (Price, 1972). His major point is that just as "certain characteristics of a congressional committee may standardize its behavior across a range of policy areas," so "a single committee may construe its responsibilities differently in different areas" (p. 180).

Still other analytic criteria are used by Schick (1981) in a broad-gauged interpretation and evaluation of the consequences of the 1974 Congressional Budget Act for the budget process itself and the operations of the House and Senate appropriations and revenue committees. The legislative process is seen as a continuing balance act between the confrontation that a decentralized committee system is likely to engender and the accommodation that a product acceptable to the Congress as a whole (or, rather, majorities in the two houses) calls for. After reviewing the 1976 tax legislation as a "case" (pp. 319-324), Schick suggests that "on every tax issue in Congress, the budget and tax committees can veer toward confrontation or accommodation." While in the 1976 case the *modus operandi* was more confrontational than accommodative, "no successful legislative committee could function on these terms for long. In the pluralist environment of Capitol Hill, success is not bought in the currency of war but in the deference accorded to committees (and members) by virtue of their expertise in particular areas of legislation" (p. 324).

In establishing a coordinating budget process, Schick continues elsewhere, "Congress sought to preserve its essential character as a legislative body. It sought to balance budget control with other legislative values." As a legislative body, Congress is characterized by a wide dispersion of power, multiple opportunities for access and influence, and often piecemeal, inconsistent decision making: "These characteristics are political imperatives for a legislature whose distinctive role is the representation of diverse interests" (p. 325).

Within this broad theoretical frame of reference Schick appraises the development of congressional budgeting and the conflicts between the appropriations and revenue committees which yet, for many decades, constituted "a relatively stable committee structure for making spending and revenue decisions." Schick's evaluative language is consonant with his theoretical understanding of what a legislature is about. For instance, "the Budget Act disrupted this symmetrical division of labor by vesting a third set of committees with a role in financial policy"; or, "the content of a budget resolution intrudes on the central business of these older committees" (p. 288).

To support his judgments, Schick reviews in detail the difficulties of congressional budgeting and the functions of the relevant committees. As becomes clear, the Budget Act and the establishment of the budget committees had less impact on the operations of the traditional committees than one might assume, for their "intrusion" was anticipated by earlier or contemporaneous reforms that in the 1970s "weakened" these influential committees. Schick sets forth these developments in systematic fashion for the House Appropriations Committee (pp. 297-304) and Ways and Means Committee (pp. 309-311). In this respect his account is an authoritative and perspicacious, if more condensed, update of the studies conducted in the 1960s by Fenno (1966) and Manley (1970).

By bifocal concentration on a necessarily single process like budget-ing—through the lense of appropriations, on the one hand; through the lense of taxation, on the other hand—Schick can thus compare and evaluate two (or four) committees-in-interaction. It becomes apparent that evaluation of the "success" or "failure" of any one committee is not unrelated to evaluation of another committee, precisely because their real-world operations are intertwined, much as they may presume to be "autonomous" in their specific domains. Schick's study of the emergence of the new budget com-mittees and, in turn, their relationships to the two (or four) older committees reports an almost paradigmatic instance of obsolescence in an institutional subsystem and its policy-making processes.

Oppenheimer's (1980, 1981b) studies of the role of relevant—perhaps irrelevant—committees in energy legislation during the 94th and 95th (1975-1978) Congresses are more of a monitoring than evaluative sort, but he does not eschew assessment of the process and fate of energy policy-making as it was mired in the maze of many committees. In this instance, the establishment of a coordinating ad hoc committee by the House leadership was, at best, a temporary cure and, as Oppenheimer (1980, p. 26) puts it, "just that, 'ad hoc'."

Comparing the effects of decentralization in the House and Senate, Oppenheimer identifies a significant micro-analytic difference that any further House committee reorganization should not ignore. Referring to "the problem of mobilization" being greater in the House, he writes:

when jurisdictional splits occur on legislation in the Senate it is likely that several senators serve on both committees involved in the jurisdictional claim, which facilitates commu-nication and negotiation between the two committees. In addition, senators are likely to be less concerned with jurisdictional turf than House members since the same total turf is divided among fewer members (p. 27).

Oppenheimer's observation points to the continued impasse that derives, in both academic theory and political practice, from the discrepant needs of the individual legislator, on the one hand, and of the collective institution, on the other hand. Purposive models view the institution as an aggregation of individuals whose goals and activities shape its structures, functions, and processes. And there is but little question that legislators in fact often act on the assumptions that the purposive models posit. The decentralizing tendencies in and operations of the congressional committee system, observed before, during, and after the reforms of the 1970s, document the theoretical validity of these models.

But as organizational models, properly reformulated and applied to the particular conditions of a legislature (see Froman, 1968; Cooper, 1977, 1981; Davidson and Oleszek, 1976) suggest, the institution as a whole has its own needs and objectives that cannot be reduced and may come into conflict with individual members' purposes and needs. This potential for conflict and, indeed, the many conflicts that have been observed are facts of legislative life. If individual-oriented models are insufficient to explain committees as institutions or, at a further level of organizational complexity, the committee system, institution-oriented organizational models will often and perhaps must neglect, ignore, or even violate the behavioral assumptions of the micro-analytic models. The "reform and change" literature reviewed here illustrates the nature of this dilemma. If and when the conflict between individual members' and the institution's interests occurs, it is likely to be resolved in favor of one or the other depending, as Schick suggests, more on external circumstances than internalities to the legislature itself (1981, p. 326).

Comparative Systems Studies

As this essay noted at the outset, there does not exist in the literature an explicit definition of "committee system" or any description of a "committee system as a whole" that would meet operational criteria of such a definition. Even in the much-researched congressional field there is no empirical study that deals with all committees as a set of complex interactions that could be called a "system" in any serious scientific sense. Three texts, now outdated, presumably cover the congressional "committee system," and one of them, by Lees (1967), uses the term in its title. Written by an English observer, it is descriptive of the great variety of congressional committees, but, its title notwithstanding, it cannot be considered a description or analysis of the congressional "committee system" as it may have existed in the middle 1960s.

Morrow (1969) provides descriptive data and uses a systems-analytic framework. It fails in both respects. Although it abounds in terms borrowed from systems and other sociological theories, it does not treat committees-in-interaction as one might expect, given its terminology (for a perspicacious review, see Cooper, 1971, p. 130). Goodwin (1970) is exhaustive, with almost encyclopedic coverage of congressional committees. A compilation of facts, it has no central analytic scheme to pull the information together. In the preface the author touches on the theme of party control versus committee decentralization, but the theme is not systematically pursued.

Crossnational Analysis

The problematics of research on legislative committee systems arise, paradoxically, out of the universality of the "committee phenomenon," on the one hand, and its particularity, on the other hand. There is, as a result, a strain towards highly abstract formulation to specify the "covering laws" that are required by the existence of committee systems as universal phenomena but also a strain towards highly concrete description to satisfy whatever uniqueness committee systems may exhibit at a particular place at a particular time. "A modern legislature," write Loewenberg and Patterson (1979, p. 22) in their broadly comparative internation text, "typically organizes itself into a set of committees to permit its members to specialize and to undertake a division of labor among themselves." But the covering laws of specialization and division of labor do not yield much insight into a particular system of committees. It is paradoxical, then, that intersystem comparison will stress typicality and similarity, while intrasystem comparison will stress uniqueness and difference. One might expect just the opposite—that observers of a phenomenon across systems would be impressed by uniqueness and difference, while observers of the same phenomenon within a system would emphasize typicality and commonality.

The paradox is more appearance than reality, though it is a source of confusion. Intersystem analysts, comparing the "committee phenomenon," conduct their analyses at a macro level, while intrasystem analysts work at various micro levels and make their comparisons there. In other words, intersystem analysts compare committees as wholes, while intrasystem analysts compare committees as parts or subunits, with little attention to how the parts fit together in a committee system. While intersystem structural or functional aspects of the committee phenomenon are the object of comparative macro analysis, with special attention to such global properties as specialization and the division of labor, these properties are simply taken for granted in comparative micro analysis conducted within a system. The difficulties of internation comparison are exacerbated by the unevenness of relevant scholarship. It is easy enough to inveigh against the neglect of comparison as a method to study legislative committees across systems. Nelson (1974), for instance, deplores "the seeming indifference which many students of the American Congress have toward studies done on the legislatures of other nations. By depriving themselves of this rich area of research, many congressional scholars are unable to place the American Congress in its world context" (p. 121). Nelson's central argument is that political scientists have been led astray by what he calls a "bifocal inference." By studying only the U.S. and British legislatures, congressional scholars have concluded that when party leaders are strong, committees are weak (as they presumably are in Parliament); and, conversely, that when committees are strong, party leaders are not. (Nelson refers to Polsby, Gallaher, and Rundquist, 1969.)

Nelson's is a rather curious indictment because, alas, it is taken for granted that there is, in fact, a "rich area of research" in other countries. This is not the case and Nelson's own article confirms it. The little writing he cites consists mainly of macro-analytic "description," much of it un-reliable, speculative, and judgmental. At one end of the spectrum, then, what has been reported about committees the world over seems to be based on the most casual and suspect observations of journalists, visiting scholars, or parliamentarians; or what one can only call "less than knowledge" is derived deductively from general impressions of a country's politics or formal con-stitution. Any kind of generalization, whether in regard to commonalities or differences, based on such evidence cannot be better than the evidence itself. At the other end of the spectrum, as in connection with the congres-sional committee system, scholarship concerned with individual committees is so extensive and detailed that generalization regarding the system is equally difficult.

The tension between universality and particularity as it affects research on legislative committees thus constitutes a continuing impasse. Comparative treatments across diverse systems (Blondel, 1973; Loewenberg and Patterson, 1979) are so general that they cannot give much guidance to the intranation analyst who seeks to locate his/her work in a broadly comparative frame of reference. The intensive study of committees within any one legislature, however, whether by way of case analysis or statistical treatment, is likely to be so concrete that it defies the ingenuity of generalizers who wish to provide proper classification as a precondition for comparison.

The problem can be illustrated by two recent works—one which seeks to cope with comparative internation committee analysis in the context of whole legislative systems (Mezey, 1979) and another which seeks to draw generalizations from comprehensive, specially commissioned reports on committees or committee systems in eight countries (Lees and Shaw, 1979). The country studies presented by different scholars in Lees and Shaw are more or less informative but not held together by a common framework. It was apparently the intention of the editors to "pull together" these country studies in order to arrive at generalizations that would "cover" the eight cases. But in pointing to exceptions, variations, and differences from one country to the next, the mode of juxtaposition makes for generali-zations which are so much guided by the empirical observations in each case and, in the end, are so circumscribed that one is really not better off than before (that is, having read the eight country studies). While this descrip-tive-generalizing approach presumes to see "patterns" across countries, it is more than likely that if these patterns were subjected to a hypothetical-analytic mode of analysis they would be falsified. The problems involved in this approach are well known in crosscountry comparative study that makes entire "systems" the units of analysis.

Mezey's attempt to come to grips with variety is more interesting because he is concerned with harnessing the rich historical, cultural, and

political contexts of committees or committee systems within a set of surrogate, preempirical categories. Such categories, by overcoming some country-
by-country differences, would make generalizations less disembodied. And
he evidently leaves no stone unturned in what can only be described a *tour
de force*—making use of general accounts of country political systems, studies
of legislative institutions, dissertations, unpublished papers, and articles
on any number of cases on which he could secure material. Comparative
analysis over so many diverse units can proceed only by creating relatively
abstract categories which might serve as surrogates of the "real" contexts
that constrain generalizations and save them from being unduly concrete.
Yet, whether the classification—providing for "active," "vulnerable," "reactive," "marginal," and "minimal" legislatures—is theoretically viable and,
when imposed on the "committee phenomenon," can yield new knowledge,
is open to question. The image of committee systems and structures that
emerges is highly stylized and, again, quite unlikely to withstand falsification.
Mezey's purpose, then, is to reduce particularity and advance universality,
and as a method his approach may be useful; but, like all typologies, it is
beset by the problem of fit between case and type.

Cross-state Analysis

The quandary of comparative committee analysis across nations is
partly theoretical and partly methodological but above all empirical. Yet,
there is a research arena which could be exploited more than it has been
and where access to data across several committee systems is easier and
comparison, because of possible control over exogenous variables, likely to
be more valid—the U.S. state legislatures. But there exist only a few studies
of committees in or across the states and even fewer of committee systems.
Rosenthal (1973), on the basis of informant reports from selected legislators
in the 50 states, finds that "*general* distinctions among committee systems
are not very difficult to make" (p. 254). He is concerned with the relationship
between "institutional capacity" and "institutional power," which "in
combination are closely related to committee system effectiveness" (p. 261).
As he admits, "data available are usually imprecise; when they are precise,
they may not be completely reliable. . . . The present endeavor has attempted
to map out a terrain, leaving much still to be done and a great deal still to
be explained" (p. 262).

Polsby's (1968) theory of institutionalization inspired a comparative
study of two state legislative committee systems. Characterizing the Montana
House of Representatives an "amateur" and the Wisconsin Assembly a
"professional" legislature, Chaffey (1970) predicts that the latter "will be

more likely to exhibit several characteristics of institutionalization" than the former (p. 181). Alas, the investigator encountered surprises. For instance, basing the analysis on measures of seniority violations (including perceptions of such violation) in committee appointments for several sessions, Chaffey finds that insofar as these measures symbolized institutionalization, it was more characteristic of the Montana than the Wisconsin legislature. Other measures—of relative committee autonomy and influence of chairmen—also cast "some doubt" on relevant hypotheses (p. 192). One explanation for the findings is that an amateur legislature like the Montana House "of necessity must transfer much of its decision-making to its committee structure, where the limited expertise in the body will be concentrated," while in Wisconsin the members "do have the time and resources to bring to bear on issues in either caucus or floor debate" (p. 193). The explanation does not sound convincing. Nor does another explanation to the effect that the amateur Montana legislature relies more than the professional Wisconsin legislature on committees "to overcome the handicaps of the environment" (p. 194). A final explanation—rather novel—is based on a distinction between "labor-intensive" and "labor-permissive" legislative processes.

Hamm (1980), using a longitudinal and cross-sectional "most-different systems" design, examines committee decision making in Texas and Wisconsin. Finding "large disparities in terms of 'performance', internal structure and general environmental factors," he raises the question "whether the bill-specific variables have the same effect on committee decision making in these different systems" (p. 36).[16] The method is aggregative across committees, making the state chamber committee systems the units of analysis. Not all of Hamm's findings can be treated here. And there are difficulties. For instance, Hamm reports that "the most consistent significant relationship involves the number of actors—labor, business, and so forth—opposing the proposed legislation. That is, in each session, the greater the number of actors against the legislation, the lower the probability of successfully negotiating the committee stage of the legislative process" (p. 43). But this plausible, perhaps banal finding required modification because Hamm also discovers "some unanticipated directions":

In Wisconsin during both legislative sessions, the relationship between significant actor support and committee success is positive, although significant in only three of the four sessions. However, in the Texas legislature, the relationship is the inverse, and statistically significant in one of the two cases. This unexpected finding indicates that the greater the legislative support in terms of significant actors, the lower the chance of success (p. 43).

A multivariate (discriminant function) analysis does not nullify the findings. Hamm therefore concludes on a note of caution, lest it be accepted that extralegislative opposition "may reduce intra-legislative opposition once bills reach the floor" (p. 49). In general, the author of this empirically rich and methodologically sophisticated study does not speculate beyond the many variables entered into the multivariate analysis. Nevertheless, to what extent the legislature's external (group) environment makes for similarities or differences across committee systems and shapes them remains an important problem on the research agenda here opened up.

Assuming increased reliance on committees across all U.S. state legislatures, Francis and Riddlesperger (1982) raise two questions: "First, to what extent have the committee systems, rather than the party system, become the central means of making decisions? Second, to what extent are the committee systems successful?" (p. 454). To answer these questions they develop a measure of "committee system centrality" and a measure of "procedural efficiency." Party distribution and chamber size serve as "primary structural" variables in addition to several committee-level variables such as average committee size, number of committees, type of committee system, subcommittee use, and chair dominance.

Aggregating mail questionnaire data across all 99 chambers,[17] Francis and Riddlesperger find that regular committee meetings as the most significant loci of decisions receive about two-thirds of the top three choices, almost as many as do presiding officers or majority leaders. About half of the legislators' time is reported to be given to committee work. These findings, according to the investigators, "mask rather sharp differences in committee importance among the 99 legislative chambers" (p. 455). On the "committee centrality" measure (scored from 0 to 5) aggregate scores ranged from a low of .125 in the Illinois Senate to a 3.9 in the Nevada House. "In general, house and senate scores from the same state were similar ($r = .69$, $n = 49$), but not so similar that intrastate chamber differences could be ignored" (p. 456). Scanning the lower-chamber rank-order listings reveals that

more of the states with dominant majority parties are at the head of the list, while states with rather even party splits tend to fall at the end of the list. In other words, the committee systems tend to be more central in chambers dominated by one party. The chamber level correlation between committee centrality scores and percentage of seats controlled by the majority is .38 ($n = 98$). No doubt there are other factors at work, but when the majority party controls almost all of the seats, the party caucus becomes less useful. In contrast, for example, the chamber level correlation between party caucus significance and percentage in the majority is negative ($r = -.50$).

Francis and Riddlesperger examine a number of other structural properties, finding that chamber size "has a major effect upon the optimal number and size of committees," that "the use of subcommittees offers an important refinement for the improvement of agenda processing," and that "the procedural efficiency of committee systems has an impact upon the relative influence of the legislative actors" (p. 469). A system was defined as being "more efficient procedurally if it reduces the per item costs (time and energy) of processing the agenda without an offsetting reduction in the quality of informed judgment applied to each decision" (p. 458). The authors conclude that "while committees and subcommittees bring decentralization, efficient committee/subcommittee systems may do so at the expense of party leadership control. Certainly the evidence indicates that partisanship is less apparent in the committee context" (p. 470).

Francis (1982) pursues the theme of procedural efficiency in committee systems by way of "a Buchanan/Tullock type model and through exploration of the meaning of 'optimal committee size'." Legislators are assumed to minimize both decision and external costs, and "the extent of each of these costs depends upon the number of people who must agree to particular decision outcomes, and the two types of costs are related inversely in such a manner that an 'optimal committee size' may be identified" (p. 823). The model is tested in terms of legislators' own specification of "ideal" committee size and two other structural features—the use of sub-committees and chamber size.[18] In general, legislators tend to prefer smaller committees than they experience. However, "this tendency persists until a certain threshold is reached where, say, committees have fewer than nine members. . . . [T]his threshold (or optimum) may vary, depending on the use of subcommittees and chamber size" (p. 834).

Francis's study is replete with a number of suggestive observations. The following involves the notion of the committee as an interstitial structure in the process of representation:

Closer attention to the nature of external costs may reveal that when committees become large they do become more representative and, thus, will make changes with fewer adverse repercussions. If they become too cumbersome, however, they may fail to consider much of the agenda and, thus, the external costs of retaining the *status quo* may accumulate. In essence, this second type of external cost may be part of the reason committees are either reduced in size or dissolved into subcommittees (pp. 835-836).

Francis takes exception to the view of "most scholars" who would "see a natural tension between party leaders and the committee chieftains."

A two-party system and majority rule may provide efficiencies within committees that allow them to function optimally with somewhat larger numbers than might otherwise be found. With precast lines of division between a majority and minority, the complexity of the bargaining situation to each member may be reduced substantially (p. 836).

In actuality, however, the party phenomenon in U.S. legislatures may work itself out differently: "Committees and especially small committees or subcommittees probably are much more likely to conduct business in a non-partisan, problem-solving manner. The larger and busier the committee, the greater the need to reduce the complexity of the situation. Party affiliation has a simplifying effect, most readily appreciated in full forum" (p. 836).

A study by Hamm and Moncrief (1982), comparing changes in certain structural features of committee systems and their effects on committee performance in five U.S. state chambers, is empirically the most ambitious effort of its kind yet reported.[19] As these investigators modestly point out, few of the prior studies (actually, none) "have utilized both a comparative and a longitudinal framework to determine how long it takes for the consequences of change to become apparent" (p. 384). And there are other design considerations; amount of structural change and performance level prior to change must be included as variables. Finally, "structural change in the committee system may have consequences at two separate stages of the legislative process—in committee or on the floor. Each stage should be considered in an analysis of performance levels" (p. 384).

To execute this ambitious design, the investigators measure structural change in terms of three dimensions: "(1) activity structuring (task specialization, division and distribution of labor, and formalization), (2) distribution of authority (centralized or decentralized), and (3) establishment or enlargement of support services" (p. 385). Three measures of performance—screening, shaping, and passage of legislation—serve as dependent variables in the formulation of four major propositions which compare pre- and postchange effects of system structures on performance. Space limitations do not permit detailed description of the findings. According to Hamm and Moncrief themselves their findings "indicate" that:

1. The structural changes in the committee system (i.e., activity structuring, support mechanisms, distribution of authority) had a most discernible impact on those activities the committee could control most readily, namely the screening and shaping of legislation.

2. The magnitude of the performance changes is a function of the combined effects of the magnitude of the structural changes and the screening/shaping performance levels before structural change.

3. The impact of the structural changes in the committee system on the more remote, less controllable aspects of the legislative process (i.e., floor acceptance) is indeterminate (p. 396).

Postscript

It is not uncommon and, in fact, is conventional to cap a review of research by saying that there have been significant advances in substantive knowledge, methodological development, and the construction of theories. This can certainly be said of the field of legislative studies in general and of committee studies in particular. However, the enterprise of research cannot rest on its laurels; it depends on collective self-criticism that need not be interpreted as being disrespectful of what has been accomplished.

The single most ineluctable impression left by this survey of studies on legislative standing committees is their substantive perishability. Secular changes, environmental changes, institutional changes, and changes in research fashions tend to make even the best of committee studies obsolete. But obsolescence does not mean uselessness. In the first place, even though they are time- and context-bound, many studies will remain of great evidentiary value to future chroniclers of institutional development. And, in the second place, much can be learned from both their theoretical or methodological failures, as well as successes.

In a scientific perspective, as a research arena the study of legislative committees appears fragmented, incomplete, and haphazard, in some respects additive but essentially noncumulative. The committee studies appear to be arbitrarily selective, isolated, and episodic. It is rarely clear why a particular committee or set of committees was chosen over what period of time. All of the studies were prepared by a single investigator or a pair of investigators. While, as we noted, there are research traditions or what we have called "generations" of studies, discontinuity rather than continuity—in substance especially but also in theory and method—is their most characteristic attribute. As a result, scientific fashion is often mistaken for scientific progress on the assumption, apparently, that the latest is always the best. That this is not so the survey may have shown.

Given this state of affairs, the would-be systematizer's task is formidable. To recount or summarize what has been described, recorded, found, or interpreted in a multitude of studies, yields only a disorderly enumeration of mostly disconnected and temporally limited pieces of information— fragments of some "grand design" one could imagine if professional manpower and resources were committed to building a body of cumulative and theoretically viable empirical knowledge. But as the objective of a "grand design" has been neglected or, for perhaps understandable reason, has actually been discarded—we are referring to the efforts to cope with the variegated nature of the species in terms of "systems theory"—nothing seems to be left other than the inconclusive "conclusion" reached in the most masterful of comparative committee studies that "committees differ from one another" (Fenno, 1973, p. 280). This conclusion confirms chaos rather than order. Perhaps the "real world" of legislative committees "looks like" chaos, but positing chaos would be an assumption on which no science of politics and not even a political theory can be built.

We have centered this review in theoretical and methodological issues and dealt with substantive findings only when they seemed to generate or fertilize relevant aspects of theory or method; but scholarly experiences in theorizing and methodizing, even if temporarily forgotten, neglected, or intentionally ignored may yet be rediscovered, reapplied, perhaps modified, and extended to serve further inquiry. And despite the continuing curse of discontinuity, we conclude that perhaps more has been learned about legislative committees than one might have reasonably expected 30 years ago when, with Huitt's (1954) truly path-breaking work, the modern era of legislative research can be said to have begun.

NOTES

1. There are, of course, other units that also intervene between the individual member and the legislature, such as parties, factions, cliques, delegations, caucuses, and so on, including what has recently been identified as "member-centered enterprises" (Salisbury and Shepsle, 1981a, 1981b).

2. Huitt in a footnote mistakenly refers to "preface to 1884 edition." The preface is, indeed, dated "October 7, 1884," but the book was not published until 1885.

3. We say that research "once again" sees the individual person as a purposive actor because the formulation is far from new. As in so many other respects, Lasswell (1948, p. 17) anticipates the formulation in his definition of the "social process" in which "*Man* pursues *Values* through *Institutions* on *Resources*." (Undoubtedly, a latter-day Lasswell would speak of "person" rather than "man".) A set of "purposive roles" is specified in Wahlke, Eulau, Buchanan, and Ferguson (1962, pp. 245-266).

4. These studies are treated in a separate literature review.

5. An adaptation of Bales's interaction process analysis to a "board of finance" may be found in Barber (1966).

6. There is, unfortunately, no indication in the essay or in the book on which we draw that much of the same material had previously been published in an article by Bibby (1966) dealing specifically with legislative oversight.

7. The study is based on data from the 91st to 93d (1969-1974) Congresses. Interviews with members, staff, lobbyists, and executive personnel were conducted in 1972 by a team studying the Commerce Committees for the Nader Congress Project. Additional interviews, focusing on environmental factors, were conducted by Price in 1973 and 1975. The article here reviewed (Price, 1978) was subsequently republished in an only slightly expanded version as a monograph (Price, 1979).

8. In a footnote (1978, p. 569, fn. 70) Price points out that "it may also be true that under certain conditions conflict helps produce public salience," but he argues that "conflict per se is surely no guarantee of salience."

9. Fenno (1973) himself is cautious as to the general applicability of his model: "It is tempting to press for a premature verdict by purporting to show, here and now, that our scheme is useful for understanding committees other than those we have studied. But that judgment will have to come from political scientists with a working knowledge of such other committees" (p. 280).

10. The study is based on roll-call data compiled by the Inter-University Consortium for Social and Political Research for the 10-year period 1955-1964. In addition the investigators compiled data on committee assignments as indications of committee attractiveness. They used all roll calls, regardless of their importance, and covered 20 standing committees of the House of Representatives.

11. The study is based on roll-call and other data for 15 Senate committees during the 87th (1960-1961) Congress.

12. The Virginia House for 1976, the Wisconsin Assembly for 1975-1976, and the New Mexico House for 1977-1978, all requiring the investigator's visits to examine committee records on location; the Michigan House for 1977-1978 and the Illinois House for 1977, where the data on committee voting were available in house journals; and Missouri's two chambers for 1979-1980, where committee votes could be obtained from archives.

13. Procedural roll calls and roll calls with 90 percent of members on the same side were excluded. The data were pooled for the two congresses, partly because roll calls varied in number from committee to committee, partly because pooling "insures that the defined factions demonstrate some stability" (p. 86). The latter is a poor reason for pooling: stability or change can only be observed diachronically and pooling the data obscures this question. Committee members included in the analysis were limited to those who voted on at least 70 percent of the roll calls and served in both congresses. Factional structures and issue dimensions were derived by way of several factor-analytic techniques. Regression equations representing the three best predictors of each committee faction were used to examine the impact of issues on the factional structure. The Appropriations Committee was omitted because its work is mostly done in subcommittees and few substantive roll calls are taken in the full committee.

14. The "group ratings" are those provided by such organizations as Americans for Democratic Action, Committee on Political Education, National Farmers' Union, Americans for Constitutional Action, and the U.S. Chamber of Commerce. To enhance reliability, the investigators used multiple measures to describe the factions, and their interpretation is said to be "based upon the consistency in the patterns of correlations between factional alignments and diverse group ratings" (1981, p. 88).

15. The investigators accompany the following summary with an interesting footnote to the effect that their analysis "poses complex questions of causality. While it is customary to assume that leaders, in fact, lead (e.g., Fenno, 1973; Manley, 1970), the causal flow in influence may run in the reverse direction. That is, a chairperson may actually forge a bipartisan consensus on the committee or, alternatively, may assume a bipartisan leadership posture to conform to extant committee norms and processes. Recognizing this, we use conditional language ('may,' 'apparently,' 'seemingly') where exposition permits throughout the article" (1981-1982, p. 86).

16. A random sample of nonlocal bills was drawn for each of three sessions, yielding, after exclusion of postponed bills and those for which insufficient information was available, a final sample of 509 for the 1959 Wisconsin session, 422 for the 1975-1976 Wisconsin session, and 742 for the 1977 Texas session. Extralegislative "demand patterns" were determined by "analyzing the records of committee hearings, noting the participants along with the scope and intensity of participation" (1980, pp. 36-37).

17. The study's data come from mail questionnaire responses received in 1981 from 2,028 legislators in all 99 chambers of the American states and constituting a response rate of 43 percent. The responses are aggregated either within or across the chambers. The minimum number of responses for any chamber was seven, which might worry the statistically fastidious analyst but does not seem to trouble the investigators.

18. The study, based on a 1979 nationwide sample of 511 respondents (a 38 percent return rate), asked legislators to specify the "ideal" committee size of a typical standing committee in their chamber.

19. The study covers the Louisiana Senate, Texas Senate, Kentucky House, South Dakota House, and Texas House. In each case, data were compiled for three

prechange and three postchange sessions. Development of the measures used, the investigators report, "requires an analysis of the legislative history of each bill from introduction through final disposition in the chamber. Over 29,000 bills are so analyzed" (p. 389). The range of bills and joint resolutions is from 347 in the South Dakota House to 2,300 in the Texas House. As the entire population of bills is used, no statistical tests are conducted. A change was considered "substantial if the difference in performance between prechange and postchange sessions exceeded 5 percent" (1982, p. 391).

REFERENCES

These references are only to works cited or mentioned in the article. They do not include studies of committee assignments and seniority nor of committee staffing or committee-agency-interest group relations, both of which are covered by other literature reviews.

Arnold, R. Douglas. 1979. *Congress and the Bureaucracy: A Theory of Influence.* New Haven: Yale University Press.

Bales, Robert F. 1950. *Interaction Process Analysis.* Cambridge, MA: Addison-Wesley.

Barber, James D. 1966. *Power in Committees: An Experiment in the Governmental Process.* Chicago: Rand McNally.

Bentley, Arthur F. 1908. *The Process of Government.* Chicago: University of Chicago Press.

Bibby, John F. 1966. "Committee Characteristics and Legislative Oversight of Administration," *Midwest Journal of Political Science* 10:78-98.

Bibby, John F. and Roger Davidson. 1967. "The Congressional Committee," in John F. Bibby and Roger Davidson, eds., *On Capitol Hill: Studies in the Legislative Process.* New York: Holt, Rinehart & Winston, pp. 170-196.

Black, Duncan. 1958. *The Theory of Committees and Elections.* Cambridge: Cambridge University Press.

Blalock, Hubert M., Jr. 1964. *Causal Inferences in Nonexperimental Research.* Chapel Hill: University of North Carolina Press.

Blondel, Jean. 1973. *Comparative Legislatures.* Durham, NC: Duke University Press.

Brenner, Philip. 1974. "Committee Conflict in the Congressional Arena," *Annals* 411: 87-101.

Chaffey, Douglas C. 1970. "The Institutionalization of State Legislatures: A Comparative Study," *Western Political Quarterly* 23:180-196.

Chamberlain, Joseph O. 1936. *Legislative Processes, National and State.* New York: Appleton-Century.

Cooper, Joseph. 1965. "Jeffersonian Attitudes Toward Executive Leadership and Committee Development in the House of Representatives, 1789-1829," *Western Political Quarterly* 18:45-63.

————. 1970. *The Origins of the Standing Committees and the Development of the Modern House.* Houston: Rice University Press.

————. 1971. "The Study of Congressional Committees: Current Research and Future Trends," *Polity* 4:123-133.

————. 1977. "Congress in Organizational Perspective," in Lawrence C. Dodd and Bruce I. Oppenheimer, eds., *Congress Reconsidered.* New York: Praeger, pp. 140-159.

————. 1981. "Organization and Innovation in the House of Representatives," in Joseph Cooper and G. Calvin Mackenzie, eds., *The House at Work.* Austin: University of Texas Press, pp. 319-355.

Cummings, Milton C. and Robert L. Peabody. 1963. "The Decision to Enlarge the Committee on Rules: An Analysis of the 1961 Vote," in Robert L. Peabody and Nelson W. Polsby, eds., *New Perspectives on the House of Representatives.* Chicago: Rand McNally, pp. 167-194.

Dahl, Robert A. 1960. *Who Governs?* New Haven: Yale University Press.

———. 1967. *Pluralist Democracy in the United States: Conflict and Consent.* Chicago: Rand McNally.

Davidson, Roger H. 1974. "Representation and Congressional Committees," *Annals* 411:48-62.

———. 1981a. "Two Avenues of Change: House and Senate Committee Reorganization," in Lawrence C. Dodd and Bruce I. Oppenheimer, eds., *Congress Reconsidered.* 2d ed. Washington, DC: Congressional Quarterly Press, pp. 107-133.

———. 1981b. "Subcommittee Government: New Channels for Policy Making," in Thomas E. Mann and Norman J. Ornstein, eds., *The New Congress.* Washington, DC: American Enterprise Institute, pp. 99-133.

Davidson, Roger H. and Walter J. Oleszek. 1976. "Adaptation and Consolidation: Structural Innovation in the U.S. House of Representatives," *Legislative Studies Quarterly* 1:37-65.

———. 1977. *Congress Against Itself.* Bloomington: Indiana University Press.

Deering, Christopher J. 1982. "Subcommittee Government in the U.S. House: An Analysis of Bill Management," *Legislative Studies Quarterly* 7:533-546.

Deering, Christopher J. and Steven S. Smith. 1981. "Majority Party Leadership and the New House Subcommittee System," in F. H. Mackaman, ed., *Understanding Congressional Leadership.* Washington, DC: Congressional Quarterly Press, pp. 261-292.

Dodd, Lawrence C. 1972. "Committee Integration in the Senate: A Comparative Analysis," *Journal of Politics* 34:1135-1171.

Dodd Lawrence C. and John C. Pierce. 1975. "Roll Call Measurement of Committee Integration: The Impact of Alternative Methods," *Polity* 7:386-401.

Dyson, James W. and John W. Soule. 1970. "Congressional Committee Behavior on Roll Call Votes: The U.S. House of Representatives, 1955-1964," *Midwest Journal of Political Science* 14:626-647.

Easton, David. 1953. *The Political System.* New York: Knopf.

———. 1957. "An Approach to the Analysis of Political Systems," *World Politics* 9:383-400.

Entin, Kenneth. 1973. "Information Exchange in Congress: the Case of the House Armed Services Committee," *Western Political Quarterly* 26:427-439.

Eulau, Heinz. 1969. "On Units and Levels of Analysis," in *Micro-Macro Political Analysis: Accents of Inquiry.* Chicago: Aldine, pp. 1-19.

Eulau, Heinz, John C. Wahlke, William Buchanan, and LeRoy C. Ferguson. 1959. "The Role of the Representative: Some Empirical Observations on the Theory of Edmund Burke," *American Political Science Review* 53:742-756.

Farnsworth, David N. 1961. *The Senate Committee on Foreign Relations.* Urbana: University of Illinois Press.

Feig, Douglas G. 1979. "The Stability of Congressional Committees," *Political Methodology* 6:311-341.

———. 1981. "Partisanship and Integration in Two House Committees: Ways and Means and Education and Labor," *Western Political Quarterly* 34:426-437.

Fenno, Richard F., Jr. 1962. "The House Appropriations Committee as a Political System," *American Political Science Review* 56:310-324.

_____ . 1963. "The House of Representatives and Federal Aid to Education," in Robert L. Peabody and Nelson W. Polsby, eds., *New Perspectives on the House of Representatives.* Chicago: Rand McNally, pp. 195-235.

_____ . 1966. *The Power of the Purse: Appropriations Politics in Congress.* Boston: Little, Brown.

_____ . 1973. *Congressmen in Committees.* Boston: Little, Brown.

Ferejohn, John A. and Morris P. Fiorina. 1975. "Purposive Models of Legislative Behavior," *American Economic Association Papers and Proceedings* 65:407-414.

Fiorina, Morris P. 1974. *Representatives, Roll Calls, and Constitutencies.* Lexington, MA: Heath.

Fox, Douglas M. and Charles H. Clapp. 1970a. "The House Rules Committee's Agenda-Setting Function, 1961-1968," *Journal of Politics* 32:440-444.

_____ . 1970b. "The House Rules Committee and the Programs of the Kennedy and Johnson Administrations," *Midwest Journal of Political Science* 14: 667-672.

Francis, Wayne L. 1982. "Legislative Committee Systems, Optimal Committee Size, and the Costs of Decision Making," *Journal of Politics* 44:823-837.

Francis, Wayne L. and James W. Riddlesperger. 1982. "U.S. State Legislative Committees: Structure, Procedural Efficiency, and Party Control," *Legislative Studies Quarterly* 7:453-471.

Froman, Lewis A., Jr. 1968. "Organization Theory and the Explanation of Important Characteristics of Congress," *American Political Science Review* 62:518-526.

Galloway, George B. 1946. *Congress at the Crossroads.* New York: Crowell.

Goodwin, George, Jr. 1970. *The Little Legislatures.* Amherst: University of Massachusetts Press.

Griffith, Ernest S. 1951. *Congress: Its Contemporary Role.* New York: New York University Press.

Gross, Bertram M. 1953. *The Legislative Struggle.* New York: McGraw-Hill.

Haeberle, Steven H. 1978. "The Institutionalization of the Subcommittee in the House of Representatives," *Journal of Politics* 40:1054-1065.

Hamm, Keith E. 1980. "U.S. State Legislative Committee Decisions: Similar Results in Different Settings," *Legislative Studies Quarterly* 5:31-54.

_____ . 1982. "Consistency Between Committee and Floor Voting in U.S. State Legislatures," *Legislative Studies Quarterly* 7:473-490.

_____ . 1983. "Patterns of Influence Among Committees, Agencies, and Interest Groups," *Legislative Studies Quarterly* 8:379-426.

Hamm, Keith E. and Gary Moncrief. 1982. "Effects of Structural Change in Legislative Committee Systems on Their Performance in U.S. States," *Legislative Studies Quarterly* 7:383-400.

Hinckley, Barbara. 1975. "Policy Content, Committee Membership, and Behavior," *American Journal of Political Science* 19:543-558.

Homans, George C. 1950. *The Human Group.* New York: Harcourt, Brace.

Horn, Stephen. 1970. *Unused Power: The Work of the Senate Committee on Appropriations.* Washington, DC: Brookings Institution.

Huitt, Ralph K. 1954. "The Congressional Committee: A Case Study," *American Political Science Review* 48:340-365.

Huitt, Ralph K. and Robert L. Peabody. 1969. *Congress: Two Decades of Analysis.* New York: Harper & Row.

Jones, Charles O. 1961. "Representation in Congress: The Case of the House Agriculture Committee," *American Political Science Review* 55:358-367.

_____. 1962. "The Role of the Congressional Subcommittee," *Midwest Journal of Political Science* 6:327-344.

_____. 1974. "Between Party Battalions and Committee Suzerainty," *Annals* 411: 158-168.

Kaplan, Lewis. 1968. "The House Un-American Activities Committee and its Opponents: A Study in Congressional Dissonance," *Journal of Politics* 30:647-671.

Kingdon, John W. 1966. "A House Appropriations Subcommittee: Influences on the Budgetary Process," *Southwestern Social Science Quarterly* 47:69-78.

_____. 1973. *Congressmen's Voting Decisions*. New York: Harper & Row.

Lasswell, Harold D. 1948. *Power and Personality*. New York: Norton.

_____. 1963. "The Decision Process: Seven Categories of Functional Analysis," in Nelson W. Polsby, Robert A. Dentler, and Paul A. Smith, eds., *Politics and Social Life*. Boston: Houghton Mifflin, pp. 93-105. Published as a monograph, 1950. College Park: Bureau of Government Research, University of Maryland.

Lasswell, Harold D. and Abraham Kaplan. 1950. *Power and Society*. New Haven: Yale University Press.

Lees, John D. 1967. *The Committee System of the United States Congress*. New York: Humanities Press.

Lees, John D. and Malcolm Shaw, eds. 1979. *Committees in Legislatures: A Comparative Analysis*. Durham, NC: Duke University Press.

Lewis, Anne L. 1978. "Floor Success as a Measure of Committee Performance in the House," *Journal of Politics* 40:460-467.

Linton, Ralph. 1945. *The Cultural Background of Personality*. London: Routledge and Kegan Paul.

Loewenberg, Gerhard, and Samuel C. Patterson. 1979. *Comparing Legislatures*. Boston: Little, Brown.

Lutzker, Paul. 1969. "The Behavior of Congressmen in a Committee Setting: A Research Report," *Journal of Politics* 31:140-167.

MacRae, Duncan, Jr. 1956. "Roll Call Votes and Leadership," *Public Opinion Quarterly* 20:543-558.

Manley, John. 1965. "The House Committee on Ways and Means: Conflict Management in a Congressional Committee," *American Political Science Review* 59:927-939.

_____. 1969. "Wilbur D. Mills: A Study in Congressional Influence," *American Political Science Review* 63:442-464.

_____. 1970. *The Politics of Finance: The House Committee on Ways and Means*. Boston: Little, Brown.

Mann, Thomas E. and Norman J. Ornstein, eds. 1981. *The New Congress*. Washington, DC: American Enterprise Institute.

Masters, Nicholas A. 1961. "Committee Assignments in the House of Representatives," *American Political Science Review* 55:345-357.

Matsunaga, Spark M. and Ping Chen. 1976. *Rulemakers in the House*. Urbana: University of Illinois Press.

Matthews, Donald R. 1960. *U.S. Senators and Their World*. Chapel Hill: University of North Carolina Press.

Mayhew, David R. 1974. *Congress: The Electoral Connection*. New Haven: Yale University Press.

McConachie, Lauros G. 1898. *Congressional Committees*. New York: Crowell.

Mezey, Michael L. 1979. *Comparative Legislatures*. Durham, NC: Duke University Press.

Morrow, William. 1969. *Congressional Committees*. New York: Scribners.

Munger, Frank J. and Richard F. Fenno, Jr. 1962. *National Politics and Federal Aid to Education.* Syracuse, NY: Syracuse University Press.

Murphy, James T. 1974. "Political Parties and the Porkbarrel: Party Conflict and Co-operation in House Public Works Committee Decision Making," *American Political Science Review* 68:169-185.

Nelson, Garrison. 1974. "Assessing the Congressional Committee System: Contributions From a Comparative Perspective," *Annals* 411:120-132.

Oppenheimer, Bruce I. 1977. "The Rules Committee: New Arm of Leadership in a Decentralized House," in Lawrence C. Dodd and Bruce I. Oppenheimer, eds., *Congress Reconsidered.* New York: Praeger, pp. 96-116.

———. 1980. "Policy Effects of U.S. House Reform: Decentralization and the Capacity to Resolve Energy Issues," *Legislative Studies Quarterly* 5:5-30.

———. 1981a. "The Changing Relationship Between House Leadership and the Committee on Rules," in F. H. Mackaman, ed., *Understanding Congressional Leadership.* Washington, DC: Congressional Quarterly Press, pp. 207-225.

———. 1981b. "Congress and the New Obstructionism: Developing an Energy Program," in Lawrence C. Dodd and Bruce I. Oppenheimer, eds., *Congress Reconsidered.* 2d ed. Washington, DC: Congressional Quarterly Press, pp. 275-295.

Ornstein, Norman J. 1974. "Towards Restructuring the Congressional Committee System," *Annals* 411:147-157.

———. 1975. "Causes and Consequences of Congressional Change: Subcommittee Reforms in the House of Representatives, 1970-73," in Norman J. Ornstein, ed., *Congress in Change: Evolution and Reform.* New York: Praeger, pp. 88-114.

Ornstein, Norman J. and David W. Rohde. 1977a. "Shifting Forces, Changing Rules and Political Outcomes: The Impact of Congressional Change on Four House Committees," in Robert L. Peabody and Nelson W. Polsby, eds., *New Perspectives on the House of Representatives.* 3d ed. Chicago: Rand McNally, pp. 186-269.

———. 1977b. "Revolt from Within: Congressional Change, Legislative Policy, and the House Commerce Committee," in Susan Welch and John G. Peters, eds., *Legislative Reform and Public Policy.* New York: Praeger, pp. 54-72.

Ostrom, Donald. 1979. "Consensus and Conflict in the House: A Revised Look at the Ways and Means and Education and Labor Committees," *Polity* 11:430-439.

Parker, Glenn R. and Suzanne L. Parker. 1979. "Factions in Committees: The United States House of Representatives," *American Political Science Review* 73: 85-102.

Parsons, Talcott. 1951. *The Social System.* Glencoe, IL: The Free Press.

Patterson, Samuel C. 1963. "Legislative Leadership and Political Ideology," *Public Opinion Quarterly* 27:399-410.

Payne, James L. 1982. "The Rise of Lone Wolf Questioning in House Committee Hearings," *Polity* 14:626-640.

Peabody, Robert L. 1963. "The Enlarged Rules Committee," in Robert L. Peabody and Nelson W. Polsby, eds., *New Perspectives on the House of Representatives.* Chicago: Rand McNally, pp. 129-164.

———. 1969. "Research on Congress: A Coming of Age," in Ralph K. Huitt and Robert L. Peabody, *Congress: Two Decades of Analysis.* New York: Harper & Row, pp. 3-73.

———. 1974. "Committees from the Leadership Perspective," *Annals* 411:133-146.

_____. 1981-1982. "Research on Congress," *Congress and the Presidency* 9:1-15.

Perkins, Lynette P. 1980. "Influence of Members' Goals on Their Committee Behavior: The U.S. House Judiciary Committee," *Legislative Studies Quarterly* 5: 373-392.

_____. 1981. "Member Recruitment to a Mixed Goal Committee: The House Judiciary Committee," *Journal of Politics* 43:348-364.

Plott, Charles R. 1968. "Some Organizational Influences on Urban Renewal Decisions," *American Economic Association Papers and Proceedings* 58:306-321.

Polsby, Nelson W. 1968. "The Institutionalization of the U.S. House of Representatives," *American Political Science Review* 62:144-168.

Polsby, Nelson W., Miriam Gallaher, and Barry S. Rundquist. 1969. "The Growth of the Seniority System in the U.S. House of Representatives," *American Political Science Review* 63:787-807.

Price, David E. 1972. *Who Makes the Laws? Creativity and Power in Senate Committees.* Cambridge, MA: Schenkman.

_____. 1978. "Policy Making in Congressional Committees: The Impact of 'Environmental' Factors," *American Political Science Review* 72:548-574.

_____. 1979. *Policymaking in Congressional Committees: The Impact of "Environmental" Factors.* Tucson: University of Arizona Press.

_____. 1981. "Congressional Committees in the Policy Process," in Lawrence C. Dodd and Bruce I. Oppenheimer, eds., *Congress Reconsidered.* 2d ed. Washington, DC: Congressional Quarterly Press, pp. 156-185.

Price, Douglas. 1971. "The Congressional Career," in Nelson W. Polsby, ed., *Congressional Behavior.* New York: Random House, pp. 14-27.

_____. 1977. "Careers and Committees in the American Congress," in William O. Aydelotte, ed., *The History of Parliamentary Behavior.* Princeton, NJ: Princeton University Press, pp. 28-62.

Rieselbach, Leroy N. and Joseph K. Unekis. 1981-1982. "Ousting the Oligarchs: Assessing the Consequences of Reform and Change on Four House Committees," *Congress and the Presidency* 9:83-117.

Ripley, Randall B. 1974. "Congressional Party Leaders and Standing Committees," *Review of Politics* 36:394-409.

Robinson, James A. 1963. *The House Rules Committee.* Indianapolis: Bobbs-Merrill.

Rohde, David W. 1974. "Committee Reform in the House of Representatives and the Subcommittee Bill of Rights," *Annals* 411:39-47.

Rosenthal, Alan. 1973. "Legislative Committee Systems: An Exploratory Analysis," *Western Political Quarterly* 26:252-262.

Rudder, Catherine E. 1977. "Committee Reform and the Revenue Process: The Old Ways and Means Committee and Its Transformation," in Lawrence C. Dodd and Bruce I. Oppenheimer, eds., *Congress Reconsidered.* New York: Praeger, pp. 117-139.

Rundquist, Barry S. and John A. Ferejohn. 1975. "Observations on a Distributive Theory of Policy-Making: Two American Expenditure Programs Compared," in Craig Liske, William Loehr, and John McCamant, eds., *Comparative Public Policy: Issues, Theories and Methods.* New York: Wiley pp. 87-108.

Salisbury, Robert H. and Kenneth A. Shepsle. 1981a. "U.S. Congressman as an Enterprise," *Legislative Studies Quarterly* 6:559-576.

_____. 1981b. "Congressional Staff Turnover and the Ties-That-Bind," *American Political Science Review* 75:381-396.

Schattschneider, Elmer E. 1960. *The Semi-Sovereign People.* New York: Holt.

Schick, Allen. 1981. "The Three-Ring Budget: The Appropriations, Tax, and Budget Committees in Congress," in Thomas E. Mann and Norman J. Ornstein, eds., *The New Congress*. Washington, DC: American Enterprise Institute, pp. 288-328.

Sharkansky, Ira. 1965. "Four Agencies and an Appropriations Subcommittee: A Comparative Study of Budget Strategies," *Midwest Journal of Political Science* 9:254-281.

Shepsle, Kenneth A. 1978. *The Giant Jigsaw Puzzle: Democratic Committee Assignments in the Modern House*. Chicago: University of Chicago Press.

Simon, Herbert A. 1957. *Models of Man*. New York: Wiley.

Sinclair, Barbara. 1983. "Purposive Behavior in the U.S. Congress: A Review Essay," *Legislative Studies Quarterly* 8:117-131.

Truman, David B. 1951. *The Governmental Process*. New York: Knopf.

———. 1959. *The Congressional Party*. New York: Wiley.

Unekis, Joseph K. 1978. "From Committee to the Floor: Consistency in Congressional Voting," *Journal of Politics* 40:761-769.

Unekis, Joseph K. and Leroy N. Rieselbach. 1983. "Congressional Committee Leadership, 1971-1978," *Legislative Studies Quarterly* 8:251-270.

Wahlke, John C., Heinz Eulau, William Buchanan, and LeRoy C. Ferguson. 1962. *The Legislative System: Explorations in Legislative Behavior*. New York: Wiley.

Wilson, Woodrow. 1885. *Congressional Government*. Boston: Houghton Mifflin.

Chapter 10

Voting Behavior in Legislatures

by

MELISSA P. COLLIE

The purpose of this article is to review and assess from a comparative perspective the research on voting behavior in non-American legislatures, the American Congress, and U.S. state legislatures. Essays of this type always present organizational dilemmas, since whole literatures seldom lend themselves to tightly ordered frameworks of presentation and evaluation. This is the case with the literature on legislative voting behavior. Indeed, few subfields in legislative studies have generated as eclectic and profuse a body of research.

There are several factors that have contributed to the volume and heterogeneity of this literature. One factor derives from the broader shift within the discipline away from its institutional-historical and normative-reformist traditions and toward a behavioral orientation (Kirkpatrick, 1962). To be sure, several analyses of legislative voting predated the behavioral revolution of the 1950s, notably those of Lowell (1902), Rice (1928), and Key (1949). Nonetheless, the volume of such studies in the last two decades attests to the regard of behavioral analyses as necessary and important additions to the study of legislatures in general. A second and related factor is the availability of data. Clearly, voting behavior has received greater attention than any other facet of legislative behavior. While official voting records are not as accessible for a number of legislatures as we might wish, there have been substantial data available for both longitudinal and comparative analyses. A third factor is a function of legislatures themselves. The great majority of studies have dealt with voting on the floor. Still, owing to the variety of structures and procedures within legislatures, there are several other points during the legislative process at which voting may be monitored and evaluated. The fourth and most important factor is theoretical. The study of legislative voting behavior is intimately linked with many of the most prominent questions that concern students of legislatures, including the strength of legislative parties and factions, the nature of representation, the parameters of individual decision making, and the durability of governments. Accordingly, the heterogeneity and volume of the literature are due to the breadth of the theoretical considerations and the many perspectives from which voting behavior has been examined. Studies of legislative voting behavior have assumed not only an integral but a consequential role in efforts to understand the complexities of legislative bodies and their relationships to the larger political system.

A Framework for Analysis

To varying degrees, studies of legislative voting behavior are concerned with identifying the patterns of legislative voting and establishing the determinants and implications of these patterns. Though not all studies have focused explicitly or exclusively on voting behavior as either the dependent or independent variable, one appropriate framework for review might distinguish between analyses that have dealt primarily with the determinants of legislative voting behavior and those that have dealt primarily with its implications.

Such a framework would imply that a universal conceptualization of the phenomenon, regardless of whether it has been treated as the independent or dependent variable, has been established. There have developed, on the contrary, two varieties or schools of research. To distinguish between these two varieties of research, it is helpful to draw from the terminology Eulau (1969) uses. In his discussion of the conceptual and methodological problems involved in the study of political behavior, he differentiates the "object unit" of analysis, which is the unit whose behavior is to be explained, from the "subject unit" of analysis, which is the unit whose behavior is observed in order to explain the behavior of an object unit. The distinction between the two, as Eulau suggests, is more than a matter of the different levels of analysis at which research is conducted. In addition, the distinction is not constrained to a micro or macro locus of analysis—for example, the committee as opposed to the legislature. Rather, it lies in whether individual or collective actors are the focus of the research problem.

The two schools of research that together constitute the study of legislative voting behavior are distinguished by their different "object units" of analysis. One variety takes as its object of analysis the individual and the other takes as its object of analysis some form of collective. The former focuses on patterns of individual decision making and the latter on cleavage and alignment patterns. As a whole, then, research that has sought to assess the determinants and impact of legislative voting in American and non-American legislatures has explored the behavioral patterns of two overlapping but analytically distinct object units of analysis.

This essay builds on the distinction between these two varieties of research: its first section examines research on cleavages and alignments and its second section examines research on individual decision making.

The research on cleavages and alignments is further subdivided into two domains distinguished by their different definitions of the research problem. The first domain covers analyses in which the research problem has primarily been to document and explain intraparty cohesion and interparty conflict. In these studies, the object of analysis has been party as collective actor. While the American context has traditionally generated studies of this type, analysts of non-American legislatures have not devoted nearly as much attention to the topic, largely because consistently high levels of party cohesion and conflict in these legislatures have made such investigations appear superfluous. Further, while students of party behavior in the American legislative setting have been sensitive to both cohesion and conflict, students of party behavior in other settings have focused mainly on party cohesion. The second domain covers analyses in which the research problem has been to identify the nature of voting cleavages. In the American setting, the object of analysis has been the policy coalitions associated with broad issue areas. In other settings the object of analysis has been the legislative parties, yet the research problem has been to establish the dimensionality of interparty relations rather than to document and explain party cohesion and conflict per se. Thus the two types of research on cleavages and alignments have similarities, but are separable by virtue of their different research problems. In keeping with this distinction, the section on voting cleavages and alignments considers first the analyses whose emphasis is on party cohesion and conflict and second those whose emphasis is on the dimensionality of legislative voting cleavages.

The section on individual decision making focuses on the determinants of individual voting behavior. In the non-American setting, analysts have only begun to explore the factors possibly involved in voting decisions, again because high levels of party cohesion and conflict left little variation to be explained. It seemed reasonable to conclude that a single factor (i.e., party) was the primary determinant. In the American setting, a growing number of recent analyses have been concerned with establishing the representativeness of individuals' voting behavior vis-à-vis their constituencies. Phrased explicitly in the context of the representation question, these studies have examined for the most part the correspondence between legislators' voting records and constituency opinion. Parallelling the considerable attention now devoted to individual representation, there have been developed in the last decade a variety of more general or comprehensive models of individual decision making. While the linkages and the results that have emerged in research on representation have direct implications for the more general models of individual decision making (and vice versa), the emphasis in this article is on the latter.

It must be underscored that the entire literature on legislative voting behavior does not fall neatly or exclusively into these two research modes. In the American setting, for example, the study of policy coalitions as opposed to political parties is rooted in a model of individual decision making. However, organized around these two research modes, this review evaluates analyses largely in terms of the research questions addressed.

The discussion in each section is attentive to key variables and linkages, to methodologies and measurement techniques, and to the findings both in general areas of inquiry and on more specific research questions. However, the essay does not contain a critique of the many methodologies and statistics employed by students of voting behavior, except insofar as particular methodologies are associated with particular research questions and findings. Therefore, the reader is referred to several works that do examine in detail the methodological issues of legislative voting research (Anderson, Watts, and Wilcox, 1966; Clausen, 1967b; MacRae, 1970; Weisberg, 1972, 1974; Laakso, 1975).

This review does not examine in detail studies of voting behavior cast in the framework of axiomatic theory. Research of this type has its foundation in the earlier work of Black (1958), Riker (1958, 1961, 1962), Shapley and Shubik (1954), and von Neumann and Morgenstern (1947). While most axiomatic research on legislative voting behavior deals with majority preferences, a substantial and multifaceted literature in the last decade has approached the study of coalition formation and legislative decision making from a formal perspective. Unlike most of the research examined here, these studies do not focus directly on the explanation of legislative voting behavior. Rather, based on the assumption that rationality guides legislative behavior, they focus on the relations among institutional arrangements and procedures, individual strategies, and legislative outcomes. A synthesis of the axiomatic research and the more behaviorally oriented research on legislative voting would no doubt be informative; however, a discussion of the issues engendered by such a synthesis, and more particularly those introduced in the axiomatic literature itself, is beyond the scope of this article.

As already noted, there are a variety of points in the legislative process at which voting patterns may be evaluated. Whether the focus of research has been on alignment patterns or patterns of individual decision making, legislative voting analyses have been in large part restricted to behavior in plenary sessions. However, several recent studies have begun to assess comparatively the voting behavior exhibited in American legislative committees

(Dyson and Soule, 1970; Dodd, 1972; Fenno, 1973; Dodd and Pierce, 1975; Hinckley, 1975; Parker and Parker, 1979; Hamm, 1980). Others have sought to explain also the variation in legislative voting between the committee and the floor stages (Unekis, 1978; Francis and Riddlesperger, 1982; Hamm, 1982) as well as the patterns that appear in House-Senate conference committees (Fenno, 1966; Strom and Rundquist, 1977). Such research complements the more traditional research on voting in plenary sessions and supplements a committee literature in which studies of single committees still prevail (Jones, 1961; Manley, 1970; Ferejohn, 1974; Murphy, 1974; Price, 1978; LeLoup, 1979; Gross, 1980; Perkins, 1980; Ray, 1980).

Like other subfields in legislative studies, a great many analyses of legislative voting have concerned the U.S. Congress and particularly the House of Representatives. Although the scope of this essay is not limited to research on Congress, the review will reflect that emphasis in the literature itself. Where comparative perspective has been lacking, I shall identify approaches and methodologies that have the potential for such application.

This essay describes earlier work that has shaped and defined more current investigations, but more recent research receives a more detailed treatment. This is necessary in order to address concisely the theoretical and empirical contours of this literature. Such an emphasis presents less of a problem for assessing the research on voting in non-American legislatures, since most such research is of rather recent vintage (Patterson, 1968; Blondel, 1969; Loewenberg, 1971b, 1972; Jewell, 1978). For the American Congress and state legislatures, several thorough reviews of earlier research are fortunately available (Meller, 1960; Wahlke, 1962; Dye, 1965; Eulau and Hinckley, 1966; Huitt and Peabody, 1969; Jewell and Patterson, 1966, 1973; Kessel, 1973).

Voting Cleavages and Alignments

Party Cohesion and Conflict

Traditionally, research on cleavages and alignments in legislatures has focused on the collective behavior of the legislative parties. Influenced by the classic monograph of Lowell (1902) and the subsequent work of Rice (1928), these analyses assessed the strength or importance of partisan cleavages via two measures of party behavior, the level of intraparty cohesion and the incidence of interparty conflict. Although a variety of techniques were employed, analysts typically relied on four summary statistics: the Rice index of cohesion, the party vote score, the index of likeness, and the party unity score. With these statistics it was possible to compare party cohesion and conflict across time, across policy areas, and across legislatures.

Early research in the American setting was conducted within the context of the growing interest in "responsible" parties (Schattschneider, 1942; American Political Science Association, 1950; Ranney, 1954) and sought to establish the importance of party as a basis of cleavage vis-à-vis sectional and demographic factors. In the non-American setting, the voting behavior of the legislative parties generated comparatively little research, not surprising in light of the high levels of party cohesion and conflict observed in analyses of parliaments in western Europe. With the notable exception of MacRae's (1967) investigation of the causes and impact of party behavior in the French parliament, the research on non-American legislatures had a historical/constitutional orientation rather than a behavioral one.

The American setting. At the national level, Turner's (1951) work stands as the earliest comprehensive exploration into the variations in party behavior across time and across policy areas. In this and other studies, party emerged as the predominant basis of cleavage in Congress (Truman, 1959; Matthews, 1960; Marwell, 1967; Shannon, 1968; Shapiro, 1968; Turner and Schneier, 1970). Complementing the analysis of the congressional parties, several studies presented results for particular state legislatures at particular points in time (Keefe, 1954; Derge, 1958; Flinn, 1960; Buchanan, 1963; Sorauf, 1963; Friedman and Stokes, 1965; Wiggins, 1967; Bryan, 1968; Le Blanc, 1969). As a collection, they indicated the considerable variation in the character of partisan cleavages across legislatures. Comparative state analyses further demonstrated that the degree of party cohesion and conflict tended to be higher in the more urban states; however, the variation in levels of party voting, even among urban states, was the single most important finding that emerged from these studies (Zeller, 1954; Jewell, 1955; Keefe, 1956; Lockard, 1959; Dye, 1965).

In the last decade the shifting nature of partisan cleavages in the U.S. House has been more fully documented (Clubb and Traugott, 1977; Cooper, Brady, and Hurley, 1977). The results indicate an erratic but overall decline in the levels of both intraparty cohesion and interparty conflict since the turn of the century. Although similar results on the U.S. Senate await presentation, a number of studies have examined partisan cleavages in more specific historical periods (Dauer, 1953; Young, 1956; Cunningham, 1963; Alexander, 1967; Holt, 1967; Patterson, 1967; Silbey, 1967; Russo, 1972; Bell, 1973; Bogue, 1973; Brady, 1973; Hoadley, 1980).[1] Other research on the U.S. Congress has highlighted the fluctuations in particular aspects of party behavior that have occurred within the last few decades. For example, Patterson (1978) has shown that the percentage of party votes increased during the 1950s, declined during the 1960s, and increased during the 1970s. Similarly, Deckard and Stanley (1974) have attributed the decline in party unity scores over the period 1945-1970 to the increasing importance of ideologically charged regional groups within each party. The importance of regional cleavages has been explored for other historical periods (Young, 1966; Bogue and Marlaire, 1975).

Of continuing interest to students of party cleavages in Congress have been the activities of the Conservative Coalition. As a rule, the Conservative Coalition has been regarded as a Senate phenomenon (Manley, 1973, 1977). Brady and Bullock (1980, 1981) have documented a similar pattern of activity among Republicans and Southern Democrats in the House of Representatives. In addition, they have differentiated the Conservative Coalition in the House, which they argue has been organized to block legislation, from coalitions such as the Democratic Study Group, which have been designed to pass legislation (Stevens, Miller, and Mann, 1974). Rather than focusing on coalition activity, other scholars have tracked the deviance of the Southern Democratic contingent. Abramowitz (1980) has shown that, contrary to the conclusions drawn by Bass and DeVries (1977), the overall level of Southern Democratic disloyalty has not faded in the wake of the changing character of Southern politics.

In the state legislative setting, recent research has examined the nature of voting coalitions in weak party systems (Broach, 1972; Welch and Carlson, 1973). Results have indicated that in the absence of high party cohesion and conflict cleavages are fluid, factional, and highly issue-specific, thus confirming the conclusions drawn in earlier studies (Key, 1956; Patterson, 1962). Overall, however, information on the changing (or unchanging) character of party behavior in American state legislatures has remained highly fragmentary. Despite major breakthroughs in the comparative study of state legislatures (Key, 1949, 1956; Lockard, 1959) and the early attention devoted to party voting (Jewell, 1969, pp. 106-121), even marginally longitudinal studies of party behavior in American state legislatures are noticeably absent from the literature. Perhaps as a result of the methodological criticisms levied against roll calls as a data base for the study of state legislatures (Crane, 1960; Greenstein and Jackson, 1963) and the problems encountered in the collection of such data, comparative state analysis has been dominated by "input-output" modeling (Fenton and Chamberlayne, 1969; Hofferbert, 1972; Jones, 1973) and survey research (Wahlke, Eulau, Buchanan, and Ferguson, 1962; Francis, 1967; Patterson, Hedlund, and Boynton, 1975; Uslaner and Weber, 1977).

The non-American setting. As noted earlier, little attention has been devoted to the study of party voting behavior in the non-American setting. This is not to say that partisan cleavages have held no interest to students of non-American legislatures. However, studies of party cleavages in the American setting have used behavioral concepts and measured levels of cohesion and conflict, while studies of non-American legislatures have focused on the composition of such cleavages, measuring the number of parties participating in the legislature and the strength of their memberships (Rustow, 1956; Duverger, 1959; Sartori, 1966; Blondel, 1968; Lijphart, 1968). Several single-nation and crossnational studies have been based on indices that measure fragmentation by the size and number of legislative parties (Flanagan, 1971; Rae, 1968, 1971; Rae and Taylor, 1970; Taylor and Herman, 1971; Väyrynen, 1972).

Still, several recent studies suggest an increasing attention to the behavioral variations in party cleavages in non-American legislatures. In his critique of the compositional approach, Sartori (1976, pp. 305-323) has shown that for the Netherlands, Italy, Denmark, and Norway behavioral majorities have differed from compositional majorities. In Italy, for example, the compositional majority has comprised the Christian Democratic and Communist parties which, as Sartori points out, have yet to sit together. Other studies indicate that party cohesion has varied both within and across legislatures. Mezey (1979) has organized a number of single-nation studies that deal with the variations in party cohesion within a larger framework developed for the comparative analysis of legislatures. Wilson and Wiste (1976) have shown that cohesion varied among the parties in France during the Fourth Republic but was generally higher for all parties during the Fifth Republic. Even then, left-wing parties were the most cohesive, and centrist parties the least, with Gaullists in the middle. In the Swiss parliament, party cohesion has been higher in the Socialist and Swiss Populist parties than in the Christian Democratic party (Hertig, 1978). In addition, Stjernquist and Bjurulf (1970) have shown that cohesion in the five-party Swedish parliament has varied among the parties and has been highest on votes that were party proposals or government bills.

Among countries that are noted for high levels of party cohesion, there has also been variation. Although the German legislative parties have generally been recognized as highly cohesive blocs (Loewenberg, 1967), the Christian Democratic party has been slightly less cohesive than the Social Democratic party, usually on domestic matters (Schwarz and Shaw, 1976). Similarly, several studies have shown that the level of intraparty dissent on division votes in the British House of Commons has varied between the parties and has increased since 1974 (Norton, 1975, 1980; Crowe, 1980; Schwarz, 1980).[2] At the other end of the scale, cohesion in one-party Kenya was for a period the exception rather than the rule (Stultz, 1970).

DiPalma's (1977) research on the Italian legislative parties provides an interesting complement to these recent behavioral analyses, all of which have emphasized variation in party cohesion. In the Italian legislature, parties in the majority and minority coalitions have been highly cohesive, but the minority coalition has frequently sided with the majority coalition rather than adopting the role of loyal opposition. Thus, DiPalma's analysis is sensitive both to cohesion within the parties and to conflict (or the lack of it) between the parties. Damgaard and Rusk (1976) have shown that, in contrast to the largely nonconflictual relationship between the Italian majority and minority coalitions, the Danish legislative parties from 1953 to 1972 had a left-right dimension on which a three-party "bourgeois" bloc was consistently allied against a two-party "socialist" bloc. However, the long-term stability of Danish party cleavages was arrested during 1974, when Prime Minister Poul Hartling and his government were compelled to initiate a series of ad hoc coalitions to secure passage of a variety of policy measures (Borre, 1975).

Other research on the Danish parliament has distinguished the behavior of new and old parties. With the exception of the Socialists from 1966 to 1968, "new" opposition parties have voted more frequently than "old" ones on the losing side of final divisions on government bills that were passed (Pedersen, 1967; Pedersen, Damgaard, and Olsen, 1971; Damgaard, 1973). Damgaard (1974) has confirmed these findings for all proposals that reached the floor.

Explanations of party behavior. It has frequently been observed that the levels of party cohesion and conflict in the U.S. Congress and state legislatures have seldom approximated those in most non-American legislatures (Turner, 1951; Zeller, 1954; Epstein, 1980a). The focus in such comparisons has been on differences in party cohesion, and a number of factors have been discussed as possible explanatory variables, including national size and heterogeneity, the degree of class consciousness associated with the parties, the existence of programmatically oriented mass-membership organizations, and the system of government. After examining a number of single-nation studies, Epstein (1980a, pp. 315-350) has attributed the lower levels of party cohesion in American legislatures to a system of government based on separation of powers; high levels of party cohesion have been observed in the absence of all factors except parliamentary government.

The central theoretical tenet is that in parliamentary systems of government, party cohesion is essential to government stability.[3] The rationale is clearest in the case of two-party parliamentary systems. There, each party has its own incentive for being cohesive: the majority party to maintain the government in office and the minority party to show itself capable of maintaining a government should it become the majority party. Epstein (1980a, p. 321) has argued that the same incentive applies for a majority coalition but that cohesion among parties in the minority coalition is more problematic because no single opposition party is regarded as an alternative government.

The positive relationship between parliamentary government and party cohesion has held true among the three Commonwealth nations (Epstein,

1977). However, the British experience during the 1970s suggests that parliamentary systems can tolerate greater incohesion than had been surmised previously (Epstein, 1980b). Moreover, recent research on the House of Commons has shown that government defeats on major policy matters do not necessarily result in resignation, even when backbench members of the government's parliamentary party join in the opposing coalition (Norton, 1978, 1981; Schwarz, 1980). The outstanding exceptions to the positive relationship between the parliamentary system of government and party cohesion are the Third and Fourth Republics in France. Since MacRae's (1967) classic study, several analyses have reexamined the relationship between party incohesion and government instability in France (Wood, 1973; Wilson and Wiste, 1976; Wood and Pitzer, 1979). Beyond the Western European setting, Brass (1977) has shown that a lack of party cohesion is strongly related to the instability of governments in India.

In the American setting, party behavior has been viewed as highly contingent. Although earlier research on the American Congress and state legislatures clearly reflected an interest in the variations in party behavior and depicted a number of explanatory relationships,[4] the research designs of many analyses led to predictions of individual behavior rather than to predictions of the collective behavior of parties.

A number of recent analyses have tried to explain the variations in the collective behavior of the American legislative parties; however, no consensus has emerged concerning either proximate or intermediary factors. Using the Miller-Stokes data, Norpoth (1976) has argued that party cohesion in the House of Representatives is a function of shared policy attitudes among party members. Other research has emphasized the importance of electoral factors and institutional variables. In certain historical periods, party cohesion and conflict in the House have increased as the homogeneity of the parties' constituency bases, the strength of the party leadership, and the amount of turnover increased (Brady, 1972, 1978; Brady and Althoff, 1974). Two studies have argued that the importance of electoral factors outweighs that of internal variables (Cooper, Brady, and Hurley, 1977; Brady, Cooper, and Hurley, 1979). Cooper and Brady (1981a) have argued that the institutional character of the legislature is highly circumscribed by the nature of party cleavages rather than the reverse. Controlling for trend, Sinclair (1977b) has tested for the impact of several variables—including the presidential popular vote, party size, legislative and administrative status, and change in party control—on party cohesion in the House over the period 1901-1956. The more important of her many findings is that the impact of electoral and nonelectoral factors differed by party. Finally, while recent research on Congress has deemphasized legislative status and the role of the executive, recent analyses of party behavior in state legislatures have demonstrated the importance of status and of gubernatorial pressure (Morehouse, 1973; Bernick, 1978).

The general tendency among analyses of party behavior has been to treat party cleavages and alignments as the dependent variable. Supplementing this research perspective, several studies have sought to assess the effects of varying levels of party cohesion and conflict on public policy (Cooper and Bombardier, 1968; Sinclair, 1977a; Hurley, 1979; Hurley, Brady, and Cooper, 1977). Others have highlighted the relationship between partisan turnover, party cleavages, and policy change (Fishel, 1973; Orfield, 1975; Brady and Lynn, 1973; Brady, 1978, 1980; Brady and Stewart, 1982).

The Dimensionality of Voting Cleavages

In research concerning both the American and non-American legislative settings, an increasing number of analyses have sought to characterize the overall structure of legislative cleavages and alignments. The research covered in the previous section has emphasized the documentation and explanation of party cohesion and conflict. Among analyses of the dimensional genre, the discussion has revolved around the enumeration of dimensions.

In the American setting, most of the recent dimensional analyses have been related explicitly to broad areas of public policy. In fact, substantive policy areas have been established a priori as a first step to the examination of voting cleavages. The implicit if not explicit assumption in such analyses has been that the character of voting has varied across policy areas—that is, that there are distinguishable coalitions that vary across policy areas. The validity of this assumption has been at issue among researchers. In contrast, dimensional analyses of non-American legislatures have not explicitly identified policy coalitions. Rather, reflecting the generally acknowledged importance of party in parliamentary governments as well as the frequency of multiparty legislative representation, their purpose has been to assess whether the voting behavior of the legislative parties is accommodated by a single ideological continuum or by multiple dimensions.

American policy coalitions. A number of early studies of voting behavior in the American Congress and state legislatures examined the coalitions and alignments that formed around such policy areas as civil rights (Andrain, 1964), agricultural policy (Pennock, 1956), tariff questions (Watson, 1956), and foreign policy (Grassmuck, 1951; Westerfield, 1955; Haviland, 1958; Jewell, 1959, 1962; Kesselman, 1961, 1965; Havens, 1964; Rieselbach, 1964; Carroll, 1966; Robinson, 1967). Using a number of techniques,[5] others sought to compare the alignments associated with different policy areas (Gage and Shimberg, 1949; Turner, 1951; Belknap, 1958; Farris, 1958; MacRae, 1958, 1965; Marwell, 1967; Shannon, 1968). As a group, the latter analyses testified to the variation in alignments across policy areas.

The study of policy coalitions has undergone something of a theoretical revolution in the past decade, largely due to innovative approaches proposed by Theodore Lowi and Aage Clausen. Both have argued the now familiar thesis that policy content predicts policy coalitions. In Lowi's (1964, 1970, 1972) words, "policies determine politics" and in Clausen's (1973, p. 31), "different alignments form as the policy content changes." Although Lowi and Clausen each conceptualize the variations in policies differently, both have subscribed to the view that different policies predict different voting alignments.

Most of the recent studies of policy coalitions in the U.S. Congress have relied heavily on the policy dimensional technique and classification system developed by Clausen (1967a, 1974, 1978; Clausen and Van Horn, 1977a). Previously associated with the work of MacRae (1958, 1965), the dimensional method was extended by Clausen (1967a) and first presented as a solution to the measurement identity problem encountered in the longitudinal analysis of the voting alignments associated with particular policy areas. Policy dimensional analysis is founded on the classification of votes into substantively defined policy domains and on the establishment of intradomain unidimensionality by statistical cut-off criteria. The internal validity of policy dimensions was to be based, according to Clausen, on two criteria: 1) higher correlations among individual scale positions within dimensions across time than between dimensions in either the same or succeeding legislatures and 2) differential correlations among predictor variables within dimensions over time.

In an analysis of voting in the House and Senate between 1953 and 1964, Clausen and Cheney (1970) used this method and showed that voting patterns on economic and welfare policy dimensions could be differentiated and that the patterns associated with each dimension were highly stable across time and similar in the two houses. In addition, they argued that partisan differences were more pronounced on the economic dimension and constituency differences more pronounced on the welfare dimension. In a subsequent and more extensive analysis of House and Senate voting patterns over the same period, Clausen (1973) distinguished the durability and dominance of the voting alignments associated with five policy areas: government management, social welfare, international involvment, civil liberties, and agricultural assistance. Clausen concluded that congressional voting cleavages were multidimensional and stable across time.

The five policy dimensions defined by Clausen have come to constitute the framework within which policy coalitions in the contemporary Congress are assessed. Indeed, policy dimensional analysis has become far more than a method for establishing policy content equivalence in longitudinal examinations of the relationship between public policy and voting alignments. Instead, it seems to be the preferred approach for the analysis of voting cleavages and alignments in general.

The results of several studies using this framework suggest that the distinctiveness, durability, and dominance of the voting alignments associated with these dimensions, as well as the dimensions themselves, have been more ephemeral than was suggested in the earlier applications. Sinclair (1977c) has shown that during the first three New Deal congresses (1933-1938) House voting alignments corresponding to the government managment, social welfare, and agricultural policy dimensions were all highly partisan. Moreover, stable civil liberties and international involvement dimensions, as characterized in Clausen's analysis, did not appear in the House until the 75th and 76th Congresses, respectively (Sinclair, 1978a). Clausen and Van Horn (1977b) have argued that two new dimensions—the "agricultural subsidy limitation" dimension and the "national security commitment reorientation" dimension—emerged in the 91st and 92d Congresses. In a series of studies, Sinclair (1978a, 1978b, 1981a, 1981b) has emphasized the differences that have developed over time in the support of partisan/regional groups for the legislation contained in the government management and social welfare policy dimensions. Finally, Sinclair's (1982) analysis of the House of Representatives during the period 1925-1978 represents the most comprehensive and extensive longitudinal examination of change and stability in policy coalitions conducted to date. As a group, then, these analyses testify to the changing character of voting alignments within policy dimensions as well as to the changing character of the policy agenda itself.

At least three studies have challenged both the findings derived from policy dimensional analysis and the concept of multidimensionality in congressional politics on which such analysis is based. The most direct and extensive criticism has come from Schneider (1979). He has argued that the central theoretical thrust to a policy content approach comes from a "contemporary pluralist interest group" theory of American politics that in turn suggests that "there is no coalition, durable across issues or time, with any clear common characteristic among its members" (p. 25). Based on the results of interview data, an alternative classification system of roll-call votes, and an analysis of documentary sources, Schneider has proposed that three ideologically oriented blocs—composed of legislators adhering to conservative, liberal, and progressive philosophies—have been operative across issue dimensions in Congress during the 1970s. Although a significant portion of his critique and analysis states that these individuals are ideologically motivated in their voting behavior, his general point is that the structure of congressional coalitions has in recent years been unidimensional, not multidimensional as the Clausen-type analyses of policy dimensions imply. Also challenging a multidimensional perspective of congressional coalitions, Smith (1981) has argued that over the period 1957-1976 the correlation between the voting alignments associated with different issue dimensions in the Senate has increased. Finally, Shaffer (1980) has argued that during the period 1965-1976 non-Southern Democrats and Republicans have exhibited a dramatic ideological division in both the Senate and the House, with Republicans homogeneously clustered at the right and Democrats less homogeneously clustered at the left.

Unfortunately, the results of these studies are not strictly comparable to the results derived within the Clausen framework. Shaffer's conclusions are based on an examination of ADA scores and a selection of ideologically oriented member profiles. Schneider's findings, as noted above, are based on a different policy classification system, and Smith has not applied statistical cut-off criteria to the votes categorized in the five conventional policy dimensions.

With few exceptions, the Clausen framework has been used for the analysis of policy-oriented cleavages and alignments in the post-New Deal Congresses. However, historical research has shown that at certain points congressional politics has been characterized by highly polarized and partisan conflict that transcends broadly defined policy areas and in turn generates nonincremental policy changes (Sinclair, 1977c; Brady, 1978, 1980; Brady and Stewart, 1982). At the subnational level, LeLoup (1976) has attempted to differentiate voting alignments in four of the five dimensions (the exception being foreign policy) for the 1965-1966 and 1973-1974 sessions of the Missouri and Ohio state legislatures. His findings have indicated that more than half of the votes under consideration were not structured statistically in the policy dimensions and that among the votes that were retained party was the most important predictor of the alignment within each dimension. While LeLoup's findings have provided counterevidence to the thesis that policy determines voting alignments as well as to the assumption that state legislative voting alignments are multidimensional, other research on state legislatures, already noted, has demonstrated that in the absence of strong party conflict, voting cleavages have varied across policy areas (Key, 1956; Patterson, 1962; Broach, 1972; Welch and Carlson, 1973).

Non-American interparty relations. The dimensionality of interparty relations has long been an area of dispute. Early research contended that political parties generally fell along a unidimensional continuum whether the two-party or the multiparty system prevailed (MacIver, 1926). The unidimensional perspective on interparty relations has been buttressed by Duverger's (1959) notion of the inherent "dualism" of politics as well as by Downs's (1957) formal explication of party strategy and behavior. In the most direct criticism of a unidimensional perspective and specifically of the Downsian model, Stokes (1963) has argued in favor of a multidimensional party space in which interparty relations varied across issue areas. Stokes's conception of multidimensionality has received support from scholars of both the American and non-American political systems (Sjobolm, 1957; Dahl, 1966).

In the past, most of the dimensional research has concerned voting patterns in the electorate and party competition (Converse, 1966; LaPonce, 1970; Converse and Valen, 1971; Inglehart and Klingemann, 1976; Budge and Farlie, 1978). However, complementing the growing interest in levels of party cohesion and conflict, recent studies have begun to investigate the dimensionality of interparty relations by observing legislative voting behavior.

From an institutional perspective, the stongest argument that interparty relations are unidimensional derives from the precepts of parliamentary systems, in which parties must cooperate to form a government. Accordingly, center parties are expected to ally with parties of the left or right extremes but parties at the extremes are not expected to ally with each other against the center (Axelrod, 1970; de Swaan, 1973). The most surprising finding in this still limited area of research has been that in several multiparty systems the structure of voting cleavages has not appeared to be unidimensional.

Wood (1982) has examined parliamentary voting in France and Britain, primarily on European integration issues. His findings have indicated that such issues have produced internal divisions in parties of the left and right in both legislative settings; however, only among leftist parties have moderates been clearly distinguished from extremists. In an analysis of the legislative parties in the Finnish parliament from 1951 to 1958, Nyholm (1972) has argued that voting cleavages have been multidimensional and oblique throughout the period. Similarly, Clausen and Holmberg (1977) have adapted the dimensional technique to the analysis of the Swedish legislature in 1967, eliminating the a priori classification of votes according to policy content which is standard in analyses of the American Congress. They find that a dominant left-right dimension primarily comprised votes on economic matters while votes on social welfare, decentralization, and foreign policy were more highly concentrated in "other dimensions." Stjernquist and Bjurulf's (1970) research on Swedish party relations in 1964 and 1966 has also suggested a multidimensional structure. They have shown that a small minority of votes during these years divided Socialist and non-Socialist parties; they have also identified variation in the frequency of particular party alliances.

Pedersen, Damgaard, and Olsen (1971) likewise have rejected the unidimensional model after their analysis of Danish legislative voting on final divisions and agenda motions during the period 1945-1968. In addition, the authors have differentiated the behavior of "new" and "old" parties. Old parties have tended to be consistent in their behavior vis-à-vis each other across time but the positions and distances of new parties have tended to vary considerably across issue areas and time. Other research on the modern Danish legislature has derived more ambiguous conclusions. Damgaard (1973) has concluded that a left-right model has accounted very successfully for the party coalitions formed on government bills from 1953 to 1970. But he has also found that the level of conflict within the legislature has varied by policy area. Finally Olsen's (1972) research provides a historical perspective on Danish voting cleavages. In his examination of the dimensionality of cleavages during the Danish Constitutional Convention (1848-1849), he has identified a liberal-conservative dimension and an urban-rural dimension and has concluded that the former was the more pronounced.

In an earlier examination of voting patterns in the British House of Commons during the 1840s, Aydelotte (1962-1963) found that Guttman-scaling yielded substantively hetergeneous sets of roll calls, a finding which led him to reject a policy content explanation in favor of a party strategy explanation. Olsen (1972) has concurred with Aydelotte's notion that party maneuvers rather than issue content accounted for the multidimensionality of voting cleavages during the Danish Constitutional Convention. In Nyholm's (1972) analysis of Finnish voting cleavages, multidimensionality corresponded with issue content and with the origin of the proposal. He considered two alternative explanations of group movement: "political interest motivation" and "political power motivation." According to the former explanation, a legislative party takes stands in accordance with its ideology and electoral interests and is thereby better able to realize aspects of the party program. According to the latter explanation, a party supports (if it is part of the governmental coalition) or subverts (if it is part of the opposition coalition) the government. Of the two, the former is roughly analogous to the policy thesis current in research on the U.S. Congress, while the latter corresponds to Aydelotte's party maneuver thesis. Nyholm has found that group movement has corresponded to changes in governmental coalition and therefore has attributed the multidimensional structure of Finnish legislative voting cleavages to the political power motivation of legislative parties.

Assessment

An overview of the recent research on cleavages and alignments suggests a number of observations. In order to maintain the demarcation between analyses that have focused on party cohesion and conflict and those that have focused on the dimensions of voting alignments, the following discussion considers research trends and problems in the two types of analyses separately.

Party behavior. The major distinction between analyses of partisan voting cleavages in the U.S. national and state legislatures is one of documentation. While a fairly extensive longitudinal portrait of party behavior in Congress has been developed, the possible evolution or devolution of partisan cleavages in state legislatures has been largely unexamined. In light of the evidence on long-term trends at the national level, it would seem appropriate to ask whether the highly partisan state legislatures of two decades ago have met with similar decline. In addition, given the considerable interest nowadays in the "new" South, one wonders whether Republican inroads in electoral politics have become manifest in legislative politics as well. Bass and DeVries's (1977) analysis is a case in point: in an otherwise thorough exploration into the evolution of Southern politics, there is no longitudinal or cross-sectional presentation of state legislative party behavior.

The acquisition of longitudinal documentation of state partisan cleavages is more than an end in itself. It would inevitably introduce a comparative element into the evaluation of the changing character of party cleavages in the American Congress. At a minimum, such documentation would better establish the generalizability of trends in party cleavages observed at the national level. It would also refine our understanding not only of how partisan cleavages and alignments change over time but of why they change over time.

While party voting cleavages must be documented before they can be explained, the studies conducted on the U.S. Congress indicate the complexity of explaining the contours of party behavior. Longitudinal research on Congress has suggested one conclusion—that party cleavages have varied across time. The variation in the voting behavior of the parties is indeed one of the few areas of congressional research on which diachronic results have been accumulated.[6] Overall, these variations have elicited few attempts to explain systematically why they have taken place. This is Shannon's (1970) major criticism of the historical literature on congressional party behavior, but it applies equally to analyses of contemporary patterns. For instance, to date analysts have not attempted to explain systematically one of the more prominent phenomena of the contemporary era, the decline of party as a basis of cleavage in the Congress. This phenomenon has coincided with and been linked to a number of other changes in American politics, including the erosion of party identification in the electorate (Nie, Verba, and Petrocik, 1979), the increased importance of incumbency and "particularistic" politics (Mayhew, 1974; Fiorina, 1977), the declining ideological distance between the parties (Sorauf, 1976), the growth of the bureaucracy and the increased complexity of issue networks (Dodd and Schott, 1979; Heclo, 1979), and individual legislators' ambitions in the legislature (Dodd, 1977; Jones and Woll, 1979). If, however, the emphasis is on systematic evaluation, the relationships between these factors and the decline of party as a basis of cleavage in Congress is far from clear.

Likewise, there has been no documentation of party cleavages in non-American legislatures comparable to that which has been made for the U.S. Congress. Underlying this deficiency is a difference in approach which has already been noted: analysts have tended to emphasize the behavioral aspects of party cleavages in U.S. legislatures, whereas they have emphasized the composition of party cleavages in other legislatures.

As one result of these different approaches, the terms used to describe party cleavages have different connotations to students of American and of non-American legislatures. Party "strength" to the student of American legislatures implies high levels of party cohesion and conflict; to the student of non-American legislatures it implies a numerically strong party. Thus, there is an evaluative problem when party strength in the American Congress is compared with that in non-American legislatures, as in Loewenberg and Patterson's (1979) comparison of party strength in the British, German, Kenyan, and American legislatures. Similarly, the "fragmentation" of cleavages implies to the student of American legislatures the demise of party as a basis of cleavage; to the student of non-American legislatures it implies multiple legislative parties of roughly equal size.

A second result is that the profile of party cleavages in non-American legislatures is at best partial and at worst distorted. Sartori (1976) shows that compositional and behavioral majorities are dissimilar and that a compositional approach creates a misleading picture of party cleavages. The contrast between a behavioral and a compositional depiction of party cleavages is shown by Damgaard and Rusk's (1976) analysis of Danish voting behavior. From a compositional perspective, the five-party system in the Danish parliament implies a high level of fragmentation. But the authors have shown that for 20 years a left-right dimension consistently pitted a three-party majority coalition against a two-party minority coalition. Thus, from a behavioral perspective, it is difficult to view Danish party cleavages as fragmented. By comparison, party cleavages in the French Fourth Republic were fragmented both from a compositional and a behavioral perspective (MacRae, 1967).

A third result is that students of party cleavages in non-American legislatures have tended to assume that legislative parties can be treated as cohesive blocs. Indeed, the analysis of party cleavages in compositional terms rests on the assumption that parties act as cohesive blocs regardless of their coalition partners. As the more recent research discussed here suggests, party cohesion in parliamentary systems cannot be taken for granted. The argument seems to have been not merely that parliamentary systems (and especially two-party parliamentary systems) produce more cohesive parties than the American system does but that they produce legislative parties in which cohesion is high in some absolute sense. Again, recent research suggests that party cohesion in parliamentary systems is problematic and conditional rather than static and fixed.

The variation in legislative party cleavages seems more complex than a simple compositional perspective would indicate. A more complete and meaningful analysis of party cleavages in the non-American setting would integrate the compositional and behavioral perspectives. Further, the explanation of party voting behavior in parliamentary systems is far from self-evident, especially the explanation of party cohesion.

A final point is relevant to research on party cleavages in both the American and non-American settings. The significance of party as a basis of cleavages can be evaluated only by the interface between intraparty cohesion and interparty conflict—that is, the degree to which the parties as collective actors demonstrate both cohesion and conflict (Cooper, Brady, and Hurley, 1977). In a two-party system, highly cohesive parties that are unopposed do not attest to the importance of party any more than do highly fragmented parties where slim majorities conflict. In a multiparty system, the same rationale applies to majority and minority coalitions. Research on party cleavages and alignments must first evaluate the bases (if any) of conflict in the legislature and then assess how prominently party figures in the structure of voting cleavages. Quite clearly, the basis of conflict can be evident between parties and coalitions as well as within parties and coalitions. To ignore one or the other locus of conflict in an assessment of the behavioral significance of party is to neglect the overall structure of party relations. In sum, the full character of party behavior in the legislature cannot be developed without taking into account the level of conflict both within and between majority and minority parties and coalitions.

Dimensional perspectives. Research on legislatures both within the U.S. and outside of it raises the question of whether legislative voting cleavages are more accurately represented by a multidimensional space or a single continuum. In the American setting, research has used a policy framework constructed a priori to examine the dimensionality of voting cleavages. Such research has tended to assess the factors that account for individual voting behavior within the coalitions associated with each policy area. In contrast, research in the non-American setting has used a party framework to assess the dimensionality of voting cleavages. Accordingly, the emphasis has been on the dimensionality of interparty relations rather than on policy coalitions. In research on both American and non-American legislatures, the thesis that coalitions form around policies has been considered. However, the relationship between policy and voting cleavages has been more an explanation in the non-American setting, whereas in the American setting it has supplied the conceptual and methodological framework for the analyses. As the research findings in both legislative settings suggest, the dimensionality of legislative voting cleavages should be counted as a research question rather than an unexamined assumption.

The thesis that "policies determine politics" raises the question of whether majority and minority coalitions in non-American legislatures fluctuate, either in their alliance partners or in intraparty cohesion, in a manner that is connected to broad policy areas. Indeed, the recent research on the variability of party cohesion and conflict within and across legislatures suggests that the thesis merits investigation as an alternative to the more politically oriented explanation of party strategy and maneuver. Moreover, the policy-content thesis in the most general sense conflicts with recent cross-national analyses which have tested for the impact of changes in governmental coalitions (left-wing and right-wing) on policy rather than the reverse (Hibbs, 1977; Cameron, 1978; Castles, 1979; Payne, 1979).

It is uncertain whether a policy-content framework can be constructed which is suitable for the analysis of voting cleavages in different legislative settings. Despite the widespread adoption of Clausen's five-fold classification system of votes in the American Congress, several other bases of categorization have been proposed (Froman, 1967; Salisbury and Heinz, 1970; Lowi, 1972; Hayes, 1978). When students of non-American legislatures have attempted to differentiate votes by policy content, they have tended to rely on highly discrete categories (such as housing policy), variants of Lowi's redistributive-distributive-regulatory classification system, or criteria distinguishing "important" from "nonimportant" legislation (Blondel, 1973; Blondel et al., 1969; DiPalma, 1977). As yet, there has emerged no consensus on the level of abstraction at which or the substantive boundaries within which policy-content categories are to be constructed. This has already introduced comparability problems into the discussion of the dimensionality of congressional coalitions. To be sure, alternative sets of policy categories may serve alternative theoretical purposes. Nonetheless, it seems necessary to develop policy-content categories that are generalizable beyond the American Congress if this approach to the study of legislative cleavages is to become useful in crossnational comparisons or comparative state analyses.

A related issue concerns the conceptual and statistical parameters of a policy dimension itself. Presumably, if the voting alignments associated with substantively defined policy areas cannot be differentiated, then policy dimensions do not exist. Moreover, if the voting coalitions associated with different policy areas become more related over time, then policy dimensions collapse; the multidimensional structure of cleavages collapses into a unidimensional one. This is the criticism currently directed toward the multidimensional perspective of congressional voting alignments: that policy dimensions break down when it can be shown that the structure of cleavages is unidimensional. The question becomes whether policy dimensions can also break down from within. That is, policy dimensional analysis implies that the coalitions are indeed structured, not highly structured as in the unidimensional case but structured nonetheless. However, it is conceivable not only that coalitions may become more structured and unidimensional but that they may become less structured, even more highly fluid and factionalized than the current multidimensional perspective would suggest. In other words, there is some point at which coalitions are so highly issue-specific that policy dimensions have no value. The dimensional technique would seem to provide the most useful methodological tool for discerning an increase in factional politics (MacRae, 1970). But dimensional analysts have not yet proposed conceptual or statistical criteria that would distinguish a multidimensional structure of cleavages and alignments from a less structured, ad hoc state of coalition formation that would be associated with the acute fragmentation of legislative voting cleavages.

A final point concerns the general application of dimensional analysis to the study of legislative voting cleavages. As already noted, discussion in both the American and the non-American legislative settings has centered on whether cleavages display a unidimensional or a multidimensional structure. In the American Congress, cleavages seem more emergent and flexible than in other legislatures (Polsby, 1975, 1978). In this respect, dimensional analysis has illustrated (more clearly than, for example, party voting statistics) the contours of contemporary congressional cleavages. This is not to say that the character of congressional cleavages is inherently multidimensional. On the contrary, historical analyses have shown that at certain points congressional cleavages have been characterized by highly polarized partisan conflict (Sinclair, 1977c; Brady, 1978, 1980; Brady and Stewart, 1982). Indeed, the message of the realignment literature is that abrupt and salient environmental stimuli provoke changes in electoral coalitions, creating party polarization and clusters of policy change (Burnham, 1970; Campbell and Trilling, 1980; Clubb, Flanigan, and Zingale, 1980). Therefore it would appear that a multidimensional structure of congressional cleavages is more apparent in some periods than in others. The point may apply equally to the dimensions of interparty relations in the non-American setting. Shifts in the dimensions of voting behavior in non-American legislatures do not seem altogether unlikely in light of the increasing evidence on the shifting nature of party cleavages in the electorate (Butler and Stokes, 1969; Converse and Valen, 1971; Crewe, Sarlvik, and Alt, 1977; Pedersen, 1979; Irvine and Gold, 1980). All of this leads to a broader question that concerns not whether parties and coalitions are polarized or nonpolarized, unidimensional or multidimensional, but whether and why they change over time.

Individual Decision Making

Individual decision making has been and is studied primarily in American legislatures. As has already been noted, the focus of earlier research on voting behavior in the American Congress and state legislatures was to establish the extent and variation of party cleavages; however, the research designs of many analyses led to the prediction of individual voting behavior. The theme of these and other analyses that focused more explicitly on individual voting behavior was to assess the relative impact and interrelationship of party and constituency. This purpose or theme generated a number of attendant and more specific research questions.

From the outset, there was controversy surrounding the importance of party and constituency as determinants of individual decision making. Some scholars adopted the view that the voting behavior of individual legislators was a matter of constituency influence alone (Froman, 1963a; Flinn, 1964). In contrast to what Key (1961) termed the "simple constituency pressure model," others argued that individual decisions were a function of both party and constituency "pressures" (Turner, 1951; Turner and Schneier, 1970; Mayhew, 1966; Shannon, 1968). Questions were also raised concerning the separation of party and constituency effects from an operational standpoint (Froman, 1963b; Shannon, 1968) and the need to address the relevance of legislators' personal attitudes and perceptions (Dexter, 1957; Froman, 1963c; Anderson, 1964). The latter gained additional prominence with the findings of Miller and Stokes (1963).

The approach and findings of Turner (1951) and MacRae (1952) shaped many of the subsequent investigations into party and constituency influence. Based on the examination of party, sectional, ethnic, and urban/ rural cleavages in Congress, Turner showed that members divided along lines other than party, although not as frequently as they did on party lines. In addition, he showed that constituency characteristics were related to variations in individual members' party loyalty. Based primarily on these two observations, he affirmed his original proposition that congressmen were subject to both party and constituency pressures and concluded that of the two party was the more important predictor of individual voting decisions. In an analysis of several sessions of the Massachusetts House of Representatives, MacRae confirmed that Democrats and Republicans from districts "typical" of their party's electoral base demonstrated higher party loyalty than those from "atypical" districts. In addition, he hypothesized that representatives from "marginal-competitive" districts, which for the most part were also "atypical" in their constituency makeup , were more subject to constituency influence. Since legislators from atypical and marginal districts tended to have lower party loyalty scores than legislators from typical and safe districts, atypicality and marginality were interpreted as predictors of constituency influence as opposed to party influence.

In view of Turner's and MacRae's analyses, several studies of Congress and state legislatures attempted to replicate the relationships found between constituency characteristics, electoral margins, and party loyalty (Dye, 1961; Patterson, 1961, 1962; Parsons, 1962; Froman, 1963a; Pesonen, 1963; Flinn, 1964; Shannon, 1968; Le Blanc, 1969; Turner and Schneier, 1970). Several studies, many of which employed scaling and clustering techniques, explored the impact of party and/or constituency in various policy areas (MacRae, 1958; Cnudde and McCrone, 1966; Flinn and Wolman, 1966; Mayhew, 1966; Jackson, 1967; Shannon, 1968).

The results were by no means comparable across analyses. The fairest summary of their conclusions is that the impact of party and constituency varied between Democrats and Republicans and across issue areas, legislatures, and time. To different ends, Fiorina (1974) and Cooper, Brady, and Hurley (1977) have presented the most comprehensive critiques of these studies and of some of the more recent literature. Fiorina has examined the literature in order to glean from past studies evidence of constituency influence; Cooper, Brady, and Hurley have examined it in order to determine what evidence has been shown regarding party influence. Though both analyses have found past research wanting in its conceptualization and measurement of party and constituency, the two critiques testify to the predominant theme of the earlier research: to examine the relative impact of party and constituency and the interrelationship between them.

In contrast to the party-constituency orientation of earlier research, more recent analyses of constituency influence has sought to establish the parameters of representation. At a theoretical level, the discussion has concerned the multiple aspects of district-to-legislator representation and the influence of constituency opinion on individual voting behavior rather than the correspondence between the two (Eulau and Karps, 1977; Karps and Eulau, 1978; Jewell and Loewenberg, 1979; Stone, 1979; Weissberg, 1979). At a conceptual and technical level, the discussion has revolved around creating and operationalizing clearer and more appropriate measures of constituency opinion (Markus, 1974; Achen, 1977, 1978; Kuklinski, 1977a; Fenno, 1978; Erikson, 1978; Weissberg, 1979).

Among the representation studies, several have reexamined the relationship between constituency influence, individual voting behavior, and legislative roles (Eulau, Wahlke, Buchanan, and Ferguson, 1959; Wahlke et al., 1962; Davidson, 1969; Jewell, 1970; Hedlund and Friesema, 1972; Jones, 1973; Friesema and Hedlund, 1974; Erikson, Luttbeg, and Holloway, 1975; Deckard, 1976a; Hadley, 1977; Kuklinski and Elling, 1977; Gross, 1978; Alpert, 1979; McCrone and Kuklinski, 1979). Some analyses have tested for the constancy of constituency influence across different policy areas (Miller and Stokes, 1963; Jackson, 1971, 1974; Sullivan and O'Connor, 1972; Achen, 1978; Erikson, 1978; Kuklinski, 1978; Kuklinski and McCrone, 1980). Others have examined the relationship between constituency opinion and legislators' support for presidential programs (Weinbaum and Judd, 1970; Buck, 1972; Edwards, 1976, 1977, 1978, 1980; Martin, 1976; Schwarz and Fenmore, 1977). Still others have focused specifically on the relationship between constituency characteristics and policy responsiveness to the black electorate in the South (Bullock and MacManus, 1981). Kuklinski (1978) and Elling (1982) have shown that legislators' responsiveness increases as reelection approaches. Finally, considerable attention has been devoted to the relationship between electoral margins, constituency influence, and individual voting behavior (Miller, 1970; Erikson, 1971; Fiorina, 1973, 1974, 1975; Deckard, 1976b; Kuklinski, 1977b; Wright, 1977; Sullivan and Uslaner, 1978; Bartlett, 1979).

The diversity of the studies which share this theme or research purpose demonstrates how complex the task is of establishing the determinants of individual decision making in the American legislative setting. Conducted within the parameters of the representation question, they quite naturally have tested for the impact of the extralegislative environment. Complementing this research on individual decision making, several more general models, most of which incorporate elements of the intralegislative environment, have been developed.

Legislative Decision-making Models

To date, there is no consensus on what determines individual decision making in the American setting. Indeed, a variety of models of individual decision making have been proposed in recent years.

The consensus model. According to Kingdon (1973), individual decision making is a function of the legislator's search for consensus. He has identified six main actors who influence the legislator's ultimate decision: the legislator's constituency, the legislator's House colleagues, the party leadership, interest groups, the administration, and the legislator's staff. In the "consensus mode of decision," the legislator first determines whether the impending vote has evoked any controversy in the legislative arena. If not, he votes with "the herd." If there is controversy, he determines whether there is consensus in his "perceptual field of forces," the aforementioned set of six actors plus his own policy attitude. If the field is free of conflict, he votes in that direction. If it is not, he votes with the majority of actors.

The cue-taking model. A second model has been proposed by Matthews and Stimson (1970, 1975; Stimson, 1975). They have identified nine actors from which legislators are likely to seek and to receive "cues" concerning an impending vote: the state party delegation, the Conservative Coalition, the party leadership, the president, committee chairmen and ranking minority members, the party majority, the House majority, and the Democratic Study Group. In this model, legislators develop hierarchies of cue-givers; the hierarchies may differ by legislator but are constant across time and across issue areas.

The predisposition-communication model. Cherryholmes and Shapiro (1969) have developed a third model. They have argued that legislators' "predispositions" or attitudes toward legislation predict the voting decision only if they are strongly positive or negative. A range of equally weighted variables, many of which are included in the above two models, determine the direction and strength of the legislator's predisposition. If their predisposition is weak, legislators enter a "communication phase" based on their network of "most likely contacts" among other House members.

The policy-dimension model. A fourth model is associated with the work of Aage Clausen (1973). In this model, the most important variable is the policy content of the motion itself. Legislators related specific motions to broad policy areas and, depending on the policy area, consider the positions taken by various actors. Over time, the legislator refers to the same actors with regard to each policy area; however, different actors are influential in different policy areas.

The voting-history model. Closely related to Clausen's model is that proposed by Asher and Weisberg (1978). In their model, congressmen's past decisions regarding issue areas predict future decisions; that is, congressmen develop a "voting history" within broad policy areas. Like Clausen, they view the influence of party, constituency, and the president as varying among policy areas; however, they argue that legislators' voting histories are more subject to change in some issue areas than in others.

The electoral-incentive model. Last, based on the contention that the primary goal of legislators is reelection, Fiorina (1974, 1975) has formalized a model of individual decision making based entirely on constituency influence. "Constituency opinion" is conceptualized as the group or groups, subjectively identified by the legislator, that could affect, again according to the subjective judgment of the legislator, his or her probability of reelection. So defined, constituency opinion is homogeneous when groups are consensual and heterogeneous when groups are conflictual. In addition, the relevant groups may vary with the issue.

As a group, these models testify to the variety of actors and decision rules that have appeared relevant to the decision-making process. Several reflect an emphasis found in some of the earlier research: the patterns of interaction within the legislative setting itself (Patterson, 1959; Francis, 1962; Fiellin, 1962; Kessel, 1964). The disparities in perspective have been noted in comparative evaluations of several of the models (Kingdon, 1977; Weisberg, 1978; Kuklinski, 1979).

In one of the few attempts to integrate theoretically the various components of the different models, Kingdon (1977) has also incorporated legislators' goals. The first two steps of his (1973) "consensus" model have been retained. That is, in the search for consensus the legislator still evaluates first the legislative arena and second his perceptual field of forces. Kingdon then identifies three major individual goals: maintaining constituency satisfaction, developing influence in Washington, and making "good" public policy. In the third step of his revised version of the decision-making process, these goals circumscribe the influence of various actors when there is controversy in the group.

Kozak (1982) has also attempted to synthesize the various factors that have been treated in several of the models. Based on interview data in which House members in the 97th Congress were asked to evaluate 31 votes, he has distinguished between the decision "referent" (that is, the factor cited by the member as the determinant of the voting decision) and the decision "mode" (that is, the general approach or decision rule adopted by the member). His results have indicated that both referents and modes vary according to whether the vote is controversial. Accordingly, he has concluded that legislative decision making is a highly contingent phenomenon rather than a function of a single determinant or rule. The conditional or contextual perspective is reflected variously in several analyses and models of individual decision making (Lowi, 1964, 1972; Cherryholmes and Shapiro, 1969; Clausen, 1973; Kingdon, 1973, 1977; Jones, 1974; Asher and Weisberg, 1978; Hayes, 1978; Kozak, 1982).

In addition to research that has developed comprehensive models of individual decision making, studies have focused on the role of more particular components of the decision process, such as legislative norms (Asher, 1973), ideology (Bernstein and Anthony, 1974), member policy preferences (Gross, 1979; Fry and Stolarek, 1980), and the influence of informal groups (Best, 1971; Clausen, 1972; Deckard, 1972).

Decision Making in the Non-American Setting

As has already been noted, studies of individual voting behavior have concentrated on American legislatures. Owing to the high levels of party cohesion in many non-American legislatures, it has been assumed that party predicts individual decision making. Even so, there has been some disagreement concerning what "party" is. Mezey (1979) has discussed party impact in terms of the degree to which members anticipate sanctions and disciplinary action by the party leadership. However, Epstein (1980a) has argued that in Britain the impact of party on individual voting behavior derives from the set of norms shared by MPs and that these correspond to the party solidarity necessary to parliamentary systems of government. The importance of norms is also suggested by Di Palma's (1977) analysis of decision making in the Italian parliament. He has argued that a lack of consensus among Italian legislators concerning "decisional rules"—that is, those which govern how conflicts should be resolved in the legislative arena—underlies the voting cleavages in parliament and the nature of Italian public policy.

Other recent studies have begun to examine the relationship between constituency influence and party disloyalty. As with recent research conducted in the American setting, these studies have emphasized the importance of conceptualizing and measuring constituency from the legislator's perspective (Jewell and Loewenberg, 1979). Converse and Pierce (1979) have noted that in the rare instances of party disloyalty in the French legislature members have voted in accordance with the issue preferences of their constituencies. Analysis of member voting in the British House of Commons has yielded more variegated conclusions. Earlier research had shown that rebellious MPs tended to be secure in their local associations and were likely to be readopted in spite of their rebellion (Epstein, 1964; Rasmussen, 1966). And in an examination of voting on the immigration issue in 1969, Frasure (1971) had argued that the concentration of immigrants in a constituency played no role in member disloyalty. However, Schwarz (1975) has examined member voting on education and immigration issues during the period 1957-1964 and has found an association between disloyalty and both electoral vulnerability and constituency policy interest. Party disloyalty in the House of Commons during the 1970s has been linked with members' career objectives and with their perception that they had too small a role in policymaking (Schwarz and Lambert, 1971; Crowe, 1980). Finally, in a study of British parliamentary voting from 1880-1892, Stephens and Brady (1976) have attributed the high levels of party loyalty to skillful party leadership and centralized parliamentary decision making rather than to polarized constituencies.

Assessment

In the American setting, earlier research measured the relative influence of party and constituency on legislative voting decisions. The more recent studies still attend to party and constituency factors, but their theme has shifted. In fact, there are now two themes: district representation and general models of individual decision making. This shift has had at least two implications.

First, the independent impact of party has become less specifiable, both operationally and conceptually. To be sure, the conceptualization and measurement of party influence has varied widely. In analyses that focus on or incorporate the influence of the internal environment of the legislature, party appears interactive, its effects channeled through partisan referent groups such as the party leadership or the state party delegation (e.g., Matthews and Stimson, 1970; Clausen, 1972; Deckard, 1972; Kingdon, 1973). In other analyses party influence is conceptualized as a set of shared attitudes that transcend or compete with constituency (Clausen, 1973, 1978; Norpoth, 1976). When the constituent base of parties is recognized, the tendency has been lately to view party influence as inseparable from constituency influence (Fiorina, 1975; Kuklinski, 1977b). Few would deny that party has roots in constituent groups and coalitions as well as structural manifestations in the legislative arena. The trouble is that when party influence is conceptualized as an intralegislative factor, its extralegislative or constituent component is lost; when it is acknowledged that party is tied to constituent groups, party and constituency seem one and the same.

A second and related implication concerns the manner in which the impact of the extralegislative environment has been conceptualized. Recent studies of individual decision making, especially those conducted within the framework of the representation question, have had a highly localized or district-specific orientation. Yet environmental factors other than district make-up and district opinion may affect the degree to which legislators respond to their constituencies. Specifically, party as an aggregate, extralegislative phenomenon that transcends local factors may shape constituency opinion and circumscribe constituency influence on individual voting behavior; this possibility needs to be incorporated into theoretical models of individual decision making. In other words, constituency influence on individual legislators' voting decisions may be greatest when the parties, as collectives, define and shape the political agenda in partisan terms. This would imply some polarity between the parties in their electoral capacity. The general point suggests, then, that there is both a local and a national component to the influence of the extralegislative environment on individual decision making and that, to the degree the two components are related, the correspondence between constituency opinion and individual voting behavior varies across time.

There are a number of similarities among the generalized models of legislative decision making. Several of the models assume that legislators routinely operate under conditions of decisional overload, low information, and uncertainty, conditions that necessitate decisional rules of thumb. Most attempt to incorporate a similar set of determinants, both internal and external to the legislature, and most accommodate in some form the legislator's own policy preferences. In addition, several reflect the perspective that individual decision making is a conditional process.

As there is convergence among the models in many respects, there are also noticeable differences. For example, in the cue-taking model, individual decision making is entirely a function of member interaction within the legislative arena. In the electoral incentive model, it is a function of subjectively defined constituency opinion and the extralegislative environment assumes primacy. However, in both the original and the revised consensus model, legislators turn to constituency only if they perceived conflict in the legislative setting. In the policy dimensional model, the influence of actors varies across policy areas but is fixed for all legislators within each policy area. In the cue-taking model, the influence of actors is hierarchically constant across policy areas but may vary by legislator. In the voting history model, members' policy positions may vary across time within policy areas, but in the policy dimensional model, they remain stable. In the predisposition-communication model, members' policy preferences have a direct impact on their decisions whereas in the consensus model the impact of policy preferences is conditional. Finally, while several of the models reflect the perspective that individual decision making involves a set or series of conditions, the question arises as to which conditions are the relevant ones—for example, the substantive attributes of policy measures, the strength of member policy preferences, or the degree of consensus in either the legislature or the relevant set of actors. As a group, then, the models raise these questions: whether the legislative environment or the extralegislative environment is the legislator's primary referent, whether decision making is a function of single or multiple determinants, whether the influence of various actors is circumscribed or direct, and whether decisional rules are universal or conditional.

Besides the obvious difference in volume, the most noticeable distinction between research on individual decision making in the non-American setting and in the American setting concerns the manner in which the dependent variable has been defined. In the non-American setting, analysts have sought to explain the basis of party loyalty and disloyalty, a research topic which reflects their understanding of the importance of legislative parties to parliamentary systems of government. In contrast, research in the American setting has sought to explain why and under what conditions legislators arrive at decisions in general, rather than why they have voted with or against their party.

At this point, research on individual decision making in non-American legislatures is still very limited. Certainly, the British experience since 1974 has contributed to the new interest in the determinants of individual voting decisions in parliamentary systems. Despite the highly circumscribed nature of this research, recent analysis of decision making in non-American legislatures raises several issues.

One issue is whether and to what degree the more inclusive models of decision making discussed above apply in non-American legislative systems. Quite clearly, there are a number of perspectives that may be borrowed from research on American legislatures. Moreover, increased attention to the structural or institutional context of individual decision making, which would presumably be forthcoming were one or more of these models to be considered by analysts of decision making in non-American legislatures, would likely enhance our understanding of the process and determinants of decision making in the American system.

A second issue in non-American settings, as in American legislatures, concerns the conceptual specification of the impact of party on individual decision making. As noted with regard to the analyses discussed earlier, legislators' party loyalty has been linked to a variety of factors, including the anticipation of internal sanctions and disciplinary action, shared norms among members, a centralized legislative structure, and the skills of party leaders. In addition, party disloyalty has been attributed to varying factors, including constituency preferences, electoral vulnerability, and members' policy and career objectives. Considering the many factors that have been proposed in either case, it is not implausible to suppose that the reasons behind party loyalty and disloyalty vary across legislative settings. The broader question concerns under what conditions these factors come into play.

A final and related issue in non-American research concerns the determination of the conditions under which patterns of individual voting behavior change. In the House of Commons, for example, not only have certain measures evoked higher levels of party disloyalty, but over time aggregate levels of disloyalty have increased. Parenthetically, it is tempting to infer a connection between the change in British parliamentary politics and the continued erosion of the constituent bases of the British parties. The possible relationship between partisan change in the electorate and change in the patterns of individual voting behavior in the legislature (as opposed to electoral displacement) has yet to be systematically investigated. The question is not merely what accounts for party loyalty or disloyalty but what accounts for increases (or decreases) in loyalty or disloyalty. In short, what accounts for change?

Concluding Comments

This essay has identified two schools of research that deal with legislative voting behavior and are distinguished by alternative object units of analysis. One school has focused on collective behavior and this focus has led to the analysis of cleavage and alignment patterns; the other has focused on individual behavior and this focus has led to the analysis of individual decision-making patterns. In the course of this essay, elements of change and continuity in the themes and approaches that characterize research on collective and individual voting behavior have become evident.

In both varieties of research, the American congressional referent continues to predominate. As a result, the question unavoidably arises as to whether and to what degree the findings regarding collective and individual decision making are generalizable beyond the congressional setting. Moreover, despite the considerable attention devoted to patterns of collective and individual voting behavior in Congress, there remain significant gaps in our understanding of the variations in voting cleavages and alignments as well as of individual voting behavior. These gaps are all the more apparent in our understanding of voting patterns of either type in American state legislatures.

In the American setting, the primary object unit of analysis has shifted gradually and erratically from the study of collective behavior to the study of individual behavior in particular collectivities and, most recently, to the study of individual behavior in legislatures per se. Accordingly, emphasis has shifted from the examination of cleavages to the examination of individual decisions. By contrast, research in the non-American setting has leaned toward the study of collective behavior, primarily focusing on the importance of parties and factions in the legislative setting. In the last decade scholars have begun to document and analyze the varieties of voting behavior exhibited across legislatures. In addition, the geographical scope of research in non-American legislatures has been extended beyond western Europe both in single-nation studies and in crossnational comparisons.

Also apparent is the degree to which there has been conceptual interchange and crossfertilization between these two varieties of research. The interchange, in other words, derives from the degree to which the study of cleavages and alignments has influenced conceptually and empirically the study of individual decision making and, of late, the degree to which the study of individual decision making has influenced conceptually and empirically the study of cleavages and alignments. The primary testimony to this assertion lies in the manner in which legislative voting behavior in the American as opposed to the non-American setting has been considered and evaluated. Due to the structure of cleavages and alignments in many non-American legislatures, the assumption has been that party was the most important if not the single determinant of individual decision making in these legislatures. By contrast and corresponding to the often multiple bases of cleavage evident in American legislatures, individual decision making has been considered a function of multiple if not conflicting factors.

As research on legislative voting behavior in non-American legislatures has become more sensitive to the variation in legislative voting cleavages, it has, in a parallel fashion, become more sensitive to the possibility that factors other than party enter the decisional calculus of individual legislators. Similarly, as longitudinal analyses of Congress have depicted the peaks and valleys of party cohesion and conflict, they imply that individual decision making is to greater or lesser degrees a function of multiple determinants. Perhaps the larger import of the mesh between the study of collective and individual decision making is that the parameters and determinants of individual

voting behavior vary with the overall structure of voting cleavages and alignments in the legislature.

Earlier in this review I attempted to identify some of the problems
and developments that have arisen in recent research on cleavage patterns
and patterns of individual decision making. If there is one major point that is
commendable to future research in either area, it is the need to address conceptually and empirically the parameters of longitudinal variation in both
collective and individual patterns of voting. This is especially relevant to
the study of individual decision making since theory has advanced largely
within the context of the contemporary Congress. While scholars have traditionally been attentive to the possibility that the determinants and process
of individual decision making varies across legislative systems, there has
been relatively little attention devoted to the possibility that the impact
of factors varies across time within a legislative system. This is not to deny
the importance of collective decision making. It is, after all, the collective
decision-making process that is the business of legislatures, the collective
decision that defines public policy.

Considering the unresolved issues evident in studies of legislative
voting behavior in the American setting and the new interest in legislative
cleavages and individual voting behavior in the non-American setting, there
is little reason to suspect that legislative voting research has peaked. Overall,
recent research on legislative voting behavior admits to more questions
than answers.

NOTES

I am especially grateful to John Kingdon and Samuel Patterson for their
detailed comments on the earlier version of this essay. I also wish to thank David Brady,
Joseph Cooper, Anthony King, and Rick Wilson for their suggestions.

1. Silbey (1981) has compiled a list of studies by U.S. historians on congressional and state legislative voting behavior.

2. Instead of division lists, other analysts have used Early Day Motions to
study intraparty dissent (Berrington, 1973; Finer, Berrington, and Bartholomew, 1961;
Franklin and Tappin, 1977; Leece and Berrington, 1977).

3. Loewenberg (1971a) provides a conceptual discussion of the relationship
between parliamentary behavior and government instability.

4. See especially Jewell and Patterson (1966, 1973) for a review of many of
these analyses.

5. See MacRae (1970, pp. 11-174) for a discussion of the literature and its
technical foundations.

6. See the exchange among Cooper and Brady (1981b), Patterson (1982),
and Polsby (1982).

REFERENCES

Abramowitz, Allan I. 1980. "Is the Revolt Fading? A Note on Party Loyalty among Southern Democratic Congressmen," *Journal of Politics* 42:568-572.

Achen, Christopher. 1977. "Measuring Representation: Perils of the Correlation Coefficient," *American Journal of Political Science* 21:805-815.

_____ . 1978. "Measuring Representation," *American Journal of Political Science* 22:475-510.

Alexander, Thomas. 1967. *Sectional Stress and Party Strength.* Nashville, TN: Vanderbilt University Press.

Alpert, Eugene. 1979. "A Reconceptualization of Representational Role Theory," *Legislative Studies Quarterly* 4:587-604.

American Political Science Association Committee on Political Parties. 1950. *Toward a More Responsible Two-Party System.* New York: Holt, Rinehart.

Anderson, Lee F. 1964. "Individuality in Voting in Congress: A Research Note," *Midwest Journal of Political Science* 8:425-429.

Anderson, Lee F., Meredith Watts, Jr., and Allen R. Wilcox. 1966. *Legislative Roll Call Analysis.* Evanston, IL: Northwestern University Press.

Andrain, Charles F. 1964. "A Scale Analysis of Senators' Attitudes Toward Civil Rights," *Western Political Quarterly* 27:488-503.

Asher, Herbert B. 1973. "The Learning of Legislative Norms," *American Political Science Review* 67:499-513.

Asher, Herbert B. and Herbert F. Weisberg. 1978. "Voting Change in Congress: Some Dynamic Perspectives on an Evolutionary Process," *American Journal of Political Science* 22:391-425.

Axelrod, Robert. 1970. *Conflict of Interest.* Chicago: Markham Publishing.

Aydelotte, William O. 1962-1963. "Voting Patterns in the British House of Commons in the 1840s," *Comparative Studies in Society and History* 5:134-163.

Bartlett, Robert V. 1979. "The Marginality Hypothesis: Electoral Insecurity, Self-Interest, and Voting Behavior," *American Politics Quarterly* 7:498-508.

Bass, Jack and Walter DeVries. 1977. *The Transformation of Southern Politics.* New York: Basic Books.

Belknap, George M. 1958. "A Method for Analyzing Legislative Behavior," *Midwest Journal of Political Science* 2:377-402.

Bell, Rudolph. 1973. *Party and Faction in American Politics: The House of Representatives, 1789-1801.* Westport, CT: Greenwood Press.

Bernick, E. Lee. 1978. "The Impact of U.S. Governors on Party Voting in One-Party Dominated Legislatures," *Legislative Studies Quarterly* 3:431-444.

Bernstein, Robert A. and William W. Anthony. 1974. "The ABM Issue in the Senate, 1968-70: The Importance of Ideology," *American Political Science Review* 68:1198-1206.

Berrington, Hugh. 1973. *Backbench Opinion in the House of Commons, 1945-55.* New York: Pergamon Press.

Best, James J. 1971. "Influence in the Washington House of Representatives," *Midwest Journal of Political Science* 15:547-562.

Black, Duncan. 1958. *The Theory of Committees and Elections.* Cambridge: Cambridge University Press.

Blondel, Jean. 1968. "Party Systems and Patterns of Government in Western Democracies," *Canadian Journal of Political Science* 1:180-203.

_____ . 1973. *Comparative Legislatures.* Englewood Cliffs, NJ: Prentice-Hall.

Blondel, Jean et al. 1969. "Legislative Behavior: Some Steps towards a Cross-National Measurement," *Government and Opposition* 5:67-85.

Bogue, Allan. 1973. "The Radical Voting Dimension in the U.S. Senate During the Civil War," *Journal of Interdisciplinary History* 3:449-474.

Bogue, Allan and Mark P. Marlaire. 1975. "Of Mess and Men: The Boardinghouse and Congressional Voting, 1821-1842," *American Journal of Political Science* 19:207-230.

Borre, Ole. 1975. "The General Election in Denmark, January, 1975: Toward a New Structure of the Party System?" *Scandinavian Political Studies* 10:211-216.

Brady, David W. 1972. "Congressional Leadership and Party Voting in the McKinley Era: A Comparison to the Modern House," *Midwest Journal of Political Science* 16:439-459.

———. 1973. *Congressional Voting in a Partisan Era*. Lawrence: University of Kansas Press.

———. 1978. "Critical Elections, Congressional Parties and Clusters of Policy Change," *British Journal of Political Science* 8:79-100.

———. 1980. "Congressional Elections and Clusters of Policy Change in the U.S. House: 1886-1960," in Richard Trilling and Bruce Campbell, eds., *Realignment in American Politics: Toward a Theory*. Austin: University of Texas Press.

Brady, David W. and Phillip Althoff. 1974. "Party Voting in the U.S. House of Representatives, 1890-1910: Elements of a Responsible Party System," *Journal of Politics* 36:753-775.

Brady, David W. and Charles S. Bullock III. 1980. "Is There A Conservative Coalition in the House?" *Journal of Politics* 42:549-552.

———. 1981. "Coalition Politics in the House of Representatives," in Lawrence C. Dodd and Bruce I. Oppenheimer, eds., *Congress Reconsidered*. 2d ed. Washington, DC: Congressional Quarterly, pp. 186-203.

Brady, David W. and Naomi Lynn. 1973. "Switched-Seat Congressional Districts: Their Effect on Party Voting and Public Policy," *American Journal of Political Science* 67:528-543.

Brady, David W. and Joseph Stewart, Jr. 1982. "Congressional Party Realignment and Transformations of Public Policy in Three Realignment Eras," *American Journal of Political Science* 26:333-360.

Brady, David W., Joseph Cooper, and Patricia Hurley. 1979. "The Decline of Party Voting in the U.S. House of Representatives," *Legislative Studies Quarterly* 4:381-400.

Brass, Paul R. 1977. "Party Systems and Government Stability in the Indian State," *American Political Science Review* 71:1384-1405.

Broach, Glen T. 1972. "A Comparative Dimensional Analysis of Partisan and Urban-Rural Voting in State Legislatures," *Journal of Politics* 34:905-921.

Bryan, Frank M. 1968. "The Metamorphosis of a Rural Legislature," *Polity* 1:191-212.

Buchanan, William. 1963. *Legislative Partisanship*. Berkeley: University of California Press.

Buck, Vincent. 1972. "Presidential Coattails and Congressional Loyalty," *Midwest Journal of Political Science* 16:460-472.

Budge, Ian and Dennis Farlie, 1978, "The Potentiality of Dimensional Analyses for Explaining Voting and Party Competition," *European Journal of Political Research* 6:203-231.

Bullock, Charles S. III and Susan A. MacManus. 1981. "Policy Responsiveness to the Black Electorate," *American Politics Quarterly* 9:357-368.

Burnham, Walter Dean. 1970. *Critical Elections and the Mainsprings of American Politics.* New York: Norton.

Butler, David and Donald E. Stokes. 1969. *Political Change in Britain: Forces Shaping Electoral Choice.* New York: St. Martin's Press.

Cameron, David R. 1978. "The Expansion of the Public Economy: A Comparative Analysis," *American Political Science Review* 72:1243-1261.

Campbell, Bruce A. and Richard J. Trilling, eds. 1980. *Realignment in American Politics: Toward A Theory.* Austin: University of Texas Press.

Carroll, Holbert N. 1966. *The House of Representatives and Foreign Affairs.* Pittsburgh: University of Pittsburgh Press.

Castles, Frank. 1979. "Does Politics Matter: An Analysis of the Public Welfare Commitment in Advanced Democratic States," *European Journal of Political Research* 7:169-186.

Cherryholmes, Cleo H. and Michael J. Shapiro. 1969. *Representatives and Roll Calls: A Computer Simulation of Voting in the Eighty-eighth Congress.* Indianapolis: Bobbs-Merrill.

Clausen, Aage. 1967a. "Measurement Identity in the Longitudinal Analysis of Legislative Voting," *American Political Science Review* 61:1020-1035.

_____ . 1967b. "The Measurement of Legislative Group Behavior," *Midwest Journal of Political Science* 11:212-224.

_____ . 1972. "State Party Influence on Congressional Policy Decision," *Midwest Journal of Political Science* 16:77-101.

_____ . 1973. *How Congressmen Decide: A Policy Focus.* New York: St. Martin's Press.

_____ . 1974. "Subjectivity and Objectivity in Dimensional Analysis: Illustration from Congressional Voting," in James F. Herndon and Joseph L. Bernds, eds., *Mathematical Applications in Political Science.* Vol. 7. Charlottesville: University of Virginia Press.

_____ . 1978. "Party Voting in Congress," in Jeff Fishel, ed., *Parties and Elections in An Anti-Party Age.* Bloomington: Indiana University Press, pp. 274-279.

Clausen, Aage and Richard B. Cheney. 1970. "A Comparative Analysis of Senate-House Voting on Economic and Welfare Policy: 1953-64," *American Political Science Review* 64:138-152.

Clausen, Aage and Soren Holmberg. 1977. "Legislative Voting Analysis in Disciplined Multi-Party Systems: The Swedish Case," in William O. Aydelotte, ed., *The History of Parliamentary Behavior.* Princeton: Princeton University Press, pp. 159-185.

Clausen, Aage and Carl E. Van Horn. 1977a. "How to Analyze Too Many Roll Calls and Related Issues in Dimensional Analysis," *Political Methodology* 4:313-332.

_____ . 1977b. "The Congressional Response to a Decade of Change: 1963-1972," *Journal of Politics* 39:625-666.

Clubb, Jerome M. and Santa A. Traugott. 1977. "Partisan Cleavage and Cohesion in the House of Representatives, 1861-1974," *Journal of Interdisciplinary History* 7:375-402.

Clubb, Jerome M., William H. Flanigan, and Nancy H. Zingale. 1980. *Partisan Realignment: Voters, Parties, and Government in American History.* Beverly Hills, CA: Sage Publications.

Cnudde, Charles and Donald J. McCrone. 1966. "The Linkage Between Constituency Attitudes and Congressional Voting Behavior," *American Political Science Review* 60:66-72.

Converse, Phillip E. 1966. "The Problem of Party Distances in Models of Voting Change," in M. Kent Jennings and H. Zeigler, eds., *The Electoral Process*. Englewood Cliffs, NJ: Prentice-Hall, pp. 175-207.

Converse, Phillip E. and Roy Pierce. 1979. "Representative Roles and Legislative Behavior in France," *Legislative Studies Quarterly* 4:525-562.

Converse, Phillip E. and Henry Valen. 1971. "Dimensions of Cleavage and Perceived Party Distances in Norwegian Voting," *Scandinavian Political Studies* 6: 107-152.

Cooper, Joseph and Gary Bombardier. 1968. "Presidential Leadership and Party Success," *Journal of Politics* 30:1012-1027.

Cooper, Joseph and David W. Brady. 1981a. "Institutional Context and Leadership Style: The House From Cannon to Rayburn," *American Political Science Review* 75:411-426.

—————. 1981b. "Toward a Diachronic Analysis of Congress," *American Political Science Review* 75:988-1006.

Cooper, Joseph and Patricia Hurley. 1977. "The Electoral Basis of Party Voting: Patterns and Trends in the U.S. House of Representatives, 1887-1969," in Louis Maisel and Joseph Cooper, eds., *The Impact of the Electoral Process*. Beverly Hills, CA: Sage Publications, pp. 133-165.

Crane, Wilder, Jr. 1960. "A Caveat on Roll-Call Studies of Party Voting," *Midwest Journal of Political Science* 4:237-249.

Crewe, Ivor, Bo Sarlvik, and James Alt. 1977. "Partisan Dealignment in Britain 1964-1974," *British Journal of Political Science* 7:129-190.

Crowe, Edward W. 1980. "Cross-Voting in the British House of Commons: 1945-1974," *Journal of Politics* 42:487-510.

Cunningham, Noble. 1963. *The Jeffersonian Republicans in Power: Party Operations, 1801-1809*. Chapel Hill: University of North Carolina Press.

Dahl, Robert A. 1966. *Political Oppositions in Western Democracies*. New Haven: Yale University Press.

Damgaard, Erik. 1973. "Party Coalitions in Danish Law-Making 1953-70," *European Journal of Political Research* 1:35-66.

—————. 1974. "Stability and Change in the Danish Party System over Half a Century," *Scandinavian Political Studies* 9:103-126.

Damgaard, Erik and Jerrold Rusk. 1976. "Cleavage Structures and Representational Linkages: A Longitudinal Analysis of Danish Legislative Behavior," *American Journal of Political Science* 20:179-206.

Dauer, Manning. 1953. *The Adams Federalists*. Baltimore: The Johns Hopkins Press.

Davidson, Roger H. 1969. *The Role of the Congressman*. New York: Pegasus.

Deckard, Barbara Sinclair. 1972. "State Party Delegations in the U.S. House of Representatives," *Journal of Politics* 34:199-222.

—————. 1976a. "Political Upheaval and Congressional Voting: The Effects of the 1960s on Voting Patterns in the House of Representatives," *Journal of Politics* 38:326-345.

—————. 1976b. "Electoral Marginality and Party Loyalty in House Roll Call Voting," *American Journal of Political Science* 20:469-482.

Deckard, Barbara Sinclair and John Stanley. 1974. "Party Decomposition and Region: The House of Representatives, 1945-70," *Western Political Quarterly* 27: 249-264.

Derge, David R. 1958. "Metropolitan and Outstate Alignments in Illinois and Missouri Legislative Delegations," *American Political Science Review* 52:1051-1065.

Dexter, Lewis A. 1957. "The Representative and His District," *Human Organization* 16:2-13.

de Swaan, Abram. 1973. *Coalition Theories and Cabinet Formations.* San Francisco: Jossey-Bass.

Di Palma, Giuseppe. 1977. *Surviving Without Governing: The Italian Parties in Parliament.* Berkeley: University of California Press.

Dodd, Lawrence C. 1972. "Committee Integration in the Senate: A Comparative Analysis," *Journal of Politics* 34:1135-1171.

_____ . 1977. "Congress and the Quest for Power," in Lawrence C. Dodd and Bruce I. Oppenheimer, eds., *Congress Reconsidered.* New York: Praeger.

Dodd, Lawrence C. and John C. Pierce. 1975. "Roll Call Measurement of Committee Integration: The Impact of Alternative Methods," *Polity* 7:386-401.

Dodd, Lawrence C. and Richard L. Schott. 1979. *Congress and the Administrative State.* New York: Wiley.

Downs, Anthony. 1957. *An Economic Theory of Democracy.* New York: Harper & Row.

Duverger, Maurice. 1959. *Political Parties.* 2d ed. London: Methuen.

Dye, Thomas R. 1961. "A Comparison of Constituency Influences in the Upper and Lower Chambers of a State Legislature," *Western Political Quarterly* 14:473-481.

_____ . 1965. "State Legislative Politics," in Herbert Jacob and Kenneth Vines, eds., *Politics in the American States.* Boston: Little, Brown, pp. 151-206.

Dyson, James W. and John W. Soule. 1970. "Congressional Committee Behavior on Roll Call Votes: The U.S. House of Representatives, 1955-64," *Midwest Journal of Political Science* 14:626-647.

Edwards, George C. III. 1976. "Presidential Influence in the House: Presidential Prestige as a Source of Presidential Power," *American Political Science Review* 70:101-113.

_____ . 1977. "Presidential Influence in the Senate: Presidential Prestige as a Source of Presidential Power," *American Politics Quarterly* 5:481-500.

_____ . 1978. "Presidential Electoral Performance as a Source of Presidential Power," *American Journal of Political Science* 22:152-168.

_____ . 1980. *Presidential Influence in Congress.* San Francisco: Freeman.

Elling, Richard C. 1982. "Ideological Change in the U.S. Senate: Time and Electoral Responsiveness," *Legislative Studies Quarterly* 7:75-92.

Epstein, Leon. 1964. *British Politics in the Suez Crisis.* Urbana: University of Illinois Press.

_____ . 1977. "A Comparative Study of Australian Parties," *British Journal of Political Science* 7:1-22.

_____ . 1980a. *Political Parties in Western Democracies.* New Brunswick, NJ: Transaction Books.

_____ . 1980b. "What Happened to the British Party Model?" *American Political Science Review* 74:9-22.

Erikson, Robert S. 1971. "The Electoral Impact of Congressional Roll Call Voting," *American Political Science Review* 65:1018-1032.

_____ . 1978. "Constituency Opinion and Congressional Behavior: A Reexamination of the Miller-Stokes Representation Data," *American Journal of Political Science* 22:511-535.

Erikson, Robert S., Norman R. Luttbeg, and William V. Holloway. 1975. "Knowing One's District: How Legislators Predict Referendum Voting," *American Journal of Political Science* 19:231-246.

Eulau, Heinz. 1969. "Introduction: On Units and Levels of Analysis," in Heinz Eulau, ed., *Micro-Macro Political Analysis*. Chicago: Aldine, pp. 1-22.

Eulau, Heinz and Katherine Hinckley. 1966. "Legislative Institutions and Processes," in James A. Robinson, ed., *Political Science Annual*. Vol. 1. Indianapolis: Bobbs-Merrill, pp. 85-190.

Eulau, Heinz and Paul K. Karps. 1977. "The Puzzle of Representation: Specifying Components of Responsiveness," *Legislative Studies Quarterly* 2:233-254.

Eulau, Heinz, John C. Wahlke, William Buchanan, and Leroy C. Ferguson. 1959. "The Role of the Representative: Some Empirical Observations on the Theory of Edmund Burke," *American Political Science Review* 53:742-756.

Farris, Charles C. 1958. "A Method of Determining Ideological Groupings in the Congress," *Journal of Politics* 20:308-338.

Fenno, Richard. 1966. *The Power of the Purse*. Boston: Little, Brown.

————. 1973. *Congressmen in Committees*. Boston: Little, Brown.

————. 1978. *Homestyle*. Boston: Little, Brown.

Fenton, John H. and Donald W. Chamberlayne. 1969. "The Literature Dealing with the Relationships Between Political Processes, Socio-Economic Conditions and Public Policies in the American States: A Bibliographical Essay," *Polity* 1: 388-404.

Ferejohn, John A. 1974. *Pork Barrel Politics*. Boston: Little, Brown.

Fiellin, Alan. 1962. "The Function of Informal Groups: A State Delegation," *Journal of Politics* 24:72-91.

Finer, S.E., H.B. Berrington, and D.V. Bartholomew. 1961. *Backbench Opinion in the House of Commons, 1955-59*. Oxford: Pergamon Press.

Fiorina, Morris P. 1973. "Electoral Margins, Constituency Influence, and Policy Moderation: A Critical Assessment," *American Politics Quarterly* 1:478-498.

————. 1974. *Representatives, Roll Calls, and Constituencies*. Lexington, MA: Heath.

————. 1975. "Constituency Influence: A Generalized Model and Its Implications for Statistical Studies of Roll-Call Behavior," *Political Methodology* 2:249-266.

————. 1977. *Congress: Keystone of the Washington Establishment*. New Haven: Yale University Press.

Fishel, Jeff. 1973. *Party and Opposition: Congressional Challengers in American Politics*. New York: McKay.

Flanagan, Scott C. 1971. "The Japanese System in Transition," *Comparative Politics* 3:231-254.

Flinn, Thomas. 1960. "The Outline of Ohio Politics," *Western Political Quarterly* 13:702-721.

————. 1964. "Party Responsibility in the States: Some Causal Factors," *American Political Science Review* 58:60-71.

Flinn, Thomas and Harold Wolman. 1966. "Constituency and Roll Call Voting: The Case of Southern Democratic Congressmen," *Midwest Journal of Political Science* 10:192-199.

Francis, Wayne L. 1962. "Influence and Interaction in a State Legislative Body," *American Political Science Review* 56:953-960.

————. 1967. *Legislative Issues in the Fifty States*. Chicago: Rand McNally.

Francis, Wayne L. and James W. Riddlesperger. 1982. "U.S. State Legislative Committees: Structure, Procedural Efficiency, and Party Control," *Legislative Studies Quarterly* 7:453-471.

Franklin, Mark N. and Michael Tappin. 1977. "Early Day Motions as Unobtrusive Measures of Backbench Opinion in Britain," *British Journal of Political Science* 7:49-70.

Frasure, R. 1971. "Constituency, Racial Composition and the Attitudes of British MPs," *Comparative Politics* 3:201-211.

Friedman, Robert S. and Sybil L. Stokes. 1965. "The Role of Constitution-Maker as Representative," *Midwest Journal of Political Science* 9:148-166.

Friesema, H. Paul and Ronald D. Hedlund. 1974. "The Reality of Representational Roles," in Norman R. Luttbeg, ed., *Public Opinion and Public Policy*. Homewood, IL: Dorsey Press.

Froman, Lewis A. 1963a. *Congressmen and Their Constituencies*. Chicago: Rand McNally.

_____ . 1963b. "Inter-Party Constituency Differences and Congressional Voting Behavior," *American Political Science Review* 57:57-61.

_____ . 1963c. "The Importance of Individuality in Voting in Congress," *Journal of Politics* 25:324-332.

_____ . 1967. "An Analysis of Public Policies in Cities," *Journal of Politics* 29: 94-108.

Fry, Brian R. and John S. Stolarek. 1980. "The Impeachment Process: Predisposition and Votes," *Journal of Politics* 42:1110-1117.

Gage, N.L. and B. Shimberg. 1949. "Measuring Senatorial Progressivism," *Journal of Abnormal Psychology* 44:112-117.

Grassmuck, George L. 1951. *Sectional Biases in Congress on Foreign Policy*. Baltimore: The Johns Hopkins Press.

Greenstein, Fred I. and Elton F. Jackson. 1963. "A Second Look at the Validity of Roll Call Analysis," *Midwest Journal of Political Science* 7:156-166.

Gross, Donald A. 1978. "Representational Styles and Legislative Behavior," *Western Political Quarterly* 31:359-371.

_____ . 1979. "Measuring Legislators' Policy Positions: Roll Call Votes and Preferences Among Pieces of Legislation," *American Politics Quarterly* 7:417-438.

_____ . 1980. "House-Senate Conference Committees: A Comparative-State Perspective," *American Journal of Political Science* 24:769-778.

Hadley, David J. 1977. "Legislative Role Orientations and Support for Party and Chief Executive in the Indiana House," *Legislative Studies Quarterly* 2:309-336.

Hamm, Keith. 1980. "U.S. State Legislative Committee Decisions: Similar Results in Different Settings," *Legislative Studies Quarterly* 5:31-54.

_____ . 1982. "Consistency Between Committee and Floor Voting in U.S. State Legislatures," *Legislative Studies Quarterly* 7:473-490.

Havens, Murray C. 1964. "Metropolitan Areas and Congress: Foreign Policy and National Security," *Journal of Politics* 26:758-776.

Haviland, H. Field, Jr. 1958. "Foreign Aid and the Policy Process: 1957," *American Political Science Review* 52:689-724.

Hayes, Michael T. 1978. "The Semi-Sovereign Pressure Groups," *Journal of Politics* 37:134-161.

Heclo, Hugh. 1979. "Issue Networks and the Executive Establishment," in Anthony King, ed., *The New American Political System*. Washington, DC: American Enterprise Institute, pp. 87-125.

Hedlund, Ronald D. and H. Paul Friesema. 1972. "Representatives' Perceptions of Constituency Opinion," *Journal of Politics* 34:730-752.

Hertig, Hans-Peter. 1978. "Party Cohesion in the Swiss Parliament," *Legislative Studies Quarterly* 3:63-81.

Hibbs, Douglas A. 1977. "Political Parties and Macroeconomic Policy," *American Political Science Review* 71:1467-1487.

Hinckley, Barbara. 1975. "Policy Content, Committee Membership, and Behavior," *American Journal of Political Science* 19:553-557.

_____ . 1981. *Coalitions and Politics.* New York: Harcourt Brace Jovanovich.

Hoadley, John. 1980. "The Emergence of Political Parties in Congress, 1789-1803," *American Political Science Review* 74:757-779.

Hofferbert, Richard I. 1972. "State and Community Policy Studies: A Review of Comparative Input-Output Analyses," in James A. Robinson, ed., *Political Science Annual.* Vol. 3. Indianapolis: Bobbs-Merrill, pp. 3-72.

Holt, James. 1967. *Congressional Insurgents and the Party System, 1909-1916.* Cambridge: Harvard University Press.

Huitt, Ralph K. and Robert L. Peabody. 1969. *Congress: Two Decades of Analysis.* New York: Harper & Row, pp. 3-73.

Hurley, Patricia A. 1979. "Assessing the Potential for Significant Legislative Output in the House of Representatives," *Western Political Quarterly* 32:45-58.

Hurley, Patricia A., David Brady, and Joseph Cooper. 1977. "Measuring Legislative Potential for Policy Change," *Legislative Studies Quarterly* 2:385-398.

Inglehart, Ronald and Hans D. Klingemann. 1976. "Party Identification, Ideological Preference and the Left-Right Dimension among Western Mass Publics," in Ian Budge, Ivor Crewe, and Dennis Farlie, eds., *Party Identification and Beyond.* London: Wiley.

Irvine, William P. and H. Gold. 1980. "Do Frozen Cleavages Ever Go Stale? The Bases of the Canadian and Australian Party Systems," *British Journal of Political Science* 10:187-219.

Jackson, John. 1967. "Some Indirect Evidences of Constituency Pressures on Senators," *Public Policy* 16:253-270.

_____ . 1971. "Statistical Models of Senate Roll Call Voting," *American Political Science Review* 65:451-470.

_____ . 1974. *Constituencies and Leaders in Congress: Their Effects on Senate Voting Behavior.* Cambridge: Harvard University Press.

Jewell, Malcolm E. 1955. "Party Voting in American State Legislatures," *American Political Science Review* 49:773-791.

_____ . 1959. "Evaluating the Decline of Southern Internationalism through Senatorial Roll Call Votes," *Journal of Politics* 21:624-646.

_____ . 1962. *Senatorial Politics and Foreign Policy.* Lexington: University of Kentucky Press.

_____ . 1969. *The State Legislature.* 2d ed. New York: Random House.

_____ . 1970. "Attitudinal Determinants of Legislative Behavior: The Utility of Role Analysis," in Allan Kornberg and Lloyd D. Musolf, eds., *Legislatures in Developmental Perspective.* Durham, NC: Duke University Press.

_____ . 1978. "Legislative Studies in Western Democracies: A Comparative Perspective," *Legislative Studies Quarterly* 3:537-554.

Jewell, Malcolm E. and Gerhard Loewenberg. 1979. "Toward a New Model of Legislative Representation," *Legislative Studies Quarterly* 4:485-500.

Jewell, Malcolm E. and Samuel C. Patterson. 1966. *The Legislative Process in the United States.* New York: Random House.

_____ . 1973. *The Legislative Process in the United States.* New York: Random House.

Jones, Bryan D. 1973. "Competitiveness, Role Orientations and Legislative Responsiveness," *Journal of Politics* 35:924-947.

Jones, Charles O. 1961. "Representation in Congress: The Case of the House Agriculture Committee," *American Political Science Review* 55:358-367.

_____ . 1973. "State and Local Public Policy Analysis: A Review of Progress," in *Political Science and State and Local Government*. Washington, DC: American Political Science Association, pp. 27-54.

_____ . 1974. "Speculative Augmentation in Federal Air Pollution Policy-Making," *Journal of Politics* 36:438-464.

Jones, Rochelle and Peter Woll. 1979. *The Private World of Congress*. New York: The Free Press.

Karps, Paul D. and Heinz Eulau. 1978. "Policy Representation as an Emergent: Toward a Situational Analysis," in Heinz Eulau and John C. Wahlke, eds., *The Politics of Representation*. Beverly Hills, CA: Sage Publications, pp. 207-232.

Keefe, William J. 1954. "Parties, Partisanship, and Public Policy in the Pennsylvania Legislature," *American Political Science Review* 48:450-464.

_____ . 1956. "Comparative Study of the Role of Political Parties in State Legislatures," *Western Political Quarterly* 9:726-742.

Kessel, John H. 1964. "The Washington Congressional Delegation," *Midwest Journal of Political Science* 8:1-21.

_____ . 1973. "American Political Parties: An Interpretation with Four Analytical Levels," in Cornelius P. Cotter, ed., *Political Science Annual*. Vol. 4. New York: Bobbs-Merrill, pp. 127-180.

Kesselman, Mark. 1961. "Presidential Leadership in Congress on Foreign Policy," *Midwest Journal of Political Science* 5:284-289.

_____ . 1965. "Presidential Leadership in Congress on Foreign Policy: A Replication of an Hypothesis," *Midwest Journal of Political Science* 9:401-416.

Key, V.O. 1949. *Southern Politics in State and Nation*. New York: Knopf.

_____ . 1956. *American State Politics*. New York: Knopf.

_____ . 1961. *Public Opinion and American Democracy*. New York: Knopf.

Kingdon, John W. 1973. *Congressmen's Voting Decisions*. New York: Harper & Row.

_____ . 1977. "Models of Legislative Voting," *Journal of Politics* 39:563-595.

Kirkpatrick, Evron. 1962. "The Impact of the Behavioral Approach on Traditional Political Science," in Austin Ranney, ed., *Essays on the Behavioral Study of Politics*. Urbana: University of Illinois Press, pp. 1-30.

Kozak, David C. 1982. "Decision-Making on Roll Call Votes in the House of Representatives," *Congress & The Presidency* 9:51-79.

Kuklinski, James H. 1977a. "Constituency Opinion: A Test of the Surrogate Model," *Public Opinion Quarterly* 41:34-40.

_____ . 1977b. "District Competitiveness and Legislative Roll-Call Behavior: A Reassessment of the Marginality Hypothesis," *American Journal of Political Science* 21:627-638.

_____ . 1978. "Representativeness and Elections: A Policy Analysis," *American Political Science Review* 72:165-177.

_____ . 1979. "Representative-Constituency Linkages: A Review Article," *Legislative Studies Quarterly* 4:121-140.

Kuklinski, James H. and Richard C. Elling. 1977. "Representational Role, Constituency Opinion, and Legislative Roll-Call Behavior," *American Journal of Political Science* 21:135-147.

Kuklinski, James H. and Donald J. McCrone. 1980. "Policy Salience and the Causal Structure of Representation," *American Politics Quarterly* 8:139-165.

Laakso, Markku. 1975. "Cooperativeness in a Multi-Party System: A Measure and an Application," *European Journal of Political Research* 3:181-197.

LaPonce, J.A. 1970. "Note on the Use of the Left-Right Dimension," *Comparative Political Studies* 2:481-502.

Le Blanc, Hugh. 1969. "Voting in State Senates: Party and Constituency Influences," *Midwest Journal of Political Science* 13:33-57.

Leece, John and Hugh Berrington. 1977. "Measurements of Backbench Attitudes by Guttman-Scaling of Early Day Motions: A Pilot Study, Labour, 1968-69," *British Journal of Political Science* 7:529-540.

LeLoup, Lance T. 1976. "Policy, Party, and Voting in U.S. State Legislatures: A Test of the Content-Process Linkage," *Legislative Studies Quarterly* 1:213-230.

————. 1979. "Process Versus Policy: The U.S. House Budget Committee," *Legislative Studies Quarterly* 4:227-254.

Lijphart, Arend. 1968. "Typologies of Democratic Systems," *Comparative Political Studies* 1:3-44.

Lockard, Duane. 1959. *New England State Politics*. Princeton: Princeton University Press.

Loewenberg, Gerhard. 1967. *Parliament in the German Political System*. Ithaca, NY: Cornell University Press.

————. 1971a. "The Influence of Parliamentary Behavior on Regime Stability: Some Conceptual Clarifications," *Comparative Politics* 3:177-200.

————. 1971b. "New Directions in Comparative Political Research," *Midwest Journal of Political Science* 15:741-756.

————. 1972. "Comparative Legislative Research," in Samuel C. Patterson and John C. Wahlke, eds., *Comparative Legislative Behavior: Frontiers of Research*. New York: Wiley.

Loewenberg, Gerhard and Samuel Patterson. 1979. *Comparing Legislatures*. Boston: Little, Brown.

Lowell, A. Lawrence. 1902. "The Influence of Party Upon Legislation," *Annual Report of the American Historical Association for 1901* 1:321-545.

Lowi, Theodore. 1964. "American Business, Public Policy, Case-Studies and Political Theory," *World Politics* 16:677-715.

————. 1970. "Decision Making vs. Policy Making: Toward an Antidote for Technocracy," *Public Administration Review* 30:314-325.

————. 1972. "Four Systems of Policy, Politics, and Choice," *Public Administration Review* 32:298-310.

MacIver, R.M. 1926. *The Modern State*. London: Oxford University Press.

MacRae, Duncan, Jr. 1952. "The Relation between Roll-Call Votes and Constituencies in the Massachusetts House of Representatives," *American Political Science Review* 46:1046-1055.

————. 1958. *Dimensions of Congressional Voting: A Statistical Study of the House of Representatives in the Eighty-First Congress*. Los Angeles: University of California Press.

————. 1965. "Method for Identifying Issues and Factions from Legislative Votes," *American Political Science Review* 59:909-926.

————. 1967. *Parliament, Parties, and Society in France: 1946-1958*. New York: St. Martin's Press.

————. 1970. *Issues and Parties in Legislative Voting: Methods of Statistical Analysis*. New York: Harper & Row.

Manley, John F. 1970. *The Politics of Finance*. Boston: Little, Brown.

————. 1973. "The Conservative Coalition," *American Behavioral Scientist* 17: 223-248.

_____ . 1977. "The Conservative Coalition in Congress," in Lawrence C. Dodd and Bruce I. Oppenheimer, eds., *Congress Reconsidered*. New York: Praeger.

Markus, G.B. 1974. "Electoral Coalitions and Senate Roll Call Behavior: An Ecological Analysis," *American Journal of Political Science* 18:595-607.

Martin, Jeanne. 1976. "Presidential Elections and Administration Support Among Congressmen," *American Journal of Political Science* 10:483-490.

Marwell, Gerald. 1967. "Party, Region and the Dimensions of Conflict in the House of Representatives, 1949-1954," *American Political Science Review* 61:380-399.

Matthews, Donald R. 1960. *U.S. Senators and Their World*. Chapel Hill: University of North Carolina Press.

Matthews, Donald R. and James A. Stimson. 1970. "Decision-Making by U.S. Representatives: A Preliminary Model," in S. Sidney Ulmer, ed., *Political Decision-Making*. New York: Litton.

_____ . 1975. *Yeas and Nays: Normal Decision-Making in the U.S. House of Representatives*. New York: Wiley.

Mayhew, David B. 1966. *Party Loyalty Among Congressmen: The Difference Between Democrats and Republicans, 1947-62*. Cambridge: Harvard University Press.

_____ . 1974. *Congress: The Electoral Connection*. New Haven: Yale University Press.

McCrone, Donald J. and James H. Kuklinski. 1979. "The Delegate Theory of Representation," *American Journal of Political Science* 23:278-300.

Meller, Norman. 1960. "Legislative Behavior Research," *Western Political Quarterly* 13:131-153.

Mezey, Michael L. 1979. *Comparative Legislatures*. Durham: Duke University Press.

Miller, Warren. 1970. "Majority Rule and the Representative System of Government," in E. Allart and Stein Rokkan, eds., *Mass Politics*. New York: The Free Press, pp. 284-311.

Miller, Warren and Donald Stokes. 1963. "Constituency Influence in Congress," *American Political Science Review* 57:45-56.

Morehouse, Sally McCally. 1973. "The State Political Party and the Policy-Making Process," *American Political Science Review* 67:55-72.

Murphy, James T. 1974. "Political Parties and the Porkbarrel: Party Conflict and Cooperation in House Public Works Committee Decision-Making," *American Political Science Review* 68:169-186.

Nie, Norman H., Sidney Verba, and John R. Petrocik. 1979. *The Changing American Voter*. Cambridge: Harvard University Press.

Norpoth, Helmut. 1976. "Explaining Party Cohesion in Congress: The Case of Shared Policy Attitudes," *American Political Science Review* 70:1156-1171.

Norton, Phillip. 1975. *Dissension in the House of Commons: Intraparty Dissent in the House of Commons Division Lobbies 1945-1974*. London: MacMillan.

_____ . 1978. *Conservative Dissidents: Dissent Within the Parliamentary Conservative Party, 1970-74*. London: Temple, Smith.

_____ . 1980. *Dissension in the House of Commons, 1974-1979*. Oxford: Clarendon Press.

_____ . 1981. *The Commons in Perspective*. New York: Longman.

Nyholm, Pekka. 1972. *Parliament, Government and Multi-Dimensional Party Relations in Finland*. Helsinki: Societas Scientiarum Fennica.

Olsen, P. Nannestad. 1972. "At the Cradle of a Party System: Voting Patterns and Voting Groups in the Danish Constitutional Convention 1848-1849," *Scandinavian Political Studies* 7:119-136.

Orfield, Gary. 1975. *Congressional Power: Congress and Social Change.* New York: Harcourt Brace Jovanovich.

Parker, Glenn R. and Suzanne L. Parker. 1979. "Factions in Committees: The U.S. House of Representatives," *American Political Science Review* 73:85-102.

Parsons, Malcolm B. 1962. "Quasi-partisan Conflict in a One-party Legislative System: The Florida Senate, 1947-61," *American Political Science Review* 56:605-614.

Patterson, James. 1967. *Congressional Conservatism and the New Deal.* Lexington: University of Kentucky Press.

Patterson, Samuel C. 1959. "Patterns of Interpersonal Relations in a State Legislative Group: The Wisconsin Assembly," *Public Opinion Quarterly* 23:101-109.

──────── . 1961. "The Role of the Deviant in the State Legislative System: The Wisconsin Assembly," *Western Political Quarterly* 14:460-473.

──────── . 1962. "Dimensions of Voting Behavior in a One Party State Legislature," *Public Opinion Quarterly* 26:185-201.

──────── . 1968. "Comparative Legislative Behavior: A Review Essay," *Midwest Journal of Political Science* 12:599-616.

──────── . 1978. "The Semi-Sovereign Congress," in Anthony King, ed., *The New American Political System.* Washington, DC: American Enterprise Institute.

──────── . 1982. "Understanding Congress in the Long Run: A Comment on Joseph Cooper and David W. Brady, 'Toward A Diachronic Theory of Congress'," *American Political Science Review* 76:1007-1009.

Patterson, Samuel C., Ronald D. Hedlund, and G. Robert Boynton. 1975. *Representatives and Represented: Bases of Public Support for the American Legislatures.* New York: Wiley.

Payne, James L. 1979. "Inflation, Unemployment and Left-Wing Political Parties: A Reanalysis," *American Political Science Review* 73:181-185.

Pedersen, Mogens N. 1967. "Consensus and Conflict in the Danish Folketing 1945-65," *Scandinavian Political Studies* 2:143-166.

──────── . 1979. "The Dynamics of European Party Systems: Changing Patterns of Electoral Volatility," *European Journal of Political Research* 7:1-26.

Pedersen, Mogens N., Erik Damgaard, and P. Nannestad Olsen. 1971. "Party Distances in the Danish Folketing 1945-68," *Scandinavian Political Studies* 6:87-106.

Pennock, J. Roland. 1956. "Party and Constituency in Postwar Agricultural Price-Support Legislation," *Journal of Politics* 17:167-210.

Perkins, Lynette P. 1980. "Influences of Members' Goals on their Committee Behavior: The U.S. House Judiciary Committee," *Legislative Studies Quarterly* 5:373-392.

Pesonen, Pertti. 1963. "Close and Safe Elections in Massachusetts," *Midwest Journal of Political Science* 7:54-70.

Polsby, Nelson W. 1975. "Legislatures," in F.I. Greenstein and N.W. Polsby, eds., *The Handbook of Political Science.* Vol. 5. Reading, MA: Addison-Wesley, pp. 257-319.

──────── . 1978. "Coalition and Faction in American Politics: An Institutional View," in S.M. Lipset, ed., *Emerging Coalitions in American Politics.* San Francisco: Institute for Contemporary Studies, pp. 103-123.

──────── . 1982. "Studying Congress through Time: A Comment on Joseph Cooper and David Brady, 'Toward a Diachronic Analysis of Congress'," *American Political Science Review* 76:1010-1012.

Price, David E. 1978. "Policy Making in Congressional Committees: The Impact of 'Environmental' Factors," *American Political Science Review* 72:548-575.

Rae, Douglas W. 1968. "A Note on the Fractionalization of Some European Party Systems," *Comparative Political Studies* 1:414-416.

_____ . 1971. *The Political Consequences of Electoral Laws*. Rev. ed. New Haven: Yale University Press.

Rae, Douglas W. and Michael Taylor. 1970. *An Analysis of Political Cleavages*. New Haven: Yale University Press.

Ranney, Austin. 1954. *The Doctrine of Responsible Party Government*. Urbana: University of Illinois Press.

Rasmussen, J. 1966. *The Relations of the Profumo Rebels With Their Local Parties*. Tucson: University of Arizona Press.

Ray, Bruce A. 1980. "The Responsiveness of the U.S. Congressional Armed Services Committees to Their Parent Bodies," *Legislative Studies Quarterly* 5:501-516.

Rice, Stuart A. 1928. *Quantitative Methods in Politics*. New York: Knopf.

Rieselbach, Leroy N. 1964. "The Demography of the Congressional Vote on Foreign Aid, 1939-58," *American Political Science Review* 58:577-588.

Riker, William H. 1958. "The Paradox of Voting and Congressional Rules for Voting Amendments," *American Political Science Review* 52:349-366.

_____ . 1961. "Voting and the Summation of Preferences: An Interpretative Bibliographic Review of Selected Developments During the Last Decade," *American Political Science Review* 55:900-912.

_____ . 1962. *The Theory of Political Coalitions*. New Haven: Yale University Press.

Robinson, James A. 1967. *Congress and Foreign Policy-making*. Rev. ed. Homewood, IL: Dorsey Press.

Russo, David. 1972. "The Major Political Issues of the Jacksonian Period and the Development of Party Loyalty in Congress, 1830-1840," *Transactions of the American Philosophical Society* 62, part 5.

Rustow, Dankwart. 1956. "Scandinavia: Working Multiparty Systems," in Sigmund Neumann, ed., *Modern Political Parties*. Chicago: University of Chicago Press.

Salisbury, Robert and John Heinz. 1970. "A Theory of Policy Analysis and Some Preliminary Applications," in Ira Sharkansky, ed., *Policy Analysis in Political Science*. Chicago: Markham Publishing.

Sartori, Giovanni. 1966. "European Political Parties: The Case of Polarized Pluralism," in Joseph LaPalombara and Myron Weiner, eds., *Political Parties and Political Development*. Princeton: Princeton University Press.

_____ . 1976. *Parties and Party Systems: A Framework for Analysis*. London: Cambridge University Press.

Schattschneider, E.E. 1942. *Party Government*. New York: Farrar and Rinehart.

Schneider, Jerrold. 1979. *Ideological Coalitions in Congress*. Westport, CT: Greenwood Press.

Schwarz, John E. 1975. "The Impact of Constituency on the Behavior of British Conservative MPs: An Analysis of the Formative Stages of Issue Development," *Comparative Political Studies* 8:75-89.

_____ . 1980. "Exploring a New Role in Policy-Making: The British House of Commons in the 1970s," *American Political Science Review* 74:23-37.

Schwarz, John E. and Barton Fenmore. 1977. "Presidential Election Results and Congressional Roll Call Behavior: The Cases of 1964, 1968, 1972," *Legislative Studies Quarterly* 2:409-423.

Schwarz, John E. and Geoffrey Lambert. 1971. "Career Objectives, Group Feeling and Legislative Party Cohesion: the British Conservatives, 1959-68," *Journal of Politics* 33:399-421.

Schwarz, John E. and L. Earl Shaw. 1976. *The United States Congress in Comparative Perspective.* Hinsdale, IL: Dryden.

Shaffer, William R. 1980. *Party and Ideology in the United States Congress.* Lanham, MD: University Press of America.

Shannon, W. Wayne. 1968. *Party, Constituency and Congressional Voting.* Baton Rouge: Louisiana State University Press.

——————. 1970. "Congressional Party Behavior: Data, Concept and Theory in the Search for Historical Reality," *Polity* 2:280-284.

Shapiro, Michael J. 1968. "The House and the Federal Role: A Computer Simulation of Roll Call Voting," *American Political Science Review* 62:494-517.

Shapley, Lloyd S. and Martin Shubik. 1954. " A Method for Evaluating the Distribution of Power in a Committee System," *American Political Science Review* 48: 787-792.

Silbey, Joel H. 1967. *The Shrine of Party: Congressional Voting Behavior, 1841-1952.* Pittsburgh: University of Pittsburgh Press.

——————. 1981. "Congressional and State Legislative Roll-Call Studies by U.S. Historians," *Legislative Studies Quarterly* 6:597-608.

Sinclair, Barbara. 1977a. "Who Wins in the House of Representatives: The Effect of Declining Party Cohesion on Policy Outputs, 1959-1970," *Social Science Quarterly* 58:121-128.

——————. 1977b. "Determinants of Aggregate Party Cohesion in the U.S. House of Representatives," *Legislative Studies Quarterly* 2:155-175.

——————. 1977c. "Party Realignment and the Transformation of the Political Agenda: The House of Representatives, 1925-38," *American Political Science Review* 71:940-953.

——————. 1978a. "From Party Voting to Regional Fragmentation: The House of Representatives, 1933-1956," *American Politics Quarterly* 6:125-146.

——————. 1978b. "The Policy Consequences of Party Realignment—Social Welfare Legislation in the House of Representatives, 1935-54," *American Journal of Political Science* 22:83-105.

——————. 1981a. "Agenda and Alignment Change: The House of Representatives, 1925-78," in Lawrence C. Dodd and Bruce I. Oppenheimer, eds., *Congress Reconsidered.* Washington: Congressional Quarterly, pp. 221-245.

——————. 1981b. "Coping with Uncertainty: Building Coalitions in the House and Senate," in Thomas E. Mann and Norman J. Ornstein, eds., *The New Congress.* Washington, DC: American Enterprise Institute.

——————. 1982. *Congressional Realignment 1925-1978.* Austin: University of Texas Press.

Sjobolm, Gunnar. 1957. *Party Strategies in a Multiparty System.* Lund, Sweden: Lund Political Studies.

Smith, Steven S. 1981. "The Consistency and Ideological Structure of U.S. Senate Voting Alignments, 1957-1976," *American Journal of Political Science* 25:780-795.

Sorauf, Frank J. 1963. *Party and Representation: Legislative Politics in Pennsylvania.* New York: Atherton.

——————. 1976. *Party Politics in America.* 3d ed. Boston: Little, Brown.

Stephens, Hugh W. and David W. Brady. 1976. "The Parliamentary Parties and the Electoral Reforms of 1884-85 in Britain," *Legislative Studies Quarterly* 1: 491-510.

Stevens, Arthur J., Jr., Arthur H. Miller, and Thomas E. Mann. 1974. "Mobilization of Liberal Strength in the House—1950-1970: The Democratic Study Group," *American Political Science Review* 68:667-681.

Stimson, James A. 1975. "Five Propositions about Congressional Decision-Making," *Political Methodology* 2:415-436.

Stjernquist, Nils and Bo Bjurulf. 1970. "Party Cohesion and Party Cooperation in Swedish Parliament in 1964 and 1966," *Scandinavian Political Studies* 5:129-164.

Stokes, Donald E. 1963. "Spatial Models of Party Competition," *American Political Science Review* 57:368-377.

Stone, Walter J. 1979. "Measuring Constituency-Representative Linkages: Problems and Prospects," *Legislative Studies Quarterly* 4:623-640.

Strom, Gerald S. and Barry S. Rundquist. 1977. "A Revised Theory of Winning in House-Senate Conferences," *American Political Science Review* 71:448-453.

Stultz, Newell M. 1970. "The National Assembly in the Politics of Kenya," in Allan Kornberg and Lloyd M. Musolf, eds., *Legislatures in Developmental Perspective*. Durham, NC: Duke University Press, pp. 303-332.

Sullivan, John L. and Robert E. O'Conner. 1972. "Electoral Choice and Popular Control of Public Policy: The Case of the 1966 House Elections," *American Political Science Review* 66:1256-1268.

Sullivan, John L. and Eric M. Uslaner. 1978. "Congressional Behavior and Electoral Marginality," *American Journal of Political Science* 22:536-554.

Taylor, Michael and V.M. Herman. 1971. "Party Systems and Government Stability," *American Political Science Review* 65:28-37.

Turner, Julius. 1951. *Party and Constituency: Pressures on Congress*. Baltimore: The Johns Hopkins Press.

Turner, Julius and Edward V. Schneier, Jr. 1970. *Party and Constituency: Pressures on Congress*. 2d ed. Baltimore: The Johns Hopkins Press.

Truman, David B. 1959. *The Congressional Party: A Case Study*. New York: Wiley.

Unekis, Joseph K. 1978. "From Committee to the Floor: Consistency in Congressional Voting," *Journal of Politics* 40:761-769.

Uslaner, Eric M. and Ronald E. Weber. 1977. *Patterns of Decision Making in State Legislatures*. New York: Praeger.

Vayryren, Raimo. 1972. "Analysis of Party Systems by Concentration, Fractionalization, and Entropy Measures," *Scandinavian Political Studies* 7:137-156.

von Neumann, John and Oskar Morgenstern. 1947. *The Theory of Games and Economic Behavior*. Princeton: Princeton University Press.

Wahlke, John C. 1962. "Behavioral Analyses of Representative Bodies," in Austin Ranney, ed., *Essays on the Behavioral Study of Politics*. Urbana, IL: University of Illinois Press, pp. 173-190.

Wahlke, John C., Heinz Eulau, William Buchanan, and LeRoy C. Ferguson. 1962. *The Legislative System: Explorations in Legislative Behavior*. New York: Wiley.

Watson, Richard A. 1956. "The Tariff Revolution: A Study of Shifting Party Attitudes," *Journal of Politics* 18:678-702.

Weinbaum, Marvin G. and Dennis R. Judd. 1970. "In Search of a Mandated Congress," *Midwest Journal of Political Science* 14:276-302.

Weisberg, Herbert F. 1972. "Scaling Models for Legislative Roll-Call Analysis," *American Political Science Review* 66:1306-1315.

——————. 1974. "Models of Statistical Relationships," *American Political Science Review* 68:1638-1655.

——————. 1978. "Evaluating Theories of Congressional Roll-Call Voting," *American Journal of Political Science* 22:554-577.

Weissberg, Robert F. 1979. "Assessing Legislator-Constituency Policy Agreement," *Legislative Studies Quarterly* 4:605-622.

Welch, Susan and Eric H. Carlson. 1973. "The Impact of Party on Voting Behavior in a Nonpartisan Legislature," *American Political Science Review* 67:854-867.

Westerfield, Bradford. 1955. *Foreign Policy and Party Politics*. New Haven: Yale University Press.

Wiggins, Charles W. 1967. "Party Politics in the Iowa Legislature," *Midwest Journal of Political Science* 11:86-97.

Wilson, Frank L. and Richard Wiste. 1976. "Party Cohesion in the French National Assembly: 1958-73," *Legislative Studies Quarterly* 1:467-510.

Wood, David M. 1973. "Responsibility for the Fall of Cabinets in the French Fourth Republic, 1951-1955," *American Journal of Political Science* 17:767-780.

_____ . 1982. "Comparing Parliamentary Voting on European Issues in France and Britain," *Legislative Studies Quarterly* 7:101-118.

Wood, David M. and Jack T. Pitzer. 1979. "Parties, Coalitions, and Cleavages: A Comparison of Two Legislatures in Two French Republics," *Legislative Studies Quarterly* 4:197-226.

Wright, Gerald C. 1977. "Constituency Response to Congressional Behavior," *Western Political Quarterly* 30:401-410.

Young, James. 1966. *The Washington Community*. New York: Columbia University Press.

Young, Roland. 1956. *Congressional Politics in the Second World War*. New York: Columbia University Press.

Zeller, Belle. 1954. *American State Legislatures*. New York: Crowell-Collier.

Chapter 11

Legislative-Executive Relations And Legislative Oversight

by

BERT A. ROCKMAN

Executive-legislative relations cover a wide territory, encompassing diverse actors and actions. In surveying this territory, I divide it into four major parts. First, I try to place the study of executive-legislative relations in a context of values and different perspectives of governance. Second, since to talk of "the executive" and "the legislature" is to use the language of airy abstraction, I identify the players concretely. Third, I survey the field of play and look at some of the major investigations connecting executive and legislative actors and institutions. From among these points of relationship, I focus last, but most closely, on the subset involving legislative control and supervision of executive behavior, i.e., oversight.

Since the focus on oversight represents a special thrust in this review, I pay particular attention to the various definitions provided of oversight and the implications of those definitions. I also examine legislative supervision in both quantitative and qualitative senses: how much of it is there, and how is it done? Oversight is polymorphic, but for convenience sake I will from time to time have to make reference to oversight activity as though there was an "it." Speaking this way, I will look at oversight as a dependent variable and, thus, at the conditions under which it occurs. Turning matters around, I will then examine oversight as an independent variable, that is, its impact on administrative behavior.

Much of the literature on oversight—and indeed on executive-legislative relations generally—is either straightforwardly or implicitly prescriptive, pervaded by assumptions about government and its proper institutional arrangements, activities, and norms. Images of the oversight process contain assumptions, sometimes explicit but more often casual, of the proper role of executive and legislative institutions. These assumptions, in turn, are reflective of a scholar's beliefs about how the need for delegation should be balanced against the need for accountability.

My reading of this literature suggests, too, that scholars are often partisans of the institutions they study. Those who study the executive organs of the state tend to favor broader grants of discretion and to disapprove of what they see as legislative meddling in matters better left in the hands of the knowledgeable and experienced (cf. Rourke, 1979). The latter day Hamiltonians recommend that legislatures get out of details and into broader-scale and more coordinated supervision—which, from the standpoint of exercising supervisory power, may be read as a thinly disguised hint for the legislature to get lost.

Legislative partisans, in contrast, advocate enhancing accountability and ensuring executive responsiveness to statutory guidelines. If they are often disappointed with the supervision that exists, they also believe that more of it would be better and that, if it can be done better, more of it will happen. The scholarly record on the subject of oversight is one that largely derives, for understandable reasons, from legislative enthusiasts. Perhaps this is why research on the subject has primarily examined why oversight does or does not exist and in what form it exists rather than what its impact is. Yet the last question bears most on the significance of oversight as a research subject. Students of the executive, in brief, are less apt to give priorities to the problems students of the legislature would. The former will be more concerned with problems of direction, effectiveness, and competence; the latter with problems of accountability, representation, and responsiveness. The oversight literature has so much implicit assumption as to what the state of play between executive and legislative power ought to be, that we unavoidably are led to consider the extent to which key values about the process of governing are given embodiment in executive and legislative institutions and actors.

Models and Muddles: Governance and Values

Three Values of Governance

Finer (1980) sets forth three principles of democratic governance: *representativeness, stability,* and *futurity.* The representative principle is based on the joint notions of responsiveness to public or partisan demands and accountability to elected officials. Put bluntly, it means instruction to the selected (civil servants) by the elected (political officeholders)—an unarguably democratic principle. The frame of reference for the value of stability, however, is the state and its organs rather than its temporary governors.

Stability means continuity and the observance of antecedent behaviors, principles, and agreements. As representativeness is embodied in political officialdom, so stability is the ballast given to the state by the career public service. The stereotype that politicians push while bureaucrats resist is implied by this contrast. Needless to say, both in theory and in practice there is conflict between the two principles and necessarily some tension between the officials who embody them.

Finally, "futurity" is the quality of foresight in government. Undoubtedly, neither politicians nor bureaucrats would quarrel about this value, but they would presumably differ on the criteria to be sensitive to in pursuing it. Some empirical studies of the attitudes of bureaucrats and politicians, for example, suggest that politicians are more inclined than bureaucrats toward the representative principle, and more likely to define the futurity principle in terms of an embracing political ideology. Bureaucrats, though, are apt to think that arriving at the public interest is a matter more or less of technical calculation (Suleiman, 1974; Aberbach, Putnam, and Rockman, 1981).

Executive and Legislative Perspectives on Governance

If stability and representativeness are clashing principles, does the principle of futurity clash with either of these? Bureaucrats are seen, for instance, as tending to wed stability to futurity, thus producing a future of no visible direction at all (Rose, 1969; Peters, 1981; Aberbach, Putnam, and Rockman, 1981). Huntington (1965) hints at this also in his famous essay on the role of Congress in the twentieth century, claiming, in essence, that only the president is positioned to operate on behalf of the futurity principle. According to Huntington, "particular territorial interests are represented in Congress; particular functional interests are represented in the administration; and the national interest is represented territorially and functionally in the Presidency" (p. 17).

Another perspective, however, sees politicians, especially legislators, as tending to wed ideology to futurity (thus confusing postures for policies) and/or unable to separate a national interest from the interests of groups in society. Such perspectives, one study concludes, are widely held by French civil servants toward deputies in the Assembly (Suleiman, 1974, pp. 290-296). Heclo also illustrates the politicians' discomfort with "neutral competence"; he quotes a Nixon administration official involved in the creation of the Office of Management and Budget (OMB), as saying that the old Bureau of the Budget (BOB) "was the kind of place that could make a one-term President out of anybody" (1975, p. 97).

In brief, the "representative" principle is overtly a political function, embodied in the legislature, whereas the "stability" principle is overtly an administrative function, embodied in the bureaucracy. There are, naturally, skirmishes around the borders even here. One writer (Ronge, 1974), for example, believes bureaucrats are increasingly pushed into the role of legitimizing policy to key interests precisely because so much delegation must be granted. Earlier, another writer saw the U.S. federal bureaucracy as a force that helped fill in representational lacunae (Long, 1952). From the other side of the coin, for nearly two decades until the early 1970s, one could make the argument that the then lengthy tenure of members of Congress (Bullock, 1972) combined with a rigid application of the seniority rule made for a legislature that also embodied the stability principle to an unusual degree.

Still, it is clear that the principal area of contest is the futurity principle: who do we entrust to see the future more clearly? Democracy gives us one answer, technocracy another. Neustadt eloquently, but mistakenly, saw the matter taking this form: "Bureaucracy has brought a new contestant into play: the great prospective struggle is between entrenched officialdom and politicians everywhere, White House and Hill alike" (1965, p. 119).

But the issue is not simply one of politicians vs. bureaucrats or of legislatures vs. executives, even though important differences of perspective are associated with these distinctions. In the contest over policy, shared interests frequently coalesce politicians and bureaucrats or executives and legislators. Bureaucrats often are pitted against one another (though the rules of this game differ widely across systems), or against political executives. By definition, legislators are aligned against other legislators. Wright (1974) points out this complexity by noting that while the executive was strengthened in the French Fifth Republic, the independence of the civil service was weakened. Put simply, relationships between the executive and the legislature are anything but simple, because nowhere are the executive and the legislature homogeneous entities.

Executive and Legislative Players

I distinguish four sets of players on the executive and four on the legislative side, outlined here. They are presented in Table 1. Since they appear to be largely self-explanatory, my main focus is on the characteristics of the various players and on the principal analytic relations relevant to executive-legislative intersections.

Identification and Circuitry

Executives of the government and of the state. The first obvious distinction to be drawn on the executive side of the ledger is between the officials of the government and those of the state; in other words, political and career executives. Even this distinction is not without ambiguity. For

TABLE 1
Executive and Legislative Players

Executive

The Executive Center
  −President, Prime Minister and Central Agents
  (USA) - Executive Office of the President
  (UK) - The Cabinet Office
  (FRG) - The Chancellor's Office

Ministers and Department Heads and their Staffs (e.g., French cabinets)
  −Center vs. periphery (inner and outer departments)
  −Collectivity vs. collection (British vs. U.S. cabinets)

Junior Ministers and Subcabinet Officials

Senior Civil Service

Legislative

Party Leaders
  −Government
  −Opposition

Backbench (or in U.S., junior members)

Committee Chairs (and in U.S., especially, subcommittees also)

Legislative Staffs
  −Institutional
  −Personal

Polsby (1978) argues that contemporary presidential cabinets in the United States are less and less linked to traditional political structures and instead seem to reflect key policy publics that embody policy expertise. Though Polsby's generalization may be formed from the administration of a particularly technocratic president (Jimmy Carter), his point is that cabinet members (and presumably subcabinet strata as well) are decreasingly "Red" (partisan) and increasingly "expert" (technocratic). From this he infers that cabinet officials are in business for themselves to an extent abnormal even within the traditions of the U.S. system. Heclo (1978) picks up Polsby's theme and extends it considerably. He argues that because presidential appointees are wired into sectors of policy expertise they are, if inadvertently, better able to immobilize presidential policy aspirations than to mobilize constituencies on the president's behalf—though the latter was once thought an important credential for cabinet selection. Heclo (1981) takes this analysis further, suggesting that even the president's staff tends to become committed to relationships with particular interest sectors and lobbies, thus representing their claims to him.

There is evidence of a depoliticization of this sort (evidence that may have been peculiarly associated with the technocratic tendencies and special political problems of the Carter administration), but there is far more compelling evidence that forces running in the opposite direction are considerably stronger. Elsewhere, both Polsby (1981) and Heclo (1975) have noted that high ranking civil servants have been losing ground in the constellation of forces in Washington. Polsby argues, for instance, that "senior bureaucrats have lost ground massively" (1981, p. 13), both because the functions of the federal bureaucracy have changed and because careerists are not thought sufficiently trustworthy by their superiors. Indeed, if Polsby is right, Neustadt's concern that politicians, and the criteria they bring to policy making, would be overwhelmed by the bureaucracy can be put to rest. For, in Polsby's view, "the politicians who sit at the tip of these bureaucratic icebergs like to keep control of policy planning and evaluation themselves, and will contest about it, if they must, only with other politicians" (1981, p. 11). Similarly, Heclo sees the deterioration of the neutral competence ideal at the Office of Management and Budget (OMB) in terms of the incursion of presidential policy needs; a deterioration expedited by layering in an array of political appointments near the top. As Heclo claims, "There has been a fundamental shift in OMB's role away from wholesaling advice to the Presidency and towards retailing policy to outsiders" (1975, p. 89). Subtly, but inevitably, the dynamics of executive politics will also influence developments between the executive and the legislature. How likely would Congress have been, for instance, to establish the Congressional Budgetary Office (CBO) if OMB had not been politicized?

The tradition of the "in and outer" is infinitely weaker in Europe than in the United States, but the European career service sometimes brings forth roughly equivalent officials of especially sensitive political instincts and well developed political connections. Suleiman (1974, pp. 285-286) notes that they make the genus "career official" far more heterogeneous than classical Weberian theory would allow. Such officials appear to have distinctly political orientations, unlike the main corps of civil servants. Anton (1980, p. 94), for example, finds that Swedish ministerial officials (rough equivalents of the French ministerial cabinet or U.S. subcabinet officials) trust politicians and accept popular pressures more than do their colleagues in the classic bureaucratic settings of administrative boards and public authorities. In the U.S., these differences between "in and outers" and careerists are not so clear, mostly because features of the American system tend to induce an abundance of political instinct in nearly all the executive players (Aberbach and Rockman, 1977).

It is difficult to know for sure whether there is a general tendency toward the politicization of administration or whether administrators are thrust increasingly into roles requiring them to relate successfully to the grey areas between administration and politics. If the latter is the case, then the civil service increasingly may be channeled into politics itself as, for example, in West Germany, Japan, and France. Indeed, in these and several other countries, a sizeable number of civil servants sit as members of the legislative body, confounding the classic distinction between executive and legislative.

A central question exists also as to whether "executive" refers to the government or the state. Since officials of the government presumably supervise those of the state, is it the legislature's responsibility to supervise the officials of the government, of the state, or of both? In the United States, one body of analysis posits that there are sharp differences of interest between the political executive and career executive, and that careerists work to salvage their interests in pertinent congressional subcommittees (Fiorina, 1981). Often such alliances defend against the plans and priorities of the presidential administration and its emissaries in the departments. In Britain, on the other hand, it is almost exclusively the minister with whom Parliament deals, and it is mostly the minister who deals the cards.

Central and departmental executives. In addition to the hierarchical distinction in our outline of executive and legislative players, we must also make a lateral distinction between central agencies and line or program agencies. Activity taxes coordination, and the executive uses central agencies to monitor and coordinate the activities of its implementing and policy proposing organs. Central agencies can operate under a set of informal rules that are well understood by those they have commerce with. Despite the importance of their activities, they are themselves rarely subject to legislative scrutiny. Such is the point made by Heclo and Wildavsky (1975) in their study of the British Treasury, its relations with the spending departments, and its virtual lack of relations with Parliament. The latter, though, is due partly to a calculus common to legislators. To wit: the costs of understanding are not worth the effort.

Central agencies operate with virtually no statutory guidance, as Campbell and Szablowski (1979) point out in their study of Canadian central agencies. This means that while they wield considerable clout within the executive, they are remarkably unaccountable to the legislature. This question of who will monitor these monitoring agencies is apt to become especially important as central agencies become more influential. Certainly, there are substantial differences between the supervision provided by a central agency and that provided by the legislature, differences summed up well by Campbell and Szablowski: "Central agencies . . . strongly promote quantitative measurement of bureaucratic performance and the adoption of generally applicable criteria of measurement as a rigorous and much more reliable method of control than that supposedly exercised by Parliament and parliamentary committees" (1979, p. 14).

Party leadership, the backbench, and legislative committees. On the legislative side, we can distinguish between party leaders and backbenchers, and between party leaders and committee chairs. Leaders generally do not like to share the powers they have. Kornberg and Frasure (1971), for instance, found that frontbenchers and backbenchers within each party in the British House of Commons mostly agreed on policy issues but disagreed on whether Parliament should increase the role and authority of specialized committees. Leaders want to manage, and backbenchers want leverage.

Thus, the Opposition would view a committee-oriented legislature as potentially a threat to adversarial partisanship, and the Government would view it as a threat to disciplined followership. Moreover, the more important committees become the more diverse the points of leverage in the legislative body also become—a special threat to the Government. Diverse points of leverage in both the executive and legislative realms ripen opportunities for engagement between institutions. Aberbach, Putnam, and Rockman (1981), in this regard, note the substantial contacts across institutions in those countries (the U.S., West Germany, and Italy) that lack powerful aggregating mechanisms in the executive and in the legislature. By contrast, these contacts are fewer in countries possessing more powerful centripetal elements (the U.K., Holland, and Sweden).

Staffs. A committee-oriented legislature is also likely to be staff oriented. The growth of staff and support agencies has been amply documented in the United States (Fox and Hammond, 1977; Malbin, 1980; Salisbury and Shepsle, 1981a, 1981b), but these also have grown meteorically in other legislatures known to be committee oriented. Blischke (1981) documents, for example, a spectacular increase in the parliamentary staff of the Bundestag in a 30-year period and an even larger increase in personal staffing. Staffs, in sum, represent yet another point of legislative-executive relationship.

In fact, as Heclo sees it (1978, pp. 99-100), policy professionals and technocrats in the U.S. executive establishment and in the congressional bureaucracy are becoming virtually indistinguishable from one another. Comparability does not, of course, necessarily mean cooperation, but the implication is that the circuitry between the Hill and Downtown in Washington is far more convoluted informally than formally, and even busier where it is less visible than where it is more so. Heclo's image is perhaps more superficially compelling than the reality that underlies it, but once again, what is pointed out is that to say "executive" or "legislative" is as yet to say little at all.

Role overlap. A further point in regard to executive-legislative role overlap has to do with the tendency, noted above, for positions in the civil service to be avenues to formal political activity in a number of European parliaments. In the national legislatures of West Germany, France, the Netherlands, and Sweden, among others, a substantial minority of members have come from the executive (though in the German case, frequently from state or municipal administration). In several legislatures, especially those of France and Sweden, members also can hold multiple political offices. Therefore, it is not always certain when bargaining between members of the administration and those of the legislature may be taking place. Is contact, for example, between the administration and a member of the legislature because of the latter's role in the legislature or because the member is also a mayor (Ashford, 1982, pp. 141-142)?

Attributes of Executives and Legislators

Now that we have identified legislative and executive players, we can focus on what we know of each. Here we examine studies that compare and contrast, as paired portraits, members of the executive with those of the legislature.

Three principal questions are typically raised by such comparisons. First, in what sense are executive officials and legislators unrepresentative, and what if any difference does that make? Second, how different or similar are the pathways to each institution? Third, how different or similar are the beliefs and perspectives of executives (usually civil servants) and legislative politicians?

Representativeness. Executives and legislators each come disproportionately from families of upper status. Yet their own statuses reflect a high degree of achieved social mobility. Presthus's study of Canadian and U.S. administrative and legislative elites (1974, pp. 342-343) overstates the degree of mobility to some extent, since he contrasts the backgrounds of present members of the elite with those of their families instead of contrasting the status of their families with the distribution of statuses in the general population. Still, neither executives nor legislators are drawn from representative populations, and by the time of their recruitment each comes from educational and occupational strata even more unrepresentative and rarified than those of their parents (Aberbach, Putnam, and Rockman, 1981, pp. 46-83). Comparing executives and legislators across countries *and* across national and regional governments, however, Presthus (p. 345) shows that national elites in both the United States and Canada are of higher status than state or provincial elites. Furthermore, Presthus's data indicate that U.S. federal legislators and bureaucrats have similar statuses (a finding also reported in Aberbach and Rockman, 1977), and that Canadian legislators have backgrounds comparable to theirs. Canadian administrators, however, are more substantially upper status than any of the above groups.

Except in the United States, these divergences between executive officials and legislative politicians are commonplace (Aberbach, Putnam, and Rockman, 1981, p. 63). Geographically, national administrators also are always more urban (and it is probably equally fair to say more urbane) than their legislative counterparts; administrators come very disproportionately from the metropole and are very unreflective of the periphery, small town, and rural sectors of their societies.

But what, if anything, do these differences add up to? Politicians, whose backgrounds are slightly less unrepresentative than administrators', are also slightly less unrepresentative in their politics. The more important points here, though, are two. First, each elite, executive and legislative, is biased to the right of the mass public; it is conceivable that elites more representative in background would also be more politically representative. Second, each elite is biased a good deal to the left of those in private life from the same social stratum (Aberbach, Putnam, and Rockman, 1981, p. 76). In every system, politicians in the legislature are by background, status, and politics always somewhat less unrepresentative than are bureaucrats. In short, the evidence is that the legislature more closely embodies the representative principle than the executive.

Campbell and Szablowski (1979) indicate, however, that in Canada there is an important difference in background between career officials in the line departments and those in the central agencies. Departmental officials tend to be generalists, as in the British model, and selected without regard to ascriptive criteria; central agents, on the other hand, are especially highly technically qualified but are also apparently selected with an eye toward more diversity on such characteristics as language, sex, region, and ethnicity (p. 12).

In the United States, Aberbach and Rockman (1977) show that politically appointed executives at subcabinet levels share many characteristics with senior career officials, and each in turn shares similar characteristics with members of the U.S. House. Even so, the appointed officials take a somewhat more elevated path to the top than either civil servants or members of the House. Their backgrounds are somewhat more exclusive, and they are more likely to have been educated at prestigious private institutions.

Pathways. The trip to the top appears to be more evenly paced for bureaucrats than for legislative politicians. Bureaucrats generally begin their careers at an early age and then rise through a hierarchy in fairly modulated steps, while politicians everywhere get into the fray later and their advancement is more subject to self-promoting entrepreneurial activity. Party organization is the principal channel for such activity except in the U.S., where relevant political selectorates are unusually diverse.

Senior careerists and legislators, then, are subject to very different types of selectorates. Much more, however, remains to be explored in regard to central agency officials, who seem to reflect elements of each selectorate. Some evidence (Campbell and Szablowski, 1979; Suleiman, 1974; Wright, 1974) suggests that they combine politics and technics, ambition and expertise.

Do central agents, therefore, represent a new third force with its own unique pathways and perspectives between career officialdom and legislative politicians? Or, are they merely an interface between the two traditional worlds of bureaucrat and legislator? How do they get to the top? Who are their relevant selectors? And how do they relate to executive politicians, to departmental officials, and to legislators?

To these questions, Suleiman (1974) and Campbell and Szablowski (1979) suggest some answers, and the answers depict great complexity. They do not easily comport with Neustadt's assumption (1965) that politicians, both executive and legislative, share interests which they fail only to properly perceive and which, by throwing off the institutional shackles holding them apart, could unite to further their judgmental criteria. A more frequent alignment, in fact, pits central political executives and expert central agents against the departmental interests of career officials and the more particu-larized concerns of legislators. The traditional division into "executives" and "legislators" may be crosscut by the division between integrative evaluation and budgetary criteria (i.e., central agents and central political executives) and particularized or ideological interests in administrative programs and services (department officials and legislators).

We need, therefore, to know more about the paths to the top of central agents, and their links to executive and legislative politicians and to career officials in departments. "They" may be no more homogeneous in reality than other groups within the executive and legislative realms, and how they go about their business no doubt will have much to do with what precisely their business is. The National Security Council and the Office of Management and Budget, for instance, are apt to be very different organizations doing very different things, though each is a central agency. We know as yet little about the operative perspectives and norms of officials in these agencies. In view of their likely importance, it should prove helpful to know more.

Perspectives. In a study examining the beliefs and perspectives of senior bureaucrats and legislative politicians across several Western nations, Aberbach, Putnam, and Rockman (1981) conclude that while the tasks of policy making are shared between them, bureaucrats and politicians bring different perspectives to their joint undertaking. The differences between them are more sharp in some settings (Britain and Italy, for example) and less sharp in others (the U.S. and West Germany, for instance) but, whatever the magnitude of these differences, they are consistently found (with some exception in the U.S.) across all of the countries. In their portrait, bureaucrats are painted as equilibrators, politicians as energizers and articulators of ideals; bureaucrats are accessible to the well organized and well focused, politicians are sensitive to broader currents of opinion and social forces; bureaucrats see feasibilities in technical terms, politicians in political terms; bureaucrats are politically centrist and cautious about participation, politicians are more ideologically diverse and, overall, more amenable to participation. Above all, legislative politicians naturally enough tend to see their environment and to define problems in terms of politics, conflict, and allocation, whereas bureaucrats are inclined to see things in terms of governance, consensus, and management. Everywhere (with frequent exceptions in the U.S. and lesser ones in West Germany), Finer's distinction between representativeness and stability appears to be embodied in the distinction, respectively, between legislators and bureaucrats. The more "political" attitudes of the U.S. career officials and, to a lesser extent, those in West Germany reflect systems in which bureaucrats must themselves engineer alliances to sustain their interests. Neustadt's contrast of the U.S. with the European norm is well founded: "In certain . . . well-established governments, relations are rigged to minimize as far as possible, the personal and institutional insecurities of everyone in public life. . . . Not so with us. With us it is almost the opposite: we maximize the insecurities of men and agencies alike" (1965, p. 114).

We need to refine distinctions within executive and legislative populations in order to understand how and in what ways perspectives and values are apt to either converge or diverge. But inquiries into perspectives and values are predispositional only. They do not themselves derive from inquiries into behavior or relational forms. To move from attitude to behavior, we need to understand contextual influences, but these are difficult to control. Differences of institutional role, authority, and responsibility can alert us, however, to important determinants of behavior. Kornberg and Frasure (1971) discovered, for instance, that on broad matters of policy stand, frontbenchers and backbenchers in the same party were largely in agreement but differed on matters of the concentration or dispersion of power inside Parliament. Aberbach, Putnam, and Rockman also discovered that the more immediate the issue the more relevant role becomes to it. Conversely, the more distant the issue the more philosophical the response. Put in a sentence: "With their feet on the desk, politicians and bureaucrats think more similarly than with their feet on the floor" (Aberbach, Putnam, and Rockman, 1981, p. 141). When each, in other words, holds responsibility for decision making, the philosophical range of options to be indulged in narrows. Generally, bureaucrats hold more of these day to day responsibilities than do legislative politicians; bureaucrats' feet, therefore, more often are on the floor—one of the reasons they are more politically centrist than legislators.

The connection between beliefs and behaviors is never straightforward. For the most part, studies of the structure of political beliefs and the operating ideals of executives and legislators take these as variables to be explained rather than as variables to predict from. And role itself turns out to be a major part of the explanation. In rough order, *role* (bureaucrat/ legislator), *ideology* (left/right), and *national setting* are the key explanatory variables. Role and ideology particularly predict well to operating ideals and to ways of thinking about problems and their solutions; national setting tends to define operational role relationships and behavior. This should not be surprising. While the generic labels—"bureaucrat" and "politician" and "leftist" and "rightist"—provide fairly distinctive perspectives across political systems, the actual texture of relationships depends upon institutional arrangements, informal understandings, and the structure of political power— in other words, political system characteristics.

Having identified and analyzed some of the major players in executive-legislative relations, we can now demarcate the field of play. Because of their diversity, however, not all possible relations between the executive and the legislature are discussed in the following pages. I emphasize three areas. The first is *support for the government*, which encompasses the role of the legislature in cabinet appointments, the durability of governments, and policy support. The second is the *structure of interaction* between the executive and legislative realms. The third area, and the one to which I give most attention (thereby placing in a section of its own), is the role of legislative supervision and monitoring of the executive; in other words, *legislative oversight*.

Support for the Government

Of the three elements of support to which I call attention—cabinet appointments, government durability, and policy support—the second (dura-bility) applies almost exclusively to parliamentary-cabinet governments. The autonomy of the legislature granted by the separation of powers in the U.S., however, makes the other two elements—cabinet appointment and, especially, policy support—manifestly contingent. Understandably, the literature on these two matters is overwhelmingly focused on the U.S. Congress simply because there is far more variability in the extent to which these forms of support are granted.

Cabinet Appointments

Cabinet members may be drawn from the parliamentary body exclusively, as in Britain, or rarely, as in the United States. Under which of these conditions—executive-legislative fusion or institutional separation—is the role of the legislature more critical in influencing cabinet appointment?

The answer to this question may be less obvious than it seems on the surface. The constitutional right of the U.S. Senate to affirm or disapprove of presidential nominees provides this body with exceptional legal powers to influence the process of selection. Yet, few U.S. cabinet officials have been drawn from the legislature, whereas in most cabinet systems officials are either selected from, or placed into, the legislature. Moreover, under multiparty governing coalitions, jockeying for cabinet posts gives the legislature (really the parties in it) opportunities to independently form governing coalitions unreflective of electoral outcomes. Loewenberg (1971, p. 187) warns, however, that such jockeying can delegitimize the government. He hypothesizes that without a rapid and accurate translation of electoral preferences into cabinet composition, public support will be diminished and the stability of the regime deleteriously affected. Ironically, then, the more the legislature plays an intermediary role in forming governments through the maneuvering of its parties and intraparty factions, the less support there will be for the regime. Election results and the resulting government apparently need to closely correspond.

No such issues arise on the U.S. side, since the cabinet is the product of neither interparty nor legislative bargaining. In one of the most recent and comprehensive studies of the Senate's role in passing on presidential appointments, Mackenzie (1981) suggests that criteria employed in confirmation proceedings are susceptible to few generalizations, and that temporal boundaries limit historical consistencies in the confirmation process. The confirmation process, Mackenzie argues (p. 188), is best perceived as falling along the main lines of congressional activity. When Congress is more assertive in general, the Senate is apt to be more assertive in the confirmation process as well. Some of Mackenzie's evidence on the disposition of executive appointments over the last decade shows this to be the case (p. 177).

Ultimately, the Senate has a very large capacity to influence the disposition of appointments short of outright rejection of nominees through floor votes. Mackenzie's analysis indicates here the importance of anticipated reactions: few of the nominations that fail to receive Senate approval are rejected in committee, and exceedingly few are rejected by floor vote (p. 177). In recent years, when appointments have failed to be confirmed it is because the nominee has received the appropriate message and withdrawn.

Government Durability

Closely related to the issue of how cabinets are formed is the issue of how long they will last. This, of course, is primarily relevant to governments of the cabinet-parliamentary type, which must maintain functioning majorities through interparty coalitions. The most thorough inquiry into the relationship of cabinet status and the durability of governments across many nations and over an extended period of time is Dodd's *Coalitions in Parliamentary Government* (1976). Dodd's analysis is motivated by A. Lawrence Lowell's thesis that parliamentary government will be strong and efficient only where there is a single-party majority. Although "strength" and "efficiency" are not directly defined, they are assumed to be best indicated by a government's durability. Dodd's principal argument, and also Powell's (1982), is that while durability is most directly explained by whether or not there is a coalition, it is best understood by reference to the conditions that make for particular cabinet configurations.

In this regard, Dodd stresses two important features. First, he illustrates that *minimum-winning coalitions* (those with an efficient support-to-payoff ratio) tend to produce governments that are nearly as stable as single-party majority governments. Second, he illustrates that *instability* in parliamentary representation and *hyperfractionalization* of the parties represented deter the emergence of durable minimum-winning coalitions. When there is also a high degree of party polarization, there will tend to be minority or undersized governments. But when the parties are depolarized under conditions of instability and hyperfractionalization, the tendency will be for oversized coalitions to result. In brief, stability and relatively low levels of fractionalization seem to be prerequisites for the emergence of minimum-winning coalitions, and these coalitions, in turn, tend to be fairly durable.

Powell's analysis (1982) also affirms the importance of understanding the conditions under which particular coalitions form. Powell, however, emphasizes the role of *extremist* party representation in parliament, rather than instability (volatility) or fractionalization per se. As Dodd had, Powell also found minimum-winning coalitions to be durable but less likely to appear in systems with extremist representation—a factor mitigating against the formation of majority governments generally (pp. 144-151). According to this formulation, electoral systems that emphasize representativeness will, in the presence of extremist parties, increase the probability of extremist representation; thus, they will also decrease the probability of durable governments. Empirically, therefore, Powell finds some support for the Lowell thesis that Dodd had evaluated, but the reasons are complex and to be found in the party system, the support base for extreme parties, and the electoral system.

Digging deeper still into the "conditions" making for durable government, Steiner (1982) argues that formal theories of coalitions do not take into account the formulas for cabinet formation which particular societies have arrived at historically. For example, proportionality (an oversized coalition) is a formula for generating consensus, often adopted in such ethnically and linguistically heterogeneous systems as Switzerland and Belgium but also to some extent in such relatively homogeneous societies as Sweden and Norway. Where accommodation and the procedures of syndicating risk are valued, oversized coalitions are apt to appear at least sporadically, if not persistently. Loewenberg and Patterson (1979, p. 224), in this context, note that in the 1950s and 1960s, the opposition in the West German Bundestag voted with the government on 80-90 percent of all bills. Steiner's emphasis is to move from formal theorizing and aggregated analysis to historical understandings and political culture. Steiner's plea seems to be on behalf of a deviant case analysis of a subset of oversized coalitions—an emphasis different from, but not necessarily incongruent with, the more aggregated treatments of cabinet status and government durability offered by Dodd and Powell, for instance.

Policy Support

Institutional issues. Legislative support for the policies of the executive is problematical when the legislature and the executive are independent of one another, and when party discipline is not enforced. Therefore, policy support, as an overt matter, is especially interesting in the U.S. context. Elsewhere the absence of policy support in cabinet-parliamentary systems may well bring the government down. But it also may simply produce fewer party votes when nontraditional intraparty cleavages emerge and governments choose not to risk their survival on matters that are not clearly defined along party lines.

Although the range of variation in overt policy support (floor voting) is far more limited in the cabinet-parliamentary systems, there is some variation. Over a 25-year period, for example, the proportion of government bills enacted in Britain varied by 11 percent. In a roughly similar period in West Germany, they varied by 15 percent (Loewenberg and Patterson, 1979, p. 267). These swings, of course, are mild in contrast to what may be found in the United States, where different parties may control the presidency and the houses of Congress.

The strength of the committee system also appears to affect the extent to which government bills emerge intact. While the character of the committee system and the relative autonomy of the legislature are related characteristics, bills are more likely to be substantially altered or amended or even delayed where committees are able to scrutinize government-sponsored legislation (Loewenberg and Patterson, 1979, pp. 263-268).

In sum, policy support is a variable in both the U.S. separation of powers system and the more common cabinet-parliamentary systems. Despite the more extensive range of this variable in the U.S., however, it is apparently less crucial than in the cabinet-parliamentary systems. This is because policy disagreement is less likely to make a government unstable where the executive and legislative powers are independent since such disagreement does not directly imperil the survival of the president. In cabinet-parliamentary systems, because the continuance of government depends upon the continuance of policy support, there is much effort to conceal disagreement, especially where multiparty coalitions are brittle. Numerous subterfuges may be employed, including simply a failure to submit bills that would divide the Government. The Government must make far more effort to ensure support within the coalition or to satisfy factions within the dominant party before legislation is proposed. Bargaining is equally relevant in both multiparty coalitions and separation of powers systems, but the time at which bargaining takes place distinguishes between the two. In the coalition government, most bargaining takes place before bills are proposed and before cabinets are formed, while in the U.S. system most occurs after the executive has proposed legislation.

The partisan basis of support. In the United States, where the processes of policy support (or rejection) are more open, visible, and quantifiable, research on the partisan basis of support has been extensive. Most frequently, congressional determinants of support are examined rather than presidential manipulations. Scholars have more data on the congressional side; more important, congressional factors explain most of the variability in policy support. The factors predicting to presidential support are starkly simple: seats and cohesion (Cooper and Bombardier, 1968). Even at this level, though, the indicators cry out for further elaboration. Aside from the relationship that may exist between seat distribution and party cohesion, there is the further question of the impact of historical era and of electoral effects on the size of the majority and, above all, on its cohesion. A number of studies point out, for example, that particular electoral eras have heightened party cohesion and, thus, potentially invigorated and unified support for the president or opposition to him (Brady, 1978; Clubb and Traugott, 1977). With the exception of the New Deal electoral era, however, the president's legislative leadership was far less prominent during eras of great partisan cohesion in Congress than it has been since the emergence of the modern presidency and the relative eclipse of congressional leadership.

Presidential popularity and support. Beyond the obvious elements of political arithmetic, the question of how public evaluations of the president affect congressional support for his policies has received significant attention. The hypothesis that presidential fortunes with Congress would be bolstered by favorable rankings in the polls was most prominently advanced by Neustadt (1960). The proposition, it is fair to say, has generated numerous efforts both to test and refine it. Much effort has gone into disaggregating the sources of congressional and public impact on presidential legislative success.

Edwards's analyses (1976, 1977, 1979) consider the role of party and the particular impact that presidential public standing has on the electoral supporters of members of Congress. Members of Congress, thus, mediate the effects of public approval by responding in more (or less) favorable terms in accordance with the president's standing among their natural political constituents. Overall, Edwards emphasizes that the degrees of presidential freedom are set in Congress and, therefore, that presidential manipulations are greatly overrated as a source of presidential legislative success (1979).

Both elements—the role of public approval of the president and the direct influence of the president on Congress—have been given attention. In regard to the first of these elements, Bond and Fleisher (1980) argue, as Edwards had, that the effects of public standing for the president are not undifferentiated across the parties. They conclude that a favorable public view of the president will be advantageous to him when his own party is in the majority in Congress, since it will generate more support from members of his own party. But if his party is not in the majority in Congress, his chances of success are less likely. This seems to occur because the improved support rate from his own party still will be insufficient to generate the necessary majorities on behalf of the president's favored proposals. Unlike Edwards, however, Bond and Fleisher do not disaggregate the presidential popularity variable so that partisan or other sources of public approval can be traced to kindred sources of potential support within Congress. In other words, while they have disaggregated bases of support within Congress, they have not done so within the mass public.

Looking at approval as a direct explanation for presidential legislative success, Zeidenstein (1983) concludes that there is no coherent zero-order connection between these variables. While the conclusion is apparently true, the role of presidential approval may be misspecified in this formulation, for approval is apparently mediated by other variables and is not a direct cause of a president's policy support in Congress. In any event, it is fair to say that the role of popular standing is very complex in accounting for legislative support of presidential proposals.

Policy sectors and support. Policy sectors also have been thought to have some bearing on presidential legislative success. Employing a typology developed by Lowi, a longitudinal analysis of presidential proposals (Spitzer, 1983) finds that the policy sector into which proposals fall is associated with its controversiality and with its prospects for adoption. "Constituent" proposals (administrative and organizational rearrangements) are least controversial and most likely to be adopted. "Regulatory" proposals (employing sanctions to alter conduct), in turn, are the most controversial and least successful. The argument is that the presidential agenda is a far more important consideration than presidential skill in determining the president's fortunes with Congress.

Another reputed policy sector difference is even more familiar. This thesis—"the two presidencies"—posits legislative compliance in foreign affairs and legislative recalcitrance in domestic requests (Wildavsky, 1966). However, Peppers (1975) has criticized it as time-bound, and Sigelman (1979), after an analysis of key votes, finds growing partisanship connected to foreign policy requests since 1973. Consequently, the idea of two presidencies—a foreign and a domestic one—fails to find much support. Even looking back to 1957, Sigelman found little evidence to comport with Wildavsky's thesis. Why? The answer may be in the different measures used, box scores and key votes. As with much of the quantitative research literature on congressional support, what one finds has much to do with how one measures.

Timing and support. Indeed, perplexities of this sort dot the literature on presidential policy success with Congress. For instance, Light (1981) and Shull (1983) conclude quite different things about the timing and the prospects for adoption of presidential legislative initiatives. Light emphasizes the importance of the first year in this regard, whereas Shull finds evidence that more initiatives appear at the end than at the beginning of the term and that the chances of adoption are also slightly greater then. Each had used different measures under the same conceptual umbrella, and they produce different results. No wonder few generalizations about the effects of timing on legislative success are safe.

Presidential operations. Turning from congressional constraints to presidential manipulations emphasizes the dynamic aspects of the relationship. The question thus becomes how presidents can organize and operate to influence what can be influenced. Manley's analysis of presidential lobbying (1978) finds its effects to be highly constrained by political arithmetic. Presidential lobbying is more significant in developing atmospherics than in generating direct and discrete influence. The implication is that proper atmospherics guarantee virtually nothing, but that poor atmospherics will contribute to presidential grief in dealings with Congress.

In his studies of the White House congressional liaison office, Davis (1979a, 1979b) stresses simultaneously its relevance and its limits during the Carter administration. Like the president it served, the Office of Congressional Relations was inexperienced and politically insensitive, and organized its tasks around conceptual rather than political categories. Like the president it served, the liaison office also absorbed some political lessons but the learning occurred after the atmosphere had been deleteriously, and perhaps irretrievably, affected. As deficient as the president's congressional liaison operations were, though, Carter's legislative problems, even Davis asserts, stemmed from facts of political life more fundamental than the congressional lobbying operation. "Over the years," Schick comments, "legislative-executive relations have been tranquil only when Congress has been compliant" (1983, p. 180). The Carter years were not among those tranquil moments.

Viewed quantitatively, presidential efforts seem to account for little of the outcome. But not all presidents have the same legislative needs, and they may organize their relations with Congress accordingly. In an effort to come to grips with the problem at this level, Jones (1983) projects two models of presidential relationship with Congress—an exchange model and an independence model. The exchange model emphasizes bargaining and interdependence; the independence model emphasizes the separateness of president and Congress, and in this model the president sees himself as the sole overseer of the public interest. Jones places Johnson and Ford in the exchange category, and Nixon and Carter in the independence category. However, of themselves, the models will not necessarily tell us a great deal about the outcome of presidential-congressional relations.

Johnson and Ford, by virtue of their style of relations with Congress and their long experience in leadership positions on Capitol Hill, enjoyed good relations with Congress, but hardly equivalent levels of success. The key difference surely was in the numbers. While Nixon and Carter were both viewed as "cold fish" on the Hill, their objectives insofar as Congress was concerned were entirely different—a difference relevant to the style adopted. For Nixon, his main ambition was not to ask much from Congress but to keep it out of his hair so that he could focus on grand designs in foreign policy. Carter, however, like Johnson, had a sizeable legislative agenda but a very different style of relationship with Congress. The absence of a comfortable relationship in Carter's case was certainly not helpful to his extensive ambitions. What Nixon could afford to do, Carter could not. The bottom line of Jones's analysis is that strategy is contingently important. We need to know the relationship between situation and presidential objectives in order to assess the appropriateness of a president's strategy for dealing with Congress.

In this section, three different meanings of support for the government have been elaborated. The salience and particular meaning of each is related to institutional characteristics of the legislature, the executive, and the party system. From these broad forms of support, we next consider the structure of executive-legislative interactions and the roles of institutions and party systems, of policy subsystems, and of individual motives in shaping these interactions.

The Structure of Executive-Legislative Interaction

Party Modes

Several studies have constructed paradigms of executive-legislative interaction (King, 1976; Ripley and Franklin, 1980; Aberbach, Putnam, and Rockman, 1981). King's focus on patterns of executive-legislator relations pivots essentially on three main factors: (1) the make-up of governments (coalitional or majority), (2) the constitutional arrangements defining the "executive" and "legislature," and (3) the relative power and operating patterns of the legislature itself. The basic premise behind King's analysis is so eminently sensible that it bears restating.

There are in the real world institutions called "executives" and "legislatures," and it is tempting to speak of the "relations" between them. It is tempting, but much more often than not misleading. It seldom makes sense to speak of executive-legislative relations. Rather, there are in each political system a number of distinct political relationships, each with its own "membership," so to speak, and each with its own dynamics and structure of power (1976, p. 32).

The trick, of course, is not merely to specify who interacts with whom, however necessary a beginning that is, but rather to provide a taxonomy of relations with cross-national applicability and then to develop a generic explanation for the cross-system variance in these relations. King takes us part way there and ends on a familiar, perhaps even obligatory, academician's note that "the analysis ... needs ... to be made more rigorous and to be extended" (p. 32).

In his analysis of executive-legislator relations in Britain, France, and West Germany, King sets forth several hypothetical modes of interaction and extracts from them some that actually occur: intraparty, opposition, nonparty, and crossparty. He then examines reasons for the variance in their occurrence across the three systems, primarily the considerations of governmental composition, constitutional arrangement, and legislative power outlined above.

The intraparty mode, for example, depends greatly on the extent of legislative independence. Norms of legislative independence are more powerful in West Germany than in Britain or in the French Fifth Republic, and these, as students of U.S. politics will appreciate, make intraparty relations more complicated than in Britain and France. First, legislative leadership in the Bundestag is independent of the Government and second the nonpartisan features of committee activity give members more opportunities to exert influence over legislation, independent of the Government. Party reins loosely held in committee are more taut on the floor—a circumstance also characteristic in kind, if not degree, of partisanship in the U.S. Congress. Government backbenchers in West Germany have greater opportunities than their British counterparts to inflict substantial damage on the cabinet because they are members of a more powerful and independent legislature (Loewenberg, 1967, p. 133). But they also hold these opportunities because the Government is itself an interparty coalition. Mostly, though, in times of the Government's dire need, members have withheld inflicting such damage, reflecting the importance of party as a channel for political career opportunities in both the German and British systems.

During the peak Gaullist period in France, the multiparty coalition had for the most part the appearance of a solid bloc aligned against the hostile forces of the left. The "nonpartisan" regime of DeGaulle, in fact, was a heartily cohesive force motivated less by past norms of party discipline than by present fears of the consequences of indiscipline. After the death of DeGaulle, the majority coalition inevitably splintered, leading to a president in Giscard who represented a minority tendency within the coalition, and finally to a change of both president and government altogether. In general, though, cohesion appears to have developed during the right-center governments when members had limited opportunities, in a chamber stripped of many of its past powers, to engage effectively in opposition. With the civil service molded to reflect the dominant coalition, the lines of contact between civil servants and legislators were largely asymmetric. Contact between the executive and the legislature ran along Gaullist coalition lines (Suleiman, 1974). Past may not be prologue here, however, for the executive-legislative relationship is one especially worthy of attention now in view of the Left's accession to power in France.

In the opposition mode, the powers of the legislature and its internal mechanisms dictate opportunities for the expression of opposition beyond the level of symbolism. As King asserts, opposition in the British Parliament is mostly in the form of set pieces in debate. The British Parliament being a mostly plenary body, relatively few opportunities are afforded for the Opposition, and in France the relative weakness of legislative powers similarly offers few opportunities for the Opposition. In West Germany, though, greater legislative capacity also affords greater opportunities for the Opposition to influence the legislative course. The relative importance of committees in each chamber of the West German parliament and their departisanized atmosphere gives to the Opposition opportunities within the committees that it lacks in plenary session. In other words, opposition may well be effective so long as it is not perceived as merely partisan.

Crossparty and nonparty modes are influenced substantially by the extent to which the legislative body is what Polsby (1975) calls a transformative institution. These modes of relationship may be simply different ways of saying much the same thing. They each refer to circumstances in which partisanship per se is relatively unimportant. All other things being equal, the more a legislature's activities are committee oriented, the more nonpartisan or crosspartisan modes become a significant element in the operations of the parliamentary body. The committee-oriented Bundestag, for instance, has much crossparty activity (inquiry, consultation, and bargaining amongst members, and between members and ministers of different parties). Crossparty activity, therefore, appears to be heightened by coalitional government in a transformative and internally differentiated legislative body. The nonparty mode is presumably appropriate to majority governments and to circumstances under which the legislative body is acting in relatively nonpartisan ways, principally through its committees.

Both the British and French parliaments are more plenary or less committee oriented than the West German parliament. In contrast to the West German Bundestag, therefore, the British House of Commons and French Assembly are bodies closer to the partisan arena pole than to the transformative one. Neither is as internally differentiated or as independently powerful as the Bundestag. And although there are changes taking place in each chamber that may enhance their legislative capabilities, neither approximates the extent to which the nonpartisan (or in the West German case, crosspartisan) mode colors legislative life and relations with the executive.

Important exogenous factors, however, also need to be considered. King emphasizes, in this regard, the consensual politics prevalent in the Federal Republic through the 1950s and 1960s. Inevitably, he wonders to what extent the modes of relationship are subject to changes in the broader partisan atmosphere. This is a good query and represents a point of research and theory worthy of further engagement, namely to what extent partisanship in governing institutions is relatively more or less permeated by, or impermeable to, the influence of external sociopolitical forces? Conversely, to what extent can new structures within the legislature alter its habitual patterns of conduct and norms of legislative-executive relations? These questions are pertinent if not easy to answer. They are pertinent because structures designed to give the legislature a greater say in the policy-making process (including formulating policy, overseeing implementation, and evaluating policy) may also alter, absorb, or even heighten partisan tendencies within the legislature or the polity.

In this last regard, Finer (1980) notes and fears that a growth in the powers of the select committees in the House of Commons will enable the more charged-up party backbenchers to control and direct the minister. The minister will then be assessed for his or her control and direction of the bureaucracy in accordance with the constituency party program. The real powers of Parliament vis-à-vis the executive would undoubtedly grow under such circumstances. But partisan acrimony could grow far greater and eclipse "impartial" inquiry. Finer also sees committee government as an impediment to party government, a view also held by others (Dodd and Schott, 1979, p. 66; Mackintosh, 1971, p. 61). Yet Finer fears that while committee government is an obstacle to party government, it impedes hardly at all the expression of virile partisanship within the legislature.

Policy Subsystems

While King looks at features of the executive and the legislature, Ripley and Franklin (1980) employ policy types as their frame of reference for examining patterns of executive-legislative relation. Their analysis is limited, however, to the United States, where both executive and legislative diversity make for an unusual degree of disaggregated accommodation between executive and legislative actors. Ripley and Franklin distinguish between the following six policy types: distributive, protective regulatory, redistributive, structural, strategic, and crisis (pp. 212-219). In their schema, five sets of actors are constants but their relative involvement varies significantly across the policy types. The five sets of actors are the president and central bureaucracy, Congress as a plenary institution, administrative bureaus, congressional subcommittees, and private individuals, corporations, or interest groups.

The patterns of relationship, then, are hypothesized to differ among the policy types. Distributive and structural policy each involve intense, narrow interactions between congressional subcommittees, administrative bureaus, and specifically affected interests. Regulatory policy, on the other hand, involves to some degree all five sets of actors, but principally the president and central bureaucracy, the Congress as a plenary body, and the regulated interests. In the redistributive policy type, president and central bureaucratic actors, Congress in plenary form, and peak associations become the principal actors. Strategic (national security) policy involves a close interaction between the president and central bureaucracy on the one hand and Congress on the other, and a less intense involvement by private sector interests. Finally, crisis policy making tends to be most centralized within the executive, having only a weak congressional involvement. In general, the less visible the issue (or the less pertinent to central leaders), the more disaggregated its settlement.

Ripley and Franklin's analysis, like King's, highlights the diversity of actors on each side of the fence, a particular virtue to understanding the diversity of their interests. Examining policy making is useful for understanding modal relations between actors, and Ripley and Franklin's analysis suggests the utility of starting with policy as the independent variable in such an examination. However, it is difficult to separate the policy category from the pattern of participation, a problem which may well be inherent to using policy as an independent variable. In this formulation, the process of policy making is itself used to define the policy type (pp. 90-91). Scholars must still distinguish operationally the variables of policy category from the constellation of executive, legislative, and private actors so that they are conceptualized and measured independent of one another. Moreover, Ripley and Franklin focus on the early stages of the policy process, formulation and legitimation; it is likely that at later stages, involving implementation and supervision, the constellation of actors will change, probably in the direction of constriction.

Nonetheless, policy process is an excellent vehicle for the analysis of executive-legislative relations. Ripley and Franklin's categories provide rough guides to the scope of involvement; and though the anatomical features differ across political systems, the physiology of policy making is what is in question. Looking at similar types of policy across political systems may be especially instructive for assessing points of intersection between executive and legislative sectors, and the ways in which influence is carried across them.

Systemic and Individual Patterns

Patterns of contact between executive and legislative actors may also allow us to infer the structure of their relationship. Aberbach, Putnam, and Rockman (1981, pp. 209-237) and also Anton (1980, pp. 129-133) rely upon members of the legislative body and the executive to report their contacts with a variety of actors, including one another. Data from these studies focus on two levels of causation: the systemic and the individual. At the systemic level, interchange between senior civil servants, ministers, and legislators has two main patterns. One is the mediated linkage model and the other the direct linkage model, which itself has two forms: simultaneous and end-run (Aberbach, Putnam, and Rockman, 1981, p. 234). Mediated linkage is found in Britain, the Netherlands, and, for the most part, in Sweden. Direct linkage occurs in Italy, West Germany, and the United States.

In the mediated linkage pattern, contacts are mostly through the minister. The purest version of this is found in Britain, where the traditions of ministerial responsibility and anonymous officialdom are strongest. In the Netherlands and Sweden, legislators do have more contact with the civil service, but the linchpin still is the minister.

In the direct linkage model, a heavy volume of traffic flows in pretty much all directions; all intersections of the triadic network are busy. This is especially the case in West Germany and, to a slightly lesser degree, also in Italy. These two cases, therefore, are known as simultaneous linkage models and they differ from the United States which, apparently uniquely, has a busier traffic flow between senior civil servants and legislators than between either of these and department heads. Such a pattern of interaction is called end-run.

The principal hypothesis offered for explaining these different patterns is a variant of King's: executive fragmentation and a complex legislative system of powerful committees will beget an especially heavy flow of traffic between senior bureaucrats and legislators. The splintered American executive, a product at least in part of the enormous decentralization of the U.S. Congress, seems to reflect the low level accommodations indicated by Ripley and Franklin as typical of distributive and structural policy types. Extensive bureau-subcommittee relations are not at all inconsistent with the end-run pattern of contact between senior bureaucrats and legislators. In this triangle, department heads are the party left out. Competing centers of power, the absence of strong central coordination, and the existence of complex transformative legislatures provide bureaucrats and legislators each with resources and, thus, induce mutual dependency between them (Aberbach, Putnam, and Rockman, 1981, p. 235). Whereas central aggregative mechanisms tend to enhance the gatekeeping powers of the "political" executive (the Government), weaker aggregative mechanisms intertwine the executive and legislature below ministerial levels. In the U.S., of course, with its exceptional lack of centralizing mechanisms, the legislature holds an especially powerful hand in dealing with the political executive. It is, in other words, essentially the concentration or dispersion of political authority in the system that defines the conditions of mutual dependence between executive and legislative actors. It is those conditions that, in turn, largely account for the particular pattern of interaction between executives and legislators.

Indeed, evidence that bureaucrats with attitudes favorable to politics have contacts with legislators no more frequently than their less accepting colleagues affirms clearly the powerful grip of systemic factors in motivating interactions between bureaucrats and politicians in the legislature (Aberbach, Putnam, and Rockman, 1981, pp. 219-227). In fact, bureaucrats with a zest for politics do interact more with politicians and with those administrative officials in the forefront of policy making, but they do not necessarily interact more with legislative politicians (aside from party leaders and cabinet officials who also happen to be members of the legislative body). Put somewhat differently, administrators who are movers and shakers structure their contacts, even adjusting for differences in where they sit, so as to interact with the top executive elite, not with the legislature. While evidence from among Dutch civil servants does indicate modest association between "political" thinking and contact with members of Parliament (Eldersveld, Kooiman, and van der Tak, 1981, p. 157), the tautness or looseness of authority still accounts for most of the level of interchange between senior bureaucrats and members of the legislature.

Anton (1980, pp. 95-100), in his study of Swedish bureaucrats and legislators, demonstrates one other significant aspect of administrators' dealings with the legislature: administrators are sought after rather than seeking. They more commonly receive than initiate communications. Moreover, there is no self-reporting bias as both legislators and bureaucrats agree that legislators initiate most of the contacts. Bureaucrats, it seems reasonable to infer, are not looking to move beyond their cocoons. On the other hand, legislators have a much wider and thicker array of contacts with diverse sectors of their society than do bureaucrats, indicating once again that while bureaucrats are oriented toward stability and quietude legislators are oriented toward representation.

These communication patterns help in depicting the role configurations of legislators and executive officials, and in ascertaining the pull of both individual motives and the imperatives of political dependency. King (1976) suggests that such research efforts can be enriched, which they probably should be, for contact patterns are themselves only a kind of skeletal structure. Even when only pro forma, however, a heavy volume of traffic still can tell us much about who must be communicated with in the political system. We learn, after all, from these simple quantitative patterns of executive-legislative interaction the etiquette of elite communication—what patterns of involvement are accepted and permitted.

To summarize, investigations into the structure of executive-legislative relations must first internally differentiate executive and legislative actors. The configuration of actors and of key relationships is apparently determined especially by the formal and informal dispersion of power in the governing institutions of the system and by the type of policy question involved.

The structure of relationship, however, provides by itself no evidence of the spirit in which the relationship is developed. Extensive involvement across sectors is born of necessity and is no predictor to either enmity or trust. Close involvement, though, may be osmotic. After all, U.S. career officials as a group are intimately involved with legislative politicians, the study by Aberbach, Putnam, and Rockman (1981) shows. They evidence more "political" instincts of the sort that members of Congress themselves have. In turn, the abundance of technical prowess and detailed policy information available to members of the U.S. Congress give them a more technical orientation toward policy than legislators in other countries, especially where osmotic influences are much weaker. Accordingly, Heclo and Wildavsky (1975), in assessing the parliamentary role in expenditure review, contend that while some members are moved to deal in the same language as the executive, their ranks are thin. "The closer this or that MP becomes involved, the more likely he is to be turned on by his fellow MPs and labeled a technician, accountant, empire-builder and/or Government lackey" (p. 263). Still, close involvement is no guarantee of trusting relations, and distance does not necessarily mean enmity.

A particularly interesting development to consider in this regard is the apparent decline of the plenary parliamentary body and subsequent emergence of committee powers within parliamentary bodies, a phenomenon that would appear to presage closer contacts between legislators and senior bureaucrats. How this will affect actual working relationships is as yet unknown and certainly worthy of inquiry.

One aspect of these working relationships, of course, is that of legislative monitoring of the executive, a process commonly called "oversight." This is the subject I explore in the following section.

Oversight

Justifications, Goals, and Definitions

In perusing the literature on legislative oversight, one is struck by the rituals which accompany discussions of the subject. Though the order of the rite is sometimes altered, the first paragraph (one may substitute whole pages for more prolix authors!) is typically devoted to the signal importance of the subject for democracy. This is followed by a statement of the goals of oversight, typically so abstract that it could hardly evoke dissent, perhaps not even from the most recalcitrant executive. Third, there is a statement, also invariably true, that clear terminology and standard definitions of oversight are absent, inevitably making the subject hard to handle. Fourth, there is a lament that little research has been done in the field despite its importance (see step 1) often without a precise statement of what the object of the research should be.

Justifications. How is oversight justified? Harris says that "control of administration is one of the most important functions of legislative bodies in all modern democracies" (1964, p. 1). Ogul contends that the issue of "who rules the rulers" is ultimately at stake, if in more complicated form than that stark question implies, and that "the significance of the topic provides ample justification for additional attention" to it (1976, pp. 3-4). Scher claims that "democratic ideology requires control of administrative action by elected representatives of the people" (1963, p. 526).

Moreover, the concern is not exclusive to students of the U.S. system; there is a general fear that democratic practices will erode through excessive grants of administrative discretion, and that popular and representative institutions will therefore decline. Thus, a British member of Parliament, arguing for strengthening parliamentary scrutiny, complains that "it is . . . alarming that ministers should find it so convenient to write the law long after Parliament thinks it has done so itself, and that they should have so little difficulty in ensuring a smooth passage through Parliament for what is in effect legislation by the executive" (Beith, 1981, p. 165). Another Briton notes that "popular control of bureaucratic behavior is a matter of concern in many political systems, but little research has been conducted on the contribution of representative assemblies to that control" (Lees, 1977, p. 205). The principal value of justifying legislative monitoring of the executive, it seems, is to ensure the triumph of representative government by lines of accountability running through the organ that embodies popular sovereignty. Representativeness, rather than effectiveness, is the irreducible core. So defined, oversight is, in Aberbach's words, "an intensely political activity" (1982, p. 285).

Niskanen's work (1971) is one possible exception to this stress on representativeness over effectiveness. His analysis pivots around assumed propensities for bureaus to maximize their budgets (driven by the motives of bureau chiefs to maximize their interests) and to be inadequately supervised by the appropriating authority (because the monitors have interests compatible with the bureaus). The consequence, in Niskanen's formulation, is both ineffectiveness (defined as inefficient allocation) and unrepresentativeness in the distribution of costs and benefits. In these terms, to be unrepresentative is also to be inefficient and thus presumably ineffective from the standpoint of a general welfare function.

Goals. As central as "who rules the rulers" is in any catalogue of the objectives of oversight, there are additional expectations about what legislative supervision of the executive should accomplish. The list of oversight goals enunciated by MacMahon nearly 40 years ago (1943, pp. 162-163) is still serviceable today. The objectives, MacMahon asserted, were to (1) check dishonesty and waste, (2) guard against harsh and callous, (i.e., arbitrary and unresponsive) administration, (3) evaluate implementation in accordance with legislative objectives, and (4) ensure administrative compliance with statutory intent. A more or less official version of oversight objectives emanates from a Senate Committee on Government Operations report published in 1977 and cited in recent works on the subject of oversight (Dodd and Schott, 1979, p. 156; Aberbach, 1979, p. 494). The study reveals five objectives of oversight, most equivalent to or overlapping MacMahon's. These are (1) to see that policy is implemented in accordance with intent (cf. MacMahon's fourth objective); (2) to determine whether policy is effective and its impact in accord with congressional standards (cf. MacMahon's third objective); (3) to prevent waste and dishonesty and assure efficiency (cf. MacMahon's first category); (4) to prevent discretionary abuse (cf. MacMahon's second category); and (5) to represent the public interest by monitoring and constraining agency-clientele group relations. On this last point, there appears to be a more general congressional inclination to accept close agency-clientele ties (Scher, 1960; Aberbach and Rockman, 1978; Fiorina, 1977, 1981). Members of Congress, after all, are representatives, not administrative rationalists.

Such lists have the ring of New Year's resolutions. They are unarguably admirable. They also are difficult to specify. Legislators may, and often do, disagree on what, for instance, constitutes waste, abuse, and inefficiency. Another critical complication is discerning the meaning of legislative intent. No doubt, things would be clearer if the authors of particular statutes did the later evaluating. Undeniably, too, if statutes were more precise (or inflexible), there would be less difficulty in arriving at a standard for judging administrative implementation. Fiorina (1981), in this regard, contends that it is to congressional advantage to farm out large grants of discretion to the administration and then use critical feedback as a means of fixing responsibility on the bureaucrats.

Judging intent is always problematic, though, even under the best of circumstances; "intent" is usually more a battle cry than a standard. The following vignette is instructive. In *The New York Times* of 4 August 1982, reporter Ben Franklin quoted from a speech made by the Secretary of the Interior during a ceremony honoring civil servants in the Office of Surface Mining for rewriting regulations associated with the Surface Mining Control and Reclamation Act of 1977. Secretary Watt said that while his department had "received huge abuse from Congress itself never once did we falter, never once did we back up and never once did we change our determination to bring the program into compliance with the intent of Congress." Apparently the word "intent" has highly pliable properties.

Intent might be somewhat easier to discern if Congress expressed it clearly—a task that legislative bodies have difficulty performing. "If Congress can make up its mind as to what it wants done," Hyneman wrote almost 35 years ago, "it ought to incorporate its wishes into law" (1950, p. 88). True enough. But collective bodies rarely have the clarity of a single mind. In addition, they tend to lack organic continuity. What is the intent of Congress—that which the law states or that which is defined as the mood of its present members, or even just its strategically located members? Philosophical fog is pervasive here.

Most likely, abuse will have to be flagrant to beget a concerted and nonpartisan congressional reaction. As an absolutely minimal condition, oversight activity presumably would hold down, as Aberbach asserts "flagrant abuses of power by administrators" (1979, p. 495). As defined by Webster's New Collegiate Dictionary, flagrant is said to apply "to offenses or errors so bad that they can neither escape notice nor be condoned." Defined operationally, it refers to something done within the executive that is nearly universally condemned by the Congress or by its relevant committees or subcommittees. Such circumstances are rare, and even Secretary Watt's oracular vision of congressional intent in the face of congressional expressions to the contrary might not qualify.

Definitions. In a very general sense, there is rough agreement that oversight, as a somewhat convoluted means of expressing popular sovereignty, is a good. In much the same vein there is also a consensus about the goals of oversight activity, however proverbial and internally inconsistent these may be. Definitions of oversight, however, are more problematic, and disagreement is common. Some definitions are inclusive; others focus on a narrower segment of activity. The definition, I noted earlier, depends on how many legislative activities it is seen to encompass; it also depends on the types of controls and supervision placed on the executive, the instruments employed, and the stages of legislative intervention. Moreover, the legislature may constrain the executive, in the U.S. system at least, by a very high degree of statutory precision, or, conversely by administrative delegation subject to a specific legislative approval (Fisher, 1978, pp. 241-242). This sort of statutory delegation may be thought of more properly as "foresight" than "oversight," though it is a means of legislative control over the bureaucracy. Some modes of legislative monitoring may be characterized as "after-thought"—for example, the legislative veto by which Congress, in essence, continually assesses the propriety of administrative regulations. The legislative veto and other delegations of authority subject to legislative approval have been sharply curtailed by recent Supreme Court decisions. What consequences this curtailment will have on actual supervisory behavior by Congress are, however, yet to be seen.

Given these possible channels of legislative influence on the executive, some definitions of oversight can be stupendously broad. One, for example, states that "oversight comprises activity that forces some patterned response by executive branch officials" (Halpert, 1981, p. 479). By this account, "this formulation regards any legislative activity as potentially oversight-related." Another very broad definition, and one of the most widely accepted in the oversight literature, is Ogul's: "Legislative oversight is behavior by legislators and their staffs, individually or collectively, which results in an impact, intended or not, on bureaucratic behavior" (1976, p. 11). This definition implies that oversight activity may be found in numerous and unexpected places.

Others, however, are more exclusive. Aberbach defines oversight as

congressional review of the actions of the federal departments, agencies, and commissions and of the programs and policies they administer. This includes review that takes place during program and policy implementation as well as afterwards, but excludes much of what Congress now does when it considers proposals for new programs or even for the expansion of current programs (1979, p. 494).

Schick identifies oversight also as being "review after the fact," emphasizing that "the main form of oversight is investigatory activity by Congressional committees . . . of past administrative actions" (1976, p. 125). In between these polarities is a definition advanced by Lyons and Thomas: "Oversight encompasses all activities undertaken by a legislature to influence administrative behavior, during program implementation as well as afterwards" (1982, p. 118).

A definition, by definition, is neither right or wrong, nor more or less correct. But there is no agreed upon definition in use by researchers studying the "phenomenon" of oversight. The relevance of these diverse definitions is well stated by Ogul: "Assessment of oversight is conditioned . . . by one's perception of what oversight is" (1976, p. 6). All of the above definitions incorporate formal review processes at the implementation stage and thereafter. That, it seems, is the core. The broader definitions, however, encompass more activities under the oversight rubric and, above all, some that do not constitute formal review. Thus, Ogul identifies *manifest* and *latent* (formal and informal) oversight processes.

How much evidence there is of oversight activity as well as how one evaluates the quality of it is contingent on how oversight is defined— how encompassing or restrictive the conception of it. A tour through the recent literature generates the impression that more formal oversight is occurring in the U.S. Congress (Aberbach, 1979), and perhaps generally. There is also an indication that broader definitions, since they incorporate latent forms of oversight, also consider more activity to be oversight. Moreover, Schick (1976, pp. 132-134) points out that Congress has over an even longer period moved to assert its control over administrative detail by the use of "foresight" and "afterthought" mechanisms—that is, annual authorization, sunset riders, and legislative veto provisions. How much oversight is going on is, to some degree, a function of how it is defined.

How much oversight is enough, however? Or for that matter, how much is too much? A frequent assumption is that, ceteris paribus, more is better. Aberbach states this premise straightforwardly: "I . . . assume that more oversight is usually better than less" (1979, p. 495). Four decades ago, however, when Congress was less well equipped to perform its oversight functions, and when the culture of executive vitality was a cornerstone of political science, more congressional intervention in administrative processes was not a popular position to hold. The executive bias is noteworthy in White's (1945) conclusions about the role of legislative intervention: "Congress faces a delicate problem of balance—it must control with enough certainty of touch to guarantee a responsible and responsive public service; but it must refrain from impairing the capacity of the public service to achieve the great social purposes to which it is dedicated" (p. 11). In an article published shortly before, MacMahon had contended that

no amount of legislative staffing could take the place of executive supervision. Fitful legislative intervention is no substitute for controls within administration . . . . The committees frequently disclaim competence for detailed constructive inquiry in these matters. The staff necessary for continuous inquiry could be maintained only at the risk of a harmful division of responsibility, while such a staff would still lack a first hand sense of operations (1943, pp. 413-414).

More pertinent than how much oversight should take place is the question of its quality and how it is to be done. Qualitative considerations such as the now enumerated "goals" of oversight are easier to discuss abstractly than concretely. If political factors are important motivators of oversight activity (and this is now a widely but not quite universally held assumption), it is inevitably hard to disassociate qualitative judgments from political motivations. Ogul hammers this point hard: "Most of the material published has been concerned primarily with assessing the quality of oversight or in providing descriptions of formal procedures." In it, "politics is perceived as peripheral . . . an aberration from sound principles of executive-legislative relations" (1976, p. 9).

Yet the question of quality should not be dismissed, nor should the more mundane question of identifying various dimensions of oversight activity and connecting them to changes in executive behavior. A great deal more careful empirical work needs to be done on this second question, but the former question really inquires as to whether the subject of oversight is at all important. Whether it is important or not is intimately linked to the question of quality. Assessments of quality ultimately need to be related to both the empirical study of oversight forms and the normative justifications made on behalf of studying the subject in the first place.

A Schema for the Study of Oversight

Oversight is done in many guises (the broader the definition the more guises in which it is done), but whether these various guises are complementary or exclusive is not clear. Oversight activity also is both a dependent variable (or, more properly, variables) to be explained and an independent variable. As a dependent variable we want to see whether or not the structure of explanation for the various forms "it" may assume is variant or constant across different conditions. While progress is being made in research dealing with the conditions for oversight activity, these efforts mostly have been of startlingly recent vintage. A good many, judging from their dates of publication, appear to have heeded Ogul's call for more serious research on the topic. As with legislators' motivations to engage in the activity, however, scholars too are jogged into research directions by the salience of the events around them. Much is owed to the perverse presidency of Richard Nixon. As Nixon helped spur the study of presidential character, so he also helped advance both the cause of, and scholarly inquiry into, legislative control of the executive.

Our knowledge of oversight is asymmetric. We have many more inquiries focusing on its occurrence, its forms, and explanations of it than we have on its impact. The reasons are not mysterious. Impact is a lot harder to measure and very difficult to conceptualize. Do we really know what we expect effective oversight to accomplish? And how can we measure these accomplishments and show them to be attributable to oversight? However tenuous our grasp of oversight as something to be explained, it is considerably firmer than our grasp of it as a factor explaining executive change.

FIGURE 1
Oversight as a Dependent and an Independent Variable

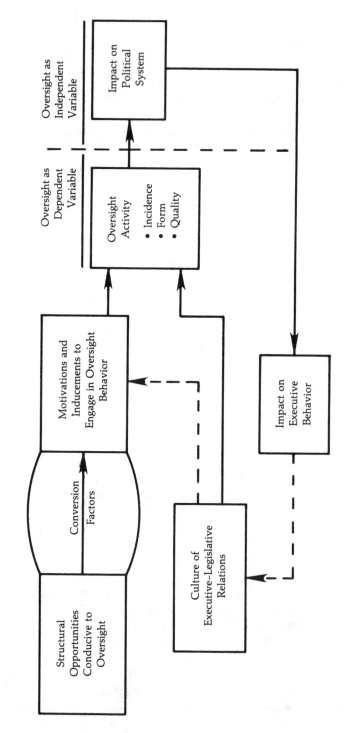

In Figure 1, I sketch out the relations discussed above. As all diagrams must be, this one is overly simple, but it helps connect the two pivotal analytic roles of oversight activity as a dependent and independent variable. Viewed as a dependent variable, oversight activity is seen in Figure 1 as a consequence of three sets of variables. The first is the culture of interelite relations. There are spectacular differences across political systems in this regard. Kelman's outstanding study of U.S. and Swedish bureaucrats involved in occupational health and safety administration makes this patently clear. As Kelman puts it: "No equivalent to congressional oversight exists in Sweden. . . . Yet if the dominant attitude in the White House and Congress can be described as close to paranoia about the bureaucracy, the dominant one in . . . Stockholm is serenity" (1981, p. 108). Elling (1979) notes, also, in a comparison of two state legislatures (Minnesota and Kentucky), that culture plays a role in determining whether case work activity is transformed into oversight activity or whether it remains at the level of a highly particularized intervention.

A second key but indirect variable is the structural opportunities available for oversight, of which I shall have more to say shortly. A third variable is the motives and incentives of members to engage in oversight, that which converts the structural opportunities and activates them.

Oversight, as I have been emphasizing, is not a single variable; it varies in incidence, form, and quality. Similarly, when seen as an independent variable, oversight has various dimensions which may affect executive behavior. The impact on executive behavior will probably reflect the form of oversight that occurs; when oversight is episodic and particularistic, the executive response is apt to be similar. Finally, we may ask, if not fully answer, how oversight-related alterations of executive behavior affect the political system and thus affect the culture of executive-legislative relations?

An arrow connects the impact of oversight on executive behavior to its impact on the political system. This connection raises the question of the quality of oversight activities. Do they help promote trust and mutual confidence? Or do they promote defensiveness and hostility, serving as a venue only for the promotion of partisan cause or personal ambition? Much, undoubtedly, depends upon the way it is done, and upon the forms of oversight that become prevalent.

Effective oversight must also be, in some measure, apolitical at least in the narrower sense, and motivated by considerations beyond personal aggrandizement, publicity, and partisan cause. Robinson, in her study of the Public Expenditure Committee in the British Parliament, quotes a committee member as saying that "good administration is not newsworthy" (1978, p. 153). Nor is effective monitoring. The paradox contained herein is given classic expression by an official interviewed by Ogul, who proclaimed: "Where there is publicity to be gained, there is oversight to be had" (1976, p. 37).

Of course, if politicians were not stimulated by publicity or were not attracted to the scent of juicy public issues, they would not be politicians. The paradox of oversight implied by this can be stated thusly:

(a) political factors tend to stimulate sporadic, but not sustained, oversight;

(b) therefore, effective and sustained oversight rests upon non-political factors;

(c) but only political factors are apt to motivate oversight at all.

This syllogism is too neat. Some systematic oversight apparently does occur, and sometimes it is facilitated by conditions that do not involve a member's raw calculation of political gain (Rosenthal, 1981; Halpert, 1981). Explanations of oversight activity, as Figure 1 indicates, are complex and involve cultural, institutional, and individual variables.

Oversight as Dependent Variable

In the broadest sense, the culture of executive-legislative relations is colored by the modalities of relationship between a Government and its rank and file supporters in the legislature. How strong or tenuous are these bonds? How closely linked, in turn, are these relationships to parliamentary power and to its presumptive decline in the face of supposed executive and technocratic dominance? The decline of parliaments, in fact, has been a much heralded nonevent through much of this century. Parliaments have not declined so much as the spirit and organization of partisanship, the yeast of democratic politics, has risen—a phenomenon discussed recently by King (1981b) and earlier by Weber. This powerful and disciplined partisan force makes for a system of relatively few sheep herders and relatively many sheep; it makes, in short, for Government dominance bolstered by the lock of party organizations on members' political careers. While this gives the illusion of parliamentary decline, what is really operative is robust political party organization. Only in the U.S. did the power of party organization peak concurrently with the power of the legislature in a system with no easily definable Government. But notably also, the power of rank and file members was then quite weak.

Ironically, the emergence of professional political organization brought with it elements that, in the shorter run, would create and, in the longer run, contest a state of affairs in which the Government governs and the backbench uncritically follows. Ultimately, professional politicians with ambitions for society or themselves (and tending often to see these ambitions coterminously) will not long stay at rest. They will act to advance their beliefs and possibly their influence. One vehicle is the committee.

As both Robinson (1978) and Heclo and Wildavsky (1975) point out, ideologues in the legislature are usually disinclined toward committee activity because, in the latter's phrase, "knowing too much can inhibit repartee" (p. 261). Party leaders are also skeptical of committee activity because subject specialization, as Loewenberg points out in the case of the West German Bundestag, inhibits leadership influence (1967, p. 217). At the same time, the growing participation from the backbenches is not due merely to a quest for knowledge (something not usually prized by politicians for its own sake) but reflects dissent, especially notable in Britain, from the view that the Government knows best. Such an altered view also, not coincidentally, derives from intraparty fractiousness, especially from within the Labour party (Norton, 1980; Schwarz, 1981). Committees may merely provide a vehicle for the expression of virulent partisanship under such circumstances. Finer (1980), for example, clearly sees the threat of an extreme partisan politicization in these developments and an erosion of governmental competence. Whatever orientation specialist committees develop—toward facts or factiousness—probably depends a great deal on the political setting and the permanence of committees in the life of the legislature (Robinson, 1978, pp. 89, 106).

Still, even the embryonic development of committee government is widely perceived as a threat to party government, to ministerial responsibility, and to civil servants' protected neutrality. The drive for involvement comes from the rank and file. A supporter of these trends in Britain has commented:

The Chairman of the Parliamentary Labour Party, Mr. Houghton, has argued that "the backbencher is now mobilizing for an advance on the concentration of Ministerial and Executive power." If this is to be successful, it must be an advance on many fronts, from looser discipline to better facilities for MPs, and one of the most important fronts . . . is that of the specialist committees (Macintosh, 1971, p. 61).

An even stronger enthusiast for reforms leading in this direction (Walkland, 1976) sees the issue straight away as adjusting the claims of an impermeable Government reliant on party unity in a plenary parliament against those of an invigorated legislative body reliant on investigating committees. Such an invigorated legislature would presumably be in a position to exercise significant independence over the course of policy. Majority party government and an effective legislative role, it is acknowledged by this advocate, are at odds.

Another advocate of a more central role for committees in the British House of Commons claims that the virtue of institutionalized specialist committees is that they tend to create a nonpartisan spirit of work and cohesiveness among members (Robinson, 1978, pp. 89-100). At the same time, she warns of the inescapable fragmentation that results. In the Public Expenditures Committee's specialized subcommittees, Robinson says, "the autonomy of the sub-committees . . . and the consequent fragmentation of their work means that the subjects examined do not allow for inter-Departmental or inter-functional comparisons of spending." Robinson's lament is (perhaps, more properly, was) a familiar one to students of the U.S. Congress.

However, Robinson points to a problem that is endemic to the oversight process. Knowledgeable oversight is promoted by committee and subcommittee organization, just as specialized knowledge is promoted by the organizational division of labor characteristic of bureaucracy. In each case, specialization also bears a price, namely integrative capacity and coordination. Dodd and Schott (1979) show particular sensitivity to this issue. For while Congress has gained many more resources to help it see the larger picture, they claim that it is ever more fragmented in its oversight structures. According to their criteria, effective oversight is not "possible so long as the pull of subcommittee government is stronger than the desire to assure effective implementation of public policy" (p. 274).

To summarize, member aspirations tend everywhere to strengthen, in varying degrees, committee government at the expense of executive autonomy and, to some degree, of party discipline. But committee government is also specialized government, and specialized government shares many of the strengths and weaknesses of bureaucratic government: knowledge without direction, and functional rather than substantive rationality. The irony is that "reform" often travels in opposing directions depending on the point of origin. In plenary parliaments, reformers wishing to strengthen legislative independence cry out for the assets associated with the specialization and consensus politics that are thought to be the primary features of committee government. In the U.S., conversely, contemporary reform pushes toward party government, greater integration, and a holistic approach to legislative supervision (Dodd and Schott, 1979; Fiorina, 1981). Some reforms proposed by Dodd and Schott—for example, giving the Senate president pro tem and the Speaker of the House the authority to appoint committee chairs—are also basically restorationist.

If administration is detail, then its oversight is also necessarily detailed (Schick, 1976). When legislators interfere with "details," executives tend to tolerate reluctantly the interference. Oversight of a broader and more coordinated nature, however, not only supervises implementation (that being a largely U.S. phenomenon to begin with) but also redefines policy. To executives, particularly cabinet ministers, that represents a threat, not a mere annoyance, because it also redefines authority.

In any case, a fine eye would discern a rise in both committee government and in members' aspirations for involvement and influence. The tendencies appear transnational, differing only in their magnitudes, threshold levels, and place vis-à-vis other parliamentary traditions.

These are general trends, but because of the separation of powers and the long tradition of legislative independence the United States constitutes a special case. Specialized committees and individualistic motives have long been present in U.S. legislative processes, for example. These specifically American conditions make oversight both important *and* problematic (Aberbach, 1982, pp. 285-286).

To summarize factors explaining the prevalence and form of oversight, it is necessary to maintain comparability in legislative structures and traditions. Therefore, the balance of this analysis focuses closely on the U.S. Congress and U.S. state legislatures.

Structural opportunities. Factors that conduce to oversight activity are extensively reviewed in the literature. Ogul (1976) provides the most general list of factors, amended slightly by Aberbach (1979). In their overlapping lists are such considerations as

(1) the legal authority to compel change—a largely American resource (see Coombes, 1975; Loewenberg and Patterson, 1979);

(2) committee structure, prestige, and leadership (see Bibby, 1966; Kaiser, 1977; Johnson, 1980; Henderson, 1970);

(3) staff resources (see Rosenthal, 1981; Kaiser, 1977);

(4) split party control of the government (see Hamm and Robertson, 1981; but for contrary evidence see Halpert, 1981);

(5) committee or subcommittee relations with an agency, its programs, and its political leadership;

(6) the role of the individual on a committee; and

(7) the nature of the subject matter and its newsworthiness.

Most writers assume that these factors require activation through individual motives. One analyst (Rosenthal, 1981), though, largely rejects this notion that structure is only a necessary and not a sufficient condition for oversight. He contends that most research on oversight is premised on an individualistic fallacy. Accordingly, researchers tend to see oversight as stimulated by individual behavior rather than by altered institutional functioning. Consequently, they also tend to rely too frequently on individual member reports of their interests and activities. He argues the need to look more at institutional resources and less at individual inducements: "Oversight," he contends, "requires the awareness and involvement of a few legislators, and only a few" (p. 130).

The key to oversight activity, according to Rosenthal, is not in the legislator but in the legislature, and independent commissions and audit staffs provide resources for oversight that are at least partly self-activating. In place of individual incentives, therefore, Rosenthal stresses institutional incentives. In state legislatures, these are (1) a more conservative and anti-bureaucratic political climate; (2) a more independent legislative posture (due perhaps to the congressional resurgence of the 1970s); (3) a growth in legislative staff and professionalism; and (4) a growth of resources specifically designed to evaluate executive compliance and behavior. In other words, Rosenthal sees an increase in oversight activity taking place in Congress and the state legislatures in the absence of a commensurate increase in individual motivation to engage in oversight activity. The analysis suggests that a small number of legislative entrepreneurs with a special interest in legislative professionalism and control of executive activity stimulate the development of institutional resources that, in turn, promote oversight.

A contrasting study across three state legislatures (Lyons and Thomas, 1982) discovers a curious relationship between structure and motivation. Nonpolitical motivation counts most when structural opportunities are absent, according to this analysis. In the state with the least structural capacity for oversight, the attitude of members that oversight should be conducted is the best direct indicator that it will be undertaken. In environments better equipped to perform the oversight function, such factors as partisan opposition to the executive and constituency interest come more into play. A theory to explain this is not advanced, nor is one likely to be forthcoming within the limiting context of institutional and individual variables alone.

Executive-legislative conflict and divided party control are also prominent factors in a study by Hamm and Robertson (1981) of methods of oversight in state legislatures. Political opposition, according to their analysis, leads to rule and regulation review as a form of oversight—essentially a form of legislative veto provision. On the other hand, limited capacity and low levels of legislative professionalism predict the use of sunset provisions on agency program authorizations. Whereas the legislative veto involves a continuous review of administrative rule making, sunset provisions are more like an alarm clock. Nothing is required between the setting and the awakening. If one employs a strict definition of oversight, neither procedure fits, since one is a form of foresight and the other legislative afterthought. In a more general sense, though, each influences executive activity. Apparently, sunset provisions are popular, at least for their symbolic value, in legislatures that are otherwise underequipped to perform continuous oversight.

Henderson's investigation (1970) of the oversight activities of the House Committee on Government Operations during an 18-year period (1947-1964) emphasizes both the potential and limits of structural considerations. Under an accommodating chairman, the committee avoided partisan fire. It was also rich in well-staffed autonomous subcommittees. While the committee enquired episodically into juicy cases of alleged maladministration, the resources available to the committee did not result in any substantial "continuing review of executive operations" (pp. 70-71).

A study by Kaiser (1977) of the House International Relations Committee discovered that a fairly active oversight profile resulted from favorable structural capacities such as committee prestige, a supportive chair, substantial staff resources, and a relatively high degree of subcommittee autonomy. These were activated by big-ticket issues and committee members' hostility to the politics of the presidential administration. What Kaiser found, however imprecise his measurement of oversight activity, is that Ogul's emphasis on the interaction of opportunities and inducements is generalizable to oversight on foreign policy as well as domestic policy jurisdictions. Kaiser conceptualizes a fairly wide range of activity, including individual member requests of support agencies such as the GAO and the Congressional Research Service (CRS), as part of his definition of oversight.

Johnson's study (1980) of the Select Committee on Intelligence in the House also emphasizes a combination of structural opportunities and motivating factors. Hostility toward "dirty tricks"—those attributed to Richard Nixon and to the Operations Division of the CIA—as well as the obvious publicity value of the topic created prime oversight conditions. The chair (and perhaps also the chamber) apparently provided a basis for either effective inquiry (as apparently occurred in the House) or publicity seeking (as apparently occurred in the Senate). Five personal factors were seen to be relevant to a member's involvement: interest, disapproval, stamina, knowledgeable background, and concentration of focus. While emphasizing member motivations, Johnson concludes, like Rosenthal (1981), that only a few persistent members are critical to an inquiry.

Some structural factors, however, may be less important than originally thought. Aberbach (1979), for example, finds no correlation between committees' structures (the number of subcommittees) and the amount of oversight activity they engaged in during the period of his investigation (the 91st through the 94th Congresses). On the other hand, another structural factor, the proliferation of congressional staff, does correlate with the growth of oversight activity in the U.S. Congress (p. 509). The direction implied by this correlation is unclear, however. Staff may be an excellent resource for members motivated to engage in oversight, but a large staff may itself lead to smoking out issues that attract the attention of members (see Malbin, 1980; Salisbury and Shepsle, 1981a, 1981b; Aberbach, 1982).

Some conditions thought to be of considerable importance either may be overrated or too gross as structural factors leading to oversight. Halpert (1981), for instance, tries to test the hypothesis that "partisan opposition is naturally translated into an adversary oversight relationship" (p. 480). His evidence is drawn from a content analysis of authorizing and appropriations subcommittees involved with several Office of Education programs and the OE budget. Halpert shows, at least insofar as review of past executive actions is concerned, very little change along party lines in the behavior of members despite a change in presidential party (from Johnson to Nixon). On the matter of instructing future executive actions, however, party did become relevant. On the basis of his content analysis, Halpert concludes that more oversight is stimulated by members' proprietary interests in particular programs than by their opposition. This conclusion coincides with Aberbach's notion that oversight can be stimulated for preemptive reasons, in order to head off inquiries that could be more damaging to the agency or favored programs.

Bibby (1966) focuses on committee factors which induce or suppress oversight activity. Focusing on the Senate Committee on Banking and Currency under two different chairmen and its relations with three noncabinet agencies, Bibby found little committee oversight. The reasons he stipulated are quite compatible with Ogul's factors: committee chairs uninterested in stimulating oversight, a simple committee structure, modest staffing, an essentially legislative rather than review orientation to the committee, and a relatively unattractive committee having few members of very senior stature, and most wishing they were on other committees.

Bibby's analysis is of one committee under different chairs. Ogul (1976), examining a low-prestige House committee (the Post Office and Civil Service Committee) and a prestigious subcommittee of the House Judiciary Committee, substantiates some of Bibby's points. A committee with little prestige, simple structure, few attractive issues, and an uninspired chairman tends to produce very little oversight activity. Evidence for the Judiciary subcommittee, however, is more complex. The committee was prestigious, its subcommittee chair quite active, and the issues very important and topical; yet it undertook little continuous or systematic inquiry, though a good bit of latent or informal oversight was to be had. In the same study, Ogul investigated a third unit, a special subcommittee, and his results for this unit further limit some of these generalizations. The special subcommittee had few opportunity factors operating on its behalf yet was fairly high on oversight performance.

Dodd and Schott (1979) assert an intimate relationship between congressional structures and congressional capacity for sustained and integrated oversight. The proliferation of subcommittees and the dispersal of power accompanying this process provide, in their view, weak capacities for control of the executive. Their principal contention is not that Congress pays less attention to the agencies but that piecemeal and uncoordinated oversight has little effect. Increasingly, agencies come under multiple jurisdictions; these increase the probability of review, but agencies can also play off against one another's subcommittees with claims to their program activity. Essentially agencies can often do comparative shopping for favorable subcommittee reviews and thus escape effective, coordinated control. From this perspective, oversight incidence could well be related inversely to its quality; indeed, the more efforts to produce accountability, perhaps the less likely broad accountability can be produced.

Conversion factors and individual inducements. Resources are there to be used. But what prompts their use and how? On the basis of structural factors the U.S. Congress has a legal authority to do far more than its sister legislatures in Europe, even the quasi-independent West German parliament. Authority and resources are necessary but not sufficient factors in most views. What turns them into sufficient factors?

Partly one answers this question in accordance with how broadly and informally or precisely and formally one defines oversight. Case work activity stimulates some degree of oversight, for instance. But it is typically of the latent variety (Johannes, 1979; Ogul, 1976; Elling, 1979), conducted informally and therefore narrowly—rarely going beyond the case that stimulated it. Conversely, Aberbach (1979) and Rosenthal (1981) point to factors which lead to very broad and necessarily systematic review. Aberbach sees scarcity, for example, and the concomitant growth of central program review in the executive as inducements to systematic program evaluation in the legislative branch. Similarly, Rosenthal sees a mood favoring small government and, in the abstract, limiting expenditures as a condition that could lead (and perhaps already has led) to more systematic legislative evaluation.

Moreover, in the U.S. federal system there may always be contagion effects, in which moods and legislative innovations get transmitted from the Congress to the states and occasionally the other way around. Just as the Watergate crisis led to a veritable epidemic of investigative reporting, state legislators may have seen the virtues of strengthening legislative prowess, building professional staff, and challenging the executive once Congress moved to stake out its claim.

Crisis, publicity, and corruption are strong external inducements to oversight. Such inducements provide opportunities for legislators to gain visibility at little cost. They also provide opportunities for them to register outrage or concern at particularly propitious moments.

Policy disagreements, of course, stimulate oversight activity (Ogul, 1976, pp. 22-23). In an interesting twist, Aberbach (1979) suggests that preemptive oversight can be stimulated indirectly by the prospect of opponents tearing away at an agency's programs unless friends get there first to perform cosmetic surgery.

Behind the motivational factors thus far noted, rational man lurks. Members will allocate their own limited resources of time and energy to activities that are salient to their preferential and political interests. As Ogul puts it: "A member who is indifferent to a program seldom presses for oversight" (1981, p. 328). Scher (1960, 1963) is especially explicit, from the standpoint of rational theory, about why more oversight does not occur. Among the many activities a member can spend his limited time on, sustained and nonparticularistic oversight activity offers little payoff. Scher's study of relations in the 83d Congress between the House Committee on Education and Labor and the National Labor Relations Board (NLRB) illustrates the importance of preferential and political criteria. When NLRB decisions adversely affect a member's larger political constituency (those groups with whom he is ideologically compatible or politically committed) or create aggrieved constituents, members are prompted to seek rectification.

These examples illustrate that most oversight is stimulated by particularistic or episodic situations that promise to generate favorable publicity for the overseers. Is it realistic, then, to expect oversight in circumstances that fail to provide some reward for the legislator? If not, and if oversight is conducted mostly under circumstances that maximize publicity and individual member objectives, can it be continuous and effective? That question leads us to look at the scant offerings on the impact of oversight activity.

Oversight as an Independent Variable

When at long last one asks what is the impact of oversight activity, there is remarkably little to say. The reason is astonishingly simple: little has been written on the subject, and even less investigated. We have arrived on the dark side of the moon.

Executive response to legislative monitoring reflects the powers a legislature has to influence the activities of the executive and the traditions that influence the use of those powers. In most of Europe, unlike the United States, these possibilities are relatively limited. Summarizing a series of investigations into the role of several European parliaments in influencing budgetary decisions, Coombes concludes that "none of the parliaments considered here devotes much time to control of regularity or expects to be able to achieve it acting alone. . . . Control of regularity is really a task entrusted to some organ of the executive, like the Treasury in Britain or the Ragioneria Generale in Italy" (1975, p. 371). Loewenberg and Patterson also point to differences in legislative independence and tradition, noting that the British select committees, unlike U.S. legislative committees, cannot use oversight powers to influence policy. They also note that the German parliament, because of its greater tradition of independence, can "go beyond oversight to supervision and occasional control over the implementation of policy" (1975, pp. 274-275).

The broader political culture, as suggested earlier, influences the quest for oversight and the forms it will take. By influencing the latter, it also may impact on executive response to legislative intervention. Elling (1979) points to the impact of U.S. state culture in determining whether casework activity will be drawn farther into oversight activity. Similarly, differences between national cultures—between consensus and adversarial politics and between systems of distinctively demarcated roles or of greatly overlapping ones—influence relations across executive-legislative boundaries and the forms of influence employed.

Studies by Anton (1980) and Kelman (1981) emphasize these differences in policy making and implementation; Kelman, especially, contrasts the Swedish and U.S. styles. The conflict avoidance that has dominated the Swedish scene and the rules of thumb employed to avoid generating opposition (Anton, pp. 171-174) reflect the self-discipline and internalized norm of accountability on which Friedrich (1940) thought a democratically accountable administration rested. In contrast, U.S. administrators often push their preferences to the boundaries of toleration. Legislation on many important subjects is the product of momentary opportunities rather than lengthy consultation. It is, thus, often grand in intent and thin in operational guidance. Congress, then, sternly reacts to administrative interpretations that generate strong constituent or group grievances. The Swedish system rests upon private and detailed deliberation in a consensual atmosphere, while the U.S. system is fueled by publicity and symbolic remonstration in an adversarial atmosphere. Much oversight activity in the U.S., from the evidence we have surveyed, appears to be the product of the latter conditions; in other words, it arises where publicity is to be gained or where opposition can be expressed. By contrast, the serenity of politicians' attitudes toward the Swedish administration is engendered by the prevalence of deliberation and consensus. That most American political scientists appear to believe that a lack of oversight is a "bad" itself reflects their culture, especially the notion that individuals will be power aggrandizers and will seek to maximize their own interests and preferences. Their ambitions presumably can be checked only by the attentiveness of others.

Backbench passivity, though, is increasingly rare in all Western legislatures. So, the major issue is probably not whether more oversight will be done but how it will be done. How will it affect the attitudes and behavior of political and career executives, their relations to one another and to the legislature, organically and in its working parts? Will oversight activity and the modalities through which it is undertaken alter (or perhaps reinforce) the prevailing culture and pattern of executive-legislative relations?

That is a large question, of course, and large questions beget indefinite answers, though that makes them no less worthy of being asked. The brief literature that exists on the impact of oversight only scratches a very large surface. Before discussing this literature, I draw again on Ogul's (1976) distinction between manifest and latent forms of oversight to characterize some of the key variables differentiating these two forms (Table 2). There is, of course, much overlap between the two. In the U.S. Congress at least, even most manifest forms of oversight activity are subsystemic. Nor, for example, is much oversight self-automating, though the development of oversight subcommittees in recent years has helped generate some degree of regular review.

TABLE 2

Alternative Modes of Oversight

	Latent Oversight	Manifest Oversight
Scope:	Almost Always Particularistic and Narrow Remedies	Sometimes Universalized Policy Objectives
Trigger:	Nearly Always Stimulus-Provoked	Sometimes Self-Automating
Approach:	Nearly Always Inductive	Sometimes Deductive
Nature of Inquiry:	Almost Always Individualistic	At least Subsystemic; May be, if rarely, Systemic

The more oversight forms reflect characteristics of the latent model, the more likely administrative responses will be of a similar sort, particularistic and narrow. This is illustrated in a study by Elling (1980) which indicates that while casework activities in two state legislatures provided useful feedback and a crude form of case justice, these virtues also came at the cost of establishing precedents and bending rules. Latent oversight that is case related apparently helps improve the particulars of administration by neglecting or destroying its universalistic and neutral competent norms.

A study by Brown (1961) also reveals how oversight can be generated by fortuitous factors and then influence, if narrowly, agency behavior. When public opinion polls appeared in the media, covertly financed by the State Department and claiming great public support for foreign aid, this alerted a lone member of the House to initiate personal queries and to diligently follow them up. Polite but evasive responses from department officials provoked him to transform a private inquiry into a public one. The member's skepticism and dogged persistence ultimately led the department to drop its covert financing of these polls. The case reflected the conditions under which it was brought to light. It involved a narrow quest to alter a narrow activity to conform to existing statutory prohibitions.

Johnson's (1980) examination of the House Select Committee on Intelligence reveals the impact of a more manifest form of oversight on the attitudes of the CIA director toward congressional inquiry. Before the formation of intelligence committees in each chamber, the executive typically withheld everything not specifically asked for and made it difficult to acquire that which was asked for. Until that time, of course, little had been requested. Johnson hypothesizes that the existence and relative effectiveness of investigation induced a positive and more forthcoming change of attitude on the part of CIA directors. This may be, though there are complications in drawing such a conclusion. For instance, the directors who were selected, and their publicly stated attitudes toward sharing information with the committees, may have been an ephemeral response to the times, reflecting the need to appear open and the priorities given to those appearances from within the White House. While Colby and Turner displayed more forthcoming attitudes, the subsequent director did not. To what do we attribute this? Changes in the effectiveness of the oversight performance? A lack of public saliency, and therefore congressional attention, toward the issues posed? A more secretive CIA director? Different priorities within the White House? In short, tracing the direct impact of investigative activity on executive behavior is an enormously complicated task.

The impact of latent oversight on executive behavior is normally easier to see than the impact of manifest oversight—unless, of course the latter is accompanied later by direct changes in the law. Latent oversight usually provokes discrete change, whereas manifest oversight is sometimes invoked as a more generalized form of inquiry (Anagnoson, 1978). Each form needs to be looked at from the executive side as well. How do executives respond? Frequently, Goodsell (1981) observes, case inequities derive from laws that "compress" the official's room to exercise judgment.

A larger set of questions have to do not only with the impact of oversight on executive behavior defined narrowly but also on the political system more broadly. Oversight, after all, is not just a matter of establishing the political sovereignty of the legislature; that can be established easily enough if Congress writes more definitive guidelines (and if "it" knows what "it" wants). It is, in the end, a matter of mutuality. Often researchers have looked only at what motivates legislators to engage in oversight rather than what is produced by the process. On this, a wise student of the executive side of the equation had an early word, but for all practical purposes also the latest one.

A hostile remark by a congressman in a committee hearing or . . . on the floor . . . induces tremors throughout the official world. But congressional wrath is not necessarily control, and official trepidation not necessarily conformity. The problem remains of translating undoubted congressional influence on administrative performance into intelligent ultimate control of standards of administrative excellence (White, 1945, p. 7).

Taking Stock

Executive-legislative relations in general, and oversight in particular, as areas of scholarly inquiry provoke large questions and unclear answers. With regard to oversight, especially, concepts and terminology are indefinite. Empirical work, while scarce, is growing. It largely remains, however, a scattering of singular case studies so that there are few opportunities for any of the "test" variables to vary. Moreover, measurement of the activity itself is frequently implicit or impressionistic or both. Additionally, what is at a minimum a bilateral (and really a complex multilateral) process of engagement is treated as though only one set of actors (legislators) was important to it. This is because the question most often posed is "what makes oversight occur?" Too little attention has been given to the question "what is its effect?" Or to the related question "how do we measure it?" Most startling of all, though, is that justification of inquiry into the subject of oversight, and perhaps more broadly the culture of executive-legislative relations, often is addressed only fleetingly. We are to assume the subject important, it seems, without it ever clearly being justified.

Debate in regard to the issue of the arrangement of accountability in the administrative state is an old one. Friedrich's (1940) emphasis on norms, values, and self-inhibition and Finer's (1941) on external legislative controls continue to be relevant. It would be fair to say, however, that those engaged in research and theorizing about oversight have been more persuaded by what Finer had to say than by what Friedrich had. To be blunt about it, a perusal of the literature suggests that there was a good deal more thinking about these basic issues 40 years ago than there has been in more recent times. There is, obviously, need for more research. But there is an even more pressing need for getting our concepts straight and reasons for research clearer. In recent years, we have witnessed progress on the research front. One can lay no such claim, however, for commensurable conceptual and theoretical progress.

The Watergate crisis and its aftermath seem to have stimulated not only more oversight but also more scholarly attention to the subject. A good sampling of research, however, mirrors the oversight processes it is presumably engaged in tracking. There is a lot of intimate detail, but no systematic or generally accepted criteria for conceptualizing the subject at hand and measuring it. More broadly, there is a need to think about the model of government implied by the emphasis on oversight. Lees argues here, as I have, for a "broader conceptual approach [to] differentiate between different types of oversight, and seek to develop realistic criteria for evaluating the impact on policy outputs" (1977, p. 205). And King rightly cautions that "legislatures are not governments and . . . their size, their composition, their internal organization, and their methods of operation make them ill-suited for the conduct of a wide range of public business" (1981a, p. 89). Finally, we need also to think about oversight in terms of experiences of other nations—not for the social engineering purpose of transplanting non-transplantable traditions and structures but for gaining perspective on models of relationship that can occur.

While there is no single definition of oversight, there does seem to be a dominant theoretical paradigm for its investigation, largely stemming from the work of Scher (1963) and especially of Ogul (1976). The paradigm conjoins inducements to oversight activity with opportunities for such activity and, with amendment here and there, constitutes a framework that most subsequent research has followed and tried to test. A paradigm exists, but the process itself has not been modeled because studies have usually focused intensively, though piecemeal, on a particular committee or subcommittee. Data from systematic designs over time, across chambers, and across a variety of committees and subcommittees are necessary to such an undertaking. Obviously, too, more attention must be expended on conceptualizing and measuring oversight activity—the dependent variable—in its various forms.

Oversight as dependent variable, however, is the bright side of the moon. A theoretical framework guides probes, and there have been numerous landings even if no one seems to stay for long. The dark side, nearly unprobed and certainly theoretically unmapped, is oversight as independent variable; its effects are likely to differ for its different forms. Aberbach (1979) asks, "Just what effects does oversight really have?" He poses it as the last, but I suspect not the least, in a series of questions that researchers need to address. It probably should be the first.

As a scientific problem, we need to know more about oversight. As a theoretical problem, however, we need even more to know what we want to know and why.

REFERENCES

Aberbach, Joel D. 1979. "Changes in Congressional Oversight," *American Behavioral Scientist* 22:493-515.

———. 1982. "Congress and the Agencies: Four Themes on Congressional Oversight of Policy and Administration," in Dennis Hale, ed., *The United States Congress.* Boston: Boston College Press, pp. 285-296.

Aberbach, Joel D. and Bert A. Rockman. 1977. "The Overlapping Worlds of American Federal Executives and Congressmen," *British Journal of Political Science* 7:23-47.

———. 1978. "Bureaucrats and Clientele Groups: A View from Capitol Hill," *American Journal of Political Science* 22:818-832.

Aberbach, Joel D., Robert D. Putnam, and Bert A. Rockman. 1981. *Bureaucrats and Politicians in Western Democracies.* Cambridge: Harvard University Press.

Anagnoson, J. Theodore. 1978. "What Kind of Oversight? The Case of Federal Grant Agencies' Project Selection Strategies." Delivered at the Annual Meeting of the American Political Science Association, New York.

Anton, Thomas J. 1980. *Administered Politics: Elite Political Culture in Sweden.* Boston: Martinus Nijhoff.

Ashford, Douglas E. 1982. *British Dogmatism and French Pragmatism: Central-Local Policymaking in the Welfare State.* London: George Allen & Unwin.

Beith, Alan. 1981. "Prayers Unanswered: A Jaundiced View of the Parliamentary Scrutiny of Statutory Instruments," *Parliamentary Affairs* 34:165-173.

Bibby, John F. 1966. "Committee Characteristics and Legislative Oversight of Administration," *Midwest Journal of Political Science* 10:78-98.

Blischke, Werner. 1981. "Parliamentary Staffs in the German Bundestag," *Legislative Studies Quarterly* 6:533-558.

Bond, Jon R. and Richard Fleisher. 1980. "The Limits of Presidential Popularity as a Source of Influence in the U.S. House," *Legislative Studies Quarterly* 5:69-78.

Brady, David W. 1978. "Critical Elections, Congressional Parties and Clusters of Policy Changes," *British Journal of Political Science* 8:79-99.

Brown, MacAlister. 1961. "The Demise of State Department Public Opinion Polls: A Study in Legislative Oversight," *Midwest Journal of Political Science* 5:1-17.

Bullock, Charles S. III. 1972. "House Careerists: Changing Patterns of Longevity and Attrition," *American Political Science Review* 66:1295-1300.

Campbell, Colin and George J. Szablowski. 1979. *The Superbureaucrats: Structure and Behavior in Central Agencies.* Toronto: Macmillan.

Clubb, Jerome M. and Santa A. Traugott. 1977. "Partisan Cleavage and Cohesion in the U.S. House of Representatives, 1861-1974," *Journal of Interdisciplinary History* 3:375-401.

Coombes, David. 1975. "The Role of Parliament in Budgetary Decisions: Some General Conclusions," in David Coombes, ed., *The Power of the Purse: A Symposium on the Role of European Parliaments in Budgetary Decisions.* New York: Praeger, pp. 364-390.

Cooper, Joseph and Gary Bombardier. 1968. "Presidential Leadership and Party Success," *Journal of Politics* 30:1012-1027.

Davis, Eric L. 1979a. "Legislative Liaison in the Carter Administration," *Political Science Quarterly* 94:287-301.

————. 1979b. "Legislative Reform and the Decline of Presidential Influence on Capitol Hill," *British Journal of Political Science* 9:465-479.

Dodd, Lawrence C. 1976. *Coalitions in Parliamentary Government.* Princeton: Princeton University Press.

Dodd, Lawrence C. and Richard L. Schott. 1979. *Congress and the Administrative State.* New York: Wiley.

Edwards, George C. III. 1976. "Presidential Influence in the House: Presidential Prestige as a Source of Presidential Power," *American Political Science Review* 70: 101-113.

————. 1977. "Presidential Influence in the Senate: Presidential Prestige as a Source of Presidential Power," *American Politics Quarterly* 5:481-500.

————. 1979. *Presidential Influence in Congress.* San Francisco: Freeman.

Eldersveld, Samuel J., Jan Kooiman, and Theo van der Tak. 1981. *Elite Images of Dutch Politics: Accommodation and Conflict.* Ann Arbor: University of Michigan Press.

Elling, Richard C. 1979. "The Utility of State Legislative Casework as a Means of Oversight," *Legislative Studies Quarterly* 4:353-379.

————. 1980. "State Legislative Casework and State Administrative Performance," *Administration and Society* 12:327-356.

Finer, Herman. 1941. "Administrative Responsibility in Democratic Government," *Public Administration Review* 1:335-350.

Finer, S. E. 1980. "Princes, Parliaments, and the Public Service," *Parliamentary Affairs* 33:353-372.

Fiorina, Morris P. 1977. *Congress: Keystone of the Washington Establishment.* New Haven: Yale University Press.

———. 1981. "Congressional Control of the Bureaucracy: A Mismatch of Incentives and Capabilities," in Lawrence C. Dodd and Bruce I. Oppenheimer, eds., *Congress Reconsidered.* 2d ed. Washington, DC: Congressional Quarterly Press, pp. 332-348.

Fisher, Louis. 1978. "A Political Context for Legislative Vetoes," *Political Science Quarterly* 93:241-254.

Fox, Harrison W., Jr. and Susan Webb Hammond. 1977. *Congressional Staffs: The Invisible Force in American Lawmaking.* New York: The Free Press.

Franklin, Ben A. 1982. "5 Year Old Mining Act is Still Bothering Watt," *The New York Times,* 4 August, p. A12.

Friedrich, Carl J. 1940. "Public Policy and the Nature of Administrative Responsibility," *Public Policy* 1:3-24.

Goodsell, Charles. 1981. "Looking Once Again at Human Service Bureaucracy," *Journal of Politics* 43:763-778.

Halpert, Leon. 1981. "Legislative Oversight and the Partisan Composition of Government," *Presidential Studies Quarterly* 11:479-491.

Hamm, Keith E. and Roby D. Robertson. 1981. "Factors Influencing the Adoption of New Methods of Legislative Oversight in the U.S. States," *Legislative Studies Quarterly* 6:133-150.

Harris, Joseph P. 1957. "Legislative Control of Administration: Some Comparisons of American and European Practice," *Western Political Quarterly* 10:465-467.

———. 1964. *Congressional Control of Administration.* Washington, DC: The Brookings Institution.

Heclo, Hugh. 1975. "OMB and the Presidency—The Problem of 'Neutral Competence'," *The Public Interest* 38:80-98.

———. 1978. "Issue Networks and the Executive Establishment," in Anthony King, ed., *The New American Political System.* Washington, DC: American Enterprise Institute, pp. 87-124.

———. 1981. "The Changing Presidential Office," in Arnold J. Meltsner, ed., *Politics and the Oval Office: Towards Presidential Governance.* San Francisco: Institute for Contemporary Studies, pp. 161-184.

Heclo, Hugh and Aaron Wildavsky. 1975. *The Private Government of Public Money.* Berkeley: University of California Press.

Henderson, Thomas A. 1970. *Congressional Oversight of Executive Agencies.* Gainesville: University of Florida Press.

Huntington, Samuel P. 1965. "Congressional Responses to the Twentieth Century," in David B. Truman, ed., *The Congress and America's Future.* Englewood Cliffs, NJ: Prentice-Hall, pp. 5-31.

Hyneman, Charles S. 1950. *Bureaucracy in a Democracy.* New York: Harper.

Johannes, John R. 1979. "Casework as a Technique of U.S. Congressional Oversight of the Executive," *Legislative Studies Quarterly* 4:325-351.

Johnson, Loch. 1980. "The U.S. Congress and the C.I.A.: Monitoring the Dark Side of Government," *Legislative Studies Quarterly* 5:477-499.

Jones, Charles O. 1983. "Presidential Negotiation with Congress," in Anthony King, ed., *Both Ends of the Avenue.* Washington, DC: American Enterprise Institute, pp. 96-130.

Kaiser, Fred. 1977. "Oversight of Foreign Policy: The U.S. House Committee on International Relations," *Legislative Studies Quarterly* 2:255-279.

Kelman, Steven. 1981. *Regulating America, Regulating Sweden: A Comparative Study of Occupational Safety and Health Policy*. Cambridge: M.I.T. Press.

King, Anthony. 1976. "Modes of Executive-Legislative Relations: Great Britain, France, and West Germany," *Legislative Studies Quarterly* 1:11-36.

————. 1981a. "How to Strengthen Legislatures—Assuming That We Want To," in Norman J. Ornstein, ed., *The Role of the Legislature in Western Democracies*. Washington, DC: American Enterprise Institute, pp. 77-89.

————. 1981b. "The Rise of the Career Politician in Britain—And Its Consequences," *British Journal of Political Science* 11:249-285.

Kornberg, Allan and Robert C. Frasure. 1971. "Policy Differences in British Parliamentary Parties," *American Political Science Review* 65:694-703.

Lees, John D. 1977. "Legislatures and Oversight: A Review Article on a Neglected Area of Research," *Legislative Studies Quarterly* 2:193-207.

Light, Paul C. 1981. "The President's Agenda: Notes on the Timing of Domestic Choice," *Presidential Studies Quarterly* 11:67-82.

Loewenberg, Gerhard. 1967. *Parliament in the German Political System*. Ithaca, NY: Cornell University Press.

————. 1971. "The Influence of Parliamentary Behavior on Regime Stability: Some Conceptual Clarifications," *Comparative Politics* 3:177-199.

Loewenberg, Gerhard and Samuel C. Patterson. 1979. *Comparing Legislatures*. Boston: Little, Brown.

Long, Norton E. 1952. "Bureaucracy and Constitutionalism," *American Political Science Review* 46:808-818.

Lyons, William V. and Larry W. Thomas. 1982. "Oversight in State Legislatures: Structural-Attitudinal Interaction," *American Politics Quarterly* 10:117-133.

Mackintosh, John P. 1971. "Reform of the House of Commons: The Case for Specialization," in Gerhard Loewenberg, ed., *Modern Parliaments: Change or Decline?* Chicago: Aldine-Atherton, pp. 33-63.

Mackenzie, G. Calvin. 1981. *The Politics of Presidential Appointments*. New York: The Free Press.

MacMahon, Arthur W. 1943. "Congressional Oversight of Administration: The Power of the Purse," Parts I and II, *American Political Science Review* 58:161-190, 380-414.

Malbin, Michael J. 1980. *Unelected Representatives: Congressional Staff and the Future of Representative Government*. New York: Basic Books.

Manley, John F. 1978. "Presidential Power and White House Lobbying," *Political Science Quarterly* 93:255-275.

Neustadt, Richard E. 1960. *Presidential Power: The Politics of Leadership*. New York: Wiley.

————. 1965. "Politicians and Bureaucrats," in David B. Truman, ed., *The Congress and America's Future*. Englewood-Cliffs, NJ: Prentice-Hall, pp. 102-120.

Niskanen, William C. 1971. *Bureaucracy and Representative Government*. Chicago: Aldine-Atherton.

Norton, Philip. 1980. "The Changing Face of the British House of Commons in the 1970s," *Legislative Studies Quarterly* 5:333-357.

Ogul, Morris S. 1976. *Congress Oversees the Bureaucracy: Studies in Legislative Supervision*. Pittsburgh: University of Pittsburgh Press.

————. 1981. "Congressional Oversight: Structures and Incentives," in Lawrence C. Dodd and Bruce I. Oppenheimer, eds., *Congress Reconsidered*. 2d ed. Washington, DC: Congressional Quarterly Press.

Peppers, Donald A. 1975. "'The Two Presidencies': Eight Years Later," in Aaron Wildavsky, ed., *Perspectives on the Presidency*. Boston: Little, Brown, pp. 462-471.

Peters, B. Guy. 1981. "The Problem of Bureaucratic Government," *Journal of Politics* 43:56-82.

Polsby, Nelson W. 1975. "Legislatures," in Fred I. Greenstein and Nelson W. Polsby, eds., *Handbook of Political Science*. Reading, MA: Addison-Wesley, pp. 257-317.

_____. 1978. "Presidential Cabinet Making," *Political Science Quarterly* 93:15-26.

_____. 1981. "The Washington Community, 1960-1980," in Thomas E. Mann and Norman J. Ornstein, eds., *The New Congress*. Washington, DC: American Enterprise Institute, pp. 7-31.

Powell, G. Bingham, Jr. 1982. *Contemporary Democracies: Participation, Stability, and Violence*. Cambridge, MA: Harvard University Press.

Presthus, Robert. 1974. *Elites in the Policy Process*. London: Cambridge University Press.

Ripley, Randall B. and Grace A. Franklin. 1980. *Congress, the Bureaucracy, and Public Policy*. Rev. ed. Homewood, IL: The Dorsey Press.

Robinson, Ann. 1978. *Parliament and Public Spending: The Expenditure Committee of the House of Commons, 1970-76*. London: Heinemann.

Ronge, Volker. 1974. "The Politicization of Administration in Advanced Capitalist Societies," *Political Studies* 22:86-93.

Rose, Richard. 1969. "The Variability of Party Government," *Political Studies* 17: 413-445.

Rosenthal, Alan. 1981. "Legislative Behavior and Legislative Oversight," *Legislative Studies Quarterly* 6:115-131.

Rourke, Francis E. 1979. "Bureaucratic Autonomy and the Public Interest," *American Behavioral Scientist* 22:537-546.

Salisbury, Robert H. and Kenneth A. Shepsle. 1981a. "Congressional Staff Turnover and the Ties-That-Bind," *American Political Science Review* 75:381-396.

_____. 1981b. "U.S. Congressman as Enterprise," *Legislative Studies Quarterly* 6:559-576.

Scher, Seymour. 1960. "Congressional Committee Members as Independent Agency Overseers: A Case Study," *American Political Science Review* 54:911-920.

_____. 1963. "Conditions for Legislative Control," *Journal of Politics* 25:526-551.

Schick, Allen. 1976. "Congress and the Details of Administration," *Public Administration Review* 36:516-528.

_____. 1983. "Politics Through Law: Congressional Limitations on Executive Discretion," in Anthony King, ed., *Both Ends of the Avenue*. Washington, DC: American Enterprise Institute, pp. 154-184.

Schwarz, John E. 1981. "Attempting to Assert the Commons' Power: Labour Members in the House of Commons, 1974-79," *Comparative Politics* 14:17-29.

Shull, Steven A. 1983. "Legislative Adoption of Presidents' Domestic Policy Initiatives," *Presidential Studies Quarterly* 13:551-555.

Sigelman, Lee. 1979. "A Reassessment of the Two Presidencies Thesis," *Journal of Politics* 41:1195-1205.

Spitzer, Robert J. 1983. "Presidential Policy Determinism: How Policies Frame Congressional Responses to the President's Legislative Program," *Presidential Studies Quarterly* 13:556-574.

Steiner, Jürg. 1982. "Switzerland: 'Magic Formula' Coalitions," in Eric C. Browne and John Dreijmanis, eds., *Government Coalitions in Western Democracies.* New York: Longman, pp. 315-334.

Suleiman, Ezra N. 1974. *Politics, Power and Bureaucracy in France: The Administrative Elite.* Princeton, NJ: Princeton University Press.

Walkland, S. A. 1976. "The Politics of Parliamentary Reform," *Parliamentary Affairs* 29:190-200.

White, Leonard D. 1945. "Congressional Control of the Public Service," *American Political Science Review* 39:1-11.

Wildavsky, Aaron. 1966. "The Two Presidencies," *Trans-Action* 4 (December): 7-14.

Wright, Vincent. 1974. "Politics and Administration Under the French Fifth Republic," *Political Studies* 22:44-45.

Zeidenstein, Harvey G. 1983. "Varying Relationships Between Presidents' Popularity and Their Legislative Success: A Futile Search for Patterns," *Presidential Studies Quarterly* 13:530-550.

Chapter 12

Legislative Committees, Executive Agencies, And Interest Groups

by

KEITH E. HAMM

This essay examines research on the patterns of influence among legislative committees, executive agencies, and interest groups. While the essay summarizes and synthesizes literature covering a number of political systems, it draws a substantial number of theoretical and descriptive statements from studies of legislatures whose policy-making powers are relatively strong (i.e., active or vulnerable legislatures [Mezey, 1979]) and whose committee systems are considered moderately important in the legislative process (see Lees and Shaw, 1979).

The literature review is organized around six major topics.[1] The essay first examines research on the conceptual characteristics of subgovernments, emphasizing different classificatory criteria. Second, the essay summarizes research on the effect of a commonality of interests or priorities among the interest groups, legislative committees, and executive agencies. The literature reviewed demonstrates the extent of commonality within and across different legislative bodies. The literature also describes the types of individuals who occupy the strategically placed decision-making positions within the subsystem and their effect on the influence patterns which develop. Finally, it describes the effects of variable committee recruiting processes, the overrepresentation of "interesteds" on committees, and the circulation of personnel among different parts of the subsystem.

A third body of literature describes interaction patterns among members of the triad. Emphasis is on information search patterns, communication networks, methods of communication, and role orientations. The research here deals with whether and how committee members differ from the non-members in their interaction patterns with interest groups and executive agency personnel. Researchers have also studied what techniques of communication are employed, what the shape of the communications network among members of the subsystem is, and what the consequences of this network may be.

The fourth area of research reviewed here examines exchange relationships—mutually beneficial transactions—among interest groups, agencies, and committee members. There are several major research questions here: What are the bases for, and behavioral consequences of, transactions between agencies and committees, and between interest groups and committees and secondarily between agencies and interest groups? To what extent do these exchanges differ in kind or magnitude from those which interest groups or agencies have with nonmembers? How does this exchange process vary by issue, level of support, or type of legislature?

A fifth area of the literature ascertains the unique contributions that committees, agencies, and interest groups make to the policy process. The influence of the participants is evaluated according to the stage in the policy making process, the type of committee, the type of issue, the type of environmental factors, and so on. Necessary conditions for agency or interest group impact are examined as well as the consequences of different strategic decisions.

The final section of this essay reviews the literature on appropriations politics. It summarizes research on agency-committee relationships, the impact of internal and external factors on committee budget decisions, variations in agencies' budget strategies, committee impact on agencies' substantive policy, methods of legislative control, and variations in subcommittees' supervision and control.

Subsystem Characteristics

Scholars have noted that in some political systems particular policy areas are dominated by an executive agency, legislative committees with the appropriate jurisdiction, and relevant interest groups. An early observer of this phenomenon commented that

the relationship among these men—legislators, administrators, lobbyists, scholars—who are interested in a common problem is a much more real relationship than the relationships between congressmen generally or between administrators generally (Griffith, 1939, pp. 182-183).

To describe these relationships, the researcher's lexicon came to include such terms as "whirlpools," "cozy triangles," "subgovernments," "subsystems," "iron triangles," and so on.

Researchers have traced the development and change in subgovernments (Dodd and Schott, 1979), the extent to which subgovernments predominate in various policy areas (Ripley and Franklin, 1980), and the extent to which legislators accept bureaucratic and clientele-group interaction (Aberbach and Rockman, 1978). Electoral security among congressmen is traced, in part, to the existence of many subgovernments.

In sum, the decentralization of congressional power has created numerous subgovernments that enable individual members to control policy decisions and influence elements of the bureaucracy which are of particular concern to their districts. Increased electoral security is the natural result (Fiorina, 1977, p. 67).

Research has also produced a plethora of single-policy studies, including studies of river development (Maass, 1950, 1951), Indian affairs (Freeman, 1965), civil aviation (Redford, 1960), agricultural policy (Lowi, 1973), sugar and military affairs (Cater, 1964), manpower programs (Davidson, 1975), and merchant shipping policies (Lawrence, 1966), to name only a few.

While most of these case studies are descriptive and limited to one topic and may be time bound, they provide a glimpse of the variety of interaction and influence patterns. Each functional subsystem falls somewhere on a continuum for several leading characteristics: (1) internal complexity (Davidson, 1975, p. 105); (2) functional autonomy (Davidson, 1975, pp. 105-106); (3) unity within type of participant (Redford, 1969, p. 97); and (4) cooperation or conflict among different participants (Freeman, 1965, pp. 113-114). "Internal complexity" refers to the number and variety of participants in the subsystem. Some are relatively simple, composed of a few key individuals in each sector, as are the sugar or Indian affairs subsystems; others are more complex, loosely defined systems involving numerous agencies and interest groups, as are the civil aviation, manpower, military-industrial, and maritime subgovernments. In some cases, change occurs within a policy area. For example, "the *cozy little triangles* which had come to characterize the development of energy policies had become *sloppy large hexagons*" (Jones, 1979, p. 105). Some argue that the complexity of the various subsystems in Congress has increased as a result of decentralization of power (Dodd and Schott, 1979, p. 124), and that "several committees could claim responsibility for particular bureaus, agencies, and programs" (p. 125).

"Functional autonomy" refers to the extent to which policies are formulated and implemented within the subsystem, "with scant attention from actors in other subsystems, much less the public at large" (Davidson, 1975, p. 105). As a later section of this essay indicates, researchers have shown that the autonomy of the subsystem can vary as a function of the type of policy (see Ripley and Franklin, 1980). Case study material also highlights this variation; for example, Freeman (1965) indicates that administrators in the

Bureau of Indian Affairs tried to obtain departmental or executive support, but Lawrence (1966) shows that the participants in merchant marine policy tried to "resolve problems through negotiation rather than referring them to the president or the Congress as a whole" (p. 331).

Third, most studies describe the unity among the individuals in each sector—agencies, interest groups, and committees. Some subsystems display considerable disunity. As Freeman (1965) shows in his analysis of Indian affairs, various positions are taken by the substantive committees and the appropriations subcommittees or by the clientele groups and the nonclientele groups. On the other hand, Maass's studies (1950, 1951) of river and harbor development suggested much more harmonious relations within each sector.

Finally, the patterns of cooperation or conflict among the interest groups, committees, and agencies vary across different policies within the same legislature. Thus, Maass presents a picture of a significantly cohesive subsystem, while Freeman indicates more disagreement and tension. In addition, analysis of the same policy in different legislatures uncovers dissimilar relationships. For example, Masters, Salisbury, and Elliot (1964) describe different patterns for education policy in different states, ranging from a significantly cooperative system in which no deep-seated controversies emerge to one in which uncertainty and conflict prevail. What factors account for these patterns of conflict or cooperation and subsequent patterns of influence? A major factor is the sharing of common interest among participants.

Commonality of Interests

An initial consideration of the influence patterns among committees, agencies, and interest groups may take into account the extent to which these sectors have similar perspectives or similar interests. To understand any similarities or variations in perspectives, it is necessary to know how committees recruit members, whether committees overrepresent a given interest, and whether the various sectors interchange personnel or have overlapping memberships.

Recruitment

Under what conditions do interest groups influence the recruitment of legislators to committees? On occasion, a particular group is said to have been involved in the appointment process. For example, the business lobby group was "directly influential in the appointments of chairmen and members of the committees considered of probable concern to the business group" (Garceau and Silverman, 1954, p. 673). Or we find that in Italy, a major objective of the interest group is to affect the appointment of the *relatore*, since this person can expedite or delay any bill he investigates (LaPalombara, 1964, p. 222).

One perspective on the interest group-committee recruitment linkage is provided in Buchanan's (1963) study of the California legislature during a relatively nonpartisan period. In this system of reciprocal influence, a set of interest groups provided campaign funds or endorsements to supporters during elections to office. Then, on the vote for speaker, lobby supporters would typically vote for the candidate recommended. The lobby would recommend supporters for powerful and strategic committee assignments, the supporters would request assignments strategic to the lobby, and the speaker would act upon the suggestions and requests. The speaker would refer relevant bills to committees controlled by supporters, the lobby would testify to provide "reasons" for supporters' actions, and the supporters would speak, make motions, act, and vote in support of the lobby (p. 46). However, given the lack of necessary data, it is impossible to test the relationships.

What if interest groups do not necessarily control the appointment process? Do the "interesteds" "gravitate to decision arenas in which their interests are promoted," thus providing "the fertile environment in which clientelism flourishes" (Shepsle, 1978, p. 248)?

This question has been studied by researchers who focus on either the legislator's articulated goals or his/her interests, as defined by constituency or background. In the former, the motivating force is the member's specific goals. Interviewing a new class of House members, Bullock (1976) used Fenno's (1973) typology of committee preference motives—reelection, policy making, and prestige—to determine among other things the relative importance of each goal and the extent to which each goal is associated with a particular committee. Because Congress has legislators with different goals and committees with varying degrees of attractiveness, its committees "are often unrepresentative of the chamber, not to mention the political system at large" (Davidson, 1974, p. 52).

Studies of the committee recruitment process also relate legislators' interests to actual committee assignment requests. Studies analyzing requests by Democratic members of the U.S. House focus on district and personal characteristics or federal spending in specific policy areas in each legislative district.

Rohde and Shepsle (1973) develop a social choice process involving requestors, the Committee on Committees, and leadership. Committees are found to differ in their relative attractiveness to various groups of legislators: for the five committees specifically studied, interesteds are at least twice as likely to apply for a specific committee position as are indifferents (pp. 895-896), and the Committee on Committees serves a management goal, satisfying requestor demands rather than trying to match individuals to committees on the basis of constituency characteristics (p. 900).

In a second study Shepsle (1978) concludes that the committee assignment process can be characterized as "an *interest-advocacy-accommodation syndrome* in which interests are articulated, advanced, and accommodated in a highly institutionalized . . . fashion" (p. 231). Request behavior is based on a member's interests—involving a set of constituency and personal background factors—plus a set of likelihood of assignment variables (pp. 64-68). The findings, while varying somewhat from committee to committee, indicate that "for all of the major legislative committees (plus Interior), 'interest' variables exert a strong independent effect on request likelihood" (p. 232). The effect is greatest where there is an obvious linkage between committee jurisdiction and constituency-clientele interests, and the effect is least for committees which have jurisdictions of general interest to many constituencies (p. 232). Individual Committee on Committee members, because of a series of factors, adopt an advocacy role (pp. 234-235); party leaders, "as they negotiate a new committee structure, give significant weight to the wishes of their followers" (p. 236); and the full Committee on Committees accommodates a substantial proportion of freshman committee requests (p. 237). The major consequence is that "the accommodation of interests at the stage at which members seek committee assignments is the necessary first step in the creation of enduring relationships among legislators, lobbyists and agency personnel in particular policy areas" (p. 247).

In the third study, Ray (1980c) examines whether "the pre-existing geographic distribution of federal spending dictates representatives' committee assignments" (p. 495). The major independent variables are the federal outlays in congressional districts for six spending areas. Findings indicate that most members who request a committee with jurisdiction over one of these spending areas represent districts in which federal spending in that area is higher-than-average; in addition, in multivariate analysis, "those whose constituencies have the highest levels of involvement in a spending area are most likely to request a matching committee assignment" (p. 505).

What effect can party leaders have on controlling the gravitation of interesteds to specific committees? In some legislatures their appointment power varies across different subject-matter committees. Thus, as Loewenberg shows, the fact that interest groups are overrepresented on some committees of domestic policy in the German Bundestag is "due to the influence of the interests within the parliamentary parties . . . and to the dependence of the party leaders on the subject expertise which often only the 'interested' member can supply" (1967, p. 199). Yet, these interests do not dominate a particular subject-matter committee since they are not distributed uniformly across all parties. The parliamentary parties are thought to encourage a heterogeneous membership on the committee, although "success varies with the pressure exerted by the interest groups" (p. 113).

Beth and Havard (1961) and Havard and Beth (1962), in their studies of committee stacking in the Florida legislature, note that presiding officers not only overrepresented some committees with members who agreed with their own political policies but also stacked certain committees whose jurisdiction included a specific economic interest so that the committee represented that interest (1961, p. 69). Thus, "legislators with personal or representative stakes in the interest with which the committee deals make up all or almost all of the membership" (1962, pp. 141-142).

Interest Overrepresentation

Some studies do not examine the process of appointment but instead focus on distribution of obvious interesteds on the committees and comment on possible consequences. For example, in one of the earliest studies, the relationship between a legislator's occupation and the topic of his/her committee assignment was explored in the Maryland and Pennsylvania legislatures, although no complete profile was provided (Winslow, 1931).

In one of the more complete studies, Damgaard (1977) systematically links sectoral politics to committee composition in the Danish Folketinget, a unicameral legislature, during the 1972-1973 and 1973-1974 periods. Examining the legislator's occupational position and experiences which may be related to a committee's jurisdiction, Damgaard finds that

in both sessions, and without exceptions, committee members are very frequently associated with the relevant sector of society and have related interests outside the legislative arena. . . . On the average it applies to at least one-half of the committee members whereas only one-fifth could be expected to have such affiliations by chance (1977, p. 301).

However, it is unclear whether the affiliations of the members always precede the appointment to the committee, an important causal question (1977, pp. 300-301). A diachronic analysis over two sessions lends further support to the idea of sectoral specialization. Among members who actually continue on a committee, 58 percent have sectoral affiliation, while among members leaving the committee, the figure is only 37 percent (1977, p. 303).

Scholars, whether focusing on an interest group perspective (Brown, 1956, 1957; Ehrmann, 1958) or concentrating on the legislative perspective (Williams, 1954, 1964; Harrison, 1958), have noted that certain interests were frequently overrepresented on specific committees during the Fourth French Republic due to defense of local interests, electoral considerations, advancement of personal interests, and previous experiences (Harrison, 1958, p. 174; Williams, 1954, p. 240). The overrepresentation effect was actually greater than it appeared since the *bureaux* of the committee and the *rapporteurs* were said to contain an excessive number of members representing the interested groups (Harrison, 1958, pp. 177-178). However, in the Fifth Republic, the discipline maintained by the majority in the committee, coupled with the increased size of the new committees, "made it harder than before for a few pressure-group spokesmen to win a majority by packing a meeting, or by skillful log-rolling" (Williams, 1968, p. 64).

Overrepresentation of a particular interest can be exacerbated by assigning committee members to subcommittees according to the interests of their constituency. Thus, Jones (1961, 1962) points out that Agriculture Committee members are assigned to subcommittees dealing with commodities mainly of concern to their constituencies; these representatives are then permitted to write legislation in the specialized commodity subcommittees (1962, p. 331).

Even in legislatures where the committees are not an important factor, legislators with perceived ties to major interest groups are sometimes accommodated. Thus, in the Japanese Diet, committee members are given assignments in order to perform an errand-running function for interest groups (Kim, 1975, p. 73). However, members serve on a committee for only a few years, since the leadership does not want strong ties to develop among committee members, relevant government personnel, and interest groups (p. 72).

Overlapping Membership and Circulation of Personnel

The circulation of personnel among interest groups, agency positions, committee staffs, and personal staffs is often seen as one way to increase access and interaction. Such circulation patterns have been described in studies of committee staff in the U.S. Congress (Fox and Hammond, 1977) and of *rapporteurs* in the French Senate Finance Committee (Lord, 1973, pp. 153-154). One case study indicates that interest group-committee ties expanded when a former chairperson and a staff member of a committee left congressional service and became staff consultants to lobbying groups (Haider, 1974, pp. 237-238); another case study showed that committee-agency ties expanded when the administrative assistant to the chairperson of a committee became administrator of the agency under its supervision (Vinyard, 1968).

Consequences of Variations in Commonality of Interests

Freeman's (1965) study of Indian affairs examines committees whose members overrepresented distinct sociocultural values, values which diverged from those of the agency administering the program. Here the substantive committees dealing with Indian affairs were overrepresented by legislators elected by white majorities in constituencies with Indian minorities. Freeman suggests that one can "better understand the committee's frequent tendencies to work counter to a Bureau that promoted the interests of Indian minorities in the face of objections by local whites" (p. 100).

By contrast, Maass's (1950, 1951) studies of river and harbor development indicate how commonality of interests affected policy decisions. Members of Congress from areas that traditionally had great need for flood protection, drainage, or river navigation requested positions on committees which had jurisdiction over the Corps of Engineers. Thus, the Committee on Public Works and the Corps developed a very close identity of interests (1951, p. 580). These legislators, strategically located, became honorary members of major relevant interest groups (1951, p. 46). Interest group-agency relations were also close (1951, p. 46). These relationships seemed to routinize a series of decision-making rules. The Projects Committee of the Rivers and Harbors Congress would not, as a general rule, endorse a project unless the Corps had given a favorable or noncommittal report (1951, p. 49), and the Committee on Public Works did not usually authorize any project which had not received a favorable survey report from the Corps (1951, p. 30). Moreover, the committees in charge of writing the navigation and flood control legislation blocked, even from the president, major initiatives (e.g., establishment of river valley authorities) which the Corps opposed (1950, p. 589).

Does overrepresentation have direct, significant effects on policy outcomes? Several studies hint at the effects, or try to describe them in very general terms without examining any alternative factors. Two studies very thoroughly investigate the overrepresentation phenomena. Oppenheimer (1974), using a comparative case study approach, focuses on the effects of the constituency-interests variable, rules and procedures, interest group competition, and policy type in two major policy areas—oil depletion allowance and water pollution legislation. After reviewing the linkages extensively and acknowledging that constituency ties are an important factor in the success of an interest group, he summarizes the material on overrepresentation.

When we compile all this evidence, we find that the level of constituency ties is in some way related to the industry's success on each issue. At best, however, it operates in a haphazard fashion. It is certainly not a sufficient explanatory variable for understanding the degree of industry success. But just as clearly it is not an unrelated variable (1974, p.60).

Studying one of the same policies but using a longitudinal design, Bond (1979) indicates the extent of overrepresentation of oil states on congressional tax committees and its relationship to the oil depletion allowance from 1900 to 1974. Two points raised in Bond's article are important. First, in testing for overrepresentation on a committee, other factors must be taken into account and controlled. When Bond controlled other factors (i.e., previous committee assignments for both tax committee equations and delegation size in the Ways and Means equation), he found "no evidence that oil states exhibit a greater preference for representation on the tax committees than non-oil states at any time in the legislative history of the oil depletion allowance" (p. 657). Second, the analysis of changes in the oil depletion allowance must be tested using a longitudinal design covering several years. Bond's longitudinal study revealed that changes in the legislation which increased the oil depletion allowance were not related to periods in which oil states were overrepresented on the tax committees nor to the number of key congressional leaders from oil states (p. 659). He suggests caution "about extending the subgovernment explanation to different types of committees and to different policy arenas" (p. 662).

Information, Communication, and Influence

Several scholars have investigated the interaction patterns of members of the triad. Most studies use only one political system, typically the national level of the United States, to test their hypotheses, and some analyze only one committee or the behavior of members of one committee or subcommittee. Therefore, additional research to test the various hypotheses in different legislative settings is necessary. Research conducted to date may be classified by whether it concentrates on information usage patterns, direct techniques of communication, committee hearings, role orientations, or the influence of communications.

Information Usage Patterns

Research on legislators' information usage patterns has produced numerous published studies (e.g., Porter, 1974, 1975; Robert B. Bradley, 1980; Wissel, O'Connor, and King, 1976; van Schendelen, 1976). As a specific subgroup, committee members have been analyzed to determine what their important information sources are, whether they have different information search patterns than nonmembers, and what role uncertainty plays in the type of source they consult.

To what extent do committee members or staff rely on interest groups and agency personnel for information? Maisel (1981), in his study of U.S. House members and patterns of using personal staff, found that "members rely most heavily on their own staffs in order to learn what they need to know to perform all aspects of their jobs" (pp. 258-259). The legislative assistants, in turn, rely most heavily on committee staff, also an important source for legislators, for committee work (pp. 259, 263). A greater percentage of legislators and their assistants indicate that lobbyists, rather than the administration, are more important as an information source for committee work (pp. 259, 263). Committee staff at the congressional level, and in some state legislatures, also rely heavily on executive agencies (Fox and Hammond, 1977, pp. 121-122; Balutis, 1975, p. 126).

Do committee and noncommittee members rely on different information sources? In interviews with 40 members of Congress, Scott and Hunt (1966) try to ascertain interest group activity in one field in which the legislators specialized and one in which they did not. Specialization was not always equated with membership on the appropriate committee, limiting the utility of the findings for this analysis. However, one useful finding is that members with low seniority on the committee generally attributed greater importance to organized groups than those with high seniority (p. 66).

Zwier (1979) compares the search processes for specialists (i.e., members who sit on the subcommittee initially considering a bill) and nonspecialists in the U.S. House by interviewing 50 members on one specialist bill and one nonspecialist bill. While nonspecialists tended to rely heavily on congressional sources, subcommittee members utilized external sources, such as executive branch personnel and interest groups. Confirmation of a loose subgovernment phenomena is forthcoming: "when legislators did mention the administration as a source of information, most of them referred to the department or agency that had proposed the legislation or would have responsibility for executing it" (p. 38); moreover, most of these contacts were with program people, not with those who specialize in liaison work (p. 38).

To what extent is uncertainty a critical variable motivating committee members to tap external sources of information (Francis, 1971)? Entin (1974), in his survey of House Armed Services Committee members and associated private groups, found that committee decision patterns are routinized, group norms further group communication, and the committee is relatively cohesive (p. 148). Thus, uncertainty is reduced and the need for outside information sources is minimal (p. 148). Most committee members stated that information provided by the private associations was of little consequence, and relatively few members rated the private groups as being part of their information environment (p. 147). Yet groups saw themselves as providing information which is important to the committee members (p. 148). Why the discrepancy? It appears to evolve from differing assumptions about the role of communications in the lobbying process: "groups consider themselves effective because they have been given the opportunity to present a case," while for committee members the "transfer of information serves to legitimate decisions already made" (p. 149).

Direct Techniques of Communication

How do lobbyists convey their messages to committee members? An initial assumption is that to be effective, lobbyists have to interact with legislators regularly and frequently (Zeigler and Baer, 1969, p. 146). Studies indicate that there are cross-national differences in interaction patterns, due in part to the political structure (Presthus, 1974; Von Nordheim and Taylor, 1976) and that there are cross-state differences and substantial intrastate differences in legislators' and lobbyists' perceptions as to the frequency of interaction (Zeigler and Baer, 1969).

What generalizations have been developed in this literature about the effectiveness of various techniques? In interviews, lobbyists in certain states and in Washington indicated direct communication techniques—personal presentation of viewpoints, presenting research results, and testifying at hearings—as being most effective, while indirect contacts via intermediaries are somewhat less effective and the wining and dining least useful (Porter, 1974, p. 718; Zeigler and Baer, 1969, p. 176; Milbrath, 1963, pp. 392-393). What are the conditions, variations, or qualifications associated with the direct personal approach? From interviews with legislators and lobbyists in four state legislatures, Zeigler and Baer (1969) found that in three of the four states, legislators and lobbyists believe that direct, personal communication is most effective the longer they have been engaged in either legislating or lobbying (p. 178). As to the effectiveness of various techniques, lobbyists, more than legislators, perceive personal presentation of requests to be more effective, while they perceive presentation of research results and testimony at hearings to be less effective (p. 175). Committee hearings provide for a substantial amount of interchange between legislators and lobbyists, although there is some variation among state legislatures (p. 162). Finally "communication unrelated to hearings is not important," although "it is probably best to look upon the formal hearing as a climax to a series of communications" (p. 165).

Under what conditions will lobbyists vary their behavior? Bacheller (1977) suggests that a key factor is the type of issue being considered. He hypothesizes that lobbyists dealing with group-defined, noncontroversial issues will concentrate lobbying efforts on the committee, rely on techniques that are most appropriate in committee, and interact primarily with committee staff. Lobbyists dealing with campaign-defined, controversial issues will be more oriented to floor activity, rely on techniques more appropriate for floor action, and will be more likely to approach members of Congress themselves. If lobbyists are dealing with a group-defined controversial issue, their behavior should fall somewhere between that for the other two cases just described (p. 254). Analysis of responses from 118 Washington lobbyists confirms these hypotheses. One interesting finding is that the use of committee specialized techniques, such as submitting statements or testifying before committees, does not vary by type of issue; but nonspecialized techniques, such as contacting congressmen or other interest groups, are utilized more by lobbyists dealing with campaign-related issues. In addition, "mass groups were found to rely more on letters and telegram campaigns, while nonmass groups rely on telephone and direct contact by a few influential constituents" (p. 262). Since few of the issues are campaign defined, Bacheller suggests that to study political outcomes, emphasis should be placed on ascertaining how committee decision makers are recruited and how committee decisions are made (p. 262).

Importance of Committee Hearings

One type of direct communication technique which is seen as important, at least in the United States, is testifying at the committee hearing. In fact, Herring ([1929], 1967) suggested that the new lobby concentrates its efforts on the hearing, not on entertaining or on unethical dealings behind the scenes. Rather, "it is at the hearings held by the committees of Congress that the lobbyist today performs his heavy work" (1967, pp. 71-72).

Aside from general statements as to the functions the hearings perform for the various legislative participants (e.g., Zeigler and Peak, 1972, p. 140; Truman, 1971, p. 372; Huitt, 1973, p. 108; Gross, 1953, pp. 284-308), there are analyses as to who testifies in a policy area (Cahn, 1974), case studies which focus on testimony on a particular bill (e.g., Schattschneider, 1935—see the fifth section of this literature review, on policy making), and general studies which use information from the hearing to find clusters of interest group cooperation patterns (Ross, 1970) or to determine attitudes of citizen witnesses (Van der Slik and Stenger, 1977).

From interviews with lobbyists, generalizations about the lobbyists' behavior emerge. Rather than have the lobbyist testify, the typical case has a "working member of the lobby group speak" (Milbrath, 1963, p. 231). In their four-state study of lobbyists, Zeigler and Baer (1969) note that generally the more experienced lobbyists spend more time at committee hearings than novices do (p. 170), but the more influential lobbyists do not rely upon committee hearings as much as do less influential ones (p. 171), and those scoring lower on the persuasibility index are more likely to rely on the hearings (p. 171).

Committee Members' Role Orientations

Legislative role orientations have been emphasized as one way to understand interest group access and influence (e.g., Wahlke, Buchanan, Eulau, and Ferguson, 1960; Davidson, 1969; Bell and Price, 1975). When role orientations have been applied to studying committee-interest group-agency relationships, different roles have been determined from interactions at committee hearings. Huitt (1954) is able to provide a description of the various roles (e.g., representatives of sectional interests) members assumed at a hearing on a controversial program, although no data on the distribution of roles is presented. In testing whether the committee is a fact finding agency or a participant in the political struggle, a major theoretical point is noted.

The Committee and its witnesses were made up of two loose groups of people who disagreed, not so much in their opinions upon what should be done about a known or ascertainable fact situation, as upon what the underlying facts themselves were. . . . The interest group orientation furnished the pattern of preconceptions through which the facts were screened (p. 367).

DelSesto (1980) ascertained, in systematic empirical fashion, whether members of the Joint Committee on Atomic Energy displayed different role behaviors toward different witnesses testifying at committee hearings. Using hearings from the 1973-1974 period, witnesses were categorized into one of four groups. Committee member roles were dichotomized into those which were cooperative—investigator, instrumentalist, and organizer/administrator—and those which were antagonistic—debunker of facts, procedural antagonist, and debunker of qualifications (pp. 231-232). The major finding is that the members' role behaviors varied tremendously, depending on the witnesses' affiliation. Antagonistic committee roles occurred less than 4 percent of the time toward the Atomic Energy Commission, nuclear power industry, or nuclear community witness groups, while for environmental and concerned citizens, the figure rises to 64 percent (p. 235). As DelSesto notes,

on the basis of the analysis there is strong evidence that the Committee appeared very closely aligned and cooperative with the subsystem, while appearing antagonistic and unresponsive to outside groups who brought their views before the Committee hoping for support (p. 240).

Communication and Influence Patterns

Research focusing on the frequency of communication has examined the structure of communication patterns, the importance of the receiver's orientation toward the group, and impact of such communication. Thomas (1970) analyzed the perceived frequencies of communication during an 18-month period among members of the U.S. national education policy system. Acknowledging that the existence of communication does not imply that an influence relationship exists, he still suggests that "the greater the frequency of communication between two individuals, the greater the probability that an influence relationship can develop" (p. 56). Using smallest space analysis, the sender and receiver of communication are arrayed along three dimensions—institutional affiliation, level of education toward which the person is oriented, and exclusiveness of contacts with governmental personnel (pp. 63-64). A major finding is that the principal operating agency occupies a central position in the communication network, confirming Freeman's contention that bureaus have a more influential role than do their departments in relationships with Congress (1965, p. 75). As to the role of legislative committees in this particular network,

as one would expect, the data reveal that there is frequent communication between key congressional figures such as committee and subcommittee chairmen and staff directors and bureaucrats having legislative liaison and program control functions. Congress does not, however, appear to be as effectively integrated with the operating agencies as are interest groups, but along with the agency, Congress does serve as a major point of access for the lobbies (p. 76).

The receptivity of the decision maker to the communicator is taken into account in Wolman's analysis of the national housing subsystem (1971). While access is related to frequency of communication, effective access requires that a group's views be represented within the decision-making elite (p. 67). While two different groups have the same amount of communication with decision makers, the receptivity of the individuals to the particular group's message may vary substantially. For the housing policy system during the 1960s, this differential response translates into the following:

it is the groups which in general terms supported the Johnson Administration programs which are best represented. Moreover, it is the more conservative groups rather than the more radical groups whose views were most rejected by members of the elite (pp. 68-69).

In the only published study to systematically link influence to communications, Kovenock (1973) utilized a communication audit technique to compile data on six representatives of the U.S. Congress, all members of the same "interest" subcommittee. This design was chosen intentionally to test Freeman's (1965) ideas regarding a policy subsystem (p. 449). Communication was defined as "premises transmitted from one relevant person to another" (pp. 410-411); influence occurs "when person B accepts an X-relevant premise communicated by person A regarding decision X" (pp. 410-411). Both legislator attribution and subsequent behavior tests were used for gauging influence. In terms of integration and autonomy of the policy-making subgovernment, nearly three out of four influential premises came from legislators, staffers, governmental officials, and interest groups with formal roles in the specific policy area, with these government officials and organized interest groups each contributing 15 percent of the influential premises (Table 7, p. 451). When communications by members within the subsystem are compared to communications with those outside, the closed nature of the process is apparent.

A representative with a formal J role (i.e., a J subcommittee member) was over 50 times as likely to receive an influential J premise from another individual with a J role than from a 'typical' House colleague without such a role. Our Ss received 25 times as many influential J legislative premises from J subcommittee and K committee staff personnel than from all other congressional committee and party staffers combined, eight times as many from governmental officials with formal roles in J matters than from all those without them, and nearly eight times as many from interest groups whose paramount legislative interests were in J policy than from all groups whose major interests lay in non-J policy fields (p. 451).

On the other hand, these individuals within the subsystem accounted for only a few percent of the influential communications in other policy areas (pp. 451-452).

Exchange Relationships

From one perspective, the operation of the subsystem is a series of exchange relationships. Since each sector of the subsystem can influence, to a certain degree, the goal attainment of the others, there is an incentive for exchanges to transpire which are mutually beneficial. Committee members provide interest groups with legislation suitable to their requests and influence the agency in the implementation of programs, particularly where discretion is available. Legislators provide agencies with secure and expanded budgets as well as programs they requested. From interest groups, committee members receive electoral support, policy information, research, and so on. From agencies, legislators receive an expeditious and favorable consideration of requests from their districts, programs which benefit their constituents, and implementation of laws to benefit their constituents. Finally, agencies provide favorable programs to interest groups in exchange for a supportive environment, including influence with the committee (e.g., Dodd and Schott, 1979, p. 103; Gryski, 1981, pp. 164-173; Arnold, 1979; Fiorina, 1977).

Interest Group Exchanges with Committees

In describing the exchange relationship between legislators and interest groups, researchers assume that committee members benefit most in the exchange, that they receive a disproportionate share of publicity, campaign workers, money, and so on. To what extent is this assumption accurate?

Ogul (1976), in his study of legislative oversight, analyzes the tactics utilized by the employee groups with members of the U.S. House Post Office and Civil Service Committee. The various postal employee organizations gave committee members recognition in their periodicals, invited them to speak at association meetings, provided campaign support, bought tickets to testimonial dinners, and provided transportation, theater tickets, and so on (pp. 65-73). In addition, the employee groups had a skilled, well-financed lobbying organization, testified before congressional committees, held breakfasts for congressmen, and had their members petition or write to their congressmen (pp. 74-81). What were the effects? To answer this question, knowledge of committee member priorities is useful. Few members sought a seat on this committee, and a substantial number sought a voluntary transfer from it. Members who stayed were concerned with an early rise to positions of power, with constituency interests, with high political salience for reelection campaigns, and with the pace of committee work (pp. 56-70). Given these conditions, Ogul finds that in this case the interest groups were able to affect the committee's agenda and time, its information sources, its staffing, and its behavior generally (pp. 81-85). Although no quantitative measurement is provided, Ogul feels he is able "to demonstrate that these groups have had a substantive impact on committee behavior" (p. 90).

Few studies provide such a complete analysis. Instead, the consequences of providing a single resource, usually money, are examined. Since "giving campaign contributions is easily the most publicized tactic of groups for access and influence in the political process" (Ornstein and Elder, 1978, p. 71) and since, behaviorally, there are some data to suggest that "campaign contributions do stimulate legislators toward interaction" (Zeigler and Baer, 1969, p. 190), the obvious question is whether interest groups provide a disproportionate share of their campaign resources to committee members who have jurisdiction over their legislation. Quantitative research published on this topic exists only for the U.S. Congress.

At the congressional level, no published academic study has documented a total distribution of funds to various committee members nor tried to link campaign contributions directly to committee behavior, although some descriptive information is provided on the extent of the contributions by a few groups. Thus, in discussing campaign contribution patterns for the dairy industry, the American Medical Association, the banking industry, and the maritime union's political action committees, Jacobson (1980) indicates that "they give overwhelmingly to incumbents in both parties who sit on committees that handle matters directly affecting their financial interests, although if the election is in doubt, they may contribute to both candidates" (p. 77). Yet, even for interest groups known to make substantial contributions, indications are that they "were not a major source of funds for any of the committee's members, except for the chairman" (Malbin, 1979, p. 36). An interesting, but untested, observation is that "if campaign contributions from Washington-based organizations were prohibited, the rest of what the Washington 'issue networks' do would remain untouched" (p. 37).

If "lobbying is conceived as a matter of bargaining" (Matthews, 1960, p. 190), then interest groups can be seen as being asked to provide a series of services for the legislator. In one perspective, "the lobbyist becomes, in effect, a service bureau for those congressmen already agreeing with him, rather than an agent of direct persuasion" (Bauer, Pool, and Dexter, 1963, p. 353). That legislators request these services of lobbyists at times is not disputed. Findings from certain state legislatures demonstrate the proportion of lobbyists who are called upon to offer their services (Zeigler and Baer, 1969). Even a moderate proportion of Washington's public interest groups provide information on a frequent basis (Berry, 1977, pp. 280-284). While it appears that committee members use a different information search pattern, no statistical evidence exists as to whether committee members request lobbyists to write speeches, prepare reports, answer correspondence, write legislative bills, and so forth at a different rate than do noncommittee members, and with what consequences.

Agency Exchanges with Committees: Geographic Distribution of Programs

Research in this area may be divided into that which concentrates on how agencies distribute resources and projects throughout the various parts of the country and that which examines the response by the agency to discrete requests from legislators for constituent services and information.

Do the relevant authorization and appropriations committee members influence the geographical distribution of benefits emanating from governmental agencies? Descriptive case study information is available (e.g., Murphy, 1971) and general theoretical work on the question of distribution rules exist (Buchanan and Tullock, 1962; Barry, 1965). Recent theoretical work, from a rational choice perspective, accounts for the inefficiency of pork-barrel distributive projects by focusing on the biases of democratic institutions, with emphases on the politicization of economic costs, representation by geographical districts, and the financing of projects through generalized taxation (Weingast, Shepsle, and Johnsen, 1981). However, for this review, two theories are most appropriate: a "distributive" theory, explicitly formulated by Rundquist and Ferejohn (1975), and Arnold's theory of influence (1979).

Distributive Theory. The greatest amount of empirical research has been given to testing the distributive theory, which does not apply to all policies, just "those which can be subdivided into many parts, each of which can be implemented in different areas of the country and regarding which separate choices can be made by legislative or bureaucratic decision-makers" (Rundquist and Ferejohn, 1975, p. 88). In this theory, it is assumed that members of Congress want to serve the economic interests of their constituencies. This objective is best obtained when legislators are assigned to a committee with jurisdiction over those activities which most affect their constituencies. In those legislatures in which the major decisions are made in the committee, the most important legislators will be found within the committee, and "this means that committee members who wish to withold their support for an agency's request until it is changed to include consideration for their constituencies will tend to obtain that objective" (Rundquist and Ferejohn, 1975, p. 89). Three hypotheses are presented.

1. Recruitment hypothesis: "Members from constituencies with a pecuniary interest in a particular form of govenment activity seek membership on a constituency-relevant authorizing committee or appropriations subcommittee."

2. Overrepresentation hypothesis: "When the districts of committee members are compared with those of other congressmen, the committees will be found to overrepresent constituencies with a stake in the matter."

3. Benefit hypothesis: "Relative to those of other congressmen, the constituencies of committee members benefit disproportionately from the distribution of expenditures under their jurisdiction" (p. 88).

In testing the benefit hypothesis, researchers have examined executive-oriented decisions, legislative-oriented decisions, and legislative-and-executive-oriented decisions. While the second set is most germane to this discussion, consideration of the other two provides comparison and contrast.

For a considerable number of programs, the formal authority for making distributional decisions resides with the executive agencies. Bureau and agency leaders, striving for budgetary growth and security, are thought to have strategic sensitivity "in recognizing the interests of powerful committee members and making necessary accommodations" (Freeman, 1965, p. 121). In doing so, the administrators are seen as responding to the influence of the various legislators. In most empirical studies, a legislator is perceived as being influential whenever "bureaucrats' allocational decisions reflect in some way the congressman's preferences regarding allocation" (Arnold, 1979, p. 73).

Research testing the benefit hypothesis has produced mixed findings. For the most studied sector—military-industrial subgovernment—the results have been generally negative. Goss (1972) investigated whether there was a relationship between military committee membership and excess benefits, benefits measured as numbers of military personnel, civilian personnel on military bases, and private defense plant personnel. The general conclusion is that the impact is variable, depending on the specific committee analyzed and type of employment examined. Using prime military contracts as the dependent variable, the benefit and overrepresentation hypotheses were rejected for the U.S. House, although the recruitment hypothesis was verified for the Armed Service Committee (Rundquist and Ferejohn, 1975). No support for the benefit hypothesis is forthcoming when a comparison is made of the ratio of disaggregated prime military contracts to manufacturing capability in the districts represented by members on the military committees and districts of nonmembers. Also, when the relative impact of the district's manufacturing capability and military committee representation are assessed using a regression analysis, the null hypothesis is accepted (Rundquist, 1978). Finally, using an interrupted time-series design, little support is found for the hypothesis that if states obtain representation on the congressional military committees, they will show increased military procurement expenditures; conversely, those states which lose representation on the same committee will exhibit a decreased amount of these expenditures (Rundquist and Griffith, 1976).

More positive results are found from analysis of programs which have more domestic content. Thus, in one of the first published studies of the geographical distribution of government programs, Plott (1968) analyzed how the Urban Renewal Agency allocated projects and spending throughout the United States. Using both state- and district-level data, he found support for the benefit hypothesis. At the district level, for example, "in all cases it was expected that about 37 percent of the expenditures should have occurred during the time of representation. However, about 70 percent of the expenditures took place at the time of representation" (p. 310).

Another study indicates some support for the proposition with modifications. Anagnoson (1980) examines the executive-oriented decision making of the Economic Development Administration, using a basic model consisting of two major factors: the need or eligibility of each area and political representation of that area (p. 70). Most of the variance is explained by need variables—number of eligible areas per congressional district, population, and income (p. 83). Anagnoson, however, suggests that "the distributive theory should not be abandoned, for there are significant benefits to some of those overseeing the agency" (p. 83). But the specific process in which influence is exercised is more complicated than it was initially thought to be.

Thus it is not simply a position overseeing the agency which produces benefits for influential congressmen, but the combination of position, choice on the part of the congressmen that these are the kinds of benefits he wishes to emphasize, and local initiative in producing good quality applications. It does not appear that the agency is favoring politically well-situated congressmen with easier standards of approval, and the decentralized EDA project selection process argues against this (p. 84).

Studies concentrating on programs in which the legislature (i.e., Congress) makes the major distributional decisions usually find an influential role for the committee. For example, Strom (1975) analyzed the distribution of funds relative to demand for the Environmental Protection Agency's waste treatment construction grant program. Using data gathered for the decade 1962 to 1971, Strom found that states represented on the House Public Works Committee received more funds from the grant relative to the demand than did states which did not have membership on the committee (p. 723). In addition, a series of other factors—party, delegation size on committee, and so on—appeared to affect the amount of positive policy benefits. Ferejohn (1974) analyzes the politics surrounding the geographical distribution of the rivers and harbors projects administered by the Corps of Engineers. In this discretionary program, most of the major decisions are made by Congress. His major findings are that

(1) members of the public works committees of both chambers get more new projects than nonmembers do; (2) members of the public works subcommittees get more new projects than nonmembers do; (3) appropriations subcommittee members receive better treatment than authorization committee members (by several different measures) in both chambers; (4) the committee leaders of the public works committees (subcommittees and full committee chairmen and ranking minority members) receive more favorable treatment for their state's budget requests than do nonleaders on the committees in both chambers and for both the authorization and appropriations committees; (5) within the appropriations subcommittee of both chambers, the budgets of states represented by Democrats fared better than those of states represented by Republicans (p. 234).

Results of a second study supported the benefit hypothesis at the state and district level for both the authorizing and appropriations committees, but it did not support the recruitment or overrepresentation hypotheses (Rundquist and Ferejohn, 1975, pp. 92-97).

A study of multiple programs indicates the variations which may exist within the same policy area. Reid (1980), in an analysis of five different health programs, tried to identify how variations in grant-in-aid programs—formula versus project type—may affect congressional influence, presidential influence, and state aggressiveness. Congressional influence, in this case, is defined as "where members of the authorizing and appropriations committees are able to direct greater shares of the grant-in-aid funds to their district" (p. 46). Findings reveal that formula grants are more tightly governed by programmatic criteria than are project grants (p. 48) and that the clearer the formula language, the less the impact of political factors (p. 48). As to congressional influence,

no single committee or subcommittee appears to exercise dominant influence over the distribution of health grant funds. Rather, the regression coefficients suggest that individual committees tend to specialize in the exercise of influence (pp. 48-49).

What is the cumulative effect of committee influence on the distribution of total expenditures for an agency? In general, research conducted at this level has not substantiated a benefit hypothesis. Three studies are pertinent. Ritt (1976) examines how committee and subcommittee assignments, seniority, party, and region affect the distribution of total expenditures and expenditures for six departments among congressional districts during 1972. Membership on the exclusive committees does not result in a higher comparative expenditure, except for Republicans on the Ways and Means Committee (p. 479). For Democrats, membership on the Public Works Committee and interest committees enhances the chances of obtaining additional funds (p. 479). When one controls for the nature of constituency, "the benefits appearing to accrue to committee members diminish substantially" (p. 479).

Membership on the subcommittee does not increase constituency benefits automatically (p. 481), and seniority on the committee is not predominately related to expeditures even when constituency effects are controlled. Thus, "although it is contrary to what is said about the operation of Congress, it would appear that seniority per se is simply not a significant factor in determining a congressman's ability to get dollars for his district" (p. 486).

What is the effect of committee position on incremental change in expenditures—that is, change from year to year? Ray addresses this question in three separate articles. In one study he tests whether constituencies of powerful representatives receive larger increases than those districts with less powerful congressmen (1980a, p. 12). His analysis covers seven budget areas for eight years of data, his unit of analysis the congressional district rather than the representative. This complex analysis includes variables which control for district characteristics, variables which deal with possibilities for logrolling, and eight variables which tap congressional influence rooted in institutional position. In summarizing the regression analysis, he states that "the most obvious conclusion is that there is little evidence of a consistent pattern of successful promotion rooted in institutional influence" (p. 18). Substantive committee assignment and appropriations subcommittee assignment exhibit no consistent pattern (p. 25). In terms of seniority, "the more seniority Democrats accrue on a committee with jurisdiction over a spending area, the more benefits their districts receive within that subsystem" (p. 26). For the minority party members, no such relationship emerges clearly.

In a second study, Ray (1980b) analyzes whether members of the appropriate legislative committees are able to prevent losses of existing federal activities in their district. The major finding is that "representation in a jurisdiction is no guarantee that a constituency will not suffer losses in federal activity within that jurisdiction" (p. 362). In a third article, he tries to ascertain the causal relationship between congressional position and federal spending, concluding that

it has been shown that congressmen are more likely to follow their districts' dependencies upon specific segments of federal activities than they are to create dependencies by exercising the influence resulting from their committee assignments. This is why committee positions positively correlate with the geographic distribution of federal spending (1982d, p. 690).

An Alternative Theory of Influence. A different theoretical perspective is developed by Arnold (1979) for he focuses explicitly on bureaucratic behavior. He theorizes that bureaucrats, in an attempt to provide budget security and growth, exchange benefits "in an effort to maintain and expand their supporting coalitions" (p. 207). In making strategic decisions regarding the distribution of benefits, bureaucrats take into account the general-benefit preferences among congressmen (that is, whether there is consensus, indifference, or a polarized distribution of preferences) and allocate accordingly. Extra consideration is given to committee members who have jurisdiction over the agencies' activities, since they determine the agenda for all legislative activity dealing with a program (p. 63), influence bureaucratic behavior through nonstatutory techniques not available to nonmembers (p. 63), and have a legislative veto. In addition, most committee members are potential coalition leaders (p. 66). Yet, bureaucrats' estimates of the probability that committee sanctions may be used "vary from committee to committee or from program to program" (p. 67) depending on the amount of oversight, committee members' willingness to approve budget requests, and the type of congressmen who are attracted to the committees (pp. 67-68).

Previous studies have employed the constituency or district. Noting the limitations with these studies (pp. 83-85), Arnold argues for the program decision as the appropriate unit. Thus, the military installation is the analytic unit for studying military employment (p. 102), while the program application is the unit for water and sewer grant programs (p. 139). Given the specific set of decision rules for the model cities program, Arnold is forced to adopt districts (rather than program decisions) as the analytic units in this case (p. 178).

As for the empirical analysis, Arnold indicates that congressional influence accounts for between 10 and 30 percent of the allocational decisions in these three public programs (p. 214). To what extent do committee members have an effect on this allocation process? Arnold's summary indicates the complex nature of bureaucratic decision making.

Ordinarily, bureaucrats choose to allocate disproportionate shares of benefits to members of those committees that have jurisdiction over their programs. But these extra shares do not come automatically. They accrue to members who have performed important services, who control resources the bureaucrats desire, or who threaten in some way the achievement of bureaucratic goals. Committees that merely have the potential to threaten bureaucrats' fortunes but fail to develop that potential do not ordinarily obtain extra benefits for their members (p. 207).

Agency-Committee Exchanges: Constituent Services

Additional studies have examined exchange strategies focusing on constituent needs or legislative needs. In this regard, Freeman's proposition that bureau leaders, in their attempts to influence committees, had to go through the legislative liaison specialists in the various departments (1965, p. 122) becomes appropriate. Specific research on these liaison operations has either focused on a single agency or department, such as the Agency for International Development, the Department of State, or NASA (e.g., DeGrazia, 1966;

Robinson, 1962; Murphy, 1972) or has concentrated on a comparative analysis of liaison activities in different departments (e.g., Pipe, 1966; Holtzman, 1970).

Studies of individual agencies indicate that legislative requests more often involve service functions than policy functions (Robinson, 1962, p. 159) and that agencies receive a disproportionate number of requests from committee members (e.g., Murphy, 1972, p. 202). To what extent and with what effects do agencies utilize a strategy which emphasizes constituent needs of committee members? Liaison officers in a number of departments "agreed that members of their substantive committees or appropriations subcommittees took precedence in time and attention as well as services and favors over other members of the legislative system" (Holtzman, 1970, p. 183). The element of partisanship was also an important factor in terms of offering services and favors (Holtzman, 1970, p. 184). It has been shown that members of the committees which have jurisdiction over NASA received marginally better treatment than other legislators, save for personnel referrals (Murphy, 1972, pp. 200-201).

Does the handling of constituent services have a noticeable effect on committee member behavior? No comparative quantitative study exists and those studies that have been completed vary in their assessment. Robinson (1962) argues that satisfaction is a necessary but not a sufficient condition for "establishing congressional support for Departmental policies" (p. 185). Murphy (1972) observes that NASA, in providing constituent services to members of Congress "cannot change any Congressman's basic position on issues, but it is likely to make him a bit more disposed to give NASA the benefit of the doubt" (1972, p. 202); however, he presents no data on this point. Replies from liaison personnel in domestic agencies indicate that "more positive results accrued to them and to their departments as a result of their employing a strategy of services and favors" (Holtzman, 1970, p. 188). On the other hand, Robinson (1962) collected data on legislators' satisfaction with the information provided them by the State Department and on their approval of State Department policies. For members of committees with foreign policy responsibilities, but not for nonmembers, he found a statistically significant relationship between satisfaction and approval (p. 186). Finally, what is the overall impact of the liaison activity? In one assessment, the "prevailing influences seem clearly to be factors relating to NASA's program relationship with Congress rather than influences of the legislative liaison office" (Murphy, 1972, p. 213).

Impact on Policy

This section examines the extent to which the committees, agencies, and interest groups affect policy outcomes. The influence of participants is evaluated in light of theoretical perspectives, issues selected, methodologies, and so on.

Interest Group-Committee Relationships

A considerable body of political science literature focuses on interest groups as "the fundamental units of analysis" (Hayes, 1981, p. 7). Research in this vein ranges from a general presentation of group theory (e.g., Truman, 1971) to an analysis of the impact of groups on a particular legislature (Zeller, 1937) to case studies of the impact of specific interest groups (e.g., Odegard, 1928) to studies of group impact on a single bill (e.g., Latham, 1952; Morgan, 1956).

One study meriting attention for this essay is Schattschneider's analysis (1935) of the role played by interest groups on tariff legislation. The pattern of interest group activity was characterized as being more or less sporadic, conflict as occasional, and pressure as enormously unbalanced (p. 109). Among several factors which account for this distribution of interests, two are worth noting. First, Schattschneider distinguishes between "insiders" and "outsiders" (p. 166); committee members would help the insiders by not adequately circulating committee hearings notices, so that only the most knowledgeable lobbyists would be informed and able to obtain necessary, but confidential, information (pp. 164-213). Second, the contestants operated under the norm of reciprocal noninterference, and committee members were inclined to enforce this policy, thus tending to reduce the level of conflict (p. 143).

Schattschneider's discussion of the conduct of the committee hearings indicates how process and interest identification are intertwined. Committee members permitted interest groups to choose what information to submit, did not check to see if material contained the requested information, and did not ask difficult questions of the protected interests (pp. 38-41). Communication between the members of the committee and those testifying was "rather in the style and manner of equals engaged in negotiation" (p. 43). The hearings were expedited, since "agreements may be reached speedily in a friendly proceeding in which every major premise of the petitioners is conceded in advance" (p. 44).

Since committee members had no workable criterion for determining tariff rates, they adopted a decision rule of universalization in which they sought political support for the system by "giving limited protection to all interests strong enough to furnish formidable resistance to it" (p. 85). Yet, the Committee on Ways and Means did not simply acquiesce to the demands of the industries for a specific tariff; instead, they "granted only a small percentage of the tariff increases desired" (p. 80).

An alternative perspective developed by Bauer, Pool, and Dexter (1963, 1972) on interest group impact downplays the role of "pressures." While pressure may occasionally be applied, there is no linear causal relationship analogous to fluid mechanics in which "the pressure is applied here and the results come out there" (1972, p. 455). These researchers see the relationship instead as transactional; that is, they view "all the actors in the situation as exerting continuous influence on each other" (1972, p. 457). All the actors are to some extent "in a situation of mutual influence and interdependence" (1972, p. 457). The authors try to merge the empirical-influence model from psychology with the teleological-maximizing model from economics (p. 472). Communications, in this perspective, tend to act "more as triggers than as forces" (1972, p. 467), becoming one factor in a sociopsychological system (1972, p. 470). In this communication process, lobbyists are seen as contacting and assisting those who agree with them (1972, p. 442).

In a study of the relative importance of interest groups and the executive branch and committees on policy making in the U.S. Congress, Price (1972) argues that it is erroneous to concentrate solely on the "causal" impact of external factors since there is sufficient "slack" in the system and substantial variations in behavior (pp. 310-311). Thus, in analyzing the impact of external actors, he suggests a different perspective.

Patterns of legislative influence were found which approximated the classic 'pressure group' model. But the characteristic relationship to sympathetic interest groups among legislative activists was 'entrepreneurial,' the initiatives taken were best seen not as a response to group demands but as an anticipation or projection of group demands and stimulation of their active concern (p. 322).

This is not to say that the groups have no impact, since interest group orientations are seen as constraining, stimulating, and shaping committee behavior (p. 323).

The lack of interest group impact is also to be seen in a study of the New Zealand Parliament. Using a sample of ten bills considered by the committees, Willie (1972) tries to determine the relationship between evidence presented to the committees by interest groups and the type of amendments subsequently proposed by the committees. For the ten bills studied, 106 groups and individuals, covering different levels of society, presented testimony (p. 112). Noting that all bills considered were amended and that most of the amendments had their origin in the group testimony, he comments that "this indicates both government sensitivity to the groups and the close attention paid by the groups to the legislation" (p. 111). At the same time, though, groups do not appear to assert a large amount of influence. "In fact, a considerable amount of evidence was given in vain" (p. 111).

Interest Group Importance in Agency-Committee Relationships

A different perspective on the role of interest groups focuses on their role in helping the agency attain its goals. Freeman's (1965) proposition serves to structure this literature: "A bureau leader generally finds it necessary to have at least the support of most of the bureau's employees and most of its clientele in order to assert his policy views successfully before committee members" (p. 124). The importance of clientele groups may be evaluated under two conditions: (1) when there is no clientele group involved and (2) when clientele groups oppose the bureau's position.

Several studies indicate that a mobilized constituency is crucial to the agency's development. Morrow (1968), in his study of foreign aid, comments that "the relative lack of support for a program from a structured constituency tends to encourage legislative limitations on administration discretion and subsequent executive-legislative conflict" (p. 1005).

Green and Rosenthal (1963) provide a complete analysis of the Joint Committee on Atomic Energy's sources of influence, including the importance of nonconstituency ties. The influence of the committee was extensive; it could achieve its program objectives "by persuasion, negotiation, and pressure, not through legislation" (p. 105). The committee in this case had unique statutory power (pp. 79-103), but its institutional bases of power were also extensive. First, the Atomic Energy Commission was in a "no-man's land" between the president and Congress (p. 77). Second, the members of the committee had longer continuity than those on the commission and a relatively stable and skilled staff. Third, because of its highly technical and secret subject area, the committee's position within the Congress increased and therefore the AEC's dependence on the committee increased (p. 78). Finally, "unlike most other government agencies, the AEC had no significant constituency; there were no important segments of American society with a special interest in the atomic-energy program which might serve as sources of strength or influence" (p. 75). This created a situation in which, aside from the Joint Committee on Atomic Energy and the committees dealing with appropriations, the AEC was relatively isolated from Congress (pp. 75-76). Thus, the concessions on legislation were made by the agency, not by the committee (p. 137).

What happens when the clientele group takes a position opposite that of the bureau? There are several case studies of this phenomenon and its consequences. We have already discussed Freeman's study of Indian affairs. An analogous situation occurs in the Federal grazing policy area (Foss, 1960). When administrators of the Federal grazing agency were in general agreement with the clientele group of stockmen, the administrators could serve as major lobbyists for the clientele. However, when the administrators acted contrary to the wishes of the stockmen, the administrators have been unsuccessful with the committees (p. 201). Levantrosser's (1967) analysis of the armed forces reserve also demonstrates that the agency must have the support of the major interest group. In his study of seven cases, he concludes, "whenever one of the two associations representing citizen soldiers has differed with a Department of Defense proposal Congress has sustained association objections in considering that proposal for enactment" (p. 220).

The importance of interest groups may be stated in a slightly different way: "the amount of bargaining and compromising of executive branch proposals in Congress varies inversely with the amount of bargaining and compromising that occurs between interest groups and the executive branch" (Manley, 1970, p. 356). Studying a particular committee, he finds that "the stronger the opposition (by interest groups) to Treasury proposals the more Ways and Means will tend to reject or seriously amend the proposals; the stronger the support the less likely Ways and Means will reject or amend the proposal" (pp. 359-360). Analyzing a series of Treasury proposals, Manley demonstrates some support for the hypothesis, although the similarity of committee response to majority demands does not indicate the exact extent to which the groups and individuals influenced the committee's decision (p. 362). In addition, the committee decision did not always agree with the position of the majority of groups testifying (pp. 365-366). Manley concludes that for executive agencies "on major policy initiatives some group support is probably necessary to gaining congressional approval, especially if there are groups in opposition to the proposals" (p. 374). It does not say, however, that the support must necessarily be a majority of all demands made.

What if agencies and interest groups oppose the legislation? Hamm (1980), in research on decision making in state legislative committees, addresses this question. Using two state legislatures, differentiating the lower house from the senate, and using two different sessions for one legislature, he calculated support and opposition scores for each bill by counting how many of seven significant sectors (e.g., state agencies or labor unions) testified at the committee hearing. In both the bivariate and multivariate analysis, he found that among eight independent variables (e.g., complexity of legislation) the most consistently significant factor is the extent of opposition expressed by the significant actors (p. 47).

Factors Affecting Variations in Relationships

Studies also indicate that agency-committee relationships vary with the type of policy, the stage in the policy process, the type of committee, environmental constraints, and issue characteristics. Recognizing that different types of policies have different characteristics and thus different political relationships, several scholars have developed policy typologies (Huntington, 1961; Lowi, 1964; Froman, 1968; Hayes, 1978; Salisbury, 1968; Edelman, 1960), although some difficulties have been noted with them (Froman, 1968, pp. 45-52). Ripley and Franklin (1980) analyze congressional-bureaucratic relationships using a hybrid of these typologies. The focus is basically on the impact which the subgovernment has in different policy areas, although some analysis is devoted to the outcomes of conflict among members of the subgovernment. In distributive policy and structural defense policy, where subgovernments are thought to hold sway, the ordinary relationship involves cooperation among members of the subgovernment. In each policy area, however, when conflict arises, its resolution is weighted slightly more toward the subcommittee preferences than toward bureaucratic preferences (pp. 92, 119, 185).

In regulatory policy, the conflict is thought to originate when members of the subcommittee want a variance from a regulation for favored constituents rather than when they want more stringent enforcement of the regulations (p. 124). However, in some cases "the Senators and representatives involved were more aggressive in asking for regulatory action than were the agencies themselves" (p. 152). In cases of disagreement, a compromise is likely between the initial specific measures, with the congressional position probably prevailing more often, particularly if the full Congress gets involved (p. 124). Generalizations regarding influence are difficult for other policy areas, since there is either minimal subsystem interaction or resolution of the issue at a higher level.

Price (1972), in trying to assess the influence exercised by different participants at different stages in the legislative policy process, conceptualized six separate stages of activity. He assessed the relative responsibility of certain actors—including members of the committees—on 13 major bills handled by three committees, all of which passed the U.S. Senate during the 89th Congress. He concludes that the committee dominates in the modification stage while the executive—mainly agencies and departments—are preeminent in information-gathering activities (pp. 293-294). For the other four stages, it is more difficult to assign responsibility. One function (formulation) may be shared, while another (interest aggregation) "generally takes place in different ways and under different conditions in the two arenas" (p. 295).

Fenno's (1973) analysis of committees presents a different conceptualization of the relationship between groups, agencies, and committees. His analytic scheme for comparing committees involves environmental constraints, along with member goals, as the major independent variables in explaining decision-making processes and decisions, with strategic premises or decision rules acting as intervening variables. For the purposes of this essay, a key point is that "each committee operates within a distinctive set of environmental constraints—most particularly the expectations of influential external groups" (p. xv).

Outside groups include clientele groups and members of the parent house, executive branch, or party leadership. Each committee is subject to influence from a specific policy coalition of these "outside groups." For some committees, clientele groups target the relevant agencies and spend little direct communication with the committee. For other committees, the policy coalitions may be described as "clientele-led." Fenno argues that "it is not possible to predict the characteristics of a committee's environment by knowing only its members' goals. Nor is it possible to predict the goals simply by knowing the environment" (p. 44). Thus, even though the two committees with a high percentage of legislators whose major goal is reelection are clientele led, the complexity of the policy coalition varies substantially (p. 44).

Committee decision-making autonomy is also variable: Fenno states that "the greater the relative influence of the members, the more autonomous the committee; the greater the relative influence of outside groups, the less autonomous the committee" (p. 137). Fenno concludes the analysis by suggesting that there are two "ideal types" of committees— "corporate and permeable." Permeable committees tend to be "more responsive but less influential than corporate committees" (p. 279).

Price (1978) elaborated on the impact of "environmental" factors on committee policy making. Rather than focusing on the entire committee, he analyzes factors associated with each issue. Legislators are assumed to be rational-economic persons trying to maximize chances of reelection and to ingratiate themselves with outside actors with whom the committee must deal (p. 549). Committee outputs are a function of individual initiatives (p. 549), and the analysis centers on how variations in environmental forces across a range of policy areas affect the level and content of committee output for one clientele-centered committee—Commerce—in each house from 1969 to 1974.

Summarizing the influence of perceived incentives and constraints, Price concludes that committee members, when deciding where to direct policy-making time and effort, take into account the degree of public salience and amount of conflict (p. 568). Thus, issues which have low conflict but high salience "offer the highest incentives to legislators calculating the likely consequences of initiative and involvement" (p. 569), while low-salience, high-conflict areas present the least incentive (p. 569). His analysis indicates that all policy areas are not equally closed in terms of particularistic groups and agencies, but rather "that the inclination of legislators to take their bearings from broader public policy will be dependent in large part on an issue's perceived public salience" (p. 569). It should be noted that these are perceptual variables, that they may tend to vary over time, between chambers, and so on (p. 570). Finally, the level and direction of the executive's involvement is seen as an intervening variable: committee initiative is more likely if there is executive neglect or if the executive's decisions run counter to the "expressed interests of the groups dominating the congressional landscape" (p. 572), a theme already developed.

Weingast's (1981) analysis of the political foundations of agency-clientele relationships in regulatory policy areas indicates another constellation of factors. The model of regulatory policy equilibrium, using social choice models of voting, produces a policy that "remains stable and beneficial to congressional-agency clientele as long as the relevant variables of public opinion, balance of power of interests groups, presidential initiative, and precedential legal decisions are stable" (p. 160). However, change in these variables may affect the operation of the subgovernment. These effects are demonstrated in an analysis of regulatory policy movement in three areas: deregulation of the airlines by CAB, broadcast and telephone regulation by FCC, and influence of the environmentalists on nuclear power. This analysis includes a discussion of the impact of judicial constraints, an overlooked topic in the literature (see Fiorina, 1982).

That influence of the participants can change over time is nicely illustrated by Bresnick's (1979) study of the national educational policy system. While the enactment of the Elementary and Secondary Education Act was a major executive policy initiative (Eidenberg and Morey, 1969), the revision of the act produced a different set of influences. In this case, the committees in each house, not the agencies or interest groups, tended to dominate the issues of formula allocation. Why didn't interest groups have greater effect in this institutionalized policy-making process? The issue of competing formulae was so divisive among the national interest groups, given their diverse geographical base, that "they became for the most part immobilized" (1979, p. 202). Moreover, the executive was relatively uninvolved due to recent defeats in educational policy and difficulty in mustering majority support in the Congress (1979, p. 200).

Appropriations Politics

Researchers have tended to treat relationships involving appropriations politics as a distinct subsystem (Dodd and Schott, 1979). And an identifiable body of literature surrounding this topic has developed (e.g., Huzar, 1943, 1950; MacMahon, 1943; Knapp, 1956; Wallace, 1960; Wildavsky, 1964; Sharkansky, 1965a, 1965b; Fenno, 1966; Kingdon, 1966; Knight, 1968; Kirst, 1969; Horn, 1970; Thomas and Handberg, 1974; Meier and Van Lohuizen, 1978a, 1978b; John P. Bradley, 1980).

Agency-Committee Relationships

What agency-committee factors tend to influence the committee budgetary decisions? In Huzar's (1943, 1950) study of the relationships between the military agencies and the appropriations committees, committee members are shown to concentrate on those areas "which fall within the experience, competence, and interest of the legislators" (1943, pp. 665-666). Huzar emphasizes that when committee members examine the agency witnesses, they place importance on the witnesses' personal relations, impressions, reputation in military circles, accuracy in previous statements, and so on (1943, p. 664). Thus, during the hearings, the extent to which the committees scrutinize agency proposals is a function of the confidence members have in a particular administrator (1943, p. 665).

Kingdon (1966) accounts for variation in subcommittee behavior toward four agencies under its jurisdiction. He emphasizes individual subcommittee members' policy values, particularly as they affect their perception that the agency is cuttable, and the members' recognition that the agency has something to offer their constituents or clientele groups (pp. 69-70). Given the emphasis on cutting the budget, a value is placed on information. Thus, agencies which make effective presentations, particularly by presenting quantifiable activities, may have greater influence. The extent to which an administrator conforms to a particular role enhances the committee members' confidence. The more an administrator is perceived as efficient and effective, as one who keeps the subcommittee informed about developments in the agency, spends the money for the appropriated purposes, and follows the directives of the committee, the greater the confidence the committee will have. Finally, agencies are seen as crafting their strategies "to values which they think the subcommittee considers important" (p. 75). However, Kingdon argues that "strategies can exploit advantages, but they cannot create them" (p. 77).

In the most complete treatment of the topic, Fenno (1966) conceives of the U.S. House Appropriations Committee as a political system, with identifiable, interdependent internal parts, existing in an identifiable external environment (p. xviii), engaged in adaptation, integration, and decision making (p. xviii). He ascertains observable behavior, expectations as to what should happen, and images (attitudes and perceptions) which participants hold (p. xx).

While Fenno uses these concepts to explain the committee's integration and its relationship to the House, for purposes of this review, their application to committee-agency relationships is most relevant. Thus, committee members have numerous goals (e.g., protecting the power of the purse) and view the typical agency with suspicion, "the natural suspicion which a legislative body . . . has for an executive body" (p. 317).

A major problem for Appropriations Committee members is uncertainty as to whether they have the necessary information to make appropriate budget judgments (p. 320). This adaptation problem of informed decision making is reflected in various types of committee behavior (e.g., collecting information via travel to the agency activity sites) (pp. 320-324), although constraints do not permit members to undertake a thorough technical information search. Rather, they develop strategies for sampling information at committee hearings which culminates, via an inductive process, in a general judgment of agency activity (pp. 332-340).

The typical agency has these goal expectations: that the Appropriations Committee accept the agency's base and focus on the incremental increase (p. 267), that it accept the entire agency budget request (p. 269), and that it deal with the budget requests in programmatic terms (pp. 269-271). In terms of maintenance expectations, agencies want predictability or certainty in committee relations, stability in these relations, and fair procedures (pp. 273-274).

A considerable portion of agency behavior is an attempt to adapt to a situation of uncertainty. To maintain a semblance of a stable relationship with the Appropriations Committee, the agency tends to obey reports, prepare for hearings, build confidence in the hearing, and maintain informal contacts (pp. 291-312).

In summary, Fenno suggests that the committee-agency relationships involve conflict, since the agency has program-oriented goals and the committee has economy-oversight goals (p. 348), and uncertainty, since the committee is concerned about relevant information and the agency about what the members will ask (p. 348). Attempts are made to reduce uncertainty and conflict via the methods previously discussed.

Internal and External Influences on Committee Decisions

To what extent do committee-agency relationships or external factors affect committee decisions on the budget and substantive policy? All major published empirical studies on these topics have been at the congressional level. Taking the individual bureaus as the unit of analysis and examining the U.S. House Appropriations Committee decisions for a 16-year period, Fenno (1966) argues that the extent of increase in the bureaus' appropriations from year to year is mainly a function of "the strength of the demands made in support of the bureau by people outside the committee" (p. 412). On the other hand, when examining the extent to which bureaus obtain their requests, he emphasizes factors "internal to the bureau, to the committee, and to the bureau-committee relationship" (p. 412).

However, the conclusions are not generalizable to the Senate, since those bureaus least successful in obtaining the requested amount from the

House Appropriations Committee are most successful in the Senate Finance Committee. This is due, in part, to the fact that the Finance Committee acts as an appeals court; in addition, however, the agencies with relatively low success in the House are "bureaus whose programs command an especially large degree of extra-Committee support" (p. 587).

Additional studies have focused on different bureaus, on different years, or on different combinations of bureaus and time periods (Knight, 1968; Fox, 1971; Thomas and Handberg, 1974). An interesting finding emerges from a study of the budgets of eight agencies from 1947 to 1962: "highly constituency oriented agencies (e.g., Corps, Bureau of Reclamation, and the TVA) were found to receive more generous treatment from both the House and Senate Appropriations Committees" (Thomas and Handberg, 1974, p. 184).

Meier and Van Lohuizen undertake actual measurement of group and bureau lobbying in two articles. While the dependent variable is not the committee decision, the findings are worth noting given the importance of the committee in each house in the appropriations process. In one study (1978a), they investigate the impact of interest group support, using as the unit of analysis the 20 bureaus in the Department of Agriculture, concluding that congressional budgeting behavior was responsive to strong (in the sense that many groups supported the bureau) interest group support for bureaus. On the other hand, the percentage of groups favorably testifying and the intensity of group support do not influence the budget process positively (p. 461), nor does the type of clientele support have much impact (p. 462).

In the second study (1978b), data were gathered from 1974 to 1976 for 107 major operating bureaus of the Federal Government. Using basically the same measurement process as they did in the other study, the authors correlate eight independent variables with bureau growth rate and bureau success rate. In none of the three years studied do they find a group measure positively and significantly correlated with a budget measure (p. 488). In addition, there is no support for the oft-stated relationship between interest group support or intensity and budgetary decisions—growth and success rates—for distributive agencies; in fact, the relationships are mostly negative. Regulatory agencies with strong interest group support have a slower growth rate, and budget success is unrelated to interest group involvement. For constituent agencies, there is a slight benefit from large interest group coalitions but no effect from intense groups. For redistributive policies, the impact is negative, although the few cases reduce confidence in the findings. Finally, when examining specific subcommittees, "even in a narrow substantive policy subfield with only nonregulatory bureaus, the size and intensity of interest group coalitions are unrelated to the growth and success rates of agency appropriations" (p. 492). From these findings, the authors conclude that "agencies with large and/or intense clientele support . . . fare no better in the appropriations process than agencies without such support" (p. 493).

That a subcommittee of the Appropriations Committee, along with the relevant interest groups, can affect an agency's substantive policies and programs can be seen in Knapp's study (1956) of the agricultural conservation policy. In this case, the members of the subcommittee had extensive personal experience and seniority and the Farm Bureau had a strong influence in the subcommittee between 1940 and 1945. However, in post-war years, "most of the major changes came from other sources and were often enacted over the objections of the Farm Bureau" (p. 269). This waning of influence coincided with changes in the leadership of the Farm Bureau and of the House appropriations subcommittee (p. 278). A conclusion is that "interest groups, it would appear, by no means controlled policy-making in the appropriations process, but tended to influence decisions most when an identity of interests existed between members of appropriations subcommittees and interest-group officials" (p. 279).

This lack of identity of interest can result in situations where bureau-committee cooperation prevails in the face of clientele group opposition. For example, John P. Bradley (1980) demonstrates that the Bureau of Health Insurance and the Senate Finance Committee cooperated on changes in Medicare policy, even with the various provider groups exhibiting opposition. In this case, neither of the cooperating participants exercised exclusive influence; instead, mutual interaction prevailed (p. 498).

Variations in Agencies' Budget Strategies

Research has also been conducted into the factors which account for variations in agency budgetary behavior. Sharkansky (1965a), using published records, focuses on the assertiveness of four agencies as they interact with one subcommittee of the House Appropriations Committee. He constructs a causal model to explain differences among agencies' budget strategies, although he performs no actual statistical testing. Stated simply, the revised model indicates that the pattern of influence is from the nature of the program to public support, administration support, and subcommittee support; from the perceptions, values, attitudes, or beliefs of agency administrators to the assertiveness of the agency budget strategy. Reciprocal interaction among the various supporting actors is also hypothesized (pp. 280-281). In addition, the nature of the budget strategy should be considered as a factor influencing the nature of its programs and its support (p. 281). One finding which runs counter to the model is that there is little or no support for the idea "that administrators have considered changing—or have actually changed—their basic strategies in response to the subcommittee's behavior" (p. 280).

Methods of Legislative Control

One technique by which committees can affect agency behavior is the use of nonstatutory controls. These include committee hearings, committee reports, floor debates, and informal meetings. The clearest statements of these have been forthcoming in the studies of the control exercised by the appropriations committees of the U.S. Congress. For example, MacMahon (1943) indicates, in a descriptive sense, how these activities operate, and the effect which they have. Kirst (1969) examines how nonstatutory controls are used in various departmental appropriations bills. For three of the four bills he examines, he finds that an overwhelming majority of the controls over a four year period are nonstatutory (p. 117). Bureaucrats typically comply with nonstatutory language, although Kirst suggests that noncompliance may be traced to either bureaucratic inertia (p. 68, 70) or to "administrators' determination that language will prevent implementation of crucial policy" (p. 67). Interest groups are able to influence language in nonstatutory devices, and they do not have to go through the requirements of legal enactment (p. 134). Finally, agencies and subcommittees cooperate on nonstatutory controls to affect higher level administrators (p. 135).

Horn (1970), in his study of the Senate Finance Committee, analyzes both statutory and nonstatutory controls. After analyzing one year of committee reports, he concludes that

the directives pertained mainly to the goals and emphasis of the agency activity (program), the distribution of costs among the programs and groups (budget procedure), and the administrative means to implement the activity (management) (pp. 187-188).

While bureaus and departments are often allied in trying to have the subcommittee provide specific nonstatutory language for implementation of a program, at times one may try to have language inserted which may offset the activities of the other (p. 187). Lobbyists often use the report as a way to influence not only executive departments and agencies, but also semiautonomous regulatory bodies (p. 189). Horn indicates that the members of the Committee are doubtful as to the effectiveness of the reports (pp. 191-192).

Variations in Subcommittee Supervision and Control

Sharkansky (1965b), studying one subcommittee and four agencies during the budget years 1949 to 1963, examines how a subcommittee divides its supervisory and control activities among the agencies under its jurisdiction. He suggests that the concept of "oversight" is not unidimensional but has numerous facets. Thus, subcommittee supervision may vary in the attention paid to agency operations, the thoroughness of supervision, the incisiveness of supervision, the frequency of independent investigations, control over expenditures, and control via committee reports. What accounts for the major oversight differences among the agencies? Subcommittee members

devote more than the average amount of supervisory and control efforts to agencies that spend the most money, whose requests have increased the most rapidly, and whose behavior toward the subcommittee has deviated most frequently from subcommittee desires (p. 628).

Conclusion

The major perspectives for analyzing the patterns of relationships among legislative committees, interest groups, and executive agencies are reviewed in this essay. Although numerous studies have been undertaken in recent years, major research gaps still exist.

One obvious difficulty is having only one or two research studies for a specific topic, covering only one committee or one narrow policy area. At the beginning of this article, I outlined the thesis that the subgovernments fall on a series of continua with regard to internal complexity, functional autonomy, unity, and cooperation or conflict. Most studies focus only on the relationships which occur at a specific point on the continuum, usually conforming to the characteristics of the "iron triangle." These studies are valuable. However, analysis of numerous and more complex subsystems should be undertaken. Then more complex, but more useful, generalizations can be developed.

The problem is exaccerbated by the tendency to focus on only one legislature—the U.S. Congress. While this may be useful for initial hypothesis testing, more resources should be devoted to comparative studies on cross-national or cross-state bases. For example, given the important role committees play in the Italian Parliament (See DiPalma, 1976; LaPalombara, 1964), it would appear most appropriate to investigate the relationships among the committees, interest groups, and administrative agencies. In addition, given the variation in the extent to which the committees are the major loci of decision making in state legislatures (Francis and Riddlesperger, 1982), some of the theories and hypotheses developed in a congressional setting could be tested in different contexts.

Several neglected research areas could also be studied. For example, the extent to which private interests of committee members affect their behavior should be explored. Initial research indicates that, at least for the U.S. House of Representatives, "members of standing committees have significantly higher financial holdings in the policy domain of the committee than nonmembers" (Welch and Peters, 1982, p. 554). In fact, "the proportion having substantial financial holdings, which we defined as over $10,000, is from 2½ to 50 times higher for members of relevant committees than for the Congress as a whole" (p. 552). Also, there has been an acknowledgement that, in some cases, the triangular metaphor is not accurate. Rather, there is a fourth actor—the courts—which has not been adequately taken into account (Fiorina, 1982, p. 8).

In summary, our knowledge of this area, while expanding, must be more comparative and take into account additional internal and external factors. Then, subsequent reviews may be able to present statements which have a wider applicability and have been tested in different contexts.

NOTES

I wish to acknowledge the helpful written comments of Morris Fiorina, Malcolm Jewell, and Samuel Patterson as well as suggestions by numerous participants at the Legislative Research Conference in Iowa City, Iowa, October 25-27, 1982.

1. Several decision rules were employed in writing this paper.

Preference was given to studies which develop theoretical statements or test relationships; descriptive case studies are cited typically only where they can be linked to some theoretical point.

Studies which treat either the committee, interest group, or agency or the individual committee members, lobbyists, or administrators as the unit of analysis are included.

Studies are not included if they only analyzed the relative importance of a particular subsystem in the policy formulation or policy implementation process; in addition, to be included, the study had to contain discussions of the conditions under which the various subsystem participants (e.g., interest groups) are able to affect the behavior of individuals in other parts of the subsystem (e.g., agencies or committees).

Given the emphasis on legislative studies, this essay does not concentrate on research which only examines the linkages between interest groups and administrative agencies. However, an expanded review could analyze the general patterns of interaction (e.g., Peters, 1977; Ehrmann, 1961), the extent of agency "capture" by interest groups (e.g., Bernstein, 1955; Sabatier, 1975; Culhane, 1981), interest group representation on agency committees (e.g., Christensen and Egeberg, 1979; Buksti and Johansen, 1979; Helander, 1979; Kvavik, 1975; Olsen, 1977; Leiserson, 1942), or parentela relationships (e.g., LaPalombara, 1964).

Given that the topic of oversight is being covered in another review piece, most studies in this area have not been included (e.g., Bibby, 1966; Scher, 1960, 1963; Cotter and Smith, 1957; Fiorina, 1981; Ogul, 1976; Kaiser, 1977; Johnson, 1980; Jahnige, 1968; Aberbach, 1979; Schubert, 1958; Kerr, 1965; Ethridge, 1981; Harris, 1964), although those which specifically focus on legislative control, interest groups, and agencies are analyzed.

Research which focuses on the entire legislature (e.g., city council) without discussing the committees is typically excluded.

Because of translation and acquisition difficulties, most studies not printed in English are excluded.

REFERENCES

Aberbach, Joel D. 1979. "Changes in Congressional Oversight," *American Behavioral Scientist* 22:493-515.

Aberbach, Joel D. and Bert A. Rockman. 1978. "Bureaucrats and Clientele Groups: A View from Capitol Hill," *American Journal of Political Science* 22:818-832.

Anagnoson, J. Theodore. 1980. "Politics in the Distribution of Federal Grants: The Case of the Economic Development Administration," in Barry S. Rundquist, ed., *Political Benefits: Empirical Studies of American Public Programs*. Lexington, MA: Lexington Books, pp. 61-91.

Arnold, R. Douglas. 1979. *Congress and the Bureaucracy: A Theory of Influence.* New Haven: Yale University Press.

Bacheller, John M. 1977. "Lobbyists and the Legislative Process: The Impact of Environmental Constraints," *American Political Science Review* 71:252-263.

Baer, M. A. 1974. "Legislative Lobbying: In Washington and the States," *Georgia Political Science Association Journal* 2:17-27.

Balutis, Alan P. 1975. "Legislative Staffing: A View From the States," in James J. Heaphey and Alan P. Balutis, eds., *Legislative Staffing: A Comparative Perspective*. New York: Sage Publications, pp. 106-137.

Barry, Brian. 1965. *Political Argument*. London: Routledge and Kegan Paul.

Bauer, Raymond A., Ithiel de Sola Pool, and Lewis A. Dexter. 1963. *American Business and Public Policy: The Politics of Foreign Trade.* New York: Atherton Press.

——————. 1972. *American Business and Public Policy: The Politics of Foreign Trade.* 2d ed. Chicago: Aldine-Atherton.

Bell, Charles G. and Charles M. Price. 1975. *The First Term: A Study of Legislative Socialization.* Beverly Hills, CA: Sage Publications.

Bernstein, Marver. 1955. *Regulating Business by Independent Commission.* Princeton: Princeton University Press.

Berry, Jeffrey M. 1977. *Lobbying for the People.* Princeton: Princeton University Press.

Beth, Loren P. and William C. Havard. 1961. "Committee Stacking and Political Power in Florida," *Journal of Politics* 23:157-183.

Bibby, John F. 1966. "Committee Characteristics and Legislative Oversight of Administration," *Midwest Journal of Political Science* 10:78-98.

Bond, Jon R. 1979. "Oiling the Tax Committee in Congress, 1900-1974: Subgovernment Theory, the Overrepresentation Hypothesis, and the Oil Depletion Allowance," *American Journal of Political Science* 23:651-664.

Bradley, John P. 1980. "Shaping Administrative Policy With the Aid of Congressional Oversight: The Senate Finance Committee and Medicare," *Western Political Quarterly* 33:492-501.

Bradley, Robert B. 1980. "Motivations in Legislative Information Use," *Legislative Studies Quarterly* 5:393-406.

Bresnick, David. 1979. "The Federal Educational Policy System: Enacting and Revising Title I," *Western Political Quarterly* 32:189-202.

Brown, Bernard E. 1956. "Pressure Politics in France," *Journal of Politics* 18:702-719.

——————. 1957. "Alcohol and Politics in France," *American Political Science Review* 51:976-995.

Brown, MacAlister. 1961. "The Demise of State Department Public Opinion Polls: A Study in Legislative Oversight," *Midwestern Journal of Political Science* 5:1-17.

Buchanan, James M. and Gordon Tullock. 1962. *The Calculus of Consent.* Ann Arbor: University of Michigan Press.

Buchanan, William. 1963. *Legislative Partisanship: The Deviant Case of California*. Berkeley: University of California Press.

Buksti, Jacob A. and Lars Norby Johansen. 1979. "Variations in Organizational Participation in Government: The Case of Denmark," *Scandinavian Political Studies* 2:197-220.

Bullock, Charles S. 1976. "Motivations for U.S. Congressional Committee Preferences: Freshmen of the 92nd Congress," *Legislative Studies Quarterly* 1:201-212.

Cahn, Anne H. 1974. *Congress, Military Affairs and (a Bit of) Information*. Beverly Hills, CA: Sage Publications.

Cater, Douglas. 1964. *Power in Washington*. New York: Random House.

Christensen, Tom and Morten Egeberg. 1979. "Organized Group-Government Relations in Norway: On the Structured Selection of Participants, Problems, Solutions, and Choice Opportunities," *Scandinavian Political Studies* 2:239-259.

Cohen, Bernard C. 1957. *The Political Process and Foreign Policy*. Princeton: Princeton University Press.

Cohen, Bernard C. 1959. *The Influence of Non-Governmental Groups on Foreign Policy Making*. Boston: World Peace Foundation.

Cole, Taylor. 1958. "Functional Representation in the German Federal Republic," *Midwest Journal of Political Science* 2:256-277.

Cotter, Cornelius P. and Malcolm J. Smith. 1957. "Administrative Accountability: Reporting to Congress," *Western Political Quarterly* 10:405-415.

Crane, Wilder, Jr. 1960. "A Test of the Effectiveness of Interest-Group Pressures on Legislators," *Social Science Quarterly* 41:335-340.

Culhane, Paul T. 1981. *Public Lands Politics: Interest Group Influence on the Forest Service and the Bureau of Land Management*. Baltimore: Johns Hopkins University Press, published for Resources for the Future, Inc.

Damgaard, Erik. 1977. *Folketinget under forandring. Aspekter af Folketingets udvikling, virkemade og stilling idet politiske system*. Copenhagen: Samfundsvidenskabeligt Forlag.

Davidson, Roger H. 1969. *The Role of the Congressman*. New York: Pegasus.

_____ . 1974. "Representation and Congressional Committees," *Annals of the American Academy of Political and Social Science* 411:48-62.

_____ . 1975. "Policy Making in the Manpower Subgovernment" in M.P. Smith et al., eds., *Politics in America*. New York: Random House.

_____ . 1977. "Breaking Up Those Cozy Triangles: An Impossible Dream?" in Susan Welch and John G. Peters, eds., *Legislative Reform and Public Policy*. New York: Praeger, pp. 30-53.

Dawson, Raymond H. 1962. "Congressional Innovation and Intervention in Defense Policy: Legislative Authorization of Weapons Systems," *American Political Science Review* 56:42-57.

de Grazia, Edward. 1966. "Congressional Liaison—An Inquiry into Its Meaning for Congress," in Alfred de Grazia, ed., *Congress: The First Branch*. Washington, DC: American Enterprise Institute, pp. 297-335.

DelSesto, Steven L. 1980. "Nuclear Reactor Safety and the Role of the Congressman: A Content Analysis of Congressional Hearings," *Journal of Politics* 42:227-241.

DiPalma, Giuseppe. 1976. "Institutional Rules and Legislative Outcomes in the Italian Parliament," *Legislative Studies Quarterly* 1:147-179.

Dodd, Lawrence C. and Richard L. Schott. 1979. *Congress and the Administrative State*. New York: John Wiley.

Edelman, Murray. 1960. "Symbols and Political Quiescence," *American Political Science Review* 54:695-704.

Ehrmann, Henry W. 1958. "Pressure Groups in France," *The Annals of the American Academy of Political and Social Science* 319:141-148.

_____ . 1961. "French Bureaucracy and Organized Interests," *Administrative Science Quarterly* 5:534-555.

Eidenberg, Eugene and Roy D. Morey. 1969. *An Act of Congress: The Legislative Process and the Making of Education Policy*. New York: Norton.

Entin, Kenneth. 1973. "Information Exchange in Congress: The Case of the House Armed Services Committee," *Western Political Quarterly* 26:427-439.

_____ . 1974. "Interest Group Communication with a Congressional Committee," *Policy Studies Journal* 3:147-150.

_____ . 1977. *Bureaucratic Politics and Congressional Decision Making: A Case Study*. Providence: Brown University Press.

Ethridge, Marcus E. III. 1981. "Legislative-Administrative Interaction and 'Intrusive Access': An Empirical Analysis," *Journal of Politics* 43:473-492.

Eulau, Heinz. 1964. "Lobbyists: The Wasted Profession," *Public Opinion Quarterly* 28:27-38.

Fenno, Richard F., Jr. 1966. *The Power of the Purse: Appropriations Politics in Congress*. Boston: Little, Brown.

_____ . 1969. "The House of Representatives and Federal Aid to Education," in Robert L. Peabody and Nelson W. Polsby, eds., *New Perspectives on the House of Representatives*. Chicago: Rand McNally.

_____ . 1973. *Congressmen in Committees*. Boston: Little, Brown.

Ferejohn, John A. 1974. *Pork Barrel Politics: Rivers and Harbors Legislation, 1947-1968*. Stanford: Stanford University Press.

Fiorina, Morris P. 1977. *Congress: Keystone to the Washington Establishment*. New Haven: Yale University Press.

_____ . 1981. "Congressional Control of the Bureaucracy: A Mismatch of Incentives and Capabilities," in Lawrence C. Dodd and Bruce I. Oppenheimer, eds., *Congress Reconsidered*. 2d ed. Washington, DC: Congressional Quarterly Press, pp. 332-348.

_____ . 1982. "Assorted Thoughts on the Study of Subgovernments," unpublished comments on Keith E. Hamm, "Patterns of Influence Among Committees, Agencies and Interest Groups." Delivered at the Legislative Research Conference, Iowa City, Iowa.

Foss, Phillip O. 1960. *Politics and Grass: The Administration of Grazing on the Public Domain*. Seattle: University of Washington Press.

Fox, Douglas M. 1971. "Congress and the U.S. Military Service Budgets in the Post-War Period: A Research Note," *Midwest Journal of Political Science* 15:382-393.

Fox, Harrison W. and Susan W. Hammond. 1977. *Congressional Staffs: The Invisible Force in American Lawmaking*. New York: Free Press.

Francis, Wayne L. 1971. "A Profile of Legislator Perception of Interest Group Behavior Relating to Legislative Issues in the States," *Western Political Quarterly* 24:702-712.

Francis, Wayne L. and James W. Riddlesperger. 1982. "U.S. State Legislative Committees: Structure, Procedural Efficiency, and Party Control," *Legislative Studies Quarterly* 7:453-371.

Freeman, J. Leiper. 1958. "The Bureaucracy in Pressure Politics," *The Annals of the American Academy of Political and Social Science* 319:10-19.

_____ . 1965. *The Political Process: Executive Bureau-Legislative Committee Relations*. Rev. ed. New York: Random House.

Froman, Lewis A., Jr. 1968. "The Categorization of Policy Contents," in Austin Ranney, ed., *Political Science and Public Policy.* Chicago: Markham Publishing, pp. 41-52.

Garceau, Oliver and Corinne Silverman. 1954. "A Pressure Group and the Pressured," *American Political Science Review* 49:672-691.

Gladieux, Lawrence E. and Thomas R. Wolanin. 1976. *Congress and the Colleges: The National Politics of Higher Education.* Lexington, MA: Lexington Books.

Goss, Carol F. 1972. "Military Committee Membership and Defense Related Benefits in the House of Representatives," *Western Political Quarterly* 25:215-233.

Green, Harold P. and Alan Rosenthal. 1963. *Government of the Atom: The Integration of Powers.* New York: Atherton Press.

Griffith, Ernest S. 1939. *The Impasse of Democracy.* New York: Harrison-Hilton Books.

Gross, Bertram M. 1953. *The Legislative Struggle: A Study in Social Combat.* New York: McGraw-Hill.

Gryski, Gerard S. 1981. *Bureaucratic Policy Making in a Technological Society.* Cambridge, MA: Schenkman.

Haider, Donald H. 1974. *When Governments Come to Washington: Governors, Mayors, and Intergovernmental Lobbying.* New York: The Free Press.

Hamm, Keith E. 1980. "U.S. State Legislative Committee Decisions: Similar Results in Different Settings," *Legislative Studies Quarterly* 5:31-54.

Harris, Joseph P. 1964. *Congressional Congress of Administration.* Washington, DC: Brookings Institution.

Harrison, M. 1958. "The Composition of the Committees of the French National Assembly," *Parliamentary Affairs* 11:172-179.

Havard, William C. and Loren P. Beth. 1962. *The Politics of Mis-Representation: Rural-Urban Conflict in the Florida Legislature.* Baton Rouge: Louisiana State University Press.

Hayes, Michael T. 1978. "The Semi-Sovereign Pressure Groups: A Critique of Current Theory and An Alternative Typology," *Journal of Politics* 40:134-161.

————. 1979. "Interest Groups and Congress: Toward a Transactional Theory," *The Congressional System: Notes and Readings.* 2d ed. North Scituate, MA: Duxbury Press, pp. 252-273.

————. 1981. *Lobbyists and Legislators: A Theory of Political Markets.* New Brunswick, NJ: Rutgers University Press.

Helander, Voitto. 1979. "Interest Representation in the Finnish Committee System in the Post-War Era," *Scandinavian Political Studies* 2:221-238.

Herring, E. Pendleton. [1929], 1967. *Group Representation Before Congress.* New York: Russell and Russell.

————. 1933. "Special Interests and the Interstate Commerce Commission, I," *American Political Science Review* 27:738-751.

————. 1933. "Special Interests and the Interstate Commerce Commission, II," *American Political Science Review* 27:899-917.

Holtzman, Abraham. 1970. *Legislative Liaison: Executive Leadership in Congress.* Chicago: Rand McNally.

Horn, Stephen. 1970. *Unused Power: The Work of the Senate Committee on Appropriations.* Washington, DC: Brookings Institution.

Huitt, R.K. 1954. "The Congressional Committee: A Case Study," *American Political Science Review* 48:340-365.

————. 1973. "The Internal Distribution of Influence: The Senate," in David B. Truman, ed., *The Congress and America's Future.* Englewood Cliffs, NJ: Prentice-Hall, pp. 91-117.

Huntington, Samuel P. 1961. *The Common Defense*. New York: Columbia University Press.

Huzar, Elias. 1943. "Congress and the Army: Appropriations," *American Political Science Review* 37:661-676.

———. 1950. *The Purse and the Sword: Control of the Army by Congress Through Military Appropriations, 1933-1950*. Ithaca, NY: Cornell University Press.

Jacobson, Gary C. 1980. *Money in Congressional Elections*. New Haven: Yale University Press.

Jahnige, Thomas P. 1968. "Congressional Committee System and the Oversight Process: Congress and NASA," *Western Political Quarterly* 21:227-239.

Johnson, Loch. 1980. "The U.S. Congress and the CIA: Monitoring the Dark Side of Government," *Legislative Studies Quarterly* 5:477-499.

Jones, Charles O. 1961. "Representation in Congress: The Case of the House Agriculture Committee," *American Political Science Review* 55:358-367.

———. 1962. "The Role of Congressional Subcommittees," *Midwest Journal of Political Science* 6:327-344.

———. 1979. "American Politics and the Organization of Energy Decision Making," *Annual Review of Energy* 4:99-121.

Kaiser, Fred. 1977. "Oversight of Foreign Policy: The U.S. House Committee on Foreign Relations," *Legislative Studies Quarterly* 2:255-279.

Kerr, James R. 1965. "Congress and Space: Overview or Oversight?" *Public Administration Review* 25:185-192.

Kim, Young C. 1975. "The Committee System in the Japanese Diet: Recruitment, Orientation, and Behavior," in G.R. Boynton and Chong Lim Kim, eds., *Legislative Systems in Developing Countries*. Durham, NC: Duke University Press, pp. 69-85.

Kingdon, John W. 1966. "A House Appropriations Subcommittee: Influence on Budgetary Decisions," *Social Science Quarterly* 47:68-78.

Kirst, Michael W. 1969. *Government Without Passing Laws: Congress' Non-Statutory Techniques of Appropriations Control*. Chapel Hill: University of North Carolina Press.

Knapp, David C. 1956. "Congressional Control of Agricultural Conservation Policy: A Case Study of the Appropriations Process," *Political Science Quarterly* 71:257-281.

Knight, Jonathan. 1968. "The State Department Budget, 1933-1965: A Research Note," *Midwest Journal of Political Science* 12:587-598.

Kovenock, David M. 1973. "Influence in the U.S. House of Representatives: A Statistical Analysis of Communciations," *American Politics Quarterly* 1:407-464.

Kvavik, Robert. 1975. *Interest Groups in Norwegian Politics*. Oslo: Universitetsforlaget.

Lane, Edgar. 1954. "Interest Groups and Bureaucracy," *The Annals of the American Academy of Political and Social Science* 292:104-110.

LaPalombara, Joseph G. 1960. "The Utility and Limitations of Interest Group Theory in Non-American Field Stations," *Journal of Politics* 22:29-49.

———. 1964. *Interest Groups in Italian Politics*. Princeton: Princeton University Press.

Latham, Earl. 1952. *The Group Basis of Politics: A Study of Point Basing Legislation*. Ithaca, NY: Cornell University Press.

Lawrence, Samuel A. 1966. *United States Merchant Shipping Policies and Politics*. Washington, DC: Brookings Institution.

Lees, John D. and Malcolm Shaw, eds. 1979. *Committees in Legislatures: A Comparative Perspective*. Durham, NC: Duke University Press.

Leiserson, Avery. 1942. *Administrative Regulation: A Study in Representation of Interests.* Chicago: University of Chicago Press.

Levantrosser, William F. 1967. *Congress and the Citizen-Soldier: Legislative Policy-Making for the Federal Armed Forces Reserve.* Columbus: Ohio State University Press.

Liske, Craig and Barry S. Rundquist. 1974. *The Politics of Weapons Procurement: The Role of Congress.* Denver: University of Colorado Press.

Loewenberg, Gerhard. 1967. *Parliament in the German Political System.* Ithaca, NY: Cornell University Press.

Lord, Guy. 1973. *The French Budgetary Process.* Berkeley: University of California Press.

Lowi, Theodore J. 1964. "American Business, Public Policy, Case Studies and Political Theory," *World Politics* 16:677-715.

————. 1967. "The Public Philosophy: Interest-Group Liberalism," *American Political Science Review* 61:5-24.

————. 1969. *The End of Liberalism.* New York: Norton.

————. 1972. "Four Systems of Policy, Politics, and Choice," *Public Administration Review* 32:298-310.

————. 1973. "How the Farmers Get What They Want," in Theodore J. Lowi and Randall B. Ripley, eds., *Legislative Politics, U.S.A.* 3d ed. Boston: Little, Brown, pp. 184-191.

Maass, Arthur A. 1950. "Congress and Water Resources," *American Political Science Review* 44:576-593.

————. 1951. *Muddy Waters.* Cambridge: Harvard University Press.

MacMahon, Arthur W. 1943. "Congressional Oversight of Administration: The Power of the Purse," *Political Science Quarterly* 58:161-190, 380-414.

Maisel, Louis Sandy. 1981. "Congressional Information Sources," in Joseph Cooper and G. Calvin MacKenzie, eds., *The House at Work.* Austin: University of Texas Press, pp. 247-274.

Malbin, Michael J. 1979. "Campaign Financing and the 'Special Interests'," *The Public Interest* 56:21-42.

Manley, John F. 1968. "Congressional Staff and Public Policy Making: The Joint Committee on Internal Revenue Taxation," *Journal of Politics* 30:1046-1067.

————. 1970. *The Politics of Finance: The House Ways and Means Committee.* Boston: Little, Brown.

Masters, Nicolas A. 1961. "House Committee Assignments," *American Political Science Review* 55:345-357.

Masters, Nicolas A., Robert H. Salisbury, and Thomas H. Eliot. 1964. *State Politics and the Public Schools: An Exploratory Analysis.* New York: Knopf.

Matthews, Donald R. 1960. *U.S. Senators and Their World.* Chapel Hill: University of North Carolina Press.

Meier, Kenneth J. and J.R. Van Lohuizen. 1978a. "Bureaus, Clients and Congress," *Administration and Society* 9:447-466.

————. 1978b. "Interest Groups in the Appropriations Process: The 'Wasted Profession' Revisited," *Social Science Quarterly* 59:482-495.

Mezey, Michael. 1979. *Comparative Legislatures.* Durham, NC: Duke University Press.

Milbrath, Lester W. 1963. *The Washington Lobbyists.* Chicago: Rand McNally.

————. 1967. "Interest Groups and Foreign Policy," in James Rosenau, ed., *Domestic Sources of Foreign Policy.* New York: The Free Press, pp. 231-261.

Mitchell, Douglas E. 1981. *Shaping Legislative Decisions: Education Policy and the Social Sciences.* Lexington, MA: Lexington Books.

Moran, Mark J. and Barry R. Weingast. 1982. "Congress as the Source of Regulatory Decisions: The Case of the Federal Trade Commission," *American Economics Association Papers and Proceedings* 72:109-113.

Morgan, Robert J. 1956. "Pressure Politics and Resources Administration," *Journal of Politics* 18:39-60.

Morrow, William L. 1968. "Legislative Control of Administrative Discretion: The Case of Congress and Foreign Aid," *Journal of Politics* 30:985-1011.

Murphy, Thomas P. 1971. *Science, Geopolitics, and Federal Spending*. Lexington, MA: Heath, Lexington Books.

————. 1972. "Congressional Liaison: The NASA Case," *Western Political Quarterly* 25:192-214.

Nelson, Garrison. 1974. "Assessing the Congressional Committee System: Contributions from a Comparative Perspective," *The Annals of the American Academy of Political and Social Science* 411:120-132.

Odegard, Peter H. 1928. *Pressure Politics: The Story of the Anti-Saloon League*. New York: Columbia University Press.

Ogul, Morris. 1976. *Congress Oversees the Bureaucracy: Studies in Legislative Supervision*. Pittsburgh: University of Pittsburgh Press.

Olsen, Marvin E. 1977. "Influence Linkages Between Interest Organizations and the Government in Sweden," *Journal of Political and Military Sociology* 5:35-51.

Oppenheimer, Bruce Ian. 1974. *Oil and the Congressional Process: The Limits of Symbolic Politics*. Lexington, MA: Heath, Lexington Books.

Ornstein, Norman J. and Shirley Elder. 1978. *Interest Groups, Lobbying and Policy-making.* Washington, DC: Congressional Quarterly Press.

Peters, B. Guy. 1977. "Insiders and Outsiders: The Politics of Pressure Group Influence on Bureaucracy," *Administration and Society* 9:191-218.

Pipe, G. Russell. 1966. "Congressional Liaison: The Executive Branch Consolidates Its Relations with Congress," *Public Administration Review* 26:14-24.

Plott, Charles R. 1968. "Some Organizational Influences on Urban Renewal Decisions," *American Econometric Review* 58:306-321.

Polsby, Nelson W. 1975. "Legislatures," in Fred I. Greenstein and Nelson W. Polsby, eds., *Government Institutions and Process, Handbook of Political Science*. Vol. 5. Reading, MA: Addison-Wesley, pp. 257-319.

Porter, H. Owen. 1974. "Legislative Experts and Outsiders: The Two-Step Flow of Communication," *Journal of Politics* 36:703-730.

————. 1975. "Legislative Information Needs and Staff Resources in the American States," in James Heaphey and Alan Balutis, eds., *Legislative Staffing: A Comparative Perspective*. New York: Halstead, pp. 39-59.

Presthus, Robert. 1971. "Interest Groups and the Canadian Parliament: Activities, Interaction, Legitimacy, and Influence," *Canadian Political Science* 4:444-460.

————. 1974. "Interest Group Lobbying: Canada and the United States," *The Annals of the American Academy of Political and Social Science* 413:44-57.

Price, David E. 1971. "Professionals and 'Entrepreneurs': Staff Orientations and Policy Making on Three Senate Committees," *Journal of Politics* 33:316-336.

————. 1972. *Who Makes the Laws?* Cambridge, MA: Schenkman.

————. 1978. "Policy Making in Congressional Committees: The Impact of 'Environmental' Factors," *American Political Science Review* 72:548-574.

————. 1979. *Policymaking in Congressional Committees: The Impact of "Environmental" Factors*. Tucson: University of Arizona Press.

————. 1981. "Congressional Committees in the Policy Process," in Lawrence C. Dodd and Bruce I. Oppenheimer, eds., *Congress Reconsidered*. 2d ed. Washington, DC: Congressional Quarterly Press, pp. 156-185.

Ray, Bruce A. 1980a. "Congressional Promotion of District Interests: Does Power on the Hill Really Make a Difference?" in Barry S. Rundquist, ed., *Political Benefits: Empirical Studies of American Public Programs*. Lexington, MA: Heath, Lexington Books, pp. 1-36.

————. 1980b. "Congressional Losers in the U.S. Spending Process," *Legislative Studies Quarterly* 5:359-372.

————. 1980c. "Federal Spending and the Selection of Committee Assignments in the U.S. House of Representatives," *American Journal of Political Science* 24:495-510.

————. 1982. "Causation in the Relationship Between Congressional Position and Federal Spending," *Polity* 14:676-690.

Redford, Emmette S. 1960. "Case Analysis of Congressional Activity: Civil Aviation 1957-1958," *Journal of Politics* 22:228-258.

————. 1969. *Democracy in the Administrative State*. New York: Oxford University Press.

Reid, J. Norman. 1980. "Politics, Program Administration and the Distribution of Grant-In-Aid: A Theory and a Test," in Barry S. Rundquist, ed., *Political Benefits: Empirical Studies of American Public Programs*. Lexington, MA: Lexington Books, pp. 37-60.

Rhode, William E. 1959. *Committee Clearance of Administrative Decisions*. East Lansing: Bureau of Social and Political Research, Michigan State University.

Riggs, Fred W. 1950. *Pressures on Congress: A Study of the Repeal of Chinese Exclusion*. New York: Columbia University, Kings Crown Press.

Ripley, Randall B. and Grace A. Franklin. 1980. *Congress, Bureaucracy and Public Policy*. Rev. ed. Homewood, IL: Dorsey Press.

Ritt, Leonard. 1976. "Committee Position, Seniority, and the Distribution of Governmental Expenditures," *Public Policy* 24:463-489.

Robinson, James A. 1962. *Congress and Foreign Policy-Making: A Study in Legislative Influence and Initiative*. Homewood, IL: Dorsey Press.

Rohde, David W. and Kenneth A. Shepsle. 1973. "Democratic Committee Assignments in the House of Representatives: Strategic Aspects of a Social Choice Process," *American Political Science Review* 67:889-905.

Ross, Robert L. 1970. "Relations Among National Interest Groups," *Journal of Politics* 32:96-114.

Rundquist, Barry S. 1978. "On Testing a Military Industrial Complex Theory," *American Political Quarterly* 6:29-54.

————. 1980. "On the Theory of the Political Benefits in American Public Programs," in Barry S. Rundquist, ed., *Political Benefits: Empirical Studies of American Public Programs*. Lexington, MA: Lexington Books, pp. 229-254.

Rundquist, Barry S. and John A. Ferejohn. 1975. "Observations on a Distributive Theory of Policy Making," in Craig Liske, William Loehr, and John McCarrant, eds., *Comparative Public Policy*. New York: John Wiley, pp. 87-108.

Rundquist, Barry S. and David E. Griffith. 1976. "An Interrupted Time Series Test of the Distributive Theory of Military Policy Making," *Western Political Quarterly* 29:620-626.

Sabatier, Paul. 1975. "Social Movements and Regulatory Agencies: Toward a More Adequate—Less Pessimistic—Theory of 'Clientele Capture'," *Policy Sciences* 6:301-342.

Salisbury, Robert H. 1968. "The Analysis of Public Policy: A Search for Theories and Roles," in Austin Ranney, ed., *Political Science and Public Policy*. Chicago: Markham Publishing, pp. 151-175.

Schattschneider, E.E. 1935. *Politics, Pressures and the Tariff*. New York: Prentice-Hall.

Scher, Seymour. 1960. "Congressional Committee Members as Independent Agency Overseers: A Case Study," *American Political Science Review* 54:911-920.

_____ . 1962. "The Politics of Agency Organization," *Western Political Quarterly* 15:328-344.

_____ . 1963. "Conditions for Legislative Control," *Journal of Politics* 25:526-551.

Schubert, Glendon. 1958. "Legislative Adjudication of Administrative Legislation," *Journal of Public Law* 7:135-161.

Scott, Andrew M. and Margaret A. Hunt. 1966. *Congress and Lobbies*. Chapel Hill: University of North Carolina Press.

Sharkansky, Ira. 1965a. "Four Agencies and an Appropriations Subcommittee: A Comparative Study of Budgeting Strategies," *Midwest Journal of Political Science* 9:254-281.

_____ . 1965b. "An Appropriations Subcommittee and Its Client Agencies," *American Political Science Review* 59:622-628.

Shepsle, Kenneth A. 1978. *The Giant Jigsaw Puzzle: Democratic Committee Assignments in the Modern House*. Chicago: University of Chicago Press.

Stephens, Herbert W. 1971. "Role of the Legislative Committees in the Appropriations Process: A Study Focused on the Armed Services Committee," *Western Political Quarterly* 24:146-162.

Strom, Gerald S. 1975. "Congressional Policy Making: A Test of a Theory," *Journal of Politics* 37:711-734.

Teune, Henry. 1967. "Legislative Attitudes Toward Interest Groups," *Midwest Journal of Political Science* 11:489-504.

Thomas, Norman C. 1970. "Bureaucratic-Congressional Interaction and the Politics of Education," *Journal of Comparative Administration* 2:52-80.

Thomas, Robert O. and Roger B. Handberg. 1974. "Congressional Budgeting for Eight Agencies, 1947-1972," *American Journal of Political Science* 78:179-185.

Thurber, James A. 1976. "Legislative-Administrative Relations," *Policy Studies Journal* 5:56-65.

Trice, Robert H. 1977. *Interest Groups and the Foreign Policy Process*. Beverly Hills, CA: Sage Publications.

Truman, David B. 1951. *The Governmental Process*. New York: Knopf.

_____ . 1971. *The Governmental Process*. 2d ed. New York: Knopf.

Van der Slik, Jack R. and Thomas C. Stenger. 1977. "Citizen Witnesses before Congressional Committees," *Political Science Quarterly* 92:465-485.

van Schendelen, M.P.C.M. 1976. "Information and Decision Making in the Dutch Parliament," *Legislative Studies Quarterly* 1:231-250.

Vinyard, Dale. 1968. "The Congressional Committees on Small Business: Patterns of Legislative Committee-Executive Agency Relations," *Western Political Quarterly* 21:391-399.

_____ . 1973. "The Senate Committee on Aging and the Development of a Policy System," *Michigan Academician* 5:281-299.

Von Nordheim, M. and R.W. Taylor. 1976. "The Significance of Lobbyist-Legislator Interaction in German State Parliaments," *Legislative Studies Quarterly* 1:511-531.

Wallace, Robert Ash. 1960. *Congressional Control of Federal Spending*. Detroit: Wayne State University Press.

Wahlke, John C., William Buchanan, Heinz Eulau, and Leroy C. Ferguson. 1960. "American State Legislators' Role Orientations Toward Pressure Groups," *Journal of Politics* 22:203-227.

Weingast, Barry R. 1980. "Congress, Regulation, and the Decline of Nuclear Power," *Public Policy* 28:231-255.

—————— . 1981. "Regulation, Reregulation, and Deregulation: The Political Foundations of Agency Clientele Relationships," *Law and Contemporary Problems* 44:147-177.

Weingast, Barry R., Kenneth A. Shepsle, and Christopher Johnsen. 1981. "The Political Economy of Benefits and Costs: A Neoclassical Approach to Distributive Politics," *Journal of Political Economy* 89:642-664.

Welch, Susan and John G. Peters. 1982. "Private Interests in the U.S. Congress: A Research Note," *Legislative Studies Quarterly* 7:547-555.

Wildavsky, Aaron B. 1964. *The Politics of the Budgetary Process*. Boston: Little, Brown.

Williams, Philip M. 1954. *Politics in Post-War France*. Hamden, CT: Archon Books.

—————— . 1964. *Crisis and Compromise: Politics in the Republic*. 3d ed. Hamden, CT: Archon Books.

—————— . 1968. *The French Parliament 1958-1967*. London: Allen and Unwin.

Willie, Frank. 1972. "Pressure Groups and Parliamentary Select Committees," in Les Cleveland, ed., *The Anatomy of Influence: Pressure Groups and Politics*. Wellington, New Zealand: Hicks, Smith, pp. 98-112.

Winslow, Clinton Ivan. 1931. "State Legislative Committees: A Study in Legislative Procedure," *Johns Hopkins University Studies in Historical and Political Science* 49:1-158.

Wissel, Peter, Robert O'Connor, and Michael King. 1976. "The Hunting of the Legislative Snark: Information Searches and Reforms in U.S. State Legislatures," *Legislative Studies Quarterly* 1:251-267.

Wolman, Harold. 1971. *Politics of Federal Housing*. New York: Dodd, Mead.

Zeigler, L. Harmon. 1961. *The Politics of Small Business*. Washington, DC: The Public Affairs Press.

—————— . 1969. "The Effects of Lobbying: A Comparative Assessment," *Western Political Quarterly* 22:122-140.

Zeigler, L. Harmon and Michael Baer. 1969. *Lobbying*. Belmont, CA: Wadsworth.

Zeigler, L. Harmon and Wayne G. Peak. 1972. *Interest Groups in American Politics*. 2d ed. Engelwood Cliffs, NJ: Prentice-Hall.

Zeller, Belle. 1937. *Pressure Politics in New York*. New York: Russell and Russell.

Zwier, Robert. 1979. "The Search For Information: Specialists and Nonspecialists in the U.S. House of Representatives," *Legislative Studies Quarterly* 4:31-42.

Chapter 13

Legislative Influence On Policy and Budgets

by

BRUCE I. OPPENHEIMER

If one had been asked 15 or 20 years ago to survey work on how legislatures shape policy and budgets, the task would have been most manageable. Until the mid-1960s, with some important exceptions, legislative policy outputs had not been a focus of most legislative researchers. Instead, research was substantially process-oriented, and policy outputs resulting from those processes tended to be treated tangentially. This situation may merely have reflected a disciplinary bias against what was labeled "policy science." As late as 1968 in *Political Science and Public Policy*, a collection of essays that developed from two conferences sponsored by the Social Science Research Council (Ranney, 1968), a number of authors expressed strong reservations about the involvement of political scientists in the study of public policy. Their fear was that political scientists would become policy advisors rather than scholars improving "the scientific quality of our special body of knowledge" (Ranney, 1968, p. 20). Despite the reservations it contained, the publication of *Political Science and Public Policy* marked a turning point in political science research. Although the first stimulus for a concern with policy as well as process may have come with Theodore Lowi's (1964) book review of Bauer, Pool, and Dexter's *American Business and Public Policy* (1963), the SSRC conferences and the subsequent book gave the necessary professional legitimacy to the study of public policy. Thus, there is a strong scholarly basis for the attention students of legislatures, and political scientists in general, have given to policy-related questions in recent years.

This intellectual legitimacy was not the only stimulus. Legislatures, most notably the U.S. Congress, have undergone a series of changes or reforms since the late 1960s that have substantially reshaped their organization and power structures (Dodd and Oppenheimer, 1977a; Ornstein, 1975; Rosenthal, 1974). Accordingly, there has been both new and renewed interest in the study of legislatures. The response to these two stimuli has been a mushrooming of policy-oriented research on legislatures. In turn, the task of surveying the relevant literature is no longer simple.

Accordingly, I will first outline what we should ideally know about how legislatures structure policies and budgets. After all, to judge where knowledge stands it is useful to measure it against some ideal. Second, I will summarize the available literature, using some broad and arbitrary categories. I will not endeavor to discuss or mention every book and article but will focus on a representative range of the literature within major areas of scholarship and cite a selected group of related writings. Because congressional, state legislative, and non-American legislative research are very different in their research concerns and in the scope of their achievements, it will be necessary to deal with them separately. Third, I will evaluate the research on legislative policy outputs against the ideal framework from which I began and suggest areas, both substantive and organizational, in need of our attention.

There is one additional matter of which the reader should be aware. For the purposes of this paper I have taken a fairly broad definition of policy, one that includes policy decisions (the actions by which legislatures give direction and content to policy activities) and policy statements (the formal expression of policy in terms of legislation) as well as actual policy outputs. Nevertheless, I do not assume that everything that legislatures do is policy-relevant and, before including a work in this essay, have looked in it for a fairly direct tie between legislative activity and public policy. This distinction has considerable significance in my analysis of non-American legislatures and excludes many of them from this literature review.

A Framework

If one wished to know fully how legislatures structure policy and budgets, one would seek concrete information on a range of dimensions. I can propose six which would form a framework: legislative actions or functions, legislative forums and actors, the stages of policy making, legislative outputs over time, the influence of legislatures in different policy areas, and the differences among legislatures.

Each of these needs some elaboration. By legislative actions or functions, I mean what legislatures can do to structure policy. This would encompass the capacity of legislatures to initiate, amend, deliberate, incubate, delay or defeat, expedite, legitimate, and oversee. Clearly some legislatures are able constitutionally or politically to do more of these than others are or to combine them in different ways when considering policy questions.

Next, one would like to have some grasp of where and by whom such activities are performed: the legislative forum and actors. What is the locus of decision making? Is it in committees and subcommittees or in party caucuses? On the floor, in informal groups, or in a combination of forums? And what actors perform in the various forums? Does the initiative belong to party leaders, committee chairs, crossparty coalitions, or individual members?

In addition, one would like to know at what stage or stages in the policy making or budget processes the legislatures affect policy outputs. For this purpose I find those policy stages useful which David Price sets forth in his book on U.S. Senate committees (1972): the stages of instigation and publicizing, formulation, information gathering, interest aggregation, mobilization, modification, and implementation. The impact of legislatures, their forums of activity, and the actions available to them may vary across the stages of the policy process. Price certainly finds ample evidence for this in his analysis of the Senate Commerce, Finance, and Labor and Public Welfare Committees and their subcommittees. One may find it useful to merge the stages with the first dimension, actions or functions. And an argument can be made that they overlap. However, I would contend that a range of legislative actions would occur in a particular policy-making stage.

The time dimension requires little elaboration. Clearly one would like to know about the stability and change in legislative outputs over time, even though time is not an easy dimension to handle. One would also like to know of any differences in the legislature's influence across policies, information which might be organized by traditional substantive policy areas or by policy typologies. Finally, one would inquire along the dimension of comparative politics: how, to what extent, where, and at what policy stages different legislatures affect policies and budgets.

However desirable it might be to have complete information about legislative outputs on all these dimensions, a six-dimensional matrix would be cumbrous to use either for storing the results of research or for directing future research. And in fact, any single piece of research is likely to add information to only a few cells of such a matrix. However, as we examine the literature, this framework can remind us of the many dimensions with which the study of outputs of legislatures should concern itself. Only at the end of each major section (U.S. Congress, state legislatures, and non-American legislatures) and in the general conclusion will this essay return to the framework to evaluate the state of the literature.

The U.S. Congress

Case Studies

Some may disagree as to when political scientists began to study how Congress makes policy. I would argue that our intellectual debt is to E.E. Schattschneider for his book on the Smoot-Hawley Tariff (1935). His primary concern was the activity of interest groups seeking the level of protection they desired in a new tariff bill, and later scholars have claimed that "what happened in 1929 is not a general model of the legislative process" (Bauer, Pool, and Dexter, 1963, p. 25). Still, Schattschneider's book was the first significant case study of a legislative policy output. In fact, until the late 1960s much of the work on Congress's policy-making role was in the form of legislative case studies. And even today many of the more valuable qualitative analyses of legislative policy making are case studies.

In particular, among the earlier case studies Stephen K. Bailey's work on the Employment Act of 1946 stands out (1950). Bailey's use of interviews and his observation of the actual process separates his work from the more traditional political science of his day. In all he made use of over 400 interviews in describing the legislative politics surrounding the act. True, as Robert Peabody notes, Bailey "was unable to divorce himself from the moral overtones of traditional political science" (1969, p. 11), but he kept the reformist positions apart from his objective description and analysis. Bailey's book became the standard against which other case studies of the congressional process have been measured.

These subsequent case studies fall into several groups. Some have used the story of a single piece or several pieces of legislation to depict how Congress works (Bibby and Davidson, 1967; Eidenberg and Morey, 1969; Peabody, Berry, Frasure, and Goldman, 1972; Gross, 1953; Redman, 1973; Reid, 1980; Levine and Wexler, 1981). From these we derive a richer feel for the congressional process and for the policy influence of Congress. We also see that Congress reacts in different ways to different legislative issues— employment, area redevelopment, campaign financing, the National Health Service Corps, and others. Thus, these case studies have a value when linked together or when considered independent of one another. In addition, although each study presents a separate picture in time, together they give one a sense of the change in the law-making process over 30 to 40 years. As we shall see, this is especially true when case studies from this group are supplemented by other case materials.

A second group of case studies analyze a particular policy issue or issue area rather than instructing the reader in how Congress works per se. These studies see congressional influence as just one of the forces which structure governmental output. Thus, we have studies on housing policy (Wolman, 1971), welfare (Bowler, 1974; Steiner, 1966), social security (Derthick, 1979), education (Thomas, 1975; Munger and Fenno, 1962), poverty (Donovon, 1967), energy (Davis, 1974), and Medicare (Marmor, 1970), among many others. In most of these cases Congress was just part of the policy puzzle, although usually an important part, and the studies are often not the work of legislative scholars. For example, Martha Derthick examined how social security policy evolved from 1935 to the early 1970s, and Congress is only one of many figures in the picture Derthick paints of constrained conflict in social policy development. By focusing on policy rather than Congress, Derthick and others establish the relative importance of Congress compared to other policy-making cores in the structuring of policy. Moreover, most of these studies cover longer periods than those in the first group. They are not merely "a bill becomes a law" stories. Thus, Fenno and Munger (1962) trace federal aid to education over nearly a century of conflict.

In addition to Schattschneider's work (1935), there are several case studies of legislative policy making whose primary concern is interest group activity and lobbying. By far the most extensive of these is *American Business and Public Policy* (Bauer, Pool, and Dexter, 1963), a study of lobbying activities and interest group opinions surrounding the Trade Expansion Act of 1962. The study is especially valuable in setting forth the linkages between opinion (elite and mass) and congressional structuring of policy decisions. More recently Norman Ornstein and Shirley Elder (1978), in addition to discussing and analyzing the interest group literature, have presented three case studies of group activity to influence congressional decision making on significant pieces of legislation—common situs picketing, the 1977 Clean Air Act Amendments, and deployment of the B-1 bomber.

The final group of case studies are to be found in the reformist literature on Congress. They illustrate the difficulties the reformers faced in making Congress an effective policy-making institution. Some of these studies (Burns, 1949, 1963; Bailey and Samuel, 1952) are part of the responsible party-government movement. Others, case studies by legislators such as Congressman Richard Bolling (1964), and Senator Joseph Clark (1964), support the need for making the institutions more effective policy-making instruments. In particular, Bolling's discussion of the Landrum-Griffin Bill and of the 1957 Civil Rights Act (1964, pp. 156-194) is written from a perspective on the structuring of policy outputs rarely, if ever before, available to the legislative scholar.

This is by no means an exhaustive list of the case materials on Congress's policy role, but it does illustrate the wealth of studies available. (Other materials, many of which develop generalizations from case studies, will be discussed in different contexts later in this paper.) Moreover, despite the fact that case studies are often denigrated as atheoretical or unscientific, legislative scholars continue to find them useful vehicles for describing the substantive impact of Congress. One realizes the value of these congressional case studies most when one discovers how thin the case materials on state and non-American legislatures are by comparison. And theory without policy substance, illustration, and qualitative richness is not very satisfying.

If there is a weakness in the case study materials on Congress, it is the cases which have been selected, mostly cases in which Congress played a significant role in structuring policy. One may correctly ask whether scholars tend to ignore cases where congressional influence is minimal. Thus, one gets the impression from these case studies that Congress had an important policy role, even though many of the studies were completed in an era when, it is generally agreed, Congress's influence over policy was on the decline. Perhaps more important, few scholars of Congress have tried to pull these case materials together systematically. Except in broad-ranged theory such as Theodore Lowi provides in *The End of Liberalism* (1969) or in a policy-oriented discussion such as Randall Ripley provides in *Congress: Process and Policy* (1978), the potential benefits of the case studies have not been realized.

Process Studies

Although case studies are one major source of information on how Congress affects policy, another source is the work of scholars whose primary interest was process, not policy, particularly studies done in the 1960s.

The following distinction has been made between earlier and later process studies. The process studies of the 1960s treated policy as the dependent variable and gave less attention to it than to the independent variables, focusing on process and variations in process presumed to affect policy decisions. More recently, scholars have considered policy or policy types as an independent variable which shapes process and in turn shapes legislative outputs.

Whether one accepts this distinction is not crucial here, but it is important to note that the earlier studies were generally less concerned with the outputs of legislatures than were the later ones. However, process-oriented studies were not devoid of findings on legislative policy roles; in the studies of congressional committees, parties and leadership, member-constituency ties, internal formal and informal groups, presidential-congressional and other interinstitutional relations, and rules and procedures, we find a good deal of information about Congress's policy functions, albeit often indirectly presented.

Because committees are important in congressional policy making, studies of committees tell us a good deal about how Congress shapes policy and budgets. However, a detailed analysis of that literature is not called for here.

Yet in the 1960s, when committee studies first flourished, they were the major source of understanding policy variations, especially in the House of Representatives. Several publications (Robinson, 1963; Peabody, 1963; Cummings and Peabody, 1963) established that the House Rules Committee could influence the course of policy. This committee's main influence came from its ability to exercise "negative" power.

Richard Fenno (1966), in his study of the appropriations committees, showed how internal relationships on the committees and their need to satisfy certain parent body expectations shaped their norms, behavior, and policy, and, in turn, the floor success of the bills and final spending decisions. Implicit in Fenno's discussion is the ideologically conservative bias of the House Appropriations Committee in the 1950s and 1960s. Along similar lines, John Manley (1969) explains how the Ways and Means Committee dominates the tax-policy arena, and Charles O. Jones (1961) shows that constituency is the central factor structuring policy decisions in the House Agriculture Committee.

Clearly not all committees studied in the 1970 era have the policy dominance of those mentioned above. Studies of the House Armed Services Committee (Dexter, 1963; Dawson, 1962) indicate a rather limited role for the committee in military policy. Its members perceived themselves as non-experts and concentrated on the "real estate" aspects of armed services policy. By contrast, both Malcolm Jewell (1962) and Holbert Carroll (1966) find ample roles for the Senate Foreign Relations and House Foreign Affairs Committees respectively in influencing foreign-policy decision making.

The work on individual congressional committees done in the 1960s is brought together and given a comparative perspective in Richard Fenno's *Congressmen in Committees* (1973). Fenno devotes one chapter to analyzing how the differences between committees affect the committees' decisions (pp. 192-279). In this section Fenno treats the committees individually and the outputs he examines are mainly committee decisions (pp. 192-193). Nevertheless, there is some discussion of the substantive content of these decisions and concern with the level of satisfaction of various actors with the decisions. The book takes a major step in linking process differences to policy output. It is ironic that the "Decisions" chapter has not received as much explicit attention from political scientists as have the earlier chapters.

The committee studies of the 1960s have some shortcomings for those with interests in policy outputs of legislatures. Yet aside from the case studies, they were the most significant of the legislative studies which attempted to discuss or at least hypothesize about the impact of process on policy outputs. It should be noted that most studied House committees, with Jewell's study of the Senate Foreign Relations Committee (1962) and Stephen Horn's book on the Senate Appropriations Committee (1970) the exceptions. Only with the publication of David Price's book, *Who Makes the Laws?* (1972), would

Senate committees receive significant treatment. Moreover, these committee studies present pictures of committees in the political and policy environments of the 1950s and early 1960s. By the mid 1970s, much of the conventional wisdom was based on research 10 to 20 years old. As we shall see later, this required scholars to reexamine the policy impact of committees in the congressional process.

Parties and Roll-Call Voting

The study of congressional parties, party leaders, and crossparty groups has also yielded some useful information about how Congress influences policy outputs. Once again, such studies have primarily described and analyzed process and organization. Thus, studies of party leaders and party committees (Bone, 1956; Truman, 1959; Huitt, 1961; Jones, 1964, 1968; Ripley, 1964, 1967; Froman and Ripley, 1965; Dodd and Oppenheimer, 1977a; Peabody, 1981) give more attention to the workings of party organizations in Congress than to the effects of those workings on policy. The linkage to policy impact is often presented in logical argument, hypothesized rather than given empirical backing. In their study of House Democrats, Froman and Ripley (1965) show inductively on what types of issues party leadership is likely to be more effective. Similarly Jones's article (1968) on House Republicans has a definite policy slant, and Dodd and Oppenheimer (1977a) do ponder the policy impact of a revitalized Democratic Steering and Policy Committee. Only in recent studies by Oppenheimer (1980) and Sinclair (1981) do we get concrete notions about the effect of party organizations and structures on House policy outputs. Otherwise, our knowledge about the policy influence of congressional party organs is either very general or absent.

Particularly valuable from the standpoint of policy have been the studies of the crossparty conservative coalition in Congress. More than just studies of the effect of ideology on members' roll-call behavior, these studies document the workings and substantive impact of the conservative coalition, using roll-call voting materials for substantiation. Clearly James T. Patterson's *Congressional Conservatism and the New Deal* (1967) provides the qualitative base and stimulus for research on the conservative coalition and congressional policy making. Subsequently, John Manley (1973) has analyzed the sources of the conservative coalition and its levels of success. Recently, David Brady and Charles Bullock (1981) have examined the coalition's activity in five issue areas from the 75th through the 94th Congresses and distinguished its policy influence as a blocking coalition. These two studies have focused on the House of Representatives; the literature on the conservative coalition in the Senate centers on an Inner Club or Establishment in the 1950s and 1960s (Clark, 1963; White, 1956; Matthews, 1960; Ripley, 1969; Polsby, 1969). If there is a weakness in this literature, it is that the coalition's tremendous success on roll-call votes seems incongruent with the fact that most of the policies it opposed have been enacted. Roll-call success can easily deceive the researcher calculating policy outputs. More attention needs to be given to the policy significance of the votes the coalition was losing and to changes in the substantive content of the coalition's roll calls over time.

Aside from party and conservative coalition studies, other research focuses on the voting behavior of members and so concerns itself with the outputs of Congress (Matthews and Stimson, 1975; Kingdon, 1981; Mayhew, 1966; Clausen,1973; Sinclair,1981). David Mayhew demonstrates that cohesion among Democratic House members varies substantially with policy area. Aage Clausen's (1973) roll-call work is particularly policy-oriented. He studies how long term forces—party and constituency primarily—rather than short term cues can affect voting on several issue dimensions—government management, social welfare, international involvement, civil liberties, and agricultural aid. From a policy outputs standpoint, Clausen makes two prime contributions: he finds that different long-term forces best predict voting on different issue dimensions and he emphasizes that House members develop relatively stable positions on policies.

Barbara Sinclair's (1981) contribution is that she links roll-call voting behavior to policy change. She attends to change in the issues on the agenda, policy change resulting from new legislation, and changes in voting alignments. Studying roll-call voting in the House of Representatives from 1925 to 1978, Sinclair documents the transformation of the policy agenda in the Great Depression, the growth of domestic policy activism in Congress in the 1950s and 1960s, and the change in the international involvement dimension in the late 1960s. She presents a dynamic picture of policy and of congressional voting alignments. For those interested in legislative outputs, this research moves in a useful direction, linking the aggregation of individual voting decisions to the change and stability of policy outputs.

Congress and the President

Before 1970, the literature on Congress and the president was one area where significant attention was given to the way Congress structures policy and budgets. James L. Sundquist's *Politics and Policy* (1968) is the most far-reaching and informative of these. Sundquist examines the internal struggle within Congress and the external struggle between Congress and three administrations to develop policy in six major domestic issue areas from 1953 to 1966. From these qualitative studies one can see the structuring of policy at various stages of the congressional process, comprehend the impact of a decentralized decision-making apparatus, learn the critical policy implications of rules and procedures, and grasp the policy significance of low cohesion legislative parties and relatively weak party leadership. In addition, because of the time span, one sees that Congress has an "incubation" function in developing public policy. Thus, Part I of Sundquist's book is a rich source of information on Congress and policy making across a range of issues and a sizeable slice of time. In Part II, Sundquist systematizes the legislative histories and argues that the development of policy proposals has been an important factor in the Democrats' electoral success and in the eventual enactment of their policies.

Although Sundquist's book is not neatly scientific, it does not merely describe process; his is one of the few major studies of the 1960s to examine legislative processes in order to understand their impact on policy outputs. As we shall see later in this essay, others (Orfield, 1975; Fisher, 1972; Dodd, 1977; Sundquist, 1981) have since examined the ongoing struggle for policy influence both within Congress and between Congress and the executive branch. In addition, Sundquist's book reenforces notions about the importance of Congress in structuring of national policy in the post-World War II era.

Before Sundquist, one must look to Lawrence Chamberlain's study (1946) to find a major statement of Congress's influence over policy. Examining the origins of 90 major legislative programs over a half century, Chamberlin finds that on 35 programs congressional influence was preponderant and that on another 29 there was joint presidential-congressional influence. Of major policy areas, only defense and business legislation were more influenced by the president than by Congress, and even there Congress had made significant contributions. In a later study Ronald Moe and Steven Teel (1970) update the Chamberlin findings and reach much the same conclusions, although they place more emphasis on joint influence.

Other work, however, tends to deemphasize Congress's importance in the struggle with the president over policy. For example, in a study of the development of the president's legislative program, Richard Neustadt (1955) analyzes the growth of legislative initiative from the executive offices. Neustadt finds that by 1954 even President Eisenhower, who had reservations about the legislative role the presidency had developed in the Roosevelt and Truman administrations, found it necessary to present a legislative program. In fact, Congress had come to expect this from the president. This is a far cry from 1897 when, despite McKinley's landslide victory, Republicans in Congress were proceeding with their legislative program and not awaiting his leadership (Brady, 1973).

Rules and Procedures

Perhaps surprisingly, the study of congressional rules and procedures has contributed substantially to our knowledge of how Congress shapes policies and budgets. The importance of rules and procedures in affecting policy outputs pops up throughout the literature, but nowhere is the connection between the rules of the game and congressional policy making made as systematically as in Lewis Froman's *The Congressional Process* (1967). Froman recognizes that rules and procedures are not neutral, that they exert a considerable conservative bias—favoring the opponents rather than the proponents of policy change. In large part this results from what Froman sees as the serial nature of the process: "a single negative action may be sufficient to defeat the bill," but passage requires a series of majorities and even extraordinary large majorities (p. 17).

In *Congressional Procedures and the Policy Process* (1978), Walter J. Oleszek updates the description of rules and procedures to take into account the many changes made in the 1970s. And others, such as those writing on the budget process (Ellwood and Thurber, 1981; Havemann, 1978; LeLoup, 1980; Ippolito, 1981; Schick, 1980) and those writing on the Rules Committee (Matsunaga and Chen, 1976; Oppenheimer, 1978), also extended our knowledge of the impact of rules and procedures on policy. More attention will be given to them at a later point in this essay.

Congress and Public Policy

Growth of a Policy Focus

It is difficult to pinpoint when policy outputs became a primary focus of congressional scholars rather than a byproduct of process-oriented research. The publication of *Political Science and Public Policy* (1968) is at best an arbitrary point, for there were those such as Sundquist who had a considerable interest in policy before that. And several scholars had stimulated interest in the study of policy some years earlier: Lowi (1964) had categorized policy into distributive, redistributive, and regulatory types; Murray Edelman (1964) had distinguished between material and symbolic politics; and Peter Bachrach and Morton Baratz (1962) had distinguished between decisions and nondecisions. In fact some of the essays in *Political Science and Public Policy* build on these policy typologies (Salisbury, 1968; Froman, 1968). But in the late 1960s, there began a slow and steady trend among congressional scholars, as well as among political scientists generally, to gear their research to policy-related inquiry.

It is much easier to pinpoint the source of the new research than the time the trend began. Many of the studies are by researchers linked directly or indirectly with the Brookings Institution, which has always emphasized public policy research. After publishing Sundquist's book (1968), Brookings produced a collection of articles under the editorship of Frederic Cleaveland,

Congress and Urban Problems (1969). In his introduction, Cleaveland acknowledges his debt to Lowi's analytical approach but rejects his formulation because "Congressmen, interest group leaders, politicians, and voters will of course continue to think and act in terms of familiar, descriptive policy fields" (pp. 6-7). The seven case studies include diverse legislative issues: airport aid, air pollution control, and food stamps, for example. Each is more concerned with what happens to policy content as the legislation moves through the congressional process than previous case studies were. And Cleaveland in a concluding chapter tries to use the case studies to generalize about Congress's policy impact. Seeing Congress as a source of policy initiation, he claims the case studies "cast considerable doubt on the stereotype of a passive legislature simply responding to presidential initiatives" even "when a young, aggressive President occupies the White House and his party is in full command" (p. 396). But because he had examined congressional policy making in the traditional policy category, Cleaveland has difficulty generalizing from the case studies about the pattern of decisions on issue context.

Three other studies focusing on Congress and policy outputs were not published by Brookings but had their origins there. John Ferejohn's examination of rivers and harbors legislation from 1947 to 1968 (1974) demonstrates the influence Congress may exercise on an almost purely distributive issue. He shows how the structure of congressional decision making affects which projects are accepted and funded. Not only does he indicate, through regression analysis, that members of certain subcommittees get more projects than do other members, but he also presents sound institutional and behavioral explanations for his statistical findings. Thus, he goes beyond the general notion that members with influence over the Corps of Engineers fare better in obtaining projects than those without such influence; he demonstrates why this is so. In addition, he offers a deductive theory to explain pork barrel decision making in Congress and in legislative bodies generally.

Like Ferejohn, Bruce Oppenheimer in *Oil and the Congressional Process* (1974) uses policy as an independent variable affecting process, which in turn structures outputs. His study focuses on depletion allowance (tax) legislation and water pollution legislation as they affect the oil industry from the end of World War II until 1970. In particular, Oppenheimer studies how congressional decision making and interest group behavior and strategy vary across issues, couching his analysis in Edelman's material-symbolic policy distinction. Among other things, he finds that as legislation contains more material and fewer symbolic components, interest groups shift their strategies, the locus of the legislative struggle shifts, and the level of conflict increases. As Michael Hayes correctly points out in his theoretical analysis of interest behavior in legislatures (1981), Oppenheimer's analysis is limited to interest groups in a defensive position, and on other links of issues the role of interest groups and the strategies they employ to influence legislative outputs may differ considerably.

A third scholar who benefitted from the Brookings environment is Arnold Kanter (1972) who reexamines the traditional view that Congress exercises little influence over defense policy (see also Dawson, 1962; Gordon, 1961). Kanter's interest in empirically testing Congress's role in defense policies was stimulated by what he saw as dissatisfaction in the 1960s with those policies (p. 129). Analyzing defense appropriations from 1960 to 1970, he finds that Congress makes significant changes from the president's requests on procurement and on research, development, testing, and evolution (RDT&E) rather than making changes across the board. Kanter concludes that Congress "also has evidenced a willingness and desire to influence the content of national security policy" (p. 142).

In a recent study, John Gist (1981) refines Kanter's findings and shows that the appropriations process is not the only place where Congress structures defense policy. Gist tests what influence annual authorization of items in the defense budget has had. He finds that since the procedure was instituted in 1964 the Armed Services Committees have had an impact on defense spending; appropriations for RDT&E have been lower than the amounts requested, whereas before 1964 the appropriations were regularly higher. Gist is able to refute other explanations for this change.

These studies, while indicating a new policy emphasis in the study of Congress, were limited to single or narrow policy areas. Thus, although individually the researchers have generalized about congressional influence over policy outputs and collectively have demonstrated range and variety in the sources and extent of congressional influence, they did not build more general theories. Two other studies of this period, however, focus on a wider range of issues and provide the scholars with a greater opportunity to generalize.

In the first of these, David Price (1972) studies how the levels of decentralization on three Senate committees—Commerce, Finance, and Labor and Public Welfare—affect their policy-making influence. In all he analyzes the role these committees play on 13 different bills, primarily during the 89th Congress. Through a combination of field research and interviewing, Price assigns legislative responsibility for each of seven functions within the policy-making process. Thus he finds, for example, that the highly decentralized Labor and Public Welfare Committee was especially influential in the functions of formulation, interest aggregation, and modification; but, depending on which of its subcommittees was involved, it performed the functions of instigation and publicizing, information gathering, mobilization, and implementation unevenly. By comparison, the centralized Finance Committee was primarily influential in interest aggregation and modification; the Commerce Committee, while it had the same strengths as Finance, was also important in mobilization (pp. 290-313). Price argues in favor of the decentralization or "pluralization" of committee organization, contending that centralization "tends to dampen committee activism and that at least a modest dispersal of prerogatives and resources is necessary if legislative initiatives are to be undertaken and sustained down through the ranks" (pp. 320-321).

Of course Price was limited to studying these committees in a single Congress, but with the exception of Fenno's work on House committees (1973) Price's is the most significant work on congressional committees and is without exception the most valuable work on the relationship between committee organization and policy outputs. Moreover, Price's subsequent work on House committees (to be discussed later), especially on the Interstate and Foreign Commerce Committee, builds on this foundation (Price, 1978a, 1978b, 1981).

In a study relying heavily on published records rather than on interviews, questionnaires, or sophisticated data analysis, Gary Orfield (1975) examines congressional influence on a range of domestic policies, providing a useful supplement to Sundquist's book (1968). In his analysis of congressional activity during the Nixon presidency he includes legislation on civil rights, education, employment, and welfare. Orfield uses these cases to argue that Congress's role in the policy process has changed: in the 1950s and 1960s, Congress exerted negative power via conservative committee chairs; in the late 1960s and early 1970s Congress became less rigidly conservative and more progressive than the Nixon administration, initiating new social programs and protecting old ones. Although one might dispute Orfield's unequivocal ideological positions and the conclusions he draws, the factual material in the case studies is most useful for understanding the changing policy role of Congress in the late 1960s and early 1970s, prior to the major reforms. Orfield also furthers our general knowledge of how Congress structures policy outputs, describing those "conditions" which contribute to congressional policy leadership and those which diminish it (pp. 260-262). Thus he provides valuable analytic tools for studying variations in Congress's policy influence.

Most studies of Congress and its policy outputs stop at the point of enactment. With growing interest in the politics of implementation, some scholars have gone beyond the enactment stage to analyze how congressional structuring of policy outputs affects the implementation of that legislation. The most notable of these is Charles O. Jones's book *Clean Air: The Policies and Politics of Pollution Control* (1975). Jones builds on Randall Ripley's analysis of the 1963 clean air legislation (1969), developing this historical context for the 1970 Clean Air Act. He then presents a detailed case study of the 1970 Act, attending particularly to the reasons Congress developed legislation which state and local governments were unable to implement. The case study indicates how large a part Congress, as opposed to the executive, played in formulating environmental policy.

Some scholars with a policy bent have even begun to study congressional activity in an area previously immune from significant congressional involvement: intelligence policy. John Elliff (1977) discusses the growth of congressional interest in intelligence community activities and Congress's struggle to develop a position in intelligence policy. Other research (Ransom, 1975, 1977; Freeman, 1977; Johnson, 1980) indicates an ongoing interest in the effectiveness of the House and Senate intelligence committees.

These studies of intelligence policy are part of a growing interest in Congress's capacity to oversee the executive branch and the federal bureaucracy in their exercise of governmental authority. Morris Ogul (1976), Lawrence Dodd and Richard Schott (1979), and Morris Fiorina (1981) have been concerned with the incentives, disincentives, means, and capacity Congress has to conduct meaningful oversight, the effectiveness of oversight activities, and their impact on policy. Joel Aberbach (1979) finds changes in congressional oversight capacities and recognizes that oversight subcommittees provide members and staff with the incentive they previously lacked to involve themselves in oversight activities. And Fred Kaiser (1977) examines the oversight activities of a particular House committee. The literature on congressional oversight is considerably more systematic and extensive now than that available in the 1960s (Bibby, 1966; Scher, 1963; Vinyard, 1968).

Some research, largely theoretical, looks at Congress's policy influence through the development of subgovernments. In recent years the discussion has perhaps been presented best by Lowi (1969) under the rubric of "interest group liberalism." It sees policy as designed in a relatively closed network of clientele interest groups, government agencies serving those groups, and congressional subcommittees with apppropriate specialized jurisdictions. Morris Fiorina further popularized the notion in *Congress: Keystone of the Washington Establishment* (1977). And Roger Davidson (1977) indicates the problems these "cozy triangles" caused in committee reorganization efforts. Yet there is only limited empirical evidence on which policy areas have such networks, and, to the extent the networks exist, they involve multiple and competing subcommittees, bureaus, and interest groups. In a recent book R. Douglas Arnold (1979) finds a fairly complex relationship between congressmen and bureaucrats on three allocation policies, although that relationship fits his model of national bureaucratic allocation, a model sympathetic to the subgovernment literature.

The Influence of Reforms

These studies of congressional policy influence represent only one segment of that literature which has become available since 1968. The changes and reforms in Congress, instituted in the 1970s, have also stimulated studies of how Congress structures policy outputs. Not only did scholars describe the reforms (Ornstein, 1974, 1975; Dodd and Oppenheimer, 1977; Welch and Peters, 1977; Mann and Ornstein, 1981), but many examined the policy implications and impacts of these reforms. A new group of committee studies appeared. Catherine Rudder in her research on the Ways and Means Committee (1977, 1978) finds the committee's organization and process different from those Manley (1969) had described and, more important, links the changes to the production of different policy outputs. She concludes that the committee "is probably more liberal in fiscal policy than the old committee" and "is willing to support a more progressive income tax system" (1977, p. 135). However, Rudder later writes that one impact of closed-rule reform and the expansion of the committee has been "to widen the number and kind of influence on committee legislation and, as a consequence, to alter the substance of tax legislation" (1978, p. 86).

Price (1981) discovers that, following reforms that mandated subcommittees, the House committees, like Senate committees at an earlier time, increased certain activities, such as hearings. These reforms have opened avenues for policy entrepreneurship which may previously have been blocked. However, he is careful to note that "it is impossible to predict the substantive effects of decentralization in a given situation without some knowledge of to whom the authority and resources are being given" (p. 179).

Even changes on a process-oriented committee such as the House Rules Committee have had policy impact (Oppenheimer, 1981). In recent Congresses this committee has spent much of its effort crafting complex rules designed to expedite floor considerations of leadership-backed legislation and to minimize the opportunities for House members to unravel legislation on the floor. The impact of this and other changes in the Rules Committee can be seen on individual bills and on the management of the majority "party's overall legislative program" (p. 102).

The effects of the reforms have not been the same on all committees. In a study of four House committees, Norman Ornstein and David Rohde (1977) demonstrate that each committee has increased its policy-oriented activities as the result of the subcommittee bill of rights but that the policy outputs do not always differ from the prereform period. On the Agriculture Committee, for example, they find that, despite the effects of the reforms and a high turnover in its membership, "little overt change in behavior or policy outputs has occurred" (p. 229). A constituency-oriented membership and subcommittee chairs, for the most part nonactive, have kept the committee in its traditional policy mold. Ornstein and Rohde found that the committee was organized differently and gave less attention to commodity subcommittees than the Agriculture Committee described in the Jones study (1961); but they also found that the committee in the mid-1970s structured policy outputs in much the same way it had in the late 1950s and early 1960s. In contrast, they found the International Relations Committee trying to expand its policy activities well beyond the limited role that Carroll (1966) analyzed.

If nothing else, these newer committee studies update the earlier work of congressional committee scholars. And clearly the changes of the 1970s were vast enough that a serious updating was needed. But beyond updating, the newer committee studies have a more explicit concern with how Congress and its committees shape policy than do the older ones.

The struggle between Congress and the president for policy-making authority has received nearly as much scholarly attention as have the effects of congressional reforms on committees. Several researchers have analyzed presidential influence in congressional decision making. Most notably, George Edwards (1980) finds that the number of seats the president's party holds in Congress, rather than a given president's legislative skills, affects the level of support he receives from Congress for his program. Unlike Edwards, whose analysis is based largely on roll-call data, Stephen Wayne (1978) examines a broad range of activities by which the "legislative presidency" has come to influence congressional decision making. Clearly Wayne sees presidential influence over legislative policy outputs in more than just the outcome of roll-call votes, for he spends as much time on policy formulation and implementation as he does on enactment of legislation.

A number of scholars have chosen to evaluate Congress's efforts to reassert its policy influence in the 1970s. A series of essays on the subject appear in *Congress Against the President* (Mansfield, 1975). They range from Richard Pious's (1975) general discussion of domestic policy initiatives to essays on executive privilege and on confirmation of presidential appointments. Collectively these pieces give the reader a sense of the range of opportunities Congress was exploring to reassert policy-making influence.

In contrast to these, Lawrence Dodd (1977) theorizes about the limits of Congress reasserting itself. He argues that the historical cycle of the presidential-congressional struggle is tipped toward an increase in executive authority because the political goals of individual members conflict with broader institutional goals. The consequence is that Congress's efforts to reassert itself in its dealing with the president will inevitably fall short.

In a recent book, James L. Sundquist (1981) takes a detailed look at the cycles of congressional decline and resurgence. After tracing the ups and downs of two centuries, Sundquist examines the more precipitous changes since the late 1960s. He places special attention on impoundment and the new budget process, war powers, foreign policy partnership, oversight, the legislative veto, and institutional professionalization. In large part he finds the congressional resurgence of the 1970s to be an overreaction to particular political circumstances and to the remaining, and in some cases inherent, institutional weaknesses "to produce a comprehensive integrated program" (p. 438). Sundquist's study provides a useful historical perspective on Congress's policy role and a useful realization: that most reform designed to strengthen Congress cuts more than one way. For example, Sundquist notes that if the legislative veto were carried to its fullest extent, Congress could not effectively handle the workload it would create and would perhaps lose policy influence. But if Congress were entirely without the veto (if, for instance, the veto were found unconstitutional in all its forms), the president might lose authority, for Congress would be unwilling to grant authority without the veto provisions.

To a degree, Sundquist's book is diagnostic and prescriptive. He gathers the available information about Congress's condition, looks at the treatments that condition has been subjected to, and recommends that Congress take things easier and resume a more normal role. Thus, it may not be typical political science, if there is such a thing. While more scholars pursue the study of details of the congressional policy role, Sundquist makes an effort to analyze the entirety.

In some ways Sundquist's study is symptomatic of much of the effort to evaluate the policy impact of the congressional reforms. Unlike earlier studies of Congress, the work carries with it either implicit or explicit recommendations. It has a reformist sense to it. This is especially true of the literature on Congress and foreign policy. A recent collection of articles edited by John Spanier and Joseph Nogee entitled *Congress, the Presidency, and American Foreign Policy* (1981) illustrates the point. The book includes case studies of a variety of foreign policy issues in the 1970s, including Middle East policy, SALT II, the Panama Canal treaties, the Turkish arms embargo, trade with the Soviet Union and Rhodesia, and energy. The studies generally support the authority of the president in foreign policy within some boundaries. Nogee concludes that "in several issues Congress made it difficult for the United States to pursue a coherent foreign policy" (p. 195), although he recognizes that Congress has tried to increase its foreign policy role and that "studies in this volume have amply documented mistakes committed by the Nixon, Ford, and Carter administrations" (p. 199).

By comparison, I.M. Destler, who takes a somewhat more positive view of Congress's participation in foreign policy decision making, notes that congressional-executive conflict on foreign policy may be desirable for democratic government but incompatible with effective foreign policy (1981a). His prescription is that the source of the conflict—substantive differences, electoral interests, institutional characteristics of Congress, and staff expansion—must be recognized and managed if both democratic government and policy goals are to be served. When the conflict can be managed, as with the multilateral trade negotiations, consensus can be arrived at; when the conflict cannot be managed, as with SALT II, stalemate is likely (1981b).

Destler finds that the institutions lack structures for managing the conflict. "The Congress," Destler observes, "continues decentralized and amply staffed; the problems will continue to cross jurisdictional lines and defy easy resolutions; presidents will continue to be vulnerable politically" (p. 359).

The diagnostic and prescriptive tone of the recent literature is by no means limited to the foreign policy area. It is evident in Oppenheimer's work on how the reforms affect Congress's capacity to develop energy legislation (1980, 1981). More significantly, the scholarship on the new congressional budget process (Ellwood and Thurber, 1981; Havemann, 1978; LeLoup, 1980; Ippolito, 1981; Schick, 1980) provides a wealth of information on Congress's changing role in budgetary matters. This research reports on the incentives and policy needs that led to the enactment of the Budget Act, the structures the Act created, the ways it should operate, and the strengths, weaknesses, and differences between the House and Senate Budget Committees. In addition, several of the scholars assess how well the new process is working, what goals it is not meeting, what some of the Act's unintended consequences are, and what can be done to improve its operation. Some of these authors, Ellwood and Schick in particular, not only are political scientists but have had significant roles in the formulation and/or implementation of the process.

No doubt with the activities on budget matters between the 97th Congress and the Reagan administration several of these researchers will take another look at a process which, designed to improve congressional control of spending, has become a tool of presidential policy leadership. In any case, it is unlikely that coverage of Congress's structuring of the budget will lapse as it did after the publication of Wildavsky's (1964) and Fenno's (1966) landmark studies.

Finally, there are a number of studies examining the effects of congressional staff growth. The ample staff resources of the House and Senate appear to be crucial ingredients for the maintenance of policy influence. When we examine non-American legislatures, where staff resources are slim, we will see how crucial staff has become for legislative policy influence.

Summary

The research on Congress over the past 15 or so years has undergone a major transformation. The study of Congress's impact on policy and budgets, which until the late 1960s was largely a by-product of process studies, has been recognized as a major area of research. Moreover, there are now an unusually large number of scholars engaging in policy-oriented research on Congress. Some have even demonstrated that political scientists have knowledge and expertise of use to legislative policy makers—something doubted and warned against by those who held reservations about political scientists engaging in policy research.

In the framework set forth at the start of this paper, congressional scholars have filled in substantial areas. We have good knowledge of the actions or functions Congress may engage in to influence policy. In terms of the arenas in which this may occur, the coverage of committees and subcommittees is particularly strong, and we increasingly understand the workings of party organizations and informal groups, the role of leadership, and the impact of enlarged staffs. There appear to be two areas in need of greater attention. One is the Senate in general, where political scientists have clearly had less access than in the House. The other, perhaps surprising, is the political process on the House and Senate floors and the policy impact the institutions have at that stage. Except in studies of roll-call votes and of floor amendments, we have learned little about what appears to be the renewed importance of floor activity in structuring policy outputs.

Our coverage of policy stages is mixed. Most of the earlier studies were focused on the mobilization of majorities. Recent work has refined our knowledge of interest aggregation and has begun to be concerned with Congress's role in policy implementation.

Perhaps most encouraging is the range and number of policy areas receiving attention. There is fine empirical work on everything from public works and agriculture to taxes and foreign policy. Some research is only in the context of traditional policy categories, but scholars are making progress in generalizing about broader policy types. Moreover, we are now developing some coverage of policy areas over time, as scholars take another look at and expand on the work of those of an earlier generation.

If there is a remaining problem with the research, it comes from the absence of central planning in its development. Attention to particular subject matter seems to wax and wane. Thus, for example, for a decade there was relatively little research on Congress and budgetary policy, until the enactment of the new congressional budget process. Suddenly we have a wealth of research. Among those studying Congress and policy outputs, there may be a tendency to complete a research project and move on to something else. The responsibility for monitoring after the project is finished may be left for some other scholar or may not be undertaken at all. Perhaps the luxury of having a large number of scholars allows for this "free market" to exist without substantial research gaps. As we shall see, the same luxury does not exist for researchers of state and non-American legislatures.

State Legislatures

In a comparison with the extensive literature on how Congress shapes policy and budgets, the work on state legislatures and policy outputs is dwarfed. This is not totally surprising, since there are fewer scholars pursuing state legislative research and they must build generalizations on 50 diverse legislatures, not just one. It is difficult enough under these circumstances even to describe the range of procedures and organization. Research on state legislatures is clearly costly and time consuming, and the research on state legislative policy outputs is accordingly slim. In a recent review essay on the state of state legislative research (1981), Malcolm Jewell does not include a separate subheading on policy outputs. Instead much of this material is subsumed under legislative decision making, budgeting, and oversight. What Jewell presents is discouraging for those interested in state legislative policy making, and my examination of the literature sustains that evaluation.

Case Studies

Whereas there are numerous case studies on Congress, there are few on state legislatures. The most recent and best is Michael BeVier's study of housing politics in California (1979). BeVier, who was a player in the legislative struggle over a housing finance agency, not only describes the battle in substantive and procedural detail but also gives excellent insight into the role of staff within the state legislature. He views staff as crucial in decreasing the reliance of state legislators on lobbyists. Of all the state legislative case studies, this one gives the best feel for the pulling and hauling of the process and for policy entrepreneurship in the legislature. Other case studies (see for example Steiner and Gove, 1960; Frost, 1961) are not nearly so detailed and focus on issues of state government organization.

Aside from these cases, few studies of state policy making in given issue areas include material on legislative influence. On education policy, Nicholas Masters, Robert Salisbury, and Thomas Eliot (1964) compare the behavior of political actors in Missouri, Illinois, and Michigan; and Mike Milstein and Robert Jennings (1973) study the New York legislature. As Samuel Patterson (1976, p. 176) summarizes these findings, the role of the state legislatures varies in these four states. In Missouri and Illinois, consensus on education policy develops outside the legislature, although some legislators participate, and then the legislature ratifies it. By comparison, in Michigan education policy is subject to partisan pressures in the legislature, and in New York it is part of a routine that makes legislative influence on education policy not all that different from influence on other policy areas.

Helen Ingram, Nancy K. Laney, and John R. McCain (1980) have written a valuable new study of water-policy decision making in the four bordering southwestern states of Utah, Colorado, Arizona, and New Mexico. The authors examine whether state legislators represent the opinions of voters on policy questions and whether legislatures can respond effectively to increased competition for scarce resources. They find that legislators' attitudes are similar to voters' in that both groups see water policy in distributive terms—that is, they believe everybody should get more. The problem the authors uncover is that policy will have to be redistributive unless water resources are greatly expanded. Given low internal professionalism—low staff resources, low salaries, short sessions, and sizeable turnover—in these four state legislatures, the members rely heavily on interest groups for expertise and develop stronger prodevelopment attitudes than their constituents on water policy. Ingram, Laney, and McCain find that the "amateur" status of these four legislatures limits their policy influence and that policy decisions relating to water get passed elsewhere—to local or federal levels (p. 198). Of course, the authors note that the legislatures may react differently on different issues. Clearly, however, the policy influence of these legislatures is markedly less than that of the California legislature as described by BeVier.

In sum, the case study literature is not very rich. A few states receive most of the coverage, and a limited range of issues have been studied. The Ingram book is a source of encouragement that state legislative scholars are recognizing the value of case materials.

State Policy Outputs—The Role of Legislatures

The more broadly theoretical work on state legislatures likewise has a weak policy-output focus. Wahlke, Eulau, Buchanan, and Ferguson, in the first chapter of their classic study of four state legislatures (1962), discuss legislative output. They note that

a major theoretical problem for legislative research . . . is therefore to achieve adequate conceptualization of legislative output, i.e., to specify the dimensions or variables of legislative output which are related to different consequences of that output. We have not attempted to deal with this problem in this book (p. 25).

Thus, one learns much about the input side of the four legislatures, the environment within which each operates, and the mix of members each contains, but the relationship of these factors to what the legislatures produce is not explicit.

Ironically, there is ample research on state policy outputs, but little of it deals with the impact of legislatures. In the late 1960s several researchers (see for example Dye, 1966; Sharkansky, 1968; Hofferbert, 1966; Sharkansky and Hofferbert, 1969) studied the relative influence of economic, sociological, and political variables on state policy outputs. These studies have substantial methodological problems. For example, they rely primarily on expenditures as policy measures. More important, the political variables they use, such as party competition indices and malapportionment measures, are not particularly imaginative. Not surprisingly, the relationships between the political variables and the policy measures in most cases are nonsignificant once economic and sociological variables are used as controls. Needless to say, these findings were not particularly comforting to those who wished to study the impact of legislature on policy.

These findings are in keeping with other writings in the 1960s which indicated a limited policy influence for state legislatures (Packenham, 1970, pp. 556-559). Thomas Dye (1965), for example, describes state legislatures as more "arbiters" than initiators of public policy, and Herbert Jacob (1966) sees them as legitimizing policy.

Two important articles suggest that the early studies of state policy output had underestimated the importance of politics. The first is Jack Walker's study of the diffusion of innovations (1969). Like earlier studies of policy output, Walker's is not particularly concerned with the impact of legislatures. But he does find that the partial correlations between two legislative-oriented political variables and composite innovation scores remain sizeable. The two political variables are urban representation, measured on the David-Eisenberg index, and political opportunity, measured on the Schlesinger index. Thus, states which fully represent urban areas in legislatures rather than discriminating against them and states where major offices change hands frequently tend to show higher levels of policy innovation. In sum, apportionment and turnover should not be ruled out as variables which affect legislative structuring of policy outputs.

More important from the standpoint of the impact of state legislatures on policy, although it has not received as much attention as Walker's work on diffusion of innovation, is Edward Carmines's study of state welfare policy determinants (1974). Carmines argues that researchers have not found a strong relationship between interparty competition and state welfare policies because they have not considered the differences among state legislatures as a mediating factor in the relationship. He claims that a state legislature has to be sufficiently well organized if it is "to convert party conflict into public policies" (p. 1119). When he groups state legislatures according to their level of professionalism, Carmines finds a strong relationship between party competition and welfare effort (measured by seven specific measures) in states with highly professional legislatures, even when he controls for socioeconomic variables. But in low professionalism states the relationship vanishes. Of all the state policy-output literature, Carmines's article most clearly points to the significance of state legislatures in influencing policy.

Other studies by Fry and Winters (1970) and Winters (1976) investigate factors affecting redistribution policies in American states. Like the Walker and Carmines articles, these offer some indication that state legislatures affect policy outputs. The measures of legislative professionalism and of legislative incentives are of particular interest because they are related to an index of redistribution. However, Winters finds no relationship between party control and redistributive policies in northern states.

The work of Wayne Francis (1967) and the follow-up study by Francis and Ronald Weber (1980) also demonstrate the significance of state legislatures in policy making. From their mailed questionnaires, Francis and Weber find both stability and change in the issues legislators view as main agenda items. Although the authors do not concern themselves with the content of legislative decisions in these areas, the studies do indicate the potentially significant role of legislators in choosing among potential agenda items.

Reform, Professionalism, and Performance

Closely related to the policy outputs literature is a sizeable body of research on the effects of reform and professionalism on state legislatures. A series of articles (Ritt, 1973; Patterson, 1974; Karnig and Sigelman, 1975; Tatalovich, 1978) discuss the usefulness and in some cases test the significance of an evaluation of state legislatures undertaken by the Citizens Conference on State Legislatures. Two of these studies (Ritt, 1973; Karnig and Sigelman, 1975) find that the relationship between the CCSL ratings and policy is nonexistent when controls for socioeconomic variables are applied. Patterson contends that the CCSL measure is methodologically unsound, although he suggests that the ratings may be "plausible" (1974, p. 114). Only Tatalovich contends that the measure is useful. He finds that higher-quality legislatures rely less on federal grants-in-aid, enact a lower percentage of bills introduced, and spend more on welfare and education than do lower-quality legislatures.

Much of the research on state legislative outputs deals with policy only in the broadest sense. These studies tend to be concerned with such outputs as the number of bills introduced and the efficiency of bill processing. Alan Rosenthal and Rod Forth (1978) look at factors affecting the number of bills introduced and the number of bills passed by state legislatures from 1963 to 1974. They find that population, urbanization, and industrialization account for 45 percent of the variation in bill introduction and 40 percent of the variation in bill enactment. In addition, two internal legislative variables, the number of members and the amount of money the legislature expends on itself, explain significant amounts of the remaining variation. The latter is, of course, a good indicator of legislative professionalism.

Similarly, two articles focus on performance outputs: Ronald Hedlund and Keith Hamm's (1978) on the Wisconsin Assembly and Hedlund and Patricia Freeman's (1981) comparing the Wisconsin and Iowa legislatures. Hedlund and Hamm find that reforms have made the Wisconsin Assembly "more productive and expeditious" (p. 127) in treating bills on certain key issues but not on all issues. By contrast, Hedlund and Freeman examine variables affecting legislative performance over a 12-year period. They discover that the reform syndrome gave an effect opposite to the expected one. But again their attention is on "the operating levels of the decision-making process in a quantitative sense" and not on "the nature, types, nor comprehensiveness of the decisions made" (p. 108).

Some attempt to evaluate the consequences of innovation for policy as well as for performance can be found in a collection James Robinson edited (1973). The studies are qualitative evaluations of legislative innovations in particular states, and the results of these studies are mixed. Samuel Gove (1973, p. 132), for example, claims the reorganization of the Illinois legislature "has not had an identifiable impact on policy," whereas James Best (1973) and Alan Wyner (1973) find innovations have significantly affected legislative policy outputs in Washington and California respectively.

Inside State Legislatures—Committees, Parties, and Interest Groups

The difference between the congressional and state legislative policy literature is most apparent in the material on committees. With the exception of a book by Alan Rosenthal (1974) and an article by Keith Hamm (1980), there has been little published on the policy impact of state legislative committees. Rosenthal's interest is primarily in the role committees play in legislative effectiveness. He classifies the committee systems in all 50 states on policy and program factors and contends that staffing has a considerable effect on the policy capacities of committees. Hamm analyzes factors that affect committee decision making in the Texas and Wisconsin legislatures. Although he finds differences between the two states, Hamm falls short of making strong policy-related conclusions. He admits "substantial work needs to be done to ascertain more refined measures of policy content" (p. 50).

There has been fairly extensive work on political party influence in state legislatures, albeit mostly roll-call analyses. Some of this literature, as Samuel Patterson describes it, does indicate that party voting is more likely on some policies or issues than on others. In particular, on labor legislation and on tax and spending bills parties are active, while on business regulation, liquor control, crime, and conservation issues party voting has not been found to be particularly strong (Patterson, 1976, p. 181; see LeBlanc, 1969; Wiggins, 1967; Goldman, 1968).

On the other hand, there is relatively little on the role of interest groups in state legislatures. Jewell (1981, p. 14) notes that there has been "no major study since Zeigler and Baer," which appeared in 1969. In general then, with the exception of work on parties, studies on the organization and structuring of state legislatures are sparse.

Budgeting and Oversight

In some areas of policy research on state legislatures, progress is being made. In particular, there is a stream of research on state legislative budgeting. Books by Thomas Anton (1966) on expenditure politics in Illinois and by D. J. Doubleday (1967) on legislative influence over the budget in California contain useful information and analysis. Anton finds that the Illinois legislature, with little staff support and with few members holding any expertise, does not play a significant role in the budgetary process. He contends that "in such circumstances, not only approval, but approval essentially without serious dissent, was perhaps unavoidable" (p. 175). Doubleday details a far more "professional" process in California, where legislative analysts evaluate the governor's budget, prepare analyses of appropriations bills, present trends, and participate in budget preparation. He does, however, note that although professionalization increases legislative influence, the process is one of "muddling through" and the policy impact is incremental (p. 192).

More recently, the Council on State Governments (1975) has published a summary of appropriations processes in 15 states. It includes data on length of sessions, budget periods, committees, staff, and procedural variation. This wealth of data is a valuable resource for testing hypotheses about legislative influence in appropriations. Similarly, a collection of articles by Balutis and Butler (1975) offers updated information on budget procedures in several states. It is worth noting that the article on Illinois (Kent, 1975) indicates that substantial professionalization and increases in legislative influence have occurred since Anton's study.

Finally, two articles—one on oversight (Hamm and Robertson, 1981) and the other on state legislative casework (Elling, 1979)—indicate a broadening policy interest in state legislative research. Hamm and Robertson examine a range of independent variables which might explain differences among state legislatures in their review of regulation and sunset policy. They find that rule-making review is associated with high legislative-executive conflict and divided party control, whereas sunset review is associated with low legislative professionalism and low level of existing oversight. They conclude that stronger legislatures can adopt more demanding oversight procedures; sunset, a less demanding procedure, is chosen by legislatures with lesser capabilities.

Elling's study of casework in Minnesota and Kentucky yields one interesting policy finding. In both states, although to a greater extent in Minnesota, legislators say that one of the main benefits of casework is that it leads the legislature to remedy the general problem that caused the constituent difficulty.

Summary

Within the framework I set forth in the beginning of this essay, the literature on state legislatures and policy outputs is spotty. Some of the research is indeed very fine, but the gaps in the literature are large. Given the area to be covered, there are simply not enough scholars actively involved. Moreover, the studies of policy in state legislatures have largely been concerned with performance and how to improve it, and not with the ways legislatures influence substantive policy areas.

Non-American Legislatures

In a thoughtful essay on the functions of legislatures, Robert Packenham writes that the principal function of most of the world's legislatures is not to make decisions. Most of them, that is to say, do not allocate values or at least do not have this as their principal function (1970, p. 522). Instead, he argues, most of them deal with legitimation, recruitment, and socialization. Packenham then illustrates his point with the functions of the Brazilian National Congress, whose policy influence is limited to rare negotiation with the executive over legislative content and to the "exit" function when there is an impasse. Since 1964, the Congress has done little, if anything, to resolve conflicts or oversee the bureaucracy (pp. 531-536).

Packenham contends that Brazil in the mid-1960s is not unique among legislatures. It is rather typical, and the U.S. Congress is the exception. To prove his point, Packenham summarizes the literature on a range of legislatures in developing countries (among which he includes Japan) to support his point that "most of the world's legislatures do not legislate very much" (p. 546).

John Wahlke (1971) holds views similar to Packenham's. He believes that political scientists have spent too much time studying the policy role of parliaments instead of their supportive functions, which he views as more critical. One may not agree with Wahlke about how worthwhile it is to study the parliamentary policy role, but it is clear that for many legislatures that role is nearly nonexistent. That is, many of the world's legislatures rarely initiate, amend, incubate, delay, defeat, expedite, or oversee public policy or budgets. Their policy function, to the degree it exists, is largely one of legitimation and deliberation, and even that may have little substantive impact.

Therefore, I distinguish here between legislatures which perform significant policy functions and those which do not, borrowing the categories of legislatures which Michael Mezey (1979) adopts to discriminate among their policy roles. He classifies legislatures into four groups according to their policy-making importance. Active and vulnerable legislatures are those which participate in policy formulation, deliberation, and oversight and have highly developed committee systems as a prerequisite for that activity (p. 52). Reactive legislatures have "a less influential policy making role" than the first group, especially in formulating policy, and are "subordinate to executive-centered elites" (pp. 57-58). Marginal legislatures are dominated by executives and may have even the "modest constraints" they try to impose resisted (p. 58). Finally, minimal legislatures play only a peripheral role and exist at the pleasure of executive elites (p. 58). When Mezey assigns legislatures to these policy groups he is indeed generous. If he errs at all, it is in assuming a larger policy role for some legislatures than they actually have. It therefore makes little sense to go beyond the reactive legislatures here. The policy roles of the others, to the degree they exist, are too minimal and too indirect to warrant significant attention, especially in comparison with the policy roles of Congress and state legislatures. As we shall see, even some of the reactive legislatures play rather minor policy roles.

Before examining the literature on the policy functions of active, vulnerable, and reactive national legislatures, I will note that many studies indicate a decline in the number of legislatures with significant policy roles. Thus, among Mezey's active and vulnerable groups, several are in countries where legislatures have since been suspended or replaced. These include the Philippines, Chile, Uruguay, and the French Fourth Republic (Mezey, 1979, p. 60). Similarly, Carlos Astiz (1973, p. 115) claims that as of 1970 only three Latin American legislatures could be categorized as having "effective participation in the decision-making process"—Chile, Costa Rica, and Uruguay. Clearly only Costa Rica would meet that criteria today. Astiz finds two others, Venezuela and Colombia, have fallen to only a limited role. In general, he views Latin American legislatures as in a state of decay because they did not perform as the constitutions led citizens to expect. His conclusion holds little hope that conditions in Latin America will improve: "Six countries have dissolved their legislatures . . . and none seems to be missing them too much" (p. 126). This trend is not universal. As we shall see, the literature indicates that in some countries the legislature's policy influence is growing or the legislature has been restored.

Active and Vulnerable Legislatures

Except for the scholarship on the U.S. Congress, there are few studies on the policy role of active and vulnerable legislatures. The quality of the research, however, is generally high.

There are two fine articles on the Costa Rican National Assembly (Baker, 1971; Hughes and Mijeski, 1973). Both describe a legislative body with substantial policy influence. Its power stems from constitutional provisions; the Assembly can initiate its own legislation, both national bills and private member bills. Baker finds that in a seven-month period it initiated 68 percent of the national bills (pp. 64-65); however, Hughes and Mijeski find in sampling 200 bills over a twelve-year period that the Assembly initiated only 37 percent of the national bills. In addition, the Assembly exercises policy influence at the committee level. It has a standing committee system, albeit guided by a few members. Committees may amend bills, although two-thirds remain unchanged, and may also delay or defeat legislation. These powers extend to money bills as well as to authorizing legislation. Further, the committees have staff support and investigatory powers. Legislation may also be altered on the Assembly floor, where members or party members are not normally bound by their respective caucuses.

Thus, the picture one gets of the Costa Rican National Assembly is one of a true policy-making institution. It does not have as much authority nor as many resources as the U.S. Congress, but it is far closer to the U.S. Congress than most legislatures are. We do not, however, have a sense of how this legislature's influence varies across different issues and over time, since both studies are in the same time period. Nevertheless, there is ample support for Baker's contention that the Assembly "does play a significant part in the allocation of values for the Costa Rican society" (p. 63).

The research on the Chilean Senate before its suspension (Agor, 1971; Hughes and Mijeski, 1973) indicates a legislative body with substantial policy influence. Legislators initiated a high percentage of important legislation except during specially called sessions. But even in those, legislator initiation was still sizeable. Agor credits the policy influence of the Senate to historical development, the support of public opinion, a standing committee system, and a highly competent professional staff "which compares favorably to the staff available to the U.S. Congress" (p. 30). The committees could delay or defeat presidential proposals and could thus bargain with the executive. Again we have little information on the influence of the Chilean Senate across policy. Agor, however, does provide some historical perspective on the general growth of its policy influence until 1970.

The legislatures of Chile, Costa Rica, and the Philippines (see Stauffer, 1975), share(d) one feature with the U.S. Congress: they lacked strong, cohesive legislative parties. Although the party caucuses might be active, members were rarely bound by caucus decisions and not normally disciplined for voting in opposition to their parties. Thus, the legislatures in these non-parliamentary systems play a more important role in policy making because party plays a diminished role.

Italy and the Fourth French Republic, however, present cases of active and vulnerable parliaments where party discipline was quite strong. The nonmajority status of parties in the two systems helped enable the parliament to play a significant policy role. But the literature indicates that neither legislature dealt with many important issues. Thus, much of the literature on the Fourth Republic deals with private bills (Williams, 1964; Leites, 1959; Mezey, 1979). Giuseppe DiPalma's excellent study of the Italian Parliament

(1977) paints the picture even more clearly. He finds that Parliament's workload and output between 1948 and 1968 were very high indeed. And compared to other Western European legislatures, the Italian Parliament is the most successful in getting its amendments on government bills accepted, although it also offers the fewest amendments. When DiPalma uses Blondel's scale (Blondel, 1969-1970) to rate the importance of the legislation with which the Italian Parliament deals, it ranks by far the lowest of the countries studied. It produces a largely disaggregated legislative product of small laws or "leggine" (p. 75). Thus, this legislature, which seems active on policy, is really not doing anything of significance. Moreover, DiPalma believes that the causes for this situation are largely external to Parliament and not readily addressable with organizational reforms (pp. 216-218).

Accordingly, as one reads Mezey's (1979) analysis of the active and vulnerable legislatures as well as the original research, one is struck by how marginal their policy roles are (or have been) compared with the role of the U.S. Congress. True, committee systems and professional staff seem a crucial prerequisite for legislatures to compete with executives and bureaucrats for policy influence, but those features alone do not guarantee a substantial voice in policy making. With one important exception, the case of the reactive legislatures is even weaker.

Reactive Legislatures

If reactive legislatures are "subordinate to executive-centered elites who, operating through disciplined majority parties, are able to minimize the legislature's policy making role" (Mezey, 1979, p. 87), then one would expect the research to find that their policy functions are even more limited than those of active legislatures. And with one important exception, the West German Bundestag, this is true. What is perhaps ironic, however, is that there appears to be a greater quantity of research on the policy roles of these legislatures than on the non-American active and vulnerable legislatures, largely because more political scientists have studied the governments of these primarily Western European countries.

By far the most extensive study of the policy-making role of a non-American legislature is Gerhard Loewenberg's work on the German Parliament (1967). Moreover, of the reactive legislatures, the Bundestag is the most influential. Although it has little legislative initiative, except as the opposition party uses the body "to demonstrate that it offers constructive alternatives" (p. 268) and although three-fourths of the government's bills are ultimately enacted (p. 269), the Bundestag retains some influence. As Loewenberg demonstrates, that influence appears to be growing with "the expanding importance of law in the political system" (p. 279). To substantiate this position, Loewenberg examines seven stages of the legislative process, from bill drafting to promulgation, to determine the role of the Parliament. Perhaps most important, he then illustrates the variation in Parliament's influence at each stage of the process, using five diverse pieces of legislation. The cases range from a rearmament bill, totally rewritten in the Bundestag, to a travel regulation bill, held captive in committee, to a child benefits bill, passed in unchanged form by the majority party. The examination of these bills and of the stages through which each passes is the most significant policy-oriented analysis of the workings of a non-American legislature. It allows Loewenberg to discuss sources of various legislative influences—"the origins of the legislation, its timing, its subject, and the pattern of political support and opposition it arouses" (p. 281).

Loewenberg's analysis makes it clear that specialized committees and staff are crucial to the Bundestag's exercise of policy influence. These allow the Bundestag to exercise informal influence, to develop internal policy expertise, to draft amendments to government bills, and, in the case of legislation hastily prepared by the government, to redraft legislation totally. Unfortunately, there has been no attempt since its publication 15 years ago to update Loewenberg's work, although Gerard Braunthal's fine case study of two transportation bills (1972) supplements Loewenberg's book nicely. Examining the struggles over a highway relief bill and a transportation finance bill in the mid-1950s, Braunthal demonstrates how political actors and institutions compete for policy influence and why the government could have very different levels of success with two closely related bills. Moreover, Braunthal places this comparative case study in the broader historical context of German transportation policy.

In a more recent collection of articles on European legislatures and budgetary matters (Coombes, 1976), it is evident that the policy role of the Bundestag is becoming more formidable. Not only does the German legislature clearly surpass its European counterparts in budgetary influence, but its capacities in the budgetary matters have grown since Loewenberg wrote. The budget committee's "deliberations on the government draft tend to be thorough and intensive" (p. 79) but its impact tends to be more in the number of amendments it makes than in their substantive effect. By comparison, the Italian Parliament has insufficient staffing and expertise to deal with the complexities of budgetary policy. And in the Netherlands, which has a reactive legislature, "parliament seems to many of its members to be a helpless victim rather than an independent political actor" (p. 311).

The literature on other reactive legislatures indicates they have far less policy influence than the German legislature. Their legislative initiative is largely reduced to private members' bills. But, as Mezey (1979, p. 89) notes, in reactive legislatures, unlike active ones, private members' bills "do not appear to be vehicles for protecting constituency interests." (The student of American legislatures is surprised that the scholars studying non-American legislatures examine private members' bills at all, since congressional scholars all but ignore them.)

The committee systems, with some exceptions, also tend to lack substantial resources for policy influence. In Britain, for example, committees are not specialized (Crick, 1965; Loewenberg and Patterson, 1979), most committee amendments are recommended by ministers (Loewenberg and Patterson, 1979, p. 255), and committee members lack the information and expertise available to a minister. At best, the committees can impose some delay (Loewenberg and Patterson, 1979, p. 256). Even in a study of specialized committees on European Communities Legislation, where factors favored parliamentary influence, the author found that the committees had little direct influence (Miller, 1977). He concludes, "Parliament has obtained a role in EC policymaking within the UK, but that has not meant actual influence.... The Committees have created the unrealized possibilities for giving back-benchers ante hoc influence over ED policy" (p. 68).

In his extensive historical analysis of parliamentary power in Britain, Ronald Butt concludes that "specialized committees are not a full answer to the main question of how to give Parliament more influence in major areas of policy" (1967, p. 441). He notes that the power of Commons comes from its ability to bring a government down and to debate matters of "high policy." Moreover, he claims that the policy influence of Parliament has not declined significantly and that many measures normally used to indicate declining influence, such as the reduced use of private bills on economic and social issues, are not valid indicators of legislative policy influence.

Recently, one of Butt's claims has been turned on its head. John Schwarz (1980) argues that in the 1970s Commons increased its policy influence precisely because it relaxed the parliamentary rule which had often required a government to resign. Parliament's influence then came less from the Government anticipating Parliament's reaction and more from the Commons's ability to amend and defeat government bills in committee and on the floor without the Government resigning. Under these conditions Commons has amended or defeated government bills much more frequently. Schwarz finds that Commons frequently makes key decisions on important policy matters and that the coalitions defeating the government have changing membership. Accordingly, he argues that Commons has become more a "transformative" or "policy-making" legislature rather than a mere "arena" or "legitimizing" legislature (p. 23). The question remains whether the trend Schwarz analyzes will continue, especially under a Conservative government, or whether it largely reflected growing divisions in the Labour Party.

The Canadian Parliament has also slightly strengthened its organizational potential. Kornberg (1970) described committees which met infrequently and had turnover, and Kornberg and Mishler (1976) note that committees remain weak and are staffed by only a single clerk. Although they later contend that individual members have policy influence (pp. 146-147), we find that this influence amounts to proposing resolutions for debate, introducing private bills, voting on the floor when there is a division, participating in debate, and asking questions during the question period. It should be noted, however, that their concern is primarily with the influence of members within the Parliament rather than with the influence of the Parliament itself. Paul Thomas (1979) finds that even the 1968 reform requiring that government bills be referred to committee has not significantly increased the Canadian Parliament's policy influence because party discipline within committees limits their activities.

If there are reactive legislatures which have significant and growing policy functions, they appear to be in relatively small countries: Israel, Denmark, Switzerland, and Portugal. In Israel (Mezey, 1979, pp. 98-99) and in Denmark (Damgaard, 1980) relatively strong parliamentary committees seem crucial to the legislature's policy influence. In response to a growing workload, the Danish Parliament has increased its professional staff and replaced ad hoc committees with permanent and specialized ones. Damgaard reports that the committees are "not as autonomous as their American counterparts" (p. 105) but provide the oversight mechanism, the expertise, and the division of labor necessary for policy influence. Thus, he finds that "the Danish parliament seems, like the German, to fall between the legislating and deliberating categories" (p. 113). However, because the committees over-represent affected constituencies there is a tendency for them to fit into a "sectoral policymaking" model, a counterpart to the subgovernments that students of American politics have described (p. 115).

Neither the Swiss nor Portuguese case is as strong as the Danish one. Nevertheless, Henry Kerr (1978) notes that the influence of the Swiss Federal Assembly varies across policy. The Swiss Parliament equitably represents minorities in its membership. Thus, on issues that are highly partisan, there is a strong tendency to reinforce broader societal splits. On such issues parliamentary interest, activity, and impact may be substantial, whereas on cross-cutting issues the parliament is often a rubber stamp for decisions made elsewhere. Along with Loewenberg, Kerr is one of the few scholars of non-American legislatures who has a strong research interest in the relationship between policy differences and variations in legislative influence.

The creation of a new legislature in Portugal has received some attention (Opello, 1978). Although much of what Opello presents is descriptive, he also reports findings which indicate that the Portuguese Parliament has the potential for policy influence. It possesses, for example, a system of standing specialized committees, responsible for working out the details of already approved legislation and for conducting oversight. Moreover, the legislature can override a presidential veto. Opello believes that this Parliament will have most opportunity for policy influence during minority governments.

Not all studies of reactive legislatures indicate that their influence is on the rise. In "The Bureaucratization of Policymaking in Postwar Japan," T.J. Pempel (1974) found a decline in the policy influence of the Japanese Diet. Pempel analyzed several measures of legislative influence: percentage of individually sponsored bills passed, success of opposition party bills, and amendments to government legislation. He contended that the Diet had lost much of its independent policy role and, in direct contrast with Schwarz's (1980) findings in Britain, that most amendments made to government legislation in Japan were "more procedural and definitional 'sops' than they were substantive alternatives" (p. 651-652). Pempel concluded that the Diet still has investigative and communications functions but that in policy making it has become "much more the reactive amender and legitimator of proposals generated by the bureaucracy and consolidated through bureaucratic-LDP cooperation" (p. 652).

In general, the literature on reactive legislatures does not demonstrate that most have significant policy roles, at least in comparison to the U.S. Congress and other active legislatures. Some scholars would disagree with this conclusion—for example, Loewenberg and Patterson (1979) in their comparison of executive-legislative relations in the United States, Britain, Germany, and Kenya. They contend that "the initiative in proposing policy belongs to the executive in all four systems" (p. 263) and that the major differences occur in policy adoption. There Congress has more influence than the other legislatures "in determining whether any particular part of the executive's program will be enacted" (pp. 267-268). My examination of the policy literature on Congress, however, leads me to conclude that substantial differences exist at the initiation and formulation stages as well as at the adoption stage. True, efforts to develop specialized committees and staff are making legislatures better able to influence policy in some of these countries, especially Germany; some may eventually be classified as active legislatures. But the differences between reactive and active legislatures in their law-making influence appears to be more than organizational.

Summary

In sum, the literature on the policy functioning of non-American legislatures is slim, in some cases because the legislature has not been amply studied. But more often the reason may be as Packenham (1970) states it: for many legislatures, a direct and comprehensive law-making function is not primary to their role in government.

In the framework constructed at the beginning of this essay, the literature is most helpful in eliminating many of the policy-making functions and activities which we might associate with the U.S. Congress. Many of these activities are simply not performed by most of the non-American legislatures. On the other hand, Mezey may be right when he says that active specialized committees are crucial for policy influence; they appear to be a prerequisite at least. If so, we need more detailed analysis of the workings of the committee systems in the active and reactive legislatures. With few exceptions, the discussion of the various committee systems remains general (Lees and Shaw, 1979). We certainly have nothing approaching the research that has been done on congressional committees.

There has also been little research on how legislative influence varies across policy areas, except for the books by Loewenberg (1967) and Butt (1967) and some comparative public policy studies (Smith, 1975; Heidenheimer, Heclo, and Adams, 1975). Again to the degree that research on non-American legislatures focuses on policy influence at all, it tends not to be issue specific or case oriented nor to consider a range of influence.

Conclusion

If bees can be found where the honey is, scholars interested in the influence of legislatures on policy are drawn to study Congress. From the standpoint of policy making, Congress remains the most influential legislature. Moreover, the relative ease of access, the availability of documents, and the substantial day-to-day coverage of its activities make Congress attractive to scholarly attention. This is likely to continue. Therefore, for future research on how Congress shapes policy, the main questions relate to the direction of that research.

In particular, this paper raises two questions which deserve careful consideration. The first is whether legislative scholars should encourage the monitoring, updating, and/or replication of earlier research findings in some organized or planned fashion. This, of course, could be asked about research in a range of areas. But with the stockpile of material now available on Congress and policy making, should we ensure that this sizeable asset not depreciate or become out-of-date? And how can we provide the incentives for congressional scholars to engage in such activity? Curiously, students of non-American legislatures appear to have their research responsibilities more clearly organized than do students of Congress. A 1976 survey of "Comparative Legislative Newsletter" subscribers provides a good indication of where they devote their research attention (Grumm, 1977). It is encouraging that the role of the legislature in policy making tied for the most frequently mentioned substantive research topic.

The second question is how to give the research on Congress a more systematic value. Unlike the policy research on state legislatures and on non-American legislatures, which is relatively meager and where each additional study adds to the knowledge base, congressional policy research is so plentiful that we might benefit from testing some of the knowledge that has thus far accumulated. Clausen (1982), commenting on the framework set forth at the beginning of this essay, noted, "The more serious component of the framework advanced is the implicit recognition of the need for approaches which define analytic phenomena so as to generate cases of sufficient number to permit meaningful induction and generalization" (p. 8). Although we may not yet be fully equipped to do this across legislatures, there is every indication that the base upon which such research is built already exists in the literature on how Congress shapes policy.

In the research on state legislatures and policy making, the situation is more enigmatic. There appears to be honey, or at least the potential for its production, but few bees interested in producing it. Whether scholars were discouraged by the literature of the late 1960s on state policy outputs or by the seemingly insurmountable task of coordinating qualitative policy research on 50 legislatures or by the fact that state legislatures and state governments may be perceived as the equivalent of baseball's minor leagues—for whatever reason, the available literature is slim. Something should be done to give scholars the incentive to do research on state legislative policy making. Not all legislative scholars need go to Washington, especially when state legislatures are in many cases just down the street from the campuses on which the scholars teach. In an era when the federal government may transfer program responsibility and choices back to the states, the policy-making role of state legislatures should be particularly exciting to study.

Regarding the role of non-American legislatures in policy making, I think that researchers are faced with a very different challenge from that facing either the congressional or state legislative scholars. For many legislatures, a significant policy role has not yet even been identified, and the research on the influence of those legislatures would probably be best pursued in a broader study of the law-making function. In countries with active or strong reactive legislatures, separate analysis of how those legislatures structure policy and budgets may prove useful. In these cases research on staff, committees, legislative leadership, constituency, and interest groups and on the effects they have on legislative policy outputs should be fruitful. But clearly most legislatures do not yet fall in this category.

The question thus remains whether the potential now exists for the comparative analysis of how legislatures shape policy and budgets. As may be evident from the preceding discussion, I am not terribly optimistic that such research can be successful or should be undertaken on a large scale. Nevertheless, there are some arenas in which comparative legislative policy analysis might fruitfully begin. For example, John Grumm (1973) in his monograph *A Paradigm for the Comparative Analysis of Legislative Systems* discusses a variety of approaches which may be useful in developing a theory for comparative study of legislative systems. He then constructs and tests a model of the responsive capacity of legislative systems. Grumm uses data on the American states and examines their responsive effectiveness on education and welfare policy. Although Grumm admits that this is only a "pilot" study, he is able to suggest some meaningful conclusions about the relationship between institutionalization and political differentiation of legislatures and their policy responsiveness.

Grumm realizes the limitations of such a comparative analysis. He notes that a "fundamental limitation of the pilot study was that it dealt exclusively with systems where the legislative function was presumed to be dominated by typically constituted legislative bodies" (p. 78). The question remains whether it is possible to conduct worthwhile comparative studies of the policy impact of legislatures, including legislatures that do not dominate the legislative function.

One answer to this question can be drawn from Joseph Cooper's application of organization theory to comparative legislative analysis (1982). Cooper describes three legislative forms—subservient, controlled, and independent—and within each form discusses three types. He discriminates among the forms and types according to mode of integration, operational characteristics, and, most important from the standpoint of policy impact, functional role. From Cooper's classificatory scheme comes the potential for testing meaningful comparative legislative hypotheses about legislatures of the same form and type or of the same form and different type. If scholars are to make meaningful comparative studies of how legislatures shape policy outputs, they must do so first among legislatures with similar functional roles.

When I examine the situation more pessimistically, however, I am not at all certain that the study of legislative policy making harmonizes with crossnational comparisons. A focus on the policy-making, budgetary, or legislative functions may prove far more profitable than a comparison of institutions which perform very different functions within different forms of government.

REFERENCES

Aberbach, Joel D. 1979. "Changes in Congressional Oversight," *American Behavioral Scientist* 22, no. 5:493-515.

Agor, Westin H. 1971. "The Decisional Role of the Senate in the Chilean Political System," in Westin H. Agor, ed., *Latin American Legislatures: Their Role and Influence*. New York: Praeger, pp. 3-51.

Anton, Thomas J. 1966. *The Politics of State Expenditure in Illinois*. Urbana: University of Illinois Press.

Arnold, R. Douglas. 1979. *Congress and the Bureaucracy: A Theory of Influence*. New Haven: Yale University Press.

Astiz, Carlos Alberto. 1973. "The Decay of Latin American Legislatures," in Allan Kornberg, ed., *Legislatures in Comparative Perspective*. New York: David McKay, pp. 114-126.

Bachrach, Peter and Morton S. Baratz. 1962. "Two Faces of Power," *American Political Science Review* 56:947-952.

Bailey, Stephen K. 1950. *Congress Makes A Law*. New York: Columbia University Press.

Bailey, Stephen K. and Howard D. Samuel. 1952. *Congress at Work*. New York: Holt, Rinehart & Winston.

Baker, Christopher E. 1971. "The Costa Rican Legislative Assembly: A Preliminary Evaluation of the Decisional Function," in Westin H. Agor, ed., *Latin American Legislatures: Their Role and Influence*. New York: Praeger, pp. 53-111.

Balutis, Alan and Daron Butler, eds. 1975. *The Political Pursestrings: The Role of the Legislature in the Budgetary Process*. New York: John Wiley.

Barton, Weldon V. 1982. "Coalition Building in the U.S. House of Representatives: Agricultural Legislation," in James E. Anderson, ed., *Cases in Public Policy*. 2d ed. New York: Holt, Rinehart & Winston, pp. 100-115.

Bauer, Raymond A., Ithiel de Sola Pool, and Lewis Anthony Dexter. 1963. *American Business and Public Policy*. New York: Atherton.

Bernstein, Robert A. and William W. Anthony. 1974. "The ABM Issue in the Senate, 1968-1970: The Importance of Ideology," *American Political Science Review* 68:1198-1206.

Best, James J. 1973. "The Impact of Reapportionment on the Washington House of Representatives," in James A. Robinson, ed., *State Legislative Innovation*. New York: Praeger, pp. 136-183.

BeVier, Michael J. 1979. *Politics Backstage: Inside the California Legislature*. Philadelphia: Temple University Press.

Bibby, John F. 1966. "Committee Characteristics and Legislative Oversight of Administration," *Midwest Journal of Politics* 10:78-98.

Bibby, John F. and Roger H. Davidson. 1967. *On Capitol Hill*. New York: Holt, Rinehart & Winston.

Blondel, Jean. 1973. *Comparative Legislatures*. Englewood Cliffs, NJ: Prentice-Hall.

Blondel, Jean et al. 1969-1970. "Legislative Behavior: Some Steps Towards a Cross-National Measurement," *Government and Opposition* 5:67-85.

Bolling, Richard. 1964. *House Out Of Order*. New York: Dutton.

Bone, Hugh A. 1956. "An Introduction to the Senate Policy Committees," *American Political Science Review* 50:339-359.

Bowler, M. Kenneth. 1974. *The Nixon Guaranteed Income Proposal: Substance and Process in Policy Change*. Cambridge, MA: Ballinger Books.

Brady, David W. 1973. *Congressional Voting in a Partisan Era*. Lawrence: University of Kansas Press.

Brady, David W. and Charles S. Bullock III. 1981. "Coalition Politics in the House of Representatives," in Lawrence C. Dodd and Bruce I. Oppenheimer, eds., *Congress Reconsidered*. 2d ed. Washington, DC: Congressional Quarterly Press, pp. 186-203.

Brady, David W., Joseph Cooper, and Patricia A. Hurley. 1979. "The Decline of Party in the U.S. House of Representatives," *Legislative Studies Quarterly* 4:381-407.

Braunthal, Gerard. 1972. *The West German Legislative Process: A Case Study of Two Transportation Bills*. Ithaca, NY: Cornell University Press.

Burns, James MacGregor. 1949. *Congress on Trial*. New York: Harper & Row.

_____ . 1963. *The Deadlock of Democracy: Four Party Politics In America*. Englewood Cliffs, NJ: Prentice-Hall.

Butt, Ronald. 1967. *The Power of Parliament*. New York: Walker.

Carmines, Edward G. 1974. "The Mediating Influence of State Legislatures on the Linkage Between Interparty Competition and Welfare Policies," *American Political Science Review* 68:1118-1124.

Carroll, Holbert. 1966. *The House of Representatives and Foreign Affairs*. Pittsburgh: University of Pittsburgh Press.

Chadwin, Mark L., ed. 1974. *Legislative Program Evaluation in the United States*. New Brunswick, NJ: Rutgers University-Eagleton Institute of Politics.

Chamberlain, Lawrence. 1946. *The President, Congress and Legislation*. New York: Columbia University Press.

Clark, Joseph S. 1963. *The Senate Establishment*. New York: Hill & Wang.

_____ . 1964. *Congress: The Sapless Branch*. New York: Harper & Row.

Clausen, Aage. 1973. *How Congressmen Decide*. New York: St. Martin's Press.

_____ . 1982. "Commentary on 'Outputs of Legislatures': How Legislatures Shape Policy and Budgets." Delivered at the Legislative Research Conference, University of Iowa.

Cleaveland, Frederic N. and associates. 1969. *Congress and Urban Problems*. Washington, DC: The Brookings Institution.

Coombes, David, ed. 1976. *The Power of the Purse: The Role of European Parliaments in Budgetary Decisions*. London: George Allen & Unwin.

Cooper, Joseph. 1982. "Applying Organization Theory to Comparative Legislative Analysis: Utilities, Limits, and Possibilities." Delivered at the Legislative Research Conference, University of Iowa.

Council of State Governments. 1975. *State Legislative Appropriations Process*. Lexington, KY.

Crabb, Cecil V., Jr. and Pat M. Holt. 1980. *Invitation to Struggle: Congress, President and Foreign Policy*. Washington, DC: Congressional Quarterly Press.

Crick, Bernard. 1965. *The Reform of Parliament*. New York: Anchor Books.

Cummings, Milton C., Jr. and Robert L. Peabody. 1963. "The Decision to Enlarge the Committee on Rules: An Analysis of the 1961 Vote," in Robert L. Peabody and Nelson W. Polsky, eds., *New Perspectives on the House of Representatives*. Chicago: Rand McNally, pp. 167-194.

Dahl, Robert. 1950. *Congress and Foreign Policy*. New York: Harcourt, Brace.

Damgaard, Erik. 1980. "The Function of Parliament in the Danish Political System: Results of Recent Research," *Legislative Studies Quarterly* 5:101-121.

Davidson, Roger H. 1977. "Breaking Up Those 'Cozy Triangles': An Impossible Dream?" in Susan Welch and John G. Peters, eds., *Legislative Reform and Public Policy*. New York: Praeger, pp. 30-53.

Davis, David Howard. 1974. *Energy Politics*. New York: St. Martin's Press.

Dawson, Raymond. 1962. "Congressional Innovation and Intervention in Defense Policy: Legislative Authorization of Weapons Systems," *American Political Science Review* 56:42-57.

Derthick, Martha. 1979. *Policymaking for Social Security*. Washington, DC: The Brookings Institution.

Destler, I. M. 1981a. "Executive-Congressional Conflict in Foreign Policy: Explaining It, Coping With It," in Lawrence C. Dodd and Bruce I. Oppenheimer, eds., *Congress Reconsidered*. 2d ed. Washington, DC: Congressional Quarterly Press, pp. 296-316.

_____ . 1981b. "Trade Consensus, SALT Stalemate: Congress and Foreign Policy in the 1970s," in Thomas C. Mann and Norman J. Ornstein, eds., *The New Congress*. Washington, DC: The American Enterprise Institute, pp. 329-359.

Dexter, Lewis Anthony. 1963. "Congressmen and the Making of Military Policy," in Robert L. Peabody and Nelson W. Polsby, eds., *New Perspectives on the House of Representatives*. Chicago: Rand McNally, pp. 305-324.

DiPalma, Giuseppe. 1977. *Surviving without Governing: The Italian Parties in Parliament*. Berkeley: University of California Press.

Dodd, Lawrence C. 1977. "Congress and the Quest for Power," in Lawrence C. Dodd and Bruce I. Oppenheimer, eds., *Congress Reconsidered*. New York: Praeger, pp. 269-307.

Dodd, Lawrence C. and Bruce I. Oppenheimer. 1977a. "The House in Transition," in Lawrence C. Dodd and Bruce I. Oppenheimer, eds., *Congress Reconsidered*. New York: Praeger, pp. 31-61.

_____ , eds. 1977b. *Congress Reconsidered*. New York: Praeger.

Dodd, Lawrence C. and Richard Schott. 1979. *Congress and the Administrative State*. New York: John Wiley.

Donovan, John C. 1967. *The Politics of Poverty*. New York: Pegasus.

Doubleday, D. J. 1967. *Legislative Review of the Budget in California*. Berkeley: University of California Press.

Dye, Thomas R. 1965. "State Legislative Politics," in Herbert Jacob and Kenneth N. Vines, eds., *Politics in the American States*. Boston: Little, Brown.

_____ . 1966. *Politics, Economics and the Public: Policy Outcomes in the American States*. Chicago: Rand McNally.

Edelman, Murray. 1964. *The Symbolic Uses of Politics*. Urbana: University of Illinois Press.

Edwards, George S. III. 1980. *Presidential Influence in Congress*. San Francisco: W. H. Freeman.

Eidenberg, Eugene and Roy D. Morey. 1969. *An Act of Congress: The Legislative Process and the Making of Education Policy*. New York: Norton.

Elliff, John T. 1977. "Congress and the Intelligence Community," in Lawrence C. Dodd and Bruce I. Oppenheimer, eds., *Congress Reconsidered*. New York: Praeger, pp. 193-206.

Elling, Richard C. 1979. "The Utility of State Legislative Casework as a Means of Oversight," *Legislative Studies Quarterly* 4:353-379.

Ellwood, John W. and James A. Thurber. 1981. "The Politics of the Congressional Budget Process Re-examined," in Lawrence C. Dodd and Bruce I. Oppenheimer, eds., *Congress Reconsidered*. 2d ed. Washington, DC: Congressional Quarterly Press, pp. 246-271.

Fenno, Richard F., Jr. 1966. *The Power of the Purse*. Boston: Little, Brown.
———. 1973. *Congressmen in Committees*. Boston: Little, Brown.
Ferejohn, John A. 1974. *Pork Barrel Politics: Rivers and Harbors Legislation, 1947-1968*. Stanford, CA: Stanford University Press.
Fiorina, Morris P. 1977. *Congress: Keystone of the Washington Establishment*. New Haven: Yale University Press.
———. 1981. "Congressional Control of the Bureaucracy: A Mismatch of Incentives and Capabilities," in Lawrence C. Dodd and Bruce I. Oppenheimer, eds., *Congress Reconsidered*. 2d ed. Washington, DC: Congressional Quarterly Press, pp. 332-348.
Fisher, Louis. 1972. *President and Congress: Power and Policy*. New York: The Free Press.
Francis, Wayne L. 1967. *Legislative Issues in the Fifty States*. Chicago: Rand McNally.
Francis, Wayne L. and Ronald E. Weber. 1980. "Legislative Issues in the 50 States: Managing Complexity Through Classification," *Legislative Studies Quarterly* 5:407-421.
Franck, Thomas M. and Edward Wiesland. 1979. *Foreign Policy by Congress*. New York: Oxford University Press.
Freeman, J. Leiper. 1977. "Investigating the Executive Intelligence. The Fate of the Pike Committee," *Capitol Studies* 5, no. 2:103-117.
Froman, Lewis A., Jr. 1967. *The Congressional Process: Strategies, Rules, and Procedures*. Boston: Little, Brown.
———. 1968. "The Categorization of Policy Contents," in Austin Ranney, ed., *Political Science and Public Policy*. Chicago: Markham Publishing, pp. 41-52.
Froman, Lewis A. and Randall B. Ripley. 1965. "Conditions for Party Leadership: The Case of the House Democrats," *American Political Science Review* 59:52-63.
Frost, Richard T., ed. 1961. *Cases in State and Local Governments*. Englewood Cliffs, NJ: Prentice-Hall.
Fry, Brian R. and Richard F. Winters. 1970. "The Politics of Redistribution," *American Political Science Review* 64:502-522.
Frye, Alton. 1975. *A Responsible Congress: The Politics of National Security*. New York: McGraw-Hill.
Gist, John R. 1981. "The Impact of Annual Authorizations on Military Appropriations in the U.S. Congress," *Legislative Studies Quarterly* 6:439-454.
Goguel, Francis. 1971. "Parliament Under the Fifth French Republic: Difficulties of Adapting to a New Role," in Gerhard Loewenberg, ed., *Modern Parliaments: Change or Decline?* Chicago: Aldine-Atherton, pp. 81-95.
Goldman, Sheldon. 1968. *Roll Call Behavior in the Massachusetts House of Representatives*. Amherst: Bureau of Government Research, University of Massachusetts.
Gordon, Bernard R. 1961. "The Military Budget: Congressional Phase," *Journal of Politics* 23:689-710.
Gove, Samuel K. 1973. "Policy Implications of Legislative Reorganization in Illinois," in James A. Robinson, ed., *State Legislative Information*. New York: Praeger, pp. 101-135.
Griffith, J.A.G. 1974. *Parliamentary Scrutiny of Government Bills*. London: Allen & Unwin.
Gross, Bertram T. 1953. *The Legislative Struggle: A Study of Social Combat*. New York: McGraw-Hill.
Grumm, John G. 1973. *A Paradigm for the Comparative Analysis of Legislative Systems*. Beverly Hills, CA: Sage Publications.
———. 1977. "Survey of Comparative Legislative Research," *Legislative Studies Quarterly* 2:481-486.

Hamm, Keith E. 1980. "U.S. State Legislative Committee Decisions: Similar Results in Different Settings," *Legislative Studies Quarterly* 5:31-54.

Hamm, Keith E. and Roby D. Robertson. 1981. "Factors Influencing the Adoption of New Methods of Legislative Oversight in the U.S. States," *Legislative Studies Quarterly* 6:133-150.

Havemann, Joel. 1978. *Congress and the Budget.* Bloomington: Indiana University Press.

Hayes, Michael T. 1981. *Lobbyists and Legislators: A Theory of Political Markets.* New Brunswick, NJ: Rutgers University Press.

Hedlund, Ronald D. and Patricia K. Freeman. 1981. "A Strategy for Measuring the Performance of Legislatures in Processing Decisions," *Legislative Studies Quarterly* 6:87-113.

Hedlund, Ronald D. and Keith E. Hamm. 1978. "Institutional Innovation and Performance Effectiveness in Public Policy Making," in Leroy Rieselbach, ed., *Legislative Reform: The Policy Impact.* Lexington, MA: Lexington Books, pp. 117-132.

Heidenheimer, Arnold, Hugh Heclo, and Carolyn Teich Adams. 1975. *Comparative Public Policy: The Politics of Social Choice in Europe and America.* New York: St. Martin's Press.

Hennis, Wilhelm. 1971. "Reform of the Bundestag: The Case for General Debate," in Gerhard Loewenberg, ed., *Modern Parliaments: Change or Decline?* Chicago: Aldine-Atherton, pp. 65-79.

Hofferbert, Richard I. 1966. "The Relationship between Public Policy and Some Structural and Environmental Variables in the American States," *American Political Science Review* 60:73-82.

Horn, Stephen. 1970. *Unused Power.* Washington, DC: The Brookings Institution.

Hughes, S.W. and K.J. Mijeski. 1973. "Legislative-Executive Policy-Making: The Case of Chile and Costa Rica," Sage Research Papers in the Social Sciences. Beverly Hills, CA: Sage Publications.

Huitt, Ralph K. 1961. "Democratic Party Leadership in the Senate," *American Political Science Review* 55:333-344.

Ingram, Helen M., Nancy K. Laney, and John R. McCain. 1980. *A Policy Approach to Political Representation: Lessons From the Four Corners.* Baltimore: The Johns Hopkins Press.

Ippolito, Dennis. 1981. *Congressional Spending.* Ithaca, NY: Cornell University Press.

Jacob, Herbert. 1966. "Dimensions of State Politics," in Alexander Heard, ed., *State Legislatures in American Politics.* Englewood Cliffs, NJ: Prentice-Hall.

Jewell, Malcolm E. 1962. *Senatorial Politics and Foreign Policy.* Lexington, KY: University of Kentucky Press.

——————. 1981. "Editor's Introduction: The State of U.S. State Legislative Research," *Legislative Studies Quarterly* 6:1-23.

Johnson, Loch. 1980. "The U.S. Congress and the CIA: Monitoring the Dark Side of Government," *Legislative Studies Quarterly* 4:477-499.

Jones, Charles O. 1961. "The Agriculture Committee and the Problem of Representation," *American Political Science Review* 55:358-367.

——————. 1964. *Party and Policy-making: The House Republican Policy Committee.* New Brunswick, NJ: Rutgers University Press.

——————. 1968. "The Minority Party and Policy-making in the House of Representatives," *American Political Science Review* 62:481-493.

——————. 1975. *Clean Air: The Policies and Politics of Pollution Control.* Pittsburgh: University of Pittsburgh Press.

Kaiser, Fred. 1977. "Oversight of Foreign Policy: The U.S. House Committee on International Relations," *Legislative Studies Quarterly* 2:255-280.

Kanter, Arnold. 1972. "Congress and the Defense Budget: 1960-1970," *American Political Science Review* 66:128-143.

Karnig, Albert K. and Lee Sigelman. 1975. "State Legislative Reform and Public Policy: Another Look," *Western Political Quarterly* 7:51-59.

Kent, James P. 1975. "Legislative Fiscal Staffing in Illinois," in Alan P. Balutis and Daron K. Butler, eds., *The Political Pursestrings*. New York: John Wiley, pp. 91-101.

Kerr, Henry H., Jr. 1978. "The Structure of Opposition in the Swiss Parliament," *Legislative Studies Quarterly* 3:51-62.

Kingdon, John. 1981. *Congressmen's Voting Decisions*. 2d ed. New York: Harper & Row.

Kolodziej, Edward. 1966. *The Uncommon Defense and Congress, 1945-1963*. Columbus: Ohio State University Press.

Kornberg, Allan. 1970. "Parliament in Canadian Society," in Allan Kornberg and Lloyd D. Musolf, eds., *Legislatures in Developmental Perspective*. Durham, NC: Duke University Press, pp. 55-128.

_____ , ed. 1973. *Legislatures in Comparative Perspective*. New York: David McKay.

Kornberg, Allan and William Mishler. 1976. *Influence in Parliament: Canada*. Durham, NC: Duke University Press.

LeBlanc, Hugh L. 1969. "Voting in State Senates: Party and Constituency Influences," *Midwest Journal of Political Science* 13:33-57.

Lees, John D. and Malcolm Shaw. 1979. *Committees in Legislatures: A Comparative Perspective*. Durham, NC: Duke University Press.

Leites, N. 1959. *On the Game of Politics in France*. Stanford, CA: Stanford University Press.

LeLoup, Lance T. 1979. "Process Versus Policy: The U.S. House Budget Committee," *Legislative Studies Quarterly* 4:227-254.

_____ . 1980. *The Fiscal Congress*. Westport, CT: Greenwood Press.

Levine, Erwin L. and Elizabeth M. Wexler. 1981. *PL 94-142: An Act of Congress*. New York: Macmillan.

Loewenberg, Gerhard. 1967. *Parliament in the German Political System*. Ithaca, NY: Cornell University Press.

_____ , ed. 1971. *Modern Parliaments: Change or Decline?* Chicago: Aldine-Atherton.

Loewenberg, Gerhard and Samuel C. Patterson. 1979. *Comparing Legislatures*. Boston: Little, Brown.

Lowi, Theodore J. 1964. "American Business, Public Policy, Case-Studies, and Political Theory," *World Politics* 16:677-715.

_____ . 1969. *The End of Liberalism*. New York: Norton.

MacKintosh, John P. 1971. "Reform of the House of Commons: The Case for Specialization," in Gerhard Loewenberg, ed., *Modern Parliaments: Change or Decline?* Chicago: Aldine-Atherton, pp. 33-63.

Manley, John F. 1969. *The Politics of Finance*. Boston: Little, Brown.

_____ . 1973. "The Conservative Coalition in Congress," *American Behavioral Scientist* 17:223-247.

Mann, Thomas E. and Norman J. Ornstein, eds. 1981. *The New Congress*. Washington, DC: American Enterprise Institute.

Mansfield, Harvey C., Sr., ed. 1975. *Congress Against the President*. New York: Praeger.

Marmor, Theodore R. 1970. *The Politics of Medicare*. Chicago: Aldine.

Masters, Nicholas A., Robert A. Salisbury, and Thomas H. Eliot. 1964. *State Politics and the Public Schools*. New York: Knopf.

Matsunaga, Spark M. and Ping Chen. 1976. *Rulemakers of the House.* Urbana: University of Illinois Press.

Matthews, Donald R. 1960. *U.S. Senators and Their World.* Chapel Hill: University of North Carolina Press.

Matthews, Donald R. and James A. Stimson. 1975. *Yeas and Nays.* New York: John Wiley.

Mayhew, David R. 1966. *Party Loyalty Among Congressmen.* Cambridge: Harvard University Press.

McDonald, Ronald H. 1971. "Legislative Politics in Uruguay: A Preliminary Statement," in Westin H. Agor, ed., *Latin American Legislatures: Their Role and Influence.* New York: Praeger, pp. 113-135.

Mezey, Michael L. 1979. *Comparative Legislatures.* Durham, NC: Duke University Press.

Miller, Harris N. 1977. "The Influence of British Parliamentary Committees on European Communities Legislation," *Legislative Studies Quarterly* 2:45-75.

Milstein, Mike M. and Robert E. Jennings. 1973. *Educational Policy-making and the State Legislature: The New York Experience.* New York: Praeger.

Moe, Ronald C. and Steven C. Teel. 1970. "Congress as Policy-Maker: A Necessary Reappraisal," *Political Science Quarterly* 85:443-470.

Munger, Frank J. and Richard F. Fenno, Jr. 1962. *National Politics and Federal Aid to Education.* Syracuse, NY: Syracuse University Press.

Murphy, James. 1974. "Political Parties and the Pork-barrel: Party Conflict and Cooperation in House Public Works Committee Decision Making," *American Political Science Review* 68:169-185.

Neustadt, Richard E. 1955. "Presidency and Legislation: Planning the President's Program," *American Political Science Review* 49:980-1021.

Ogul, Morris S. 1976. *Congress Oversees the Bureaucracy: Studies in Legislative Supervision.* Pittsburgh: University of Pittsburgh.

Oleszek, Walter J. 1978. *Congressional Procedures and the Policy Process.* Washington, DC: Congressional Quarterly Press.

Opello, Walter C., Jr. 1978. "The New Parliament in Portugal," *Legislative Studies Quarterly* 3:309-324.

Oppenheimer, Bruce I. 1974. *Oil and the Congressional Process.* Lexington, MA: Lexington Books.

_____ . 1978. "Policy Implications of Rules Committee Reforms," in Leroy Rieselbach, ed., *Legislative Reform: The Policy Impact.* Lexington, MA: Lexington Books, pp. 91-104.

_____ . 1980. "Policy Effects of U.S. House Reform: Decentralization and the Capacity to Resolve Energy Issues," *Legislative Studies Quarterly* 5:5-30.

_____ . 1981. "Congress and the New Obstructionism: Developing an Energy Program," in Lawrence C. Dodd and Bruce I. Oppenheimer, eds., *Congress Reconsidered.* 2d ed. Washington, DC: Congressional Quarterly Press, pp. 275-295.

Orfield, Gary. 1975. *Congressional Power: Congress and Social Change.* New York: Harcourt Brace Jovanovich.

Ornstein, Norman J., ed. 1974. *Changing Congress: The Committee System.* The Annals of the American Academy of Political and Social Science, vol. 411. Philadelphia.

_____ , ed. 1975. *Congress in Change: Evolution and Reform.* New York: Praeger.

Ornstein, Norman J. and Shirley Elder. 1978. *Interest Groups, Lobbying, and Policymaking.* Washington, DC: Congressional Quarterly Press.

Ornstein, Norman J. and David W. Rohde. 1977. "Shifting Forces, Changing Rules, and Political Outcomes," in Robert L. Peabody and Nelson W. Polsby, ed., *New Perspectives on the House of Representatives.* 3d ed. Chicago: Rand McNally, pp. 186-269.

Packenham, Robert A. 1970. "Legislatures and Political Development," in Allan Kornberg and Lloyd D. Musolf, eds., *Legislatures in Developmental Perspective*. Durham, NC: Duke University Press, pp. 521-582.

Patterson, James T. 1967. *Congressional Conservatism and the New Deal*. Lexington: University of Kentucky Press.

Patterson, Samuel C. 1974. "Legislative Research and Legislative Reform: Evaluating Regime Policy," *Publius* 4:109-115.

_____. 1976. "American State Legislatures and Public Policy," in Herbert Jacob and Kenneth N. Hines, eds., *Politics in the American States: A Comparative Analysis*. 3d ed. Boston: Little, Brown, pp. 139-195.

Peabody, Robert L. 1963. "The Enlarged Rules Committee," in Robert L. Peabody and Nelson W. Polsby, eds., *New Perspectives on the House of Representatives*. Chicago: Rand McNally, pp. 129-164.

_____. 1969. "Research on Congress: A Coming of Age," in Ralph K. Huitt and Robert L. Peabody, *Congress: Two Decades of Analysis*. New York: Harper & Row.

_____. 1981. "House Party Leadership in the 1970s," in Lawrence C. Dodd and Bruce I. Oppenheimer, eds., *Congress Reconsidered*. 2d ed. Washington, DC: Congressional Quarterly Press, pp. 137-155.

Peabody, Robert L., Jeffrey M. Berry, William G. Frasure, and Gerry Goldman. 1972. *To Enact a Law: Congress and Campaign Financing*. New York: Praeger.

Pempel, T.J. 1974. "The Bureaucratization of Policymaking in Postwar Japan," *American Journal of Political Science* 18:647-664.

Pious, Richard M. 1975. "Sources of Domestic Initiatives," in Harvey C. Mansfield, Sr., ed., *Congress Against the President*. New York: Praeger, pp. 98-111.

Platt, Alan. 1978. *The U.S. Senate and Strategic Arms Policy, 1969-1977*. Boulder, CO: Westview Press.

Polsby, Nelson W. 1969. "Goodbye to the Inner Club," *Washington Monthly* 1:30-34.

Price, David E. 1972. *Who Makes the Laws?* Cambridge, MA: Schenkman Publishing.

_____. 1978a. "Policy Making in Congressional Committees: The Impact of 'Environmental' Factors," *American Political Science Review* 72:548-574.

_____. 1978b. "The Impact of Reform: The House Commerce Committee Subcommittee on Oversight and Investigations," in Leroy Rieselbach, ed., *Legislative Reform: The Policy Impact*. Lexington, MA: Lexington Books, pp. 133-157.

_____. 1981. "Congressional Committees in the Policy Process," in Lawrence C. Dodd and Bruce I. Oppenheimer, eds., *Congress Reconsidered*. 2d ed. Washington, DC: Congressional Quarterly Press, pp. 156-185.

Ranney, Austin, ed. 1968. *Political Science and Public Policy*. Chicago: Markham Publishing.

Ransom, Harry Howe. 1975. "Congress and the Intelligence Agencies," *Proceedings of the Academy of Political Science* 32, no. 1:153-166.

_____. 1977. "Congress and the Reform of the C.I.A.," *Policy Studies Journal* 5:476-480.

Ray, Bruce A. 1980. "The Responsiveness of U.S. Congressional Armed Services Committees to Their Parent Bodies," *Legislative Studies Quarterly* 4:501-516.

Redman, Eric. 1973. *The Dance of Legislation*. New York: Simon and Schuster.

Reid, T.R. 1980. *Congressional Odyssey*. San Francisco: W.H. Freeman.

Ripley, Randall B. 1964. "The Party Whip Organizations in the United States House of Representatives," *American Political Science Review* 58:561-576.

_____. 1967. *Party Leaders in the House of Representatives*. Washington, DC: The Brookings Institution.

————. 1969. "Congress and Clean Air: The Issue of Enforcement, 1963," in Frederic N. Cleaveland and Associates, *Congress and Urban Problems.* Washington, DC: The Brookings Institution, pp. 224-278.

————. 1969. *Power In the Senate.* New York: St. Martin's Press.

————. 1978. *Congress: Process and Policy.* New York: Norton.

Ritt, Leonard B. 1973. "State Legislative Reform: Does It Matter?" *American Politics Quarterly* 1:499-510.

Robinson, James A. 1963. *The House Rules Committee.* Indianapolis: Bobbs-Merrill.

————, ed. 1973. *State Legislative Innovation: Case Studies of Washington, Ohio, Florida, Illinois, Wisconsin, and California.* New York: Praeger.

Rosenthal, Alan. 1974. *Legislative Performance in the States.* New York: The Free Press.

Rosenthal, Alan and Rod Forth. 1978. "The Assembly Line: Law Production in the American States," *Legislative Studies Quarterly* 3:265-291.

Rudder, Catherine E. 1977. "Committee Reform and the Revenue Process," in Lawrence C. Dodd and Bruce I. Oppenheimer, eds., *Congress Reconsidered.* New York: Praeger, pp. 117-134.

————. 1978. "The Policy Impact of Reform of the Committee on Ways and Means," in Leroy Rieselbach, ed., *Legislative Reform: The Policy Impact.* Lexington, MA: Lexington Books, pp. 73-89.

Salisbury, Robert H. 1968. "The Analysis of Public Policy: A Search for Theories and Rules," in Austin Ranney, ed., *Political Science and Public Policy.* Chicago: Markham Publishing, pp. 151-175.

Schattschneider, E.E. 1935. *Politics, Pressures and the Tariff.* Englewood Cliffs, NJ: Prentice-Hall.

Scher, Seymour. 1963. "Conditions for Legislative Control," *Journal of Politics* 25: 526-551.

Schick, Allen. 1980. *Congress and Money: Budgeting, Spending and Taxing.* Washington, DC: The Urban Institute.

Schwarz, John E. 1980. "Exploring a New Role in Policy Making: The British House of Commons in the 1970s," *American Political Science Review* 74:23-37.

Sharkansky, Ira. 1968. *Spending in the American States.* Chicago: Rand McNally.

Sharkansky, Ira and Richard I. Hofferbert. 1969. "Dimensions of State Politics, Economics, and Public Policy," *American Political Science Review* 63:867-879.

Sinclair, Barbara. 1981. "The Speaker's Task Force in the Post-Reform House of Representatives," *American Political Science Review* 75:397-410.

————. 1981. "Agenda and Alignment Change: The House of Representatives, 1925-1978," in Lawrence C. Dodd and Bruce I. Oppenheimer, eds., *Congress Reconsidered.* 2d ed. Washington, DC: Congressional Quarterly Press, pp. 221-245.

Smith, T. Alexander. 1975. *The Comparative Policy Process.* Santa Barbara, CA: ABC-Clio Press.

Spanier, John and Joseph Nogee. 1981. *Congress, the Presidency and American Foreign Policy.* New York: Pergamon Press.

Stauffer, Robert B. 1970. "Congress in the Philippine Political System," in Allan Kornberg and Lloyd D. Musolf, eds., *Legislatures in Developmental Perspective.* Durham, NC: Duke University Press, pp. 334-365.

————. 1975. "The Philippine Congress: Causes of Structural Change." Sage Research Papers in the Social Sciences. Beverly Hills, CA: Sage Publications.

Steiner, Gilbert Y. 1966. *Social Insecurity: The Politics of Welfare.* Washington, DC: The Brookings Institution.

Steiner, Gilbert Y. and Samuel K. Gove. 1960. *Legislative Politics in Illinois.* Urbana: University of Illinois Press.

Stephens, Herbert. 1971. "The Role of the Legislative Committees in the Appropriations Process: A Study Focused on the Armed Services Committees," *Western Political Quarterly* 24:146-162.

Sundquist, James L. 1968. *Politics and Policy.* Washington, DC: The Brookings Institution.

——————. 1981. *The Decline and Resurgence of Congress.* Washington, DC: The Brookings Institution.

Tatalovich, Raymond. 1978. "Legislative Quality and Legislative Policy Making: Some Implications for Reform," in Leroy Rieselbach, ed., *Legislative Reform: The Policy Impact.* Lexington, MA: Lexington Books, pp. 223-231.

Thomas, Norman C. 1975. *Education in National Politics.* New York: David McKay.

Thomas, Paul G. 1979. "The Influence of Standing Committees of Parliament on Government Legislation," *Legislative Studies Quarterly* 3:683-704.

Truman, David. 1959. *The Congressional Party.* New York: John Wiley.

Turner, Julius. 1951. *Party and Constituency: Pressures on Congress.* Baltimore: The Johns Hopkins Press.

——————. 1970. *Party and Constituency: Pressures on Congress.* Rev. ed. by Edward V. Schneier. Baltimore: The Johns Hopkins Press.

Vinyard, Dale. 1968. "The Congressional Committees on Small Business: Pattern of Legislative Committee-Executive Agency Relations," *Western Political Quarterly* 21:391-399.

Wahlke, John C. 1971. "Policy Demands and System Support: The Role of Parliament," in Gerhard Loewenberg, ed., *Modern Parliaments: Change or Decline?* Chicago: Aldine-Atherton, pp. 141-171.

Wahlke, John C., Heinz Eulau, William Buchanan, and LeRoy C. Ferguson. 1962. *The Legislative System.* New York: John Wiley.

Walker, Jack L. 1969. "The Diffusion of Innovations Among the American States," *American Political Science Review* 63:880-899.

Wayne, Stephen J. 1978. *The Legislative Presidency.* New York: Harper & Row.

Welch, Susan and John G. Peters, eds. 1977. *Legislative Reform and Public Policy.* New York: Praeger.

White, William S. 1956. *Citadel: The Story of the United States Senate.* New York: Harper.

Wiggins, Charles W. 1967. "Party Politics in the Iowa Legislature," *Midwest Journal of Political Science* 11:86-97.

Williams, Philip M. 1964. *Crisis and Compromise: Politics in the Fourth Republic.* Hamden, CT: Archon Books.

——————. 1971. "Parliament Under the Fifth French Republic: Patterns of Executive Domination," in Gerhard Loewenberg, ed., *Modern Parliaments: Change or Decline?* Chicago: Aldine-Atherton, pp. 97-109.

Wildavsky, Aaron. 1964. *The Politics of the Budgetary Process.* Boston: Little, Brown.

Winters, Richard. 1976. "Party Control and Policy Change," *American Journal of Political Science* 20:597-637.

Wolman, Harold. 1971. *Politics of Federal Housing.* New York: Dodd, Mead.

Wyner, Alan J. 1973. "Legislative Reform and Politics in California: What Happened, Why, and So What?" in James A. Robinson, ed., *State Legislative Innovation.* New York: Praeger, pp. 46-100.

Zeigler, Harmon and Michael A. Baer. 1969. *Lobbying: Interaction and Influence in American State Legislatures.* Belmont, CA: Wadsworth Publishing.

Chapter 14

Formal Models
Of Legislative Processes

by

WILLIAM H. PANNING

Over two decades ago Richard Fenno argued that for students of Congress "the sheer generation of data has proceeded so much faster than the generation of theory, that we are woefully short-handed for ways of relating one set of facts to another" (1964, p. 975). Two years later, Eulau and Hinckley concluded that for legislative research "the next step toward maturity must be accelerated theoretical advance" (1966, p. 179). In another influential review published three years later, Robert Peabody likewise asserted that "the critical need is for theory" (1969, p. 70). Today, many political scientists would agree that the need for "more and better theory" is just as pressing.

Formal analysis is distinguished as a mode of inquiry by the kind of theory to which it aspires and by the means it employs in developing it. In this essay I review those portions of formal theory that pertain to legislative phenomena and evaluate the theory's success in providing theoretical understanding of these phenomena. I begin with studies of coalitions, studies which were stimulated in large part by Riker's *Theory of Political Coalitions* (1962) but whose intellectual origins are found in Von Neumann and Morgenstern's *Theory of Games and Economic Behavior* (1944). I then turn to studies that pertain to voting in legislatures and committees. For the most part, these studies are the direct or indirect intellectual progeny of Arrow's *Social Choice and Individual Values* (1951) and Black's *Theory of Committees and Elections* (1958; see also Black, 1948) and comprise a portion of the vast area of study known as social choice. Next, I discuss the emerging research agenda in formal theory, an agenda principally concerned with accounting for the considerable discrepancy between the characteristics of legislative processes that are predicted by extant social choice theory and those that are in fact observed. Here I discuss the role of assumptions in formal theorizing and argue that the discrepancy between theory and observation may well result from the assumptions employed and the questions addressed by theorists. However, I also discuss a number of studies that exemplify in both respects a different kind of theorizing with considerable promise. I conclude with a brief discussion of the relationship between formal theory and empirical research.

Throughout the essay my exposition is nontechnical, in some cases at the expense of the precision and detail rightly considered important by formal theorists. I consequently focus almost exclusively on the substantive implications of formal analyses rather than upon the procedures by which they were derived. More technical treatments are readily available in several excellent texts and reviews (Brams, 1973, 1975; Abrams, 1980; Shepsle, 1974b; Ferejohn and Fiorina, 1975; Frohlich and Oppenheimer, 1978; Hinckley, 1981; Riker and Ordeshook, 1972) as well as in the original sources.

Coalitions

Coalition theory owes its existence to the theory of games developed by Von Neumann and Morgenstern (1944). Much of the subsequent work in game theory, especially recently, has been concerned with coalitions. However, most of this work is abstract and consists of proposals or critiques of solution concepts, criteria for identifying stable configurations of payoffs in particular classes of games with three or more actors. Yet another large literature is concerned with coalitions that form in experimental games. Here I shall focus on those studies that aim instead to explain the characteristics of coalitions in legislative bodies.

First among these is Riker's *Theory of Political Coalitions* (1962). Riker argues that "in social situations similar to n-person, zero-sum games with side-payments, participants create coalitions just as large as they believe will ensure winning and no larger" (1962, pp. 32-33; see also Riker, 1967). To see what this statement implies, consider a parliamentary system in which there are three parties, with 25, 30, and 45 members respectively. Von Neumann and Morgenstern (1944) predicted that in such a situation a government would be formed by a coalition consisting of any two of the three parties, since any two would together comprise a majority. In their terminology, each of the three possible coalitions is "minimal winning," since the removal of a single party from each of them would change its status from winning to losing. Their prediction, then, is that only minimal winning coalitions will occur.

Riker, by contrast, focuses attention upon the sizes or "weights" of each party and predicts that only coalitions of minimal size will occur—in this case, the coalition consisting of the parties with 25 and 30 members. Riker's hypothesis is therefore aptly named the "size principle." A similar hypothesis was independently proposed by Gamson (1961).

Riker's hypothesis is more specific than that of Von Neumann and Morgenstern. Coalitions of minimal size are a subset of minimal winning coalitions. Riker's aim is therefore to predict which of the several minimal winning coalitions will occur. Suppose, however, that there are five parties, each with 20 members. In this and other cases in which the parties or other actors have identical sizes or weights, the set of coalitions of minimal size is identical to the set of minimal winning coalitions.

Riker claims that his size principle applies to situations that can be represented as zero-sum games—situations in which the gains of the winners are exactly equal to the losses of the losers—in which participants have perfect and complete information concerning the weights and actions of others. However, Koehler (1972, 1975a) has argued that this principle can be extended to coalitions on congressional roll-call votes, which are not usually considered zero-sum contests and concerning which actors' information is typically imperfect and incomplete. Koehler argues that since turnout on roll-call votes is uncertain, party leaders will tend to create coalitions consisting of an absolute majority of the membership rather than simply a majority of those present and voting. In his view, this satisfactorily accounts for the fact that roll-call votes are won by coalitions that exceed minimum size. (He rules out of consideration roll calls that approach unanimity, on the ground that they are "uncontested.") Koehler's argument is consistent with Riker's (1962, pp. 88-89) claim that coalitions exceeding minimal size will form when actors' information is imperfect and incomplete and presumes (as does Riker) that coalitions exercise control over their membership.

The theoretical validity of the size principle has been challenged by Butterworth (1971a, 1971b; see also Riker, 1971), who argued that the possibility of side-payments would enable some members of the losing coalition to bribe the winners into including them in their coalition, thereby creating a coalition that exceeds minimum size. Shepsle (1974a) replied, however, that competition among the losers for such inclusion would ultimately restore the coalition to minimum size. Later critiques by Frohlich (1975) and Hardin (1976) demonstrated more serious problems: coalitions of minimum size are inherently unstable and can be expected to form only in a very restricted class of situations (cp. Riker, 1977; Hardin, 1977). Under most conditions what can be expected is an unending series of coalitions, each created by bargains in which losers induce a member of the winning coalition to defect and join them in forming a new coalition.

Alternative theories of coalitions have been proposed by Leiserson, Axelrod, and DeSwaan. Leiserson (1968, 1970) argues that since bargaining costs among coalition members increase with their number, those coalitions will form that are minimal winning (in the sense of Von Neumann and Morgenstern) and that also have the fewest members. If, for example, there are three parties with 20 members each and four others with 10 each, Leiserson predicts that the coalition that forms will consist of the three large parties rather than, say, two of the large parties and two of the small ones.

Axelrod (1970) incorporates into his model the ideological positions of parties, as represented by their locations on some policy dimension. He predicts that coalitions will consist of parties that are connected—adjacent to one another on this policy dimension—and, of those that are connected, minimal winning. For example, if parties A through E, each with 20 members, are located from left to right on the policy dimension, then the coalitions consistent with Axelrod's prediction are (A, B, C), (B, C, D), and (C, D, E). The coalition (A, B, C, D) is connected but not minimal winning, whereas (A, C, D) is minimal winning but not connected. Hence, Axelrod predicts that neither would form.

DeSwaan's (1970, 1973) proposed theory, like Axelrod's, takes into account the ideological positions of parties but presumes that parties strive to join coalitions whose policies they expect to be most similar to their own. For example, party C may prefer to be a member of coalition (B, C, D) rather than of coalitions (A, B, C) or (C, D, E) if it expects the policies adopted by the former to be closer to its position on the policy dimension.

These various coalition theories are of two general types. Those of Riker, Gamson, and Leiserson imply that coalitions will be minimal winning and attempt to specify which of the possible minimum winning coalitions will form. By contrast, the theories of Axelrod and DeSwaan predict that coalitions will consist of members that are ideologically compatible and will be minimal winning only with respect to the set of compatible coalitions, not with respect to all possible coalitions. Despite these differences, all of them presume that coalitions exercise control over their membership and can therefore eject "surplus" members. This presumption thus renders these theories more applicable to the formation of parliamentary governing coalitions than to voting coalitions on roll calls in legislatures that lack disciplined parties. It is not surprising, then, that none of them has proved satisfactory in accounting for the observed sizes of voting coalitions in the U.S. Congress or in state legislatures (see, e.g., Hinckley, 1972, 1981; Lutz and Williams, 1976; Lutz and Murray, 1975; Uslaner, 1975; Hardin, 1976; but see Thompson, 1979 for a different conclusion).

Although there exist numerous case studies designed to establish the plausibility of particular coalition theories (see, e.g., Groennings, Kelley, and

Leiserson, 1970), and a few studies comparing selected rival theories (Browne, 1971, 1973), the only comprehensive crossnational tests of rival theories in all their variants are DeSwaan (1973) and Browne and Dreijmanis (1982). With regard to 90 parliamentary governing coalitions in the nonwar period since 1918 in nine countries (Denmark, Finland, France, Israel, Italy, the Netherlands, Norway, Sweden, and the Weimar Republic), DeSwaan found Axelrod's theory superior to its alternatives. Similarly, in studies of postwar governing coalitions in European democracies, Browne and Dreijmanis found no general tendency for coalitions to be of minimal winning size but a pervasive tendency for coalitions to consist of actors that are adjacent on relevant policy dimensions.

Particular coalition theories have thus proved successful in accounting for important characteristics of parliamentary governing coalitions. But oddly enough, these empirical successes appear to have had little impact on the most recent work on coalitions. For reasons discussed later on, this recent work has consisted of proposals of new solution concepts and tests of rival solution concepts in experimental situations (see, e.g., Fiorina and Plott, 1978; McKelvey, Ordeshook, and Winer, 1978; Ordeshook and Winer, 1980; and the studies collected in Ordeshook, 1978).

Legislative Voting

The study of collective choice is concerned with the procedures by which collectivities such as legislative bodies or committees choose from among multiple alternatives that are mutually exclusive. Typically, neither the collectivity nor the alternatives from which it chooses are specified empirically in such research. The conclusions obtained are intended to be applicable to any decision-making body that possesses the relevant properties posited by the theorist. Here I shall review those portions of the literature on collective choice that pertain most directly to legislatures and legislative committees.

The Paradox of Voting

Much research concerning legislative strategies is concerned with circumstances that occur when legislation is adopted by simple majority rule. Under simple majority rule in which three or more mutually exclusive alternatives are voted on pairwise, there may exist no alternative that can secure majority support against all its rivals. The alternatives here may be the status quo and rival bills or rival versions of a single bill. Suppose, for example, that there exist three factions, each less than a majority, and that they rank alternatives A, B, and C from most preferred to least as follows:

Faction 1: A, B, C
Faction 2: B, C, A
Faction 3: C, A, B.

A majority (factions 1 and 3) will support A in a pairwise choice against B, and a different majority (factions 1 and 2) will support B when it is pitted against C. Nonetheless, in a contest between A and C, a majority (factions 2 and 3) will support alternative C. This phenomenon of cyclical majorities, most widely known as the "paradox of voting," was first discovered by the Marquis de Condorcet (1785) but is now most closely associated with the work of Black (1958) and Arrow (1951).

In this case the collective or social ordering of alternatives produced by simple majority rule is intransitive: A is socially preferred to B, and B to C, but C is socially preferred to A. No matter which is ultimately chosen, a majority will be dissatisfied (Shepsle, 1974b). Remarkably, Arrow (1951) proved that in producing a social ordering from individual preferences neither majority rule nor any other procedure that meets certain very mild conditions of reasonableness can preclude the possible occurrence of such paradoxes. Consequently, so long as parliamentary rules permit choice between any pair of alternatives, the possibility of such a paradox is universal. [For useful expositions and guides to the enormous subsequent literature, see Sen (1970) and MacKay (1980). The early literature is reviewed by Riker (1961), and the historical background by Black (1958).]

Numerous studies have attempted to determine the actual likelihood that the paradox will occur (Bjurulf, 1972; Black, 1958; Campbell and Tullock, 1965; DeMeyer and Plott, 1970; Garman and Kamien, 1968; Gleser, 1969; Guilbaud, 1952; Klahr, 1966; May, 1971; Niemi, 1969; Niemi and Weisberg, 1968; Pomerantz and Weil, 1970; Tullock and Campbell, 1970; Weisberg and Niemi, 1972). Most of these estimates rest upon a priori assumptions concerning the relative frequency of possible individual preference orderings. Despite differences in these assumptions, however, there is general agreement that the probability of a paradox depends upon the number of alternatives being considered and to a lesser degree on the number of individuals in the group making the choice among them. With three alternatives, the probability of there being no majority winner rises with the number of individuals to a maximum of about 9 percent. But when the number of individuals is large, the probability increases rapidly with the number of alternatives, from about 0.25 when there are 5 alternatives to more than 0.8 when there are 40 (Niemi and Weisberg, 1968; Garman and Kamien, 1968).

These estimates may be misleading, however, for the actual distribution of preferences in particular societies is affected by a variety of social conditions—a common culture or class antagonisms—not taken into account in these calculations (Williamson and Sargent, 1967; Sen, 1970). The actual occurrence of the paradox may therefore be higher or lower than these estimates suggest. If legislators' preferences are to some extent homogeneous, so that some preference orderings occur more frequently than others, then the likelihood of the paradox is considerably reduced (Abrams, 1976; Fishburn, 1973; Fishburn and Gehrlein, 1980; Gehrlein and Fishburn, 1976a, 1976b; Jamison and Luce, 1972; Kuga and Nagatani, 1974). A useful measure of homogeneity is the Kendall-Smith coefficient of concordance applied to legislators' preference orderings (Kendall and Smith, 1939).

Especially important is the case in which legislators' preferences are single-peaked. This means, roughly, that the alternatives can be ordered in such a way that the rank of an alternative in each legislator's preference ordering decreases with its ordinal distance from his most preferred alternative. Black (1958) has demonstrated that occurrence of the paradox is precluded when legislators' preferences are single-peaked and can therefore be represented unidimensionally. When this condition holds, legislators' votes will be Guttman scalable (Coombs, 1964). However, Niemi and Weisberg (1974) demonstrate that Guttman scalability does not necessarily guarantee single-peakedness of preferences.

If legislators' preferences over a set of motions are not unidimensional, is there a condition analogous to single-peakedness that guarantees against occurrences of the paradox? This question was explored by Black and Newing (1951) and subsequently given a precise answer by Plott (1967): there is indeed a set of conditions that precludes the paradox when preferences are multidimensional, but these conditions are so stringent that they are unlikely to be satisfied in actual situations. Essentially, these conditions require that pairs of legislators have utility functions that are mirror images, opposite in direction and intensity, and that they be symmetrically arrayed about a single point that is itself occupied by a single remaining legislator. Kramer (1973) demonstrated that the conditions for equilibrium (i.e., avoidance of the paradox) are so restrictive as to be incompatible with even a very modest heterogeneity of preference orderings. Schloss (1973) showed that in a game theoretic representation the conditions identified by Plott define the core (roughly, the set of stable outcomes), which Rubinstein (1979) later demonstrated to be empty when the set of alternatives and legislators' preferences over them are continuous. For all practical purposes, then, there is no set of conditions pertaining to legislators' preferences that precludes the occurrence of the paradox so long as their preferences are multidimensional.

Since complete information on legislators' preference orderings is rarely obtainable, the actual likelihood of the paradox is extremely difficult to ascertain. Marz, Casstevens, and Casstevens (1973) provide a rule for determining the number of votes needed to identify the existence of cyclical majorities. Shepsle (1972) argues that the likelihood of the paradox is considerably reduced when the alternatives from which legislators choose have uncertain consequences, thus introducing considerations of risk into legislators' decisions. Bowen (1972) demonstrates that when the alternatives consist of the status quo, a bill, and an amended bill, the paradox cannot have occurred if the bill was passed. Weisberg and Niemi (1972) extend this result to the case of two amendments: when either the unamended bill or the bill as modified by only the first amendment is adopted, the paradox cannot have occurred.

Even when the underlying conditions for the paradox exist, its actual occurrence can be prevented by particular legislative rules and practices. Blydenburgh (1971) argues that underlying preferences leading to cyclical majorities are especially likely with regard to revenue bills and explains the use of the closed rule (preventing floor amendments) on tax measures in the U.S. House of Representatives as a device for avoiding the paradox. Sullivan (1976) extends this argument to the norms of behavior that characterize congressional committee and floor behavior. Riker (1958, 1965) describes several fascinating instances of the paradox in congressional voting and proposes a specific change in the rules of the U.S. House and Senate that would resolve paradoxes that occur.

Agenda Influence

When the conditions of the paradox exist, then the actual choice among the alternatives will be determined by some factor other than legislators' preferences—e.g., the order in which motions are voted on, as determined by parliamentary rules. In the example given above, suppose that C is the status quo, B is a bill, and A is an amendment or substitute bill. Since a majority prefers the amended or substitute bill to the original, it will be adopted, but then subsequently defeated in a vote on final passage (i.e., when pitted against C, the status quo). But an alternative sequence is one in which bill A is proposed and defeated (by C, the status quo), and then bill B is subsequently proposed and therefore pitted against C, in which case B will be the eventual outcome (Luce and Raiffa, 1957, p. 359). Parliamentary rules governing the order of voting may therefore become crucial when conditions for the paradox exist.

That this is so makes it advantageous for legislators to create a paradox under certain circumstances (Riker, 1965). Suppose, for example, that a majority is expected to support bill A against the rival bill B. The supporters of B may then introduce a third motion C such that the supporters of A are split into two minorities, one which orders the alternatives (A, B, C) and the other which orders them (C, A, B). If the supporters of B assert their own preference ordering as (B, C, A), then the paradox has been contrived. If the supporters of B can now arrange the order of voting as well, so that A is pitted against C and the winner against B, the outcome will be B. By creating a paradox and controlling the order of voting, B's supporters have converted defeat to victory.

As this example demonstrates, control of the agenda—the set of motions from which choice is to be made and the order in which they are voted on—can be an important means of influencing legislative outcomes. Tullock (1967a) argued that cyclical majorities resulting from the paradox would typically be confined to a small number of motions at or near the top of most legislators' preference orderings and that the importance of these cycles in permitting the manipulation of outcomes would vary inversely with the size of the legislature. This conjecture, if true, would imply that control of the agenda is typically not very important. However, McKelvey (1976, 1979) subsequently demonstrated the opposite to be the case: when preferences over alternatives are multidimensional, then if cycles exist they include within them all possible alternatives. An analogous result is proven by Schofield (1978). Bell (1978) showed that for a large number of legislators among whom all possible preference orderings are equally likely, as the number of alternatives increases the probability that all alternatives are included in the top cycle approaches one. These results imply that a legislator who controls the agenda could, by introducing a suitable sequence of motions and determining the order in which they are voted on, bring about any final outcome whatsoever. Consequently, in the multidimensional case, control over the agenda is the ultimate political resource.

If, as formal theorists believe, multidimensional preference orderings are typical in legislative situations, the series of investigations from Arrow to McKelvey tell us that legislative outcomes are usually not determined solely by legislators' preferences and the relevant decision rule. Instead, the prevalence of the paradox of voting and its cyclical majorities renders outcomes inherently unstable and unpredictable. The alternative that is eventually chosen depends crucially on the particular set of alternatives that are proposed and the order in which they are voted on, as experimental studies of committee decisions have shown (Plott and Levine, 1978; Levine and Plott, 1977). To understand legislative outcomes, then, we must understand the particular institutional arrangements that affect this agenda (Shepsle, 1979a, 1979b; Riker, 1980a; see also Ordeshook, 1980; Rae, 1980; and Riker, 1980b). For example, Gross (1979) argues that if there are similar cyclical majorities in both chambers of a bicameral legislature but different orders of voting, then the chambers will choose different versions of a bill, making a conference committee necessary. The existence of cyclical majorities will likewise give the conference committee considerable latitude in its decisions and effective control over the outcome, for the committee's report is always voted on last and will therefore be victorious if legislators vote sincerely.

Strategic Voting

In the example in the preceding section, the supporters of bill B saved it from defeat by bill A by introducing a new motion C that split the supporters of bill A into two groups: those with preference ordering (A, B, C) and those with ordering (C, A, B). If the supporters of B have the preference ordering (B, C, A) and if the voting first pits A against C and the winner against B, B will be the outcome. But suppose that B's supporters instead had the preference ordering (B, A, C). Were they then to vote sincerely—in accordance with their preference over bills—then bill A would win. Anticipating this, B's proponents may choose instead to vote insincerely—contrary to their preference ordering—in order to bring about a more preferred outcome than would otherwise occur. Although they prefer A to C, they must support C in the first of the two votes if B is to win in the second.

This is also an instance of strategic or sophisticated voting, since the votes cast by B's proponents at each stage of the procedure reflect their anticipated effect on the final outcome. Sophisticated voting need not be insincere, however. In the original example, in which the preferences of B's supporters were (B, C, A), a sophisticated vote in the choice between A and C was the sincere vote for C. Rather, sophisticated voting requires that the choice at each stage of the voting procedure be made in light of its effect on the eventual outcome and therefore in light of the choices of other voters (whose choices may also be sophisticated). However, insincere voting is an indication that voting is sophisticated.

Enelow and Koehler (1980) have shown that incentives for at least some legislators to vote insincerely are created whenever amendments are introduced either to save a bill that would otherwise lose or to kill a bill that would otherwise win. By reconstructing the preferences of U.S. representatives on the 1977 Common Site Picketing Bill and of U.S. senators on the Panama Canal neutrality treaty, Enelow and Koehler are able to infer that sophisticated voting was widespread in those two cases. Similar instances occurring in Scandinavian parliaments have been described by Bjurulf and Niemi (1978).

A systematic procedure for theoretically analyzing strategic voting was first developed by Farquharson (1969) in his analysis of an incident in the Roman Senate. Farquharson's procedure presumes that legislators possess complete information, that they can therefore accurately predict how each vote in a series of votes will turn out, and that all participants vote sophisticatedly. An analytic procedure less cumbersome than Farquharson's has been independently developed by McKelvey and Niemi (1978) and Miller (1977a, 1977b).

A procedure for identifying some forms of sophisticated voting in roll-call data has been developed by McCrone (1977).

Farquharson was concerned with proving that sophisticated voting by all participants individually would lead to a determinate outcome. Kramer (1972) extends this result to cases in which sophisticated voting can result from collaborative agreements. Enelow (1981) extends Farquharson's analysis to situations in which legislators have only probability estimates of these outcomes rather than certain knowledge and uses this extended procedure to account for patterns of voting on two amendments in the U.S. House of Representatives.

Strategic voting can be either noncooperative or cooperative. Cooperative strategic voting results from explicit agreement among two or more legislators to vote insincerely and includes vote trading and logrolling. In vote trading two or more legislators agree to vote insincerely, each on a different motion, thus reversing their preferred outcome on that motion but bringing about their preferred outcome on a motion they consider more important. In logrolling, legislators likewise collaborate in bringing about an outcome other than the one that would occur under sincere voting, but in this case the collaborators constitute a majority of the legislature. Much of the literature on strategic voting is concerned with identifying the conditions under which logrolling and vote trading can occur and determining their relationship to the paradox of voting (Bernholz, 1973, 1974, 1975; Coleman, 1966; Enelow, 1979; Enelow and Koehler, 1979; Haefele, 1970, 1971; Hillinger, 1971; Kadane, 1972; Koehler, 1975b, 1975c; Miller, 1975; Mueller, 1967; Oppenheimer, 1975; Park, 1967; Riker and Brams, 1973; Schwartz, 1975, 1977; Uslaner and Davis, 1975; Wilson, 1969). Miller (1977a, 1977b) synthesizes earlier studies and resolves many of the conflicting claims and differences in terminology that abound in this literature.

Two early presumptions in the analysis of vote trading were that such trades would necessarily benefit all participants and that trading provided a means for circumventing voting paradoxes (Buchanan and Tullock, 1962; Tullock, 1967a). Both have been shown to be illusory. Riker and Brams (1973) provide an example of a series of trades in which all traders are ultimately made worse off. What makes such an eventual outcome possible is the fact that each trade alters the outcomes on two motions and thereby creates gains or losses for legislators other than the traders. In the Riker-Brams example, each trader gains from his own trading but suffers even greater losses as a consequence of trades made by others. Riker and Brams infer from their example that trading should be discouraged. However, Tullock (1974) argues that the Riker—Brams analysis is misleading in that legislators with sufficient information would collaboratively agree to avoid trading when a series of trades would result in ultimate losses for all. Furthermore, Schwartz (1975) demonstrates that there can also be sequences of trades that make all participants better off.

Vote trading and logrolling can also lead to paradoxical situations in which there is a cycle of outcomes similar to the cyclical majorities in the paradox of voting. In the absence of enforceable trading agreements, the situation described by Riker and Brams results in an endless cyclical sequence of trades as the legislators attempt to recoup the losses imposed on them by other traders (for another example see Abrams, 1980, pp. 104-108). Although, as Miller (1977a, 1977b) has shown, the relationship between vote trading or logrolling and the paradox of voting is a tenuous one, under rather broad conditions logrolling situations are those in which there exists a voting paradox. In general, there is no guarantee that logrolling or vote trading will lead to determinate outcomes.

These conclusions dash the hope expressed by Buchanan and Tullock (1962) that logrolling and vote trading might provide a means for minorities with intense preferences to avert defeat. The use of such strategies was in their view a potential solution to the intensity problem (Dahl, 1956; Kendall and Carey, 1968). But, as has been demonstrated, the outcomes produced by vote trading and logrolling are not necessarily invulnerable to defeat, nor are these outcomes necessarily beneficial ones even to the traders themselves. Under some circumstances these and other varieties of strategic voting produce outcomes less desirable to all participants than the outcome produced by sincere voting. However, as Gibbard (1973) and Satterthwaite (1975) have shown, neither majority voting nor any other voting scheme in which outcomes depend upon the expression of individual preferences can avoid the possibility of such pathological results, for all are vulnerable to strategic manipulation under some circumstances.

The Emerging Research Agenda

As formal theorists themselves have increasingly recognized, social choice theory as it pertains to legislative voting is unsatisfactory in ways that are not easily dismissed. The immediate focus of dissatisfaction is the radical inconsistency between what the theory implies and what is in fact observed. Extant theory implies that stable outcomes typically do not exist, that the outcomes which do occur are inherently unpredictable, and that consistent policy choices by legislatures are not to be expected due to the prevalence of cyclical majorities. Schofield (1980), for example, concludes from his survey of social choice theory that political processes are fundamentally chaotic and unpredictable, that almost anything can happen. But these theoretical expectations are clearly at odds with what we know empirically about most legislatures (Tullock, 1981). Unless the observed stability of legislative processes is simply dismissed as illusory, this inconsistency between theory and observation poses awkward problems for formal theorists. How this inconsistency can be remedied is consequently a principal question on the research agenda now emerging in formal theory.

One response to the problem is to develop extant theory even further in the hope that conditions of equilibrium will be discovered. Underlying this alternative is the view that existing theory is not flawed but merely incomplete. Presumptive support for this view is given by Miller (1980), who points out that McKelvey's (1976, 1979) theorem concerning agenda manipulation presumes that legislators vote sincerely. If voting is sophisticated, however, the number of alternatives over which majority cycles can occur are relatively few. The set of possible outcomes is therefore limited, rather than infinite as McKelvey's theorem implies.

Yet another way to extend existing theory is to adopt a somewhat less restrictive notion of stability than the one heretofore employed. In extant theory an alternative is unstable if it can be defeated by other proposals, stable if it cannot. However, as Ferejohn, Fiorina, and Packel (1980) point out, alternatives that are unstable can differ substantially in the number of winning coalitions or in the number of alternatives by which they can be defeated. That is, even though there may exist no equilibrium outcome among a set of motions, some motions are less vulnerable to defeat than others and are therefore, they propose, more likely to be the eventual outcome of the decision-making process. A majority rule equilibrium is thus a special case in which some motion exists which has a probability equal to one of being the eventual outcome.

Institutional Rules

Shepsle and Weingast (1981; Shepsle, 1979a, 1979b) argue that extant theory should be extended in a different way, namely, by taking into account the internal organization and rules of legislatures. They distinguish between stable outcomes resulting from particular patterns of legislators' preferences (preference-induced equilibria) and those resulting from constraints imposed by legislative rules and organization (structure-induced equilibria). In particular, they point out, the existence of a system of committees with nonoverlapping jurisdictions and of rules governing the types of amendments that are introduced and the order in which they are considered preclude the comparison of certain pairs of alternatives with each other, thereby precluding or restricting cyclical majorities as well. For example, the procedural rules in most legislatures and committees require that the status quo be considered last. That is, whatever the preceding sequence of votes, the final vote always pits a surviving motion against the status quo (i.e., defeat of the motion). Consequently, only those motions or amendments that can defeat the status quo will survive, and any majority cycling will be effectively constrained to that subset of possible proposals (Shepsle and Weingast, 1982).

The concept of structure-induced equilibria suggests that the inadequacies of existing theory can be remedied by extending that theory so as to incorporate additional known characteristics of legislatures. However, the viability of this solution is questioned by Denzau and Mackay (1981), who argue that legislators may learn to anticipate how the outcome of a particular vote affects the outcomes of subsequent votes and take such effects into account in their voting decisions. If this occurs, then structure-induced equilibria will not necessarily exist. To guarantee their existence requires constraints in addition to those considered by Shepsle and Weingast—for example, restrictions on the kinds of amendments that can be proposed. Exactly what properties such constraints must have are yet to be determined.

Formal Theory and Empirical Phenomena

An alternative diagnosis of formal theory as it pertains to legislative voting is that the theory is not just incomplete but in large part fundamentally misdirected. But to develop this argument requires that we first examine somewhat more carefully the relationship of formal theory to empirical phenomena.

I begin by example. The legislature of a newly-independent nation is about to convene for the first time. Its 62 members, two elected from each of 31 districts, begin to take their seats. By agreement, members from the same district are to sit adjacent to one another—either side by side, or one in front of the other, as they choose. The seats in the chamber, a converted theater, had originally numbered 64, in eight rows of eight, but the two seats nearest the doors have been removed, one at the left end of the front row and another at the right end of the back row. Suddenly there is confusion. Only two members remain to be seated, but although both are from the same district, no two adjacent seats are available. As the problem becomes apparent, members who are already seated rise and begin to reassemble, laughing good-naturedly. But when nearly all the legislators have seated themselves anew, it turns out that the problem has not been solved, so again the members reassemble, this time somewhat more impatiently. But once again the problem appears. Finally, after several fruitless attempts to seat themselves by district, the legislators find themselves genuinely puzzled. Why are they apparently unable to seat themselves by district in this configuration of seats?

How can formal analysis contribute to our understanding of this phenomenon? The initial objective of the formal theorist is to discover a way of thinking about it that will permit him to infer what he has in fact observed. This way of thinking consists of a representation of the phenomenon together with a principle for applying that representation in answering the question just raised. In the case at hand he may think of the first arrangement of seats as a checkerboard in which each square represents a seat and in which the squares in the upper left and lower right corners have been removed, as were the corresponding seats. He may then regard a pair of legislators from the same district, seated together, as a domino that fits precisely over two adjacent squares on this checkerboard, either horizontally (as in side-by-side seating) or vertically (front-to-back). Thinking of the phenomenon in this way translates our original problem—how to place 31 pairs of legislators, seated adjacently, into the arrangement of 62 chairs—into an analogous one— how to fit 31 dominos, each covering two squares, onto a mutilated checkerboard with 62 squares.

He now reasons as follows. Each domino covers one white square and one black one. Thirty-one dominos must therefore cover an equal number of black and white squares. But the mutilated checkerboard on which they must be placed does not have an equal number of black and white squares, since the squares that were removed, being at opposite corners, were necessarily of the same color. Consequently the dominos cannot be fitted onto the checkerboard and, analogously, the 31 pairs of legislators cannot be seated in adjacent pairs by district.

Crucial to his new understanding was the recognition of an underlying principle: that the checkerboard can be covered by dominos only if it has an equal number of black and white squares. Call this the "parity principle." The seating arrangement was impractical because, when represented as a checkerboard, it violated this requirement. Notice that this principle is stated in terms of the checkerboard representation and makes little sense without it. Similarly, the checkerboard representation is of little use in the absence of one or more principles that guide its application to the problem at hand.

The sequence of steps exhibited in this simple example occurs in every formal analysis of a phenomenon. First, the observed entities and their relations are translated into an appropriate representation. Seats become squares, pairs of legislators become dominos, adjacency becomes "having a common border." This translation is called "mapping"—appropriately so, since the representation is to the objects and their relations as a map is to geographic locations and the distances between them. Second, accepted principles are used to draw implications concerning the representation, just as one determines that two points lie one inch apart on a geographic map. This step is often facilitated when the representation is mathematical, for then mathematical principles can be used in drawing implications. Third, these implications are translated back into statements about the original phenomena, a process called "inverse mapping." In the analogous case of a geographic map, this inverse mapping is made possible by the fact that points are given names—e.g., Chicago—and a scale shows the conversion of inches to miles. In the seating problem the conclusion about dominos and squares was translated back into a conclusion about pairs of legislators and seats.

This mode of inquiry has three principal goals. The first is the discovery of principles that account for our empirical generalizations. Further unsuccessful attempts by the legislators to seat themselves by district in this particular arrangement of chairs would have reinforced our belief that doing so was impossible, but would not have explained why this was so. The discovery of the parity principle provided this missing explanation.

The second is the use of such principles to generate new hypotheses. For example, the parity principle permits us to infer whether a particular alternative configuration of seats is practical even before it has been tried out. Such inferences can, of course, be tested empirically. But if a particular principle has been repeatedly successful in generating new hypotheses that are confirmed by observation, our confidence in it may lead us to doubt observations that are inconsistent with it. Suppose, for example, that the parity principle tells us that legislators can seat themselves by pairs in a particular configuration of chairs, even though all their actual attempts to do so have failed. If the principle has proven fruitful, we may be justified in regarding the available evidence as misleading and reject the apparent implication of our data that pairwise seating is impossible for that arrangement. Consistency with known principles can thus become a criterion of valid generalization, just as is consistency with observation.

A third aim of formal analysis is to lend coherence to what we know. We may discover empirically that pairwise seating is possible in some arrangements of chairs and impossible in others. The checkerboard representation and parity principle permit us to see these separate findings as components of a larger pattern or structure, rendering them "cumulative" in a way that is far more compelling than simple agglomeration.

The Premise Problem

These, then, are the aspirations of formal theory, in order of increasing ambition. But achieving even the first of them—accounting for what we have observed—requires that the three steps of a formal analysis be carried out correctly. Of these, the most crucial is mapping, the translation of the observed characteristics of a process or phenomenon onto a representation. Whether the implications drawn from that representation can be translated back into valid conclusions concerning the original phenomenon depends crucially upon the appropriateness of the representation chosen—that is, its consistency with the most important relevant characteristics of that phenomenon. If the representation chosen is inappropriate, then the conclusions we draw from it are likely to be inapplicable to the phenomenon we seek to explain.

How appropriate to legislative phenomena are the representations typically used by formal theorists? Underlying much of social choice theory as it pertains to legislatures are four fundamental assumptions. First, the principal goal of legislators is to obtain the policies that they prefer. What matters most to them, it is claimed, is the set of outcomes that results from legislative decision making. Second, in order to obtain the outcomes they prefer, legislators readily vote contrary to their preferences on one or more motions in order to obtain more preferred outcomes on still other motions that they regard as more important. Their decisions to do so may be either unilateral, as in individualistic sophisticated voting, or part of an explicit exchange, as in vote trading. Third, the environment of decision is one in which legislators possess perfect and complete information concerning the preferences and chosen strategies of their colleagues. In the absence of such information legislators could not rationally choose the optimal strategy for achieving the set of outcomes they prefer. Given such information, the decisions of legislators indeed warrant the term "sophisticated." Not only do they strategically alter their votes in response to their knowledge of colleagues' preferences, but indeed in response to their colleagues' strategic decisions as well, through as many levels of complexity as are necessary to reach a stable voting decision. Fourth, the structure of the legislature is quite simple, consisting only of undifferentiated members—no committees, no parties, no leaders—and a single decision rule, typically simple majority rule. This is the representation that formal theorists have typically used to infer legislators' optimal strategies and to predict the outcomes that result from particular configurations of legislators' preferences.

With regard to most legislatures each of these assumptions is highly dubious. First, a substantial empirical literature strongly supports the view that the principal goal of legislators is reelection and that, except for pork-barrel bills, legislative victories contribute little towards the achievement of this end. As David Mayhew aptly points out, "We can all point to a good many instances in which congressmen seem to have gotten into trouble by being on the wrong side in a roll-call vote, but who can think of one where a member got into trouble by being on the losing side?" (1974, p. 118).

Second, one way in which legislators seek to maintain or enhance their probability of reelection is voting in accordance with the preferences of their supporting coalition. Since their failure to do so may be used as effective ammunition by rival candidates, legislators will typically vote sincerely. Voting contrary to the preferences of supporters thus has costs quite distinct from the effect of doing so on the voting outcome (Panning, 1982).

Third, the legislative environment is typically one of incomplete information and uncertainty. For most bills the information that legislators possess concerning their colleagues' preferences is necessarily incomplete and imperfect, for the preferences of others are inherently unobservable and can only be inferred from their behavior. Indeed, the norms and practices that characterize vote trading in the U.S. Congress are means of coping with the consequent possibility that legislators can advantageously conceal or misrepresent their preferences (Panning, 1982). The practice of cue taking, both in the U.S. Congress (Kingdon, 1973, 1977) and in other legislatures (van Schendelen, 1976) is likewise an adaptation to uncertainty, in this case legislators' uncertainty concerning the preferences of voters in their supporting coalitions.

Fourth, legislatures are typically complex institutions with a high degree of internal differentiation and numerous rules that govern the consideration of legislation. To say more would belabor the obvious.

Each of these alternative assumptions is supported by a substantial number of empirical studies surveyed in other chapters of this *Handbook*. Together they imply that the analyses of legislative voting described earlier are simply inapplicable to most legislatures most of the time. That is, the puzzling contrast between extant theory and reality rests upon the mistaken belief that extant theory is widely applicable.

To be sure, representations that are known to be too simple or even counterfactual can be useful nonetheless, for they may provide important clues to the development of more adequate representations. Moreover, the belief that a particular characteristic of a legislature is crucial to our understanding of it may simply be false. These defenses of the assumptions typically employed in formal theory would be more convincing, however, if formal theorists were appropriately cautious in drawing conclusions about the world from their representations of it, were more assiduous in rigorously testing those implications, or—and this is especially important—more frequently checked the sensitivity of those implications to changes in the assumptions from which they were derived. For example, formal theorists typically presume that slight departures from their assumed condition of perfect and complete information will bring about only slight departures from the consequences implied by their models (see, e.g., Tullock, 1981). Rarely, however, has this presumption been seriously examined (an exception is Brams, 1975, pp. 78-82). Rarer still are analyses of the possible consequences of deliberate concealment or misrepresentation of preferences (but see Brams, 1977a, 1977b). Yet there are both theoretical and empirical grounds for believing that these phenomena occur and that the implications of extant theory fail to hold when they do (Panning, 1982).

The persistent use of assumptions that render formal theory inapplicable to most legislatures actually points to a more fundamental limitation of that theory. In the checkerboard example the starting point for formal analysis was a phenomenon in need of explanation. But in many theoretical studies of social choice and coalitions it is not at all clear what phenomena, if any, are being addressed. In much of this work the puzzles that motivate inquiry are puzzles generated by previous theoretical studies rather than by observed phenomena or empirical generalizations. Although there is nothing wrong with this in principle, in fact the research agenda in formal theory is still dominated to a remarkable extent by questions originating either in welfare economics (to which Arrow's work was directed) or in mathematics (specifically, in game theory). Welfare economics is concerned with the possible ways in which social choices can be derived from individual preferences and with identifying which of these ways, if any, meet certain criteria of desirability. This accounts for the prevalence in the social choice literature of possibility and impossibility theorems and the lack of concern over the realism of basic assumptions. In game theory a central aim is to discover a solution concept for n-person games (games with three or more players) that is as elegant and persuasive as is the minimax theorem for two-person zero-sum games (games in which the payoffs to the winner exactly match the losses to the loser). The empirical evidence that ideological constraints limit the possible coalitions that may form has had only a modest impact on these inquiries, for such constraints are considered extrinsic to game theory (a fact deplored by Luce and Raiffa, 1957, p. 164). It is thus the persistent influence of its historical origins that accounts for the prevalence of counterfactual assumptions in formal theorizing and the secondary importance attached by many theorists to explaining observed phenomena.

But there is no reason for believing that the kinds of models appropriate to welfare economics or game theory will necessarily account for observed legislative phenomena as well. This is not to say that the accomplishments of formal theory are uniformly irrelevant to our understanding of legislative processes. It is to say, however, that the relevance of many formal analyses to legislative phenomena remains to be demonstrated and cannot simply be taken for granted by their proponents. To be sure, some formal theorists have taken pains to establish the empirical applicability of their work (e.g., Riker, 1958, 1962, 1965; Enelow and Koehler, 1980; Enelow, 1981; Leiserson, 1968; Axelrod, 1970; DeSwaan, 1970, 1973). But these instances are unfortunately atypical.

Needed: A Different Kind of Formal Theory

These limitations of existing work by no means imply that formal theory can necessarily contribute little to our understanding of legislatures.

What they do imply is the need for a different kind of formal theory, a theory that is principally directed towards explaining legislative phenomena and that is shaped much more strongly by what we know empirically. Happily, a growing body of work in formal theory, some of it very recent, does have these characteristics.

Although the size and composition of governing coalitions has been the principal focus of coalition theory, Dodd (1974, 1976) investigates the relationship of these and other variables to coalition (cabinet) durability. Dodd establishes both theoretical and empirical support for the proposition that cabinet durability is a function of its minimum winning status: durability decreases as governing coalitions deviate from being minimum winning. In turn, the likelihood that a minimum winning cabinet will form depends upon the willingness of parties to bargain with one another and upon the certainty of their information, and these two conditions depend upon the fractionalization, instability, and cleavage intensity of the party system in a country. Dodd finds support for his hypotheses in data for 17 countries from 1918 to 1972, excluding wartime.

Fiorina (1974) is concerned with the relationship of legislators to their constituents. From his model of legislators' voting decisions, which assumes that representatives aim to maintain or increase their probability of being reelected, he draws several implications that are empirically supported. One is that homogeneous constituencies will tend to be electorally safe, whereas heterogeneous districts tend to be marginal. Another is that representatives from marginal districts will not, as is sometimes alleged, take moderate positions on issues, but will instead align themselves consistently with the strongest constituency group. These implications provide persuasive theoretical ground for choosing among the many conflicting empirical findings concerning marginality and moderation. A particular virtue of Fiorina's model is its consistency with our empirical knowledge in the motivations it ascribes to legislators and in the uncertainty it claims accompanies their decisions.

In a series of papers Weingast, Shepsle, and Johnsen seek to explain the practice of universalism, the tendency of congressional leaders to seek nearly unanimous support for distributive programs by including projects for all legislators who want them. Weingast (1979) shows that legislators can reasonably expect to benefit more from universalism than from bills benefitting a bare majority whose composition is uncertain, provided that the benefits offered by such bills exceed their cost. Shepsle and Weingast (1981) extend this argument to bills that are more costly than beneficial. These analyses imply the emergence in Congress of an informal rule or norm prescribing universalism. Finally, Weingast, Shepsle, and Johnsen (1981) argue that this phenomenon together with the geographic basis of representation, the financing of projects by general taxation, and the divergence between economic and political evaluations of project costs creates a bias towards inefficient (pork-barrel) projects. Their conclusions nicely complement those of Ferejohn's (1974) earlier empirical study.

These studies have two characteristics in common. First, each aims to account for an observed phenomenon: the longevity of coalition governments, the relationship of electoral marginality to political moderation, and the prevalence of universalism. Second, each takes into account our relevant existing empirical knowledge. In both these respects the studies just described are models for emulation by formal theorists.

Conclusion

The notion that politics is a game is a very old one. What is relatively new is the attempt by political scientists to transform this metaphor into a rigorous scientific theory. To understand political phenomena, it is claimed, we must first identify the players, their goals or preferences, the rules that constrain them, and the strategies from which they can choose, and then demonstrate how the outcome of the game results from the preferences of the players. Substantiating this claim constitutes the research program of social choice theory.

It has become increasingly evident, however, that the theoretical results achieved by the formal analysis of legislative choice are markedly inconsistent with our empirical knowledge of legislatures such as the U.S. Congress. This puzzling inconsistency results, I have argued, from mistaken conceptions of the game that legislators are playing and from the prevalent (although not universal) study of questions originating in welfare economics and mathematics. If formal theorizing is to fulfill its considerable promise as a mode of inquiry, there must be a more widespread realization among formal theorists of the relevance and importance to their research of existing empirical knowledge and a greater concern with explaining observed phenomena. Fortunately, this is a direction in which recent work in the field appears to be steadily moving.

These criticisms should by no means be interpreted as a dismissal of what formal theorists have already accomplished as useless or irrelevant. As a distinguished historian of science points out,

the business of science involves more than the mere assembly of facts: it demands also intellectual architecture and construction. Before the actual building comes the collection of materials; before that, the detailed work at the drawing-board; before that, the conception of a design; and, before that even, there comes the bare recognition of possibilities. No wonder science has included, and must include, a much *a priori* study of possible forms of theory, developed without immediate regard to the particular facts (Toulmin, 1961, p. 108).

However keen our retrospective awareness of its limitations, much formal theorizing in political science has played precisely this essential role. In doing so it has brought to our discipline a healthy infusion of clarity and rigor. That in itself is no mean achievement, for as Francis Bacon, that patron saint of empiricists, recognized, "Truth will sooner come out from error than from confusion."

NOTE

I am indebted to John Ferejohn, Phil Schrodt, Ken Shepsle, and Gerhard Loewenberg for helpful comments on portions of the manuscript; they are, however, absolved from responsibility for its conclusions.

REFERENCES

Abrams, Robert. 1976. "The Voter's Paradox and the Homogeneity of Individual Preference Orders," *Public Choice* 16:19-27.

————. 1980. *Foundations of Political Analysis*. New York: Columbia University Press.

Arrow, Kenneth J. [1951], 1963. *Social Choice and Individual Values*. 2d ed. New York: John Wiley.

Axelrod, Robert. 1970. *Conflict of Interest*. Chicago: Markham.

Bell, Colin E. 1978. "What Happens When Majority Rule Breaks Down? Some Probability Calculations," *Public Choice* 33:121-127.

Bernholz, Peter. 1973. "Logrolling, Arrow Paradox and Cyclical Majorities," *Public Choice* 15:87-95.

————. 1974. "Logrolling, Arrow-Paradox and Decision Rules: A Generalization," *Kyklos* 27:49-62.

————. 1975. "Logrolling and the Paradox of Voting," *American Political Science Review* 69:961-962.

Bjurulf, Bo H. 1972. "A Probabilistic Analysis of Voting Blocs and the Occurrence of the Paradox of Voting," in Richard G. Niemi and Herbert F. Weisberg, eds., *Probability Models of Collective Decision Making*. Columbus, OH: Charles Merrill.

Bjurulf, Bo H. and Richard G. Niemi. 1978. "Strategic Voting in Scandinavian Parliaments," *Scandinavian Political Studies* 1:5-22.

Black, Duncan. 1948. "On the Rationale of Group Decision-Making," *Journal of Political Economy* 56:22-34.

————. 1958. *The Theory of Committees and Elections*. Cambridge: Cambridge University Press.

Black, Duncan and R. A. Newing. 1951. *Committee Decisions with Complementary Valuation*. London: William Hodge.

Blydenburgh, John. 1971. "The Closed Rule and the Paradox of Voting," *Journal of Politics* 33:57-71.

Bowen, Bruce D. 1972. "Toward an Estimate of the Frequency of Occurrence of the Paradox of Voting in U.S. Senate Roll Call Votes," in Richard G. Niemi and Herbert F. Weisberg, eds., *Probability Models of Collective Decision Making*. Columbus, OH: Charles Merrill.

Brams, Steven J. 1973. "Positive Coalition Theory: The Relationship Between Postulated Goals and Derived Behavior," in Cornelius P. Cotter, ed., *Political Science Annual*. Vol. 4. Indianapolis: Bobbs-Merrill.

_____ . 1975. *Game Theory and Politics*. New York: Free Press.

_____ . 1977a. "Deception in 2 x 2 Games," *Journal of Peace Science* 2:171-203.

_____ . 1977b. "Deception in Simple Voting Games," *Social Science Research* 6:257-272.

Brams, Steven J. and William H. Riker. 1972. "Models of Coalition Formation in Voting Bodies," in James F. Herndon and Joseph L. Bernd, eds., *Mathematical Applications in Political Science*. Vol. 6. Charlottesville: University Press of Virginia, pp. 79-124.

Browne, Eric C. 1971. "Testing Theories of Coalition Formation in the European Context," *Comparative Political Studies* 3:391-412.

_____ . 1973. *Coalition Theories: A Logical and Empirical Critique*. Sage Professional Papers in Comparative Politics 01-043. Beverly Hills, CA: Sage Publications.

Browne, Eric C. and John Dreijmanis, eds. 1982. *Government Coalitions in Western Democracies*. New York: Longman.

Buchanan, James M. and Gordon Tullock. 1962. *The Calculus of Consent*. Ann Arbor: University of Michigan Press.

Butterworth, Robert L. 1971a. "A Research Note on the Size of Winning Coalitions," *American Political Science Review* 65:741-748.

_____ . 1971b. "Rejoinder to Riker's 'Comment'," *American Political Science Review* 65:747-748.

Campbell, Colin and Gordon Tullock. 1965. "A Measure of the Importance of Cyclical Majorities," *Economic Journal* 75:853-857.

Coleman, James S. 1966. "The Possibility of a Social Welfare Function," *American Economic Review* 56:1105-1122.

de Condorcet, M. 1785. *Essai sur l'Application de l'Analyse à la Probabilité des Décisions Rendues à la Pluralité des Voix*. Paris.

Coombs, Clyde. 1964. *A Theory of Data*. New York: John Wiley.

Dahl, Robert A. 1956. *A Preface to Democratic Theory*. Chicago: University of Chicago Press.

Davis, Morton D. 1970. *Game Theory: A Non-Technical Introduction*. New York: Basic Books.

DeMeyer, Frank and Charles Plott. 1970. "The Probability of a Cyclical Majority," *Econometrica* 38:345-354.

Denzau, Arthur T. and Robert J. Mackay. 1981. "Structure-Induced Equilibria and Perfect-Foresight Expectations," *American Journal of Political Science* 25: 762-779.

DeSwaan, Abram. 1970. "An Empirical Model of Coalition-Formation as an n-Person Game of Policy Distance Minimization," in Sven Groennings, E. W. Kelley, and Michael Leiserson, eds., *The Study of Coalition Behavior: Theoretical Perspectives and Cases from Four Continents*. New York: Holt, Rinehart & Winston, pp. 424-444.

_____ . 1973. *Coalition Theories and Cabinet Formations*. San Francisco: Jossey-Bass.

Dodd, Lawrence C. 1974. "Party Coalitions in Multiparty Parliaments," *American Political Science Review* 68:1093-1117.

_____ . 1976. *Coalitions in Parliamentary Government*. Princeton, NJ: Princeton University Press.

Dummett, Michael and Robin Farquharson. 1961. "Stability in Voting," *Econometrica* 29:33-42.

Enelow, James M. 1979. "Noncooperative Counter-threats to Vote Trading," *American Journal of Political Science* 23:121-138.

_____ . 1981. "Saving Amendments, Killer Amendments, and an Expected Utility Theory of Sophisticated Voting," *Journal of Politics* 43:1062-1089.

Enelow, James M. and David H. Koehler. 1979. "Vote Trading in a Legislative Context: An Analysis of Cooperative and Noncooperative Strategic Voting," *Public Choice* 34:157-175.

_____ . 1980. "The Amendment in Legislative Strategy: Sophisticated Voting in the U.S. Congress," *Journal of Politics* 42:396-413.

Eulau, Heinz and Katherine Hinckley. 1966. "Legislative Institutions and Processes," in James A. Robinson, ed., *Political Science Annual*. Vol. 1. Indianapolis: Bobbs-Merrill, pp. 85-189.

Farquharson, Robin. 1969. *Theory of Voting*. New Haven: Yale University Press.

Fenno, Richard. 1964. Review of Daniel M. Berman, *In Congress Assembled. American Political Science Review* 58:975-976.

Ferejohn, John A. 1974. *Pork Barrel Politics: Rivers and Harbors Legislation, 1947-1968*. Stanford, CA: Stanford University Press.

Ferejohn, John A. and Morris P. Fiorina. 1975. "Purposive Models of Legislative Behavior," *American Economic Review* 65:407-414.

Ferejohn, John A., Morris P. Fiorina, and Edward W. Packel. 1980. "Nonequilibrium Solutions for Legislative Systems," *Behavioral Science* 25:140-148.

Fiorina, Morris. 1974. *Representatives, Roll Calls, and Constituencies*. Lexington, MA: D.C. Heath.

Fiorina, Morris and Charles Plott. 1978. "Committee Decisions under Majority Rule: An Experimental Study," *American Political Science Review* 72:575-598.

Fishburn, Peter C. 1973. "Voter Concordance, Simple Majorities, and Group Decision Methods," *Behavioral Science* 18:364-376.

Fishburn, Peter C. and William V. Gehrlein. 1980. "Social Homogeneity and Condorcet's Paradox," *Public Choice* 35:403-419.

Frohlich, Norman. 1975. "The Instability of Minimum Winning Coalitions," *American Political Science Review* 69:943-946.

Frohlich, Norman and Joe Oppenheimer. 1978. *Modern Political Economy*. Englewood Cliffs, NJ: Prentice-Hall.

Gamson, William A. 1961. "A Theory of Coalition Formation," *American Sociological Review* 26:373-382.

Garman, Mark B. and Morton I. Kamien. 1968. "The Paradox of Voting: Probability Calculations," *Behavioral Science* 13:306-316.

Gehrlein, William V. and Peter C. Fishburn. 1976a. "The Probability of the Paradox of Voting: A Computable Solution," *Journal of Economic Theory* 13:14-25.

_____ . 1976b. "Condorcet's Paradox and Anonymous Preference Profiles," *Public Choice* 26:1-18.

Gibbard, Alan. 1973. "Manipulation of Voting Schemes: A General Result," *Econometrica* 41:587-601.

Gleser, Leon. 1969. "The Paradox of Voting: Some Probabilistic Results," *Public Choice* 7:47-64.

Groennings, Sven, E.W. Kelley, and Michael Leiserson, eds. 1970. *The Study of Coalition Behavior*. New York: Holt, Rinehart & Winston.

Gross, Donald A. 1979. "Conference Committees, Sophisticated Voting, and Cyclical Majorities," *Legislative Studies Quarterly* 4:79-94.

Guilbaud, G. Th. [1952], 1966. "Theories of the General Interest and the Logical Problem of Aggregation," in Paul F. Lazarsfeld and Neil W. Henry, eds., *Readings in Mathematical Social Science*. Cambridge, MA: MIT Press.

Haefele, Edwin. 1970. "Coalitions, Minority Representation, and Vote Trading Probabilities," *Public Choice* 8:75-90.

_____ . 1971. "A Utility Theory of Representative Government," *American Economic Review* 61:350-367.

Hardin, Russell. 1976. "Hollow Victory: The Minimum Winning Coalition," *American Political Science Review* 70:1202-1204.

_____ . 1977. Reply to Riker. *American Political Science Review*. 71:1060-1061.

Hillinger, Claude. 1971. "Voting on Issues and Platforms," *Behavioral Science* 16:564-566.

Hinckley, Barbara. 1972. "Coalitions in Congress: Size and Ideological Distance," *Midwest Journal of Political Science* 16:197-207.

_____ . 1981. *Coalitions and Politics*. New York: Harcourt Brace Jovanovich.

Jamison, D. and E. Luce. 1972. "Social Homogeneity and the Probability of Intransitive Majority Rule," *Journal of Economic Theory* 5:79-87.

Kadane, Joseph B. 1972. "On Division of the Question," *Public Choice* 13:47-54.

Kendall, M. G. and B.B. Smith. 1939. "The Problem of m Rankings," *Annals of Mathematical Statistics* 10:275-287.

Kendall, Willmoore and George W. Carey. 1968. "The 'Intensity Problem' and Democratic Theory," *American Political Science Review* 62:5-24.

Kingdon, John W. 1973. *Congressmen's Voting Decision*. New York: Harper & Row.

_____ . 1977. "Models of Legislative Voting," *Journal of Politics* 39:563-595.

Klahr, David. 1966. "A Computer Simulation of the Paradox of Voting," *American Political Science Review* 60:384-390.

Koehler, David H. 1972. "The Legislative Process and the Minimal Winning Coalition," in Richard G. Niemi and Herbert F. Weisberg, eds., *Probability Models of Collective Decision Making*. Columbus, OH: Charles Merrill.

_____ . 1975a. "Legislative Coalition Formation: The Meaning of Minimal Winning Size with Uncertain Participation," *American Journal of Political Science* 19:27-39.

_____ . 1975b. "Vote Trading and the Voting Paradox: A Proof of Logical Equivalence," *American Political Science Review* 69:954-960.

_____ . 1975c. "Vote Trading and the Voting Paradox: Rejoinder," *American Political Science Review* 69:967-969.

Kramer, Gerald H. 1972. "Sophisticated Voting over Multidimensional Choice Spaces," *Journal of Mathematical Sociology* 2:165-181.

_____ . 1973. "On a Class of Equilibrium Conditions for Majority Rule," *Econometrica* 41:285-297.

_____ . 1977. "A Dynamical Model of Political Equilibrium," *Journal of Economic Theory* 16:310-334.

Kuga, K. and H. Nagatani. 1974. "Voter Antagonism and the Paradox of Voting," *Econometrica* 42:1045-1067.

Leiserson, Michael. 1968. "Factions and Coalitions in One-Party Japan: An Interpretation Based on the Theory of Games," *American Political Science Review* 62:770-787.

—————— . 1970. "Game Theory and the Study of Coalition Behavior," in Sven Groennings, E.W. Kelley, and Michael Leiserson, eds., *The Study of Coalition Behavior: Theoretical Perspectives and Cases from Four Continents.* New York: Holt, Rinehart & Winston, pp. 255-272.

Levine, Michael E. and Charles R. Plott. 1977. "Agenda Influence and its Implications," *Virginia Law Review* 63:561-604.

Luce, R. Duncan and Howard Raiffa. 1957. *Games and Decisions.* New York: John Wiley.

Lutz, Donald and Richard Murray. 1975. "Coalition Formation in the Texas Legislature: Issues, Payoffs, and Winning Coalition Size," *Western Political Quarterly* 28:296-315.

Lutz, Donald and James Williams. 1976. *Minimum Coalitions in Legislatures: A Review of the Evidence.* Sage Professional Paper 04-028. Beverly Hills, CA: Sage Publications.

MacKay, Alfred F. 1980. *Arrow's Theorem: The Paradox of Social Choice.* New Haven: Yale University Press.

Marz, Roger H., Thomas W. Casstevens, and Harold T. Casstevens. 1973. "The Hunting of the Paradox," *Public Choice* 15:97-102.

May, Robert. 1971. "Some Mathematical Remarks on the Paradox of Voting," *Behavioral Science* 16:143-151.

Mayhew, David R. 1974. *Congress: The Electoral Connection.* New Haven: Yale University Press.

McCrone, Donald J. 1977. "Identifying Voting Strategies from Roll-Call Votes: A Method and an Application," *Legislative Studies Quarterly* 2:177-191.

McKelvey, Richard D. 1976. "Intransitivities in Multidimensional Voting Models and Some Implications for Agenda Control," *Journal of Economic Theory* 12:472-482.

—————— . 1979. "General Conditions for Global Intransitivities in Formal Voting Models," *Econometrica* 47:1085-1111.

McKelvey, Richard D. and Richard G. Niemi. 1978. "A Multistage Game Representation of Sophisticated Voting for Binary Procedures," *Journal of Economic Theory* 18:1-22.

McKelvey, Richard D., Peter Ordeshook, and Mark Winer. 1978. "The Competitive Solution for N-Person Games Without Transferable Utility, With an Application to Committee Games," *American Political Science Review* 72:599-615.

Miller, Nicholas. 1975. "Logrolling and the Arrow Paradox: A Note," *Public Choice* 21:107-110.

—————— . 1977a. "Logrolling, Vote Trading, and the Paradox of Voting: A Game Theoretical Overview," *Public Choice* 30:51-73.

—————— . 1977b. "Graph-Theoretical Approaches to the Theory of Voting," *American Journal of Political Science* 21:769-803.

—————— . 1980. "A New Solution Set for Tournaments and Majority Voting: Further Graph-Theoretical Approaches to the Theory of Voting," *American Journal of Political Science* 24:68-96.

Mueller, Dennis C. 1967. "The Possibility of a Social Welfare Function: Comment," *American Economic Review* 57:1304-1311.

—————— . 1976. "Public Choice: A Survey," *Journal of Economic Literature* 14: 395-433.

—————— . 1979. *Public Choice.* Cambridge: Cambridge University Press.

Niemi, Richard G. 1969. "Majority Decision-Making With Partial Unidimensionality," *American Political Science Review* 62:488-497.

Niemi, Richard G. and Herbert F. Weisberg. 1968. "A Mathematical Model for the Probability of the Paradox of Voting," *Behavioral Science* 13:317-323.

_____ . 1972. "The Effects of Group Size on Collective Decision Making," in Richard G. Niemi and Herbert F. Weisberg, eds., *Probability Models of Collective Decision Making*. Columbus, OH: Charles Merrill.

_____ , eds. 1972. *Probability Models of Collective Decision Making*. Columbus, OH: Charles Merrill.

_____ . 1974. "Single-Peakedness and Guttman Scales: Concept and Measurement," *Public Choice* 20:33-45.

Oppenheimer, Joe. 1975. "Some Political Implications of 'Vote Trading and the Voting Paradox: A Proof of Logical Equivalence'," *American Political Science Review* 69:963-966.

Ordeshook, Peter, ed. 1978. *Game Theory and Political Science*. New York: New York University Press.

_____ . 1980. "Political Disequilibrium and Scientific Inquiry: A Comment on William Riker's 'Implications from the Disequilibrium of Majority Rule for the Study of Institutions'," *American Political Science Review* 74:447-450.

Ordeshook, Peter and Mark Winer. 1980. "Coalitions and Spatial Policy Outcomes in Parliamentary Systems: Some Experimental Results," *American Journal of Political Science* 24:730-752.

Panning, William H. 1982. "Rational Choice and Congressional Norms," *Western Political Quarterly* 35:193-203.

Park, R. E. 1967. "The Possibility of a Social Welfare Function: Comment," *American Economic Review* 57:1300-1304.

Peabody, Robert L. 1969. "Research on Congress: A Coming of Age," in Ralph K. Huitt and Robert L. Peabody, *Congress: Two Decades of Analysis*. New York: Harper & Row.

Plott, Charles R. 1967. "A Notion of Equilibrium and Its Possibility Under Majority Rule," *American Economic Review* 57:787-806.

Plott, Charles R. and Michael E. Levine. 1978. "A Model of Agenda Influence on Committee Decisions," *American Economic Review* 68:146-160.

Pomerantz, John and Roman Weil, Jr. 1970. "The Cyclical Majority Problem," *Communications of the ACM* 13:251-254.

Rae, Douglas. 1980. "An Altimeter for Mr. Escher's Stairway: A Comment on William H. Riker's 'Implications from the Disequilibrium of Majority Rule for the Study of Institutions'," *American Political Science Review* 74:451-455.

Riker, William H. 1958. "The Paradox of Voting and Congressional Rules for Voting Amendments," *American Political Science Review* 52:349-366.

_____ . 1961. "Voting and the Summation of Preferences: An Interpretive Bibliographic Review of Selected Developments During the Last Decade," *American Political Science Review* 55:900-912.

_____ . 1962. *The Theory of Political Coalitions*. New Haven: Yale University Press.

_____ . 1965. "Arrow's Theorem and Some Examples of the Paradox of Voting," in John Claunch, ed., *Mathematical Applications in Political Science*. Dallas: Southern Methodist University Press, pp. 41-60.

_____ . 1967. "A New Proof of the Size Principle," in Joseph Bernd, ed., *Mathematical Applications in Political Science*. Vol. 2. Dallas: Southern Methodist University Press, pp. 167-174.

_____ . 1971. "Comment on Butterworth, 'A Research Note on the Size of Winning Coalitions'," *American Political Science Review* 65:745-747.

_____ . 1977. Comment on Hardin. *American Political Science Review* 71: 1056-1059.

_____ . 1980a. "Implications from the Disequilibrium of Majority Rule for the Study of Institutions," *American Political Science Review* 74:432-446.

_____ . 1980b. "A Reply to Ordeshook and Rae," *American Political Science Review* 74:456-458.

Riker, William H. and Peter C. Ordeshook. 1972. *Positive Political Theory*. Englewood Cliffs, NJ: Prentice-Hall.

Riker, William H. and Steven Brams. 1973. "The Paradox of Vote Trading," *American Political Science Review* 67:1235-1247.

Rubinstein, Ariel. 1979. "A Note about the 'Nowhere Denseness' of Societies Having an Equilibrium under Majority Rule," *Econometrica* 47:511-514.

Satterthwaite, Mark. 1975. "Strategy-proofness and Arrow's Conditions: Existence and Correspondence Theorems for Voting Procedures and Social Welfare Functions," *Journal of Economic Theory* 10:187-217.

Schloss, Judith. 1973. "Stable Outcomes in Majority Voting Games," *Public Choice* 15:19-48.

Schofield, Norman J. 1978. "Instability of Simple Dynamic Games," *The Review of Economic Studies* 45:575-594.

_____ . 1980. "Formal Political Theory," *Quality and Quantity* 14:249-275.

Schwartz, Thomas. 1975. "Vote Trading and Pareto Efficiency," *Public Choice* 24: 101-109.

_____ . 1977. "Collective Choice, Separation of Issues, and Vote Trading," *American Political Science Review* 71:999-1010.

_____ . 1981. "The Universal-instability Theorem," *Public Choice* 37:487-501.

Sen, Amartya. 1970. *Collective Choice and Social Welfare*. San Francisco: Holden Day.

Shepsle, Kenneth A. 1972. "The Paradox of Voting and Uncertainty," in Richard G. Niemi and Herbert F. Weisberg, eds., *Probability Models of Collective Decision Making*. Columbus, OH: Charles Merrill.

_____ . 1974a. "On the Size of Winning Coalitions," *American Political Science Review* 68:505-518.

_____ . 1974b. "Theories of Collective Choice," in Cornelius P. Cotter, ed., *Political Science Annual*. Vol. 5. Indianapolis: Bobbs-Merrill, pp. 1-87.

_____ . 1979a. "Institutional Arrangements and Equilibrium in Multidimensional Voting Models," *American Journal of Political Science* 23:27-59.

_____ . 1979b. "The Role of Institutional Structure in the Creation of Policy Equilibrium," in D.W. Rae and T.J. Eismeier, eds., *Public Choice and Public Policy*. Beverly Hills, CA: Sage Publications, pp. 249-283.

Shepsle, Kenneth A. and Barry R. Weingast. 1981. "Structure-induced Equilibrium and Legislative Choice," *Public Choice* 37:503-519.

_____ . 1981. "Political Preferences for the Pork Barrel: A Generalization," *American Journal of Political Science* 25:96-111.

_____ . 1982. "Institutionalizing Majority Rule: A Social Choice Theory with Policy Implications," *American Economic Review* 72:367-371.

Sullivan, Terry. 1976. "Voter's Paradox and Logrolling: An Initial Framework for Committee Behavior on Appropriations and Ways and Means," *Public Choice* 25:31-44.

Taylor, Michael. 1975. "The Theory of Collective Choice," in Fred I. Greenstein and Nelson W. Polsby, eds., *Handbook of Political Science*. Vol. 3. Reading, MA: Addison-Wesley, pp. 413-481.

Thompson, Fred. 1979. "American Legislative Decision Making and the Size Principle," *American Political Science Review* 73:1100-1108.

Toulmin, Stephen. 1961. *Foresight and Understanding*. New York: Harper & Row.

Tullock, Gordon. 1967a. "The General Irrelevance of the General Impossibility Theorem," *Quarterly Journal of Economics* 81:256-270.

——————. 1967b. *Toward a Mathematics of Politics*. Ann Arbor: University of Michigan.

——————. 1970b. "A Simple Algebraic Logrolling Model," *American Economic Review* 60:419-426.

——————. 1974. Comment on Riker and Brams. *American Political Science Review* 68:1687-1688.

——————. 1981. "Why So Much Stability," *Public Choice* 37:189-205.

Tullock, Gordon and Colin Campbell. 1970. "Computer Simulation of a Small Voting System," *Economic Journal* 80:97-104.

Uslaner, Eric. 1975. "Partisanship and Coalition Formation in Congress," *Political Methodology* 2:381-414.

——————. 1981. "Manipulation of the Agenda by Strategic Voting: Separable and Nonseparable Preferences," in M. J. Holler, ed., *Power, Voting, and Voting Power*. Wurzburg: Physica-Verlag, pp. 135-152.

Uslaner, Eric and J. Ronnie Davis. 1975. "The Paradox of Vote Trading: Effects of Decision Rules and Voting Strategies on Externalities," *American Political Science Review* 69:929-942.

van Schendelen, M. 1976. "Information and Decision Making in the Dutch Parliament," *Legislative Studies Quarterly* 1:231-250.

Von Neumann, John and Oskar Morgenstern. [1944], 1964. *Theory of Games and Economic Behavior*. New York: John Wiley.

Weingast, Barry R. 1979. "A Rational Choice Perspective on Congressional Norms," *American Journal of Political Science* 23:245-262.

Weingast, Barry R., Kenneth A. Shepsle, and Christopher Johnsen. 1981. "The Political Economy of Benefits and Costs: A Neoclassical Approach to Distributive Politics," *Journal of Political Economy* 89:642-664.

Weisberg, Herbert F. and Richard G. Niemi. 1972. "Probability Calculations for Cyclical Majorities in Congressional Voting," in Richard G. Niemi and Herbert F. Weisberg, eds., *Probability Models of Collective Decision Making*. Columbus, OH: Charles Merrill.

Williamson, Oliver and Thomas Sargent. 1967. "Social Choice: A Probabilistic Approach," *Economic Journal* 77:797-813.

Wilson, Robert B. 1969. "An Axiomatic Model of Logrolling," *American Economic Review* 59:331-341.

PART FOUR

Cross-National
And Longitudinal Perspectives

Chapter 15

Historical Research
On 19th-Century Legislatures

by

MARGARET SUSAN THOMPSON
JOEL H. SILBEY

Born in western Europe during the Middle Ages, national legislatures came by the nineteenth century to occupy positions of prominence throughout the western world. In several places, especially Great Britain, France, and the United States, they were their nations' dominant governmental institutions and their major arenas of political action. Given their place and role, scholars naturally have focused much attention on them; the British Parliament, the U.S. Congress, and their sister bodies elsewhere became and have remained fertile areas of research activity (Bogue, 1974, p. 99; Baker, 1977; Henneman, 1982). From the beginning, historians, with their special commitments, perspectives, and methods, took the lead in such research. The original impluse, so well represented in the great works of Bishop Stubbs and S.R. Gardiner in late nineteenth-century Britain and of Frederick Jackson Turner and his students in the United States at the same time, forged a trail that many others have since traveled to describe our legislative past (Stubbs, 1874-1878; Gardiner, 1883; Turner, 1932).

This tradition has continued in the twentieth century and has been fortified by the contributions of several research consortiums. Both the History of Parliament Trust in Great Britain, founded in 1932 under the leadership of Sir Lewis Namier and vigorously active since the end of World War II, and the International Commission for the History of Representative

701

and Parliamentary Institutions, founded in 1935, have stimulated efforts to understand such topics as the origins and recruitment of European parliamentary institutions since the Middle Ages, the changing relationship between king and legislature, and most particularly the growth of parliamentary power. A similar body, the *Kommission für die Geschichte des Parlimentarismus und der Politischen Parteien*, has existed in the Federal Republic of Germany for the past 30 years, organizing and stimulating work like its sister institutions elsewhere (Loewenberg, 1966).

As one suggestion of the research vitality of all of this effort, more than 60 volumes of research studies have been published under the auspices of the ICHRPI since the 1930s. In addition, it has organized regular international conferences and published a semiannual journal.[1] A recent special issue of *Legislative Studies Quarterly*, "Studies in the History of Parliaments," reported on some of these efforts and contained articles on England, France, Spain, Holland, and Sweden at different moments, as well as references to additional work covering still other times and places (Henneman, 1982).

Collectively, these studies reflect the evidence contained in the plethora of surviving documents from the parliamentary experience. Henneman's introduction to the special issue of *Legislative Studies Quarterly* noted above effectively sets out the research record and the epistemological tradition undergirding it and ably captures the nature and state of the art within this particular tradition. These studies, he argues,

deal with aspects of the history of assemblies and representative institutions over a span of eight centuries. They focus primarily on why assemblies were convened and what they did. . . . The nature of the source material has influenced the way in which scholars have studied them. Scholars who lack the documentation that would permit statistical analysis are nonetheless able to describe many important functions of such assemblies and, sometimes, to observe their political behavior. Those who have the sources to analyze assemblies by statistical techniques must remain mindful of the long tradition of ceremonial, constitutional, social, and legal behavior that have given political institutions a complexity which statistics can describe but not necessarily explain (1982, p. 176).

The European-focused research is primarily concerned with a number of themes already alluded to, most particularly the growth of parliamentary authority, usually through conflict with centralized executive power. For the United States Congress, scholars have pursued similar themes, modified appropriately to the different historical and political environment in which they work. They have, from the beginning, undertaken highly detailed studies of great leaders, individual bills, and momentous confrontations among legislative blocs—efforts that have produced a stunning corpus of work. A recent bibliography compiled by the Office of the Historian of the United States Senate records more than 800 books, articles, and theses that reflect these traditional concerns. They range from Kammen's *Deputyes and Libertyes* (1969), about the colonial era, and Rakove's *The Beginning of American National Politics* (1979), focusing on the revolutionary period, to Patterson's (1967) study of the conservative coalition in Congress during the New Deal years, all of which have added much highly specific, often useful, data to our arsenals. At the same time, a few masterful overviews have also appeared, ranging in scope from MacNeil's *Forge of Democracy* (1963) and Wise's revision (1976) of Galloway's *History of the House of Representatives* to Haynes's (1938) still useful history of the Senate from the beginning to the New Deal years.

Biography has become one of the most persistent of traditional scholarly interests in the U.S. Congress. Many nineteenth-century members, including James G. Blaine and John Sherman, produced autobiographic accounts of their experiences and ever since biography has been a frequent and effective genre of legislative inquiry. The Senate Historian's bibliography lists works by or about senators from Ralph Izard, Aaron Burr, and William Blount in the 1790s to J. William Fulbright and Margaret Chase Smith in the 1960s and 1970s (Baker, 1977). Few senators of any prominence have been ignored, while some of the most notorious have received repeated attention. In the last year or so alone, two additional biographies of the interesting and controversial Joseph R. McCarthy have appeared alongside the six others already in print (Oshinsky, 1983; Reeves, 1981; see also Baker, 1977, p. 57). In addition, many lesser lights—Herbert R. O'Connor, H. Alexander Smith, Thurston B. Morton, and Thomas C. Hennings come to mind—have also been subjects of biographic treatment. If these and similar studies of House members were added to the many analyses of bills, sessions, and great moments, it would not be hard to dig out a running history of the United States Congress. It would be highly detailed, interesting, and important. But it would be incomplete.

Origins and Development of
Empirical Social Science Historical Research

Some of the traditional works completed on both European and American subjects stand as imaginative behavioral forays that have advanced our understanding of legislative activity over time. Nonetheless, most work of this sort has been limited, anecdotal, and ridden with gaps, weaknesses that have only lately begun to be overcome. Henneman's (1982) reference to statistical weapons in parliamentary historiography underscores the fact that empirical, social scientific investigation of legislative behavior over past time, employing a full range of statistical tools and specific theoretical and behavioral orientations, is of relatively recent origin. Yet in less than three decades the latter approach has produced a very full record and an extensive and suggestive literature on legislative behavior and development. Here, too, historians have undertaken and accomplished much, although not all, of the work.

Underlying their efforts has been, as one recent analyst noted, a belief that systematic quantitative research in congressional and state legislative history has the same virtues as similar research in other areas: "the ability to examine the behavior of large masses of individuals with great precision and to uncover insights and relationships hitherto unknown or only partially understood. History of this kind attempts to refine crude generalizations and impressionistic hunches, to clarify old and contentious problems, and to open up new ideas and problems" (Silbey, 1983, p. 603). And while some of this empirical research by historians is atheoretical and reflective of uneven methodological sophistication, collectively it forms solid ground for understanding the nature of the historical legislature as well as the roots of modern legislative behavior.

Portents of such historical scholarship were discernible as early as 1896 with the publication of Libby's seminal "A Plea for the Study of Votes in Congress," buttressed a few years later by Lowell's (1901) original analysis of party voting in the Commons and in Congress. But it took another 60 years before Libby's challenge and Lowell's pioneering efforts inspired significant or systematic response. The origins of modern legislative research among historians can be located in Aydelotte's work at The University of Iowa. Informed by his reading of the political science and sociological literature on legislative behavior and on the systematic measurement of political phenomena, Aydelotte's work on the British House of Commons (1971, 1977) impelled many others to follow in his footsteps. His analysis of parliamentary roll calls in the middle of the nineteenth century has been supplemented by Berrington (1968), Bylsma (1968), Lubenow (1971), Heyck and Klecka (1973), and Cromwell (1982), works which together cover most of the last 60 years of the nineteenth century in British politics.

Aydelotte's role was not confined to the British sphere, however; his edited collection, *The History of Parliamentary Behavior* (1977), suggests the reach of his influence. It contains essays not only on Britain and the United States, but also on Denmark, France, and Mexico, while its notes and introductory material indicate much of the additional material extant in the field. In virtually all of these pioneering efforts, the legislative roll call is the principal data resource and, as Aydelotte and others have explained, there are many reasons for this. Floor votes are more readily available than any other evidence on pre-twentieth-century situations, they are empirical reports of actual behavior, and they have the great virtue of being complete records—an unusual phenomenon in historical research (Aydelotte, 1977; Bogue, 1974; Silbey, 1983). Consequently, historians have performed extensive manipulations of computer tapes filled with ayes and nays in their attempts to illuminate patterns of legislative activity.

Investigations of this sort have been especially extensive among students of the political process in the United States. While the legislative histories of other countries, even England, have at best received intensive but sporadic empirical coverage, literature on the United States Congress is quite different in reach, scope, coverage, and completeness. The first book-length roll-call studies of congressional behavior appeared in 1967 (Alexander, Silbey), with some additional books, several articles and many doctoral dissertations written since, treating various parts of the American experience. Works ranging chronologically from Henderson's (1974) study of the Continental Congress to James Hilty's study of the New Deal (1973), Gary Reichard's analysis of Dwight Eisenhower's first congress (1975), and Barbara Sinclair's new analysis of congressional voting and political realignment from the 1920s to the 1970s (1982), have since touched on every period of U.S. history since the late colonial era.[2]

The preponderance of this empirical research has been accomplished by practitioners of the so-called "new political history," following guidelines set down by their colleagues in political science and adapted by historians such as Aydelotte (1971, 1977) and Bogue (1968, 1974, 1978, 1980, 1981b). While these scholars have varied widely in their objectives, in the main they have demonstrated strong commitment to traditional sensibilities of the historical craft. They have focused their efforts primarily on refining crude generalizations and impressionistic hunches that relate to persistently contentious interpretive problems: the importance of sectionalism (Silbey, 1967; Alexander, 1967), the identification of Civil War Radical Republicans (Bogue, 1981a; Benedict, 1974; Gambill, 1965; Linden, 1966, 1967, 1968, 1976), patterns of support for the War of 1812 (Bell, 1973, 1979; Fritz, 1977; Hatzenbuehler, 1972, 1976; Hatzenbuehler and Ivie, 1980), bases of partisanship in the Age of Jackson (Davis, 1970; Ershkowitz and Shade, 1971; Levine, 1977; Bogue and Marlaire, 1975), the impact of Populism (Parsons, 1973; Wright, 1974), partisan performance in eras of realignment (Brady, 1973; Shade, Hopper, Jacobson, and Moiles, 1973), and so on.[3] Topically, there has been heavy emphasis upon foreign affairs in studies of the War of 1812, economic affairs during Reconstruction (Seip, 1983), and Southern behavior at many different moments throughout U.S. history. These traditional issues of historical concern have been subjected for the first time to scientific testing, which removes them from the realm of speculative assumption where most had been lodged before. And roll-call analysis, with its comprehensive data base and potential for rigor, has been found to be not only particularly appropriate to such corrective efforts but highly revealing as well.

The historiography is particularly impressive in its coverage of the nineteenth century. Of the more than 70 books, articles, and unpublished dissertations involving roll-call analysis at the state or federal level, 40 fall between 1800 and 1900. Every session of the House of Representatives in those years has been subject to some work, while treatment of the Senate is just a little less complete, missing only the years 1800-1807 and 1825-1937 (Silbey, 1981). Cumulatively, this scholarship has replaced the nonempirical, impressionistic, and narrowly conceived studies with a scientific canon of rigorous, data-based analysis. Similar studies of state legislative behavior also exist and are growing in number. They are less extensive in coverage than congressional research, strong on the revolutionary period and the Jacksonian era, but sparse elsewhere (Silbey, 1981). At the same time, as has been noted, the research accomplished on all other societies, even Great Britain, seems scattered and diffuse in comparison with that on the United States. For this reason, and because the focus, direction, and conceptualization of nineteenth-century research, regardless of country, tend to follow similar lines of inquiry, the balance of this essay will explore research on U.S. legislatures as fully as possible, with occasional references to research on legislatures outside the U.S., where that is particularly appropriate.

We believe that such limited focus will be neither narrow nor distortive. A number of scholars have identified the presence of important qualities unique to the legislative experience in the United States; others have begun to engage in some comparative analysis seeking to measure and fix the similarities and differences between the U.S.' and other nation's experience. But it is still a truism that in most research, regardless of country, themes and approaches are being essayed (with suitable contextual refinement) that are similar to those so well documented in the historiography of the United States (Patterson, 1968; Loewenberg, 1973; Graham, 1982). Therefore, we believe that our exclusive and intensive concentration on one particularly well-analyzed part of the research record can help illuminate the accomplishments, the needs, and the promise of the vast subject of western legislatures generally.

Findings of Roll-Call Analysis

Early roll-call studies of U.S. legislative bodies tended to investigate all behavior during an individual session of a single congress or in series of congresses. Thus, Silbey (1967) and Alexander (1967) began with all members and all roll calls in the era they considered and tried to delineate the patterns exhibited in the voting. But not all subsequent scholarship has attempted such coverage. Often its focus has been on a single bloc within the Congress, such as Radical Republicans in the 1860s (Bogue, 1981a); on a single bill, such as the Kansas-Nebraska Act of 1854 (Wolff, 1977); or on specific policy areas, such as agriculture (Erickson, 1971). Unlike the pioneering efforts, these sacrificed comprehensiveness and breadth for depth and intensity.

"The American state legislatures," Campbell wrote in 1976, "are an underdeveloped historical resource" (p. 185). Nevertheless, much more has begun to appear recently than had been the norm. Since Davis's important

1970 article, several other scholars—Ershkowitz and Shade (1971), Erickson (1971), Wright (1974), Levine (1977), Campbell (1980), and Kousser (1980b)—have all made important contributions. Yet this literature does not now offer broad or systematic coverage of all states or periods in U.S. history. At the same time, the divergent foci, methodologies, data bases, and environments of these studies make comparisons difficult.

Whether it is conducted at the state or federal level, nearly all of the roll-call research employs quantitative techniques largely borrowed from the other social sciences. And while these techniques have ranged widely in degrees of sophistication and application, historians have moved well beyond simple percentaging or adding up of yeas and nays in unsystematic fashion as once was routinely done. Unfamiliar names, such as Rice, Guttman, and Yule, linked to their particular indices, scales, and measurements, have been heard in more and more graduate seminars and have appeared in increasing numbers of the books and essays dealing with nineteenth-century legislative behavior (Aydelotte, 1977). Cluster blocs, indices of cohesion, agreement, and disagreement, factor analysis, and, particularly, Guttman scaling, became the main methodological tools of these efforts. Most of the early studies employed only one of these methods. But recent works have often tended to incorporate several complementary quantitative techniques.

Moreover, historians' efforts have not been limited to laying out voting patterns; most have gone beyond the delimiting and ordering of behavior to examine, classify, and evaluate the patterns they reveal. Here the underlying premise is that roll-call behavior generally reflects some personal and/or group attribute in combination with institutional constraints of some kind. Accepted wisdom has it that the United States contains a pluralism of political forces, each capable of influencing an individual legislator's or bloc's behavior (Silbey, 1967). The important question for the roll-call analyst, then, is to discover which elements—personal, geographic, or partisan, alone or in combination—best explain the discernible quantitative patterns.

Sectionalism and partisanship were the principal foci of the early congressional studies (Silbey, 1967; Alexander, 1967). Then came consideration of subsectional and regional groupings as well as of factions within the larger party blocs (Seip, 1983; Bogue, 1981b). At the same time, a number of scholars also tried to relate voting patterns to other forces: to the economic and social dimensions of specific constituencies or to levels of partisan competition within districts (Wolff, 1977; Donald, 1965). Underlying all this work has been the assumption that congressmen, members of an elite though they may be, reflect or at least interact with the popular will as they perceive it (Bogue, 1980; Silbey, 1983). In sum, this literature has constantly linked voting alignments to the social and political dynamics likely to shape the behavior of congressmen.

Such efforts have paid off handsomely; a cumulative perspective is emerging out of the quantitative legislative historiography of the last decade and a half. One scholar, for example, recently referred to the existence of a "party period" in U.S. history, stretching from the 1830s to the end of the nineteenth century, when partisan loyalties and behavior dominated the existing political norms, persistently penetrating, primarily shaping, and thoroughly organizing the polity at most moments (McCormick, 1979). Analyses of U.S. legislative behavior both at specific times and in longer segments of those years strongly support that description, suggesting that the rhythms both of Congress and of most state legislatures were usually partisan. Party divisions dominated Congress's vote for war in 1812, for instance, as Hatzenbuehler (1972a, 1972b) has shown, with Republican unity as the determining factor in the decision to fight Great Britain. Nor was this pattern surprising, sudden, or new. Bell argues that in 1812 federal roll-call behavior "was substantially the same . . . as it had been over two decades"—often if intermittently, partisan (1979, p. 90; see also Bell, 1973).

Even as the Federalist party collapsed after 1812, thereby ending serious two-party competition in the United States for a time, party memories continued to have influence and to affect some legislative decisions well into the Era of Good Feelings, although such commitments did not play the same critical role that they often had earlier. Partisan clues were always abundant, even in the absence of a highly developed party structure in either Congress or the electorate. Certainly, much more than randomness or accident explained behavior on the floor. Representative Churchill Cambreleng of New York reflected the persistence of traditional loyalties when he declared in 1827 that parties were "indispensible to every Administration . . . essential to the existence of our institutions" (U.S. Congress, *Register of Debates*, 1826, p. 1546). And as these protopartisan elements of the 1820s evolved into wide-ranging, powerful structures—at first fitfully and then with a rush through the 1830s—their impact was clear: partisanship permeated everywhere, on and off Capitol Hill. Congressmen were elected and served as partisans, reflecting party-oriented battles over issues and candidates at the local level. Unsurprisingly, similar forces shaped contemporary state legislatures as well. They, too, reflected the strong partisan currents emerging throughout the political system.

Partisan behavior in the 1840s exceeded all previous levels. Despite extensive differences among districts and regions, "in the actual roll-call voting, the heterogeneity was compressed, with only a few dissenters, within a stable, wide-ranging, and large-scale system of national parties" (Silbey, 1967, p. 142). Divisions were substantive; parties diverged from one another on a whole range of issues, consistently and repeatedly, including the economy, social policy, and foreign affairs. These votes contained strong ideological content. Nineteenth-century Americans embodied varied policy mind-sets (i.e., ideologies), and parties reflected, organized, and articulated them. Party members in legislative bodies did so as well, repeatedly and consistently, as they moved on and off the floor. Certainly, party representatives consistently took positions that were congruent with those taken by others in the same bloc and that differed sharply from those expressed and acted upon by members of other partisan legislative groupings. And these policy preferences were not isolated from the rest of the political environment. Generally, legislators' positions agreed with the stances that their parties and their supporters advocated in election campaigns, in newspaper editorials, and in day-to-day expressions of position and belief.

Once established, comparable partisan patterns remained evident throughout the antebellum era. Even during the growing sectional tensions of the 1850s, party continued to play an important role in congressional behavior. Wolff (1977) found that partisan commitments remained important during the session of the 33d Congress that produced the Kansas-Nebraska Act, as they did thereafter. These deep-seated divisions displayed remarkable longevity; one study sums up the years after the Civil War as an era of "continuous, high, and fairly stable partisanship in the United States Senate running up to the turn of the century" (Shade et al., 1973, pp. 198-199). Of course, partisan voting varied somewhat in intensity and amount, from issue area to issue area. Other pressures appeared on almost every vote. There were only a few times when everything in a given session fell onto a single, partisanly-defined, voting dimension. In the antebellum era, parties cohered most in voting on banking and currency, for example, while at critical moments partisanship dropped sharply in votes on federally-financed internal improvements legislation and was replaced by higher quotients of regional influences. Sectional issues such as slavery usually received sectional responses in Congress—although even then some partisan cast often appeared as well (Silbey, 1967). Thus, there were blocs based on extrapartisan criteria in every period of legislative history: Southerners, Scalawags, regional cohorts, radical and moderate Republicans, and so on. And, depending upon what policy questions were temporarily dominant, these could supersede party as voting determinants, even in periods of normally high partisanship.

Critically and centrally, however, nonpartisan blocs usually were neither so prevalent nor so important as parties in ordering individual and group behavior. Rather, they were likely to appear as exceptions or deviations from the norm, emerging intermittently, if often importantly, but without the persistence or reach of party loyalties (Silbey, 1983). In short, while historians have expended much effort correctly and fruitfully in studying nonpartisan legislative behavior, the fact remains that party almost always prevailed as the dominant force at any given moment in U.S. politics after the 1820s. Despite deviations, then, most recent scholarship suggests that party remained more, and more consistently, important than was acknowledged generally before the days of systematic quantitative analysis. Consequently, roll-call studies have deemphasized the significance that sectionalism assumed in the earlier historical analytic literature. In substantive terms, this may be the most important finding to have emerged from the roll-call aspect of the new legislative historiography.

Before the Floor:
Recruitment, Position, and Decision Making

Some scholars have argued vigorously that the influential emphasis on describing roll-call behavior, while it does much to establish the contours of the nineteenth-century system, is not in itself sufficient to illuminate all of the system's details, dynamics, and nuances. There is much activity still not covered by the research we have been describing, such as the dynamics before the floor and off the floor that contribute to and shape the ultimate outcome of legislative conflicts. Behind the partisan blocs in nineteenth-century legislative institutions lay a dense network of individual and group relationships, beliefs, pressures, and forces, all affecting in some way the ultimate decisions made by the individual members. These networks, unfortunately, remain largely unknown to scholars, due to a lack of systematic research into their nature (Thompson, 1976).

Students of nineteenth-century U.S. legislatures have responded to this suggestion by moving beyond the study of roll calls alone and exploring other aspects of congressional and state legislative life as well. But they usually have done so with much less reach and energy than the roll-call behavior studies have. They have sought to flesh out the rather bloodless categories reported in the voting patterns so as to understand all that went into the making of a partisan political culture. Scholars have asked, for example, about the characteristics of legislative membership: the social background, wealth, ethnoreligious identification, and previous political experience of individual legislators; the structure of different constituencies; and the locational and regional qualities potentially influencing the members of Congress and the state legislatures. Such efforts continue a long and honorable tradition reaching back at least to the work of Namier and Neale on the British Parliament—research that, in turn, stimulated other British historians and led to the development of the ongoing History of Parliament project (Namier, 1929, 1930; Neale, 1951; Brooke and Namier, 1964). Such scholars assume that biographical information about each legislator can be a key indicator of legislative conflict and of individual and group behavior and that biographical data provide some basis for understanding both representative institutions themselves and the social environments in which they operate (Main, 1967; Alexander and Beringer, 1971; Bogue, 1973; Bogue, Clubb, and Flanigan, 1977).

Work of this sort on U.S. legislative bodies in the nineteenth century, while not extensive, has already produced two useful conclusions. The first is that "modern legislatures are populated by individuals who are not representative of the population at large, in that they are not collectively a mirror of the population sociologically. Recruitment to legislatures is characterized by the selection of persons of high social status and intense political experience" (Brady, 1973, p. 141). This is hardly surprising since it agrees generally with the existing findings in studies of the origins of political leadership in the United States (Benson, 1974).

The second point is more compelling, however. Since the days of Beard's (1913, 1915) research into the economic status of delegates to the Constitutional Convention and of other early political leaders, Americans have usually assumed a correspondence between partisanship and socioeconomic identification. Yet recent systematic analyses have produced different, more complex, and less symmetrical results. Goodman (1968), for example, found some socioeconomic differences between Republicans and Federalists from the Middle Atlantic and New England states from 1797 to 1804, and Campbell (1980) located significant ethnic distinctions among state legislatures in the late nineteenth-century Midwest. At the same time, though, Goodman saw no comparable breakdown among Southerners, and Campbell found little in the way of occupational disparity between legislators of different parties. The most far-reaching of these studies—that by Bogue, Clubb, McKibbin, and Traugott (1976) on recruitment to the national House of Representatives from 1789 to 1970—revealed no clear or well-articulated socioeconomic differences between partisan groupings at the national level.

These studies suggest that there are some sociopartisan distinctions among legislators which help to define differences between parties and/or other legislative blocs, but that such distinctions are more intermittent and milder than was assumed previously. Those elite divisions that do exist seem to fall more along ethnocultural than economic lines, thereby prefiguring and reflecting those of the party coalitions they represent. In short, the basic partisan differences, rather than class distinctions, have generally been the larger influence upon legislative recruitment. This has been the case over time and in most locales as well.

American legislative behavior has not, of course, been shaped solely by forces in the external environment that interplay with the individual legislator. Congress and the state legislatures often contain complex internal mechanisms, for instance. There are leadership positions, committee structures, and related processes, all of which also influence the decisions of members.

From the nation's beginning, some senators and representatives have had more power than others, and lobbying and similar activities have contributed to the final shape of legislation, too. But while political scientists have filled shelves with studies of these matters and the impact they have on congressional behavior in recent times, students of the past have barely touched on them in any systematic fashion (Polsby, 1975; Bogue, 1974). Nevertheless, a few efforts of this sort have been made. And these prove to be both interesting and stimulative for further work.

Some of these institutional analyses have, for the most part, utilized traditional methodology, although at least some of their findings proved to be testable and assimilable into more explicitly social scientific contexts. Rakove (1979) and Cunningham (1978), for example, both have studied the operations of Congress during the early national period. Young's (1966) work on *The Washington Community, 1800-1828*, suggests the importance of informal and social mores for explaining legislative coalitions, although this work has since been challenged (see Bogue and Marlaire, 1975). And Rothman's (1966) study of the late nineteenth-century Senate constitutes a useful initial effort to articulate and describe internal structuring of its individual and group behavior in the Gilded Age.

Other scholars of the nineteenth century have tried to adapt relevant guidelines from political science as they looked at the internal structure and locus of power in different congresses. Polsby's work has been most influential in this respect, largely through the pair of articles he published on legislative institutionalization and the regularization of careers (Polsby, 1968; Polsby, Gallaher, and Rundquist, 1969). He found that the history of the House since 1789 reveals a general trend toward "impersonal, automatic, and universalistic methods of conducting business" associated with movement toward "institutional maturity" (Polsby, 1968, p. 145). There was growth in internal complexity, in seniority as a norm defining leadership, in increasing numbers of specialized committees and subcommittees and, finally, in longer terms for members—all of which contrasted with the underdeveloped, haphazard, and erratic patterns at the beginning of the nineteenth century.

Bogue's (1981b) study of the distribution of legislative power in the Civil War Senate, meanwhile, serves as a model for such endeavors within a single or two contiguous congresses. Bogue asked a simple question: Who, among the Republicans on the scene, had the most power from 1861 to 1865? Bogue borrowed a number of measuring techniques from political scientists and isolated a number of senators who possessed substantial power, which enabled them to shape and direct the Senate's operation more than most of their colleagues. Bogue also made judgments about the relative power of different Republican factions, why certain things did or did not ensue from such power relationships, and, finally, how such relationships shifted to affect legislation and Republican behavior in successive sessions of the Senate. Many shrewd guesses had been made about these matters previously, but Bogue was the first to apply quantitative methods to focus and sharpen understanding of a number of elusive concepts.

Other aspects of the off the floor world of the nineteenth-century Congress have begun to be examined in some detail by one of Bogue's students. Thompson's (1979) examination of Congress in the Grant era suggests a world in which congressmen were overworked and underinformed, with almost no staff assistance and little effective guidance available. Dozens (and sometimes hundreds) of inexperienced freshmen legislators clogged the policy machinery. Of 47 standing committees, only 3 or 4 retained more than one or two members from term to term. As a result, not only did officeholders fail to develop substantive expertise, but the committees as units were unable to serve as agencies of institutional continuity. The largest single category of legislation consisted of private pension bills, and the typical representative was hounded by dozens of constituents who wanted him to visit the executive departments, procure patronage positions, and defend himself against charges of falling prey to the corruption that—if one was to believe the popular press—eventually subsumed everyone in the Capitol.

Lobbyists were an omnipotent and potent force in the congressional world. They were not necessarily corrupt, or even competent, but since they usually knew more about the issues they worked on than anybody in the House, their influence over congressional life could be, and often was, tremendous. In the absence of a seniority system, and with all of the committee seats up for grabs every two years, it was within the lobbyists' power to influence the creation of sympathetic panels in areas that touched upon their clients. Even an incumbent speaker as shrewd as James G. Blaine had to seek out their advice. How else was he to determine where to put all the indistinguishable novices who appeared routinely on Capitol Hill? All in all, the Gilded Age House emerged as a body with profound systemic weakness, without permanent form or clear lines of authority, a body in which a handful of professionals worked against all odds to produce minimal amounts of absolutely essential policy. In such a world, to underline the obvious once more, partisan cues had to play a major role in shaping action and response. But some crosspressures may have existed along functional economic and regional lines to shape bills before they reached the floor or to determine which bills moved out of committee for roll-call action at all. Such possibilities, coupled with further explorations of formal and informal power relationships, need to be subjected to a great deal of additional testing and analysis by historians.

The Changing Shape of the American Legislative Universe[4]

Gaps and shortcomings exist in this research, but as a result of the studies already done, scholars have started to tease out a great deal about the nineteenth-century American legislative world. Analysts have begun, for example, to develop middle-range understandings of the legislative process and of some of the larger aspects of politics and society itself. They have found consistent, pluralist conflict on the floor and in committee rooms despite the social homogeneity among members, a legislative politics that reflected patterns of continuity more than change, and an organizational structure primarily rooted in parties of tremendous strength, ideologically different from and interactive with the electorate (Silbey, 1983). Most of all, they have uncovered a highly partisan legislative arena quite distinct in character from its twentieth-century counterpart. Nineteenth-century legislative research underscores the notion of a different political universe in the period before the 1890s, along the lines that Burnham (1965) discerned almost 20 years ago.

The increasingly prolific research about Congress and the state legislatures in the twentieth century, beginning with Turner (1951), Truman (1959), and MacRae (1958) and continuing through Reichard (1975) and Sinclair (1982), has found that partisan structuring of representatives' behavior has remained an important feature of the period since 1900, but that it has exhibited a steady decline from its nineteenth-century levels. Before 1900, it is clear, partisan cohesion was the central fixed fact. In the twentieth century, in its weakened state, partisanship has had to share place with other, nonpartisan factors in the political environment. The central thrust of the roll-call pattern has, as a result, shifted markedly. And all of that, in turn, has reflected the reality of a much changed political universe (see also Silbey, 1981, 1983).

Other, less direct, evidence also suggests a shift over time in the nature of the legislative universe. Here, too, scholars have moved beyond reliance on roll-call analysis alone. The outlines of the nineteenth-century legislative world and the ways that it differed from today's have been specifically articulated in a particularly provocative body of recent research already noted: the longitudinal studies of "professionalism" and "institutionalization" by political scientists (Polsby, 1968; Polsby, Gallaher, and Rundquist, 1969; Price, 1971, 1975, 1977; Nelson, 1975, 1977; Abram and Cooper, 1968; Cooper, 1970; Fiorina, Rohde, and Wissel, 1975; Swenson, 1982). Collectively, these works provide documentation of the ways and degree to which Congress has changed over time, and therefore they serve as an appropriate starting point for those who want a context in which to think about the past. But more has happened.

Just as they have been aware of the methodological advances of the social scientists in political studies, historians have also become conscious of the body of theoretical constructs that has developed among students of contemporary legislatures and that is reported in the companion essays to this one. More than that, they have become particularly conscious of this literature's potential and usefulness as a means to enhance scholarly understanding of the nineteenth-century legislative world.

Two groups of historians have sought to benefit from this literature. First are those who want to understand particular events or outcomes at particular moments. To do so, they have borrowed such theories as seem appropriate to illuminate specific situations. Campbell (1980), for example, effectively drew on a number of models of legislative voting and theories of coalition building that had been developed by political scientists working on the late twentieth-century Congress; these models helped him decipher the behavior of three state legislatures at the end of the nineteenth century. In particular, Campbell found Clausen's (1973) policy-dimension theory useful to classify and illuminate interrelationships among voting blocs in different policy areas. His careful application of such organizing ideas helped Campbell to extend his understanding of how a particular process worked and to refine several hypotheses about the late nineteenth-century political and legislative world in the United States.

Campbell's approach was microcosmic; that is, his explanatory concerns were highly focused on a short chronological period. Other historians, meanwhile, have tried to apply theories originating in political science to longitudinal investigations of the legislative experience and how it has changed. In 1973, Bogue argued that since "dozens of scholars have been working upon aspects of American legislative history during the last fifteen years," it was now time "to fit the findings into a theory of the historical development of legislative behavior in America" (p. 81). Zemsky (1973) and Silbey (1983), among others, issued similar calls, but Bogue was among the first to heed his own advice. In his work with Clubb, McKibbin, and Traugott (1976) on modernization in the House, his goal was to see whether a pattern of modernization had occurred in congressional recruitment over two centuries. Legislative modernization was defined to include long-range movement toward complexity in organization, regularity in service and promotion, a pattern of structured career development, and different sources of legislative personnel over time, as the United States moved from a colonial-rural landscape to a postindustrial megalith. Bogue and his colleagues did discern some evolution, but the amount of change appeared surprisingly "unimpressive" to the authors and occurred at a glacial rather than a sudden or dramatic rate. Great external events—national growth, civil war, the industrial revolution, and great electoral overturns—did not immediately or seriously affect recruitment to the Capitol; the tides were calmer and slower than expected (Bogue et al., 1976).

social science theory, which is derived primarily from observations of the contemporary scene. Most of the authors of applicable social scientific theories about legislative behavior, in fact, have been political scientists whose objective is principally to illuminate the present. The very terminology these scholars employ reveals this unmistakably; the past is explored, not for its own sake, but in order to locate the roots and trace the evolution of current practices. Thus, historians are likely to find that the institutionalization literature is more suggestive than directly applicable to their own work—although, at least in this instance, the power of suggestion should not be underestimated.

But what is crucial is that, stated simply, these longitudinal studies demonstrate the danger of borrowed theory; that which is designed for the late twentieth century cannot be imposed indiscriminately on the past, as it depends upon the presence of intrinsically "modern" legislative characteristics. When the required preconditions of legislative activity and institutional structure do not exist, the twentieth-century models will probably lose most or all of their explanatory powers. At a minimum, the contextual problem suggests the need to subject such theories to rigorous and extensive testing before their appropriateness can be assumed. Perhaps even more, historians of the nineteenth-century legislative process might be better off concentrating on the development of explanatory models of their own—ones that are predicated explicitly upon the historical conditions of the period they are investigating.

To construct such theory does not mean that students of the past must ignore the work of their present-minded colleagues. An intrinsically historical approach cannot be constructed in a vacuum, after all. On the contrary, historians can profit greatly from the modernists' efforts—and particularly from the kinds of questions that they ask. What facets of the legislative process do scholars of the modern legislative process consider to be important and why? What do they want to know about the membership? How do different domains in the arena contribute to its overall operation? Asking such questions of the earlier period does help direct inquiry, but only if the queries are cast in historically contingent terms, appropriate to conditions prevailing in the nineteenth century. Here, for example, are a number of additional questions of this sort. They encompass and are informed by much of what occupies the current agenda of political science's legislative research. But each item has been expressed in a way that reflects the peculiarities of nineteenth-century circumstances. Each, in other words, ought to produce answers that will illuminate explicitly historical phenomena.

1. How were nineteenth-century legislative candidates recruited? In the absence of primaries and the other regularized access modes of today, how did aspirants for office call attention to themselves? Did potential

candidates or party leaders exercise greater power over the selection process? By what criteria were would-be legislators evaluated?

2. How were freshmen socialized into the legislative community, especially after boardinghouses were no longer their likely places of residence? Did nineteenth-century novices exhibit the sort of group spirit that is manifest in the "election-class" caucuses of today? What, if anything, did senior colleagues do to facilitate assimilation? Who were the senior colleagues who may have helped in the assimilation process—party leaders, members of state delegations, or fellow committee members?

3. Given the fact that most members' legislative service was very brief, what distinguished the handful of careerists from the majority of their amateur colleagues? Did they arrive in the legislature with the intention of becoming professionals, or did this intention develop after they came into office? Do they exhibit different political or professional backgrounds or come from different sorts of districts? Are their early experiences in the legislature in any way distinctive (e.g., better committee assignments, protegé relationships with established members)?

4. Once they assumed their seats, how did premodern legislators spend their time? What significance did they attach to business on and off the chamber floor? How, for example, did they allocate their energies among competing demands?

5. In the absence of an established seniority system, what norms governed the distribution of committee assignments? What relative significance did the speaker attach to such matters as legislative experience, substantive expertise, issue positions, geographic distribution, and personal and party loyalty? Did initial assignments determine later ones?

6. In any given term, several thousand bills were introduced but only a few hundred eventually reached the floor. How were those proposals distinguished from those that failed?

7. In the absence of modern transportation and communication, how did members keep in touch and maintain a working relationship with their constituents? How did they define their representational obligations to their districts; how explicitly did they try to act upon the wishes of constituents?

8. The vast majority of modern legislators consider "constituent service" to be one of their most important responsibilities. How important was constituent service as a component in the pre-modern legislator's job and what forms did it take?

9. If high proportions of long-tenured members are assumed to lend stability to the late twentieth-century legislature, what were the institutional and programmatic ramifications of large numbers of inexperienced members in the past? How did their presence affect the efficiency of government?

10. Contemporary research suggests that legislative staffs make important contributions to institutional efficiency and competence. What implications did the lack of staff and other support machinery have in the premodern era, especially in light of the membership's general inexperience? How did members inform themselves on the issues? What, if any, alternative sources of expertise and assistance were they able to locate?

11. What roles did outside actors—lobbyists, the press, etc.—play in the premodern legislative process? Was their impact relatively greater or less than it is now; did it take similar or different forms?

12. What was the nature of legislative-executive relations in the premodern era? To what extent did legislative control over executive patronage inform this relationship? Does it help to explain the relatively greater power of the representative branch? How, if at all, did legislators exercise oversight over policy implementation?

13. What factors went into the selection of a speaker of the House? Given his extensive formal authority over the committee system, agenda, and floor activities of the body, what would convince a party caucus to choose a particular individual? In the absence of today's hierarchical leadership structure, through which leaders are able to mature gradually, how did a hopeful go about preparing for the job?

Collectively, these questions suggest a broad and potentially rewarding agenda for the study of pre-twentieth-century legislative behavior. They provide guidelines for extending knowledge of the legislative institution itself: its personnel, rules, procedures and informal norms, workload, and responsibilities. Second, in their inclusion of nonlegislative matters such as patronage and, especially, ombudsmanship, they raise issues that receive considerable attention from today's political scientists, but that historians usually do not incorporate into their analyses of representative bodies. They incorporate the legislature into the larger political system and, therefore, offer the basis for linkages between legislative analysis and contiguous subfields: those that look at elections, political socialization, public opinion, policy implementation, and so on (Kousser, 1982). Similarly, as the list consists of queries that parallel those posed by students of contemporary legislative processes and behavior, the historical findings that emerge should be compatible with theirs. Answering such questions, therefore, can be steps toward a theory of legislative behavior that will allow, as current theories do not, the taking into account of significant differences between the nineteenth- and twentieth-century legislative universes and the larger polities in which they operate (Thompson, 1982; McCormick, 1979). As a result, historians' contributions can be assimilated more easily by those scholars who are interested in longitudinal analysis and "diachronic" legislative theory (Cooper and Brady, 1981).

Finally, although we have expressed the questions specifically in reference to the nineteenth-century Congress, they should also prove quite applicable to other legislatures that exhibit similar institutional characteristics and serve similar functions. It may be, for example, that such questions will call attention to parallels between the U.S. House of Representatives in the nineteenth century and some of the less institutionally-developed U.S. state legislatures in the twentieth century—those legislatures with high membership turnover, powerful speakers, inadequate internal expertise, influential lobbyists, and other attributes reminiscent of Washington in days gone by.

Answers to some of these questions should also cast new light on the sorts of research that already is underway, as well as on the developmental insights that currently are almost exclusively the products of political science. They should, in any event, place that work in better perspective. Examination of the entire legislative process, for example, may lead to some reassessment of the significance of roll calls. Are they, in fact, always the best, or the only reliable indicators of policy alignments? Or are these revealed as tellingly in committees or elsewhere? Can we confine definitions of a legislative agenda to matters that become subject to voting? Or should we look as well to those matters that were filtered out at earlier stages of the process? Does floor behavior provide sufficient opportunity by itself to discern the complex dimensions of nineteenth-century partisanship or of its perhaps largely imperceptible decline in substance and power over time? In 1872, for instance— a year which fell well within the era in which parties appeared to be quite strong—Republican House leader James A. Garfield could express the view that "we are rapidly reaching that period when the two great political parties must dissolve their present organizations. . . . [Both] still have great organization, but out of which the informing life has nearly departed" (Brown, 1978, p. 271). Perhaps, at certain times (i.e., in the late nineteenth century), floor votes only occurred on questions that obscured or evaded the fluidity and imprecision that Garfield noticed. At any rate, he grounded his opinion on something more than observable activity in the chamber. Contemporary impressionistic evidence demonstrates, moreover, that Garfield's assessment of the two-party system was not unique (Merriam, 1923, pp. 201-205; Robinson, 1924, pp. 193-194; Bryce, 1888, Vol. 1, pp. 653-661).

Similarly, a broader base of intrinsically historical research might challenge the belief among some scholars that the nineteenth century constituted a sort of "golden age" of federal governance, especially in legislative responsibility and legislative-executive relations (Fiorina, 1977; Sundquist, 1977, 1981a, 1981b; Dodd, 1981). Although the raw material is around to challenge it, there remains a tendency to accept Woodrow Wilson's (1885) anglophilic and prescriptive *Congressional Government* as descriptive of the Gilded Age. Those inured to Josephson's descriptions (1934, 1938) of the Gilded Age, for instance, might be surprised to learn that some of their colleagues—with a contemporary perspective jaded by today's political action committees and single issue voters, federal entitlements and pork-barrel measures, by Watergate, Ronald Reagan's 1981 "reconciliation" of the budget, and so on—now look back on the Congress of a century ago with something approaching nostalgia. Is this view appropriate—or the whole story?

Other anachronisms also structure too much of our understanding. The still standard work by McConachie on nineteenth-century congressional committees first appeared in print in 1898, and Mary P. Follett's *Speaker of the House of Representatives* (1896) remains authoritative on that subject for the period before its publication. Alexander (1916) published what turned out to be the last full-length effort to provide an overview of activities in the turn-of-the-century House, just six years after the overthrow of Speaker Joe Cannon. And many collateral topics are explored in books of vintages comparable to that of Fish's *Civil Service and the Patronage* (1904). Clearly, we have to move beyond these. Both Josephson's image of a "robber baron" era and that of a golden age need to be modified, but that will not be possible until historians look explicitly and more fully at the intrinsically nineteenth-century nature of relationships between government's elected branches. And that, too, is addressed in the questions listed above.

Beyond Roll-Call Data

There is more to implementing this suggested agenda than posing the right questions about the models that currently dominate work on the history of the legislative process in the U.S. Congress. Today's historians have both the resources and the competence to generate a kind of legislative literature that goes beyond the current mainstream work. Historians of the nineteenth-century legislative arena have, in their work, developed something of a "feel" for various periods and their boundaries, for political culture and for behavioral quality. That "feel" has always been rooted first, in hard, quantifiable data, beginning, in the case of Congress and the state legislatures, with a thorough examination of the roll-call record. But such a "feel" needs to encompass still other things, as well. Thompson's (1979) study of the 43d and 44th Congresses, referred to earlier, suggests what some of them are.

The heart of Thompson's study involved scholarly penetration of an important part of the way into the corridors, committee and caucus rooms, cloak rooms, lodgings, and informal meeting places of members of Congress, in a more thorough and detailed way than anyone has been able to do before. Critically, she did so without the benefit of or even primary reliance on any great amount of the detailed quantitative materials that roll-call analysts have so readily at hand. She began by scavenging everywhere possible, especially from political scientists' studies of the House and of the larger political system as they now exist—from the insights of Fenno (1973, 1978), Truman (1971), Dahl (1956, 1982), Davidson (1969), and Davidson and Oleszek (1977)—among others. Yet, all the while, something more was needed; the nature of congressional behavior had to be addressed comprehensively and with particular sensitivity to the contextual dimensions of the Grant years.

This necessitated moving off the legislative floor and beyond the roll call as the main focus of analysis, to consideration of traditional historical material lately left untouched, with an eye on its behavioral possibilities. There may not be many committee records for the nineteenth century, but there are complete rosters of committee membership for the congresses then, located in the *Globe*, the *Record*, and the House and Senate *Journals*. When combined with biographical data of the sort now available from the ICPSR archive, it was possible to investigate interrelationships between legislators' precongressional careers, for example, and the substantive jurisdictions of the committees on which they served. The committee experiences of professionals could be traced over time; freshman assignments of future professionals could be compared with those of men who did not stay long. Similarly, the House and Senate *Journals* contain lists of all bills that were introduced, their sponsors, and their committees of reference.

From such information, a picture emerged of the range of issues that legislation might have addressed, of committee and institutional workloads, of the relationship between members' districts or institutional responsibilities and the kinds and numbers of bills they submitted, and of the connection between other manifestations of legislative power and the ability to get legislation through. The patronage records for various departments, now located in the National Archives, also are sources with great analytic potential. Which types of patronage were routinized and which were open to competition among members? When competition occurred, what sorts of candidates or legislative sponsors were most likely to win out? And did members of appropriate oversight committees enjoy greater success in obtaining jobs for their constituents than did other, more randomly located colleagues?

The National Archives also possess voluminous petition files that, while incomplete, nonetheless contain more than enough raw material for suggestive statistical analysis. There are 61 linear feet of them for the 43d and 44th Congresses alone. What sorts of issue, inspired petition campaigns, and what sorts of citizens signed them? What, if anything, distinguished successful campaigns from failures? Does persistence over time have any effect on eventual outcomes? What evidence do these documents provide of organized interest groups? What sorts of clienteles organized early and why? What distinguished organized campaigns from those that were more diffused?

Legislators' correspondence is among the least reliable types of data: none is extant for many very important members (such as the first speaker of the 44th Congress, Michael Kerr) and even some very large collections have been subjected to significant editing (e.g., those of James G. Blaine and John A. Logan). Nonetheless, if one looks at enough collections, one can discern regular patterns of mail distribution and see what types of legislative issues and other business usually predominated. From mail, historians do get a good idea of the demands upon legislators' time, of the types of services that citizens wanted and expected from them, and of the kinds of appeals that were more likely to impel representatives into action.

Even these few examples should indicate the variety of data that exist and that can be used creatively to investigate a wide range of legislative phenomena. And when they are added to the election figures, census information, and roll calls, one realizes in how many areas even more extensive quantitative methods can be used to illuminate further the world of nineteenth-century legislatures.

Still, this is only one aspect of the historically contingent enterprise. Another set of descriptive qualities is still required if we are to explicate the nineteenth-century legislatures. Some of the best current research already reflects these qualities. Bogue's recent *The Earnest Men* (1981a), while fundamentally a study of roll-call voting behavior, also reveals a good deal more. Before he describes how the senators cast their votes on legislation pending between 1861 and 1865, Bogue reveals a great deal about them and their environment. The book opens with a short and colorful portrait of Civil War Washington and its Capitol, and proceeds through a series of very brief yet perceptive vignettes of every senator who participated in the Civil War sessions. We then learn about the committee system, how it fit into the legislative process, and how the membership fit into it. By the time the senators enter the chamber (which is described and illustrated through seating charts), we have a sense of a whole set of stages—on the floor and off—on which the actors performed. Without minimizing either the value or the complexity of Bogue's roll-call analysis, we can say that an equally important long-term contribution is his ability to convey a textured "feel" for what the Senate was all about at the beginning of the 1860s. Bogue has assimilated theoretical frameworks and rigorous methodology and interwoven them with an intimate familiarity with the kinds of impressionistic sources that traditionally have been the signs of well-written history.

Indeed, some of the best of traditional legislative history does contribute to a behavioral understanding of the nineteenth-century systems and the differences between it and that of our own day. Brown, for example, has illuminated the inner workings of the Gilded Age House through his masterful editing of the *Garfield Diaries* (Brown and Williams, 1967-1981), his superb congressional chapter in *The Garfield Orbit* (Leech and Brown, 1978), and a delightful essay on "Garfield's Congress" that is likely to be overlooked because it appears in the rather obscure *Hayes Historical Journal* (Brown, 1981). Welch's (1971) biography of George Frisbie Hoar recounts the career of a maverick who became an institution and never quite lost sight of his ideals. In some respects, it is reminiscent of Ralph Huitt's (1957) classic essay on Wayne Morse. And although it is carelessly edited in spots and contains too many unfinished cases, Norris and Shaffer's (1970) compendium of Garfield's correspondence with his unofficial "home secretary," Charles E. Henry, documents the "home style" of a harassed and overworked national leader who, despite frequent complaints about the burden it entailed, was diligent in serving his district and in obtaining federal jobs for as many of his constituents as he could.

These items suggest that, if looked for well and widely, a body of basic source material exists from which to construct an intrinsically historical set of theories on precontemporary legislative behavior and practices. Problems remain, of course; just as the past differs from the present, so do different periods and different legislative and political arenas in the past differ among themselves. Scholars may not yet be able to articulate a model that will organize the full range of phenomena that comprise the legislative process, even at a single moment. For the time being, the primary task of concerned scholars has to be the creation of relevant building blocks. But the more such blocks are informed by the long-term objective of developing a body of historical theory, the more likely it is that they all will be able to fit together when the time for aggregation arrives.

Conclusion

Twenty years of research has produced a substantial if incomplete picture of the nineteenth-century legislative world in the United States. Our pictures of it at other times and of legislative arenas outside of the United States in the same and different periods remain similarly unfinished. Roll-call studies have not yet completed their descriptive possibilities—for the U.S. Congress, for the state legislatures, and certainly not for all of the legislatures outside the United States. We are still deficient in describing a great deal of actual behavior, let alone in understanding the full range of before-the-floor activities in legislatures, the internal dynamics, cue-giving mechanisms, external pressures, from lobbyists and from constituents that make up the decision-making complex. Linkages remain unclear among various aspects of legislative activities, between internal and external realities, and between the legislative arena and the rest of the political system. The meaning of all of these activities in a larger framework is still elusive.

But we have noted all of this already. Scholars of noncontemporary legislatures, especially of the U. S. Congress, can be content that they have mastered certain topics and established a quantitative bedrock of useful information. They have begun the difficult process of framing models for further analysis. They can hope and expect that more will be accomplished subsequently as a result. Historians of the legislative process are far from where they started and much better off than they were 20 years ago. Their sights are much more clearly focused than they were, as is their expertise and the base on which they stand. That is significant in its own right and highly promising for the future. The energy and will have always been there; the ability to focus and engage in hard and subtle thinking is improving. The legislative world that existed before our own, in all of its many ramifications, lies within our abilities to understand.

NOTES

1. The history of the commission, with a listing of its publications, can be found in Henneman, 1982.
2. There is a complete list of these works in Silbey, 1981.
3. This discussion of research accomplished relies heavily on Silbey, 1983.
4. With apologies and thanks to Walter Dean Burnham.
5. The numbers of political scientists interested in the past happily appear to be growing. At the 1983 annual meetings of both the American Political Science Association and the Social Science History Association, there were sessions, peopled primarily by political scientists, on methodological issues confronting students of nineteenth-century legislatures.

REFERENCES

Abram, Michael and Joseph Cooper. 1968. "The Rise of Seniority in the House of Representatives," *Polity* 1:53-85.

Alexander, DeAlva S. 1916. *History and Procedure of the House of Representatives*. Boston: Houghton Mifflin.

Alexander, Thomas B. 1967. *Sectional Stress and Party Strength: A Study of the Influence of Member Characteristics on Legislative Voting Behavior, 1861-1865*. Nashville, TN: Vanderbilt University Press.

Alexander, Thomas B. and Richard E. Beringer. 1971. *The Anatomy of the Confederate Congress: A Study of the Influence of Member Characteristics on Legislative Voting Behavior, 1861-1865*. Nashville, TN: Vanderbilt University Press.

Aydelotte, William O. 1971. *Quantification in History*. Reading, MA: Addison-Wesley.

————, ed. 1977. *The History of Parliamentary Behavior*. Princeton: Princeton University Press.

Baker, Richard. 1977. *The United States Senate: A Historical Bibliography*. Washington, D.C.: U.S. Government Printing Office.

Beard, Charles A. 1913. *An Economic Interpretation of the Constitution of the United States*. New York: Macmillan.

_____. 1915. *Economic Origins of Jeffersonian Democracy*. New York: Macmillan.

Bell, Rudolph. 1973. *Party and Faction in American Politics: The House of Representatives, 1789-1801*. Westport, CT: Greenwood Press.

_____. 1979. "Mr. Madison's War and Long Term Congressional Voting Behavior," *William and Mary Quarterly* 36:373-395.

Benedict, Michael Les. 1974. *A Compromise of Principle: Congressional Republicans and Reconstruction, 1863-1869*. New York: Norton.

Benson, Lee. 1974. "Political Power and Political Elites," in Lee Benson, Allan G. Bogue, J. Rogers Hollingsworth, Thomas J. Pressly, and Joel H. Silbey, eds., *American Political Behavior: Historical Essays and Readings*. New York: Harper & Row, pp. 281-334.

Berrington, Hugh, 1968. "Partisanship and Dissidence in the Nineteenth Century House of Commons," *Parliamentary Affairs* 21:338-374.

Bogue, Allan G. 1968. "United States: The 'New Political History'," *Journal of Contemporary History* 3:5-27.

_____. 1973. "Review of Thomas B. Alexander and Richard Beringer, *Anatomy of the Confederate Congress*," *Historical Methods Newsletter* 6:76-81.

_____. 1974. "American Historians and Legislative Behavior," in Lee Benson, Allan G. Bogue, J. Rogers Hollingsworth, Thomas J. Pressly, and Joel H. Silbey, eds., *American Political Behavior: Historical Essays and Readings*. New York: Harper & Row, pp. 99-197.

_____. 1978. "Recent Developments in Political History: The Case of the United States," in Torgny T. Segerstedt, ed., *Frontiers of Human Knowledge*. Uppsala: Uppsala University Press, pp. 79-109.

_____. 1980. "The New Political History in the 1970s," in Michael C. Kammen, ed., *The Past Before Us: Contemporary Historical Writing in the United States*. Ithaca, NY: Cornell University Press, pp. 231-251.

_____. 1981a. *The Earnest Men: Radical and Moderate Republicans in the U.S. Senate During the Civil War*. Ithaca, NY: Cornell University Press.

_____. 1981b. "Quantification in the 1980s," *Journal of Interdisciplinary History* 12:137-175.

Bogue, Allan G. and Mark P. Marlaire. 1975. "Of Mess and Men: The Boardinghouse and Congressional Voting, 1821-1842," *American Journal of Political Science* 19:207-230.

Bogue, Allan G., Jerome M. Clubb, Carroll R. McKibbin, and Santa A. Traugott. 1976. "Members of the House of Representatives and the Process of Modernization," *Journal of American History* 63:275-302.

Bogue, Allan G., Jerome M. Clubb, and William Flanigan. 1977. "The New Political History," *American Behavioral Scientist* 21:201-220.

Brady, David W. 1973. *Congressional Voting in a Partisan Era: A Study of the McKinley Houses and a Comparison to the Modern House of Representatives*. Lawrence: University of Kansas Press.

_____. 1978. "Critical Elections, Congressional Parties and Clusters of Policy Changes," *British Journal of Political Science* 8:79-99.

_____. 1980. "Elections, Congress, and Public Policy Changes: 1886-1960," in Bruce A. Campbell and Richard J. Trilling, eds., *Realignment in American Politics: Toward a Theory*. Austin: University of Texas Press, pp. 176-201.

Leech, Margaret and Harry J. Brown. 1978. *The Garfield Orbit: The Life of President James A. Garfield*. New York: Harper & Row.

Levine, Peter. 1977. *The Behavior of State Legislative Parties in the Jacksonian Era: New Jersey, 1829-1844*. Rutherford: Fairleigh Dickinson University Press.

Libby, Orrin G. 1896. "A Plea for the Study of Votes in Congress," *Annual Report of the American Historical Association* 1:323-334.

Linden, Glenn M. 1966. " 'Radicals' and Economic Policies: The Senate, 1861-1873," *Journal of Southern History* 32:189-199.

_____ . 1967. " 'Radicals' Political and Economic Policies: The House of Representatives, 1873-1877," *Civil War History* 13:51-65.

_____ . 1968. " 'Radicals' Political and Economic Policies: The Senate, 1873-1877," *Civil War History* 14:240-249.

_____ . 1976. *Politics or Principle? Congressional Voting on the Civil War Amendments and Pro-Negro Measures, 1838-1869*. Seattle: University of Washington Press.

Loewenberg, Gerhard. 1966. *Parliament in the German Political System*. Ithaca, NY: Cornell University Press.

_____ . 1973. "The Institutionalization of Parliament and Public Orientations to the Political System," in Allan Kornberg, ed., *Legislatures in Comparative Perspective*. New York: McKay, pp. 142-156.

Lowell, A. Lawrence. 1901. "The Influence of Party Upon Legislation in England and America," *American Historical Association Annual Report for the Year 1901* 1:319-550.

Lubenow, William. 1971. *The Politics of Government Growth: Early Victorian Attitudes toward State Intervention, 1833-1848*. Hamden, CT: Archon Books.

MacNeil, Neil. 1963. *Forge of Democracy: The House of Representatives*. New York: McKay.

MacRae, Duncan, Jr. 1958. *Dimensions of Congressional Voting: A Statistical Study of the House of Representatives in the 81st Congress*. Berkeley: University of California Press.

Main, Jackson T. 1967. *The Upper House in Revolutionary America, 1763-1788*. Madison: University of Wisconsin Press.

McConachie, Lauros G. 1898. *Congressional Committees: A Study of the Origins and Development of Our National and Local Legislative Methods*. Reprint ed., 1973. New York: Burt Franklin.

McCormick, Richard L. 1979. "The Party Period and Public Policy: An Exploratory Hypothesis," *Journal of American History* 66:279-298.

Merriam, Charles E. 1923. *The American Party System: An Introduction to the Study of Political Parties in the United States*. New York: Macmillan.

Namier, Lewis. 1929. *The Structure of Politics at the Ascension of George III*. London: Macmillan.

_____ . 1930. *England in the Age of the American Revolution*. London: Macmillan.

Neale, J.E. 1951. "The Biographical Approach to History," *History* 36:193-203.

Nelson, Garrison. 1975. "Change and Continuity in the Recruitment of U.S. House Leaders, 1789-1975," in Norman J. Ornstein, ed., *Congress in Change: Evolution and Reform*. New York, Praeger, pp. 155-183.

_____ . 1977. "Partisan Patterns of House Leadership Change, 1789-1977," *American Political Science Review* 71:918-939.

Norris, James D. and Arthur H. Shaffer. 1970. *Politics and Patronage in the Gilded Age: The Correspondence of James A. Garfield and Charles E. Henry*. Madison: State Historical Society of Wisconsin.

Oshinsky, David M. 1983. *A Conspiracy So Immense: The World of Joe McCarthy.* New York: The Free Press.

Parsons, Stanley B. 1973. *The Populist Context: Rural Versus Urban Power on a Great Plains Frontier.* Westport, CT: Greenwood Press.

Patterson, James T. 1967. *Congressional Conservatism and the New Deal: The Growth of the Conservative Coalition in Congress.* Lexington: University of Kentucky Press.

Patterson, Samuel C. 1968. "Comparative Legislative Behavior: A Review Essay," *Midwest Journal of Political Science* 12:599-606.

Peabody, Robert L. 1969. "Research on Congress: A Coming of Age," in Ralph K. Huitt and R.L. Peabody, eds., *Congress: Two Decades of Change.* New York: Harper & Row, pp. 3-73.

_____. 1981. "Research on Congress: The 1970s and Beyond," *Congress and the Presidency* 9:1-15.

Polsby, Nelson W. 1968. "The Institutionalization of the U.S. House of Representatives," *American Political Science Review* 62: 144-168.

_____. 1975. "Legislatures," in Fred I. Greenstein and Nelson W. Polsby, eds., *Handbook of Political Science.* Reading, MA: Addison-Wesley Publishing Co., 5:257-319.

Polsby, Nelson W., Miriam Gallaher, and Barry S. Rundquist. 1969. "The Growth of the Seniority System in the U.S. House of Representatives," *American Political Science Review* 63:787-807.

Price, H. Douglas. 1971. "The Congressional Career—Then and Now," in Nelson W. Polsby, ed., *Congressional Behavior.* New York: Random House, pp. 14-27.

_____. 1975. "Congress and the Evolution of Legislative 'Professionalism'," in Norman J. Ornstein, ed., *Congress in Change: Evolution and Reform.* New York: Praeger, pp. 2-23.

_____. 1977. "Careers and Committees in the American Congress: The Problem of Structural Change," in William O. Aydelotte, ed., *The History of Parliamentary Behavior.* Princeton: Princeton University Press, pp. 28-62.

Rakove, Jack N. 1979. *The Beginnings of National Politics: An Interpretative History of the Continental Congress.* New York: Knopf.

Reeves, Thomas C. 1981. *The Life and Times of Joe McCarthy.* New York: Stein and Day.

Reichard, Gary. 1975. *The Reaffirmation of Republicanism: Eisenhower and the 83rd Congress.* Knoxville: University of Tennessee Press.

Robinson, Edgar Eugene. 1924. *The Evolution of American Political Parties: A Sketch of Party Development.* New York: Harcourt, Brace.

Rothman, David J. 1966. *Politics and Power: The United States Senate, 1869-1901.* Cambridge: Harvard University Press.

Seip, Terry L. 1983. *The South Returns to Congress: Men, Economic Measures and Intersectional Relationships, 1868-1879.* Baton Rouge: Louisiana State University Press.

Shade, William G., Stanley D. Hopper, David Jacobson, and Stephen E. Moiles. 1973. "Partisanship in the United States Senate, 1869-1901," *Journal of Interdisciplinary History* 4:185-205.

Silbey, Joel H. 1967. *The Shrine of Party: Congressional Voting Behavior, 1841-1852.* Pittsburgh: University of Pittsburgh Press.

_____. 1981. "Congressional and State Legislative Roll-Call Studies by U.S. Historians," *Legislative Studies Quarterly* 6:597-607.

_____. 1983. "'Delegates Fresh from the People': American Congressional and Legislative Behavior," *Journal of Interdisciplinary History* 13:603-627.

Sinclair, Barbara. 1982. *Congressional Realignment, 1925-1978*. Austin, Texas: University of Texas Press.

Stubbs, William. 1874-1878. *The Constitutional History of England and its Origin and Development*. 3 vols. Oxford: Clarendon Press.

Sundquist, James L. 1977. "Congress and the President: Enemies or Partners?" in Lawrence C. Dodd and Bruce I. Oppenheimer, eds., *Congress Reconsidered*. New York: Praeger, pp. 222-243.

_____. 1981a. "Congress, The President and the Crisis of Competence in Government," in Lawrence C. Dodd and Bruce I. Oppenheimer, eds., *Congress Reconsidered*. 2d ed. Washington, DC: Congressional Quarterly Press, pp. 351-370.

_____. 1981b. *The Decline and Resurgence of Congress*. Washington, DC: The Brookings Institution.

Swenson, Peter. 1982. "The Influence of Recruitment on the Structure of Power in the U.S. House, 1870-1940," *Legislative Studies Quarterly* 7:7-36.

Thompson, Margaret Susan. 1976. "Before the Floor: Preliminary Stages in the Legislative Decision Making Process." Unpublished paper delivered before the Social Science History Association, Philadelphia.

_____. 1979. "The 'Spider Web': Congress and Lobbying in the Age of Grant." Ph.D. Dissertation, University of Wisconsin-Madison.

_____. 1982. "Ben Butler Versus the Brahmins: Patronage and Politics in Early Gilded Age Massachusetts," *New England Quarterly* 55:163-186.

Truman, David. 1959. *The Congressional Party*. New York: John Wiley.

_____. 1971. *The Governmental Process: Political Interests and Public Opinion*. 2d ed. New York: Knopf.

Turner, Frederick Jackson. 1932. *The Significance of Sections in American History*. New York: Holt.

Turner, Julius. 1951. *Party and Constituency: Pressures on Congress*. Baltimore: The Johns Hopkins University Press.

United States Congress. 1826. *Register of Debates*. Nineteenth Congress, 1st Session. Washington, DC: Gales and Seaton, p. 1546.

Welch, Richard E., Jr. 1971. *George Frisbie Hoar and the Half-Breed Republicans*. Cambridge: Harvard University Press.

Wilson, Woodrow. 1885. *Congressional Government: A Study in American Politics*. Reprint ed., 1956. Cleveland: World Publishing.

Wise, Sidney. 1976. Revision of George Galloway, *History of the House of Representatives*. New York: Crowell.

Wolff, Gerald. 1977. *The Kansas-Nebraska Bill: Party, Section and the Coming of the Civil War*. New York: Revisionist Press.

Wright, James. 1974. *The Politics of Populism: Dissent in Colorado*. New Haven: Yale University Press.

Young, James Sterling. 1966. *The Washington Community, 1800-1828*. New York: Columbia University Press.

Zemsky, Robert. 1973. "American Legislative Behavior," in Allan G. Bogue, ed., *Emerging Theoretical Models in Social and Political History*. Beverly Hills, CA: Sage Publishing, pp. 57-76.

Chapter 16

The Functions of Legislatures In the Third World

by

MICHAEL L. MEZEY

The literature on Third World[1] legislatures is of relatively recent vintage, emerging for the most part in the period since 1960, when the new states of Africa and Asia were created and when American and European scholars first began to take seriously the politics of "developing areas." It is a remarkably diverse body of literature, composed largely of case studies of individual legislatures executed by scholars working independently of one another and at geographically dispersed research sites. In addition, these scholars have represented several different research traditions, each with its own concepts, research questions, and data collection categories.

Originally, most of the work was done by country or area specialists—historians as well as political scientists—who studied legislative institutions as a way of understanding more completely the politics of the nations with which they were concerned. They were soon joined by scholars interested primarily in political and economic development who approached the legislature by asking what it contributed to the process of change. Most recently, specialists in legislative studies have sought an understanding of how these legislatures operated internally, how they were affected by and in turn affected other political and social institutions, and (at least implicitly) how they compared with American and western European legislatures.

As we shall see, the intellectual and geographical breadth of this scholarly community has meant that the literature generated on Third World legislatures is somewhat less coherent, and also much more resistant to

733

cumulation and synthesis, than the literature on Western legislatures. Nonetheless, there are certain discernible categories to this literature, the identification of which can serve as an introduction to the more detailed discussion that follows.

At the outset, nearly everyone who studied Third World legislatures agreed that most of these institutions were at best marginal to the law-making processes of the nations in which they existed. While this conclusion was often based primarily on structural and legal data or, in some cases, on highly impressionistic evidence and was always heavily influenced by a narrow, culture-bound view of what an effective legislature should be, it nonetheless became the point of departure for subsequent research efforts.

Thus, some scholars dealt only with those few Third World legislatures that did seem to be effective law-making bodies. Others, however, took the weak-legislature conclusion as a research hypothesis and produced evidence that some legislatures that had been thought to be ineffectual were in fact somewhat more important than had previously been assumed. The most significant response to the weak-legislature conclusion proceeded on a functionalist assumption: if legislatures were not central to law making yet continued to exist, they had to be performing some other functions for the political systems in which they persisted. Such a line of inquiry yielded several alternative nonlawmaking functions, the most important of which centered on the legitimizing effects of the legislative institution and on the representational activities of individual legislators.

The next set of questions asked how, if at all, these newly identified functions contributed, along with the more traditional law-making functions, to legislatures solving the compelling political and human problems that Third World nations confronted. This work concentrated on the legislature's capacity to link citizens with their political leaders, a link which would presumably enable the political system to respond to mass wishes and to generate both support for the regime and compliance with its policies.

Finally, some scholars, convinced that strong legislatures were desirable either because they were democratic institutions or because they were of instrumental value to Third World nations, turned to the question of how such legislatures evolved and persisted. This approach tacitly accepted the weak-legislature conclusion and sought to discover the causes for the legislature's status and the conditions under which its status could be improved.

In sum, the research and writing on Third World legislatures has been concerned with these broad tasks: mapping the structural and functional characteristics of these institutions, assessing the legislature's effect on political and social change, and identifying the factors that influence how legislatures themselves change.

Legislative Structure

The earliest work on Third World legislatures, executed for the most part by country and area specialists, employed a structural approach; it concentrated on describing the characteristics and activities of those institutions constitutionally defined as legislatures. Most such discussions assumed that the structure and operation of Third World legislatures should be analyzed in the same way as one would analyze Western legislatures and that therefore the decision-making authority of these legislatures should be the primary focus of inquiry.

In the decade immediately following the emergence of the newly independent states of Africa, many such studies found their way into periodicals such as the *Journal of Modern African Studies, Parliamentary Affairs,* and the *Journal of Commonwealth Political Studies.* (See Austin, 1958; Proctor, 1960; Lee, 1963; Engholm, 1963; Proctor, 1965; Kraus, 1965; Tordoff, 1965; Gupta, 1965-1966; Gertzel, 1966; Markakis and Beyene, 1967.) As a rule, such articles contained descriptions of the legislature's constitutional structure and powers and its internal operation; often some background data on members and a discussion of the method for their selection was included. Comparisons with the Westminster model or, less frequently, with the American Congress ran throughout such discussions. Although some of these pieces were written by indigenous scholars, most were done by foreign scholars who visited these countries, collected the appropriate documents, observed the legislature in action, and perhaps did some unstructured informant interviewing.

Stultz (1968), in a useful article on "Parliaments in Former British Black Africa," summarized the findings of many of these studies and added his own observations on African legislatures. He identified 11 structural and performance characteristics which, with certain exceptions, the legislatures of 12 nations seemed to share. These included the popular election of legislators, presidentialism, constitutional supremacy, impotent second chambers or unicameralism, the absence or ineffectiveness of parliamentary opposition, significant independence of government back-benchers during question period, the absence of lobbying by private interests, uninformed debate often focusing on parochial concerns of legislators, executive dominance, and a functional ambiguity proceeding from a limited decision-making role. This last point led Stultz to speculate on alternative functions for such legislatures.

An effort similar to Stultz's is Weston Agor's (1971a) collection of essays on Latin American legislatures. Although some of these essays consider alternative functions of legislatures, most describe the constitutional

World legislatures, providing those who were studying these institutions with a more sensitive conceptual apparatus for identifying legislative involvement in policy making. In brief, the possibility was now open that even if a legislature could not say no, it still could affect the shape of policies by using more subtle techniques to resist the executive.

Decision-Making Authority: Practice

The range of variation in legislative decisional authority became clearer through case studies of specific legislatures. One group of studies indicated that not all Third World legislatures were wanting even by the narrow Western standards of decisional authority. Although he acknowledges its other functions, Stauffer's (1970) discussion of the pre-martial-law Philippine Congress indicated that legislators, through their negotiations with the president, had a quite influential role in shaping public policy and that they could and did reject presidential policy initiatives. Similarly, Agor's (1971b) book-length analysis of the pre-1973 Chilean Senate demonstrates its considerable involvement in all aspects of policy making. Even in situations where presidents had used their urgency powers, the Senate was able "to delay or reject a presidential measure" (1971b, p. 36). Unlike Stauffer's more impressionistic assessment of the influence of the Philippine Congress, Agor's discussion of the Chilean Senate is based on analyses of legislation and extensive interviews with members of that body.

A somewhat more complete perspective on the Chilean Congress's policy-making power is offered by Hughes and Mijeski (1973). Their comparative treatment of Chile and Costa Rica draws on an analysis of bills introduced in both legislative bodies over an extended period of time, and is further enhanced by a partitioning of the policy-making process into four phases: initiation, modification, acceptance-rejection, and review. They concluded that in Chile the president tended to dominate the acceptance-rejection and review phases of the policy-making process and that he and the Congress were on a par in the first two phases. They detected a trend toward even greater executive control, though they predicted that the Congress would retain a significant say in the process. They found that this contrasted with the situation in Costa Rica, where the Congress seemed to deal on much more even terms with the executive branch at each stage of the policy-making process (see also Baker, 1971).

All three of these country studies, then, find substantial legislative policy-making authority even by Western standards and therefore demonstrate that executive dominance cannot be taken as a given in the Third World. The fact that shortly after the publication of these studies two of these legislatures were abolished (in Chile and the Philippines) speaks to another issue— the durability of legislatures—which will be taken up at a later point.

Other case studies provided illustrations of a more subtle form of legislative involvement in policy making. Hopkins's (1970) interviews with 56 Tanzanian MPs allowed him to identify certain informal rules governing the policy-making activities of members of the Parliament. These rules suggested that MPs could express criticism or opposition to government policies only on practical grounds and not on principle, that MPs could not publicly oppose a policy decision taken by the party's National Executive Committee, and that MPs could oppose government policy in party discussions or within the Assembly before the Assembly voted but that once the policy passed members had to support it among their constituents. These "rules" led Hopkins to conclude that the Parliament, while clearly restricted in its policy-making role, could not be considered "a mere showcase for propaganda purposes" and that criticisms voiced by MPs "have affected some policies" (pp. 768-771).

Hopkins's finding suggested that private rather than public opposition was likely to be the mode of legislative influence in many Third World legislatures. This was confirmed in the comparative study of Kenya and Zambia published by Hakes and Helgerson (1973). Their findings, based on interviews and personal observations, suggest that bargaining was a regular part of the relationship between the president and legislators in both countries. However, in Zambia this bargaining was more likely to take place in private and therefore would not be as apparent from the public records of questions and legislative debates as it was in Kenya, where a somewhat more open pattern of opposition was permitted.

This notion of private rather than public influence on policy decisions recurs in various discussions of committee systems in Third World legislatures. The consistent theme is that while legislative influence is not very great, it is likely to be greatest when exercised in the relative privacy of committee meetings. Thus, it was reported that the final shape of agrarian reform legislation in Colombia and in Peru was significantly influenced by deliberations in the committees to which this legislation was assigned (McCoy, 1971, p. 349; Duff, 1971, pp. 384-386). Studies of the Lebanese and Afghanistani Parliaments done during the 1960s produced evidence that frequent and substantial changes were made in government-sponsored legislation in committee (Crow, 1970, p. 292; Weinbaum, 1972, p. 68).

Further illustrations of legislative influence on policy decisions will be offered at a later point. For now, it should be noted that Third World legislatures, while more constrained in their policy-making activities than Western legislatures, are nonetheless involved. Compared with Western legislatures, they are likely to be more involved at the deliberative stage of the policy-making process than at the formulation or decision stages, more involved on narrow, practical matters than on major policy questions, and more active in private arenas such as party caucuses or committees than in public debates and votes on the floor of the legislature. Thus, while these institutions do have functions other than the decisional, the research cited here should caution against the mistake of assuming that a restricted decisional influence means no decisional influence at all.

Representation

When those studying Third World legislatures began to seek alternative, nondecisional functions for these institutions, representation seemed an obvious place to begin. However, studies of representation in Western legislatures had been closely tied to decision making, with the major works on representation in the American Congress concerned with the relationship between constituency views and the roll-call voting behavior of legislators. Such a perspective was hardly relevant to legislatures where roll-call votes seldom occurred and, when they did, were usually unanimous.

The analytic tool that yielded a broader concept of representation was role analysis. As originally developed by Wahlke, Eulau, Buchanan, and Ferguson in the *Legislative System* (1962), representational role orientations also had a strong decisional content. Legislators were asked to say, for example, how important constituency views were when they made their voting decisions. This approach addressed what Eulau and Karps (1977) were to call the policy-responsiveness dimension of representation.

The Wahlke-Eulau concept of purposive roles proved to be a more useful way to get at other aspects of representation. The approach here was simply to ask legislators "to describe the job of being a legislator—what are the most important things you should do here?" (Wahlke et al., 1962, p. 249). The question was originally designed to distinguish among different role orientations held by members of the same body, but when these orientations were taken in the aggregate, conclusions about the functions of these institutions could be drawn. The findings of the studies that followed this approach pointed quite clearly to the importance of the representational activities of Third World legislators.

Thus, when Hopkins asked his sample of Tanzanian MPs to describe their responsibilities, the responses most frequently emphasized working with the constituency, explaining government policy, encouraging compliance, and bringing the needs and demands of the constituency to the attention of the government. Hopkins concluded that "the role emerging for an MP in Tanzania emphasizes his functions as a communicator rather than either a deliberator or a law-maker" (1970, p. 764).

In Hoskin's role analysis of the Colombian Congress, published shortly after Hopkins's work, the purposive role orientation that Wahlke and Eulau had labeled "ritualist"—emphasizing work in committees and the studying of legislative proposals—dominated.[2] However, approximately 25 percent of the respondents spoke of representing the people, or the department from which they were elected, as their primary job. Hoskin followed the purposive question by asking all of his respondents to indicate exactly what they did to represent their constituents. The three tasks most frequently mentioned were helping constituents deal with government ministries, identifying regional problems and bringing them to public attention, and serving as a broker between the constituency and the government.

Mezey's (1972) findings on the Thai legislature were congruent with those of Hopkins and Hoskin. The ritualist orientation was once again the dominant response to the open-ended purposive role question, but the other responses emphasized intervention with the bureaucracy on behalf of constituents and the articulation of constituency demands. Thai legislators also reported that they were besieged by requests that they perform various political and personal services for individual constituents as well as by demands that they secure funds from the central government for local projects. Most members indicated that they felt frustrated by their inability to deal effectively with many of these demands.

Several conclusions can be drawn from these role analyses of three different Third World legislatures. First, they suggest that the behavior of legislators outside the legislature should be an important research focus. Second, these studies suggest the possibility that these representational activities by individual legislators might have policy consequences that are worth exploring. Substantively, these studies identified two categories of representational activities that Eulau and Karps (1977) were later to label "allocation responsiveness" and "service responsiveness," the former referring to legislators' efforts to ensure that their constituencies got their share of expenditures from the national treasury and the latter referring to the particularized services that legislators were asked to perform for their constituents. Subsequent studies of Third World legislatures would emphasize these aspects of representation, rather than policy responsiveness, as the most important manifestations of the representative function of these bodies.

Allocation responsiveness appears to be a concern of all legislators everywhere (Mezey, 1979, Ch. 9), but in the Third World such activities seem a way of life. Joel Barkan (1979b) defined the role of the legislator in Africa as that of "an entrepreneur" whose job was to mobilize the resources of his constituency for community development projects and to extract resources from the central government to finance such undertakings. The projects run the gamut "from schools, health centers, cattle dips, and irrigation works to feeder roads, crop and settlement schemes, and various forms of cottage industries" (p. 270). In Chile, according to Valenzuela and Wilde (1979), members of the Congress were able to amend budget legislation on behalf of local interests and regularly attempted "to have the money allotted for a particular line in the budget destined to their own particular projects" (pp. 201-202). After the legislation was passed, there was regular contact between legislators and bureaucrats aimed at diverting public works funds to the constituency of the intervening legislator. Similarly, Morell (1979) notes that Thai legislators regularly intervened with the bureaucracy on matters relating to the nature and implementation of local development projects. Finally, there is evidence from the only crossnational study of Third World legislatures that most MPs in Kenya, Korea, and Turkey believe that they have been effective in getting resources to their districts (Kim, Barkan, Turan, and Jewell, 1983).

The service responsiveness aspect of representation frequently found the legislator in an ombudsmanic role of intervening with the bureaucracy on behalf of individual constituents. Maheshwari (1976) reports that members of the Indian Lok Sabha regularly engage in such activities, and Marvin Weinbaum (1977) indicates that such work was the most important aspect of the job of members of the Afghanistan Parliament. Those asking for such legislative intervention seek a wide variety of bureaucratic responses. In India, for example, legislators were asked to help constituents get government jobs (Maheshewari, 1976, p. 338). In South Vietnam (Goodman, 1975, p. 185) and Afghanistan (Weinbaum, 1977, p. 112), legislators were asked to intervene in judicial proceedings. In Chile (Valenzuela and Wilde, 1979, pp. 200-201) a great deal of constituency casework involved efforts to get the nation's overburdened social security system to respond to individual complaints, while in Thailand (Mezey, 1972, p. 696) some legislators reported that they were asked to help the children of constituents gain admission to desirable state-run schools.

While these allocative and service relationships between legislators and their constituents have been commented on extensively in studies of the American Congress (Olson, 1967; Saloma, 1969; Mayhew, 1974; Fiorina, 1977) and other Western legislatures (Barker and Rush, 1970; Cayrol, Parodi, and Ysmal, 1976), for several reasons the volume of such demands was found to be much greater in Third World nations. Therefore, dealing with these demands emerged as a primary function of such institutions and their members (see Mezey, 1979, pp. 147ff). First, the patron-client relationship that represents the more generic case of service is ingrained in many "non-Western" cultures. Quite simply, legislators are expected to offer something concrete to constituents in return for their votes, and responsiveness to their particularized concerns is an obvious thing to offer (see Hopkins, 1975, p. 216; Grossholtz, 1964, p. 97). One of the first to comment on this expectation was Bailey (1960) in his study of legislators in the Indian state of Orissa.

He observed that voters view the member of the Legislative Assembly (MLA) as "an effective broker who can get a man out of trouble, or win a favor for him, or so manipulate matters that the benefits of the welfare state are diverted away from others toward his own people" (p. 123).

Second, because interest groups are not very strong in these political systems, individual demands are not readily aggregated. Thus, as Styskal (1969) discovered in his survey of Philippine legislators, weak interest groups means that "a more frequent source of demands of legislators are constituents—individuals unaffiliated with groups—who come in large numbers to press their representatives to help with personal needs and wants" (p. 421).

Third, in nations undergoing rapid social and political changes, severe dislocations engendered by centrally contrived plans are likely to be the order of the day. In many nations where legislators are the only elected officials and where civilian and military bureaucracies are likely to be quite inaccessible and unresponsive (see Mezey, 1976), citizens will turn to the legislator to seek redress of their grievances.

Fourth, because in many non-Western cultures the political realm is not as well differentiated from the nonpolitical (see Pye, 1958), Third World legislators have had to deal with requests that their Western counterparts seldom confront. Thus, in Bangladesh, MPs were asked to mediate private disputes among their constituents (Jahan, 1976, p. 367). In India, MPs were regularly asked to lend or give money to constituents in need (Maheshwari, 1976, p. 338). In Thailand, legislators reported that they were asked to act as go-betweens in arranging marriages (Mezey, 1972, p. 697), while in Singapore some MPs indicated that they had been asked to help find run-away spouses (Chee, 1976, p. 436).

While these findings make clear that all Third World legislators have to cope with a large volume of particularized constituency demands, some are more willing than others to define their role in these terms. Three studies have sought to explain differences in the attitudes of Third World legislators toward their representational roles. Kim and Woo (1975, p. 282) subjected their role data on the Korean legislature to causal analysis and concluded that those legislators who represented rural districts, who won by a narrow margin, who had been politically active for a relatively short period of time, and whose careers were sponsored by political parties or by other organized groups were more oriented toward their constituency than their colleagues. Comparable findings result from Kumbhat and Marican's (1976) analysis of the attitudes of Malaysian state legislators, with freshman members from rural districts displaying the strongest orientation toward their constituency. Similarly, Hoskin (1971) found that Colombian legislators from more rural and less developed departments, although they were more likely to be trustees, were also more oriented toward the constituency as a focus of representation than their colleagues from more developed and more metropolitan areas.

On the whole, these findings suggest that legislators who represent the more traditional sectors of society are more likely to be oriented toward their constituency than those who represent the more modernized sectors. This lends some support to the notion that the large volume of particularized demands that come to Third World legislatures are at least in part a product of the dominantly traditional cultures within which these institutions and their members operate.

Legislatures and Development

As indicated earlier, the functions of Third World legislatures that were of primary concern to a number of scholars had to do with the role of the institution in the process of societal change. More specific research questions involved the role of the legislature in recruiting political elites, in facilitating political integration, in mobilizing support for government policies, in legitimizing political regimes, and in designing legislation aimed at bringing about socioeconomic change.

Elite Recruitment

Perhaps the first coincidence between the interests of development scholars and the legislature was in the literature on political elites.

This research described the backgrounds of people who held elite positions, their differences from mass publics, and the process by which they were recruited to these positions. While legislators were not always the most influential elites, information on them was usually more available than information on members of partisan or military bureaucracies. Also, in some systems, legislatures were the training ground for future members of executive elites, so to study the characteristics of legislators meant to study the characteristics of future holders of more influential positions. These studies, then, were less directly concerned with the legislature and more interested in what the legislature and its membership indicated about political change.

The first and most complete study of this sort was Frey's (1965) analysis of the Grand National Assembly of Turkey. Explaining why he had undertaken the study, he observed that "when one examines the social backgrounds of deputies . . . one obtains, ipso facto, information on the backgrounds of all the cabinets and ministers, on the formal leadership of the Assembly, and on the top political party leaders as well" (p. 6). This rationale led him to collect information on the education, occupation, family backgrounds, religious beliefs, age, and sex of 2,210 deputies serving in the 10 Assemblies that convened between 1920 and 1957. In addition, he analyzed these data to determine the characteristics of leadership and party groups within the legislature. Finally, the longitudinal aspect of his data set allowed for analyses of change over time on all of these dimensions. This permitted him to arrive at conclusions about the nature of elites in Turkey and the developing world and about the process of political development as it is reflected in the changing composition of elites.

The scope of Frey's data and the breadth of his analysis makes his book the model for future studies of this sort. One such study was executed by Stauffer (1966) who looked at the backgrounds of members of the Philippine Congress during five sessions spanning the period between 1921 and 1962. He sought to determine both how the composition of the Congress had changed and whether social and political changes in the nation were reflected in the changing membership of the legislature and, more importantly, in the composition of interests represented in the legislature. The impact of political change on legislative composition was also the focus of Le Vine's (1968) analysis of recruitment to the legislatures of French-speaking Africa. More specifically, he assessed the impact of independence, military coups, and the emergence of one-party systems on the composition of legislatures and the nature of recruitment to these bodies.

An alternative approach to these longitudinal analyses is to look at the composition of the legislature at a particular time and ask what that has to tell us about the politics of the nation. For example, Ranis's interview data on the backgrounds and attitudes of Argentine legislators indicate that experiences such as university training and education abroad are associated with greater ideological flexibility (1970, p. 225). Similarly, Verner's (1970) data on Guatemalan legislators detects certain background differences between leftist and rightist legislators, with the latter more likely than the former to have traveled and been educated abroad. The implication of both of these studies then is that the backgrounds of legislators in developing nations affects the nature of political conflict in the legislature.

Schulz's (1973) study brought this research tradition an important step forward by examining the impact of "changing political contexts upon legislative recruitment patterns" through a comparison of the backgrounds of legislators in "transitional" systems, such as Iran, Syria, India, and Turkey, with the backgrounds of legislators in several Western nations. She concludes that there are systematic background differences between the two groups. Those from transitional systems are likely to be from governmental and agricultural occupations, are young and highly educated, and do not spend a great deal of time in legislative careers. The Western legislator, in contrast, is either a professional or a businessman, is more likely than his Third World counterpart to resemble his constituents in his educational background, and may well spend much of his working lifetime in the legislature (Shulz, 1973, p. 589).

The perhaps obvious message of Shulz's cross-national analysis as well as the over-time single nation studies of Frey, Stauffer, and Le Vine is that as a political system changes, the composition of its legislative elite will change accordingly. To the extent that significant political interaction takes place in the legislature, the cross-sectional studies of Ranis and Verner suggest that different types of legislators mean different patterns of conflict.

In addition to being affected by the stage of development, the composition of the legislature may be affected by the environment within which its members gain and lose their seats. In an important theoretical essay, Seligman (1975) makes the point that service in most Third World legislatures entails significant political and, sometimes, personal risk. In such high risk systems, "the deprivation that results from the loss of political status generates political outlooks that contrast sharply with those found in low risk systems. Since political careers are hazardous vocations, politics is viewed as life or death, total power or total humiliation, and nothing in between" (p. 96). In brief, the cost of gaining office (in money and perhaps danger) and the cost of losing (status loss, the end of one's political career, or, in some cases, imprisonment and death) are very high. Therefore, two types of legislators predominate in such systems: "cautious sycophants who are flexible in pursuing safety and opportunity, fearing severe sanctions that disfavor brings" and "the political demagogue and adventurer" who seeks high stakes and is willing to risk safety to achieve them (p. 97). Because incumbents in high risk systems need to provide themselves with "cushions" to protect against "high recruitment and career risks" their behavior is likely to be characterized by "nepotism, cliquism, corruption, and empire building" (p. 103).

Some empirical support for Seligman's theory is found in Chong Lim Kim's (1971) comparative study of Korean legislators and American state legislators. He finds that the loss of political status among losing Korean candidates was much greater than among Americans who had lost elections. Information from several other political systems also tends to confirm Seligman's view that Third World legislatures, especially those vulnerable to extraconstitutional attack, are high risk institutions characterized by the opportunistic member behavior patterns predicted by Seligman (Mezey, 1979, Ch. 11).

Integration

The backgrounds of legislators also may indicate the extent to which the political system is integrated. Political integration involves "the penetration of the primary, occupational, or geographical groups" of a nation "by a broader national identification" (Grossholtz, 1970, p. 94). One way to ensure diverse ethnic or regional groupings that their particular identities and needs are to be respected is by providing the group with adequate representation in the legislature.

In Lebanon, perhaps more than in any other nation, the history of the legislature was intimately tied to the challenge of creating and maintaining national unity in an ethnically divided nation. The story of how the Lebanese Parliament became the central element for providing equitable representation for the various regional groups and religious sects of that country is told in Baaklini's *Legislative and Political Development in Lebanon* (1976). The Lebanese Parliament was the place where these groups "were brought together to plan and chart the future path" and "to lay down the principles of coexistence in the newly created Lebanese State." The constitutional provisions and subsequent electoral laws designed to provide "each community a fair representation in political authority" were devised in the legislature (pp. 276-277).[3]

In *Legislatures in Plural Societies* (1977) Eldridge collects several essays on political integration. Jewell's contribution to this volume is a general treatment of how electoral laws and their associated party systems can facilitate or hinder equitable representation. Drawing on the extant literature, Jewell assesses the comparative effects of separate electorates, reserved seats, single-member plurality systems, multimember plurality systems, and proportional representation on the achievement of appropriate representation for minorities. He also makes the point that the effect of particular electoral systems on minority representation depends to a large extent "on the strategy of party and group leaders concerning the nomination of legislative candidates" as well as upon "the voting behavior of both minority and majority members of the electorate" (p. 40).

In another article in the Eldridge book, Sisson and Shrader utilize background and attitudinal data on members of the Legislative Assembly of the Indian state of Rajasthan. They find great disparities in education, mobility, occupation, and caste between the legislators and the electorate whom they represent. But they also find that the MLAs "have close associations with the constituencies they represent. Most have close familial and ancestral ties; most spend most of their time actively engaged in politics. The language which most legislators consider to be their mother tongue is that spoken by their constituencies" (1977, p. 89).

Weinbaum's analysis of the Afghanistan Parliament, also in the Eldridge volume, argues that the activities of individual members of the legislature serve an integrative function because, as agents of local elites, the legislators embody the "penetration of national decision arenas" and "carried most of the burden of communications between the periphery and the center" (1977, p. 118). In a society beset by regional, religious, and ethnic animosities, the capacity of individual legislators to assure these groups of representation at the center was, in Weinbaum's view, in no small measure responsible for holding the political system together.

Weinbaum's discussion suggests that legislatures are also places where the integration of national elites takes place. This point was also made by Stauffer, who observed that in the Philippines "the existence of a 'national' legislature long before the nation achieved independence, and regular congressional elections throughout the nation, greatly contributed to the creation of a political class that was national in geographic spread and integrated in political outlook" (1970, p. 355). Similarly, Proctor (1968) describes how the creation of a House of Chiefs as a second chamber in the Parliament of Botswana provided a partial solution to the problem of integrating traditional elites with modernizing elites.

These discussions attest to the inherent integrative capacities of the legislature. Because it is a multimember institution, seats can be apportioned among different groups, thereby facilitating integration at the mass level. Because its members are locally elected and have ties to parochial groups, it facilitates mass-elite integration. Because it is a central political institution where representatives of different groups and regions meet regularly, it is a vehicle for elite integration. However, as the history of countries such as Lebanon, Pakistan, and Nigeria demonstrate, the integrative potential of legislatures is not unlimited. Especially when it is the only integrative agent in a society subject to strong disintegrative forces, the legislature is quite unlikely to maintain stability.

Mobilization

If Third World legislators link citizens with central leaders by articulating the needs of the former to the latter, legislators can also communicate with citizens on behalf of central leaders to gain popular support for and compliance with specific policies.

It should not be surprising that executive elites look more fondly upon this role for legislators than the legislators themselves do. Therefore, the extent to which legislators perform this function of mobilizing support depends in large measure on the capacity of the government to coerce them into doing it. This point is neatly demonstrated in two comparative discussions of the Kenyan and Tanzanian Parliaments published in the same year by Barkan (1979b) and Hopkins (1979).

In Kenya, even though former President Kenyatta had told MPs that they had a duty to urge citizens to follow the advice of the government technicians, many Kenyan legislators either did not perform this activity or accorded a much lower priority to it than they did to generating resources for their constituency. The capacity of Kenyatta and his party to force their compliance was minimal. In comparison, both Barkan and Hopkins note that Tanzanian legislators are more restricted by the strong political organization of President Nyerere. As Barkan says, Tanzanian legislators "are expected to confine their activities in their home communities to being agents of the center—primarily by explaining government policies to those residing at the grass roots" (1979b, p. 75). An earlier finding by Hopkins (1970, p. 765) suggests that legislators respond to this expectation: when asked what was the most important aspect of their job, twice as many said explaining government policies to their constituency as said advocating the interests of the constituency to the government.

That the strength of the mobilization expectations of executive leaders will vary with the sanctions at their disposal is also suggested by Musolf and Springer (1977, pp. 126-128), who found that Malaysian legislators who were members of the Government party emphasized the importance of explaining government policies to their constituents, while opposition legislators were more oriented toward representing their districts to the government.

Legitimization

While some legislators in Third World nations generate support for government programs through direct mobilization activities, in most instances the legislature creates support for the government through its legitimization function. In an influential essay, Packenham (1970), writing specifically about the Brazilian Congress as well as more generally about Third World legislatures, argued that legitimization was a basic latent function of legislatures: "Simply by meeting regularly and uninterruptedly, the legislature produced, among the relevant populace and elites, a wider and deeper sense of the government's moral right to rule than would otherwise have obtained" (pp. 527-528). Legitimization also has its manifest component when the legislature puts its "stamp of approval on initiatives taken elsewhere" (p. 529). Packenham goes on to survey the then-existing descriptions of Third World legislatures in action and concludes that few have any real decisional influence and that legitimization is the most important function of each. He further suggests that even in those Western and Third World nations where legislatures do have a significant decisional role, they also have important legitimization functions which had hitherto been ignored.

Packenham's point of view is at once persuasive and elusive. It is persuasive in that it seems clear that legislative institutions, by providing the symbols if not always the reality of democracy, can engender support for the regime. On the other hand, it is not at all clear how this function can be demonstrated. The only attempt to do so has been made by Hakes (1973).

He studied seven African nations and found that in the three in which military coups had taken place, the annual number of parliamentary meetings tended to decline in the period preceding the coups. In the four countries in which coups did not take place, the annual number of meetings either remained constant or increased.

While findings of this sort seem to show an association between legislative saliency and regime stability, no causal connection is demonstrated. Perhaps the strongest argument for such a connection lies in the fact that when legislatures are abolished in particular countries as the result of regime changes or coups, they are usually reestablished relatively quickly and seldom with their authority significantly altered from that which they possessed when they were disbanded. It is possible to argue that this institutional resiliency implies that the legislature performs a useful function even for the most authoritarian political elites, a function which is very likely to be that of legitimizing their rule. The limit to this line of reasoning, however, is suggested by the prolonged period during which the leaders of countries such as Chile and the Philippines have done without a legislature.

Legislatures and Socioeconomic Change

In the same article in which he discusses legitimization, Packenham also offers the following hypothesis:

Legislatures tend to represent, all over the world, more conservative and parochial interests than executives, even in democratic polities. . . . In societies that need and want change . . . it may not make much sense to strengthen the decision-making function of an institution that is likely to resist change (1970, p. 578).

While the idea had been suggested previously (Huntington, 1968, pp. 388ff) and while Packenham noted that there were exceptions to his generalization, this "conservative legislature" hypothesis was a recurrent theme in subsequent research on the contributions that legislatures could make to solving the social and economic problems of the Third World.

Investigations of Packenham's hypothesis fell into three categories. One group focused on the activities relevant to development that legislators engaged in outside the legislature. Put differently, the issue here was the policy consequences of the representational activities of legislators. A second research category consisted of studies of the fate of development policies during the formal legislative phases of the policy-making process. A third approach, drawing on cross-national data, asked whether or not the existence of a legislature made any difference to the ultimate shape of development policies.

Much of the best work representing each of these approaches can be found in an anthology edited by Musolf and Smith entitled *Legislatures in*

Development (1979). The book resulted from a conference in which the paper writers had been expressly asked to address the consequences of legislative activities for development.

The strongest concensus is that the activities of its members outside the legislature have the greatest impact on development. The most comprehensive statement of this view is offered by Barkan (1979a). Drawing upon interview data with Kenyan MPs and his observations of the activities of legislators in other nations of sub-Saharan Africa, he concludes that the activities of the legislature in rural development projects are best seen as "the individual efforts through which legislators attempt to establish linkages between the periphery and the center." Viewed from this perspective, legislators do not have much effect on the major decisions regarding the allocation of resources, but "the members of most Third World legislatures can and do affect their distribution." When relatively free from party control and when subject to popular election, Third World legislators "will spend a substantial amount of their time promoting rural development in their constituencies because it is in their interest to do so." It is also in the interests of the society that they do so because such activities "create linkages between the center and the periphery that are qualitatively different and autonomous from the linkages created by other potential linkers" and thereby serve to "increase the level of vertical integration in these societies." Rural development therefore is likely to proceed at a faster rate because legislators recognize that such projects will mitigate some of the hardships under which the rural population lives and render it "more receptive to other government-initiated efforts at changing their conditions." Barkan also suggests the possibility that such entrepreneurial activities may have long-term negative consequences. They may increase the level of intraelite conflict, as MPs compete with each other for scarce resources; such grass roots efforts may also reduce the prospect of a coordinated development plan for the entire society (Barkan, 1979a, pp. 286-287).

Although Barkan's identification of an entrepreneurial role for Third World legislators is not supported in all of its details in the other essays in Musolf and Smith, his emphasis on the legislator's role as a link between the constituency and the central government is substantiated. Musolf and Springer, drawing on interviews with Malaysian MPs, conclude that legislators had no role in deciding the provisions of government programs designed to foster housing and to improve agricultural productivity in rural areas. Rather, the MPs reported that their role was "to educate their constituents about the development programs, to listen attentively to complaints, to attend meetings in their constituencies at which suggestions and complaints can be processed, and to communicate back to the center those matters that resist settlement at local levels" (1979, p. 307).

Two additional studies in the Musolf and Smith volume argue that
while linkage and entrepreneurial activities are the most important aspects
of legislative involvement in development programs, the legislature as a whole
has some impact. Thus, Hopkins, in his comparative analysis of the impact
of Kenyan and Tanzanian legislators on development strategies, concludes
that speeches in the legislature and committee activities, especially in Kenya,
have had some impact on "clarifying goals, promoting alternatives, or reinforcing implementation. . . . The legislator's contribution has been to call
attention to problems, e.g., limited educational opportunities, flagrant elite
privileges, unemployment, and land pressure, thereby implicitly helping
to set priorities" (1979, p. 179). Similarly, Morell reports that on occasion
the speeches and votes that took place in the Thai legislature forced the
government to be more responsive to constituency demands. However, the
most significant involvement of MPs in development programs was on "issues
of project implementation, especially in altering the locations of development
projects" and in advocating a shift of resources away from large infrastruc-
ture projects toward smaller projects such as "village level irrigation canals
and feeder roads" that presumably had a more immediate impact on the lives
of people living in the countryside. Morell suggests that there was some degree
of personal opportunism and ambition rather than pure altruism on the part
of the MPs. Like Barkan, he notes that the expenditure of funds in this manner might not have been the most rational and effective deployment of development resources (Morell, 1979, pp. 359-363).

Several case studies suggest, as do Hopkins and Morell, that legislatures may affect policy by their collective action as well as through the
extralegislative activities of their members. For example, Duff (1971) describes the efforts to pass a land reform measure through the Colombian
Congress. Over a 13-month period, extensive negotiations took place between
the government and those parliamentarians opposed to particular aspects
of the legislation, confirming "Congress' role as a delayer and modifier of
government initiatives" (Duff, 1971, p. 396) but also confirming Packenham's
view that Congress would respond in a conservative manner to such proposals.
On the other hand, Baaklini and Abdul-Wahab (1979, p. 326) find that debates in the Kuwaiti legislature "played a major role in setting the guidelines
for the country's oil policy" and that in many respects the Assembly was
more assertive and nationalistic in its views than the executive branch.

A difficulty with all of these studies is that because each is based
for the most part on data drawn from one particular nation, it is difficult
to generalize their findings to other Third World systems. Some scepticism
about generalizations may be in order simply because this literature, like
that in many other areas, is usually not designed to encourage negative
findings. One notable exception is Jain's (1979) analysis of the role of the

Indian Lok Sabha in the development of economic plans. He concludes that the legislature "has neither seriously sought nor played a significant role in plan formulation and plan implementation and, thereby, in socio-economic development" (p. 232).

To develop conclusions of general applicability, researchers look at a large number of nations. One such undertaking is McCoy's (1979) attempt to assess the impact of Third World legislatures on population policy. For 107 "less developed countries," McCoy coded information on the existence and strength of the legislature and the nature of their population policies. This aggregate data is supplemented by evidence from various case studies. While he finds some association between the existence of a legislature and the existence of a population policy, he concludes that "legislatures have taken a back seat to executives and bureaucracies in the shaping of national population policies. . . . Where there has been legislative intervention, it has come often in the form of either symbolic legitimization of executive proposals or occasionally obstructionist opposition to standard policy measures" (1979, p. 252).

Verner (1981) takes a more ambitious approach to the assessment of the differences that Third World legislatures make for development policy, analysing data on 78 developing countries for the 1960-1970 period. His data set includes measures of such socioeconomic indicators as wealth, industrialization, communications, and the quality of life and measures of such political variables as the strength of the military, the openness of the system, and government instability. He also includes several legislative variables grouped into three factors: legislative institutionalization, fractionalization within the legislature, and the degree of party competitiveness. All these independent variables are then correlated with 20 public expenditure variables to test the hypothesis that "countries that have institutionalized, stable legislatures and that are party competitive, polyarchic, and effective will spend more" on various categories of development projects. The multivariate analysis leads Verner to conclude that socioeconomic factors are more important predictors of expenditure policies than either political or legislative factors. The legislative factors, however, were far more important than the political system variables, especially in regard to levels of gross expenditures.

Although Verner's analysis is limited by the impressionistic quality of many of his independent variables as well as by his exclusive concentration on expenditure policies, it is to date our hardest comparative assessment of legislative impact on public policy in Third World nations. The conclusion that legislative systems do "mediate to some extent between the socioeconomic environment and the policy variables" (Verner, 1981, p. 293) needs to be taken as a hypothesis in need of further testing with more complete data.

Where does this leave us in assessing the impact of legislatures on the socioeconomic problems of Third World nations? The most obvious point is that legislatures are not the place where such policies are designed and decided upon, although there is some evidence that their presence and strength has an effect on the nature of the policies adopted. Second, legislatures are arenas within which needs can be articulated and, on occasion, bargaining can take place which will have some marginal influence on aspects of development policies. Third, the clearest examples of legislative influence lie in the activities of individual legislators in their constituencies as they link local residents and elites with central decision makers, seeking on the one hand to sensitize decision makers to the needs of the constituency and on the other to encourage local support for and compliance with central decisions.

The Development of Legislatures

Our final category of research on Third World legislatures includes work on the conditions that promote or inhibit the strengthening of such institutions. Such research deals with the legislature's relationship with civilian and military bureaucracies, with political parties, and with the people. Theoretical work on the institutionalization of legislatures and on legislative types is also included.

The Legislature and the Bureaucracy

When political scientists began to study the politics of Third World nations, they directed much of their attention toward bureaucracies because these institutions seemed to be the focus of the policy-making process and also seemed to be more "developed" than other political institutions. In a seminal article, Riggs (1963) was the first to point to the connection between these strong bureaucracies and the weak legislatures that seemed to accompany them. Riggs argued that overdeveloped bureaucracies undermined the electoral, party, and interest group systems which he viewed as essential sources of support for legislative bodies. He further suggested that the tendency of such bureaucracies to control public revenues and expenditures and the general failure of the legislature even to oversee this process weakened that traditional pillar of legislative authority, the power of the purse. The weakness of fiscal supervision reflected a more general failure of oversight which rendered these legislatures for the most part incapable of ensuring that their legislation was implemented honestly and efficiently.

Riggs's themes have been sharpened and elaborated by more recent theoretical and empirical discussions. For example, O'Donnell (1979) argues that military and civilian bureaucracies in Third World nations tend to establish systems of "political exclusion" guided by "a determination to impose a particular type of order on society." Such a system of exclusion inevitably involves the "suppression of the institutional roles and channels of access to the government characteristic of political democracy" (p. 292). Such elites wish to preserve their dominance of the political system and have a techno-cratic and oligopolistic vision of economic development that brings them into conflict with legislative institutions.

This phenomenon is illustrated by Valenzuela and Wilde (1979) in their discussion of the decline of the Chilean Congress between 1964 and 1970. Among other things, the Christian Democrats who controlled the executive during this period attempted to institute central economic planning through a strengthened budget bureau. This provoked opposition from legis-lators who saw in such a proposal the elimination of their opportunity to influence specific budget items for their own political advantage. Although legislators argued that they knew the needs of their provinces better than central planners, the executive tried to protect its plan. Their goal then was "to do away with particularistic considerations in order to rationalize national planning" (p. 207). The executive even attempted to eliminate small subsidies that legislators arranged "for the benefit of particular hospitals, convents, sports clubs, orphanages and the like within their constituencies." Although this last proposal failed, the move to central planning, in Valenzuela and Wilde's view, "undermined the informal mechanism for compromise within the legislature" (p. 208).

In Thailand, as Mezey (1973) and Morell (1979) suggest, the conflict between the bureaucracy and the legislature was in some respects similar to that in Chile, as legislators sought to protect their particularized projects against the ostensibly more rational development plans that came from tech-nocratic elites. In the case of the military, the conflict was a more straight-forward one between the expenditure needs of the military and the economic development priorities of legislators. According to Kornberg and Pittman (1979), such conflict over chronically scarce resources, along with a dissensus on political values and norms and an endemic crisis environment, explains the prevalence of military intervention in developing states.

In his study of the demise of the Philippine Congress, Stauffer (1975) adds an additional perspective to this view of inevitable conflict between bureaucrats and legislators. While he too discusses the tension between tech-nocratic elites and legislators overly concerned with their particular demands, he argues further that the strength of the bureaucratic and military elites surrounding the president had increased before the Marcos coup partly be-cause the United States had tried to strengthen these sectors at the expense of the more democratic and popular institutions. Of course, the information on Chile that came to light after the military coup in that country indicated that the United States was also influential in undermining the democratic institutions of that country. Stauffer's analysis anticipates O'Donnell who, in his explication of the bureaucratic-authoritarian system, makes the point that elites in such systems typically have strong ties to foreign capital (O'Donnell, 1979, p. 293).

In sum, one source of legislative fragility in Third World nations is the hostility of bureaucratic elites, who view their presumably rational development plans as threatened by the particularism that characterizes the representational activities of legislators. This tension between the bureaucratic and the legislative perspective is not peculiar to the Third World. However, while more established legislatures have equipped themselves with committee systems and with staff support to assist them in exercising at least some control over the bureaucracy, comparable resources and structures are generally absent in the Third World (see Baaklini and Heaphey, 1976; Loewenberg and Patterson, 1979, pp. 159ff; Mezey, 1979, Ch. 6). Finally, as Stauffer and O'Donnell suggest, the bureaucratic-legislative struggle in Third World nations is influenced to a significant degree by transnational actors whose activities usually work to the disadvantage of the legislature.

The Legislature and the People

If legislatures are to survive and prosper, especially in the face of hostility from military and civilian bureaucracies, they need to maintain the support of the population. While there is reason to believe that legislators are in a demographic sense more representative of the population than bureaucrats (see Hopkins, 1971, pp. 75-77), there is also evidence that legislators are not always the objects of popular affection. Stauffer (1975) notes that in addition to its other problems, the Philippine Congress, in the period prior to its closure, was not very well thought of by either mass or attentive publics. Stories of legislative graft and corruption, along with other critical reports on legislative behavior, filled the Manila newspapers (p. 38). In addition, the reputation of the institution was not enhanced by its favoritism toward the landed and industrial interests, manifested by its resistance to policy initiatives in land reform and the taxation of exports. Not surprisingly, then, "any resistance to martial law was not to be occasioned by regret over the closing of Congress" (p. 6). Similarly, Astiz (1973) says that the fact that they are dominated by wealthy interests contributes to the "decay of Latin American legislatures." He asserts that these bodies "fail to be representative of the lower class, and particularly of its rural sectors. . . . [T]he lower middle class is grossly underrepresented in many of these bodies" (p. 122).

Although the discussions by Astiz and Stauffer seem persuasive, neither one has any hard data that demonstrates the supposedly low levels of support for these institutions. In contrast, those few studies that do provide such data suggest a somewhat different picture.

One of the first such data sets, discussed by Hopkins (1975), comes from a survey done in Nairobi and Mombassa. Although these urban respondents viewed members of the Kenyan Parliament as primarily representative of elite interests and as marginal to the policy-making process, they recognized that these MPs performed valuable services for their constituencies and they were generally supportive of them (pp. 220-227).

Most of the data that we have on attitudes toward Third World legislatures have been generated by the University of Iowa's Comparative Legislative Research Center study of the Parliaments of Kenya, Korea, and Turkey. This work has been reported in a series of articles (Jewell and Kim, 1976; Kim and Loewenberg, 1976; Kalaycioglu, 1980) as well as in a recent book (Kim et al., 1983). These data suggest that the legislature in these countries is, in general, the object of popular support. However, different population sectors support the legislature for different reasons; the attitudes of the more modernized sectors are based on satisfaction with legislative performance, while the views of the more traditional sectors of society reflect, for the most part, diffuse support. For citizens classified as more modern, the legislature is more salient; their support turns on evaluations of the job done by the legislature or by individual legislators. More traditional citizens know less about the institution but are nonetheless supportive, perhaps out of a basic loyalty or an ingrained deferential attitude toward authority. While many traditional respondents favorably evaluated their MP, they appeared to make no consistent connection between the legislator's performance and the legislature as an institution.

Thus, our information on how Third World legislatures are perceived is sparse and to some extent contradictory. While impressionistic accounts of several legislatures make it easy to believe that these institutions and their members are viewed as corrupt and incompetent, the hardest data that we have from three rather diverse countries suggest a relatively high level of support for the legislature and for individual legislators. It may be that these support questions are picking up a diffuse commitment to the symbols of the regime as well as the respect for authority that is a part of traditional political cultures. This raises the question of what these findings mean for Third World legislatures. The presumption is that the high levels of support for the Kenyan, Korean, and Turkish Parliaments will discourage executive leaders from intimidating or suspending these institutions, but that has not been the case in either Korea or Turkey in recent years. Certainly, since support for the legislature, at least from some segments of society, tends to be based on its performance, charges by elites that the legislature is performing incompetently or dishonestly may significantly detract from support. Ultimately situations similar to those in the Philippines and Chile may result; there the demise of once strong congresses provoked no mass resistance at first and little over the 10 years that these suspensions have been in effect.

Legislatures and Political Parties

As Riggs (1963) implied, the status and survival of a legislature may also be related to the condition of the nation's political party system. Mezey (1975) argues that legislatures are most vulnerable to extraconstitutional attacks on their prerogatives in systems whose political parties are very weak. Stronger parties will help the legislature to generate from mass publics the support it needs to withstand challenges from bureaucratic elites. He supports this claim with a case study of the connection between the weak party system in Thailand and that legislature's continued vulnerability to military coups.

At the other extreme, very strong parties will subordinate the legislature, although they usually maintain it as a functioning entity within parameters defined by the party. Thus, the Tanzanian Bunge remains an operating part of that political system, although it is clearly under the control of the governing party (see Hopkins, 1970; Kjekshus, 1974). Le Vine's (1979) assessment of the fate of legislatures in Francophone Africa is also suggestive. Although it is not the main point of his analysis, his data indicate that in one-party systems the legislature has survived.

It is important to note this role of strong political parties in the survival of legislatures. While most discussions of the party-legislature relationship have focused on the capacity of strong parties to reduce the autonomy of the legislature (see Jewell, 1973), it may be just as important to look at such party domination as an alternative to the abolition of the legislature.

The Institutionalization of Legislatures

There have been some attempts at speculative theory seeking to tie together the several variables that we have discussed as conditions for the establishment and survival of viable legislatures. Riggs (1975), for example, begins with the contexts under which what he refers to as "national elected assemblies" originate and acquire "salience" and "durability." He discusses the emergence of "constitutive systems" composed of three interdependent components: one or more national elected assemblies, an electoral system designed to select its members, and a party system. He offers several propositions about the relationships among these three elements and then develops a categorization of constitutive systems based upon the system's relationship with the bureaucracy. He develops four different genetic patterns for the origin of constitutive systems based on whether or not the system emerged by displacing an incumbent elite, and on the strength of the bureaucracy under the constitutive system. Different genetic patterns produce different types of constitutive systems with legislatures of varying degrees of salience and durability. To illustrate the various possibilities, Riggs offers case studies of the emergence of constitutive systems in 10 southeast Asian nations. On the basis of these discussions, he concludes that variables such as the nature of the indigenous culture, geography, levels of industrialization, urbanization, and social mobilization "do not seem to be as highly correlated with the kind of polity that emerges or the roles assumed by elected assemblies as the structural mode of genesis. [In southeast Asia, a] basic factor affecting the genetic mode seems to be the policies followed by imperial rulers in dealing with their dependencies" (Riggs, 1975, p. 72).

The terminology and implications of Riggs's full model are complex, but his essential point seems reasonable: the conditions under which new nations come to independence influence the type of legislative structure that will emerge. Similarly, Sisson and Snowiss (1979) write that viable legislative institutions require a supportive ideology involving constitutionalism and individual rights. In new nations where "parliamentary institutions are either borrowed or inherited from colonial regimes, supportive ideologies are not likely to be well-developed" (p. 57). There are exceptions: nations like India, where the legislature was instrumental in securing independence from colonial domination, or like Kenya, where mass parties have led the fight for independence in cooperation with parliamentary institutions. Without such conditions or a supportive ideology, Sisson and Snowiss argue, legislatures in new nations will be viable only to the extent that they are able to serve the interest of dominant classes.

However, in an earlier formulation, Sisson (1973) took a somewhat different approach. Although he emphasized the importance of the relationship between the legislature and the external environment, he said that the institutionalization of legislatures depends in part on the degree to which their structure is congruent with the traditional cultural structure of the society, a factor that Riggs discounts. He concludes that both these structural and cultural perspectives need to be related to the willingness of mass and elite publics to comply with the judgements and decisions of legislative institutions.

Weinbaum's (1975) historical case studies of parliamentary institutions in Iran, Turkey, and Afghanistan offer another view of the conditions for transformation of legislative institutions. Unlike Riggs and Sisson, Weinbaum is concerned with identifying conditions that can lead toward either diminished or enhanced legislative viability. He concludes that a transformed legislature follows one of several events: an abrupt expansion or contraction in executive powers, a radical modification in the configuration of parliamentary parties, a revision in formal constitutional procedures, a change in societal norms regarding the legislature, a change in the level of support accorded to the legislature by attentive publics.

Weinbaum's analysis complements Riggs's (1975) by emphasizing the importance of party and executive power in determining the status of legislatures. Also, as Sisson (1973) does, Weinbaum notes the importance of societal norms. However, Weinbaum offers no discussion of the relative importance of the various factors that he identifies or of how they interact with each other. Instead, he concludes his discussion with a statement that summarizes the approach that he, as well as Riggs and Sisson, have taken. He asserts that changes in the status of legislatures, "especially modifications in their decisional and integrative capacities, were the results of events elsewhere in the political system and largely beyond their control" (Weinbaum, 1975, p. 63).

In sum, these analyses of the institutionalization of legislatures view them as exclusively dependent variables, shaped and controlled by their cultural and political environments. This to some extent conflicts with much of the other literature that we have cited, which argues implicitly that legislatures, by virtue of the things they do and, more importantly, the things their members do, can increase their utility to the political systems of which they are a part.

The extreme version of the argument that legislatures can, in effect, institutionalize themselves is found in work advocating the strengthening of the internal structure of the legislature. Drawing on the legislative reform tradition, this approach has been most closely associated with the Graduate School of Public Affairs at the State University of New York at Albany. Examples of this work are found in *Comparative Legislative Reforms and Innovations,* edited by Baaklini and Heaphey (1977). Baaklini's essay on reforms undertaken by the Brazilian Chamber of Deputies concludes that the chamber has been able to increase its importance in the Brazilian political system "by adopting structures and procedures that are ostensibly rational and efficiency-oriented rather than political" (p. 259), thereby making the legislature more acceptable to the dominant technocratic elites. In the same volume, Jain surveys reforms of the Indian Lok Sabha designed to ensure the effective utilization of time, improve the committee system, increase the institution's legislative oversight capacity, and improve the effectiveness of individual members of parliament.

If the lessons of the institutionalization literature seem overly abstract, the reform approach may strike some as too simplistic. The conclusion that legislatures may make themselves viable by improving their performance and making themselves more useful to dominant elites appears to avoid too easily the political and cultural variables that others have discussed and also to strain the meaning of the term "viable." On the other hand, if viability means adaptability and survival, then reforms of the sort discussed here may be effective means to that end.

Categories

Riggs's (1975) work on the origin of legislatures suggests the need to develop categories of legislatures reflecting the different positions that the institution might occupy in a political system. Traditionally, such classification schemes have focused on the legislature's role in making public policy and more specifically on its formal relationship with the executive branch. Thus, the presidential-parliamentary dichotomy has been with us for some time, as have more sophisticated gradations of legislative-executive relationships based on constitutional provisions (see Blondel, 1973).

The fragility and formality of constitutional provisions led some to look at what the legislature does rather than at what the constitution says about the legislature. Thus, Polsby (1975) constructed a continuum with "transformative" legislatures at one end and "arena" legislatures at the other. The former "possess the independent capacity, frequently exercised, to mold and transform proposals from whatever source into laws"; the latter "serve as formalized settings for the interplay of significant political forces in the life of a political system" (p. 277). Similarly, Weinbaum (1975) distinguished among legislatures on the basis of their "decisional role," indicated by the institution's capacity to initiate legislation; to modify, delay, or defeat bills; to influence administrative actions through parliamentary questions, interpellations, and investigations; and to alter departmental budgets, authorizations, and personnel (p. 43).

However, Weinbaum recognized that classifying legislatures simply on the basis of their decisional roles would create a concentration of institutions at the low end of the scale, some quite different from each other on criteria other than the decisional. Another criterion that Weinbaum suggested was the success of the legislature in performing "integrative" functions, measured by its ability to create and/or disseminate "symbols and goals that identify common interests," to "focus competing interests and furnish mechanisms leading to the containment and resolution of conflict," and to "facilitate the control of disintegrative elements, actual and potential" (p. 45). Using the criteria of decisional and integrative activities, Weinbaum developed five categories of legislatures which he labeled coordinate, subordinate, submissive, indeterminate, and competitive-dominant; and he speculated on how each might differ from the other. Weinbaum suggested that most Third World legislatures were "submissive" institutions with weak decisional capacities and only modest integrative capacities.

Similarly, Mezey (1979) developed a classification scheme based on the decisional role of the legislature, conceived in much the same way as Weinbaum's but with "the degree of support accruing to the institution" as a second dimension and with support defined as "a set of attitudes that look to the legislature as a valued and popular political institution" (p. 27). Using these two dimensions, legislatures are classified into five categories: active legislatures, with strong decisional capacities and high levels of support; vulnerable legislatures, with strong decisional capacities and low levels of support; reactive legislatures, with moderate decisional capacities and high levels of support; marginal legislatures, with moderate decisional capacities and low levels of support; and minimal legislatures, with little or no decisional capacities and high levels of support. Although at least one Third World legislature could be found in each category, most legislatures were either marginal or minimal.

The utility of any classification scheme lies in its capacity to explain variance across a large number of cases. When Mezey's categories are used to analyze the activities of legislatures all over the world, many instances of substantial intracategory variation are found; however, there are also indications of recurring patterns of policy-making, representational, and system-maintenance activities among legislatures within the same category. Ultimately, determining whether or not any classification actually does explain variance among Third World nations will depend on whether or not we can gather better and more comparable data than is currently available.

Summary

What we know about legislatures in the Third World can be summarized as follows.

1. Such institutions, while seldom dominant in their political systems, usually are able to exert some influence on the public policy process. Such influence is likely to be manifested in private rather than in public arenas, on lesser rather than greater decisions, and through the efforts of legislators working individually rather than collectively.

2. The individual members of Third World legislatures, like their counterparts elsewhere, spend a great deal of their time attending to the allocative and service concerns of their constituencies; such activities often have policy consequences.

3. The membership of these legislatures reflects the nature of conflict and risk within the political system as well as the stage of development that the system has reached.

In sum, the study of Third World legislatures has been something of an orphan among different political science subdisciplines, with none willing to accept or fully integrate its findings. The result is a literature that is a part of, yet apart from, each of the research traditions from which it has emerged. The noncumulative nature of this work is therefore not surprising.

The situation is further exacerbated by the case study approach that is typical of this literature. Because what we know about Third World legislatures is in large measure derived from geographically diverse and time-bound case studies, it has been difficult to generalize to a universe populated by many unique and rapidly changing cases. The fact that this inability to generalize is viewed as a failure reflects another important distinction between this literature and that on Western legislatures. Those studying the U.S. Congress have never been asked to generalize their findings to other legislative institutions. The Congress is viewed as an important institution and therefore simply understanding how it alone operates has been deemed to be important. Because legislatures in Third World countries and, by implication, these countries themselves, have not been seen as very important, the worth of knowledge about these institutions has not been self-evident. Instead, the major virtue of any work on any one Third World legislature is what it had to tell us about Third World legislatures in general, or what it had to tell us about its political system, and seldom what it had to tell us about itself.

The problem is that the consensus on the concepts and, more significantly, the data-gathering capacities required to produce findings which are generalizable have been and likely will continue to be beyond the reach of those working in this field. The specific barriers to the necessary data are painfully obvious: an international group of scholars that communicates infrequently and with great difficulty, variable levels of research accessibility to different legislatures, language problems, and persistent idiosynchratic national characteristics which inevitably frustrate the development of cross-national research designs. Thus, this literature is based on case studies because, ordinarily, that is all that is feasible. Therefore, it is of utility only to those who are particularly interested in the nation that provides the case or to those who are willing to pick through the findings of many such studies in order to unearth similarities and differences.

When the latter use is made of this literature, it will be found that the work on Third World legislatures often complements, and in some cases leads, the findings on more established legislatures. For example, the importance of constituency concerns to Third World legislators was discovered concurrently with similar findings concerning the service activities of members of the U.S. Congress. When taken together with the later findings from European and Marxist legislatures (see Mezey, 1979, Ch. 9), such activities provide one of the few constants that apply to all legislative settings.

Similarly, while most Third World legislatures have only marginal policy-making influence, it is not at all clear that any legislature outside Washington, DC exercises a great deal more authority than the modal Third World case. And the challenge to legislative authority posed by the ascendance of technocrats is a worldwide phenomenon, as apparent in Washington as it is in Brasilia or Nairobi. In this context, the emphasis in studies of Third World legislatures on their symbolic function of legitimizing political regimes and on linking citizens with executive-centered elites seems increasingly relevant to Western systems. It is difficult, for example, to read works such as Fenno's *Home Style* (1978) without coming to the conclusion that the most significant impact of the representational activities of American legislators is symbolic.

What these parallels suggest is the necessity to fully integrate the study of Third World legislatures into the field of legislative studies if we are serious about developing general theories of legislatures and legislative behavior. In this connection, it is important to note those areas where the work on Third World legislatures has lessons for those of us who study Western legislatures.

While it is a diverse, noncumulative, and, at times "soft" body of research, if there is one common denominator to the research on Third World legislatures it is this: a persistent concern with the relationship between the legislature—as a whole and as composed of individual legislators—and the larger political and social system within which the legislature operates. Because of our ready access to Western legislatures and because of our concern with the details of how they operate, we have as a rule neglected to discuss the functions of such institutions for their political and social systems and the reciprocal effects of larger system variables upon the legislature.

Also, we have not of late been very critical of these institutions. We have not discussed seriously their limitations and failings, and considered carefully the changes that would be desirable. Ironically, because we know less about Third World legislatures and because we have found them less accessible, we have not been at all hesitant about being critical of them and their operation. And the greatest irony of all is that our criticisms have often been based upon our own unexamined premises about what constitutes a successful legislature.

NOTES

1. By "Third World" I refer to all of the nations of Africa except South Africa, all of the nations of Asia except Israel and Japan, and all of the nations of Central and South America. Compared with North America, Europe, and the Soviet Union, these nations are generally less urbanized and industrialized, poorer by most economic measures, and less socially developed in terms of such things as literacy and health care. Many but not all of these nations are also characterized by high levels of political instability. I use the term "Third World" not because it is a model of clarity but because the other adjectives conventionally used to describe this group of nations are less satisfying. Thus, the term "non-Western" is geographically inaccurate if Latin America is to be included. The term "developing" and its "underdeveloped" and "less-developed" variants have been criticized on two counts: first, because they impute a political inferiority to these nations and, presumably, a political superiority to the "developed" world; and second, because they erroneously imply that the part of the world not so labeled is no longer "developing" or changing.

2. Wahlke et al. (1962, p. 261) suggest that the ritualist orientation is an automatic response that may not be as revealing as the other purposive role orientations evoked by this question.

3. It is perhaps too easy to say that current events in Lebanon demonstrate the failure of this constitutional design. In conversations with me, Baaklini points out two major causes of Lebanon's current travail: the presence of a sizable refugee group that was not a part of the original arrangement and the intervention of external forces, i.e., Syria and Israel.

REFERENCES

Agor, Weston H. 1971a. "The Decisional Role of the Senate in the Chilean Political System," in Weston H. Agor, ed., *Latin American Legislatures: Their Role and Influence.* New York: Praeger.

_____ . 1971b. *The Chilean Senate.* Austin: University of Texas Press.

Astiz, Carlos A. 1973. "The Decay of Latin American Legislatures," in Allan Kornberg, ed., *Legislatures in Comparative Perspective.* New York: McKay.

Austin, D.G. 1958. "The Ghana Parliament's First Year," *Parliamentary Affairs* 11: 350-360.

Baaklini, Abdo I. 1976. *Legislative and Political Development: Lebanon, 1842-1972.* Durham, NC: Duke University Press.

_____ . 1977. "Legislative Reforms in Lebanon," in Abdo I. Baaklini and James J. Heaphey, eds., *Comparative Legislative Reforms and Innovations.* Albany: Comparative Development Studies Center, Graduate School of Public Affairs, State University of New York at Albany.

Baaklini, Abdo I. and Alia Abdul-Wahab. 1979. "The Role of the National Assembly in Kuwait's Economic Development: National Oil Policy," in Lloyd D. Musolf and Joel Smith, eds., *Legislatures in Development.* Durham, NC: Duke University Press.

Baaklini, Abdo I. and James J. Heaphey. 1976. *Legislative Institution Building in Brazil, Costa Rica, and Lebanon.* Beverly Hills, CA: Sage Publications.

Bailey, F.G. 1960. "Traditional Society and Representation: A Case Study of Orissa," *Archives Europeenes de Sociologie* 1:121-141.

Baker, Christopher E. 1971. "The Costa Rican Legislative Assembly: A Preliminary Evaluation of the Decisional Function," in Weston H. Agor, ed., *Latin American Legislatures: Their Role and Influence.* New York: Praeger.

Barkan, Joel D. 1979a. "Bringing Home the Pork: Legislator Behavior, Rural Development, and Political Change in East Africa," in Lloyd D. Musolf and Joel Smith, eds., *Legislatures in Development.* Durham, NC: Duke University Press.

————. 1979b. "Legislators, Elections and Political Linkage," in Joel D. Barkan and John J. Okumu, eds., *Politics and Public Policy in Kenya and Tanzania.* New York: Praeger.

Barker, Anthony and Michael Rush. 1970. *The British Member of Parliament and His Information.* Toronto: University of Toronto Press.

Blondel, Jean. 1973. *Comparative Legislatures.* Englewood Cliffs, NJ: Prentice-Hall.

Blondel, Jean et al. 1969-1970. "Comparative Legislative Behaviour," *Government and Opposition* 5:67-85.

Cayrol, Roland, Jean-Luc Parodi, and Colette Ysmal. 1976. "French Deputies and the Political System," *Legislative Studies Quarterly* 1:67-99.

Chee, Chan Heng. 1976. "The Role of Parliamentary Politicians in Singapore," *Legislative Studies Quarterly* 1:423-441.

Crow, Ralph E. 1970. "Parliament in the Lebanese Political System," in Allan Kornberg and Lloyd D. Musolf, eds., *Legislatures in Developmental Perspective.* Durham, NC: Duke University Press.

Duff, Ernest A. 1971. "The Role of Congress in the Colombian Political System," in Weston H. Agor, ed., *Latin American Legislatures: Their Role and Influence.* New York: Praeger.

Engholm, G.F. 1963. "The Westminster Model in Uganda," *International Journal* 18: 468-487.

Eulau, Heinz and Paul D. Karps. 1977. "The Puzzle of Representation: Specifying Components of Responsiveness," *Legislative Studies Quarterly* 2:233-254.

Fennell, Lee C. 1971. "Congress in the Argentine Political System: An Appraisal," in Weston H. Agor, ed., *Latin American Legislatures: Their Role and Influence.* New York: Praeger.

Fenno, Richard F. 1978. *Home Style: House Members in Their Districts.* Boston: Little, Brown.

Fiorina, Morris P. 1977. *Congress: Keystone of the Washington Establishment.* New Haven: Yale University Press.

Frey, Frederick W. 1965. *The Turkish Political Elite.* Cambridge, MA: MIT Press.

Gertzel, Cherry. 1966. "Parliament in Independent Kenya," *Parliamentary Affairs* 19:486-504.

Goodman, Allan E. 1975. "Correlates of Legislative Constituency Service in South Vietnam," in G.R. Boynton and Chong Lim Kim, eds., *Legislative Systems in Developing Countries.* Durham, NC: Duke University Press.

Grossholtz, Jean. 1964. *The Philippines.* Boston: Little, Brown.

————. 1970. "Integrative Factors in the Malaysian and Philippine Legislatures," *Comparative Politics* 3:93-114.

Gupta, Anirudha. 1965-1966. "The Zambian National Assembly: A Study of an African Legislature," *Parliamentary Affairs* 19:48-64.

Hakes, Jay E. 1973. *Weak Parliaments and Military Coups in Africa: A Study in Regime Instability.* Sage Research Papers in the Social Sciences, Comparative Legislative Studies Series No. 90-004. Beverly Hills, CA: Sage Publications.

Hakes, Jay E. and John Helgerson. 1973. "Bargaining and Parliamentary Behavior in Africa: A Comparative Study of Zambia and Kenya," in Allan Kornberg, ed., *Legislatures in Comparative Perspective.* New York: McKay.

Hopkins, Raymond. 1970. "The Role of the M.P. in Tanzania," *American Political Science Review* 64:754-771.
_____. 1971. *Political Roles in a New State: Tanzania's First Decade*. New Haven: Yale University Press.
_____. 1975. "The Kenyan Legislature: Political Functions and Citizen Perceptions," in G. R. Boynton and Chong Lim Kim, eds., *Legislative Systems in Developing Countries*. Durham, NC: Duke University Press.
_____. 1979. "The Influence of the Legislature on Development Strategy: The Case of Kenya and Tanzania," in Lloyd D. Musolf and Joel Smith, eds., *Legislatures in Development*. Durham, NC: Duke University Press.
Hoskin, Gary W. 1971. "Dimensions of Representation in the Colombian National Legislature," in Weston H. Agor, ed., *Latin American Legislatures: Their Role and Influence*. New York: Praeger.
Hughes, Steven W. and Kenneth J. Mijeski. 1973. *Legislative-Executive Policy-Making: The Case of Chile and Costa Rica*. Sage Research Papers in the Social Sciences, Comparative Legislative Studies Series No. 90-007. Beverly Hills, CA and London: Sage Publications.
Huntington, Samuel P. 1968. *Political Order in Changing Societies*. New Haven: Yale University Press.
Jahan, Rounaq. 1976. "Members of Parliament in Bangladesh," *Legislative Studies Quarterly* 1:355-370.
Jain, R. B. 1977. "Innovations and Reforms in Indian Parliament," in Abdo I. Baaklini and James J. Heaphey, eds., *Comparative Legislative Reforms and Innovations*. Albany: Comparative Development Studies Center, Graduate School of Public Affairs, State University of New York at Albany.
_____. 1979. "The Role of the Indian Parliament in Economic Planning," in Lloyd D. Musolf and Joel Smith, eds., *Legislatures in Development*. Durham, NC: Duke University Press.
Jewell, Malcolm E. 1973. "Linkages Between Legislative Parties and External Parties," in Allan Kornberg, ed., *Legislatures in Comparative Perspective*. New York: McKay.
_____. 1977. "Legislative Representation and National Integration," in Albert Eldridge, ed., *Legislatures in Plural Societies*. Durham, NC: Duke University Press.
Jewell, Malcolm E. and Chong Lim Kim. 1976. "Sources of Support for the Legislature in a Developing Nation," *Comparative Political Studies* 8:461-489.
Kalaycioglu, Ersin. 1980. "Why Legislatures Persist in Developing Countries: The Case of Turkey," *Legislative Studies Quarterly* 5:123-140.
Kelley, R. Lynn. 1971. "The Role of the Venezuelan Senate," in Weston H. Agor, ed., *Latin American Legislatures: Their Role and Influence*. New York: Praeger.
Kim, Chong Lim. 1971. "Toward a Theory of Individual and Systemic Effects of Political Status Loss," *Journal of Developing Areas* 4:193-206.
Kim, Chong Lim and Gerhard L. Loewenberg. 1976. "The Cultural Roots of a New Legislature: Public Perceptions of the Korean National Assembly," *Legislative Studies Quarterly* 1:371-388.
Kim, Chong Lim and Byung-Kyu Woo. 1975. "Political Representation in the Korean National Assembly," in G. R. Boynton and Chong Lim Kim, eds., *Legislative Systems in Developing Countries*. Durham, NC: Duke University Press.

Kim, Chong Lim, Joel D. Barkan, Ilter Turan, and Malcolm E. Jewell. 1983. *The Legislative Connection: The Politics of Representation in Kenya, Korea and Turkey.* Durham, NC: Duke University Press.

Kjekshus, Helge. 1974. "Parliament in a One-Party State–the Bunge of Tanzania, 1965-1970," *The Journal of Modern African Studies* 12:19-43.

Kornberg, Allan and Kenneth Pittman. 1979. "Representative and Military Bodies: Their Roles in the Survival of Political Systems in New States," in Lloyd D. Musolf and Joel Smith, eds., *Legislatures in Development.* Durham, NC: Duke University Press.

Kraus, Jon. 1965. "Ghana's New 'Corporate' Parliament," *Africa Report* 10 (August): 6-11.

Kumbhat, M. C. and Y. M. Marican. 1976. "Constituent Orientation Among Malaysian State Legislators," *Legislative Studies Quarterly* 1:389-404.

Lee, J. M. 1963. "Parliament in Republican Ghana," *Parliamentary Affairs* 16:376-395.

Le Vine, Victor T. 1968. "Political Elite Recruitment and Political Structure in French Speaking Africa," *Cahiers d'Etudes Africaines* 8:369-389.

_____ . 1979. "Parliaments in Francophone Africa: Some Lessons From the Decolonization Process," in Lloyd D. Musolf and Joel Smith, eds., *Legislatures in Development.* Durham, NC: Duke University Press.

Loewenberg, Gerhard L. and Samuel C. Patterson. 1979. *Comparing Legislatures.* Boston: Little, Brown.

McCoy, Terry L. 1971. "Congress, the President, and Political Instability in Peru," in Weston H. Agor, ed., *Latin American Legislatures: Their Role and Influence.* New York: Praeger.

_____ . 1979. "Legislatures and Population Policy in the Third World," in Lloyd D. Musolf and Joel Smith, eds., *Legislatures in Development.* Durham, NC: Duke University Press.

McDonald, Ronald H. 1971. "Legislative Politics in Uruguay: A Preliminary Statement," in Weston H. Agor, ed., *Latin American Legislatures: Their Role and Influence.* New York: Praeger.

Maheshwari, Shriram R. 1976. "Constituency Linkage of National Legislators in India," *Legislative Studies Quarterly* 1:331-354.

Markakis, John and Asmelash Beyene. 1967. "Representative Institutions in Ethiopia," *Journal of Modern African Studies* 5:193-220.

Mayhew, David R. 1974. *Congress: The Electoral Connection.* New Haven: Yale University Press.

Mezey, Michael L. 1972. "The Functions of a Minimal Legislature: Role Perceptions of Thai Legislators," *Western Political Quarterly* 25:686-701.

_____ . 1973. "The 1971 Coup in Thailand: Understanding Why the Legislature Fails," *Asian Survey* 13:306-317.

_____ . 1975. "Legislative Development and Political Parties: The Case of Thailand," in G. R. Boynton and Chong Lim Kim, eds., *Legislative Systems in Developing Countries.* Durham, NC: Duke University Press.

_____ . 1976. "Constituency Demands and Legislative Support: An Experiment," *Legislative Studies Quarterly* 1:101-128.

_____ . 1979. *Comparative Legislatures.* Durham, NC: Duke University Press.

Morell, David. 1979. "Thailand's Legislature and Economic Development Decisions," in Lloyd D. Musolf and Joel Smith, eds., *Legislatures in Development.* Durham, NC: Duke University Press.

Musolf, Lloyd D. and J. Fred Springer. 1977. "Legislatures and Divided Societies: The Malaysian Parliament and Multi-Ethnicity," *Legislative Studies Quarterly* 2:113-136.

_____ . 1979. "The Parliament of Malaysia and Economic Development: Policy-making and the MP," in Lloyd D. Musolf and Joel Smith, eds., *Legislatures in Development.* Durham, NC: Duke University Press.

O'Donnell, Guillermo. 1979. "Tensions in the Bureaucratic-Authoritarian State and the Question of Democracy," in David Collier, ed., *The New Authoritarianism in Latin America.* Princeton: Princeton University Press.

Olson, Kenneth G. 1967. "The Service Function of the United States Congress," in Albert de Grazia, ed., *Congress: The First Branch of Government.* Garden City, NY: Doubleday.

Packenham, Robert A. 1970. "Legislatures and Political Development," in Allan Kornberg and Lloyd D. Musolf, eds., *Legislatures in Developmental Perspective.* Durham, NC: Duke University Press.

Polsby, Nelson W. 1975. "Legislatures," in Fred I. Greenstein and Nelson W. Polsby, eds., *Handbook of Political Science.* Vol. 5. Reading, MA: Addison-Wesley.

Proctor, J. Harris. 1960. "The Legislative Activity of the Egyptian National Assembly of 1957-1958," *Parliamentary Affairs* 13:213-226.

_____ . 1965. "The Role of the Senate in the Kenya Political System," *Parliamentary Affairs* 18:389-415.

_____ . 1968. "The House of Chiefs and the Political Development of Botswana," *The Journal of Modern African Studies* 6:59-79.

Pye, Lucian W. 1958. "The Non-Western Political Process," *Journal of Politics* 20: 468-486.

Ranis, Peter. 1970. "Profile Variables Among Argentine Legislators," in Weston H. Agor, ed., *Latin American Legislatures: Their Role and Influence.* New York: Praeger.

Riggs, Fred W. 1963. "Bureaucrats and Political Development: A Paradoxical View," in Joseph J. LaPalombara, ed., *Bureaucracy and Political Development.* Princeton: Princeton University Press.

_____ . 1975. *Legislative Origins: A Comparative and Contextual Approach.* International Studies Association, Occasional Paper No. 7. Pittsburgh, PA: International Studies Association.

Saloma, John S. 1969. *Congress and the New Politics.* Boston: Little, Brown.

Schulz, Ann T. 1973. "A Cross-National Examination of Legislators," *The Journal of Developing Areas* 7:571-590.

Seligman, Lester G. 1975. "Political Risk and Legislative Behavior in Non-Western Countries," in G. R. Boynton and Chong Lim Kim, eds., *Legislative Systems in Developing Countries.* Durham, NC: Duke University Press.

Sisson, Richard. 1973. "Comparative Legislative Institutionalization: A Theoretical Exploration," in Allan Kornberg, ed., *Legislatures in Comparative Perspective.* New York: McKay.

Sisson, Richard and Lawrence L. Shrader. 1977. "Social Representation and Political Integration in an Indian State: The Legislative Dimension," in Albert Eldridge, ed., *Legislatures in Plural Societies.* Durham, NC: Duke University Press.

Sisson, Richard and Leo M. Snowiss. 1979. "Legislative Viability and Political Development," in Lloyd D. Musolf and Joel Smith, eds., *Legislatures in Development.* Durham, NC: Duke University Press.

Stauffer, Robert B. 1966. "Philippine Legislatures and Their Changing Universe," *Journal of Politics* 28:556-591.

——————. 1970. "Congress in the Philippine Political System," in Allan Kornberg and Lloyd D. Musolf, eds., *Legislatures in Developmental Perspective.* Durham, NC: Duke University Press.

——————. 1975. *The Philippine Congress: Causes of Structural Change.* Sage Research Papers in the Social Sciences, Comparative Legislative Studies Series, No. 90-024. Beverly Hills, CA and London: Sage Publications.

Stultz, Newell M. 1968. "Parliaments in Former British Black Africa," *The Journal of Developing Areas* 2:479-494.

Styskal, Richard A. 1969. "Philippine Legislators' Reception of Individuals and Interest Groups in the Legislative Process," *Comparative Politics* 2:405-422.

Tordoff, William. 1965. "Parliament in Tanzania," *Journal of Commonwealth Political Studies* 3:85-103.

Valenzuela, Arturo and Alexander Wilde. 1979. "Presidential Politics and the Decline of the Chilean Congress," in Lloyd D. Musolf and Joel Smith, eds., *Legislatures in Development.* Durham, NC: Duke University Press.

Verner, Joel G. 1970. "The Guatemalan National Congress: An Elite Analysis," in Weston H. Agor, ed., *Latin American Legislatures: Their Role and Influence.* New York: Praeger.

——————. 1981. "Legislative Systems and Public Policy: A Comparative Analysis of 78 Developing Countries," *The Journal of Developing Areas* 15:275-296.

Wahlke, John C., Heinz Eulau, William Buchanan, and LeRoy Ferguson. 1962. *The Legislative System.* New York: Wiley.

Weinbaum, Marvin G. 1972. "Afghanistan: Non-Party Parliamentary Democracy," *Journal of Developing Areas* 7:57-74.

——————. 1975. "Classification and Change in Legislative Systems: With Particular Application to Iran, Turkey, and Afghanistan," in G. R. Boynton and Chong Lim Kim, eds., *Legislative Systems in Developing Countries.* Durham, NC: Duke University Press.

——————. 1977. "The Legislator as Intermediary: Integration of the Center and Periphery in Afghanistan," in Albert Eldridge, ed., *Legislatures in Plural Societies.* Durham, NC: Duke University Press.

Contributors

DAVID W. BRADY is the Herbert Autrey Professor of Social Sciences at Rice University. He received his Ph.D. in political science from the University of Iowa in 1970. His publications include *Congressional Voting in a Partisan Era: A Study of the McKinley Houses* (1973), *Public Policy and Politics in America*, 2d ed. (1984), *Public Policy in the Eighties* (1983), and numerous articles in professional journals. He has recently completed a Project 87-funded manuscript on critical elections in the U.S. House of Representatives.

CHARLES S. BULLOCK, III is the Richard Russell Professor of Political Science at the University of Georgia. His research on congressional committee assignments, roll-call voting, and civil rights policy has appeared in a number of political science, education, and sociology journals, including the *American Political Science Review, Journal of Politics, American Journal of Political Science,* and *Social Science Quarterly.*

MELISSA P. COLLIE has been an Assistant Professor of Political Science at Rice University and Visiting Assistant Professor of Political Science at Stanford University. She is the author of articles in the *American Political Science Review* and *Legislative Studies Quarterly* and is presently engaged in an analysis of voting alignments in the contemporary House of Representatives.

HEINZ EULAU is the William Bennett Munro Professor of Political Science at Stanford University. He is the co-author of *The Legislative System* (1962) and *Labyrinths of Democracy* (1973). He is a former president of the American Political Science Association and presently working on a book, *Representation in America.*

KEITH E. HAMM is Associate Professor of Political Science at Texas A&M University. He has published articles on the impacts of legislative change and committee decision making in the *Journal of Politics,* the *Legislative Studies Quarterly,* and the *Social Science Quarterly.* He is currently working on comparative studies of committee decision making and interest group influence in U.S. state legislatures.

SUSAN WEBB HAMMOND is Professor of Political Science at American University. She has written on congressional organization, change and reform, legislative staffing, and congressional recruitment. She is co-author of *Congressional Staff: The Invisible Force in American Lawmaking* (1977), and is currently working on a study of informal caucuses in the United States Congress.

RONALD D. HEDLUND is Professor of Political Science and Associate Dean for Research in The Graduate School at the University of Wisconsin-Milwaukee. He is co-author of *Representatives and Represented* (1975) and "A Strategy for Measuring Legislative Processing of Decisions" (1981), and is a member of the *Legislative Studies Quarterly* Editorial Board. He is currently studying the applicability of organization theories to legislative bodies.

MALCOLM E. JEWELL is Professor of Political Science at the University of Kentucky. He is co-author of *The Legislative Process in the U.S.*, 4th ed. (1985), and author of *Representation in State Legislatures* (1982), and *Parties and Primaries* (1984). He is co-editor of the *Legislative Studies Quarterly* and former president of both the Midwest and Southern Political Science Associations.

GERHARD LOEWENBERG is Professor of Political Science and Dean of the College of Liberal Arts at the University of Iowa. He is author of *Parliament in the German Political System* (1967), co-author of *Comparing Legislatures* (1979), and is managing editor of the *Legislative Studies Quarterly*. He is doing research on the Belgian, Italian, and Swiss Parliaments.

VERA E. MCCLUGGAGE is a technical writer at Four-Phase Systems in Cupertino, California. She has a Master's degree in Political Science from Yale University and is working on a dissertation on U.S. Senate committees.

DONALD R. MATTHEWS is Professor of Political Science at the University of Washington. His best known work is *U.S. Senators and Their World* (1960). He has written extensively on political recruitment, decision making by Congressmen, Black politics, and presidential nominating politics in the United States. His current research is on recruitment and representation in the U.S. and Norway.

MICHAEL L. MEZEY is Professor of Political Science and Associate Dean of the College of Liberal Arts and Sciences at DePaul University in Chicago. He is the author of *Comparative Legislatures* (1979), and of several scholarly articles and papers on American and comparative legislative behavior. He is currently writing in the area of presidential-congressional relations.

BRUCE I. OPPENHEIMER is Associate Professor of Political Science at the University of Houston. He received his Ph.D. at the University of Wisconsin and has been both a Brookings Fellow (1970-1971) and an APSA Congressional Fellow (1974-1975). He is the author of *Oil and the Congressional Process* (1974), and is co-editor of *Congress Reconsidered*, 3d ed. (1985).

WILLIAM H. PANNING is Senior Research Consultant at the Hartford Insurance Group in Hartford, Connecticut. His work has appeared in the *American Political Science Review,* the *American Journal of Political Science, Political Methodology, Political Behavior,* and in several edited collections. His current research on corporate finance has appeared in several business journals.

SAMUEL C. PATTERSON is Roy J. Carver Distinguished Professor of Political Science at the University of Iowa. He is the author or co-author of *Representatives and Represented* (1975), *The Legislative Process in the United States,* 4th ed. (1985), and *Comparing Legislatures* (1979). He has been a co-editor of the *Legislative Studies Quarterly,* and is managing editor of the *American Political Science Review.* Currently he is working on a book on *The Congressional Parties.*

ROBERT L. PEABODY is Professor of Political Science at The Johns Hopkins University. He is the author of *Leadership in Congress* (1976), and co-editor of *New Perspectives on the House of Representatives,* 3d ed. (1977). Associate Director of the APSA Study of Congress, his major field of research interest is congressional leadership change and performance.

LYN RAGSDALE is Assistant Professor of Political Science at the University of Arizona. She is the author of several articles that have appeared in scholarly journals, including the *American Political Science Review.* Her current research interests are the American presidency and congressional elections.

BERT A. ROCKMAN is Professor of Political Science at the University of Pittsburgh. He is co-author of *Bureaucrats and Politicians in Western Democracies* (1981) and author of *The Leadership Question: The Presidency and the American System* (1984). He is presently working on a study of changing roles and norms within national executive systems.

JOEL H. SILBEY is Professor of American History at Cornell University. Author of *The Shrine of Party: Congressional Voting Behavior, 1841-1852* (1967), *A Respectable Minority: The Democratic Party, 1860-1868* (1977), and *The Partisan Imperative: The Dynamics of American Politics Before the Civil War* (1985), he is currently examining the origins of the Republican party in Congress.

MARGARET SUSAN THOMPSON is Assistant Professor of History in the Maxwell School, Syracuse University, and author of *The "Spider Webb": Congress and Lobbying in the Age of Grant* (1985) and several essays on the nineteenth-century Congress. The only historian to have been an academic APSA Congressional Fellow, she is currently working on a book about nineteenth-century American nuns.

Index